Ellis Wasson

The British and Irish Ruling Class 1660-1945

Volume 1

Ellis Wasson

The British and Irish Ruling Class 1660-1945

Volume 1

Managing Editor: Katarzyna Michalak

Associate Editor: Łukasz Połczyński

DE GRUYTER
OPEN

ISBN 978-3-11-054836-5
e-ISBN 978-3-11-054837-2

Published by De Gruyter Open Ltd, Warsaw/Berlin
Part of Walter de Gruyter GmbH, Berlin/Boston
The book is published with open access at www.degruyter.com.

Library of Congress Cataloging-in-Publication Data
A CIP catalog record for this book has been applied for at the Library of Congress.

Managing Editor: Katarzyna Michalak
Associate Editor: Łukasz Połczyński

www.degruyteropen.com
Cover illustration: © Thinkstock/bwzenith

Contents

Acknowledgements —— XIII
Preface —— XIV
The Entries —— XV
Abbreviations —— XVII
Introduction —— 1
List of Parliamentary Families —— 5

Dedicated to the memory of my parents

Acknowledgements

A full list of those who helped make my research possible can be found in *Born to Rule*. I remain deeply in debt to the inspiration and mentorship of David Spring.

Preface

In this list cadet, associated, and stem families are arranged in a single entry when substantial property passed between one and the other providing continuity of parliamentary representation (even, as was the case in a few instances, when no blood or marriage relationship existed). Subsidiary/cadet families are usually grouped under the oldest, richest, or most influential stem family.

Female MPs are counted with their birth families, or, if not born into a parliamentary family, with their husband's family. Females who held peerages in their own right were barred from taking a seat in the House of Lords until legislation was passed in 1958 and 1963.

Illegitimate children who became MPs are included if the gaining of their seat was assisted by a family connection.

Relationships based on marriage are not counted unless they involved the transfer of estates.

Members of the European Parliament (MEPs), of the Northern Irish Parliament, the Irish Senate, and of the Welsh Assembly have not been incorporated into the list, although selection for such offices is usually mentioned in the Notes section of the appropriate entry. A small number of parliamentary families continued to gain election to the *Dáil* after 1922. Those "TDs" (*Teachta Dála*) are included.

Cromwellian and Jacobite peers are not included. A few families would have qualified for inclusion had a bishop with a seat in the House of Lords been allowed to count along with two MPs. I have not, however, incorporated them into the list with the exception of the Huttons of Marske.

Members of families mentioned in the new *Oxford Dictionary of National Biography* are noted, in part to recommend a source for further information and in part to indicate the role of the family in national life.

Information about the origins of medieval and early modern families is often extremely hard to interpret with precision. Sometimes it was clearly a judge, royal official, warrior, or merchant who launched a dynasty's ascent, but many families rose slowly, sometimes over a number of centuries in the manner of a coral reef, gradually accumulating landed estates through calculation, luck, patronage, and marriage to heiresses. For the purposes of my research on social origins any family that entered the gentry before 1660 the source of whose wealth was uncertain was counted as "landed". Information for families that rose after 1660 is usually (though not always) easier to identify. Most of the time one "founder" stands out, and his profession or business is the clear launching pad for future success. Detailed information about how social origins were identified and incorporated into the study may be found in my book, *Born to Rule: British Political Elites* (2000).

The Entries

"ORIGINS": Where reliable information is available about the first entry of the family into the gentry, the date of the purchase of land or holding of office is provided. When possible, the source of the wealth that enabled the family's election to Parliament for the first time is identified. Inheritance of property that supported participation in Parliament is delineated. The date of the election of the first MP (or peer), if this occurred before 1660, is given and the number and dates of subsequent MPs elected before 1660 follow. **These are printed in bold**. The information available about pre-1660 MPs varies considerably in quality. When possible, data are taken from the printed volumes of the Histories of Parliament for England and Wales, Scotland, and Ireland (see "Reference Works" in the Bibliography). Other sources include the printed list of MPs issued by Parliament in the nineteenth century, Stenton and Lees, *Who's Who*, online sources, and local and family histories. The dates and numbers of pre-1660 MPs in such sources are not always accurate, so that data should be used with caution.

"SEAT(S)": This category does not necessarily include all residences that belonged to a family. Most seats sold or abandoned before 1660 or inherited or purchased after 1945 are not included. Some houses were only used temporarily or by junior members of the family. Information about many seats was difficult to trace and no heroic efforts were made to find out about every building associated with a family. Information concerning current ownership was accumulated at various times over the past twenty years and, therefore, is sometimes out of date. The architectural data is as accurate as I can make it, but the quality of sources varies enormously and even respected authorities often contradict each other about dates. However, following the history of country houses is one of the surest means of keeping track of landed families.

"ESTATES": Data about wealth is drawn from the Bateman compendium of great landowners published in the 1870s (John Bateman, *The Great Landowners of Great Britain and Ireland*, 1876, 1883). Bateman based his numbers on a government survey of landownership. The first figure in the entry lists acreage, the initials in parentheses identify the location of estates, and the second figure is income in pounds (the entry usually does not include urban property or some other non-landed sources of wealth). Data has also been collected from Rubinstein's *Who Were the Rich*, the History of Parliament volumes, the *ODNB*, obituaries, magazines and, sometimes polemical, books, and works of reference. Families extinct before the survey of landowners was conducted often passed their estates on to other parliamentary families via heiresses. In that case data may be included further down the entry in the section on estates of a successor family. However, in some cases estates were sold or divided up among multiple heirs.

"TITLES": The dates of creation and extinction of all subsidiary peerages and all baronetcies are included in this category. The highest rank in the peerage achieved by a member of the family (1660-1945) is placed at the head of the entry, even if it was not held for long.

"PEERS": Dates (1660-1945) when peerages were held provide years of legal access to the Houses of Lords (in London and Dublin - the Scottish Parliament was unicameral but included title holders) and do not mean a seat in the chamber was actually occupied unless direct evidence shows it was not assumed (due, for example, to insanity, religious disqualification, exile, imprisonment, or other known causes). Years served by elected Irish or Scottish Representative Peers in the British House of Lords are included.

"LD LT": The number of family members appointed to serve as Lord Lieutenant of a county after 1660. Until the twentieth century the office retained a considerable amount of power as well as prestige, especially in times of emergency or war. The power to nominate JPs was used to exercise control over the gentry by the magnates.

"CABINET": Dates provided for senior office holders, including Secretaries of State, etc. before the modern Cabinet emerged.

"KG, KT, KP": The number of family members who were holders of the most prestigious orders of knighthood in England and Wales, Scotland and Ireland after 1660: Knight of the Garter, Knight of the Thistle, and Knight of St. Patrick. The "Garter" was of considerable significance. An eighteenth-century magnate could be thrown into a rage and even move into political opposition by being denied one. Nineteenth-century magnates were so enamored of membership in these orders that they could be seen wearing the insignia on their dressing gowns. The Garter was the nation's reward to Winston Churchill for his service in the Second World War.

Brackets

Brackets are used to differentiate members of the English/Welsh Parliament from the Scottish and Irish Parliaments. The dates of service of English and Welsh MPs are not enclosed in brackets.

[dates] = membership in the Scottish Parliament in Edinburgh

{dates} = membership in the Irish Parliament in Dublin or TDs after 1922

Abbreviations

acq.	acquired
add.	addition
BLG	*Burke's Landed Gentry*
BP	*Burke's Peerage*
Bt	Baronet
c.	*circa* or century
CL	*Country Life*
CP	*Complete Peerage*
cr.	creation
d.	died
DNB	*Dictionary of National Biography*
E	England
EI	East India
fl.	flourishing
GB	Great Britain
HP	*History of Parliament*
I	Ireland
IoW	Isle of Wight
inher.	inherited
KC	King's Counsel
KG	Knight of the Order of the Garter
KP	Knight of the Order of St. Patrick
KT	Knight of the Order of the Thistle
Kt	Knight
Kted	Knighted
Ld Lt	Lord Lieutenant
mar.	marriage, married
MP	Member of the House of Commons
NT	National Trust
ODNB	*Oxford Dictionary of National Biography*
pa	*per annum*
PC	Privy Councilor
purch.	purchased
QC	Queen's Counsel
r.	reign
Rep	Representative
RE	Royal Engineers
remod.	remodeled
repurch.	repurchased
RN	Royal Navy

S	Scotland
TD	Member of the Irish *Dáil*
UK	United Kingdom of Great Britain and Ireland
W	Wales
WI	West Indies

Corrections or Additions

Please forward any suggestions for corrections or additions to:
Ellis Wasson ewasson@udel.edu or ewasson@towerhill.org

Introduction

"The world of the British governing class was not only small, but one of blood."
Patrick Joyce[1]

Nearly forty years ago I began collecting information about parliamentary families in the British Isles. I had both motive and opportunity. My ambition was to analyze the social origins of the ruling elite over the course of centuries; the means was provided by the accelerating publication program of the History of Parliament Trust and new biographical works on the Scottish and Irish Parliaments.[2] The arrival of data-crunching computers to do the sums also helped. The fruits of my research appeared in a series of articles in *The English Historical Review*, *The Historical Journal*, *The Economic History Review*, and *Parliamentary History*.[3] In 2000 my analysis was consolidated and extended in the book *Born to Rule: British Political Elites*. As it happened, Lawrence Stone and Jeanne Fawtier Stone, using an alternative approach based on ownership of country houses in three English counties, also published an analysis of the ruling class in *An Open Elite? England 1540-1880* (1984). In the company of a number of distinguished historians such as W. D. Rubinstein and David Spring we were able to make considerable advances in the understanding of modern Britain. The centrality of Parliament and of the great landowners in shaping the state and society in England (and also in Wales, Scotland, and Ireland) made understanding the dynamics of those "born to rule" fundamental to following the interactions of different parts of the archipelago and in tracing pathways to modernity.

My hope had always been to make the data I assembled about parliamentary families available to scholars. Other projects intervened and it has only been recently that I have had the opportunity to gather together the information in an accessible form. This compendium is the result of those labors.

These volumes contain a comprehensive account of all families in the British Isles who had at least one member sit in either house of Parliament between 1660 and 1945 and was represented in Parliament by at least three members at any time between the Middle Ages and 2015. A person who served as both a peer and a MP is counted only once for the purpose of inclusion in the list. Membership in the Scottish Parliament before abolition in 1707 or after the reconstitution in 1999 is also counted, as is membership in the Irish Parliament before 1801 or after 1922.

---

1 Patrick Joyce, *The State of Freedom: A Social History of the British State since 1800*, Cambridge, 2013, 296.

2 See the bibliography under the heading "Reference Works" for those and other sources providing data for this study.

3 Collected for publication in *The Role of Ruling Class Adaptability in the British Transition from Ancien Regime to Modern State*, Lewiston, 2010.

The total number of British and Irish families with at least one MP or peer serving in the period 1660 to 1945 connected by lineage or inheritance with a member of a "three MP/peer" family is 2937. Of these, 2352 elected a minimum of three MPs or produced three peers, or a combination of the two. The remaining 585 families were either related by blood or passed property to or from one of the 2352 stem families but produced only one or two MPs (or peers) one of who served in the period 1660 to 1945. Broken down by nationality the numbers look like this, divided between stem families and associated secondary or cadet lines with fewer than three MPs/peers.[4]

Table 1. Number of families with at least one MP or peer 1660-1945 included in this study[5]

	three or more MPs/peers	cadet/secondary families
ENGLAND	1523	331
WALES	75	22
SCOTLAND	310	131
IRELAND	444	101

The families listed here constituted the political elites of England, Wales, Scotland, and Ireland between 1660 and the First World War. Many were also leading families in the sixteenth century and even earlier, and quite a few remained active and influential until the end of the Second World War. For a variety of reasons ownership of large blocks of land and membership in Parliament ceased to be the *sine qua non* for elite status as the nineteenth century progressed, although even late in the period a core of traditional grandees were richer than the most successful industrialists, and many

4 Identifying the nationality of some families is not easy due to ownership of estates spread between several countries or parliamentary service in multiple capitals. In general, the place where the largest part of the family estate lay in the years 1660-1945 was the determining factor in assigning nationality.
5 During the years since *Born to Rule* (2000) was issued, I been able to refine and correct the pool of data published in it. A small number of families have been added to the list. Most of these were uncovered thanks to the publication of new volumes of the History of Parliament and other sources that revealed pre-1660 MPs that I had not identified. I also came across evidence relating to the transfer of landed estates via heiresses while doing further genealogical studies. The discovery of additional MPs has not significantly altered the original findings, but the percentage of English MPs in the period 1660-1715 that were members of the elite was larger than I originally portrayed. Thus the proportion of the Commons composed of MPs from the families listed in this volume (around 80% during the later seventeenth, the eighteenth, and the early nineteenth centuries) is slightly more consistent across the years 1660 to 1820 than portrayed in Figure 2.1 on page 42 of *Born to Rule*.

rising families continued to purchase landed estates and aspire to a peerage long after these ceased to be the essential foundations of wealth and power. Parliamentary families also, by and large, constituted the social elite until 1945. For an extended explanation and analysis of the evidence supporting these statements see *Born to Rule: British Political Elites*. The distinctive histories and cultures of Wales, Scotland, and Ireland meant that membership of Parliament functioned uniquely in each country and that is also studied in depth in my book.

I chose the minimum of three members of (either) house of Parliament as the standard for inclusion in the study even though this could be regarded as an arbitrary minimum. I found, however, that it was almost unknown for three or more brothers to be elected MPs or gain a peerage without at least one other generation of the family also serving in Parliament. Hence the three-MP/peer criterion ensured that only families capable of projecting status and power over more than a single generation are included.[6]

Power was tied closely to land until the twentieth century. In this list of parliamentary families, descent is traced through ownership of estates, which often passed via the female line. In many cases a husband adopted his wife's name on inheriting property and extinct titles were revived to ensure continuity and paper over the cracks. Thus the modest Smithson family founded by a London haberdasher in the 17th century ascended to the dizzying heights of wealth and power associated with the Earldom of Northumberland through a union in 1740 with the heiress to the ancient Percy patrimony. The marriage sustained a dynasty established in England in 1066. For the purpose of this study the Percys and Smithsons are treated as a single, continuous family. The Smithson/Percy Dukes of Northumberland ensconced in their new seat at medieval Alnwick Castle sent family members to Parliament (the last to serve in 1937) in an unbroken line that began in 1297. Many (usually far more prosaic) instances of such inheritances meant parliamentary families were centered in a locality for many generations. These mergers to achieve continuity were made all the more powerful by the practice of primogeniture, which generally ensured the bulk of a family's wealth and political influence remained intact over long periods. Often marriage to an heiress created a family that adopted a double-barreled name suggesting the merger of equals and multiplied the acreage available to exploit for social and political purposes.

6 A handful exceptions to the 3 MP/peer rule have been included in this volume. For example, the Huttons produced two Archbishops and two MPs, and were clearly a family of rank and influence over multiple generations. The Dixons (Lord Glentoran) produced only two MPs but also a NI Senator, a NI Assembly MP, and a Speaker of the NI Assembly, while the 3 Baron Glentoran was elected to the House of Lords in the new system established after 1999. These were families of political, social, and economic importance over multiple generations. A few other families fall into a similar category, producing, for example multiple generations of MPs and an MEP. No more than half a dozen exceptions are included in the list and none were incorporated into the data used in *Born to Rule*.

Some important families are missing from this study. Those that remained Roman Catholic in the seventeenth and eighteen centuries either do not appear or produced far fewer MPs or peers with free access to the House of Lords than their social status and wealth should have guaranteed, due to legal exclusion from Parliament and/or financial penalties imposed because of their religious faith.[7] (Wealthy families with fewer than three MPs/peers are listed in Appendix I.)

Some families (usually with only a small number of MPs) are included on the list due to their prominence in a parliamentary borough where the local commercial elite determined the outcome of elections. The number of such families is small, and a number of them went on to acquire landed estates and join the mainstream of the elite over time. Those that remained completely parochial in their origins and interests, however, were not important members of the national social and political elite.

In the several decades that have passed since I published my findings, I have had no reason to revise the conclusions relating to social mobility laid out in *Born to Rule*. If anything, the role of entrepreneurship and business in the rise of elite families was even greater than I depicted. When I have been able to find out more about generations earlier in the history of families that appeared to emerge through skilful or lucky management of landed property, I have often found some sort of commercial or business figure in the background.

---

7 Systematic suppression and dispossession of important Irish Catholic families completely removed a number of them from high social, economic, and political status. Some, including Jacobites and "wild geese", moved abroad. A few entered the titular aristocracies of Spain, Austria, and France.

List of Parliamentary Families

ABBOT

Baron Colchester (1817-1919 UK)

Origins: 1 Baron was the son of a clergyman. He was a politician and Speaker of the House of Commons 1802.

1. Charles Abbot, 1 Baron Colchester – Helston 1795-1802 Woodstock 1802-06 Oxford University 1806-17

Seat: Kidbrooke Park, Sussex (built 1733, purch. 1803, remod. c. 1805, add. 1814-15, sold 1874)
Estates: Bateman under 2000 acres. 1 Baron granted an annuity of £4000, and £3000 for his successor.
Peers: 3 peers 1817-1919
Notes: 1 Baron in ODNB.

ABBOTT

Baron Tenterden (1827-1939 UK)

Origins: 1 Baron was the son of a hairdresser. He became a barrister and Chief Justice of the King's Bench. Kt 1816.

No MPs

Seat: Hendon Place, Middlesex (purch. 1824, sold 1862)
Estates: Bateman under 2000 acres. Rubinstein - 1 Baron left £120,000 in probate in 1832.
Peers: 4 peers 1827-1939
Notes: 1 and 3 Barons in ODNB.

ABDY [Rutherford]

Origins: Alderman, London 1630 (a merchant, married the daughter of a Lord Mayor 1610, Director of East India Company). Three of his sons created Baronets.

1. Sir Robert Abdy 3 Bt – Essex 1727-48
2. Sir John Abdy 4 Bt – Essex 1748-59
3. Sir Anthony Abdy 5 Bt – Knaresborough 1763-75

4. Sir William Abdy 7 Bt – Malmesbury 1817-18
5. Sir Thomas Abdy 1 Bt – Lyme Regis 1847-52

Seats: Albyns, Essex (built c. 1587, remod. 1620, purch. c. 1654, remod. 1754, remod. 1898-1901, sold 1926, bomb damage in 1945, demolished 1954); Chobham Place, Surrey (built 17th c., acq. by mar. 1721 from a family who had held it since the later 16th c., remod. later 18th c., sold 1809, flats); Felix Hall, Essex (built 16th c., purch. 1630, rebuilt c. 1710, add. c. 1750, sold 1790, ruin)
Estates: Bateman 3121 (E) 9710
Titles: Baronets 1641-1868; 1660-1759; 1660-62; 1850-
Notes: The eldest line was seated at Felix Hall and Chobham Place. This branch eventually succeeded to Albyns on the extinction of the second line in 1759. When the senior line became extinct, the estates passed to the Rutherford family by marriage via a daughter of the 4 Baronet, and they took the name Abdy, created Baronets in 1850.

ABERCROMBY [Ogilvie] *SCOTLAND*

<u>Abercromby</u>

Origins: Acquired landed estates by the early 14th century. Held a peerage for life under James II, King of Scots. The father of the 1 Baronet was Grand Falconer in Scotland to Charles II.

1. Sir Alexander Abercromby 1 Bt – [Banffshire 1641 1643-4 1646-7 1648-51 1661-63]
2. Sir James Abercromby 2 Bt – [Banffshire 1693-1702]
3. Alexander Abercromby – [Banffshire 1706-07] Scotland 1707-08 Banffshire 1708-27
4. James Abercromby – Banffshire 1734-54
5. Sir Robert Abercromby 5 Bt – Banffshire 1812-18

Seats: Forglen House, Banffshire (medieval, rebuilt c. 1800, acq. by mar. 1803, new house built 1839-42, sold 1974); Glasshaugh House, Banffshire (old house, purch. c. 1650, rebuilt 1770, passed out of family 1781, ruinous); Birkenbog House, Banffshire (built 16th c., purch. late 16th c., rebuilt c. 1730-40, replaced by Glasshaugh as principal seat later in 18th c., abandoned later 20th c., derelict); Dunlugas House, Banffshire (old house, rebuilt c. 1680, rebuilt 1793, purch. 1877, abandoned 1970s?)
Estates: Bateman 11768 (S & I) 12395
Title: Baronet 1636-2003
Notes: Purchased Irish estates in the early 19th c.

Baron Abercromby (1801-1924 UK)

Origins: Cadet of above.

1. Alexander Abercromby – [Clackmannanshire 1703-07]
2. James Abercromby – Clackmannanshire 1761-68
3. Sir Ralph Abercromby – Clackmannanshire 1774-80 1796-98
4. Burnett Abercromby – Clackmannanshire 1788-90
5. Sir Robert Abercromby – Clackmannanshire 1798-1802
6. George Abercromby 2 Baron Abercromby – Edinburgh 1805-06 Clackmannanshire 1806-07 1812-15
7. James Abercromby 1 Baron Dunfermline – Midhurst 1807-12 Calne 1812-30 Edinburgh 1832-39
8. Sir John Abercromby – Clackmannanshire 1815-17
9. Alexander Abercromby – Clackmannanshire 1817-18
10. George Abercromby 3 Baron Abercromby – Clackmannanshire 1824-26 1830-31 Stirlingshire 1838-41 Clackmannan & Kinrosshire 1841-42

Seats: Tullibody House, Clackmannanshire (built c. 1650, purch. 1679, rebuilt 1725-43, repaired 1803, sold 1906, fire and demolished 1961); Airthrey Castle, Stirlingshire (built 1790-91, purch. 1798, sold c. 1889, institutional use); Menstrie Castle, Clackmannashire (built c. 1560, purch. 1719, sold c. 1924); Lord Dunfermline and his son lived at Colinton House, Edinburghshire (built c. 1800-06, purch. 1839, remod. c. 1840, sold c. 1924, institutional use)
Estates: Bateman 15264 (S) 14959. The first four holders of the Barony of Abercromby were granted an annuity of £2000 pa.
Title: Baron Dunfermline 1839-68 UK
Peers: 6 peers 1821-52 1839-68 1859-1924
2 Lds Lt
1 in Cabinet 1834
Notes: 1 Baron Dunfermline was Speaker of the House of Commons and in ODNB, along with a number of other family members.

Baron Banff (1642-1803 S)

Origins: A cadet line of the Earls of Airlie (see Ogilvy) that broke off in the mid-15th century. Seated in Banffshire by 1500. Kt. 1503.

1. Sir Alexander Ogilvy 1 Bt – [Banff 1702-07]

Seats: Forglen House, Banffshire (medieval castle, purch. 1637, rebuilt c. 1800, passed by mar. to Abercrombys 1803); Inchdruer (Inchdrewer) Castle, Banffshire (purch.

and built mid-16th c., fire 1713, passed to Abercrombys by mar. 1803, derelict, recently rebuilt); Dunlugas House, Banffshire (old house, rebuilt 1680 and 1793, sold c. 1780)
Title: Baronet 1627-1803; 1701-1803
Peers: [3 peers 1660-68 1706-07]
Notes: Family extinct 1803. The senior line was seated at Pitmeddan in the 14th century. The Barons Abercromby descended from a younger son of the 1 Baronet. On the death of the 8 Baron Banff, Forglen House passed to his eldest sister, wife of Sir George Abercromby 4 Bt of Birkenbog, Banffshire. 1 Baron Banff in ODNB.

ACHESON [Sparrow] *IRELAND*

Earl of Gosford (1806- I)

Origins: A burgess in Edinburgh (Gosford) 1605, JP for Haddington 1610. **First [MP 1625].** To Ireland 1610, held legal office and created Bt. 1628, acquired estates there by 1634. High Sheriff of Armagh 1657.

1. Sir Nicholas Acheson 4 Bt – {County Armagh 1695-99}
2. Sir Arthur Acheson 5 Bt – {Mullingar 1727-49}
3. Archibald Acheson 1 Viscount Gosford {Dublin University 1741-60 County Armagh 1761-76 Enniskillen 1776}
4. Arthur Acheson 1 Earl of Gosford – {Old Leighlin 1783-90}
5. Archibald Acheson 2 Earl of Gosford – {County Armagh 1797-1800} 1801-07
6. Archibald Acheson 3 Earl of Gosford – County Armagh 1830-47

Seats: Gosford Castle, Armagh (acq. and built early 17th c., destroyed 1641, rebuilt later 17th c., remod. 1780s, burned 1805, rebuilt 1819-52, add. 1859-63, abandoned 1921, sold 1958, institutional use); Worlingham Hall, Suffolk (built late 17th c., purch. by Sparrows 1755, inher. by mar. with Sparrow heiress 1822 by 2 Earl, sold 1849)
Estates: Bateman 18594 (I) 17934. Owned 3000 acres in 2001.
Titles: Baron Gosford 1776 I; Viscount Gosford 1785 I; Baron Worlingham 1835- UK; Baron Acheson 1847- UK; Baronet 1628-
Peers: {2 peers 1776-1800} 1 Irish Rep peer 1811-49 4 peers 1835-49 1847-1945
3 Lds Lt 19th, 20th
2 KP 19th, 20th
Notes: The rebuilding of the castle 1819-50 cost £80,000. Land sales began in 1876, and the estate was largely gone after 1903. Contents of Gosford Castle sold 1921. 2 Earl in ODNB.

Sparrow

Origins: From Ipswich. The 2 Earl of Gosford married Mary, daughter and heiress of Robert Sparrow of Worlingham in 1805.

1. Robert Sparrow – Bedford 1774-75

Seat: Worlingham, Suffolk (older house, purch. 1755, rebuilt c. 1800, passed by mar. to 2 Earl of Gosford 1822)

ACLAND [Dyke, Palmer, Troyte]

Origins: Settled at Akeland (Accolem) in Devon in 12th century. **First MP 1586 (for Devon 1607-11).** Kt 1604.

1. Sir Hugh Acland 5 Bt – Barnstaple 1679 Tiverton 1685
2. Arthur Acland – Barnstaple 1679-80
3. John Acland – Callington 1702-03
4. Richard Acland – Barnstaple 1708-13
5. Sir Hugh Acland 6 Bt – Barnstaple 1721-27
6. Sir Thomas Dyke-Acland 3 Bt – Devon 1746-47 Somerset 1767-68
7. John Dyke-Acland – Callington 1774-78
8. John Acland-Palmer – Bridgwater 1781-84
9. Sir Thomas Dyke-Acland 10 Bt – Devon 1812-18 1820-31 N. Devon 1837-57
10. Sir Thomas Dyke-Acland 11 Bt – W. Somerset 1837-47 N. Devon 1865-85 Wellington Div. Somerset 1885-86
11. Sir Thomas Dyke Acland 12 Bt – E. Cornwall 1882-85 Launceston Div. Cornwall 1885-92
12. Sir Arthur Dyke Acland 13 Bt – Rotherham Div. W. R. Yorkshire 1885-99
13. Sir Francis Dyke Acland 14 Bt – Richmond Div. N. R. Yorkshire 1906-10 Camborne Div. Cornwall 1910-22 Tiverston Div. Devon 1923-24 N. Cornwall 1932-39
14. Sir Gilbert Acland Troyte – Tiverton Div. Devon 1924-45
15. Sir Richard Dyke Acland 15 Bt – Barnstaple 1935-45 Gravesend Div. Kent 1947-55

Seats: Killerton Park (House), Devon (built later 16th c., acq. later 16th c., rebuilt 1778-79, add. c. 1830, donated to NT with 17,000 acres 1943); Wooleigh (Woodleigh), Devon (medieval, acq. by mar. later 16th c., declined to farm house status in the 18th c.); Holnicote, Somerset (medieval, rebuilt early 18th c., acq. 1745, fire 1799, rebuilt early 19th c., fire 1851, rebuilt 1873, sold 1944 and to NT, hotel); Sprydoncote Lodge, Devon (acq. later 16th c., NT 1943); Trerice, Cornwall (medieval, rebuilt 1570-73, acq. by mar. from the Arundells 1802, NT 1943)
Estates: Bateman 39896 (E) 34785; Troyte property after 1852 6807 (E) 7408

Titles: Baronet 1644- ; 1677- ; 1890-
1 in Cabinet 1892-95
Notes: Succeeded to the Wroth estates in 1721 (see Wroth). The 10, 11, 13, and 15 Bts and other members of the family in ODNB.

ACTON

Baron Acton (1869-UK)

Origins: Family at Aldenham from the 14th century. **First MP 1378 for Shropshire.** High Sheriff 1383. **Several other MPs 1449-1644, one for county.** Bt 1643. A line of lawyers purchased some ex-monastic land 1546 but later sold it. Also an ironmaster in the mid-16th century. A junior line of Elmley Lovatt, Worcestershire produced **two MPs in the 16th century**.

1. Sir Walter Acton 2 Bt – Bridgnorth 1660
2. Sir Edward Acton 3 Bt – Bridgnorth 1689-1705
3. Sir Whitmore Acton 4 Bt – Bridgnorth 1710-13
4. John Dalberg-Acton 1 Baron Acton – Carlow 1859-65 Bridgnorth 1865-66

Seats: Aldenham Hall, Shropshire (acq. and built 14th c., rebuilt 1691, rebuilt 1713-14, remod. 1820s, sold 1947); Acton Round Hall, Shropshire (built c. 1695, sold 20th c.)
Estates: Bateman 6335 (E) 7596
Title: Bt 1643-
Peers: 3 peers 1869-1945
Notes: Estates were divided among heiresses in 1621. Aldenham passed in 1791 to a younger branch descended from a younger son of the 2 Bt who coverted to Roman Catholicism and was prime minister of the Kingdom of the Two Sicilies with large estates in Calabria. He married the Duchess of Dalberg in 1832. Lord Acton was perhaps the most celebrated academic historian of the 19th century. 1 Baron and other members of the family in ODNB.

ADAIR (Adare) *ENGLAND & IRELAND*

Baron Waveney (1873-86 UK)

Origins: Scots at Kinhilt, Wigtownshire in the 15th century who went to Ireland c. 1620s. Married the daughter of a Baronet 1608. Kt and **first [MP 1639 for Wigtownshire]**. Sheriff 1695. Continued to hold estates in Scotland and Ireland. An Army agent made a fortune and purchased the estate at Flixton in Suffolk in the 18th century.

1. Sir Robert Adair – {Antrim 1692-93}
2. Robert Adair – {Philipstown 1727-37}

3. Robert Adair 1 Baron Waveney – Cambridge 1847-52 1854-57
4. Sir Hugh Adair 3 Bt – Ipswich 1847-74

Seats Flixton Hall Suffolk (medieval, rebuilt 1615, purch. 1753, rebuilt after fire 1846-55, remod. 1888-92, sold 1950, demolished 1952); Ballymena Castle, Antrim (acq. 1620, built c. 1626, fire 1740, new house built 1865-70s, most of estate sold 1904, castle sold and demolished 1957)
Estates: Bateman 19252 (E & I) 23395. Rubinstein – Alexander Adair left £700,000 in probate in 1834.
Title: Baronet 1838-1988
Peer: 1 peer 1873-86
1 Ld Lt 19th

ADAM *SCOTLAND*

Origins: William Adam and his sons made a fortune in ordnance contracts, coal, salt, brickmaking, ironmaking, glassmaking, building, and, supremely, architecture. Purchased almost 4000 acres early 18th century.

1. Robert Adam – Kinross-shire 1768-74
2. William Adam – Gatton 1774-80 Wigtown Burghs 1780-84 Elgin Burghs 1784-90 Ross-shire 1790-94 Kincardineshire 1806-12
3. Sir Charles Adam – Kinross-shire 1831-32 Clackmannan & Kinross 1832-41 1846-47
4. William Adam – Clackmannan & Kinross 1859-80

Seats: Blair Adam, Kinross-shire (purch. 1731, built 1733, remod. 1775, remod. 1815-16 and 1833 and 1859, still own); Woodstone, Kincardineshire
Estates: Bateman 4277 (S) 3739
Title: Baronet 1882-1922
3 Lds Lt 19th, 20th
Notes: Serious financial setbacks led to Blair Adam standing empty 1785-96; fortunes recouped by a lawyer in the first half of the 19th c. First MP and other members of the family in ODNB.

ADDERLEY [Bowyer, Gresley]

<u>Baron Norton</u> (1878- UK)

Origins: Gentry family of medieval origins. Humphrey Adderley (1512-98) rose to prominence as Master of the Wardrobe to Henry VIII. High Sheriff under Elizabeth I. Lawyer purchased estates 1558. Kt reign of Charles I.

1. Sir William Adderley – New Windsor 1690-93
2. Charles Adderley 1 Baron Norton – N. Staffordshire 1841-78

Seats: Hams Hall, Warwickshire (acq. 1637, built house, rebuilt 1764, fire 1890, estate sold 1911, house demolished 1920 and partly rebuilt, site a power station); Norton, Staffordshire (medieval hall, family not resident in modern period); Fillongley Hall, Warwickshire (purch. c. 1820, built 1824-25, add. 1840-41, still own but offered for sale)
Estates: Bateman 4515 (E) 16225
Peers: 6 peers 1878-1945
1 in Cabinet 1874-78
Notes: Owned urban property in Birmingham and coal mines in Staffordshire. 1 Baron Norton and two others in ODNB.

<u>Bowyer</u>

Origins: First Bowyer of Knipersley **MP (Newcastle-u-Lyme) 1411**. Grocer in London mid-Tudor period. **At least a dozen further Bowyer MPs in 16th and 17th centuries**.

1. Sir John Bowyer 1 Bt – Staffordshire 1646 Newcastle-u-Lyme 1656, 1660
2. Sir John Bowyer 2 Bt – Warwick 1677-79 Staffordshire 1679-81

Seats: Norton-le-Moors Hall, Staffordshire (medieval hall became farm house, passed by mar. to Adderleys); Knipersley (Knypersley) Hall (Park), Staffordshire (medieval, acq. by mar. 14th c., passed 1702 by mar. to Gresleys)
Title: Baronet 1627-80; 1660-1702
Notes: On the death of the 4 Baronet of Norton his estates passed to his daughter Mary, who married Charles Adderley, ancestor of the Lords Norton. The 4 Baronet's youngest daughter, Dorothy, succeeded to Knipersley and married Sir Thomas Gresley 4 Bt (see below).

<u>Gresley</u>

Origins: Descended from Nigel de Stafford, a genuine "baron" of the William the Conqueror era and held Drakelow from Norman times until 1931. Kt 15th century. (Craven and Stanley, *Derbyshire Country House*, 72) **First MP (Derbyshire) 1340. Seven further MPs for Derbyshire and Staffordshire 15th, 16th, 17th centuries**.

1. Sir Thomas Gresley 5 Bt – Lichfield 1753
2. Sir Roger Gresley 8 Bt – Durham 1830-31 New Romney 1831 S. Derbyshire 1835-37
3. Sir Thomas Gresley 10 Bt – S. Derbyshire 1868

Seats: Drakelow Park (Hall), Derbyshire (acq. by 1100, medieval house, rebuilt c. 1543, rebuilt 1723, rebuilt 1806, remod. 1830, remod. 1870s, remod. 1901-04, sold 1931-33, demolished 1934); Netherseal Hall, Derbyshire (acq. by mar. 17th c., built 1620, add. c. 1860s, remod. 1908-11, sold 1927, demolished 1938); Knypersley Hall, Staffordshire (medieval, acq. 1702 by mar., rebuilt 18th c., sold 1809, demolished 20th c.)
Estates: Bateman 3747 (E) 8511. In 1600 held 14,500 acres.
Title: Baronet 1611-1978
Notes: One of the most ancient families in the English landed elite. Sir Thomas Gresley (MP Derbyshire 1401-21, Staffordshire 1413-19) went on the Agincourt campaign. The grandson of the 9 Bt, Sir H. N. Gresley, was a great locomotive engineer. Several members of the family are in the ODNB.

ADDINGTON

<u>Viscount Sidmouth</u> (1805- UK)

Origins: Father of first MP was a well-known doctor in the 18th century. First MP was a professional politician.

1. Henry Addington 1 Viscount Sidmouth – Devizes 1784-1805
2. John Addington – Truro 1787-90 Winchslsea 1794-96 Wendover 1796-1802 Bossiney 1802 Harwich 1803-18
3. William Addington 3 Viscount Sidmouth – Devizes 1863-64

Seats: Up Ottery Manor, Devon (old house, purch. c. 1780, rebuilt 1845-47, sold 1954, demolished 1962); Early (Erleigh) Court, Berkshire (built 16th c., rebuilt 17th c., remod. 18th c., acq. by mar. 1836, sold 1932, demolished 1935)
Estates: Bateman 5905 (E) 8220
Peers: 5 peers 1805-1945
1 in Cabinet 1801-07 1812-24
Notes: 1 Viscount was Prime Minister. (See Christie, *Non-Elite MPs*, 102) A number of members of the family including the father of the 1 Viscount and the 1 Viscount in ODNB.

ADEANE [Jones]

<u>Baron Adeane</u> (1972-84 UKLife)

Origins: Claimed old descent. Main property in 18th century at Chalgrove. First MP was a general. He married the heiress of an East India Director who purchased and built Babraham in 1770.

1. James Adeane – Cambridge 1780-89 Cambridgeshire 1789-1802
2. Henry Adeane – Cambridgeshire 1830-32
3. Henry Adeane – Cambridgeshire 1857-65

Seats: Babraham Hall, Cambridgeshire (see Jones below, acq. by mar. 1774 from Jones, rebuilt 1833-37, add. 1864, house and some land sold 1948 and rest of estate c. 1982); Chalgrove, Oxfordshire (acq. 17th c., sold 1839)
Estates: Bateman 3448 (E) 5003
2 Lds Lt 19th, 20th
Notes: Royal secretaries in the 20th century. 1 Baron in ODNB.

Jones

Origins: East India Company merchant purchased Brabraham 1770. Rose from lowly origins to a Director of East India Company. Robert Jones MP daughter and heiress married James Adeane who succeeded to estates.

1. Robert Jones – Huntingdon 1754-74

Seat: Brabraham Hall, Cambridgeshire (medieval, rebuilt c. 1580, demolished 1767, purch. and built new house 1770, passed to Adeanes by mar. 1774)
Estates: Purchased Brabraham for £27,500 and had wealth in funds worth £88,000.

AFFLECK

Origins: First MP was the son of an East India Company official who purchased Dalham 1714. First Bt was a naval officer.

1. Gilbert Affleck – Cambridge 1722-27 1737-41
2. John Affleck – Suffolk 1743-61 Amersham 1767-68
3. Sir Edmund Affleck 1 Bt – Colchester 1782-88

Seats: Dalham Hall, Suffolk (built 1704-05, purch. 1714, sold 1901); Fingringhoe Hall, Essex (built 16th c., remod. 1660s and 1740s, purch. 1765, sold 1929, fire 1970s)
Estates: Bateman 3764 (E) 4776
Title: Baronet 1782-1939
Notes: Family ran into serious financial trouble in 1890s in part due to fraud. In Australia in 20th c. 1 Bt and brother in ODNB.

AGAR [Ellis, Hunt, Robartes] *IRELAND & ENGLAND*

Viscount Clifden (1781-1974 I)

Origins: Moved from Yorkshire to Kilkenny mid-17th century with Cromwell and acquired estates. Purchased additional land in the early 18th century. Archbishop in 18th century.

1. James Agar – {Old Leiglin 1703-13 Gowran 1713-14 Callan 1715-27 St. Canice 1727-33}
2. Henry Agar – {Gowran 1727-46}
3. James Agar 1 Viscount Clifden – {Gowran 1753-60 County Kilkenny 1761-76 Gowran 1776}
4. James Agar {Gowran 1747-60 Tulsk 1768-69}
5. George Agar 1 Baron Callan – {Callan 1776-90}
6. Henry Welbore Ellis Agar 2 Viscount Clifden – {County Kilkenny 1783-88} Heytesbury 1793-1802
7. Sir Emanuel Agar – Sudbury 1807-12
8. George Welbore Agar Ellis 1 Baron Dover – Heytesbury 1818-20 Seaford 1820-26 Ludgershall 1826-30 Okehampton 1830-1
9. Thomas Agar-Robartes 1 Baron Robartes – E. Cornwall 1847-68
10. Leopold Agar Ellis 5 Viscount Clifden – County Kilkenny 1857-74
11. Thomas Agar Ellis Robartes 6 Viscount Clifden – E. Cornwall 1880-82
12. Thomas Agar Ellis – Bodmin Div. Cornwall 1906 St. Austell Div. Cornwall 1908-15

Seats: Gowran Castle, Kilkenny (old castle, acq. c. 1660, fire and new house 1713, demolished 1816, new house 1817-19, add. c. 1840, passed by mar. to the Lords Annaly 1944, sold 1955, derelict 1990s); Ringwood (The Rower), Kilkenny (resident 18th c.); Lanhydrock House, Cornwall (acq. by mar. from Robartes via the Hunts 1798, fire 1881, rebuilt, 1953 given to NT); Tylney Hall, Hampshire (tenanted by 1 Baron Mendip 18th c.); Wimpole House, Cambridgeshire (built c. 1640-70, remod. 1693-1705, add. 1713-30, remod. 1742-47 and 1791-1806, add. c. 1840, purch. 1894, sold 1938, NT 1976); Holdenby House, Northamptonshire (late 16th c., passed to the Crown 1607, dismantled 1651, purch. 1802, rebuilt 1873-75, add. 1887-88, passed by inher. to Lowthers 1945)
Estates: Bateman 49017 (E & I) 38915. Rubinstein – 1 Baron Callan left £160,000 in probate 1815 and 2 Viscount Clifden £180,000 in 1836.
Titles: Earl of Brandon 1758-89 I; Baron Gowran 1776-1974 I; Baron Callan 1790-1815 I; Baron Mendip 1794- GB; Baron Dover 1831-99 UK; Baron Robartes 1869-1974 UK
Peers: {3 peers 1777-1800 1790-1800} 1 Irish Rep peer 1801-15 8 peers 1802-36 1833-66 1884-99 1869-1930 1882-1945
1 Ld Lt 20th
Notes: Henry Agar married Anne Ellis, sister and heiress of Welbore Ellis, Baron Mendip of Tylney Hall, Hampshire. Their son was created 1 Viscount Clifden. The 2 Viscount succeeded by special remainder as Baron Mendip and took the additional

name Ellis. A younger son of the 1 Viscount married the daughter of Thomas Hunt and grandniece and heiress of Henry Robartes 3 Earl of Radnor. Their son was created 1 Baron Robartes. His son succeeded as 6 Viscount Clifden. Holdenby House passed to the 4 Viscount's sister, Lady Annaly. Family extinct 1974. 1 Baron Dover in ODNB.

Baron Mendip (1794-1974 GB)

Origins: The Ellis family rose through the church and politics in the 17th century. Bishop of Meath, Secretary of State to James II and William III.

1. Welbore Ellis 1 Baron Mendip – Cricklade 1741-47
   Weymouth & Melcombe Regis 1747-61 Aylesbury 1761-68
   Weymouth 1774-90 Petersfield 1791-94

Seat: Tylney Hall, Hampshire (tenanted in 18th c.)
Peer: 1 peer 1794-1802
1 in Cabinet 1762-65 1777-94
Notes: 1 Baron in ODNB.

Earl of Radnor (1679-1757 E)

Origins: The Robartes family acquired great wealth in the Tudor period in the tin trade as merchants and bankers in Truro. Purchased estates late 16th and early 17th centuries. Sheriff 1614. Kt 1616. **First MP 1623.** 1 Baron Robartes a merchant and userer in Truro. Purchased his peerage via the Duke of Buckingham in 1625.

1. Robert Robartes Viscount Bodmin – Cornwall 1660 Bossiney 1661-79
2. Francis Robartes – Bossiney 1673-79 Cornwall 1679-81 1685-87 Lostwithiel 1689-90 Cornwall 1690-95 Tregony 1695-1702
3. Charles Robartes 2 Earl of Radnor – Bossiney 1679-81 Cornwall 1685
4. Russell Robartes – Bodmin 1693-1702 Lostwithiel 1702-08 Bodmin 1708-13
5. Hender Robartes – Bodmin 1753-83

Seats: Lanhydrock, Cornwall (purch. 1620, built c. 1634-42, passed by mar. to the Hunts 1758 and in 1798 to the Lords Clifden, see above); Wimpole Hall, Cambridgeshire (built c. 1640-70, remod. 1693-1705, purch. 1686, sold 1710)
Estates: Bateman 22234 (E) 30730; est. worth £7000 pa post 1660.
Title: Baron Robartes 1625-1757 E
Peers: 4 peers 1660-1757
1 Ld Lt 17th-18th
1 in Cabinet Council 1661-73 1679-84
Notes: 1 Earl and one of his sons in ODNB.

Hunt

Origins: Alderman in Shrewsbury 1613. High Sheriff 1656. Barrister late 17th century.

1. George Hunt – Bodmin 1753-84
2. Thomas Hunt – Bodmin 1784-89
3. George Ward Hunt – N. Northamptonshire 1857-77
4. Rowland Hunt – Ludlow Div. Shropshire 1903-18

Seats: Mollington Hall, Cheshire (purch. 1699, rebuilt 1756-7, sold 1796, demolished 1937); Boreatton Park, Shropshire (purch. 1664, built 1850s, sold c. 1986, school); Wadenhoe House, Northamptonshire (built 1617, Wards purch. c. 1714, remod. 1858, passed to Hunts, who owned into 20th c., sold, conference center); Boreatton Old Hall, Shropshire (purch. 1664, old house, still own)
Estates: Bateman 3919 (E) 7046
1 in Cabinet 1868 1874-77
Notes: Sir Edward Ward of Wadenhoe was Chief Baron of the Exchequer 1695. His heiress married a Hunt. The 4th and last Earl of Radnor left 1758 Lanhydrock to his nephews Thomas and George Hunt, sons of his sister by Thomas Hunt of Mollington. In 1798 it passed to the Agars. George Ward Hunt is in ODNB.

Earl of Normanton (1806- I)

Origins: Descended from a younger brother of the 1 Viscount Clifden. 1 Earl was Archbishop of Dublin and amassed a large fortune through clerical preferment and income.

1. James Agar 3 Earl of Normanton – Wilton 1841-52

Seat: Somerley, Hampshire (built 1792-95, purch. 1825, add. 1850-51, add. 1868-70, still own)
Estates: Bateman 42961 (E & I) 48280; 1 Earl died worth £400,000 in 1809. Owned 6000 acres in 2001.
Titles: Baron Somerton 1795- I; Viscount Somerton 1800- I; Baron Somerton 1873- UK
Peers: {1 peer 1795-1800} 3 peers 1873-1945
Notes: 1 Earl in ODNB.

AGLIONBY [Bateman, Yates]

Origins: First recorded in Cumberland in the 12th century. Rose through the law in early 16th century. High Sheriff under Henry VIII. **First MP Carlisle 1368. Seven additional MPs all but one sitting for Carlisle 1529-1625.**

1. Henry Aglionby – Carlisle 1721-27
2. Henry Bateman Aglionby – Cockermouth 1832-54
3. Francis Aglionby Yates – E. Cumberland 1837-40
4. Henry Aglionby Bateman – Cockermouth 1832-54

Seats: (The) Nunnery, Cumberland (medieval, acq. 1694, rebuilt c. 1727, passed to Yates family by mar. 1785, took name Aglionby, then by mar. to the Bateman family in 1840 who also took name Aglionby, sold 1919); Newbiggin Hall, Cumberland (medieval, rebuilt c. 1720, remod. 1820-26, sold 1855).
Notes: Estates divided among four daughters in 1785. They eventually passed to an American branch of the family in the second half of the 19th century. One in ODNB.

AGNEW [Vans, Vanse, Vaus] *SCOTLAND*

Agnew

Origins: Medieval landowners. Acquired Lochnaw 1426. Hereditary Sheriff of Wigtown 1451-1747. First knight 16th century, father of 1st Bt. **First [MP for Wigtownshire 1628-44].**

1. Sir Andrew Agnew 2 Bt – [Wigtownshire 1644 1645-7 1648-9 1665 1667 1669-70]
2. Sir Andrew Agnew 3 Bt – [Wigtownshire 1685-6 1689-1700]
3. Sir Andrew Agnew 7 Bt – Wigtonwshire 1830-37
4. Sir Andrew Agnew 8 Bt – Wigtownshire 1856-68
5. Sir Andrew Agnew 9 Bt – S. Edinburgh 1900-06

Seat: Lochnaw Castle, Wigtownshire (acq. 1426, built later 15th/early 16th c., add. 1663 and 1704, add. 1819-22, sold 1921, institutional use, part demolished 1953)
Estates: Bateman 14000 (S) 11100
Title: Baronet 1629-
Notes: 5 and 7 Bts in ODNB. A cadet line established a famous firm of art dealers in London with many members in ODNB. Of that line seated at Rougham Hall, Suffolk (purch. 1904- still own): Sir William Agnew 1 Bt (cr. 1895) **MP S E Lancashire 1880-85 Stretford 1885-86** and Sir George Agnew 2 Bt **MP W. Salford 1906-18**.

Vans-Agnew

Origins: The Vans family claimed descent from a Provençal family who came over with William the Conqueror. Prominent judge and ambassador **[MP for Wigtownshire 1593]. A second [MP also for the county 1617].**

1. Patrick Vans(e) – Wigtownshire 1710-11 Wigtown Burghs 1715-22
2. Robert Vans-Agnew – Wigtownshire 1873-80

Seats: Barnbarroch House, Wigtownshire (built 1780, remod. 1806-08, fire 1941, ruin); Stranraer Park, Wigtownshire (acq. 17th c., demolished later 19th c.)
Estates: Bateman 6777 (S) 6696
Notes: A descendent of a younger son of the 1 Agnew Bt married John Vans of Barnbarroch. Their son took the name Vans-Agnew. Two in ODNB.

AITKEN

Baron Beaverbrook (1917- UK)

Origins: 1 Baron Beaverbrook, son of a Canadian Presbyterian minister, was a self-made banker and newspaper proprietor who settled in England in 1910 and also became a politician. Kt 1911.

1. William Maxwell Aitken 1 Baron Beaverbrook – Ashton-u-Lyme 1910-16
2. John William Aitken 2 Baron Beaverbrook – Holborn 1945-50
3. Sir William Aitken – Bury St. Edmonds Div. Suffolk 1950-64
4. Sir Jonathan Aitken – Thanet E. 1974-83 Thanet S. 1983-97

Seat: Cherkly, Surrey (built c. 1870, fire, rebuilt 1894, purch. 1911, bomb damage 1943, family departed 1994, sold 2011)
Title: Baronet 1916-
Peer: 1 peer 1917-45
1 in Cabinet 1918-19 1940-45
Notes: 1 Baron in ODNB.

AKERS-DOUGLAS *ENGLAND & SCOTLAND*

Viscount Chilston (1911- UK)

Origins: The original Douglas was a younger son of a knightly family who acquired Baads in 1551. Soldiers, ministers, and merchants in the 18th century. The daughter and eventual heiress of Alexander Douglas of Baads married in 1752 Aretas Akers of Malling Abbey. Their great-great-grandson succeeded to Baads and was created 1 Viscount Chilston (a barrister and politician). The Akers family emerged in the West Indies c. 1620 as planters, where they stayed for six generations before returning to England and purchasing landed estates.

1. John Douglas – Hindon 1768-74 Weobly 1774-83
2. James Stoddart Douglas – Rochester 1841-47
3. Aretas Akers-Douglas 1 Viscount Chilston – E. Kent 1880-85 St. Augustine's Div. Kent 1885-1911

Seats: Chilston Park, Kent (built c. 1500, add. c. 1710-28, add. 1782, purch. by Douglas family 1821, inher. by Akers family 1875, add. 1880, sold 1983); Baads, Edinburghshire (acq. and built 1551, sold 1720, castle burned 1736, repurchased 1787, sold 20th c.?); (West) Malling Abbey, Kent (medieval, fell into ruin 17th and early 17th c., rebuilt mid-18th c., purch. c. 1850, sold 1892); Craigs, Dumfriesshire
Estates: Bateman 15687 (E & S) 13090. Rubinstein - George Douglas left £160,000 in probate in 1833.
Peers: 2 peers 1911-45
1 in Cabinet 1895-1905
Notes: 1 and 2 Viscounts in ODNB.

ALCOCK *IRELAND*

Origins: A merchant family that rose to wealth in the eighteenth century and came to dominate the city of Waterford. Entered the gentry by mid century. Sheriff 1740. Kt. 1785.

1. Henry Alcock – {Clomines 1761-68}
2. Henry Alcock – {Waterford 1783-97 Fethard 1797-99}
3. William Alcock – {Fethard 1764-68}
4. William Alcock – {Waterford 1797-1800} 1801-03 County Wexford 1807-12

Seat: Wilton Castle (House), Wexford (castle built 1247, purch. 1658, house built c. 1700, rebuilt 1837-44, burned 1923, sold 1920s, part restored 2009)
Estates: Bateman 9121 (I) 4672. Reduced to 2,000 acres by 1923, sold 1920s. Family lived in England post 1922.

ALEXANDER *IRELAND & ENGLAND*

<u>Earl of Caledon</u> (1800- I)

Origins: A Presbyterian minister from Scotland to Ireland by 1613 and granted land 1663. Merchants in Londonderry in the early 18th century. A nabob returned from India and purchased estates worth £600,000 c. 1770. Sheriff 1780. Other family members also East India merchants and Dublin bankers.

1. James Alexander 1 Earl of Caledon – {Londonderry 1775-90}
2. Robert Alexander – {Dingle 1777-83 Newton 1797-1800}
3. Henry Alexander – {Newton 1788-90 Askeaton 1790-97 Londonderry 1797-1800} County Londonderry 1801-02 Old Sarum 1802-06
4. DuPre Alexander 2 Earl of Caledon – {Newton 1800}
5. James Alexander – Old Sarum 1812-32

6. Josias Alexander – Old Sarum 1820-28 1830-32
7. Robert Alexander – Barnstaple 1826-30
8. James Alexander 3 Earl of Caledon – Tyrone 1837-39
9. Nathaniel Alexander – Antrim 1841-53

Seats: Caledon (House), Tyrone (medieval, rebuilt 17th c., demolished later 18th c., purch. 1776 for £96,400, new house rebuilt 1779-84, remod. 1806-13, add. 1825, remod. 1832-33, still own); Tyttenhanger Park, Hertfordshire (built 16th c., rebuilt 1654-55, remod. early and late 18th c., Alexanders acq. by mar. 1834, sold 1973, commercial use); Portglenone House, Antrim (built 1823, add. 1850, sold 1854, repurch. 1865, sold 1948, now an abbey); Forkhill (Forkill) House, Armagh (built c. 1780s, add. c. 1800, purch. c. 1840, burned 1920s); Acton House, Armagh (built 1619, rebuilt 1790, acq. later 19th c., still own); Boom Hall, Londonderry (purch. 1770, rebuilt c. 1772, sold 1849, now a ruin)
Estates: Bateman 34060 (I & E) 22321; 8850 (I) 6272; 8324 (I) 5151; 3165 (I) 3192. In 1817 the Irish estate was valued at £200,000 and that in Wiltshire at nearly £74,000. Rubinstein – Josias Alexander MP left £250,000 in probate in 1839. Owned 9400 acres in 2001.
Titles: Baron Caledon 1790- I; Viscount Caledon 1797- I; Viscount Alexander 1946- UK; Earl Alexander of Tunis 1952- UK
Peers: {1 peer 1790-1800} 4 Irish Rep peers 1805-39 1841-55 1877-98 1898-1945
2 Ld Lt 19th, 20th
2 KP 19th
1 KG 20th
1 in Cabinet 1952-54
Notes: Tyttenhanger came to the Alexanders via the Pope family. The founder of the Popes rose in the Tudor bureaucracy under Henry VIII and Mary I and acquired land at the Dissolution of the Monasteries. Granted arms 1535, **first MP 1536**, Privy Council 1544. His nephew was created Earl of Downe in 1628 (see North). No subsequent MPs. His seat at Tyttenhanger, Hertfordshire (acq. 1547) descended through the female line to the Blounts and then to the Earls of Caledon. A younger son of the 4 Earl of Caledon was a senior commander in the Second World War and later Minister of Defence, created Earl Alexander of Tunis in 1952. Three members of the family are in the ODNB.

Alexander

Origins: descended from a common ancestor (18th c.) with the Earls of Caledon. Operated the largest flour mill in Ireland in the mid-19th c.

1. John Alexander – Carlow 1853-59

Seats: Milford House, Carlow (acq. c. 1790, built c. 1820, still resident); Roe Park (Daisy Hill), Londonderry (rebuilt 1743, add. 1782, acq. c. 1850, sold, hotel)
Estates: Bateman 2375 (I) 2809; 5733 (I) 4236

ALFORD

Origins: Gentry family that held manorial land from 1220. Raised to prominence in the mid-16th century. Entered the service of Lord Burghley 1547. Branches in Sussex and Yorkshire. **First MP 1558. Seven additional members of the family were elected to the Commons between 1563 and 1648**. Kt mid-17th century.

1. John Alford – Midhurst 1679-81 Bramber 1689-90

Seats: Offington, Sussex (medieval, purch. 1601, passed out of family by mar. sec. half 17th c.); Holt Castle, Denbighshire (built c. 1282, demolished late 17th c.)
Notes: Two members of the family in ODNB.

ALLEN I [Mayne] *IRELAND*

Viscount Allen (1717-1845 I)

Origins: A master builder went to Ireland towards the end of the 16th century and acquired the large Stillorgan estate. Merchant in Dublin in 17th century, Lord Mayor 1673. Sheriff 1709. The latter's son was elected {MP 1692} and raised to the peerage in 1717.

1. John Allen 1 Viscount Allen – {County Dublin 1692-93 County Carlow 1695-99 County Dublin 1703-13 County Wicklow 1713-14 County Dublin 1715-17}
2. Joshua Allen 2 Viscount Allen – {County Kildare 1709-26}
3. Robert Allen – {Carysfort 1713-14 County Wicklow 1715-41}
4. Francis Allen – {County Kildare 1725-27}
5. Richard Allen – {Athy 1715-27 County Kildare 1727-45}
6. John Allen 3 Viscount Allen – {Carysfort 1733-42}
7. John Allen 4 Viscount Allen – {County Wicklow 1742-45}
8. Joshua Allen 5 Viscount Allen – Eye 1762-70
9. Richard Allen – {Harristown 1776-83}

Seat: Stillorgan House (Park), Dublin (acq. later 17th c., built 1695, passed by mar. to Probys (see) 1745, demolished 1860)
Worth £4500 pa in 1713 and £15,000 pa in 1799.
Peers: {5 peers 1717-1800}
Notes: Estates passed on the death of the 3 Viscount through the marriages of his sisters to the Maynes of Arnos Grove (see below) and to the Earls of Carysfort (see Proby). The last Viscounts in the 19th century were poor.

<u>Baron Newhaven</u> (1776-94 I)

Origins: Lisbon merchants in the 18th century. The 1 Baron Newhaven married the sister of the 3 Viscount Allen.

1. William Mayne 1 Baron Newhaven – {Carysfort 1761-76} Canterbury 1774-80 Gatton 1780-90
2. Robert Mayne – Gatton 1774-82

Seats: Arnos Grove, Middlesex (old house, rebuilt 1720-23, add. c. 1762, purch. 1767, sold 1775, institutional use); Upper Gatton Park, Surrey (purch. 1774, sold 1786); Gidleigh Park, Devon (leased?)
Title: Baronet 1763-94
Peers: {1 peer 1776-94}
Notes: On the death of the 3 Viscount Allen a major portion of his estates passed to the Maynes. The rest went to the Probys, (see Proby).

ALLEN II *WALES*

<u>Allen</u>

Origins: Acquired land in the 17th century. High Sheriff 1693. Acquired Cresselly by marriage to an heiress 1729. Owned coal mines. The first MP was a barrister.

1. John Allen – Pembroke Borough 1818-26
2. H. G. Allen – Pembroke District 1880-86

Seat: Cresselly House, Pembrokeshire (medieval or Tudor house, owned by Bartletts, passed by mar. 1729 to Allens, demolished and rebuilt 1769-71, remod. 1815-16, enlarged 1869, still own)
Estates: Bateman 4654 (W) 4088

<u>Allen</u>

Origins: Descended from a younger brother of the ancestor of the Cresselly line in the 18th century.

1. C. F. E. Allen – Pembroke 1892-95

Seat: Bicton, Pembrokeshire (acq. c. 1694, sold mid-20th c.)

ALLESTRY (Allestre[e])

Origins: Merchant and professional family in the West Midlands descended from a villein given his freedom in 1141 (Craven and Stanley, *Derbyshire Houses*, 66). Descent from three ironmongers/woolstaplers who were **MPs for Nottingham 1393-1468** is probable but not established. Confirmed **MP for Derby 1542-55** was a yeoman and innholder, with **another MP for Derby in the 1640s**. Heralds denied gentility 1611.

1. Roger Allestry – Derby 1660-65
2. William Allestry – Derby 1685-87

Seats: Walton-on-Trent, Derbyshire (sold c. 1691); Alveston (Alvaston) Grange (Hall), Derbyshire (built early 17th c., passed out of family 1740s, demolished 1935); Darley Hall (House), Derbyshire (medieval, rebuilt 16th c.,acq. 1666, sold early 18th c., demolished 1934)
Estates: Worth £372 p.a. in later 17th century. Serious indebtedness c. 1700.

ALLSOPP

Baron Hindlip (1886- UK)

Origins: Merchants and brewers in Burton-upon-Trent and Derby from the early 18th century onwards. World's third largest brewery in the 1870s. Baronet 1880, High Sheriff 1881. His son, created a baron 1886 (part of what became known as the "beerage").

1. Samuel Allsopp 2 Baron Hindlip – E. Staffordshire 1872-80 Taunton 1882-87
2. Henry Allsopp 1 Baron Hindlip – E. Worcestershire 1874-80
3. George Allsopp – Worcester 1885-1906
4. Alfred Allsopp – Taunton 1887-95

Seats: Hindlip Hall, Worcestershire (built 1572, fire 18th c., demolished 1818, new house 1820, purch. c. 1862, add. 1864-67, sold 1939, institutional use); Doveridge Hall, Derbyshire (built 1769, purch. c. 1891, sold 1935, demolished 1938)
Estates: Owned 1158 acres in later 19th century. 1 Baron's will proved at £557,577. Family firm was sold for over 3 million pounds in the 1880s.
Title: Baronet 1880-
Peers: 4 peers 1886-1945
Notes: 1 Baron in ODNB.

ALSTON

Origins: Minor gentry. Founder a successful barrister - High Sheriff 1641, Kt 1641, Bt 1642.

1. Sir Thomas Alston 3 Bt – Bedford 1698-1700
2. Sir Rowland Alston 4 Bt – Bedfordshire 1722-41
3. Sir Thomas Alston 5 Bt – Bedfordshire 1747-61
4. Rowland Alston – Hertfordshire 1835-41

Seats: Odell Castle, Bedfordshire (medieval, ruin by 17th c., purch. and rebuilt 1633, remod. 18th c., fire 1931, sold 1933, new house built); Harrold Hall, Bedfordshire (built 1608-10, inher. by mar. 1763, remod. 1816, sold 1933, demolished 1961)
Title: Baronet 1642-1791

AMCOTTS [Cracroft, Emerson, Hall, Ingilby]

Cracroft/Hall/Amcotts

Origins: The Cracrofts were old gentry by 1600. Robert Cracroft married in 1608 the daughter of Sir Richard Amcotts (that family purchased Harrington Hall in 1673) and inherited Hackthorn(e). The Halls acquired Kettlethorpe by marriage in the early 17th century. The families were much intertwined by marriage.

1. Charles Hall – Lincoln 1727-34
2. Charles Amcotts – Boston 1754-61 1766-77
3. Sir Wharton Amcotts 1 Bt – East Retford 1780-90 1796-1802
4. Weston Cracroft Amcotts – Mid-Lincolnshire 1868-74

Seats: Hackthorn(e) Hall, Lincolnshire (medieval, acq. by mar. and built by Cracrofts 1618, rebuilt early 18th c. and again in the 1790s, still own); Kettlethorpe Hall, Lincolnshire (medieval house, acq. by Halls early 17th c., mostly demolished, rebuilt 1720s, acq. by mar. later 17th by Amcotts, acq. by mar by Cracrofts 1814, demolished and rebuilt second half 19th c., sold post 1945); Harrington Hall, Lincolnshire (medieval, rebuilt 1535, add. later 16th c., purch. by Amcotts 1673, sold 1919, fire 1991, restored)
Estates: Bateman 10811 (E) 14727
Title: Baronet 1796-1854
Notes: Cracroft-Amcotts were still at Hackthorn later 20th century.

Ingilby

Origins: The daughter and heiress of Sir Wharton Amcotts 1 Bt married 1780 Sir John Ingilby 1 Bt. Their son, the 2 Bt, died without children. His sister Augusta married Robert Cracroft, who succeeded to the Amcotts estates in 1854 and took the additional name Amcotts. The Ingilbys came to England with William the Conqueror and acquired Barton Manor, Yorkshire in 1330 (held until 1579). Sir Thomas Ingilby, Justice of the King's Bench 1361, married an heiress in 1320 (inherited in 1352) and the family remained seated at Ripley for over 650 years. **First MP 1350 for Yorkshire.**

1. Sir John Ingilby 1 Bt – East Retford 1790-96
2. Sir William Amcotts-Ingilby 2 Bt – East Retford 1807-12 Lincolnshire 1823-32 Lindsey Div. Lincolnshire 1832-34

Seats: Ripley Castle, Yorkshire (acq. by mar. 1352, built 15th c., add. 1548-55 and 1783-86, still own); Kettlethorpe, Lincolnshire (inherited for a period before passing to the Cracrofts, see above)
Estates: Bateman 11880 (E) 13538. Estate 1750 acres c. 2000.
Titles: Baronet 1642-1772; 1781-1854; 1866-
Notes: The Inglibys were Roman Catholics and thus debarred from Parliamentary participation from the 16th century until they became Anglicans in 1771. The Baronets of the second and third creations were illegitimate sons of the last Baronet of the previous creation. A 15th century Ingilby bishop in ODNB.

AMHERST

Earl Amherst (1826- UK)

Origins: Claimed descent from 1230. Held property in West Kent since at least the 15th century. Rose to prominence in the 17th century, clergymen and barristers. Made a great fortune in the 18th century as Paymaster General. **First MP 1614.**

1. Jeffery Amherst – Bletchingly 1689-90
2. William Amherst – Hythe 1766-68 Launceston 1768-74
3. William Amherst 2 Earl Amherst – East Grinstead 1829-32
4. William Amherst 3 Earl Amherst – W. Kent 1859-68 Mid Div. Kent 1868-80

Seats: Montreal (Riverhead), Kent (built 1760s, add. 1829 demolished 1938); Linton Park, Kent (acq. by mar. 1852 to a Cornwallis but passed back to Conrwallis family in the 1880s – see Wykeham); Bay Hall, Kent (acq. early 17th c., passed by mar. to Brownes first half 18th c., heirs sold it 1790)
Estates: Bateman 7633 (E) 8781

Titles: Baron Amherst (1776-97 GB); Baron Amherst (1788- GB)
Peers: 6 peers 1776-1945
1 in Cabinet 1793-1801
Notes: 1 Baron, brother and nephew (1 Earl) in ODNB.

Baron Amherst of Hackney (1892- UK)

Origins: Descended from an elder brother of John Amherst, ancestor of the 1 Earl Amherst.

1. William Amherst 1 Baron Amherst of Hackney – W. Norfolk 1880-85 S. W. Norfolk 1885-92

Seats: Didlington Hall, Norfolk (built 17th c., add. 1774 and 1816, purch. 1852, add. 1856, rebuilt 1883-85, sold 1911, demolished 1950); Foulden Hall, Norfolk (built 16th c., rebuilt 19th c., purch. mid-19th c.?, incorporated into the Didlington estate)
Estates: Bateman 9775 (E) 6976
Peers: 3 peers 1892-1919 1933-45
Notes: 1 Baron in ODNB and another family member.

ANNESLEY *IRELAND & ENGLAND*

Earl of Anglesey (1661-1761 E)

Origins: At Annesley, Nottinghamshire by 12th century if not before (Roskell, Clark, and Rawcliffe, *The House of Commons 1386-1421*, ii, 38). Edward I granted them rights of free warren. **Four MPs for Nottinghamshire between 1295 and 1388**. To Ireland as a soldier later 16th c., and acquired estates 1606 onwards, Irish Privy Council, and Kt 1616. 1 Bt **{MP in Ireland 1613} and for English and Welsh seats 1620s**.

1. Arthur Annesley 1 Earl of Anglesey – Radnorshire 1647-53 {Dublin 1659} Carmarthen 1660
2. James Annesley 2 Earl of Annesley – {County Waterford 1666} Winchester 1679-81
3. Maurice Annesley – {Clomines 1695-99}
4. Arthur Annesley 5 Earl of Anglesey – University of Cambridge 1702-10 {New Ross 1703-10}
5. Francis Annesley – Reading 1774-1806
6. Arthur Annesley – Oxford 1790-96
7. George Annesley – Yarmouth (I of W) 1808-10
8. George Annesley – County Wexford 1830-31
9. Arthur Annesley 11 Viscount Valentia – Oxford 1895-1917

Seats: Bletchington Park, Oxford (medieval, rebuilt c. 1630, purch. 1716, add. 1782, sold 1948); Arley Castle, Worcestershire (built 16th c., add. early 17th c., on the death of 2 Baron Lyttelton in 1779 the house passed to his sister, Viscountess Valentia, add. 1844, sold 1852, demolished 1958); Camolin Park, Wexford (built early 18th c., acq. by mar. to Donovan heiress 1741, rebuilt c. 1770s, sold 1852, became a ruin and was demolished 1974); Gaynes Park, Essex (medieval, acq. c. 1660, sold 1781 or 1792); Eydon Hall, Northamptonshire (old house, purch. 1788, rebuilt 1788-89, sold before 1858)
Estates: Bateman 7050 (E & I) 8884: Estates worth as much as £40,000 pa in 1730s, but divided among three heirs.
Titles: Viscount Valentia (1621- I); Baron Mountnorris (1628- I); Baron Altham (1680-1844 I); Earl of Mountnorris (1793-1844 I); Baron Annesley (1917-49 UK); Baronet 1620-
Peers: 8 peers 1661-90 1695-1761 1917-45 {5 peers 1661 1681-89 1695-99 1711-61 1765-93}
1 in Cabinet Council 1660 1673-82
Notes: 2 Viscount, 1,5, and 6 Earls in ODNB.

Earl Annesley (1789- I)

Origins: Junior line descended from the 1 Viscount Valentia created Earls Annesley. On the death of the 9 Viscount Valentia, that title passed to the junior line.

1. Francis Annesley – {Bangor 1692-93}
2. Francis Annesley – {New Ross 1695-99}
3. Francis Annesley – {Downpatrick 1692-99 1703 1713-14} Preston 1705-08 Westbury 1708-15 1722-34
4. William Annesley 1 Viscount Glerawly – {Middleton 1741-58}
5. Francis Annesley 1 Earl Annesley – {Downpatrick 1761-70}
6. Richard Annesley 2 Earl Annesley – {Coleraine 1776-83 St. Canice 1783-90 Newton 1790-97 Blessington 1797-1800 Middleton 1800}
7. William Annesley 3 Earl Annesley – Downpatrick 1815-20
8. William Annesley 4 Earl Annesley – Great Grimsby 1852-67
9. Hugh Annesley 5 Earl Annesley – County Cavan 1857-74

Seats: Castlewellan (Cloghmahericall), Down (purch. 1741, rebuilt 1856-58, sold 1956); Mount Panther, Down (built 1750s, sold 19th c., now ruin); Donard Lodge, Down (acq. 18th c., built c. 1830, demolished 20th c.); Thorganby Hall, Yorkshire (medieval, purch. 1641-42, sold 1801)
Estates: Bateman 51060 (I) 29539
Titles: Baron Annesley (1758- I); Viscount Glerawly (1766- I)
Peers: {2 peers 1758-1800} 2 Irish Rep peers 1867-74 1877-1908

ANSON [Adams]

Earl of Lichfield (1831- UK)

Origins: Eminent lawyer purchased manors, including Shugborough, 1624. House begun 1693, but largely paid for by 1 Baron, an eminent admiral, from his prize money 1740s.

1. George Anson 1 Baron Anson – Hedon 1744-47
2. Thomas Anson – Lichfield 1747-70
3. George Adams Anson – Saltash 1761-68 Lichfield 1770-89
4. Thomas Anson 1 Viscount Anson – Lichfield 1789-1806
5. Sir George Anson – Lichfield 1806-41
6. Thomas Anson 1 Earl of Lichfield – Great Yarmouth 1818
7. George Anson – Great Yarmouth 1819-34 Stoke-upon-Trent 1836-37 S. Staffordshire 1837-53
8. Augustus Anson – Lichfield 1859-68 Bewdley 1869-74
9. Thomas Anson 2 Earl of Lichfield – Lichfield 1847-54
10. Sir William Anson 3 Bt – University of Oxford 1899-1914

Seats: Shugborough Park, Staffordshire (purch. 1624, built 1693, add. c. 1743, add. c. 1760, add. 1790-1806, acq. Staffordshire County Council 1960, NT); Ranton Abbey, Staffordshire (purch. c. 1819, built 1820, burned 1942, demolished 1992, sold 2008); Orgreave Hall, Staffordshire; Rushall Hall, Staffordshire (medieval, add. late 15th c. and 16th c., demolished c. 1845, rebuilt mid-19th c., leased ?)
Estates: Bateman 21530 (E) 42042. Rubinstein – 1 Viscount left £120,000 in probate 1818. Owned 4500 acres in 2001.
Titles: Baron Anson (1747-72 GB); Viscount Anson (1806- UK); Baronet 1831-
Peers: 6 peers 1747-62 1806-1945
1 Ld Lt 19th
1 in Cabinet 1751-62
Notes: George Adams MP 1761-89 married the heiress of Admiral Anson and took the name Anson. 1 Baron and 5 Earl and other members of the family in ODNB.

ANSTRUTHER [Carmichael, Craig, Gibson, Gray, Lloyd, Paterson] *SCOTLAND & ENGLAND*

Anstruther

Origins: Family established at Dreel Castle near Anstruther in 12th century. Kt and Master of the Royal Household of Scotland 1592.

1. Sir Philip Anstruther – [Fifeshire 1665 1667 1678]
2. Sir William Anstruther – [Fifeshire 1681 1689-1701 1703-07]
3. Sir John Anstruther 1 Bt – [Anstruther Easter Burghs 1702-07] 1708-41
4. Philip Anstruther – Anstruther 1715-41 1747-54
5. Sir John Anstruther 2 Bt – Anstruther 1766-74 1780-82 1790-93
6. Sir Philip Anstruther-Paterson 4 Bt – Anstruther 1774-77
7. Sir John Anstruther 1 Bt – Anstruther 1783-90 Cockermouth 1790-96 Anstruther 1806-11
8. Robert Anstruther – Anstruther 1793-94
9. Sir John Carmichael-Anstruther 2 Bt – Anstruther 1811-18
10. Sir Wyndham Anstruther 5 Bt – S. Lanarkshire 1874-80

Seats: Carmichael House, Lanarkshire (built 17th and 18th c., partly demolished c. 1955); Anstruther Place, Fife (built later 17th c., demolished 1811); Dreel Castle (Anstruther), Fife (built 1663, demolished) Elie House, Fife (rebuilt 1697, add. c. 1740, remod. 1854-55, became a convent in 20th c.)
Estates: Bateman 12398 (S) 9534
Titles: Baronet 1700- ; 1798-
Notes: Three in ODNB.

Earl of Hyndford (1701-1817 S)

Origins: At Carmichael by c. 1350. Kt 1436. Ambassador to England 1590. **First [MP 1504]. Four additional [MPs 1560-1645].** Sir John Anstruther 1 Bt [MP 1702-41] married the daughter and heiress of the 2 Earl of Hyndford and the Carmichael estates passed to the Anstruthers 1817.

1. Sir Daniel Carmichael – [Lanarkshire 1649-50 1689-90]
2. William Carmichael – [Lanark 1703-07]
3. James Carmichael – Linlithgow Burghs 1734-41 1748-5

Seats: Carmichael House, Lanarkshire (see above); Maudsley (Mauldslie) Castle, Lanarkshire (built 1792-96, demolished 1935)
Titles: Baron Carmichael 1647-1710 S; Baronet 1627-1710
Peers: [2 peers 1660-72 1701-07] 1 Scottish Rep peer 1738-67
1 Ld Lt 18th
1 in Cabinet 17th-18th
1 KT 18th
Notes: 1 Baron and 1 and 3 Earls and one other Carmichael in ODNB.

Baron Carmichael (1912-26 UK)

Origins: The Gibsons were an old Fife family. Lord of Session 1532. Several more high judges in the 17th century. The sister of the 4 Earl of Hyndford married the 6th Gibson Bt, and he inherited the Skirling estate. The Gibsons took the additional name Carmichael.

1. Sir Alexander Gibson – [Fifeshire 1661]
2. Sir William Gibson-Craig 2 Bt – Midlothian 1837-41
3. Thomas Gibson-Carmichael 1 Baron Carmichael – Midlothian 1895-1900

Seats: Castle Craig (Castlecraig), Peebleshire (built 1798, sold c. 1904); Skirling, Peebleshire (medieval, Carmichaels inher. by mar. c. 1691, passed to Gibsons 1787, rebuilt 1912)
Estates: Bateman 9488 (S) 10419
Titles: Baronet 1702- ; 1831-
Peers: 1 peer 1912-26
1 Ld Lt 20th
Notes: 1 Baron and three other Gibson-Craigs in ODNB.

Paterson

Origins: Bishop 1662. 1 Bt was lawyer, Clerk of the Privy Council 1679. Purchased estates 1688. The daughter of Sir John Paterson 3 Bt married Sir Philip Anstruther 4 Bt, who succeeded to the Paterson estates and took the additional name Paterson.

1. John Paterson – Ludgershall 1761-68
2. Sir John Paterson 3 Bt – Berwickshire 1779-80

Seat: Eccles, Berwickshire
Title: Baronet 1687-1782

Anstruther

Origins: The descendants of the second son of Sir Philip Anstruther in the 17th century whose eldest son was seated at Anstruther (see above).

1. Sir Robert Anstruther 1 Bt – [Anstruther Easter Burghs 1681-2 Anstruther Wester Burghs 1703-07] Fifeshire 1710
2. Sir Robert Anstruther 5 Bt – Fifeshire 1864-80 St. Andrews District Burghs 1885-86
3. Henry Anstruther – St. Andrews District Burghs 1886-1903
4. Robert Lloyd-Anstruther – S. E. Suffolk 1886-92

5. William Anstruther-Gray – St. Andrews Burghs 1906-18
6. William Anstruther-Gray 1 Baron Kilmany – N. Div. Lanarkshire 1931-45 Berwick & East Lothian 1951-66

Seats: Balcaskie House, Fife (built c. 1629, add. 1668-74, purch. 1698, remod. mid-18th c. and 1830-32 and 1856-58, still own); Kilmany House, Fife (built 1914-19 and 1927, now subdivided); Watten, Caithness; Hintlesham Hall, Suffolk (Lloyd-Anstruther) (acq. by mar. to Lloyds 1837, sold 1909)
Estates: Bateman 24718 (S) 9062
Titles: Baron Kilmany 1966-85; Baronet 1694- ; 1956-85
2 Lds Lt 19th and 20th
Notes: Two in ODNB.

Lloyd

Origins: First MP was the son of a soldier. He became a lawyer and judge who in 1745 was left the estate of the widow of the 3 Earl of Winchelsea (to whom he was not related) and became rich. Kt 1745. The Lloyd estates passed 1837 by marriage to the Anstruthers of Blacaskie.

1. Sir Richard Lloyd – Mitchell 1745-47 Maldon 1747-54 Totnes 1754-59
2. Richard Lloyd – Totnes 1759-68

Seat: Hintlesham Hall, Suffolk (built later 16th c., remod. 1724, purch. 1747, passed by mar. to Anstruthers above)
Estates: Bateman 3612 (E) 4539
Notes: First MP in ODNB.

ANTROBUS [Crawford]

Antrobus

Origins: Old (at Antrobus Hall 15th c.) Cheshire family raised to great wealth by a banker (partner in Coutts) in the later 18th and first half of the 19th centuries. A junior branch produced an **MP in 1604**.

1. Gibbs Antrobus – Aldborough 1820-26 Plympton Erle 1826-32
2. Sir Edmund Antrobus – E. Surrey 1841 Wilton 1855-77

Seats: Eaton Hall (Congleton), Cheshire (built 18th c., purch. early 19th c., rebuilt 1827-31, sold early 20th c., demolished 1981); Amesbury Abbey, Wiltshire (medieval, new house 1660, purch. 1824 for £145,000, estate sold 1915, house sold 1979)

Estates: Bateman at Amesbury 10673 (E & S) 13224 and at Eaton 3051 (E) 5806; Rubinstein – Philip Antrobus left £100,000 in probate 1816 and the 1 Bt left £250,000 in 1824. The Amesbury Abbey estate sold in 1915 included 6,400 acres. Uncle of Gibbs Antrobus MP worth £700,000
Title: Baronet 1815-
Notes: The Eaton branch of the family emigrated to South Africa. Sir Reginald Antrobus in ODNB.

Crawford

Origins: Family came to England from Scotland early 18th c. The first MP a government official. The father of Gibbs Antrobus MP married the heiress of Gibbs Crawford MP.

1. Gibbs Crawford – Queenborough 1790-93

Seat: Saint Hill Manor, Sussex (purch. and built 1733, demolished and rebuilt 1792, sold later 19th c.)

APSLEY

Origins: Held land in Sussex in the reign of Edward III. Owned ironworks. **First MP 1459. Four additional MPs in the 15th and 16th centuries, including two shire kts for Sussex 1472 and 1563.**

1. Sir Allen Apsley – Thetford 1661-79

Seats: Thakenham Place, Sussex (acq. in Middle Ages, passed out of family c. 1660, demolished by 19th c., farm house); Ore Place, Sussex (medieval, acq. by mar. 15th-16th c., built early 17th c. passed out of family by mar. 1682 or earlier)
Notes: Two in ODNB.

ARBUTHNOT (Arbuthnott) [Maitland] *SCOTLAND*

Viscount Arbuthnott (1641- S)

Origins: At Arbuthnot by 1206. **First [MP 1560. An additional MP 1621].**

1. Alexander Arbuthnott Maitland – [Kincardineshire 1689-1702]
2. Alexander Arbuthnott – [Inverbervie 1703-07] Scotland 1707-08
3. Charles Arbuthnott Maitland – Aberdeen Burghs 1748-51
4. Sir Hugh Arbuthnott – Kincardineshire 1826-65

Seats: Arbuthnott House, Kincardineshire (built 1242, add. 1420, add. later 15th c., remod. 1580, 1650, and c. 1682-85, remod. 1754-57, remod. 1795-1800, still own); Castle of Fiddes, Kincardineshire (acq. 1553, built 1592, sold late 17th c., became a farm house, restored 1930s)
Estates: Bateman 13560 (S) 13036
Peers: [3 peers 1660-94 1707] Scottish Rep peer 1818-20 1821-47
2 Lds Lt 19th, 20th

Maitland

Origins: Lawyer granted arms and a Bt 1672. Claimed to be a cadet of the Maitlands of Thirlestane 14th c. The sister and heiress of Sir Charles Maitland 3 Bt married Alexander Arbuthnot MP. Their son took the name Maitland.

1. Sir Charles Maitland 3 Bt – [Aberdeenshire 1685-86]

Seat: Pitrichie, Aberdeenshire (acq. 17th c., passed by mar. out of family 1757)
Title: Baronet 1672-1704

ARCHDALL [Archdale] *IRELAND*

Origins: Merchant in London to Ireland late 16th c., granted land 1612. Sheriff of Tyrone 1616.

1. Nicholas Archdall – {County Fermanagh 1731-60}
2. Mervyn Archdall – {County Fermanagh 1761-1800} 1801-02
3. Richard Archdall – {Ardfert 1790-97 Killibegs 1797-1800} Kilkenny 1801-02 Dundalk 1802-06
4. Mervyn Archdall – Fermanagh 1802-34
5. Mervyn Archdall – Fermanagh 1834-74
6. William Archdall – Fermanagh 1874-85
7. Sir Edward Archdale 1 Bt – N. Fermanagh 1898-1903 1916-22 Tyrone & Fermanagh 1922-29

Seats: Castle Archdale, Fermanagh (acq. 1612, built 1615, demolished 1641, rebuilt, fire 1689, abandoned, rebuilt 1773, family departed 1942, RAF WW II, derelict since 1959, ruin, demolished c. 1970); Riversdale, Fermanagh (acq. c. 1800-17 and built house, remod. c. 1840-60, sold house and estate 1947, demolished 1960, retained stables); Trillie (Trillick, Trelick), Tyrone (acq. by mar. from Mervyns (see) 1776)
Estates: Bateman 33015 (I) 16991 and 5627 (I) 3182. Worth £3000 to £4000 pa in 1753, £13,000 pa in c. 1800.
Title: Baronet 1928-
1 Ld Lt 20th
Notes: One member of family in ODNB.

ARCHER [Cheeke, Cheke]

<u>Baron Archer of Umberslade</u> (1747-78 GB)

Origins: Rose by farming into the gentry in the 13th and 14th centuries (Carpenter, *Locality and Polity*, 135). Kt. 1624. **First MP 1640.** On the death of the 2 Baron Archer in 1778 without a male heir, his estates were divided among four daughters.

1. Thomas Archer – Warwick 1659 Warwickshire 1660
2. Andrew Archer – Warwickshire 1690-98 1705-10 1713-22
3. Henry Archer – Warwick 1735-68
4. Thomas Archer 1 Baron Archer – Warwick 1735-41 Bramber 1741-47
5. Andrew Archer 2 Baron Archer – Coventry 1761-68

Seats: Umberslade Hall, Warwickshire (held at least since 13th c., medieval house demolished and rebuilt 1695-1700, passed to the Earl of Plymouth – see Clive – by mar. 1778, sold 1826); Hale Park, Hampshire (purch. c. 1713-20, rebuilt c. 1715, sold after 1778, remod. c. 1782); Pyrgo Park, Essex (medieval, owned 16th-17th c.?, demolished before 1814, new house, demolished c. 1940)
Estates: Worth £1,000 pa c. 1660; £2,015 pa in 1693. (In later 16th c. family owned agricultural land, an iron mill, shares in the East India Co., and gained a dowry from a London merchant's daughter. The estate produced bricks and timber as well. Tyack, *Warwickshire Country Houses*, 189)
Peers: 2 peers 1747-78
Notes: The Chekes (Cheekes) were old gentry (at Mottistone, IoW, by 1325, held until 1618) on the Isle of Wight rose with Sir John who was an academic and tutor to Edward VI. He became a Secretary of State. His grandson, Sir Thomas Cheke purchased Pyrgo. **First Cheke MP 1547. Two further MPs 1571-84 and 1604-28. Two further Cheke MPs 1363-73 and 1460-61 may be related.** Thomas Archer MP mar. 1726 the daughter of Sir Thomas Tipping 1 Bt by Anne, daughter and heiress of Thomas Cheeke of Pirgo (Pyrgo). 1st MP in ODNB. Thomas Archer MP, the distinguished architect also in ODNB.

ARKWRIGHT

Origins: Industrialists (cotton) in the second half of the 18th century. The great inventor and founder of the family, Sir Richard Arkwright, was the son of a tailor. Kt 1786. High Sheriff 1787.

1. Richard Arkwright – Rye 1813-18 1826-30
2. George Arkwright – Leominster 1842-56
3. Richard Arkwright – Leominster 1866-75

4. Augustus Arkwright – N. Derbyshire 1868-80
5. Francis Arkwright – E. Derbyshire 1874-80
6. Sir John Arkwright – Hereford 1900-12

Seats: Hampton Court, Herefordshire (built 1435, purch. 1810, remod. 1834-45, sold 1912); Kinsham Court, Herefordshire (built 18th c., purch. early 20th c., still own); Sutton Scarsdale, Derbyshire (rebuilt 1724-27, purch. 1824, family did not return after WWI, sold 1920, gutted 1921, ruins donated to the nation 1969); Coton House, Warwickshire (built 1784, purch. c. 1870, sold 1948, now offices); Willersley Castle, Derbyshire (built 1789-90, there until 1923, sold 1936)
Estates: Bateman: 15652 (E) 21579 (Sir Richard Arkwright died 1792 worth £500,000; 1st MP worth £3,250,000 in 1832). Arkwrights of Kinsham owned 2,000 acres in 2001.
1 Ld Lt 20th
Notes: Sir Richard Arkwright and his son in ODNB, as are Sir John, MP, and Sir Joseph, the bacteriologist.

ARMSTRONG [Heaton, MacDonnell] *IRELAND*

Armstrong

Origins: From Holland. Granted land in Ireland c. 1620s. **First {MP 1647}**. Kt 1660s.

1. John Armstrong – {Fore 1768-76 Kilmallock 1783-91}
2. William Armstrong – {Wicklow 1798-1800}
3. William Heaton-Armstrong – Sudbury Div. Suffolk 1906-10

Seats: Mount Heaton (Ballyskennagh), King's County (built early 18th c., acq. by mar. from Heatons 1731, sold 1817); Farney Castle, Tipperary (old tower house, acq. c. 1670, sold 1834)
Estates: Owned 133,460 acres in 1817.
Notes: William Armstrong MP moved abroad in 1816 and began to sell his estates in Ireland and England. All sold by 1850.

MacDonnell

Origins: Claimed common ancestry with the Earls of Antrim (*Burke's Landed Gentry 1879*, 1021)(see Kerr). Seated in Clare in 17th century. Became Protestants 1690 and gained office c. 1700. Sheriff 1728. New Hall devolved in 1850 on William Armstrong, second son of William Armstrong of Mount Heaton, maternal nephew of John MacDonnell, who took the additional name MacDonnell.

1. Charles MacDonnell – {County Clare 1765-68 Ennis 1768-73}
2. Charles MacDonnell – {Taghmon 1796-97 Rathcormack 1797-1800} Yarmouth (IoW) 1803

Seats: Liscrona House, Clare (acq. 17th c., ceased to be principal seat 1764); New Hall (Killone Abbey), Clare (built c. 1750, purch. 1764, add. c. 1764, passed by mar. of 1809 to Armstrongs in 1850, remod. mid-19th c., sold early 20th c.); Kilkee, Clare
Estates: Bateman 6601 (I) 2947

ARNOLD *WALES & ENGLAND*

Origins: Claimed descent from the Kings of Gwent. Merchants in Bristol, rose as Tudor officials - lawyer and clerk to Cromwell, then Lord Justice of Ireland 1564. Kt Edward VI. **First MP 1545 for Gloucestershire. Three other MPs 1547-1628 (Monmouthshire 1626 and 1628).**

1. John Arnold – Monmouth 1680-81 Southwark 1689-95 Monmouth 1695-98

Seats: Llanthony Abbey, Monmouth (acq. at Dissolution, sold 1702); Llanfihangel (Llanvihangel) Court, Monmouthshire (medieval, rebuilt 16th and 17th c., purch. 1623, sold 1702); Highnam Court (Churcham), Gloucestershire (medieval house, acq. at Dissolution, passed by mar. to Cooke (II) family 1605)
Notes: Family ran into serious financial difficulties in the 17th c. Nicholas Arnold MP 1626-28 was imprisoned for over 20 years for debt. Extinct on last MP's death and estates sold 1726. The Lord Justice of Ireland and John Arnold MP are in ODNB.

ARSCOTT

Origins: Rising slowly in the medieval period over several centuries at Holsworthy from freeholders to gentry by accumulation of property mainly through marriage. Moved to Devon 16th c. **First MP 1547** the younger son of a lawyer and local office holder. Purchased monastic land in the 1550s.

1. Arthur Arscott – Tiverton 1722-47
2. John Arscott – Ashburton 1741-54

Seats: Tetcott House, Devon (medieval, acq. c. 1550, rebuilt house 1603, rebuilt c. 1700, passed to Molesworth (see) family by mar. 1788, demolished 1831); Dunsland (Holsworthy), Devon (acq. by mar. 1522, passed by mar. to Bickford family mid-17th c.)
Notes: Family extinct 1788.

ARTHINGTON

Origins: Held manor of Arthington since 14th century.

1. Henry Arthington – Pontefract 1646 W. R. Yorkshire 1656 Ripon 1660
2. Henry Arthington – Aldborough 1679
3. Cyril Arthington – Aldborough 1701-02

Seat: Arthington Hall, Yorkshire (acq. 14th c., new house built 1st half 17th c., rebuilt by later owner 18th c.)
Estates: Worth £2,200 pa in late 17th c.

ASBURNHAM [Crowley, Vaughan] *ENGLAND & WALES*

Earl of Ashburnham (1730-1924 GB)

Origins: "A family of stupendous antiquity". (Shirley, *Noble and Gentle Men*, 253) Claimed Saxon descent. Owned Asburnham at least by 1166. Kt Henry III. Enhanced fortune as ironmasters in the 16th century. **First MP 1397 for Sussex. At least three additional MPs in the 16th century.**

1. John Ashburnham – Hastings 1628 1640-44 Sussex 1661-67
2. William Ashburnham – Ludgershall 1640-41 1661-79
3. John Ashburnham 1 Baron Ashburnham – Hastings 1679-81 1685-87 1689
4. William Ashburnham 2 Baron Ashburnham – Hastings 1702-10
5. John Ashburnham 1 Earl of Ashburnham – Hastings 1710
6. George Ashburnham Viscount St. Asaph – New Romney 1807-12
7. Percy Ashburnham – Berealston 1825-30

Seats: Ashburnham Place, Sussex (acq. at least by 1166, old house, rebuilt 1757-61, add. 1813-17, remod. 1853-55, sold 1953-57, most demolished 1959, institutional use); Barking Hall, Suffolk (acq. by mar. 1756 from Crowley family who purch. early 17th c., built 17th c., rebuilt early 18th c., add. later 18th c., sold c. 1913 with Suffolk estate of 3,400 acres for £60,000 – Roberts, *Lost Country Houses of Suffolk*, 21 - demolished 1926); Pembrey House (Court), Carmarthenshire (estate acq. by mar. to Vaughans – who held it by descent from medieval owners - later 17th c., new house built 18th or 19th c., family departed 1920s, burned c. 1960)
Estates: Bateman 24489 (E & W) 24136
Titles: Baron Ashburnham 1689-1924 E; Viscount St. Asaph 1730-1924 GB
Peers: 8 peers 1689-1737 1745-1924
1 Ld Lt 18th
1 KG 19th

Notes: The daughter of Sir Charles Vaughan (**MP Breconshire 1614, 1625, another MP 1606**) of Porthamel and Pembrey married the 1 Baron Ashburnham and brought him Welsh estates. The Ashburnhams acquired great wealth from their Wealdian iron works from an early period. Two family members in ODNB.

Crowley (Crawley)

Origins: Owned large iron works 17th and 18th c. The 2 Earl of Ashburnham married the daughter and heiress of John Crowley of Barking.

1. Sir Ambrose Crowley – Andover 1713
2. John Crowley – Okehampton 1722-27 Queenborough 1727-28

Seat: Barking Hall, Suffolk (purch. early 17th c., built 17th c., rebuilt early 18th c., passed to Ashburnhams by mar. 1756)
Estates: Worth well over £100,000 c. 1715. Estate worth £70,000 in 1728.

Ashburnham

Origins: In the 15th century a younger son of the progenitor of the Earls of Ashburnham settled at Broomham. **The first MP of this line was elected in 1593.**

1. Sir Denny Ashburnham 1 Bt – Hastings 1660 1661-79 1685-87
2. Sir William Ashburnham 2 Bt – Hastings 1710-13 Seaford 1715-17
3. William Ashburnham 5 Bt – Hastings 1761-74

Seat: Broomham Park, Sussex (acq. by mar. 15th c., built 16th c., rebuilt 18th c., enlarged 1927, now a school)
Title: Baronet 1661-

ASHBY

Origins: Acquired Quenby in mid-13th century. A branch of the family seated at Losely, Leicestershire **elected two MPs between 1529 (Leicestershire) and 1597.**

1. George Ashby – Leicestershire 1695-98 1707-08
2. Shukburgh Ashby – Leicester 1784

Seat: Quenby Hall, Leicestershire (estate owned by the Ashbys since the 13th century, new house built 1615-30, remod. 19th c., sold 1904)
Estates: 1,023 acres in 2012.

ASHE [A'Court, Holmes, Repington] *ENGLAND & IRELAND*

Baron Heytesbury (1828- UK)

Origins: West Country industrialists steadily rising since the mid-16th century. Became the greatest clothiers in England before the Civil War when they were worth £3,000 pa. **Elected two MPs for the first time in 1640, including one for Heytesbury, which they represented into the 19th century. Of the three MPs elected before 1660, two sat as Kts of the shire for Somerset (1654) and Wiltshire (1654).** An Ashe heiress married an A'Court in the early 18th century who took the additional name Ashe and succeeded to Heytesbury.

1. William Ashe – Heytesbury 1668-81 1685-87 1689-1701 Wiltshire 1701-02
2. Edward Ashe – Heytesbury 1679-81 1685-87
3. Edward Ashe – Heytesbury 1695-1747
4. William Ashe – Heytesbury 1708-13 1715-22
5. Pierce A'Court – Heytesbury 1713-15 1722-25
6. Pierce A'Court Ashe – Heytesbury 1734-68
7. William Ashe – Heytesbury 1747-50
8. William A'Court Ashe – Heytesbury 1751-81
9. Sir William Ashe A'Court 1 Bt – Heytesbury 1781-90 1806-07
10. William A'Court 1 Baron Heytesbury – Dorchester 1812-14
11. Charles A'Court Repington – Heytesbury 1820
12. Edward A'Court Repington – Heytesbury 1820-32 Tamworth 1837-47
13. William A'Court Holmes 2 Baron Heytesbury – Isle of Wight 1837-47
14. Charles A'Court Repington – Wilton 1852-55

Seats: Heytesbury House, Wiltshire (medieval, purch. 1641, rebuilt 1782, remod. 1820, sold 1926); Westover Hall, Hampshire (acq. early 19th c.?, sold 1897); Amington Hall, Warwickshire (medieval, acq. by Repingtons 1422, rebuilt early 19th c., passed by mar. to A'Courts 1837, sold 1925, demolished)
Estates: Bateman 13303 (E & I) 15465
Title: Baronet 1795-
Peers: 4 peers 1828-1945
1 in Cabinet 1844-46
Notes: Amington Hall was inherited from the Repington family in 1837 and some members of the family took the additional name Repington. Members of the family adopted the name A'Court in the early 18th century. The current heir to the peerage is a wealthy Australian. John and Edward Ashe MPs 17th c. and 1 Baron in ODNB.

Baron Holmes (1760-64 1797-1804 I)

Origins: Soldier to Ireland under Elizabeth I. Kt 1666. Settled on Isle of Wight later 17th century. The daughter and heiress of the 1 Baron Holmes of the second creation married Sir Henry Worsley 8 Bt of Appuldurcombe, Hampshire (see that family), who took the additional name Holmes. His granddaughter and heiress, Elizabeth, married the 2 Baron Heytesbury, who took the additional name Holmes.

1. Sir Robert Holmes – Winchester 1669-79 Newport (IofW) 1678-79 1685-87 Yarmouth (IofW) 1689-90 Newport 1690-92
2. Sir John Holmes – Newtown (IofW) 1677-81
3. Henry Holmes – Yarmouth 1695-1717
4. Thomas Holmes 1 Baron Holmes – Newtown 1727-29 1734-41 Yarmouth 1747-64
5. Henry Holmes – Newtown 1741-47 Yarmouth 1747-62
6. Charles Holmes – Newport 1758-61

Seat: Thorley Manor, Hampshire (IoW) (previous houses, purch. 1679, rebuilt 1712, passed to Lord Heytesbury 1860, still owned 1912)
Peers: {2 peers 1760-64 1797-1800}

Ashe

Origins: The Ur-Ashe was James Ashe living in the mid-17th century. His second son established the Heytesbury line above. Other junior lines combined here (they were close cousins) from two other sons.

1. Sir Joseph Ashe 1 Bt – Downton 1670-81
2. Samuel Ashe – Heytesbury 1659 Chippenham 1679-81
3. John Ashe – Westbury 1681
4. Sir James Ashe 2 Bt – Downton 1701-05
5. Joseph Ashe – Chippenham 1710-11

Seats: Heywood House, Wiltshire (built early 17th c., acq. later 17th c., sold c. 1700-15); Langley Burrell, Wiltshire (acq. c. 1655, new house or rebuilt c. 1780, still own)
Estates: The Baronets of Langley Burrell were worth £4,000 pa in 1733.
Title: Baronet 1660-1734
Notes: The estates of the Langley Burrell line devolved in 1733 on a son-in-law, Joseph Windham Ashe MP (see Wyndham).

Ashe

Origins: Another younger son of James Ashe (see above) and uncle of Sir Joseph Ashe 1 Bt went to Ireland in the early 17th century and married the heiress of Nicholas Bailey of Abbey St. John's, Meath (the Bailey's settled in Ireland under Elizabeth I, Kt 1603). **Three Ashes were elected {Irish MPs between 1613-42}**.

1. Thomas Ashe – {Cavan 1661-66}
2. Thomas Ashe – {Cavan 1692-93 1695-99 1703-13}
3. Thomas Ashe – {Swords 1695-99 Clogher 1713-14 1715-22}
4. Richard Ashe – {Trim 1713-14 1727-28 Athboy 1721-27}
5. Joseph Ashe – {Trim 1735-60}

Seat: Ashfield, Meath (acq. and built 17th c., resident 18th c.)
Estates: Worth £1,500 pa in 1722

ASHHURST (Ashurst)

Origins: Minor gentry early 17th century. Father of 1 Bt was a wealthy woolen draper and London Alderman, younger son of a gentry family. Sir William Ashhurst MP was also a woolen draper, great merchant, Director of the Bank of England, and Lord Mayor of London 1693. **First MP 1640 (Lancashire 1654)**.

1. Sir Henry Ashhurst 1 Bt – Truro 1681 1689-95 Wilton 1698-1702
2. Sir William Ashhurst – London 1689-90 1695-1702 1705-10
3. Henry Ashhurst – Preston 1698-1702
4. Sir Henry Ashhurst 2 Bt – New Windsor 1715-22
5. William Ashhurst – Oxfordshire 1815-30

Seats: Waterstock House, Oxfordshire (purch. 1691 and built, held into 20th century, demolished 1953); Ashhurst Hall, Lancashire (acq. and built mid-17th c., sold 1751)
Title: Baronet 1688-1732
Notes: Family continued in the later 19th century but not in Parliament. 1 Bt and father and another member of the family, a judge, in ODNB.

ASHLEY-COOPER *ENGLAND & IRELAND*

Earl of Shaftesbury (1672- E)

Origins: The Ashleys acquired Wimborne St. Giles c. 1460s by marriage to the heiress of Sir John Hamelyn (whose family owned it from 1301 by inheritance from the Plecys, who acquired it soon after the Conquest. The estate has not be bought or sold for nearly one thousand years – *Country Life*, 93, p. 464). **First MP (1547) kt of shire for Dorset 1554. Four other MPs 1572-1625.** The Coopers were gentry from the 1530s based on the fortune of an official under Henry VIII. **First MP 1584. Two further MPs in the 17th century.** Succeeded to the Ashley estates by marriage in the 17th century after the father of the first Earl married the daughter and heiress of the 1st Ashley Bt.

1. Anthony Ashley-Cooper 1 Earl of Shaftesbury – Tewkesbury 1640 Wiltshire 1653 1654 1656 1659 Downton 1660 Wiltshire 1660
2. George Cooper – Poole 1654 1660 1673
3. Anthony Ashley 2 Earl of Shaftesbury – Weymouth & Melcombe Regis 1670-79
4. Anthony Ashley 3 Earl of Shaftesbury – Poole 1695-98
5. Maurice Ashley – Weymouth & Melcombe Regis 1695-98 1701 Wiltshire 1701-02 Weymouth 1705-13
6. C. Ashley-Cooper 6 Earl of Shaftesbury – Dorchester 1790-1811
7. Anthony Ashley-Cooper 7 Earl of Shaftesbury – Woodstock 1826-30 Dorchester 1830-31 Dorset 1831-46 Bath 1847-51
8. Anthony Ashley-Cooper – Dorchester 1826-30
9. Anthony Ashley-Cooper – Gatton 1831-32
10. Anthony Ashley-Cooper – Dorchester 1831-47
11. Anthony Ashley-Cooper 8 Earl of Shaftesbury – Hull 1857-59 Cricklade 1859-65
12. Evelyn Ashley-Cooper – Poole 1874-80 Isle of Wight 1880-85
13. Wilfred Ashley 1 Earl Mount Temple – Fylde Div. Lancashire 1918-22 New Forest and Christchurch Div. Hampshire 1922-32

Seats: St. Giles's House, Dorset (acq. by mar. c. 1460 from family who held it by 1301, built mid-16th c., rebuilt c. 1651, remod. 1740-44, remod. 1854, contents sold 1980, restored 2010, still own); Belfast Castle, Antrim (built 1867, acq. by mar. 1883, donated to Belfast Corporation 1934)
Estates: Bateman 34221 (E & I) 21884; 12436 (I) 5801. Worth £3,000 pa in the 1680s. Estate stood at 15,500 acres in 1947 and only 5,500 in 2007. (Russell and Grindrod, *Manor Houses of Dorset*, 202) Coopers held 7,000 acres in 1610.
Titles: Baron Ashley 1661- E; Earl Mount Temple 1932-39 UK; Baronet 1622-
Peers: 9 peers 1661-1711 1732-71 1785-1886 1890-1945 1932-39
4 Lds Lt 17th, 18th, 19th, 20th
1 in Privy Council 1660-74 1679
1 KG 19th
1 KP 20th
Notes: Belfast Castle and the Irish estates came by marriage with an heiress of the Marquess of Donegal. The third son of the 7 Earl succeeded to the estates of the Prime Minister, Viscount Palmerston and his son became Earl Mount Temple (see Grenville). 1, 3, 7 Earls of Shaftesbury in ODNB, as are a number of Ashleys and the 1 Baron Mount Temple.

ASTLEY [Blake, Calthorpe, Delaval]

Astley

Origins: Landowners by the early 12th century. At Melton Constable since 1236 by marriage to the heiress Edith Constable. Thomas de Astley was killed at Evesham in 1265. Created Baron Astley by writ 1295 (not summoned after 1370). **First MP 1304. Two subsequent MPs in the 15th and 16th centuries.** Senior line (since 13th century) at Patshull.

1. Sir John Astley 2 Bt – Shrewsbury 1727-34 Shropshire 1734-71
2. Sir John Astley 1 Bt – Wiltshire 1820-32 N. Wiltshire 1832-34
3. Sir John Astley 3 Bt – N. Lincolnshire 1874-80

Seats: Patshull House (Hall), Staffordshire (acq. 13th c., built 1730s, sold 1756); Everley (Everleigh) House (Manor), Wiltshire (built 17th c., purch. 1736 and 1765, add. c. 1765, leased out from 1856, fire 1882, remod later 19th c., sold c. 1917); Elsham Hall, Lincolnshire (built early 17th c., rebuilt 1760, inher. by mar. by Astleys in 19th c., sold 1936)
Estates: Bateman 15567 (E) 22057. The Patshull estate was sold for £100,000 in the 18th century.
Titles: Baronet 1662-1772; 1821-
Notes: 3 Bt of sec. cr. dissipated much of the family's wealth in the pursuit of sport, in ODNB.

Baron Hastings (1290- E)

Origins: The 1 Baron Hastings (family name Hastings) was one of the three contenders for the throne of Scotland in 1290. Earls of Pembroke 1339. The fifth Astley Bt of the junior line seated at Melton Constable (see above) married the daughter and heiress of Sir N. L'Estrange, who was co-heir to the Barony of Hastings (see Rawdon Hastings). The 6 Bt succeeded as 16 Baron Hastings in 1841.

1. Sir Jacob Astley 1 Bt – Norfolk 1685-87 1690-1701 1702-05 1710-22
2. Sir Edward Astley 4 Bt – Norfolk 1768-90
3. Sir Jacob Astley 5 Bt – Norfolk 1797-1806 1807-17
4. Jacob Astley 16 Baron Hastings – W. Norfolk 1832-37

Seats: Melton Constable, Norfolk (acq. by mar. 1236, built 16th c., rebuilt 1664-70, add. 20th c., sold 1948); Seaton Delaval, Northumberland (rebuilt 1718-28, acq. by mar. from Delavals 1814, fire 1822, still own); Hillmorton, Warwickshire (acq. 13th c., sold later 18th c.); East Barsham Manor, Norfolk (built early 16th c., acq. by mar. 1762, sold 1915)

Estates: Bateman 19558 (E) 44452
Titles: Baron Astley 1644-88 E; Baronet 1641-59; 1660-
Notes: 1 Baron and a Tudor courtier in ODNB.

Calthorpe

Origins: The family has held manorial property in Norfolk since 1376. They acquired East Barsham by marriage to a Fermor heiress, a family prominent since the reign of Richard II. **First MP kt of the shire for Norfolk 1445 and another in 1491. Two further MPs in the 16th century.**

1. Sir Christopher Calthorpe – Norfolk 1679

Seat: East Barsham Manor, Norfolk (built early 16th c., passed by mar. to Calthorpes 1628, passed by mar. to the L'Estranges 1720)
Notes: Tudor judge and a lawyer in ODNB. The Calthorpe estates passed to the L'Estranges in 1720 and thence to the Astleys in 1762.

Baron Delaval (1783 I and 1786 GB, both extinct 1808)

Origins: The Delaval family arrived in England at the Conquest or shortly thereafter. Manorial lords of a small estate and a coal mine by 1219. Later gained wealth through salt pans and were both landowners and industrialists for many centuries. Kt 1519. High Sheriff 1527. Acquired Seaton in the reign of Henry I. **First MP 1373, for Northumberland. Two additional MPs 1626-1658.** The Blakes were minor gentry and office holders. First MP and **Kt 1689**. Edward Delaval married Mary, daughter and heiress of Sir Francis Blake of Ford Castle, Northumberland (acq. by marriage to a Carr heiress in 1667). The Blakes descended from the Irish family seated at Menlo Castle, Galway. Their descendants took the name Blake-Delaval. Rhoda Blake-Delaval married the fourth Astley Baronet of Melton Constable and brought with her Seaton Delaval.

1. Sir Ralph Delaval 1 Bt – Northumberland 1659 1660 1677-81
2. Sir Francis Blake – Berwick-on-Tweed 1689-95 1698-1700 Northumberland 1701-05
3. Sir Ralph Delaval – Great Bedwyn 1695-98
4. Sir John Delaval 3 Bt – Morpeth 1701-05 Northumberland 1705-08
5. George Delaval – West Looe 1715-23
6. Francis Blake-Delaval – Northumberland 1716-22
7. Sir Francis Blake-Delaval – Hindon 1751-54 Andover 1754-68
8. John Hussey-Delaval 1 Baron Delaval – Berwick-on-Tweed 1754-61 1765-74 1780-86
9. George Delaval – Northumberland 1757-74

Seats: Seaton Delaval, Northumberland (acq. 12th c., medieval house, rebuilt 1718-28, passed to Astleys by mar. 1814); Ford Castle, Northumberland (built 13th c., rebuilt c. 1338, ruined and rebuilt by 1509, ruined c. 1648, acq. by mar. 1667, remod. 1694, rebuilt 1761-1800, passed by mar. to the Beresfords 1822); South Dissington, Northumberland (acq. medieval period, sold 1673); Doddington Hall, Lincolnshire (built 1593-1607, acq. by mar. from the Husseys 1749, remod. 1761-62, bequeathed in 1829 to Javis family – Col. George Ralph Payne Jarvis was the friend and possibly lover of Sarah Hussey-Delaval (Gunman) who left her estates to him, still own)
Estates: 8,000 acres in early 17th c. Northumberland estates under Baron Hastings; Doddington (Jarvis) estates 4720 (E) 5824. Rubinstein – Sarah Hussey-Delaval (Gunman) ledt £120,000 in probate in 1825. Worth £1990 pa in the 1620s.
Titles: Baronet 1660-1729; 1761-1808
Peers: 1 peer 1786-1808
Notes: A Blake-Delaval married the heiress to Doddington Hall, Lincolnshire. Ford Castle (acquired from the Blakes via marriage in 1718 – see that family) later passed by marriage to the Beresfords (see that family). Doddington eventually passed to the Jarvis family. A Delaval heiress in 1471 married a stonemason (Horsley) whose descendants carried on the Delaval name. Delavals extinct in the male line 1814. The Delaval family has an entry in the ODNB as well as eight individual members.

ASTOR

Viscount Astor (1917- UK)

Origins: Fur traders in 19th century. The first was a butcher's son from Germany. Established in Canada and the United States (arrived 1783) and millionaires by 1830. Then made a great fortune in Manhattan real estate. Moved to England in 1890 and became newspaper proprietors.

1. Waldorf Astor 2 Viscount Astor – Plymouth 1910-18 Sutton Div. Plymouth 1918-19
2. Nancy Astor Viscountess Astor – Sutton Div. Plymouth 1919-45
3. John Jacob Astor 1 Baron Astor – Dover Div. Kent 1922-45
4. William Astor – East Fulham 1935-45 Wycombe Div. Buckinghamshire 1951-52
5. Michael Astor – E. Surrey 1945-51
6. John Jacob Astor – Plymouth Sutton 1951-59
7. John Astor – Newbury 1964-74

Seats: Cliveden, Buckinghamshire (built late 17th c., fire 1795, rebuilt after 1824, fire c. 1850, rebuilt 1850-51, add. 1862, purch. 1893, remod. 1893-97, NT 1942, family in residence until 1966); Hever Castle, Kent (built c. 1270 and 1384, purch. 1903, add. 1906-07, sold 1983, conference center)

Estates: The father of the 1 Viscount Astor left a fortune estimated at $100,000,000 in 1890. Viscount Astor was worth £100,000,000 in 1990 and Lord Astor of Hever £20,000,000. Owned 21,500 acres in 2001.
Title: Baron Astor 1916- UK; Baron Astor of Hever 1956- UK
Peers: 2 peers 1916-1945
Notes: 1 Viscount and four other Astors in ODNB.

ATHERTON [Gwillym]

Origins: The family held Atherton, Lancashire from the 13th century. Prominent gentry into the 18th century. **First MP kt of the shire for Lancashire 1373. Three subsequent MPs for the county 15th and 16th centuries**. On the extinction of the male line in the late 17th century the estates passed via an heiress to the Gwillyms of Langstone.

1. Richard Atherton – Liverpool 1677-79 1685-87
2. Robert Vernon Atherton Gwillym – Newton 1774-80

Seats: Atherton Hall, Lancashire (medieval, rebuilt c. 1600, acq. by mar. 1675, rebuilt 1723-43, passed to Powys family by mar. 1820, demolished 1825); Bewsey Hall, Lancashire (medieval, acq. by mar. 1675, passed to Powys family by mar. 1820, demolished c. 1950); Langstone Court, Herefordshire (built c. 1700, sold 1794)
Estates: Rebuilding of Atherton Hall 1723-43 cost £63,000. (*Country Houses in Great Britain*, 37)
Notes: The eldest daughter of Robert Atherton Gwillym married 1797 Thomas Powys 2 Lord Lilford and the Atherton and Gwillym estates passed to the 3 Lord Lilford in 1820 (see Powys). See F. and K. Wood, eds., *A Lancashire Gentleman*, 1-114 and 395.

ATKINSON [Farrand, Savile]

Origins: The first MP was a very successful corn factor. He had two illegitimate sons who took the names Savile and Farrand.

1. Christopher Atkinson – Hedon 1780-83 1796-1806 Okehampton 1818-19
2. Albany Savile – Okehampton 1807-20
3. Robert Farrand – Hedon 1818-26 1830-32 Stafford 1837-41

Seat: Hill Hall, Norfolk (built later 16th c., leased 19th c.?)
Estates: First MP left £60,000 and real estate

ATKYNS (Atkins)

Origins: Practiced law and served as judges in unbroken succession since the 14th century. An Atkyns who was a merchant at Chepstow purchased land for his sons at the Dissolution and raised the family to gentry status. (Joan Johnson, *Gloucestershire Gentry*, 41). **Possible relative MP 1571.**

1. Edward Atkyns – New Woodstock 1660
2. Robert Atkyns – Carmarthenshire 1656 Evesham 1659 East Looe 1661-72 Middlesex 1681
3. Sir Robert Atkyns – Cirencester 1679-81 Gloucestershire 1685-87

Seats: Sapperton Manor, Gloucestershire (medieval, rebuilt early 17th c., purch. 1667, sold 1730, demolished soon after); Pinbury Park, Gloucestershire (built 15th c., rebuilt late 16th c., purch. 1660s, remod. late 17th c., sold 18th c.); Hensington, Oxfordshire (acq. later 16th c.); Albury Hall, Hertfordshire (purch. 1661); Swell Bowl, Gloucestershire (purch. 1659, rebuilt 1671, demolished c. 1778)
Cabinet: Lord Chancellor 1690
Notes: Family extinct in the male line and estates sold by heiress 1730. A number of entries in ODNB.

ATTWOOD

Origins: Pioneering ironmasters in the 18th century. Father of the first MP made a fortune in iron production and banking. First MP a banker. High Sheriff 1811.

1. Matthias Attwood – Fowey 1819 Callington 1820-30 Boroughbridge 1830-32 Whitehaven 1832-47
2. Thomas Attwood – Birmingham 1832-40
3. Matthias Attwood – Greenwich 1837-41
4. John Attwood – Harwich 1841-49

Seat: Sion Hill, Worcestershire
Estates: Rubinstein – Matthais Attwood left £120,000 in probate in 1836 and the widow of James Attwood left £250,000 in 1838.
Notes: Charles and Thomas Attwood MP, the celebrated reformer, in ODNB.

AUBREY [James, Rede]

Origins: Tudor lawyer, (**first MP 1554**) Master of Requests 1595 purchased land in Breconshire and died worth £2,500 pa from land alone. **Another MP early 17th century**. His son was a Kt, High Sheriff 1685.

1. Sir John Aubrey 2 Bt – Brackley 1698-1700
2. Sir John Aubrey 3 Bt – Cardiff 1701-06
3. Sir John Aubrey 6 Bt – Wallingford 1768-74 Aylesbury 1774-80 Wallingford 1780-84 Buckinghamshire 1784-90 Clitheroe 1790-96 Aldeburgh 1796-1812 Steyning 1812-20 Horsham 1820-26
4. Thomas Aubrey – Wallingford 1784-90

Seats: Boarstall, Buckinghamshire (built c. 1312, acq. 18th c., family departed 1777, part demolished, sold early 20th c., NT 1943); Llantrithyd (Llantriddyd) Place, Glamorganshire (built 16th c., acq. by mar. 1586, changed main seat to Boarstall in the later 18th c., fell into ruin); Dorton, Buckinghamshire (built 1626, purch. 1777, now a school)
Estates: Worth £3,000 pa c. 1700
Title: Baronet 1660-1856
Notes: Boarstall built by the FitzNigels and descended through a number of heiresses. Among the families through whom it passed were the Jameses, who rose through royal service in the 14th century. **They elected 2 MPs in the 14th and 15th centuries.** From them it passed to the Redes, who rose through law, **elected two kts of the shire in the 14th and 15th centuries**. It descended from the Redes in the 16th century. Edward Lewis of Van, Glamorganshire inherited it (see under Clive). His daughter had no children. Boarstall passed to the heirs of her husband, the Aubreys (2 Bt). The 6 Bt was the last to live there. The Aubreys became extinct in the male line and their estates were dispersed among relatives after 1856. First MP, William Aubrey MP, John Aubrey the antiquary, and the 6 Bt in ODNB.

AUSTEN

<u>Austen</u>

Origins: Minor gentry since Tudor times. London merchant in the 17th century.

1. Robert Austen – Winchelsea 1666-79 1689-96
2. Sir John Austen 2 Bt – Rye 1667-79 1689-99
3. Robert Austen – Hastings 1695-98 Winchelsea 1701-02
4. Sir Robert Austen 3 Bt – Rye 1699-1701
5. Sir Robert Austen 4 Bt – New Romney 1728-34 1736-41

Seats: Hall Place, Kent (medieval house, rebuilt 1469, rebuilt 1540s, purch. c. 1640, add. 1649-53, passed by mar. to Dashwoods later 18th c.); Heronden (Hernden), Sussex (purch. mid-17th c., passed out of family 1742)
Estates: Worth £559 pa (but heavily in debt) in 1706.
Title: Baronet 1660-1772

Austen

Origins: Cadet branch were clothiers c. 1600.

1. Thomas Austen – W. Kent 1845-47

Seat: Kippington House (Park), Kent (rebuilt early 18th c., purch. later 1796, sold 1865)
Estates: Bateman 2980 (E) 6802
Notes: Edward Austen of this branch of the family, brother of the novelist Jane Austen, succeeded to the Knight estates at Chawton and Godmersham – see Peachey. Extinct 1893.

AYLWARD *IRELAND*

Origins: Settled in Waterford in the Middle Ages. Mayor of Waterford 1650. **Two MPs for County Waterford 1559 and 1585**.

1. Nicholas Aylward – {Thomastown 1727-56}

Seats: Faithlegg House, Waterford (confiscated 17th c.); Aylwardstown House, Kilkenny (acq. 1400s, rebuilt 1609, confiscated mid-17th c.); Shankill Castle, Kilkenny (old house, acq. by mar. 1685, rebuilt 1713, remod. c. 1828, sold 1991)
Notes: Roman Catholic family. Conformed 1711. Succeeded to Kearney estates 1876 and took the additional name Kearney. Took name Toler in 1884.

AYSCOUGH [Boucherett]

Ayscough

Origins: Settled in Lincolnshire in the 15th century. Chief Justice of the Common Pleas 15th c. **First MP (Great Grimsby 1529)** a soldier. **Kt of shire for Lincolnshire 1640-48. Two other MPs 17th century**. "A great county family". (Keeler, *The Long Parliament*, 93)

1. Sir Edward Ayscough – Great Grimsby 1685-87 1689-99

Seats: South Kelsey Hall, Lincolnshire (acq. by mar. and built 16th c., demolished); Nuthall, Nottinghamshire (sold later 17th c. or early 18th c.); Stallingborough Hall, Lincolnshire (medieval, acq. by mar. 15th c., passed by mar. to Boucheretts c. 1700, demolished first half 19th c.)
Estates: Worth £1,400 pa in 1680s.

Boucherett

Origins: Huguenot merchants settled in England 1644 who purchased Lincolnshire estates in the 18th century, and acquired Ayscough estates by marriage.

1. Ayscough Boucherett – Great Grimsby 1796-1803

Seats: Stallingborough Hall, Lincolnshire (acq. by mar. c. 1700, sales from 1789, demolished first half 19th c.); Willingham Hall (House), Lincolnshire (acq. 18th c., built 1790, demolished c. 1962)
Estates: Bateman 5834 (E) 7823; wealth in 1905 £38,500.
Notes: Family extinct 1905 upon the death of Jessie Boucherett (in ODNB).

BABINGTON

Origins: Landowners at Bavington, Northumberland by 1274. William Babington had a spectacular legal career, Chief Justice of Common Pleas 1423-36. (Payling, *Political Society in Lancastrian England*, 36-39) **Five MPs between 1399 and 1536, several kts of the shire.**

1. Matthew Babington – Leicestershire 1660
2. Thomas Babington – Leicester 1685-87 1689-90
3. Philip Babington – Berwick-on-Tweed 1689-90
4. Thomas Babington – Leicester 1800-18

Seat: Rothley Temple (Temple Hall), Leicestershire (medieval, purch. c. 1550 and add. 1565, sold 1845, remod. later 19th c., hotel)
Estates: Worth £2,000 pa in 1776.
Notes: Four members of the family in ODNB.

BACON [Frank]

Bacon

Origins: The first Bacon of note was son of a sheepreeve, although ancestors were recorded as early as 1286. He was a lawyer, **MP 1542**, Lord Keeper of the Great Seal 1558. Estates were purchased at the Dissolution. His brother was a London merchant. Eldest son created the first baronet 1611. Younger son Lord Chancellor 1618, created a viscount 1621. **Eight further MPs in the 16th and 17th centuries, including kts of the shire for Norfolk and Suffolk.**

1. Sir Edmund Bacon 4 Bt – Orford 1700-08
2. Sir Edmund Bacon 6 Bt – Thetford 1710-13 Norfolk 1713-15 1728-41
3. Sir Edmund Bacon 5 Bt – Thetford 1722-38

Seats: Thonock Hall, Lincolnshire (built mid-18th c., acq. by mar. 1826, family depart 1945, demolished 1964); Raveningham Hall, Norfolk (acq. by Castells c. 1235 from whom it passed by mar. to the Bacons 1735, built c. 1800, add. c. 1900, still own); Garboldisham Old Hall, Norfolk (built 16th c., purch. later 17th c., sold c. 1755); Gillingham Hall, Norfolk (purch. early 17th c., built early 17th c., remod. 18th c., passed by mar. to Schutz family 1750, thence to the Kenyons and other descendents, still own); Redgrave Hall, Suffolk (medieval, acq. 1545, add. 1560s, sold 1702, demolished 1947/1970); Gainsborough Old Hall, Lincolnshire (built c. 1460-80, acq. by mar. 1826, leased to museum 1952)
Estates: Bateman 3377 (E) 5358. Estates worth at least £3,000 in 1614. Worth £28,000,000 in 1990s with 14,000 acres.
Titles: Baron Verulam 1618-26 E; Viscount St. Albans 1621-26 E; Baronet 1611- ; 1627-
1 KG 20th
Notes: Many members of the family the in ODNB.

Bacon

Origins: A cadet line in the 16th century.

1. Waller Bacon – Norwich 1705-10 1715-34
2. Edward Bacon – Kings Lynn 1742-47 Callington 1748-54 Newport 1754-56 Norwich 1756-84

Seat: Earlham Hall, Norfolk (built early 17th c., passed by mar. to Bacons, sold 1925)
Notes: Earlham passed by marriage to the Frank family.

Frank

Origins: Leading tradesmen in Pontefract.

1. Robert Frank – Pontefract 1710-16

Seat: Campsall Hall, Yorkshire (acq. early 17th c., coverted into flats after 1945, demolished 1983)
Estates: Bateman 4009 (E) 5761

Bacon

Origins: Descended from a younger son of the Lord Keeper.

1. Francis Bacon – Ispwich 1646 1654 1656 1659 1660
2. Nathaniel Bacon – Ipswich 1654 1659 1660
3. Sir Nicholas Bacon – Ipswich 1685-87

Seat: Shrubland Park, Suffolk (acq. by mar. c. 1580s, rebuilt 1770-72, sold c. 1796)

Bacon

Origins: Cousins of the Bacons of Shrubland.

1. Thomas Bacon – Suffolk 1654 Aldeburgh 1660

Seat: Friston Hall, Suffolk (purch. and possibly built c. 1570, sold c. 1680s)
Notes: Nathaniel Bacon, the Virginia rebel, in ODNB.

BAGOT [Chester]

Baron Bagot (1780- GB)

Origins: Resident in Staffordshire from the time of the Conquest. (Thrush and Ferris, *House of Commons*, iii, 113-14) Bagot land listed in the Domesday Book 1086. Medieval barons, warriors and landowners. Kt c. 1250. **First MP 1348**. Lucrative marriages in the 14th c. **Five additional MPs, kts of the shire through to 1644**. Senior line took the name Stafford and became Dukes of Buckingham 1444 (attainted 1521).

1. Sir Edward Bagot 2 Bt – Staffordshire 1660
2. Sir Walter Bagot 3 Bt – Staffordshire 1679-81 1685-87 1689-90 1693-95
3. Sir Edward Bagot 4 Bt – Staffordshire 1698-1708
4. Charles Bagot – Staffordshire 1712-13
5. Sir Walter Bagot 5 Bt – Newcastle-u-Lyme 1724-27 Staffordshire 1727-54 University of Oxford 1762-68
6. William Bagot 1 Baron Bagot – Staffordshire 1754-80
7. Charles Bagot-Chester – Castle Rising 1794-1807
8. Sir Charles Bagot – Castle Rising 1807-08
9. William Bagot 3 Baron Bagot – Denbighshire 1835-52
10. Josceline Bagot – S. Westmorland 1892-1906 1910-13

Seats: Blithfield, Staffordshire (medieval, acq. by mar. before 1357 to Blithfield family heiress, built 1390s, add. 15th c., rebuilt late 16th c., add. 1740, add. 1820-24, still own); Levens Hall, Westmorland (medieval, rebuilt c. 1580-86, add. 1690s, acq. by Bagots by mar. 1783, add. 1820, still own); Pype Hayes Hall, Warwickshire (built c. 1600, acq. by mar. 1643, add. mid-19th c., sold 1919, municipal uses)
Estates: Bateman 30543 (E & W) 22212. Worth £1,400 pa in 1639 and £4,000 pa in 1690s. Owned 6,000 acres in 2001.
Titles: Baronet 1627- ; 1913-20
Peers: 5 peers 1780-1945
Notes: The head of the family was in France on the Agincourt campaign. A Bagot inherited great estates from the Earls of Berkshire and Suffolk 1783 (see Howard I). The Bagot family has an entry in ODNB with numerous members discussed.

Chester

Origins: A merchant in London granted arms 1472. Kt 1557. Son of a draper, a merchant was elected Lord Mayor of London 1560. **First MP 1563**. Inherited Chicheley from the Caves (rich merchants). Frances Bagot, daughter of the 4 Bagot Bt married in 1719 Sir John Chester 6 Bt. Her nephew, Charles Bagot, son of the 5 Bt, succeeded to the Chester estates in 1755 and took the name Chester.

1. Sir Anthony Chester 3 Bt – Bedford 1685-87
2. Sir John Chester 6 Bt – Bedfordshire 1741-47

Seats: Chicheley Hall, Buckinghamshire (purch. by Caves 1545, passed by mar. to Chesters under Eliz. I, built 1713-25, rented out 1880s, sold 1952); Lidlington Park, Bedfordshire (purch. 1630s, sold 1769)
Estates: Bateman 3129 (E) 4000
Title: Baronet 1620-1769
Notes: Family set up the first sugar refinery in England in the 16th century. John Chester, grandson of Charles Chester Bagot succeeded in 1863 to the St. Leger estate of Park Hill Yorkshire, which he sold. (see St. Leger). Sir Charles Chester Bagot cut off the entail to his estates to exclude his sister and his son and heir and left his estates to his maternal cousin Charles Bagot then working as a wine merchant in Oporto on condition he took the name Chester. Hence the estate and baronetcy were separated. (*Country Life*, 157, p. 501). First Kt in ODNB.

BAGWELL *IRELAND*

Origins: Quaker bankers from the early 18th century making £20,000 pa in the mid-century. Purchased landed estate beginning in 1729. Sheriff 1763.

1. William Bagwell – {Clonmell 1756}
2. John Bagwell – {Tulske 1761-68}
3. John Bagwell – {County Tipperary 1792-1800} 1801-06
4. William Bagwell – {Rathcormack 1798-1800} Clonmell 1801-19 County Tipperary 1819-26
5. Richard Bagwell – {Cashel 1799-1800} 1801
6. John Bagwell – Cashel 1801-02
7. John Bagwell – Clonmell 1857-74

Seats: Marlfield, Tipperary (purch. 1781 and rebuilt 1784, burned 1890s, rebuilt, burned 1923, rebuilt 1925, sold 1970s, flats); Eastgrove, Cork (acq. by inher. 19th c., sold c. 1958); Kilmore, Tipperary (purch. and built mid-18th c., sold c. 1851)
Estates: Bateman 4806 (I) 9433. Worth £2,000 pa in 1755.
Notes: John Bagwell was a Senator of the Free State in the 1920s. One in ODNB.

BAILEY *ENGLAND & WALES*

Baron Glanusk (1899- UK)

Origins: Rich ironmasters 18th century, purchased the 22,000 acre Glanusk estate for c. £500,000 in the early 19th century. (Thompson, "Desirable Properties", 164.)

1. Sir Joseph Bailey 1 Bt – Worcester 1835-47 Breconshire 1847-58
2. Joseph Bailey – Herefordshire 1841-50
3. Crawshaw Bailey – Monmouth District 1852-68
4. Joseph Bailey 1 Baron Glanusk – Herefordshire 1865-85 Hereford 1886-92

Seats: Glanusk Park, Breconshire (purch. 1826, built 1825, demolished 1954, still own estate); Maindriff Court, Monmouthshire (built 1877, donated as a hospital 1924); Easton Court, Herefordshire (built early 19th c., rebuilt early 19th c., purch. c. 1840, sold 1909, now derelict); Hay Castle, Herefordshire (medieval, new house built 1660, purch. 1844, fire 1939, sold)
Estates: Bateman 28308 (E & W) 25559 and 13649 (E & W) 12888. In 2015 16,500 acres.
Title: Baronet 1852-
Peers: 3 peers 1899-1945
3 Lds Lt 19th, 20th
Notes: Richard Crawshay of Cyfartha, one of the first industrial millionaires and a great Welsh ironmaster, left two-eighths share of his ironworks to his nephew Sir Jospeh Bailey 1 Bt in 1810. Rubinstein – William Crawshay left £700,000 in probate in 1834.

BAILLIE *SCOTLAND & ENGLAND*

Baillie

Origins: Kt living in the 15th century. Small lairds at Dochfour in the 17th century. Became successful land speculators. Owned a plantation in Grenada (purchased 1765). First MP a lawyer. Director of the East India Company and family members were bankers in Bristol in the late 18th and 19th centuries.

1. James Baillie – Horsham 1792-93
2. Evan Baillie – Bristol 1802-12
3. Peter Baillie – Inverness Burghs 1807-11
4. James Baillie – Tralee 1813-18 Bristol 1830-34
5. John Baillie – Hedon 1820-30 Inverness Burghs 1830-33
6. Hugh Baillie – Rye 1830-31 Honiton 1835-47
7. Henry Baillie – Inverness-shire 1840-68
8. James Baillie – Inverness-shire 1895-1900

Seats: Dochfour House, Inverness-shire (acq. 1442, medieval, burned 1745, rebuilt 1780, add. 19th c., still own); Redcastle, Ross-shire (built 1179, rebuilt 16th c., add. 1641, purch. 1838, unroofed and ruin after WWII); Leys Castle, Inverness-shire (acq. 1712, sold 1926)
Estates: Bateman 92648 (S) 11881 and 11959 (S) 7038
1 Ld Lt 19th
Notes: Rubinstein – James Baillie, probably a relative, possibly illegitimate, left £250,000 in probate in 1828. John Baillie MP and one other in ODNB.

Baillie

Origins: Cadet of the Dochfour line. Member of the Court of Session 1550, a judge, Lord Polkemmet 1793. Sheriff of County Down 1767.

1. James Bailie – {Hillsborough 1777-87}
2. Sir William Baillie 2 Bt – Linlithgowshire 1845-47
3. Charles Baillie – Linlithgowshire 1859
4. Sir Adrian Baillie 6 Bt – Linlithgowshire 1931-35 Tonbridge Div. Kent 1937-45

Seats: Polkemmet House, Linlithgowshire (built 17th c., add. 19th c., add. 1912, demolished, country park 1971); In(n)ishargie (Inishargy) House, Down (resident 18th c., sold 1785)
Estates: Bateman 4320 (S) 2825
Title: Baronet 1823-
Notes: Lord Polkemmet in ODNB.

BAINES

Origins: The first MP was the son of a grocer who became a printer and newspaper proprietor in Leeds 19th century.

1. Edward Baines – Leeds 1834-41
2. Matthew Baines – Hull 1847-52 Leeds 1852-59
3. Sir Edward Baines – Leeds 1859-74

Seat: The Hall, Bawtry, Yorkshire (built c. 1785, resident sec. half 19th c. into early 20th c., sold)
1 in Cabinet 1855-58
Notes: The three MPs and one other Baines in ODNB.

BAIRD I *SCOTLAND*

Viscount Stonehaven (1938- UK)

Origins: Farmers and millers in the 18th century, became coal mine managers, leaseholders, and then owners from the 1820s onwards. Became rich as ironmasters (first blast furnace built 1830) and purchased estates.

1. William Baird – Falkirk District Burghs 1841-46
2. James Baird – Falkirk District Burghs 1851-57
3. John Baird – N. W. Div. Lanarkshire 1885-86
4. John Baird – Central Div. Glasgow 1886-1906
5. John Baird 1 Baron Stonehaven – Rugby Div. Warwickshire 1910-22 Ayr Burghs 1922-25

Seats: Ury (Urie) House, Kincardineshire (built late 17th c., purch. 1853, rebuilt 1855, add. 1884, derelict after 1945, demolished 1956); Lockwood (House), Lanarkshire (purch. 1825); Adamton House, Ayrshire (built 1888, sold by 1939, hotel); Strichen House, Aberdeenshire (built 1818-21, purch. mid-19th c., partly demolished 1954, ruin); Durris House, Kincardineshire (built 16th c., burned, rebuilt c. 1650, add. 1824, add. 1835-38, purch. 1890, sold post WWII, flats)
Estates: Bateman 11018 (S) 12630; at Elie House, Fife 3575 (S) 8815; at Knoydart (purch 1857), Inverness-shire 68000 (S) 5800; at Cambusdoon, Ayrshire (fire 1970) 19599 (S) 9043; at Closeburn, Dumfriesshire 13573 (S) 11298; at Stichill, Aberdeenshire 23141 (S) 23199. James Baird MP died in 1876 worth £1,190,000.
Titles: Baron Stonehaven 1925- UK; Baronet 1897-
Peers: 2 peers 1925-45
1 Ld Lt 19th-20th

1 in Cabinet 1922-24
Notes: The Baird firm had 10,000 employees in the 1860s. James Baird gave a staggering £500,000 to the Kirk in 1873 to build new churches. James Baird MP in ODNB.

BAIRD II *SCOTLAND*

Origins: Gentry 16th century. Father of the 1 Bt was a prominent judge (himself the son of a lawyer) and politician. Said to have been created Baron Doveran by Charles I but died before the patent was issued. Purchased Newbyth in the reign of Charles I. 1 Bt a Lord of Session.

1. Sir John Baird 1 Bt – [Aberdeenshire 1665 1667]
2. Sir James Baird – [Banffshire 1665 1669-74]
3. James Baird – [Banffshire 1678]
4. Sir John Baird 2 Bt – Edinburghshire 1715-22
5. Robert Baird – Haddington Burghs 1796-1802

Seats: Newbyth House, Haddingtonshire (purch. mid-17th c., rebuilt 1817, now flats); Auchmedden, Banffshire (purch. 1539, forfeited 1746); Sauchton Hall, Edinburghshire (acq. and built 17th c., sold by 1929, demolished)
Estates: Bateman 2771 (S) 8354
Titles: Baronet 1680-1745; 1680-1745; 1695- ; 1809-
Notes: The Lord of Session, Lord Newbyth, in ODNB.

BAKER [Littlehales (Littlehaye)]

Origins: The father of the first MP was a great London builder, who laid out Baker Street. Sheriff 1787. On the death of the first MP he left Ranston to his cousin, Sir Edward Baker Littlehales 1 Bt. This line assumed the name Baker in 1814.

1. Peter Baker – Arundell 1781-84 Wootton Bassett 1802-06 Corfe Castle 1807-15
2. Sir Randolf Littlehales Baker 4 Bt – N. Dorset 1910-18
3. Sir Nicholas Baker – N. Dorset 1979-97

Seat: Ranston, Dorset (built 16th c., new house 1753, purch. 1781, partially demolished c. 1960, new house built, still own)
Estates: Rubinstein – Peter Baker left £150,000 in probate in 1815 and 1 Bt left £160,000 in 1825.
Title: Bt 1802-1959

BALCH

Origins: Merchants in Bridgwater in the 17th-18th centuries.

1. Robert Balch – Bridgwater 1692-95
2. George Balch – Bridgwater 1701-10
3. Robert Balch – Bridgwater 1753-61

Seat: [Nether] Stowey Court, Somerset (medieval, add. late 16th c., acq. 1627 by maternal ancestors, passed by mar. to Balches 1745, passed out of male line by mar. 1814, sold 1838)

BALDWIN

Earl Baldwin (1937- UK)

Origins: Iron and steel manufacturers from the 18th century. Gentry by mid-19th century but remained active in the firm.

1. Enoch Baldwin – Bewdley 1880-85
2. Alfred Baldwin – W. Worcestershire 1892-1908
3. Stanley Baldwin 1 Earl Baldwin – Bewdley Div. Worcestershire 1908-37
4. Oliver Baldwin 2 Earl Baldwin – Dudley 1929-31 Paisley 1945-47

Seat: Astley Hall, Worcestershire (built c. 1830s, purch. 20th c. by 1 Earl Baldwin, bequeathed to City of Birmingham as a school 1947)
Estates: Baldwin firm worth £1,000,000 in 1900
Peers: 1 peer 1937-45
1 in Cabinet 1921-23 1924-29 1931-37
1 KG 20th
Notes: Alfred and Stanley in ODNB

BALDWYN [Childe, Pytts]

Baldwyn/Childe

Origins: The Baldwyns settled in Shropshire by the 14th century. A lawyer elected **MP for Ludlow 1640 and another in 1659**, Kt. A Childe heiress married a Baldwyn who took the name Childe.

1. Charles Baldwyn – Ludlow 1681 1689-90 1695-98
2. Acton Baldwyn – Ludlow 1705-15 1722-27

3. William Childe – Shropshire 1727-34
4. Charles Baldwyn – Shropshire 1766-80
5. William Childe – Wenlock 1820-26

Seats: Kinlet Hall, Shropshire (acq. by mar. 1640, built 1727-29, now leased as a school, sold c. 1975); Brockleton, Shropshire; Aqualate Hall, Shropshire (now in Staffordshire) (built 16th c., rebuilt 1808, resident part of 19th c., fire 1910); Stokesay Castle, Shropshire (built c. 1291-1305, leased 1648 by Baldwyns, farm house after c. 1728, ruin 19th c.); Elsich (Elsych) Manor, Shropshire (built 16th c., sold 1779); Kyre Park, Worcestershire (medieval, remod. 1588, rebuilt 1753-76, inher. by mar. 1807, sold 1930s, now institutional use)
Estates: Bateman 14234 (E) 13183 and 3364 (E) 4696
Notes: The Kinlet estate originally belonged to the Cornewalls and Brampstons from whom it passed to Sir George Blount and through him to the Lacons, who mar. Childe in 1640. The Lacons (Roman Catholics) were an old family with 11,000 acres, much of it in Shropshire. **Six MPs 1413-1614**. William Lacon Childe MP heiress married Charles Baldwyn MP, and their son took the name Childe.

<u>Pytts</u>

Origins: Yeomen in the 15th century who moved into the gentry due to profitable legal office (Kt, Chief Justice of the Common Pleas 1563) under Elizabeth I. Purchased Kyre 1576.

1. Edward Pytts – Worcestershire 1654 1656 Bewdley 1659 Leominster 1660
2. James Pytts – Weobley 1660 Leominster 1679 Worcestershire 1685-86
3. Samuel Pytts – Hereford 1699-1700 Worcestershire 1710-15
4. Edmund Pytts – Worcestershire 1741-53
5. Edmund Pytts – Worcestershire 1753-61

Seat: Kyre Park, Worcestershire (medieval, purch. 1576 and rebuilt, add. early 17th c., add. 18th c., passed to Childes 1807)
Notes: On the extinction of the Pytts family in 1807 Kyre Park passed to their relatives (a grandson of an aunt, 1832), the Childes of Kinlet Hall.

BALFOUR I [Ramsay] *SCOTLAND*

<u>Earl Balfour</u> (1922- UK)

Origins: George Balfour (d. 1665) made a fortune as a clothier in London and Edinburgh and purchased Balbirnie in 1642. A younger son went to India and returned a nabob with £300,000 (Harris, *Whittinghame*, 15). He purchased the Whittinghame estate.

1. James Balfour – Anstruther Easter Burghs 1826-31 Haddingtonshire 1831-34
2. James Balfour – Haddington District 1841-47
3. Arthur Balfour 1 Earl Balfour – Hertfordshire 1874-85 E. Manchester 1885-1906 City of London 1906-22
4. Gerald Balfour 2 Earl Balfour – Leeds Central Div. 1885-1906
5. Charles Balfour – Hornsey Div. Middlesex 1900-07

Seat: Whittinghame, East Lothian (built 1817, sold 1980, flats)
Estates: Bateman 87196 (S) 19833. First MP died worth over £1,000,000.
Peers: 3 peers 1922-45
1 Ld Lt 20th
2 in Cabinet 1886-92 1895-1905 1902-05 1915-22 1925-29
1 KG 20th
Notes: 1 Earl, three siblings, and a niece in ODNB.

Balfour/Ramsay

Origins: Senior line of the Balfours succeeded by marriage to the Ramsey estates at Whitehill in the 18th century.

1. Robert Balfour Ramsay – Edinburghshire 1751-54

Seats: Balbirnie, Fife (medieval, purch. 1642, rebuilt 1777-82, add. 1815-19, sold 1968, now hotel); Whitehill, Edinburghshire (acq. by mar. 18th c.)
Estates: Bateman 10600 (S) 14718. Income was £1,722 pa in 1777. Coal and improved farming raised this to £7,697 pa in 1813 (*Country Life*, 151 p. 1670). Rubinstein - James Balfour Ramsay left £250,000 in probate 1823. Owned 5,000 acres in 1996.

BALFOUR II [Bethune, Bruce, Townley] *SCOTLAND & IRELAND*

Baron Balfour of Burleigh (1607- S)

Origins: Landowners 15th century. President of the Court of Session 1590s. Sir Michael Balfour **sat in the [Convention 1599]. Another [Member of Parliament 1643-44].** The daughter of the 4 Baron married Alexander Bruce of Kennet (owned since the mid-16th century). Their great-great-grandson succeeded as 6 Baron.

1. Henry Balfour – [Fifeshire 1703-07]
2. Nisbet Balfour – Wigtown Burghs 1790-96 Arundel 1797-1802
3. Robert Bruce – Clackmannanshire 1820-41

Seats: Kennet (House), Clackmannanshire (acq. 16th c., house built, rebuilt 1793-94, sold 1946, demolished 1967); Brucefield House, Clackmannashire (built 15th c.?, add. c. 1690, rebuilt 1714, sold c. 1759, later repurch., restored c. 1936-58, still own); Burleigh Castle, Kinross-shire (acq. 1446, built early 16th c., add. 1582, ruin); Dunbog House, Fife (built c. 1540, partly demolished 20th c.)
Estates: Bateman 2715 (S) 3364
Peers: [3 peers 1661-1707] 2 Scots Rep peers 1876-1921 1922-45
1 in Cabinet 1895-1903
1 KT 20th
Notes: The Barony was attainted 1715 and restored 1869. The daughter of the 1 Baron married Robert Arnot, son of Sir Robert Arnot. He changed his name to Balfour and the barony descended through this line. 2, 3, 5, and 6 Barons and the latter's daughter in ODNB.

Bethune

Origins: Descended from Sir William Balfour, brother of Sir Michael de Balfour, ancestor of the Balfours of Balfour. **First [MP 1572]. Three further [MPs 1612-41 one for Fifeshire].**

1. George Bethune – [Kilrenny Burgh 1689-93]
2. David Bethune – [Fifeshire -1703-07]
3. James Bethune – [Kilrenny Burgh 1703-07]

Seat: Balfour Castle, Fife (acq. 1196, ruin)

Balfour

Origins: A cadet (16th c.) of Balfour of Burleigh.

1. Sir David Balfour – [Fifeshire 1685-86]

Seat: Forret, Fife (purch. c. 1650, passed out of family 1712)

Townley-Balfour

Origins: A nephew of the 1 Baron Balfour of Burleigh served under Essex, acquired large estates in County Fermanagh under Elizabeth I and James VI, and was created an Irish peer (Baron Balfour of Glenawley 1619-c.1636 I). A Balfour heiress married Blayney Townley in the 1692, and the Townleys succeeded to Castle Balfour in 1738. His brother married in 1734 his cousin and heiress to Townley Hall and succeeded to both estates. The Townleys emerged in the 17th c. Sheriff 1694.

1. Blayney Townley – {Dunleer 1692-93 1695-99 1703-14 Carlingford 1715-22}
2. William Balfour – {Carlingford 1705-13 Augher 1713-39}
3. Henry Townley – {Carlingford 1727-41}
4. William Townley-Balfour – {Carlingford 1757-59}
5. Blayney Townley-Balfour – {Carlingford 1760-76}
6. Blayney Townley-Balfour – {Belturbet 1800}

Seats: Townley Hall, Louth (acq. and built early 18th c., add. 1771-73, new house built 1794, sold 1956, institutional use); Castle Balfour, Fermanagh (built 1618, Towneley's inherit 1739, sold 1823, ruin by late 19th c.); Piedmont, Louth (built early 18th c., abandoned in favor of Townley Hall, now a ruin)
Estates: Bateman 6952 (I) 6555. Balfours owned 8,000 acres in 1739 down to 4,000 acres sold for £86,000 in 1823.

BALL *IRELAND*

Origins: Legal family. The first two MPs were sons of a military chaplain and curate of Drogheda. The first two MPs were lawyers, the third MP was a Judge of Common Pleas, and fourth MP Lord Chancellor of Ireland 1875.

1. John Ball – {Drogheda 1796-1800}
2. Charles Ball – {Clogher 1800}
3. Nicholas Ball – Clonmell 1836-39
4. John Ball – County Carlow 1852-57

Notes: Nicholas Ball MP and his son John Ball MP were Roman Catholics and both in the ODNB. There seems to be some confusion between the ODNB and the entries for the two MPs in the Irish Parliament as listed in Johnston-Liik, *History of the Irish Parliament*. It is possible the second two MPs were not related to the first two.

BAMPFYLDE (Bampfield) [Warre]

Baron Poltimore (1831- UK)

Origins: At Poltimore by the reign of Edward I. **First MP 1429 for Devon. Three further MPs 1597-1650 (two kts of the shire for Devon).**

1. Thomas Bampfield – Exeter 1654-1656 1659 1660
2. Sir Coplestone Bampfylde 2 Bt – Tiverton 1659 Devon 1671-79 1685-87
3. Sir Coplestone Bampfylde 3 Bt – Exeter 1710-13 Devon 1713-27
4. John Bampfylde – Exeter 1715-22 Devon 1736-41
5. Sir Richard Bampfylde 4 Bt – Exeter 1743-47 Devon 1747-76
6. Sir Charles Bampfylde 5 Bt – Exeter 1774-90 1796-1812

Seats: Poltimore Park (House), Devon (acq. 1298, built c. 1550, add. c. 1810, estate sold 1920, institutional use for house, sold 1945. derelict, under restoration); Court Hall, Devon (inher. by mar. later 15th c. from St. Maurs and Zouches owners since 12th c., built early 17th c., add. 1835 and 1902, demolished later 20th c., some property still owned by descendents)
Estates: Bateman 19883 (E) 21800. Owned 9,000 acres in 1626.
Title: Baronet 1641-
Peers: 4 peers 1831-1945
Notes: 4 Baron sold most of his estates and moved to Rhodesia in the 1950s. A large part of the Devon estate sold. Five members of the family in ODNB.

<u>Warre</u> (Weare)

Origins: At Hestercombe since the late 14th century. **First MP 1449, kt of the shire for Wiltshire. Three other MPs 1553-1624.** The daughter and heiress of the 1 Baronet brought Hestercombe to her husband Sir Copleston Bampfylde 2 Bt in 1718.

1. Sir John Warre – Somerset 1665-69
2. Sir Francis Warre 1 Bt – Bridgwater 1685-87 1689-95 1699-1700 Taunton 1701-15

Seat: Hestercombe House, Somerset (acq. and built c. 1400, remod. 1680s, passed to Bampfyldes 1718, rebuilt 1730, sold 1873)
Title: Baronet 1673-1718

<u>Warre</u>

Origins: Cadet of the Hestercombe family descended from Thomas Warre (1576-1617).

1. John Warre – Lostwithiel 1812-18 Taunton 1820-26 Hastings 1831-34 Ripon 1857-60

Seats: Cheddon Fitzpayne, Somerset; West Newton Manor, Somerset

BANKES

Origins: Modest yeoman family in Cumberland. Father of first MP a merchant. Lawyers and royal officials in the 17th century. Fortune made by a Chief Justice of the Common Pleas under Charles I, who purchased estates in Dorset. Kt 1630. **First MP 1624**.

1. Sir Ralph Bankes – Corfe Castle 1659 1660-77
2. John Bankes – Corfe Castle 1698-1714
3. John Bankes – Corfe Castle 1722-41
4. Henry Bankes – Corfe Castle 1741-62

5. Henry Bankes – Corfe Castle 1780-1826 Dorset 1826-31
6. William Bankes – Truro 1810-12 University of Cambridge 1822-26 Marlborough 1829-32 Dorset 1832-34
7. George Bankes – Corfe Castle 1816-23 1826-32 Dorset 1841-56

Seat: Kingston Lacy, Dorset (medieval, ruin by 15th c., purch. 1632-36 for £11,400 - A. Mitchell, *Kingston Lacy*, London, 1994, 8 - built 1663-66, remod. 1780s, remod. 1835-41, given to NT 1981 with 16,000 acres)
Estates: Bateman 19228 (E) 14985. 16,000 acres in 1981. Ralph Bankes left an estate of £23 million in 1981. (Legg, *Dorset Families*, 76-77)
Notes: Three members of the family in ODNB.

BANKS (Bankes)

Origins: Originally goldsmiths and bankers in Wigan. The first MP's grandfather was a London goldsmith. Rapidly became gentry. Judge mid-17th c. Intermarried with the magnate family the Leghs of Lyme.

1. William Banks – Newton 1660 Liverpool 1675-76
2. William Banks – Wigan 1679 1689-90
3. Legh Banks – Newton 1695-98

Seat: Winstanley Hall, Lancashire (purch. and built 1596, remod. 1785 and 1818-19, family departed 1980s)
Notes: Male line extinct 1784, carried on by a cousin who took the name Banks.

BANNATYNE *SCOTLAND*

Origins: At Kames by 13th c. **[First MP sat for Buteshire 1617, another MP 1628-48]**.

1. Ninian Bannatyne – [Buteshire 1667 1669-74 1678 1681]

Seat: Kames Castle, Buteshire (built c. 16th, later add., sold 1810)
Notes: A 19th-century Lord of Session in ODNB.

BARCLAY [Allardice] *SCOTLAND & ENGLAND*

Barclay Allardice

Origins: The Allardice family was landed from at least the 15th century. Father of the **first MP [1560, 1607 for the county, second MP for the county 1612]** was a merchant. In the 18th century made a fortune in the West Indian slave trade and purchased estates on return from the WI in 1780. Continued as an investor and speculator.

1. Sir George Allardyce – [Kintore Burghs 1702-07] Scotland 1707-08
2. Robert Barclay Allardice – Kincardineshire 1788-97

Seats: Ury (Urie) House, Kincardineshire (Barclay seat, acq. 1647, built late 17th c., sold 1853, derelict after 1945, demolished 1956); Allardice (Allardyce) Castle, Forfarshire (there by 15th c., medieval, built late 16th c., add. 1695, passed to Barcalys 1776, became a farm house, sold 1854)
Notes: The Barclay's took the name Allardice on marriage to an heiress in 1776. The family became extinct 1854. Heiress left for America. An 18th century Barclay laird of Ury and several cadets in the ODNB.

Allardyce

Origins: Cadet line.

1. Alexander Allardyce – Aberdeen Burghs 1792-1801

Seat: Dunottar House, Kincardineshire (built c. 1800, demolished 1957)

Barclay

Origins: Younger son of the laird of Ury born 1682 succeeded to the family religious tradition of Quakerism and eventually the estates. Became merchants, bankers, and brewers in London. Acquired Thrale's brewery 1781. Also owned land with coal in Pennsylvania where an early 18th-century ancestor had been a customs official in Philadelphia. Succeeded to the Barclay Allardice estates in 1854.

1. Charles Barclay – Southwark 1815-18 Dundalk 1826-30 West Surrey 1835-37
2. David Barclay – Penryn 1826-30 Sunderland 1835-37 1841-47
3. Alexander Barclay – Taunton 1865-80

Seats: Eastwick Park, Surrey (purch. 1833, sold); Bury Hill, Surrey; Higham Hall, Suffolk (built early 19th c., still own)
Estates: Bateman 3816 (E) 4766. Rubinstein – Robert Barclay left £160,000 in probate in 1830.
Notes: Two 18th century Barclays in ODNB.

BARING [Dunning, Wall]

Earl of Northbrook (1876-1929 UK)

Origins: Academics, officials and merchants in Germany. One emigrated to England and was apprenticed in Exeter 1717. (Ziegler, *The Sixth Great Power*, 14-16) He purchased land and left £40,000. A son went to London 1750s and became Chairman of the East India Company and a merchant banker (Barings Bank founded 1762), followed by successive generations late into the 20th century. Held great wealth in several branches both in land (very large estates assembled from the 1790s onwards) and business.

1. John Baring – Exeter 1776-1802
2. Sir Francis Baring 1 Bt – Grampound 1784-90 Chipping Wycombe 1794-96 Calne 1796-1802 Chipping Wycombe 1802-06
3. Sir Thomas Baring 2 Bt – Chipping Wycombe 1806-32 Hampshire 1832
4. Henry Baring – Bossiney 1806-07 Colchester 1820-26
5. Charles Baring-Wall – Guildford 1819-26 Wareham 1826-30 Guildford 1830-31 Weymouth & Melcombe Regis 1831-32 Guildford 1832-47 Salisbury 1847-53
6. Francis Baring 1 Baron Northbrook – Portsmouth 1826-65
7. Thomas Baring – Great Yarmouth 1835-37 Huntingdon 1844-73
8. Thomas Baring 1 Earl of Northbrook – Penryn & Falmouth 1857-66
9. Thomas Baring – S. Essex 1874-85 London 1887-91
10. Francis Baring 2 Earl of Northbrook – Winchester 1880-85 N. Bedfordshire 1886-92

Seats: Stratton Park, Hampshire (built 1731, purch. 1801, rebuilt 1803, demolished c. 1961, rebuilt 1963-65, still own); Norman Court, Hampshire (built 1752, purch. 1815, add. 1820, school since 1952)
Estates: Bateman 18937 (E) 19596. The founder of the bank left £625,000 at his death in 1810 (Ziegler, *The Sixth Great Power*, 51; see also Rubinstein)
Titles: Baron Northbrook 1866- UK; Baronet 1793-
Peers: 4 peers 1866-1945
1 Ld Lt 19th-20th
2 in Cabinet 1839-41 1849-52 1880-85
Notes: Charles Wall's (MP) mother was a Baring. She left him Norman Court, and he took the name Baring. Rubinstein – Charles Wall, banker, left £125,000 in probate in 1815. Over a dozen Barings in the ODNB.

Earl of Cromer (1901- UK)

Origins: Cadet of 1 Baronet. Succeeded to Cromer Hall by marriage to a Windham heiress. His eldest son was created a baronet, the second son Baron Revelstoke, and the third son Earl of Cromer. An exceptionally active branch in banking, imperial governance, and diplomacy.

1. Henry Baring – Callington 1831-32 Marlborough 1832-68
2. Sir Godfrey Baring 1 Bt – Isle of Wight 1906-10 Barstaple Div. Devonshire 1911-18

Seats: Cromer Hall, Norfolk (purch. and built 1827, fire, rebuilt 1829, sold 1852); Membland Hall, Devon (built 18th c., purch. and add. 1877-79, sold in parcels from 1890 onwards, demolished c. 1952); Revelstoke Manor, Devon (purch. mid-19th c., sold 20th c.); Lambay Castle, Dublin (built 15-16th c., purch. and new house built 1904-08, still own)
Estates: Bateman under 3000 acres
Titles: Baron Revelstoke 1885- UK; Baron Cromer 1892- UK; Viscount Cromer 1899- UK; Baronet 1911-
Peers: 6 peers 1885-1945 1892-1945
Notes: Lord Revelstoke was bankrupted during the panic of 1890.

<u>Baron Ashburton</u> (1782-1823 E and 1835- UK)

Origins: The Dunnings were country lawyers in the 18th century. The 1 Baron made a fortune at the Bar, and as a legal official. He married the sister of Sir Francis Baring 1 Bt. The latter's second son was created Baron Ashburton.

1. John Dunning 1 Baron Ashburton – Calne 1768-82
2. Alexander Baring 1 Baron Ashburton – Taunton 1806-26 Callington 1826-31 Thetford 1831-32 N. Essex 1832-35
3. William Baring 2 Baron Ashburton – Thetford 1826-30 Callington 1830-31 Winchester 1832-37 N. Staffordshire 1837-41 Thetford 1841-48
4. Francis Baring 3 Baron Ashburton – Thetford 1830-31 1832-41 1848-57
5. Alexander Baring 4 Baron Ashburton – Thetford 1857-67
6. Guy Baring – Winchester 1906-16

Seats: The Grange, Hampshire (built c. 1670, rebuilt 1804-25, purch. 1817, add. 1852, remod. 1880, abandoned 1940, part demolished 1975, opera house); Buckenham Tofts Hall, Norfolk (built later 17th c., purch. c. 1830, sold later 19th c., demolished 1946); Ashburton, Devon (purch. early 19th c.); Sandridge Park, Devon (purch. by Dunning 2nd half 18th c., passed by mar. to Barings, new house built c. 1810, sold 1935); Rosehall House, Sutherlandshire (acq. and built 1806, fire 1817, rebuilt rebuilt 1818-25, sold later 19th c.)
Estates: Bateman 36772 (E) 46685; The first Baring Baron spent between £800,000 and £1,000,000 on the purchase of land 1816-48 (Ziegler, *The Sixth Great Power*, 88)
Peers: 8 peers 1782-83 1803-23 1835-1945
1 Ld Lt 20th
2 in Cabinet 1782-83 1835-1945

BARKER I

Origins: Clothiers and merchants in Ipswich since the reign of Edward III. Achieved gentry status under Elizabeth I. **First MP 1559 for Ispwich. Two further MPs for the town between 1584-93.**

1. Sir John Barker 4 Bt – Ipswich 1680-81 1685-87 1689-96
2. Sir William Barker 5 Bt – Ipswich 1708-13 Thetford 1713-15 Suffolk 1722-31

Seat: Grimston Hall, Suffolk (acq. and built 1597, rebuilt 18th c., passed to Nassaus 1766, now a farm house)
Title: Baronet 1622-1766
Notes: The 7th and last Baronet left his estates to George Nassau of Easton Park, Suffolk in 1766 (see Pitt).

BARKER II

Origins: Established in Berkshire under the Tudors, rose by law in Wallingford, and became gentry 17th century. Kt 1608. **First MP 1621. A second for Wallingford 1640-41.**

1. Scorie Barker – Wallingford 1679-81 Middlesex 1705-10
2. William Barker – Berkshire 1679-81

Seats: Sonning, Berkshire (medieval, acq. mid 16th c., demolished c. 1574, new house late 17th c., demolished 1760); Grove House, Chiswick, Middlesex (built early 17th c., sold 1682, demolished 1928)

BARKER III [Raymond]

Origins: The **first MP for Bristol 1624** was a merchant and the son of a prominent Bristol merchant. Fairford purchased 1650. Estates passed to Raymond of Hatchlands in 1789; took name Raymond-Barker.

1. Samuel Barker – Cricklade 1702-08
2. John Raymond – Weymouth & Melcombe Regis 1741-47

Seat: Fairford Park, Gloucestershire (built early 16th c., purch. 1650, new house 1661-62, remod. 18th c., sold 1945, demolished c. 1955)
Estates: Bateman 3395 (E) 4500

BARNARDISTON

Origins: Gentry at least since the mid-13th century. **First MP for Suffolk 1298 and a further MP 1358 for Lincolnshire. Two further MPs 1512-1654**.

1. Sir Samuel Barnardiston 1 Bt – Suffolk 1674-81 1690-1702
2. Sir Thomas Barnardiston 2 Bt – Great Grimsby 1685-87 1689-90 Sudbury 1690-98
3. Sir Samuel Barnardiston 2 Bt – Ipswich 1698-1700

Seats: Ketton Hall, Suffolk (leased?); Brightwell Hall, Suffolk (built 16th c., demolished late 18th c.); The Ryes, Essex (built 1810, add. 1884, sold 1970s)
Estates: Bateman 2932 (E) 2672. Worth £2,000 pa in 1660.
Titles: Baronet 1663-1712; 1663-1750
Notes: An old gentry family raised to a title by a son who entered the East India Company and made a fortune. Three members of the family in ODNB.

BARNE

Origins: The father of the first MP was a London merchant and Director of the East India Company, descended from a Lord Mayor of London 1552. Purchased estates in Suffolk 1744.

1. Miles Barne – Dunwich 1747-54 1764-77
2. Barne Barne – Dunwich 1777-91
3. Miles Barne – Dunwich 1791-96
4. Snowdon Barne – Dunwich 1796-1812
5. Michael Barne – Dunwich 1812-30
6. Frederick Barne – Dunwich 1830-32
7. Frederick Barne – E. Suffolk 1876-85

Seats: Sotterley Hall, Suffolk (built early 17th c, purch. 1744, rebuilt soon after, add. c. 1820, still own); May Place, Kent (medieval, acq. early 18th c., add. later 18th c., partially destroyed WWII, fire 1959); Grey Friars, Suffolk (built in Victorian period)
Estates: Bateman 7642 (E) 9471. Rubinstein – Miles Barne left £400,000 in probate 1825.

BARNES

Baron Gorell (1909- UK)

Origins: Purchased coal mines 1846 and later railways. The father of the 1 Baron was a shipowner in Liverpool. Other family members in business.

1. Alfred Barnes – Derbyshire 1880-85 Chesterfield Div. Derbyshire 1885-92
2. Frederick Barnes – N. E. Kent 1895-1900

Seat: Ashgate Lodge, Chesterfield, Derbyshire (19th c.)
Peers: 3 peers 1909-45
Notes: 1 Baron Gorell, a judge, in ODNB.

BARNEWALL *IRELAND*

Baron Trimleston (1461- I)

Origins: The de Barnewalls came to Ireland in the medieval period. Settled at Drimnagh Castle, County Dublin in the early 13th century. Kt 14th century. Warriors, landowners, judges. 1 and 3 Barons Lord Chancellors of Ireland. **First {MP 1585}. Three subsequent {MPs 1615-39}.**

No MPS post 1660

Seats: Trimleston Castle (Trimblestown), Meath (acq. and built later 15th c., add. 18th c., remod. early 19th c., abandoned 1813, ruin mid-19th c.); Bloomsbury House, Meath (built c. 1700, acq. early 19th c., remod. 1858, family left c. 1916 and sold); Lara (Laragh), Kildare (built early-mid 18th c., passed out of family late 18th c.); Roebuck Castle, Dublin (acq. and built sec. half 16th c., damaged 17th c., rebuilt c. 1790, sold early 19th c.); Turvey House, Dublin (16th c. built tower house, add. late 17th c., remod. 1725-50, acq. by inher. 1800, demolished 1987)
Estates: Bateman 6759 (I) 7656
Peers: {4 peers 1661-87 1795-1800}
Notes: A Roman Catholic family, which debarred them from the Irish Parliament for much of the 17th and 18th centuries. The title was attainted 1691, reversed 1795. The 13 Baron conformed to the Established Church 1795. Family lived in England by 1930s. 3 and 12 Barons and son of the 11 Baron in ODNB.

Viscount Barnewall of Kingsland (1646-1834 I)

Origins: Cadet of the Barnewall family. The 13 Baron Trimleston succeeded to the estates of the 5 Viscount Barnewall in 1800. **First {MP 1559 for County Meath}. Three other {MPs 1585-1641}.**

No post-1660 MPs

Seat: Turvey House, Dublin (16th c. acq. and built tower house, add. late 17th c., remod. 1725-50, passed to kinsmen, Lords Trimleston, 1800, demolished 1987)

Estates: Worth c. £3500 pa in 1725.
Peers: {3 peers 1660-63 1689 1787-1800}
Notes: Roman Catholic family. Title dormant 1800-14. Last Viscount died poor. Father of 1 Viscount and the 1 and 3 Viscounts in ODNB.

Barnewall

Origins: Descended from the elder brother of the 1 Baron Trimleston. **First {MP 1585 for County Meath}. One other {MP 1639}.**

1. Sir Patrick Barnewall 3 Bt – {County Meath 1680 1690}

Seat: Crickstown, Meath (acq. and built c. 1400, rebuilt c. 1600, destroyed 1640s, passed out of the family 19th c.)
Estates: 2,000 acres worth £1,261 pa c. 1800.
Title: Baronet 1622-
Notes: Lost much land in the mid-17th c. Regained Crickstown 1661. The remaining land was divided among female descendants on the death of the 4 Bt in 1735. The 12 Bt lived in Australia in the 20th c.

BARRAN

Origins: The 1 Baronet was the son of a London gunmaker who became a tailor and clothes manufacturer, a pioneer of the ready-made clothing industry in the 1850s. Mayor of Leeds 1870, MP 1876, and a baronet in 1895.

1. Sir John Barran 1 Bt – Leeds 1876-85 Otley Div. Yorkshire 1886-95
2. Sir Rowland Barran – N. Leeds 1902-18
3. Sir John Barran 2 Bt – Hawick Burghs 1909-18

Seats: Sawley Hall, Yorkshire (built 1770, remod. mid-19th c., owned well into 20th c.); Chapel Allerton Hall, Yorkshire; Leathley Hall, Yorkshire (built c. 1800, purch. or leased late 19th c.)
Title: Baronet 1895-
Notes: Barran family has an entry in the ODNB. Sir David Barran was President of Shell Oil 1967-72.

BARRINGTON I [Shute, Wildman]

Viscount Barrington (1720- I)

Origins: The Shutes were a legal family who rose high through the career of a judge appointed 1579. **First MP 1571. One additional MP 1621.** 1 Viscount was a barrister. The Shutes inherited estates in Berkshire from John Wildman in 1710 (**first MP 1654** a lawyer), whose family purchased estates worth £1,500 pa in the 1650s. Finally they inherited Tofts, Essex from Francis Barrington and took the name Barrington (for that family, see Barrington II).

1. Sir John Wildman – Scarborough 1654 Great Bedwyn 1681 1689
2. John Wildman – Wootton Basset 1689-95
3. John Barrington 1 Viscount Barrington – Berwick-on-Tweed 1715-23
4. William Barrington-Shute 2 Viscount Barrington – Berwick-on-Tweed 1740-54 Plymouth 1754-78
5. George Barrington – Sunderland 1832-33
6. William Barrington 6 Viscount Barrington – Berkshire 1837-57
7. George Barrington 7 Viscount Barrington – Eye 1866-80

Seats: Becket House (Hall), Berkshire (purch. by Wildmans 1666, inherited by Shutes 1710, sold 1938); Tofts, Essex (acq. 17th c., sold 1778)
Estates: Bateman 6387 (E) 17087. Rubinstein – Shute Barrington left £120,000 in probate in 1826.
Title: Baron Shute 1880- UK
Peers: {1 peer 1745-93} 4 peers 1880-1945
1 in Cabinet 1755-78
Notes: 1 Viscount and four of his sons in ODNB.

BARRINGTON II [Simeon]

Barrington

Origins: The Barringtons held property in Essex since the early 13th century. Acquired Swainstown, Isle of Wight by marriage to an heiress c. Mary I. **First MP 1572 for Essex. Four additional MPs 1589-1644.**

1. Sir John Barrington 3 Bt – Newtown (IofW) 1645-48 1660-79
2. Sir Charles Barrington 5 Bt – Essex 1694-1705 1713-15
3. Sir John Barrington 7 Bt – Newtown 1729-34 1741-75
4. Sir John Barrington 9 Bt – Newtown 1780-96

Seats: Swainstown (Swainston), Hampshire (IoW) (medieval, acq. by mar. c. 1550s, became principal seat early 18th c., rebuilt 1775-80, passed by mar. to Simeons mid-19th c.); Barrington Hall, Essex (acq. early Middle Ages, medieval house, demolished and rebuilt 1564, new house demolished c. 1640, new house 1734, add. c. 1790, sold c. 1834)
Estates: Worth at least £3,000 pa in 1628, £4,000 pa in c. 1660. Possibly worth £6,000 pa c. 1700.
Title: Baronet 1611-1833
Notes: 1 and 2 Bts in ODNB.

Simeon

Origins: The 1 Baronet was a Master of the Court of Chancery. Sir Richard Simeon 2 Bt married the daughter and heiress of the 10th and last Barrington Baronet.

1. Sir John Simeon 1 Bt – Reading 1797-1802 1806-181
2. Sir Richard Simeon 2 Bt – Isle of Wight 1832-37
3. Sir John Simeon 3 Bt – Isle of Wight 1847-51 1865-70
4. Sir John Simeon 4 Bt – Southampton 1895-1906

Seats: Walliscote House, Oxfordshire (acq. by 1 Bt, sold later in 19th c.); Swainstown, Hampshire (IoW) (built c. 1750, acq. by mar. mid-19th c., family in residence until bombed 1941, rebuilt 1950-54, school and then hotel)
Estates: Bateman 8724 (E) 8056. Rubinstein – Edward Simeon left £150,000 probate in 1812.
Title: Baronet 1815-
Notes: 1 Bt and his brother, the famous Evangelical preacher, in ODNB.

BARRINGTON III *IRELAND*

Origins: Settled in Ireland at the end of the 16th century and acquired more land with successive confiscations. **First {MP 1613}. One additional {MP Queen's County 1646}**. Sheriff 1697.

1. John Barrington – {Ballynakill 1692-93 1703-14 1727-56}
2. Jonah Barrington – {Ballynakill 1747-60}
3. Sir Jonah Barrington – {Tuam 1790-97 Clogher 1798-1800}

Seats: Cullenagh Castle (Timoge), Queen's County (acq. 1554, resident through 18th c.); Knapton, Queen's County (acq. 1562, sold 18th c., demolished 20th c.)
Estates: Worth £400 in 1713. Impoverished gentry in 18th century.
Notes: Sir Jonah Barrington MP, a judge, died in disgrace as a possible embezzler from court funds, in ODNB.

BARRY [Cusack, Purdon, Smith] *IRELAND*

Earl of Barrymore (1628-1823 I)

Origins: The Norman lord Philip de Barry and his brother Robert were granted vast estates in Ireland and went there in 1169 and 1183. A great Anglo-Norman family. Baron 1261. **Two {MPs 17th century}.**

1. Richard Barry – {Enniscorthy 1692-93 1695 1697-99 Baltimore 1713-14}
2. James Barry 4 Earl of Barrymore – Stockbridge 1710-13 1714-15 Wigan 1715-27 1734-47
3. James Barry – {Dungarvon 1713-14 1721-27 Rathcormack 1727-43}
4. Redmond Barry – {Dungarvon 1717-27 Tallow 1727-50}
5. David Barry – {Belfast 1727-45}
6. Arthur Barry – {Belfast 1757-60}
7. Richard Barry – Wigan 1747-61
8. Richard Barry 7 Earl of Barrymore – Heytesbury 1791-93
9. Arthur Smith-Barry 1 Baron Barry – County Cork 1867-74 S. Huntingdonshire 1886-1900

Seats: Fota Island, Cork (old castle, small house c. 1714, enlarged c. 1820, add. 1856, add. c. 1900, sold 1975, institutional use); Marbury Hall, Cheshire (acq. and built 1714, remod. 1856-58, demolished 1968); Belmont Hall, Cheshire (purch. 1749, built 1755, sold 1801); Castle Lyons, Cork (built 1204, acq. 1578, new house 16th c., rebuilt 17th c., chief seat of the Earls 17th century to 1771, burned 1771, sold c. 1800, ruin); Barry's Court, Cork (medieval castle, rebuilt 1588, chief seat until c. 1650, ruin 19th c.); Annegrove (Ballinsperrig), Cork (built late 17th c., acq. 1720, later leased out, passed out of family 19th c., demolished c. 1965); Wargrave-on-Thames, Berkshire; Belmont Hall, Cheshire (purch 1749, sold 1801); Buttevant Castle, Cork (built and acq. c. 1200, sold early 19th c.)
Estates: Bateman 26792 (I & E) 37279; 6273 (I) 6050; 8406 (I) 5552. The estates of the 7 Earl included 140,000 acres in County Cork sold 1790s for an annuity of £4,000 pa.
Titles: Baron Barry 1261-1823 I; Viscount Buttevant 1534-1823 I; Baron Barrymore 1902-25 UK
Peers: {3 peers 1661-99 1704-48} 1 peer 1902-25
Notes: The Barrys held Cork estates until 1975.
Earl Rivers acq. Marbury, Cheshire in 1684. His daughter married the 4 Earl of Barrymore and he inherited the estate in 1714. At his death in 1748 the eldest son inherited Fota and the second son Marbury. The latter's younger son, John, married a wealthy Essex heiress Dorothy Smith and he took the additional name Smith. He acquired Belmont Hall, Cheshire (de Figueirdo and Treuherz, *Cheshire Country Houses*, 31). Three 12th-century Barrys, the 3 Viscount, the 1,4, and 7 Earls, and a Smith-Barry in ODNB.

The M'Adam Barry

Origins: Cadet of the Barrys. Conformed mid-17th century.

1. Redmond Barry M'Adam Barry – {Fethard 1666}
2. James Barry M'Adam Barry – {Rathcormack 1692-93 1695-99 Dungarvon 1703-13 Rathcormack 1713-14}
3. James Barry M'Adam Barry – {Rathcormack 1768-76}

Seats: Lisnagar (Lisnegar), Cork (acq. 12th c., medieval castle, rebuilt early 18th c., sold c. 1771); Ballyclough House (Castle), Cork (castle built 1591, acq. 1666 by mar. to a Purdon heiress, rebuilt early 19th c., passed out of family first half 20th c., most demolished 20th c.); Rathcormack, Cork (acq. by mid-17th c., resident 18th c.)
Estates: Bateman 3910 (I) 2631

Purdon

Origins: Settled in Lurgan, County Louth (from Cumberland) in the reign of Henry VIII. Arms conferred 1585. Sheriff 1663. James Barry of Lisnegar married the Purdon heiress to Ballyclough in 1666.

1. Sir Nicholas Purdon – {Baltimore 1661-66}
2. Simon Purdon – {Ennis 1703-13}
3. Bartholomew Purdon – {Mallow 1699 1703-13 Doneraile 1713-14 Castlemartyr 1715-37}
4. Henry Purdon – {Charleville 1721-27}
5. George Purdon – {County Clare 1725-27}

Seats: Ballyclough House, Cork (acq. mid-17th c., castle passed by mar. 1666 to Barrys, derelict mid-20th c.); Tinerana (Tincrana), Clare (acq. 1659, sold 1901)
Estates: Bateman 8802 (I) 4381. At one point held 60,000 acres in Clare, sold out 1901.

Cusack-Smith (Smyth)

Origins: Erasmus Smyth was a merchant in London and contractor to the Parliamentray army in Ireland in the 1640s. Acquired estates there in the 1650s. Later became an important legal family over a number of generations.

1. Erasmus Smyth – {Ardee 1665-66}
2. Sir Michael Smith 1 Bt – {Randalstown 1783-93}
3. Sir William Cusack-Smith 2 Bt – {Lanesborough 1794-97 Donegal 1797-1800}
4. Thomas Cusack-Smith – Ripon 1843-46

Seat: Newton, King's County (acq. 1670, resident in 19th c.)
Title: Baronet 1799-
Notes: 1 Bt was Master of the Rolls in Ireland. The 2 Baronet married the daughter of James Cusack of County Wicklow. 2 Bt and a son in ODNB.

<u>Baron Barry of Santry</u> (1661-1739 I)

Origins: Cadet of the Barrys. Became wealthy merchants in Dublin in late 16th and early 17th centuries. Kt 1640. First Baron was Chief Justice of the King's Bench 1660. **One {MP Dublin 1613, 1634, 1639}**.

No post-1660 MPs

Seat: Santry Court, Dublin (built 1703, add. 1740-50, passed by mar. 1751 to Domviles, demolished 1940s)
Peers: {4 peers 1661-1739}
Notes: 4 Baron convicted of the murder of a footman and his title forfeited 1739, but he was reprieved from beheading. His estates passed to his cousins the Pocklingtons (see Domvile). Extinct 1751. 1 Baron in ODNB.

BARTTELOT

Origins: Gentry at least since the 14th century. **First MP (for Sussex) 1435. Second MP 1625-26.**

1. Sir Walter Barttelot 1 Bt – W. Sussex 1860-8 Horsham 1885-93

Seat: Stopham House (Ford House), Sussex (acq. by mar. from the Stophams 14th c. possible Domesday tenants, medieval house, rebuilt 1485, remod. 16th c., part demolished 1638, remod. 1842-65, rebuilt 1887, add. 1898, still own, flats)
Estates: 3633 (E) 4793
Titles: Bt. 1875-
Notes: Two in ODNB.

BASS

<u>Baron Burton</u> (1886-1909 1897- UK)

Origins: Brewers. Business founded 1777.

1. Michael Bass – Derby 1848-83

2. Michael Bass 1 Burton – Stafford 1865-68 E. Staffordshire 1868-85 Burton Div. Staffordshire 1885-86
3. Hamar Bass – Tamworth 1878-85 W. Staffordshire 1885-98

Seats: Rangemore Hall, Staffordshire (built 1822, acq. and rebuilt 1850s, remod. 1898-1901, sold 1949); Glen Quoich (Glenquoich) Lodge, Inverness-shire (built 1838, leased 1873-1905, add. c. 1900); Byrkley Lodge, Staffordshire (built 1887-91, demolished 1952)
Estates: Bateman 2283 (E) 17317. Millionaires by 1900. Worth £31,000,000 in 1990 and owned 58,000 acres, much of it in Scotland.
Title: Baronet 1882-1952
Peer: 1 peer 1886-1909
Notes: 1 Baron and father in ODNB.

BASSET (Bassett)

<u>Basset</u>

Origins: An early Norman family, possibly at Hastings in 1066. Justiciars of England and barons in the 12th and 13th centuries. **First MP 1553, for Devon 1554-58. Three further MPs 1563-1626, for Devon 1572**.

1. John Basset – Barnstaple 1677-81 1685-86
2. John Basset – Barnstaple 1718-21
3. John Basset – Barnstaple 1740-41
4. Francis Basset – Barnstaple 1780-84

Seats: Heanton Court, Devon (acq. by mar. 15th c., passed to Davie-Bassets by mar. 1802, sold c. 1852 but came back into Basset ownership by female descent later 19th c., farm house, see Williams V, hotel); Pilton House, Devon (built 1746, acq. later 19th c. by Williams/Bassets, sold by 1890); Watermouth Castle, Devon (built by Davie-Bassets mid-19th c., passed to Williams/Bassets, sold c. 1945); Umberleigh, Devon (acq. by mar. 15th c., passed with other estates to Davie-Bassets and Williams-Bassets in later 19th c.)
Estates: Bateman 6973 (E) 6105
Notes: Extinct in the male line late 18th century. Charles Williams married in 1858 the Basset heirss and took the name Basset (see Williams V). Numerous medieval Bassets and a Tudor Basset in ODNB.

<u>Baron Dunstanville</u> (1796-1835 GB)

Origins: A cadet line descended from a younger son. **First MP 1332. Two other MPs 1563 and 1640.**

1. John Basset – St. Ives 1661
2. Francis Basset – Mitchell 1702-05
3. Francis Basset – Penryn 1766-69
4. Francis Basset 1 Baron Dunstanville – Penryn 1780-96
5. John Basset – Helston 1840-41

Seats: Tehidy Park, Cornwall (acq. by mar. medieval period, rebuilt 1734-35, add. 1869, sold 1916, fire 1918); St. Michael's Mount, Cornwall (medieval, purch. 1640, sold to the St. Aubyns 1647)
Estates: Bateman 16969 (E) 32854. Huge mineral wealth in Cornwall.
Titles: Baron Basset 1797-1855 GB; Baronet 1779-1835
Peer: 1 peer 1796-1835
Notes: Sir Francis Basett (d. 1645) and 1 Baron in ODNB.

BASSETT I

Origins: Emerged in the Middle Ages. **First MP under Edward III for Gloucestershire. Another MP 1640-44.**

1. Sir William Bassett – Bath 1669-79 1681 1685-87 1689-93

Seat: Claverton, Somerset (purch. early 17th century, sold 1701)
Estates: 1,300 acres in later 17th century worth £1,800 pa. Sold 1693 for £19,000.
Notes: Main line extinct 1693. Estates sold to pay off debts.

BASSETT II (Basset) *WALES*

Origins: A landed family in Glamorganshire in the 13th century. **First MP 1542. Two other MPs 1547-71.**

1. Sir William Bassett – Cardiff Boroughs 1661

Seat: [Old] Beaupré Castle, Glamorganshire (acq. by mar. and built by 1330, add. mid/later-16th c., add. c. 1600, sold 1709, decayed into a ruin, state guardianship 1952)
Estates: Worth £800 pa in c.1660.
Notes: Finances damaged by Civil War. Gradually abandoned Beaupré and then sold it.

BASTARD

Origins: Claim descent from 850 AD but only emerged in the 16th century. **First MP 1597**, a lawyer. **Another MP 1654**. High Sheriff 1676, Kt 1677.

1. Sir William Bastard – Bere Alston 1679-81
2. John Bastard – Truro 1783-84 Devon 1784-1816
3. Edmund Bastard – Dartmouth 1787-1812
4. Edmund Bastard – Dartmouth 1812-16 Devon 1816-30
5. John Bastard – Dartmouth 1816-32

Seats: Kitley, Devon (built 16th c., rebuilt early 18th c., rebuilt c. 1820-25, leased out 1987); Buckland Court, Devon (acq. and built early 19th c., resident into 20th c.); Sharpham House, Devon (purch. 1765 by Pownolls, built c. 1770, passed by mar. to Bastards 1783, sold 1841, institutional use)
Estates: Bateman 7639 (E) 11259
Title: Baronet in 1779 but not assumed
Notes: A Bastard married a Pollexfen (pronounced Poulson) heiress to Kitley and succeeded to the estate 1710. Philemon Pownoll, a naval officer, won £60,000 in prize money during the Seven Years War and purchased Sharpham House in 1765. His grandson, John Bastard inherited the estate but gambled away his wealth and sold it 1841. John Bastard (d. 1816) in ODNB.

BATESON [Yarburgh] *IRELAND & ENGLAND*

Baron Deramore (1885- UK)

Origins: From Lancashire, emerged 17th century; to Ireland early 18th c.; purchased estates mid-18th century. Sheriff 1761.

1. Sir Robert Bateson 1 Bt – County Londonderry 1830-42
2. Sir Robert Bateson – County Londonderry 1842-43
3. Thomas Bateson 1 Baron Deramore – County Londonderry 1844-57 Devizes 1864-85

Seats: Belvoir Park, Down (built 1740s, purch. 1811, remod. 1820, renovated c. 1865, demolished 1961); Heslington Hall, Yorkshire (built 1568, acq. from an heiress in the later 19th century, remod. 1903, family departed 1939, institutional use); Magherafelt (Ballymaguigan), Londonderry (leased from 1754); Fort Breda, Down (purch. 1870, sold 1896)
Estates: Bateman 17373 (I) 14888
Titles: Baronet 1789-1825 1818-
Peers: 4 peers 1885-1945
1 Ld Lt 19th-20th

Yarburgh

Origins: **First MP 1325**. JP and Kt Charles I. At Snaith early 18th century. Mary Elizabeth Yarburgh married 1862 the 2 Baron Deramore, whose descendants succeeded to Heslington.

1. Sir Thomas Yarburgh – Pontefract 1685-87 1689-90

Seats: Snaith Hall, Yorkshire (acq. by mar. 1625, ceased to be occupied 1692 as chief seat, passed to Lloyd-Greames later 19th c.); Heslington Hall, Yorkshire (built 1568, acq. by mar. 1692, passed to Batesons later 19th c.); Blane (Balne) Hall, Yorkshire (acq. mar. 1625, passed with Snaith)
Estates: Bateman 9364 (E) 10010
Notes: Heslington was originally a Hesketh seat and passed by marriage in 1692 to the Yarburghs.

BATHURST [Bragge]

Earl Bathurst (1772- GB)

Origins: Clothiers in Canterbury in the 15th century. Alderman in London in the 16th century and entered the gentry by the reign of Elizabeth I. Married an heiress 1610. First MP was a Governor of the East India Company and Kt.

1. Sir Benjamin Bathurst – Bere Alston 1685-87 New Romney 1702-04
2. Allen Bathurst 1 Earl Bathurst – Cirencester 1705-12
3. Peter Bathurst – Wilton 1711-13 Cirencester 1727-34 Salisbury 1734-41
4. Benjamin Bathurst – Cirencester 1713-27 Gloucester 1728-54 Monmouth 1754-67
5. Benjamin Bathurst – Gloucestershire 1734-41 Cirencester 1754-61
6. Henry Bathurst 2 Earl Bathurst – Cirencester 1735-54
7. Henry Bathurst 3 Earl Bathurst – Cirencester 1783-94
8. Peter Bathurst – Eye 1784-90 1792-95
9. Henry Bathurst 4 Earl Bathurst – Weobly 1812 Cirencester 1812-34
10. William Bathurst 5 Earl Bathurst – Weobly 1812-16
11. Thomas Bathurst – St. Germans 1818-26
12. Allen Bathurst 6 Earl Bathurst – Cirencester 1857-78
13. Allen Bathurst – E. Gloucestershire 1895-1906 1910-18
14. Allen Bathurst Viscount Apsley – Southampton 1922-29 Central Div. Bristol 1931-42
15. Violet Bathurst Viscountess Apsley – Central Div. Bristol 1943-45

Seat: Cirencester House (Oakley Park/House), Gloucestershire (built c. 1590, purch. 1695, rebuilt 1715-18, add. 1810-11 and 1830, still own)

Estates: Bateman 13663 (E) 21168. Worth £30,000,000 in 1990 with 15,000 acres.
Titles: Baron Bathurst 1712- GB; Baron Apsley 1771- GB; Baronet 1643-c. 1750
Peers: 7 peers 1712-1943
2 in Cabinet 1771-78 1779-82 1807-27 1828-30
1 KG 19th
Notes: 1, 2, and 3 Earls and several other members of the family in ODNB.

Viscount Bledisloe (1935- UK)

Origins: Anne Bathurst, daughter of a younger brother of the 1 Earl Bathurst, married Charles Bragge. Their great-great-grandson was 1 Baron Bledisloe.

1. Charles Bragge-Bathurst – Monmouth 1790-96 Bristol 1796-1812 Bodmin 1812-18 Harwich 1818-23
2. Charles Bathurst 1 Viscount Bledisloe – Wilton Div. Wiltshire 1910-18

Seat: Lydney Park, Gloucestershire (built c. 1590, rebuilt c. 1677, purch. 1723, remod. 1833, demolished, rebuilt 1875-77, still own); Cleve (Cleeve) Hill House, Gloucestershire (built 17th c., remod. early 18th c., inherit. from Players (who purch. 1625) in 1736, sold 1790, demolished 1930)
Estates: Bateman 4098 (E) 5189
Title: Baron Bledisloe 1918- UK
Peer: 1 peer 1918-45
1 in Cabinet 1812-23
Notes: 1 Viscount in ODNB.

Bathurst

Origins: Kinsmen of the Bathursts of Kent. **First MP 1656-58** was Oliver Cromwell's physician.

1. Theodore Bathurst – Richmond 1690-95
2. Charles Bathurst – Richmond 1727-28

Seats: Clints Hall, Yorkshire (Willance seat passed by mar. to Bathursts 2nd half 17th c., sold 1747, later demolished); Marske Hall, Yorkshire (Willance seat acq. by mar. 2nd half 17th c., sold 1747)
Estates: Said to be worth £2,000 pa 1659.

BAYNE *SCOTLAND*

Origins: Merchants in Tulloch at least by the 16th century. **First [MP for Dingwall 1593].**

1. Alexander Bayne – [Dingwall 1661-63 1669-70]
2. Sir Donald Bayne – [Dingwall 1681 Ross-shire 1685-86]
3. John Bayne – [Dingwall 1703-07]

Seat: Resident in the burgh of Tulloch, Ross-shire

BAYNTUN-ROLT

Bayntun

Origins: Seated in Wiltshire from at least the 14th century. **First MP 1445 for Wiltshire. Eight further MPs 1472-1653 including four kts of the shire.**

1. Sir Edward Bayntun – Devizes 1640-48 1654 Calne 1659 1660 Devizes 1675-79
2. Henry Bayntun – Chippenham 1661-72
3. Nicholas Bayntun – New Woodstock 1679-81 Chippenham 1689-90
4. Henry Bayntun – Chippenham 1685-87 1689-90 Calne 1690-91
5. Edward Bayntun – Calne 1705-10
6. Sir Edward Bayntun-Rolt 1 Bt – Chippenham 1737-80
7. Sir Andrew Bayntun-Rolt 2 Bt – Weobley 1780-86
8. Samuel Bayntun – York 1830-33

Seats: Spye Park, Wiltshire (remod. c. 1749, sold 1863, fire 1974, demolished 1985); Sacombe Park, Hertfordshire (Rolt seat, see below); Browfront House, Wiltshire
Estates: Worth £4000 pa in 1657. Estates disbursed and sold mid-19th c.
Title: Baronet 1762-1816
Notes: The family greatly increased its wealth in the mid- 16th century when Sir Edward Bayntun was a royal favorite and acquired large estates at the Dissolution. Male line extinct 1816. Estates sold and remnants of family emigrated to New Zealand. Bayntun family has an entry in the ODNB.

Rolt

Origins: The original Rolt was a lawyer in the later 16th century in Bedford. One of his sons married the daughter of Lord Protector Cromwell's uncle. Their son went with the East India Company (of which he became President) to Persia and India, returning in 1682 to purchase Sacombe. In 1716 the Rolt family succeeded to the Baynton estates via an heiress and took the additional name Bayntun.

1. Samuel Rolt – Bedford 1701 1713-15
2. Edward Rolt – St. Mawes 1713-15 Grantham 1715-22 Chippenham 1722

Seat: Sacombe Park, Hertfordshire (purch. 1688, passed to Caswells via an heiress 1758, remod. 1st half 18th c., demolished c. 1780 and new house built c. 1803, sold by Caswells 1825)
Notes: Two in ODNB.

BEAUCHAMP [Proctor]

Origins: The Beauchamps were merchants in the early 18th century. The Proctors purchased Langley Park in 1742. Estates passed by marriage to the Beauchamps 1745.

1. Sir William Beauchamp Proctor 1 Bt – Middlesex 1747-68
2. Sir Edward Beauchamp 1 Bt – Lowestoft Div. Suffolk 1906-22
3. Sir Brograve Beauchamp 2 Bt – East Walthamstow 1931-45

Seats: Langley Park (Hall), Norfolk (built early 18th c., purch. 1742, built 1742-46, sold 1953); White Hall, Tottenham, Middlesex (built early 17th c., purch. 1720s, rebuilt mid-18th c., sold 1790)
Estates: Bateman 7146 (E) 10634
Titles: Baronet 1744- ; 1911-76

BEAUCLERK [de Vere, Topham]

Duke of St. Albans (1683- GB)

Origins: The 1 Duke of St. Albans was an illegitimate son of King Charles II and Nell Gwyn.

1. Charles Beauclerk 2 Duke of St. Albans – Bodmin 1718-22 New Windsor 1722-26
2. Lord William Beauclerk – Chichester 1724-33
3. Vere Beauclerk 1 Baron Vere – New Windsor 1726-50
4. Lord Sidney Beauclerk – New Windsor 1733-44
5. Lord Henry Beauclerk – Plymouth 1740-41 Thetford 1741-61
6. Lord George Beauclerk – New Windsor 1744-54 1768
7. Aubrey Beauclerk 5 Duke of St. Albans – Thetford 1761-68 Aldborough 1768-74
8. Aubrey Beauclerk 6 Duke of St. Albans – Hull 1790-96
9. Charles Beauclerk – Richmond 1796-98
10. Aubrey Beauclerk – E. Surrey 1832-37

Seats: Redbourne Hall, Linconshire (built 18th c., inher. by mar. to Carter (II) heiress before 1773, sold 20th c.); Hanworth Place, Middlesex (medieval, acq. by mar. 1736, fire 1797); Ardglass Castle, Down (built late 18th c., passed to Beauclerks mid-19th c., remod. later 19th c., became a golf club 1911); Little Grimsby, Lincolnshire (built early 18th c., passed by marriage from the Nelthorpes to the Beauclerks 19th c.?); Bestwood Lodge, Nottinghamshire (medieval, acq. 1683, demolished and rebuilt 1862-64, fire 1893, sold 20th c., hotel)
Estates: Bateman 12472 (E & I) 16515. Owned 4,000 acres in 2001.
Titles: Earl of Burford (1676- E); Baron Vere (1750- GB)
Peers: 12 peers 1691-1849 1750-81 1861-1945
5 Lds Lt 18th, 19th
2 KG 18th
Notes: Seven in ODNB.

Earl of Oxford (1142-1703 E)

Origins: The 1 Earl was Lord Great Chamberlain to Henry I. **First MP 1404 was a kt of the shire for Leicestershire. Three additional MPs 1455-1624.** The 1 Duke of St. Albans married the heiress of the 20th and last Earl of Oxford (de Vere).

No post-1660 MPs

Seats: Bentley Hall, Essex (built early 17th c., acq. by mar., later dismantled, sold by 1680); Castle Camps, Cambridgeshire (acq. 11th c., built c. 1068, add. late 15th c., rebuilt late 16th c., sold 1607, ruin c. 1738); Castle Hedingham, Essex (built mid-12th c., ruin, house built 18th c., leased?)
1 peer 1660-1703
1 Ld Lt 17th-18th
1 KG 17th-18th
Notes: The 17 Earl of Oxford (d. 1632) dissipated most of the family fortune (Stone, *The Crisis of the Aristocracy*, 172). Fourteen de Vere Earls of Oxford in ODNB.

Topham

Origins: Rose through office and law in the second half of the 17th century. The family estate passed after the death of the first and only MP to Lord Sidney Beauclerk MP.

1. Richard Topham – New Windsor 1698-1713

BEAUMONT I [Blackett, Calverley, Douglas, Macaulay, Trevelyan]

Viscount Allendale (1911- UK)

Origins: Sir Robert de Bellomont, granted lands by Richard I for services on the Third Crusade, was the common ancestor of the Beaumonts (Roebuck, *Yorkshire Baronets*, 109ff.). The senior line seated at Whitley Beaumont became extinct in 1631, when the estates passed to a junior line. Another branch was seated at Bretton Park, which has never changed hands by sale from the early Middle Ages onwards, passing through heiresses including the Wentworths (see Wentworth), seated there 1407-1792 and then to the Beaumonts of Oaks, Yorkshire.

1. Thomas Beaumont – Northumberland 1795-1818
2. Thomas Wentworth Beaumont – Northumberland 1818-26 Stafford 1826-30 Northumberland 1830-32 S. Northumberland 1832-37
3. Wentworth Beaumont 1 Baron Allendale – S. Northumberland 1852-85 Tyneside Div. Northumberland 1886-92
4. Somerset Beaumont – Newcastle-upon-Tyne 1860-65 Wakefield 1868-74
5. Frederick Beaumont – S. Durham 1868-80
6. Wentworth Beaumont 1 Viscount Allendale – Hexham Div. Northumberland 1895-1907
7. Hubert Beaumont – Eastborne Div. Sussex 1906-10
8. Michael Beaumont – Aylesbury Div. Buckinghamshire 1929-38
9. Ralph Beaumont – Central Div. Portsmouth 1931-45

Seats: Bretton Park, Yorkshire (built c. 1815, sold 1948); Hexham Abbey (Prior's House), Northumberland (medieval, purch. by Blacketts 1689, remod. 1736, fire 1775 and rebuilt, passed to Beaumonts by mar. later 18th c., fire 1817-18, not reoccupied by family, donated to county council); Bywell Hall, Northumberland (medieval, purch. in 1820 for £132,000, still own); Dilston Hall, Northumberland (medieval castle and house of 16th-18th c., mostly demolished 1765, new house 1835, purch. 1875, now institutional use)
Estates: Bateman 24098 (E) 34670. In 1805 reputedly made £100,000 pa. out of lead and coal mines. Rubinstein – Diana (Blackett) Beaumont, grandmother of 1 Viscount, left £180,000 in probate in 1831 and Thomas Beaumont left £120,000 in 1833. Worth £40,000,000 in 1990 with 20,000 acres.
Title: Baron Allendale 1906- UK
3 peers 1906-45
Notes: One of the wealthiest untitled families in England until finally granted a barony in 1906. One in ODNB.

Beaumont

Origins: Descended from Sir Robert de Bellomont 14th century, see above. **First MP 1624.**

1. Henry Beaumont – S. Div. W. R. Yorkshire 1865-74 Colne Valley Div. W. R. Yorkshire 1885-92

Seat: Whitley Beaumont (Whitley Hall), Yorkshire (acq. 12th century, rebuilt 1560, early 17th c., and 1704, sold 1924, demolished 1950)
Estates: Bateman 5306 (E) 12022 (2,000 acres in the first half of the 17th c. worth c. £1,200 pa)
Title: Baronet 1628-31
Notes: On the extinction of the Beaumonts of Whitley Beaumont in 1857, the estates passed to a junior branch of the Wentwoth-Blacketts (see below).

Blackett

Origins: The Blackets claimed descent from a hero at the Battle of Agincourt and to have been substantial landowners in the 16th century. They became rich as merchants in Newcastle by the 1630s and were involved in coal and lead mining on a grand scale and in the shipping of their own products. An unusually complex series of inheritances led the Blackett estates to the Beaumonts. The son of Sir William Blackett of Wallington (purch. 1684) and Hexham (purch. 1689) died in 1728 and left Hexham to his illegitimate daughter Elizabeth Ord who married his nephew Walter Calverley of Calverley. On her death her husband took the name Calverley-Blackett. His estates passed to Diana Blackett, sister of Sir William's son, who married Sir William Wentworth 4 Bt of Bretton Hall. Their son Sir Thomas Wentworth Bt succeeded to the Blackett estates in 1777 and took the additional name Blackett. He died and left his estates including Wallington to his illegitimate daughter Diana, who married Thomas Beaumont MP above. (*A History of Northumberland*, Newcastle, 1896, iii, 62-3) The senior Blackett line, cousins of the Blacketts of Wallington, were seated at Wylam.

1. Christopher Blackett – Bere Alston 1830-31 S. Northumberland 1837-41
2. John Blackett – Newcastle-upon-Tyne 1852-56

Seat: Wylam Hall, Northumberland (medieval castle, acq. 17th c., rebuilt c. 1880, add. 1914, sold 1971, now flats)
Notes: Extinct 1971.

Blackett

Origins. See above. A younger brother of the Wylam line was created a Baronet 1673.

1. Sir William Blackett 1 Bt – Newcastle-upon-Tyne 1673-80
2. Sir Edward Blackett 2 Bt – Ripon 1689-90 Northumberland 1698-1700
3. Sir Edward Blackett 4 Bt – Northumberland 1768-74

Seats: Matfen Hall, Northumberland (acq. by mar. 1757, new house built 1828—40, leased out from 1965, now hotel); Newby Hall, Yorkshire (purch. later 17th c. for £32,000, built 1690s, sold 1748)
Estates: Bateman 17476 (E) 16183
Title: Baronet 1673-
Notes: Three in ODNB.

Douglas

Origins: The first MP a lawyer. His daughter and heiress married Sir Edward Blackett 4 Bt MP.

1. Oley Douglas – Morpeth 1713-15

Seat: Matfen Manor House, Northumberland (purch. 1680, passed by mar. to Blacketts 1757)

Blackett

Origins: A younger brother of Sir Edward Blackett 2 Bt of Matfen (see above) established the Blackett line at Wallington (see also Wentworth).

1. Sir William Blackett 1 Bt – Newcastle-upon-Tyne 1685-87 1689-90 1695-1700
2. Sir William Blackett 2 Bt – Newcastle-upon-Tyne 1710-28

Seats: Wallington Hall, Northumberland (medieval castle, mid-16th c. house, purch. 1684, demolished and rebuilt c. 1688, remod. c. 1740-43, passed to Trevelyans 1777); Anderson Place, Northumberland (built 1580, purch. 1675, add. 1680, sold 1782, demolished 1834)
Title: Baronet 1685-1728

Calverley

Origins: The Calverleys claimed to have emigrated from Scotland to England in the reign of Henry I and married a daughter of the Lord of Calverley. They took the name Calverley c. 1350. Kt under Richard II. Acquired landed estates with money made in fulling cloth and the iron industry. Existence of related MPs before 1660 unclear. For the passage of their estates to the Blacketts see above.

1. William Calverley – Newcastle-upon-Tyne 1660
2. Sir Henry Calverley – Northallerton 1679-81
3. Sir Walter Calverley-Blackett 2 Bt – Newcastle-upon-Tyne 1734-77

Seats: Calverley Hall, Yorkshire (built c. 1400, remod. c. 1485-95, mid-16th c., and 17th c., ceased to be seat of the Calverley family 1709, sold 1754 for £112,000, broken up into farm houses); Eryholme, Yorkshire (acq. 1580, passed out of family 1696); Oulton Hall, Yorkshire (purch. by Blayds, a Leeds banker, built sec. half 18th c., passed to Calverleys by inher., add. early 19th c., sold 1820, ruin); Esholt Hall, Yorkshire (acq. by mar. 17th c., built 1706-10 and became chief seat, sold 1775)
Estates: Bateman 2401 (E) 83334 (Oulton line)
Title: Baronet 1711-77
Notes: Three in ODNB.

Trevelyan

Origins: The Trevelyans were Cornish landowners in the Middle Ages, Kt and High Sheriff under Henry VI. **First MP, a lawyer, 1442, kt of the shire 1453. Another {MP 1613}.** In the late 15th century they acquired Nettlecombe through the heiress of a family that had held it since the reign of Henry II. Sir Walter Calverley-Blackett 2 Bt MP left his estates to his nephew Sir John Trevelyan 4 Bt in 1777. A brother of the 4 Bt married the heiress of James Thornton of Netherwitton (originally Newcastle merchants in the 14th c.).

1. Sir John Trevelyan 2 Bt – Somerset 1695-98 1701 Minehead 1708-15 1717-22
2. Sir John Trevelyan 4 Bt – Newcastle-upon-Tyne 1777-80 Somerset 1780-96
3. Anne-Marie Trevelyan – Berwick on Tweed 2015-

Seats: Nettlecombe Court, Somerset (acq. by Raleghs and passed to Trevelyans by mar. late 15th c., rebuilt end 16th c., left by family 1939, sold 1965); Netherwitton, Northumberland (medieval castle, new house built c. 1700, acq. later 18th c., still own); Wallington, Northumberland (inher. from Blacketts (see above) 1777, remod. 1853-54, NT 1942)
Estates: Bateman 9656 (E) 11616
Titles: Baron Treveylan 1968-85 UKLife; Baronet 1662-
Notes: Four in ODNB.

Trevelyan

Origins: A nephew of the 5 Bt succeeded to Wallington.

1. Sir George Otto Trevelyan 2 Bt – Tynemouth 1865-68 Hawick District 1868-86 Bridgeton Div. Glasgow 1887-97
2. Sir Charles Trevelyan 3 Bt – Elland Div. Yorkshire 1899-1918 Central Div. Newcastle-upon-Tyne 1922-31

Seats: Wallington, Northumberland (built c. 1700, acq. 1777, donated to NT 1942); Welcombe House, Warwickshire (built 1866-68, acq. by mar. 1890, sold 1931, hotel)
Estates: Bateman 22058 (E) 15448
Title: Baronet 1874-
1 Ld Lt 20th
2 in Cabinet 1882-86 1892-95 1924 1929-30
Notes: Wallington was the largest property ever given to the NT. Six in ODNB.

Baron Macaulay (1857-59 UK)

Origins: Presbyterian ministers in Scotland in the 17th and 18th centuries. The 1 Baron a politician and author. He also succeeded in 1836 to the estate of his uncle, a Lt. Gen. in the East India Company service and MP. He left his very considerable literary earnings to his sister, Hannah, whose son was Sir George Otto Trevelyan MP (see above).

1. Colin Macaulay – Saltash 1826-30
2. Thomas Babington Macaulay 1 Baron Macaulay – Calne 1830-32 Leeds 1832-34 Edinburgh 1839-47 1852-56

Peer: 1 peer 1857-59
1 in Cabinet 1846-47
Notes: Five in ODNB.

BEAUMONT II [Stapleton, Stapylton]

Baron Beaumont (1309-1507 1840-1895 1896- E)

Origins: The 1 Baron Beaumont was a grandson of the King of Jerusalem and the younger son of a French nobleman who emigrated to England in the early 14th century. Barons 1309 and granted a large estate. The Stapletons rose via a noble servant in the mid to late 13th century who built up estates. Barons by writ 1313. Sir Brian Stapleton (d. 1496) married the daughter of the 2 Viscount Beaumont. **First MP 1416 for Yorkshire. Three further MPs in the 15th and 16th centuries (and see also below for further**

pre-1660 MPs). Sir Brian's son became co-heir to the Barony of Beaumont, which fell into abeyance 1507.

1. John Stapleton – Berwick 1852-53 1857-59 1868-74

Seat: Carlton Towers (Hall), Yorkshire (Stapletons acq. by marriage 1301 from a family that held it from the Conquest, rebuilt early 17th c., rebuilt c. 1873-77, in 1975 passed by mar. to Duke of Norfolk, still own)
Estates: Bateman 5754 (E) 25400. Much of estate sold to pay debts 1888-89.
Title: Viscount Beaumont 1440-1507 E
Peers: 3 peers 1840-54 1869-95
Notes: A staunch Roman Catholic family. Held their estates intact through the Civil War because the head of the family was a lunatic. (Roebuck, *Yorkshire Baronets*, 20-21) The Beaumonts also inherited the estates of the Barons Bardolf (1299-1406 1437-1441 E) and through them the lands of the ancient parliamentary family of Erpingham. MPs early 15th century. Seven Stapletons in ODNB.

Viscount Beaumont of Swords (1622-1702 I)

Origins: Cadet of the Beaumonts (above). Astute purchases of land at the Dissolution. Master of the Rolls 1550. Judge 1592. **First MP 1429. Seven additional MPs 1539-1654. Several kts of the shire for Leicestershire.**

1. Sir Henry Beaumont 2 Bt – Leicester 1679-81 1685-87
2. John Beaumont – Nottingham 1685-87 Hastings 1689-95
3. Sir George Beaumont 4 Bt – Leicester 1702-37
4. Sir George Beaumont 7 Bt – Bere Alston 1790-96

Seats: Stoughton Grange, Leicestershire (built 15th c., acq. by mar. by Beaumonts 1584, passed by mar. to the Kecks 18th c., see Legh, demolished 1926); Cole Orton (Coleorton) Hall, Leicestershire (medieval, acq. by mar. 1426, rebuilt c. 1804, remod. 1862, sold 1948, now flats); Buckland Court, Surrey (old manor house, acq. by mar. 1750, rebuilt c. 1835, sold and divided into several houses in 1940s)
Estates: Bateman 3556 (E) 4660
Title: Baronet 1619-1702 1627-80 1661-
Notes: Ten in ODNB.

Stapylton (Stapleton)

Origins: Descended from Sir Brian Stapylton **MP 1416. Five further MPs 1437-1648.**

1. Sir Henry Stapylton 1 Bt – Boroughbridge 1647-48 1660

2. Sir Bryan Stapylton 2 Bt – Aldborough 1679-81 Boroughbridge 1690-95 1698-1705 1708-15
3. Sir John Stapylton 3 Bt – Boroughbridge 1705-08
4. Sir Miles Stapylton 4 Bt – Yorkshire 1734-50

Seats: Myton Hall, Yorkshire (acq. 17th c., rebuilt c. 1693 or 1680s, sold 1933); Wighill Park, Yorkshire (purch. 1375, built 1580, sold 1811, demolished 1950s)
Estates: Bateman 5119 (E) 8280. Worth £900 pa in 1631.
Title: Baronet 1660-1817

BECKETT [Denison]

Baron Grimthorpe (1886- UK)

Origins: Bankers in Leeds in the 18th century. Also acquired wealth in the 19th century through inheritance, the law, and railway entrepreneurship. Inherited by marriage the fortune of Sir Thomas Denison (d. 1765) a judge on the King's Bench.

1. Sir John Beckett 2 Bt – Cockermouth 1818-21 Haslemere 1826-32 Leeds 1835-37
2. Sir William Beckett 1 Bt – Leeds 1841-52 Ripon 1852-57
3. Sir Edmund Beckett-Denison 4 Bt – W. R. Yorkshire 1868-80
4. Christopher Beckett-Denison – E. Div. W. R. Yorkshire 1868-80
5. William Beckett-Denison – E. Retford 1876-80 Bassetlaw Div. Nottinghamshire 1885-90
6. Sir Gervase Beckett 1 Bt – Whitby Div. N. R. Yorkshire 1906-18 Scarborough and Whitby Div. N. R. Yorkshire 1918-22 N. Div. Leeds 1923-29
7. Ernest Beckett 2 Baron Grimthorpe – Whitby Div. N. R. Yorkshire 1885-1905

Seats: Easthorpe Hall, Yorkshire (acq. and enlarged c. 1926?, sold 1965, burned 1971); Kirkstall Grange, Yorkshire (acq. and built 1830, sold 1912, institutional use); Grimthorpe (Manor), Yorkshire (medieval, demolished late 18th c., acq. mar. to Denison heiress 1814); Meanwood Park (Hall), Yorkshire (built 1762, acq. by mar. Denison heiress 1814, remod. 1834, sold 1919, residential); Batchwood, Hertfordshire (built 1874-76, part demolished, sold, nightclub); Somerby Park (Hall), Lincolnshire (built later 18th c., demolished c. 1960)
Estates: Bateman 8473 (E) 15554. The 1 Baron left over £2,100,000 in 1905.
Titles: Baronet 1813– ; 1921-
Peers: 3 peers 1886-1945
Notes: 1 Baron and three others in ODNB.

BEDINGFIELD

Origins: Seated at Bedingfield soon after the Conquest. Charter c. 1100. Kt 13th c. Succeeded to Oxburgh 1462 by marriage to Tuddenham heiress (**two MPs 1431-61**). **First Bedingfield MP for Suffolk 1553. Four additional MPs 1586-1654, three kts of shire.**

1. Sir Henry Bedingfield 2 Bt – Dunwich 1660 Aldeburgh 1685-87
2. Daniel Bedingfield – Kings Lynn 1690-95
3. Sir Robert Bedingfield – Hedon 1701

Seat: Oxburgh Hall, Norfolk (medieval, acq. 1462 by mar. from a descent established at Oxburgh in 1274, rebuilt 1482, damaged 1647, restored 1725, remod. 1775, add. 1830-65, estates sold 1951, house to NT 1952)
Estates: Bateman 5638 (E) 5844. Estates worth £1,551 pa in 1715.
Title: Baronet 1661-
Notes: Roman Catholic family, which prevented MPs being elected and reduced the family's wealth and power. The Bedingfield family with numerous members mentioned has an entry in ODNB.

BEECHER (Becher)

Origins: Founder a London haberdasher and Alderman d. 1571. His grandson was elected an MP and married the sister of the Earl of Bolingbroke. **First MP 1601; another 1614-28**. Kt 1622.

1. Sir William Beecher – Bedford 1667-79

Seat: Howbury Hall, Bedfordshire (acq. c. 1624, sold 1781, rebuilt early 19th c.)
Estates: Worth £1,600 pa in 1660.
Notes: One in ODNB.

BEKE (Beake)

Origins: Mayor of Reading 1458, purchased Whiteknights. **First MP for Reading 1450. An additional MP 1572**.

1. Richard Beke – [Elgin and Nairn 1656] Amersham 1659 Aylesbury 1689-90 Wendover 1690-1700

Seats: Whiteknights, Berkshire (acq. 1412, sold mid-17th c.); Ford, Dinton, Buckinghamshire (acq. 1682)

BELASYSE (Bellasis) [Wombwell]

Earl of Fauconberg (1689-1701 E; 1756-1802 GB)

Origins: Acquired land in Durham by mid-14th century. Expanded estates at the Dissolution, the head of the rural family aided with the support of a brother in London, a Chancery clerk working for Thomas Cromwell who became Cardinal Wolsey's agent in Durham and Constable of the Castle. A grandson became a peer in 1627. (James, *Family, Lineage, and Civil Society*, 36-7) **First MP 1586. Three further MPs 1597-1644, one for Yorkshire.**

1. Sir Henry Belasyse – Great Grimsby 1666-67
2. Sir Henry Belasyse – {Galway 1692-93} Morpeth 1695-1701 Durham 1701-08 1710-12 Mitchell 1713-15
3. Richard Belasyse – Mitchell 1710-13
4. Henry Belasyse 2 Earl of Fauconberg – Peterborough 1768-74

Seats: Newburgh (Newborough) Park (Priory), Yorkshire (medieval monastic buildings, acq. c. 1540 and remod. 1568, remod. c. 1615 and c. 1725-75, passed by mar. to Wombwells 1825, fire 1947, part decayed, restored 1960s); Worlaby, Lincolnshire (built 17th c., demolished 1807)
Estates: Acquired 5,000 acres at Dissolution. Worth £4,000 pa in 1627 and c. £6,000 pa in 1700 (*Country Life*, 155, p. 483).
Titles: Baron Fauconberg (1627-1815 E); Viscount Fauconberg (1643-1815 E); Baron Belasyse (1645-91 E); Baronet 1611-1815
Peers: 5 peers 1660-1718 1660-78 1736-1802
3 Lds Lt 17th, 18th, 19th
Notes: The Fauconbergs were Roman Catholic in the early 18th century but confomed to the Church of England in 1737. Bellasis family with numerous members has an entry in ODNB.

Wombwell

Origins: Claimed medieval descent and expanded their estate under Elizabeth I. However, much of the land was sold owing to extravagance and unsuccessful litigation. Became lawyers in Leeds. One was a Barnsley grocer. His son became a London merchant and Chairman of the East India Company. He amassed great wealth from government victualling contracts and repurchased the Wombwell estates. (Roebuck, *Yorkshire Baronets*, 28-29) Lady Anne Belasyse, daughter and heiress of the last Earl of Fauconberg married (1791) the 2 Wombewell Baronet, and the estates passed to the Wombwells in 1825.

1. Sir George Wombwell 1 Bt – Huntingdon 1774-80

Seats: Newburgh Park (Priory), Yorkshire (see above, leased to a school 20th c., reoccupied by family 1969, still own); Wombwell Hall, Yorkshire (acq. 13th c., let to tenants from the 18th c., demolished late 19th c.)
Estates: Bateman 12226 (E) 14500
Title: Baronet 1778-

BELL *SCOTLAND*

Origins: Glasgow merchants 17th century. **First [MP for Glasgow 1612]. Two further MPs for the city [1625-44].** Kt. 1679.

1. Sir John Bell – [Glasgow 1661-63 1681]

Seat: Hamilton Ferme, Renfrewshire

BELLEW [Bryan, Grattan] *IRELAND*

Baron Bellew (1686-1770 I; 1848- I)

Origins: One of the oldest Anglo-Norman families in Ireland arriving in the 12th century. Transferred by Cromwell from Louth to Galway. Regained some estates after 1660. (Burke, *Visitation of Seats*, II, 2nd ser., 176) **First {MP 1585}. Two further kts of the shire for {Louth 1634-39}.**

1. Richard Bellew 3 Baron Bellew – Steyning 1712
2. Thomas Bellew – {Mullingar 1713-27}
3. Patrick Bellew – County Louth 1831-32 1834-37
4. Richard Bellew – Louth 1832-52

Seats: Mount Bellew, Galway (built late 18th c., remod. before 1820, sold and demolished c. 1938); Castletown Castle, Louth (acq. and built late 15th-early 16th c., passed to Viscounts Boyne 1694, see Hamilton I); Barmeath Castle, Louth (old castle, acq. 1670s, remod. mid-18th c., add. 1839, still own)
Estates: Bateman 4314 (I) 5092
Title: Baronet 1838-
Peers: {2 peers 1686-91 1707-15} 2 Irish rep peers 1904-11 1914-35
2 Lds Lt 19th, 20th
Notes: Married Grattan heiress 1858. Roman Catholics. The 3 Baron Bellew of the first creation conformed to the established Church.

Grattan

Origins: The Grattans acquired an estate by the mid 17th century. The first MP was Recorder of Dublin and married the daughter of the Lord Chief Justice of Ireland. Thomas Bellew, descended from a younger son of Sir John Bellew of Louth, married in 1858 the heiress of Henry Grattan and took the additional name Grattan.

1. James Grattan – {Dublin 1761-66}
2. Henry Grattan – {Charlemont 1775-90 Dublin 1790-97 Wicklow 1800} Malton 1805-06 Dublin 1806-20
3. James Grattan – County Wicklow 1821-41
4. Henry Grattan – Dublin 1826-30 County Meath 1831-52
5. Thomas Grattan-Bellew – County Galway 1852-57

Seats: Tinnehinch, Wicklow (built 18th c., acq. 1782, passed by mar. to Bellews 1858, fire 1950s, ruin); Mount Bellew, Galway (see above); Moyanna, Queen's County (purch. 1782, passed to Bellews 1858, sold 1937); Moyrath, Meath (passed to Bellews by mar. 1858, sold 1937)
Estates: Bateman 23004 (I) 11974. The great "Patriot", Henry Grattan, was voted £50,000 by the Irish Parliament in 1782 for services to the country.
Title: Baronet 1838-
Notes: Henry Grattan the "Patriot" and a cousin in ODNB.

Bryan

Origins: Became landed in the later 16th century. James Bryan sat in King James II's Parliament 1689. The sister and heiress of George Bryan MP 1865-80 married the 2 Baron Bellew and their second son took the name Bryan and settled at Jenkinstown 1880.

1. George Bryan – County Kilkenny 1837-43
2. George Bryan – County Kilkenny 1865-80

Seat: Jenkinstown Park, Kilkenny (built early 19th c., add. later 19th c., part demolished 19th c., passed to Bellews by mar. 1880, part demolished 20th c., sold 1970s)
Estates: Bateman: 12891 (I) 8897
Notes: The Bryans were Roman Catholic and thus long debarred from sitting in Parliament.

BELLINGHAM *IRELAND & ENGLAND*

Origins: Established in the 14th century in Westmorland. **First MP for Cumberland 1449. Seven additional MPs between 1545 and 1645 including four kts of the shire for Westmorland.** Kt 1562. Lord Deputy of Ireland 1548.

1. Henry Bellingham – {County Louth 1661-66}
2. Alan Bellingham – Westmorland 1678-81 1685-87
3. Thomas Bellingham – {County Louth 1692-93 1695-99 1703-13}
4. Henry Bellingham – {Dundalk 1703-14}
5. Henry Bellingham – {County Louth 1741-53}
6. Sir William Bellingham 1 Bt – Reigate 1784-89
7. Sir Alan Bellingham 4 Bt – County Louth 1880-85

Seats: Castle Bellingham (Gernonstown), Louth (old castle, purch. c. 1660, burned 1689, new house built c. 1690-1700, remod. later 18th c., remodeled early 19th c., sold 1956, hotel); Levens, Westmorland (purch. 1489, sold 1686)
Estates: Bateman 15996 (I) 4586. Estates worth £1,500 pa c. 1640.
Titles: Baronet 1620-50; 1666-99; 1796-
2 Lds Lt 20th
Notes: Acquired estates in Ireland under O. Cromwell. The family wealth was heavily damaged by the spendthrift Alan Bellingham, forcing the sale of Levens in 1686. Free State Senator 1925-36. One in ODNB.

BELLOT (Bellott)

Origins: The family held Moreton from the mid-15th century. **First MP 1597. Two subsequent MPs between 1601-53, one for Staffordshire.**

1. Sir Thomas Bellot 2 Bt – Newcastle-u-Lyme 1679-81 1690-95 1698-99
2. Sir Thomas Bellot 3 Bt – Newcastle-u-Lyme 1705-06 1708-09

Seats: Great Moreton Hall, Cheshire (acq. mid-15th c., built 1602-06, sold c. 1714); The Ashes, Staffordshire (acq. by mar. c. 1615, rebuilt mid-17th c., remod. early 18th c., sold 1711)
Estates: Worth £500 pa in 1660. Great Moreton estate sold 1793 for £57,107. (de Figueirdo and Treuherz, *Cheshire Country Houses*, 103)
Title: Baronet 1663-1714
Notes: One in ODNB.

BENCE

Origins: Prominent merchants in Aldeburgh since Tudor period. **First MP 1589.** His son was a London grocer mid-17th century. Purchased landed estates late 16th c., early 17th and early 18th century. **Four subsequent MPs 1604-54.**

1. John Bence – Aldeburgh 1659 1669-81 1685-87
2. John Bence – Dunwich 1691-95 Ipswich 1702-08

Seats: Heveningham, Suffolk (purch. c. 1700, sold 1718); Thorington Hall, Suffolk (purch. 1691, rebuilt 1817-20, sold 1945, demolished 1949)
Estates: Bateman 3929 (E) 5164
Notes: Thorington passed through the female line several times, with the inheriting family taking the name Bence. Two in ODNB.

BENETT (Bennett) [Lambert]

Benett

Origins: Clothiers in the early Tudor period. Emerge as gentry under Elizabeth I. **First MP 1554. A possible second MP 1586-89.**

1. John Bennett – Shaftesbury 1667-77
2. Thomas Bennett – Shaftesbury 1677-81
3. John Benett – Wiltshire 1819-32 S. Wiltshire 1832-52
4. Vere Fane-Benett-Stanford – Shaftesbury 1873-80
5. Charles Thomas-Stanford 1 Bt – Brighton 1914-22

Seats: Pythouse, Wiltshire (acq. 1225, medieval house, rebuilt 16th c., sold 1669, repurch. 1725, new house 1725, remod. c. 1805, add. 1891, sale of contents 1919, inher. by Rumbolds by inher. 1956, house leased and then sold 1959, flats); Hatch House, Wiltshire (built 16th c., decayed, purch. 1805, remod. c. 1806, remod. 1908, passed to Rumbolds by inher. 1956) Norton Bavant, Wiltshire (leased from 1519); Preston Place (Manor), Sussex (medieval and 16th c., remod. 18th c., purch. by Stanfords 1794, passed by mar. to Benetts 1867, passed to Brighton Corporation 1932)
Estates: Bateman 6997 (E) 25306. Much urban property in Hove became very valuable after marriage to Stanford heiress in 1862.
Title: Baronet 1929-32
Notes: Benett estates passed by mar. 1852 to Fanes. Additional name Stanford taken in 1862 after succession to the Preston estate. Family extinct in male line 1947. Two in ODNB.

Lambert

Origins: Held land in Wiltshire since 1560. One Lambert, a grocer, was a London Alderman and Sheriff who purchased Boyton 1572. **First MP 1625 for Hindon**. The Lambert male line became extinct in 1842. An heiress married John Benett of Pythouse. The elder son succeeded to Boynton and the second son to the Benett estates.

1. Thomas Lambert – Hindon 1679 1685-87
2. Edmund Lambert – Hindon 1708-13 Salisbury 1715-22

Seat: Boyton, Wiltshire (purch. 1572, house completed 1618, passed by mar. to Benetts 1842).

BENN

Viscount Stansgate (1942- UK)

Origins: Emerged in the later-19th century as publishers.

1. Sir John Benn 1 Bt – Tower Hamlets 1892-95 Devonport 1904-10
2. Wedgwood Benn 1 Viscount Stansgate – Tower Hamlets 1906-18 Leith 1918-27 Aberdeen N. 1928-31 Gorton Div. Manchester 1937-42
3. Anthony Wedgwood Benn 2 Viscount Stansgate – Bristol S.E. 1950-61 1963-83 Chesterfield 1984-2001
4. Hilary Wedgwood Benn – Leeds Central 1991-

Seat: Stansgate, Essex (purch. and built early 20th c., still own)
Title: Baronet 1914-
3 in Cabinet 1945-46 1964-70 2003-10
Notes: Emily Benn, the granddaughter of the 2 Viscount, stood for Parliament in 2010, but she was defeated. 3 in ODNB.

BERESFORD [Pack, Power (Le Poer, De la Poer), Peirse] *IRELAND & ENGLAND*

Marquess of Waterford (1789- I)

Origins: The Beresfords originated in Staffordshire in the 14th century. A younger son went to Ireland in the early 17th century and became manager of the Ulster plantation of Londonderry. **First MP 1634**. The heiress of the 3 Earl of Tyrone (d. 1703), head of a great Anglo-Norman family established in Ireland in the 12th century and at Curraghmore c. 1452, barons 1535, married 1717 Sir Marcus Beresford 4 Bt who succeeded to the Le Poer estates. He was created Earl of Tyrone in 1746.

1. Sir Tristram Beresford 1Bt – {County Londonderry 1634 1661-66}
2. Sir Randal Beresford 2 Bt – {Coleraine 1661-66}
3. Sir Tristram Beresford 3 Bt – {Londonderry 1692-93 1695-99}
4. Sir Marcus Beresford 1 Earl of Tyrone – {Coleraine 1715-20}
5. George Beresford 1 Marquess of Waterford – {County Waterford 1757-60 Coleraine 1761-63}
6. John Beresford – {County Waterford 1761-1800} 1801-05
7. Marcus Beresford – {Dungarvon 1783-97}
8. Henry Beresford 2 Marquess of Waterford – {County Londonderry 1790-1800}
9. John Beresford – {Swords 1790-97 Dublin 1797-1800} 1801-04 County Waterford 1806-11
10. Marcus Beresford – {St. Canice 1790-94 Swords 1798-1800}
11. John Horsley-Beresford 2 Baron Decies – {Coleraine 1797-1800}
12. Lord George Beresford – County Londonderry 1802-12 Coleraine 1812-14 County Waterford 1814-26 1830-31
13. William Beresford 1 Viscount Beresford – County Waterford 1811-14
14. William Beresford – Harwich 1841-47 N. Essex 1847-65
15. John Beresford 5 Marquess of Waterford – County Waterford 1865-66
16. Marcus Beresford – Southwark 1870-80
17. George Beresford – Armagh 1875-85
18. Charles Beresford 1 Baron Beresford – County Waterford 1874-80 E. Marylebone 1885-89 York 1898-1900 Woolwich 1902-03 Portsmouth 1910-16

Seats: Curraghmore, Waterford (Powers acq. and built by 15th c., passed by mar. to Beresfords 1717, rebuilt, remod. 1750-60, remod. 19th c., still own); Ford Castle, Northumberland (medieval, ruined and rebuilt by 1509, ruined c. 1648, acq. by mar. 1667, remod. 1694, rebuilt 1761-1800, acq. by mar. to Delaval heiress 1822, rebuilt 1861-65, sold 1907); Aubawn, Cavan; Bolam Hall, Northumberland (built 1810, acq. by mar. mid-19th c., now divided into multiple houses); Learmount Park (Castle), Londonderry (built c. 1710, passed by mar. to Beresfords 1774, rebuilt c. 1850, abandoned by family 1925, sold 1944); Bedgebury Park, Kent (built early 18th c., Viscount Beresford acq. 1836, rebuilt c. 1836, passed to Hopes 1854, add. 1854-55)
Estates: Bateman 121388 (E, I & S) 70459. Worth £13,000 pa in 1777. Owned 10,000 acres in 2001.
Titles: Baron Le Poer 1535-1688 I; Viscount Tyrone 1720- I; Earl of Tyrone 1746- I; Baron Tyrone 1786- GB; Baron Decies 1812- I; Baron Beresford 1814-54 I; Viscount Beresford 1823-54 UK; Baron Beresford 1916-19 UK; Baronet 1665-
Peers: {1 peer 1763-1800} 9 peers 1786-1826 1823-54 1832-1911 1916-19 1922-34 1 Irish Rep peer 1912-44
1 Ld Lt 19th
1 in Cabinet 1828-30
5 KP 18th, 19th, 20th
Notes: Eight members of the family in ODNB.

Earl of Tyrone (1672-1704 I)

Origins: Granted arms 1273. Eustace le Poer (d. 1311) was called to the Parliament of Kilkenny in 1295. His son was Lord Chief Justice of the King's Bench. **Several Powers were elected to the Irish Parliament in the 17th century**.

1. Richard Power 1 Earl of Tyrone – {County Waterford 1661-66}

Seat: Curraghmore, Waterford (see above)
Title: Baron Le Poer (Power) 1535-1704 I
Peers: {3 peers 1661-93 1695-1704}
Notes: 1 Earl in ODNB.

Power (De La Poer)

Origins: Cadet of Richard Poer, Baron Curraghmore (1535 I). The head of this branch claimed the Barony after the death of the last Earl of Tyrone in 1704, but he had been outlawed in 1688. Took name de la Poer in lieu of Power 1863.

1. Roger Power – {Dungarvon 1703-09}
2. Richard Power – {Monaghan 1767-68 Tuam 1768-72}
3. Patrick Power – County Waterford 1826-36
4. John Power – Dungarvon 1837 County Waterford 1837-40
5. Maurice Power – County Cork 1847-51
6. Edmund De la Poer (Count De la Poer) – County Waterford 1863-73
7. Richard Power – Waterford 1874-91

Seats: Gurteen la Poer, Waterford (acq. and built later 17th c., rebuilt 1866, sold 1969 but estate still owned by family); Glen Poer House, Waterford (built c. 1820, add. c. 1870, institutional use); Ringacoltig, Cork (purch. 1860s); Pembrokestown House, Waterford (resident 19th c.); Newtown House, Waterford (purch. 1858)
Estates: Bateman 13460 (I) 4971
Title: (Baron Le Poer (Power) 1535- I)
2 Lds Lt 20th
Notes: This line remained Roman Catholic, although some members conformed. Changed name to de la Poer in 1863. Created Papal Counts in 1864.

Power

Origins: Junior line of above.

1. Richard Power – {County Waterford 1798-1800} 1801-02
2. Richard Power – County Waterford 1814-30
3. Robert Power – County Waterford 1831-32

Seats: Clashmore House, Waterford; Whitechurch House, Waterford (built 1737, now flats)

Pack-Beresford

Origins: The Packs claimed descent from the Packs of Prestwold, Leicester (founded by a merchant in London in the early 17th century, Lord Mayor 1654). Came to Ireland with Cromwell's army. One descendent became a Dean of Ossory. His son, Major General Sir Denis Pack married in 1816 Lady Elizabeth Beresford, daughter of the 1 Marquess of Waterford. One of their sons took the name Beresford after inheriting the estates of Viscount Beresford in 1854.

1. Denis Pack-Beresford – County Carlow 1862-68

Seat: Fenagh House, Carlow (acq. and built mid-19th c., still resident 1950s)
Estates: Bateman 7679 (I) 6936

Peirse-Beresford

Origins: The Peirses were gentry by the early 17th century and purchased Bedale mid-century. Sir John Beresford 1 Bt, an illegitimate son of the 1 Marquess of Waterford, married in 1815 the Peirse heiress and succeeded to Bedale and Hutton Bonville in 1824.

1. Henry Peirse – Northallerton 1713-15 1722-54
2. Henry Peirse – Northallerton 1774-1824
3. Sir John Beresford 1 Bt – Coleraine 1809-12 1814-23 Berwick 1823-26 Northallerton 1826-32 Coleraine 1832-33 Chatham 1835-37
4. Marcus Beresford – Northallerton 1824-26 Berwick 1826-32
5. Sir George Beresford 2 Bt – Athlone 1841-42

Seats: Bedale Hall, Yorkshire (purch. 1638, built 17th c. add.1760 and 1777, leased after 1918, sold 1951, institutional use); Hutton Bonville, Yorkshire (acq. 17th c., rebuilt 18th c., acq. by mar. 1824, sold 1859, demolished 1921 and 1970, ruins)
Estates: Bateman 6199 (E) 7500
Title: Baronet 1814-

BERKELEY [Fitz-Hardinge, Portman, Thompson]

Earl of Berkeley (1679-1942 E)

Origins: One of the very few credible claimants to Saxon origin among the political elite. The manor of Berkeley was granted to Robert FitzHarding, a rich Bristol merchant, c. 1153-54, for financial backing given to the Angevins. (Saul, *Knights and Esquires*, 62) The family took the name of the manor. His son married the daughter of the previous owner whose family had held it before the Conquest. Barons by tenure from 1160. **First MP 1290s for Gloucestershire**. They were the only family in England through male descent by the 19th century still in possession of their feudal castle. (Shirley, *Noble and Gentle Men*, 1866, 89) The family **elected at least 17 MPs from various branches in every century between 1328 and 1656.**

1. Sir Rowland Berkeley – Worcester 1661-79
2. Charles Berkeley 2 Earl of Berkeley – Gloucester 1679-81
3. James Berkeley 3 Earl of Berkeley – Gloucester 1701-02
4. Henry Berkeley – Gloucestershire 1720-34
5. George Berkeley – Dover 1720-34 Hedon 1734-41 1742-46
6. Rowland Berkeley – Droitwich 1774
7. Sir George Berkeley – Gloucestershire 1783-1810
8. William Fitz-Hardinge Berkeley 1 Earl Fitz-Hardnge – Gloucestershire 1810
9. Maurice Berkeley 1 Baron Fitz-Hardinge – Gloucester 1831-33 1835-37 1841-57
10. Craven Fitz-Hardinge Berkeley – Cheltenham 1832-47 1848 1852-55
11. George Fitz-Hardinge – W. Gloucestershire 1832-52
12. Francis Fitz-Hardinge Berkeley – Bristol 1837-70
13. Charles Berkeley – Cheltenham 1848-52 Evesham 1852-55 Cheltenham 1855-56
14. Sir George Berkeley – Devonport 1852-57
15. Francis Fitz-Hardinge Berkeley 2 Baron Fitz-Hardinge – Cheltenham 1856-65
16. Charles Fitz-Hardinge Berkeley – 3 Baron Fitz-Hardinge – Gloucester 1862-65

Seats: Berkeley Castle, Gloucestershire (built c. 1070, add. 1153-56 and c. 1320-46, remod. 1637, 1805-07 and 1920-30, passed to Spetchley Park line 1943, still own); Spetchley Park, Worcestershire (built 16th c., purch. 1605 by a Berkeley clothier of a junior line, burned 1651, rebuilt 1811, still own); Cotheridge Court, Worcestershire (built 16th c., remod. 1770, add. Victorian, now flats)
Estates: Bateman 27386 (E) 45168 and a valuable London estate. Worth £1,150 pa in 1347 (Emery, *Greater Medieval Houses of England and Wales 1300-1500*, III, 64) Worth £20,000,000 in 1990. 10,000 acres in 2016
Titles: Baron Berkeley by tenure 1160 E; Baron Berkeley 1321 E; Marquess of Berkeley 1482-92; Baron Seagrave 1831-57 UK; Earl Fitz-Hardinge 1841-57 UK; Baron Fitz-Hardinge 1861-1916 UK

Peers: 10 peers 1660-98 1689-1710 1705-55 1766-1810 1831-57 1861-1916 1891-1942
5 Lds Lt 17th, 18th, 19th
2 in Cabinet Council 1699 1717-27
1 KG 18th
1 KT 18th
Notes: On the death of the 5 Earl of Berkeley the family estates passed to his illegitimate children (the heir was created Earl Fitz-Hardinge). This line became extinct in 1916 when the Castle returned to the 8 and last Earl of Berkeley. Twenty-one family members listed in ODNB.

Baron Botetourt (1305- E)

Origins: Sir Maurice Berkeley of Stoke Gifford, Gloucestershire, descended from the 2 Baron Berkeley, married Catherine the daughter of the 2 Baron Botetourt. He died in 1361. The title was dormant from 1385 to 1764 when the abeyance was terminated in favor of Norborne Berkeley of Stoke Gifford. Charles Thompson 1 Bt was said to be his illegitimate son. The Barony passed to the 4 Baron's sister, who married the Duke of Beaufort (see Somerset). **Two MPs of this Berkeley line sat in the 14th century. Three MPs sat for the county 1604-25.**

1. John Berkeley – Gloucestershire 1710-15
2. Norborne Berkeley 4 Baron Botetourt – Gloucestershire 1741-63
3. Charles Thompson 1 Bt – Monmouth 1796-99

Seat: Stoke Gifford (Stoke Park), Gloucestershire (acq. 14th c., rebuilt later 16th c., remod. 1749-52 and 1760-64, estates passed by mar. to the Dukes of Beaufort 1770 – see Somerset, sold 1915)
Estates: The Stoke estate began to produce large mineral revenues from coal mines in the 18th c.
Title: Baronet 1797-1868
1 Ld Lt 18th
Notes: 1 Baron and 1 Bt in ODNB.

Earl of Falmouth (1664-65 E)

Origins: Sir Maurice Berkeley of Bruton Abbey descended from a cadet line of the Berkeleys who inherited the Barony of Botetourt. One of his grandsons was created Earl of Falmouth and Viscount Fitzhardinge. The Earldom became extinct on his death but the Viscountcy passed first to his father and then to his brothers and became extinct in 1712. Bruton then passed to the descendents of Sir Maurice's younger son, John, who had been created Baron Berkeley of Stratton. On the extinction of this line in 1773 all of the estates, including London property, passed to the Earls of Berkeley. This line produced **seven MPs between 1584 and 1641.**

1. Charles Berkeley 1 Earl of Falmouth – New Romney 1661-65
2. Charles Berkeley 2 Viscount Fitzhardinge – Somerset 1621 Bodmin 1624 Heytesbury 1625 1626 1628 Bath 1640 Heytesbury 1661-68
3. Maurice Berkeley 3 Viscount Fitzhardinge – Wells 1661-79 Bath 1681 1685-87 1689-90 {Lanesborough 1665-66}
4. John Berkeley 4 Viscount Fitzhardinge – Hindon 1691-95 New Windsor 1695-1710
5. John Berkeley 5 Baron Berkeley of Stratton – Stockbridge 1735-41

Seat: Bruton Abbey (Priory), Somerset (medieval, rebuilt after Dissolution when acq. by Berkeleys, demolished 1786)
Titles: Viscount Fitzhardinge 1633-1712 I; Baron Berkeley of Stratton 1658-1773 E; Baron Berkeley of Rathdowne 1663-1712 I; Baron Botetourt 1664-65 E; Baronet 1660-90
Peers: 8 peers 1660-78 1663-68 1681-83 1692-1712
2 Lds Lt 17th and 18th
2 in Cabinet Council 1670-72 1710-15
Note: 1 Earl and seven others in ODNB.

Berkeley

Origins; An Irish branch of the family **elected two {MPs 1585 and 1613}**.

1. Hugh Berkeley – {Lifford 1661-66}

Viscount Portman (1873- UK)

Origins: Minor gentry since the reign of Edward I. **First MP 1302**. Married the heiress to the Orchard estate in mid-15th century. Acquired substantial estates, including large acreage in London, in 1533. Lord Chief Justice 1555. Baronet 1611. **Seven additional MPs 1362-1644. Several kts of the shire for Somerset in the 16th and 17th centuries**. On the death of Sir William Portman 6 Bt in 1690 the Portman estates passed to a cousin, Sir Edward Seymour 4 Bt (see Seymour). On the extinction of this line in 1728, William Berkeley of Pylle (cadet of the Berkeleys of Berkeley) succeeded by right of his descent from Joan Portman, daughter and heiress of the last Baronet.

1. Sir William Portman 6 Bt – Taunton 1661-79 Somerset 1679-81 Taunton 1681-87 1689-90
2. Henry Seymour Portman 6 Bt – St. Mawes 1679-90 Totnes 1690-95 St. Mawes 1696-98 Taunton 1698-70 Wells 1701-08 Somerset 1708-10 Taunton 1710-15

3. Edward Berkeley – Wells 1679-80 1685-87 1689-1700
4. Maurice Berkeley – Wells 1705-08 1710-16
5. Henry Berkeley Portman – Taunton 1734-41 Somerset 1741-47
6. Henry Berkeley Portman – Wells 1790-96
7. Edward Berkeley Portman – Boroughbridge 1802-06 Dorset 1806-23
8. Edward Portman 1 Viscount Portman – Dorset 1823-32 Marylebone 1832-33
9. William Portman 2 Viscount Portman – Shaftesbury 1852-57 Dorset 1857-85
10. Edwin Portman – N. Dorsetshire 1885-92

Seats: Bryanston, Dorset (purch. 1660, rebuilt on new site 1778, new house 1889-94, school from 1927); Orchard Portman, Somerset (acq. by mar. mid 15th c., demolished c. 1700?, estate sold 1944); Pylle, Somerset (acq. 15th c., built 17th c., add. 18th c., sold 1924?)
Estates: Bateman 33891 (E) 45972 and a large, very valuable, London estate. Estimated income in 1883 was £100,000 pa (Fisher, *The House of Commons 1820-32*, VI, 856). Worth £1.2 billion in 2006. Owned 9,100 acres in 2001, valued at two billion pounds.
Titles: Baron Portman 1837- UK; Baronet 1611-95
6 peers 1837-1945
1 Ld Lt 19th
Notes: The rebuilding of Bryanston in c. 1890 cost £200,000. (Franklin, *The Gentleman's Country House and Its Plan 1835-1914*, 257). Maurice Portman (d. 1888) was an MP in Canada. 1 Viscount and two others in ODNB. For the Seymour connection with the Portmans see Seymour.

BERMINGHAM *IRELAND*

Earl of Louth (1319-29 I; 1759-99 I)

Origins: Anglo-Norman family that arrived in Ireland late 12th century. Great medieval lords. Baron 1280. Summoned as Lord Athernry 1284-95. One was Archbishop of Tuam in 1289 and two others Justiciars of Ireland in 1294 and 1346. Granted Ardee in Louth 1318. Lord Justice of Ireland 1321.

1. Thomas Bermingham 1 Earl of Louth – {County Galway 1745-50}

Seat: Bermingham House, Galway (acq. c. 1200, rebuilt c. 1730s, sold c. 1800)
Titles: Baron Athernry 1280-1691 I; 1698-1799 I
Peers: 4 peers 1661-91 1700-09 1713-99
Notes: Roman Catholic family. Conformed 1713. On the death of the 1 Earl of Louth in 1799 his estates were divided between his daughter, Lady Elizabeth Duffield, the daughter of Viscountess St. Lawrence, and Lady Louisa Blake. Two medieval members of the family in ODNB.

BERNARD I *IRELAND*

Earl of Bandon (1800-1979 I)

Origins: Settled in Ireland under Elizabeth I and acquired large estates 1611-41. The first MP was Solicitor General of Ireland 1692 and a judge under Queen Anne.

1. Francis Bernard – {Clonakilty 1692-93 Bandon 1695-99 1703-27}
2. Arthur Bernard – {Bandon 1713-14}
3. Francis Bernard – {Clonakilty 1725-60 Bandon 1766-76}
4. Stephen Bernard – {Bandon Bridge 1727-60}
5. Francis Bernard 1 Earl of Bandon – {Ennis 1778-83 Bandon 1783-90}
6. James Bernard – {County Cork 1781-90}
7. James Bernard 2 Earl of Bandon – Youghal 1806-07 County Cork 1807-18 Youghal 1818-20 Bandon Bridge 1820-26 1830
8. Richard Bernard – Bandon Bridge 1812-15
9. Francis Bernard 3 Earl of Bandon – Bandon 1831 1842-56
10. William Bernard – Bandon 1832-35 1857-63
11. Henry Bernard – Bandon 1863-68
12. Percy Bernard – Bandon 1880

Seats: Castle Bernard, Cork (old castle, acq. early 17th c., built 1715, add. 1731, rebuilt 1798-1815, burned 1921, new house 1960s, family extinct 1979); Bassingborne Hall, Essex (purch. 1773, sold late 18th c.)
Estates: Bateman 40941 (I) 19215. Worth £8,000 pa in 1779, £18,000 pa in 1791, and £30,000 pa in 1810.
Titles: Baron Bandon 1793-1979 I; Viscount Bandon 1795-1979 I
Peers: {1 peer 1793-1800} 4 Irish Rep peers 1801-30 1835-56 1858-77 1881-1924
3 Lds Lt 19th, 20th
1 KP 20th
Notes: Much land was sold after 1903, but the family still own c. 500 acres surrounding the ruined Castle Bernard in Bandon. They were paid £80,000 in compensation for the destruction of Castle Bernard. 5 Earl, an Air Chief Marshal in the RAF 1959, in ODNB.

BERNARD II [Bigg]

Bernard

Origins: Sir Nicholas Lylling made his fortune in London and purchased the manor of Abington in c. 1390. His heiress brought the estate to the Bernards by mar. c. 1450. A successful Bernard lawyer purchased Brampton 1653. **First MP 1640**. Bt 1662. High Sheriff 1688.

1. Sir John Bernard 2 Bt – Huntingdon 1654 1656 1659 1660
2. Sir Robert Bernard 3 Bt – Huntingdonshire 1689-90
3. Sir Robert Bernard 5 Bt – Huntingdonshire 1765-68 Westminster 1770-74

Seat: Brampton Park, Huntingdonshire (medieval, later 16th c., purch. 1653, rebuilt after purch., rebuilt c. 1820, sold 1870s or 1880s, institutional use, fire 1907)
Title: Baronet 1662-1789
Notes: 5 Bt in ODNB.

<u>Bernard</u>

Origins: Senior line of the family from whom the Brampton line was descended from a younger son. Kt 1661.

1. Sir John Bernard – Northampton 1664

Seat: Abington Manor, Northamptonshire (medieval, acq. c. 1390 by Lyllings from whom it passed to the Bernards by mar. c. 1450, rebuilt c. 1530, add. 1670, sold 1669, now a museum)
Estates: Sold Abington for £13,750.
Notes: Extinct 1670.

<u>Bernard</u>

Origins: Most junior line of the family. 1 Bt was Governor of New Jersey in 1758 and Massachusetts Bay 1760. The 4 Bt married 1785 a banking heiress (Morland) and took the additional name Morland.

1. Sir Scrope-Morland Bernard 4 Bt – Aylesbury 1789-1802 St. Mawes 1806-30
2. Sir Thomas Bernard 6 Bt – Aylesbury 1857-65

Seat: Winchendon Priory (Nether Winchendon), Buckinghamshire (medieval, remod. mid-16th c., acq. 1571, inher. from Tyringhams by mar. 1771, remod. 1790, still own)
Title: Baronet 1769-1883
Notes: Tyringhams of Tyringham, (see Mackworth). 1 and 2 Bt in ODNB.

<u>Morland</u>

Origins: The father of the MP was a merchant in Woolwich, Kent. The MP was a banker in London. His daughter and heiress married Sir Scrope Bernard.

1. William Morland – Taunton 1786-1806

Seat: Lee, Kent
Estates: Rubinstein – William Morland left £100,000 in probate 1815.

Bigg

Origins: The first MP was a merchant tailor and Sheriff of London 1653. High Sheriff of Cambridgeshire and Huntingdonshire 1682. John Bigg MP left his estates to his kinsman the 4th Bernard Bt on his death in 1748.

1. John Bigg – Huntingdon 1689-90
2. John Bigg – Huntingdonshire 1715-34

Seat: Grafham, Huntingdonshire (purch. first half 17th c., passed into the Brampton estate 1748, see above)

BERRY I

Viscount Camrose (1941- UK)

Origins: Father of 1 Baron was a station master in the 1870s and later sold tea. He was an estate agent and auctioneer, and Mayor of Tydfil 1912. His sons were successful in the coal, steel, and newspaper businesses.

1. Seymour Berry 2 Viscount Camrose – Hitchin Div. Hertfordshire 1941-45
2. Lionel Berry 2 Viscount Kemsley – Buckingham Div. Buckinghamshire 1943-45
3. Anthony Berry – Enfield Southgate 1964-84

Seats: Hackwood Park, Hampshire (built 1683, add. c. 1800, purch. 1935, sold 1997); Farnham Park, Buckinghamshire (add. c. 1865, purch. 20th c., add. c. 1920); Dropmore, Buckinghamshire (built 1792-94, purch. 1943, sold 1968, demolished 1990)
Estates: 1 Viscount Camrose left one and a half million pounds in 1954. Worth £120,000,000 in 1990.
Titles: Baron Buckland 1926-28 UK; Baron Camrose 1929- UK; Baron Kemsley 1936- UK; Viscount Kemsley 1945- UK; Baron Hartwell 1968-2001 UKLife; Baronet 1921- ; 1928-
Peers: 3 peers 1926-28 1929-45 1936-45
Notes: Four Berrys in ODNB.

BERRY II

Origins: Minor gentry since the 13th century. **Three MPs 1529-1656.**

1. Sir Thomas Berry – Totnes 1673-79

Seat: Burrough, Devon

BERTIE [Burrell, Drummond, Heathcote, Jephson, Norreys (Norris), Willoughby] *ENGLAND & IRELAND*

Duke of Ancaster (1715-1809 GB)

Origins: Emerge in the early Tudor period through the law and then marriage to heiresses. Richard Bertie, gentleman usher to Baroness Willoughby de Eresby, married her in 1552 and acquired Grimsthorpe (for the ancestry of the Willoughbys see Willoughby below). Their son married an heiress of the Earl of Oxford. His son was raised to an earldom. Robert Bertie 1 Earl of Lindsey and 13 Baron Willoughby de Eresby was the common ancestor of the Bertie clan. **First MP 1563 for Lincolnshire, another in 1614, and a subsequent MP for the county 1624-26.**

1. Robert Bertie 3 Earl of Lindsey – Boston 1661-66
2. Peregrine Bertie – Stamford 1665-79 1685-87 Westbury 1689-95
3. Charles Bertie – Stamford 1678-79 1685-87 1689-1711
4. Robert Bertie 1 Duke of Ancaster – Boston 1685-87 1689-90
5. Richard Bertie – New Woodstock 1685-86
6. Peregrine Bertie – Boston 1685-87 1690-98 1701-05 Truro 1705-08 Boston 1708-11
7. Philip Bertie – Stamford 1694-98
8. Charles Bertie – New Woodstock 1705-08
9. Albemarle Bertie – Lincolnshire 1705-08 Cockermouth 1708-10 Boston 1734-41
10. Peregrine Bertie 2 Duke of Ancaster – Lincolnshire 1708-15
11. Lord Vere Bertie – Boston 1741-54
12. Lord Robert Bertie – Whitechurch 1751-54 Boston 1754-82
13. Brownlow Bertie 5 Duke of Ancaster – Lincolnshire 1761-79
14. Gilbert Heathcote-Drummond-Willoughby 1 Earl of Ancaster – Boston 1852-56 Rutland 1856-67
15. Gilbert Heathcote-Drummond-Willoughby 2 Earl of Ancaster – Horncastle Div. Lincolnshire 1894-1910
16. George Heathcote – Brighton 1910
17. Claud Heathcote-Drummond-Willoughby – Stamford Div. Lincolnshire 1910-18 Rutland & Stamford Div. Lincolnshire 1918-22
18. Gilbert Heathcote-Drummond-Willoughby 3 Earl of Ancaster – Rutland & Stamford Div. Lincolnshire 1933-50

Seats: Grimsthorpe Castle, Lincolnshire (built early 13th c., acq. 1516 by Willoughbys, passed by mar. to Berties mid-16th c., add. 1541, remod. 1680s, add. 1722-26, remod. 1811, still own); Swinestead Hall (House), Lincolnshire (built early 17th c., rebuilt c. 1720, demolished mid-19th c.); Eresby, Lincolnshire (medieval, new house 1533, destroyed by fire 1796); Gwydir Castle, Caernarvonshire (built c. 1500, add. 1540 and c. 1600, acq. by mar. 1678, remod. c. 1828, passed to Marquess of Lincolnshire by mar.

1895); Uffington House, Lincolnshire (old house, purch. 1673, built 1681-87, destroyed by fire 1904)
Estates: Bateman 163495 (E & W) 120900 (includes the Willoughby de Eresby estates). Estates said to be worth £60,000 pa in 1778. Rubinstein – 5th Duke left £175,000 probate 1809 and the 3 Duke's daughter left £100,000 in 1828. Owned 78,200 acres worth 121 million pounds in 2001.
Titles: Baron Wiloughby de Eresby 1313- E; Earl of Lindsey 1626- E; Marquess of Lindsey 1706-1809 E; Earl of Ancaster 1892-1983 UK; Baronet 1733-
Peers: 9 peers 1660-1701 1690-1723 1715-1809 1867-1945
8 Lds Lt 17th, 18th, 19th, 20th
1 in Cabinet Council in the 17th century
1 KG 17th
Notes: The 1 Duke of Ancaster married the daughter of Richard Wynne 4 Bt of Gwydir (see Williams-Wynn) and succeeded to the Gwydir Castle estates. These descended to Priscilla Bertie, sister of the 4 Duke, who married Peter Burrell, created 1 Baron Gwydir (see below). The Bertie estates passed by marriage in the 19th century to Sir Gilbert Heathcote 5 Bt of Normanton. His son was created Earl of Ancaster and the family assumed the name Heathcote-Drummond-Willoughby. The 28 Baroness Willoughby de Eresby is still seated at Grimsthorpe. Seven members of the family in ODNB.

Earl of Lindsey (1626- E)

Origins: The second son of the 2 Earl of Lindsey was seated at Uffington. His great-grandson succeeded as 9 Earl on the death of the 5 Duke of Ancaster in 1809.

1. Charles Bertie – Stamford 1711-27
2. Albemarle Bertie 9 Earl of Lindsey – Stamford 1801-09

Seat: Uffington House, Lincolnshire (built 1691, burned 1904)
Estates: Bateman 4790 (E) 9286
Peers: 4 peers 1809-1818 1835-1945

Earl of Abingdon (1682- E)

Origins: The third son of the 2 Earl of Lindsey was created Earl of Abingdon. The 2 Earl married Bridget Baroness Norris in her own right. Their son succeeded as 5 Baron Norreys. The descendents of the fourth son of the 2 Earl of Lindsey seated at Chesterton, Oxfordshire are included here.

1. Henry Bertie – Westbury 1678-80 New Woodstock 1681 Oxford 1685-87 1689-95 Westbury 1701-15

2. Montagu Venables-Bertie 2 Earl of Abingdon – Berkshire 1689-90 Oxfordshire 1690-99
3. Robert Bertie – Westbury 1695-1708
4. James Bertie – Woodstock 1695-1705 Middlesex 1710-34
5. Henry Bertie – Beaumaris 1705-27
6. Willoughby Bertie 3 Earl of Abingdon – Westbury 1715
7. Norreys Bertie – Oxfordshire 1743-54
8. Peregrine Bertie – Westbury 1753-54
9. Peregrine Bertie – Oxford 1774-90
10. Montagu Bertie 6 Earl of Abingdon – Oxfordshire 1830-52 Abingdon 1852-54

Seats: Wytham House (Abbey), Oxfordshire (medieval, acq. by mar. 1648 from a family that held it from 1539, rebuilt 17th c., remod. early 19th c., sold 1920, institutional use); Kinderton Lodge, Cheshire (acq. by mar. 1687, built late 17th, demolished c. 1860); Rycote, Oxfordshire (built 1st part 16th c., acq. by mar. 1648, remod. 1768, demolished 1807, stable converted into current house, sold 1911)
Estates: Bateman 18182 (E) 25760
Titles: Baron Norreys 1572- E; Baron Bertie of Thame 1915- UK; Viscount Bertie of Thame 1918- UK
Peers: 10 peers 1675-1799 1805-1945 1915-45
4 Lds Lt 17th, 18th, 19th
Notes: 1 Viscount in ODNB.

<u>Baron Gwydir</u> (1796-1915 GB)

Origins: See notes under Duke of Ancaster. The Burrells emerged as merchants and bankers in the later 17th century. Bt 1766. This entry includes cousins, who inherited Valentines House, Essex by marriage to the heiress of Sir Charles Raymond 1 Bt, banker and shipowner.

1. Peter Burrell – Haslemere 1722-54 Dover 1755-56
2. Sir Merrick Burrell 1 Bt – Great Marlow 1747-54 Grampound 1754-68 Haslemere 1774-80 Great Bedwyn 1780-84
3. Peter Burrell – Launceston 1759-68 Totnes 1768-74
4. Sir William Burrell 2 Bt – Haslemere 1768-74
5. Peter Burrell 1 Baron Gwydir – Haslemere 1776-80 Boston 1782-96
6. Sir Charles Burrell 3 Bt – New Shoreham 1806-62
7. Peter Drummond-Burrell 2 Baron Gwydir and Baron Willoughby de Eresby – Boston 1812-20
8. Walter Burrell – Sussex 1812-31
9. Sir Percy Burrell 4 Bt – New Shoreham 1862-76
10. Sir Walter Burrell 5 Bt – Shoreham 1876-85

Seats: Langley Park, Kent (purch. 1684, fire 1913); West Grinstead Park, Sussex (built c. 1806, sold 1912, demolished 1968); The Deepdene, Surrey (built early 17th c., rebuilt 1769-75, purch. c. 1800, sold 1807); Knepp Castle, Sussex (old house, acq. c. 1800, rebuilt 1809-11, fire 1832, still own); Valentines House, Essex (built 1696-97, purch. 1754 by Raymonds, remod. c. 1769, passed to Burrells, sold 1788); Ockenden House (Manor), Sussex (original seat, now hotel); Stoke Park, Suffolk (purch. 1840, rebuilt c. 1840, sold 1919, demolished c. 1930)
Estates: The 1 Baron Gwydir had an income of £18,000 pa in the late 18th century. Rubinstein – 1 Baron Gwydir left £120,000 in probate 1820 and Elizabeth Burrell Bennet left £120,000 in 1837. The West Grinstead and Knepp estates stood at about 5,000 acres in 1831 and 4,000 acres in the 1980s.
Titles: Baronet 1766-1915; 1774-
Peers: 5 peers 1796-1915
1 Ldt Lt 19th
Notes: 2 Bt and 1 Baron in ODNB.

Baron Aveland (1856- UK)

Origins: The founder was the son of an ironmonger and Alderman of Chesterfield in the later 17th century. He apprenticed in the wine trade in London and became an East and West Indian merchant, government contractor, and Governor of the Bank of England. Kt 1702, Lord Mayor of London 1711, Bt 1732. At his death he was said to be the richest commoner in England. He purchased Normanton in 1729. (*Country Life*, 33, p. 198) The marriage with the Berties brought Grimsthorpe and an earldom (see Duke of Ancaster).

1. Sir Gilbert Heathcote 1 Bt – London 1701-10 Helston 1715-22
2. Sir John Heathcote 2 Bt – Grantham 1715-22 Bodmin 1733-41
3. George Heathcote – Hindon 1727-34 Southwark 1734-41 London 1741-47
4. Sir Gilbert Heathcote 3 Bt – Shaftesbury 1761-68
5. Sir Gilbert Heathcote 4 Bt – Lincolnshire 1797-1807 Rutland 1812-41
6. Gilbert Heathcote 1 Baron Aveland – Boston 1820-32 S. Lincolnshire 1832-41 Rutland 1841-56

Seats: Normanton Park, Rutland (built later 16th c., purch. 1729, rebuilt 1735-40, add. 1763-67, passed by mar. of 1827 to 23 Baroness Willoughby d'Eresby, fire, sold, and demolished 1925); Stockton Hall, Rutland (built early 17th c., purch. c. 1708, remod. early 18th c., leased out, sold 1907)
Estates: 1 Bt worth c. £700,000 at death in 1733. Estates under Duke of Ancaster. Junior line at Lobthorpe, Lincolnshire and Lenton, Lincolnshire 4933 (E) 7276
Title: Baronet 1733-
Peer: 1 peer 1856-67
1 Ld Lt 19th
Notes: 1 Bt in ODNB.

Heathcote

Origins: Descended from the second son of the 2 Heathcote Bt of Normanton.

1. John Heathcote – Rutland 1790-95
2. John Heathcote – Gatton 1796-98 Ripon 1798-1806

Seat: Conington Castle, Huntigdonshire (medieval, rebuilt later 16th c., add. early 17th c., abandoned and became a ruin by beginning of the 18th c., acq. 2nd half 18th c., rebuilt by Heathcotes c. 1800, family departed after 1946, demolished c. 1953)
Estates: Bateman 7144 (E) 11386

Heathcote

Origins: Descended from a brother of the 1 Bt of Normanton.

1. Sir William Heathcote 1 Bt – Buckingham 1722-27 Southampton 1729-41
2. Samuel Heathcote – Berealston 1740-47
3. Sir William Heathcote 3 Bt – Hampshire 1790-1806
4. Sir Thomas Freeman-Heathcote 4 Bt – Bletchingley 1807-08 Hampshire 1808-20
5. Sir William Heathcote 5 Bt – Hampshire 1826-31 N. Hampshire 1837-49 Oxford University 1854-68

Seat: Hursley Park, Hampshire (purch. 1718, rebuilt c. 1720, estate broken up and sold before 1900, house now business offices)
Estates: Bateman 14189 (E) 14154
Title: Baronet 1733-
Notes: 5 Bt in ODNB.

Baron Norreys (1572- E) (Norris)

Origins: Royal servant granted a manor in Berkshire 1267. Rose higher as an official and courtier under Henry VI. **First MP 1547 for Berkshire. Six further MPs 1572-1654, most kts of the shire**. The 2 Baron was created Earl of Berkshire, extinct 1621. The Earl's granddaughter, Baroness Norreys in her own right, married the 2 Earl of Lindsey and the title and estates were merged with the Earldom of Abingdon (see above).

1. Sir Edward Norreys – Oxfordshire 1675-79 Oxford 1689-1700
2. Francis Norreys – Oxford 1701-06

Seat: Rycote (Ryecote), Oxfordshire (built 1st half of 16th c., acq. by mar. c. 1544, passed by mar. to Berties (Abingdon) 1648, demolished 1807)
Notes: (See also Wykeham under Wenman). Six in ODNB.

Jephson

Origins: Founder acquired the manor of Froyle, Hampshire at the Dissolution and held it until 1652. Went to Ireland with the Earl of Essex and acquired Irish estates in the early 17th century. **First MP 1604 for Hampshire. One additional MP in the 1621 for the county and one other MP 1640s. First Irish {MP 1656}.** The daughter of the 1 Baron Norreys married the heir of Sir John Jephson and succeeded to Mallow Castle, Cork by a marriage of 1607. Sheriff 1681.

1. Alexander Jephson – {Trim 1661-66}
2. William Jephson – East Grinstead 1679-81 Chipping Wycombe 1689-91
3. John Jephson – {Mallow 1692-95}
4. John Jephson – {Blessington 1703-24}
5. William Jephson – {Mallow 1695-98}
6. William Jephson – {Mallow 1713-16}
7. Anthony Jephson – {Mallow 1713-55}
8. Denham Jephson – {Mallow 1756-81}
9. William Jephson – {Mallow 1761-68}
10. Denham Jephson – {Mallow 1768-1800} 1802-12
11. Robert Jephson – {St. Johnstown 173-76 Old Leighlin 1776-83 Granard 1783-90}
12. Anthony Jephson – {Mallow 1781-83}
13. Sir Richard Jephson 1 Bt – {Charlemont 1794-98}
14. Sir Charles Jephson-Norreys 1 Bt – Mallow 1826-59

Seats: Mallow Castle, Cork (built 1185, acq. 1588 by Norreys, rebuilt late 16th c., passed by mar. of 1607 to Jephsens, damaged 1645, burned 1689, ruin, new house built from stables c. 1700, add. 18th c., add. 1837, add. 1954, sold 1984); Froyle Place, Hampshire (medieval, purch. and rebuilt 1542, sold by 18th c.)
Estates: "Great estate" in Ireland 17th c. (Thrush and Ferris, *History of Parliament*, IV, 890). Worth £12,000 pa in 1803.
Titles: Baronet 1815-1900; 1838-88
Notes: Estates heavily indebted by the mid-19th century and passed to a daughter of the last Bt in 1888. One in ODNB.

Baron Middleton (1711- GB)

Origins: The origins of the family can be traced to Ralph Bugge (d. c. 1250) a wool merchant in Nottingham who purchased piecemeal a manorial estate in Willoughby-on-the-Wolds and took the name of the land. A grandson was a lawyer who rose to Chief Justice of the King's Bench 1323. He purchased Wollaton. His son married an heiress. (Payling, *Political Society in Lancastrian England*, 33-34) **The first Bugge MP 1397. Six additional MPs, many kts of the shire, 1425-1654.**

1. Thomas Willoughby 1 Baron Middleton – Nottinghamshire 1698-1702 1705-10 Newark 1712-12
2. Francis Willoughby 2 Baron Middleton – Nottinghamshire 1713-22 Tamworth 1722-27
3. Thomas Willoughby – University of Cambridge 1720-27 Tamworth 1727-34
4. Thomas Willoughby 4 Baron Middleton – Nottinghamshire 1762-74
5. Henry Willoughby – Newark 1805-31

Seats: Wollaton Hall, Nottinghamshire (acq. c. 1312, old manor house, new house built 1580-88, sold 1925 to Nottingham City Council, museum); Birdsall House, Yorkshire (acq. by mar. early 18th c., built later 18th c., add. early and late 19th c., still own); Settrington House, Yorkshire (built late 18th c., purch. 1826, sold 1938, fire 1963); Middleton Hall, Warwickshire (medieval, passed by inher. from 12th c. owners to the Willoughbys 1418 and 1493, leased out from 1800, sold 1924, derelict, restored 1980); Applecross House, Ross-shire (built c. 1675, rebuilt c. 1730-40, purch. 1862, sold 1929)
Estates: Bateman 99576 (E & S) 54014. Estates worth £140 in 1325, £500 by 1326, and £1000 in 1528. (Payling, *Political Society in Lancastrian England*, 33-34). Already growing rich on coal in the 16th c. Worth £30,000,000 in 1990 and still own most of the Yorkshire estate and some land in Nottinghamshire, Lincolnshire, and Warwickshire. Wollaton sold for £200,000 in 1925.
Peers: 11 peers 1712-1945
1 Ld Lt 20th
Notes: The family became Tudor courtiers and gained a large income from coal from the 1530s onwards. The Willoughby (Bugge) heiress to Wollaton married Robert Willoughby of Bore Place Kent, who descended from the 5 Baron Willoughby de Eresby (a separate family, see below). Willoughby family has an entry in ODNB and five others.

<u>Willoughby</u>

Origins: The Willoughbys de Eresby claimed Norman descent. They were first recorded in the 12th century, were knighted in the 13th century, and created Barons in 1313. This line descended from a younger son of the 4 Baron Willoughby de Eresby. They became Bristol merchants in the later 17th century (Mayor 1665) and purchased Baldon c. 1754.

1. Sir Henry Willoughby 3 Bt – Yarmouth (I of W) 1831-32 Newcastle-u-Lyme 1832-34 Evesham 1847-65
2. Sir John Willoughby 4 Bt – Leominster 1857-58

Seats: Baldon House, Oxfordshire (built 17th c., purch. c. 1754, add. late 18th c., sold 1921); Fulmer Hall, Buckinghamshire (rebuilt 1833, purch. c. 1861, sold 20th c.)
Estates: Bateman 2282 (E) 3926

Title: Baronet 1794-1918
Notes: Willoughby de Eresby family have an entry in ODNB and several other individuals are listed.

Baron Willoughby of Parham (1547-1779 E)

Origins: Descended from a younger brother of the 10 Baron Willoughby de Eresby. Ancestors by marriage held Parham since the reign of Henry III. **First MP 1545 for Lincolnshire**.

1. William Willoughby 6 Baron Willoughby – Midhurst 1660

Seats: Parham Hall, Suffolk (acq. 13th c., rebuilt 1630-50, sold 1687, much demolished and became a farm house); Shaw Place, Lancashire (acq. by mar. 18th c., sold 1765?); Hunsdon House, Hertfordshire (built 15th c., acq. 1653, sold 1671); Knaith Hall, Lincolnshire (medieval monastic buildings, remod. c. 1540s, acq. mar. of 1535, sold 1761)
Estates: 12 Baron owned only 550 acres in 1712.
Peers: 10 peers 1666-1765 1767-79
Notes: 5, 6, 12, 15 Barons in ODNB. They became colonial governors and West Indian plantation owners in the 17th century, but met with financial ruin. Were Presbyterians in 17th and 18th centuries.

BEST

Baron Wynford (1829- UK)

Origins: The founder was Chief Justice of the Common Pleas 1824. Kt 1819. Baron 1829.

1. William Best 1 Baron Wynford – Petersfield 1802-06 Bridport 1812-17 Guildford 1818
2. William Best 2 Baron Wynford – Mitchell 1831-32

Seats: Wynford Eagle Manor, Dorset (medieval, rebuilt 1630, purch. 1829, still own); Leasons, Kent (owned 19th c.); Toller Fratrum, Dorset (built mid-16th c., purch. 1867)
Estates: Bateman 3460 (E) 4179
Peers: 8 peers 1829-1945
Notes: 1 Baron in ODNB.

BETHELL I

Bethell

Origins: Rose by leasing and purchase of land in the late Tudor period. Leased Rise c. 1591. Bought more land in the early and mid-17th century. Kt r. Charles I. It is unclear how they obtained the money to make large purchases of land in the 18th century. (English, *The Great Landowners of East Yorkshire*, 56-61) **One MP pre-1660 (1658).**

1. Sir Hugh Bethell – E. R. Yorkshire 1654 1656 Hedon 1660-79
2. Henry Bethell – Knaresborough 1660
3. Hugh Bethell – Hedon 1695-1700
4. Hugh Bethell – Bevereley 1768-72
5. Richard Bethell – Yorkshire 1830-31 E. Yorkshire 1832-41
6. George Bethell – Holderness Div. E. R. Yorkshire 1885-1900

Seats: Rise Park, Yorkshire (leased c. 1591, rebuilt 1815-20, still own); Watton Abbey, Yorkshire (acq. 1605, passed to Bethells by marriage c. 1700, now a farm house)
Estates: Bateman 13395 (E) 17234
Notes: The male line of the Bethells died out in 1799. The last Bethell selected a vicar's son named Bethell, sent him to Eton and on the grand tour and made him his heir. No blood connection can be traced. (English, *The Great Landowners of East Yorkshire*, 23)

Bethell

Origins: Cousins of the Bethells of Rise mid-17th century.

1. Hugh Bethell – Pontefract 1716-22
2. Slingsby Bethell – London 1747-58

Seat: Swindon Hall, Yorkshire (acq. mid-17th c., passed by mar. to the Codringtons later 18th c.)
Estates: Worth c. £1,500 pa in 1685.
Notes: One in ODNB.

BETHELL II

Baron Westbury (1861- UK)

Origins: Founder was the son of a physician in Bristol who worked his way through Oxford. Lord Chancellor 1861.

1. Richard Bethell 1 Baron Westbury – Aylesbury 1851-59 Wolverhampton 1859-61

Seat: Westbury House, Wiltshire (built early 18th c., purch. late 18th c., sold later 19th c.)
Estates: Bateman under 2000 acres. 1 Baron left c. £300,000 in 1873.
Peers: 4 peers 1861-1945
1 in Cabinet 1861-65
Notes: 1 Baron in ODNB.

BETHELL III

Baron Bethell (1922- UK)

Origins: 1 Baron was a stockbroker and politician.

1. John Bethell 1 Baron Bethell – Romford 1906-18 E. Ham 1918-22

Estates: The 4 Baron left £4,500,000 in 2007.
Title: Baronet 1911-
Peers: 2 peers 1922-45
Notes: The 4 Baron was an MEP 1979-94 1999-2003. One in ODNB.

BINDON *IRELAND*

Origins: David Bindon settled in County Tipperary at the end of the 16th century. Merchants in the 17th and 18th centuries. Mayor of Limerick c. 1664. Sheriff 1694.

1. David Bindon – {Ennis 1715-27}
2. Samuel Bindon – {Ennis 1715-60}
3. David Bindon – {Ennis 1731-60}

Seat: Clooney (Cloony) House, Clare (purch. 1670, remodeled c. 1765, add. c. 1840, fire c. 1850, sold 1853, fire 1924, ruin)
Notes: The family encountered financial difficulties in the mid-19th century and sold Clooney for £8,000 through the Encumbered Estates Court and emigrated to Australia. A married daughter returned and her husband repurchased Clooney in 1859. (Blake, *Abandoned Mansions of Ireland*, 32) Two in ODNB.

BINGHAM *IRELAND & ENGLAND*

Earl of Lucan (1795- I)

Origins: The family came from Dorset, at Melcombe in the early 13th century. Bishop of Salisbury 1229. **MP for Dorset 1654**. A younger son went to Ireland as a military commander from 1579. **First Irish {MP 1585}**. Governor of Connaught 1584, Marshall of Ireland 1598. Sheriff 1607. **Two further Irish {MPs 1613-39}.** The elder brother of the founder of the Irish family retained Melcombe, where his descendants lived until 1895, resident for more than 600 years.

1. Sir George Bingham 2 Bt – {Castlebar 1661-66}
2. John Bingham – {Castlebar 1692-93 County Mayo 1695-99 1703-06}
3. Sir Henry Bingham 3 Bt – {County Mayo 1692-93 1695-99 1703-14}
4. Richard Bingham – Bridport 1702-05 Dorset 1711-13
5. John Bingham – {Castlebar 1715-27}
6. Sir John Bingham 5 Bt – {County Mayo 1727-49}
7. Sir John Bingham 6 Bt – {County Mayo 1749-50}
8. Henry Bingham – {Tuam 1761-68}
9. Charles Bingham 1 Earl of Lucan – {County Mayo 1761-76} Northampton 1782-84
10. Richard Bingham 2 Earl of Lucan – St. Albans 1790-1800
11. George Bingham 3 Earl of Lucan – County Mayo 1826-30
12. George Bingham 4 Earl of Lucan – County Mayo 1865-74
13. George Bingham 5 Earl of Lucan – Chertsey Div. Surrey 1904-06

Seats: Castlebar House, Mayo (acq. and built early 17th century, burned later in c., new house built 18th c., destroyed in 1798 rebellion, new house early 19th c., sold post WWI, later burned); Laleham House (Abbey), Surrey (purch. 1803, built c. 1804, remod. c. 1828, contents sold 1922, sold 1931, flats); Melcombe Bingham House (Bingham's Melcombe), Dorset (medieval, acq. by mar. early 13th c., remod. mid-16th c., sold 1895)
Estates: Bateman 62936 (I & E) 17423. Worth £10,000 pa early 19th c.
Titles: Baron Lucan 1776- I; Baron Bingham 1934- UK; Baronet 1634-
Peers: {1 peer 1776-99} 4 Irish Rep peers 1801-39 1840-88 1889-1914 1914-34 1 peer 1934-45
2 Lds Lt 19th, 20th
1 KP 19th-20th
Notes: 3 and 7 Earls and five others in ODNB.

Baron Clanmorris (1800- I)

Origins: Descended from a younger brother of the 1 Bingham Bt. Sheriff 1686.

1. Henry Bingham – {County Mayo 1707-14 Castlebar 1715-43}

2. John Bingham – {Tuam 1739-60}
3. Henry Bingham – {Tuam 1750-68}
4. John Bingham 1 Baron Clanmorris – {Tuam 1797-1800}

Seats: Newbrook, Mayo (acq. early 17th c., built mid to late 18th c., fire 1837, not rebuilt); Creg Clare, Galway (purch. 1855, sold 1909 to land commission, principal seat 1855-1909); Foxford, Mayo (acq. mid-17th c., sold 1916)
Estates: Bateman 18111 (I) 8263. Worth £10,000 pa in early 19th c.

BIRCH [Peploe]

Origins: The younger son of minor gentry became a wine merchant. He purchased an estate 1636. **First MP 1646. One MP before 1660**. The Peploes succeeded to the Birch estates by marriage in 1752.

1. John Birch – Leominster 1646-48 1654-55 1656-58 1660 Penryn 1661-79 Weobley 1679-81 1689-91
2. John Birch – Weobley 1701-02 1705-32 1734-35
3. Daniel Peploe – Herefordshire 1874-80

Seats: Garnstone Manor (Castle), Herefordshire (built 17th c., purch. 1661, rebuilt c. 1806, demolished 1951); The Homme, Herefordshire (purch. c. 1648, passed to the Harcourts by mar.)
Estates: Bateman 5848 (E) 9025
Notes: Two in ODNB.

BISSE [Richards]

Origins: Clerical origins. **First MP 1584. Another MP 1625**. Stephen Bisse was a Director of the East India Company and a victular to the Royal Navy. Bisse Richards succeeded to his uncle's property and took the name Bisse.

1. Stephen Bisse – Great Bedwyn 1715-22 New Romney 1734-41
2. Bisse Richards – Hindon 1747-55

Seat: Martlock (Mortlock, Matlock), Somerset (numerous Bisses owned property in the neighborhood and the Richards family owned manorial land there 18th and 19th c.)

BISSHOPP (Bysshopp, Bishopp) [Tate, Zouche]

Baron Zouche (1308- E)

Origins: The Zouches were a Breton family that came to England in the reign of Henry II. Summoned as Barons 1308. KG 1415. **First MP 1305. Ten further MPs 1390-1624, most kts of the shire**. The Bisshopps acquired estates in Sussex in the 16th century (a lawyer and noble servant) by marriage and purchase. **First MP 1542. Two other MPs 1584-1640.** The heiress of the 11 Baron Zouche married Sir Cecil Bisshopp 7 Bt of Parham and the barony was revived in that family in 1815.

1. Sir Cecil Bisshopp 4 Bt – Bramber 1662-79
2. Sir Cecil Bisshopp 6 Bt – Penryn 1727-34 Boroughbridge 1755-68
3. Cecil Bisshopp 12 Baron Zouche – New Shoreham 1780-90 1796-1806
4. Cecil Bisshopp – Newport (I o W) 1811-12

Seat: Parham Park, Sussex (built 1577, purch. 1601, sold 1922)
Estates: Bateman 6893 (E) 6223. Worth £1,500-2,000 pa in 1626.
Title: Baronet 1620-1870
Peer: 1 peer 1816-28
Notes: The Zouche barony was in abeyance from 1625 to 1815. The daughter and heiress of the 6 Bt was said to have an income of £18,000 pa on her marriage to Sir Nathaniel Holland 1 Bt in 1783. Her wealth passed to her nephew the Earl of Cardigan in 1825. The Zouche family has an entry in ODNB.

Tate

Origins: The Tates were brewers and mercers in the 15th century, Lord Mayor of London 1473; then officials and soldiers. **First MP 1483. Five further MPs 1504-1648. Kt of the shire for Northamptonshire 1614.** Sheriff 1603. Katherine Tate, heiress of Delapre Abbey and of the 11 Baron Zouche, had a daughter, Susan Hedges, who married the 7th Bisshopp Bt of Parham.

1. Bartholomew Tate – Northampton 1702-04

Seat: Delapre Abbey, Northamptonshire (medieval, purch. 1548, add. soon after, remod. early 17th c. and early 18th c., sold for £22,000 in 1764)
Estates: Worth £1,500-2,000 pa in the mid-17th century.
Notes: One in ODNB.

BLACKBURNE [Ireland]

Blackburne

Origins: The founder was a Russia merchant in the 16th century who purchased estates. High Sheriff 1763.

1. John Blackburne – Lancashire 1784-1830
2. John Ireland-Blackburne – Newton 1807-18 Warrington 1835-47
3. John Blackburne – S. W. Lancashire 1875-85

Seats: Orford Hall, Lancashire (purch. 1637, remod. 1716, demolished 1935); Hale Hall, Lancashire (built by Irelands early 17th c., remod. 1674, add. for Blackburnes 1806, largely demolished 1935, ruin)
Estates: Bateman 3148 (E) 8490
Notes: Two in ODNB.

Ireland

Origins: Held landed property since 1279. **First MP 1336. Three other MPs 1572-1656.** The Ireland estates passed to the Blackburnes by inheritance.

1. Sir Gilbert Ireland – Lancashire 1654 1656 Liverpool 1659 1660-75

Seats: Hale Hall, Lancashire (acq. and built in the Jacobean period, passed to Blackburnes 1675); Bewsey Hall, Lancashire (medieval, purch. 1586, rebuilt c. 1600, passed from Irelands to Powys family)

BLAGRAVE

Origins: Acquired property in 16th century by inheritance including half the town of Reading. **First MP 1601 for Reading. An additional MP 1648-58.**

1. John Blagrave – Reading 1660 1679-81
2. Anthony Blagrave – Reading 1701-02 1708-10 1722-27
3. John Blagrave – Reading 1739-47

Seats: Southcote, Berkshire (purch. early 16th c., sold and demolished c. 1921); Bulmershe Court (Park), Berkshire (acq. mid-16th century, sold 1789, demolished); Calcot Park, Berkshire (purch. and rebuilt 1759, sold 1929, golf club)
Notes: Three in ODNB

BLAKE *IRELAND & ENGLAND*

Blake

Origins: The family descended from merchants in Galway, Mayor of Galway c. 1300. Progenitor of many lines; most remained Roman Catholic and thus debarred from Parliament in the 17th and 18th centuries.

1. John Blake – Waterford 1857-69 County Waterford 1880-84 County Carlow 1886-87

Seat: Renvyle (Renville) Castle, Galway (medieval castle, add. 18th c., acq. 1681, add. 19th c. sold 20th c., burned 1923)
Estates: 4682 (I) 1011 in 1878

Blake

Origins: See above. Conformed to the established church. Mayor of Galway 1611, 1637, 1643. **First {MP 1613}. Two further {MPs 1634-39}.**

1. Sir Walter Blake 6 Bt – {County Galway 1689}
2. Sir Valentine Blake 12 Bt – Galway 1813-20 1841-47

Seats: Menlough (Menlo) Castle, Galway (acq. and built 1622, remod. 18th c., remod. 19th c., burned 1910, ruin); Towerhill (Clooneen), Mayo (purch. c. 1636, rebuilt c. 1790, sold late 1940s, ruin); Bunowen Castle, Galway (purch. 1853, sold early 20th c., now ruined).
Estates: 3403 (I) 763 in 1878. Most land sold by 1909.
Title: Baronet 1622-

Blake

Origins: The Blakes of Tillmouth descended from Robert Blake of Menlough (d. 1734). Bankers in Newcastle in the 18th century; later coal owners and inherited an East Indian fortune.

1. Sir Francis Blake 3 Bt – Berwick 1820-26 1827-34
2. Sir Francis Blake 1 Bt – Berwick Div. Northumberland 1916-22

Seats: Tillmouth Park, Northumberland (purch. c. 1740, rebuilt c. 1810, demolished 1880); Twizel(l) (Twisell), Northumberland (medieval castle, ruin, purch. 1685, vastly rebuilt c. 1770-1830, demolished 1880, now a ruin); Fowberry Tower, Northumberland (built before 1513, burned 1541, acq. after 1666 and rebuilt, add. 1776, sold 1807)

Estates: Bateman 2083 (E) 4726
Titles: Baronet 1774-1860; 1907-
Notes: The family was encumbered by debt in the 1820s, and the bank collapsed. Recovered later. It is said Sir Francis Blake spent £80,000 rebuilding Twizell Castle. For this family see also Blake-Delaval under Astley. Two members of the family in ODNB.

Blake

Origins: Roman Catholic cadet line. Merchants in the 18th century.

1. Martin Blake – Galway 1833-57

Seats: Ballyglunin Park (House), Galway (purch. 1671, built 18th c., add. mid-late 19th c., sold 1964, institutional use); Brooklodge, Galway (purch. 1813, family departed c. 1890s)
Estates: Bateman 10452 (I) 3968

Blake

Origins: Acquired a fortune in the West Indies in the 18th century.

1. Sir Patrick Blake 1 Bt – Sudbury 1768-84

Seat: Langham Hall, Suffolk (built 18th c., purch. mid-18th c., sold 1832)
Title: Baronet 1772-

Blake

Origins: Roman Catholic cadet line. Sheriff 1838.

1. Mark Blake – Mayo 1840-46

Seat: Ballinafad House, Galway (acq. early 17th c., new house 1827, sold 1908, institution)
Estates: 3443 (I) 1797 in 1878.

Baron Wallscourt (1800-03 I; 1806-1920 I)

Origins: Cadet line that conformed to the established church. **First MP for {County Galway 1634}**.

1. Joseph Blake 1 Baron Wallscourt – {County Galway 1792-1800}

Seats: Ardfrey (Ardfry), Galway (castle, acq. 17th c., new house c. 1770, remod. 1826, deroofed early 20th c., ruin, demense still owned by family 1990s); Ballinacourt (Wallscourt), Galway (acq. 1612, sold 1795)
Estates: 2827 (I) 1970 in 1878. Worth £4502 pa in 1790.
Peer: {1 peer 1800}
Notes: Roman Catholic until the 1780s. Heavily indebted in the 19th c.

BLAKENEY *IRELAND*

Baron Blakeney (1756-61 I)

Origins: English gentry 16th century, to Ireland later 16th c.. Granted land as a Cromwellian soldier. **One pre-1660 {MP}.** Sheriff 1709. 1 Baron a general.

1. Robert Blakeney – {Athenry 1721-33}
2. William Blakeney 1 Baron Blakeney – {Kilmallock 1725-56}
3. John Blakeney – {Athenry 1727-47}
4. Robert Blakeney – {Athenry 1747-62}
5. John Blakeney – {Athenry 1763-89}
6. Theopholis Blakeney – {Athenry 1768-76 Carlingford 1776-83 Athenry 1783-1800}
7. John Blakeney – {Athenry 1776-81}
8. William Blakeney – {Athenry 1781-83 1790-1800}

Seats: Castle Blakeney (Mount Blakeney), Limerick (acq. c. 1666, fire 1720s, passed out of the family by mar. early 19th c.); Abbert Castle, Galway (purch. 1734, resident into early 20th c., ruin)
Estates: Bateman 7504 (I) 2579
Peer: {1 peer 1756-61}
Notes: Much land sold 1860s onwards, with 1,500 acres sold in 1911. 1 Baron and one other in ODNB.

BLAKISTON

Origins: At Blakiston in the 14th century. An **MP for Newcastle 1472** was a merchant and shipowner (related?) **One MP 1640 for Newcastle**, a younger son and mercer. Many members of the family were Roman Catholic.

1. William Blakiston – Durham 1679-81
2. Nathaniel Blakiston – Mitchell 1715-22

Seats: Blakiston Hall, Northumberland (or Durham) (held for 300 years until sold 1615); Old Malton, Yorkshire (branch extinct 1684); Pittington Hall, Durham (branch male line extinct 1684); Newton Hall, Durham (built c. 1730 for another family, perhaps only tenanted, demolished 1926); Black Callerton, Northumberland
Notes: One in ODNB.

BLAND

Origins: Founder an official under Elizabeth I. Married an heiress. Sir Thomas Bland (d. 1612) built Kippax. Bt 1642.

1. Sir John Bland 4 Bt – Appleby 1681 Pontefract 1690-95 1698-1713
2. Sir John Bland 5 Bt – Lancashire 1713-27
3. Sir John Bland 6 Bt – Ludgersall 1754-55

Seats: Kippax Park, Yorkshire (purch. 1595, new house built 1590s; contents sold 1929 and house abandoned, derelict by 1953, later destroyed by open cast mining); Hulme Hall, Lancashire (medieval, acq. by mar. 1695, sold 1751, demolished c. 1840 during construction of a canal)
Estates: Bateman 4320 (E) 8500
Title: Baronet 1642-1756
Notes: On the death of the 6 Bt, a profligate gambler who died in exile, the estates passed to sisters and then in 1786 to a cousin Thomas Davison who took the name Bland. This line became extinct in 1928.

BLAYNEY *IRELAND*

Baron Blayney (1621-1874 I)

Origins: 1 Baron went to Ireland with Essex in 1598 as a soldier. Kt 1603. **First {MP for County Monaghan 1613}. One additional {MP 1634}.**

1. Richard Blayney 4 Baron Blayney – {County Monaghan 1634, 1661-66}
2. Andrew Blayney 11 Baron Blayney – Old Sarum 1806-07
3. Cadwallader Blayney 12 Baron Blayney – Monaghan 1830-34

Seat: Castle Blayney (Balyney Castle) (aka Hope Castle), Monaghan (acq. 1611 and built soon after, new house 18th c., sold 1853)
Estates: Bateman 2074 (I) 2323
Peers: {6 peers 1661-69 1689 1692-1706 1713-33 1735-75} 1 Irish Rep peer 1841-74

Notes: Severe financial difficulties required the sale of most of the family estate in 1646, but these were recovered by the 4 Baron marrying the heiress of the purchaser. 11 Baron in ODNB.

BLENNERHASSETT *IRELAND*

Blennerhassett

Origins: **First MP for Carlisle 1381. Four subsequent MPs, three for Carlisle, 1413-1604**. Sir John Blennerhassett went to Ireland c. 1611 as a Baron of the Exchequer and acquired estates. **First {MP Belfast 1613}.** Sheriff 1622.

1. Henry Blennerhassett – {County Fermanagh 1662-66}
2. Robert Blennerhassett – {Clonmell 1692-93 1695-99 Limerick 1703-12}
3. Conway Blennerhassett – {Tralee 1723-24}
4. Arthur Blennerhassett – {Tralee 1727-43}
5. Sir Rowland Blennerhassett 4 Bt – Galway 1865-74 Kerry 1880-85
6. Rowland Blennerhassett – Kerry 1872-85

Seats: Churchtown House, Kerry (built c. 1740, sold 1860); Blennerville House, Kerry (built c. 1700, sold later 19th c.); Flimby Lodge (Hall), Cumberland (acq. 1547, sold to Lowthers 1772); Kells (Mount Holly), Kerry (acq. and built 1837, sold 1949); Killorgin (Kilorgin) Castle, Kerry (aka Castle Conway) (built 13th c., acq. by mar. late 17th c. and new house built, sold late 18th c. and dismantled)
Estates: Bateman 8393 (I) 2145
Title: Baronet 1809-

Blennerhassett

Origins: Cadet of the Blennerhassetts of Cumberland. **First {MP} Robert Blennerhassett {Tralee 1613)** settled in Ireland c. 1600.

1. John Blennerhassett – {County Kerry 1661-66}
2. John Blennerhassett – {Tralee 1661-66 1692-93 Dingle 1695-99 County Kerry 1703-08}
3. John Blennerhassett – {County Kerry 1709-13 Tralee 1713-14 County Kerry 1715-27 Tralee 1727-60 County Kerry 1761-75}
4. John Blennerhassett – {County Kerry 1751-60 1762-63
5. Arthur Blennerhassett – {Tralee 1743-60 County Kerry 1775-83}
6. John Blenerhassett – {County Kerry 1790-94}
7. Arthur Blennerhassett – County Kerry 1837-41

Seat: Ballyseedy House, Kerry (acq. 1611-28, built c. 1760, remod. 1816, remod. late 19th c., sold 1967, hotel); Elmgrove, Kerry (built early 18th c., fire c. 1800)
Estates: Bateman 12621 (I) 4159

BLIGH [Williamson] *IRELAND & ENGLAND*

Earl of Darnley (1725- I)

Origins: A merchant in Plymouth and then London. His son an agent for Landed Adventurers in Ireland 1641. First MP (1660) a London merchant who acquired substantial estates in Meath.

1. John Bligh – {Athboy 1660-66}
2. Thomas Bligh – {Athboy 1692-93 County Meath 1695-99 1703-10}
3. John Bligh 1 Earl of Darnley – {Trim 1709-13 Athboy 1713-21}
4. Thomas Bligh – {Athboy 1715-75}
5. John Bligh 3 Earl of Darnley – {Athboy 1739-47} Maidstone 1741-47
6. Thomas Bligh – {Athboy 1783-1800} County Meath 1802-12
7. Edward Bligh – {Athboy 1800}
8. Edward Bligh 5 Earl of Darnley – Canterbury 1818-30

Seats: Cobham Hall, Kent (built c. 1550s, add. c. 1582-1603, acq. by Dukes of Lennox and Richmond c. 1603, add. 1660s, acq. by Blighs by mar. 1713, remod. 1760s-70s, 1789-90, and 1811-1831, sold 1961, became school); Clifton Lodge, Meath (acq. 17th c., resident 19th c.); Rathmore, Meath (acq. 17th c., original seat in Ireland 18th c., sold early 20th c.); Brittas, Meath (acq. and built 1672, rebuilt 1732, add. post 1800, sold c. 1920s)
Estates: Bateman 34872 (E & I) 37350. Cadet line at Brittas, Meath 7443 (I) 5968 (not in Bateman but listed under "Trustees" in Return of Irish landowners). Irish estates worth an estimated £12,000 pa in 1800.
Titles: Baron Clifton (1608- E); Baron Clifton (1721 I); Viscount Darnley (1723 I)
Peers: {3 peers 1737-47 1760-81 1789-1800} 7 peers 1722-81 1788-1835 1848-1900 1937-45
1 Irish Rep peer 1905-27
1 Ld Lt 19th
Notes: The 1 Earl of Darnely married 1713 the 10 Baroness Clifton in her own right. A Clifton MP (see below) was elected in 1597. 8 Earl and two others in ODNB.

Williamson

Origins: The first MP was the son of a vicar. He rose through the legal profession and outstanding ability to high office (Secretary of State 1674-79).

1. Sir Joseph Williamson – Thetford 1669-81 1685-87 Rochester 1690-1701 {County Clare 1692-93 Limerick 1695-99}

Seat: Cobham Hall, Kent (purch. £45,000 c. 1672, see above)
Notes: Sir Jospeh married the 7 Baroness Clifton in her own right. Cobham passed through her descendants to the Darnleys. One in ODNB.

BLOIS (Bloys) [Brooke]

Origins: The grandfather of Sir Robert Brooke MP was a merchant who purchased estates in Suffolk in 1597. **First MP 1624**. Sir Robert entailed his property to his nephew Sir Charles Blois 1 Bt. The Blois family were at Grundisburgh in the reign of Henry VII. Merchants in Ipswich in the 17th century. First Kt d. 1675.

1. Sir Robert Brooke – Aldeburgh 1660-69
2. William Bloys – Suffolk 1654 1656 Ipswich 1661-73
3. Sir Charles Blois 1 Bt – Ipswich 1689-95 Dunwich 1700-09

Seats: Cockfield Hall, Suffolk (Brooke seat) (built early 16th c., rebuilt 1613, acq. by Blois 1693 by mar. from Brooke family, remod. c. 1770, add. 1896, bomb damage WWII, sold 1990s); Grundisburgh Hall, Suffolk (Blois seat) (built c. 1500, acq. c. 1510-20, sold 1771)
Estates: Bateman 6307 (E) 8212
Title: Baronet 1686-

BLOOMFIELD [Douglas]

<u>Baron Bloomfield</u> (1825-79 I 1871-79 UK)

Origins: The son of a soldier the 1 Baron was a barrister, diplomat, courtier, and soldier.

1. Benjamin Bloomfield 1 Baron Bloomfield – Plymouth 1812-18

Peers: 1 peer 1871-79
Notes: 1 and 2 Barons in ODNB.

<u>Douglas</u>

Origins: The first MP was the son of a wealthy industrialist (cotton mills) and landowner. John Douglas MP left his estates to his nephew (sister's son) to the 2 Baron Bloomfield.

1. John Douglas – Orford 1818-21 Minehead 1822-26

BLOUNT

Blount

Origins: The family claimed Norman descent, were warriors, royal advisors, and peers (Baron Blount 1330) from the 13th century. The Bounts of Sodington descended from Sir John Blount and his first wife, the daughter and heiress of Sir Thomas Mountjoy (**first MP 1318**). Sir Walter Blount was in France with Henry V on the Agincourt campaign. **First MP 1399. Four additional MPs 1399-1624. A further eight MPs 1461-1572 including a number of kts of the shire** were seated at Kinlet, Shropshire.

1. Edward Blount – Steyning 1830-32

Seats: Sodington Hall, Worcestershire (medieval, acq. by mar. mid-14th c., burned 1646, rebuilt 1660s, rebuilt 1806, sold 1958); Shabbington, Buckinghamshire (medieval, purch. 1827, still owned 1920s); Mawley Hall, Shropshire (built 1730, add. late 18th c., sold 1950s)
Estates: Bateman 5482 (E) 5069
Titles: Baronet 1642-
Notes: Owned coal mines. Numerous early Blounts in ODNB.

Earl of Newport (1628-79 E)

Origins: Descended from Sir John Blount and his second wife, Eleanor Beauchamp. They became Lords Mountjoy (1465-1660) and Earls of Devonshire (1603-06). An illegitmate son was also created Baron Mountjoy and Earl of Newport (1628-79). **First MP 1318. Fifteen further MPs 1397-1601 with a number of kts of the shire**. The surviving line at Mapledurham was Roman Catholic and hence elected no further MPs.

No post-1660 MPs

Seat: Mapledurham, Oxfordshire (purch. 1490, house built 1580s, heirs still own, although the male line became extinct in 1908)
Estates: Bateman 5276 (E) 7528
Peer: 1 peer 1660-79
Notes: 1, 3, 4, and 5 Barons and 2 Earl in ODNB.

BLUDWORTH

Origins: Founder was a mid-17th century Turkey merchant in London. First MP 1660. Kt 1660.

1. Sir Thomas Bludworth – Southwark 1660-79
2. Sir Thomas Bludworth – Bramber 1685-87
3. Thomas Bludworth – Bodmin 1741-47

Seat: Thorncroft Manor, Surrey (acq. mid-17th c., built 1772)

BLUNDEN *IRELAND*

Origins: A London cloth bleacher turned Cromwellian adventurer arrived in Ireland in the 1650s. Acquired 254 acres in 1660. Sheriff 1716.

1. John Blunden – {Kilkenny 1727-52}
2. Sir John Blunden 1 Bt – {Kilkenny 1761-76}
3. Overington Blunden – Kilkenny 1812-14

Seats: Castle Blunden, Kilkenny (old house, acq. 1667, rebuilt c. 1750, still own); Bonnettstown Hall, Kilkenny (built 1737, acq. 19th c.)
Estates: In the later 19th century 2,592 acres in Ireland worth £1,993. Estates worth £5,000 pa in the mid 18th century. The 2 Bt married an heiress worth £8,000 pa. Held 1,846 acres in 1883.
Title: Baronet 1766-

BODVELL (Bodville, Bodfel, Gwyn) *WALES*

Origins: Old Welsh family. **First MP for Caernarvonshire 1553. Two additional MPs 1589-1644.**

1. William Bodvell – Caernarvonshire 1741-54 Montgomery 1754-59

Seats: Bodvel (Bodfel) Castle, Caernarvonshire (medieval, remod. mid. 17th c., most of estate sold 1671); Llanigrad Park, Anglesey (resident 17th c.)
Estates: Worth £1,800 pa in 1644.

BOLES

Origins: The first MP a vicar's son. Landed 19th century.

1. Sir Dennis Boles 1 Bt – Wellington 1911-18 Taunton 1918-21
2. Dennis Boles – Wells 1939-51
3. Nicholas Boles – Grantham and Stamford 2010-

Seats: Ryll Court, Devon; Rackenford Manor, Devon (old manor house, rebuilt 18th c., add. 1928)
Title: Baronet 1922-

BOLLES

Origins: Settled in Lincolnshire since the 13th century. **First MP for Lincolnshire in the reign of Edward III.** Lord Mayor of London 1617-18.

1. Sir Robert Bolles 1 Bt – Lincoln 1661-63
2. Sir John Bolles 4 Bt – Lincoln 1690-1702

Seat: Scampton, Lincolnshire (built 16th c., acq. by marriage 1642, sold c. 1714)
Estates: Worth £3,000 pa in the later 17th century.
Title: Baronet 1628-1714
Notes: On the death of the 4 Bt the estates were sold by his sister.

BOND

Origins: At Lutton by 1510. **First MP 1529. Second MP (1640)** was a linen draper and Mayor of Dorchetser (1635). He became President of the Council of State 1652. **Another MP 1658.**

1. Nathaniel Bond – Corfe Castle 1679-80 Dorchester 1681 1695-98
2. Denis Bond – Dorchester 1709-10 Corfe Castle 1715-27 Poole 1727-32
3. John Bond – Corfe Castle 1721-22 1727-44
4. John Bond – Corfe Castle 1747-61 1764-80
5. John Bond – Corfe Castle 1780-1801
6. Nathaniel Bond – Corfe Castle 1801-07
7. John Bond – Corfe Castle 1823-28
8. George Bond – E. Dorset 1886-91

Seats: Creech Grange, Dorset (built c. 1540, purch. 1691, remod. 1738-41, remod. 1846, estate sold 1967 and house 1979); Tyneham House, Dorset (built c. 1350, rebuilt 1567-83, purch. 1683, rebuilt 1820, requisitioned 1943, family did not return after the war, sold c. 1945, partially demolished 1967); Lutton, Dorset (medieval, acq. by marriage to an heiress by 1510, transferred seat to Creech Grange c. 1691)
Estates: Bateman 8794 (E & W) 5614
Notes: Bond Street in London is named after the family. Four in ODNB.

BONHAM

Origins: Gentry family in the 13th century. **First MP 1529 for Essex. Two further MPs in the 16th century**. Henry Bonham MP (1806-30) was grandson of a captain in the slave trade, and he and his father were merchants and shipowners.

1. Henry Bonham – Leominster 1806-12 Sandwich 1824-26
   Rye 1826-30

Seats: High Canons, Hertfordshire (built c. 1800, purch. 1806, sold 1812); Titness Park, Berkshire (old house, purch. c. 1820, rebuilt 1823, sold by 1838, demolished mid-20th c.?); Rochetts, Essex (built 18th c., leased 19th c.?, fire 1975); Kelvedon Hall, Essex (built 16th c., rebuilt c. 1743, leased or purchased later 19th c., sold ? 1932)

BORROWES [Dixon] *IRELAND*

Borrowes

Origins: Settled in Ireland in the reign of Elizabeth I. Married the heiress to Gilltown in 1585. Their son was High Sheriff of Kildare 1641. **First {MP 1642}.**

1. Sir Kildare Borrowes 3 Bt – {County Kildare 1703-09}
2. Sir Walter Borrowes 4 t – {Harristown 1721-27 Athy 1727-41}
3. Sir Kildare Borrowes 5 Bt – {County Kildare 1745-76}

Seats: Gilltown, Kildare (acq. by mar. of 1585, sold c. 1918); Barrettstown (Barretstown) Castle, Kildare (old tower house, acq. by mar. 17th c., add. Victorian, sold 1918); Colverstown, Kildare (acq. by mar. 1725, sold 1748)
Estates: Bateman 4818 (I) 2594 and 6089 (I) 4103
Title: Baronet 1646-1939
Notes: Resident in England after WWI.

Dixon

Origins: Sir Robert Dixon was Lord Mayor of Dublin 1634. **First {MP 1639}.** High Sheriff 1709. Sir Walter Borrowes 4 Bt succeeded to the estates of his maternal uncle Robert Dixon of Colverstown in 1725.

1. Sir William Dixon – {Jamestown 1661-66}
2. Robert Dixon – {Randalstown 1692-93 1713-14 1715-26 Harristown 1703-13}
3. Hugh Dixon – {Lismore 1725-27 Cork 1727-38}
4. Robert Dixon – {Kildare 1727-31}

Seat: Colverstown (Calverstown), Kildare (acq. 17th c., passed by mar. to Borrowes 1725)

BORTHWICK *SCOTLAND*

Baron Borthwick (c. 1452- S)

Origins: Medieval barons from an early period. Ambassador to Rome 1424 and to England 1459. The date of the title is uncertain, and it has fallen into disuse a number of times. The 9 Baron sat in the Scottish Parliament before and after the Civil War. **First [MP 1458].**

1. James Borthwick – [Edinburgh 1649-50 1661-62]

Seats: Borthwick Castle, Edinburghshire (built 1430, sold later 17th c., repurch. 1813, restored 1890s, leased for commercial use 1984); Ravenstone Castle, Wigtownshire (built 16th c., add. 17th c., add. 19th c., purch. 1870, add. 1875, abandoned 20th c., ruin); Crookston House, Edinburghshire (acq. by 15th c., rebuilt 17th c., new house 1816-17, remod. 1860-64, still own)
Estates: 9723 (S) 5850. Owned 10,400 acres in 2001.
Peers: 2 Scottish Rep peers 1880-85 1906-10
Notes: The title was called out of abeyance most recently in 1986. Borthwick family and 4 Baron has an entry in the ODNB.

BOSCAWEN [Griffith, Stapleton]

Earl of Falmouth (1821-52 UK)

Origins: Acquired Tregothnan in 1334 by marriage to the Tregothan family heiress. The Boscawens were unambitious squires until the 17th century when their position was raised by Hugh Boscawen (1578-1641) a courtier and pensioner.

1. Hugh Boscawen – Cornwall 1646-48 1659 1660 Grampound 1660 Tregony 1661-81 Cornwall 1689-1701
2. Edward Boscawen – Tregony 1659 Truro 1660-79 1681
3. Robert Boscawen – Tregony 1679
4. William Boscawen – Truro 1679-81
5. Charles Boscawen – Cornwall 1654 Truro 1659 Tregony 1689
6. Hugh Boscawen 1 Viscount Falmouth – Tregony 1702-05 Cornwall 1705-10 Truro 1710-13 Penryn 1713-20
7. Hugh Boscawen 2 Viscount Falmouth – Truro 1727-34
8. Edward Boscawen – Truro 1742-61
9. George Boscawen – Penryn 1743-61 Truro 1761-74

10. John Boscawen – Truro 1747-67
11. Edward Boscawen – Truro 1767-74
12. George Boscawen – St. Mawes 1768-74 Truro 1774-80
13. Hugh Boscawen – St. Mawes 1774-90
14. William Boscawen – Truro 1784-92
15. Edward Boscawen 1 Earl of Falmouth – Truro 1807-08
16. George Boscawen-Rose 2 Earl of Falmouth – W. Cornwall 1841
17. Robert Boscawen – Wells 1970-83 Somerton and Frome 1983-92

Seats: Tregothnan, Cornwall (medieval, acq. by 1334, built early 16th c., rebuilt 1650s and 1845-48, still own); Mereworth Castle, Kent (built 1720-30, inher. from Stapletons 1831, sold 1924); Hatchlands Park, Surrey (purch. c. 1750, rebuilt 1754-60, sold 1770)
Estates: Bateman 30606 (E) 42904. Income of £1,000 pa in 1641. Large interest in mines. Owned 42,000 acres in 2001.
Titles: Baron le Despencer 1264- E; Viscount Falmouth 1720- GB
Peers: 8 peers 1720-1945
Notes: The 6 Viscount married in 1845 Mary Baroness le Despencer in her own right. The 7 Viscount succeeded as 24 Baron. Five in ODNB.

Griffith-Boscawen

Origins: Thomas Griffith married in 1830 Elizabeth Boscawen, heiress of the Trevelyan Hall estate by the marriage of her grandfather (a son of the 1 Viscount Falmouth) to Anne Trevor of Trevelyan (see Hill I).

1. Sir Arthur Griffith-Boscawen – Tunbridge Div. Kent 1892-1906 Dudley 1910-21 Taunton Div. Somerset 1921-22

Seat: Trevalyn Hall, Denbighshire (built c. 1576, acq. by mar. 1830, sold 1980s, flats)
1 in Cabinet 1921-23
Notes: One in ODNB.

Stapleton

Origins: Originally from Tipperary. 1 Bt was Governor of the Leeward Islands under Charles II. Acquired a West Indian fortune. The 4 Bt was born on Nevis and married a Berkshire heiress, Catherine Paul, daughter of Catherine Fane, daughter of the 4 Earl of Westmorland. Through this marriage the 6 Bt succeeded as 22 Baron le Despencer in 1788. His granddaughter married the 6 Viscount Falmouth.

1. Sir William Stapleton 4 Bt – Oxfordshire 1727-40
2. Sir Thomas Stapleton 5 Bt – Oxford 1759-68

Seats: Rotherfield Greys (Grey's Court or Greys Court), Oxfordshire (built c. 12th c., add. c. 1347, add. c. 1450-51, add. c. 1559-87, rebuilt early 17th c., acq. by mar. c. 1740, remod. c. 1750, sold 1934, NT 1969); Mereworth Castle, Kent (built 1720-30, inher. by mar. 1781, passed by mar. 1831 to 6 Baron Falmouth)
Estates: Property on St. Kitts and Nevis was worth £85,000 in 1776 (*Country Life*, 164, p. 158)
Title: Baronet 1776-
Peer: 1 peer 1788-1831
Notes: The Conwy estates passed through this family (see Taylour).

BOTELER (Butler) [Farrer]

Boteler

Origins: Began as grocers in London. The family was settled in Hertfordshire by the reign of Edward III. Kt 14th century. **First MP 1445 for Hertfordshire.** Lord Mayor of London 1515 (merchant). **Six further MPs 1529-1626, all but one kts of the shire.**

1. Sir Francis Boteler – Hertford 1685-87
2. John Boteler – Hertford 1715-22 Wendover 1734-35

Seat: Woodhall Park (Watton Woodhall), Hertfordshire (acq. 14th century, sold 1777)

Boteler

Origins: Cadet of Watton line. At Biddenham early 14th century. **First MP 1378. An additional MP 1563.**

1. William Boteler – Bedfordshire 1685-87

Seat: Biddenham, Bedfordshire (acq. early 14th c., passed by mar. and sale to Farrers c. 1709)
Estates: Owned c. 2,000 acres in 1660.
Notes: Family extinct 1703. Estates divided among multiple heiresses.

Boteler

Origins: Cadet of the Biddenham line.

1. Sir Philip Boteler 3 Bt – Hythe 1690-1708
2. John Boteler – Hythe 1701-15

Seat: Barham Court, Kent (acq. c. 1600, sold early 18th c.)

Title: Baronet 1641-1772
Notes: The 3 Bt married a Bouverie (see Pleydell-Bouverie) and the estates passed to that family in 1772. One in ODNB.

Farrer

Origins: A legal family that acquired Harrold in 1556 and married a Boteler heiress (daughter of Willam MP 1685-87) of Biddenham.

1. William Farrer – Bedford 1695-98 1701-02 1705-13 1715-27

Seats: Harrold, Bedfordshire (purch. 1556, built 1608-10, sold 1714); Biddenham, Bedfordshire (acq. by mar. and purch. c. 1709, sold mid-18th c.)
Notes: See also Hillersden.

BOUGHTON [Johnes, Knight, Rous(e)] *ENGLAND & WALES*

Boughton

Origins: The family was landed by the 15th century. **First MP 1453 for Warwicksire. Three additional MPs 1472-1584**.

1. Sir Edward Boughton 2 Bt – Warwickshire 1679-81
2. Sir William Boughton 4 Bt – Warwickshire 1712-13
3. Sir Charles Rouse Boughton 9 Bt – Evesham 1780-90 Bramber 1796-1800
4. Sir William Boughton 10 Bt – Evesham 1818-26

Seats: Downton Hall, Shropshire (built late 17th c., add 1730, acq. by mar. in 1781, remod. 1824, still own); Lawford Hall, Warwickshire (acq. by mar. c. 1440, demolished 1780, sold 1793); Poston House, Herefordshire (medieval, purch. by Earl of Worcester, passed by mar. to Boughtons c. 1760s, rebuilt c. 1775, add. c. 1882, passed by mar. to the Robinsons late 19th c., sold c. 1960); Brownsover Hall, Warwickshire (acq. 15th c.?, passed by mar. to Leighs c. 1787 and then by mar. to the Wards 1818, rebuilt c. 1857, sold before WWII, now hotel); Rous Lench Court, Worcestershire (medieval, add. early 17th c. and early 18th c., acq. by mar. 1721 from Rouses, remod. 19th c., sold 1876)
Estates: Bateman 5456 (E) 7645 and (under Ward-Boughton-Leigh) 4400 (E) 9000
Titles: Baronet 1641-1963; 1791- ; 1794-
Notes: The Leighs, who inherited Brownsover Hall descended from the Leighs of High Leigh (see Legh). The 9 Bt was a nabob. 9 Bt in ODNB.

Rous(e)

Origins: A landed family from the 14th century. **First MP 1332. Another MP 1436 for the county**. Kt 1607. **An additional MP 1626 for Worcestershire**. On the death of the 4 Bt in 1721 Rouse Lench passed to the Boughtons by marriage.

1. Sir Thomas Rous 1 Bt – Worcestershire 1654 1656 Evesham 1660
2. John Rous – Warwick 1660

Seat: Rous Lench Court, Worcestershire (acq. 1380s, add. early 16th c. and early 17th c., passed to Boughtons by mar. 1721)
Title: Baronet 1641-1721
Notes: Rous family has an entry in the ODNB.

Rouse-Boughton-Knight

Origins: Knights were ironmasters whose business grew large in the 1740s and 1750s. Richard Payne Knight (d. 1746) who purchased a landed estate at Downton was the grandson of a Shropshire iron maker (later 17th century). The Knights formed business partnerships with the Foleys (see that family) and the Lytteltons (see also). His niece and heiress married the second son of Sir William Boughton 10 Bt (see above).

1. Richard Payne Knight – Leominster 1780-84 Ludlow 1784-1806

Seats: Downton Castle, Herefordshire (built 1772, remod. 1850 and 1861, sold 1979); Henley Hall, Shropshire (rebuilt c. 1725, purch. 1770, add. 1772, sold 1884); Croft Castle, Herefordshire (built 14th c., acq. 1746, passed to Johnes family by mar. 1765); Wormsley Grange, Herefordshire (early Georgian, Victorian add., became a farm house, sold 1850s); Lea Castle, Worcestershire (built early 19th c., sold, demolished c. 1945)
Estates: Bateman 10518 (E) 12042
Notes: Knight family has an entry in ODNB. Two additional listed.

Knight

Origins: Descended from a younger brother of Richard Payne Knight (see above). Continued to manage the ironworks into the early 20th century.

1. Sir Frederick Knight – W. Worcestershire 1841-85
2. Eric Knight – Kidderminster 1910-18 Kidderminster Div. Worcestershire 1918-22

Seats: Wolverley House, Worcestershire (built 1750s, donated to an educational trust and contents sold 1944); Simmonsbath, Devon (built 1654, purch. with 10,000 acres 1818, sold 1879)
Estates: Bateman 22031 (E) 9852. Rubinstein – Edward Knight left £125,000 probate in 1812.

Johnes

Origins: The Johnes were an old Carmarthenshire family descended from a Prince of Gower and were seated at Dolau Cothy from the time records exist. **First MP 1542-58 for Carmarthenshire.** The daughter of an uncle of Richard Payne Knight (see above) married Thomas Johnes and brought Knight estates to that family.

1. Thomas Johnes – Cardiganshire 1713-15
2. Thomas Johnes – Cardigan Boroughs 1775-80 Radnorshire 1780-96 Cardiganshire 1796-1816
3. Thomas Johnes – Radnorshire 1777-80

Seats: Llanfair, Cardiganshire (sold 1833); Hafod (Dyfed), Cardiganshire (purch. in the 18th century, built 1786, fire and rebuilt 1807, add. early 19th c., sold 1833, demolished 1958); Croft Castle, Herefordshire (built 14th c., acq. through the Knight inheritance 1756, sold 1785); Dolau Cothy (Dolaucothy), Carmarthenshire (acq. and built medieval period, sold 1833, demolished 1954)
2 Lds Lt 18th, 19th
Notes: The Welsh estates of the family were sold in 1833 by an only daughter and heiress because of a financial crash during the last years of her father's life due to overspending. One in ODNB.

BOWYER [Stonhouse]

Baron Denham (1937- UK)

Origins: Cadet of the Bowyers of Knipersley **First MP (Newcastle-u-Lyme) 1411**. (See under Adderley) Merchants, Mayor of Chichester 1532 and then in business in London. Settled in Surrey in the mid-16th century. **First MP of this line 1563 for Westminster. Two further MPs 1593-1624.**

1. Sir William Bowyer 1 Bt – Amersham 1659 Buckinghamshire 1660-179
2. Sir Edmund Bowyer – Gatton 1660 Surrey 1661-79
3. Anthony Bowyer – Southwark 1685-87 1690-98
4. Sir George Bowyer 5 Bt – Queenborough 1784-90
5. Sir George Bowyer 6 Bt – Malmesbury 1807-09 Abingdon 1811-18

6. Henry Bowyer – Abingdon 1809-11
7. Sir George Bowyer 7 Bt – Dundalk 1852-68 Wexford 1874-80
8. George Bowyer 1 Baron Denham – Buckingham Div. Buckinghamshire 1918-37

Seats: Denham Court (not Place), Buckinghamshire (medieval, acq. c. 1660, rebuilt 1667, sold 1935, now golf club); Camberwell Manor, Surrey (purch. 1583, demolished 1861); Radley Park, Berkshire (acq. by mar. 1792, sold 1889)
Estates: Bateman 4451 (E) 9412
Titles: Baronet 1660- ; 1794- ; 1933-
Peer: 1 peer 1937-45
Notes: Three in ODNB.

<u>Stonhouse</u>

Origins: Tudor merchants gained land at the Dissolution. Royal official under Elizabeth I. High Sheriff 1606. **First MP 1628**. On the death of the 9 Bt in 1792 Radley Park passed to the Bowyers of Denham.

1. Sir George Stonhouse 3 Bt – Abingdon 1640-44 1660-75
2. Duke Stonhouse – Great Bedwyn 1661-63
3. Sir John Stonhouse 2 Bt – Abingdon 1675-81 1685-87 1690
4. Francis Stonhouse – Great Bedwyn 1679-81 1694-1705
5. Sir John Stonhouse 3 Bt – Berkshire 1701-33

Seats: Radley Park, Berkshire (purch. 1560, passed to Bowyers 1792); Stock House, Wiltshire
Estates: Worth £2,000 pa in the 1660s
Titles: Baronet 1628- ; 1670-
Notes: One in ODNB.

BOYLE [Gardiner, Stewart] *IRELAND & ENGLAND*

<u>Earl of Cork and Orrery</u> (1620- and 1660- I)

Origins: Perhaps the most famous story of a rapid social and economic rise of a family on record. The 1 Earl of Cork went to Ireland in 1588 to make his fortune with £27 to his name. His brother also came and ended up as Bishop of Cork in 1617. They were from a gentry background and well educated but of comparatively humble station. The 1 Earl rose in government service with Cecil's favor: Kt 1603, PC Ireland 1612, Baron 1616, Earl 1620, and Lord Justice of Ireland 1629. He accumulated a vast estate in Cork at first by manipulating control over confiscated land and became an industrial entrepreneur. Lawrence Stone called him the richest landowner in the British Isles in 1640 with an income of £18,000-20,000 pa. (Stone, *The Crisis of the Aristocracy*, 140, 268) "The old nobility queued up to marry his eight daughters." (Mark Girouard noted: *Country Life*, 136, p. 336) **First {MP 1613}. Two other MPs pre-1660**. The 1 Earl of Orrery was Lord President of the Council of Scotland 1656. The family established a great landed presence in England as well.

1. Roger Boyle 1 Earl of Orrery – {County Cork 1654 1656-57} [Edinburgh 1656] Arundel 1660-79
2. Richard Boyle – {County Cork 1661-65}
3. Roger Boyle 2 Earl of Orrery – {County Cork 1665-66}
4. Charles Boyle Viscount Dungarvon – Tamworth 1670-79 Yorkshire 1679-81 1685-87
5. Charles Boyle 2 Earl of Burlington – Appleby 1690-94
6. Henry Boyle 1 Baron Carleton – Tamworth 1689-90 Cambridge University 1692-1705 {County Cork 1692-93} Westminster 1705-10
7. Henry Boyle – {Youghal 1692-93}
8. Lionel Boyle 3 Earl of Orrery – East Grinstead 1695 1698-1702
9. Charles Boyle 4 Earl of Orrery – {Charleville 1695-99} Huntingdon 1701-05
10. Bellingham Boyle – {Bandon Bridge 1731-60 Youghal 1761-68}
11. Charles Boyle Viscount Dungarvon – {County Cork 1756-59}
12. Charles Boyle – {Lismore 1758}
13. Hamilton Boyle 6 Earl of Cork – {Charleville 1759-60} Warwick 1761-62
14. Charles Boyle – {Charleville 1797-1800}
15. Sir Courtney Boyle – Bandon Bridge 1806-07
16. John Boyle – County Cork 1827-30 Cork 1830-32
17. Robert Boyle – Frome 1847-54
18. Richard Boyle 9 Earl of Cork – Frome 1854-56
19. William Boyle – Frome 1856-57
20. William Boyle – Mid Div. Norfolk 1910-18

Seats: Marston House, Somerset (medieval house, purch. and rebuilt 1641, remod. mid-18th c., add 1770s, sold 1905); Lismore Castle, Waterford (medieval castle, purch. 1602, rebuilt c. 1610, passed by mar. to Dukes of Devonshire 18th c., still own); Ballymallow House, Cork; Londesborough, Yorkshire (built c. 1589, inher. by mar. from the Clifford Earls of Cumberland 1643, add. before 1700, passed to Dukes of Devonshire, demolished 1818); Stalbridge Park, Dorset (built 1638, fire and demolished 1822)
Estates: Bateman 38313 (I & E) 17343. The 3 Earl held 42,000 acres in Cork worth £20,000 pa.
Titles: Baron Boyle 1616- I; Viscount Dungarvon 1820- I; Viscount Boyle 1627- I; Baron Broghill 1628- I; Baron Clifford 1644-1753 E; Earl of Burlington 1664-1753 E; Baron Boyle 1711- GB; Baron Carleton 1714-25 GB
Peers: {6 peers 1660-82 1663-94 1697-1731 1735-62} 4 peers 1660-98 1689-1753 1711-31 1711-1945

6 Lds Lt 17th, 18th, 19th, 20th
2 in Cabinet Council 1660 1708-10 1721-25
1 KG 18th
2 KP 19th, 20th
1 KT 18th
Notes: 1, 2, 4, 5, and 12 Earls of Cork, 1 Earl of Orrery, and seven others in ODNB.

Earl of Shannon (1756- I)

Origins: The youngest son of the 1 Earl of Cork was created Viscount Shannon 1660. On the death of the 2 Viscount the estates passed to a descendent of a younger son of the 1 Earl of Orrery.

1. Joshua Boyle – {Clonakilty 1661-66}
2. Henry Boyle – {Youghal 1695-99}
3. Richard Boyle 2 Viscount Shannon – {Old Leighlin 1695-99} Arundel 1708-10 Hythe 1710-15 East Grinstead 1715-34
4. Henry Boyle 1 Earl of Shannon – {Midleton 1707-13 Kilmallock 1713-14 County Cork 1715-56}
5. William Boyle – {Charleville 1715-25}
6. Henry Boyle Walsingham – {Tallow 1751-56}
7. Richard Boyle 2 Earl of Shannon – {Dungarvon 1749-60 County Cork 1761-64}
8. Robert Boyle Walsingham – {Dungarvon 1758-68} Knaresborough 1758-61 Fowey 1761-68 Knaresborough 1768-80
9. Richard Boyle – {Tallow 1782-83}
10. Henry Boyle 3 Earl of Shannon – {Clonakilty 1793-97 County Cork 1797-1800} County Cork 1801-07 Bandon Bridge 1807
11. Richard Boyle 4 Earl of Shannon – County Cork 1830-32

Seats: Castle Martyr, Cork (old castle, purch. early 17th c., remod. mid-late 17th c., ruin from 1690, new house built early 18th c., add 1764-71, sold 1905, now a college); Ashley Park, Surrey (built c. 1500, purch. 1718, passed out of family by inher. mid 18th c., demolished 1920)
Estates: Bateman 11232 (I) 12319
Titles: Viscount Shannon (1660-1740 I); Baron Carleton (1786- GB)
Peers: {4 peers 1660-1740 1756-1800} 6 peers 1786-1907 1921-45
1 Ld Lt 19th
2 KP 18th, 19th
Notes: 1 Earl in ODNB.

Viscount Blesington (1673-1732 I)

Origins: Descended from a younger son of Roger Boyle, great-grandfather of the 1 Earl of Cork. Archbishop of Armagh second half 17th c.

1. Morragh Boyle 1 Viscount Blesington – {Kilmallock 1665-66}
2. Charles Boyle 2 Viscount Blesington – {Blesington 1711-18}

Seat: Blesington (Blessington), Wicklow (acq. 1669, built c. 1670, passed to Stewarts by mar. 1732, burned 1798)
1 in Cabinet Council 1696

Earl of Blesington (1745-69 I)

Origins: On the extinction of the Boyles of Blesington their estates passed to a sister of the 2 Viscount, wife of the 2 Viscount Mountjoy, whose son was created Earl of Blesington. Stewarts from Wigtownshire early 17th c.

1. Richard Stewart – {County Tyrone 1703-14 Strabane 1715-27 County Tyrone 1727-28}
2. Charles Stewart – {County Tyrone 1715-27} Malmesbury 1723-27 Portsmouth 1737-41
3. James Stewart – {County Tyrone 1733-48}

Seats: Ramalton (Ramelton), Donegal (acq. 1610); Blesington, Wicklow (built c. 1670, acq. by mar. 1732, passed by mar. to Dunbars 1769, burned 1798); Mountjoy Forest (Cottage), Tyrone (purch. 1631, passed by mar. to Gardiners 1738, see below)
Titles: Baron Stewart and Viscount Mountjoy 1683-1769 I; Baronet 1623-
Peers: {2 peers 1695-1728 1731-69}

Earl of Blesington (1816-24 I)

Origins: Luke Gardiner, the grandson of a footman, made a fortune in land speculation, banking, and the profits of office. (Connolly, *Religion, Law and Politics*, 64) The Gardiners succeeded by marriage to estates through a brother of the 2 Viscount Mountjoy (see above).

1. Luke Gardiner – {Tralee 1725-27 Thomastown 1727-55}
2. Charles Gardiner – {Taghmon 1742-60}
3. Luke Gardiner 1 Viscount Mountoy – {County Dublin 1773-89}
4. William Gardiner – {Thomastown 1800}

Seats: Monkstown Castle, Cork (built 1636, acq. by Boyles 1685, passed by mar. to Gardiners, sold later 18th c., now a ruin); Mountjoy Forest (Cottage), Tyrone (inher. by mar. from Stewarts 1738, sold 1854)
Estates: Worth £14,000 pa in 1799.
Titles: Baron Mountjoy 1789-1824 I; Viscount Mountjoy 1795-1824 I
Peers: {1 peer 1789-98} 1 Irish Rep peer 1809-24
Notes: 1 Earl squandered the family wealth by 1824 and all the estates were sold in pieces by 1854. 1 Viscount and brother in ODNB.

Stewart

Origins: The grandfather of the 1 Viscount Mountjoy (see above) was an undertaker for the plantation of Ulster and a soldier in the Civil War. He acquired property in Tyrone and Donegal. The 1 Viscount was a soldier and Master of the Ordinance 1684. On the extinction of the Earldom of Blesington in 1769 the Stewart Baronetcy of 1623 passed to the descendents of a younger son of Sir William Stewart 1 Bt, grandfather of the 1 Viscount Mountjoy.

1. Sir Annesley Stewart 6 Bt – {Charlemont 1763-97}
2. Sir James Stewart 7 Bt – {Enniskillen 1783-90} County Donegal 1802-16

Seat: Fort Stewart (Ramelton), Donegal (acq. and built 1610, burned 1641, rebuilt 18th c., remod. early 19th c., resident later 20th c., sold)
Estates: Bateman 7547 (I) 4486
Title: Baronet 1623-
Notes: Bankers in the 18th century.

BOYNTON

Origins: Landowners in Yorkshire since 12th century. **First MP 1309 and another, both knights of the shire. Two further MPs in the 16th century and another 1645-47**.

1. William Boynton – Hedon 1680-81
2. Sir Francis Boynton 4 Bt – Hedon 1734-39
3. Sir Griffith Boynton 6 Bt – Beverley 1772-74

Seat: Burton Agnes Hall, Yorkshire (rebuilt by Griffiths, who inher. a late 12th c. house in 1355, rebuilt c. 1598-1610, Boyntons inher. 1654, remod. 1730s, still own)
Estates: Bateman 9300 (E) 10000
Title: Baronet 1618-
Notes: One of the top ten landowning families in East Yorkshire 1580 through the 18th century. (English, *Landowners of East Yorkshire*)

BOYSE *IRELAND*

Origins: Probably founded by a Cromwellian officer. Purchased Bannow House 1677, Sheriff 1677.

1. Nathaniel Boyse – {Clomines 1661-66}
2. Nathaniel Boyse – {Bannow 1692-93 1695-99 1703-14}
3. James Boyse – {Bannow 1715-24}
4. Samuel Boyse – {Bannow 1725-30}

Seat: Bannow House, Wexford (purch. 1677, rebuilt c. 1816, sold 1948)
Estates: Bateman 7120 (I) 6041

BRABAZON [Chambre] *IRELAND*

Earl of Meath (1627- I)

Origins: The family asserts one of the few credible claims to have come over accompanying the Conqueror, perhaps at Hastings 1066. Settled in Leicestershire and attended the Parliament of 1291. **MPs 14th and 16th centuries**. To Ireland as Vice Treasurer 1534, Lord Deputy 1543. Baron 1616. **Three Irish {MPs 1585-1634}**.

1. Edward Brabazon 4 Earl of Meath – {County Wicklow 1666}
2. Chambre Brabazon 5 Earl of Meath – {County Meath 1692-93}
3. Chaworth Brabazon 6 Earl of Meath – {County Dublin 1713-14}
4. Edward Brabazon 7 Earl of Meath – {County Dublin 1715-60}
5. Anthony Brabazon 8 Earl of Meath – {County Wicklow 1745-60 County Dublin 1761-72}
6. William Brabazon – {County Wicklow 1765-83}
7. William Brabazon 9 Earl of Meath – {County Dublin 1789-90}
8. William Brabazon 11 Earl of Meath – County Dublin 1830-32 1837-41

Seats: Killruddery Castle, Wicklow (acq. 1618, built 1619, fire 1645, rebuilt 1651, add. 18th c., add. 1820-27, add. 1852, reduced in size 1950s, still own); Eaton Court, Herefordshire
Estates: Bateman 15448 (I) 9398. Worth £6,000 pa in 1713. Owned 4,800 acres, some of it near Dublin, worth possibly 400 million pounds in 2001 before the property crash in Ireland. (Cahill, *Who Owns Britain*, 383).
Title: Baron Ardee 1616- I; Baron Chaworth 1831- UK
Peers: {9 peers 1661-75 1665-1800} 4 peers 1831-1945
3 Lds Lt 19th, 20th
2 KP 19th, 20th

Notes: The Earls of Meath have been able to hold on to Kilruddery thanks to the sale of development land near Dublin. 12 Earl and two others in ODNB.

Baron Brabazon of Tara (1942- UK)

Origins: John Moore of Dublin acquired land in Louth in 1721. His son was a barrister. A younger son of the 7 Earl of Meath had a daughter and heiress who married John Moore of New Lodge, Hertfordshire in 1788. From this union descended the Moore-Brabazons.

1. John Moore-Brabazon 1 Baron Brabazon – Chatham Div. Rochester 1918-29 Wallasey 1931-42

Seat: Tara House (Hall), Meath (built early-mid-18th c., passed by mar. to Brabazons, resident 20th c.)
Estates: 642 acres worth £612 pa in 1878.
Peer: 1 peer 1942-45
Notes: 1 Baron in ODNB.

Brabazon

Origins: Cadet line.

1. Sir William Brabazon 2 Bt – County Mayo 1835-40

Seat: Brabazon Park (New Park), Mayo (19th c., passed out of the family by mar. 1840)
Estates: Bateman 6857 (I) 2081
Title: Baronet 1797-1840

Chambre

Origins: From Wales, to Ireland 1612. Established iron making business first half of 17th century in Wicklow. **First MP 1626 and first Irish {MP 1642}.** A Chambre heiress married the 2 Earl of Meath who succeded to Carnowe.

1. Robert Chambre – {Ardee 1703-13}

Seat: Carnowe (Carnew), Wicklow (leased from 1619, passed to Earls of Meath later in the 17th c.)

BRADDYLL [Gale]

Origins: The Braddylls were land speculators and proto-industrialists in the later 17th century. They rented properties to hand-loom weavers. Wilson Gale succeeded to the Braddyll estates in 1776 and took the name Braddyll. The Gales were merchants in Whitehaven, and rich Virginia tobacco importers in the 17th and 18th centuries.

1. Dodding Braddyll – Lancaster 1715-22
2. Wilson Gale-Braddyll – Lancaster 1780-84 Horsham 1790-91 Carlisle 1791-96
3. Thomas Gale-Braddyll – Bodmin 1818-20

Seats: Highhead (High Head) Castle, Cumberland (Richmonds purch. early 16th c., passed to Gales late 17th c., rebuilt 1740-48, sold 1902, fire 1956, ruin); Conishead Priory, Lancashire (medieval, Braddyll seat built later 16th c., acq. by mar. 1683, passed to Gales by mar. 1776, rebuilt 1821-36, sold 1847, institutional use); Bardsea Hall, Lancashire (built 18th c., Braddyll seat passed by mar. to Gales 1776, remod. 1840, sold 1918, demolished 1927); Samlesbury Old Hall, Lancashire (built 14th c., add. 15th c., purch. 1697, sold 1846, school); Cleator Hall, Cumberland (Gale seat, bult 17th c.?, sold 1842, demolished)
Estates: Worth £1,500 pa in 1810. Depleted the family fortune by overbuilding at Conishead in 1820s and 1830s and forced to begin to sell estates.
Notes: Thomas Gale-Braddyll (d. 1862) went bankrupt 1840s.

BRADSHAW I

Origins: The first MP was of humble origins and served as a Treasury official and agent for the Duke of Grafton. The second MP was an agent of the Duke of Bridgewater and superintended his canals.

1. Thomas Bradshaw – Harwich 1767-68 Saltash 1768-74
2. Robert Bradshaw – Brackley 1802-32
3. James Bradshaw – Brackley 1825-32

Seat: Lifton Park, Devon (built 1815, remod. 1857, acq. mid-later 19th c. resident into 20th c.)
Estates: Bateman 8122 (E) 10342. The third MP sold estates in Lancashire for £127,000 in 1834. His will was sworn at £350,000.

BRADSHAW II

Origins: The Ellerkers acquired Risby by marriage to the Risby heiress in 1401. Became Kts in the 15th century. Official appointed in 1522. Entered the group of top 10 landowners in the East Riding of Yorkshire (English, *The Great Landowners of East Yorkshire*). **First MP 1529. Two other MPs 1558-71.** However, they remained Roman Catholics and lost much of their property. The Bradshaws rose through the law and office in the first half of the 17th century. Sir James Bradshaw married the daughter and heiress of the last Ellerker of Risby. Family later took the name Ellerker.

1. Ellerker Bradshaw – Beverley 1727-29 1734-41

Seat: Risby Hall, Yorkshire (Ellerkers acq. 1401, rebuilt 16th c., 1655 passed by mar. to Bradshaws, remod. c. 1680, new house built c. 1685, burned later 1770s and rebuilt, inherited by Onslows, sold 1883, demolished)
Estates: Onslows held the remains of the estate in the 1870s: 2303 (E) 3475
Notes: The estates passed to four heiresses and were broken up in the later 18th century.

BRAMSTON [Berney]

Bramston

Origins: Became landed in the early 17th century. Chief Justice of the King's Bench 1635. The first MP was a lawyer.

1. Sir John Bramston – Essex 1660-79 Maldon 1685-87
2. Thomas Bramston – Maldon 1712-27 (error in Sedgwick corrected in Hayton)
3. Thomas Bramston – Maldon 1727-34 Essex 1734-47
4. Thomas Bramston – Essex 1779-1802
5. Thomas Bramston – Essex 1830
6. Thomas Bramston – S. Essex 1835-65

Seat: Skreens, Essex (purch. 1635 for £8,000, built 1728, sold c. 1910, demolished c. 1920)
Estates: Bateman 5426 (E) 6665
Notes: Four in ODNB.

Berney

Origins: Norwich merchants who entered the gentry in the 14th century as a lawyer and agent for the Black Prince. **First MP for Norfolk 1346. Another MP 1390-1414.** The family lost much of its wealth before the heiress of the last male married 1733 Thomas Bramston MP.

1. Richard Berney – Norwich 1710-15

Seats: Langley Hall, Norfolk (acq. 1577, built early 18th c., sold 1739); Westwick House, Norfolk (built 18th c., passed from Berneys to Petres after 1731); Barton Bendish Hall, Norfolk (purch. 1665, remod. 1856, sold 1935); Kirby Bedon Hall, Norfolk (purch. c. 1700, sold 1817, demolished 1841); Hockering House, Norfolk (house built 1968 on land owned by family since 1655)
Estates: 3148 (E) 4181 (at Morton Hall 5429 (E) 6977)
Title: Bt 1620-

BRANDLING

Origins: The **first MP (1545 for Newcastle)** was the son of a merchant and mayor, Kt. Entered gentry by late 16th century. In the 17th century they became industrialists and coal owners (mining from c. 1670). **Two MPs 1621-25, one for Northumberland.**

1. Charles Brandling – Newcastle-upon-Tyne 1784-97
2. Charles Brandling – Newcastle-upon-Tyne 1798-1812 Northumberland 1820-26

Seats: Gosforth House (Hall), Northumberland (acq. by mar. 1509, rebuilt 18th c., sold 1852, fire 1947, partially demolished); Felling, Durham (acq. by mar. 1509, sold c. 1850)
Estates: Claimed an income of £2,000 pa in c. 1630 (much from the coal trade) (Thrush and Ferris, *House of Commons*, III, 295).
Notes: Male line extinct 1826.

BRASSEY

Earl Brassey (1911-1919 UK)

Origins: The father of the 1 Earl was the son of a farmer (Rubinstein, *Men of Property*, 131) who became a road surveyor. (The family were yeomen in Cheshire in the 16th c.) By 1841 he had earned half a million pounds building railway lines and became a great civil engineer and entrepreneur.

1. Thomas Brassey 1 Earl Brassey – Devonport 1865 Hastings 1868-86
2. Henry Brassey – Sandwich 1868-85
3. Albert Brassey – Banbury Div. Oxfordshire 1895-1906
4. Robert Brassey – Banbury Div. Oxfordshire 1910
5. Henry Brassey 1 Baron Brassey – N. Northamptonshire 1910-18 Peterborough Div. Northamptonshire 1918-29

Seats: Preston Hall, Kent (medieval, rebuilt 1850, purch. 1867, sold 1906, institutional use); Apethorpe Hall, Northamptonshire (medieval, rebuilt 1490s, add. 16th c. and 1620s, remod. 1693 and 1846, purch. 1904, sold 1947); Heythrop(e) Hall (Park),

Oxfordshire (old house burned 1831, purch. 1870, rebuilt 1870, sold 1922, now hotel); Normanhurst, Sussex (built 1867, demolished 1951); The Grange, Bulkeley, Cheshire (built by an ancestor c. 1600, rebuilt by 1 Earl 1860s); Copse Hill (Copsehill), Gloucestershire (acq. and built 1872-75, remod. 1906, sold 1973); Cottesbrooke Hall, Northamptonshire (built 1702-12, remod. 1775-79, purch. 1911, remod. 1911, sold 1937)
Estates: Bateman 4061 (E) 11253; 3617 (E) 4417; 4275 (E) 5100. The father of the 1 Earl left an estate in the UK of £3,200,000 and considerable assets abroad in 1870.
Titles: Baron Brassey 1886-1919 UK; Baron Brassey 1938- UK; Baronet 1922-
Peers: 3 peers 1886-1919 1938-45
Notes: Brasseys were gentry in Cheshire in the 17th century. (de Figueirdo and Treuherz, *Cheshire Country Houses*, 220) Two in ODNB.

BRETT

Viscount Esher (1897- UK)

Origins: Landowning gentry in the 18th century. 1 Viscount was a successful lawyer and Master of the Rolls 1883.

1. William Brett 1 Viscount Esher – Helston 1866-68
2. Reginald Brett 2 Viscount Esher – Falmouth and Penryn 1880-85

Seat: Watlington Park, Oxfordshire (purch. 1877, partially demolished 1955)
Title: Baron Esher 1885- UK
Peers: 3 peers 1885-1945
Notes: 1,2, and 4 Viscounts in ODNB.

BRIDGEMAN [Addison, Newport]

Earl of Bradford (1694-1762 E; 1815- UK)

Origins: The Newports emerged in the 13th century. **First MP 1380 for Shropshire. Five further MPs 1547-1644, three of them for Shropshire**. Baron 1642. On the death of the 4 Earl his estates passed to the husband of his sister, Sir Orlando Bridgeman 4 Bt. The Bridgemans reached prominence in the later 16th century. High Sheriff 1578. Bishop of Chester 1619. Lord Chief Justice 1660 and Lord Keeper of the Great Seal 1667. **First MP 1625. Two further MPs 1628-42.**

1. Andrew Newport – Montgomeryshire 1661-79 Preston 1685-87 Shrewsbury 1689-98
2. Sir Orlando Bridgeman 1 Bt – Horsham 1669-79
3. Richard Newport 2 Earl of Bradford – Shropshire 1670-81 1689-98
4. William Bridgeman – Bramber 1685-87

5. Thomas Newport 1 Baron Torrington – Ludlow 1695-98 1699-1700 Winchelsea 1701 Much Wenlock 1715-16
6. Orlando Bridgeman – Wigan 1698-1705
7. Sir Orlando Bridgeman 2 Bt – Coventry 1707-10 Calne 1715-22 Lostwithiel 1724-27 Bletchingley 1727-34 Dunwich 1734-38
8. Henry Newport 3 Earl of Bradford – Bishop's Castle 1706-08 Shropshire 1708-10 1713-22
9. Richard Newport – Much Wenlock 1714-15
10. Orlando Bridgeman – Ipswich 1714-15
11. Sir Orlando Bridgeman 4 Bt – Shrewbury 1723-27
12. Henry Bridgeman 1 Baron Bradford – Ludlow 1748-68 Wenlock 1768-94
13. Henry Bridgeman – Wigan 1780-82
14. John Bridgeman Simpson – Wenlock 1784-85 1794-1820
15. Orlando Bridgeman 1 Earl of Bradford – Wigan 1784-1800
16. Orlando Bridgeman 3 Earl of Bradford – S. Shropshire 1842-65
17. George Bridgeman 4 Earl of Bradford – N. Shropshire 1867-85
18. Francis Bridgeman – Bolton 1885-95
19. William Bridgeman 1 Viscount Bridgeman – Oswestry Div. Shropshire 1906-29

Seats: Weston Park, Staffordshire (built 1671, principal seat from 1762, remod. 1802-8 and 1830-31, add. 1866, passed to foundation with help of National Heritage Memorial Fund 1986); Castle Bromwich Hall, Warwickshire (medieval, new house 1599, purch. 1657, remod. 1685-1702, ceased to be principal seat 1762, remod. 1825 and 1840, family departed 1936, engulfed by suburbia, leased, sold 1969, offices); Bilton Hall (built 1623, acq. by mar. 1797, sold 1898, now flats); High Ercall Hall, Shropshire (acq. 1391, built 1608); Tong Castle, Shropshire (medieval, rebuilt c. 1500, acq. 1760, rebuilt for the Durants 1765, passed to Bridgemans, abandoned c. 1908, fire 1913, demolished 1954)
Estates: Bateman 21710 (E & W) 41982 and 5593 (E) 7810. Newport estates worth £2,200 pa in 1646. Worth £50,000,000 in 1990 with 13,000 acres.
Titles: Baron Newport 1642-1762 E; Baron Torrington 1716-19 GB; Baron Bradford 1794- GB; Viscount Bridgeman 1929- UK; Baronet 1660- ; 1673-1740
Peers: 11 peers 1661-1734 1716-19 1794-1945 1929-45
5 Lds Lt 17th, 18th, 19th
2 in Cabinet 1667-72 1922-29
Notes: Three Newports and eight Bridgemans in ODNB.

Addison

Origins: Landed since the 16th century. Secretary of State 1717-18. The first MP's daughter and heiress left her estates 1797 to the third son of Lord Bradford.

1. Joseph Addison – Lostwithiel 1708-09 Malmesbury 1710-19

Seats: Holland House, Middlesex (inher. by his wife, his residence 1716-19, see Rich II for house details); Bilton Hall, Warwickshire (built 1623, purch. 1711, passed by mar. 1797 to the Bridgemans)
Notes: Two in ODNB.

BRIGHT I [Meyler]

Bright

Origins: The family held land in Herefordshire since the 17th century, but made their fortune as merchants and bankers in Bristol in the later 18th century. The first MP was a barrister.

1. Henry Bright – Bristol 1820-30
2. Richard Bright – E. Somerset 1868-78
3. Alan Bright – Oswestry Div. Shropshire 1904-06

Seats: Brockbury Hall, Herefordshire (purch. early 17th c., rebuilt 1698, remod. 1738, still own); Barton Court, Herefordshire (built c. 1790, purch. 1870s, still own)
Estates: Rubinstein – Lowbridge Bright left £100,000 in probate 1818.

Meyler

Origins: West Indian merchants in Bristol and plantation owners. The estates of Richard Meyler MP passed on his death in 1818 to his cousin Henry Bright MP.

1. Richard Meyler – Winchester 1812-18

Seat: Crawley House, Hampshire
Estates: Estimated to be worth £30,000 pa in 1805.

BRIGHT II

Origins: The first MP was the son of a Rochdale miller. Became businessmen in Manchester and Rochdale.

1. John Bright – Manchester 1847-57 Birmingham 1857-88
2. Jacob Bright – Manchester 1867-74 1876-85 S. W. Manchester 1886-95
3. William Bright – Stoke-on-Trent 1885-90
4. John Bright – Central Div. Birmingham 1889-95 Oldham 1906-10

Seat: The Ash, Lancashire

Estates: John Bright left £86,000 in 1889.
1 in Cabinet 1868-70 1873-74 1880-82
Notes: Three in ODNB.

BRINCKMAN [Broadhead]

Origins: The Brinckmans were Hanoverian nobles who came to England with George I and acquired estates in Yorkshire. A Broadhead (brewers) heiress of Monk Bretton married John Brinckman. Their son Theodore took the name Broadhead. His grandson resumed the name Brinckman and was created a Baronet.

1. Theodore Broadhead-Brinckman – Wareham 1812-18 Yarmouth (I of W) 1820
2. Sir Theodore Brinckman 1 Bt – Yarmouth 1821-26
3. Sir Theodore Brinckman 2 Bt – Canterbury 1868-74

Seat: Monk Bretton (Burton, Bretton), Yorkshire (Broadheads acq. 1609, departed by 1880s)
Estates: Bateman 2301 (E) 3857
Title: Baronet 1831-

BRISCOE (Bristowe)

Origins: The family was established in the 13th century on a manor from which they took their name. They acquired Crofton by marriage and began to represent Carlisle in the reign of Richard II. **First MP 1365. Four further MPs 1386-1553.**

1. William Briscoe – Cumberland 1654 1656 1659 Carlisle 1660

Seats: Crofton Hall, Cumberland (acq. by mar. later 14th c., sold 1908, demolished c. 1958); Briscoe, Cumberland (alienated to the church in the 14th century but repurch. in the 17th century)
Estates: Bateman 3540 (E) 5229
Notes: Richard Briscoe married the Lamplugh heiress and succeeded to Lamplugh Hall 1737 (see Lamplugh).

BRISTOW

Origins: Made a great fortune in Virginia from the 1660s and returned to purchase estates in England. The first MP was a grocer and merchant in London.

1. Robert Bristow – Winchelsea 1698-1701
2. Robert Bristow – Winchelsea 1708-37

3. John Bristow – Bere Alston 1734-41 St. Ives 1741-54 Bere Alston 1754-61 Arundel 1761-68
4. Robert Bristow – Winchelsea 1738-41 New Shorham 1747-61

Seat: Micheldever, Hampshire (acq. late 17th c.)

BROADLEY [Harrison]

Origins: Merchants in Hull from the later 17th century, spread into shipowning, insurance, banking and land speculation in the 18th and 19th centuries. Invested profits in landed estates. (English, *Great Landowners of East Yorkshire*, 31-32) High Sheriff 1867. William Harrison married the daughter and heiress of Henry Broadley MP.

1. Henry Broadley – E. R. Yorkshire 1837-51
2. William Harrison-Broadley – E. R. Yorkshire 1868-85
3. Henry Harrison-Broadley – Howdenshire Div. E. R. Yorkshire 1906-14

Seat: Welton House, Yorkshire (purch. 1848, demolished 1952)
Estates: Bateman 14877 (E) 23378

BROCKLEHURST

Baron Rankesborough (1914-21 UK)

Origins: Gentry by the 17th century. Became silk manufacturers and bankers in Macclesfield in the 19th century.

1. John Brocklehurst – Macclesfield 1832-68
2. William Brocklehurst – Macclesfield 1868-80 Macclesfield Div. Cheshire 1885-86
3. William Brocklehurst – Macclesfield Div. Cheshire 1906-18

Seats: Swythamley Park (Hall), Staffordshire (medieval, add. c. 1690, burned 1813 and rebuilt, purch. 1832, sold 1977); Butley Hall, Cheshire (built 17th c., rebuilt 1777, add. 19th c., purch. 1861, sold early 20th c., now flats); Tytherington House (Hall), Cheshire (built mid-19th c., sold later 19th c., demolished 1960s)
Estates: Bateman 5320 (E) 4600
Title: Baronet 1903-
Peer: 1 peer 1914-21
1 Ld Lt 20th

BRODIE *SCOTLAND*

Brodie of Brodie

Origins: First recorded laird c. 1285. Acquired Brodie 1311. **First [MP 1643 for Elgin and Forres].**

1. James Brodie – [Elgin and Forres 1689-1702 1703-4]
2. George Brodie – [Nairnshire 1693-1702 Forres Burgh 1703-07]
3. James Brodie – Elginshire 1720
4. Alexander Brodie – Elginshire 1720-41 Caithness-shire 1741-47
5. Alexander Brodie – Nairnshire 1785-90 Elgin Burghs 1790-1802

Seat: Brodie Castle, Elginshire (acq. 1311 or earlier, rebuilt 1567, add. early 17th c., burned 1645, restored later 17th c., add. 1824 and 1846, renovated 1980, NT 1978, still own estate)
Estates: Bateman 9135 (S) 4758. Rubinstein - Alexander Brodie MP, nabob, left £120,000 in probate 1818.
4 Lds Lt 18th, 19th, 20th
Notes: Three in ODNB.

Brodie

Origins: Cadet established at Lethen in the 16th century. **First [MP 1646 for Nainrnshire].**

1. David Brodie – [Nairnshire 1689]
2. Alexander Brodie – Nairnshire 1735-41
3. James Brodie – Elginshire 1796-1807

Seat: Lethen House, Nairnshire (purch. 1634, built 1788, add. later 18th and 19th c., still own)
Estates: Bateman 23682 (S) 6067. Owned 12,800 acres in 1996.
1 Ld Lt 19th

BRODRICK *IRELAND & ENGLAND*

Earl of Midleton (1920- UK)

Origins: Gentry in Surrey by the 16th century. Kt 1625 was Lt. Gov. of the Tower of London. Settled in Ireland 1641 onwards and acquired estates in Cork 1653. Sheriff 1662. A Commissioner for settling the affairs of Ireland at the Restoration when additional land was gained (Burns, *Irish Parliamentary Politics*, I, 28). Lord Chancellor of Ireland 1714.

1. Sir Allen (Alan) Brodrick – Orford 1660-79 {Dungarvon 1661-65}
2. Sir St. John Brodrick – {Kinsale 1661-66 County Cork 1692-93 1695-99}
3. Thomas Brodrick – {Midleton 1692-93 County Cork 1695-99 1703-13 Midleton 1715-27}
4. Alan Brodrick 1 Viscount Midleton – {Cork 1692-93 1695-99 1703-10 County Cork 1713-14} Midhurst 1717-28
5. St. John Brodrick – {Midleton 1695 1703-07}
6. St. John Brodrick – {Castlemartyr 1709-13 Cork 1713-14 County Cork 1715-28} Bere Alston 1721-27
7. William Brodrick – {Mallow 1716-27}
8. George Brodrick 3 Viscount Midleton – Ashburton 1754-61 New Shoreham 1761-65
9. Thomas Brodrick – {Midleton 1761-68}
10. Edward Brodrick – {Midleton 1768-76}
11. George Brodrick 4 Viscount Midleton – Whitechurch 1774-96
12. Thomas Brodrick – {Midleton 1776-83}
13. Henry Brodrick – {Midleton 1776-83}
14. William Brodrick – Whitechurch 1796-1818
15. William Brodrick 8 Viscount Midleton – Mid Surrey 1868-70
16. William Brodrick 1 Earl of Midleton – W. Surrey 1880-85 Guildford Div. Surrey 1885-1906

Seats: Peper Harrow, Surrey (purch. 1713, rebuilt 1765-75, sold 1944, institutional use); Cahirmone (Cahermore), Cork (acq. mid-17th c., owned into 20th c. but rarely occupied by Brodricks); Ballyanan (Ballyanahan) Castle, Cork (acq. 1653, built soon afterwards, abandoned 18th c., ruin early 19th c.)
Estates: Bateman 9580 (E & I) 10752. Worth £8,000 pa in 1805.
Titles: Baron Brodrick 1715- I; Viscount Midleton 1717- I; Baron Brodrick 1796- GB
Peers: {4 peers 1715-28 1733-47 1751-65 1775-1800} 7 peers 1796-1945
2 Lds Lt 19th, 20th
1 in Cabinet 1900-05
Notes: 1 Viscount and 1 Earl and three others in ODNB.

BROKE [De Saumarez, Vere]

Broke

Origins: The Brokes came to London from Cheshire in the early 16th century. **First MP 1512** a lawyer. Chief Baron of the Exchequer 1526. **Another MP 1542**.

1. Sir Robert Broke 1 Bt – Suffolk 1685-87
2. Philip Broke – Ipswich 1730-34
3. Sir Charles Broke Vere – E. Suffolk 1835-43

Seats: Broke Hall, Suffolk (purch. and built early 16th c., remod. 1773-75 and 1791-92, sold 19th c., now school); Nacton, Suffolk (acq. 1514); Livermere Hall (Park), Suffolk (built early 18th c., add. 1790-97, acq. by mar. 1860, passed later to the de Saumarez family 1882, see below)
Estates: Bateman 3550 (E) 3927
Titles: Baronet 1661-94; 1813-87
Notes: A naval family with admirals in the 18th and 19th centuries. Three in ODNB.

Middleton

Origins: Gentry background. A Middleton went to South Carolina as Governor 1730. He returned in the 1760s on succeeding to Crowfield. The daughter of the 1 Bt married Admiral Sir Philip Vere Broke of Nacton, and the Brokes succeeded to Shrubland in 1860.

1. Sir William Middleton 1 Bt – Ipswich 1784-90 1803-06 Hastings 1806-07

Seats: Crowfield Hall, Suffolk (rebuilt 1728, demolished 1819); Shrubland Park (Hall), Suffolk (rebuilt 1770-72, purch. c. 1796, remod. 1830-32, rebuilt c. 1830-33, Brokes succ. 1860, de Saumarez succ. by mar. 1882, institutional use after WWII, sold 2010)
Estates: Bateman 9500 (E) 9000 (under Broke-Middleton)
Title: Baronet 1813-87

Baron De Saumarez (1831- UK)

Origins: Landowners in the Channel Islands by the Tudor period. Naval officers in the 17th and 18th centuries. 1 Baron an admiral (with Nelson). The Broke heiress married the 4 Baron De Saumarez in 1882 and succeeded to the Broke and Middleton estates.

No MPs

Seats: Shrubland Park (Hall), Suffolk (built 1770-72, remod. 1830-32, rebuilt c. 1830-33, acq. by mar. 1882, institutional use after 1945, sold 2010, still own estate); Saumarez Park, Guernsey; Broke Hall, Suffolk (see above); Livermere Hall (Park), Suffolk (see above, acq. by mar. 1882, sold 1919, demolished 1923)
Titles: Baronet 1801- ; 1928-1941
Peers: 5 peers 1831-1945
Notes: Six in ODNB.

BROMLEY [Davenport, Ward]

Baron Montfort (1741-1851 GB)

Origins: The Bromleys held land in Shropshire from the 13th century. A legal family in the 16th century. The Bromley Lord Chancellor (1579) purchased Holt Castle. **First MP 1529. Seven further MPs 1553-1628 including several kts of the shire for Shropshire and Worcestershire.**

1. Henry Bromley – Worcestershire 1660
2. William Bromley – Worcester 1685-87 1700 Worcestershire 1701-02 1705-07
3. John Bromley – Cambridgeshire 1705-07
4. John Bromley – Cambridgeshire 1707-18
5. Henry Bromley 1 Baron Montfort – Cambridgeshire 1727-41
6. Thomas Bromley 2 Baron Montfort – Cambridge 1754-55

Seats: Horseheath Hall, Cambridgeshire (rebuilt 1663-65, purch. 1701 for £42,000 from Lord Alington (999 year lease) £30,000 was spent on improvements, sold 1776, c. demolished 1792); Holt Castle, Worcestershire (medieval, purch. 1579, remod. 1680-c. 1700, sold c. 1760)
Estates: 5,000 acres worth £3,050 pa sold in 1777.
Peers: 3 peers 1741-1851
1 Ld Lt 18th
Notes: John Bromley MP 1707-18 (son of John Bromley MP 1705-07, who was self-made and of obscure origins, became a Barbados sugar planter) married the daughter and heiress of William Bromley MP 1685-1707 with whom he was not related, but their son succeeded to the estates. The 1 Baron became heavily indebted and shot himself 1754. Three in ODNB.

Bromley

Origins: Cadet descended from Sir Henry Bromley (d. 1615) of Holt. William Bromley was Speaker of the House of Commons 1710. Moved to Warwickshire 1618.

1. William Bromley – Warwickshire 1690-98 University of Oxford 1701-32
2. Clobery Bromley – Coventry 1710-11
3. William Bromley – Fowey 1725-27 Warwick 1727-35 University of Oxford 1737
4. William Bromley – Warwickshire 1765-69
5. William Bromley Chester – Gloucestershire 1776-80

Seats: Baginton Hall, Warwickshire (medieval, purch. 1618, rebuilt 2nd half 17th c., fire 1706, new house 1714-23, passed to Davenports by mar. 1822, fire 1889); Cleve (Cleeve) Hill House, Gloucestershire
1 in Cabinet Council 1713-14
Notes: Two in ODNB.

Davenport

Origins: Claim uninterrupted male descent from a Saxon Davenport alive at the time of the Conquest. (Angus-Butterworth, *Old Cheshire Families*, 49) Appointed Chief Forester of Leek and Macclesfield 1166. Owned part of the Capesthorne estate from 1176. Became Liverpool merchants and slave-traders in the 18th century. The Davenports succeeded to the Bromley estates and took the additional name Bromley in 1822.

1. Sir Thomas Davenport – Newton 1780-86
2. Davies Davenport – Cheshire 1806-30
3. Edward Davenport – Shaftesbury 1826-30
4. William Bromley-Davenport – N. Warwickshire 1864-84
5. Sir William Bromley-Davenport – Macclesfield Div. Cheshire 1886-1906
6. Sir Walter Bromley-Davenport – Knutsford 1945-70

Seats: Capesthorne Hall, Cheshire (Davenports purch. 1176, passed to Wards by mar. 1386, rebuilt 1720s, acq. Davenports again by mar. 1748, remod. 1837 and 1843, fire 1861 and rebuilt, still own); Woodford, Cheshire (acq. 1355, rebuilt early 17th c., left for Capesthorne early 18th c.); Wootton Hall, Staffordshire (resident 18th and 19th c., demolished 1931); Baginton Hall, Warwickshire (18th c. house, inher. by mar. 1822, fire 1889, site sold 1918, ruins demolished); Bramall Hall, Cheshire (acq. and built late 14th c. by Davenports, remod. 1592-1609, add. c. late 17th c. and 1810-19, sold 1877)
Estates: Bateman 15647 (E) 26876. Rubinstein – Davies Davenport left £120,000 in probate in 1837.
1 Ld Lt 20th
Notes: Three in ODNB.

Ward

Origins: Wards settled at Capesthorne 1386. Davies Davenport married 1721 Mary Ward, heiress to Capesthorne and succeeded to the Ward estates on the extinction of the male line in 1748

1. John Ward – Newton 1703-15 Thetford 1715-22

Seat: Capesthorne Hall, Cheshire (acq. by mar. 1386, medieval, rebuilt house 1720s, passed to Davenports 1748, see above)
Notes: A cadet went to Ireland and founded the Wards of Castle Ward, Down (see Ward II).

Bromley

Origins: a cadet of the Baginton line.

1. William Bromley – Tewkesbury 1710-13

Seat: Upton, Worcestershire (purch. 1593, 1756 passed out of family by mar.)

BROOKE I *IRELAND*

Viscount Brookeborough (1952- UK)

Origins: The founder was an English soldier who went to Ireland in 1598. Kt 1616. He gained a large estate in 1623. Sheriff 1669.

1. Henry Brooke – {Donegal 1661-71}
2. Thomas Brooke – {Antrim 1695-96}
3. Henry Brooke – {Dundalk 1713-27 County Fermanagh 1727-60}
4. Sir Arthur Brooke 1 Bt – {County Fermanagh 1761-83 Maryborough 1783-85}
5. Henry Brooke – {Donegal 1777-83 County Donegal 1783-1800} County Donegal 1801-02 1806-07
6. Sir Arthur Brooke 2 Bt – Fermanagh 1840-54

Seats: Colebrooke Park, Fermanagh (acq. 1666, house built 18th c., rebuilt 1825, unlived in post WWII, remod. recently, still own); Donegal Castle, Donegal (built 1505, acq. 1623, long a ruin)
Estates: Bateman 27994 (I) 15288. Worth £13,000 pa in c. 1800.
Titles: Viscount Alanbrooke (1946- UK); Baronet 1764-85; 1822- ; 1903-
Notes: The 1 Viscount Brookeborough was an MP in the Ulster Parliament and became a notorious Unionist Prime Minister of Northern Ireland. A younger son was Chief of the Imperial General Staff during World War II, Churchill's pincipal military adviser, and created Viscount Alanbrooke. Three in ODNB.

BROOKE II

Baron Brooke (1966-84 UKLife)

Origins: The 1 Baron was the son of a professional artist, and grandson of a manufacturer. He was a lecturer in Philosophy at Oxford who went into politics. His wife was also a peeress in her own right.

1. Henry Brooke 1 Baron Brooke of Cumnor – W. Lewisham 1938-45 Hampstead 1950-66
2. Peter Brooke 1 Baron Brooke of Sutton Mandeville – London and City of Westminster 1977-2001

Titles: Baroness Brooke of Ystradfellte (1966-2000 UKLife); Baron Brooke of Sutton Mandeville (2001- UKLife)
Notes: 2 in Cabinet 1957-64 1989-94. Three in ODNB.

BROOKE III

Brooke

Origins: Emerged under Henry VIII. A Vice Admiral acquired Norton at the Dissolution. 1 Bt was **first MP 1654**.

1. Thomas Brooke – Newton 1786-1807

Seats: Ashton Hayes, Cheshire (built 1780, sold 1809, demolished 1950s); Norton Priory, Cheshire (medieval, acq. 1540s, new house 1730s-40s, remod. c. 1775, add. 1868, family departed 1928 due to industrial encroachment and house was demolished); Hallwood, Cheshire (rebuilt 1655-60, remod. c. 1720, purch. 1800, leased out from 1834, bomb damage WWII, now a pub)
Estates: Bateman 6397 (E) 13367
Title: Baronet 1662-

Brooke

Origins: A cadet of the Norton line. **First MP 1646**. Married an heiress in 1756 and inherited the West Indian estates of the Langfords.

1. Thomas Brooke – Newton 1797

Seat: Mere Hall, Cheshire (old hall purch. 1652, built later 17th c., remod. 1809-15, reduced in size c. 1836, leased out much of 19th c., new hall built 1834 on new site and sold 1970s, fire c. 1975, old hall sold 1994)

BROOKE-PECHELL

Origins: Pechells were Huguenot nobles who fled France after the revocation of the Edict of Nantes. Soldiers in the 18th century. The 1 Bt was a general.

1. Sir Thomas Brooke-Pechell 2 Bt – Downton 1813-26
2. Sir Samuel Brooke-Pechell 3 Bt – Helston 1830-31 Windsor 1832-34
3. Sir George Brooke-Pechell 4 Bt – Brighton 1835-60

Seats: Pagglesham (Paglesham), Essex (Brooke seat, acq. by mar. by Pechells 18th c.); Alton House, Hampshire; Aldwick, Sussex (purch. and built 1802, sold 1827); Castle Goring, Sussex (built 1790s, acq. 1825, passed out of family by mar. mid-19th c.)
Estates: Bateman 2469 (E & I) 3107
Title: Baronet 1797-
Notes: The 2 Bt was also a general and the 3 and 4 Bts were admirals. The 3 and 4 Bts in ODNB.

BROOKS

<u>Baron Crawshaw</u> (1892- UK)

Origins: The founder was a banker d. 1846. Owned great calico printing works in Manchester and quarries and coal mines in Lancashire second half of the 19th century.

1. Sir William Brooks 1 Bt – E. Cheshire 1869-85 Altrincham Div. Cheshire 1886-92
2. John Brooks – Altrincham Div. Cheshire 1885-86

Seats: Whatton House, Leicestershire (built 1802, purch. 1870s, fire and rebuilt 1876, part demolished 1950s, still own); Barlow Hall, Lancashire (built 1574, add. 17th c., purch. 1848, burned 1879, reconstructed, now golf club); Crawshaw Hall, Lancashire (built 1831-33, sold 1976, institutional use); Portal (Lodge), Cheshire (built early 19th c., acquired 2nd half 19th c., house demolished 1900, new house c. 1900-05, sold); Wanlass How, Westmorland (built 1841, sold late 19th c.)
Estates: Bateman 2488 (E) 14663
Title: Baronet 1891- ; 1886-1900
Peers: 3 peers 1892-1945

BROUGHAM

Baron Brougham and Vaux (1830- UK)

Origins: Minor gentry who purchased Brougham in 1726 which they claimed to have owned in the Middle Ages. 1 Baron a barrister and Lord Chancellor 1830.

1. Henry Brougham 1 Baron Brougham – Camelford 1810-12 Winchelsea 1815-30 Knaresborough 1830 Yorkshire 1830
2. James Brougham – Tregony 1826-30 Downton 1830-31 Winchelsea 1831-32 Kendal 1832-33
3. William Brougham 2 Baron Brougham – Southwark 1831-34

Seat: Brougham Hall, Westmorland (built 12th c., purch. 1726, rebuilt late 18th c. and c. 1830-44, sold c. 1930s, demolished c. 1935)
Estates: Bateman 5076 (E) 7138
Peers: 4 peers 1830-1927 1931-45
1 in Cabinet 1830-34
Notes: 1 and 2 Barons in ODNB.

BROUGHTON [Delves]

Origins: The Broughtons were old gentry seated at Broughton in the Middle Ages. The 3 Bt married the heiress of Sir Thomas Delves (at Doddington since the reign of Edward III, Justice of the King's Bench 14th c., served under the Black Prince at Poitiers, Bt 1621-1727) and the 4 Bt took the additional name Delves. **The first Delves MP 1388 for Staffordshire. Four additional MPs 1425-1572 three kts of the shire**.

1. Sir Bryan Broughton 3 Bt – Newcastle-u-Lyme 1715-24
2. Sir Bryan Delves Broughton 4 Bt – Wenlock 1741-44

Seats: Broughton Hall, Staffordshire (medieval, rebuilt 1637, sold 1914); Doddington Hall, Cheshire (Delves purch. 1352, built 1365, add. mid-17th c., passed by mar. to Boughtons 1727, new house 1776-98, leased to a school after WWII to 1980s, now unoccupied, still own); Weston Hall, Cheshire (Delves acq. by mar. 14th c., built c. 1677, fire 2005)
Estates: Bateman 15154 (E) 21774
Title: Baronet 1660-
Notes: 11 Bt in ODNB.

BROWN [Clifton]

Viscount Ruffside (1951-58 UK)

Origins: Merchants and bankers in the 18th and 19th centuries.

1. Sir William Brown 1 Bt – S. Lancashire 1846-58
2. Sir Alexander Brown 1 Bt – Wenlock 1868-85 Wellington Div. Shropshire 1885-1906
3. James Brown – Horsham 1876-80
4. Douglas Clifton-Brown 1 Viscount Ruffside – Hexham Div. Northumberland 1918-23 1924-51
5. Howard Clifton-Brown – Newbury Div. Berkshire 1922-23 1924-45
6. Geoffrey Clifton-Brown – Bury St. Edmunds 1945-50
7. Geoffrey Clifton-Brown – Cirencester and Tewkesbury 1992-97 Cotswolds 1997-

Seats: Astrop House, Northamptonshire (built c. 1740, later add., resident 19th c., demolished 1961); Holmbush House, Sussex (built 1826, purch. c. 1864, sold 1951, institutional uses); Ruffside Hall, Durham (possibly 17th c., add. 19th c.); Broome Hall, Surrey (built 1830, purchased mid-19th c., sold 1945); Flempton Hall, Suffolk (built 16th and 17th c., remod. 19th c.)
Estates: Bateman 2089 (E) 4925; 1 Bt left £900,000 in 1864.
Titles: Baronet 1863- ; 1903-
Notes: 1 Bt and 1 Viscount in ODNB.

BROWNE I [Grant, Sheridan] *ENGLAND & IRELAND*

Browne

Origins: Rose from yeomen to gentry and purchased Frampton 1572. Enriched during the Civil War. **First MP 1614. Another MP 1621 (Dorset 1641), and another 1624.**

1. Thomas Browne – Dorset 1678-79 Weymouth & Melcombe Regis 1679-80
2. Robert Browne – Dorchester 1720 1737-41
3. John Browne – Dorchester 1727-50
4. Francis Browne – Dorset 1784-1806

Seats: Frampton Court, Dorset (tenants from r. Henry VI, purch. 1572, rebuilt 1704, enlarged 19th c., passed by inher. to the Sheridans 1833, partially demolished 1935); Forston Manor, Dorset (purch. 1572, built 1698, add. 1750, donated as an asylum 1827); Nethercerne Manor, Dorset (purch. c. 1660, built late 17th c., add. late 18th c., passed by inher. to Sheridans 1833)

Estates: c. 5,000 acres worth £1,000 pa in the 1640s. Rubinstein – Francis Browne MP left £100,000 in probate in 1833.
Notes: Male line extinct 1833. Some of the estates passed to Colquhoun-Grants but must have been sold.

Sheridan

Origins: Clergymen and schoolmasters in the 17th and 18th centuries in Ireland. The father of Richard B. Sheridan MP was a lawyer and Chief Secretary for Ireland to James II. Two uncles were Bishops in the 1680s. Richard Brinsley Sheridan, son of the playwright, married the niece of John Browne MP, and he inherited Frampton Court.

1. Charles Sheridan – {Belturbet 1776-83 Rathcormack 1783-90}
2. Richard B. Sheridan – Stafford 1780-1806 Westminster 1806-07 Ilchester 1807-12
3. Richard Sheridan – {Charlemont 1790-93}
4. Richard Sheridan – Shaftesbury 1845-52 Dorchester 1852-68

Seats: Frampton Court, Dorset (built 1704, inher. from Brownes 1833, enlarged 19th c., demolished 1931); Polesden Lacey, Surrey (built 1632, leased 1796, lease sold 1818); Nerthercerne, Dorset (built 17th and 18th c., inher. 1833, sold c. 1900)
Estates: Bateman 11468 (E) 12765
Notes: Five in ODNB.

Grant

Origins: A cadet of the Grant clan. The first MP was a Lt. General. He inherited his wife's sister's husband's (Francis Browne) estate of Frampton in 1833. His daughter married Richard B. Sheridan and inherited Frampton in 1835.

1. Sir Colquhoun Grant – Queenborough 1831-32

Seat: Frampton Court, Dorset (acq. 1833, see above)

BROWNE II [Poyntz] *ENGLAND & IRELAND*

Viscount Montague (1554-1797 E)

Origins: The Brownes rose to eminence during the 16th century through heiresses and royal favor. Sir Anthony Browne inherited Cowdray in 1543 from the Fitzwilliams (**four MPs 1529-63**, Earl of Southampton 1537-43, royal favorite) and gained further wealth from his mother, co-heiress of John Neville, Marquess of Montagu. However, Browne acquired most of his estates through royal favor and at the Dissolution. The family was originally from Newcastle-upon-Tyne and then became London merchants from the late 14th century. **First Browne MP 1439** (a royal official). **Five further MPs 1449-1547 including kts of the shire for Kent and Surrey**.

No MPs post 1660

Seats: Cowdray House, Sussex (medieval house, rebuilt c. 1520s, purch. 1528 by Fitzwilliams, add. 1530s, passed to Brownes 1543, fire 1793, passed by mar. to Poyntz family 1793, sold 1843, ruin); Battle Abbey, Sussex (medieval monastic buildings, acq. and remod. 1538, sold 1719)
Estates: Held 20,000 acres worth £1,200 in c. 1548.
1 Ld Lt 17th
1 KG 16th century
Notes: The Brownes remained Roman Catholic and hence were debarred from electing further MPs. They were also spendthrifts who dissipated their fortune by the 18th century. The remaining estate passed to a cadet line at Betchworth. Two in ODNB.

Browne

Origins: Cadet line descended from a merchant and Lord Mayor of London 1439. One served as Treasurer of the Household to Henry VI and married an heiress to Betchworth, inherited 1437. **First MP 1478 for Surrey. Five subsequent MPs 1559-1648 with several kts of the shire for Surrey**.

1. Sir Adam Browne 2 Bt – Surrey 1661 1685-87
2. Ambrose Browne – Bletchingly 1685-87

Seat: Betchworth Castle, Surrey (medieval, acq. by mar. from Arundells in 1437, add. late-16th c., sold c. 1690)
Estates: Worth £1,600 pa c. 1660
Title: Baronet 1627-90
Notes: One in ODNB.

Poyntz

Origins: The founder came to England with the Conqueror. Summoned to Parliament as Barons 1295 until the direct male line failed in 1359. (Roskell, Clark, and Rawcliffe, *The House of Commons*, IV, 132). Seated at Iron Acton, of North Ockenden in 1618 and acquired further estates at the Dissolution. **At least nine MPs 1368-1628 with numerous kts of the shire**. The last Poyntz of Iron Acton, Gloucestershire (owners from c. 1344) died in 1680 and the estate was sold. The family regained a footing among the elite in the 18th century through the career of Stephen Poyntz of a cadet line who served as a diplomat and courtier. John Poyntz married a Browne heiress and succeeded to Cowdray.

1. William Poyntz – St. Albans 1800-07 Callington 1810-18 Chichester 1823-30 Ashburton 1831-34 Midhurst 1835-37

Seats: Cowdray House, Sussex (see above, sold 1843 to the Earl of Egmont); Midgham House, Berkshire (purch. 1735, sold 1842).
Notes: Cowdray sold in 1843 for £300,000. (See Thompson, "The Poyntz Family", *Trans. of the Bristol and Glouc. Arch. Soc.*, 4, 1879-80, 73-85. The male line extinct 1840. Some Poyntz estates passed to the Lytteltons of North Ockenden 1618 (see). Two "modern" Poyntzs in ODNB.

Baron Kilmaine (1789- I)

Origins: Sir John Browne 1 Bt of The Neale was *probably* descended from the illegitimate brother of the 1 Viscount Browne (see above). To Ireland by 1583 when he was appointed Sheriff of Mayo. **First Irish {MP for County Mayo 1585}.** Bt 1636.

1. George Browne – {Castlebar 1713-14}
2. John Browne 1 Baron Kilmaine – {Newtown 1776-83 Carlow 1783-89}
3. John Browne 2 Baron Kilmaine – {Carlow 1790}
4. Robert Browne – Mayo 1836-50

Seats: Gaulstone Park, Westmeath (built 1770s, purch. 1784, sold 1918, burned 1920); The Neale, Mayo (acq. c. 1580, rebuilt early 18th c., add. early 19th c., remod. 1860s, add. c. 1907, sold 1925, demolished c. 1939); Glencorrils, Mayo
Estates: Bateman 14665 (I) 7499
Title: Baronet 1636-
Peers: {2 peers 1789-1800} 3 Irish Rep peers 1849-73 1890-1907 1911-46
Notes: 6 Baron in ODNB.

Marquess of Sligo (1800- I)

Origins: Descended from a younger son of Sir John Browne 1 Bt of The Neale. His grandson married the heiress of the 3 Viscount Bourke (descended originally from the O'Malleys who owned Westport from very early times) and acquired a vast estate.

1. John Browne 1 Earl of Altamount – {Castlebar 1744-60}
2. Peter Browne-Kelly 2 Earl of Altamount – {County Mayo 1761-68}
3. Arthur Browne – {Gowran 1769-76 County Mayo 1776-79}
4. James Browne – {Jamestown 1768-76 Tuam 1776-83 Castlebar 1783-90}

5. James Browne 1 Marquess of Sligo – {Jamestown 1776-80}
6. George Browne – {County Mayo 1779-80}
7. Denis Browne – {County Mayo 1782-1800} County Mayo 1801-18 Kilkenny 1820-26
8. James Browne – County Mayo 1818-31
9. Peter Browne – Rye 1818-26
10. John Browne – County Mayo 1831-34
11. Sir John de Beauvoir (Browne) – Windsor 1835
12. John Browne 4 Marquess of Sligo – Mayo 1857-68

Seats: Westport House, Mayo (O'Malley castle, passed by mar. to Brownes late 17th c., new house built 1730, add. 1778, remod. 1781, add. 1816-19, add. 1845, remod. 1857-59 still own); Claremount House, Mayo (acq. and built later 18th c., sold 1854); Mount Browne, Mayo (acq. late 17th c., built early 18th c., demolished 20th c.); Claremorris, Mayo (acq. late 17th c., burned 1798)
Estates: Bateman 114881 (I) 19000. Worth £11,389 pa in 1796. Owned 5,000 acres in 2001.
Titles: Baron Mounteagle 1760- I; Viscount Westport 1768- I; Earl of Altamount 1771- I; Earl of Clanricarde 1800- I; Baron Mounteagle 1806- UK
Peers: {3 peers 1761-76 1778-1800} 1 Irish Rep peer 1800-06 8 peers 1806-1945
2 Lds Lt 19th, 20th
2 KP 19th
Notes: The Brownes of Westport were Roman Catholic and supported James II. They were obliged to sell over 100,000 acres between 1698 and 1708 to pay fines and debts. The last Catholic head of the family died in 1724. His son conformed but was worth only £700 pa. He married the daughter of the Earl of Arran and the family fortunes rose. His son married the heiress of Denis Kelly, Chief Justice of Jamaica, and they inherited his West Indian plantations 1757. (M. Girouard, *County Life*, 137, p. 1010)

Browne

Origins: A brother of Sir John Browne 1 Bt of The Neale was the ancestor of this family.

1. George Browne – Mayo 1870-80

Seat: Brownestown (Brownstown), Mayo (there by 18th c., held into 20th c.)
Estates: Held 2809 (I) 1121 in the 1870s

BROWNE III *IRELAND*

Baron Oranmore and Browne (1836- I)

Origins: An Anglo-Norman family that acquired land in Ireland from 1316. Rich merchants 16th century. Married the Prendergast (to Ireland 1169) heiress to Castle Macgarret in 1564. Conformed to the Established Church 1754. {**First MP 1634, and another 1639**}

1. Geoffrey Browne – {Tuam 1661}
2. Dominick Browne 1 Baron Oranmore – Mayo 1814-26 1830-36

Seats: Castle Macgarrett, Mayo (built 13th c., acq. by mar. 1564, ruin by 1690s, new house built 1694, fire 1811, rebuilt, sold 1964, institutional use); Carrabrowne (Carra Browne, Carrowbrowne) Castle, Galway; Ashford Castle, Mayo (built 1228, acq. 14th c., new house c. 1750, sold 1855); The Mount, Ayrshire; Boutree Hill (Boutreehill) House, Ayrshire (built early 17th c., acq. by mar. 1852, fire and rebuilt 1879, now a ruin); Mereworth Castle, Kent (built 1720-30, purch. 1923, sold 1928)
Estates: Bateman 6963 (S & I) 8460. 23,000 acres worth £20,000 in 1807. (O'Byrne, *Luggala Days*, 101-02)
Title: Baron Mereworth 1926- UK
Peers: 2 Irish Rep peers 1869-1900 1902-27 2 peers 1926-45
1 Ld Lt 19th
1 KP 20th
Notes: Family finances damaged by the Famine and heavy indebtedness. Large sales of the estate took place through the Encumbered Estates Commission 1852-55. More sales after 1903. The final portion of the estate (1,750 acres) sold 1964. Senator in the Irish Republic 1921.

BROWNE IV *IRELAND*

Earl of Kenmare (1801- UK)

Origins: Founder came from Linclonshire to Ireland as a pay official with the Elizabethan army from the 1550s. Auditor General of Ireland 1583. **First MP 1571 for Berwick-on-Tweed. Also an Irish {MP 1585}. Three other MPs in the early 17th century both in England and Ireland including a kt of the shire for Lincolnshire 1610**. Bt 1622.

1. William Browne – County Kerry 1830-31 1841-47
2. Valentine Browne 4 Earl of Kenmare – County Kerry 1852-71

Seats: Kenmare House (Killarney House), Kerry (old castle, acq. 1588, add. 1688, Kenmare new house built 1726, add. 1775-78, demolished c. 1872, Killarney House built 1870s, burned 1879 and 1913, rebuilt 1936, sold and demolished 1956-57); Lisnagree, Cork (built early 20th c.); Molaliffe, Kerry; Rosse (Ross) Castle, Kerry (built 15th c., acq. c. 1580s, house built 17th c., abandoned post-1688); Woodlawn, Kerry
Estates: Bateman 118606 (I) 34473. Still owned 25,000 acres when estates sold 1956.
Titles: Viscount Kenmare 1798- I; Baron Kenmare 1841-53 UK; Baron Kenmare 1856- UK; Baronet 1622-
Peers: {1 peer 1798-1800} 4 peers 1841-53 1856-1945
3 Lds Lt 19th, 20th
1 KP 19th-20th
Notes: The family was Roman Catholic and thus debarred from electing MPs, although two Brownes attended James II's Irish Parliament in 1689. Created Viscounts in the Jacobite peerage 1689. Family virtually bankrupt in the 1880s. 4 Viscount in ODNB.

BROWNLOW *IRELAND*

Baron Lurgan (1839- UK)

Origins: Moved to Ireland 1610 and acquired 3,500 acres in Armagh. Kt 1622. Sheriff 1667. **First {MP 1639 for County Armagh}.**

1. Authur Chamberlain Brownlow – {County Armagh 1692-93 1695-99 1703-11}
2. William Brownlow – {County Armagh 1711-39}
3. William Brownlow – {County Armagh 1753-94}
4. Willam Brownlow – {County Armagh 1795-97} 1807-15
5. Charles Brownlow 1 Baron Lurgan – County Armagh 1818-32

Seat: Brownlow House (aka Lurgan Castle), Armagh (Lurgan Castle acq. and built 1610, destroyed 1640s, rebuilt 1833-36, sold 1903, institutional use)
Estates: Bateman 15276 (I) 20589. Held 22,720 acres in the 1790s.
Peers: 4 peers 1839-1945
1 Ld Lt 19th
1 KP 19th
Notes: Arthur Bronwlow MP was born a Chamberlain of Nizelrath, Louth, the son of the heiress Lettice Brownlow and he took the name Brownlow. The Brownlows founded a bank in 1806. One in ODNB.

BROXHOLME

Origins: Gentry by 16th c. **First MP 1571. One additional MP 1640.**

1. William Broxholme – Great Grimsby 1673-81

Seat: Broxholme Place, Lincolnshire
Estates: Worth £1,000 pa in 1660.
Notes: William Broxholme MP above was the last of the line.

BRUCE *WALES*

Baron Aberdare (1873- UK)

Origins: Were parish gentry at Duffryn raised to great wealth through coal, steel, and railways. Gained the first true industrial peerage.

1. Henry Bruce 1 Baron Aberdare – Merthyr Tydvil 1852-68 Renfrewshire 1869-73

Seat: Duffryn (Dyffryn), Glamorganshire (built 17th c., purch. 1747, rebuilt 1870, sold 1926, institutional use)
Estates: Bateman 3950 (W) 12113
Peers: 3 peers 1873-1945
1 in Cabinet 1868-74
Notes: The family's original name was Knight. The 1 Baron's father, who succeeded to Duffryn in 1837, changed it to Bruce in 1805. The Scottish Bruce family moved to Wales and purchased Duffryn in the mid-18th century. Large seams of coal were discovered under the Duffryn estate in the mid-19th century. 1 and 3 Barons and two others in ODNB.

BRUDENELL [Bruce] *ENGLAND & SCOTLAND*

Earl of Cardigan (1661- E)

Origins: The Brudenells were small landowners who by the 15th century had acquired large estates through marriages to two heiresses and the profits of the distinguished legal career (Attorney General) of Edmund Brudenell (d. 1425). **First MP 1404 for Buckinghamshire.** A younger son became a judge 1505, Kt 1516, PC 1520, Chief Justice of the Common Pleas 1521. He purchased the estates of his indebted cousins of the senior line. The Brudenells did well as Tudor sheepmasters and in the wool trade. Bt 1611. Baron 1628 (Finch, *The Wealth of Five Northamptonshire Families*, 135-64). Sir Thomas Brudenell married a Bussy heiress in 1539 (**two MPs 14th century**). The father of the 1 Earl of Cardigan married the Tayland heiress (**four MPs 15th and 16th century**).

1. James Brudenell – Chichester 1713-15 Andover 1715-34 Chichester 1734-46
2. George Brudenell – Rutland 1754-61 Stamford 1761-68 Rutland 1768-90
3. James Brudenell 5 Earl of Cardigan – Shaftesbury 1754-61 Hastings 1761-68 Great Bedwyn 1768 Marlborough 1768-80
4. Robert Brudenell – Great Bedwyn 1756-61 Marlborough 1761-68
5. John Brudenell Montagu Marquess of Monthermer – Marlborough 1761-62
6. Robert Brudenell 6 Earl of Cardigan – Marlborough 1797-1802
7. James Brudenell 7 Earl of Cardigan – Marlborough 1818-29 Fowey 1830-32 N. Northamptonshire 1832-37

Seat: Deene Park, Northamptonshire (medieval, purch. 1514, add. 1532-49, remod. 1571-72 and early 17th c., add. early 19th c., still own)
Estates: Bateman 15724 (E) 35357. Income £3,500 pa in 1635 (Heward and Taylor, *The Country Houses of Northamptonshire*, 155). Rubinstein – 5th Earl left £175,000 probate in 1811 and the Countess of Cardigan left £100,000 in 1823 and the 6 Earl left £350,000 in 1837.
Titles: Baron Brudenell 1628- E; Duke of Montagu 1766-90 GB; Baron Brudenell 1780-1811 GB; Baron Montagu 1786-1845 GB
Peers: 8 peers 1660-88 1709-90 1762-70 1780-1868
1 Ld Lt 18th
1 KG 18th
Notes: Remained Roman Catholic into the 17th c. Tudor judge, 1 Duke, and 7 Earl in ODNB.

Marquess of Ailesbury (1821- UK)

Origins: The Bruce and Brudenell families became closely intertwined in the 18th century. The Bruce family were cadets of the medieval Bruce Kings of Scots. Gained estates in the 12th century. Chancellor of Scotland 14th century. Edward Bruce, Baron Kinloss (1601 S), was a younger son of a Lord of Session (1597) and Master of the Rolls in England 1603, who accompanied James VI to London. His son was created Earl of Elgin. The 2 Earl was created Earl of Ailesbury in England 1664. The daughter of the 3 Earl of Elgin married the 3 Earl of Cardigan (see above). The eldest son of this marriage married the daughter of the 2 Duke of Montagu (see Montagu I). On the death of his father-in-law he was created Duke of Monatgu in 1766. His daughter married the 3 Duke of Buccleuch, which carried his estates to that family (see Monatgu I). However, his youngest brother was created Earl of Ailesbury of the second creation in 1776. The Cardigan title passed to another brother until that line became extinct in 1868 when the Cardigan and Ailesbury titles were merged. Deene Park (see above) passed to a younger son of the 3 Marquess of Ailesbury.

1. Charles Brudenell-Bruce 1 Marquess of Ailesbury – Marlborough 1796-1814
2. George Brudenell-Bruce 2 Marquess of Ailesbury – Marlborough 1826-29
3. Ernest Brudenell-Bruce 3 Marquess of Ailesbury – Marlborough 1832-78
4. Lord Charles Brudenell-Bruce – N. Wiltshire 1865-74 Marlborough 1878-85
5. Henry Bruce 5 Marquess of Ailesbury – N. W. Wiltshire 1886-92

Seats: Tottenham Park (House) (aka Savernake Forest), Wiltshire (built c. 1570, fire 1675, fire 1712, rebuilt 1731-39, add. 1737, rebuilt 1823-26, damaged WWII, long unoccupied, sold 2014); Houghton Park (House), Bedfordshire (built 1615-21, acq. c. 1624, sold 1738, gutted 1790s, ruin)
Estates: Bateman 55051 (E) 59716. Rubinstein – 1 Earl left £150,000 in probate 1814. Owned 4,500 acres in 2001.
Titles: Baron Bruce 1746- GB; Earl of Ailesbury 1776- GB; Baronet 1611-
Peers: 7 peers 1747-1856 1838-1945
3 Lds Lt 18th and 19th
1 KG 19th
2 KT 18th and 19th
Notes: Hereditray Wardens of Savernake Forest since the Middle Ages. The current holder is 31st in succession. 2 Earl in ODNB.

<u>Earl of Elgin</u> (1633- S), <u>Earl of Kincardine</u> (1647- S) and <u>Earl of Ailesbury</u> (1664-1747 E)

Origins: For the Bruce ancestry see above under the Marquess of Ailesbury. When the Earldom of Ailesbury of the first creation became extinct in 1747, the Earldom of Elgin passed to a cousin, the 9 Earl of Kincardine.

1. Robert Bruce 2 Earl of Elgin and 1 Earl of Ailesbury – Bedfordshire 1660-63
2. Alexander Bruce 4 Earl of Kincardine – [Culross Burgh 1661-63 1669-74 1678 1685-86 Sanquhar Burgh 1693-1702]
3. Thomas Bruce 3 Earl of Elgin and 2 Earl of Ailesbury – Marlborough 1679-81 Wiltshire 1685
4. James Bruce – Great Bedwyn 1702-05 Marlborough 1708-10
5. Robert Bruce – Marlborough 1702-05 Ludgershall 1708-10 Marlborough 1710-15 Great Bedwyn 1722-27
6. Charles Bruce 4 Earl of Elgin and 3 Earl of Ailesbury – Great Bedwyn 1705-08 Marlborough 1710-11
7. Thomas Bruce – Marlborough 1790-96 Great Bedwyn 1796-97
8. James Bruce – Marlborough 1796-97
9. James Bruce 8 Earl of Elgin and 12 Earl of Kincardine – Southampton 1841
10. Thomas Bruce – Portsmouth 1874-85
11. Robert Bruce – Fifeshire 1880-85 W. Fifeshire 1885-89

Seats: Broomhall, Fife (acq. estate by 16th c., built c. 1650, add. 1702, rebuilt 1796-99, remod. 1865-66, still own); Houghton Park, Bedfordshire (see above); Culross Abbey House, Perthshire (built 1608, add. 1670, passed out of the Bruce family late 18th c., acq. by Earl of Elgin later 19th c., dismantled late 19th c., restored 20th c., Elgins still resident 1950s)
Estates: Bateman 18503 (S) 13120 (includes part of B. Thurlow and son's property). Owned 1,000 acres in 1996.
Titles: Baron Kinloss 1601- S; Baron Bruce of Kinloss 1633- S; Baron Bruce of Whorlton 1641- E; Baron Bruce and Viscount Bruce 1664-1747 E; Baron Bruce of Tottenham 1756- GB; Baron Elgin 1849- UK
Peers: [5 peers 1660-63 1660-1707] 6 peers 1660-95 1711-1747 1849-63 1870-1917 1 Scottish Rep peers 1790-1807
6 Lds Lt 17th, 18th, 19th, 20th
2 in Cabinet 1859-60 1905-08
1 KG 19th-20th
1 KT 19th
Notes: The Earls of Kincardine had prospered from the 17th and 18th centuries from salt works, stone and marble quarries, and coal mines operated by successive Earls. 2 Earl of Kincardine and two others and the 2, 7, 8, and 9 Earls of Elgin and one other and 1 Baron Kinloss in ODNB.

Bruce

Origins: Descended from the eldest son of the eldest son of the father of the 1 Baron Kinloss. **Two [MPs for Culross 1593-1625].**

1. Sir William Bruce 1 Bt – [Fifeshire 1669-74 Kinross-shire 1681-82 1685-86]
2. Sir John Bruce 2 Bt – [Kinross-shire 1702-07] Scotland 1707-08

Seats: Balcaskie House, Fife (built c. 1629, purch. 1665, add. 1668-74, sold 1684); Kinross House, Kinross-shire (built c. 1554, purch. 1675, new house built 1685-93, old house demolished 1723; new house built 1685-93, sold c. 1777)
Title: Baronet 1668-1711
Notes: This family enjoyed great wealth from coal in the 16th and 17th centuries. On the extinction of the male line in 1711 the estates passed to the Hopes of Craighall, Fife (see that family). 1 Bt in ODNB.

Bruce

Origins: Descended from a younger son of the eldest son of the father of the 1 Baron of Kinloss (see above). **First [MP 1617 for Clackmannanshire].**

1. Sir Henry Bruce – [Clackmannanshire 1661-63 1667 1669-74]
2. David Bruce – [Clackmannanshire 1678 1685-86 1689-93]

Seats: Blairhall, Clackmannanshire (medieval house, purch. 1541, passed by mar. to Stewarts of Bute early 18th c.); Clackmannan Tower, Clackmannanshire (medieval house, purch. 1359, rebuilt c. 1360s, add. 15th c., add. late 16th c., finally abandoned by family 1791, ruin)
Notes: Sir Henry Bruce fell deeply in debt due to poor management of his collieries. David Bruce declared bankrupt 1708 and most estates sold before his death 1712. His son came "out" in 1745. Male line extinct 1772.

BRUEN *IRELAND*

Origins: To Ireland in military service with with Cromwell. Acquired estates in Carlow in the 1770s. Sheriff 1785.

1. Henry Bruen – {Jamestown 1783-90 County Carlow 1790-95}
2. Henry Bruen – County Carlow 1812-31 1835-37 1840-52
3. Francis Bruen – Carlow 1835-37 1839
4. Henry Bruen – County Carlow 1857-80

Seats: Oak Park (orig. Painestown), Carlow (built early 18th c., purch. c. 1775, remod. 1832, remod. 1876-79, fire 1902, restored 1903, sold c. 1957, institutional use); Coolbawn, Wexford (acq. 19th c., built 1820-39, sold 1917, burned 1923)
Estates: Bateman 23627 (I) 17481

BUCHANAN *SCOTLAND*

Buchanan

Origins: Lairds by the 15th century. **First [MP 1560]. A [MP for Stirlingshire 1644-51].**

1. John Buchanan – [Stirlingshire 1662-63]

Seat: Buchanan Castle, Stirlingshire (medieval, acq. by 1231, sold late 17th c.)
Note: Male line failed 1682.

Buchanan

Origins: Cadet of the Buchanans of Buchanan (15th century). Family became successful tobacco merchants in Glasgow in the 18th century. Provost 1740.

1. Neil Buchanan – Glasgow Burghs 1741-44
2. Arthur Buchanan – Coatbridge Div. Lanarkshire 1918-22

Seat: Drumpellier House, Lanarkshire (purch. 1735, built 1741, donated to town 1919, demolished)
Estates: Bateman 31331 (S) 15870 and 16424
Notes: Bankrupted by the American Revolution, but Drumpellier later repurchased with a second fortune. Two in ODNB.

BUCHANAN-SMITH *SCOTLAND*

Baron Balerno (1963-1984 UKLife)

Origins: Glasgow merchants in the 19th century.

1. Walter Buchanan – Glasgow 1857-65
2. Alick Buchanan-Smith – North Angus and Mearns 1964-83 Kincardine and Deeside 1983-91

Seat: Eriska House, Argyllshire (built 1884, purch. 1973)
Peer: 1 peer 1963-84

BULKELEY [Williams] *WALES, ENGLAND, & IRELAND*

Viscount Bulkeley (1644-1822 I)

Origins: The Bulkeleys from Cheshire began in Beaumaris, Angelsey as merchants from the mid-14th century. They acquired a large landed estate in the 15th century. Dominated the island from the reign of Henry VII. **First MP 1545 for Angelsey. Seven additional MPs 1553-1628**. Bishop of Bangor 1541. Archbishop of Dublin 1613. Irish peer 1644.

1. Robert Bulkeley 2 Viscount Bulkeley – Anglesey 1660 Caernarvonshire 1675-79 Anglesey 1685-87
2. Thomas Bulkeley – Caernarvonshire 1679-81 1685-87 Angelsey 1689-90 Beaumaris 1690-95 Caernarvonshire 1697-1705 Caernarvon 1705-08
3. Richard Bulkeley 3 Viscount Bulkeley – Beaumaris 1679 Anglesey 1680-81 1690-1704
4. Henry Bulkeley – Anglesey 1679 Beaumaris 1679-81 1685-87
5. Robert Bulkeley – Beaumaris 1701-02
6. Richard Bulkeley 4 Viscount Bulkeley – Anglesey 1704-15 1722-24
7. Richard Bulkeley 5 Viscount Bulkeley – Beaumaris 1730-39

8. James Bulkeley 6 Viscount Bulkeley – Beaumaris 1739-52
9. Thomas Warren-Bulkeley 7 Viscount Bulkeley – Anglesey 1774-84

Seats: Baron Hill, Anglesey (acq. and built 1618, rebuilt 1776 and 1830, family depart 1920s, requisitioned WWII, fire, ruin); Dynas (Dinas), Caernarvonshire (acq. mid-17th c. by mar.)
Estates: Worth £4,300 pa in the 1570s. Rubinstein – 7 Viscount left £100,000 in probate 1822 and his widow left £250,000 in 1826. She inherited the Warren estates (see Leicester).
Title: Baron Bulkeley (1802-22 UK)
Peer: 1 peer 1802-22
1 Ld Lt 18th-19th
Notes: Six in ODNB.

Williams

Origins: A medieval family. One an Archbishop of York (d. 1650). High Sheriff 1650. **First MP 1656**. Sir Richard Williams 10 Bt succeeded to the Bulkeley estates through marriage in 1822 and took the additional name Bulkeley.

1. Coningsby Williams – Beaumaris 1701 1703-05
2. Sir Hugh Williams 8 Bt – Beaumaris 1768-80 1785-94
3. Sir Richard Williams-Bulkeley 10 Bt – Beaumaris 1831-32 Anglesey 1832-37 Flint 1841-47 Anglesey 1847-68

Seats: Nant (Plas y Nant), Caernarvonshire (built 1671, owned by the Williams family during the 19th c., add. 19th c., sold later 19th c.); Caerau, Anglesey (built 17th, add. 1730, acq. by Bulkeleys by mar. 1749); Baron Hill, Anglesey (see above); Friars, Anglesey; Penhryn, Caernarvonshire
Estates: Bateman 29878 (W) 21138. Owned 2,000 acres in 2001.
Title: Baronet 1661-
2 Lds Lt 19th, 20th

Williams

Origins: Cadet of the Williams line above (16th century)

1. Sir Willliam Williams 6 Bt – Caernarvonshire 1689-96

Seats: Vaynol (Vaenol, Faenol), Caernarvonshire (acq. and built c. 1550, c., passed to Crown 1696); Penhryn, Caernarvonshire
Title: Baronet 1622-96

Notes: On the extinction of this line the estates passed to the Crown and were granted to the Assheton-Smiths (see). Penhryn passed via heiresses to the Douglas family (see)

Bulkeley

Origins: Descended from a younger son in the 15th century.

1. John Bulkeley – Yarmouth (IoW) 1640 Newton 1645 Hampshire 1654 1656 Christchurch 1659 Hampshire 1660 Lymington 1661-63
2. Bartholomew Bulkeley – Lymington 1679
3. Sir Dewey Bulkeley – Bridport 1719-27

Seat: Nether Burgate, Hampshire (acq. by inher. c. 1439, later passed by mar. to Earls of Coventry 1801)
Notes: The estates passed to a younger son of the Earl of Coventry (see Coventry) in 1801 by marriage.

Bulkeley

Origins: Descended from the Bulkeley Archbishop of Dublin (see above). Settled in Wicklow 1650s.

1. Sir Richard Bulkeley 1 Bt – {Baltinglas 1665-66}
2. Sir Richard Bulkeley 2 Bt – {Fethard 1692-93 1695-99 1703-10}

Seats: Dunlavin, Wicklow (acq. by mar. 1702, sold c. 1710); Old Bawn, Dublin (acq. and built c. 1635, passed by mar. to Worth (see Tynte under Wharton) family 1710, demolished 1970s); Ewell, Surrey
Title: Baronet 1672-1710
Notes: Extinct in male line 1710.

BULLER [Gould, Manningham, Yarde]

Buller

Origins: The Bullers were landed by the 14th century. Established gentry by the early 16th century. **First MP 1555. Four further MPs in the first half of the 17th century, kt of the shire for Cornwall 1640**. They succeeded to Morval in 1637 from the Coodes, who had inherited it from the Glynns, who held it in the Middle Ages. Two lines at Shillingham and Morval were merged in 1707. In the 18th century four brothers established separate lines at Downes, Down Hall, Morval, and Churston.

1. John Buller – East and West Looe 1656-58 E. Looe 1659 W. Looe 1660 Saltash 1661-79 Liskeard 1679-81 1689-90 Grampound 1692-95
2. Anthony Buller – Callington 1659 Saltash 1660
3. Francis Buller – Cornwall 1659 Saltash 1660-79
4. Francis Buller – Saltash 1695-98
5. James Buller – Saltash 1699-1701 Cornwall 1701-05 Saltash 1705-08 Cornwall 1708-10
6. John Buller – Lostwithiel 1701
7. Benjamin Buller – Saltash 1702 (probable kin)
8. John Buller – Saltash 1718-22
9. James Buller – East Looe 1741-47 Cornwall 1748-65
10. John Buller – East Looe 1747-86
11. Francis Buller – West Looe 1761-64
12. John Buller – Exeter 1768-74 Launceston 1774-80 West Looe 1780-82 1784
13. James Buller – Exeter 1790-96 East Looe 1802 Exeter 1802-18
14. John Buller – West Looe 1796 1826-27
15. John Buller – East Looe 1796-99 1802-07
16. Frederick Buller – East Looe 1798-1802
17. James Buller – West Looe 1802-05 1806-12
18. Sir Edward Buller 1 Bt – East Looe 1802-20
19. Sir Anthony Buller – West Looe 1812-16 1831-32
20. Charles Buller – West Looe 1812-16 1826-30
21. James Buller – Exeter 1830-34 N. Devon 1857-65
22. Charles Buller – West Looe 1830-31 Liskeard 1832-48
23. Sir Arthur Buller – Devonport 1859-65 Liskeard 1865-69

Seats: Downes House, Devon (built 1692, acq. by mar. 1726, remod. 1794, still own); Morval, Cornwall (built 16th c., acq. by mar. 1637, remod. 18th c., passed to Tremaynes 1890); Shillingham, Cornwall (acq. by mar. c. 1555, built 1613, demolished early 19th c., sold mid-19th c.); Erle Hall, Devon (resident 19th and 20th c.)
Estates: Bateman 5089 (E) 14137 (at Morval 4594 (E) 5014 – acq. by Bullers by mar. 1637, passed by mar. to Tremaynes 1890 – and at Down Hall 2005 (E) 7151). Worth £3,000 pa in 1660.
Title: Baronet 1808-24
Notes: Seven in ODNB.

<u>Gould</u>

Origins: The Goulds, seated at Downes, were an old family. Jame Buller of Morval married the Gould heiress.

1. William Gould – Dartmouth 1670-72

Seat: Downes, Devon (passed by mar. to Bullers 1726, see above)

Baron Churston (1858- UK)

Origins: The youngest brother in the 18th century Buller division, Sir Francis Buller 1 Bt, married the Yarde heiress of Churston Ferrers. Their grandson was created Baron Churston. In 1824 his brother married the Manningham heiress. The 4th Manningham-Buller Baronet was Lord Chancellor 1962-64 and created Viscount Dilhorne.

1. Sir Francis Buller-Yarde-Buller 2 Bt – Totnes 1790-96
2. Sir Edward Manningham Buller 1 Bt – N. Staffordshire 1832-41 Stafford 1841-47 N. Staffordshire 1865-74
3. John Yarde-Buller 1 Baron Churston – S. Devon 1835-58
4. Sir Mervyn Manningham-Buller 3 Bt – Kettering Div. Northamptonshire 1924-29 Northampton 1931-40
5. Sir Reginald Manningham-Buller 4 Bt – Daventry 1943-50 S. Div. Northamptonshire 1950-62

Seats: Lupton House, Devon (built 1772, fire 1926, rebuilt, family depart 1939, sold post 1945, school); Churston Ferrers (Churston Court), Devon (acq. by mar. 1788, sold 1967, now hotel); Dilhorne Hall, Staffordshire (rebuilt c. 1830, passed by mar. to Feildens 1910, demolished 1925)
Estates: Bateman 10903 (E) 11464
Titles: Baron Dilhorne 1962- UK; Viscount Dilhorne 1964- UK; Baronet 1790- ; 1866-
Peers: 4 peers 1858-1945
Notes: Dame Eliza Manningham-Buller was Director General of MI5 2002-07. 1 Viscount in ODNB.

Yarde

Origins: Held Churston since marriage with a Ferrers heiress in the reign of Edward IV. **First MP 1559**. Estates passed to Bullers (see above).

1. Edward Yarde – Dartmouth 1679-81 Ashburton 1685-87
2. Edward Yarde – Totnes 1695-98
3. Gilbert Yarde – Ashburton 1705-07

Seat: Churston Ferrers (Churston Court), Devon (medieval, acq. by mar. 15th c., passed by mar. to Bullers 1788)

BULLOCK

Origins: Merchants 17th century.

1. Edward Bullock – Essex 1698-1700 Colchester 1705
2. John Bullock – Maldon 1699-1700
3. John Bullock – Maldon 1754-74 Steyning 1780-84 Essex 1784-1809

Seats: Faulkbourne Hall, Essex (built c. 1437-89, purch. 1637, add. 17th c., rebuilt 1832, sold post 1897); Dynes Hall, Essex (built c. 1580, rebuilt c. 1670, purch. 1690?, sold 1765?)
Estates: Bateman 2865 (E) 4661

BURDETT I [Jones]

Burdett

Origins: Landed family in Warwickshire since the 11th century (Hayton, *The House of Commons*, III, 410). **First MP early 14th century. Five further MPs 1380-1601, most kts of the shire.** Baron Latymer 1432 by writ. In 1602 married the heiress of William Frauncys, heiress to Foremark. The latter family acquired the estate in 1387. **Five Frauncys MPs in the 1337-1626.** The Barony of Latymer was called out of abeyance in 1913, the representation of which had passed through several families to the Burdetts, for the son of a sister of the 6 Bt.

1. Sir Robert Burdett 3 Bt – Warwickshire 1679-81 Lichfield 1689-98
2. Sir Robert Burdett 4 Bt – Tamworth 1748-68
3. Sir Francis Burdett 5 Bt – Boroughbridge 1796-1802 Middlesex 1802-04 1805-06 Westminster 1807-37 N. Wiltshire 1837-44

Seats: Foremark Hall, Derbyshire (acq. by Frauncys 1387, passed by mar. to Burdetts 1602, rebuilt 1650s, rebuilt 1759-61, sold 1951); Bramcote, Warwickshire (acq. 15th c., rebuilt c. 1720s, family departed mid-20th c., derelict); Ramsbury Manor, Wiltshire (built c. 1681-86, acq. by mar. of 1766, sold 1965)
Estates: Bateman 20984 (E) 29385
Title: Baronet 1681-1951
Peers: 2 peers 1913-45
Notes: The MPs listed in Burdett II may well be related to the Burdetts of Foremarke. Two American brothers, who were adventurers, named Ashmead-Bartlett, entered the Commons between 1880-1921. William married Baroness Burdett-Coutts and assumed her name. (Lubenow, *Parliamentary Politics*, 184-85 n. 71). Rubinstein - she inherited the Coutts fortune of £600,000 in 1837 from her step-grandmother, Harriot, Duchess of St. Albans. Two in ODNB.

Jones

Origins: Ironmasters acquired a landed estate under Elizabeth I (Stowey Court, Somerset), **one elected MP for Somerset 1654**. Attorney General 1675, purchased Ramsbury 1681. A Jones heiress married 1766 a Burdett of Foremark, and Ramsbury passed to them in 1800.

1. Sir William Jones – Plymouth 1680-81
2. Robert Jones – Glamorgan 1712-15

Seat: Ramsbury Manor, Wiltshire (purch. 1681, built 1681-86, passed to Burdetts by mar. of 1766, see above)
Title: Baronet 1774-91
One in ODNB.

BURDETT II [Weldon] *IRELAND*

Burdett

Origins: This family may well be descended from the Burdetts of Foremarke. To Ireland c. 1650. Sheriff 1701

1. Thomas Burdett – {Carlow 1661-63}
2. Sir Thomas Burdett 1 Bt – {County Carlow 1704-13 Carlow 1713-14 County Carlow 1715-27}
3. George Burdett – {Gowran 1783-90 Thomastown 1790-97 Gowran 1797-1800}
4. Arthur Burdett – {Harristown 1790-97}

Seats: Longtown House, Kildare (built early 18th c., add. late 18th c., sold 1829, demolished); Coolfin, King's County (purch. 1836, resident 20th c.); Garryhill (Garahill) Castle, Carlow (resident 18th c., passed by mar. to Weldons)
Estates: 3238 (I) 1816 in 1878. Worth £1,000 pa in 1713.
Title: Baronet 1723-
Note: The 2 Bt was poor.

Weldon

Origins: To Ireland late 16th century. Rose as merchants and officials. **First {MP 1613}.** A sister of the 1st Burdett Bt married Walter Weldon of Rahinderry, and the Baronetcy passed through the sister by special remainder. Sheriff 1729.

1. William Weldon – {Athy 1661-63}
2. Walter Weldon – {Carlow 1692-93 1703-27 Ballynakill 1695-99}

3. Walter Weldon – {Athy 1745-60}
4. Stewart Weldon – {Ennis 1783-90}

Seats: Kilmorony, Queen's County (acq. 18th c., built c. 1800, family still resident 1930s, now demolished); Rahinderry (Raheen), Queen's County (acq. early 17th c., still owned 1930s)
Estates: Bateman 2739 (I) 2206
Title: Baronet 1723-
1 Ld Lt 20th

BURGH (Bourke, De Burgh) [Canning, Downes] *IRELAND*

Marquess of Clanricarde (1646-57 1789-97 1825-1916 I)

Origins: The de Burghs claimed descent from Charlemagne and from Baldwin de Burgh, King of Jerusalem (Bourke, *Burke, Bourke, and De Burgh*, 4) They were with certainty Anglo-Normans who arrived in Ireland and were granted land by 1185. Chief Justiciar 1215. Summoned to Parliament as feudal lords in England in 1308 and 1318 and in Ireland 1310, 1326. (Earls of Ulster 1264, extinct 1333). William de Burgo married Elizabeth, daughter of King Edward I before he came to Ireland. (Chambers, *Chieftain to Knight*, 12-25) He married secondly the daughter of the last King of Cashel. He was granted all of Connaught by King John. Two lines of great chieftans emerged: The Upper MacWilliam and the Lower MacWilliam. **Several Irish MPs in 16th century**. The 2 Marquess of the third creation took the additional name Canning in compliance with the will of his maternal uncle Earl Canning in 1862.

1. Ulrick Canning De Burgh Baron Dunkellin – Galway 1857-65 County Galway 1865-67
2. Hubert De Burgh-Canning 2 Marquess of Clanricarde – County Galway 1867-71

Seat: Portumna Castle, Galway (acq. by mar. 1601, built 1602-13, neglected 18th c., fire 1826, ruin, new house 1862, passed to Earl of Harewood 1916, burned 1922, sold 1947)
Estates: Bateman 56826 (I) 24358. Rental in the early 17th century was estimated at £29,000. The 2 Marquess left £2,500,000 in 1916.
Titles: Baron Dunkellin and Earl of Clanricarde 1543- I; Viscount Tunbridge 1624-57 I; Earl of St. Albans 1628-57 I; Baron Tyaquin and Viscount Galway 1687-91 I; Baron Dunkellin 1711-97 I; Earl of Clanricarde 1800- I; Baron Somerhill (1826-1916 UK)
Peers: {7 peers 1661-87 1689-91 1711-26 1743-1800} 1 Irish Rep peer 1801-08 2 peers 1826-1916
1 Ld Lt 19th
1 in Cabinet 1846-52 1858
2 KP 18th and 19th

Notes: The family conformed to the Established Church c. 1630 and again in 1709 and took its seat in the House of Lords. The Earldom of Clanricarde passed by marriage to the 6 Marquess of Sligo in 1916. The estates passed to the Earl of Harewood (see Lascelles). A number of medieval Burghs, the 4 Earl and 1 Marquess of first creation, 1 and 2 Marquess of second creation in ODNB.

Viscount Mayo (1627-1767 I)

Origins: A cadet line of the Marquesses of Clanricarde. The head of the family was known as The MacWilliam until raised to the peerage. **Three {MPs 1613-39}.**

No post-1660 MPs

Seat: Castle Bourke (Castle Burke, Castleburke), Mayo (medieval, held in 17th c., most of remaining estate sold late 17th c., castle sold 1862 for £1,800, ruin)
Estates: 50,000 acres in the 1670s
Title: Baronet 1638-1767
Peers: {5 peers 1661-81 1638-1767}
Notes: Estates confiscated by Cromwell; a portion returned 1660.

Earl of Mayo (1785- I)

Origins: A cadet of The Macwilliam (early 16th century).

1. Theobald Bourke – {Naas 1713-26}
2. John Bourke 1 Earl of Mayo – {Naas 1727-60 Old Leighlin 1761-68}
3. John Bourke 2 Earl of Mayo – {Naas 1763-90}
4. John Bourke 4 Earl of Mayo – {Naas 1790-94}
5. Richard Bourke 6 Earl of Mayo – County Kildare 1847-52 Coleraine 1852-57 Cockermouth 1857-68
6. Robert Bourke 1 Baron Connemara – King's Lynn 1868-86

Seats: Palmerstown House, Kildare (acq. mid-17th c., built c. 1660, rebuilt c. 1872, burned 1923, rebuilt, sold later 1920s); Kill, Kildare (acq. 17th c., abandoned later in the century for Palmerstown)
Estates: Bateman 7834 (I) 7690
Titles: Baron Naas 1766- I; Viscount Mayo 1781- I; Baron Connemara 1887-1902 I
Peers: {4 peers 1776-1800} 3 Irish Rep peers 1816-49 1852-67 1890-1927 1 peer 1887-1902
1 in Cabinet 1852-53 1858-59 1866-68
2 KP 19th, 20th
1 Ld Lt 19th

Notes: 6 Earl assassinated in the Andaman Islands while Viceroy of India 1872. 6 Earl and one other in ODNB.

Baron Downes (1822-63 I)

Origins: Descended from a younger son of William De Burgh, ancestor of the Claricarde line. The grandfather of the 2 Baron married Anne Downes and the Barony by special remainder passed through her. The Downes family descended from an early 18th century bishop and the 1 Baron was Lord Chief Justice of Ireland 1803-22. The 2 Baron married the heiress of Walter Bagenall of Killedmonde, Carlow and Bert House, Kildare (see Paget I).

1. John Burgh – Brackley 1711-15
2. William Burgh – {Lanesborough 1713-14}
3. Robert Donwnes – {Kildare 1735-54}
4. Thomas Burgh – {Lanesborough 1727-58}
5. William Burgh – {Athy 1768-76}
6. Walter Hussey Burgh – {Athy 1769-76 Dublin University 1776-82}
7. Thomas Burgh – {Athy 1776-90 Kilbeggan 1790-97 Clogher 1797-1800 Fore 1800}
8. William Downes 1 Baron Downes – {Donegal 1790-92}
9. Ulysses Bagnel De Burgh 2 Baron Downes – County Carlow 1818-26 Queenborough 1826-30

Seats: Donnybrook Castle, Dublin (built 16th c., Downes acq. by mar. 1737, demolished 1759, rebuilt 1795, sold 1816); Bert House, Kildare (built 1725-30, enlarged early 19th c., passed by mar. to De Burghs 19th c., passed to Colbornes by mar. 1863); Donore House, Kildare (acq. by Husseys later 17th c./early 18th c., new house built c. 1750, leased after 1850, sold 1874, now a ruin); Dromkeen House, Limerick (built 18th c., Husseys acq. by mar. mid-18th c. from Burghs, became principal seat, resident into mid-20th c.)
Peers: 1 Irish Rep peer 1833-63
Notes: 1 and 2 Barons in ODNB. On the death of the 2 Baron Downes his estates were divided between the husbands of his daughters, the 3 Earl of Clonmell and the 2 Baron Seaton (see Colborne). The intertwining of the Burgh, Foster and Downes families in the 18th and 19th century is extrordinarily difficult to disentangle. (See Malcolmson, *John Foster: the Politics of the Anglo-Irish Ascendancy*, Table 3.)

Burgh

Origins: Descended from a younger son of the ancestor of the 2 Baron Downes. Sheriff 1711

1. Thomas Burgh – {Naas 1713-30}
2. Thomas Burgh – {Naas 1731-59}

3. Thomas Burgh – {Naas 1759-62}
4. Thomas Burgh – {Harristown 1775-76 Athy 1776-90}

Seat: Oldtown, Kildare (acq. later 17th c., burned 1691, rebuilt c. 1709, fire 1950s, one wing still occupied by family, sold c. 2000)
Estates: Worth £500 pa in 1713.
Notes: One in ODNB.

BURGOYNE

Origins: Gentry since the 15th century. Acquired more estates at the Dissolution. **First MP for Cambridgeshire 1413. Four additional MPs 1442-1648, all kts of the shire.**

1. Sir Roger Burgoyne 6 Bt – Bedfordshire 1735-47
2. John Burgoyne – Midhurst 1761-68 Preston 1768-92

Seats: Sutton Park, Bedfordshire (medieval, acq. 1544, rebuilt, fire 1825, rebuilt 1859, sold 1948, now golf club); Wroxall Abbey, Warwickshire (medieval, acq. c. 1530s, add. 1580s, sold 1713)
Estates: Bateman 2375 (E) 3547
Titles: Baronet 1641-1921; 1856-71
Notes: Seven members of the family in ODNB.

BURKE [Haviland]

Origins: The family claimed descent from the De Burghs. The father of the first MP was an attorney in Dublin. The first MP was a politician and philosopher. The Havilands succeeded to the Burke property and took the name Burke in 1816.

1. Edmund Burke – Wendover 1765-74 Bristol 1774-80 Malton 1780-94
2. William Burke – Great Bedwyn 1766-74
3. Richard Burke – Malton 1794
4. Edmund Haviland-Burke – Christchurch 1868-74
5. Edmund Haviland-Burke – Tullamore Div. King's County 1900-14

Seat: Gregories, Buckinghamshire (built c. 1712, purch. 2nd half 18th c., remod. later 18th c., fire and demolished 1813)
Notes: Three in ODNB.

BURNS

Baron Inverclyde (1897- UK)

Origins: Merchants in Glasgow early 19th century, then mining and shipowning. Founder and Chairmen of the Cunard Line.

No MPs

Seats: Castle Wemyss, Renfrewshire (built c. 1850, purch. and add. 1860, sold 1957, demolished 1984); Kilmahew House (Castle), Dumbartonshire (castle built 16th c., remod. 1744, remod. early 19th c., purch. 1839, new house 1865-68, sold 1919)
Estates: The 1 Baron left over £1,000,000 in 1901.
Title: Baronet 1889-
Peers: 5 peers 1897-1945
Notes: Five in ODNB.

BURRARD [Neale]

Burrard

Origins: Mayor of Lymington 1599. Owned salt works and town property.

1. John Burrard – Lymington 1679-81 1685-87 1689-98
2. George Burrard – Lymington 1698-1700
3. Paul Burrard – Lymington 1701-05
4. Paul Burrard – Lymington 1705-13 1722-27 Yarmouth (IoW) 1727-35
5. Sir Harry Burrard 1 Bt – Lymington 1741-78
6. Sir Harry Burrard 1 Bt – Lymington 1780-88 1790-91 1802
7. Sir Harry Burrard-Neale 2 Bt – Lymington 1790-1802 1806-07 1812-23 1832-34
8. Sir George Burrard 4 Bt – Lymington 1828-32

Seat: Walhampton House, Hampshire (purch. 1668, built 1711, sold 1888, now school)
Titles: Baronet 1769-1965; 1807-1870
Notes: Two in ODNB.

Neale

Origins: Father of the first MP was a wealthy clothier who acquired landed estates. The heiress of Robert Neale MP married Sir Harry Burrard 2 Bt who took the additional name Neale in 1795.

1. Robert Neale – Wootton Bassett 1741-54

Seat: Shaw House, Wiltshire (medieval, rebuilt 1711, acq. by mar. 1759, passed to Burrards 1776, sold 1844, institutional use)

BURRIDGE

Origins: Wine and linen merchants in Lyme Regis. Mayor 1689

1. John Burridge – Lyme Regis 1689-95 1701-10
2. Robert Burridge – Tiverton 1702-08
3. John Burridge – Lyme Regis 1710-28

Seat: Thorn Falcon (Thornfalcon), Somerset (purch. 1679, sold 1753)

BUSFIELD

Origins: Busfields were Leeds businessmen. Mayor 1673. Purchased landed estates 1672. Currier Busfield married in 1805 Sarah Ferrand heiress to St. Ives (there were several intermarriages among the families from 1686 onwards).

1. Walker Ferrand – Tralee 1831-32
2. William Busfield – Bradford 1837-51
3. William Busfield Ferrand – Knaresborough 1841-47 Devonport 1863-65

Seats: St. Ives, Yorkshire (acq. 1712, new house 1759, renamed Harden Grange 1854, most demolished 1859, sold 1927); Ryshworth Hall, Yorkshire (built early 16th c., purch. 1672, add. early and mid-18th c.); Harden Grange, Yorkshire (Ferrand seat prior to 1712 – purch. 1636; they abandoned St. Ives and moved back to Harden Grange, which they renamed St. Ives in 1854, sold early 20th c.)
Estates: Bateman 3906 (E) 7698
Notes: One in ODNB.

BUSHE (Bush) *IRELAND*

Origins: The first MP, who was appointed Judge Advocate General in 1702, was the son of an English Colonel granted Kilfane in 1670. Glencairn (known as Castle Richard) was the seat of the Gumbletons (settled in Ireland under Charles II) whose heiress married Henry A. Bushe.

1. Arthur Bushe – {Thomastown 1695-99 1703-14}
2. Amyas Bush – {New Ross 1703-13 Thomastown 1713-14}

3. Gervase Bushe – {Granard 1767-76 Kilkenny 1778-83 Fore 1783-90 Lanesborough 1790-93}
4. Charles Bushe – {Callan 1796-99 Donegal 1799-1800}

Seats: Kilmurry, Kilkenny (acq. and built mid-17th c., sold 1788, repurch. 1814, remod. early 19th c., sold later 19th c.); Kilfane, Kilkenny (acq. 1670, rebuilt c. 1800, passed by mar. to the Power Bts mid-19th c., sold c. 1967); Glencairn Abbey (Castle Richard), Waterford (built c. 1814, passed by mar. to Bushes 1819, sold c. 1930, fire 1973)
Estates: Bateman 2366 (I) 2051
Notes: Charles Bushe MP was the son of the much indebted Rev. Thomas Bushe of Kilmurry, who revived his family fortunes as Lord Chief Justice of Ireland 1822. Two in ODNB.

BUTLER I [Ferguson, Johnstone, Munro, Wandesford] *IRELAND, ENGLAND, & SCOTLAND*

Duke of Ormonde (1661-1758 I)

Origins: Anglo-Norman lords who settled in Ireland c. 1185. One was Archbishop of Canterbury and Lord Chancellor 1199. Summoned as an Irish baron by Edward I. Lord Deputy of Ireland 1312. Earl 1328. The head of the family is the "Chief Butler" of Ireland, the most ancient hereditary dignity still enjoyed by the heirs male of any family in the British Isles, if not in Europe. (Dunboyne, *Butler Family History*, 6). **At least two and possibly as many as 10 Irish MPs between 1585-1639** (not all of the genealogical information is clear or accurate). A number of younger sons were created peers in their own right.

1. Thomas Butler Earl of Ossory – Bristol 1661-66 {Dublin University 1661-62}
2. Ricahrd Butler 1 Earl of Arran – Wells 1661-73
3. John Butler 1 Earl of Gowran – {Dublin University 1662-66}
4. Sir James Butler – Tavistock 1685-87
5. John Butler 17 Earl of Ormonde – {Gowran 1776-83 Kilkenny 1783-91}
6. Walter Butler 1 Marquess of Ormonde – {County Kilkenny 1789-95}
7. John Butler Wandesford – {Kilkenny 1791-96 County Kilkenny 1796}
8. James Butler 2 Marquess of Ormonde – {County Kilkenny 1796-1800} 1801-20
9. Charles Butler-Clarke-Southwell-Wandesford – Kilkenny 1802-09 1814-20 County Kilkenny 1820-30
10. John Butler 2 Marquess of Ormonde – County Kilkenny 1830-32

Seats: Kilkenny Castle, Kilkenny (built 1192, purch. 1391, remod. c. 1660, rebuilt c. 1826, remod. 1859-62, damaged 1922, family departed 1935, given to a trust 1967); The Castle, Carrick-on-Suir, Tipperary (built 15th c., add. 1598, family departed 17th c., leased until 19th c., now owned by government); Dunmore House (Palace), Kilkenny

(acq. and built 17th c., demolished 18th c.); Ballykene, Waterford; Kilcash Castle, Tipperary (medieval tower house, fell into decay after 1716, lodge built 1867, held into 20th c.); Castlecomer, Kilkenny (purch. by Wandesford 1637, new house 18th c., acq. by mar. 1820, passed to Priors by mar. 1881, burned 1965); Kenure (Rush House), Dublin (acq. 1315, rebuilt c. 1703, confiscated 1715)
Estates: Bateman 27725 (I) 15431. Worth £20,000 pa in 1799.
Titles: Earl of Ormonde 1328- I; Earl of Ossory 1527- I; Viscount Thurles 1536- I; Earl of Arran 1662-86 I; Baron Butler 1673-86 E; Earl of Gowran 1676-76 I; Earl of Arran 1693-1758 I; Baron Butler 1694-1758 E; Baron Butler 1801-20 UK; Marquess of Ormonde 1816-20 I; Baron Ormonde 1821- UK; Marquess of Ormonde 1825-1997 I; Baronet 1645-1762
Peers: {10 peers 1660-88 1661-67 1662-86 1662-80 1676 1689-91 1693-1758 1697-1715 1791-1800} 11 peers 1660-88 1666-80 1673-86 1685-1715 1694-1758 1801-54 1865-1945
4 Lds Lt 17th, 18th, 19th, 20th
3 in Cabinet 1662-69 1669 1677-85 1703-07 1710-13
3 KG 17th, 18th
4 KP 18th, 19th, 20th
Notes: The 2 Duke was attainted in 1715. His brother, the Earl of Arran, was empowered to buy his estates. The 1 Earl of Arran, a younger son of the 1 Duke, was created Duke of Arran in the Jacobite peerage. 1, 2, 3, 4, 6, 8, 9, and 10 Earls, 1, 2 Dukes, and five others in ODNB.

<u>Viscount Galmoye</u> (1646-97 I)

Origins: The 1 Viscount's father was the illegitimate son of the 10 Earl of Ormonde. **First {MP 1639}.**

No post-1660 MPs

Seats: Barrowmount (Duiske), Kilkenny (acq. at Dissolution of the monasteries, confiscated 1697); Grange, Kilkenny
Peers: {2 peers 1661-67 1672-97}
Notes: Roman Catholic family. The Viscount was attainted and his estates forfeited in 1697. Created Earl of Newcastle in the Jacobite peerage. Three in ODNB.

<u>Butler</u>

Origins: Descended from a younger son of the 3 Earl of Ormonde. **First {MP 1634}.**

No post-1660 MPs

Seat: Polestown (Poolestown, Paulstown) Castle, Kilkenny (acq. and built 15th c., confiscated 1697)

Title: Baronet 1645-1762
Notes: Fled to France 1689 and estates attainted 1697.

Earl of Carrick (1748- I)

Origins: Descended from the senior line of the Butlers (14th century). Earl 1315. The 2 Viscount Ikerrin conformed to the Established Church.

1. Henry Butler 2 Earl of Carrick – {Killileagh 1768-74}
2. Pierce Butler – {Killileagh 1774-76 Callan 1776-83}

Seats: Mount Juliet, Kilkenny (purch. 1750, built 1760, remod. 1780s, sold 1914, hotel); Newtown House, Kilkenny
Estates: Bateman under 2000 acres. Worth £5,000 to £6,000 pa c. 1800. Serious financial difficulties from the 1830s led to sales of the contents of Mount Juliet in 1838 and land in the 1850s. The rest of the estate sold 1914.
Titles: Viscount Ikerrin 1629- I; Baron Butler 1912- UK
Peers: {5 peers 1661-88 1698-1711 1739-1800} 1 Irish Rep peer 1819-38 3 peers 1912-45

Earl of Kilkenny (1793-1846 I)

Origins: The 1 Viscount Mountgarret was the second son of the 8 Earl of Ormonde. **First {MP 1634}.** The 11 Viscount conformed to the Established Church.

1. Edmund Butler 11 Viscount Mountgarret – {County Kilkenny 1776-79}
2. Pierce Butler – County Kilkenny 1832-46
3. Pierce Butler – County Kilkenny 1843-52

Seats: Ballyconra House, Kilkenny (built early 18th c., family departed 1846, sold later 19th c.); Ballyragget Castle, Kilkenny (built 1495, family abandoned c. 1700); Nidd Hall, Yorkshire (acq. by mar. 1891, sold c. 1970); Stainley House, Yorkshire (acq. 1891, built 1906, sold 2004)
Estates: Bateman 14698 (I) 9606 and 9071 (E) 12045. Owned 11,492 acres in 1698, worth £8,000 pa c. 1800. Worth £32,000,000 in 1990 with 20,000 acres in Yorkshire.
Titles: Baron Kells and Viscount Mountgarret 1550- I; Baron Mountgarret 1911- UK
Peers: {7 peers 1660-79 1689 1735-36 1749-1800} 3 peers 1911-18 1924-45
Notes: The 13 Viscount married Frances only daughter and heiress of Thomas Rawson of Nidd Hall in 1844 and succeeded to the Rawson estates in 1891 and moved permanently to England. The Rawsons held the manor of Bradford in Yorkshire from the early 16th c. They made a fortune in iron-working and eventually abandoned Bradford Manor House (demolished 1860s) for Nidd Hall. (Waterson and Meadows, *Lost Houses of the West Riding*, 37) Three in ODNB.

Butler

Origins: The 1 Baronet was the illegitimate son of Sir Edmund Butler, second son of the 9 Earl of Ormonde. **{Two MPs 1559 and 1634,1639 for County Carlow}.**

1. Sir Thomas Butler 3 Bt – {County Carlow 1692-93 1695-99 1703-04}
2. Sir Pierce Butler 4 Bt – {County Carlow 1703-14}
3. Sir Richard Butler 5 Bt – {County Carlow 1730-60}
4. Sir Thomas Butler 6 Bt – {County Carlow 1761-68 Portarlington 1771-72}
5. Sir Richard Butler 7 Bt – County Carlow {1783-90 1796-1800} 1801-02

Seats: Ballin Temple, Carlow (acq. 17th c., built later 18th c., add. early 19th c., fire 1917 and later demolished, still own a part of estate); Clogrenane Castle, Carlow (built 16th c., abandoned by c. 1800); Garryhundon House, Carlow (resident 17th-20th c.)
Estates: Held 1562 acres worth £1,200 pa in 1713.
Title: Baronet 1628-

Earl of Wandesford (1758-84 I)

Origins: Gentry in Yorkshire since the 14th century. To Ireland as Master of the Rolls in 1633. Purchased estates in 1630s and appointed Lord Deputy of Ireland 1640. **First MP 1621 and first Irish {MP 1634}. Four additional Irish MPs in the 1630s and 1640s (one sitting also for Richmond in 1640).** Lady Anne Wandesforde, heiress of the last Earl of Wandesford married the 17 Earl of Ormonde in 1769. The Wandesford estates passed 1820 to his second son, who took the name Butler-Clarke-Southwell-Wandesford.

1. John Wandesford – Richmond 1624 Hythe 1640 Richmond 1662-64
2. Christopher Wandesford 1 Viscount Castlecomer – Ripon 1679-81 {St. Canice 1707}
3. Christopher Wandesford 2 Viscount Castlecomer – {St. Canice 1692-93 1695-99 1703-07} Morpeth 1710-13 Ripon 1715-19

Seats: The Hall, Kirklington, Yorkshire (acq. by mar. c. 1370, built c. 1570, remod. early 18th c., passed by mar. to Butlers 1820, remod. 19th c., held beyond mid-20th c.); Castlecomer House, Kilkenny (purch. 1637, new house 18th c., fire 1798, rebuilt 1802, passed to Earls of Ormonde 1820, burned 1965)
Estates: Bateman 27032 (E & I) 16745 and 13031 (E & I) 8141. Estates worth £2,000 pa in the 17th century (Cliffe, *Yorkshire Gentry*, 87), £5,000 pa in 1742, and £10,000 pa in c. 1810.
Titles: Baron Wandesford and Viscount Castlecomer 1706-84 I; Baronet 1662-1784
Peers: {4 peers 1707-19 1736-84}

Notes: The Wandesford estates eventually passed through a Butler heiress to John Prior of Mount Dillon, Dublin. Three in ODNB.

Baron Dunboyne (1324- and 1541- I, attainted 1660, resumed 1827)

Origins: Descended form a younger brother of the Earl of Carrick in the 14th century. At Dunboyne by the reign of Edward III. Henry Butler, younger son of the 13 Baron married on 1843 Isabella Munro-Johnstone, daughter of Sir Alexander Munro of Novar and niece and heiress of General Johnstone of Corehead (Auchen Castle). The Butlers took the additionl name Johnstone.

1. Henry Butler-Johnstone – Canterbury 1852-53 1857-62
2. Henry Munro-Butler-Johnstone – Canterbury 1862-78

Seats: Knoppogue Castle, Clare (tower house built 1467, purch. early 19th c. for £8,500, add. 1856, sold 1927); Dunboyne Castle, Meath (acq. 14th c., built 1476, new house 1768-85, passed to heiress on death of 12 Baron, convent in later 20th c.) Auchen Castle, Dumfriesshire (medieval castle, built 1869, passed by inher. to Younger Bts. (see Younger) c. 1900, now hotel); Culcairn, Ross-shire
Estates: Bateman 1979 (I) 537 and 2435 (S) 3294
Peers: 2 Irish Rep peers 1868-81 1901-13
Notes: The family was Roman Catholic, conformed 1768. One in ODNB.

Viscount Novar (1920-34 UK)

Origins: See previous entry. Jean Munro, illegitimate daughter and heiress of Sir Hector Munro of Novar, married in 1773 Sir Ronald Ferguson of Raith House. Their grandson took the additional name Munro and succeeded to Novar in 1798. The Munros emerged in the 12th century (see Munro).

1. Sir Hector Munro – Inverness Burghs 1768-1802
2. Sir Ronald Ferguson – Dysart Burghs 1806-30 Nottingham 1830-41
3. Robert Ferguson – Fifeshire 1806-07 Dysart Burghs 1831-32 Kirkaldy Burghs 1832-34 Haddingtonshire 1835-37 Kirkaldy Burghs 1837-40
4. Robert Munro-Ferguson – Kirkaldy Burghs 1841-62
5. Ronald Munro-Ferguson 1 Viscount Novar – Ross and Cromarty 1884-85 Leith Burghs 1886-1914

Seats: Raith House, Fife (tower medieval, built 1693-96, Fergusons purch. 1707, remod. 1785, still own); Novar House, Ross-shire (Munros acq. 1589, built c. 1634, add. 1720, add. 1897, still own); Culcairn House, Ross-shire (occupied 18th c.)
Estates: Bateman 25506 (S) 20317. Owned 22,000 acres in 1996.

Peer: 1 peer 1920-34
1 in Cabinet 1920-24
1 KT 20th
Notes: The Munros were related to the Munros of Foulis, see that family. Three in ODNB.

Earl of Glengall (1816-58 I)

Origins: Cahir was granted to the 3 Earl of Ormonde in 1375. It passed to an illegitimate son (legitimized by the Irish Parliament). Richard Charteris, second son of the 9 Earl of Wemyss married in 1858 Lady Margaret Butler heiress of the last Earl of Glengall (see Wemyss).

1. Richard Butler 2 Earl of Glengall – County Tipperary 1818-19

Seat: Cahir Castle (House, Park), Tipperary (keep built 13th c., acq. 1375, add. 15th and 16th c., family abandoned castle and built new house 18th c., passed 1858 to heiress mar. to a Charteris (see Wemyss) who built new house 1861, estate sold 1961: Castle intact, 18th c. house a hotel, and Charteris house burned 1960s)
Estates: Bateman 16629 (I) 11662
Title: Baron Cahir 1543-1858 I
Peers: {4 peers 1689-1700 1709-86 1796-1800} 2 Irish Rep peers 1810-19 1829-58
Notes: Serious financial difficulties by mid-19th c. led to substantial land sales in 1855.

BUTLER II

Origins: London merchants and clothiers who married into the Sussex gentry. High Sheriff 1677.

1. Jame Butler – Arundel 1679-81 1690-95
2. James Butler – Arundel 1705-08 Sussex 1715-22 1728-41
3. John Butler – East Grinstead 1742-47 Sussex 1747-66

Seats: Warminghurst Park, Sussex (old house, purch. 1707 and 1721, sold 1805); Patcham, Sussex (acq. by mar. 1673, held into 19th c.)

BUTLER III

Baron Butler of Saffron Walden (1965-82 UKLife)

Origins: Clergy in the 18th century. Chaplain to the Duke of Kent early 19th century. Scholars in the 19th century, Headmaster of Harrow.

1. Sir James Butler – Cambridge University 1922-23
2. Sir Geoffrey Butler – Cambridge University 1923-29
3. Richard Butler 1 Baron Butler – Saffron Walden 1929-65
4. Sir Adam Butler – Bosworth 1970-87

Seat: Stanstead Hall, Essex (built 1540-50, part demolished 1653, purch. and restored c. 1907 by Samuel Courtauld, whose daughter mar. Baron Butler of SW, who inherited the house, sold 1976)
1 in Cabinet 1941-45 1951-64
Notes: Two Masters of Trinity College, Cambridge, early and later 20th century. A staggering fifteen members of the family in ODNB.

BUTLER IV [Danvers] *IRELAND & ENGLAND*

<u>Earl of Lanesborough</u> (1756- I)

Origins: From Huntingdonshire, settled in Ireland in the early 17th century. Sheriff 1703.

1. Stephen Butler – {Belturbet 1661-62}
2. Francis Butler {Belturbet 1662-66 1692-93 1695-99}
3. Brinsley Butler 1 Viscount Lanesborough – {Kells 1703-13 Belturbet 1713-24}
4. James Butler – {Clomines 1703-13 Newcastle 1735-42}
5. Theophilus Butler 1 Baron Newton-Butler – {County Cavan 1703-13 Belturbet 1713-14}
6. Humphrey Butler 1 Earl of Lanesborough – {Belturbet 1727-36}
7. Thomas Butler – {Belturbet 1727-53}
8. Robert Butler – {Belturbet 1736-63}
9. John Butler – {Newcastle 1743-83}
10. Brinsley Butler 2 Earl of Lanesborough – {County Cavan 1751-68}
11. Humphrey Butler – {Donegal 1790-97}

Seats: Lanesborough Lodge, Cavan (built c. 1810, add. 1840s, resident into 20th c., burned early 1920s, ruin); Swithland Hall (Park), Leicestershire (acq. by mar. 1796, fire 1822, rebuilt 1834-52, much of estate sold after 1950, still own)
Estates: Bateman 16397 (I & E) 17419
Titles: Baron Newton-Butler 1715- I; Viscount Lanesborough 1728- I
Peers: {5 peers 1715-1800} 3 Irish Rep peers 1849-66 1870-1905 1913-29
1 Ld Lt 19th-20th

Danvers

Origins: Minor gentry since the 13th century. At Swithland since the early 15th century, by marriage to a Walcote heiress. The father of the 5 Earl of Lanesborough married the heiress of Sir John Danvers 2 Bt of Swithland.

1. Sir Joseph Danvers – Boroughbridge 1722-27 Bramber 1727-34 Totnes 1734-47

Seat: Swithland Hall, Leicestershire (acq. by 1412, medieval manor house, passed to Butlers above 1796, see above)
Title: Baronet 1746-96

BUTTON (Bitton)

Origins: Gentry by 1150. Two bishops in the 13th century. **First MP 1529. Five additional MPs 1553-1628.** Baronet 1621. **Kt of the shire for Wiltshire 1628**.

1. John Button – Lymington 1625 1640-48 1660
2. John Button – Lymington 1679

Seats: Buckland, Hampshire (acq. by mar. mid-16th c., estates divided among co-heirs 1679); Alton Priors, Wiltshire (acq. 12th c., vacated 1652); Tockenham Court, Wiltshire (acq. and probably built 1560, passed out of the family 1712); Wilcot, Wiltshire (acq. 1521, passed out of the family 1712)
Title: Baronet 1621-1712
Notes: Several branches combined here. Three in ODNB.

BUXTON I

Earl Buxton (1920-34 UK)

Origins: Made a fortune in brewing in the 18th century.

1. Sir Thomas Fowell Buxton 1 Bt – Weymouth & Melcombe Regis 1818-37
2. Sir Edward Buxton 2 Bt – S. Essex 1847-52 E. Norfolk 1857-58
3. Charles Buxton – Newport 1857-59 Maidstone 1859-65 E. Surrey 1865-71
4. Sir Thomas Fowell Buxton 3 Bt – King's Lynn 1865-68
5. Francis Buxton – Andover 1880-85
6. Sydney Buxton 1 Earl Buxton – Peterborough 1883-85 Poplar Div. Tower Hamlets 1886-1914
7. Edward Buxton – Walthamstow Div. Essex 1885-86

8. Noel Buxton 1 Baron Noel-Buxton – Whitby Div. N. Riding Yorkshire 1905-06 N. Norfolk 1910-18 1922-30
9. Charles Buxton – Ashburton Div. Devon 1910 Accrington 1922-23 Elland Div. W. R. Yorkshire 1929-31
10. Lucy, Lady Noel-Buxton – N. Norfolk 1930-31 Norwich 1945-50

Seats: Warlies, Essex (built 17th-18th c., acq. mid-19th c., add. 1879, sold 1915); Northrepps Hall, Norfolk (built 16th c.?, rebuilt 19th c., occupied 19th c.); Colne Hall, Norfolk (acq. sec. half 19th c., sold 1947); Newtimber Place, Sussex (medieval, rebuilt 16th c., rebuilt 1681, remod. 19th c., purch. 1909, still own); Catton Hall, Norfolk (built c. 1780, purch. 1866, sold 1948)
Estates: Bateman 3160 (E) 4769
Titles: Viscount Buxton 1914-34 UK; Baron Noel-Buxton 1930- UK; Baronet 1840-
Peers: 2 peers 1914-34
2 in Cabinet 1905-14 1924 1929-30
Notes: Nine members of the family in ODNB.

BUXTON II

Origins: Robert Buxton, a steward to the 4 Duke of Norfolk, acquired a lease to Shadwell in 1580 and purchased it in 1602 for £2,000. Rose to gentry status. Over the next 200 years increased the estates by judicious marriages. (*Country Life*, 136, p. 19)

1. Sir Robert Buxton 1 Bt – Thetford 1790-96 Great Bedwyn 1797-1806
2. Sir John Jacob Buxton 2 Bt – Great Bedwyn 1818-32
3. Sir Robert Buxton 3 Bt – S. Norfolk 1871-85

Seats: Shadwell Park, Norfolk (purch. 1602, built 1727-29, add. 1840-43 and 1856-60, sold 1898); Channons (Channonz) Hall, Norfolk (built c. 1569, demolished 1784, property sold c. 1935); Tockenham, Wiltshire (built c. 1604, acq. by mar. 1776, descendents still owned 1968); Earsham Hall, Norfolk (built 1704-08, sold within a decade or two)
Estates: Bateman 10190 (E) 7260
Title: Baronet 1800-88

BYNG

Viscount Torrington (1721- GB)

Origins: The family was settled at Wrotham, Kent fom the 15th century. The estate was sold by the father of the 1 Viscount in 1666 due to indebtedness. The latter started in the Royal Navy as a cabin boy in 1678 (through the influence of well-connected relations) and rose to admiral and recovered the family fortunes. (Hayton, *The House of Commons*, III, 426) A younger son of the 5 Viscount inherited Quendon Hall in 1853 and took the name Cranmer-Byng. **First MP in the 15th century. Four further MPs 1555-1614**.

1. George Byng 1 Viscount Torrington – Plymouth 1705-21
2. Patee Byng 2 Viscount Torrington – Plymouth 1721-27 Bedfordshire 1727-33
3. Robert Byng – Plymouth 1728-39
4. John Byng – Rochester 1751-57

Seats: Southill Park, Bedfordshire (built 17th c., purch. 1693, rebuilt 1724-32, sold 1795); Yotes Court, Kent (acq. by mar. to Master heiress, who acq. it 1543, built 1656-58, acq. by Byngs in 1813, sold 1861); Quendon Hall, Essex (built mid-16th c., remod. 1670-80, acq. by Cranmer-Byngs by mar. 1853, add. 1866, sold 1907)
Estates: Bateman Lord Torrington is listed as under 2000 acres; Cranmer-Byng 3751 (E) 3604
Title: Baronet 1715-
Peers: 10 peers 1721-50 1761-1831 1833-89 1907-44
1 in Cabinet 1727-33

Earl of Strafford (1847- UK)

Origins: The younger son of the 1 Viscount Torrington established a cadet line. His son married Anne Connolly, daughter of Lady Anne Wentworth, heiress of the Earl of Strafford. The Strafford Earldom was revived for Lady Anne's grandson, John Byng.

1. George Byng – Wigan 1768-80 Middlesex 1780-84
2. George Byng – Newport (IoW) 1790 Middlesex 1790-1847
3. George Byng 2 Earl of Strafford – Milbourne Port 1830-32 Chatham 1834-35 1837-52
4. John Byng 1 Earl of Strafford – Poole 1831-35
5. George Byng 3 Earl of Strafford – Tavistock 1852-57 Middlesex 1857-74

Seat: Wrotham Park, Middlesex (purch. 1748, built 1754, add. 1811, remod. 1854, fire 1883, rebuilt, still own)
Estates: Bateman 14994 (E & I) 16349
Titles: Baron Strafford 1835- UK; Baron Byng of Vimy 1919-35 UK; Viscount Byng of Vimy 1928-35 UK
Peers: 7 peers 1835-60 1853-86 1874-1945 1919-35
1 Ld Lt 19th
Notes: Six members of the family in ODNB.

BYSSHE

Origins: Family emerged in the 12th century. **First MP 1426**. Decline set in. In the Tudor period the head of the family was a miller. His son revived the family fortunes as a lawyer and was **elected an MP 1624**. His son, the MP below, was also Garter King of Arms. Kt 1660.

1. Sir Edward Bysshe – Bletchingley 1640-53 Reigate 1654 Gatton 1659 Bletchingley 1661-79

Seat: Smallfield Place, Surrey (medieval, acq. 15th c., rebuilt c. 1600, add. 17th c., reduced to a farm house 18th c. and passed out of the family)
Notes: Two in ODNB.

CADOGAN [Sloane, Stanley]

Earl Cadogan (1718-26 GB; 1800- UK)

Origins: Descended from Welsh farmers. A soldier of fortune went to Ireland 1633 as private secretary of the Lord Deputy. **First {MP 1639}** was seated at Liscarton, Meath. His son was a lawyer, and his grandson a successful general who was made an earl. A successful marriage in the 18th century brought the family its fortune in the form of 90 acres in Chelsea.

1. William Cadogan 1 Earl Cadogan – New Woodstock 1705-16
2. Charles Cadogan 2 Baron Cadogan – Reading 1716-22 Newport (IoW) 1722-26
3. Charles Cadogan 1 Earl Cadogan – Cambridge 1749-54 1755-76
4. Henry Cadogan 4 Earl Cadogan – Reading 1841-47 Dover 1852-57
5. Frederick Cadogan – Cricklade 1868-74
6. George Cadogan 5 Earl Cadogan – Bath 1873-74
7. Henry Cadogan Viscount Chelsea – Bury St. Edmunds 1892-1900
8. Sir Edward Cadogan – Reading 1922-23 Finchley Div. Middlesex 1924-35 Bolton 1940-45

Seats: Culford Hall, Suffolk (built 17th c., remod. 1790-96 and 1806-08, purch. 1889, add. later 19th c., sold 1934); Caversham Park, Oxfordshire (old house, acq. 1714, rebuilt 1723, remod. 1761, sold later 18th c.); Downham Hall, Suffolk (purch. later 18th c., sold 1825, demolished 1923); Liscarton Castle, Meath (built 15-16th c., acq. 1653, sold 1719)
Estates: Bateman under 2000 acres. However, the Earls owned one of the largest and most valuable urban estates in London. Rubinstein – Sarah D'Oyly left £100,000 in probate 1821 along with the Sloane estate of her maternal grandfather to Lord Cadogan. Rubinstein – 2 Earl left £100,000 in probate in 1832. Urban income estimated

at £180,122 pa in 1890s. Total wealth £450,000,000 in 1990. Owned 6,300 acres in 2001. Worth 2 billion pounds 2009.
Titles: Baron Cadogan 1716- GB; Viscount Caversham 1718-26 GB; Viscount Chelsea 1800- UK; Baron Oakley 1831- UK
Peers: 8 peers 1716-1807 1831-1933 1935-45
1 in Cabinet 1886-92 1895-1902
1 KG 19th-20th
1 KT 18th
Notes: Acquired 57,000 acres in Ireland in the mid-17th c. The Culford estate had 11,000 acres attached to it when purch. in 1889 (Pearman, *The Cadogan Estate*, 34, 95). Seven in ODNB.

Sloane-Stanley

Origins: The Sloane family originated probably in Ayrshire, and moved to Ireland in the 17th century as planters. The founder became agent to Viscount Clandeboye and a Receiver of Taxes. His son was a successful barrister and {MP 1692}. A younger son Hans was a physician, President of the Royal Society, and Baronet. The latter purchased the manor of Chelsea in London 1712. Sir Hans Sloane divided his property between two granddaughters. One married Lord Cadogan (see above) and the other a Stanley of Paultons who took the additional name Sloane. The Stanleys began as merchants in Chichester and Southampton in the late 16th and early 17th centuries. The first MP was a shipowner, pawnbroker, and merchant in the Newfoundland trade. Purchased Paultons in 1646.

1. William Stanley – Southampton 1660
2. James Sloane – {Killyleagh 1692-93 1695-99} Thetford 1696-1700
3. Hans Stanley – St. Albans 1743-47 Southampton 1754-80
4. Hans Sloane-Stanley – Newport (IoW) 1768-180 Southampton 1780-84 Christchurch 1788-96 Lostwithiel 1796-1806
5. William Sloane-Stanley – Orford 1807-12 Stockbridge 1830-31

Seat: Paultons, Hampshire (purch. 1646, passed to Sloanes 1780, sold 1944?, fire 1963)
Estates: Bateman 8730 (E) 6270
Title: Baronet 1716-53
Notes: Hans Sloane and Hans Stanley in ODNB.

CAESAR

Origins: Came from Italy to England, naturalized 1558, a physician to Mary I and Elizabeth I. His son was Master of the Rolls and Kt 1603. **First MP 1589. Four further MPs in the early 17th century.**

1. Sir Henry Caesar – Hertfordshire 1660-68
2. Sir Charles Caesar – Hertford 1679 Hertfordshire 1679-81 1689-90
3. Charles Caesar – Hertford 1701-08 1710-15 1722-23 Hertfordshire 1727-34 1736-41

Seat: Bennington (Benington) Place, Hertfordshire (purch. 1616, sold 1744)
Notes: Estates worth £3,500 pa in 1701, but the family was heavily in debt by 1744, and the estates were sold. Eight in ODNB.

CALCRAFT

Origins: Father of the first MP a lawyer and town clerk of Grantham. The first MP made a fortune as an official, sinecure holder, and election agent.

1. Thomas Calcraft – Poole 1761-74
2. John Calcraft – Calne 1766-68 Rochester 1768-72
3. John Calcraft – Wareham 1786-90 1800-06 Rochester 1806-18 Wareham 1818-31 Dorset 1831
4. Sir Granby Calcraft – Wareham 1807-08
5. John Calcraft – Wareham 1820-26 1832-41 1857-59
6. Granby Calcraft – Wareham 1831-32
7. John Calcraft – Wareham 1865-68

Seats: Rempstone Hall, Dorset (medieval, add. 17th c., purch. 1757, passed to descendents in the female line 1901, still own); Ingress Abbey, Kent (purch. 1760, sold 1796)
Estates: Bateman 4854 (E) 6410. Estates said to be worth over £10,000 pa in 1772.
Notes: They made a forune from clay-mining on their estate. Male line extinct 1901. Three in ODNB.

CALMADY

Origins: Landed in Devon since the 14th century. They took the name of Calmady from the village where they originally settled. Lawyers and local officials in the Tudor period. **First MP 1554**. Kt 1630s.

1. Josias Calmady – Okehampton 1660
2. Josias Calmady – Okehampton 1679-81
3. Shilston Calmady – Saltash 1715-22

Seat: Langdon Court, Devon, (medieval, purch. 1555, rebuilt 1577, sold 1876)

CAMPBELL I [Garden, Hume, Mure (Muir)] *SCOTLAND, WALES, & ENGLAND*

Duke of Argyll (1701- S and 1892- UK)

Origins: Sir Colin Campbell was knighted in 1280. His son married the sister of Robert Bruce. Prominent from the early 14th century. Barons 1445. The Campbells became among the most powerful clans in Scotland of which the Dukes of Argyll were and remain Chiefs.

1. James Campbell – [Renfrew 1700-02] Ayr Burghs 1708-10
2. Charles Campbell – [Campbelltown Burgh 1700-07]
3. John Campbell – [Argyllshire 1700-02 1703-07] Scotland 1707-08 Dumbartonshire 1708-22 1725-27
4. John Campbell 4 Duke of Argyll – Buteshire 1713-15 Elgin Burghs 1715-22 1725-27 Dumbartonshire 1727-61
5. William Campbell – Glasgow Burghs 1734-41
6. Charles Campbell – Argyllshire 1736-41
7. John Campbell 5 Duke of Argyll – Glasgow Burghs 1744-61 Dover 1765-66
8. Lord Frederick Campbell – Glasgow Burghs 1761-80 Argyllshire 1780-99 {Thomastown 1767-68 St. Canice 1768-76}
9. Lord William Campbell – Argyllshire 1764-66
10. George Campbell 6 Duke of Argyll – St. Germans 1790-96
11. John Campbell – Ayr Burghs 1794-1807
12. John Campbell 7 Duke of Argyll – Argyllshire 1799-1822
13. John Campbell 9 Duke of Argyll – Argyllshire 1868-78 S. Manchester 1895-1900
14. Lord Colin Campbell – Argyllshire 1878-85

Seats: Inveraray Castle, Argyllshire (held since 1434, medieval, rebuilt 1745-61, remod. 1770-72, fire 1877, remod. 1877-78, still own); Roseneath House (Castle), Dumbartonshire (acq. 1470, remod. 1630, remod. 1784, old house burned 1802, rebuilt 1803-06, contents sold 1940, gutted 1947, demolished 1961); Kilkatrine, Argyllshire; Coombe Bank, Kent (purch. and built 1720, sold c. 1816, now school); Lyston Hall, Essex (purch. 1727 by William Campbell, built c. 1730, owners became Campbell-Lamberts, demolished 1951); Whim House (Hall), Peeblesshire (acq. 1730, built 1734, add. 1759-61, sold 1763, institutional use); Brunstane House (Gilberton), Edinburghshire (built 1565, remod. c. 1639, add. 1672, inher. by mar. early 18th c., remod. 1744, sold 1747); Sudbrook Park, Surrey (purch. 1715, built 1715-19, sold 1767, golf club)
Estates: Bateman 175114 (S) 50842. Worth £87,000,000 in 1990 with 81,000 acres.
Titles: Baron Campbell 1445- S; Earl of Argyll 1457- S; Baron Lorne 1470- S; Baron Kintyre 1626- S; Marquis of Argyll 1641-61 S; Earl of Greenwich 1705-43 E; Earl of Ilay 1706-61 S; Duke of Greenwich 1719-43 GB; Baron Sandridge 1766- GB; Baron Hamilton 1776- GB; Baronet 1627-

Peers: [3 peers 1664-81 1689-1707] 2 Scottish Rep peers 1707-13 1715-70 7 peers 1705-43 1766-1945
7 Lds Lt 18th, 19th, 20th
2 in Cabinet 1767-68 1853-66 1868-74 1880-81
3 KG 18th, 19th, 20th
4 KT 18th, 19th, 20th
Notes: The Campbell family has its own entry in the ODNB. Additionally, the 1st through 9th Earls, 1, 2, 3, 8, and 9 Dukes and six others in ODNB.

Campbell

Origins: Descend from the Breadalbane family (see below) early 17th century.

1. Robert Campbell – Argyllshire 1766-71
2. Alexander Campbell – Anstruther Easter Burghs 1797-1806 Stirling Burghs 1807-1818

Seats: Monzie Castle, Perthshire (built 1634, add. c. 1795-1800, fire 1817, sold 1869); Fonab Castle, Perthshire (resident 17th and 18th c.); Inverawe House, Argyllshire (acq. and built c. 1550s, add. 18th c., remod. 1850-52, sold 1912)
Notes: One in ODNB.

Campbell

Origins: Descended from the 1 Baron Campbell. **First [MP 1628 for Argyllshire]. Another [MP for the county 1628-44].**

1. Sir Duncan Campbell 4 Bt – [Argyllshire 1689-98]
2. Sir James Campbell 5 Bt – [Argyllshire 1703-07] Scotland 1707-08

Seats: Auchinbreck, Argyllshire (acq. 1452, fire 1641); Carnasserie Castle (built 1565-72, purch. 1643, add. 1681, destroyed 1685, sold 19th c.)
Title: Baronet 1628-

Earl of Cawdor (1827- UK)

Origins: Founded by the third son of the 2 Earl of Argyll. **First [MP 1572]. Two further [MPs 1599-1630, one for Nairnshire].** Succeeded in 1698 to Pembrokeshire estates by marriage to a Lort heiress. The Lorts purchased Stackpole Court in 1611. **MP for Pembroke Borough 1659**. Baronets 1662-98.

1. Sir Hew Campbell – [Nairnshire 1661-63 1669-74 1678 1681 1685-86 1689]
2. Alexander Campbell – [Nairnshire 1693-95]

3. John Campbell – Pembrokeshire 1727-47 Nairnshire 1747-54 Inverness Burghs 1754-61 Corfe Castle 1762-68
4. Pryse Campbell – Inverness-shire 1754-61 Nairnshire 1761-68 Cardigan Boroughs 1780-96
5. Alexander Campbell – Nairnshire 1784-85
6. Henry Campbell – Nairnshire 1796-1802 1806-07
7. Sir George Campbell – Carmarthen Boroughs 1806-13
8. John Campbell 1 Earl of Cawdor – Carmarthen Boroughs 1813-21
9. George Pryse Campbell – Nairnshire 1820-26 1830-31
10. John Campbell 2 Earl of Cawdor – Pembrokeshire 1841-60
11. Frederick Campbell 3 Earl of Cawdor – Carmarthenshire 1874-85

Seats: Cawdor Castle, Nairnshire (established there by 1295, medieval castle, add. 1663-85, still own); Stackpole Court, Pembrokeshire (medieval building, purch. by Lorts 1611, passed to Campbells by mar. 1698, rebuilt 18th c., enlarged 1821, demolished 1962 and Welsh estates sold); Golden Grove, Carmarthenshire (inherited from John Vaughan MP c. 1700, no relation, see Vaughan Earls of Carbery, sold mid-1980s)
Estates: Bateman 101657 (W & S) 44662. Worth £60,000,000 in 1990 with 56,000 acres (sold 36,000 acres in Wales in 1976, 21,000 acres in 1980s).
Titles: Baron Cawdor 1796- GB; Viscount Emlyn 1827- UK
Peers: 6 peers 1796-1914 1921-45
3 Lds Lt 19th, 20th
1 in Cabinet 1905
Notes: The Campbells of Cawdor family have their own entry in ODNB. Additionally two others in ODNB.

Campbell

Origins: Descended from the second son of the 3 Earl of Argyll.

1. Sir Duncan Campbell – Argyllshire 1747-54
2. Dugald Campbell – Argyllshire 1754-63
3. Duncan Campbell – Ayr Burghs 1809-18

Seats; Lochnell, Argyllshire (built late 17th c, add. 1737-39 and 1816-28, sold 1912); Ballimore House, Argyllshire (rebuilt c. 1832, remod. 1898-99, sold 1899, ruin)
Estates: Bateman 35000 (S) 6801. Junior lines in Bateman at Stonefield Castle, Argyllshire (acq. 18th c., new house 1836-40, sold 1949); Barbreck House, Argyllshire (acq. by Campbells 15th c., forfeited 1732 and acquired by another branch later 18th c., built 1790, add. 19th c., sold 19th c.), and Jura, Argyllshire (acq. 1506, sold 20th c., Jura house sold 1938) total 100555 (S) 11188
Notes: Barbreck line in financial difficulties mid-19th c.

Marquis of Breadalbane (1806-62 UK; 1885-1922 UK)

Origins: Descended from a younger son of the 1 Baron Campbell. Acquired considerable wealth by diverting government funds for personal purposes in the 17th and 18th centuries. **First [MP 1560] Two other [MPs 1592-1647 for Argyllshire].**

1. John Campbell 1 Earl of Breadalbane – [Argyllshire 1661-63 1669-74]
2. Alexander Campbell – [Argyllshire 1678]
3. John Campbell 3 Earl of Breadalbane – Saltash 1727-41 Orford 1741-45
4. John Campbell 2 Marquis of Breadalbane – Okehampton 1820-26 Perthshire 1832-34

Seats: Taymouth Castle (Balloch Castle), Perthshire (built 1559, rebuilt c. 1742, rebuilt 1806-10 add. 1818-21, remod. 1842, sold 1920, hotel); Glenorchy (Kilchurn Castle), Argyllshire (acq. 1432, built c. 1450, add. 16th and 17th c., remod. c. 1690-98, abandoned c. 1760, ruin); Ardmaddy Castle, Argyllshire (built 15th c., purch. 1692, restored 1737, add. 1790 and 1837, remod. 1862, sold 1933, part demolished 1979); Langton House, Berwickshire (medieval, purch. c. 1860, rebuilt 1860-62, family departed 1920, unroofed 1930, demolished c. 1950)
Estates: Bateman 438358 (S) 58292. Rubinstein – the 1 Marquis left £300,000 in probate in 1834.
Titles: Earl of Breadalbane 1677- S; Baronet 1625-
Peers: [1 peer 1677-1707] 4 Scottish Rep peers 1713-15 1736-47 1752-68 1774-80 1784-1806
3 peers 1806-62 1873-1922
3 Lds Lt 18th, 19th, 20th
1 KG 19th-20th
1 KT 19th
Notes: The family has an entry in ODNB plus one other. The 1 and 3 Earls and the 2 Marquis and four others also in ODNB.

Campbell

Origins: Cadet of the Earls of Breadalbane.

1. John Campbell - [Argyllshire 1644 1661-63]
2. Alexander Campbell – Fowey 1819-20

Seats: Barcaldine Castle (House), Argyllshire (built 1601-09, castle abandoned 1724, new house c. 1724, add. 1733, rebuilt c. 1759, remod. 1830s, sold 1842, repurch. 1896, restored 1910, sold, now hotel); Ardchattan(e) Priory, Argyllshire (built c. 1230, add. late 15th-early 16th c., acq. 1580, converted to a house c. 1602, remod. mid-19th c.)
Estates: Bateman 20000 (S) 2078

Title: Baronet 1831-
Notes: Due to financial difficulties 30,000 acres were sold 1842 (Forman, *Scottish Country Houses and Castles*, 142).

Baron Colgrain (1946- UK; Life Peerage 1966-94)

Origins: Cadet of the Campbells of Ardchattan(e). West India merchants and shipowners in Glasgow 18th and 19th centuries. Manchester merchants mid-19th century.

1. Alexander Campbell – Launceston 1865-68

Seats: Possil, Lanarkshire (built c. 1700, acq. 1808, later sold c. 1849); Werrington Park, Cornwall (built 1730s, purch. 1864, sold 1868); Camis Eskan, Dumbartonshire (built 1648, purch. 1836, remod. 1915, sold 1946)
Estates: Bateman 2124 (S) 2429. The family owned cane fields in British Guiana worth over one million pounds in the 1930s.

Garden

Origins: The Gardens were an old family that came to office in the 16th century. Fortunes revived c. 1650s by a soldier of fortune who fought in Sweden. The Gardens succeeded by marriage in the 18th century to the estates of the Campbells of Glenlyon, a cadet line of Sir Colin Campbell of Glenorchy (see Breadalbane), and took the name Campbell.

1. Alexander Garden – Aberdeenshire 1768-85

Seats: Troup House, Banffshire (purch. 1654, rebuilt 1763, rebuilt 1897, now a school); Glenlyon, Perthshire (acq. by mar. 18th c., sold 1885)
Estates: Bateman 20063 (S) 7414

Campbell

Origins: Cadet of Sir Colin Campbell of Glenorchy in the 16th century (see Breadablane).

1. Sir Colin Campbell 1 Bt – [Inverary Burgh 1669-74 Perthshire 1690-1702]

Seats: Kilbryde Castle, Perthshire (built c. 1460, rebuilt 17th c., acq. 1643/59, add. 1861, still own); Aberuchil(l) Castle, Perthshire (acq. 1596, built 1602, sold 1642)
Title: Baronet 1668-

Baron Blythswood (1892-1940 UK)

Origins: A cadet of the Ardkinglas line (see below). Merchants and Provosts of Glasgow in the 17th century. Blythswood followed a tangled genealogical course in the 18th and 19th centuries. Mary Campbell heiress to Blythswood, married Colin Douglas of Mains (cadet of the Earls of Morton, see that family) who took the name Campbell. On the extinction of the main line Blythswood passed in 1767 to Douglas cousins. The 17th Douglas laird of Mains succeeded a cousin as 12th laird of Blythswood in 1838. His son was created Baron Blythswood. His second son succeeded to Douglas Support as heir in entail of Margaret Duchess of Douglas, sister of the Blythswood heir.

1. Colin Campbell – [Renfrew Burgh 1703-07]
2. Archibald Campbell – Glasgow Burghs 1806-09 Elgin Burghs 1812 Perth Burghs 1818-20 Glasgow Burghs 1820-31
3. Archibald Campbell 1 Baron Blythswood – Renfrewshire 1873-74 W. Renfrewshire 1885-92

Seats: Blythswood House, Renfrewshire (purch. 1634, built 1820-21, demolished 1935); Douglas Support (orig. Rosehall, renamed Douglas Support later 18th c.), Lanarkshire (built 17th and 18th c., add. 19th c., demolished 20th c.)
Estates: Bateman 15886 (S) 6455. This income does not reflect the great value of the urban property in Glasgow over which the city expanded in the 19th century that the family owned.
Title: Baronet 1880-1908
Peer: 1 peer 1892-1940
1 Ld Lt 20th
Notes: 1 Baron in ODNB.

Campbell of Carrick

Origins: Cadet of the Dukes of Argyll. The head of the family bore the honorific “Captain of Carrick”. **First [MP 1639].**

1. John Campbell Captain of Carrick – [Argyllshire 1669-74 1678 1681 1689-1702]

Seat: Carrick Castle, Argyllshire (built late 14th c., add. 16th c and early 17th c., burned 1685, ruin)

Campbell

Origins: Cadet of Colin Campbell of Lochow. **First [MP 1650].**

1. John Campbell – [Argyllshire 1681]
2. Sir Ilay Campbell 1 Bt – Glasgow Burghs 1784-89
3. John Campbell – Dumbartonshire 1826-30
4. Sir Archibald Campbell 3 Bt – Argyllshire 1851-57

Seats: Garscube House, Dumbartonshire (built 17th c., acq. 1687, new house 1827, sold 1948, demolished 1955); Succoth, Dumbartonshire (purch. 1616, moved to Garscube 1687)
Estates: Bateman 10601 (S) 17916. Owned 12,200 acres in 1996.
Title: Baronet 1808-
Notes: A famous legal family in the 18th and 19th centuries in the Court of Session. One in ODNB.

Earl of Loudon (1633- S)

Origins: A cadet of Sir Colin Campbell of Lochow (13th century). **First [MP 1571]. Another [MP 1579-99].** Succeeded to the Mure (Muir) of Rowallan estates by marriage. The Muirs were soldiers by 1263. One fell at Flodden in 1513 and another at Pinkie. **First [MP 1560], and another for [Ayrshire 1643-44].** William Muir [MP 1690-98] was the 16th and last laird. For a time the Earldom was merged with the Marquessate of Hastings (see Rawdon-Hastings).

1. William Muir – [Ayrshire 1690-98]
2. John Campbell – [Ayrshire 1700-02]
3. James Campbell – Ayrshire 1727-41
4. James Mure-Campbell 5 Earl of Loudon – Ayrshire 1754-61

Seats: Loudoun (Loudon) Castle, Ayrshire (medieval, add. 1601, rebuilt 1804-11, fire 1941, ruin, still own); Rowallan Castle, Ayrshire (acq. by Muirs 1263, rebuilt c. 1560, add. mid. 17th c., acq. by mar. by Campbells 1698, passed by mar. to Cunninghams in 19th c.); Lawers House, Perthshire (built 1724-26 and 1737-44, sold later 18th c.)
Estates: Bateman 18638 (S) 17545. Owned 4,400 acres in 1996.
Title: Baron Loudon 1601- S
Peers: [1 peer 1696-1707] 2 Scottish Rep peers 1707-31 1734-82
1 Ldt Lt 18th
1 in the Cabinet Council 1705-08
1 KT 18th
Notes: 1, 3, 4 Earls and one other in ODNB.

Campbell

Origins: Ardkinglas was granted by Sir Colin Campbell to his son Caileeen Oig in 1396. **First [MP for Argyllshire 1646-49].**

1. Sir Colin Campbell 1 Bt – [Argyllshire 1693-1702]
2. Sir James Campbell 2 Bt – [Argyllshire 1703-07] Scotland 1707-08 Argyllshire 1708-34 Stirlingshire 1734-41

Seats: Ardkinglas, Argyllshire (acq. and built 1396, passed to Livingstones of Glentirran (see) 1752, who took the additional name Campbell); Gargunnock House, Stirlingshire (built 1580, add. 17th c., remod. 1794, sold 1835)
Title: Baronet 1679-1752
Notes: The laird was attainted in 1662, but the Duke of Argyll secured restoration for the 10th laird, 1 Baronet. The male line failed with the 11th laird, and the estates were broken up among a number of heirs. A cadet line (of Dunoon) succeeded to English estates in 1843 (see Wyndham).

Campbell

Origins: Distant kinsmen of the Dukes of Argyll, with whom they became close again in the early 18th century as bankers and great Atlantic trade merchants in Glasgow. (Hayton, *The House of Commons*, III, 444)

1. Daniel Campbell – [Inverary 1703-07] Scotland 1707-08 Glasgow Burghs 1716-27 1728-34
2. John Campbell – Edinburgh 1721-34
3. Daniel Campbell – Lanarkshire 1760-68
4. John Campbell – Ayr Burghs 1807-09
5. Walter Campbell – Argyllshire 1822-32 1835-41

Seats: Shawfield, Lanarkshire (purch. 1706, sold c. 1800); Skipness Castle, Argyllshire (built 13th c., acq. 1502, add. 16th c., abandoned end of 17th c., much demolished 18th c.); Ardentinny, Argyllshire; Islay House, Argyllshire (built 1677, purch. 1726, add. c. 1731, add. c. 1760, add. 1841-45, sold 1852); Woodhall House, Lanarkshire (built 1711-27, burned early 20th c., demolished 1924)
Notes: Campbells bankrupt 1848.

Campbell

Origins: Cadet of the Dukes of Argyll.

1. Sir Archibald Campbell – Stirling Burghs 1774-80 1789-91
2. Sir James Campbell – Stirling Burghs 1780-89

Seats: Tuerechan, Argyllshire (acq. 17th c.); Inverneil House, Argyllshire (estate acq. 1480, built 18th-19th c., add. c. 1890, sold 1955)
Estates: Bateman 11810 (S) 2977
Title: Baronet 1818-19
Notes: The heads of the family are Hereditary Ushers of the White Rod for Scotland. Two in ODNB.

CAMPBELL II *SCOTLAND*

<u>Baron Stratheden and Campbell</u> (1836- and 1859- UK)

Origins: Claimed medieval descent from the Campbell's Argyll - dubious. Clergymen in 18th century. The first MP and Baron was a lawyer and Lord Chancellor.

1. John Campbell 1 Baron Stratheden – Stafford 1830-32 Dudley 1832-34 Edinburgh 1834-41
2. William Campbell 2 Baron Stratheden – Cambridge 1847-52 Harwich 1859-60
3. Sir George Campbell – Kirkcaldy 1875-92

Seat: Hartrigge House, Roxburghshire (built 1854, add. 1938, demolished)
Estates: 1 Baron left £100,000 in 1861.
Peers: 4 peers 1841-1918 1920-45
1 in Cabinet 1846-50 1859-61
Notes: Two in ODNB.

CAMPION

Origins: A lawyer purchased monastic property under Elizabeth I. Also London merchants and clothiers and continued as merchants into the 18th-19th centuries. **First MP 1586. One other MP 1621-48.**

1. William Campion – Seaford 1689-98 Kent 1701-02
2. Henry Campion – East Grinstead 1708-10 Bossiney 1710-13 Sussex 1713-15
3. William Campion – Lewes Div. Sussex 1910-24

Seat: Danny (Park), Sussex (medieval house, rebuilt 1595, passed to Campions from Courthorpes by mar. 1725, remod. c. 1725-28, sold 1955, flats)
Estates: Bateman 6832 (E) 7891. Rubinstein - William Campion left £140,000 in probate 1818 and Henry Campion left £140,000 in 1836.

CANNING *IRELAND & ENGLAND*

Earl Canning (1859-62 UK)

Origins: Mechants and mayors of Bristol in the 14th and 15th centuries. **First MP for Bristol 1383. Two further MPs 1439-61,** including a grocer in London. Kt and Lord Mayor of London 1456. A younger son went to Ireland under Elizabeth I and acquired Garvagh. A barrister in the later 18th century, who was disinherited, produced a son who became Prime Minister (and thence the earldom). Various branches combined here.

1. George Canning – Newton (IoW) 1793-96 Wendover 1796-1802 Tralee 1802-06 Newton 1806-07 Hastings 1807-12 Liverpool 1812-22 Harwich 1823-26 Newton 1826-27 Seaford 1827
2. George Canning 1 Baron Garvagh – Sligo 1806-12 Petersfield 1812-20
3. Stratford Canning 1 Viscount Stratford – Old Sarum 1828-30
4. C. J. Canning 1 Earl Canning – Warwick 1836-37

Seats: Garvagh House, Londonderry (acq. later 16th century, built early 17th c., add. 18th c., sold and demolished 20th c.); Frant Court, Kent (acq. and built 1858, remod. c. 1870, sold late 19th c.); Foxcote, Warwickshire (acq. by mar. 15th c., built early 18th c., add. late 18th c., passed by mar. to Howards 1843)
Estates: Bateman 15406 (I) 8725
Titles: Baron Garvagh 1818- I; Viscount Canning 1826-62 UK; Viscount Stratford de Redcliffe 1852-80 UK
Peers: 2 peers 1837-62 1852-80
1 Ld Lt 19th
2 in cabinet 1807-09 1816-27 1855
2 KG 19th
Notes: Resident in England post WWI. The branch of the Cannings at Foxcote were Roman Catholic. 3 in ODNB.

CAPEL (Capell) [Coningsby]

Earl of Essex (1661- E)

Origins: Gentry in the 12th century. Merchants and drapers in London and Lord Mayor of London and Kt 1503. Purchased estates in Essex and Hertfordshire where three generations became High Sheriffs. **First MP 1491. Seven further MPs 1547-1626, including kts of the shire for Essex, Somerset, and Hertfordshire.** The 1 Baron Capel inherited Cassiobury by marriage with a Morrison heiress. The first Morrison acquired wealth as an official and diplomat under Henry VIII. **Three MPs 1539-1628.** Baronet 1611-28.

1. Henry Capel 1 Baron Tewkesbury – Tewkesbury 1660-81
2. George Capel-Coningsby 5 Earl of Essex – Westminster 1779-80 Lostwithiel 1781-84 Okehampton 1785-90 Radnor Boroughs 1794-99

Seats: Cassiobury Park (House), Hertfordshire (Morrisons acq. 1545, built 1540s-50s, acq. by Capels 1632 by mar., add. 1674-75, rebuilt c. 1800, sold 1922, demolished c. 1927); Hampton Court, Herefordshire (built 1435, inher. by mar. 1781, sold 1810)
Estates: Bateman 14870 (E & I) 18936. Worth c. £7,000 pa in 1649. Rubinstein - 5 Earl left £120,000 in probate in 1839.
Titles: Baron Capel of Hadam and Viscount Maldon 1641- E; Baron Capel of Tewkesbury 1692-96 E
Peers: 9 peers 1660-83 1691-1710 1692-96 1718-43 1753-1945
5 Lds Lt 17th, 18th, 19th
2 in Cabinet Council 1672-77 1679 1679-81 1693-96
1 KG 18th
1 KT 18th
Notes: 3 in ODNB.

Earl Coningsby (1719-61 GB)

Origins: Landowners since the reign of Edward I. A Lord Chief Justice (d. 1535) purchased lands at the Dissolution. Developed a local weaving industry in the mid-16th century. **First MP 1344 for Warwickshire. Nine further MPs 1536-1641, some kts of the shire**. The Coningsby estates passed by marriage to the 5 Earl of Essex in 1781.

1. Thomas Coningsby 1 Earl Coningsby – Leominster 1679-81 1685-87 1689-1710 1715-16

Seat: Hampton Court, Herefordshire (built 1435, purch. 1509, remod. c. 1680 and 1706-10, passed by mar. to the Earl of Essex 1781, see above)
Estates: Worth £4000 pa in c. 1660.
Peers: {1 peer 1692-1729} 1 peer 1716-29
1 Ld Lt 18th
1 in Cabinet Council 1690-92
Notes: Six in ODNB.

CAREW I [Pole]

Carew

Origins: Originally Welsh and dated from a very early period. Justiciar of Ireland in the 14th century. Knighted at Bosworth and rose high under the Tudors. **First MP 1529. Fourteen further MPs 1542-1643 including five kts of the shire.** Baron 1605.

1. Thomas Carew – Callington 1659 Mitchell 1660 Exeter 1681
2. Sr John Carew 3 Bt – Cornwall 1660 Bodmin 1661-79 Lostwithiel 1679-81 Cornwall 1689-90 Saltash 1690-92
3. Richard Carew – Callington 1679-81 Saltash 1690-91
4. Thomas Carew – Saltash 1701-05
5. Sir William Carew 5 Bt – Saltash 1711-13 Cornwall 1713-44
6. Sir Coventry Carew 6 Bt – Cornwall 1744-48
7. Reginald Pole-Carew – Penryn 1782-84 Reigate 1787-90 Lostwithiel 1790-96 Fowey 1796-99 1802-12 Lostwithiel 1812-16
8. William Pole-Carew – E. Cornwall 1845-52
9. Sir Reginald Pole-Carew – Bodmin Div. Cornwall 1910-16

Seat: Antony House, Cornwall (acq. by mar. late 15th c., rebuilt 1711-24, passed to Poles by mar. 1772, add. 1905, NT 1962)
Estates: Bateman 4288 (E) 6401
Titles: Baron Carew 1605-29 E; Earl of Totnes 1626-29 E; Baronet 1641-1748
Notes: For a cadet line see Throckmorton. Fifteen in ODNB.

Pole

Origins: The family held land in Devon from the 14th century. **First MP 1545. Three additional MPs 1586-1646.** On the death of Sir Coventry Carew 6 Bt in 1772 Antony passed to Reginald Pole, great-great-grandson on the maternal side of Sir John Carew 3 Bt. He took the name Pole-Carew. In 1926 the Poles of Shute became extinct and their estates passed to the Pole-Carews of Antony.

1. Sir Courteny Pole 2 Bt – Honiton 1661-79
2. Sir John Pole 3 Bt – Lyme Regis 1685-87 1689-90 Bossiney 1698-1700 Devon 1701-02 East Looe 1702-05 Newport 1707-08
3. Sir William Pole 4 Bt – Newport 1701-02 Camelford 1704-08 Newport 1708-10 Devon 1710-12 Bossiney 1713-15 Honiton 1716-27 1731-34
4. Sir John Pole 6 Bt – West Looe 1790-96
5. Sir Charles Pole 1 Bt – Newark 1802-06 Plymouth 1806-18

Seats: Shute (Barton), Devon (built c. 1380, add. late 15th c., leased from 1560 by Poles, add. 1560s, purch. 1780, new house built 1787, passed to Carews 1926, NT 1955); Aldenham Abbey, Hertfordshire (purch. 1812, passed by marriage to William Stuart – Bute)
Estates: Bateman 5846 (E) 7786
Titles: Baronet 1628-1926; 1801-30
Notes: The Poles had Irish estates (Ballyfin) left to a cousin, William Wellesley (Pole) in 1781. See Wellelsey. Two in ODNB.

Carew

Origins: A cadet line 14th century.

1. Sir Thomas Carew 1 Bt – Tiverton 1661-73
2. Charles Carew – N. E. Div. Devon 1915-22

Seats: Haccombe House, Devon (acq. by mar. by 15th c., old house, rebuilt 18th c., held into 20th c.); Bickleigh Castle, Devon (medieval, acq. early 16th c., slighted 1640s, part rebuilt c. 1660, sold 1923); Tiverton Castle, Devon (medieval castle, remod. 17th c., acq. by mar. 1728, sold 1922); Marley House, Devon (built 18th c., acq. by ma. 1806, remod. 19th c., sold c. 1920s)
Estates: Bateman 10889 (E) 15148
Title: Baronet 1661-

Carew

Origins: A cadet of the Carews of Antony. It is claimed that Crowcombe has never been bought or sold since the Conquest. The de Crowcombes lasted until Edward III. Their heiress married a Bickham, who carried it to a Carew of Camerton in the mid-16th century. (*Country Life*, 73, p. 414)

1. Thomas Carew – Minehead 1739-47

Seat: Crowcombe Court, Somerset (acq. mid-16th c., rebuilt 1723-39, passed to Myddeltons 1886, fire 1963, restored)
Estates: Bateman 6991 (E & W) 7758
Notes: The last male Carew died in 1886, when the estates passed by marriage to a younger son of the 1 Lord Kesteven (see Myddelton).

CAREW II *IRELAND*

Baron Carew (1834- I and 1838- UK)

Origins: Claimed descent from the Carew I family. Obtained estates in Wexford 1668. Waterford merchants in the 17th and 18th century. Sheriff 1686.

1. Robert Carew – {Dungarvon 1713-21}
2. Robert Carew – {Waterford 1739-40}
3. Shapland Carew – {Waterford 1748-76}
4. Robert Carew – {Waterford 1776-1800} County Wexford 1806-07
5. Robert Carew 1 Baron Carew – County Wexford 1812-30 1831-34
6. Robert Carew 2 Baron Carew – County Waterford 1840-47

Seats: Castle Boro (Castleborough), Wexford (acq. 1668, new house 1787, burned 1840, new house 1848 cost £84,000, contents sold 1919, burned 1923, ruin); Woodstown, Waterford (older house, acq. 19th c., add. 1823, sold 1905)
Estates: Bateman 20966 (I) 11862. Worth £6,000 pa in c. 1800. Owned 700 acres in 2001.
Peers: 6 peers 1838-1945
2 Lds Lt 19th
2 KP 19th

Carew

Origins: Descended in the 18th century from a younger son of Robert Carew, ancestor of the Barons Carew.

1. Thomas Carew – {Dungarvon 1761-68}
2. Robert Carew – {Dungarvon 1768-76}

Seat: Ballinamona Park, Waterford (built 1488, acq. and rebuilt mid-18th c., add. 1866, fire and rebuilt 1894, still resident 1950s)
Estates: 2315 (I) 1578 in 1878. Worth £1,000 pa c. 1790.

CARLETON I *IRELAND & ENGLAND*

Baron Dorchester (1786-1897 GB 1899-1963 UK)

Origins: In Ireland in the late 17th century. 1 Baron rose by ability to be a general and Governor in Canada 1766.

No MPs

Seat: Greywell Hill House, Hampshire (built 17th c., purch. 1787, rebuilt c. 1824, passed by mar. to Earl of Malmesbury 1963)
Estates: Bateman 14521 (I) 2955
Peers: 4 peers 1786-1808 1832-97 1926-45
Notes: The daughter of the 3 Baron was created Baroness Dorchester in her own right in 1899 and she succeeded to the estates. Two in ODNB.

CARLETON II *IRELAND*

Viscount Carleton (1797-1826 I)

Origins: Merchants in Cork in the 18th century. Sheriff 1717. The 1 Viscount became Chief Justice of the Common Pleas in Ireland.

1. George Carleton – {Enniscorthy 1662-66}
2. Christopher Carleton – {Wicklow 1695-99 1703-04}
3. Hugh Carleton 1 Viscount Carleton – {Tuam 1772-76 Philipstown 1776-83 Naas 1783-87}

Seat: Clare, Tipperary (acq. 18th c., resident until c. 1826)
Estates: 994 (I) 720 in 1878.
Title: Baron Carleton 1789-1826 I
Peers: {1 peer 1789-1800} 1 Irish Rep peer 1801-26
Notes: The 1 Viscount had no issue. Family resident in England post 1918. One in ODNB.

CARNEGIE *SCOTLAND*

Earl of Southesk (1633- S)

Origins: First granted land in Forfarshire 1358. Married heiress to Kinnaird Castle and succeeded to the estates 1410. **First [MP 1591]. Four additional [MPs 1600-47], including two for Forfarshire and one for Kincardineshire.**

1. Sir David Carnegie 1 Bt – [Kincardineshire 1667 1669-74]
2. Sir James Carnegie 3 Bt – Kincardineshire 1741-65
3. Sir David Carnegie 4 Bt – Aberdeenshire 1784-90 Forfarshire 1796-1805
4. Sir James Carnegie 5 Bt – Aberdeen Burghs 1830-31
5. Charles Carnegie – Forfarshire 1860-72

Seats: Kinnaird Castle, Forfarshire (acq. 1410, built 15th c., add. 1610, roofless by 1855); Pittarrow House, Kincardineshire (medieval, purch. 1631 for £3277, demolished 1802); Crimonmogate, Aberdeenshire (built 1825, add. 1860, acq. by mar. to Bannerman

heiress 1891, sold 1996); Elsick House, Kincardineshire (medieval, acq. by mar. to Bannerman heiress 1891, rebuilt c. 1900, still own – see Duff)
Estates: Bateman 22699 (S) 21917. 4,500 acres in 1996.
Titles: Baron Carnegie 1616- S; Baron Balinhard 1869- UK; Baronet 1663-
Peers: [3 peers 1660-88 1690] 3 peers 1869-1945
2 Lds Lt 18th, 19th
1 KT 19th
Notes: The 5 Earl was "out" in 1715. The title was attainted and estates forfeited 1716. Estates bought back 1740. Attainder on Earldon reversed 1855. The 11 Earl of Southesk married Princess Maud of Fife in 1923, the daughter of the Duke of Fife and the Princess Royal. The 3 Duke of Fife became 12 Earl of Southesk (see Duff). Four in ODNB.

<u>Earl of Northesk</u> (1666- S)

Origins: Cadet line descended from a younger brother of the 1 Earl of Southesk.

1. James Carnegie – [possibly Forfar Burghs 1669-74 1678 Forfarshire 1686 1698-1701 1703-07]
2. Swynfen Carnegie – Stafford 1841-47
3. Douglas Carnegie – Winchester 1916-18

Seats: Ethie House (Castle), Forfarshire (built by early 16th c., acq. 1549, sold 1928); Inglismaldie, Kincardineshire (built late 16th c., acq. 1635, sold 1693); Longwood House (Rosehill), Hampshire (acq. by mar. 1788, rebuilt 1879-80, sold c. 1939, demolished 1960s)
Estates: Bateman 7735 (S & E) 9758
Titles: Baron Lours, Rosehill, & Inglismaddie 1639- S; Earl of Ethie 1647-66 S
Peers: [4 peers 1660-67 1669-79 1681-88 1698-1707] 4 Scottish Rep peers 1708-15 1796-1807 1830-31 1885-91 1900-21
Notes: Two in ODNB.

<u>Carnegie</u>

Origins: Descended from a younger son of the 1 Earl of Northesk.

1. Sir John Carnegie – [Forfarshire 1661-63]
2. John Carnegie – Forfarshire 1708-16

Seats: Boysack, Forfarshire (purch. 17th c., resident 19th c.); Kimblethmont, Forfarshire (purch. 1678)
Estates: Bateman 3670 (S) 5171

Carnegie

Origins: Descended for the youngest brother of the 1 Earl of Southesk

1. James Carnegie – [Forfarshire 1669-74 1681 1685-86]

Seat: Balnamoon, Forfarshire (medieval, acq. 16th c., passed by mar. to Arbuthnots later 19th c.)
Estates: Bateman 8066 (S) 5204. 3,500 acres in 1996

CARR [Buckworth] *IRELAND*

Carr

Origins: Founder went to Ireland from Yorkshire in the early 17th century as an official.

1. George Carr – {Naas 1661-62}
2. Thomas Carr – {Carrick 1661-66}
3. Thomas Carr – {Newtown Limavady 1703-13}
4. William Buckworth Carr – {Cashel 1739-53}

Seat: Donore House, Kildare (acq. 17th c., sold 18th c., now a ruin)

Buckworth

Origins: Richard Buckworth was a soldier. The Carr estates passed by marriage to the Buckworths in the early 18th century, and they took the additional name Carr.

1. Richard Buckworth – {Cashel 1715-38}

Seat: Lisheen, Tipperary (acq. late 17th or early 18th c., sold pre-1840, burned 1900)

CARR ELLISON

Ellison

Origins: Merchants in Newcastle from the 14th century. Acquired coal mines in the 18th and 19th centuries. Estates passed to the James family in the mid-19th century (see James) and then (due to a Carr/Ellison marriage of 1813) to the Carrs in 1870 (from a marriage of 1758).

1. Robert Ellison – Newcastle-upon-Tyne 1647 1660

2. Cuthburt Ellison – Shaftesbury 1747-54
3. Cuthburt Ellison – Newcastle-unpon-Tyne 1812-30

Seats: Hebburn Hall, Durham (medieval, add. 16th and 17th c., purch. c. 1650, rebuilt 1790, remod. 19th c., family departed but retained estate, house became a hospital); Gateshead Park, Durham (acq. by mar. 1729 from Cotesworths who purch. 1716, leased out from 1825, sold 1857, burned 1891)
Notes: Cadet branch of the Ellisons went to Ireland, see Macartney.

Carr

Origins: Merchants in Newcastle from the 14th century, Mayor 1481. **First MP 1491 for Newcastle. An additional MP for Newcastle 1571**. Grew richer in the 1660s and became mining engineers and acquired mines.

1. Sir Ralph Carr – Newcastle-upon-Tyne 1679-81 1689-95
2. William Carr – Newcastle-upon-Tyne 1690-1710
3. William Carr – Newcastle-upon-Tyne 1722-27 1729-34

Seats: Dunston Hill Hall, Durham (old house, purch. 1704, add. mid-18th c., later became a hospital); Hebburn Hall, Durham (see above); Hedgeley Hall, Northumberland (old house, purch. and rebuilt 1786, remod. 19th c., and add. 1910-14, still owned by Carr-Ellison family 2015)
Estates: Bateman 10135 (E) 12137. Rubinstein – Ralph Carr left £140,000 in probate in 1837.
Notes: One in ODNB.

CARTER I [Shaen, Tilson] *IRELAND*

Carter

Origins: The founder served at the Battle of Boyne under William III 1690. His son was Master of the Rolls 1732.

1. Thomas Carter – {Fethard 1695-99 Portarlington 1703-13}
2. Thomas Carter – {Trim 1719-27 Hillsborough 1727-60}
3. Thomas Carter – {Old Leighlin 1745-60}

Seats: Castle Martin, Kildare (built c. 1720, acq. 1730, sold 1854); Robertstown, Meath (purch. 1702, sold 1830); Watlington Park, Oxfordshire (sold 1877); Shaen Manor, Mayo (built 17th c., acq. by mar. 1750, resident 19th c.)
Estates: 42538 (I) 4153. Worth £4,000 pa in the 18th c. £2500 pa in 1850.
Notes: The Carters emigrated to South America in the late 19th century. One in ODNB.

<u>Shaen</u> (Shane)

Origins: Sir James Shaen, reputedly the son of a blacksmith, was knighted in the late 16th century by Lord Deputy Chichester for assistance as a lawyer in land conveyancing. The family acquired considerable estates during and after the Civil War. Sheriff 1655. Sir James's grandson was appointed Receiver General for Leinster 1660, Surveyor General 1668 and was Farmer General of the Revenue 1662. In supervising land transfers much clung to the Shaen's fingers. (*The Irish Builder*, July 1, 1893, vol. 35, p. 150) The heiress of Sir Arthur Shaen 2 Bt married in 1750 Henry Carter of Castle Martin, who succeeded to the Shaen estates.

1. Sir James Shaen 1 Bt – {Clonmell 1661-66 Baltinglass 1692-93 1695}
2. Sir Arthur Shaen 2 Bt – {Lismore 1692-93 1695-99 1703-25}

Seats: Shaen Manor, Mayo (acq. and built 17th c., passed to Carters by mar. 1750); Kilmore, Roscommon (acq. mid-17th c., passed by mar. to Carters 1750); Bishopstone, Westmeath (acq. mid 17th c., passed to Carters 1750)
Estates: Worth £1600 pa in 1725.
Title: Baronet 1663-1725
Notes: One in ODNB.

<u>Tilson</u>

Origins: Bishop of Elphin in the 17th century. Civil servants in the 18th century. Purchased estates 1723. The heiress of John Tilson married Thomas Shaen Carter in 1842, and the Carters succeeded to the Tilson estates.

1. Christopher Tilson – Cricklade 1727-34

Seats: Watlington Park, Oxfordshire (built 1675, purch. 1758 by Tilson for £15,100, new house c. 1750, passed by mar. to Carters 1842, sold 1877); Hampton Poyle, Oxfordshire (purch. 1723, sold 1795 for £25,000)
Notes: One in ODNB.

CARTER II *WALES & ENGLAND*

Origins: John Carter was a linen draper and soldier in the Civil War. High Sheriff 1650, Kt 1660. He acquired Kinmel by marriage 1647 from the Holland family.

1. John Carter – Denbigh 1654 1656 1659 1660
2. William Carter – Kingston-u-Hull 1741-44
3. Thomas Carter – Kingston-u-Hull 1747-54

Seats: Kinmel, Denbighshire (acq. by mar. 1647, sold 1789); Redbourne Hall, Lincolnshire (built 18th c., passed to the Dukes of St. Albans via a Carter heiress 18th c.)

CARTER III [Bonham]

Carter

Origins: The father of the first MP was a brewer in Portsmouth in the 18th century. John Carter MP succeded to the estates of his cousin Thomas Bonham in 1826 (a brewer in Petersfield who left £120,000 in probate) and took the additional name Bonham. The Carters were also brewers. Kt 1773. The family produced many mayors of Portsmouth.

1. John Bonham Carter – Portsmouth 1816-38
2. John Bonham Carter – Winchester 1847-74
3. Mark Bonham Carter 1 Baron Bonham-Carter – Torrington Div. Devon 1958-59

Seats: Adhurst St. Mary, Hampshire (purch. and built 1858, sold 1993); Buriton Manor (then House), Hampshire (built c. 1600, remod. early 18th c., purch. by the Bonhams 1798, passed by mar. to Carters 1826, rebuilt 1910, sold 1927 and 1957)
Bateman 5622 (E) 6260. Thomas Carter (d.1826) left £120,000. John Bonham Carter MP (d. 1838) also left £120,000. The Bonham estate was 6,500 acres. (Rubinstein, "The Structure of Wealth-holding in Britain 1809-39", 81)
Title: Baron Bonham Carter 1986-94 UKLife. The daughter of Herbert Asquith, 1 Earl of Oxford, Lady Helen Violet Bonham Carter was created Baroness Asquith (UKLife 1964-69).
Notes: Five in ODNB.

CARTWRIGHT

Origins: The son of a yeoman became a successful lawyer and purchased land in the late 16th century. **First MP 1650s?**

1. Thomas Cartwright – Northamptonshire 1695-98 1701-48
2. William Cartwright – Northamptonshire – 1754-68
3. William Cartwright – Northamptonshire 1797-1831 S. Northamptonshire 1832-46
4. Henry Cartwright – S. Northamptonshire 1858-68
5. Fairfax Cartwright – S. Northamptonshire 1868-81
6. William Cartwright – Oxfordshire 1868-85

Seats: Aynhoe Park, Northamptonshire (purch. late 16th c., built c. 1616, damaged 1640s, remod. 1660, add. 1707-22, remod. c. 1800-05, sold 1955, flats); Flore House, Northamptonshire (built 1608, resident 19th c.); Eydon Hall, Northamptonshire (rebuilt 1788-89, purch. mid 19th c. sold late 19th c.); Edgcote (Edgecote), Northamptonshire (medieval, rebuilt 16th c., rebuilt 1748-54, inher. by mar. 1847, sold 1924)

Estates: Bateman 8538 (E) 17003. Edgcote House and 1,700 acres sold for £25,000,000 in 2005 though no longer owned by the Cartwrights.
Notes: The male line became extinct in 1950s with the death of father and son in a car accident. Two in ODNB.

CARY *IRELAND*

Origins: At Londonderry by 1660. Merchants and Mayors of Londonderry 1740s. Married into the aristocracy 1743.

1. Henry Cary – {Coleraine 1727-56}
2. Edward Cary – {County Londonderry 1742-90}
3. Frederick Hamilton-Cary – {Londonderry 1743-46}

Seat: Pellipar Manor, Londonderry (leased 1742-1803)
Estates: Worth £4,000 pa in 1756.
Notes: Male line extinct 1797.

CASWALL

Origins: Burgesses in the 17th century. One married the daughter of a London banker in the early 18th century and became a banker himself.

1. Sir George Caswall – Leominster 1717-41
2. John Caswall – Leominster 1741-42
3. Timothy Caswall – Hertford 1761-68 Brackley 1771-89

Seat: Sacombe Park, Hertfordshire (acq. by mar. mid-18th c., rebuilt early 19th c., sold c. 1825)

CATELYN (Catlin, Catline)

Origins: A Norwich family, Tudor lawyer, established as gentry in the later 16th century. **First MP 1542. Two additional MPs 1571-1644.**

1. Sir Neville Catelyn – Norfolk 1679-81 Norwich 1685-87 1689-90

Seats: Kirby Cane, Norfolk (purch. 1604, built 17th and 18th c., sold early 18th c.); Wingfield Castle, Suffolk (built 1384, part demolished 1525, add. 1544, purch. c. 1630, passed out of the family 1702)
Notes: One in ODNB.

CATHCART *SCOTLAND*

Earl of Cathcart (1814- S)

Origins: Medieval family. Kt 14th century. Baron 1452.

1. Charles Cathcart – Clackmannanshire 1784-88

Seats: Cathcart House (Castle), Renfrewshire (acq. 12th c., built 15th c., passed out of family 1546, unroofed c. and new house built 1740, repurch. 1814, ruin, sold 1927); Schawpark (Schaw Park House), Clackmannanshire (built c. 1700, acq. by mar. 1752, sold 1826, unroofed 1925, demolished 1961); Wood End, (aka Thornton-le-Street Hall), Yorkshire (built 16th c., purch. by Cromptons 1793, acq. by mar. 1850 by Cathcarts, leased out from 1911, sold and demolished 1921)
Estates: Bateman 5564 (E & S) 5129
Titles: Baron Cathcart 1452- S; Viscount Cathcart 1807- UK
Peers: [1 peer 1660-1707] 3 Scottish Rep peers 1734-40 1752-76 1788-1812 6 peers 1807-1927 1940-45
1 Ldt Lt 18th-19th
2 KT 18th, 19th
Notes: The 3 Earl married 1850 the daughter and heiress of Sir Samuel Crompton 1 Bt of Wood End, Thornton-le-Street, Yorkshire (banking family from Derby) and succeeded to his estates. (See Crompton). Six in ODNB.

Cathcart

Origins: Descended from a younger son of the 2 Baron Cathcart. **First [MP Ayrshire 1625].**

1. Sir Hew Cathcart 1 Bt – [Ayrshire 1703-07]

Seats: Carelton House (Castle), Ayrshire (built 15th c., add. 1872, ruin); Killochan Castle, Ayrshire (acq. 14th c., built 1586, add. 18th c., sold 1950s)
Estates: Bateman 13118 (S) 7000
Title: Baronet 1703-1916
Notes: The 6th and last Baronet left his estates in 1916 to his nephew Ivo Walker-Heneage (see Heneage).

CAULFIELD *IRELAND*

Earl of Charlemont (1763-1892 I)

Origins: From Oxfordshire. To Ireland with the Earl of Essex 1598 as a soldier. Kt 1603. Receiver of Rents of the Earl of Tyrone's forfeited estates 1607. Gained 1,000 acres by 1610. Member of the Commission of parceling out lands c. 1615. **First MP for English seats 1584-1601. First {MP 1613}.** Baron {1620}.

1. Thomas Caulfield – {Charlemont 1661-65}
2. William Caulfield – {Tulske 1692-93 1695-99 1703-14}
3. James Caulfield 3 Viscount Charlemont – {Charlemont 1703-05 1715-26}
4. John Caulfield – {Charlemont 1703-07}
5. Henry Caulfield – {Tulske 1715-27}
6. John Caulfield – {Charlemont 1723-60}
7. St. George Caulfield – {Tulske 1727-51}
8. Toby Caulfield – {Tulske 1727-40}
9. Francis Caulfield – {County Armagh 1758-60 Charlemont 1761-75}
10. Thomas Caulfield – {Tulske 1715-27 1741-47}
11. William Caulfield – {Tulske 1761-68 1769-71}
12. William Caulfield – {Tulske 1769-86}
13. Toby Caulfield – {Tulske 1771-72}
14. Francis Caulfield 2 Earl of Charlemont – {County Armagh 1797-99}
15. Henry Caulfield – County Armagh 1802-07 1815-18 1820-30
16. James Caulfield 3 Earl of Charlemont – County Armagh 1847-57

Seats: Roxborough (Roxburgh) Castle, Tyrone (acq. fort 1602, new house built 1774, add. 1842-46, add. 1864, sold 1920, burned 1922); Drumcairn, Tyrone (acq. later 18th c., built early 19th c., departed 1936); Coney Island, Armagh (purch. 1890s, built 1895, sold, now NT); Marino House (and Casino), Dublin (purch. 1755, built 1758-76, house demolished 1921); Donamon Castle, Roscommon (castle built 15th c., acq. and remod. later 18th c., add. mid-19th c., sold 20th c., religious institution)

Estates: Bateman 26820 (I) 26334 and 14132 (I) 7421. Worth £3,034 pa in 1760 and £7,685 pa in 1798. Owned 20,186 acres in 1721.

Title: Baron Caulfield 1620- I; Viscount Charlemont 1665- I; Baron Charlemont 1837-92 UK

Peers: {4 peers 1660-71 1692-1734 1754-99} 2 Irish Rep peers 1806-63 1918-45 2 peers 1837-92

2 Ldts Lt 19th

3 KP 18th, 19th

Notes: The 8 Viscount was a Senator in the Northern Irish Parliament in 1925. Four in ODNB.

Caulfield

Origins: Descended from a younger son of the Earl of Charlemont.

1. James Caulfield – Abingdon 1852

Seat: Copeswood (Copswood), Limerick (built mid-19th c., estate dispersed 1852)
Estates: Bateman 3350 (I) 2513

CAVE [Locke, Otway] *ENGLAND & IRELAND*

Baron Bray(e) (1529-57 1839-62 1879- E)

Origins: Rose to wealth and titles in royal service under the Tudors. Acquired land after the Dissoultion. **First MP 1545 for Leicestershire. Two additional MPs 1547-71.**

1. Sir Roger Cave 2 Bt – Coventry 1685-87 1689-90
2. Sir Thomas Cave 3 Bt – Leicestershire 1711-19
3. Sir Thomas Cave 5 Bt – Leicestershire 1741-47 1762-74
4. Sir Thomas Cave 7 Bt – Leicestershire 1790-92
5. Robert Otway Cave – Leicester 1826-30 County Tipperary 1832 1835-44

Seat: Stanford Hall, Leicestershire (acq. 1430, old house, rebuilt 1697-1700, remod. 1745 and 1880, still own)
Estates: Bateman 4658 (E) 8317
Title: Baronet 1641-
Peers: 2 peers 1879-1945
Notes: The Barony of Braye [family name Bray(e)] fell into abeyance on the death of the 2 Baron in 1557 (see also Crewe). The sister of the 7 Bt, who had no children (the Baronetcy went to an uncle), succeeded to the estates and had the Barony of Bray(e) called out of abeyance in her favor in 1839. Two in ODNB.

Otway

Origins: Gentry by the Tudor period in Westmorland. One to Ireland in the 1640s and another as chaplain to the Lord Lieutenant 1670, Bishop of Ossory 1680, and acquired Clohonan Castle (later Castle Otway). The Baroness Braye of 1839 (see above) married Henry Otway of Castle Otway 1790.

1. Sir Arthur Otway 2 Bt – Stafford 1852-57 Chatham 1865-74 Rochester 1878-85

Seats: Castle Otway, Tipperary (Clohonan, Cloghanane Castle) (old castle, acq. 1685, add. later 17th c., add. mid-18th c., add. 19th c., burned 1922, much of the estate sold, Otways continued to own some land at least until 1950); Lissenhall, Tipperary (acq. 18th c., built mid-18th c., sold 1853, ruin by 1967)
Estates: Held 4,362 acres worth £1,830 pa in 1878.
Title: Baronet 1831-
Notes: The Westmorland estates of the Otways passed by marriage to the Uptons of Devon in the later 17th century (see Upton). Three in ODNB.

Locke

Origins: Richard Locke's daughter and heiress married Thomas Otway of Lissenhall, Tipperary. Their son succeeded to Castle Otway.

1. Richard Locke – {Athy 1692-93 1695-99 Kildare 1703-14}

Seat: Tullagory, Kildare (resident 17th c.)

CAVENDISH [Bentinck, Bradshaw, Clifford, Moore, Ogle] *ENGLAND & IRELAND*

Duke of Devonshire (1694- E)

Origins: Judge in 1371, but then William Cavendish (d. 1433) became a mercer in London. His great-grandson served Wolsey and Cromwell under Henry VIII. Gained land at the Dissolution. Kt 1546. Courtiers. Acquired great estates by marriage to "Bess of Hardwick" (Hardwicks acq. Hardwick Hall c. 1330). **First MP 1379 for Suffolk. Seven additional MPs 1547-1626, several kts of the shire**. Baron 1605.

1. William Cavendish 1 Duke of Devonshire – Derbyshire 1661-81
2. William Cavendish 2 Duke of Devonshire – Derbyshire 1695-1701 Castle Rising 1702 Yorkshire 1702-07
3. Lord Henry Cavendish – Derby 1695-1700
4. Lord James Cavendish – Derby 1701-02 1705-10 1715-42
5. William Cavendish 3 Duke of Devonshire – Lostwithiel 1721-22 Grampound 1722-27 Huntingdonshire 1727-29
6. Philip Cavendish – Bere Alston 1721 St. Germans 1722-27 Portsmouth 1734-43
7. Lord Charles Cavendish – Heytesbury 1725-27 Westminster 1727-34 Derbyshire 1734-41
8. Lord James Cavendish – Malton 1741
9. William Cavendish 4 Duke of Devonshire – Derbyshire 1741-51
10. Lord Frederick Cavendish – Derbyshire 1751-54 Derby 1754-80

11. Lord George Cavendish – Weymouth & Melcombe Regis 1751-54 Derbyshire 1754-80 1781-94
12. Lord John Cavendish – Weymouth & Melcombe Regis 1754-61 Knaresborough 1761-68 York 1768-84 Derbyshire 1794-96
13. Richard Cavendish – Wendover 1761-68
14. James Cavensdish – {Lifford 1773-76 Banagher 1776-83}
15. Lord Richard Cavendish – Lancaster 1773-80 Derbyshire 1780-81
16. George Cavendish 1 Earl of Burlington – Peterborough 1775-80 Derby 1780-96 Derbyshire 1797-1831
17. George Cavendish – {St. Johnstown 1790-97 Cavan 1798-1800}
18. William Cavendish – Knaresborough 1804 Aylesbury 1804-06 Derby 1806-12
19. George Cavendish – Aylesbury 1806-09
20. Sir Augustus Clifford 1 Bt – Bandon Bridge 1818-20 Dungarvon 1820-22 Bandon Bridge 1831-32
21. William Cavendish 7 Duke of Devonshire – University of Cambridge 1829-31 Malton 1831 Derbyshire 1831-32 N. Derbyshire 1832-34
22. Lord George Cavendish – N. Derbyshire 1834-80
23. Sir Charles Clifford 4 Bt – Isle of Wight 1857-65 Newport 1870-85
24. Spencer Cavendish 8 Duke of Devonshire – N. Lancashire 1857-68 Radnor District 1869-80 N. E. Lancashire 1880-85 Rossevale Div. Lancashire 1885-91
25. Lord Edward Cavendish – E. Sussex 1865-68 N. Derbyshire 1880-82
26. Victor Cavendish 9 Duke of Devonshire – W. Derbyshire 1891-1908
27. Lord Richard Cavendish – Lonsdale Div. Lancashire 1895-1906
28. Edward Cavendish 10 Duke of Devonshire – W. Div. Derbyshire 1923-38

Seats: Chatsworth, Derbyshire (built 14th c., purch. 1549, new house 1560-76, rebuilt 1687-96 and 1703-04, add. 1820s, still own); Hardwick Hall, Derbyshire (acq. by Hardwicks c. 1330 - old hall demolished 1746, 1789, 1870s - new house 1587-97, NT 1950s); Bolton Abbey, Yorkshire (Clifford acq. 1310, rebuilt c. 1378, acq. by mar. from Cliffords 1748, still own); Compton Place, Sussex (built 1726-29, acq. by mar. 1782, leased to a school 1954 onwards, still own); Lismore Castle, Waterford (medieval castle, acq. and rebuilt c. 1610 by Boyles, acq. by mar. 1753, rebuilt 1812, add. 1849-58, still own); Chiswick House, Middlesex (built early 17th c., purch. by Earl of Burlington 1682, add. 1727-32, passed to Duke of Devonshire by mar. of 1748, old house demolished 1788, add. c. 1788-90, leased out and part of estate sold from 1858 onwards, house sold to County Council 1929, owned by Ministry of Works from 1956, wings demolished 1956-57); Holker Hall, Lancashire (acq. and built c. 1610 by Prestons, Cavendishes acq. from Lowthers, who acq. by mar. to Prestons 1697 – see Earls of Lonsdale - by marriage 1756, remod. 1783-89, rebuilt 1838-42, fire and rebuilt 1873-74, 1908 given to younger son of 9th Duke, and his grandson, Lord Cavendish of Furness still owns)
Estates: Bateman 198572 (E & I) 180750. Owned 100,000 acres in the late 1620s. Landed income of £36,000 pa in 1764. The Hon. Henry Cavendish, scientist, left

nearly a million pounds in 1810. The Hon. William Cavendish left £150,000 probate in 1812. Rubinstein – 5 Duke left £300,000 probate in 1811. The 1 Earl of Burlington left £140,000 in probate in 1834. Worth £120,000,000 in 1990 with 73,000 acres.
Titles: Baron Cavendish 1605- E; Earl of Devonshire 1618- E; Marquess of Hartington 1694- E; Earl of Burlington 1831- UK; Baron Cavendish of Furness 1990- UKLife, Baronet 1838-95
Peers: 12 peers 1660-1755 1751-64 1769-1858 1831-1945
14 Lds Lt 17th, 18th, 19th, 20th
8 in Cabinet 1716-18 1725-30 1731-33 1737-45 1755-57 1782-83 1827 1866-74 1880-85 1882 1895-1903 1922-24
10 KG 17th, 18th, 19th, 20th
Notes: Sir Augustus Clifford 1 Bt was the illegitimate son of the 5 Duke of Devonshire. Sir Charles Clifford 4 Bt was his descendent. The Cavendishes succeeded to the Yorkshire estates (Bolton Abbey) of the Clifford Earls of Cumberland through an heiress in the 17th century. The 4 Duke married Lady Charlotte Boyle in 1748. She inherited immense estates in England and Ireland from her father the 2 Earl of Burlington. A younger son was created Earl of Burlington in 1831, but the title later merged with the Dukedom. The 1, 2, 3 Earls and 1, 2, 4, 5, 6, 7, 8, 9, 11 Dukes and 12 others in ODNB.

Baron Waterpark (1792- I)

Origins: Illegitimate descendents of Sir Henry Cavendish, Bess of Hardwick's oldest son. Given Doveridge Hall 1611. Augustus Cavendish succeeded to the Bradshaw estates (Ford Hall) through his mother and took the additional name Bradshaw. Moved to Ireland for a time in the 18th century.

1. Sir Henry Cavendish 1 Bt – {Tallow 1756-60 Lismore 1761-76}
2. Samuel Bradshaw – {Tallow 1761-62}
3. Sir Henry Cavendish 2 Bt – {Lismore 1766-68 1776-90 Killibegs 1790-97 Lismore 1798-1800} Lostwithiel 1768-74
4. Richard Cavendish 2 Baron Waterpark – {Portarlington 1790-97}
5. Augustus Cavendish Bradshaw – {Carlow 1790-96} Honiton 1805-12 Castle Rising 1812 Castle Rising 1812-17
6. Henry Cavendish 3 Baron Waterpark – Knaresborough 1830-32 S. Derbyshire 1832-35 Lichfield 1854-56

Seats: Doveridge Hall, Derbyshire (acq. 1552 by Cavendishes, built 1650s, rebuilt 1769 onwards, sold c. 1891, demolished 1938); Ford Hall (House), Derbyshire (demolished c. 1961); Waterpark, Cork (built c. 1692, acq. by mar. 18th c., sold 19th c., demolished 1981)
Estates: Bateman 8291 (E & I) 8319
Title: Baronet 1755-
Notes: 2 Bt in ODNB.

Baron Chesham (1858- UK)

Origins: Descended from a younger son of the Earl of Burlington of the second creation.

1. Henry Cavendish – Derby 1812-34
2. Charles Cavendish 1 Baron Chesham – Aylesbury 1814-18 Newton (IoW) 1821-30 Yarmouth (IoW) 1831-32 E. Sussex 1832-41 Youghal 1841-47 Buckinghamshire 1847-57
3. William Cavendish 2 Baron Chesham – Peterborough 1847-52 Buckinghamshire 1857-63

Seat: Latimer House, Buckinghamshire (purch. c. 1625, built later 16th c., fire 1830s, rebuilt 1838, sold 1924)
Estates: Bateman 11487 (E) 15625
Peers: 4 peers 1858-1945

Duke of Portland (1716-1990 GB)

Origins: The Bentincks were Dutch nobles of medieval lineage one of whom accompanied William III to England in 1688 as a page. He served at the Battle of the Boyne and became a diplomat and courtier. Baron 1689, KG 1697. The 2 Duke of Portland married the heiress to Welbeck Abbey, which descended from the Cavendishes, and the Bentincks took the additional name Cavendish. Welbeck passed through a series of heiresses beginning with the third son of Bess of Hardwick, who married the co-heiress of Lord Ogle (see below), who became Baroness Ogle in her own right. Their son succeeded as Baron Ogle and was created Duke of Newcastle-upon-Tyne. The 2 Duke left a daughter, Lady Margaret Cavendish, who married John Holles, Earl of Clare. He was created Duke of Newcastle and also left only a daughter, Lady Henrietta Cavendish-Holles. She married the 2 Earl of Oxford and Mortimer. They left an only daughter, who married the 2 Duke of Portland. The Holles estates passed to the Pelham Dukes of Newcastle (see Pelham) but Welbeck and the Cavendish property went to the Portlands. This Cavendish line **elected three pre-1660 MPs 1614-40s**.

1. Henry Cavendish 2 Duke of Newcastle-upon-Tyne – Derbyshire 1660 Northumberland 1661-76
2. Henry Bentinck 1 Duke of Portland – Southampton 1705-08 Hampshire 1708-09
3. Lord George Bentinck – Droitwich 1742-47 Grampound 1747-54 Malmesbury 1754-59
4. William Cavendish-Bentinck 3 Duke of Portland – Weobley 1761-62
5. John Bentinck – Rye 1761-68
6. Lord Charles Bentinck – Lewes 1766-68 Carlisle 1768-74 Nottinghamshire 1775-96 Clitheroe 1796-1802
7. William Cavendish-Scott-Bentinck 4 Duke of Portland – Petersfield 1790-91 Buckinghamshire 1791-1809

8. Lord William Cavendish-Bentinck – Camelford 1796 Nottinghamshire 1796-1803 1812-14 1816-26 King's Lynn 1826-28 Glasgow 1836-39
9. Lord William Cavendish-Bentinck – Ashburton 1807-12
10. Lord Frederick Cavendish-Bentinck – Weobley 1816-24 Queenborough 1824-26
11. William Cavendish-Bentinck Marquess of Tichfield – Bletchingley 1819-21 King's Lynn 1822-24
12. William Cavendish-Bentinck 5 Duke of Portland – King's Lynn 1824-26
13. Lord William Cavendish-Bentinck – King's Lynn 1828-48
14. William Cavendish-Bentinck – Glasgow 1836-39
15. Lord Henry Cavendish-Bentinck – N. Nottinghamshire 1846-57
16. George Bentinck – W. Norfolk 1852-68 1871-84
17. George Cavendish-Bentinck – Taunton 1859-65 Whitehaven 1865-91
18. William Cavendish-Bentinck Penryn & Falmouth 1886-95
19. Lord Henry Cavendish-Bentinck – N. W. Div. Norfolk 1886-92 S. Nottinghamshire 1895-1906 1910-29
20. William Cavendish-Bentinck 7 Duke of Portland – Newark Div. Nottinghamshire 1922-43

Seats: Welbeck Abbey, Nottinghamshire (acq. by Cavendishes at the Dissolution, Bentincks acq. 1755 by mar. to Cavendish heiress, huge rebuilding operations underground 1860s-70s, add. 1889-96, remod. c. 1900-02, became a school after WWII until 2005, descendents still own); Bulstrode (Park), Buckinghamshire (built c. 1676-85, acq. by 1 Earl early 18th c., sold 1810); Bothal Castle, Northumberland (built 1343, passed by mar. to Ogles 1363, then to Cavendishes 1591, restoration and add. 1830-31, 1857-59, and 1909, still own); Langwell House, Caithness-shire (built 18th c., purch. 1860 for £90,000, add. 19th c., still own); Terrington St. Clement, Norfolk (owned c. 18th c.-1920); Bolsover Castle, Derbyshire (12th c. castle, purch. 1608 by the Cavendish Duke of Newcastle, built 1612-21, rebuilt c. 1635-42, add. 1663-66, passed by mar. to Harleys 1711, unroofed 1713-15, later passed to Dukes of Portland, passed to government 1945); Skeldon House, Ayrshire (medieval, rebuilt 1780-99, purch. 1867, sold 1926)
Estates: Bateman 186001 (E & S) 112711. Worth £50,000,000 in 1990 with 16,000 acres. One of the Welbeck settlement heirs owned 45,000 acres in Scotland in 1996.
Titles: Baron Ogle 1461- E; Baron Ogle and Viscount Mansfield 1620-91 E; Baron Cavendish and Earl of Newcastle-upon-Tyne 1628-91 E; Marquess of Newcastle 1643-91 E; Duke of Newcastle 1665-91 E; Earl of Portland 1689- E; Marquess of Tichfield 1716-1990 GB; Baron Bolsover 1880-1977 UK
Peers: 10 peers 1660-91 1689-1726 1730-1945
7 Lds Lt 17th, 18th, 19th, 20th
2 in Cabinet 1782-83 1794-1805 1807-09 1809-12 1827-28
6 KG 17th, 18th, 19th, 20th
Notes: 1 and 2 Dukes of Newcastle, 1 Earl, and 3, 5, and 9 Dukes of Portland and seven others in ODNB.

Baron Ogle (1461- E)

Origins: Owned Ogle manor by the mid-12th century. **First MP 1298 for Northumberland. Six additional MPs 1435-1654, most for Northumberland.** The MPs listed below descended from a younger son of the 3 Baron Ogle (d. 1513). (For the senior line see Duke of Devonshire above).

1. William Ogle – Northumberland 1685-87
2. Samuel Ogle – Berwick-on-Tweed 1690-1710 {Belfast 1707-13}
3. Sir Chaloner Ogle 1 Bt – Rochester 1746-50
4. Sir Charles Ogle 2 Bt – Portarlington 1830-31
5. Saville Ogle – S. Northumberland 1841-52

Seats: Kirkley Hall, Northumberland (medieval tower house, house built 1632, fire 1928 and rebuilt, now an agricultural collge); Causey Park, Northumberland (acq. by mar. 14th c., built 1589, remod., 18th and 19th c., sold 1854); Coupland, Northumberland (built c. 1585, purch. 1713, add. early 18th c., sold 1806)
Estates: Bateman 7408 (E) 7895
Title: Baronet 1816-
Notes: The Barony fell into abeyance in 1597 and again in 1691. Some of the pre-1660 MPs took the name Bertram from whom the family had inherited Bothal Castle, Northumberland. Eight in ODNB.

Ogle/Moore

Origins: George Ogle, son of Samuel Ogle MP above moved to Ireland as a Commissioner of Revenue. He left his estates to a nephew George Ogle Moore in 1814. The Moores were Irish officials in the later 18th and early 19th centuries.

1. George Ogle – {Bannow 1727-46}
2. George Ogle – {County Wexford 1769-97 Dublin 1798-1800} 1801-02
3. Lorenzo Moore – {Dungannon 1783-90 Ardfert 1798-1800}
4. George Ogle Moore – Dublin 1826-31

Seats: Bellevue (Belview), Wexford (built 1737, passed by mar. to Moores 1814, sold 1825, burned 1923); Dean's Castle, Wexford; Richfield, Wexford
Estates: Possibly 1,397 acres in the 18th c.
Notes: One of George Ogle Moore MP's sons became Dean of Cashel and another emigrated to Australia. The Ogle estates were sold. One in ODNB.

CAWLEY

Baron Cawley (1918- UK)

Origins: the 1 Baron was a Manchester bleacher and dyer who entered politics.

1. Frederick Cawley 1 Baron Cawley – Prestwich Div. S. E. Lancashire 1895-1918
2. Harold Cawley – Heywood Div. Lancashire 1910-15
3. Oswald Cawley – Prestwich Div. S. E. Lancashire 1918

Seats: Berrington Hall, Herefordshire (built 1778-81, purch. 1900, NT 1957); Brooklands, Lancashire (acq. late 19th c., demolished 20th c.)
Title: Baronet 1906-
Peers: 2 peers 1918-45
1 in Cabinet 1916-18

CAYLEY

Origins: Emerged as gentry and purchased Brompton in the late 16th century. Kt 1630. Created a Baronet 1661 for services in the Civil War.

1. William Cayley – Dover 1752-55
2. Sir George Cayley 6 Bt – Scarborough 1832-34
3. Edward Cayley – N. R. Yorkshire 1832-62

Seats: Brompton (High Hall), Yorkshire (purch. late 16th c., resident into 20th c., now a school, still own estate); Llannerch Park, Denbighshire (acq. by mar. 1878)
Estates: Bateman 8459 (E) 9126
Title: Baronet 1661-
Notes: Six in ODNB.

CAYZER

Baron Rotherwick (1939- UK)

Origins: First MP was the son of a schoolmaster and started as an office clerk. Owned a steamship line.

1. Sir Charles Cayzer 1 Bt – Barrow-in-Furness 1892-1906
2. Herbert Cayzer 1 Baron Rotherwick – Portsmouth S. Div. 1910-22 1923-39
3. Sir Charles Cayzer 3 Bt – Chester 1922-40

Seats: Gartmore House, Stirlingshire (built early 18th c., add. 1779-80, purch. 1900, remod. 1901-02, family departed 1940, sold c. 1950, now conference center); Kinpurnie Castle, Forfarshire (purch. and rebuilt 1907-11, still own, for sale 2012); Cornbury Park (House), Oxfordshire (built late 16th c., remod. 1632-33 and 1663-77, remod. c. 1850, purch. 1960s, still own)
Estates: 1 Bt left over £2,000,000 in 1916. Family worth in excess of £350,000,000 in 1990. Owned 3,000 acres in Suffolk and 43,000 acres in Scotland in 2001.
Titles: Baron Cayzer 1982-99 UKLife; Baronet 1904- ; 1921- ; 1924-
Peer: 1 peer 1939-45
Notes: The Cayzer family has an entry in the ODNB. In addition one other member of the family is listed separately.

CECIL [Gascoyne]

Marquess of Exeter (1801- UK)

Origins: The grandfather of the 1 Baron Burghley was the younger son of a poor Welsh squire. He followed Henry VII in his campaign for the throne and rose in office under the new King. He purchased property at Stamford and became an **MP 1504**. The family rose high under Elizabeth I. **Seven further MPs 1539-1640, kts of the shire 1553, 1584**.

1. John Cecil 5 Earl of Exeter – Northamptonshire 1675-78
2. John Cecil 6 Earl of Exeter – Rutland 1695-1700
3. William Cecil – Stamford 1698-1705
4. Charles Cecil – Stamford 1705-22
5. Brownlow Cecil 8 Earl of Exeter – Stamford 1722
6. Brownlow Cecil 9 Earl of Exeter – Rutland 1747-54
7. Thomas Cecil – Rutland 1761-68
8. Henry Cecil 1 Marquess of Exeter – Stamford 1774-90
9. Thomas Cecil – Stamford 1818-32
10. William Cecil 3 Marquess of Exeter – S. Lincolnshire 1847-57 N. Northamptonshire 1857-67
11. Brownlow Cecil 4 Marquess of Exeter – N. Northamptonshire 1877-95
12. Lord John Joicey-Cecil – Stamford Div. Lincolnshire 1906-10
13. David Cecil 6 Marquess of Exeter – Peterborough Div. Northamptonshire 1931-43

Seat: Burghley House, Northamptonshire (purch. c. 1540, built 1556-87, remod. 1682-97, still own)
Estates: Bateman 28271 (E) 49044
Titles: Baron Burghley 1571- E; Earl of Exeter 1605- E
Peers: 11 peers 1660-1804 1816-1945

5 Lds Lt 17th, 18th, 19th, 20th
2 KG 19th, 20th
Notes: 1 Baron, 1, 2 Earls, 6 Marquess, and one other in ODNB.

Marquess of Salisbury (1789- GB)

Origins: The junior line of the family descended from a younger son of the 1 Baron Burghley. **Four MPs 1584-1656.**

1. James Cecil 3 Earl of Salisbury – Hertfordshire 1668
2. Robert Cecil – Castle Rising 1701 Wootoon Basset 1708-10
3. James Cecil 1 Marquess of Salisbury – Great Bedwyn 1774-80 Launceston 1780
4. James Gascoyne-Cecil 2 Marquess of Salisbury – Weymouth & Melcombe Regis 1813-17 Hertford 1817-23
5. Robert Gascoyne-Cecil 3 Marquess of Salisbury – Stamford 1853-68
6. Lord Eustace Cecil – S. Essex 1865-68 W. Essex 1868-85
7. James Cecil 4 Marquess of Salisbury – N. E. Lancashire 1885-92 Rochester 1893-1903
8. Hugh Cecil 1 Baron Quickswood – Greenwich 1895-1906 University of Oxford 1910-37
9. Evelyn Cecil 1 Baron Rockley – E. Hertfordshire 1898-1900 Aston Manor 1900-18 Aston Div. Birmingham 1918-29
10. Robert Cecil 1 Viscount Cecil of Chelwood – E. Marylebone 1906-10 Hitchin Div. Hertfordshire 1911-23
11. Robert Cecil 5 Marquess of Salisbury – S. Div. Dorset 1929-41
12. Robert Cecil 6 Marquess of Salisbury – Bournemouth West 1950-54
13. Robert Cecil 7 Marquess of Salisbury – S. Dorset 1979-87

Seats: Hatfield House, Hertfordshire (old house built c. 1497, acq. and new house built 1607-12, fire 1835, restored 1830s, still own); Cranborne Manor, Dorset (built 12th c., acq. c. 1603, remod. 1606-11, restored 1863, still own)
Estates: Bateman 20202 (E) 33413. Owned 7,020 acres worth 245 million pounds in 2001.
Titles: Baron Cecil 1603- E; Viscount Cranborne 1604- E; Earl of Salisbury 1605- E; Viscount Cecil of Chelwood 1923- UK; Baron Rockley 1934- UK; Baron Quickswood 1941- UK; Baron Gascoyne-Cecil 1999- UKLife
Peers: 13 peers 1660-83 1687-89 1692-94 1712-28 1734-1945 1923-45 1934-45 1941-45
3 Lds Lt 18th, 19th
6 in Cabinet 1852-53 1858-59 1866-67 1874-80 1885-92 1895-1902 1903-05 1916 1922-29 1923-26 1940-45 1994-97
5 KG 17th, 18th, 19th 20th
Notes: 1, 2, 3, 4 Earls and 3, 4, 5 Marquesses and six others in ODNB.

Gascoyne

Origins: Brewers early, mid-18th century. Lord Mayor of London 1752. The first MP entered the gentry. The heiress of Bamber Gascoyne married the 2 Marquess of Salisbury, who took the additional name Gascoyne.

1. Bamber Gascoyne – Malden 1761-63 Midhurst 1765-68 Weobley 1770-74 Truro 1774-84 Bossiney 1784-86
2. Bamber Gascoyne – Liverpool 1780-96
3. Isaac Gascoyne – Liverpool 1796-1831

Seats: Childwall Hall (Abbey), Lancashire (purch. and built 1806-13, passed by mar. to Marquess of Salisbury and leased to tenants, sold, demolished 1949); Bifrons, Essex (built early 17th c., purch. mid 18th c., rebuilt 18th c., demolished and sold 1815-16)
Estates: Worth £4,000 pa in 1791.
Notes: Three in ODNB.

CHAFIN (Chaffin)

Origins: Began as burgesses and then purchased land later 16th c. Several branches in various towns. **First MP 1472. Four additional MPs 1529-1628.**

1. Thomas Chafin – Poole 1679-81 1685-87 Dorchester 1689-90 Hindon 1690-91
2. Thomas Chafin – Shaftesbury 1699-1701 Dorset 1702-11
3. George Chafin – Dorset 1713-54

Seat: Chettle House, Dorset (purch. 1576, built c. 1710-15, sold 1826, now flats)
Estates: Worth £500 pa in c. 1650.
Notes: The family was in increasing financial difficulties by the mid-18th century. (Hayton, *The House of Commons*, III, 507). Male line extinct 1818.

CHAMBERLAIN

Origins: Manufacturers in 19th-century Birmingham.

1. Joseph Chamberlain – Birmingham 1876-85 W. Birmingham 1885-1914
2. Richard Chamberlain – W. Islington 1885-92
3. Sir Austen Chamberlain – E. Worcestershire 1892-1914 W. Birmingham 1914-37
4. Neville Chamberlain – Ladywood Div. Birmingham 1918-29 Edgbaston Div. Birmingham 1929-40

Seats: Moor Green (Moorgreen) Hall, Worcestershire (purch. and built later 19th c., sold 20th c.); Highbury Hall, Worcestershire (purch. and built 1878-80, donated to city of Birmingham 1919)
3 in Cabinet 1880-85 1895-1905 1915-17 1919-22 1924-29 1931 1931-40
1 KG 20th
Notes: Four in ODNB

CHAPLIN

Viscount Chaplin (1916- UK)

Origins: The first MP's father and grandfather were yeomen. Alderman of Bury St. Edmunds. Clothier in London, Lord Mayor and Kt 1677. 1 Bt was a Director of the South Sea Company. Purchased estates.

1. Thomas Chaplin – Bury St. Edmunds 1659 1660
2. John Chaplin – Great Grimsby 1690-95 1702-05
3. Sir Robert Chaplin 1 Bt – Great Grimsby 1715-21
4. John Chaplin – Lincoln 1754-61 Stamford 1761-64
5. Charles Chaplin – Lincolnshire 1802-16
6. Charles Chaplin – Stamford 1826-31 1832-38
7. Henry Chaplin 1 Viscount Chaplin – Mid Lincolnshire 1868-85 Kesteven Div. Lincolnshire 1885-1906 Wimbledon Div. Surrey 1907-16
8. Edward Chaplin – Lincoln 1874-80

Seats: Blankney Hall, Lincolnshire (built early 17th c., purch. 1719, rebuilt mid-18th c., add. 1825, sold 1896, burned 1945, demolished 1960); Uppat House, Sutherland (built mid-18th c., leased later 19th c.)
Estates: Bateman 23370 (E) 30517
Title: Baronet 1715-30
2 peers 1916-45
1 in Cabinet 1885-86 1889-92 1895-1900
Notes: 1 Viscount bankrupted himself. 1 Viscount in ODNB.

CHAPMAN *IRELAND*

Origins: To Ireland in the mid-17th century as a Cromwellian soldier.

1. Sir Benjamin Chapman 1 Bt – {Fore 1772-76 County Westmeath 1776-83}
2. William Chapman – {Athboy 1776-83}
3. Sir Montagu Chapman 3 Bt – County Westmeath 1830-41
4. Sir Benjamin Chapman 4 Bt – County Westmeath 1841-47

Seats: Killua Castle, Westmeath (old house acq. mid-17th c., rebuilt 1780, remod. c. 1830, sold 1930s, ruin); Southill (South Hill), Westmeath (built c. 1810, inher. by mar. from Tighes (see Tighe) later 19th c., sold 1949, hospital)
Estates: Bateman 13357 (I) 6799 and 9092 (I) 4703
Title: Baronet 1782-1919
1 Ld Lt 19th
Notes: T. E. Lawrence "of Arabia" was an illegitimate son of the family.

CHAWORTH

Viscount Chaworth (1628-93 I)

Origins: Claimed Norman descent, and it is probable that one was with William I at the Battle of Hastings. Accumulated significant estates by the end of the 13th century. **Summoned as a Baron 1299**. Rose to preeminence through a series of profitable marriages concluded over a period of centuries. Became one of the richest families in England by the 15th century. Sir Thomas Chaworth served in the Agincourt campaign with Henry V. (Payling, *Political Society in Lancastrian England*, 20, 25, 139) **Elected nine MPs 1399-1624**. A junior line became Viscounts Chaworth (1628-93 I).

1. Patrick Chaworth – East Retford 1722-27

Seat: Annesley Hall, Nottinghamshire (inherited by mar. 15th c., sold 1896)
Estates: Bateman 8211 (E) 13787 (passed in 1693 to the Musters family)
Notes: The 3 Viscount Chaworth left some of his estates via an heiress to the 5 Earl of Meath (see Brabazon). The Chaworth family has an entry in ODNB.

CHAYTOR

Origins: Minor gentry until the marriage to an heiress of Croft Hall and Clervaux Castle (Clervaux family) in the later 16th century. (Roebuck, *Yorkshire Baronets*, 24) Owned coalfields, lead mines, and a spa.

1. William Chaytor – Penryn 1774-80 Hedon 1780-90
2. Sir William Chaytor 2 Bt – Durham 1831-34
3. Sir William Chaytor 1 Bt – Sunderland 1832-35

Seats: Witton Castle, Durham (built c. 1410, remod. later 18th c., fire 1797, purch. 1816, sold 1839 but later reacq., sold 1963); Croft Hall, Yorkshire (built 15th c., acq. by mar. 1590, remod. 18th and 19th c., sold after 1980?); Clervaux Castle, Yorkshire (acq. by mar. later 16th c., new house built 1839-44, abandoned c. 1935, demolished 1950)
Estates: Bateman 2401 (E) 9803 and 2902 (E) 4226
Titles: Baronet 1671-1721; 1831-

CHEETHAM

Origins: Cotton manufacturers 19th century.

1. John Cheetham – S. Lancashire 1852-59 Salford 1865-68
2. Joshua Cheetham – Oldham 1892-1895
3. John Cheetham – Stalybridge 1905-10

Seats: Eastwood Hall, Cheshire (acq. 19th c., donated to Stalybridge 1932, demolished 1950); Eyford Park, Gloucestershire (built late 17th c., add. late 18th c., demolished and rebuilt c. 1870, purch. 1885, rebuilt 1910, part of estate sold 1959, house sold 1972)

CHERNOCK

Origins: Held Holcot since 1541 as gentry. **First MP 1623.**

1. Sir Villiers Chernock 2 Bt – Bedfordshire 1685-87
2. Sir Pynsent Chernock 3 Bt – Bedfordshire 1705-08 1713-15
3. Sir Boteler Chernock 4 Bt – Bedford 1740-47

Seat: Holcot (Hulcote), Bedfordshire (purch. 1541, passed by mar. to Herveys 1779 and later divided among heirs)
Title: Baronet 1661-1779

CHETWODE

Baron Chetwode (1945- UK)

Origins: Gentry by the 14th century and probably earlier. **First MP 1386 for Buckinghamshire. Two further MPs 1559-1653.**

1. Sir John Chetwode 4 Bt – Newcastle-u-Lyme 1815-18 Buckingam 1841

Seats: Chetwode, Buckinghamshire (may have held manor by time of Domesday book and possibly before the Conquest, medieval manor house, rebuilt c. 1600, add. 18th c., sold 1966); Oakley Hall, Staffordshire (acq. c. early 13th c., medieval, rebuilt c. 1710, sold 1919)
Estates: Bateman 4105 (E) 7071 and 11649 (E & W) 13672
Title: Baronet 1700-
Peer: 1 peer 1945
Notes: One in ODNB.

CHEYNE

Viscount Newhaven (1681-1728 S)

Origins: Held Chenies, Buckinghamshire from the 12th century. **First MP 1372 for Bedfordshire. Sixteen other MPs 1372-1641, a majority of them kts of the shire**. Baron 1487.

1. Charles Cheyne 1 Viscount Newhaven – Amersham 1660 Great Marlow 1666-79 Harwich 1690-95 Newport 1695-98

Seats: Chesham Bois (House), Buckinghamshire (acq. by 1430, sold 1735, demolished); Cogenhoe, Northamptonshire (acq. by mar. 1399 from a family that may have held manor at Domesday Book time 1086, sold 1655)
Titles: Baron Cheyne 1487-99 E; Baron Cheyne 1572-87 E
Peers: [2 peers 1681-1728]
1 Ld Lt 18th
Notes: John Cheyne, Lord Cheyne (MP 1478-86) fought at Bosworth. Purchased the manor of Chelsea in 1657. The family became extinct in 1728. Estates passed to the wife of the 1 Viscount. 1 and 2 Viscounts and two others in ODNB.

CHICHESTER [Dawson] *IRELAND & ENGLAND*

Marquess of Donegall (Donegal) (1791- I)

Origins: Large landowners in North Devon since the 13th century. A Chichester served in the Agincourt campaign (*Country Life*, 129, p. 1084). Kt 13th century. Sir John Chichester and Sir Arthur Chichester went to Ireland as administrators and soldiers under Elizabeth I, and one of them was appointed Lord Deputy of Ireland 1605-16. Baron 1612. **First {MP 1634}. A further {MP 1639}.**

1. Charles Chichester – {Belfast 1695-99}
2. Arthur Chichester 2 Earl of Donegall – {Dungannon 1661-66}
3. John Chichester – {Gorey 1692-93 1695-99 1703-13 1715-21}
4. John Chichester – {Belfast 1725-27 1745-46}
5. John Chichester – {Belfast 1761-68 Carrickfergus 1768-76}
6. Arthur Chichester 1 Marquess of Donegall – Malmesbury 1768-74
7. Lord Spencer Chichester – {Belfast 1797-98} Carrickfergus 1802-07
8. George Chichester 2 Marquess of Donegall – {Carrickfergus 1798-1800}
9. George Chichester 3 Marquess of Donegall – Carrickfergus 1818-20 Belfast 1820-30 County Antrim 1830-37 Belfast 1837-38
10. Lord Arthur Chichester – Belfast 1832-35

11. Lord John Chichester – Belfast 1845-52
12. Robert Chichester – S. Londonderry 1921

Seats: Joymount Palace, Antrim (acq. later 16th c., built 1611-18, abandoned 1724, ruin by 1760, demolished 1768), Belfast Castle, Antrim (built early 17th c., fire 1708, new house on new site 1867, passed to Ashley-Coopers 1883, now public ownership); Ormeau House, Down (built late 18th c. add. 1823, abandoned 1860s, demolished 1869, became a public park); Fisherwick Park, Staffordshire (built late 16th c., purch. 1755, built 1766-79, sold 1808 and pulled down); Fisherwick Lodge, Antrim (built 18th c., rebuilt c. 1805, sold c. 1847)
Estates: Bateman 22996 (I) 41649; 1 Baron held 100,000 acres worth £6,000 pa in 1625. Owned 250,000 acres in mid-18th c. Worth £20,000 pa in 1800 and £30,000 pa in 1838.
Titles: Baron Chichester 1612-25 I; Viscount Chichester 1625- I; Earl of Donegall 1647- I; Baron Fisherwick 1791- GB; Baron Ennishowen and Carrickfergus 1841-83 UK
Peers: {3 peers 1660-75 1692-1706 1765-99} 4 peers 1791-99 1841-83 1889-1904 1924-45
2 Lds Lt 19th
2 KP 19th
Notes: The Chichesters originally owned c. 250,000 acres in Ireland. (*Country Life*, 174, p. 250) By the mid-19th century the family had accrued huge debts and much property was sold. The 8 Earl of Shaftesbury married the daughter and heiress of the 3 Marquess of Donegall taking with her the most valuable property still in the family in 1883 (see Ashley-Cooper). The 5 Baron Templemore succeeded as 7 Marquess in 1975 (see below). 1 Baron, 1 Earl, and one other in ODNB.

Baron Templemore (1831- UK)

Origins: the 1 Baron was a grandson of the 1 Marquess of Donegal. The 5 Baron succeeded as 7 Marquess of Donegall in 1975.

1. Arthur Chichester 1 Baron Templemore – Milborne Port 1826-30 County Wexford 1830-31

Seats: Preston House, Hampshire (built 1720, purch. 1877, sold c. 1900); Dunbrody Park, Wexford (built but incomplete c. 1600, acq. by mar. 1660 from the Itchinghams who acq. Dunbrody in 1595, new house later 18th c., still own estate)
Estates: Bateman 26642 (E & I) 18793. Worth £5,000 pa in 1800.
Peers: 4 peers 1831-37 1842-1945

Chichester

Origins: The eldest son of Sir John Chichester, grandfather of the 1 Viscount Chichester, was the progenitor of this line. **First MP 1547 for Devon. One further MP 1624.**

1. Sir John Chichester 1 Bt – Barnstaple 1661-67
2. Sir Arthur Chichester 3 Bt – Barnstaple 1685-87 1689-90 1713-18
3. Sir John Chichester 4 Bt – Barnstaple 1734-40
4. Arthur Chichester – Honiton 1835-37

Seats: Youlston, Devon (acq. by mar. 1490, remod. 17th c., add. 18th c., sold 1920); Raleigh, Devon (medieval house, acq. by mar. 14th c. from a family who owned it from at least the 12th c., family moved to Youslton 1689, sold c. 1701)
Estates: Bateman 7022 (E) 6051. Rubinstein £100,000 probated estate 1808.
Title: Baronet 1641-
Notes: One in ODNB.

Chichester

Origins: A younger brother of the founder of the Youlston line founded a cadet line at a subsidiary seat at Arlington.

1. Sir John Chichester 1 Bt – Barnstaple 1831-41

Seat: Arlington Court, Devon (acq. 1384, medieval house, demolished 1783, new house 1790, demolished 1820, new house c. 1822-23, add. 1860s, given to NT 1949)
Estates: Bateman 6014 (E & W) 5343
Title: Baronet 1840-81
Notes: A Roman Catholic family that did not "conform" until 1793. Became heavily indebted and most estates sold c. 1880s. One in ODNB.

Chichester

Origins: Cadet line.

1. Sir Arthur Chichester 1 Bt – Carrickfergus 1812-18 Belfast 1818-20 Carrickfergus 1820-30 Belfast 1830-32

Seat: Greencastle (Green Castle), Donegal
Title: Baronet 1821-47

Baron Moyola (1971-2002 UKLife)

Origins: Dawsons came to Ireland in 1601 from Westmorland. Bishop of Clonfert 1627. Property developer and banker in Dublin and official in the Irish administration later 17th century. Bankers 18th century. The third son of the 4 Marquess of Donegall married the Dawson heiress to Moyola Park. The estates passed from the Dawsons back to a

Chichester heiress (daughter of a son of the 4 Marquess of Donegall), whose husband took the name Chichester-Clark.

1. Thomas Dawson – {Antrim 1695-99}
2. Joshua Dawson – {Wicklow 1705-14}
3. Arthur Dawson – {County Londonderry 1729-42}
4. Gerge Dawson – County Londonderry 1815-30 Harwich 1830-32
5. Robert Dawson – County Londonderry 1859-74
6. Sir Robert Chichester-Clark – Londonderry 1955-74

Seats: Moyola Park (Dawson's Bridge), Londonderry (purch. c. 1660, rebuilt 1768, passed by mar. to Chichesters 1872, still own); Castle Dawson, Londonderry (purch. 1633, destroyed 1689)
Estates: Bateman 3735 (I) 3594
1 Ld Lt 19th
Notes: *The Irish Genealogist* (vol. 6, Nov. 1985, 711-23) states the Dawsons came to Ireland in 1611 from Acorn Bank in Westmorland and purchased the lands at Castle Dawson in 1633. James Chichester-Clark was MP in the Northern Ireland Parliament 1929-33, as was his son, James Chichester-Clark 1960-72, Prime Minister of Northern Ireland 1969-71 and created Baron Moyola. One in ODNB.

CHOLMONDELEY (Cholmley, Cholmeley) [Harris, Harrison, Tuckfield, Walpole]

<u>Marquess of Cholmondeley</u> (1815- UK)

Origins: Norman marcher barons at Cholmondeley before the Domesday Book survey. Have held Cholmondeley since the 12th century in direct line. **First MP 1547 for Cheshire. Three further MPs 1547-1625, two for Cheshire**. Baronet 1611, Viscount 1628.

1. George Cholmondeley 2 Earl Cholmondeley – Newton 1690-95
2. George Cholmondeley 3 Earl Cholmondeley – East Looe 1724-27 New Windsor 1727-33
3. James Cholmondeley – Bossiney 1731-34 Camelford 1734-41 Montgomery 1741-47
4. George Cholmondeley Viscount Malpas – Bramber 1754-61 Corfe Castle 1761-64
5. George Cholmondeley 2 Marquess of Cholmondeley – Castle Rising 1817-21
6. William Cholmondeley 3 Marquess of Cholmondeley – Castle Rising 1822-32 S. Hampshire 1852-57

Seats: Cholmondeley Castle (Hall), Cheshire (acq. 11th c., medieval house, rebuilt 1571, remod. 1701, rebuilt 1801-05, add. 1817-19 and 1829-30, still own); Houghton Hall, Norfolk (built 1721-35, inher. by mar. from Walpoles 1797, still own)

Estates: Bateman 33991 (E) 41288. Worth £8,000-£10,000 pa in the 1640s. Worth £45,000,000 in 1990 with 12,000 acres. Rubinstein – 1 Marquess left £140,000 in probate in 1827 and George Cholmondeley £180,000 in 1830. Rubinstein says the late Marquess of Cholmondeley left an estate worth £100,000,000 in the 1980s.
Titles: Viscount Cholmondeley 1628-59 I; Baron Cholmondeley 1645-59 E; Earl of Leinster 1646-59 I; Viscount Malpas 1661- I; Baron Cholmondeley 1689- E; Viscount and Earl of Cholmondeley 1706- E; Baron Newburgh 1715- I; Baron Newburgh 1716- GB; Earl of Rocksavage 1815- UK; Baronet 1611-59
Peers: {2 peers 1661-89} 8 peers 1689-1725 1716-1827 1822-1945
4 Lds Lt 18th
1 in Cabinet 1736-44
1 KG 19th
Notes: The Marquesses of Cholmondeley succeeded to the Cheshire estates of the Savage family (Earl Rivers – see Pitt) by the marriage of James Cholmondeley to the daughter of the 4 Earl Barrymore and his wife Elizabeth Savage, sister and heiress of the 5th and last Earl Rivers. The Marquesses of Cholmondeley share with the Ancaster family the hereditary post of Lord Great Chamberlain, which entails making the ceremonial arrangements for the State Openings of Parliament. The family received a large infusion of weath through marriage into the Sassoon family in the 20th century (see Sassoon). 1 and 2 Earls and three others in ODNB.

Baron Delamere (1821- UK)

Origins: Cadet (16th century).

1. Thomas Cholmondeley – Cheshire 1670-79 1685-87
2. Francis Cholmondeley – Newton 1689-90
3. Charles Cholmondeley – Cheshire 1710-15 1722-56
4. Thomas Cholmondeley – Cheshire 1756-68
5. Thomas Cholmondeley 1 Baron Delamere – Cheshire 1796-1812
6. Hugh Cholmondeley 2 Baron Delamere – Denbighshire 1840-41 Montgomerey Burghs 1841-47

Seat: Vale Royal, Cheshire (medieval, purch. 1616 for £9,000, abbey buildings remod. as a house, remod. 18th c., add. 1796, 1810, 1833-34, 1848, 1860-61, 1877, requisitioned 1939, sold 1947, derelict).
Estates: Bateman 12319 (E) 20240 (includes the Cholmondeleys of Condover, Shropshire) Most English estates sold off by 1928; acq. 100,000 acres in Kenya c. 1902 where they still own large amounts of property.
Peers: 4 peers 1821-87 1891-1945
Notes: The family became resident primarily in Kenya in the 20th century. Still there. 3 Baron in ODNB.

Cholmeley

Origins: Descended from a younger son of Richard de Cholomdely, an ancestor of the Marquesses of Cholmondeley early 15th century.

1. Sir Montague Cholmeley 1 Bt – Grantham 1820-26
2. Sir Montague Cholmeley 2 Bt – Grantham 1826-41 Grantham Div. Lincolnshire 1847-52 1857-74
3. Sir Hugh Cholmeley 3 Bt – Grantham 1868-80

Seats: Easton Hall, Lincolnshire (purch. and built 1592, rebuilt 1805, uninhabitable after military use in WWII, demolished c. 1951, still own estate); Norton Place, Lincolnshire (built 1776, acq. 1811, enlarged 1836, still own)
Estates: Bateman 11452 (E) 15723
Titles: Baronet patent prepared but not confirmed 1642; 1806-

Harrison

Origins: The first MP was a barrister and Director of the Bank of England. May have been gentry. On his death in 1811 the Harrison estates passed to his son-in-law Sir Montague Cholmeley.

1. John Harrison – Great Grimsby 1780-96 Thetford 1796-1806

Seat: Norton Place, Lincolnshire (built 1776, passed to Cholmeleys 1811, see above)

Cholmley

Origins: Descended from a younger son of Hugh de Cholomdely (see above) 15th century. Acquired estates in Yorkshire in the late 15th century, much expanded after the Dissolution. **First MP 1529. Seven additional MPs 1558-1648, including three kts of the shire**. Bt 1641.

1. Sir Henry Cholmley – Malton 1641-48 Appleby 1660
2. Sir Hugh Cholmley 4 Bt – Northampton 1679 Thirsk 1685-87
3. John Cholmley – Southwark 1698-1711
4. Hugh Cholmley – Hedon 1708-21
5. Nathaniel Cholmley – Aldborough 1756-68 Boroughbridge 1768-74

Seats: Whitby Abbey (Whitby Hall, Cholmley House), Yorkshire (medieval, purch. 1539, add. 1672, family moved to Howsham 1743, passed out of family by mar. 1778, unroofed and part demolished, now museum); Howsham Hall, Yorkshire (built

c. 1610, acq. by mar. 1743, remod. c. 1775, passed out of family by mar. 1788, later a school) (see *Country Life*, 72, pages 196 and 224); Roxby, Yorkshire (acq. and built 1519, add. 1560s, later demolished)
Estates: Bateman 2320 (E) 2761 (Cholmeley of Brandsby House, Yorkshire (acq. late 16th c., sold 1912) – Roman Catholic cousins). Purchased 26,000 acres c.1540s and 1550s.
Title: Baronet 1641-89
Notes: Estates passed in 1778 to the Stricklands of Boynton (see that family). Two in ODNB.

Earl of Orford (1742-97 GB)

Origins: Merchants at Lynn in the Middle Ages. The Walpoles were established by a Bishop of Ely (d. 1302) (Plumb, *Sir Robert Walpole*, 81). Richard de Walpole c. 1130 married the daughter of Walter de Howelton whose estates at Houghton passed to the Walpoles by the end of the 12th century. **First MP 1315 for Norfolk. A further MP 1553.** Raised into the aristocracy by Robert Walpole, the first "Prime Minister". On the death of the last Earl of Orford, Houghton passed by inheritance to the Cholmondeleys of Cholmondeley in 1797.

1. Sir Edward Walpole – King's Lynn 1660-68
2. Robert Walpole – Castle Rising 1689-1700
3. Robert Walpole 1 Earl of Orford – Castle Rising 1701-02 King's Lynn 1702-42
4. Galfridis Walpole – Lostwithiel 1715-21
5. Sir Edward Walpole – Lostwithiel 1730-34 Great Yarmouth 1734-68 {Ballyshannon 1737-60}
6. Horatio Walpole 4 Earl of Orford – Callington 1741-54 Castle Rising 1754-57 King's Lynn 1757-68

Seat: Houghton Hall, Norfolk (acq. 12th c., built 1721-35, passed to Cholmondeleys in 1797 by mar.)
Estates: Worth £2,000 pa in 1700, £8,000 pa in 1745. (Hussey, *English Country Houses: Early Georgian 1715-1760*, 72)
Titles: Baron Walpole 1723-97 GB; Baron Houghton and Viscount Walpole 1742-97 GB
Peers: 3 peers 1723-91 1742-45
2 in Cabinet 1708-11 1714-17 1721-42 1737-39
1 KG 18th
Notes: 1 and 4 Earls and eight others in ODNB.

Earl of Orford (1806-1931 UK)

Origins: Horatio Walpole, brother of Sir Robert Walpole 1 Earl of Orford, built Wolterton Park. His son was created 1 Baron Walpole. The earldom was recreated for this line.

1. Horatio Walpole – Castle Rising 1702-13
2. Horatio Walpole 1 Baron Walpole – Lostwithiel 1710 Castle Rising 1713-15 Berealston 1715-17 East Looe 1718-22 Great Yarmouth 1722-34 Norwich 1734-56
3. Horatio Walpole 1 Earl of Orford – King's Lynn 1747-57
4. Thomas Walpole – Sudbury 1754-61 Ashburton 1761-68 King's Lynn 1768-84
5. Richard Walpole – Great Yarmouth 1768-84
6. Horatio Walpole 2 Earl of Orford – Wigan 1780-84 King's Lynn 1784-1809
7. George Walpole – Derby 1797-1806 Dungarvan 1806-20
8. Horatio Walpole 3 Earl of Orford – King's Lynn 1809-22
9. John Walpole – King's Lynn 1822-31
10. Horatio Walpole 4 Earl of Orford – E. Norfolk 1835-37
11. Spencer Walpole – Midhurst 1846-56 University of Cambridge 1856-82
12. Frederick Walpole – N. Norfolk 1868-76

Seats: Wolterton Hall (Park), Norfolk (purch. c. 1720, built 1727-41, remod. 1828, still own); Mannington Hall, Norfolk (built c. 1460, purch. 1736, add. 1860s, still own); Rainthorpe Hall, Norfolk (medieval, remod. c. 1600, purch. 1852, sold c. 1880)
Estates: Bateman 12341 (E) 15313
Titles: Baron Walpole 1723- GB; Baron Walpole 1756- GB
Peers: 7 peers 1747-1931 1756-57 1934-45
2 in Cabinet 1720-21 1852 1858-59 1866-68
Notes: 1 Baron and five others in ODNB.

Tuckfield

Origins: Clothiers at Raddon since the 16th century. Roger Tuckfield left his estates in 1754 to his granddaughter, the wife of the 2 Earl of Orford.

1. Roger Tuckfield – Ashburton 1708-11 1713-39
2. John Tuckfield – Exeter 1747-67

Seats: Raddon Court, Devon (old house, acq. c. 1700, declined to a farm house, ruins); Shobrooke House (Park) (Little Fulford), Devon (built 16th c., purch. later 16th c., rebuilt 1815, acq. by mar. 1807, remod. 1850, passed out of family by mar. 1880, fire 1945)

Harris

Origins: Gentry by the 18th century. John Harris married the daughter of Roger Tuckfield as her second husband (it was her daughter who became Countess of Orford), and he enjoyed the income of her estates during his lifetime before they passed to the Walpoles.

1. John Harris – Barnstaple 1741-47 1754-61

Seats: Pickwell Manor, Devon; Wrotham, Kent

CHOWNE [Westbrook]

Chowne

Origins: Settled in Kent in the early 15th century. **First MP 1553. One additional MP 1593.** Kt 16th century.

1. Henry Chowne – Horsham 1659 1661-68
2. Thomas Chowne – Seaford 1702 1710-13

Seats: Horsham, Sussex; Alfriston, Sussex (acq. early 17th c. and built house, partly burned, passed out of family 1787)
Notes: Extinct in male line 1787.

Westbrook (Westbrooke)

Origins: Settled at Godalming in the early 15th century. The daughter and heiress of the last Westbrook (d. 1703) married Thomas Chowne MP.

1. John Westbrook – Haslemere 1659 1660
2. William Westbrook – Arundel 1685-87 Bramber 1698-1700

Seats: Ferring (West Ferring), Sussex (acq. c. 1661, passed out of family c. 1734); Witley, Surrey (acq. early 17th c., sold 1674)

CHRISTIE [Burton, Peters]

Origns: The Burtons held some land in the 17th century but emerged due to the career of a general in the 1740s. The Peters started with a Russia merchant and Governor of the Bank of England 1785, father of the first MP. The daughter and heiress of Ralph Burton of Hull Bank and Hotham married in 1784 Napier Christie. Their daughter married in 1819 Henry Peters (Russia merchants and banking family) of Betchworth Castle, who took the name Burton.

1. Ralph Burton – Wareham 1768
2. Henry Peters – Oxford 1796-1802
3. Napier Christie-Burton – Beverley 1796-1806
4. Robert Christie-Burton – Beverley 1818-20
5. Henry Burton-Peters – Beverley 1830-37

Seats: Hull Bank House, Yorkshire (acq. 1740s, sold early 19th c.); Hotham Hall, Yorkshire (acq. and built c. 1720, add. 1772, passed out of the family 1865); Betchworth Castle (Place), Surrey (medieval, add. late-16th c., rebuilt 1808, sold c. 1815)
Estates: Henry Burton-Peters was worth £7,000 pa in 1827 and he left £140,000 in probate. Due to improvidence financial difficulties forced sales of land beginning in 1793.
Notes: Family extinct 1875.

CHRISTMAS *IRELAND*

Origins: Bristol merchants in the 17th century. Came to Ireland in the 1660s. Mayors of Waterford 1664, 1695, 1715, 1725. Sheriff 1685. Gradually cut links with trade and purchased estates late 17th and early 18th centuries.

1. Richard Christmas – {Waterford 1695-99 1703-13}
2. Thomas Christmas – {Waterford 1713-47}
3. Thomas Christmas – {County Waterford 1743-49}
4. William Christmas – {Kilmallock 1776-83}
5. William Christmas – Waterford 1832-35

Seat: Whitfield Court, Waterford (built 1st half 18th c., became ruinous 1840s, new house 1830s, sold 1916 - M. Girourd, *Country Life*, 142, 522)
Estates: Bateman 4605 (I) 3473. Worth £3,000 pa in 1713.

CHUTE (Chewte, Choute) [Wiggett]

<u>Chute</u>

Origins: Minor gentry in the Middle Ages. Rose as a soldier under Hnery VIII. Standard bearer to the King in France 1544. Purchased estates in Kent. Lawyers under Elizabeth I. **First MP 1542. Two additional MPs 1593-1614**. The Wiggetts succeeded to The Vyne and took the name Chute in 1827.

1. Chaloner Chute – Middlsex 1659 Haslemere 1661
2. Anthony Chute – Yarmouth (IoW) 1737-41 Newport (IoW) 1741-47
3. Francis Chute – Hedon 1741-42
4. William Chute – Hampshire 1790-1806 1807-20
5. William Wiggett-Chute – W. Norfolk 1837-47

Seats: The Vyne, Hampshire (built early 16th c., purch. 1653, remod. mid-17th c. and mid-18th c., NT 1956); Pickenham Hall, Norfolk (built c. 1680, purch. c. 1700, rebuilt 1829, sold 1830s)
Estates: Bateman 3416 (E) 4010
Title: Baronet 1952-56
Notes: Three in ODNB.

Choute

Origins: Cadet line.

1. Sir George Choute 1 Bt – Winchelsea 1696-98

Seat: Hinxhill Place (Court), Kent (acq. mid-17th c., demolished and sold c. 1721)
Title: Baronet 1684-1721

CLARGES

Origins: Father of the first MP was a London farrier. The first MP was a politician, official, and brother-in-law of General Monck 1 Duke of Albemarle.

1. Sir Thomas Clarges – Sutherland, Ross & Cromarty 1656-58 Aberdeen and Lauder 1659 Westminster 1660 Southwark 1666-79 Christchurch 1679-81 1685-87 University of Oxford 1689-95
2. Sir Walter Clarges 1 Bt – Colchester 1679-81 1685-87 Westminster 1690-95 1702-05
3. Sir Thomas Clarges 2 Bt – Lostwithiel 1713-15
4. Robert Clarges – Reading 1713-16
5. Sir Thomas Clarges 3 Bt – Lincoln 1780-82

Seats: Stoke Poges, Buckinghamshire (purch. 1661, sold 1740); Aston, Hertfordshire (leased?)
Estates: Worth £5,000 to £6,000 pa in 1695, £10,000 pa in 1834.
Title: Baronet 1674-1834
Notes: One in ODNB.

CLARK *ENGLAND & SCOTLAND*

Baron Clark (1970-83 UKLife)

Origins: Farmers in the mid-18th century became great thread manufacturers in Paisley from 1812.

1. Stewart Clark – Paisley 1884-85
2. Alan Clark – Plymouth Sutton 1974-92 Kensington and Chelsea 1997-99

Seats: Kilnside House, Renfrewshire (built 1836, purch. mid-19th c., remod. 1880s, used for business purposes from 1911, sold 1985); Saltwood Castle, Kent (medieval, damaged 1580, restored and add. 1885, restored 1936-39, purch. 1953, still own)
Estates: 1 Baron died worth over £5,000,000 in 1983. Owned 17,500 acres in Scotland in 1996.
Notes: The peerage was conferred on Kenneth Clark the art historian and Director of the National Gallery. Three in ODNB.

CLARKE [Bohun, Clerke]

Clarke

Origins: Merchants in Chesterfield, acquired landed estates in the later 16th century.

1. Sir Gilbert Clarke – Derbyshire 1685-87 1689-98
2. Godfrey Clarke – Derbyshire 1710-34
3. Godfrey Clarke – Derbyshire 1768-74

Seats: Somershall Hall, Derbyshire (acq. 16th c., rebuilt 1763, add. early 19th c., leased out 19th c., passed out of family 1824); Chilcote House, Derbyshire (purch. 1672, passed out of family 1824); Sutton Scarsdale Hall, Derbyshire (purch. 1740, passed out of family 1824)
Notes: Estates broken up in 1824 on the extinction of the family.

Clerke (Clarke)

Origins: Old family. One killed at the Battle of Spurs 1513. Grocers in London in the mid-17th century. **First MP 1621**, a lawyer and recorder. **An additional MP 1640.** The daughter and heiress of George Clerke MP married in 1671 Sir Gilbert Clarke MP, and the Kent estates passed to the Clarkes in 1691.

1. George Clerke – Northamptonshire 1661-79
2. Sir Francis Clerke – Rochester 1661-79 1681 1685-87
3. Francis Clerke – Rochester 1690-91

Seat: Ulcombe, Kent (passed to Clarkes 1691, passed out of the family 18th c.)
Estates: Worth £3,000 pa in 1660.

<u>Bohun</u>

Origins: Acquired Coundon in the 1570s. Coundon passed to the daughter and heiress of George Bohun MP who married the son of Sir Gilbert Clarke MP.

1. George Bohun – Coventry 1695-98

Seat: Coundon, Warwickshire (acq. 1570s, passed to Clarkes in the early 18th c.)
Notes: One in ODNB.

CLAVELL (Clavill)

Origins: Old gentry in Dorset. Claimed to have held land in the county from the time of the Conquest (Oswald, *Country Houses of Dorset*, 163). **First MP 1491. Second MP 1584**. In the 17th century the Clavells were heavily involved in the alum and glass industries. One went to India in the mid-17th century to make another fortune and returned a nabob.

1. Edward Clavell – Weymouth & Melcombe Regis 1709-10
2. George Clavell – Dorchester 1752-54

Seat: Smedmore, Dorset (Clavells inher. by mar. 1427 from a family who purch. in 1391, built 1620, remod. c. 1700, add. 1761, passed by mar. to Mansels 1833, still own)
Estates: Rubinstein – William Clavill left £100,000 in probate in 1817.
Notes: Smedmore has not changed hands by sale since the reign of Richard II. However, much of the estate was sold to pay debts 1623. The senior male line became extinct in 1774 but the remaining estates passed to the current owners through heiresses.

CLAYTON I [Courthorpe, Gethin] *IRELAND & ENGLAND*

<u>Clayton</u>

Origins: Gentry in Cheshire in the 14th century. Acquired monastic lands at the Dissolution. Sold estates in the late 16th century and moved to Ireland. Official in Ireland (d. 1636), gained estates there. Col. Randolph Clayton MP granted further land for military service (d. 1684).

1. Randolph Clatyon – {Kinsale 1661-66}
2. Laurence Clayton – {Mallow 1692-93 1695-99 1703-13}
3. Courthorpe Clayton – {Mallow 1727-60} Eye 1749-61

Seat: Mallow, Cork

Gethin

Origins: To Ireland 1630s. Officials granted land in Cork 1661. Sheriff 1679. The daughter and heiress of Courthorpe Clayton MP married Arthur Gethin, son of Sir Richard Gethin 1 Bt, who succeded to the estates.

1. Sir Richard Gethin 1 Bt – {Clonmell 1639-49 Newtown Limavady 1661-66}
2. Percy Gethin – {Sligo 1692-93 1695-99 1703-13}

Seats: Gethin's Grove (Court), Cork (acq. c. 1661, sold mid-19th c.); Earlsfield, Sligo (built 18th c., rebuilt c. 1870)
Title: Baronet 1665-
Notes: Lived in England post WWI.

Lord Courthorpe (Courthope) (1945-55 UK)

Origins: At Wadhurst, Sussex 1272. **First MP 1420**. The daughter and heiress of Sir Peter Courthorpe MP married Laurence Clayton MP.

1. Sir Peter Courthorpe – {Cork 1661-66}
2. Sir George Courthorpe – Sussex 1656 East Grinstead 1659 1661-79
3. John Courthorpe – Bramber 1699
4. Sir Peter Courthorpe 1 Bt – Rye Div. Sussex 1906-45

Seats: Whiligh, Sussex (acq. by marriage 1512, built 1586, remod. 1840, descendants still own); Danny Park, Sussex (medieval house, rebuilt 1595, purch. 1652, passed to Campions by mar. 1725)
Estates: Bateman 3656 (E) 4477
Title: Baronet 1925-55
Notes: Trees used to build the roof of Westminster Hall under Richard II were taken from Wadhurst, and more trees were harvested from the same place to repair war damage 1945-50.

CLAYTON II [Browne] *IRELAND & ENGLAND*

Clayton

Origins: A Liverpool merchant purchased Adlington 1690.

1. William Clayton – Liverpool 1698-1708 1713-15
2. Richard Clayton – Wigan 1747-54

Seat: Adlington Hall, Lancashire (purch. 1690, rebuilt 1770, acq. by Browne by mar. 1839 see below)
Estates: Bateman 7186 (I & E) 5980
Title: Baronet 1774-1839
Notes: One in ODNB.

Browne

Origins: Established in Carlow by the mid-17th century from England. Robert Browne married 1803 the only daughter and heiress of Sir Richard Clayton 1 Bt. The Brownes succeeded to the Adlington estates in 1839 and took the additional name Clayton.

1. William Browne – {Portarlington 1790-97}

Seats: Browne's Hill, Carlow (acq. early 18th c., built 1763, remod. 1842, sold 1951); Adlington Hall, Lancashire (acq. by Brownes by mar. from Claytons 1839, sold c. 1883, demolished c. 1955)
Estates: Bateman 5194 (I) 6488

CLAYTON III [East, Kenrick]

Clayton

Origins: The first MP was a carpenter's son who became the richest man in London as a conveyancer and land agent. Lord Mayor and Kt 1671.

1. Sir Robert Clayton – London 1679-81 1689-90 Bletchingley 1690-95 London 1695-98 Bletchingley 1698-1700 London 1701-02 Bletchingley 1702-05 London 1705-07
2. Sir William Clayton 1 Bt – Bletchingley 1715-44
3. Sir Kenrick Clayton 2 Bt – Bletchingley 1734-69
4. William Clayton – Bletchingley 1745-61 Great Marlow 1761-83
5. Sir Robert Clayton 3 Bt – Bletchingley 1768-83 Surrey 1783-84 Bletchingley 1787-96 Ilchester 1796-99

6. Sir William Clayton 4 Bt – Great Marlow 1783-90
7. Sir William Clayton 5 Bt – Marlow 1832-42
8. Richard Clayton – Aylesbury 1841-47

Seats: Harleyford Manor, Buckinghamshire (acq. 18th c., built 1753, sold 1950, fire mid-20th c.); Hedgerley Park, Buckinghamshire (purch. mid-19th c., sold 1881, demolished 1935); Marden Park (Place), Surrey (purch. 1672, sold c. 1911); Manor House, Kennington, Surrey (medieval house, Claytons leased from 1661-1834, demolished 1875)
Estates: Bateman 11165 (E) 12126
Title: Baronet 1732-
Notes: The family owned the lease of Kennington south of the Thames and developed the land as London expanded in the later 18th and early 19th centuries. The lease reverted to the Crown in 1834.

East

Origins: William East MP, son of a barrister, was a legal official who purchased Hall Place in 1728. Mary East, heiress of Sir Gilbert East 2 Bt, married in 1785 Sir William Clayton 4 Bt. A younger son took the name East and was created a Bt in 1838. On the extinction of the senior line of the Claytons in 1914, the 3rd East Bt succeeded as 7th Clayton Bt.

1. William East – St. Mawes 1728-35

Seat: Hall Place, Berkshire (purch. and built after 1728, passed by mar. to Claytons 1818, institutional use post-WWII)
Estates: Bateman 3224 (E) 5869. Rubinstein – 1 Bt left £200,000 in probate 1819 and 2 Bt left £300,000 in 1828.
Titles: Baronet 1766-1828; 1838-1932

Kenrick

Origins: The Kenricks were Clayton cousins. The first MP was the son of a barrister and was himself a lawyer.

1. John Kenrick – Bletchingley 1780-90
2. William Kenrick – Bletchingley 1806-14

CLEMENTS [Lucas] *IRELAND*

Earl of Leitrim (1795- I)

Origins: Merchants in Leicester in the early 17th century. To Ireland with Cromwell. Made a fortune in urban land speculation, banking, and the profits of office in the later 17th and early-mid 18th centuries. Sheriff 1694.

1. Henry Clements – {Carrickfergus 1692-93}
2. Theophilus Clements – {Cavan 1713-28}
3. Robert Clements – {Newry 1715-22}
4. Nathaniel Clements – {Dunleek 1728-60 Cavan 1761-68 County Leitrim 1768-76 Carrick 1776-77}
5. Robert Clements – {Cavan 1745-47}
6. Robert Clements 1 Earl of Leitrim – {County Donegal 1765-68 Carrick 1768-76 County Donegal 1776-83}
7. John Clements – {Cavan 1777-83}
8. Nathaniel Clements 2 Earl of Leitrim – {Carrick 1790-97 County Leitrim 1797-1800} 1801-04
9. Robert Clements Viscount Clements – County Leitrim 1826-30 1832-39
10. William Clements 3 Earl of Leitrim – Leitrim 1839-47
11. Charles Clements – County Leitrim 1847-52

Seats: Mulroy House, Donegal (acq. mid-19th c., built c. 1865, add. 1890s, descendents still own); Killadoon, Kildare (built c. 1770, remod. c. 1820, still own); Phoenix Lodge, Dublin (built 1751, sold 1780s); Rathkenny, Cavan (acq. 17th c., built 1820s, partly demolished 1920)
Estates: Bateman 59910 (I) 13196 including the Rathkenny line. Nathaniel Clements acquired c. 85,000 acres mid-18th century.
Titles: Baron Leitrim 1783- I; Viscount Leitrim 1793- I; Baron Clements 1831- UK
Peers: {1 peer 1783-1800} 1 Irish Rep peer 1801-04 4 peers 1831-92 1900-45
4 Lds Lt 19th, 20th
1 KP 19th
Notes: 3 Earl murdered by terrorists 1878. One in ODNB.

Clements

Origins: Cadet line descended from a younger brother of the 1 Earl of Leitrim.

1. Henry Clements – {Cavan 1729-45}
2. Williams Clements – {Baltimore 1761-68}

3. Henry Clements – {Cavan 1769-76 County Leitrim 1776-83 Cavan 1783-90 County Leitrim 1790-95}
4. Henry Clements – County Leitrim 1805-18 County Cavan 1840-43
5. John Clements – Leitrim 1820-26 1830-32

Seats: Ashfield Lodge, Cavan (acq. and built late 18th c., sold 1952, demolished); Lough Rynn, Leitrim (built 1833, add. 1889, sold 1990); Glenboy, Cavan
Estates: Bateman 45504 (I) 14243

Lucas

Origins: To Ireland in the early 17th century. A soldier in the 1650s. Granted and purchased land c. 1657. Sheriff 1673. Clements cousins descended from an uncle of the 1 Earl of Leitrim seated at Rathkenny. A Clements heiress married 1852 Edward Lucas of the Castle Shane family. They also inherited the estates of the Scudamores of Kentchurch Court (see Scudamore).

1. Francis Lucas – {County Monaghan 1695}
2. Francis Lucas – {Monaghan 1713-46}
3. Edward Lucas – {County Monaghan 1761-75}
4. Edward Lucas – County Monaghan 1834-51

Seat: Castle Shane, Monaghan (castle built 1591, purch. c. 1678, rebuilt 1836, burned 1920 and sold)
Estates: Bateman 9955 (I) 7934. Worth £2,000 pa in mid-18th c.

CLERK *SCOTLAND*

Origins: Merchants in Paris and Edinburgh in the early 17th century then lawyers and officials. Purchased landed estates mid-17th century.

1. Sir John Clerk 1 Bt – [Edinburghshire 1690-1702]
2. Sir John Clerk 2 Bt – [Whithorn Burgh 1703-07] Scotland 1707-08
3. Sir George Clerk 6 Bt – Midlothian 1811-32 1835-37 Stamford 1838-47 Dover 1847-52

Seats: Penicuik House, Edinburghshire (purch. 1646, new house late 1761-78, add. 1857, fire 1899, family lived in the converted stables from 1902, still own); Mavisbank, Edinburghshire (built 1723-27, remod. c. 1840, late 19th c. became a hospital, fire 1973, ruin)
Estates: Bateman 13196 (S) 11424.
Title: Baronet 1679-
Notes: Coal mines brought in additional income. 1, 2, 4, 6 Bts and the scientist James Clerk Maxwell in ODNB.

CLERKE

Origins: Old Warwickshire family settled in Buckinghamshire in the early 16th century. **First MP late 15th or early 16th century**.

1. Sir John Clerke 4 Bt – Haslemere 1710-13
2. Francis Clerke – Oxfordshire 1710-15

Seat: Shabbington, Buckinghamshire (medieval, purch. c. 1515, sold 1716)
Title: Baronet 1660-
Notes: 8 Bt in ODNB.

CLEVLAND [Christie, Hay]

Clevland (Cleveland)

Origins: The Clevland founder was the son of a naval officer and was himself an officer and administrator in the Royal Navy, who purchased Tapeley. William Christie of Glyndeborne (acq. by the Christies through mar. in the 19th c.) married in 1855 Agnes Clevland heiress of Tapeley Park.

1. John Clevland – Saltash 1741-43 Sandwich 1747-61 Saltash 1761-63
2. John Clevland – Barnstaple 1766-1802
3. William Christie – Lewes 1874-85

Seats: Tapeley Park, Devon (old house purch. and rebuilt 1704, passed by mar. 1855 to Christies, remod. mid-19th c. and early 20th c., still own); Glyndebourne, Sussex (acq. by mar. mid-19th c., remod. 1876, add. to theater from 1930s onwards, still own)
Estates: Bateman 11614 (E) 13382. Tapeley estate still consists of c. 6,000 acres
Notes: The Christies operated a famous opera house at Glyndebourne from the 1930s onwards. Two Clevlands and one Christie in ODNB.

Hay

Origins: **First MP 1640** was a lawyer who married Mary Morley, the heiress to Glynde. His father was Mayor of Hastings. Later a Hay heiress married a Langham through whom Glyndebourne passed to the Christies.

1. William Hay – Rye 1641-53 Sussex 1654 Rye 1656 1659 1660
2. William Hay – Seaford 1734-55
3. Thomas Hay – Lewes 1768-80

Seats: Little Horsted, Sussex (resident 17th c.); Glyndebourne, Sussex (medieval or early 16th c., acq. by inher. 1679, remod. 17th c., passed by mar. to Langhams 1824 and Christies mid-19th c., see above)
Notes: Glyndebourne has passed only by inheritance since Norman times. The de Glyndes acquired it soon after the Conquest. Their heiress c. 1300 took it to the Walleys, who held it until 1490. Their heiress married Nicholas Morley (see Hill I and Stanley) who owned it until 1679. A Morley heiress passed it to the Hays. (*Country Life*, 45, 554-58) One in ODNB.

CLIFFORD [Aston, Constable] *ENGLAND, SCOTLAND, & IRELAND*

Baron Clifford of Chudleigh (1672- E)

Origins: The Cliffords were a Norman family. The first Lord Clifford died at Bannockburn in 1274 (see Tufton and Southwell). **First MP 1545 for Westmorland. Four further MPs 1547-1621, two for Westmorland.** The ancestor of the 1 Baron Clifford of Chudleigh was a younger son of the 5 Baron de Clifford (Earls of Cumberland, extinct 1633). A daughter of the 2 Baron succeeded by marriage to Burton Constable, and it passed to a younger son. The Constables were paramount lords of Holdernesse from the 12th century. **First MP 1379 for Yorkshire. Three further MPs 1439-1604, all sitting for Yorkshire.**

1. Thomas Clifford 1 Baron Clifford – Totnes 1660-72
2. Sir Thomas Clifford-Constable 2 Bt – Hedon 1830-32

Seats: Ugbrooke Park, Devon (built 16th c., inher. early 17th c., rebuilt 1763-68, remod. mid-19th c., family still resident); Burton Constable Hall, Yorkshire (owned by Constables from 12th c., rebuilt house c. 1570 and 1600, add. 1730-36 and 1757-87, passed by inher. to Cliffords 1823, charitable trust 1992); Tixall Hall, Staffordshire (inherited 1768, rebuilt 1770s, demolished 1927-29)
Estates: Bateman 26374 (E) 33490. Still own 3,900 acres at Burton Constable (Sayer, *The Disintegration of a Heritage*, 107). Constables held 50,000 acres later 16th c.
Title: Baronet 1815-94
Peers: 5 peers 1831-1945
1 in Cabinet 1672-73
Notes: The 1 Baron Clifford of Chudleigh was Lord Chancellor 1672-73. The Constables and Cliffords were both Roman Catholic families in the 17th and 18th centuries, which debarred the 2 through 6 Barons from sitting in the Lords. The Cliffords claimed descent from Lady Godiva, Fair Rosamund, Rollo Duke of Normandy, and Ramsdal the Mighty, King of Denmark. 1 and 7 Barons Clifford and two others and three Constables as well as an entry on the Constable family in ODNB.

Baron Aston (1627-? S)

Origins: Old family that acquired manors in Staffordshire by 1260. Sheriff and Kt under Henry VI. **First MP for Staffordshire 1344. Three additonal MPs 1388-1553 all for Staffordshire.** Bt 1611 and Baron 1627. The 5 Baron (d. 1751) had two daughters. Barbara Aston inherited the Tixall estate and married Thomas Clifford (of Chudleigh). Their son succeeded to Tixall and took the name Constable. The right to the Barony descended to a distant cousin, who was poor. His line never claimed the peerage and the title probably became became extinct in 1769.

1. William Aston – {Dunleer 1721-27 County Louth 1727-44}
2. Tichborne Aston – {Ardee 1741-48}

Seats: Tixall Hall, Staffordshire (built 1555, rebuilt 1729-51, passed to Cliffords 1768); Standon, Hertfordshire [inherited from the Sadleir (Sadler) family (acq. 1544, built 1546) by marriage 1660, sold by heirs 1767, most demolished]; Beaulieu, Louth (built 1660-67, acq. by mar. 1st half 18th c., passed by mar. to Tippings later 18th c.); Richardstown Castle, Louth (medieval castle, occupied 18th c., sold)
Estates: Worth over £10,000 pa in the 17th century.
Titles: Baronet 1611-1751
1 Ld Lt 17th
Notes: A Roman Catholic family. William Aston MP married the Tichborne heiress to Beaulieu (1 Baron Ferrard see Montgomerie). His son, Tichborne Aston MP, left Beaulieu to his brother-in-law, Thomas Tipping, MP, (see Montgomerie). Astons extinct in male line 1751. 1 Baron and one other in ODNB.

CLIFTON

Baron Clifton (1608-18 E)

Origins: The first definitive ancestor was Sir Gervase Clifton, granted the manor of Clifton in 1280 and died 1323. (Payling, *Political Society in Lancastrian England*, 20) **He sat in the Commons for Nottinghamshire 1295. Five further MPs 1402-1601 all kts of the shire.**

1. Sir Gervase Clifton 1 Bt – Nottinghamshire 1614 1621 1624 1625 Nottingham 1626 Nottinghamshire 1628 East Retford 1640-46 Nottinghamshire 1661-66
2. Sir Clifford Clifton – East Retford 1659 1661-70
3. Sir William Clifton 3 Bt – Nottinghamshire 1685-86
4. Sir Robert Clifton 5 Bt – East Retford 1727-41
5. Sir Robert Juckes-Clifton 9 Bt – Nottingham 1861-66 1868-69

Seats: Clifton Hall, Nottinghamshire (acq. c. 1280, rebuilt 1560s, rebuilt c. 1750, remod. c. 1780, sold 1958, institutional use, now a residence again); Hodsock, Nottinghamshire (sold 1765)
Estates: Bateman 4288 (E) 8682. Rubinstein – 7 Bt left £160,000 in probate in 1837.
Title: Baronet 1611-1869
Notes: A Clifton was killed at the Battle of Shrewsbury fighting for Henry IV. The Barony passed through the female line from 1618 to numerous other families. The 4 Bt was a Roman Catholic. The 9 Baronet was the last of the male line. He built up large debts before his death in 1869. The remaining estate passed to the Bruce Bts (see Hervey). The barony did not become extinct in 1618 but passed through a series of female holders of the title to the Earls of Darnley (see Bligh).

CLIVE [Herbert, Hickman, Lewis, Windsor] ENGLAND & WALES

Earl of Powis (1804- UK)

Origins: The Clives were modest gentry seated at Styche from the Middle Ages onwards. Chancellor of the Exchequer in Ireland and Kt under Elizabeth I. **First MP 1553. Another MP 1645.** The family became prominent due to the efforts of Robert Clive (of India) whose military and civil leadership secured much of the subcontinent for the East India Company and brought him great wealth.

1. Edward Clive – Mitchell 1741-45
2. Robert Clive 1 Baron Clive – Mitchell 1754-55 Shrewsbury 1761-74
3. Richard Clive – Montgomery 1759-71
4. William Clive – Bishop's Castle 1768-70 1779-1820
5. Edward Clive 1 Earl of Powis – Ludlow 1774-94
6. Robert Clive – Ludlow 1794-1807
7. Edward Clive 2 Earl of Powis – Ludlow 1806-39
8. Robert Clive – Ludlow 1818-32 S. Shropshire 1832-54
9. Edward Herbert 3 Earl of Powis – N. Shropshire 1843-48
10. Henry Clive – Ludlow 1847-52
11. Sir Percy Clive Herbert – Ludlow 1854-60 S. Shropshire 1865-76

Seats: Powis Castle, Montgomeryshire (medieval, purch. by Herberts 1587, remod. 17th c. and 18th c., passed by mar. of 1784 to the Clives, NT 1952, still resident); Styche Hall, Shropshire (medieval, acq. by c. 1600, rebuilt 1762-66, flats, still own estate); Walcot Hall, Shropshire (purch. 1763, built 1764-69, add. early 19th c., sold 1933); Claremont, Surrey (built 1708, add. c. 1714, purch. 1768, rebuilt 1769-1772, sold 1774, school 1931); Oakly Park, Shropshire (built early 18th c., remod. 1748-58, 1784-90, and 1819-40, passed to Earls of Plymouth by mar. 19th c., see below)

Estates: Bateman 60539 (E & W) 57024. Rubinstein – 1 Earl left £120,000 in probate in 1839. Owned 30,000 acres in 2001.
Titles: For earlier Powis titles, see Herbert. Baron Clive 1762- I; Baron Clive 1794- GB
Peers: {2 peers 1762-1800} 5 peers 1794-1945 1929-45
5 Lds Lt 18th, 19th, 20th
1 KG 19th
Notes: The son of the 1 Baron married the sister of the last Herbert (see that family) Marquess of Powis (extinct 1748). They succeeded to the Powis estates and were created Earl and Countess of Powis 1804. The 2 Earl took the name Herbert in 1807. 1 Baron and 1 and 2 Earls and one other in ODNB.

<u>Clive</u>

Origins: Descended from a younger son of the 1 Baron Clive.

1. George Clive – Bishop's Castle 1763-79
2. Henry Clive – Ludlow 1807-18 Montgomery 1818-32
3. Edward Clive – Hereford 1826-45
4. George Clive – Herefordshire 1857-69 1874-80
5. Edward Clive – Herefordshire 1869-71
6. Percy Clive – S. Herefordshire 1900-06 1908-18

Seats: Whitfield, Herefordshire (built 1755-60, add. c. 1775-80, purch. late 18th c., add. c. 1850, still own); Wormbridge, Herefordshire (built 17th c., demolished 1798); Perrystone Court, Herefordshire (built 18th c., remod. in 1860s, purch. 1865, fire 1959); Claggan, Ballycroy, Mayo (resident 19th c.)
Estates: Bateman 13560 (E & I) 10130; Perrystone branch 41389 (E & I) 6250
Notes: Two in ODNB.

<u>Earl of Plymouth</u> (1682-1843 E 1905- UK)

Origins: The Windsors held the manor of Stanwell, Middlesex at the time of the Domesday Book. (Bindoff, *The House of Commons*, III, 634) **First MP 1295 for Berkshire**. Summoned as a Baron in the Parliament of Richard II. Baron 1529. **Six further MPs 1470-1555, three of them kts of the shire**. A brother of the 2 Earl of Powis married Baroness Windsor, sister and heiress of the 6 Earl of Plymouth. Their grandson, the 14 Baron Windsor, was created Earl of Plymouth of the second creation in 1905.

1. Thomas Windsor 1 Viscount Windsor – Droitwich 1685-87 Bramber 1705-08 Monmouthshire 1708-12
2. Dixie Windsor – University of Cambridge 1705-27

3. Andrews Windsor – Bramber 1710-15 Monmouth 1720-22
4. Herbert Windsor 2 Viscount Windsor – Cardiff Boroughs 1734-38
5. Robert Windsor-Clive – Ludlow 1852-54 S. Shropshire 1854-59
6. George Windsor-Clive – Ludlow 1860-85
7. Ivor Windsor-Clive 2 Earl of Plymouth – Ludlow Div. Shropshire 1922-23
8. George Windsor-Clive – Ludlow Div. Shropshire 1923-45

Seats: Oakly Park, Shropshire (see above, acq. by mar. 19th c., still own); Hewell Grange, Worcestershire (acq. 1542, built 1712, remod. 1816, demolished 1887, new house 1884-92, sold 1947, now an institution); Peel Hall, Cheshire (built 1637); St. Fagan's Castle, Glamorganshire (medieval castle, new house built c. 1620, acq. by mar. 1736, farm house by 1815, restored as a family residence post 1850, donated to National Museum of Wales 1946)
Estates: Bateman 37454 (E & W) 63778. In the 19th c. the family owned a lot of urban property in Cardiff. Owned 4,500 acres in 2001.
Titles: Baron Windsor 1529-1843 E; Viscount Windsor 1699-1758 I; Baron Mountjoy 1712-58 GB
Peers: 11 peers 1660-87 1700-25 1712-58 1728-32 1752-99 1810-43 1878-1945
5 Lds Lt 17th, 18th, 19th, 20th
Notes: The rebuilding of Hewell Grange 1884-91 cost £250,000. (Dakers, *Clouds*, 247) Earl in ODNB.

Hickman

Origins: The Hickmans were farmers before the Reformation, and later prospered in London as merchants. Purchased landed estates 1596. **First MP 1601. Another MP 1614.** Bt 1643. The sister and heiress of the 6 Baron Windsor married a Hickman. Their son, Thomas Hickman Windsor, succeeded as Baron Windsor and was created Earl of Plymouth in 1682.

1. Sir William Hickman 2 Bt – East Retford 1660-81
2. Sir Willoughby Hickman 3 Bt – Kingston-upon-Hull 1685-87 East Retford 1698-1706 Lincolnshire 1713-20
3. Willoughby Hickman – East Retford 1711-12

Seats: Gainsborough Old Hall, Lincolnshire (built c. 1460-80, purch. 1596, family departed 1720, passed by mar. to the Bacons 1826, leased to a museum 1952); Thonock Hall, Lincolnshire (built mid-18th c., purch. 1714, passed to the Bacons through an heiress 1826, demolished 1964)
Title: Baronet 1643-1781
Notes: One in ODNB.

Lewis

Origins: Authentic Welsh lineage dating to the 10th century. Purchased estates after the Reformation. The family had "a marvelous aptitude for the acquisition of property". (*Dictionary of Welsh Biography*, 546). **First MP 1555 for Monmouthshire. Three further MPs 1586-1601**. Courtiers under James I and Charles I. The only daughter and heiress of Thomas Lewis married in 1730 the 3 Earl of Plymouth, who succeeded to the Lewis estates in Wales.

1. William Lewis – Devizes 1660
2. Richard Lewis – Westbury 1660-80 1685-87 1689-1701
3. Edward Lewis – Devizes 1669-74
4. Thomas Lewis – Whitchurch 1708 Winchester 1710-13 Hampshire 1713-15 Southampton 1715-27 Salisbury 1727-34 Portsmouth 1734-36

Seats: St. Fagan's Castle, Glamorganshire (medieval castle, purch. 1616, new house c. 1620, passed by mar. to 4 Earl of Plymouth 1736, see above); The Van (Y Fan), Glamorganshire (purch. and built c. 1529, add. late 16th, add. early 17th c., passed by inher. to the 4 Earl of Plymouth and allowed to decay from 1736, ruin, sold 1991); Edington Priory, Wiltshire (medieval, acq. 1629, passed out of family c. 1694); Boarstall, Buckinghamshire (acq. by mar. 1649, later passed to the Aubreys by mar. – see that family); Soberton, Hampshire (acq. by mar. 1678, passed out of family after 1736)
Estates: Worth £5,000 pa mid 17th c. Earls of Plymouth owned c. 17,000 acres in Glamorgan in the 1940s.

Lewis

Origins: Cadet of the family above founded by an eighteenth-century ironmaster, main partners of the Dowlais Iron Company 1759-1848.

1. Wyndham Lewis – Cardiff Boroughs 1820-26 Aldeburgh 1827-29 Maidstone 1835-38

Seats: Greenmeadow (Green Meadow), Glamorganshire (resident let 18th and 19th c., demolished 1940s); Newhouse (New House), Glamorganshire (built c. 1735, remod. c. 1790, add. 19th c., passed out of family by mar. late 19th c., now hotel)
Estates: Bateman 3549 (W) 5520 plus income from ironworks. Wyndham Lewis inherted 1/16th share of the Dowlais Iron Company.

CLOPTON

Origins: Resided at Clopton since the 13th century. Lord Mayor of London, 15th c. **First MP 1346 for Gloucestershire. Two additional MPs in the 15th century**.

1. Sir John Clopton – Warwick 1679

Seat: Clopton House, Warwickshire (acq. 13th c., medieval, rebuilt 1662-70, sold 1831, now flats)
Notes: The Clopton heiress married 1580 George Carew, created Baron Carew of Clopton 1605 and Earl of Totness 1626, extinct 1629 (see Carew I). One in ODNB.

COATS *SCOTLAND*

Baron Glentanar (1916- UK)

Origins: Industrialists in the mid-19th century. Threadmakers in Paisley.

1. Sir Thomas Glen-Coats 1 Bt – West Renfrewshire 1906-10
2. Sir Stuart Coats 2 Bt – Wimbledon 1916-18 E. Surrey 1918-22

Seats: Glen Tanar, Aberdeenshire (built later 19th c., purch. 1905, descendents still own); Dunselma, Dumbartonshire (purch. 1884, built 1885-86, sold 1941); Castle Toward, Argyllshire (medieval, demolished, 1646, rebuilt 1820-21, acq. 1920s, add. 1920s, sold 1948)
Estates: The 1 Baron left £4,324,000 in 1918. (Rubinstein, *Men of Property*, 84)
Titles: Baronet 1894-1954; 1905-
Peers: 2 peers 1916-45
Notes: One in ODNB.

COBBE (Cobb) *IRELAND*

Origins: Emerged in the 15th century in Hampshire. A younger son went to Ireland 1717. Archbishop of Dublin 1743. Purchased estates 1730s and 1740s. Sheriff 1785. **First MP for Hampshire 1656.**

1. Thomas Cobbe – {Swords 1759-60 1761-68 1776-83}
2. Charles Cobbe – {Swords 1783-90 1798}

Seat: Newbridge House, Dublin (purch. 1736, built 1749, add. 1765, sold 1986)
Estates: 11367 (I) 4635. Worth £3,000-£4,000 pa in 1776. Owned 900 acres in 2001.
Notes: Two in ODNB.

COBBOLD

Baron Cobbold 1960- UK

Origins: Brewers since the mid-18th century.

1. John Cobbold – Ipswich 1847-68
2. John Cobbold – Ipswich 1874-75
3. Thomas Cobbold – Ipswich 1875-83
4. Felix Cobbold – Stowmarket Div. Suffold 1885-86 Ipswich 1906-09

Seats: Holywells, Suffolk (purch. 1812, built 1820s, rebuilt 1840s, donated to Ipswich as a park 1936, house demolished); Glemham Hall, Suffolk (medieval, rebuilt c. 1560 c., remod. 1712 and 1720, purch. 1923, still own)
Estates: Owned 2,000 acres in 2001.
Notes: Two in ODNB.

COCHRANE [Baillie, Carmichael, Wishart] *SCOTLAND*

Earl of Dundonald (1669- S)

Origins: Acquired estates in the 15th century. Kt mid-17th century. **First [MP 1644 for Ayrshire]**. Baron 1647.

1. Sir John Cochrane – [Ayrshire 1667 1669-74 1681]
2. William Cochrane – [Renfrew Burgh 1689-95 Dumbartonshire 1703-07] Wigtown 1708-13
3. Thomas Cochrane 8 Earl of Dundonald – Renfrewshire 1722-27
4. Andrew Cochrane-Johnstone – Stirling Burghs 1791-97 Grampound 1807-08 1812-14
5. Sir Alexander Cochrane – Stirling Burghs 1800-02 1803-06
6. Thomas Cochrane 10 Earl of Dundonald – Honiton 1806-07 Westminster 1807-18
7. George Cochrane – Grampound 1807-12
8. Sir Thomas Cochrane – Ipswich 1839-41
9. Thomas Cochrane 1 Baron Cochrane of Cults – N. Ayrshire 1892-1910
10. Archibald Cochrane – E. Fife 1924-29 Dumbartonshire 1932-36

Seats: Gwrych Castle, Denbighshire (built by Hesketh 1819, passed by mar. to the Dundonalds later 19th c. sold 1946, derelict, restored, hotel); Ochiltree Castle, Ayrshire (medieval, demolished, rebuilt, acq. by mar. 1675, forfeited 1685, repurch. 1686, sold 1737, fire, demolished); Wester Stanley, Renfrewshire; Lochnell Castle, Argyllshire (built late 17th c, add. 1737-39 and 1816-28, purch. 1912, still own); Auchans Castle, Ayrshire (acq. 1640, built 1644, fell into ruin after 1780)

Estates: Bateman under 2000 acres
Titles: Baron Cochrane 1647- S; Baron Cochrane of Cults 1919 UK
Peers: [2 peers 1660-90] 3 Scottish Rep peers 1713-14 1879-85 1886-1922 1 peer 1919
Notes: The 1, 9, 10, and 12 Earls and four others in ODNB.

Baillie

Orgins: William Baillie received a charter 1367 from King David II. **First [MP 1560]. Three additional [MPs 1560-1640, two for Lanarkshire]**. Mary Baillie heiress to Lamington married the 4th Carmichael Baronet of Bonnington. Their daughter married Robert Dundas. His daughter married Sir John Lockhart-Ross 6 Bt. Their granddaughter married Sir Thomas Cochrane.

1. William Baillie – [Lanarkshire 1689 1698-1701 1703-07]

Seat: Lamington (Tower) House, Lanarkshire (acq. in the medieval period by the Bradfute family, built 16th c., passed by mar. to Baillies, demolished c. 1780)
Notes: Four in ODNB.

Baron Lamington (1880-1951 UK)

Origins: The son of the 8 Earl of Dundonald married into the Ross-Wisharts. Their son took the name Cochrane-Wishart-Baillie and was created Baron Lamington.

1. Alexander Cochrane-Wishart-Baillie 1 Baron Lamington – Bridport 1841-46 1847-52 Lanarkshire 1857 Honiton 1859-68 Isle of Wight 1870-80
2. Charles Cochrane-Baillie 2 Baron Lamington – N. St. Pancras 1886-90

Seat: Lamington, Lanarkshire (Baillies acq. and built 16th c., new house 19th c., still resident 1940)
Peers: 3 peers 1880-1945
Notes: 1 and 2 Barons in ODNB.

Carmichael

Origins: See Baillie. The Carmichaels took the additional name Baillie 1727.

1. Sir James Carmichael 4 Bt – Linlithgow Burghs 1713-15

Seat: Bonnington House, Lanarkshire (acq. and built 17th c., fire c. 1900, demolished 1950s)
Title: Baronet 1676-1738

Wishart

Origins: At Pittarrow since the 13th century. **First [MP 1560]. One other [MP 1592-97].**

1. Sir James Wishart – Portsmouth 1711-15

Seats: Bedale, Yorkshire (acq. by mar. 1678, sold 1706); Pittarro (Pitarow), Kincardine (acq. 13th c., demolished 1802)
Notes: One in ODNB.

COCKBURN *SCOTLAND*

Cockburn

Origins: Prominent from 1375 onwards. Lord Keeper of the Great Seal 1389-96. Bt 1627. **First [MP 1612 Berwickshire]. Another [MP 1640-41 also for Berwickshire**].

1. Sir Archibald Cockburn 4 Bt – [Berwickshire 1678 1685-86 1689-98]
2. Archibald Cockburn – [Berwickshire 1685-86]
3. Sir James Cockburn 8 Bt – Linlithgow Burghs 1772-84
4. Sir George Cockburn 10 Bt – Portsmouth 1818-20 Weobley 1820-28 Plymouth 1828-32 Ripon 1841-47
5. Sir Alexander Cockburn 12 Bt – Southampton 1847-56

Seat: Langton, Berwickshire (medieval, acq. 1594, sold 1745)
Titles: Baronet 1627-1880; 1628-1782
Notes: Heritable Ushers of the White Rod. Cadet lines produced **three additional [MPs 1560-1648].** Two in ODNB.

Cockburn

Origins: Cadet line. **First [MP 1560]. Another [MP 1649].**

1. Adam Cockburn – [Haddingtonshire 1678 1681 1689-90]
2. John Cockburn – [Haddingtonshire 1703-07] Scotland 1707-08 Haddingtonshire 1708-41

Seat: Ormiston House, Haddingtonshire (new house 1745, sold 1747, partly demolished 1940)
Notes: Financial difficulties forced the sale of estates in 1747. Family extinct with death of the last MP's son.
Notes: Two in ODNB.

COCKS (Cox) [Somers]

Earl Somers (1821-83 UK)

Origins: The Cocks were landowners in Kent during the Middle Ages. They emerged into prominence under the Tudors and acquired Eastnor Castle c. 1600. The Somers were lesser gentry in the 17th century who rose to prominence in the law. The father of the 1 Baron, who became Lord Chancellor and was created a peer in 1697, was a local attorney in Worcester. Mary Somers, sister of the 1 Baron Somers married Charles Cocks. Her grandson was created Baron Somers in 1784. The Cocks were bankers in the later 18th and early 19th century.

1. John Somers 1 Baron Somers – Worcester 1689-93
2. Charles Cocks – Worcester 1694-95 Droitwich 1695-1708
3. Sir Richard Cocks 2 Bt – Gloucestershire 1698-1702
4. James Cocks – Reigate 1707-10 1713-47
5. Charles Cocks 1 Baron Somers – Reigate 1747-84
6. John Cocks 1 Earl Somers – West Looe 1782-84 Grampound 1784-90 Reigate 1790-1806
7. Philip Cocks – Reigate 1806
8. Edward Cocks – Reigate 1806-12
9. James Cocks – Reigate 1808-18 1823-31
10. John Somers-Cocks 2 Earl Somers – Reigate 1812-18 Hereford 1818-32 Reigate 1832-41
11. James Cocks – Reigate 1818-23
12. Charles Somers-Cocks 3 Earl Somers – Reigate 1841-47
13. Thomas Somers-Cocks – Reigate 1847-57

Seats: Eastnor Castle, Herefordshire (acq. c. 1600 and built soon after, rebuilt 1810-24 at a cost of £85,923, still own); Reigate Priory, Surrey (medieval, rebuilt as house 1541, remod. c. 1704, remod. 1779, purch. 1807, sold 1920-21); Dumbleton Hall, Gloucestershire (acq. by mar. early 17th c., rebuilt c. 1690, part demolished 1779 and the rest in 1830, sold 1828); Castleditch, Herefordshire (purch. c. 1600, demolished 1815)
Estates: Bateman 13067 (E) 16849
Titles: Baron Somers 1697-1716 E; Baron Somers 1784- GB; Baronet 1662-1765
Peers: 8 peers 1697-1716 1784-1899 1908-45
3 Lds Lt. 19th, 20th
1 in Cabinet 1693-1700 1708-10
Notes: Two in ODNB.

COCKAYNE

Viscount Cullen (1642-1810 I)

Origins: Gentry by the mid-12th century at Ashbourne, Derbyshire. **First MP 1332. Five further MPs 1335-1628 including several kts of the shire.** Chief Baron of the Exchequer (d. 1438). Younger sons merchants, one Lord Mayor of London 1619. One who was a skinner became involved in the plantation of Londonderry 1612 and became the first Governor. His daughter married the Earl of Nottingham and purchased Rushton 1614. Viscount 1642. On the death of the 6 Viscount Cullen in 1810 his estates passed to his niece Mary Cokayne who married William Adams. Their grandson took the name Cokayne and was created Baron Cullen in 1920.

No post-1660 MPs

Seats: Rushton Hall, Northamptonshire (built early 16th c., purch. 1614, add. 1626-31, sold 1828); Ashbourne Hall, Derbyshire (acq. early 12th c., built early 16th c., sold 1671)
Estates: Rent roll in early 17th century was £12,000 pa.
Titles: Baron Cullen of Ashbourne 1920- UK
Peers: {1 peer 1662-87} 2 peers 1920-45
Notes: Three in ODNB.

CODDINGTON *IRELAND*

Origins: The first known Coddington (1607-57) was High Sheriff of County Dublin in 1655 and County Wicklow 1656. One served at the Battle of the Boyne. His grandson was Sheriff of Dublin in 1695. The first MP was a lawyer and High Sheriff of Meath 1754. (Crosleigh, *Descent and Alliances of Crosleigh and Coddington and Evans*.)

1. Dixie Coddington – {Dunleer 1762-76}
2. Henry Coddington – {Dunleer 1783-90 1797-1800}
3. Nicholas Coddington – {Dunleer 1790-97}

Seats: Oldbridge, Meath (leased from 1703, purch. 1729, built 18th c., add. c. 1832, departed 1970s); Tankardstown House, Meath (purch. 1710, sold mid-18th c., now hotel)
Estates: Bateman 3737 (I) 2925
Notes: One in ODNB.

CODRINGTON

Origins: At Codrington since the reign of Edward I and acquired the manor in the mid-15th century. Standard bearer to Henry V in the Agincourt campaign. **First MP 1593.**

Purchased Dodington 1597. A younger son and his descendents gained a great fortune in Barbados from 1628 onwards as planters. Returned to England and purchased Dodington in c. 1700 from less prosperous cousins.

1. John Codrington – Bath 1710-27 1734-41
2. Sir William Codrington 1 Bt – Minhead 1737-38
3. Sir William Codrington 2 Bt – Beverley 1747-61 Tewkesbury 1761-92
4. Christopher Codrington-Bethell – Tewkesbury 1797-1812
5. Sir Edward Codrington – Devonport 1832-39
6. Christopher Codrington – E. Gloucester 1834-64
7. Sir William Codrington 5 Bt – Greenwich 1857-59

Seats: Dodington Park, Gloucestershire (medieval, new house 1557-60, purch. 1597, demolished and rebuilt 1796-1813, sold 1984); Codrington Court, Gloucestershire (acq. and built mid-15th c., remod. 16, 17, and early 18th c., family moved permanently to Dodington in the 18th c. and Codrington declined into a farm house); Didmarton, Gloucestershire (acq. by mar. 1571, sold c. 1750); Charlton House, Somerset (inher. 1694 from the Gorges, remod. 1st half 17th c., passed out of family by mar. of 1742)
Estates: Bateman 5023 (E) 7201; Christopher Codrington d. 1710 worth £80,000-£100,000. The family became the richest planters in the Leewards Islands, owners of the entire island of Barbuda. (Parker, *The Sugar Barons*, 185, 205). £122,000 was spent on construction and furnishings at Dodington Park 1796-1810 (Kingsley, *The Country Houses of Gloucester*, II, 119)
Titles: Baronet 1721- ; 1876-
Notes: Five in ODNB.

COGHILL *IRELAND & ENGLAND*

Origins: Minor gentry possibly of medieval origins at Coghill Hall, Yorkshire. A lawyer went Ireland after 1660 and was appointed as a Master in Chancery. The first {MP} was Chancellor of the Irish Exchequer. Sheriff 1756. The daughter and heiress of James Coghill {MP} married John Mayne of Richings, Buckinghamshire who took the name Coghill in 1779 and was created a Baronet.

1. Marmaduke Coghill – {Armagh 1692-93 1695-99 1703-13 Dublin University 1713-39}
2. James Coghill – {Clogher 1723-27 Newcastle 1727-34}
3. Sir John Cramer Coghill 1 Bt – {Belturbet 1755-76}
4. Sir John Mayne Coghill 1 Bt – Newport 1780-85

Seats: Glen Barrahane, Cork (built 19th c., still resident 20th c.); Coghill Hall, Yorkshire (medieval, rebuilt 1555, rebuilt later 18th c., inher. from English cousins 1789, sold 1796)
Estates: Bateman 6305 (I) 4552

Titles: Baronet 1778- ; 1781-85
Notes: Two in ODNB.

COKE I [Roberts]

Earl of Leicester (1744-59 GB; 1837- UK)

Origins: The founder of the family was Sir Edward Coke, Speaker of the House of Commons 1592 and Chief Justice 1613. He was the son of a London barrister. **First MP 1589. Three additional MPs 1614-42.** On the death of the 1 Earl of Leicester of the first creation, the Coke estates passed to his sister and heiress Anne, wife of Philip Roberts. Their son, Wenman Roberts, took the name Coke. His son was created Earl in 1837.

1. Richard Coke – Dunwich 1661-69
2. John Coke – King's Lynn 1670-71
3. Robert Coke – King's Lynn 1675-79
4. Sir Robert Coke 2 Bt – Derbyshire 1685-87
5. Gabriel Roberts – Marlborough 1713-15 1717-27 Chippenham 1727-34
6. Thomas Coke 1 Earl of Leicester – Norfolk 1722-28
7. Edward Coke Viscount Coke – Norfolk 1741-47 Harwich 1747-53
8. Wenman Coke – Harwich 1753-61 Okehampton 1761-68 Derby 1772-74 Norfolk 1774-76
9. Thomas Coke 1 Earl of Leicester – Norfolk 176-84 1790-1807 Derby 1807 Norfolk 1807-32
10. Edward Coke – Derby 1780-1807 Norfolk 1807 Derby 1807-18
11. Thomas Coke – Derby 1818-26
12. Edward Coke – W. Norfolk 1847-52
13. Wenman Coke – E. Norfolk 1858-65

Seats: Holkham Hall, Norfolk (purch. c. 1600 by Wheatleys through whom it passed by mar. to the Cokes 1612, built 1734-64, still own); Longford Hall, Derbyshire (built early 16th c., purch. 1622, remod. 1762, sold 1920, part destroyed by fire 1942); Godwick Hall, Norfolk (purch. 1580, built 1586, became a ruin); Weasenham Hall, Norfolk (acq. estate c. 1600, built 1905, still own); Minster Lovell Hall, Oxfordshire (built mid-15th c., purch. 1602, dismantled 1747)
Estates: Bateman 44090 (E) 59578 and 2442 (E) 4959. Worth £10,000 pa in 1718; Worth £50,000,000 in 1990. Owned 25,000 acres in 2013 (*Country Life*, Dec. 4, 2013, 48)
Titles: Baron Lovel (1728-59 GB); Baronet 1641-1727
Peers: 5 peers 1728-59 1837-42 1844-1945
3 Lds Lt 19th, 20th
1 KG 19th
Notes: Four in ODNB.

COKE II [Lamb]

Coke

Origins: Rose from medieval lesser gentry through office-holding in the later 16th and early 17th centuries. **First MP 1621. Two others in the 1640s.**

1. Thomas Coke – Derby 1685-87 1689
2. Thomas Coke – Derbyshire 1698-1700 1701-10 Grampound 1710-15
3. Daniel Coke – Derby 1776-80 Nottingham 1780-1802 1803-12

Seats: Trusley Manor, Derbyshire (acq. and built early 15th c., reduced to farm house 1718-1818, rebuilt 1902, most demolished 1946, "Old Hall" now residence, still own estate); Melbourne Hall, Derbyshire (built by early 13th c., acq. 1629, rebuilt 1630s, rebuilt 1706-27, passed to Lambs by mar. 1750); The College, Derby, Derbyshire (sold, institutional use); Brookhill Hall, Derbyshire (medieval, acq. 16th c.?, rebuilt c. 1630, add. 1742 and 1770, sold 1973, still own estate)
Estate: Less than 2000 acres by the 1870s.
Notes: Male line extinct 1945. Four in ODNB.

Viscount Melbourne (1781-1853 I)

Origins: The 1 Baronet, a lawyer, was the son of a solicitor, who was legal advisor to the Cokes of Melbourne Hall. The 1 Bt inherited £100,000 from a barrister uncle. He became a land agent and moneylender to the aristocracy. He married the Coke heiress and succeeded to Melbourne Hall in 1750.

1. Sir Matthew Lamb 1 Bt – Stockbridge 1741-47 Peterborough 1747-68
2. Peniston Lamb 1 Viscount Melbourne – Ludegrshall 1768-84 Malmesbury 1784-90 Newport (IoW) 1790-93
3. Peniston Lamb – Newport 1793-96 Hertfordshire 1802-05
4. William Lamb 2 Viscount Melbourne – Leominster 1806 Haddington Burghs 1806-07 Portarlington 1807-12 Peterborough 1816-19 Hertfordshire 1819-26 Newport (IoW) 1827 Bletchingley 1827-28
5. George Lamb – Westminster 1819-20 Dungarvan 1822-34

Seats: Brocket Hall, Hertfordshire (purch. 1746, rebuilt c. 1765-68, passed to Cowpers 1853); Melbourne Hall, Derbyshire (acq. by marriage – see above – 1750, passed to Cowpers by mar. 1853)
Estates: Bateman (under Mount Temple) 8145 (E & I) 16270 The 1 Baronet left an estate of £1,000,000 in 1768. Estates worth £19,000 pa in 1848.

Titles: Baron Melbourne 1770-1853 I; Baron Melbourne 1815-53 UK; Baron Beauvale 1839-53 UK; Baronet 1755-1853
Peers: {1 peer 1770-1800} 3 peers 1815-48 1839-53
1 in Cabinet 1827-28 1830-34 1835-41
Notes: On the death of the last Viscount in 1853 his estates passed to his sister Countess Cowper and then to her son the 6 Earl Cowper. Three in ODNB.

COKER

Origins: Medieval gentry. At Mappowder since the reign of Henry V. **First MP 1559.**

1. Robert Coker – Dorset 1656 1660
2. Henry Coker – Hindon 1722-27

Seats: Hill Deverill, Wiltshire (medieval, acq. by mar. 1624, sold 1738); Mappowder Court, Dorset (acq. early 15th c., old house rebuilt 1654, sold 1745, demolished mid-18th c. and rebuilt)
Notes: Family in financial difficulties 18th c. One in ODNB.

COLBORNE

Baron Seaton (1839- UK)

Origins: 1 Baron rose by merit and without purchase through the ranks of the army becoming Governor General of Canada 1839.

No MPs

Seats: Beechwood House, Devon (built 1780, purch. and remod. c. 1850, sold by 1920s); Valetta House, Torquay, Devon (resident 1850s and 60s); Bert House, Kildare (built 1725-30, enlarged early 19th c., passed to Colbornes by mar. 1863, sold 1909)
Estates: Bateman 5890 (E & I) 2341
Peers: 4 peers 1839-1945
Notes: Three in ODNB.

COLCLOUGH *IRELAND & ENGLAND*

Origins: Prominent burgesses in Newcastle-u-Lyme in the 14th century. **First MP 1360. Five further MPs (all for Newcastle) 1384-1454**. Acquired Tintern in Ireland under the Tudors. Bt 1628. Sheriff 1630.

1. Sir Caesar Colclough 2 Bt – Newcastle-under Lyme 1661-79

2. Patrick Colclough – {Enniscorthy 1689}
3. Caesar Colclough – {Taghmon 1719-26}
4. Caesar Colclough – {County Wexford 1727-60 1761-66}
5. Sir Vesey Colclough Bt – {County Wexford 1766-90 Enniscorthy 1790-94}
6. John Colclough – County Wexford 1806-07
7. Caesar Colclough – County Wexford 1806 1818-20

Seat: Tintern Abbey, Wexford (built 15th c., acq. 1577, given to nation 1958, still resident 1970s)
Estates: Bateman 13329 (I) 7124. Owned 16,992 acres in 1749. Worth £6,000 pa in 1800.
Title: Baronet 1628-87
Notes: Sir Vesey Colclough assumed the rank of Baronet without authorization. One possible relation in ODNB.

COLE *IRELAND*

<u>Earl of Enniskillen</u> (1789- I)

Origins: Perhaps a gentry family. The **first MP 1572** was a mercer. **Two further MPs 1601-60**. First Cole to Ireland 1601 came from London as an undertaker in the plantation of Fermanagh under James I and was granted one-third of the townland of Enniskillen 1612. **First {MP 1634}.** Sheriff 1670.

1. Sir Michael Cole – {Enniskillen 1661-63}
2. Sir John Cole 1 Bt – {County Fermanagh 1661-66}
3. Robert Cole – {Enniskillen 1661-66}
4. Arthur Cole 1 Baron Ranelagh – {Enniskillen 1692-95 Roscommon 1695-99}
5. Sir Michael Cole – {Enniskillen 165-66 1692-93 1695-99 1703-11}
6. John Cole – {Enniskillen 1703-26}
7. Richard Cole – {St. Canice 1703-13 Enniskillen 1713-30}
8. John Cole 1 Baron Mountflorence – {Enniskillen 1730-60}
9. William Cole 1 Earl of Enniskillen – {Enniskillen 1761-67}
10. Arthur Cole-Hamilton – {County Fermanagh 1783-90 Enniskillen 1790-1800} 1801-02
11. John Cole 2 Earl of Enniskillen – {County Fermanagh 1790-1800} 1801-03
12. Sir Galbraith Lowry Cole – {Enniskillen 1797-1800} County Fermanagh 1803-23
13. Arthur Cole – Enniskillen 1828-44
14. William Cole 3 Earl of Enniskillen – Fermanagh 1831-40
15. Henry Cole – Enniskillen 1844-51 Fermanagh 1854-80
16. John Cole – Enniskillen 1859-68
17. Lowry Cole 4 Earl of Enniskillen – Enniskillen 1880-85

Seats: Florence Court, Fermanagh (acq. early 17th c., built c. 1719, expanded 1740s, add. c. 1770s, NT 1953); Enniskillen Castle, Fermanagh (built 15th c., acq. 1607, fire 1710, abandoned by family 1739, became a barracks); Newlands (Castle), Dublin (acq. and built early 18th c., sold later 18th c., demolished 1976)
Estates: Bateman 30204 (I) 19290. Held 1,000 acres in 1612. Worth £1,070 pa in 1688 and £13,000 pa in 1805. Owned 5,000 acres in 2001.
Titles: Baron Ranelagh 1715-54 I; Baron Mountflorence 1760- I; Viscount Enniskillen 1776- I; Baron Grinstead 1815- UK; Baronet 1661-1754
Peers: {3 peers 1715-54 1761-1800} 1 Irish Rep peer 1804-15 4 peers 1815-1945
1 Ld Lt 19th
2 KP 19th, 20th
Notes: A cadet line (brother of the 1 Earl of Enniskillen) at Beltrim Castle, Tyrone (Cole-Hamilton) inherited estates from the 1 Earl of Abercorn (Hamilton) 16811 acres worth £3146 in the 1780s and £4890 in the 1880s. Two in ODNB.

COLEBROOKE *ENGLAND & SCOTLAND*

Baron Colebrooke (1906-39 UK)

Origins: Mercers and then bankers early 18th century. Purchased Chilham c. 1725. 1 Bt a nabob. 2 Bt (brother of 1 Bt) was Chairman of the East India Company.

1. Robert Colebrooke – Maldon 1741-68
2. Sir James Colebrooke 1 Bt – Gatton 1751-61
3. Sir George Colebrooke 2 Bt – Arundel 1754-74
4. Sir Edward Colebrooke 4 Bt – Taunton 1842-52 Lanarkshire 1857-68

Seats: Abington House, Lanarkshire (purch. late 18th c. estate gradually sold off early 20th c.); Chilham Castle, Kent (medieval, rebuilt 1616, purch. c. 1725, sold 1775)
Estates: Bateman 30023 (S & E) 9986
Title: Baronet 1759-1939
Peer: 1 peer 1906-39
1 Ld Lt 19th
Notes: Chilham was sold to pay the debts of Robert Colebrooke MP. Two in ODNB.

COLERIDGE

Baron Coleridge (1876- UK)

Origins: 1 Baron was the son of a judge.

1. John Duke Coleridge 1 Baron Coleridge – Exeter 1865-73

2. Bernard Coleridge 2 Baron Coleridge – Attercliffe Div. Sheffield 1885-94

Seat: The Chantry (Chanter's House), Ottery St. Mary, Devon (built 18th c., add. 1881-82, sold 2006)
Peers: 3 peers 1876-1945
Notes: 1 Baron's father was nephew of the poet. Six in ODNB.

COLLETON [Garth]

Origins: The Colletons were merchants in the 16th century. Planters in Barbados 1650. 1 Bt a soldier in the Civil War gained estates in South Carolina and was active in the Royal Africa Company. Thomas Garth (father of John Garth MP) married Elizabeth Colleton and the Garths succeeded to the Colleton estates in 1790. The uncle of the first Garth MP was Physician-General to the army and a personal doctor to George I.

1. Sir Peter Colleton 2 Bt – Bossiney 1681 1689-94
2. John Garth – Devizes 1740-64
3. James Colleton – Lostwithiel 1747-68 St. Mawes 1772-74
4. Charles Garth – Devizes 1765-80

Seats: Haines Hill, Berkshire (built mid-17th c., purch. 1736, add. 1760 and 1825, part demolished 1963, descendents still own); Brownston House (Garth House), Wiltshire (built early 18th c., purch. c. 1740, sold 1779)
Estates: Bateman 2581 (E) 4082
Title: Notes: The family continued to own property in Barbados at least until 2011. Baronet 1661-1938

COLLETT

Origins: Minor gentry. The first MP was the son of a hop merchant who became rich.

1. Ebenezer Collett – Grampound 1814-18 Cashel 1819-30
2. William Collett – Lincoln 1841-47
3. John Collett – Athlone 1843-47

Seat: Lochers (Lockers) House, Hertfordshire (purch. 1799, sold later 19th or early 20th c., school)
Estates: Rubinstein - Ebenezer Collett MP left £300,000 in probate in 1833.
Notes: First MP's estate was divided among eight children.

COLLIER

Baron Monkswell (1885- UK)

Origins: The first MP was a shipowner and merchant. 1 Baron was a judge. Kt 1863.

1. John Collier – Plymouth 1832-41
2. Robert Collier 1 Baron Monkswell – Plymouth 1852-71

Estates: The 1 Baron left £83,000 in 1886.
Peers: 3 peers 1885-1945
Notes: Two in ODNB.

COLMAN

Origins: Tiverton merchants c. 1500s. Became minor gentry; made a good marriage in the late 17th century.

1. Roger Colman – Tiverton 1660
2. William Colman – Tiverton 1685-87 1689-90
3. Edward Colman – Orford 1768-71

Seat: Gornhay, Devon (purch. early 17th c., sold 1812)

COLSTON

Baron Roundway (1916-44 UK)

Origins: Bristol merchants in the second half of the 17th century.

1. Edward Colston – Wells 1708-13
2. Edward Colston – Bristol 1710-13
3. Charles Colston 1 Baron Roundway – S. Gloucestershire 1892-1906

Seats: Roundway Park, Wiltshire (built early 18th c., rebuilt c. 1783, purch. 1840, remod. 1840s, remod. 1892, sold 1949, demolished 1954-55); Says Court, Gloucestershire (resident 19th c.); Filkins (Filkin's) Hall, Oxfordshire (passed out of family 1703 by mar., reacquired 18th c., ruin in early 20th c.)
Estates: Bateman 8364 (E) 13726; Edward Colston MP 1710-13 left £170,000 in 1721.
Peers: 2 peers 1916-44

COLT

Origins: Rose as royal official and noble servants in the mid-15th century. Acquired estates in Suffolk and Essex at that time. **First MP 1449. Another MP 1491.**

1. John Dutton Colt – Leominster 1679-81 1689-98 1701
2. Sir Henry Colt 1 Bt – Newport (IoW) 1695-98 Westminster 1701-02 1705-08

Seats: Colt Hall, Suffolk (acq. mid-15th c., sold late 17th c.); Clay Hall, Suffolk (acq. mid-15th c., sold late 17th c.); Parndon Hall, Essex (acq. mid-15th c., sold late 17th c.); Stafferton House (Dutton House), Herefordshire (acq. by mar. 1670, still resident c. 1900); Trawscoed, Radnor (resident 18th and 19th c.)
Title: Baronet 1694-
Notes: The Baronets in the 19th century were clergymen and a physician. One in ODNB.

COLTHURST [Jeffreys] *IRELAND*

Colthurst

Origins: Military officer in Ireland from 1607.

1. John Colthurst – {Tallow 1734-56}
2. Sir John Colthurst 1 Bt – {Doneraile 1751-60 Youghal 1761-68 Castlemartyr 1768-75}
3. Sir Nicholas Colthurst 3 Bt {St. Johnstown 1783-90 Clonakilty 1792-95}
4. Sir Nicholas Colthurst 4 Bt – Cork 1812-29
5. Sir George Colthurst 5 Bt – Kinsale 1863-74
6. David Colthurst – County Cork 1879-85

Seats: Blarney Castle, Cork (acq. by marriage 1846 from Jeffreys, new house 1874, still own); Ardrum, Cork (acq. and built 18th c., abandoned c. 1850, demolished)
Estates: Bateman 31260 (I) 9664 and 4301 (I) 4138
Title: Baronet 1744-

Jeffreys

Origins: First {MP} was an adventurer and Governor of Cork 1698. Purchased Blarney Castle 1703. Sir George Colthurst 5 Bt married in 1846 Louisa daughter and heiress of St. John Jeffreys.

1. Sir James Jeffreys – {Lismore 1703-14}
2. James St. John Jeffreys – {Midleton 1758-76 Randalstown 1776-80}

Seat: Blarney Castle, Cork (built 1446, purch. 1703, add. mid-18th c., fire 1820, passed to Colthursts by mar. 1846)
Estates: Worth £500 pa in 1713.

COLVILLE [Aytoun] *SCOTLAND & IRELAND*

Viscount Colville (1902- UK)

Origins: The Colvilles emerged in Scotland in the 12th century. Sir Robert Colville was Master of the Household to James IV and fell at Flodden 1513. Further soldiers, officials, and judges. **First [MP 1525]. Two further [MPs 1590-96]**. The 10 Baron Colville was a railway tycoon in the later 19th century and was created a Viscount.

No post-1660 MPs

Seat: Culross Abbey, Perthshire (sold 1630)
Titles: Baron Colville of Culross 1604- S; Baron Culross 1609- S; Baron Colville 1885- UK
Peers: 1 Scottish Rep peer 1818-49 3 peers 1885-1945
Notes: 1 and 7 Barons and five others in ODNB.

Baron Colville of Ochiltree (1651-1728 S)

Origins: The 1 Baron descended from an illegitimate son of the senior line 16th century. Sir John Aytoun of Aytoun married Margaret Colville daughter of the 2 Baron. He succeded to the estates of the 3 Baron in 1728 and took the name Colville.

1. Robert Colvile – Kinross-shire 1754-61

Seat: Ochiltree, Ayrshire (demolished)
Notes: Two in ODNB.

Aytoun

Origins: Established 12th c. **First [MP 1644].**

1. Roger Sinclair-Aytoun – Kirkaldy Burghs 1862-74

Seats: Aytoun, Fife (sold 1725); Inchdairnie House, Fife (acq. 1539, sold 1901, demolished)
Estates: Bateman 4328 (S) 6256
Notes: Two in ODNB.

Colvill

Origins: This branch of the Colvilles was founded by a brother of the 3 Baron Colville of Culross, a Professor of Divinity who came to Ireland in 1630. He acquired land through inheritance and nepotism. Purchased the Galgorm estate and renamed it Mt. Colville. (Dickson, "The Colvill Family of Ulster", 139-45.)

1. Sir Robert Colvill – {Hillsborough 1661-66 County Antrim 1692-93
2. Hugh Colvill – {County Antrim 1697-99}
3. Robert Colvill – {Antrim 1727-49 Killybegs 1719-27}
4. William Colvill – {Newton Limavady 1777-83 Killybegs 1783-90}

Seat: Mount Colville (Galgorm Castle), Antrim (old castle, purch. c. 1640, rebuilt c. 1645, sold 1851).

COLYEAR [Dawkins]

Earl of Portmore (1703-1835 S)

Origins: Soldiers in the Dutch service. 1 Baron came to England in 1688 and became a general and a peer.

1. Charles Colyear 2 Earl of Portmore – Chipping Wycombe 1726-30
2. James Colyear 4 Earl of Portmore – Boston 1796-1802

Seat: Portmore House, Weybridge, Surrey (acq. by mar. 1696, sold 1835)
Titles: Baron Portmore and Blackness 1699-1835 S; Baron Colyear and Viscount Milsington 1703-1835 S; Baronet 1677-1835
Peers: [1 peer 1700-07] 2 Scottish Rep peers 1713 1743-47
2 KT 18th
Notes: 1 Earl in ODNB.

Dawkins

Origins: The father of the first MP was one of the first settlers in Jamaica in the late 16th century, where the family came to own 25,000 acres by the mid-18th century. The daughter of the 2 Earl of Portmore married Henry Dawkins. Her eldest son succeeded to the Portmore estates on the death of the 4 Earl in 1835.

1. James Dawkins – New Woodstock 1734-47
2. James Dawkins – Hindon 1754-57

3. Henry Dawkins – Southampton 1760-68 Chippenham 1769-74 Hindon 1776-80 Chippenham 1780-84
4. James Dawkins-Colyear – Chippenham 1784-1806 1807-12 Hastings 1812-16 Wilton 1831-32
5. Henry Dawkins – Boroughbridge 1806-08 Aldborough 1812-14
6. Henry Dawkins – Boroughbridge 1820-30

Seats: Over Norton Park, Oxfordshire (purch. 1726, rebuilt 1879, still own); Standlynch Park, Wiltshire (built 1731-33, purch. 1766 for £22,000, rebuilt c. 1766-70, sold 1814); Laverstoke House, Hampshire (built late 16th c., purch. 1754 for £9,500, sold 1759)
Estates: Bateman 2512 (E) 4010; an income of possibly £60,000 pa in the mid-18th century from the Jamaica plantations (ODNB); Rubinstein – Henry Dawkins left £150,000 in probate 1814. Over Norton estate today is 400 acres.
Notes: One in ODNB.

COMPTON [Clephane, MacLean] *ENGLAND & SCOTLAND*

Marquess of Northampton (1812- UK)

Origins: Held Compton Wynyates possibly since the Conquest, certainly there by 1204. **First MP 1331 for Warwickshire. Four additional MPs 1563-1643.** Baron 1527. Earl 1618. The Comptons inherited the vast commercial fortune and properties of Sir John Spencer (Lord Mayor of London 1594) in 1610.

1. Sir William Compton – Cambridge 1661-63
2. Sir Charles Compton – Northampton 1661
3. Sir Francis Compton – Warwick 1664-79
4. Spencer Compton 1 Earl of Wilmington – Eye 1698-1710 East Grinstead 1713-15 Sussex 1715-28
5. James Compton 5 Earl of Northampton – Warwickshire 1710-11
6. George Compton 6 Earl of Northampton – Tamworth 1727 Northampton 1727-54
7. Charles Compton – Northampton 1754-55
8. Spencer Compton 8 Earl of Northampton – Northampton 1761-63
9. Charles Compton 1 Marquess of Northampton – Northampton 1784-96
10. Spencer Compton 2 Marquess of Northampton – Northampton 1812-20
11. William Compton 5 Marquess of Northampton – Warwickshire 1885-86 Barnsley Div. W. R. Yorkshire 1910-11
12. Lord Alwyne Compton – N. Div. Bedfordshire 1895-1906 Brentford Div. Middlesex 1910-11

Seats: Castle Ashby, Northamptonshire (medieval, purch. 1512, rebuilt 1574, remod. c. 1589 and 1624-34, remod. 1705-22, still own); Compton Wynyates, Warwickshire (acq.

by 1204, built late 15th c., rebuilt early 16th c., still own); Torloisk, Argyllshire (built 1770s, inher. by mar. c. 1840, remod. 1850-60, still own); Canonbury House, Middlesex (medieval, rebuilt 1509-32, acq. by Spencer family 1570, passed to Comptons by mar. of 1599, leased most of the time thereafter, partially demolished 1770s, house sold c. 1945 but surrounding urban property still owned by Comptons); Compton Place, Sussex (acq. 1618 and built by 1 Earl of Wilmington 1726-29, passed by mar. 1782 to Cavendishes)
Estates: Bateman 23501 (E & S) 23870. Worth £50,000,000 in 1990. Owned 30,000 acres in 2001. Owned extensive London property in Canonbury and Islington that rose greatly in value from the mid-19th c.
Titles: Baron Compton 1527- E (passed to the Marquesses Townshend); Earl of Northampton 1618- E; Earl of Wilmington 1730-43 GB; Baron Wilmington and Earl Compton 1812- UK
Peers: 13 peers 1660-81 1685-1727 1711-1945 1728-43
5 Lds Lt 17th, 18th, 19th, 20th
1 in Cabinet 1730-43
3 KG 18th, 19th, 20th
Notes: Earl of Wilmington and 2 Earl and 2 Marquess of Northampton and seven others in ODNB.

Compton

Origins: A cadet line descended from a younger son in the 17th century.

1. Henry Compton – S. Hampshire 1835-57
2. Francis Compton – S. Hampshire 1880-85 New Forest Div. Hampshire 1885-92
3. Henry Compton – New Forest Div. Hampshire 1905-06

Seat: Minstead Manor, Hampshire (acq. by mar. c. 1500, rebuilt 1719, add. 1802, demolished and sold 1949)
Estates: Bateman 4876 (E) 6411

Clephane

Origins: The 2 Marquess married the daughter and heiress of William Clephane MacLean and succeeded to their Scottish estates. David Clephane MP was 21st laird in his family lineage.

1. William Clephane MacLean – Kinross-shire 1802-03
2. David Clephane – Kinross-shire 1803-06 1807-11

Seats: Kirkness House, Kinross-shire (medieval, acq. by Clephanes in the 1780s by mar. from the Douglases who acq. it in the 16th c., passed by inheritance to the Marquess of Northampton in the 19th c. and sold 1900, roof removed 1920, ruin); Torloisk, Argyllshire (inher. by mar. from the MacLeans 1790, passed to the Comptons 1840, see above)

Baron MacLean of Duart (1971-90 UKLife)

Origins: The MacLeans were warriors seated at Duart on Mull by the 14th century. The chief was killed at Flodden in 1513. **First [MP 1628].** The Clephanes married a Maclean heiress to Torloisk in the 18th century, a cadet (c. 1600) of Duart.

1. Lachlan MacLean – [Argyllshire 1685-86]
2. Donald MacLean – Oxford 1835-47

Seats: Duart Castle, Argyllshire (medieval MacLean fortress, remod. 16th and 17th c., held by Campbells after 1691, ruin, repurch. 1911 and restored, still own); Brolas(s) (Brollace), Argyllshire (acq. mid-17th c., lost to Campbells in 1691)
Baronet 1631-
1 Ld Lt 20th
Notes: The MacLean of Duart estates were forfeited in 1691. The MacLeans of Duart have a family entry in the ODNB and a further four members of the family are also listed.

CONNER (O'Conner, O'Connor) *IRELAND*

Origins: Descended from a London merchant in the 18th century. Married the sister of the 1 Viscount Longueville (see Longfield), who was an heiress in her own right.

1. William Conner – {Bandon 1761-66}
2. Arthur O'Conner – {Philipstown 1790-95}
3. Feargus O'Connor – County Cork 1832-35 Nottingham 1847-52

Seat: Connerville, Cork (purch. 1703, built 1727, sold 1842, later called Carrigmore House); Fort Robert, Cork (built 1788, deserted by 1854, ruin by late 19th c.)
Estates: Worth £5,000 pa in 1761.
Notes: Arthur O'Conner was a rebel and exile. Feargus became a leading Chartist. Four members of the family in ODNB.

CONNOCK (Cannock)

Origins: A yeoman and tanner was appointed Receiver of the Duchy of Cornwall (a royal official) and acquired property at the Dissolution. **First MP 1554. Another MP 1593-1614**.

1. John Connock – Liskeard 1660
2. John Connock – Liskeard 1679 1685-87

Seat: Tregworgey House, Cornwall (medieval, purch. mid-16th c., rebuilt 18th c., passed by mar. 1757 to Marshall family who took the additional name Connock, fire 1938 and sold)

CONYERS

Origins: Originally from Durham and Yorkshire, the family came south to London in the 17th century and became merchants, then a lawyer, appointed a judge 1654. **First MP 1614**. Progressively entered the gentry.

1. Tristram Conyers – Maldon 1660
2. John Conyers – East Grinstead 1695-1708 1710-25 West Looe 1708-10
3. Edward Conyers – East Grinstead 1725-27 1734-41
4. John Conyers – Reading 1747-54 Essex 1772-75

Seat: Copt (Copped) Hall, Essex (built 16th c., purch. c. 1740, rebuilt 1753-58, remod. 1775-77, add. c. 1795, sold, fire 1916, ruin)
Notes: The medieval family has an entry in the ODNB.

COOKE I [Davies] *ENGLAND & WALES*

<u>Cooke</u>

Origins: Leading merchants in Doncaster 16th and 17th centuries. One was a barrister in the first half of the 17th century. The merchant father of the 1 Baronet purchased landed estates in the 1650s.

1. Sir George Cooke 3 Bt – Aldborough 1698-1700
2. Sir Bryan Cooke 4 Bt – East Retford 1711-13

Seats: Wheatley Hall, Yorkshire (purch. c. 1650, built c. 1680-83, abandoned c. 1914, golf club, demolished 1934); Ranby Hall, Lincolnshire (resident 18th c.); Campsmount, Yorkshire (inher. 1802, abandoned 1920s, demolished 1959)
Estates: Bateman 3638 (E) 6228; cadet at Campsmount 2894 (E) 4240
Title: Baronet 1661-

Cooke

Origins: Descended from a younger son of the 2 Baronet. Inherited Davies (medieval family) estates in Wales early 19th c. and took the name Davies-Cooke.

1. Bryan Cooke – Malton 1798-1807 1808-12

Seats: Owston Hall, Yorkshire (purch. 1685, sold 1981, golf club); Hafod-y-Wern, Denbighshire (Puleston estate, passed by mar. to Cookes early 19th c., became a farm house c. 1820); Gwysaney, Flintshire (medieval Davies seat passed via an heiress to Pulestons of Hafod-y-Wern 1785, and by a Puleston heiress to the Cookes early 19th c., still own)
Estates: Bateman 6862 (E & W) 12740. Estate reduced to 500 acres in the later 20th c. (Sayer, *The Disintegration of a Heritage*, 120)
Notes: Estates in Wales in the 19th c. included lead and coal mines, potteries and brick-works.

Davies

Origins: Seated "time out of mind" at Gwysaney, Flintshire (at least since the 13th century). (*Country Life*, 93, p. 880) The male line became extinct 1785. The estates passed via an heiress to Mary Davies who married Philip Puleston of Hafod-y-Wern. Their daughter Frances married Bryan Cooke MP of Owston.

1. Mutton Davies – Flintshire 1678-81

Seats: Gwysaney, Flintshire (medieval, see above); Llannerch Park, Denbighshire (built c. 1600, acq. by mar. 17th c., passed out of family by mar. 1785)
Notes: Llannerch Park belonged to Sir Peter Mutton, Chief Justice of Wales in the early 17th century and passed to another heiress after 1785. Family settled in Flintshire in the 14th c. Held 2,000 acres in 1565. **One Mutton MP 1604-24.**

COOKE II

Origins: Founded by a successful draper, Lord Mayor of London, and Kt in the 15th century. Purchased Gidea Hall, Essex c. 1460. **First MP 1460. Five additional MPs 1553-1640, several kts of the shire**. A cadet line established itself at Highnam Court. **First MP (and Kt) 1597**.

1. William Cooke – Gloucester 1679 1689-95
2. William Cooke – Gloucester 1705-09

Seats: Highnam Court, Gloucestershire (medieval house, acq. in 1605 by mar. of 1597, damaged 1643, rebuilt 1658, passed to Guise family via an heiress after 1747); Gidea Hall, Essex (purch. c. 1460, built 15-16 c., sold 17th c., demolished 1930)
Estates: Worth c. £1,000 pa in 1660.
Notes: Family extinct in the male line 1747. Estates passed via an heiress to the Guise Baronets, who purchased the interest of the other co-heiress to Highnam.

COOPER *IRELAND*

Origins: A soldier settled in Ireland and acquired estates from the mid-17th century. Sheriff 1698.

1. Joshua Cooper – {County Sligo 1719-57}
2. Joshua Cooper – {Castlebar 1761-68 County Sligo 1768-83}
3. Joshua Cooper – {County Sligo 1790-1800} 1801-06
4. Edward Cooper – County Sligo 1806-30
5. Edward Cooper – County Sligo 1830-41 1857-59
6. Edward Cooper – County Sligo 1865-68
7. Bryan Cooper – S. Dublin 1910 {TD 1923-30}

Seats: Markree Castle, Sligo (acq. and built 1650s, rebuilt 18th c., add 1802 and 1866, still resident 1950s, later derelict, hotel); Boden Park, Westmeath
Estates: Bateman 35238 (I) 12735. Worth £3,334 pa in 1785. Holdings reduced to 1,000 acres in 20th century.
1 Ld Lt 19th-20th
Notes: Four in ODNB.

COOTE [Nanfan] *IRELAND & ENGLAND*

Earl of Mountrath (1661-1802 I)

Origins: The 1 Baronet came from Norfolk to Ireland early in the 17th century as a military adventurer and later official. It was said of him that he "uniformly appears on the empurpled stage of civil contest as an avenging spirit, dealing forth woe and desolation." (*Country Life*, 154, p. 703) He acquired estates and operated ironworks. He died at the Battle of Trim 1642 after having acquired vast estates. **First {MP 1634} and additional {MP 1642}.**

1. Chidley Coote – {County Galway 1661-66}
2. Charles Coote 2 Earl of Mountrath – {County Roscommon 1661}
3. Thomas Coote – {Dublin 1692-93 County Monaghan 1723-27 1733-41}
4. Chidley Coote – {Kilmallock 1695-99}

5. Chidley Coote – {County Sligo 1713-19}
6. Sir Philips Coote – {Kilmallock 1713-14}
7. Henry Coote 5 Earl of Mountrath – Knaresborough 1715-20
8. Charles Coote – {Castlemartyr 1715-27}
9. Algernon 6 Earl of Mountrath – {Jamestown 1715-20} Castle Rising 1724-34 Hedon 1742-44
10. Charles Coote – {Granard 1723-27 County Cavan 1727-50}
11. Charles Coote 2 Baron Castle Coote – {Queen's County 1776-83 Maryborough 1783-97 Queen's County 1797-1800} 1801-02
12. Sir Charles Coote 9 Bt – Queen's County 1821-47 1852-59

Seats: Ballyfin, Queen's County (built 1778, purch. 1812, rebuilt 1821-26, sold 1923, now college); Woodhill, Hertfordshire; Castle Cuffe, Queen's County (owned 17th c.); (West?) Dereham Abbey, Norfolk (acq. mid-18th c., passed out of family 1802, demolished c. 1810); Ash Hill, Limerick (acq. later 17th c., sold 1794); Mount Coote, Limerick (acq. and built 18th c., remod. 19th c., sold c. 1925)
Estates: Bateman 49686 (I) 19255 and 2840 (I) 3050
Titles: Baron Castle Coote 1800-27 I; Baronet 1621-
Peers: {6 peers 1661-72 1692-1709 1711-20 1723-44 1753-1800}
1 in Cabinet Council 1696-97
Notes: On the death of the last Earl the estates were divided. The Baronetcy descended to a line founded by a younger son of the 1 Baronet. Two in ODNB.

<u>Coote</u>

Origins: Descended from a younger brother of the 2 Earl of Mountrath.

1. Sir Eyre Coote – Leicester 1768-74 Poole 1774-80
2. Sir Eyre Coote – {Ballynakill 1790-97 Maryborough 1797-1800} Queen's County 1802-06 Barnstaple 1812-18
3. Eyre Coote – Clonmell 1830-32

Seats: West Park, Wiltshire (purch. 1762, resident into 20th c., demolished c. 1945); Portrane House, Queen's County (built mid-18th c., sold 1925)
Estates: Bateman 13282 (E & I) 12695. Worth £2,000 pa in 1779.
Notes: Two in ODNB.

<u>Earl of Bellomont</u> (1689-1766 I) and <u>Earl of Bellamont</u> (1767-1800 I)

Origins: Descended from a younger son of the father of the first Coote Baronet who became a judge. Acquired confiscated O'Reilly estates in 1662.

1. Thomas Coote – {County Cavan 1661-71}
2. Richard Coote – {County Kilkenny 1692-93}
3. Richard Coote 1 Earl of Bellomont – Droitwich 1689-95
4. Charles Coote 1 Earl of Bellamont – {County Cavan 1761-66}
5. Guy Coote – {Clonmell 1769-83}

Seats: Bellamont Forest (Coote Hill), Cavan (acq. mid 17th c., built 1720s, remod. 1775, sold 1874); Coloony (Collooney), Sligo (acq. 17th c., sold 1729); Birtsmorton, Worcestershire (acq. by mar. 1764, fire, sold 1771)
Estates: Worth £2,500 pa in 1677. 5,321 acres worth £6,504 in mid-19th c.
Titles: Baron Coote 1660-1766 I; Baron Coloony (Collooney) 1764-1800 I; Baronet 1774-1897
Peers: {5 peers 1661-82 1696-1701 1707-1800}
Notes: Legitimate male line died out 1874. The baronetcy was conferred on an illegitimate line, which died out in poverty in 1897. One in ODNB.

Nanfan

Origins: The Nanfans, a Cornish family, held Birtsmorton from the reign of Henry VI. **First MP 1426. Four additional MPs 1445-1656, including three kts of the shire.** The male line became extinct in 1764. A daughter and heiress married the 1 Earl of Bellamont, whose son succeeded to the Nanfan estates.

1. Bridges Nanfan – Worcestershire 1681 Worcester 1685

Seats: Birts Morton (Birtsmorton), Worcestershire (built 14th c., acq. mid-16th c., remod. c. 1580, passed to Earls of Bellamont 1764); Trethewell, Cornwall (purch. mid-15th c., passed out of the family by mar.)
Notes: Two in ODNB.

COPE *ENGLAND & IRELAND*

Cope

Origins: Settled in Northamptonshire in the 14th century. Royal officials and courtiers under the Tudors from Henry VII onwards. **First MP 1397 for Northamptonshire. Six further MPs 1491-1625, including three kts of the shire.** Bt 1611.

1. Sir Anthony Cope 4 Bt – Banbury 1660 Oxfordshire 1661-75
2. Sir John Cope 5 Bt – Oxfordshire 1679-81 1689-90 Banbury 1699-1700
3. Jonathan Cope – Stafford 1690-94

4. Sir John Cope 6 Bt – Plympton Erle 1705-08 Tavistock 1708-27 Hampshire 1727-34 Lymington 1734-41
5. Sir Jonathan Cope 1 Bt – Banbury 1713-22
6. Sir Monoux Cope 7 Bt – Banbury 1722-27 Newport (IoW) 1741-47
7. John Cope – Queenborough 1722-27 Liskeard 1727-34 Orford 1738-41
8. James Cope – Downton 1754-56

Seats: Bramshill Park, Hampshire (built 1605-12, acq. 1700, remod. 18th c., sold 1936); Hanwell Hall (Castle), Oxfordshire (acq. 1498, built c. 1510, pulled down 1778); Bruern Abbey, Oxfordshire (medieval, purch. 1593, rebuilt c. 1710-20, fire 1780, estates divided among heiresses 1781, rebuilt)
Estates: Bateman 5442 (E) 6797
Titles: Baronet 1611- ; 1714-1821
Notes: The list above includes cadets from Ranton Abbey, Staffordshire (demolished 1992), Orton Longueville, Oxfordshire, and Bruern Abbey, Oxfordshire. Three in ODNB.

Cope

Origins: A younger son of Sir Anthony Cope 1 Bt emigrated to Ireland and established a family at Loughgall in the 17th c. Sheriff 1736.

1. Robert Cope – {Lisburn 1711-13 County Armagh 1713-14 1727-53}
2. Henry Cope – {Donegal 1779-83 Philipstown 1783-90 Tulsk 1790-97}
3. Robert Cope – {County Armagh 1799-1800} 1801-02

Seat: The Manor, Loughgall, Armagh (acq. 1st half 17th c., burned 1643, add. 1840, passed to descendents who sold out in 1947)
Estates: Bateman 9367 (I) 12463

CORBET [Kynaston] *ENGLAND & WALES*

Viscount Corbet (1679-82 E)

Origins: The Corbets had estates in Normandy, and were in Shropshire before the Conquest. Granted large estates 1070-71. **First MP 1290. At least two dozen MPs 1309-1654 including the Norfolk branch (see below).** Summoned as a Baron c. 1295 (tile extinct 1347). **Numerous of the MPs were kts of the shire for Shropshire.**

1. Sir Vincent Corbet 2 Bt – Shropshire 1679-80
2. Richard Corbet – Shropshire 1701-05
3. Andrew Corbet – Shrewsbury 1715-22

Seats: Moreton Corbet Castle, Shropshire (acq. 1239, castle built, rebuilt 1570s-80s, resident until mid-18th c., ruin, still own); Acton Reynald, Shropshire (built 17th c., add. 17th c., passed to Knyastons 1688, leased as school); Stanwardine Hall, Shropshire (acq. by mar., built 1580s, sold early 18th c., became a farm house)
Estates: Bateman 7080 (E) 8548. The Moreton estate reached 12,000 acres by 1600 with a further 7,000 acres in other counties.
Peers: 1 peer 1679-82
Titles: Baronet 1642-1788; 1808-1996
Notes: The story that a Corbet fought at Hastings is not supported by any evidence. It is possible that they were the hereditary standard bearers of the Dukes of Normandy from the time of Rollo, but, again, this cannot be proved. (Meisel, *Barons of the Welsh Frontier 1066-1272*, p. 3ff and 60ff.) Two in ODNB.

Corbet

Origins: A cadet of the Moreton Corbet family. **First MP 1604. An additional MP 1640.**

1. Sir Robert Corbet 4 Bt – Shropshire 1705-10 1715-22
2. Sir William Corbet 5 Bt – Montgomery 1728-41 Ludlow 1741-48

Seat: Adderley Hall, Shropshire (acq. by marriage to Gratewood heiress, principal seat from early 17th century, fire mid-19th c., rebuilt 1877-81, demolished 1955)
Estates: Bateman 8983 (E) 14008
Titles: Baronet 1627-1750; 1786-1823
Notes: Two in ODNB.

Corbet

Origins: Descended from a younger son of Vincent Corbet of Moreton Corbet (d. 1606).

1. Thomas G. Corbet - N. Lincolnshire 1835-37

Seats: Darnhall, Cheshire (acq. by mar. later 16th c., sold 17th c., repurch. early 18th c., sold 1860); Elsham Hall, Lincolnshire (built early 17th c., rebuilt 1760, inher. by mar. from Thompsons (see Thompson II) 1788, passed by mar. to Astleys in 19th c.)
Estates: 1,700 acres in Cheshire in 1860.

Corbet

Origins: Descended from a younger son of Roger Fitz-Corbet in the 12th century.

1. John Corbet – Shrewbury 1775-80

Seat: Sundorne Castle, Shropshire (built c. 1740, add. early 19th c., mostly demolished 1955)

Corbet

Origins: A cadet of the Moreton Corbet line. The male line became extinct in 1774. The estates passed to a kinsman named Flint who took the name Corbet and then to a nephew, Jospeh Plumley. His family also took the name Corbet in 1804.

1. Sir Richard Corbet 2 Bt – Shrewsbury 1677-81
2. Sir Richard Corbet 4 Bt – Shrewsbury 1723-27 1734-54
3. Panton Corbet – Shrewsbury 1820-30
4. Edward Corbet – S. Div. Shropshire 1868-77

Seats: Longnor Hall, Shropshire (held since reign of Henry VI, medieval, rebuilt 1670, sold 1948, but see Acton); Leighton, Montgomery
Estates: Bateman 4767 (E & W) 5920. Owned 15,000 acres in 2001.
Title: Baronet 1642-1774

Corbet

Origins: Cadet line of the Moreton Corbets. Settled in Norfolk in the 16th c. **First MP 1607. One other MP 1624-26**.

1. Miles Corbet – Great Yarmouth 1628 1640-55 1660

Seat: Sprowston Hall, Norfolk (acq. 1545, built 1560, sold c. 1661, now hotel)
Title: Baronet 1623-61
Notes: Miles Corbet was executed 1662 as a regicide. Two in ODNB.

Kynaston

Origins: The Kynastons, descended from the 11th century Princes of Powys (Bindoff, *The House of Commons*, II, 486), were settled in Shropshire in the 14th century. **First MP 1512. Five additional MPs 1554-1621**. John Kynaston married the daughter of the 2nd Corbet Bt of Moreton Corbet and inherited Acton Reynald in 1688.

1. Edward Kynaston – Shrewsbury 1679-81 1685-87
2. Edward Kynaston – Shropshire 1685-87 1689-99
3. John Kynaston – Shrewsbury 1695-1709 Shropshire 1710-15 1722-27
4. Corbet Knyaston – Shrewsbury 1714-23 Shropshire 1734-40
5. Edward Kynaston – Bishop's Castle 1734-41 Montgomeryshire 1747-72

6. William Kynaston – Shrewsbury 1734-49
7. Sir John Kynaston-Powell 1 Bt – Shropshire 1784-1822

Seats: Hardwick Hall, Shropshire (built c. 1720, passed by mar. to Owens in 1868 who took name Kynaston, still own); Acton Reynald, Shropshire (inher. by mar. 1688, rebuilt 1800, now school); Garth, Montgomeryshire; Hordley, Shropshire (medieval, acq. by mar. 15th c., abandoned for Hardwick 1712, became a farm house); Bryngwyn Hall, Montgomeryshire (passed to Mostyns early 18th c.); Ruyton Hall, Shropshire (built 1574, acq. 1707, passed to Corbets 1740)
Estates: Bateman 4484 (E & W) 6390
Title: Baronet 1818-66
Notes: The Knyaston's inherited Moel-y-Garth, Montgomeryshire from the Lloyds on the death of the last Bt in 1743 (Bt 1661-1743). The Lloyds were an ancient Welsh family. One fought at Agincourt. (*Dictionary of Welsh Biography*, 572) **First MP 1545. Three further MPs 1554-1659**. One in ODNB.

CORDELL [Firebrace]

Cordell

Origins: The founder was a noble servant who married the boss's heiress. His son was a lawyer and businessman, a founder of the Russia Company. He was granted arms 1548 and acquired former monastic property in 1554. **First MP 1553** was Speaker of the House of Commons. **One additional MP 1558**.

1. Sir Robert Cordell 1 Bt – Sudbury 1662-79
2. Sir John Cordell 2 Bt – Sudbury 1685-87 Suffolk 1689-90
3. Sir John Cordell 3 Bt – Sudbury 1701

Seat: Melford Hall, Suffolk (purch. 1554, built 1550s-60s, passed to Firebraces 1704)
Estates: Worth £3500 pa in 1710.
Title: Baronet 1660-1704
Notes: One in ODNB.

Firebrace

Origins: Father of the 1 Bt was a London vintner. The 1 Baronet acquired estates by marriage. The sister and heiress of the 3rd Cordell Bt married Sir Charles Firebrace 2 Bt and succeeded to the Cordell estates.

1. Sir Basil Firebrace 1 Bt – Chippenham 1690-92
2. Sir Cordell Firebrace 3 Bt – Suffolk 1735-59

Seats: The Old Hall, Stoke Golding, Leicestershire (purch. 1678, sold later 18th c., demolished 1850); Melford Hall, Suffolk (inher. by mar. 1704, sold 1786)
Title: Baronet 1698-1759

CORNEWALL [Amyand, Vaughan] *ENGLAND & WALES*

Cornewall (Cornwall)

Origins: The founder was the illegitimate son of the Earl of Cornwall, King of the Romans, brother of King Henry III. Granted lands by Edward I. **First MP 1369 for Shropshire. Eight additional MPs 1390-1621, most kts of the shire**.

1. Humphrey Cornewall – Leominster 1661-79
2. Robert Cornewall – Leominster 1685-87
3. Charles Cornwall – Bewdley 1709-10 Weobley 1715-18
4. Sir Robert De Cornewall 1 Bt – Leominster 1747-54
5. Charles Cornwall – Grampound 1768-74 Winchelsea 1774-80 Rye 1780-89

Seats: Berrington Castle, Herefordshire (acq. by 14th c., sold 1774); Barton Priors, Hampshire (acq. by mar. early 18th c.)
Estates: Worth £6,000 pa c. 1660.
Title: Baronet (assumed 1746-54)
Notes: Three in ODNB.

Cornewall

Origins: Cadet (c.1650s) of the Berrington family.

1. Frederick Cornewall – Montgomery 1771-74
2. Frederick Walker-Cornewall – Leominster 1776-80 Ludlow 1780-83
3. Frederick Cornewall – Bishop's Castle 1830-31

Seat: Delbury Hall, Shropshire (earlier house rebuilt 1750s, passed out of the family in 1904 as a result of inept legal work – Fisher, *The House of Commons*, IV, 754)
Estates: Bateman 2917 (E) 3398
Notes: One in ODNB.

Cornewall

Origins: Cadet of the Berrington line (17th c.). Edward Cornewall of Breadwardine Castle, Herefordshire married the widow of Sir Roger Vaughan of Moccas. Their eldest son succeded to Moccas and a younger son took the name Vaughan and inherited

Breadwardine. The Vaughans won estates and renown before the reign of Edward III. **First MP 1455. At least ten additional MPs in several branches between 1542 and 1614.** The grandson of the Moccas line had a daughter who married in 1771 Sir George Amyand 2 Bt, who succeded to Moccas. The Amyands were Huguenot refugees c. 1688. The son of the first exile was a surgeon to George I. His son was an official. However, the founder of the family fortunes was a successful merchant, banker, and West Indian planter who left an estate worth £158,000 and property in the West Indies, created a Baronet 1764. (*Country Life*, 160, p. 1475)

1. Roger Vaughan – Hereford 1662-72
2. Henry Cornewall – Weobley 1685-87 Hereford 1689-95 Herefordshire 1698-1700 Weobley 1701-08 1710-13
3. Velters Cornewall – Herefordshire 1722-68
4. James Cornewall – Weobley 1732-34 1737-41
5. Henry Cornewall – Hereford 1747-54
6. Sir George Amyand 1 Bt – Barnstaple 1754-66
7. Sir George Amyand Cornewall 2 Bt – Herefordshire 1774-96 1802-07
8. John Amyand – Camelford 1774-80
9. Claudius Amyand – Tregony 1747-54 Sandwich 1754-56

Seat: Moccas Court, Herefordshire (built 1775-81, family departed 1916, sold 1940)
Estates: Bateman 7314 (E) 8104
Title: Baronet 1764-1962
Notes: One Cornewall in ODNB.

CORRANCE

Origins: Acquired a small estate in Essex and granted arms 1620. The first MP was the son of a merchant tailor in London.

1. John Corrance – Aldeburgh 1679-81
2. Clement Corrance – Orford 1708-22
3. Frank White Corrance – E. Suffolk 1867-74

Seats: Parham Hall, Suffolk (purch. 1687, sold 1921?); Rougham Hall, Suffolk (built 16th c., purch. c. 1705 sold 1792, still owned mid-19th c., bombed 1940)
Notes: Frank White married 1782 the Corrance heiress and took the name Corrance in 1837 on succeeding to the estates.

CORRY *IRELAND*

Origins: The first MP was a merchant in Newry. His son Isaac, also an MP, was a barrister and Chancellor of the Exchequer in Ireland 1799.

1. Edward Corry – {Newry 1774-76}
2. Isaac Corry – {Newry 1776-1800} Dundalk 1801-02 Newry 1802-06 Newport (IoW) 1806-07
3. Edward Corry – {Randalstown 1794-97}
4. Thomas Corry – County Monaghan 1807-12 1813-18

Seats: Derrymore House, Down (acq. 1771, built c. 1780s, sold 1810, NT 1952); Rockcorry Castle, Monaghan; Bailieborough Castle, Cavan (acq. by mar. 1793, sold 1814)
Notes: One in ODNB.

CORYTON

Origins: Landed family in Devon by the reign of Henry III. **First MP 1558. An additional MP 1624-41.**

1. Sir John Coryton 1 Bt – Callington 1660 Cornwall 1661-79 Callington 1679 Launceston 1679-80
2. Sir John Coryton 2 Bt – Newport 1679 Callington 1685 1689-90
3. Sir William Coryton 3 Bt – Bossiney 1679 Newport 1679-81 Callington 1681 1685-87 Mitchell 1689 Callington 1695-1701 1703-11
4. Sir John Coryton 4 Bt – Callington 1713-22 1727-34

Seat: Pentillie Castle, Cornwall (built 1698, add. 1810, part demolished 1968, still own); Newton Ferrers House, Cornwall (acq. by mar. 1314, rebuilt 1686-95, part passed by mar. to Helyers 1739, sold 1834)
Estates: Bateman 9385 (E) 9944. 9,000 acres in 1603.
Title: Baronet 1662-1739
Notes: One in ODNB.

COSBY (Crosbie) *IRELAND*

Baron Sydney (1768-74 I)

Origins: To Ireland in 1548 as a soldier and official. Acquired monastic land and married well. **First {MP 1559}. One additional {MP 1639}.** Sheriff 1702.

1. Dudley Cosby – {Queen's County 1703-29}
2. Dudley Cosby 1 Baron Sydney – {Carrick 1763-68}

Seat: Stradbally Hall, Queen's County (acq. 1562, new house 1699, add. 1714, add. 1730s, demolished 1768, new house 1772, add. 1866-69, still own)
Estates: Bateman 10110 (I) 7077. Worth £1,200 pa in 1713.
Peer: {1 peer 1768-74}
Notes: Six in ODNB.

COTES

Origins: Medieval gentry, possibly very ancient. At Cotes from an early period.

1. John Cotes – Lichfield 1708-15
2. Charles Cotes – Tamworth 1735-41 1742-47
3. Thomas Cotes – Great Bedwyn 1761-67
4. John Cotes – Wigan 1782-1802 Shropshire 1806-21
5. John Cotes – N. Shropshire 1832-34
6. Charles Cotes – Shrewsbury 1874-85

Seats: Woodcote Hall, Shropshire (acq. by 1450 and built c. Henry VIII, rebuilt early 19th c. fire c. 1875, sold after fire, rebuilt late 1870s); Cotes, Shropshire (owned from the Middle Ages into 20th c.)
Estates: Bateman 6470 (E) 8860

COTTER *IRELAND*

Origins: In Ireland from the 15th century. The first {MP} was a Governor in the West Indies and attended James II's Parliament of 1688. He was executed for treason in 1720. His son created a Baronet 1763.

1. Sir James Cotter 1 Bt – {Askeaton 1761-68}
2. Sir James Cotter 2 Bt – {Taghmon 1771-76 Mallow 1783-90 Castlemartyr 1790-1800}
3. Rogerson Cotter – {Charleville 1783-1800}
4. Sir James Cotter 3 Bt – Mallow 1812-18

Seats: Rockforest, Cork (acq. 1679, rebuilt late 18th c., sold 1916, half demolished); Annegrove (Ballinsperrig), Cork (acq. c. 1600, built late 17th c., sold 1720, demolished c. 1965)
Estates: Bateman 7873 (I) 2461
Title: Baronet 1763-
Notes: The 2 Bt was a partner in a Cork bank that failed in 1807. Family lived in England 20th c. Three in ODNB.

COTTON I [Salusbury, Van] *ENGLAND & WALES*

Viscount Combermere (1827- UK)

Origins: Minor gentry rose as Comptroller of the Royal Household under Henry VIII. A major purchaser of monastic land.

1. Sir Robert Cotton 1 Bt – Cheshire 1679-81 1689-1702
2. Sir Robert Salusbury Cotton 3 Bt – Cheshire 1727-34 Lostwithiel 1741-47
3. Sir Lynch Salusbury Cotton 4 Bt – Denbighshire 1749-74
4. Sir Robert Salusbury Cotton 5 Bt – Cheshire 1780-96
5. Stapleton Cotton 1 Viscount Combermere – Newark 1806-14
6. Wellington Cotton 2 Viscount Combermere – Carrickfergus 1847-59
7. Sir Edward Cotton-Jodrell – Wirral Div. Cheshire 1885-1900

Seats: Combermere Abbey, Cheshire (medieval, acq. c. 1540, built 1563, remod. 1795 and 1814-21, sold 1919); Llewenny (Llewenni, Lleweni), Denbighshire (acq. by mar. 1684, sold 1776, part demolished 19th c., became farm house); Llanwern Park, Monmouthshire (built 1760, acq. by mar. from the Salusburys 19th c., sold 1900, demolished 1952); Reaseheath Hall, Cheshire (built c. 1830, rebuilt 1878, add. 1892, purch. 1904, sold 1920, now an institution); Shallcross Manor (Hall), Derbyshire (Jodrell seat: medieval, rebuilt 17th c., rebuilt 1723-25, passed by mar. to Jodrells c. 1800?, sold 1925, demolished 1968)
Estates: Bateman 13679 (E) 30779
Title: Baron Combermere 1814- UK; Baronet 1677-
Peers: 4 peers 1814-1945
1 Ld Lt 19th
Notes: 1 Viscount and two others in ODNB.

Salusbury

Origins: English family established at Lleweny (Llewnni) in Denbighshire by 1334. In the female line probably descended from the Princes of Gwynedd of the 11th century. (*Country Life*, 174, 906, 986) Gained Welsh estates during the English conquest. Increased wealth and power through the 15th century and supported the Tudors. Through the profits of office became the richest family in Denbighshire. The sister and heiress of Sir John Salusbury 4 Bt married Sir Robert Cotton 1 Bt, who succeeded to Llewenny in 1684, which was later sold for £110,000. **First MP 1542. Eleven other MPs 1545-1640.**

1. Sir John Salusbury 4 Bt – Denbigh 1661-81
2. Sir Robert Salusbury 1 Bt – Monmouthshire 1792-96 Brecon 1796-1812

Seats: Llewenny (Llewenni), Denbighshire (there by 1334, passed to Cottons 1684); Llanwern Park, Monmouthshire (built 1760, acq. by mar. from Van 1778, passed by mar. to Cottons 19th c.)
Title: Baronet 1619-84; 1795-1868
Notes: Salusbury family has an entry in ODNB plus four others.

Van

Origins: In Monmouthshire from the 14th century. Held manorial property from the reign of Edward III. Sir Robert Salusbury 1 Bt married Mary Van the heiress of Llanwern by whom it eventually passed to the Cottons.

1. Charles Van – Brecon 1772-78

Seat: Llanwern Park, Monmouthshire (purch. 1630, rebuilt 1760, passed to Salusburys by mar. 1778)

Cotton

Origins: Cadet of the Cottons of Combermere. Inherited Conington Castle in 1460. **First MP 1554 for Huntingdonshire. Two additional MPs 1601-40, both for Huntingdonshire.**

1. Sir John Cotton 3 Bt – Huntingdon 1661-79 Huntingdonshire 1685-87
2. Sir John Cotton 4 Bt – Huntingdon 1705-06 Huntingdonshire 1710-13

Seats: Conington (Connington) Castle, Huntingdonshire (medieval, acq. by mar. 1460 through medieval owners, rebuilt later 16th c., add. 1620, abandoned and became a ruin by beginning of the 18th c., demolished mid-18th c., acq. by Heathcotes later 18th c., demolished c. 1953); Conington Hall, Cambridgeshire (old house, purch. 1652, rebuilt c. 1700, passed out of family 1781); Stratton Park, Bedfordshire (acq. by mar. 1640, sold 1764)
Estate: Worth between £4,000-£9,000 pa c. 1700.
Title: Baronet 1611-1752
Notes: The family ended in Jacobite exile post 1745.
Notes: 1, 2, 3, 4, 5 Bts in ODNB.

Cotton

Origins: Cadet of the Cheshire Cottons. Bishop of Exeter 1598.

1. William Cotton – Camelford 1660

2. John Cotton – Bossiney 1685-87

Seat: Botreaux (Boscastle) Castle, Cornwall (medieval, acq. by mar. 1611, passed out the family 1703, demolished)
Estates: Worth £800 pa c. 1673.

COTTON II

Origins: A wealthy London mercer acquired landed estates 1420. **First MP 1439, a lawyer, sat for Cambridgeshire. Two additional MPs 1553-1601 both kts of the shire**.

1. Sir Robert Cotton – Cambridgeshire 1679-81 1689-95 Newport (IoW) 1695-1700 Truro 1702
2. Sir John Cotton 2 Bt – Cambridge 1689-1702 1705-08
3. Sir John Cotton 3 Bt – Cambridge 1708-22 1727-41 Cambridgeshire 1722-27 Marlborough 1741-52
4. Sir John Cotton 4 Bt – St. German 1741-47 Marlborough 1752-61 Cambridgeshire 1764-80

Seats: Madingley Hall, Cambridgeshire (built 1543-47, add. 1589-96, remod. 1724-34, sold 1871); Hatley St. George (Hatley Park), Cambridgeshire (built 1635-41, acq. after 1641, rebuilt c. 1700, add. c. 1750, passed out of family later 18th c.); Landwade Hall, Cambridgeshire (acq. 15th c., bult 1559, remod. 17th c., main seat until mid-18th c., new house 1846 which was demolished 1870)
Estates: 2 Bt had an income of £2,000 pa.
Title: Baronet 1641-1863
Notes: Family extinct 1863. 3, 5, 6 Bts in ODNB

COTTON III

Origins: Gentry by the 15th century. **First MP 1553 for Hampshire. Another MP 1605-28, sat for Shropshire**.

1. Rowland Cotton – Newcastle-u-Lyme 1699-1706 1708-15

Seats: Alkington Hall, Shropshire (acq. by mar. 15th c., built 1592, sold, became a farm house); Bellaport Hall, Shropshire (medieval, rebuilt early 17th c., acq. 1634, sold 1827, part demolished 19th c., declined into a farm house); Etwall Hall, Derbyshire (acq. by mar. 1695, rebuilt 1713-27, acq. by mar. mid-18th c., sold c. 1920, demolished c. 1955)
Notes: Three in ODNB.

COURTENAY [Kelland]

Earl of Devon (1335-1461 E; 1553-56 E; 1831- E)

Origins: The first Courtenay came to England with Eleanor of Aquitaine in 1152 and acquired a great estate. Baron by writ 1299 and Earl in 1335, attainted 1461. Fought at Crecy and Agincourt. Marquess of Exeter 1525-39. **First MP 1377. Fifteen additional MPs including twelve kts of the shire.** The Earldom of 1553 became dormant in 1556 but was restored in 1831. The heads of the family during this time were *de jure* Earls of Devon but did not assume the title.

1. Sir William Courtenay 1 Bt (15 Earl of Devon) – Ashburton 1660 1679-81
2. Richard Courtenay – Honiton 1689-90
3. Francis Courtenay – Devon 1689-99
4. George Courtenay – East Looe 1702 Totnes 1708-10 Newport 1710-13
5. Sir William Courtenay 2 Bt (16 Earl of Devon) – Devon 1701-10 1712-35
6. William Courtenay 1 Viscount Courtenay (17 Earl of Devon) – Honiton 1734-41 Devon 1741-62
7. Henry Courtenay – Honiton 1741-47 1754-63
8. Thomas Courtenay – Totnes 1811-32
9. William Courtenay 10 (20) Earl of Devon – Exeter 1812-26
10. William Courtenay 11 (21) Earl of Devon – S. Devon 1841-49
11. Edward Courtenay 12 (22) Earl of Devon – Exeter 1864-68 E. Devon 1868-70

Seats: Powderham Castle, Devon (acq. by marriage 1391 and built c. 1392-1406, remod. 1710-27, 1754-56, 1766-70, 1794-98 and 1835-48, still own); Walreddon Manor, Devon (built 15th c., acq. by mar. 1671, sold 1953); Forde House, Devon (built c. 1610, acq. by mar. 1648, leased out from 1762, sold 1936); The Castle, Newcastle, Limerick (built 15th c., acq. later 16th c., fell into ruin 17th c.)
Estates: Bateman 53075 (E & I) 45520. 21,000 acres in 1630. 4,000 acres in 1968.
Titles: Viscount Courtenay 1762-1835 GB; Baronet 1645-
Peers: 11 peers 1762-1831 1835-1935 1937-45
1 Ld Lt 18th
1 in Cabinet 1866-67
Notes: Thirteen members of the family in ODNB.

Courtenay

Origins: A younger son of the Earls of Devon married an heiress in the 15th century. **First MP 1553.**

1. Sir Peter Courtenay – Mitchell 1640 Tregony 1660

2. Nicholas Courtenay – Saltash 1679 Camelford 1685-87
3. Humphrey Courtenay – Mitchell 1689-96
4. William Courtenay – Mitchell 1701-02
5. Kelland Courtenay – Truro 1734-41 Huntingdon 1747-48

Seats: Trethurfe, Cornwall (acq. by mar. 16th c., passed out of family 1761); Tremeer (Tremere), Devon (acq. by mar. 16th c., passed out of family 1761)
Estates: Worth £1,200 pa in 1660.

Kelland

Origins: Totnes merchants who purchased landed estates in the mid-17th century. The Courtenays of Trethurfe succeeded to the Kelland estates by marriage.

1. John Kelland – Totnes 1679 1681 1685
2. Charles Kelland – Totnes 1681

Seat: Painsford, Devon (purch. 1647, passed to Courtenays 1695)

COVENTRY

Earl of Coventry (1697- E)

Origins: London merchants, Lord Mayor 1416. Justice of the Common Pleas purchased estates late 16th century. 1 Baron Lord Keeper of the Privy Seal 1625. **First MP 1621. Two other MPs 1625-42.**

1. Thomas Coventry 1 Earl of Coventry – Droitwich 1660 Camelford 1661-79 Warwick 1681 1685-87
2. Sir William Coventry – Great Yarmouth 1661-79
3. Henry Coventry – Droitwich 1661-81
4. Sir John Coventry – Weymouth & Melcombe Regis 1667-81
5. William Coventry 5 Earl of Coventry – Bridport 1708-19
6. Thomas Coventry – Bridport 1742-44
7. George Coventry 6 Earl of Coventry – Bridport 1744-47
8. John Coventry-Bulkeley – Worcestershire 1751-61
9. Thomas Coventry – Bridport 1754-80
10. William Coventry 8 Earl of Coventry – Worcestershire 1816-26

Seats: Croome Court, Worcestershire (purch. 1592, built 1751, sold 1948); Postlip Hall, Gloucestershire (built mid-16th c., purch. 1628, sold 1819); Snitterfield House (Park), Warwickshire (purch. 1668, rebuilt soon afterwards, sold 1816); Earls Croome Court,

Worcestershire (built c. 1600, still own); Springhill House, Worcestershire (built 18th c., sold 1830)
Estates: Bateman 14419 (E) 24878
Title: Baron Coventry 1628-1719 E
Peers: 12 peers 1660-1710 1712-1843 1859-1940
5 Lds Lt 18th, 19th, 20th
1 in Cabinet Council 1672-80
Notes: Five in ODNB.

COVERT

Origins: Emerged in Sussex in the 13th c. Profited from the iron industry. **First MP 1384. Two further MPs 1529-1626, both sat for Sussex**.

1. Sir John Covert 1 Bt – Horsham 1661-78

Seat: Slaugham Place, Sussex (acq. and built 1494, new house c. 1600, estates divided among heirs 1679, both MP families, now a ruin)
Title: Baronet 1660-79

COWPER [Clavering]

Earl Cowper (1718-1905 GB)

Origins: Father of the 1 Baronet was a London dyer. 1 Earl was Lord Chancellor.

1. James Cowper – Hertford 1656 1659 1660
2. Sir William Cowper 2 Bt – Hertford 1680-81 1689-1700
3. William Cowper 1 Earl Cowper – Hertford 1695-1700 Bere Alston 1701-05
4. Spencer Cowper – Bere Alston 1705-10 Truro 1715-27
5. George Clavering-Cowper 3 Earl Cowper – Hertford 1759-61
6. William Cowper – Hertford 1768-69
7. Edward Cowper – Hertford 1802-17
8. George Cowper 6 Earl Cowper – Canterbury 1830-34
9. William Cowper-Temple 1 Baron Mount-Temple – Hertford 1835-68 S. Hampshire 1868-80
10. Henry Cowper – Hertfordshire 1865-85

Seats: Panshanger, Hertfordshire (old house, purch. c. 1700, remod. 1704, rebuilt 1806, passed to Lord Desborough 1913, estate broken up and sold from 1919, house sold and demolished 1958); Hertford Castle, Hertfordshire (medieval, much demolished 1608, leased 18th c.); Hertingfordbury Park, Hertfordshire (rebuilt mid-17th c., purch.

1785, sold c. 1920); Brocket Hall, Hertfordshire (old house, rebuilt c. 1765-68, acq. by Cowpers by mar. 1853, sold 1923); Broadlands, Hampshire (built c. 1540, purch. by Temples 1736, rebuilt 1765-74, remod. 1788-92, add. 1859, passed by mar. to Cowpers 1865, passed by mar. in 1922 to Lord Louis Mountbatten, still own); Chopwell Hall, Durham (acq. by mar. 1706, sold c. 1830); Melbourne Hall, Derbyshire (acq. by mar. 1853, passed by mar. 1905 to the Kerrs, Marquises of Lothian)
Estates: Bateman 37869 (E) 60392 and 5720 (E) 6333. Estates worth £2,500 pa in 1706. Inherited coal mines in Durham in the 18th c.
Titles: Baron Cowper 1706-1905 GB; Baron Mount-Temple 1880-88 UK; Baronet 1642-1905
Peers: 7 peers 1706-23 1730-89 1798-1905
4 Lds Lt 18th, 19th, 20th
2 in Cabinet 1705-08 1714-18 1880-82
1 KG 19th-20th
Notes: The 2 Earl married the heiress to the Barony of Dingwall. The 6 Earl married the Baroness Lucas in her own right. On the extinction of the Earldom in 1905 both baronies passed to the Herberts (see that family). The second son of the 5 Earl Cowper and his wife, the daughter of the 1 Viscount Melbourne, was created Baron Mount-Temple. The 3 Earl Cowper was made a Prince of the Holy Roman Empire. 1, 3 and 7 Earls and four others in ODNB.

Clavering

Origins: A Norman family that emerged to prominence 13th century. **Two possible MPs 1386-1406. MP for County Durham 1656.** 1 Bt a lawyer. Owned collieries. John Clavering left his estates to the 2 Earl Cowper.

1. John Clavering – Great Marlow 1727-31 Penryn 1734-41
2. Sir Thomas Clavering 7 Bt – St. Mawes 1753-54 Shaftesbury 1754-60 County Durham 1768-90

Seats: Axwell Park, Durham (medieval, acq. 1629, rebuilt 1758, sold 1920, institutional use); Chopwell Hall, Durham (acq. by mar. 17th c., passed to Cowpers by mar. 1706); Greencroft Hall, Durham (purch. 1670, demolished 1960); Callaly Castle, Northumberland (medieval, acq. by early 15th c., rebuilt 1670s, add. 1707, sold 1877, now flats)
Estates: Bateman 13686 (E) 10498
Title: Baronet 1661-1893
Notes: One in ODNB.

Cowper

Origins: Cadet of the Earls Cowper.

1. Henry Cowper – Horsham 1701-07

Seat: Strood Park, Sussex (acq. by mar. 1465, passed out of the family 1725)

COZENS-HARDY

Baron Cozens-Hardy (1914-75 UK)

Origins: The Cozens were farmers who gradually built up an estate that reached 500 acres in the later 18th century. Became lesser gentry and JPs. The first Hardy was a self-made man and Methodist, beginning as a farmer and then brewer. In 1842 his estates and brewery went to his nephew William Cozens, who took the additional name Hardy. (Cannadine, *Aspects of Aristocracy*, 184ff)

1. Herbert Cozens-Hardy 1 Baron Cozens-Hardy – N. Norfolk 1885-99
2. William Cozens-Hardy 2 Baron Cozens-Hardy – S. Div. Norfolk 1918-20

Seats: Letheringsett Hall, Norfolk (purch. 1803 by Hardys, rebuilt c. 1808, leased out for institutional use 1975, sold 1992); Cley Hall, Norfolk (built c. 1800, purch. by Hardys 1839, sold 1946); Oak Lodge, Norfolk (built 18th c., purch. 1802, add. early 19th c., passed out of family later 19th c.)
Estates: Bateman 2929 (E) 3764; 1 Baron left £123,000 in 1920.
Peers: 3 peers 1914-45
Notes: 1 Baron Master of the Rolls 1907. 1 Baron in ODNB.

CRADOCK

Origins: Claim old lineage. Father of the first MP was spiritual Chancellor of Durham 1619.

1. Sir Joseph Cradock – Richmond 1661-62
2. Thomas Cradock – Richmond 1679-81 1685-87
3. Sheldon Cradock – Camelford 1822-32

Seats: Cradock Hall, Yorkshire; Hartforth, Yorkshire (acq. 1730, sold 1985, flats); Gainford Hall, Durham (medieval, acq. 1594, new house built c. 1603, abandoned mid-19th c. and ruinous)
Estates: Bateman 4413 (E) 5231. Estates worth £600 pa in 1686.
Notes: One in ODNB.

CRAIGIE *SCOTLAND*

Origins: Registered arms 1673. 1 Baronet a tacksman to the Earldom of Orkney and made a fortune.

1. Hugh Craigie – [Orkney & Zetland 1661-62]
2. Sir William Craigie – [Orkney & Zetland 1681 1689-1701]
3. David Craigie – [Kirkwall Burgh 1681 1685-86]

Seat: Langskaill, Gairsay, Orkney (built c. 1690s, ruin by 1840s)
Title: Baronet 1707-c.1760

CRAUFURD (Crawfurd) [Pollock] *SCOTLAND*

Craufurd

Origins: Medieval origins. The first MP's father a wealthy merchant who married an heiress.

1. Patrick Craufurd – Ayrshire 1741-54 Renfrewshire 1761-68
2. John Craufurd – Berwick-on-Tweed 1761-64
3. John Craufurd – Old Sarum 1768-74 Renfrewshire 1774-80 Glasgow Burghs 1780-84 1790
4. Sir Patrick Craufurd – Arundel 1781
5. James Craufurd – Horsham 1783-84
6. Edward Craufurd – Ayr District 1852-74

Seat: Auchenames (Auchinames), Renfrewshire (medieval tower house, purch. 1715, sold 1904)
Estates: Bateman 3440 (S) 3950
Notes: Two in ODNB.

Craufurd

Origins: Cadet of the Auchenames line (15th c.)

1. Robert Craufurd – East Retford 1802-06
2. Charles Craufurd – East Retford 1806-12

Seats: Newark Castle, Ayrshire (built 16th c., purch. and add. 1687, sold 1763); Kilbirney, Stirlingshire
Title: Baronet 1781-
Notes: Two in ODNB.

Craufurd

Origins: Cadet of the Newark line.

1. Sir John Crawfurd – [Ayrshire 1644 1661-62]

Seat: Kilbirnie (Old Place of), Ayrshire (built c. 15th c., acq. by mar. 1470, add. c. 1627, fire 1757, became a ruin)
Estates: Bateman 3145 (S) 3941
Title: Baronet 1628-62; 1765-1885
Notes: One in ODNB.

Pollock (Pollok)

Origins: The Pollocks, dating to the 12th century, were one of the oldest families in Renfrewshire. The 2nd Crawfurd Bt of Kilbirnie married the Pollock heiress and succeeded to the estates, taking the name Pollock.

1. Sir Robert Pollock 1 Bt – [Renfrewshire 1700-07] Scotland 1707-08 Renfrewshire 1710-22

Seat: Pollock (Pollok) Castle, Renfrewshire (acq. and built medieval period, add. 1686-94, rebuilt 1710, fire 1882, restored, family depart 1944, demolished 1952)
Estates: Bateman 3645 (S) 3941
Title: Baronet 1703-83

CRAVEN

Earl of Craven (1664-97 E 1801- UK)

Origins: The founder began as an apprentice to a merchant tailor second half of the 16th century, and was elected Lord Mayor of London 1610. Purchased estates 1618. His son was a soldier and created a peer 1627. **First MP 1640**.

1. Robert Craven – Coventry 1710
2. William Craven Lord Craven – Warwickshire 1746-64
3. Thomas Craven – Berkshire 1766-72

Seats: Ashdown House (Park), Berkshire (built 1660s, 1956 NT); Combe (Coombe) Abbey, Warwickshire (medieval abbey converted to house late 16th c., purch. 1622, add. 1682-9, add. 1861-72, sold 1923, part demolished c. 1923, now hotel); Benham Park (Benham-Valence), Berkshire (purch. 1630, built 1775, sold 1801, offices); Winwick

Manor House, Northamptonshire (built c. 1569, purch. before 1635, remod. c. 1700, rented out later 18th c., part demolished); Hamstead (Hampstead) Marshall (Park), Berkshire (medieval, purch. 1620, rebuilt 1663, fire 1718, rebuilt 1740s (Lodge), remod. 1825, sold 1984)
Estates: Bateman 30789 (E) 37593
Titles: Baron Craven 1627-97 E; Baron Craven 1642-67 E; Baron Craven 1666- E
Peers: 12 peers 1660-1711 1721-1825 1830-83 1889-1932 1938-45
7 Lds Lt 17th, 18th, 19th, 20th
Notes: Five in ODNB.

CRAWLEY

Origins: The founder was a Judge of the Common Pleas 1632, son of a husbandman.

1. Richard Crawley – Wendover 1701-05
2. John Crawley – Marlborough 1737-47
3. Samuel Crawley – Honiton 1818-26 Bedford 1832-41

Seats: Stockwood Park, Bedfordshire (purch. 1708, demolished 1964); Ragnall Hall, Nottinghamshire (built early 17th c., purch. 1790s, sold 1819)
Estates: Bateman 8355 (E) 7056. Estates worth £1,000 pa c. 1675.
Notes: One in ODNB.

CREWE [Gaskell, Harpur, Milnes, Offley]

Marquess of Crewe (1911-45 UK)

Origins: **First MP 1597** was of humble origin, son of a tanner in Nantwich, who rose as an official and became Chief Justice of the King's Bench 1625. Kt 1614. **Three further MPs 1624-54.** A Crewe heiress married John Offley of Madeley Manor, who took the name Crewe in 1709. The Offleys were founded by a merchant tailor in the mid-16th century who purchased estates. Lord Mayor of London and Kt 1557. The heiress of the 2 Baron Crewe married Richard Monckton-Milnes, 1 Baron Houghton (see below). Their son was 1 Marquess of Crewe.

1. Joseph Offley – Rye 1698-1702
2. John Crewe Offley – Newcastle-under-Lyme 1703-04 Cheshire 1704-10 1722-27
3. Crewe Offley – Newcastle-under-Lyme 1706-10 1715-22 Bewdley 1722-34
4. John Crewe – Cheshire 1734-52
5. John Offley – Bedford 1747-54 Orford 1754-68 East Retford 1768-74
6. Charles Crewe – Cheshire 1753-54
7. John Crewe 1 Baron Crewe – Stafford 1765-68 Cheshire 1768-1802

Seats: Crewe Hall, Cheshire (purch. 1609, built 1615-36, remod. c. 1710, remod. 1837-42, fire 1866, rebuilt 1866-71, sold 1931, offices); Madeley Manor, Staffordshire (medieval, purch. by Offley 1547, became a ruin and new house built early 19th c., sold 1936); West Horsley Place, Surrey (medieval, 16th c. and 18th c., purch. 1931, descendents still own)
Estates: Bateman 23094 (E) 35888. Offley estates worth £2,500 pa in c. 1662.
Titles: Baron Crewe 1806-93 UK; Earl of Crewe 1895-1945 UK
Peers: 4 peers 1806-93 1885-1945
1 Ld Lt 20th
1 in Cabinet 1892-95 1905-16 1931
1 KG 20th
Notes: 1 Baron and 1 Marquess, five others and one Offley in ODNB.

<u>Baron Houghton</u> (1863-1945 UK)

Origins: The Milnes family emerged in the later 17th century in the woolen trade. They were Unitarian cloth merchants, exporters second only to the Denisons in wealth in the West Riding by the 1770s, when they began to purchase estates. Robert Milnes of Fryston Hall and Bawtry Hall married Henrietta Monckton, daughter of the 4 Viscount Galway (see Monckton). Their son Richard inherited Houghton from his mother (the family taking the additional name Monckton) and married a merchant heiress worth £100,000. (Ward and Wilson, *Land and Industry*, 162ff.)

1. Richard Milnes – York 1784-1802
2. Robert Milnes – Pontefract 1806-18
3. Richard Monckton Milnes 1 Baron Houghton – Pontefract 1837-63

Seats: Fryston Hall, Yorkshire (purch. 1788, rebuilt c. 1800, sold c. 1914, dismantled 1931); Bawtry Hall, Yorkshire (purch. 1770s, built c. 1785, sold first half 19th c.)
Estates: Bateman 7599 (E) 11787
Peer: 1 peer 1863-85
Notes: For the 2 Baron Houghton, 1 Marquess of Crewe, see under Crewe above). Two in ODNB.

<u>Milnes-Gaskell</u>

Origins: Mary Milnes, the daughter and heiress of a younger son, married into the Gaskell family of business origins in the 18th and early 19th centuries.

1. James Milnes – Bletchingley 1802-05
2. Benjamin Gaskell – Maldon 1806-07 1812-26
3. Daniel Gaskell – Wakefield 1832-37
4. James Milnes-Gaskell – Wenlock 1832-68
5. Charles Milnes-Gaskell – Morely Div. W. R. Yorkshire 1885-92

Seats: Clifton Hall, Lancashire (old house, purch. 1652, rebuilt 18th c., sold after 1911); Wenlock Abbey, Shropshire (medieval, purch. 1857, still own); Thornes House, Yorkshire (Milnes built 1779-81, sold 1919, fire 1951); Lupset Hall, Yorkshire (built 1716)
Estates: Bateman 4393 (E) 10732
Notes: One in ODNB.

Baron Crew(e) (1661-1721 E)

Origins: Descended from a younger brother of the first Crewe MP (see above). **First MP 1604**. He married the heiress of Reginald Bray, who had inherited that estate from Baron Bray(e) (1529-57 E), of an old family with **several MPs 1478-1571** (see Cave).

1. John Crew 1 Baron Crew – Amersham 1624 1625 Brackley 1626 Banbury 1628-29 Northamptonshire 1640 Brackley 1640-48 Northamptonshire 1654 1660
2. Thomas Crewe 2 Baron Crewe – Northamptonshire 1656 Brackley 1659 1660-79

Seat: Stene (Steane) Park, Northamptonshire (medieval, purch. by Bray family 1574, add. late 16th c., passed by mar. to Crewes 1583, sold 1744, became ruinous)
Estates: Worth £4,000 pa in 1679 and £6,000 pa in 1697
Peers: 3 peers 1661-1721
Notes: The 1 Baron summoned to Cromwell's House of Lords. 1 and 3 Barons in ODNB.

Harpur

Origins: Minor gentry 14th century. **First MP 1419 a lawyer and kt of the shire for Staffordshire 1431**. Married the heiress to Derbyshire estates in 1558 and became major landowners. Judge 1567. **Two additional MPs 1467-1611**. The heiress of the 2 Baron Crewe of Stene married the 4 Harpur Bt. The family took the name Crewe in 1818.

1. John Harpur – Derby 1701-05 1710-13
2. Sir Henry Harpur 5 Bt – Worcester 1744-47 Tamworth 1747-48
3. Sir Henry Harpur 6 Bt – Derbyshire 1761-68
4. Sir George Crewe 8 Bt – S. Derbyshire 1835-41

Seats: Calke Abbey, Derbyshire (built 16th c., purch. 1622, rebuilt 1620s, add. c. 1650, rebuilt c. 1701, NT 1984, family still resident); Warslow Hall, Derbyshire (built 1515, purch. 1593, rebuilt 1830, sold 20th c.); Swarkestone Manor, Derbyshire (built by Harpurs 1558, remod. 1630-31, demolished 1746, ruins remain, sold 1984); Repton Park, Derbyshire (purch. 1622, built c. 1630, remod. 1811, demolished 1893)
Estates: Bateman 28056 (E) 36366. 33,000 acres c. 1700, reduced to 12,300 by the 1970s (Craven and Stanley, *The Derbyshire Country House*, 51, 53)

Title: Baronet 1626-dormant 1924
Notes: Electricity was not installed at Calke until the 1960s. One in ODNB.

CRIPPS

Baron Parmoor (1899- UK)

Origins: Martin Wiener calls the Crippses "an ancient gentry family" (Wiener, *English Culture and the Decline of the Industrial Spirit*, 125), but in fact they made their fortune operating cloth mills in the 18th and 19th centuries. In the 19th century they also became brewers, carpet-makers, and bankers while purchasing landed estates.

1. Joseph Cripps – Cirencester 1806-12 1818-41
2. William Cripps – Cirencester 1841-48
3. Charles Cripps 1 Baron Parmoor – Stroud Div. Gloucestershire 1895-1900 Stretford Div. Lancashire 1901-06 Wycombe Div. Buckinghamshire 1910-14
4. Sir Stafford Cripps – S. Bristol 1931-50 S. E. Bristol 1950

Seats: Parmoor House, Buckinghamshire (purch. 1791, sold 1947); Ampney Park, Gloucestershire (built 1628, purch. 1891, sold 1982)
Estates: 2,000 acres c. 1900.
Peers: 2 peers 1914-45
2 in Cabinet 1924 1929-31 1942-50
Notes: Four in ODNB.

CROFT

Baron Croft (1940- UK)

Origins: Claim Saxon origin. Established family of substance since the 11th century mentioned in the Domesday Book at Croft. **First MP 1307**. Kt 13th century. **At least ten MPs 1314-1628, four kts of the shire. At least one MP in each of seven centuries from the 14th to the 20th**.

1. Sir Herbert Croft 1 Bt – Herefordshire 1679 1690-98
2. Sir Archer Croft 2 Bt – Leominster 1722-27 Bere Alston 1728-34
3. Sir Herbert Croft 9 Bt – Herefordshire 1868-74
4. Henry Croft 1 Baron Croft – Christchurch Div. Hampshire 1910-18 Bournemouth 1910-40

Seat: Croft Castle, Herefordshire (acq. 11th century, castle built 14th c., sold 1746, part rebuilt c. 1760, repurch. 1923, NT 1957)
Estates: Worth £2,000 pa in 1661, but not in Bateman.

Titles: Baronet 1671-; 1924-
Peers: 1 peer 1940-45
Notes: 1 Baron and twelve others in ODNB.

CROFTS (Croftes)

Baron Crofts (1658-77 E)

Origins: Said to have held manorial lands since the reign of Edward I. Minor gentry until the 16th century when they acquired Little Saxham. Kt 1553. **First MP 1597. Another MP 1624**.

1. Sir Henry Crofts – Eye 1624 Derby 1626 Bury St. Edmunds 1660
2. William Crofts – Bury St. Edmunds 1685-87
3. Richard Crofts – Petersfield 1767-68 Downton 1768-71 University of Cambridge 1771-80

Seat: Little Saxham Hall, Suffolk (built 1513, purch. 1551, family departed c. 1730, demolished 1773, estate sold 1789)
Estates: Little Saxham estate sold for somewhat over £16,000 in 1789.
Title: Baronet 1661-64
Peer: 1 peer 1661-77
Notes: 1 Baron in ODNB.

CROMPTON [Stansfield]

Origins: Bankers and Mayor of Derby in the 18th century. A son of the Mayor became a country gentleman. The uncle of the 1 Bt married the daughter and heiress of William Rookes of Roydes Hall, whose wife was the sister and heiress of Robert Stansfield of Esholt Hall. Their son took the additional name Stansfield.

1. Sir Samuel Crompton 1 Bt – East Retford 1818-26 Derby 1826-30 Thirsk 1834-41
2. Joshua Crompton – Ripon 1832-35
3. William Crompton Stansfield – Huddersfield 1838-53

Seats: Wood End (aka Woodhall and Thornton-le-Street Hall – Old Hall), Yorkshire (built 16th c., purch. 1793, remod. 1828, passed out of family 1850); Esholt Hall (Priory, Park), Yorkshire (Stansfields purch. 1755, acq. by Cromptons by mar. 1786, resident at least until 1936); Buckden Hall, Yorkshire (built mid-18th c., add. 19th c., purch. 1879, sold 1945); Zion (Sion) Hill, Yorkshire (acq. 18th c., sold late 19th or early 20th c.)
Title: Baronet 1838-48
Notes: The 1 Baronet's only surviving child married the 3 Earl of Cathcart, who succeeded to the Yorkshire estates. One in ODNB.

CROMWELL *ENGLAND & IRELAND*

Earl of Ardglass (1645-87 I)

Origins: The Cromwells were related, but it is not certain how, to Lord Cromwell (cr. 1375, extinct 1455) of Tattersall, Lincolnshire. A cadet line emerged from a Nottinghamshire fuller who went to London c. 1452. His son was a blacksmith in Putney. His son was a solicitor and servant of Cardinal Wolsey who rose to the Earldom of Essex in 1540 as a royal official. His son was created Baron Cromwell after his father's attainder. **First MP 1523. Two further MPs 1539-89.**

1. Vere Essex Cromwell – {County Down 1634 1662}

Seats: Throwlwy (Throwleigh) Hall, Staffordshire (medieval, acq. by mar. mid-17th c., leased out from 1687 and passed out of the family 1709, partially demolished 1830, ruin from 1921); Booncastle (Lecale), Down (purch. and built 1606, sold after 1687)
Titles: Baron Cromwell 1536-40 E; Earl of Essex 1540-40 E; Baron Cromwell 1540-1697 E; Viscount Lecale 1624-87 I
Peers: 3 peers 1660-68 1674-87
Notes: 1 Earl of Essex, 3 Baron, 1 Earl of Ardglass and one other in ODNB.

Cromwell

Origins: The sister of the 1 Earl of Essex married Morgan Williams of a Welsh family, innkeepers in Putney, who acquired large estates in Huntingdonshire after the Dissolution but before his brother-in-law's fall. The family took the name Cromwell. Morgan's great-grandson was Oliver Cromwell, the Lord Protector. **First MP 1563. Eight additional MPs 1572-1657.**

1. Henry Cromwell – Huntingdonshire 1654 1656 1659 1660 1661-73

Seats: Bodsey House, Huntingdonshire (medieval monastic buildings, acq. after Dissolution and converted for domestic use by Cromwells, rebuilt c. 1600, sold 1676); Ramsey Abbey, Huntingdonshire (purch. c. 1530s, sold 1676)
Notes: The family was in financial decline in the mid-17th century, and the estates were sold in the 1670s after passing to heiresses. Oliver's son, Lord Richard Cromwell, died in 1712. Eleven in ODNB.

CROOKSHANK *IRELAND & SCOTLAND*

Viscount Crookshank (1956- UK)

Origins: The first {MP} was a Justice of the Common Pleas in Ireland 1784. The father of the 1 Viscount was a physician in Ulster. The son was a politician.

1. Alexander Crookshank – {Belfast 1777-84}
2. George Crookshank – {Belfast 1797-1800}
3. Chichester Crookshank – Berwick & Haddington 1924-29 Bootle 1931-35
4. Harry Crookshank 1 Viscount Crookshank – Gainsborough Div. Lincolnshire 1924-56

Seats: Johnstoun, East Lothian; Drumhalry, Longford (owned 19th c.); Newtown Park, Dublin (acq. 1792, sold 1805)
Estates: 1,214 acres in Ireland in 1870s.
Notes: 1 Viscount in ODNB.

CROSBIE *IRELAND*

Earl of Glandore (1776-1815 I)

Origins: To Ireland from Lancashire as soldiers and clerics. The founder was granted estates in Kerry by Elizabeth I for military services. His brother was Bishop of Ardfert 1600. Baronet 1630. A descendent was a colonel during the Civil War. Further estates acquired in 1702 from the forfeitures of the 1690s. Sheriff 1712. **First {MP 1634}. One additional {MP 1634-41}**.

1. Maurice Crosbie 1 Baron Branden – {County Kerry 1713-58}
2. William Crosbie – {Ardfert 1713-43}
3. Sir Thomas Crosbie – {Dingle 1713-31}
4. Lancelot Crosbie – {County Kerry 1759-60 1762-76}
5. William Crosbie 1 Earl of Glandore – {Ardfert 1735-62}
6. John Crosbie 2 Earl of Glandore – {Athboy 1775-76 Ardfert 1776-81}
7. John Crosbie – {County Kerry 1794-97}
8. James Crosbie – {County Kerry 1797-1800} 1801-06 1812-26

Seats: Ardfert Abbey (House), Kerry (acq. late 16th c., built 1633-35, rebuilt 1711, remod. 1720, passed by mar. to Talbots 1815, remod. 1830, burned 1922, demolished); Ballyheigue (Ballyheigh) Castle, Kerry (medieval castle, acq. 17th c., new house c. 1758, rebuilt 1806-12, burned 1921, ruin); Tubrid House, Kerry (acq. 17th c., passed by mar. to Baylys, demolished 20th c.)

Estates: Bateman 10039 (I) 4638. Worth £300 pa in 1713, succeeded to larger estates c. 1810 worth £3,000 pa.
Titles: Baron Branden 1758-1832 I; Baronet 1630-1936
Peers: {3 peers 1758-1800} 1 Irish Rep peer 1801-15
Notes: Lady Anne Crosbie, heiress of the last Earl, married William Talbot of Mount Talbot, Roscommon, who took the name Crosbie (see Talbot I).

CROSS

Viscount Cross (1886- UK)

Origins: Legal officials and squires in the 18th century. Married an heiress in 1813. 1 Viscount abandoned a legal career to become a banker and politician.

1. Richard Assheton Cross 1 Viscount Cross – Preston 1857-62 S. W. Lancashire 1868-85
2. William Cross – W. Derby Div. Liverpool 1888-92

Seats: Ecclc Riggs, Lancashire (purch. 1860, built 1865, add. 1880, contents sold 1935, now hotel); Red Scar, Lancashire (purch. 18th c., older house remod. 1798 and 1840, demolished 1930s); Ash House, Cumberland (built 17th c., purch. and add. 1894)
Estates: 1 Viscount left £91,000 in 1914.
Peers: 3 peers 1886-1945
1 in Cabinet 1874-80 1885-92 1895-1900
Notes: 1 Viscount in ODNB.

CROSSLEY

Baron Somerleyton (1916- UK)

Origins: Carpet manufacturers on a huge scale. The business was founded in Halifax by John Crossley (1772-1837) father of the first MP, a weaver, then foreman, and finally owner, a self-made man. The eldest son went to Eton and became a landowner and Baronet. The founder's sons introduced steam looms in the 1850s. By 1869 the mills employed 4,400 workmen. (Girouard, *The Victorian Country House*, 205-12)

1. Sir Francis Crossley 1 Bt – Halifax 1852-59 W. R. Yorkshire 1859-65 N. Div. W. R. Yorkshire 1865-72
2. John Crossley – Halifax 1874-77
3. Savile Crossley 1 Baron Somerleyton – Lowestoft Div. Suffolk 1885-92
4. Edward Crossley – Sowerby Div. E. R. Yorkshire 1885-92

Seats: Somerleyton Hall, Suffolk (built c. 1610, rebuilt 1844-51, purch. 1863, still own); Herringfleet Hall, Suffolk (built c. 1730, add. 1778-88, remod. c. 1830s, add. 1873, purch. 1919, still own)
Estates: Bateman 3294 (E) 5324. The firm had carpet sales of over £1,000,000 a year by the 1870s.
Title: Baronet 1863-
Peers: 2 peers 1916-45
Notes: Six in ODNB.

CROWLE

Origins: Merchants and Mayor of Hull in the 17th century.

1. George Crowle – Kingston-upon-Hull 1724-47
2. Richard Crowle – Kingston-upon-Hull 1754-57
3. Charles Crowle – Richmond 1769-74 {Harristown 1781-83}

Seat: Fryston Hall, Yorkshire (acq. 17th c.?, sold 1788, demolished 1931)

CUBITT

Baron Ashcombe (1892- UK)

Origins: The founder began as a ship's carpenter and rose to Lord Mayor of London 1860. Became great urban developers and house builders.

1. William Cubitt – Andover 1847-61 1862-63
2. George Cubitt 1 Baron Ashcombe – W. Surrey 1860-85 Mid Surrey 1885-92
3. Henry Cubitt 2 Baron Ashcombe – Reigate Div. Surrey 1892-1906

Seat: Denbies, Surrey (built 1754, purch. and rebuilt 1850, demolished 1953)
Estates: Bateman 6789 (E) 8509. Worth £1,000,000 in 1855. Worth £30,000,000 in 1990.
Peers: 2 peers 1892-1945
1 Ld Lt 20th
Notes: Three in ODNB.

CUFFE *IRELAND*

Earl of Desart (1793-1934 I)

Origins: To Ireland from Somerset with the Earl of Essex in 1598. Granted large estates soon afterwards and in the 1640s.

1. Joseph Cuffe – {Knocktopher 1665}
2. Agmondisham Cuffe – {County Kilkenny 1695-99}
3. Gerald Cuffe – {Castlebar 1703-14}
4. John Cuffe 1 Baron Desart – {Thomastown 1715-27}
5. Maurice Cuffe – {Kilkenny 1715-27}
6. Thomas Cuffe – {Wexford 1735-42}
7. William Cuffe – {Kilkenny 1783-92}
8. John Cuffe 2 Earl of Desart – Bossiney 1808-17
9. Otway Cuffe 3 Earl of Desart – Ipswich 1842

Seats: Desart Court, Kilkenny (built c. 1733, burned 1923, rebuilt, sold, demolished 1943 and 1957); Castle Inch, Kilkenny (purch. 1678)
Estates: Bateman 8932 (I) 6278. Worth £5,000 to 6,000 pa in 1804. Estates sold after 1903 except for the house and demense.
Titles: Baron Desart 1733-1934 I; Viscount Castle Cuffe 1781-1934 I; Baron Desart 1909-34 UK
Peers: {3 peers 1733-49 1751-1800} 2 Irish Rep peers 1801-04 1846-65 1 peer 1909-34
1 Ld Lt 20th
1 KP 20th
Notes: The Countess of Desart was a Senator in the Free State in the 1920s. 5 Earl in ODNB.

Baron Tyrawley (1797-1821 I)

Origins: Also from Somerset and probably related to the Earls of Desart. To Ireland 1621 and acquired land in Mayo and Galway. Sheriff 1681.

1. Sir James Cuffe – {County Mayo 1661-66}
2. Francis Cuffe – {County Mayo 1692-93}
3. Francis Cuffe – {County Mayo 1715-17}
4. Michael Cuffe – {County Mayo 1719-27 Longford 1727-44}
5. James Cuffe – {County Mayo 1742-60}
6. James Cuffe 1 Baron Tyrawley – {County Mayo 1768-97}
7. James Cuffe – {Tulsk 1800} Tralee 1819-28

Seats: Ballinrobe, Mayo (acq. 1667, sold 1821); Castle Lacken (Lackin), Mayo (built late 18th c., acq. 1814, passed by mar. in 1857 to Knox of Creagh, ruin in 20th c.); Elm Hall, Mayo (acq. and built 17th c., resident 18th c., ruin by 1830)
Estates: Worth £8,000 pa 1799.
Peer: {1 peer 1797-1800}

Notes: The last MP was the illegitimate son of the 1 Baron, who inherited the family estate, although property acquired by marriage from the Gore family reverted to the Earls of Arran (see Gore).

CUNINGHAM [Dick] *SCOTLAND*

Cuningham (Cunyngham)

Origins: Claim descent from the Earls of Glencairn (see Cunninghame). Lairds in the 14th century. **First [MP 1560]. An additional [MP 1617] for Ayrshire**.

1. Sir John Cuningham 1 Bt – [Ayrshire 1665 1681]
2. William Cuningham – [Ayr Burghs 1661-63 1665 1667 1669-74 1681]

Seats: Caprington Castle, Ayrshire (acq. by mar. 1425, built 1829, still own); Prestonfield House, Midlothian (built mid-17th c., burned 1681, rebuilt 1687, acq. by mar. late 17th c., remod. 1816, now hotel)
Estates: Bateman 7656 (S) 12657
Title: Baronet 1669-
Notes: It is claimed that Sir Richard Wallace acquired Caprington c. 1177, and that it then passed to the Cuninghams.
Notes: One in ODNB.

Dick

Origins: A merchant and tax farmer in the late 16th century became very rich (worth £200,000 Scots in c. 1640). A merchant and banker was elected Provost of Edinburgh 1638 and Kt 1646. 1 Bt was also a merchant. Janet Dick, heiress of the 1 Bt married Sir William Cuningham 1 Bt and brought Prestonfield to that family who took the additional name Dick.

1. Sir James Dick 1 Bt – [Edinburgh 1681]

Seat: Prestonfield, Midlothian (purch. 1677, burned 1681, rebuilt 1687, passed to Cuninghams by mar. late 17th c. see above)
Title: Baronet 1707-1941

CUNLIFFE-LISTER

Earl of Swinton (1955- UK)

Origins: The Cunliffes were Liverpool merchants and gentry in the 17th century. A younger son of John Cunliffe invented a railway brake in 1848, later a wool-combing machine, and then became a silk-plush manufacturer. The fortune made in industry was invested in an estate that made the family the largest landowners in North Yorkshire. They gained a barony in 1891. Philip Lloyd-Graeme, a politician, married the Cunliffe heiress and took the name Cunliffe-Lister and gained an Earldom in 1955.

1. Ellis Cunliffe-Lister-Kay – Bradford 1832-41
2. William Cunliffe-Lister – Bradford 1841
3. Philip Cunliffe-Lister 1 Earl of Swinton – Hendon Div. Middlesex 1918-35

Seats: Swinton Park, Yorkshire (built 1695, rebuilt early 19th c., purch. and add. 1882, sold 1980, repurch. 2000 to operate as a hotel, still own); Manningham Hall, Yorkshire (built 1690s, Listers rebuilt c. 1764, add. c. 1800, remod. 1821, purch. 1882, demolished 1900) Fairfield Hall, Yorkshire (built late 17th c., Lister purch. c. 1870, sold early 20th c.)
Estates: Bateman 24569 (E) 17253. Samuel Cunliffe-Lister spent three-quarters of a million pounds on land in the 1880s. Estates eventually totaled 34,000 acres. (Thompson *English Landed Society in the Nineteenth Century*, 297). Still own 20,000 acres.
Title: Baron Masham 1891-1924 UK
Peers: 2 peers 1891-1906 1935-45
1 in Cabinet 1922-29 1931-38 1951-52
Notes: The Kay(e)'s inherited the Lister estates in 1745 (see Kaye). Two in ODNB.

Cunliffe-Offley

Origins: See above. The senior line descended from the eldest son of John Cunliffe.

1. Sir Ellis Cunliffe 1 Bt – Liverpool 1755-67
2. Foster Cunliffe-Offley – Chester 1831-32
3. Sir Robert Cunliffe 5 Bt – Flint 1872-74 Denbigh Boroughs 1880-85

Seats: Acton Park (Hall), Denbighshire (purch. and built 1786-87, demolished 1952); Madeley, Staffordshire (see Crewe)
Estates: Bateman 2025 (W) 4150. The income listed does not include wealth derived from rich mineral deposits.
Title: Baronet 1759-
Notes: One in ODNB.

CUNNINGHAME (Cuninghame) [Bontine, Burton, Cairns, Conyngham, Denison, Denys, Fairlie, Montgomery, Murray, Westenra] *SCOTLAND, IRELAND, & ENGLAND*

Earl of Glencairn (1488-1796 S)

Origins: The Cunninghames were a medieval family, having held Cunningham in Ayrshire since the 12th century. The 1 Earl of Glencairn was also a decendent of a Constable of Scotland in the 12th century. Prominent from the mid-14th century onwards. Robert Graham of Gartmore, son of N. Graham and Lady Margaret Cunninghame, daughter of the 11 Earl of Glencairn, succeeded to the 15 Earl's estates and took the name Cunninghame in 1796. He had also succeeded his cousin William Bontine of Ardoch in 1770 and took the name Bontine.

1. Robert Graham Bontine Cunninghame – Stirlingshire 1794-96
2. William Cunninghame Bontine – Dumbartonshire 1796-97
3. Robert Bontine Cunninghame Graham – N. W. Lanarkshire 1886-92

Seats: Finlaystoun House (Finlaystone), Renfrewshire (medieval, acq. by mar. 1399, remod. 1746, sold 1863); Coates House, Edinburghshire (resident 18th c., sold early 19th c.); Kilmaurs Place, Ayrshire (acq. medieval period, built c. 1620, sold 1720 and 1786); Gartmore House, Stirlingshire (Graham house, old house, rebuilt early 18th c., add. 1779-80, sold 1900); Ardoch House, Dumbartonshire (acq. by Bontines 1398, passed to Grahams 1770, built c. 1780, sold early 19th c., repurch. 1901, sold 1987)
Peers: [4 peers 1661-1707] 1 Scottish Rep peer 1780-84
Notes: Robert Cunninghame MP 1794-96 was a Jamaica planter.
The Cunnigham family has an entry in the ODNB and five others. Robert Bontine Cunninghame Graham MP joined the Labour Party and attended the Second Marxist International. One Graham also in ODNB.

Baron Rossmore (1796- I; 1838- UK)

Origins: A younger son of Sir Robert de Cunninghame of Kilmaurs, ancestor of the Earls of Glencairn, established a family raised to the Irish peerage in 1796. The first in Ireland was a soldier, politician, and distributor of patronage who married an heiress in the mid-18th century. His seat was at Mount Kennedy (purch. 1769), which passed to a daughter of his sister. The title went by special remainder to the son of his wife's (Elizabeth Murray) sister (Harriet Murray who married Henry Westenra). The Murrays had succeeded to the estates of the Cairns through a daughter of Sir Alexander Cairns 1 Bt who married John Murray MP 1727-43. The Cairns family came from Kirkcudbright to Donegal in the later 17th century. Sir Alexander was a Dublin banker. The Westenras were a commercial family of Dutch origin who settled in Ireland in the later 17th century. The families have been merged in a single line here.

1. Peter Westnera – {Athboy 1692-93}
2. William Cairns – {Belfast 1703-07}
3. Sir Alexander Cairns 1 Bt – {County Monaghan 1709-27 Monaghan 1727-32}
4. John Murray – {County Monaghan 1741-43}
5. Warner Westenra – {Maryborough 1730-60}
6. Sir Henry Cairns 2 Bt – {Monaghan 1732-43}
7. Robert Cuninghame 1 Baron Rossmore – {Tulske 1751-60 Armagh 1761-68 Monaghan 1768-96} East Grinstead 1788-89
8. Henry Westenra – {Monaghan 1771-76 1796-1800}
9. William Westenra 2 Baron Rossmore – County Monaghan {1800} 1801
10. Henry Westenra 3 Baron Rossmore – County Monaghan 1818-30 1831-32 1834-42
11. John Westenra – King's County 1835-52

Seats: Rossmore Park (Castle), Monaghan (acq. by Cuninghames 18th c., built 1824-27, add. 1858, unroofed post WWII, demolished 1975); Camla Vale, Monaghan (built late 18th c., purch. early 19th c. by uncle of 3 Baron Rossmore, to whom it passed, sold 1962, demolished); Sharavogue Castle, King's County (purch. 1683, rebuilt mid-19th c., passed out of the family via an heiress 1894); Donaghmore, Donegal (Cairns owned in the 18th c., passed to Westenras 19th c.); Mount Kennedy, Wicklow (built 1670, fire 1680s, purch. 1769, new house built c. 1782-84, passed by mar. to Gun-Cuninghames 19th c.)
Estates: Bateman 14839 (I) 13427 and 4483 (I) 2091. Cairns worth £2,000 pa in 1713. Held 64,000 acres in later 18th c. (Guinness and Ryan, *Irish Houses and Castles*, 315).
Title: Baronet (Cairns) 1708-43
Peers: {1 peer 1796-1800} 1 Irish Rep peer 1800-01 6 peers 1838-60 1872-1945
3 Lds Lt 19th, 20th
Notes: A cadet line of the Cairns family was granted the Earldom of Cairns (see below). One Westenra in ODNB.

Cuninghame

Origins: Descended from a sister of the 1 Baron Rossmore.

1. James Cuninghame – East Grinstead 1786-88

Seat: Mount Kennedy, Wicklow (see above, passed to niece of 1 Baron Rossmore in 19th c., sold 1930)
Estates: Bateman 10479 (I) 5809

Earl Cairns (1878- UK)

Origins: Merchants and bankers in Dublin and Belfast. 1 Earl a Lord Chancellor. See under Baron Rossmore.

1. Hugh Cairns – Belfast 1852-66

Seats: Parkmount House, Antrim (built 17th c., purch. and rebuilt 1796, add. 19th c., sold 1828, demolished 1932); Farleigh House, Somerset (built 18th and 19th c., purch. 1906, sold after WWII)
Title: Baron Cairns 1870- UK
Peers: 4 peers 1867-1945
1 in Cabinet 1868 1878-80
Notes: One in ODNB

Cuninghame

Origins: Cadet of the Earls of Glencairn (second son of the 1 Earl of Glencairn). Held Craigends from 1479, but made a fortune as ironmasters in the 19th century. (Rubinstein, *Men of Property*, 216, 225) **First [MP 1643].**

1. William Cuninghame – [Renfrewshire 1689-95]
2. Alexander Cuninghame – Renfrewshire 1734-42

Seat: Craigends House, Renfrewshire (acq. 1479, built 1857, family departed 1951, sold and demolished 1966-67)
Estates: Bateman 33948 (S) 19122

Cuningham Fairlie

Origins: Cadet of Cuninghame of Craigends.

1. Sir William Cuningham Fairlie 7 Bt – Leominster 1818-26

Seat: Robertland, Ayrshire (sold 1696)
Title: Baronet 1630-
Note: Impoverished in the 19th century

Montgomery-Cuninghame

Origins: Descended from the second son of the 4 Earl of Glencairn.

1. Sir William Montgomery-Cuninghame 9 Bt – Ayr Burghs 1874-80

Seats: Corsehill House, Ayrshire (acq. and built 1532, abandoned after 1770); Glenmoor House (aka Kirkbride House), Ayrshire (replaced Corsehill, sold 20th c.)
Estates: Bateman 3370 (S) 3329
Title: Baronet 1672-

<u>Marquess Conyngham</u> (1816- I)

Origins: A cadet branch of the Earls of Glencairn. The first to Ireland was a Protestant minister in Donegal 1611. His son was a Lt. General of the Ordnance in Ireland. Fought with William III at the Boyne and acquired estates.

1. William Conyngham – {Bangor 1661-66}
2. Henry Conyngham – {Killybegs 1692-93 County Donegal 1695-99 1703-06}
3. Henry Conyngham 1 Earl Conyngham – {Killybegs 1727-53} Tiverton 1747-54 Sandwich 1756-74
4. William Conyngham – {Killybegs 1727-38}
5. Henry Conyngham – {Killybegs 1741-49}
6. William Conyngham – {Dundalk 1776-83}
7. William Conyngham – {Ennis 1776-83 Killybegs 1783-90 Ennis 1790-96}
8. Francis Conyngham 2 Marquess Conyngham – Westbury 1818-20 County Donegal 1825-31
9. Henry Conyngham Earl of Mount Charles – County Donegal 1818-24
10. Lord Francis Conyngham – County Clare 1857-59 1874-80

Seats: Bifrons, Kent (purch. early 19th c., demolished 1948); Slane Castle, Meath (medieval castle, purch. 1703, new house 1785, fire 1991, restored, still own); The Hall, Mount Charles, Donegal (acq. early 17th c., rebuilt early to mid-18th c., leased out 19th c., still own); Amat Lodge, Ross-shire (purch. 1924, sold 1945); Minster (Court), Kent (acq. by mar. 1688, leased out from 1787, sold 1928); Conyngham Hall (aka Coghill Hall), Yorkshire (medieval, rebuilt 1555, rebuilt later 18th c., purch. 1796, sold 1856)
Estates: Bateman 166710 (E & I) 50076. Rubinstein – the Dowager Countess left £140,000 in probate in 1816. Owned 5,000 acres in 2001 in England and 1,000 acres in Ireland.
Titles: Baron Conyngham 1753-81 I; Viscount Conyngham 1756-81 I; Earl Conyngham 1781-81 I; Baron Conyngham 1781- I; Viscount Slane 1789- I; Earl of Mount Charles 1797- I; Baron Minster 1821- UK
Peers: {3 peers 1765-1800} 1 Irish Rep peer 1801-16 6 peers 1816-97 1904-45
1 Ld Lt 19th
2 KP 19th
Notes: 1 Marquess in ODNB.

Burton

Origins: The family was settled in Shropshire for many centuries. Kt 15th century. Granted arms 1478. **First MP 1597**. The estates of the senior branch passed to the Lingens (see Lingen). A younger son's son went to Ireland 1610. Bankers in Dublin. Acquired Buncraggy 1666 and other estates in 1685. Sheriff 1691. Francis Burton purchased vast acreage of confiscated estates in Clare in 1702. Lord Mayor of Dublin 1706. It is unclear where the money came from. [The senior line remained at Longnor Hall, (Atcham) Shropshire (Bateman 2244 (E) 4653). (see Acton)] The sister of the 1 Earl Conyngham married Francis Burton of Burton Hall, Carlow and their son was the 2 Baron Conyngham. His son was created Marquess Conyngham. A younger son of Francis Burton (MP 1703) purchased Burton Hall and established a cadet line.

1. Thomas Burton – {Killybegs 1661-65}
2. Francis Burton – {Ennis 1692-93 1695-99 1703-14}
3. Benjamin Burton – {Burton 1703-27}
4. Samuel Burton – {Sligo 1713-14 1715-27 Dublin 1727-33}
5. Francis Burton – {Coleraine 1721-27 County Clare 1727-44}
6. Robert Burton – {County Carlow 1727-60 Carlow 1761-65}
7. Benjamin Burton – {Knocktopher 1741-60 County Carlow 1761-67}
8. Benjamin Burton – {County Sligo 1757-60 Boyle 1761-63}
9. Francis Burton – {Killybegs 1753-60 County Clare 1761-76}
10. William Burton – {Gowran 1761-68 County Carlow 1768-1800} Carlow 1801-02
11. William Burton – {Newtown 1761-76 Ennis 1776-83 Killybegs 1783-90 Ennis 1790-96}
12. Francis Burton – {County Clare 1790-1800} 1801-08

Seats: Burton Hall, Carlow (purch. and built 1712, remod. 1840-44, remod. late 19th c., sold 1927, demolished 1930); Goltho Hall, Lincolnshire (old house, acq. by mar 1850 and 1868, rebuilt c. 1900, demolished); Buncraggy, Clare (purch. 1666, built early 18th c., passed to Armstrongs early 19th c.)
Estates: Bateman 7370 (I) 5005. Worth £2,500 pa in 1713.
Notes: Minster Court belonged to the Williams Bts (1642-80) and passed to the Conynghams by marriage. One in ODNB.

Burton

Origins: Charles Burton, a younger son of Samuel Burton of Burton (see above) was created a Baronet and was seated at Pollacton. The niece of the 5 Bt succeeded to the estates in 1902. She married Sir Francis Denys 3 Bt who took the name Burton. The Denys family had little known lineage. Developed lead mines. High Sheriff of Northamptonshire 1812, who married a daughter of the 2 Earl of Pomfret. His son was created a Baronet 1813 and was a courtier.

1. Sir Charles Burton 1 Bt – {Dublin 1749-60}
2. Sir George Denys 1 Bt – Hull 1812-18

Seats: Pollacton, Carlow (built c. 1802, remod. later 19th c., passed by mar. to Denys and Tubbs families, demolished 1970); Draycot Hall, Yorkshire (acq. and built by Denys family late 18th c., now flats)
Estates: Owned about 1,000 acres in Kilkenny and Carlow.
Titles: Baronet 1758-1902; 1813-1960

Earl of Londesborough (1887-1937 UK)

Origins: The 1 Marquess of Conyngham married Elizabeth, sister and heiress of W. J. Denison. The second son of this marriage succeeded to the Denison estates and was created 1 Baron Londesborough. The Denisons were great Leeds woolen cloth merchants in the 18th century. A son became a London banker.

1. William Denison – Camelford 1796-1802 Hull 1806-07 Surrey 1818-32 W. Surrey 1832-49
2. Albert Conyngham Denison 1 Baron Londesborough – Canterbury 1835-41 1847-50
3. William Denison 1 Earl of Londesborough – Beverley 1857-59 Scarborough 1859-60

Seats: Londesborough Lodge (Hall), Yorkshire (old house, see under Boyle, new house 1839, purch. 1849 for c. £450,000, add. 1853, sold 1919); Blankney Hall, Lincolnshire (purch. 1896, burned 1945, demolished 1960); Denbies, Surrey (built c. 1754, purch. 1787, sold 1850); Seamer, Yorkshire (built 17th c., purch. 1790, remod. early 19th c., sold 1923, hotel); Grimston Park, Yorkshire (old house, built c. 1840, purch. 1850, add. c. 1850, sold 1872)
Estates: Bateman 52655 (E) 67876. The first MP left £2,300,000 in 1849. 1 Baron had an income of c. £100,000 pa in the mid-19th century.
Title: Baron Londesborough 1850- UK
Peers: 5 peers 1850-1937
Notes: 1 Baron in ODNB three Denisons.

CUNYNGHAME *SCOTLAND*

Origins: Claimed descent from the Earls of Glencairn. At Milncraig by early 17th century. 1 Bt a successful lawyer.

1. Sir David Cunynghame 1 Bt – [Lauder Burghs 1703-07]
2. Sir James Cunynghame 2 Bt – Linlithgowshire 1715-22
3. Sir William Augustus Cunynghame 4 Bt – Linlithgowshire 1774-90

Seats: Livingston(e) Place, Linlithgowshire (old house, acq. by mar. 1671, demolished and rebuilt late 17th c., sold 1828, demolished 1840); Milncraig, Ayrshire (acq. by mar. 17th c.)
Title: Baronet 1702-
Notes: One in ODNB.

CURRIE

Baron Currie (1899-1906 UK)

Origins: Bankers in London mid-18th and the 19th century and also owned a gin distillery.

1. William Currie – Gatton 1790-96 Winchelsea 1796-1802
2. John Currie – Hertford 1831-32
3. Raikes Currie – Northampton 1837-57
4. Henry Currie – Guildford 1847-52

Seats: Seafield House, Sussex; Sandling Park, Kent (built 1779, demolished c. 1945-46, new house); Minley Manor, Hampshire (purch. 1846, built 1858-60, fire 1871, rebuilt and add. 1886-87 cost £55,000 – Franklin, *The Gentleman's Country House*, 265 - add. 1898, sold 1934); East Horsley Park (Place, Towers), Surrey (old house, purch. 1784, rebuilt 1834, sold before 1847); Coombe Warren, Surrey (purch. and built 1861, fire 1870, rebuilt 1870-75, demolished 1920s)
Estates: Rubinstein – William Currie MP left £140,000 in probate in 1829. Raikes Currie MP left £285,000 in 1881. Owned 2,500 acres in 1934.
Peer: 1 peer 1899-1906.
Notes: Family suffered serious financial reverses in business after 1929. Three in ODNB.

CURTEIS

Origins: Claimed descent from Robert Curthose, eldest son of William the Conqueror, seated in Sussex "from time immemorial." (Burke, *Visitation of Seats*, sec. series, I, 73). In fact the first MP was an attorney and banker who married an heiress. The family purchased £90,000 worth of land in Sussex in the late 18th and early 19th centuries.

1. Edward Curteis – Sussex 1820-30
2. Edward Curteis – Rye 1832-37
3. Herbert Curteis – Sussex 1830-32 E. Sussex 1832-37 Rye 1841-47
4. Herbert Curteis – Rye 1847-52

Seat: Windmill Hill Place, Sussex (purch. later 18th c., sold 1920)
Estates: Bateman 2747 (E) 3252 and 3486 (E) 6055
Notes: Despite the first MP (and his father, also a lawyer and banker) establishing a gentry family, he divided his estates in a bourgeois manner among three sons on his death in 1835.

CURWEN

Origins: Claimed descent from Ethelred the Unready. (Roskell, Clark, and Rawcliffe, *The House of Commons*, II, 725) Almost certainly descended in the male line from pre-Norman landowners. The longest established family in Cumberland; held Workington since the 12th century. **First MP 1371 (for Cumberland). Seven further MPs 1371-1628 all sitting for the county**. Sir Christopher Curwen MP (1397-1432) served in the Agincourt campaign. Bt 1627.

1. Sir Patricius Curwen 1 Bt – Cumberland 1625 1626 1628 1640-43 1644 1661-64
2. Eldred Curwen – Cockermouth 1738-41
3. Henry Curwen – Carlisle 1761-68 Cumberland 1768-74
4. John Christian-Curwen – Carlisle 1786-90 1791-1812 1816-20 Cumberland 1820-28

Seats: Workington Hall, Cumberland (acq. 12th c., medieval, add. 1538 and late 16th c., remod. 1777-82 and 1828, family departed after 1929, donated to municipality 1930s, fire WWII, part demolished 1973); Ewanrigg (Unerigg), Cumberland (medieval, purch. c. 1638, remod. later 17th c., remod. late 18th c., sold 1886, part demolished 1903); Sella Park, Cumberland (built 14th c., acq. 16th c., rebuilt 17th c., sold c. 1800); Catterlen Hall, Cumberland (acq. by the Vaux family late 12th c., medieval building, add. 1577, add. 1652, passed to the Curwens and sold in the mid-18th c.); Belle Isle, Westmorland (purch. 1781, built c. 1780-82, sold 1991)
Estates: Bateman 7128 (E) 10054
Title: Baronet 1627-64
Notes: Curwens were recusants in early 17th c. John Christian of the Isle of Man married a Curwen heiress and took the name Curwen in 1790. The main line of the Christian family purchased Ewanrigg in c. 1638, went bankrupt and their estates forclosed upon 1886. The Curwen fortune was partly based on coal, but financial troubles with the collieries cropped up in the 1820s. The Curwen family has an entry in the ODNB and two others are also listed.

CURZON [Assheton, Howe]

Marquess Curzon (1921-25 UK)

Origins: At Kedleston before 1150, probably by 1100. **First MP 1379 for Derbyshire. At least one MP in each successive century, most kts of the shire, 1423-1648.**

1. Sir John Curzon 3 Bt – Derbyshire 1701-27
2. Sir Nathaniel Curzon 4 Bt – Derby 1713-15 Clitheroe 1722-27 Derbyshire 1727-54
3. William Curzon – Clitheroe 1734-47
4. Nathaniel Curzon 1 Baron Scarsdale – Clitheroe 1748-54 Derbyshire 1754-61
5. Nathaniel Curzon 2 Baron Scarsdale – Derbyshire 1775-84
6. George Curzon 1 Marquess Curzon – Southport Div. Lancashire 1886-98
7. Lady Cynthia Curzon Mosley – Stoke Div. Stoke on Trent 1929-31

Seats: Kedleston Hall, Derbyshire (acq. and built c. 1100, rebuilt late 16th c., rebuilt 1700, rebuilt 1758-81, NT 1984, family still own estate); Lockington Hall, Derbyshire (built 17th c., purch. 1872, add. 1870s, coverted to offices 1973)
Estates: Bateman 15228 (E) 29632. Coal income surged in the mid-18th c. Owned 6,050 acres worth 36 million pounds in 2001.
Titles: Baron Scarsdale 1761- GB; Baron Curzon 1898-1925 I; Earl Curzon 1911-25 UK; Baronet 1636- ; 1641-
Peers: 1 Irish Rep peer 1908-11 4 peers 1761-1837 1856-1916 1911-45
1 in Cabinet 1915-25
1 KG 20th
Notes: 1 Marquess and five others in ODNB.

Earl Howe (1788-99 GB; 1821- UK)

Origins: Acquired estates during Tudor period; granted arms 1625. Sophia Baroness Howe in her own right married the son of the 1 Viscount Curzon (see above). She was the daughter of the 1 Earl Howe, brother of the 3 Viscount Howe. The son of the marriage took the name Howe and was created 1 Earl Howe of the second creation.

1. Scrope Howe 1 Viscount Howe – Nottinghamshire 1673-81 1689-98 1710-13
2. Emanuel Howe – Morpeth 1701-02 Wigan 1705-08
3. Emanuel Howe 2 Viscount Howe – Nottinghamshire 1722-32
4. George Howe 3 Viscount Howe – Nottingham 1747-58
5. Assheton Curzon 1 Viscount Curzon – Clitheroe 1754-80 1792-94
6. Richard Howe 1 Earl Howe – Dartmouth 1757-82
7. William Howe 5 Viscount Howe – Nottingham 1758-80
8. Thomas Howe – Northampton 1769-71

9. Penn Assheton Curzon – Leominster 1784-90 Clitheroe 1790-92 Leicestershire 1792-97
10. George Howe 2 Earl Howe – S. Leicestershire 1857-70
11. Montagu Howe Curzon – N. Leicestershire 1883-85
12. Richard Curzon-Howe 4 Earl Howe – Wycombe Div. Buckinghamshire 1885-1900
13. Francis Curzon 5 Earl Howe – S. Div. Battersea 1918-29

Seats: Gopsall Hall, Leicestershire (built c. 1750s, acq. by mar. later 18th c., demolished 1951); Penn House, Buckinghamshire (acq. and built c. 1540, rebuilt 1760, add. c. 1880, still own); Langar Hall, Nottinghamshire (acq. by mar. 1677, sold 1818, hotel)
Estates: Bateman 33669 (E) 37032. Rubinstein – 1 Viscount Curzon left £140,000 in probate 1820. Owned 4,000 aces in 2001.
Titles: Viscount Howe 1701-1814 I; Viscount Howe 1782-99 GB; Baron Howe 1788- GB; Earl Howe 1788-99 GB; Baron Curzon 1794- GB; Viscount Curzon 1802- UK; Baronet 1660-1814
Peers: {5 peers 1701-13 1720-35 1745-1800} 7 peers 1782-99 1794-1945
2 Lds Lt 17th, 18th, 19th, 20th
1 in Cabinet 1765-70 1783-88
1 KG 18th
Notes: Gopsall was built by a wealthy merchant, Charles Jennens, and passed on his death to a grandnephew, Penn Assheton Curzon, who married Lady Sophia Howe, Baroness Howe. The Curzons also inherited Acton Place (Hall), Suffolk (demolished 1961) from the Jennens (built 1720s, inher. 1816, demolished 1825 and 1961). 1, 3 and 5 Viscounts and 1 Earl and three others in ODNB.

Baron Zouche (1308- E)

Origins: See Bisshopp. Harriet 13 Baroness Zouche married Robert Curzon second son of the 1 Viscount Curzon. Their son succeeded as 14 Baron Zouche.

1. Robert Curzon – Clitheroe 1796-1831
2. Robert Curzon 14 Baron Zouche – Clitheroe 1831-32

Seat: Parham Park, Sussex (see Bisshopp)
Peers: 2 peers 1870-1914
Notes: One in ODNB.

Baron Chedworth (1741-1804 GB)

Origins: Sir John Howe 1 Bt of Cassey Compton had two sons. The 2 Bt, seated at Great Wishford, had a son who left his property to a great nephew. The latter was descended from the 1 Bt's second son John of Langer, Nottinghamshire. The eldest son of the latter was the ancestor of the Earls Howe. The younger son, seated at Stowell, was ancestor of the Barons Chedworth.

1. John Howe – Gloucestershire 1654 1656 1659 1661-79
2. Sir Richard Howe 2 Bt – Wiltshire 1656-58 1659 Wilton 1660 Wiltshire 1675-79 Hindon 1679-81 Wilton 1690-95
3. Sir George Howe 1 Bt – Hindon 1660-76
4. Sir Richard Howe 3 Bt – Hindon 1679-81 Tamworth 1685-87 Cirencester 1690-98 Wiltshire 1701-27
5. John Howe – Cirencester 1689-98 Gloucestershire 1698-1705
6. Sir James Howe 2 Bt – Hindon 1698-1705 1708-09
7. John Howe 1 Baron Chedworth – Gloucester 1727 Wiltshire 1729-41

Seats: Great Wishford, Wiltshire (medieval, acq. by mar. c. 1646, part demolished 1785, sold 1808, demolished mid-19th c.); Cassey Compton, Gloucestershire (medieval, purch. late 16th c., rebuilt c. 1700, sold 1811, part demolished by 1812); Stowell Park, Gloucestershire (built early 17th c., purch. 1685, sold 1811); Berwick St. Leonard, Wiltshire (medieval, new house built early 17th c., acq. by mar. c. 1646, passed out of family 1736, abandoned early 19th c., became a farm building, demolished c. 1902)
Estates: 7600 acres in 1811.
Title: Baronet 1660-1814
Peers: 4 peers 1741-1804
1 Ld Lt 18th
Notes: Male line extinct and estates sold 1811. 4 Baron in ODNB.

<u>Baron Clitheroe</u> (1955- UK)

Origins: One of the oldest families in Lancashire. Landowners since 1115. Rose to prominence with the patronage of John of Gaunt. One on the Agincourt campaign (*Country Life*, 183, p. 108), and another at Flodden. **First MP 1375 for Lancashire. Nine additional MPs 1382-1648, five kts of the shire**.

1. Sir Ralph Assheton 2 Bt – Clitheroe 1625 1626 1640-48 1660-62 1679-80
2. Sir Ralph Assheton 2 Bt – Liverpool 1677-79 Lancashire 1694-98
3. Edmund Assheton – Clitheroe 1685-87
4. Richard Assheton – Lancashire 1703-05
5. Ralph Assheton – Clitheroe 1868-80
6. Ralph Assheton 1 Baron Clitheroe – Rushcliffe Div. Nottinghamshire 1934-45 London 1945-50 Blackburn W. 1950-55

Seats: Downham Hall, Lancashire (purch. 1558, remod. 1834-35, add. 1880, still own); Whalley Abbey, Lancashire (medieval, purch. 1553, rebuilt 1588, add. 1660s, remod.

c. 1840, passed to Curzon-Howes by mar. early 18th c., sold 1836); Middleton Tower, Lancashire (medieval, acq. 15th c., demolished 1845); Cuerdale Hall, Lancashire (old house, built 17th c., still own but a farm house); Chadderton Hall, Lancashire (medieval, acq. by mar. 1454, new house 1620, sold 1684, demolished 1939)
Estates: 3741 (E) 4800
Titles: Baronet 1620-96; 1660-1765
1 Ld Lt 20th
Notes: Three in ODNB.

CUST [Brownlow, Drury, Hume]

Earl Brownlow (1815-1921 GB)

Origins: The Brownlows were founded by a lawyer who married an heiress under Elizabeth I who purchased Belton c. 1617. He set himself up as a county gentleman but was looked down upon by the aristocracy. (Jackson-Stops, *The Country House in Persepctive*, 56). The Custs succeeded to the Brownlow estates and to Belton in 1754. They were yeomen who had owned land in Lincolnshire since the 14th century but did not become armigerous until 1642. The **first MP (1653**) and 1 Bt (1641) was a barrister.

1. Sir Richard Cust 1 Bt – Lincolnshire 1653 Stamford 1679-81
2. Sir William Brownlow 4 Bt – Peterborough 1689-98 Bishop's Castle 1698-1700
3. Sir John Brownlow 3 Bt – Grantham 1689-97
4. John Brownlow 1 Viscount Tyrconnel – Grantham 1713-15 Lincolnshire 1715-22 Grantham 1722-41
5. Sir John Cust 3 Bt – Grantham 1743-70
6. Peregrine Cust – Bishop's Castle 761-68 New Shorham 1768-74 Ilchester 1774-75 Grantham 1776-80 Ilchester 1780-85
7. Brownlow Cust 1 Baron Brownlow – Ilchester 1768-74 Grantham 1774-76
8. Francis Cockayne Cust – Grantham 1770-74 Helston 1775-80 Grantham 1780-91
9. John Cust 1 Earl Brownlow – Clitheroe 1802-07
10. William Cust – Lincolnshire 1816-18 Clitheroe 1818-22
11. Peregrine Cust – Honiton 1818-26 Clitheroe 1826-32
12. Sir Edward Cust 1 Bt – Grantham 1818-26 Lostwithiel 1826-32
13. John Hume-Cust Viscount Alford – Bedfordshire 1835-51
14. Charles Cust – N. Shropshire 1865-66
15. Adalbert Cust 3 Earl Brownlow – N. Shropshire 1866-67
16. Henry Cockayne-Cust – Grantham 1874-80
17. Henry Cockayne-Cust – Stamford Div. Lincolnshire 1890-95 Bermondsey Div. Southwark 1900-06

Seats: Belton House, Lincolnshire (purch. c. 1617, rebuilt 1684-89, NT 1984); Great Humby Hall, Lincolnshire (medieval, acq. c. 1600, rebuilt 17th c., passed from Brownlows to Custs by mar. 1754, sold later 18th c.); Leasingham Hall, Lincolnshire (built 17th c., new house 19th c.); Cockayne Hatley Hall (House), Bedfordshire (medieval, inher. from Cokaynes 1745, sold 1897); Arthingworth, Northamptonshire (acq. by mar. 1770, sold); Ashridge Park, Hertfordshire (medieval, purch. by Egertons 1605, rebuilt 18th c., rebuilt 1808-14, Custs succ. by mar. 1849, remod. 1855-63, sold 1928, institutional use); Leasowe Castle, Cheshire (built 1593, remod. 1818, acq. by mar. from Boodes early 19th c., remod. c. 1834, sold 1893, institutional use)
Estates: Bateman 75457 (E, S & W) 112,122. Income £9,000 pa in 1680s. Owned 22,000 acres worth 130 million pounds in 2001.
Titles: Viscount Tyrconnel 1718-54 I; Baron Brownlow 1776- GB; Baronet 1641-79; 1641-1754; 1677- ; 1876-1931;
Peers: {1 peer 1718-54} 6 peers 1776-1853 1863-1945
3 Lds Lt 19th, 20th
Notes: The Custs succeeded to the Hertfordshire estates of the Dukes of Bridgewater in 1849 (see Egerton). The Custs acq. Leasowe Castle from the Boodes by mar. early 19th c. The Boode fortune was made in the West Indies. One Brownlow and nine Custs in ODNB.

Hume

Origins: The founder was a naval victular in the 17th century. His son was a Director of the East India Company 1737. In 1839 Wormleybury passed to Viscount Alford (Cust).

1. Alexander Hume – Southwark 1743-54 Steyning 1754-61 Southwark 1761-65
2. Sir Abraham Hume 1 Bt – Steyning 1747-54 Tregony 1761-68
3. Sir Abraham Hume 2 Bt – Petersfield 1774-80 Hastings 1807-18

Seat: Wormleybury, Hertfordshire (purch. 1739, passed to Custs by mar. 1839, sold 1853)
Title: Baronet 1769-1839
Notes: 2 Bt in ODNB.

Drury

Origins: Brewers in the 18th century. 1 Viscount Brownlow married the Drury heiress in 1770 and sold Overstone in 1791.

1. Sir Thomas Drury 1 Bt – Maldon 1741-47

Seats: Overstone, Northampstonshire (sold 1791, burned 2001); Wickham Hall, Essex; Arthingworth, Northamptonshire (passed to Brownlows by mar. 1770, sold later)
Estates: Brewery worth £230,000 in the early 18th century.
Title: Baronet 1739-59

CUTTS

Baron Cutts (Cuttte) (1690-1707 I)

Origins: The great grandfather of 1 Baron rose through office under Henry VIII. **First MP 1584 for Cambridgeshire. Another MP 1604, also for the county**.

1. John Cutts 1 Baron Cutts – Cambridgeshire 1693-1702 Newport (IoW) 1702-07

Seats: Childerley Hall, Cambridgeshire (built mid-16th c., passed to Calverts 1686); Horham Hall, Essex (built c. 1450, acq. and rebuilt after 1502, rebuilt 1560s, sold 1599); Shenley Hall, Hertfordshire (acq. by purch. and inher. 1507 and 1521, sold 1600); Wood Hall (Woodhall), Essex (built 1652, sold early 18th c.)
Estates: Worth £2,000 pa c. 1690.
Notes: Family extinct 1707. Estates left to 1 Baron's wife's family. 1 Baron in ODNB.

DALRYMPLE [Elphinstone, Hay, Makgill] *SCOTLAND*

Earl of Stair (1703- S)

Origins: Small lairds until the 1 Viscount, a statesman and Lord of Session.

1. James Dalrymple 1 Viscount Stair – [Wigtownshire 1672-74 1678 1681 Ayrshire 1690]
2. John Dalrymple 1 Earl of Stair – [Stranraer Burgh 1689]
3. Sir David Dalrymple 1 Bt – [Culross Burgh 1698-1702 1703-07] Scotland 1707-08 Haddington Burghs 1708-21
4. William Dalrymple – [Ayrshire 1703-07] Scotland 1707-08 Clackmannanshire 1708-10 Wigtown Burghs 1722-27 Wigtownshire 1727-41
5. George Dalrymple – [Stranraer Burgh 1703-07]
6. John Dalrymple – Wigtown Burghs 1728-34
7. William Dalrymple – Wigtown Burghs 1784-90 {Dunleek 1796-97}
8. John Dalrymple 8 Earl of Stair – Midlothian 1833-34
9. John Dalrymple 10 Earl of Stair – Wigtownshire 1841-56
10. John Dalrymple 12 Earl of Stair – Wigtownshire 1906-14
11. Hew Dalrymple – Wigtownshire 1915-18

Seats: Lochinch Castle, Wigtownshire (acq. estate 1674, built 1864-67, still own); Oxenfoord Castle, Edinburghshire (built 16th c., inher. 1780, add. 1782, add. 1840-42, became a school 1931); Bardlands, Wigtownshire; Newliston, Linlithgowshire (acq. by mar. 1669, sold c. 1750)
Estates: Bateman 116349 (S) 67834; Rubinstein – 6 Earl left £180,000 in probate 1821. Worth £44,000,000 with 45,000 acres in 1990.
Titles: Viscount Stair 1690- S; Baron Oxenfoord (1841- UK; Baronet 1664- ; 1698-
Peers: [3 peers 1690-95 1700-07 1707] 3 Scots Rep peers 1707-08 1715-34 1744-47 1771-74 1790-1807 1820-21 5 peers 1841-1945
2 Lds Lt 19th, 20th
1 in Cabinet Council 1691-95
5 KT 18th, 19th, 20th
Notes: The 4 Countess of Dumfries in her own right married the 1 Earl of Stair. Their son succeeded as Earl of Stair and their daughter inherited the Dumfries title. Her granddaughter married Lord Mount Stuart, and their son succeeded as 2 Marquis of Bute and 7 Earl of Dumfries. (see Stuart I).
Notes: 1 Viscount and 1, 2, 5, 6, and 8 Earls and four others in ODNB.

Dalrymple

Origins: The 1 Bt was the fifth son of the 1 Viscount Stair.

1. Sir James Dalrymple 2 Bt – Haddington Burghs 1722-34

Seat: Hailes (Newhailes), Haddingtonshire (built 1686, purch. 1707, add. 1719-33, remod. 1839, NT 1997)
Title: Baronet 1701-1829
Notes: 3 Bt and one other in ODNB.

Fergusson (Ferguson)

Origins: In Ayrshire by the 12th century. Consolidated holdings in the 16th and 17th centuries. Impoverished by the Civil War. A lawyer restored the family fortunes at the end of the 17th century. Judge 1735. The Dalrymple of Hailes estates passed by marriage to the Fergussons of Kilkerran in 1849.

1. Sir James Fergusson 2 Bt (Lord Kilkerran) – Sutherlandshire 1734-35
2. Sir Adam Fergusson 3 Bt – Ayrshire 1774-80 1781-84 Edinburgh 1784-90 Ayrshire 1790-96
3. Sir James Fergusson 6 Bt – Ayrshire 1854-57 1859-68 N. E. Div. Manchester 1885-1906
4. Sir Charles Dalrymple 1 Bt – Buteshire 1868-85 Ipswich 1886-1906

Seat: Kilkerran, Ayrshire (built 15th c., acq. 1646, new house c. 1730, remod. c. 1760, add. 1818 and 1854, still own)
Estates: Bateman 22630 (S) 13334. Owned 8,000 acres in 1996.
Titles: Baron Ballantrae (1972-80 UKLife); Baronet 1703-
1 Ld Lt 20th
1 KT 20th
Notes: 2, 5, 6, 7, and 8 Bts and 1 Baron in ODNB.

Hamilton-Dalrymple

Origins: The 1 Baronet was a grandson of the 1 Viscount Stair. John Dalrymple married the daughter and heiress of the 2 Baron Bargeny in 1736 and took the additional name Hamilton. The family succeeded to the Hamilton estates in 1796. The father of the 1 Baron Bargany was an illegitmate son of the 1 Marquis of Hamilton (see Hamilton).

1. Sir Hew Dalrymple 1 Bt – [New Galloway 1690-1702 N. Berwick 1703-07]
2. Sir Hew Dalrymple 2 Bt – Haddington Burghs 1742-47 Haddingtonshire 1747-61 Haddington Burghs 1761-68
3. John Dalrymple – Wigtown Burghs 1754-61 Wigtownshire 1761-62 Wigtown Burghs 1762-68
4. Sir Hew Dalrymple 3 Bt – Haddingtonshire 1780-86
5. Sir Hew Dalrymple 4 Bt – Haddingtonshire 1795-1800 Ayrshire 1803-07 1811-18 Haddington Burghs 1820-26
6. Sir John Hamilton-Dalrymple 5 Bt – Haddington Burghs 1805-06
7. Sir Adolphus Dalrymple 2 Bt – Weymouth & Melcombe Regis 1817-18 Appleby 1819-26 Haddington Burghs 1826-32 Brighton 1837-41
8. Sir Godfrey Dalrymple White 1 Bt – Southport 1910-31

Seats: Leuchie (Luchie) House, Haddingtonshire (old house, purch. 1701, rebuilt 1779-85, remod. 1859, institutional use from 1960s, still own estate); Walltower House, (North Berwick House), Haddingtonshire (leased 1694, add. 1747, purch. 1774, sold 1939, NT 1968); Bargany, Ayrshire (built 16th c., rebuilt 1681, acq. by mar. from Hamiltons 1737, remod. 1747, add. mid-19th c., sold 1985); High Mark, Wigtownshire
Estates: Bateman 3039 (S) 8856. Owned 6,000 acres in 1996.
Title: Baron Bargeny (Bargany) 1641-1736 S; Baronet 1698- ; 1815-66; 1926-
Peers: [2 peers 1662-93 1695-1707]
Notes: 1 and 2 Bts and two others in ODNB.

Dalrymple-Elphinstone

Origins: A younger son of the 1 Earl of Stair married in 1754 the daughter and heiress of Sir James Elphinstone 3 Bt of Logie. He was not related to Lord Elphinstone. The 1 Bt was a lawyer and Receiver General 1701.

1. Sir James Elphinstone 1 Bt – [Aberdeenshire 1693-1702]
2. Sir James Dalrymple-Elphinstone 2 Bt – Portsmouth 1857-65

Seat: Logie (Elphinstone), Aberdeenshire (purch. 1492, built 1680, remod. 17th and 18th c., sold 1903, fire 1975, restored)
Estates: Bateman 5524 (S) 5107
Titles: Baronet 1701-43; 1828-

Dalrymple-Hay

Origins: Descended from a younger son of John Dalrymple ancestor of the 1 Viscount Stair. The 1 Baronet married Susan Hay heiress of Park Place.

1. Sir John Dalrymple-Hay 3 Bt – Wakefield 1862-65 Stamford 1866-80 Wigtown Burghs 1880-85

Seat: Park Place (Castle of Park), Wigtownshire (built by Hays 1596-99, add. 18th c., abandoned 1830, sold 1875, ruin, some recent restoration)
Baronet 1798-
Notes: Two in ODNB.

Viscount Oxfurd (1651-1705 S)

Origins: The Makgills were of medieval descent. Kt and Provost of Edinburgh under James V. Lords of Session 1580s, 1597, 1629. Baronet 1627. The Makgill estates passed through several families to John Dalrymple later 8 Earl of Stair in 1780.

No MPs

Seats: Cranston Riddell, Edinburghshire (acq. mid-16th c., passed out of family 18th c.); Oxenfoord Castle, Edinburghshire (see Earl of Stair)
Title: Baronet 1627-1705
Peers: [2 peers 1661-63 1672-89]
Notes: 1 Viscount in ODNB.

DALSTON

Origins: At Dalston since the 13th century. Did well out of the Dissolution and fortunate marriages. **First MP 1383, for Cumberland. Five additional MPs 1547-1644, two kts of the shire.** Bt 1641.

1. John Dalston – Appleby 1661-79
2. John Dalston – Westmorland 1747-59
3. Sir George Dalston 4 Bt – Westmorland 1754-61

Seats: Dalston Hall, Cumberland (leased from 1301, add. 1498, add. early 17th c., sold 1761); Acorn Bank, Westmorland (purch. 1544, built house c. 1600, add. 1656, remod. 18th c., sold 1761, now NT); Heath Hall, Yorkshire (built c. 1584-98, sold 1761, demolished 1961)
Estates: Worth £3,000 pa c. 1640.
Title: Baronet 1641-1765

DALWAY *IRELAND*

Origins: Came from Devon to Ireland in 1573 as a cornet in the English army. Constable of Carrickfergus Castle 1603. Granted land early 17th century. **First {MP 1613}.**

1. Robert Dalway – {Antrim 1696-99}
2. Alexander Dalway – {Carrickfergus 1715-18}
3. Marriot Dalway – {Carrickfergus 1761-68}
4. Noah Dalway – {Carrickfergus 1799-1800} 1801-02
5. Marriot Dalway – Carrickfergus 1868-80

Seat: Bella Hill (Bellahill), Antrim (acq. 18th c.)
Estates: 2477 (I) 2098. 2,287 acres worth £2,000 pa in the 18th c.
Notes: Active in Carrickfergus town affairs 1580s to the 1880s.

DALY [Coghlan(e)] *IRELAND*

Baron Dunsandle and Clanconal (1845-1911 I)

Origins: Claimed descent from an ancient Irish sept. Justice of the Common Pleas (d. 1720). Sheriff 1743.

1. James Daly – {Athenry 1741-68 Galway 1768-69}
2. Charles Daly – {County Galway 1753-68}
3. Denis Daly – {Galway 1767-68 County Galway 1768-90 Galway 1790-91}

4. Anthony Daly – {Galway 1771-90}
5. Denis Daly – {Galway 1776-90 King's County 1790-1800} County Galway 1801-02 Galway 1802-05 County Galway 1805-18
6. Peter Daly {Galway 1792-97}
7. Sir St. George Daly – {Galawy 1797-1800} 1801
8. James Daly 1 Baron Dunsandle – Galway 1805-11 County Galway 1812-30 1832-34

Seats: Dunsandle, Galway (built mid-18th c., sold 1954, demolished 1958); Dalystown, Galway (built mid-18th c., sold 1818, now ruin); Thomastown Castle, Tipperary (built 1670, acq. later 19th c. decayed, sold 20th c.); Coghlan Castle, King's County (acq. by mar. 1794, sold 1821)
Estates: Bateman 37057 (I) 17193.
Peer: 1 Irish Rep peer 1851-93
Notes: Inherited Coghlan estates 1790s. Estates worth £100,000 sold in 1815-24. Two in ODNB.

Coghlan(e) (The Mac Coughlan)

Origins: Old Irish Catholic family that managed to hold on to land. Chiefs of Lower Devlin. Regranted Kilcolgan 1632. Granted arms 1654. **First {MP 1634} for King's County. Another {MP 1639}**. The estates of the last MP passed via marriage by an heiress to the Dalys of Dalystown.

1. Thomas Coghlan – {Banagher 1768-76 Castlebar 1776-83 Carlingford 1783-90 Augher 1790-94}

Seats: Garry Castle, King's County (medieval castle, new house 18th c., passed by mar. to Dalys 1790s, sold 19th c.); Kilcolgan (Coghlan) Castle, King's County (medieval castle, rebuilt 1630s, burned 1691, passed to Dalys by mar. 1794)
Estates: Worth £5,000 pa in 1794.
Notes: Coghlans extinct in male line 1794.

DAMER [Dawson] *ENGLAND & IRELAND*

Earl of Dorchester (1792-1808 GB)

Origins: The founder was an officer from Dorset under Cromwell in Ireland who purchased estates there in the 1660s. He became a merchant, moneylender, and miser who left his estates to a nephew in 1720. The latter purchased Milton Abbey.

1. Jospeh Damer – Dorchester 1722-27 {County Tipperary 1735-37}

2. Joseph Damer 1 Earl of Dorchester – Weymouth & Melcombe Regis 1741-47 Bramber 1747-54 Dorchester 1754-62
3. George Damer – Dorchester 1751-52
4. John Damer – Dorchester 1762-80
5. George Damer 2 Earl of Dorchester – Cricklade 1768-74 Anstruther Easter Burghs 1778-80 Dorchester 1780-91 Malton 1792-98 {Naas 1795-97}
6. John Damer – {Portarlington 1761-68 Swords 1768-76} Gatton 1768-74
7. Lionel Damer – Peterborough 1786-1802

Seats: Milton Abbey, Dorset (medieval monastic buildings, add. 1498-1525, purch. 1752, remod. 1771-76, passed to Dawsons in 1829, sold 1852, school); Shronell, Tipperary (purch. c. 1662, resident 18th c.); Damer House, Tipperary (old castle, purch. and built 1715, barracks in the 19th c., now offices); Came House (Winterborne Came), Dorset (purch. early 18th century, new house 1754, passed by mar. 1829 to Dawsons, see below)
Estates: Milton Abbey estate was 8,600 acres. Worth £18,000 pa in 1779.
Titles: Baron Milton 1753-1808 I; Baron Milton 1762-1808 GB
Peers: {1 peer 1753-98} 2 peers 1762-1808
1 Ld Lt 19th
1 in Cabinet 1794-95

<u>Earl of Portarlington</u> (1785- I)

Origins: The founder was a diplomat and soldier under Cromwell and settled in Ireland after the Restoration. He became a collector of revenue and later a banker. His son purchased the Portarlington demense in the early 18th century. Mary Damer, sister of the 1 Earl of Dorchester, married William Dawson 1 Viscount Carlow in 1737. On the death of the last daughter of the 1 Earl in 1829 the Damer estates passed to the Dawsons.

1. Ephriam Dawson – {Portarlington 1713-14 Queen's County 1715-46}
2. Wiliam Dawson 1 Viscount Carlow – {Portarlington 1733-60 Queen's County 1761-68 Portarlington 1769-70}
3. John Dawson 1 Earl of Portarlington – {Portarlington 1766-68 Queen's County 1768-79}
4. Joseph Dawson – {Portarlington 1773-83}
5. George Dawson-Damer – Portarlington 1835-47 Dorchester 1847-52
6. Lionel Dawson-Damer 4 Earl of Portarlington – Portarlington 1857-65 1868-80

Seats: Emo Court (Park) (Dawson's Court), Queen's County (built early 18th c., acq. by mar. from Prestons early 18th c., new house c. 1790, remod. 1834-36, add. c. 1860, sold 1930, institution); Came House, Dorset (acq. by mar. 1829, passed through female line of succession from 1900 to present); Milton Abbey, Dorset (inher. 1829, sold 1852)

Estates: 19928 (I) 10797 and 3847 (E & I) 3733. Income in 1848 was £30,000 pa.
Titles: Baron Dawson 1770- I; Viscount Carlow 1776- I
Peers: {2 peers 1770-98} 2 Irish Rep peers 1855-89 1896-1900
1 KP 19th
Notes: Debts reached £600,000 in the 1850s.

DANBY

Origins: The **first MP in 1453** was a mercer in York. By 1500 the family was landed and later further increased the size of their estates. **Two further MPs 1554-1640**.

1. Thomas Danby – Malton 1661
2. Sir Abstrupus Danby – Aldborough 1698-1700

Seats: Farnley Hall, Yorkshire (medieval, acq. by mar. from descendants of the Domesday tenant 1497, rebuilt later 16th c., sold 1799, public park); Thorpe Perrow, Yorkshire (medieval, purch. 15th c., sold 1798)
Estates: Worth £2,500 pa in 1660.
Notes: Extinct in the male line in 1833. Danby family and one individual have entries in the ODNB.

DANIEL I

Origins: Prominent Truro merchants in the 16th and 17th centuries. Owned mines in the 18th century and became bankers. **First MP 1601 for Truro. One additional MP 1624.**

1. Ralph Daniel – West Looe 1805-12

Seat: Trelissick, Cornwall (purch. early 17th c., built 18th c., acq. 1800, rebuilt 1825, sold 1866)
Notes: The Daniels went bankrupt 1832. The head of the family died in exile 1866.

DANIEL II (Daniell)

Origins: A Cheshire family that moved to Wiltshire in the reign of Henry VIII. One became a court official and acquired monastic land in 1540. **First MP 1545. One additional MP 1558 for Marlborough.** Judge under James I.

1. Jeffrey Daniel – Marlborough 1660-79
2. William Daniell – Marlborough 1695-98

Seat: St. Margaret's, Preshute, Wiltshire (sold 1714)
Notes: Extinct on the death of the last MP.

DARELL [Nightingall]

Origins: An old Kentish family that claimed to have come over with the Conqueror and served at the Battle of Hastings. Recorded in Yorkshire in the 13th century. Acquired Kent estates by marriage in the r. Henry IV. **First MP 1407 for Kent.** A younger son married a Wiltshire heiress and succeeded to the Collingbourne of Collingbourne estates there. **Two Collingbourne MPs and two Darrell MPs all in the 15th century.**

1. Sir John Darell – Maidstone 1679 Rye 1679-81 1689-94
2. Sir Lionel Darell 1 Bt – Lyme Regis 1780-84 Hendon 1784-1802

Seat: Calehill Park, Kent (acq. c. 1400, rebuilt 1763-64, demolished 1952)
Estates: Bateman 2890 (E) 3868
Title: Baronet 1795-
Notes: The 1 Bt made a fortune as a nabob and was Chairman of the East India Company. One in ODNB.

<u>Nightingall</u>

Origins: The first MP was the commander of the army of the East India Company in the subcontinent 1816. He married Sir Lionel Darell's (see above) daughter. He left his estates to his wife with reversion to his Darell nephews.

1. Sir Miles Nightingall – Eye 1820-29

Seat: Redgrave Hall, Suffolk (leased, owned by Holt-Wilsons, see Smith I)
Notes: One in ODNB.

DARRELL

Origins: The family was resident at Lillingstone in the 12th century, lord of the manor there in the 13th century. **First MP 1388 for Buckinghamshire. Three further MPs 1559-1604.**

1. Henry Darrell – Liskeard 1696-1701

Seats: Lillingstone (Dayrell) House, Buckinghamshire (acq. 13th c., rebuilt 1693-97, house sold 1796, estate sold 1885); Trewornan, Cornwall (inher. 1658, sold 1706)
Notes: One in ODNB.

DASHWOOD [Peyton]

Baron Le Despencer (1295, called out of abeyance 1763-81 E)

Origins: The Dashwoods were yeomen in Dorset in the 1500s. They became wealthy mercers in the early 17th century, and moved to London by the middle of that century. After 1660 they became involved in the saddlery and silk trades, brewing, and shipowning. Lord Mayor 1684. Became prominent in the East India Company by 1700. Began to purchase large landed estates in the late 17th century. They made good marriages and pulled out of business affairs in the early 18th century. (Dashwood, *The Dashwoods of West Wycombe*, 11-17) The 2 Bt succeeded to the Barony of Le Despencer by marriage to an heiress. The title passed out of the family at his death.

1. Sir Samuel Dashwood – London 1685-87 1690-95
2. Sir Francis Dashwood 1 Bt – Winchelsea 1708-13
3. George Dashwood – Stockbridge 1710-13
4. Francis Dashwood 11 Baron Le Despencer – New Romney 1741-61 Weymouth & Melcombe Regis 1761-63
5. Sir John Dashwood King 3 Bt – Bishop's Castle 1753-61
6. Sir John Dashwood King 4 Bt – Wycombe 1796-1831
7. Sir George Dashwood 5 Bt – Buckinghamshire 1832-35 Wycombe 1837-62

Seats: West Wycombe Park, Buckinghamshire (purch. 1698 and built soon after, rebuilt 1748-71, NT 1944, family still resident); Halton House, Buckinghamshire (medieval, purch. 1720, sold 1853); Mereworth Castle, Kent (built 1720-30, inher. by mar. 1762, passed to Stapletons by mar. 1781); Hall Place, Kent (medieval house, rebuilt 1469, rebuilt 1540s, purch. c. 1640, add. 1649-53, acq. by mar. later 18th c., sold 1926)
Estates: Bateman 5032 (E) 7019
Title: Baronet 1707-
Peer: 1 peer 1763-81
2 Lds Lt 18th, 19th
1 in Cabinet 1762-63
Notes: 1 Bt and 11 Baron and one other in ODNB.

Dashwood

Origins: A younger son established a separate branch of the family at Kirtlington.

1. Sir Robert Dashwood 1 Bt – Banbury 1689-98 Oxfordshire 1699-1700
2. George Dashwood – Sudbury 1703-05
3. Sir James Dashwood 2 Bt – Oxfordshire 1740-54 1761-68
4. Sir Henry Dashwood 3 Bt – Wigtown Burghs 1775-80 New Woodstock 1784-1820

5. James Dashwood – Gatton 1802-03
6. Sir George Dashwood 4 Bt – Truro 1814-18

Seats: Kirtlington Park, Oxfordshire (acq. by mar. 1728, built 1742-78, sold 1909); Cockley Cley Hall, Norfolk (built c. 1698, acq. 1700, sold 1817)
Estates: Bateman 7630 (E) 12507. Worth £2,300 pa in 1682.
Title: Baronet 1684-
Notes: One in ODNB.

Peyton

Origins: Descended from the Peytons of Suffolk and Cambridgeshire (see Peyton). This branch founded by the son of a customs official in Plymouth late 16th century. A naval officer was knighted in 1606. The brother of Sir Robert Dashwood 1 Bt of Kirtlington married Algerina Peyton. Their son took the name Peyton and succeeded to Doddington.

1. Sir Henry Peyton 1 Bt – Cambridgeshire 1782-89
2. Sir Henry Peyton 2 Bt – Cambridgeshire 1802
3. Sir Henry Peyton 3 Bt – Woodstock 1837-38

Seats: Doddington, Cambridgeshire (acq. 1602, abandoned as a residence by 1808, became a farm house, sold c. 1900); Swifts (Swift's) House, Oxfordshire (built c. 1800, acq. c. 1830, still owned 1950s)
Estates: Bateman 3958 (E) 6793
Titles: Baronet 1660-60; 1667-1771; 1776-
Notes: Two in ODNB.

DAVIDSON [Vickers] *SCOTLAND*

Origins: The first MP a rich West India merchant, plantation owner, and East India Company stockholder. The son of Douglas Vickers MP succeeded to Tulloch Castle by marriage.

1. Duncan Davidson – Cromartyshire 1790-96
2. Duncan Davidson – Ross & Cromarty 1826-30 1831-32
3. Douglas Vickers – Hallam Div. Sheffield 1918-22

Seat: Tulloch Castle, Ross-shire (built mid-16th c., purch. 1762, add. 1891, remod. 1919, passed via heiress to the Vickers [aircraft] family and sold 1957, hotel)
Estates: Bateman 36130 (S) 6093; first MP left £500,000 in 1826.
1 Ld Lt 19th

Notes: In Bateman p. 121 the Davidsons claimed to have held Tulloch since 1300 in the female line (they were related to the previous owners, but the grant was made in 1542).

DAVIE (Davye) [Ferguson]

Origins: Gentry family. This line established by a younger son, a merchant, who purchased landed estates of his own. Mayor of Exeter 1584. **First MP 1621**. Bt 1641. Sir Henry Ferguson married in 1823 the only sister and heiress of Sir John Davie Bt. On the death of her uncle, Sir Humphrey Davie, he assumed the name, obtaining the revival of the baronetcy.

1. Sir John Davie 2 Bt – Tavistock 1661
2. Sir John Davie 3 Bt – Saltash 1679-81
3. Sir Henry Ferguson-Davie 1 Bt – Haddington 1847-78
4. Sir John Ferguson-Davie 2 Bt – Barnstaple 1859-65

Seat: Creedy Park (House), Devon (acq. and built c. 1600, fire 1915, new house built 1916-21, sold c. 1982, flats)
Estates: Bateman 16543 (E & W) 13678
Titles: Baronet 1641-1846; 1847-

DAVYS I *IRELAND*

<u>Viscount Mountcashell</u> (1706-36 I)

Origins: **First {MP 1634}**. Sir William Davys {MP} was Chief Justice of the King's Bench in Ireland. He married 1682 the widow of the 3 Earl of Clancarty (see MacCarty), who was also 4 Viscount Muskerry. The MacCarthy estates were forfeited in 1691, but the Davys family was granted a title. Sheriff 1700.

1. Sir William Davys – {Dublin 1661-66}
2. Sir Paul Davys – {County Kildare 1661-66}

Seat: St. Catherine's Park, Dublin (acq. later 17th c., sold 1736?)
Peers: {2 peers 1707-16 1733-36}

DAVYS II (Davis) *IRELAND*

Origins: Burgesses, aldermen, mayors, and officials in Carrickfergus.

1. John Davys – {Carrickfergus 1639 County Antrim 1661-66}

2. Henry Davys – {Belfast 1661-66 Carrickfergus 1692-93 1695-99 1703-08}
3. Hercules Davys – {Carrickfergus 1661-66 Roscommon 1692-93 1695-99}
4. William Davys – {County Fermanagh 1661-62}
5. John Davys – {Coleraine 1692-93}
6. John Davys – {Coleraine 1692-93 Kildare 1695-99 Charlemont 1705-13}
7. Arthur Davys – {Carrickfergus 1713-14}

Seat: Resident in Carrickfergus, Antrim
Notes: Relationships among MPs are uncertain.

DAWNAY (Dawney)

<u>Viscount Downe</u> (1681- I)

Origins: Another family that claimed to have come over with the Conqueror. They were one of the oldest families in Yorkshire, at Cowick in the 14th century. They were rewarded for supporting Henry VII at Bosworth. **First MP 1571.** Bt 1642.

1. John Dawnay 1 Viscount Downe – York 1660 Pontefract 1661-81
2. Henry Dawnay 2 Viscount Downe – Pontefract 1690-95 Yorkshire 1698-1700 1707-27
3. John Dawnay – Aldborough 1713-15 Pontefract 1715-16
4. Henry Dawnay 3 Viscount Downe – Yorkshire 1750-60
5. John Dawnay 4 Viscount Downe – Cirencester 1754-68 Malton 1768-74
6. John Dawnay 5 Viscount Downe – Petersfield 1787-90 Wootton Bassett 1790-96
7. William Dawnay 7 Viscount Downe – Rutland 1841-46
8. Lewis Dawnay – Thirsk 1880-85 Thirsk & Malton Div. N. R. Yorkshire 1885-92
9. Guy Dawnay – N. R. Yorkshire 1882-85

Seats: Danby Hall (Lodge, Castle), Yorkshire (built 14th c., partially ruined, purch. 1656, still own); Baldersby Park, Yorkshire (built 1718-21, purch. 1854, sold c. 1900, now a school); Wykeham Abbey, Yorkshire (inherit. 1817, main seat from 1910, still own); Cowick Hall, Yorkshire (acq. 14th c., rebuilt c. 1660-90, add. c. 1752-60, sold 1869, later institutional use); Beningborough Hall, Yorkshire (built c. 1714-16, inher. 1827, sold 1917, NT 1957)
Estates: Bateman 46252 (E) 56105. Owned 20,000 acres in 2001.
Titles: Baron Dawnay 1796-1832 UK; Baron Dawnay 1897- UK; Baronet 1642-57
Peers: 4 peers 1796-1832 1897-1945
Notes: The heiress of Beninghborough Hall, who died in 1826, left the estate to the 6 Viscount Downe because he was a friend of her son's in college and also her friend with no blood relationship. (*Country Life*, 62, p. 829). One in ODNB. Wykeham Abbey (purch. 1544) descended 1817 to Dawnays from the Hutchinsons (arms 1581, who later changed their name to Langley). **First MP 1586. Another MP 1626.**

DAWSON *IRELAND*

Earl of Dartrey (1866-1933 UK)

Origins: The family moved from Yorkshire to Armagh in the later 16th century. One married an heiress in the mid-17th century. The first MP was a banker in Dublin and Lord Mayor 1737.

1. Richard Dawson – {St. Canice 1727-60 Monaghan 1761-66}
2. John Dawson – {Monaghan 1743-47}
3. Thomas Dawson 1 Viscount Cremorne – {County Monaghan 1749-68}
4. Richard Dawson – {County Monaghan 1797-1800} 1801-07
5. Richard Dawson 2 Viscount Cremorne – County Monaghan 1812-13
6. Thomas Dawson – County Louth 1841-47 Monaghan 1847-52
7. Vesey Dawson 2 Earl of Dartrey – County Monaghan 1865-68

Seat: Dartrey House (Dawson's Grove), Monaghan (acq. by mar. c. 1655, built c. 1770, rebuilt 1844-46, demolished 1948)
Estates: Bateman 30108 (I) 21614
Titles: Baron Dartrey 1770-1813 I; Viscount Cremorne 1785-1813 I; Baron Dartrey 1797-1933 I; Baron Dartrey 1847-1933 UK
Peers: {2 peers 1785-1800} 3 peers 1847-1933
1 Ld Lt 19th
1 KP 19th

Dawson

Origins: Gained lands by military service in the mid-17th century. Remote kinsmen of the Earls of Dartrey.

1. Thomas Dawson – {County Armagh 1776-83 Sligo 1783-90 Enniscorthy 1800}
2. Alexander Dawson – Louth 1826-31

Seat: Riverstown, Louth (occupied 18th and 19th c.)
Notes: The last MP died unmarried with no direct heirs in 1831.

DE COURCY [Essington] *IRELAND & ENGLAND*

Baron Kingsale (Baron Courcy of Kinsale) (c.1223- / 1340- I)

Origins: Went to Ulster c. 1176. Earls in 1181. Outlawed in 1691, reversed 1692.

No MPs

Seats: Old Head, Kinsale, Cork (medieval castle, new house late 17th c., abandoned post-1759, ruins disappeared); Lea Castle, Worcestershire (built early 19th c., leased later 19th c.)
Estates: Bateman 4492 (I & E) 4226
Peers: {6 peers 1660-62 1665-67 1686-91 1692-1759 1762-1800}
Notes: Said to have been granted the right to remain covered in the presence of the monarch by King John. One in ODNB.

Essington

Origins: Gentry and business in the 17th century. The daughter and heiress of the MP married in 1725 the 19 Baron Kingsale.

1. John Essington – Aylesbury 1710-15

Seat: Gossington Hall, Gloucestershire (purch. c. 1675, new house c. 1695, passed to Lord Kingsale by mar. 1740, sold?)
Estate: John Essington MP said to be worth £100,000 c. 1725.

DE CRESPIGNY

Origins: Claimed medieval noble descent. Huguenot exiles came to England 1687. Soldiers and officials.

1. Philip Champion De Crespigny – Sudbury 1774-75 Aldborough 1780-90
2. Thomas Champion De Crespigny – Sudbury 1790-96
3. William Champion De Crespigny 2 Bt – Southampton 1818-26

Seats: Ufford Hall (Park), Suffolk (built late 17th c.); Kingscrew, Hampshire; Champion Lodge, Surrey (acq. and built 1717, demolished 1841); Champion Lodge (Hill House), Essex (acq. and built mid-19th c., sold 1935?) Anspach House, Hampshire (resident early 19th c., later burned); Wivenhoe Hall, Essex (resident mid-19th c., demolished c. 1929)
Estates: 4th Baronet bankrupt 1881.
Title: Baronet 1805-1952
Notes: 4 Bt in ODNB.

DE GREY

Baron Walsingham (1780- GB)

Origins: Landowners by the middle of the 13th century. Acquired Merton by marriage in the 14th century. **First MP 1545.**

1. William de Grey – Thetford 1685-87
2. Thomas de Grey – Thetford 1708-10 Norfolk 1715-27
3. William de Grey 1 Baron Walsingham – Newport 1761-70 University of Cambridge 1770-71
4. Thomas de Grey – Norfolk 1764-74
5. Thomas de Grey 2 Baron Walsingham – Wareham 1774 Tamworth 1774-80 Lostwithiel 1780-81
6. Thomas de Grey 6 Baron Walsingham – W. Norfolk 1865-70

Seat: Merton Hall, Norfolk (acq. by mar. c. 1337 from the Baynards who were Domesday tenants, built 1610-13, remod. 1832, add. 1846, leased to a school, fire 1956 destroyed much of house, still own)
Estates: Bateman 19148 (E) 16578. Rubinstein – 2 Baron left £200,000 in probate 1818.
Peers: 8 peers 1780-1945
Notes: 1 Baron a judge. 1, 2, and 6 Barons in ODNB.

DE LA BERE (Barre)

Origins: Old Herefordshire family. Rose to gentry by early 14th century. **First MP 1355 for Herefordshire. Seven additional MPs most kts of the shire.**

1. Kinard De La Bere – Gloucestershire 1722-27
2. Sir Rupert De la Bere 1 Bt – Evesham Div. Worcestershire 1935-50 Worcestershire 1950-55

Seats: Rotherwas, Herfordshire (medieval, sold c. 1732, gutted 1913); Southam Delabere, Gloucestershire (built c. 1500, acq. by marriage 1609, sold 1839)
Title: Baronet 1953-

DEANE *IRELAND*

Origins: Founder originally from Gloucester, brother of a judge, served as a major in Ireland with Cromwell. Acquired land 1666 and 1670. Sheriff 1677.

1. Joseph Deane – {Innistiogue 1661-66}

2. Edward Deane – {Innistiogue 1692-93 County Dublin 1695-99 Innistiogue 1703-17}
3. Joseph Deane – {County Dublin 1703-14}
4. Edward Deane – {Newcastle 1713-14 Innistiogue 1715-27 1728-48}
5. Stephen Deane – {Innistiogue 1717-27}
6. Edward Deane – {Innistiogue 1745-51}
7. Joseph Deane – {Innistiogue 1751-60}
8. Joseph Deane – {Innistiogue 1761-68 County Dublin 1768-76 County Kilkenny 1779-83}

Seat: Terenure, Dublin (purch. 1670, rebuilt 18th c., sold early 19th c.);
Estates: Estate purchased for £4,000 in 1670. Worth £600 pa in 1713. Held 4,645 acres in the mid-18th c.

DEEDES

Baron Deedes (1986-2007 UKLife)

Origins: The first MP was the son of a mercer in Hythe. Granted arms 1653.

1. Julius Deedes – Hythe 1679 1685 1689-90
2. William Deedes – Hythe 1807-12
3. William Deedes – E. Kent 1845-62
4. William Deedes – E. Kent 1876-80
5. William Deedes 1 Baron Deedes – Ashford 1950-74

Seats: Saltwood Castle, Kent (medieval, damaged 1580, restored and add. 1885, sold c. 1936); Sandling Park, Kent (built 1779, sold 1896, demolished 1945-46)
Estates: Bateman 4904 (E) 5539
1 in Cabinet 1962-64.
Notes: 1 Baron in ODNB.

DENISON

Viscount Ossington (1872-73 UK)

Origins: A long line of West Riding clothiers and woolen merchants. They made a great fortune from c. 1700 onwards as exporters of Yorkshire cloth in Leeds.

1. John Denison – Wootton Bassett 1796-1802 Colchester 1802-06 Minehead 1807-12
2. John Denison 1 Viscount Ossington – Newcastle-under-Lyme 1823-26 Hastings 1826-30 Nottinghamshire 1831-32 S. Nottinghamshire 1832-37 Malton 1841-57 N. Nottinghamshire 1857-72

3. Edward Denison – Newark 1868-70
4. William Denison – Nottingham 1874-80

Seat: Ossington Hall, Nottinghamshire (built 1729, purch. 1768, add. c. 1790, demolished 1963, still own estate)
Estates: Bateman 6309 (E) 10170 and 8247 (S) 16978. William Denison spent at least £100,000 on land purchased in the 1750s-80s. (Ward and Wilson, *Land and Industry*, 147, 157, 168). He left well over half a million pounds at his death 1782.
Peer: 1 peer 1872-73
Notes: William Denison's estates were left his daughter's heiress (Wilkinson, who took the name Denison). The 1 Viscount was Speaker of the House of Commons. 1 Viscount and four others in ODNB.

DENMAN

<u>Baron Denman</u> (1834- UK)

Origins: Mayor of Hull 1634. The father of the 1 Baron was an eminent physician. 1 Baron was a politician and judge.

1. Thomas Denman 1 Baron Denman – Wareham 1818-20 Nottingham 1820-26 1830-32
2. George Denman – Tiverton 1859-65 1866-72
3. Sir Richard Denman 1 Bt – Carlisle 1910-18 Central Leeds 1929-45

Seats: Balcombe Place, Sussex (built 1856, purch. late 19th c., sold 1954, institutional use); Staffield Hall, Cumberland (older house, rebuilt 1848, purch. early 20th c., sold mid-20th c., flats); Middleton Hall, Derbyshire (built mid-17th c., acq. by mar. 1790, remod. mid-19th c., sold 1953)
Estates: Bateman under 2000. The 1 Baron divided his estate among his children. 2 Baron left £12,000 in 1894.
Title: Baronet 1945-
Peers: 3 peers 1834-1945
Notes: 1 and 2 Barons and two others in ODNB.

DENNE

Origins: Armigerous since r. Henry III. **First MP 1320 for Kent. Another MP 1624**.

1. Vincent Denne – Canterbury 1656 1681

Seat: Denne Hill, Kent (acq. by 13th c., sold 1694)
Estates: Worth possibly £800 pa in 1656.

DENNIS [Swift] *IRELAND*

Baron Tracton (1781-82 I)

Origins: The father of the 1 Baron was a timber merchant. The 1 Baron was a successful lawyer and official.

1. John Dennis 1 Baron Tracton – {Rathcormack 1761-68 Youghal 1768-77}
2. John Dennis – {Clonmell 1800}

Seats: Fort Granite (Fortgranite), Wicklow (acq. by Pendred family and built c. 1730, passed by mar. to Dennis family 1810, remod. 1810-15, remod. 1870-71, still own); Tracton Abbey, Cork (acq. mid-18th c., passed out of the family 1782, demolished)
Estates: 3801 (I) 1300 in 1878.
Peer: 1 peer 1781-82

Swift

Origins: The sister and heiress of the 1 Baron Tracton married Thomas Swift of Lynnburg, Westmeath. His great uncle was the MP below. The Swifts were English minor gentry by 16th c. To Ireland as lawyers and clergy mid-17th century.

1. Adam Swift – {Newry 1703-13}

Seat: Green Castle, Down (acq. later 17th c.)

DENNY *IRELAND*

Earl of Norwich (1626-37 E)

Origins: The founder acquired substantial property in London by marriage in the mid-14th century. His son was a fishmonger and citizen of London. **His son was knight of the shire for Cambridgeshire 1391 (1st MP). Four additional MPs 1529-1625, one for Essex**. Chief Baron of the Exchequer early 16th century, and acquired more estates at the Dissolution. Baron 1604 and Earl 1629. A younger son went to Ireland as a soldier in the 1574, Sheriff of Kerry 1588, and gained large grants of confiscated land in the late 16th and early 17th centuries. **First {MP 1639 for County Kerry}.**

1. Sir Arthur Denny – {County Kerry 1661-66}
2. Edward Denny – {County Kerry 1692-93 1695-99}
3. Barry Denny – {Tralee 1696-99}
4. Edward Denny – {Doneraile 1695-99}

5. Edward Denny – {County Kerry 1703-14 Askeaton 1715-27}
6. Arthur Denny – {County Kerry 1727-42}
7. Edward Denny – {Tralee 1768-75}
8. Sir Barry Denny 1 Bt – {County Kerry 1768-76 1783-94}
9. Sir Barry Denny 2 Bt – {County Kerry 1794}
10. Sir Edward Denny 4 Bt – Tralee 1818-19
11. Sir Edward Denny 3 Bt – Tralee 1828-29

Seats: Tralee Castle, Kerry (built early 13th c., acq. 1583, rebuilt late 16th/early 17th c., partly destroyed 1641, rebuilt later 17th c., new house 1802, abandoned by family early/mid-19th c., decayed, old castle demolished 1826); Kingsend House, Worcestershire (acq. early 19th c., sold c. 1831)
Estates: Bateman 21479 (I) 9685. Worth £1,600 in 1713. Worth £5,000 in 1767. Held 18,000 acres in 1804.
Titles: Baron Denny 1604-60 E; Baronet 1782-
Notes: Family in Canada in 20th c. Three in ODNB.

DENTON [Chamberlayne]

Origins: An old Buckinghamshire family settled at Hillesdon from 1547. **First MP 1536 (kt of the shire)** prospered as a barrister and purchased large amounts of land after the Dissolution. **Three additional MPs 1558-1644, one for Buckinghamshire.** Bt 1680. George Chamberlayne of Wardington succeeded to his uncle Denton's estates in 1740 and took the name Denton. The Chambelaynes claimed to have come over with the Conqueror (Burke, *Extinct and Dormant Baronetcies*, 105), and to have been Chamberlains to Kings Stephen and Henry I and II. Seem to have been a family of medieval origins. **First MP 1529. Six additional MPs 1553-97, one for Oxfordshire** (see also Dummer). Bt 1643.

1. Alexander Denton – Buckingham 1690-98
2. Sir Edmund Denton 1 Bt – Buckingham 1698-1708 Buckinghamshire 1708-13
3. Alexander Denton – Buckingham 1708-10 1715-22 {Carrickfergus 1709-13}
4. George Chamberlayne Denton – Buckingham 1728-47

Seats: Hillesdon, Buckinghamshire (purch. 1547, burned down and not rebuilt during the 1640s); Wardington, Oxfordshire (built mid-16th c., purch. by Chamberlaynes 1602 and 1623, remod. 1665, sold 1789)
Estates: Dentons worth c. £1,000 or more pa 1630s.
Titles: Baronet 1643-1776; 1680-1714
Notes: Two Dentons and two Chamberlaynes in ODNB.

DERING

Origins: Possibly of Saxon descent (Henning, *The House of Commons*, II, 208). Sheriff first half 12th century. **First MP 1542. Four additional MPs 1547-1642 (some from a cadet line), one for Kent.**

1. Sir Edward Dering 2 Bt – Kent 1660 {Lisburn 1662-66} East Retford 1670-79 Hythe 1679-81
2. Sir Edward Dering 3 Bt – Kent 1679-81
3. Charles Dering – {Monaghan 1692-93 1695-99 Carlingford 1703-13}
4. Sir Cholmeley Dering 4 Bt – Kent 1705-08 Saltash 1708-10 Kent 1710 11
5. Sir Edward Dering 5 Bt – Kent 1733-54
6. Sir Edward Dering 6 Bt – New Romney 1761-70 1774-87
7. Cholmeley Dering – New Romney 1817-18
8. Sir Edward Dering 8 Bt – Wexford 1830-31 New Romeny 1831-32 E. Kent 1852-57 1863-68

Seat: Surrenden Dering, Kent (medieval, acq. by mar. 1430, rebuilt c. 1630s, add. c. 1840, sold 1928, fire 1952)
Estates: Bateman 7280 (E) 12000
Title: Baronet 1626-
Notes: Three in ODNB.

DEWAR *SCOTLAND*

Baron Dewar (1919-30 UK)

Origins: Whiskey distillers in the 19th century (firm founded in 1846). Annual profits of over one million pounds by 1925.

1. Arthur Dewar – S. Edinburgh 1899-1900 1906-10
2. Thomas Dewar 1 Baron Dewar – St. George Div. Tower Hamlets 1900-06
3. John Dewar 1 Baron Forteviot – Inverness-shire 1900-16

Seats: Dupplin Castle, Perthshire (built 1828-32, purch. 1911 for £249,000, fire 1934, demolished 1967, rebuilt c. 1970); Vogrie House, Edinburghshire (old house, rebuilt 1875, sold 1924, hospital)
Estates: 1 Baron Forteviot left £4,400,000 in 1929. Owned 11,600 acres in 1996.
Titles: Baron Forteviot 1917- UK; Baronet 1907- ; 1917-30
Peers: 3 peers 1917-45 1919-30
Notes: Two in ODNB.

DICKINSON I

Origins: The father of the first MP was a Quaker and Bristol merchant. The son owned plantations in Jamaica.

1. William Dickinson – Great Marlow 1768-74 Rye 1777-90 Somerset 1796-1806
2. William Dickinson – Ilchester 1796-1802 Lostwithiel 1802-06 Somerset 1806-31
3. Francis Dickinson – W. Somerset 1841-47
4. Robert Dickinson – Wells Div. Somerset 1899-1906

Seat: Kingweston House (Park), Somerset (built 16th c., purch. 1741, rebuilt 1785-88, family ceased to use 1946, donated to school 2006)
Estates: Bateman 4279 (E) 5843
Notes: Family became extinct in 20th c.

DICKINSON II [Hyett]

Baron Dickinson (1930- UK)

Origins: The founder a Captain in the Royal Navy in the later 18th century; General in the Royal Engineers in the early 19th century.

1. Sebastian Dickinson – Stroud 1868-74
2. Willoughby Dickinson 1 Baron Dickinson – N. St. Pancras 1906-18
3. Frances Dickinson Viscountess Davidson – Hemel Hempsted Div. Hertfordshire 1937-59

Seats: Washwell House, Gloucestershire (built late 19th c., still own); Brown's Hill (Brownshill) Court, Gloucestershire (enlarged 1660, add. early 18th c., rebuilt c. 1760, add. c. 1791, purch. 1853, sold c. 1880)
Estates: The Brownshill property consisted of about 600 acres. (Kingsley, *The Country Houses of Gloucestershire*, II, 92)
Peer: 1 peer 1930-45
Notes: Viscountess Davidson was created a life peer in her own right in 1964. She had married John Davidson 1 Viscount Davidson (cr. 1937) in 1919. He died 1970. Her son succeeded as 2 Viscount Davidson. The 1 Baron Dickinson was designated heir to Painswick by 1930.

Hyett

Origins: Old Gloucestershire family, purchased landed estate early 18th century.

1. Charles Hyett – Gloucester 1722-27
2. William Hyett – Stroud 1832-34

Seat: Painswick House, Gloucestershire (purch. 1733 and built soon afterwards, add. c. 1820s, passed to Dickinsons by inher. 1955, still own)
Notes: Painswick was one of the most celebrated gardens of the 18th c. and has recently been restored.

DIGBY [Baker, Wingfield] *ENGLAND & IRELAND*

Earl Digby (1790 1856 GB)

Origins: Old landed family. **First MP 1373**. High Sheriff of Rutland 1434. **Twelve further MPs 1439-1642 (two of them Irish and eight were kts of the shire)**.

1. John Digby 3 Earl of Bristol – Dorset 1675-77
2. Robert Digby 3 Baron Digby – Warwick 1677
3. Simon Digby 4 Baron Digby – Warwick 1685-86
4. William Digby 5 Baron Digby – Warwick 1689-98
5. John Digby – Newark 1705-08 East Retford 1713-22
6. Robert Digby – Warwickshire 1722-26
7. Edward Digby – Warwickshire 1726-46
8. Edward Digby 6 Baron Digby – Malmesbury 1751-54 Wells 1754-57
9. Henry Digby 1 Earl Digby – Ludgersall 1755-61 Wells 1761-65
10. Robert Digby – Wells 1757-61
11. Edward Digby 10 Baron Digby – Dorset 1876-85

Seats: Minterne House, Dorset (medieval, add. 17th c., purch. 1768, Victorian house demolished, rebuilt 1903-06, still own): Geashill Castle, King's County (orig. built 1203 by FitzGeralds, passed by mar. 1598- c. 1600 to Digbys, new house built c. 1800, remod. mid-19th c., burned 1922); Mansfield Woodhouse, Nottinghamshire (medieval, purch. c. 1480-1512, sold 1736, now flats); Sherborne Castle, Dorset (medieval castle, house built 1594, acq. 1616, enlarged 1625, inher. 1698 by senior branch of family, passed to Wingfield Digbys 1856); Coleshill Hall (Park), Warwickshire (medieval, acq. 1495, new house built 16th c., principal seat 16th and 17th c., family departed as residents mid-18th c., demolished 1810, passed to Wingfield Digbys 1856, see below); Caradoc Court, Herefordshire (built 16th c. and c. 1620, inher. by mar. from the Scudamores 1716, sold 1864)
Estates: Bateman 39505 (I & E) 15968. Rubinstein – Robert Digby left £100,000 in probate in 1814. Owned 15,000 acres worth 55 million pounds in 2001.
Titles: Baron Digby of Sherborne 1618-98 E; Baron Digby of Geashill 1620- I; Earl of Bristol 1622-98 E; Baron Digby 1765- GB

Peers: {1 peer 1661} 6 peers 1677-98 1765-1945
4 Lds Lt 17th, 18th, 19th, 20th
Notes: This family rose higher and higher in wealth and status over the centuries. For example, Simon Digby, Constable of the Tower, was granted the attainted estate of Coleshill in 1495. Sherborne was acquired as a reward for diplomatic services in 1616. The daughter of the 13 Earl of Kildare (see FitzGerald) married Robert Digby c. 1600 and brought Irish estates to the family. Minterne was purchased in 1768 by a younger son of the 6 Baron who made a fortune in the RN. Another Admiral, H. Digby, made £120,000 out of the Napoleonic Wars. (*Country Life*, 168, p. 574). 1, 2 Earl of Bristol, 5 Baron Digby of Geashill, and eight others in ODNB, including the amazingly successful Pamela Digby, daughter of the 11 Baron, who among many other things married both Randolph Churchill and Averill Harriman, became a Washington political hostess, and was President Bill Clinton's Ambassador to France 1993-97.

Digby

Origins: A cadet line established in Ireland. Bishop in the 18th century. Sheriff 1732.

1. John Digby – {Kildare 1732-60}
2. Simon Digby – {Kildare 1769-96}
3. Kenelm Digby – Queen's County 1868-80

Seat: Laundenstown (Landenstown) Lodge, Kildare (built mid-18th c., resident 18th-19th c.)
Estates: Bateman 3580 (I) 2382
Notes: One in ODNB.

Wingfield-Digby

Origins: The Wingfields were an old family seated in Northumberland and Lancashire. **First MP 1541**. The daughter and heiress of the 1 Earl Digby married in 1796 William Wingfield-Baker. That family succeeded to much of the Digby property and took the name Digby.

1. William Wingfield-Baker – Bodmin 1813
2. Richard Wingfield-Baker – S. Essex 1857-59 1868-74
3. Sir Charles Wingfield – Gravesend 1868-74
4. John Wingfield-Digby – Mid-Somerset 1885 N. Dorset 1892-1904
5. Simon Kenelm Wingfield-Digby – W. Dorset 1941-74

Seats: Sherborne Castle, Dorset (inherited on death of 2 Earl Digby 1856, still own); Coleshill Park, Warwickshire (inherited from the Digbys 1856 - see above - new house

built 1873, now a hospital, still own estate); Orsett Hall, Essex (built 17th c., remod. 18th c., purch. by Bakers 1746, passed by mar. to Whitmores 1884)
Estates: Bateman 26882 (E) 46092; Orsett estate 8545 (E) 11791; Coleshill estate 9086 (E) 15449
Notes: William Wingfield (MP 1813) assumed the additional name Baker on succeeding to the estates of Richard Baker of Orsett in 1849.

DILKE

Origins: Sir Thomas Dilke purchased Maxstoke in 1589. There is no clear evidence about how he acquired a fortune.

1. Sir Charles Dilke 1 Bt – Wallingford 1865-68
2. Sir Charles Dilke 2 Bt – Chelsea 1868-86 Forest of Dean Div. Gloucestershire 1892-1911
3. Ashton Dilke – Newcastle-upon-Tyne 1880-83

Seats: Wolston (Priory), Warwickshire (built 16th c., Wentworth seat acq. 1608, passed to Dilkes by inher. 1690, sold by 1712); Maxstoke Castle, Warwickshire (built 1346, add. 1440s, purch. 1589, remod. early 17th c., fire 1762, add. 1820, still own); Packwood House, Warwickshire (acq. by Fetherstons 15th c., built house c. 1575, passed to Dilkes 1769, sold 1869, NT 1941)
Estates: Bateman 2731 (E) 3845
Title: Baronet 1862-
1 in Cabinet 1882-85
Notes: William Dilke (1734-1800) married the Fetherston heiress of Packwood House who owned 600 to 700 acres (inherited by Dilkes 1769). The senior line held Maxstoke, and a younger son took Packwood and the name Fetherston, a process repeated several times when the senior line ended. 1 and 2 Bt and one other in ODNB.

DILLINGTON [Bockland (Bocland)]

Dillington

Origins: A customs official in Poole under Mary I acquired Knighton and entered the gentry later in the century. **First MP 1553. One further MP 1586 for Newport.**

1. Sir Robert Dillington 2 Bt – Newport (IoW) 1659 1660 1670-81
2. Sir Robert Dillington 3 Bt – Newport 1689-90
3. Edward Dillington – Newport 1689-90
4. Sir Tristram Dillington 5 Bt – Newport 1707-10 1717-21

Seat: Knighton Gorges, Hampshire (IoW) (medieval, acq. 1563, rebuilt soon after, demolished 1821)
Title: Baronet 1628-1721
Notes: Male line extinct 1721.

Bockland (Bocland)

Origins: Became landed in the mid-16th century. The daughter of Sir Robert Dillington 3 Bt married Maurice Bockland, and her sister left Knighton to the son of that marriage in 1749.

1. Walter Bockland – Downton 1661-70
2. Maurice Bockland – Downton 1678-81 1685-87 1689-95 1698
3. Maurice Bockland – Yarmouth (IoW) 1733-34 Lymington 1734-41 Yarmouth 1741-47 Newtown (IoW) 1747-54

Seats: Standlynch House, Wiltshire (purch. 1572, sold 1726); Knighton Gorges, Hampshire (acq. by mar. 1749, demolished 1821)
Estates: Worth £900 pa in the 1660s
Notes: From the Boclands the estates passed by marriage to the Bissets who died out in 1821.

DILLON [Lee] *IRELAND & ENGLAND*

Viscount Dillon (1622- I)

Origins: The Dillons claimed Norman descent. They acquired estates in Ireland in 1185. Summoned to Parliament as feudal lords. Kt 12th century. **First {MP 1634}. Four additional {MPs 1634-42}. An English MP from a cadet branch was elected in 1589**. A line of French Counts also descended from this family.

1. Henry Dillon 8 Viscount Dillon – {County Westmeath 1689}
2. Charles Dillon-Lee 12 Viscount Dillon – Westbury 1770-74
3. Henry Dillon-Lee 13 Viscount Dillon – Harwich 1799-1802 County Mayo 1802-13

Seats: Ditchley Park, Oxfordshire (rebuilt 1730s, inher. 1776, sold 1933); Loughglinn House, Roscommon (acq. mid-17th c., built early 18th c., add. c. 1830, fire 1904, rebuilt, sold post WWI, institutional use)
Estates: Bateman 94824 (I & E) 28762 (Irish estate sold 1899)
Peers: {4 peers 1660-74 1689-91 1694-1715}
1 KP 18th-19th

Notes: The 4 Viscount conformed to the Established Church in 1630. A younger son of the 7 Viscount was created Earl Dillon in the Jacobite peerage and several of his descendents living in France are in the ODNB, as are several other exiled Dillons bearing French titles. Dillons encountered financial difficulties in the early 19th c. The 4, 13, and 17 Viscounts and one other in the ODNB.

Earl of Lichfield (1674-1776 E)

Origins: The Lees came originally from Cheshire. They were farming at Quarrendon by the 14th century. Wealth based on sheep ranching. **First MP 1467. Six additional MPs 1542 1659.** (See also Lee for another branch of the family.) The 12 Viscount Dillon succeeded to the English estates, including Ditchley, of his great uncle the 4 Earl of Lichfield and took the additional name Lee in 1776.

1. Sir Francis Lee 4 Bt – Malmesbury 1660-67
2. George Lee 3 Earl of Lichfield – Oxfordshire 1740-43
3. Robert Lee 4 Earl of Lichfield Oxford 1754-68

Seats: Ditchley Park, Oxfordshire (purch. c. 1550, built 16th c., rebuilt 1720-26, passed to Dillons by mar. 1776); Quarrendon, Buckinghamshire (medieval, 1499, part demolished early 18th c., sold 1802)
Estates: Worth £3000 pa in 1660. Bankrupt 18th c.
Title: Baronet 1611-1776
Peers: 4 peers 1674-1776
1 Ld Lt 17th
Notes: 3 Earl and two others in ODNB.

Earl of Roscommon (1622-1746; 1799-1816; 1828-50 I)

Origins: Chief Justice of the Common Pleas in Ireland 1532. The 1 Earl conformed in 1619 to the Established Church. A younger son of Gerald Dillon, ancestor of the Viscounts Dillon, James Dillon of Proudstown was ancestor of the Earls of Roscommon, Barons Clonbrock, and the Dillon Bts of Lismullen. **First {MP 1634}. One additional {MP 1639, County Longford}**. The father and grandfather of the 1 Earl were judges.

1. Carey Dillon 5 Earl of Roscommon – {Banagher 1661-66}

Seat: Riverston, Meath (acq. by mar. 16th c., passed out of family 1639)
Estates: Worth £2,118 pa in 1689.
Title: Baron Dillon 1620-1746 I; 1799-1816 I; 1828-50 I
Peers: {5 peers 1661-89 1703-15 1717-46}
Notes: The 4 Earl and three others in ODNB.

Baron Clonbrock (1790-1926 I)

Origins: Cadet of the Earls of Roscommon. **First {MP 1585 for Roscommon}**.

1. Robert Dillon – {Dungarvon 1728-46}
2. Robert Dillon 1 Baron Clonbrock – {Lanesborough 1776-90}

Seat: Clonbrock House, Galway (acq. c. 1580s and built castle, new house built 1780-88, castle burned 1807, add. 1824 and 1832, add. 1855, sold 1976, burned 1984)
Estates: Bateman 29550 (I) 11873. Worth £1,631 pa in 1750, £3,155 pa in c. 1780, and £7,925 pa in 1802. Majority of estate sold 1909-14 for £250,000 (Hicks, *Irish Country Houses*, 245).
Peers: {1 peer 1790-95} 2 Irish Rep peers 1838-93 1895-1917
2 Lds Lt 19th, 20th
1 KP 20th
Notes: Roman Catholic until 1728/34.

Dillon

Origins: See Earls of Roscommon.

1. Arthur Dillon – {Trim 1663-66}
2. Sir John Dillon – {Kells 1692-93 County Meath 1695-99 1703-08}
3. Sir John Dillon 1 Bt – {Wicklow 1771-76 Blessington 1776-83}

Seat: Lismullen, Meath (old house, purch. 1703, rebuilt c. 1720, remod. 19th c., burned 1923, rebuilt on smaller scale, still own)
Estates: Bateman 3209 (I) 3106
Title: Baronet 1801-
Notes: Barons of the Holy Roman Empire 1782. One in ODNB.

DILLWYN *WALES*

Origins: An Old Breconshire family, originally from Herefordshire. One went to America in 1699. His grandson returned to England and settled near London. They were merchants in the 18th century. Became pottery manufacturers (Cambrian Potteries in Swansea) in the 19th century and later became involved in the steel industry. The first MP married the heiress to Penllergare c. 1810. High Sheriff Glamorganshire 1818.

1. Lewis Weston Dillwyn – Glamorganshire 1832-37
2. Lewis Llewelyn Dillwyn – Swansea 1855-92
3. Sir John Dillwyn-Llewelyn 1 Bt – Swansea 1895-1900
4. Sir Charles Dillwyn-Venables-Llewelyn 2 Bt – Radnorshire 1910

Seat: Penllergare (Penlle'r-gaer), Glamorganshire (built early 16th c., acq. by mar. from Llewelyns 1817, rebuilt 1835-36, demolished 1961)
Estates: Bateman 14867 (W) 9939
Title: Baronet 1890-
1 Ld Lt 20th
Notes: Four in ODNB.

DIMSDALE

Origins: Three generations of surgeons in the 18th century. Created Baron Dimsdale in Russia 1762. Bankers 19th century.

1. Thomas Dimsdale – Hertford 1780-90
2. Nathaniel Dimsdale – Hertford 1790-1802
3. Robert Dimsdale – Hertford 1866-74 Hitchin Div. Hertfordshire 1885-92

Seats: Essenden Place, Hertfordshire (built early 19th c., purch. first half 19th c., still owned 1912, sold); The Priory, Hertford, Hertfordshire (leased late 18th - early 19th c.)
Estates: Bateman 2382 (E) 3641. Rubinstein – 2 Baron left £140,000 in probate 1820 and the 1 Baron's daughter Anne Dimsdale left £250,000 in 1832.
Notes: A Quaker family. One in ODNB.

DIXON *IRELAND*

Baron Glentoran 1939- UK

Origins: 19th century merchants and shipowners. Lord Mayor of Belfast 1893. Sheriff 1896.

1. Sir Daniel Dixon 1 Bt – Belfast North 1905-07
2. Herbert Dixon 1 Baron Glentoran – Belfast Pottinger 1918-22 Belfast East 1922-39

Seats: Drumadarragh House, Antrim (built 1742, add. 1827, purch. 1891, add. 1903, still own); Ballyalloy, Down (acq. 19th c., sold 1961)
Titles: Baronet 1903-
Peers: 1 peer 1939-45
2 Ld Lt 20th
Notes: 2 Bt NI Senator and 2 Baron Speaker of the NI Senate. 1 and 3 Barons NI MPs. 3 Baron elected to membership in the UK House of Lords as a representative peer 1999- .

DOBBS *IRELAND*

Oigins: To Ireland 1599, military officer. Married local heiress. Sheriff Antrim 1664. (Clarke, *Arthur Dobbs*, 9-16)

1. Arthur Dobbs – {Carrickfergus 1727-60}
2. Conway Dobbs – {Carrickfergus 1768-90}
3. Francis Dobbs – {Charlemont 1798-1800}
4. Conway Dobbs – Carrickfergus 1832-33
5. William Dobbs – Carrickfergus 1857-59

Seat: Castle Dobbs, Antrim (castle built early 17th c., acq. 1660, new house built 1750, remod. 19th c., still own)
Estates: Bateman 13031 (I) 7489. Owned 5,000 acres in 2001.
Notes: Acquired 200,000 acres in North Carolina in 1738. Three in ODNB.

DOCMINIQUE [Humphrey]

Origins: The father of the first MP was a Huguenot who emigrated from France, naturalized 1662. The first MP was a merchant who purchased landed property. Paul Humphrey was the nephew of Paul Docminique who succeeded to the latter's estates on the death of Charles Docminique in 1745.

1. Paul Docminique – Gatton 1705-35
2. Charles Docminique – Gatton 1735-45
3. Paul Humphrey – Gatton 1745-51

Seat: Chipstead Place, Kent (acq. early 18th c., Humphrey family succ. 1745, later in the century, passed to distant relatives, sold 1788, demolished c. 1930)

DODINGTON [Bubb, Bull]

Baron Melcombe (1762-62 GB)

Origins: The Dodingtons were an ancient but impoverished family when George Dodington, a successful government contractor, left his estate to his nephew George Bubb, son of a captain in the army. The first George Dodington had made a great fortune as an army clothing contractor, ship owner, and financier c. the 1690s. Bubb took the name Dodington in 1717 and was created a peer.

1. Jeremiah Bubb – Carlisle 1689-92

2. George Dodington – Winchelsea 1705-15 {Charlemont 1707-13} Bridgwater 1708-13 Winchelsea 1713-15 Bridgwater 1715-20
3. George Bubb Dodington 1 Baron Melcombe – Winchelsea 1715-22 Bridgwater 1722-54 Weymouth & Melcombe Regis 1754-61
4. George Dodington – Weymouth & Melcombe Regis 1730-41 1747-54

Seats: Eastbury Park, Dorset (purch. 1709 and built 1717-38, left to a Dodington nephew 1762, Earl Temple, see Grenville, largely demolished 1788, sold 1806); Dodington (Hall), Somerset (acq. 13 c., medieval, add. 1581, became a farm house in 17th c., left to Earl Temple 1762, sold by Grenvilles 1837); Horsington (House, Park) Somerset (medieval, rebuilt 1633, acq. by mar. mid-17th c., passed 1728 by inher. to Jacksons and then to other descendents, some of whom took the name Dodington, part demolished 1870s, sold 1919-23, hotel)
Estates: Bateman 3353 (E) 6982. George Dodington left the 1 Baron estates worth £4,000 pa and £100,000 in money in 1720.
Peer: 1 peer 1762
2 Lds Lt 18th
1 in Cabinet 1707-08
Notes: Eastbury was the greatest house in Dorset until it was dismantled. It was said to have cost £140,000 to build (Oswald, *Country Houses of Dorset*, 149). Designed by Vanburgh. Lord Temple blew up two-thirds of it in 1788 because he could not maintain it. (Cecil, *Dorset Houses*, 44) 1 Baron in ODNB.

<u>Bull</u>

Origins: The founder was a lawyer in the 17th century. Henry Bull MP's estate was left in 1692 to his daughter, the wife of George Dodington MP above.

1. Henry Bull – Wells 1660-79 Milborne Port 1679-81 1685-87 Bridgwater 1689-92

Seat: Shapwick, Somerset (Bulls acq. 1616, passed by mar. to Dodingtons 1692, passed to other Bull descendents 1714)

DODSON

<u>Baron Monk Bretton</u> (1884- UK)

Origins: Descended from a London family that settled in Cornwall in the 16th century. Kt 1680. The first MP was a lawyer and government official. 2nd MP a judge.

1. Thomas Dodson – Liskeard 1701-07
2. Sir John Dodson – Rye 1819-23

3. John Dodson 1 Baron Monk Bretton – E. Sussex 1857-74 Chester 1874-80 Scarborough 1880-84

Seats: Conyboro' (Coneyborough) Park, Sussex (built late 17th c., destroyed 1816, new house early 19th c., acq. 1856, still owned 1930s, sold, still own estate in Sussex); Hayee, Cornwall
Estates: Bateman 3097 (E) 3467
Peers: 2 peers 1884-1933
Notes: Two in ODNB.

DOMVILE [Pocklington] *IRELAND*

Origins: To Ireland in the reign of James I. **First {MP 1613 for Kildare}**. On the extinction of the male line of the Domviles in 1768 the estates passed to Elizabeth Domvile, who married Charles Pocklington. Their grandson assumed the name Domvile and the Baronetcy was recreated. Charles Pocklington also inherited 1751 the property of his first cousin Henry Barry, the last Lord Barry of Santry (see Barry), which quadrupled the value of the Domvile estate.

1. Sir William Domvile {County Dublin 1661-63 Antrim 1665-66}
2. Sir Thomas Domvile 1 Bt – {Mullingar 1692-93}
3. John Pocklington – Huntingdon 1695-98 Huntingdonshire 1705-13
4. Sir William Domvile – {County Dublin 1717-27}
5. Sir Compton Domvile 2 Bt – {County Dublin 1727-68}
6. Charles Pocklington Domvile – {County Dublin 1768}
7. Sir Compton Pocklington Domvile 1 Bt – Bossiney 1818-26 Okehampton 1826-30 Plympton Erle 1830-32

Seats: Santry Court, Dublin (built 1703, add. 1740-50, inher. by mar. from Barrys 1751, fire 1940s, demolished); Templeogue House, Dublin (old castle, acq. 1686, built late 17th c., main seat at Santry from about 1780, sold 20th c.); Thornhill, Wicklow (acq. and sold 19th c.); Heywood, Queen's County (built 1773, inher. by mar. from Trench family 1815, add. mid-19th c., passed via heiress to the Poë family 1886, fire 1950, demolished); Loughlinstown House, Dublin (acq. and built 1660s, rebuilt 1770s, sold 1963)
Estates: Bateman 6262 (I) 17374. Worth £6,700 pa c. 1780.
Titles: Baronet 1686-1768; 1815-1935; 1912-
1 Ld Lt 20th
Notes: The estates later passed to the Poe family, who went to Ireland in the 1650s, for whom the Baronetcy was recreated in 1912. The 1 Bt mar. 1815 the daughter and heiress of the Trenchs (see Trench) of Heywood, Queen's County. The daughter and heiress of the 3 Bt married a Poë in 1886.

DONNELAN (Donnellan, Donelan) *IRELAND*

Donnelan

Origins: A native Irish family claiming descent from ancient princes. Conformed to Protestantism. Archbishop of Tuam 1609. His son was Lord Chief Justice of Ireland. **First {MP 1634}**.

1. Nehemiah Donnellan – {Galway 1692-93}
2. John Donnelan – {Ardee 1727-41}
3. Nehemiah Donnelan – {County Tipperary 1737-60}
4. Nehemiah Donnelan – {Clogher 1757-60}

Seat: Ballydonellan Castle, Galway (old castle, rebuilt 1412, add. late 17th c., add. 18th c., remod. c. 1787, passed to Mahons by mar. mid. 19th c., fire 1913, now a ruin)

Donelan

Origins: Cadet line.

1. Anthony Donelan – E. Cork 1892-1911 E. Wicklow 1911-18

Seat: Ballymona, Cork

DOPPING [Hamilton] *IRELAND*

Dopping

Origins: John Dopping of Frampton Court, Gloucestershire had a son Anthony who was Clerk of the Privy Council in Ireland and purchased estates there in 1636 and was elected **first {MP 1613}.** A Bishop of Meath 17th and a Bishop of Ossory in the 18th century. A Dopping married a Hepenstal heiress in 1858 and succeeded to that family's estates in Wicklow and Dublin.

1. Samuel Dopping – {Armagh 1695-99 1703-14 Dublin University 1715-20}

Seat: Dopping Court, Dublin (acq. 17th c., resident 18th c.); Derrycassen House, Longford (acq. and built early 18th c., sold 1929 and demolished)
Estates: under Hepenstal 3269 (I) 2034. Acquired Hamilton estates in Tyrone and Longford by mar. early 18th c. of 14,000 acres, sold 1776.
Notes: Severe financial difficulties late 19th c. Most estates sold 1903-09. One in ODNB.

Hamilton

Origins: Descended from a cadet of the Earls of Haddington (see Hamilton). The father of the first {MP} was an attorney who gained estates in Ireland. The first {MP's} daughter and heiress married Anthony Dopping, Bishop of Ossory, grandson of Anthony Dopping above.

1. John Hamilton – {Dungannon 1692-93 1695-99 Augher 1703-13}

Seat: Caledon, Tyrone (acq. 1665, sold 1776)
Estates: 6,000 acres in Tyrone and 8,000 acres in Longford.

DOUGLAS [Pennant, Steuart] *SCOTLAND*

Duke of Queensberry (1684- S)

Origins: Emerged in the 12th century and became great lords and warriors. Regent of Scotland 1333. Duke of Touraine 1420. One of the historic dynasties of Scotland, married eleven times into the royal family. The head of the house enjoyed the privilege of leading the van of the Scottish army into battle, of carrying the crown at the coronation, and of giving the first vote in Parliament. (Taylor, *Great Historic Families of Scotland*, I, 34.) All Douglases share a common descent from Archibald Douglas in the 13th century. From his eldest son derived the Dukes of Douglas and Queensberry, while the Earls of Morton were the issue of a younger son. An illegitimate grandson of the 1 Earl of Douglas was seated at Drumlanrig. **First [MP 1560]. Three additional [MPs 1609-51]**.

1. James Douglas – [Peebleshire 1685-86]
2. Charles Douglas Earl of Drumlanrig – Dumfriesshire 1747-55

Seats: Drumlanrig Castle, Dumfriesshire (medieval, rebuilt mid-16th c., rebuilt 1675-90, passed by mar. to Scotts 1810); Kellwood, Dumfriesshire (built 1572)
Estates: Vast. (see under Montagu, Dukes of Buccleuch). The 4 Duke left an estimated one million pound estate.
Titles: Baron Douglas 1628- S; Viscount Drumlanrig 1628- S; Earl of Queensberry 1633- S; Marquis of Queensberry 1681- S; Earl of Solway 1706-78 E; Marquess of Beverley and Duke of Dover 1708-78 GB; Baron Douglas 1786-1810 GB
Peers: [3 peers 1660-71 1684-1707] 1 Scottish Rep peer 1707-08 2 peers 1708-11 1786-1810
1 Ld Lt 18th-19th
1 in Cabinet Council 1702-04 1709-11
1 KG 18th
1 KT 18th-19th

Notes: The 5 Lord Drumlanrig married Janet Scott, and the Dukedoms of Queensberry and Dover and the Marquisate of Queensberry passed to her family in 1810 on the death of the 4 Duke (see Montagu under Dukes of Buccleuch). The descendant of a younger son of the 1 Earl of Queensberry succeeded in 1810 as Marquis of Queensberry. The Douglas family has an entry in the ODNB. 1 Earl of Queensberry, 1, 2, 4 Duke Of Queensberry and one other in ODNB.

Marquis of Queensberry (1681- S)

Origins: The descendents of the younger son of the 1 Earl of Queensberry (see above) seated at Kelhead succeeded to the Marquisate in 1810 on the death of the 4 Duke of Queensberry.

1. Sir John Douglas 3 Bt – Dumfriesshire 1741-47
2. Sir William Douglas 4 Bt – Dumfries Burghs 1768-80
3. William Douglas – Dumfries Burghs 1812-32
4. Archibald Douglas 8 Marquis of Queensberry – Dumfriesshsire 1847-56

Seats: Kinmount, Dumfriesshire (acq. 1633, old house, rebuilt 1812 at a cost of £40,000, sold 1896); Kelhead, Dumfriesshire; Glen Stenart, Dumfriesshire
Estates: Bateman 13243 (S) 13384
Titles: See Dukes of Queensberry above; Baron Solway 1833-37 UK; Baron Kelhead 1893-94 UK; Baronet 1668-
Peers: 3 Scottish Rep peers 1812-32 1872-80 1922-29 2 peers 1833-37 1893-94
3 Lds Lt 19th
1 KT 19th
Notes: 9 Marquis and one other in ODNB.

Earl of March (1697- S)

Origins: The 1 Earl of March was the second son of the 1 Duke of Queensberry. The 2 Earl married the Countess of Ruglen in her own right (see Hamilton). Their son, the Earl of March and Ruglen, succeeded as 4 Duke of Queensberry. On his death in 1810, the Earldom of March passed to the 8 Earl of Wemyss as heir male of his great-great grandmother, Lady Anne Douglas, daughter of the 1 Duke of Queensberry and wife of the 3 Earl of Wemyss (see Wemyss).

1. John Douglas – Peeblesshire 1722-32

Seat: Broughton, Peeblesshire (built 17th c., burned 1783)
Titles: Baron Douglas and Viscount Peebles 1687- S
Peer: [1 peer 1698-1705]

Douglas

Origins: Descended from the Drumlanrig Queensberrys.

1. William Douglas – [Dumfriesshire 1703-07]
2. Archibald Douglas – Dumfries Burghs 1754-61 Dumfriesshire 1761-74

Seat: Dornock (Darnock), Dumfriesshire (acq. 17th c.)
Notes: Air Marshal William Douglas "of Dornock" was created 1 Baron Douglas in 1948, extinct 1969. One in ODNB.

Douglas

Origins: Descended from an illegitimate son of James 2 Earl of Douglas, who obtained Cavers in 1412. **First [MP 1612] for Roxburghshire**.

1. Sir Archibald Douglas – [Roxburghshire 1661-63]
2. Sir William Douglas – [Roxburghshire 1690-96]
3. Archibald Douglas – [Roxburghshire 1700-07] Scotland 1707-08 Dumfries Burghs 1727-34
4. William Douglas – Roxburghshire 1715-22 Dumfies Burghs 1722-27 Roxburghshire 1727-34 1742-47

Seat: Cavers (House), Roxburghshire (castle 13th c., rebuilt c. 1500, burned 1542, remod. 17th c., remod. 1750, add. 1885-87, part demolished and unroofed 1953)
Estates: Bateman 9840 (S) 7937

Douglas

Origins: A cadet of the 5th laird of Cavers. A barrister raised the family fortunes in the early 18th century, helped further by an admiral, the 1 Bt.

1. James Douglas – St. Mawes 1741-47 Malmesbury 1747-51
2. Sir James Douglas 1 Bt – Orkney and Shetland 1754-68
3. Sir George Douglas 2 Bt – Roxburghshire 1784-1806
4. Sir George Scott-Douglas – Roxburghshire 1874-80

Seats: Springwood Park, Roxburghshire (built 1756, remod. 1820s, add. 1850-53, demolished 1954); Frairshaw, Roxburghshire (sold 1788)
Estates: Bateman 5568 (S) 6771
Title: Baronet 1786-
Notes: One in ODNB.

Duke of Douglas (1703-61 S)

Origins: The senior line descended from Archibald Douglas (see above) became Earls of Douglas 1358. This family (Black Douglas) died out in the male line in 1488 and the estates were forfeited to the Crown. Some of these were granted to a junior line, Earls of Angus (Red Douglas), descended from an illegitimate son of the 1 Earl of Douglas. This dynasty went through a second extinction and recreation. The 10 and 11 Earls of Angus (the latter created Marquis of Douglas by Charles I in 1633) were Roman Catholics in the early and mid-17th century. The 2 Marquis conformed to Presbyterianism. The 3 Marquis was created 1 Duke of Douglas 1703. The Dukedom became extinct 1761. The other titles passed by descent to the Dukes of Hamilton (see that family). The, possibly, illegitimate son of the daughter of the 2 Marquis of Douglas, Archibald Steuart (Stewart) of Grantully Castle, inherited Douglas Castle (upheld by the House of Lords 1767) and was created Baron Douglas in 1790. **First Douglas [MP 1526]. Two additional [MPs] in the 16th century. Two Steuarts [sat in Parliament between 1560 and 1617].** The Steuarts were a family of considerable antiquity.

1. Sir Thomas Steuart 1 Bt – [Fifeshire 1685-86]
2. Archibald Steuart Douglas 1 Baron Douglas – Forfarshire 1782-90
3. Charles Douglas 3 Baron Douglas – Lanarkshire 1830-32

Seats: Douglas Castle, Lanarkshire (medieval, razed 1644, fire 1758, rebuilt 1758-61, add. c. 1790, passed to Earl of Home by mar. 1877, demolished 1938); Bothwell Castle, Lanarkshire (medieval castle, acq. by Douglas mar. 1362, new house 17th c., passed to Stewarts 1715, demolished 1926, old castle a ruin); Balcaskie House, Fife (built c. 1629, add. 1668-74, purch. by Steuarts 1684, sold 1698); Grantully (Grandtully) Castle, Perthshire (Steuart) (acq. 14th c., built 15th c., add. 16th c., remod. 1626, add. c. 1890); Murthly (Merthly, Murthley) Castle, Perthshire (built c. 1450, add. 16th c., acq. by Steuarts 1615, add. c. 1660s, add. early 18th c., rebuilt 1829-32, remd. 1850, passed to Fothringhams by mar. 1890, add. 1893 still own - new house 1828-31, abandoned as an empty shell 1832 unfinished, demolished 1949)
Estates: Bateman 33274 (S) 18040
Titles: Earl of Angus 1389-1488 S; Marquis of Douglas 1633- S; Earl of Forfar 1661-1715 S; Earl of Dumbarton 1675-1749 S; Marquis of Angus 1703-61 S; Baron Douglas of Douglas 1790-1857 GB; Baronet (Steuarts) 1683-1890
Peers: [3 peers 1661-1707 1667-1707 1675-88] 4 peers 1790-1857
2 Lds Lt 18th, 19th
1 KT 17th
Notes: Two sons of the 1 Marquis of Douglas were created Earls in their own right: the Earl of Ormond and the Earl of Dunbarton. The son of the Earl of Ormond was created Earl of Forfar. On the extinction of the Barony of Douglas (cr. 1790) in 1857 the daughter of the 1 Baron inherited Douglas Castle. She married the Earl of Home, who

took the additional name Douglas and was created Baron Douglas (see that family). 1, 4 Baron Douglas, 1, 2, 3, 4, 5, 6, 7, 8, 9 Earls of Douglas, 1, 2 Marquis, 1 Duke, 1, 2 Earl of Forfar, 1 Earl of Dumbarton, and 1, 2, 3, 4, 5, 6, 9, and 10 Earl of Angus and nine others and four cadets in ODNB.

Douglas

Origins: Cadet of the Douglases of Douglas. **First [MP 1639].**

1. William Douglas – [Orkney & Shetland 1667]
2. Alexander Douglas – [Elgin & Forresshire 1669-74]'
3. Sir Alexander Douglas – [Orkney & Shetland 1702-07] Scotland 1707-08 Orkney & Shetland 1708-13

Seats: Spynie Castle, Elginshire (medieval, acq. estate 1606, sold late 17th c.); Howan House, Egilshay, Orkney (acq. by mar. 17th c., built late 17th c., decayed 20th c.)

Baron Glenbervie (1800-23 I)

Origins: Descended from a younger brother of the 10 Earl of Angus. John Douglas married the daughter and heiress of James Gordon of Fechil (see Gordon).

1. Sylvester Douglas 1 Baron Glenbervie – {St. Canice 1794-96} Fowey 1795-96 Midhurst 1796-1800 Plympton Erle 1801-02 Hastings 1802-06
2. Frederick Douglas – Banbury 1812-19

Seat: Fechil, Aberdeenshire (resident 18th and 19th c.)
Notes: Two in ODNB.

Earl of Morton (1458- S)

Origins: Descended from a younger son of Archibald Douglas (see above). Baron 1381. James Douglas, who was perhaps the 2 Earl of Morton, **sat for [Haddingtonshire 1479]. Two further [MPs 1612 and 1617]**.

1. Robert Douglas 12 Earl of Morton – [Kirkwall Burgh 1703-07] Tain Burghs 1709-10
2. George Douglas 13 Earl of Morton – Linlithgow Burghs 1708-13 Orkney & Shetland 1713-15 Linlithgow Burghs 1715-22 Orkney & Shetland 1722-30
3. William Douglas – Kinross-shire 1715-22
4. Robert Douglas – Orkney & Shetland 1730-45

Seats: Conaglen House, Argyllshire (purch. 1858, sold after 1935); Aberdour Castle (House) Fife (medieval, acq. 14th c., add. 15th c. and 17th c., castle abandoned 1725, house built 17th c., purch. 1725, remod. 18th c., ruinous 19th c., abandoned in 20th c.); Dalmahoy House, Edinburghshire (acq. and built 1750, remod 1787, 1830s, and 1851, became a hotel in 1927)
Estates: Bateman 65161 (S & E) 22288.
Titles: Baron Dalkieth 1381-1672 S; Baron Douglas 1791-1827 GB
Peers: [3 peers 1661-1707] 6 Scottish Rep peers 1730-34 1739-68 1784-90 1828-58 1859-84 1886-1935 1 peer 1791-1827
4 Lds Lt 18th, 19th
2 KT 18th, 19th
Notes: The 4 Earl of Morton was Regent of Scotland. The Earls of Morton owned much of Orkney and Shetland in the 18th century and sold 45,000 acres to Sir Lawrence Dundas 1766 for £60,000. 1, 4, 5, 6, 7, 14 Earls and two others in ODNB.

Baron Penrhyn (1783-1808 I; 1866- UK)

Origins: A younger brother of the 16 Earl of Morton married Juliana Pennant, heiress to Penrhyn Castle and took the name Pennant. The Pennants were large-scale Jamaican planters from the late 17th century and Liverpool merchants. From the Pennants Penrhyn passed to cousins, the Dawkinses also a West Indian family, who took the name Pennant.

1. Richard Pennant 1 Baron Penrhyn – Petersfield 1761-67 Liverpool 1767-80 1784-90
2. George Dawkins-Pennant – Newark 1814-18 New Romney 1820-30
3. Edward Douglas Pennant 1 Baron Penrhyn – Caernarvonshire 1841-66
4. George Pennant 2 Baron Penrhyn – Caernarvonshire 1866-68 1874-80
5. Edward Pennant 3 Baron Penrhyn – S. Div. Northamptonshire 1895-1900

Seats: Penhryn Castle, Caernarvonshire (acq. 13th c., by Pennants in 1765 by mar., new castle built from 1782, 1827-37, NT 1951); Winnington Hall, Cheshire (acq. by Warburtons in the 16th c., built c. 1600, passed by marriage through families to owners of Penhryn, add. 1775, sold 1809, now part of an industrial works); Wicken Park, Northamptonshire (lesaed from 1830s, purch. 1877, sold 1944)
Estates: Bateman 49548 (W & E) 71018. Jamican plantations sold 1808. Rubinstein – the Dowager Baroness Penrhyn left £120,000 in probate 1816. 36,718 acres were donated to the NT in 1951 along with Penhryn Castle.
Peers: 4 peers 1866-1945
2 Lds Lt 19th, 20th
Notes: The Williams family (see Bulkeley) originally owned Penhryn from the 13th century. It passed by heiresses several times including to the Warburtons of Winnington, Cheshire and eventually to the Pennants in the 18th century. With the

opening of immense slate quarries in the mid-18th century the estate became very valuable. (de Figueirdo and Treuherz, *Cheshire Country Houses*, 197). The estates of Lady Penrhyn passed in 1816 to the Leycesters of Toft (see Leicester). 1 and 2 Barons and one other in ODNB.

DOWDESWELL

Origins: The family lived near Tewkesbury since the later 16th century where they held local offices. The father of the first MP was a successful lawyer who purchased Pull Court. The first MP was also a lawyer.

1. Richard Dowdeswell – Tewkesbury 1660-73
2. Richard Dowdeswell – Tewkesbury 1685-87 1689-1710
3. William Dowdeswell – Tewkesbury 1712-22
4. Charles Dowdeswell – Tewkesbury 1713-14
5. William Dowdeswell – Tewkesbury 1747-54 Worcestershire 1761-75
6. William Dowdeswell – Tewkesbury 1792-97
7. John Dowdeswell – Tewkesbury 1812-32
8. William Dowdeswell – Tewkesbury 1835-47
9. William Dowdeswell – Tewkesbury 1865-66 W. Worcestershire 1866-76

Seat: Pull Court, Worcestershire (built 16th c., purch. 1628, rebuilt 1834-46, sold c. 1960s, now school)
Estates: Bateman 3960 (E) 7529
1 in Cabinet 1765-66
Notes: Two in ODNB.

DOWNING

Origins: Elizabethan landowners. **First MP 1572. One other MP 1586. An Irish {MP 1634}** was later a Cromwellian soldier. Another family member went to New England in the 1620s. The 1 Baronet attended Harvard College, and became a government official and diplomat.

1. Sir George Downing 1 Bt – Edinburgh 1654 Carlisle 1656 1659 Morpeth 1660-81
2. Sir George Downing 3 Bt – Dunwich 1710-15 1722-49
3. Sir Jacob Downing 4 Bt – Dunwich 1741-47 1749-61 1763-64

Seats: Gamlingay Park, Cambridgeshire (acq. before c. 1700, built 1712-13, divided among heirs 1717, donated to found Dowing College 1800, house demolished 1776); East Hatley, Cambridgeshire (acq. by 1700, donated 1800); Mount Prospect, Surrey (acq. early 18th c., passed out of family late 18th c.)

Title: Baronet 1663-1764
Notes: A cadet line took the name Fullerton on marriage to an heiress to Ballintoy Castle, Antrim (in Bateman 6861 (E & I) 5158). The fortune of the 3 Bt (d. 1749) was used to found Downing College, Cambridge. Two in ODNB.

DOYLEY (D'Oyly)

<u>Doyley</u>

Origins: Authentically descended from a Norman baron who came over with the Conqueror. Owned Hambledon, Buckinghamshire 1354-1651. **First MP 1572. Three further MPs 1601-48.**

1. Sir John Doyley 1 Bt – New Woodstock 1689-90
2. Christopher D'Oyly – Wareham 1774-80 Seaford 1780-84

Seat: Chiselhampton, Oxfordshire (acq. 1536, sold 1746)
Title: Baronet 1666-1773
Notes: Ran up debts and ruined in the mid-18th century. (*Country Life*, 115, pp. 216 and 284) Three in ODNB.

<u>Doyley</u>

Origins: Cadet line.

1. Sir William Doyley 1 Bt – Norfolk 1654 1656 1659 Great Yarmouth 1660-77
2. Sir John D'Oyly – Ipswich 1790-96

Seats: Shotesham Park, Norfolk (acq. 16th c., sold 1731); D'Oyly Park, Hampshire; Blackford Hall, Norfolk (medieval house, acq. after 1610, rebuilt c. 1620, demolished)
Title: Baronet 1663-

DOYNE (Dunne) *IRELAND*

<u>Doyne</u> (O'Doinn, O'Duinn)

Origins: Descended from an ancient Irish sept (The O'Duinn of Hy Regan) reaching back to the High Kings, and from the elder line of Teig O'Duinne in the 16th century. **First {MP 1613 Dublin University}**. Sheriff 1623. Robert Doyne {MP 1692-93} was raised as a Protestant and elevated to Lord Chief Justice of Ireland and refounded the fortunes of the family.

1. Robert Doyne – {New Ross 1692-93}
2. Philip Doyne – {Clomines 1715-27 Fethard 1733-54}
3. Robert Doyne – {Wexford 1743-60 Donegal 1761-68}
4. Robert Doyne – {Carlow 1765-68}

Seat: Wells, Wexford (acq. and built 1702, rebuilt c. 1840, sold c. 1964)
Estates: Bateman 10855 (I) 7552

Dunne (O'Doinn, O'Duinn)

Origins: Descended from a younger son of Teig O'Duinne.

1. Edward Dunne – {Maryborough 1800}
2. Francis Dunne – Portarlington 1847-57 Queen's County 1859-68

Seat: Brittas, Queen's County (acq. 17th c., rebuilt 1869, fire 1942, ruin); Dunsoghty Castle, Dublin (Plunkett's acq. 1426, built 15th c., add. 1573, passed by mar. 1751 to Dunne in 1870s, resident 20th c., abandoned)
Estates: Bateman 11342 (I) 4335. Worth £1,986 pa in 1776.

DRAKE [Garrard, Stradling, Tyrwhitt] *ENGLAND & WALES*

Drake

Origins: The Drakes rose as courtiers under Elizabeth I. Francis Drake was a Gentleman of the Privy Chamber to James I. He married an heiress (Tothill family, rose through a Clerk in Chancery). (Cousins of the Drakes of Buckland, see under Elliott). **First Drake MP 1572. Two further MPs 1624-59 both for Amersham**.

1. Sir William Drake 1 Bt – Amersham 1640-48 1661-69
2. Sir William Drake – Amersham 1669-81 1685-87 1689-90
3. Montague Drake – Amersham 1695-98
4. John Drake – Amersham 1699-1705 1707-08 1710-13
5. Montague Drake – Amersham 1713-22 Buckinghamshire 1722-27 Amersham 1727-28
6. William Drake – Amersham 1746-96
7. William Drake – Amersham 1768-95
8. Thomas Tyrwhitt-Drake – Amersham 1795-1810
9. Charles Drake-Garrard – Amersam 1796-1805
10. Thomas Tyrwhitt-Drake – Amersham 1805-32
11. William Tyrwhitt-Drake – Amersham 1810-32

Seats: Shardeloes, Buckinghamshire (old house, inher. by Drakes 1626, rebuilt 1758-66, family departed 1939, house sold 1953, now flats, still own estate); St. Donat's Castle, Glamorganshire (built 13th c., add. 16th c., acq. by mar. 1738/1755, sold 1862, now school)
Estates: Bateman 18463 (E) 24686
Baronet 1641-69
Notes: One in ODNB.

Drake

Origins: The grandfather of the Shardeloes line was a younger son of the Ashe line. **First MP 1572. One additional MP 1614-26.**

1. Sir John Drake 1 Bt – Bridport 1660
2. Sir William Drake 4 Bt – Honiton 1690-1713 Honiton and Dartmouth 1713-15

Seats: Ash(e) House, Devon (medieval, acq. by mar. 15th c., burned 1640s, rebuilt later 17th c., passed out of family 1733, sold); Mount Drake, Devon (acq. and built in medieval period, passed out of family 1733)
Title: Baronet 1660-1733
Notes: Male line extinct 1733. Estates passed to the Earls of Guildford (North) by inheritance by whom they were sold. One in ODNB.

Tyrwhitt

Origins: Held land in Lincolnshire from 1322. The father of the first MP was a judge of the King's Bench 1408. **First MP 1416. Eight further MPs 1491-1604**. Sir John Tyrwhitt 6 Bt left his estates to his kinsman Thomas Drake of Shardeloes. (Related to other families of this name, see Tyrwhitt).

1. Sir Philip Tyrwhitt 4 Bt – Great Grimsby 1667
2. Sir John Tyrwhitt 5 Bt – Lincoln 1715-27 1727-34
3. Sir John Tyrwhitt 6 Bt – Lincoln 1741-47

Seat: Stainfield Hall, Lincolnshire (built 2nd half 16th c., reduced in size 18th c., destroyed by fire 1855, sold after 1945)
Estates: Worth £2,500 pa in the late 17th century.
Title: Baronet 1611-1760

Garrard

Origins: Lord Mayor of London 1555. **First MP 1539**, a Kt. Purchased Lamer in the early 17th century. Bt 1622. **Two further MPs in the 16th century**. The 6 Bt left his estates to his kinsman, Charles Drake of Shardeloes, who took the name Garrard.

1. Sir John Garrard 3 Bt – Ludgershall 1679-81 Amersham 1698-1701
2. Sir Samuel Garrard 4 Bt – Amersham 1701-10
3. Sir Benet Garrard 6 Bt – Amersham 1761-67

Seats: Lamer Park (Lamers), Hertfordshire (purch. 1597, rebuilt 1761, passed to Drakes 1767, sold 1948, demolished 1950); Mackerye End, Hertfordshire (built later 16th c., add. c. 1665, purch. 1681, sold 1919)
Estates: Bateman 2543 (E) 3185
Title: Baronet 1622-1767
Notes: The 4 Bt was a grocer. Two in ODNB.

Stradling

Origins: Of Swiss origin. First appeared in England as landowners in the 13th century, and at St. Donat's by the 14th century. Built the Castle in the 15th century. **First MP 1343 for Somerset. Five additional MPs 1553-1640**. The last Stradling left his estates to his kinsmen the Drakes of Shardeloes in 1738.

1. Sir Edward Stradling 5 Bt – Cardiff Boroughs 1698-1701 1710-22
2. Edward Stradling – Cardiff Boroughs 1722-26

Seat: St. Donat's Castle, Glamorganshire (built 13th c., acq. by mar. before 1317, add. 16th c., passed out of family c. 1738/1755)
Estates: Worth £5,000 pa in 1690s.
Title: Baronet 1611-1738
Notes: The family became extinct in the male line in 1738, and the estates were partitioned among claimants. The family has an entry in the ODNB and six additional biographies.

DREWE (Drew)

Origins: Purchased Broadhambury in the late 16th century. **First MP 1584** was an eminent lawyer and judge**. One additional MP 1589**.

1. Francis Drewe – Exeter 1713-34
2. Thomas Drewe – Devon 1699-1700

Seat: The Grange, Broadhembury, Devon (medieval monastic building, purch. c. 1540, remod. mid-16th c., add. c. 1600, remod. c. 1660, part demolished 1770s, sold mid-19th c.)
Estates: Bateman 3684 (E) 4756. Rubinstein – William Drewe left £120,000 in probate in 1823.

DRUMMOND *SCOTLAND*

Earl of Perth (1605- S)

Origins: Came to prominence in the mid 14th century when close connections to the King led to grants of land. The common ancestor of the family was the 2 Baron Drummond. His grandson was created Earl of Perth. The 2 Earl married a daughter of the 1 Earl of Roxburghe. Their younger son succeeded as 2 Earl of Roxburghe (see Kerr). A younger son of the 3 Earl of Perth was created Earl of Melfort in 1686. The Perth Earldom was attainted in 1715 and the Melfort title in 1695. The Earls of Perth were created Dukes in the Jacobite peerage, as were the Earls of Melfort. The Perth Earldom was restored in 1853. The Perth estates passed by marriage to Lord Willoughby de Eresby (see Bertie) via the marriage of the 11 Earl's daughter. A younger son of the 2 Baron Drummond established a family that acquired the title Viscount Strathallan (attainted 1746 and restored 1824). The 11 Viscount succeeded as 15 (6th) Earl of Perth in 1902.

1. John Drummond – [Perthshire 1665 1667]
2. William Drummond 1 Viscount Strathallan – [Perthshire 1669-74 1678 1681 1685-86]
3. John Drummond – [Fifeshire 1678]
4. John Drummond – Thetford 1768-74
5. Henry Drummond – Wendover 1774-80 Midhurst 1780-90
6. Henry Drummond – Castle Rising 1790-94
7. Henry Drummond – Plympton Erle 1810-12 W. Surrey 1847-60
8. George Drummond – Kinardineshire 1812-20
9. James Drummond 6 Viscount Strathallan – Perthshire 1812-24

Seats: Strathallan Castle, Perthshire (castle, rebuilt 1817-18, sold 1910); Drummond Castle, Perthshire (purch. 1487, built c. 1490, add. 1630-36, damaged mid-17th c., add. 1689, add. 18th c., rebuilt mid-19th c., passed to Berties 1820s, fire and add. early 1900s); Stobhall, Perthshire (acq. 1368, built late 14th c., ceased to be main seat 1491, passed to the Berties in 19th c., and then post-WWII back to Earls of Perth as their main seat again, for sale 2012); The Grange, Hampshire (built c. 1670, purch. 1787, rebuilt 1804, sold 1817); Drumtochy Castle, Kincardineshire (built 1813-16, sold 1822); Cromlix Castle, Perthshire (acq. by mar. 16th c., passed to Earls of Kinnoul by mar. 1711, hotel);

Albury Park, Surrey (medieval, rebuilt mid-later 17th c. and 1697, remod. c. 1800 and c. 1815, purch. 1819, remod. 1846-52, passed to Percys by mar. of 1860 in 1890, sold 1969, institutional use)
Estates: Bateman 7208 (S) 7611; 7683 (S) 5239
Titles: Baron Drummond 1488- S; Baron Maderty 1609- S; Viscount Melfort 1685-95 S; Earl of Melfort 1686-95 S; Viscount Strathallan 1686- S; Baron Perth 1797-1800 GB
Peers: [7 peers 1660-88 1660-92 1685-89 1686-88 1700-02] 3 Scottish Rep peers 1825-51 1853-86 1890-93 1 peers 1797-1800
1 in Cabinet Council 1684-88
2 KT 17th
Notes: Became eminent bankers and very rich in the later 18th century. The 6 Viscount Strathallan was the nephew of the great banker Robert Drummond of Cadland and himself worked in China for the East India Company. The 17 Earl of Perth was Minister of State for Colonial Affiars 1957. The Drummond family has an entry in the ODNB and twenty additional biographies.

Drummond

Origins: A cadet of the 2 Earl of Perth.

1. William Drummond – St. Mawes 1795-96 Losthwithiel 1796-1802

Seat: Logie House, Perthshire (acq. and built 17th c., add. 18th c., add. c. 1800, ruin by end of 19th c., demolished 1970)
Estates: The wife of the above MP inherited £500,000 in 1819.
Notes: One in ODNB.

Drummond

Origins: Cadet line.

1. Sir George Drummond – [Edinburghshire 1685-86]

Seat: Milnenab, Edinburghshire

Drummond

Origins: Cadets of the Stobhall family. Claimed to have owned the Abercairny estate since 1300. The first MP was a younger son who became a merchant and Director of the East India Company.

1. John Drummond – Perth Burghs 1727-42

2. Henry Home-Drummond – Stirlingshire 1821-31 Perthshire 1840-52
3. Henry Stirling-Home-Drummond-Moray – Perthshire 1878-80

Seats: Blair Drummond, Perthshire (built c. 1490, rebuilt 17th c., rebuilt 1515, rebuilt 1868-72, remod. 1920s, family trust established 1978); Abercairney Abbey, Perthshire (Moray family held from 1300, new house 1804-10 and 1840s, add. 1869, demolished 1960, new house c. 1960, still own); Millearne House, Perthshire (purch. by Home Drummonds 1821, new house 1821-35, demolished 1969); Ardoch House, Perthshire (old house owned by Stirlings, rebuilt c. 1793, acq. by mar. by Drummonds 1850, sold 1975, demolished 1980s)
Estates: Bateman 40668 (S) 32014
Title: Bt 1666-1808 (Stirling)
Notes: One in ODNB.

Drummond

Origins: Henry Drummond, grandson of the 1 Baron Drummond, mar. in the 1530s Janet Crichton, daughter and heiress of Henry Crichton of mm. **First [MP 1628-40 for Linlithgowshire]**.

1. Thomas Drummond – [Linlithgowshire 1661-63 1665]
2. Thomas Drummond – [Linlithgowshire 1685-86 1689-98]

Seat: Riccarton, Linlithgowshire (occupied in the 17th c.)

Drummond

Origins: Cadets in the 14th century.

1. Adam Drummond – [Perthshire 1690-1702]
2. John Drummond – Perthshire 1727-34
3. Adam Drummond – Lymington 1761-68 St. Ives 1768-78 Aberdeen Burghs 1779-84 Shaftesbury 1784-86
4. John Drummond – Shaftesbury 1786-90

Seats: Megginch Castle, Perthshire (built 15th c., purch. 1640, add. 1707, add. 1780s, add. 1809, add. 1820, still own); Lennoch, Perthshire (acq. late 14th c., sold later 18th c.)
Notes: One in ODNB.

DUCANE

Origins: The family was of Flemish extraction. They fled their homeland in the late 16th century and became eminent Huguenot merchants in London. Alderman of London 1666. Governors of the Bank of England early and mid-18th century. They acquired estates in Essex by marriage to an heiress in 1710. High Sheriff of Essex 1745.

1. Richard Ducane – Colchester 1715-22
2. Peter Ducane – Steyning 1826-30
3. Sir Charles Ducane – Maldon 1852-53 N. Essex 1857-68

Seats: Braxted Park, Essex (purch. 1751, built 1760, sold 1919); Coggeshall, Essex (inher. 1737, sold 1919)
Estates: Bateman 5409 (E) 7044

DUCKETT

Origins: Old gentry family. The father (Lord Mayor 1573) of the **first MP (1584)** was a mercer in London and partner of Sir Thomas Gresham. Purchased much former monastic land. An uncle bought Calne in 1579. **Two further MPs 1601-24. All MPs for Calne.**

1. William Duckett – Calne 1659-78
2. Lionel Duckett – Calne 1679-81 1689-90
3. George Duckett – Calne 1705-10 1722-23
4. William Duckett – Calne 1727-41
5. Thomas Duckett – Calne 1754-57 1761-66
6. Sir George Duckett 1 Bt – Weymouth & Melcombe Regis 1786-88 Colchester 1788-89 1790-96
7. Sir George Duckett 2 Bt – Lymington 1807-12 Plympton Erle 1812

Seats: Hartham House, Wiltshire (acq. 16th c., sold 18th c.); Calstone House, Wiltshire (purch. 1572, sold 1763)
Estates: Worth £1,000 pa in the 1660s.
Title: Baronet 1791-1902
Notes: George Jackson took the name Duckett in 1797 under the will of his second wife's maternal uncle, Thomas Duckett of Hartham. He was created a Baronet. Four in ODNB.

DUFF [Gordon, Skene] *SCOTLAND*

Duke of Fife (1889-1912; 1900- UK)

Origins: The father of the first [MP] was a shrewd lawyer who purchased the estates of impoverished lairds. The vast Duff properties were accumulated over three generations. The 1 Duke gained his title by marrying Princess Louise, daughter of King Edward VII.

1. Alexander Duff – [Banffshire 1689-1702 1703-05]
2. William Duff 1 Earl of Fife – Banffshire 1727-34
3. James Duff 2 Earl of Fife – Banffshire 1754-84 Elginshire 1784-90
4. Arthur Duff – Elginshire 1774-79
5. Sir James Duff – Banffshire 1784-88
6. James Duff 4 Earl of Fife – Banffshire 1818-27
7. Sir Alexander Duff – Elgin Burghs 1826-31
8. James Duff 5 Earl of Fife – Banffshire 1837-57
9. George Duff – Elgin District Burghs 1847-57
10. Sir Mountstuart Duff – Elgin 1857-81
11. Alexander Duff 1 Duke of Fife – Elgin & Nairn 1874-79
12. James Duff – N. Norfolk 1876-78

Seats: Duff House, Banffshire (acq. and built 1735-49 for £70,000, new house built 1829, add. 1870, rebuilt 1895, abandoned by family 1906, public uses); Mar Lodge, Aberdeenshire (built late 18th c., demolished late 19th c., new lodge built mid-19th c., rebuilt 1895, became principal seat 1906, now guest flats); Skene House (Castle), Aberdeenshire (castle built 1217, add. 1680, inher. by mar. 1827, sold 1905); Balvenie Castle, Banffshire (built 12th-13th c., add. 15th and 16th c., purch. 1687, abandoned 1720s, new house built 1722-25, demolished 1929); Elsick House, Kincardineshire (medieval, acq. by Earl of Southesk by mar. to Bannerman heiress 1891, rebuilt c. 1900, passed to Duke of Fife 1923, still own)
Estates: Bateman 249220 (S) 72563. Rental in 1722 was £6,500 pa, one of the largest in Scotland. The Dukes of Fife sold much land from 1889 onwards and now own very few acres. The passage of the title through the female line merged what remained with the Earldom of Southesk. It is likely that large investments with Cecil Rhodes in South Africa in the late 19th century has left the family rich. (Cahill, *Who Owns Britain*, 110)
Titles: Baron Braco 1735-1912 I; Earl of Fife 1759-1912 I; Baron Fife 1790-1809 GB; Baron Fife 1827-57 UK; Baron Skene 1860-1912 UK; Earl of Fife 1885- UK
Peers: {1 peer 1782-1800}; 4 peers 1790-1809 1827-1912
6 Lds Lt 18th, 19th, 20th
1 KG 20th
3 KT 19th, 20th

Notes: The 11 Earl of Southesk married Princess Maud of Fife in 1923, the daughter of the Duke of Fife and the Princess Royal. The 3 Duke of Fife became 12 Earl of Southesk (see Carnegie). 2 and 4 Earls and four others in ODNB.

Skene

Origins: An ancient family that claimed prominence since the 11th century. Granted Skene in the 12th century. **First [MP 1646]**. The 4 Earl of Fife succeeded his uncle George Skene to Skene in 1827.

1. George Skene – Aberdeenshire 1786-90 Elgin Burghs 1806-07

Seats: Skene, Aberdeenshire (acq. 12th c., passed to Duffs 1827, see above); Careston (Cariston, Carraldson) Castle, Forfarshire (built c. 1582, acq. 17-18th c., passed to Duffs 1827)
Notes: Extinct 1827. Six in ODNB.

Skene

Origins: A cadet of the Skenes of Skene.

1. Robert Skene – Fifeshire 1779-87

Seats: Pitlour House, Fife (old house purch. c. 1699, rebuilt 1783-84, sold later 20th c.); Halyards (Hallyards) Palace, Fife (built 16th and 17th c., acq. c. 1633, sold 1715, demolished 1847, ruin)
Estates: Bateman 3415 (S) 4702
Notes: One in ODNB.

Gordon-Duff

Origins: Cadet of the Duffs of Duff. The first [MP] was a merchant in Inverness.

1. William Duff – [Inverness Burghs 1681]
2. Alexander Duff – [Inverness Burghs 1703-07] 1708-10
3. Lachlan Gordon-Duff – Banffshire 1857-61

Seats: Drummuir Castle, Banffshire (purch. 1621 or 1684, built 1670, rebuilt c. 1700, rebuilt 1847, still own); Park (House), Banffshire (built 1536, add. c. 1723, remod. c. 1750, passed by mar. from Gordons to Duffs later 18th c., add. early 19th c.)
Estates: Bateman 17938 (S) 10447. Owned 10,000 acres in the 1980s and 7,400 acres in 2001.

Duff

Origins: Cadet of Duff of Duff from c. 1600.

1. Robert Duff – Banff 1861-93

Seats: Fetteresso Castle, Kincardineshire (built early 16th c., destroyed 1645, rebuilt 1671, purch. 1782, remod. 1808, roofless 1954, restored and now flats); Culter House, Aberdeenshire (built c. 1640, purch. 1725, add. c. 1730, add. 1910, institutional use)
Estates: Bateman 13181 (S) 9803. Owned 7,400 acres in 1996.
Notes: One in ODNB.

DUGDALE

Origins: The founder of the family was a Garter King of Arms (1677), whose father had been the steward of an Oxford College's estate. The next two generations were also heralds, followed by a great-grandson who was a barrister. The family acquired estates by marriage and inheritance.

1. Dugdale Dugdale – Warwickshire 1802-31
2. William Dugdale – Shaftesbury 1830-31 Bramber 1831-32 N. Warwickshire 1832-47
3. John Dugdale – Nuneaton Div. Warwickshire 1886-92

Seats: Merevale Hall, Warwickshire (built later 17th c., acq. by mar. mid-18th c. from the Stratford family, rebuilt 1838-44, still own); Blyth Hall, Warwickshire (purch. 1625, remod. 1626, 1692, 1833, still own)
Estates: Bateman 5694 (E) 10433
Title: Baronet 1936-
Notes: Rebuilding of Merevale in 1838-44 cost £35,565 funded by coal mines on the estate. (Franklin, *The Gentleman's Country House*, 264). Three in ODNB.

Stratford

Origins: From Nuneaton in Warwickshire. The purchaser of Merevale in 1649 was a successful sheep farmer and colliery owner who entered the gentry. A younger son was a Hamburg merchant in London (Francis MP). Merevale passed via a Stratford heiress to the Dugdales in the mid 18th century.

1. John Stratford – Coventry 1679-81 1689-95
2. Francis Stratford – Newport 1699-1701

Seats: Merevale Hall, Warwickshire (purch. 1649, built house soon after, passed to Dugdales mid-18th c., see above); Horston Grange, Warwickshire (built 16th c., purch. 1648, passed to Dugdales 18th c., still owned 1940s)
Estates: Valued at £1,000 pa in 1660.

DUKE I

Origins: Settled in Suffolk from the reign of Edward III. **First MP 1640**. Kt 1641.

1. Sir John Duke 2 Bt – Orford 1679-81 1689-90 1697-98
2. Sir Edward Duke 3 Bt – Orford 1721-22

Seat: Benhall, Suffolk (old house, purch. 1610, rebuilt 1638, sold c. 1740, demolished and rebuilt 1790)
Title: Baronet 1661-1732

DUKE II [Heath]

Origins: Merchants in Exeter in the 15th century. They purchased estates and entered the gentry by mid-century. **First MP 1461. An additional MP 1545**. John Heath MP's mother was the Duke heiress to Otterton. He succeeded in 1751 and took the name Duke. The Heaths were also originally a merchant family.

1. Richard Duke – Ashburton 1679 1695-1701
2. John Heath Duke – Honiton 1747-54 1761-68

Seat: Otterton, Devon (Dukes purch. 1530s, converted monastic buildings into a house c. 1540, Heaths acq. by mar. 1751, sold 1786)
Estates: Sold for £72,000 in 1786.

DUMMER [Chamberlayne]

<u>Dummer</u>

Origins: The father of the first MP was Deputy Master of the Great Wardrobe. It is unclear how the family accumulated so much wealth.

1. Thomas Dummer – Southampton 1737-41 Newport (IoW) 1747-65
2. Thomas Dummer – Newport 1765-68 Yarmouth (IoW) 1769-74 Downton 1774-75 Wendover 1775-80 Lymington 1780-81

Seat: Cranbury Park, Hampshire (built 16th c., purch. 1737, rebuilt 1780, passed to Chamberlaynes 1825)
Estates: It was claimed that the Dummer/Chamberlayne income exceeded £20,000 pa in 1789 (*Country Life*, 120, p. 946). Thomas Dummer's estate was worth £7,000 pa in land and £100,000 in money.
Notes: Sir Nathaniel Holland 1 Bt MP (Rubinstein – left £250,000 in probate 1811) married the widow of both Thomas Dummer (d. 1781) of Cranbury and Thomas Chamberlayne the income from whose estates said to be £18,000 pa from land she enjoyed during her lifetime.

Chamberlayne

Origins: Claimed to have come over with the Conqueror and served as Chamberlains to Henry I and Henry II. (see Denton). Thomas Dummer left his estate to Edward Chamberlayne, a solicitor, who acted as his steward in 1781. The two MPs here were both solicitors to the Treasury, posts that at least in the first MP's case contributed to the family fortune. Their seat was originally Coley Park.

1. William Chamberlayne – Christchurch 1800-02 Southampton 1818-29
2. Tankerville Chamberlayne – Southampton 1892-95 1900-06

Seats: Cranbury Park, Hampshire (acq. by inher. 1825, still own); Coley Park, Berkshire (built c. 1555, purch. 1792, sold 1802)
Estates: 12363 (E) 19000. Rubinstein – William Chamberlayne left £250,000 in probate 1829.

Dummer

Origins: Cadet line.

1. Edmund Dummer – Arundel 1695-98 1701-08

Notes: One in ODNB.

DUNBAR *SCOTLAND & IRELAND*

Dunbar

Origins: Descended from the Earl of Moray (extinct 1430). The family achieved prominence in the 13th century. Estates passed to the Sutherlands in 1711, who took the name Dunbar.

1. Sir William Dunbar 1 Bt – [Caithness-shire 1678]
2. Sir Patrick Dunbar 3 Bt – Caithness 1727-34

Seats: Hempriggs Castle, Caithness-shire (built c. 1450, acq. and rebuilt 1692, passed to Sutherlands 1711, demolished); Ackergill Tower, Caithness-shire (built c. 1500, acq. 1699, passed to Sutherlands 1711, remod. 1845, still own); Northfield, Caithness-shire
Estates: Bateman 26880 (S) 11045
Title: Baronet 1700-
Notes: For the Sutherlands see Leveson Gower. The Dunbar family has an entry in the ODNB and one other biography.

Dunbar

Origins: A cadet of the Hempriggs family. George Dunbar (d. 1779) was the first to go to Ireland. His grandson, a Belfast mill owner, built Woburn.

1. George Orr Dunbar – Belfast 1835-41

Seats: Woburn House, Down (acq. late 18th c. and built 1797-1830, add. mid-19th c., passed to Bullers later 19th c. and to the Pack-Beresfords in 1924, sold 1949, institutional use); Trerissome, Cornwall
Estates: Bateman 9789 (I & E) 7823
Notes: Dunbar heiress married a younger son of the Bullers of Bake, Cornwall in 1890 who took the additional name Dunbar.

Dunbar

Origins: Descended from an illegitmate son of the 4 Earl of Moray (15th c.).

1. Patrick Dunbar – [Elgin & Forreshsire 1665]
2. Alexander Dunbar – [Elgin & Forresshire 1698-1701]
3. Sir William Dunbar 7 Bt – Wigtown District 1857-65

Seats: Westfield, Morayshire (acq. 15th c., sold 1724); Merton Hall, Wigtownshire (sold 18th c.?); Mochrum Park, Wigtownshire (acq. 15th c., sold 20th c.)
Estates: Bateman 3688 (S) 3603
Title: Baronet 1694-
Notes: In 1744 the estates passed via an heiress to the Dunbars of Grangehill (see below). One in ODNB.

Dunbar

Origins: Descended from a younger son of the Westfield family separated in the 16th century.

1. Sir David Dunbar 1 Bt – [Wigtownshire 1650-51 1665 1681]

Seat: Baldoon Castle, Wigtownshire (built 16th c., passed to Earls of Selkirk c. 1682, see Hamilton)
Title: Baronet 1664-c. 1682

Dunbar

Origins: Descended from a younger son of the 5 Earl of Moray (later 15th c.). **First [MP for Elgin & Forres 1646-47].**

1. Sir Robert Dunbar – [Elgin & Forresshire 1669-74]
2. Thomas Dunbar – [Elgin & Forresshire 1681 1689 1689-1693]
3. Robert Dunbar – [Elgin & Forresshire 1703-04]

Seats: Dalvey (Grangehill), Elginshire (purch. 1608, sold 1749); Blervie Castle, Elginshire (medieval, rebuilt c. 1600, sold early 18th c.)

DUNCH

Dunch

Origins: **First MP (1563)** an auditor of the Royal Mint. Purchased monastic property 1552. **Six additional MPs 1571-1656, several kts of the shire**.

1. Hungerford Dunch – Cricklade 1660 1679-80
2. Edmund Dunch – Cricklade 1701-02 1705-13 Boroughbridge 1713-15 Wallingford 1715-19

Seats: Down Ampney House, Gloucestershire (built 15th c., sold c. 1719); Little Wittenham, Berkshire (purch. and built 1546, divided among heirs 1719, sold 1788, demolished)
Estates: Worth £2,000 pa c. 1660 and £4,000 pa c. 1713.
Notes: Cromwellian peer. Down Ampney inherited from a Hungerford heiress in the mid-17th century (see Hungerford). Male line extinct 1719. Two in ODNB.

Dunch

Origins: Wharton Dunch MP was a third cousin of Edmund Dunch MP above.

1. Wharton Dunch – Appleby 1701-02 Richmond 1705

Seat: Pusey, Berkshire (leased?)

DUNCOMBE

Earl of Feversham (1868-1963 UK)

Origins: Goldsmiths and bankers in the City in the 17th century. Major financiers in the 18th century. Lord Mayor 1708. Estates passed to nephew, Thomas Browne, in 1711, who took the name Duncombe.

1. Sir Charles Duncombe – Hedon 1685-87 Yarmouth (IoW) 1690-95 Downton 1695-98 Ipswich 1701 Downton 1702-11
2. Anthony Duncombe – Hedon 1698-1708
3. Edward Duncombe – Appleby 1708-13
4. Francis Duncombe – Amersham 1708-13
5. Thomas Duncombe – Downton 1711-13 Ripon 1734-41
6. Anthony Duncombe 1 Baron Feversham – Salisbury 1721-34 Downton 1734-47
7. Thomas Duncombe – Downton 1751-54 Morpeth 1754-68 Downton 1768-75 1779
8. Henry Duncombe – Yorkshire 1780-96
9. Charles Duncombe 1 Baron Feversham – Shaftesbury 1790-96 Aldborough 1796-1806 Heytesbury 1812-18 Newport (IoW) 1818-26
10. William Duncombe 2 Baron Feversham – Grimsby 1820-26 Yorkshire 1826-31 N. R. Yorkshire 1832-41
11. Thomas Duncombe – Hertford 1826-32 Finsbury 1834-61
12. Arthur Duncombe – East Retford 1830-31 1835-51 E. R. Yorkshire 1851-68
13. Octavius Duncombe – N. R. Yorkshire 1841-59 1867-74
14. William Duncombe 1 Earl of Feversham – East Retford 1857-59 N. R. Yorkshire 1859-67
15. William Duncombe Viscount Helmsley – N. R. Yorkshire 1874-81
16. Arthur Duncombe – Howdenshire Div. E. R. Yorkshire 1885-92
17. Hubert Duncombe – W. Div. Cumberland 1895-1900
18. Charles Duncombe 2 Earl of Feversham – Thirsk & Malton Div. N. R. Yorkshire 1906-15

Seats: Duncombe Park, Yorkshire (purch. 40,000 acres of Helmsley estate for £90,000 in 1695, new house built 1713, add. 1843, fire 1879, rebuilt 1891-94, family departed

1924, school, reoccupied by 6 Lord Feversham c. 1990); Kilnwick Percy Hall, Yorkshire (built 1574, completed 1720, purch. 1840, sold 1919, educational center); Nawton Tower, Yorkshire (built 1855); Helmsley (Castle), Yorkshire (medieval, add. 1580s, purch. 1695, burned 1879, rebuilt, still own)
Estates: Bateman 47614 (E) 46981. Worth c. £400,000 in 1711. Worth £20,000,000 in 1990 with 12,000 acres.
Titles: Baron Feversham and Downton 1747-63 GB; Baron Feversham 1826- UK
Peers: 6 peers 1747-63 1826-1916 1927-45
Notes: Two in ODNB.

Duncombe

Origins: Kin of Sir Charles Duncombe MP 1685-1711 above. **First MP 1604**.

1. Sir John Duncombe – Bury St. Edmunds 1660-79
2. William Duncombe – Bury St. Edmunds 1673-79 Bedfordshire 1689-90 1695-98

Seat: Battlesden, Bedfordshire (acq. mid-16th c., sold 1706)
Estates: Worth c. £2,000 pa mid-17th century.
Notes: One in ODNB.

DUNDAS [Loder, Saunders] *SCOTLAND & ENGLAND*

Marquess of Zetland (1892- UK)

Origins: The Dundases of Dundas were an old family, but the founder of this line began with the younger son of a woolen draper in Edinburgh, whose family had lost their estates due to royalism during the Civil War. Sir Lawrence Dundas MP built up a huge fortune (perhaps as much as one million pounds) as a merchant and contractor of supplies for the British Army during the Seven Years War, which was used to gain a powerful Parliamentary interest that created further opportunities for taking patronage and sinecures from the state.

1. Sir Lawrence Dundas 1 Bt – Linlithgow Burghs 1747-48 Newcastle-under-Lyme 1762-68 Edinburgh 1768-80 1781 Richmond 1780-81
2. Thomas Dundas 1 Baron Dundas – Richmond 1763-68 Stirlingshire 1768-94
3. Thomas Dundas – Orkney & Shetland 1768-70
4. Thomas Dundas – Orkney & Shetland 1771-80 1784-90
5. Charles Dundas 1 Baron Amesbury – Richmond 1775-80 Orkney & Shetland 1781-84 Richmond 1784-86 Berkshire 1794-1832
6. Lawrence Dundas 1 Earl of Zetland – Richmond 1790-1802 York 1802-07 Richmond 1808-11 York 1811-20

7. Charles Dundas – Malton 1798-1805 Richmond 1806-10
8. George Dundas – Richmond 1802-06 1812 Orkney & Shetland 1818-20 1826-30
9. Sir Robert Dundas – Malton 1807-12 East Retford 1826-27 Richmond 1828-34 1839-41
10. Thomas Dundas 2 Earl of Zetland – Richmond 1818-30 York 1830-32 1833-34 Richmond 1835-39
11. John Dundas – Richmond 1830-34 York 1835-41 Richmond 1841-47 1865-66
12. James Whitley Dean Dundas – Greenwich 1832-35 Devizes 1835-38 Greenwich 1841-52
13. Charles Whitley Dean Dundas – Flint District 1837-41
14. Frederic Dundas – Orkney & Shetland 1837-47 1852-73
15. Lawrence Dundas 1 Marquess of Zetland – Richmond 1872-73
16. John Dundas – Richmond 1873-85
17. Lawrence Dundas 2 Marquess of Zetland – Hornsey Div. Middlesex 1907-16

Seats: Aske Hall, Yorkshire (built 15th c., purch. 1763, rebuilt 18th c., remod. 1960s, still own); Fingask, Stirlingshire (acq. 1364 or earlier, sold 1650); Kerse House, Stirlingshire (built 14th c., rebuilt c. 1640, purch. 1759, add. 1830-31, demolished c. 1958); Marske Hall, Yorkshire (built 1625, purch. 1762, family departed 1943, donated 1961 for institutional use); Letterewe House, Ross-shire (built late 18th c., many add., purch. later 19th c., sold 20th c.); Castlecary, Stirlingshire (medieval, purch. early 18th c., sold 20th c.); Carronhall (Carron Hall), Stirlingshire (purch. c. 1749, still resident 1900); Barton Hall (Court), Berkshire (purch. and rebuilt c. 1680, acq. by mar. 18th c., sold 1875); Waplington Hall, Yorkshire (purch. 18th c. resident 19th c.); Upleatham Park (Hall), Yorkshire (purch. 1762-3; demolished 1897); Aston Hall, Flintshire (acq. by mar. later 18th c.); Loftus Hall, Yorkshire (purch. 1764, rebuilt 1840); Moor Park, Hertfordshire (built 1460s, remod. c. 1617, rebuilt 1679-84, rebuilt c. 1720-28, purch. 1763, add. 1763-65, sold 1781)
Estates: Bateman 68169 (E & S) 49324; Sir Lawrence Dundas purchased 45,000 acres in Shetland and Orkney in 1766 from the Earl of Morton for £60,000. Rubinstein – 1 Earl left £113,781 in probate in 1839. Owned 14,000 acres in 2001.
Titles: Baron Dundas 1794- GB; Baron Amesbury 1832-32 UK; Earl of Zetland 1838- UK; Baronet 1762-
Peers: 6 peers 1794-1945 1832
7 Lds Lt 18th, 19th, 20th
2 in Cabinet 1889-92 1935-40
2 KG 19th, 20th
1 KT 20th
Notes: The Dundas family has an entry in the ODNB and five others.

Viscount Melville (1802- UK)

Origins: The first Dundas of Arniston was a younger son of George Dundas of Dundas (d. 1589). The family rose through office and the law in the 17th century. Five successive generations were Lords of Session, including one Lord President, between 1662 and 1802. **First [MP 1612 for Edinburghshire]. One further [MP 1648].**

1. Sir James Dundas – [Linlithgow 1669-74]
2. Robert Dundas – [Edinburghshire 1700-01 1703-07]
3. Robert Dundas – Edinburghshire 1722-37
4. Robert Dundas – Edinburghshire 1754-60
5. Henry Dundas 1 Viscount Melvile – Edinburghshire 1774-82 Newtown (IoW) 1782 Edinburghshire 1783-89 Edinburgh 1790-1802
6. Robert Dundas – Edinburghshire 1790-1801
7. Robert Dundas-Saunders 2 Viscount Melville – Hastings 1794-96 Rye 1796-1801 Edinburghshire 1801-11
8. William Dundas – Anstruther Easter Burghs 1794-96 Tain Burghs 1796-1802 Sutherlandshire 1802-08 Elgin Burghs 1810-12 Edinburgh 1812-31
9. Philip Dundas – Gatton 1803-05
10. Robert Dundas Nisbet Hamilton – Ipswich 1827-31 Edinburgh 1831-32 Ipswich 1835 N. Lincolnshire 1837-57

Seats: Melville Castle, Edinburghshire (castle, inher. 1765, demolished 1780s, new house built 1786-91, add. late 19th c., sold 1983, derelict, 2003 restored, hotel); Arniston, Edinburghshire (acq. 1571, built 1595, rebuilt 17th c., rebuilt 1726-58, add. c. 1800 and 1877, still own); Polton House, Edinburghshire (built c. 1730, resident 19th and 20th c.); Kirkhill, Edinburghshire (purch. and built 18th c., sold 1792); Cotterstock Hall, Northamptonshire (medieval, remod. 16th c., remod. mid-17th c., acq. mid-19th c., remod. 1856, leased out from 1912, sold 1926); Dunira House, Perthshire (built 1798, rebuilt 1851-52, remod. 1864, fire 1948, most demolished)
Estates: Bateman 16242 (S & I) 17705. Owned 10,100 acres in 1996.
Title: Baronet 1898-
Peers: 8 peers 1802-1945
2 in Cabinet 1784-1801 1804-05 1807-09 1812-30
1 KT 19th
Notes: 1, 2, and 3 Viscounts and eight others in ODNB.

Saunders

Origins: Sir Charles Saunders made a fortune as an Admiral. 1 Viscount Melville married the heiress of Sir Charles.

1. Sir Charles Saunders – Plymouth 1750-54 Hedon 1754-75

Seat: Hambledon, Hampshire (acq. 18th c. and passed to Dundases by mar., sold 19th c.)
1 in Cabinet 1766
Notes: One in ODNB.

Dundas

Origins: The Dundases claimed to have been at Dundas from c. 1170. They acquired Dundas Castle 1416. **First [MP 1560]. Two additional [MPs 1609-50 both for Linlithgowshire].** Two other cadet lines at Duddingstone and Newliston produced **three [MPs for Linlithgowshire between 1617-50].**

1. George Dundas – Linlithgowshire 1722-27 1741-43
2. James Dundas – Linlithgowshire 1770-74
3. George Dundas – Linlithgowshire 1847-60

Seats: Dundas Castle, Linlithgowshire (built 1416-24, add. 16th c., new house 1818, sold 1875); Inchgarvie House, Linlithgowshire (acq. 1491, sold 1882, ruin)
Estates: Bateman 2094 (S) 4783. Rubinstein – James Dundas left £116,156 in probate in 1833.

Loder

Origins: The 1 Baron Amesbury (see under Zetland above) inherited the estates of Sir Jonathan Raymond, a brewer who had inherited the estate from his son-in-law, Thomas Loder MP. The Loders rose from yeomen.

1. Thomas Loder – Great Bedwyn 1685-87

Seats: Prince's Harwell, Berkshire (acq. 1557, passed out of family by mar. second half 17th c.); Basildon Park, Berkshire (leased mid-17th c.)

DUNLOP *SCOTLAND*

Origins: The family first appears in records as lairds in the 13th century. The first MP was a Lt. General under Wellington.

1. James Dunlop – Kirkcudbright Stewartry 1812-26
2. Sir John Dunlop 1 Bt – Kilmarnock 1832-35 Ayrshire 1835-39
3. John Dunlop – Glasgow 1835-36

Seat: Dunlop House, Ayrshire (acq. and built 13th c., rebuilt c. 1600, rebuilt 1834, sold 1858)
Title: Baronet 1838-53
Notes: One in ODNB.

DUNN (Dun, Dunne) *IRELAND*

Origins: The first MP was the son of a dyer in Scotland. Sir Patrick Dun was educated in Scotland and made his career as a military physician in the 1670s onwards.

1. Sir Patrick Dun – {Killileagh 1692-93 Mulligar 1695-99 1703-13}
2. James Dunn – {Dublin 1758-60}
3. John Dunn – {Randalstown 1783-97}
4. Michael Dunne – Queen's County 1852-65

Notes: The precise relationship between the individuals here is hard to identify.
Notes: One in ODNB.

DUNNE

Origins: Welsh landowners in the Middle Ages, purchased estates in Herefordshire in the 17th century.

1. Edward Dunne – Walsall 1906-10
2. Philip Dunne – Stalybridge and Hyde 1935-37
3. Philip Dunne – Ludlow 2005-

Seats: Gatley Park, Herefordshire (built 16th c., purch. 1679, add. c. 1827, still own); Bircher Hall, Herefordshire (built mid-18th c., acq. by mar. 1814, add. early 19th c.)
Estates: 2,500 acres in 2015.
1 Ld. Lt. 20th
1 KG 20th
Notes: Current MP estimated to be worth 5 million pounds.

DU PRE (Dupre)

Origins: The founder was Governor of Madras, returned a nabob. Purchased landed estates in 1760. High Sheriff 1825.

1. James Dupre – Gatton 1800-02 Aylesbury 1802-06 Chichester 1807-12
2. Caledon Du Pre – Buckinghamshire 1839-71
3. William Du Pre – Wycombe Div. Buckinghamshire 1914-23

Seats: Wilton Park, Buckinghamshire (purch. c. 1760s, built 1779, leased 1939 and then sold to government, demolished 1968); Quarrendon, Buckinghamshire (medieval and 16th c., purch. 1802, held into 1920s at least)
Estates: Bateman 6876 (E) 10500

DYKE [Hart]

Dyke

Origins: Acquired estates in Sussex by marriage in c. 1620. The 1 Bt was a Commissioner of Public Accounts.

1. Thomas Dyke – Seaford 1660-69
2. Thomas Dyke 1 Bt – Sussex 1685-87 East Grinstead 1689-98
3. William Dyke 7 Bt – W. Kent 1865-68 Mid Kent 1868-85 N. W. Kent 1885-1906

Seat: Lullingstone Castle, Kent (medieval, acq. by Peche family 1361, add. 1497, passed by mar. to the Harts 1543, rebuilt later 16th c., and then went by mar. to the Dykes in the 18th c., remod. 18th c., still own)
Estates: Bateman 8865 (E) 11474
Title: Baronet 1677-
1 in Cabinet 1885-86
Notes: The medieval Peche was a London Alderman. Lullingstone only called "Castle" from the 18th c. One in ODNB.

Hart

Origins: Courtiers and office holders in the mid to late-Tudor period. **First MP 1559. Another MP 1597**. The daughter and heiress of the last MP married Sir Thomas Dyke 2 Bt and Lullingstone passed to the Dykes 1728.

1. Percival Hart – Kent 1710-15

Seat: Lullingstone, Kent (acq. by mar. 1543 from a Peche heiress, see above).

DYMOKE

Origins: The Marmions (Baron 1313) were Norman lords. They were granted Scrivelsby by William the Conqueror and were Hereditary Champions to the Dukes of Normandy. **First MP 1298 for Lincolnshire. Two further MPs 1307-1447**. Philip Marmion, the last of the direct line died in 1292. Scrivelsby passed to his daughter and heiress and to her daughter who married Sir John Dymoke, who succeeded as King's Champion.

(Denholm-Young, *The Country Gentry in the Fourteenth Century*, 88 and n.) **First MP 1372 for Lincolnshire. Three further MPs in the 16th century**.

1. Charles Dymoke – Lincolnshire 1698-1703
2. Lewis Dymoke – Lincolnshire 1703-05 1710-13

Seat: Scrivelsby Court, Lincolnshire (inherited from the Marmions before 1380, add. 1574, add. 18th c., fire 1761, rebuilt 1805, most demolished 1956, still own).
Estates: Bateman 3605 (E) 4955
Title: Baronet 1841-65
Notes: The Dymokes (pronounced dimick) continued to carry out the duties of the King's Champions on horseback at coronations until 1821 and still carried a standard in the crowning ceremony in 1953. The Dymoke family has an entry in the ODNB. Four additional biographies.

DYOTT

Origins: A barrister purchased an estate 1553, granted arms 1563. **First MP 1601 for Lichfield. An additional MP 1621-40**. Kt. 1635.

1. Richard Dyott – Lichfield 1667-77
2. Richard Dyott – Lichfield 1690-95 1698-1708 1710-15
3. Richard Dyott – Lichfield 1865-80

Seat: Freeford Hall, Staffordshire (medieval, purch c. 1563-1606, rebuilt c. 1730, remod. mid-19th c., still own)
Estates: Bateman 5427 (E & I) 8444. Worth £500 pa in the 1660s.
Notes: One in ODNB.

EARLE

Earle

Origins: Originally yeomen. The father of the first MP purchased Eastcourt. The first MP was apprenticed to a Bristol merchant 1647. High Sheriff 1671. Kt 1681.

1. Sir Thomas Earle – Bristol 1681
2. Joseph Earle – Bristol 1710-27
3. Giles Earle – Chippenham 1715-22 Malmesbury 1722-47
4. William Earle – Malmesbury 1727-47 Cricklade 1747-61 Newport (IoW) 1762-68

Seat: Eastcourt House, Wiltshire (purch. c. 1658, built 1658-62, sold c. 1807)
Notes: One in ODNB.

Earle

Origins: A distant cousin.

1. William Earle – Cricklade 1774

ECHLIN [Stafford] *IRELAND*

Echlin

Origns: A younger son of a laird came from Scotland and settled in Ireland under James I. Bishop of Down 1613. Kt 1692.

1. Robert Echlin – {Newtown 1692-93 Newry 1695-99 1703-06}
2. Robert Echlin – {Monaghan 1695-99 County Monaghan 1703-13} Sudbury 1710-15
3. Charles Echlin – {Dungannon 1727-54}

Seats: Clonagh Castle, Kildare (acq. later 17th c., resident in the 18th c., sold late 18th c.?); Echlinville, Down (acq. and built mid-18th c., passed to Clelands and rebuilt c. 1850); Rush House (Kenure Park), Dublin (purch. 1716, sold c. 1760); Castle Hacker, Mayo
Estates: 1510 (I) 1618 in 1878
Title: Baronet 1721-
Notes: The 3 Bt became heavily indebted in the second half of the 18th c.

Stafford

Origins: The Rev. John Echlin married the daughter of Sir Francis Stafford of Mount Stafford. His second son inherited the Stafford estates and took the name Stafford. **First Stafford {MP 1559}. An additional {MP 1639}.**

1. Edmund Echlin Stafford – {Randalstown 1692-93 1695-99 1703-13 Lisburn 1715-24}

Seat: Mount Stafford, Antrim (resident 17th-18th c.)

EDGCUMBE

Earl of Mount Edgcumbe (1789- GB)

Origins: Emerged 14th century. Acquired Cotehele by marriage 1353. **First MP 1447 for Plymouth. Seven additional MPs 1467-1644. Four kts of the shire for Cornwall.** Sir Richard Edgcombe MP killed at Bosworth.

1. Piers Edgcumbe – Newport 1628 Camelford 1640-44 Newport 1662-67
2. Richard Edgcumbe – Launceston 1661-79 Cornwall 1679-81
3. Richard Edgcumbe 1 Baron Edgcumbe – Cornwall 1701 St. Germans 1701-02 Plympton Erle 1702-34 Lostwithiel 1734-41 Plympton Erle 1741-42
4. Richard Edgcumbe 2 Baron Edgcumbe – Plympton Erle 1742-47 Lostwithiel 1747-54 Penryn 1754-58
5. George Edgcumbe 1 Earl of Mount Edgcumbe – Fowey 1746-61
6. Richard Edgcumbe – 2 Earl of Mount Edgcumbe – Fowey 1786-90 Lostwitheil 1790-91 Fowey 1791-95
7. William Edgcumbe Viscount Vallctort Lostwithiel 1816-18
8. George Edgcumbe – Plympton Erle 1826
9. Ernest Edgcumbe 3 Earl of Mount Edgcumbe – Fowey 1819-26 Lostwithiel 1826-30 Plympton Erle 1830 Lostwithiel 1830-32
10. William Edgcumbe 4 Earl of Mount Edgcumbe – Plymouth 1859-61

Seats: Mount Edgcumbe, Cornwall (located in Devon until 1844) (acq. by mar. early 16th c., built 1549-53, remod. 18th and early 19th c., bombed 1941, rebuilt 1958, sold to public ownership 1971, family departed 1987); Cotehele House, Cornwall (medieval, acq. by mar. 1353, add. 16th c., remod. 1650s, not much used 1667-1861, add. 1861-62, NT 1947)
Estates: Bateman 18229 (E) 24181
Titles: Baron Edgcumbe 1742- GB; Viscount Mount Edgcumbe and Valletort 1781- GB
Peers: 6 peers 1742-1945
5 Lds Lt 18th, 19th, 20th
1 in Cabinet 1743-58
Notes: Over four ceturies separated the family's first and last MP for Plymouth. 1 and 2 Barons and 1 and 2 Earls in ODNB and five others.

EDGEWORTH *IRELAND*

Origins: From England to Ireland 1582, settled in County Longford in the 1590s. Bishop of Down and Conor 1593. Acquired a fortune. Officials and soldiers in the first half of the 17th century. Sheriff 1646. **First {MP 1646 for County Longford}.**

1. Sir John Edgeworth – {St. Johnstown 1661-66 1692-93 1695-99}
2. Francis Edgeworth – {Longford 1703-09}
3. Ambrose Edgeworth – {St. Johnstown 1703-11}
4. Henry Edgeworth – {Mullingar 1703-13 County Longford 1713-14 St. Johnstown 1715-20}
5. Robert Edgeworth – {St. Johnstown 1713-27}
6. Henry Edgeworth – {St. Johnstown 1721-51}
7. Richard Edgeworth – {Longford 1737-60}
8. Richard Edgeworth – {St. Johnstown 1798-1800}

Seats: Edgeworthstown House, Longford (old house, purch. 1670, rebuilt c. 1725, add. c. 1782-1812, sold 1935, institution); Lissard House (Firmount House), Longford (acq. before 1736, sold by 1780, demolished c. 1860); Cranallagh Castle, Longford (acq. first half 17th c.)
Estates: Bateman 3255 (I) 2536 and 1659 (I) 1264. Worth £500 pa in 1713.
Notes: Relationships between MPs not always clear. Six in ODNB.

EDMONSTONE *SCOTLAND & IRELAND*

Origins: An ancient family that purchased an estate in Ulster during the Plantation and divided their interests between Scotland and Ireland. **First [MP 1560]. Three additional [MPs 1593-1633], two kts of the shire.**

1. Archibald Edmonstone – {Carrickfergus 1715-27}
2. Sir Archibald Edmonstone 1 Bt – Dumbartonshire 1761-80 Ayr Burghs 1780-90 Dumbartonshire 1790-96
3. Sir Charles Edmonstone 2 Bt – Dumbartonshire 1806-07 Stirlingshire 1812-21
4. Sir William Edmonstone 4 Bt – Stirlingshire 1874-80

Seats: Duntreath Castle, Stirlingshire (built 14th c., acq. 1434, add. 16th c., family departed to Ireland 1740, unroofed, became ruinous, family returned 1857, remod. 1857-63, reconstruction 1890, reduced in size 20th c., still own); Red Hall, Antrim (acq. and built 1609, sold for £24,500 in 1783); Colzium House, Stirlingshire (old castle, acq. 18th c., new house built 1783, sold 1930s)
Estates: Bateman 9778 (S) 7677 plus 8451. Held 2,780 acres in 1609. Worth £1,062 pa in 1777. Owned 5,600 acres in 1996.
Title: Baronet 1774-
Notes: Four in ODNB.

EGERTON [Docura, Eyles, Haynes, Warburton]

Duke of Bridgewater (1720-1803 GB)

Origins: The Egertons held land in Cheshire from the 11th century. High Sheriff under Henry III. Master of the Rolls 1594. Lord Chancellor 1603. **First MP 1429. Five additional MPs from 1478-1601.** The 1 Earl of Ellesmere was the younger son of the Marquess of Stafford (see Leveson Gower) who inherited a large part of his great uncle the 3 Duke of Bridgewater's estates. His descendents took the name Egerton.

1. Sir William Egerton – Brackley 1679-81 Aylesbury 1685-87 Brackley 1690-91
2. John Egerton 3 Earl of Bridgewater – Buckinghamshire 1685-86
3. Charles Egerton – Brackley 1695-1711
4. William Egerton – Buckinghamshire 1706-08 Brackley 1708-32
5. Charles Egerton – Chipping Wycombe 1722-i25
6. William Egerton – Brackley 1768-80
7. John Egerton 7 Earl of Bridgewater – Morpeth 1777-80 Brackley 1780-1803
8. Francis Leveson-Gower-Egerton 1 Earl of Ellesmere – Bletchingly 1822-26 Sutherlandshire 1826-31 S. Lancashire 1835-46
9. George Egerton 2 Earl of Ellesmere – N. Staffordshire 1847-51
10. Algeron Egerton – S. Lancashire 1859-68 S. E. Lancashire 1868-80 Wigan 1882-85
11. Francis Egerton – E. Derbyshire 1868-85 N. E. Duv. Derbyshire 1885-86
12. Alfred Egerton – Eccles Div. Lancashire 1885-90

Seats: Ashridge Park, Hertfordshire (medieval, purch. 1605, rebuilt 18th c., rebuilt 1808-14, passed by mar. to Custs 1849); Worsley Hall, Lancashire (built 1837-46, passed to the Dukes of Sutherland, demolished c. 1927, still own); Brackley Manor House, Northamptonshire (acq. by mar. late 16th c. and built early 17th c., rebuilt 1875-78, sold 1921, now a school); Stetchworth Park, Cambridgeshire (built c. 1800, add. 1870, purch. 1883, passed by inher. 20th c. to the Duke of Sutherland); Old Hall, Worsley, Lancashire (built 17th c., restored 1855, ceased to be occupied 1940)
Estates: Bateman 13222 (E) 71290 (Earl of Ellesmere). The Bridgewater estates were said to be worth £90,000 pa. c. 1803. Rubinstein – 7 Earl of Bridgewater left £700,000 in probate in 1823.
Titles: Baron Ellesmere 1603-1829 E; Viscount Brackley 1616-1829 E; Earl of Bridgewater 1617-1829 E; Earl of Ellesmere 1846- UK
Peers: 11 peers 1660-1745 1757-1829 1846-1862 1868-1945
5 Lds Lt 17th, 18th, 19th
1 in Cabinet Council 1696-1701
1 KG 19th

Notes: The Earls Brownlow (see Cust) succeeded to the Hertfordshire estates of the Dukes of Bridgewater in 1849. 3 Duke and 1, 2, and 3 Earls of Bridgewater and 1 Viscount, and 1 Earl of Ellesmere and four others in ODNB.

Earl Egerton of Tatton (1897-1909 UK)

Origins: Descended from a younger son of the 3 Earl of Bridgewater. An Egerton heiress married William Tatton in 1747. He was possibly a descendant of the original medieval (acq. c. 1100) owners of the Tatton estate inherited by marriage by the Egertons in 1598. He took the name Egerton, although a younger son kept the name Tatton and lived at Wythenshawe.

1. Randolph Egerton – Staffordshire 1661-79
2. Samuel Egerton – Cheshire 1754-80
3. William Tatton-Egerton – Hindon 1784-90 Newcastle-under-Lyme 1792-1802 Cheshire 1802-06
4. William Tatton-Egerton – Beverley 1796-99
5. Wilbraham Egerton – Cheshire 1812-31
6. William Egerton 1 Baron Egerton – Lymington 1830-31 N. Cheshire 1832-58
7. Edward Egerton – Macclesfield 1852-68 E. Cheshire 1868-69
8. Wilbraham Egerton 1 Earl Egerton – N. Cheshire 1858-68 Mid Cheshire 1868-83
9. Alan Egerton 3 Baron Egerton – Mid Cheshire 1883-85 Knutsford Div. Cheshire 1885-1906

Seats: Tatton Park, Cheshire (built 15th c., acq. by mar. 1598, new house c. 1677, add. c. 1760, 1789-1822, add. 1861-62, NT 1958); Wythenshawe Hall, Cheshire (medieval, fire, rebuilt by Tattons 1579, passed by mar. to Egertons 1746, add later 19th c., Egerton-Tattons 1806, sold 1926, museum); Rostherne Manor, Cheshire (acq. by mar. 1598, demolished 20th c., still own estate)
Estates: Bateman 14179 (E) 39028. The 1 Baron Tatton left legacies of between £30,000 and £40,000 to each of his four surviving younger children. Held a large estate in Kenya in 20th c.
Title: Baron Egerton of Tatton 1859-1958 UK
Peers: 4 peers 1859-1945
2 Lds Lt 19th, 20th
Notes: Extinct in the male line in 1958. The estates passed by mar. to the Earls of Albemarle while the house at Tatton went ot the NT. One in ODNB.

Earl of Wilton (1801- UK)

Origins: Descended from the common Egerton ancestor, Philip Egerton (fl. r. Edward IV). Bt 1617. The heiress of the Barons Grey of Wilton (1290 E) married the 1 Bt. The title was revived in 1784. The daughter of the 1 Earl of Wilton married the 1 Marquess of Westminster. The eldest son of that marriage became the 1 Duke of Westminster (see Grosvenor). The younger son inherited the Egerton estates and title by special remainder and took the name Egerton.

1. Sir Thomas Egerton 6 Bt – Newton 1747-54
2. Thomas Egerton 1 Earl of Wilton – Lancashire 1772-84
3. Arthur (Grosvenor) Egerton 3 Earl of Wilton – Weymouth 1859-65 Bath 1873-74

Seat: Heaton Hall, Lancashire (inher. by marriage from medieval ancestors 1684, rebuilt 1750, rebuilt 1772, sold 1902 to city of Manchester, museum)
Estates: Bateman 9871 (E) 65000
Titles: Baron Grey de Wilton 1784-1814 GB; Baron Grey de Radcliffe 1875-85 UK
Peers: 7 peers 1784-1814 1820-82 1875-1927 1942-45
Notes: Seven in ODNB.

Grey-Egerton

Origins: The Grey-Egertons were descended from the 1 Bt and the Grey de Wilton heiress (see above). On the death of the 1 Earl of Wilton (7 Bt) the baronetcy passed to the Grey-Egertons. **The first Egerton MP of this line 1601 for Staffordshire. Two additional MPs 1601-24.**

1. Sir Philip Egerton – Cheshire 1679 1685-87
2. Sir John Grey-Egerton 8 Bt – Chester 1807-18
3. Sir Philip Grey-Egerton 10 Bt – Chester 1830-31 S. Cheshire 1835-68 W. Cheshire 1868-81

Seats: Oulton Park (Hall), Cheshire (acq. by mar. to Done heiress 15th c., built 16th c., burned and rebuilt 1715-16, remod. c. 1816-20, burned 1926, family still lives on estate); Broxton Old Hall, Cheshire (built 1590s, enlarged 1873, sold 20th c.)
Estates: Bateman 8840 (E) 14676. The Egertons of Oulton held 23,000 acres 1590s.
Title: Baronet 1617-
Notes: Two in ODNB.

Egerton-Warburton

Origins: The Warbutons held Arley from at least 1346. **First MP 1584. Another MP 1601.** The heiress of the Warburton Bts of Arley married in 1803 a nephew of the 9th Grey-Egerton Bt. In 1813 he succeeded to Arley and took the additional name Warburton.

1. Sir George Warburton 3 Bt – Cheshire 1702-05 1710-22
2. Philip Henry Warburton – Chester 1742-54
3. Piers Egerton-Warburton – Mid Cheshire 1876-85

Seats: Arley Hall, Cheshire (acq. by 1346, built 1469, remod. 1758, built 1832-45 – cost £30,000, de Figueiredo and Treuherz, *Cheshire Country Houses*, 23 – still own); Warburton, Cheshire (acq. 12th c.); Grafton Hall, Cheshire (built 1613, add. 1883 for the Stanleys of Alderley, passed to Egertons 1903, demolished 1963); Hefferstone Grange, Cheshire (purch. late 16th c., rebuilt 1700, rebuilt 1741, sold mid-18th c.)
Estates: Bateman 7562 (E) 14834
Title: Baronet 1660-1813
Notes: Five in ODNB.

Docwra

Origins: The Docwras purchased landed estates in 1525. **First MP 1572**. Thomas Docwra MP left his estates to his grandson Sir George Warburton 3 Bt MP (see above).

1. Thomas Docwra – St. Albans 1685-87

Seat: Putteridge, Hertfordshire (purch. 1525, built 1556, passed to Warburtons by mar. 1710, sold 1729, burned 1808)
Estates: Said to be worth £3,000 pa c. 1700.
Title: Baron Docwra 1621-47

Eyles

Origins: Merchants in the early 17th century. A woolstapler became involved in the slave trade with the Barbados. Alderman of London 1687. The 1 Bt was a haberdasher. The sister and heiress of the 4th Eyles Bt married in 1766 her cousin Philip Egerton of the Grey-Egerton family. Their son, Sir John Grey-Egerton succeeded as 8 Bt.

1. Sir John Eyles – Devizes 1679-81
2. Sir John Eyles 2 Bt – Chippenham 1713-27 London 1727-34
3. Francis Eyles – Devizes 1715-21
4. Sir Joseph Eyles – Devizes 1722-27 Southwark 1727-34 Devizes 1734-40
5. Francis Eyles – Devizes 1727-42

Seat: Earnshill, Somerset (built 1720, sold 1720-22)
Title: Baronet 1714-68
Notes: Two in ODNB.

Haynes

Origins: The first MP was the son of a clergyman. Engaged in business? His daughter and heiress became Countess of Bridgwater. (see above)

1. Samuel Haynes – Brackley 1789-1802

Seat: Sunninghill, Berkshire (built late 17th c., remod. 1805, demolished 1947)

ELFORD

Origins: Acquired estate by marriage before 1500. **First MP 1504**. A younger son was a merchant in Plymouth. His grandson was a clergyman and great-grandson, the 1 Bt, started a bank in Plymouth. Mayor of Plymouth 1797.

1. Jonathan Elford – Saltash 1710-15 Fowey 1715-22
2. Sir William Elford 1 Bt – Plymouth 1796-1806 Rye 1807-08
3. Jonathan Elford – Westbury 1820

Seat: Bickham, Devon (acq. later 17th c., built 1680, sold c. 1825)
Title: Baronet 1800-37
Notes: The bank collapsed and 1 Bt was ruined 1825.

ELIOT

Earl of St. Germans (1815- UK)

Origins: Gentry in the 15th century. Privateers under Henry VIII. Purchased estates at the Dissolution. **First MP 1572. Another MP 1614**. Kt 1618.

1. John Eliot – St. Germans 1640 1660-79
2. Edward Eliot – Launceston 1660 St. Germans 1661-79
3. Daniel Eliot – St. Germans 1679-81 1685-87 1689-1701
4. Richard Eliot – St. Germans 1679-81
5. Edward Eliot – St. Germans 1705-15 Lostwithiel 1718-20 Liskeard 1722
6. Richard Eliot – St. Germans 1733-34 Liskeard 1734-47 St. Germans 1747-48
7. Edward Craggs-Eliot 1 Baron Eliot – St. Germans 1748-68 Liskeard 1768-74 St. Germans 1774-75 Cornwall 1775-84
8. Edward Eliot – St. Germans 1780-84 Liskeard 1784-97
9. John Eliot 1 Earl of St. Germans – Liskeard 1784-1804
10. William Eliot 2 Earl of St. Germans – St. Germans 1791-1802 Liskeard 1802-23
11. Edward Eliot 3 Earl of St. Germans – Liskeard 1824-32 E. Cornwall 1837-45

12. William Eliot 4 Earl of St. Germans – Devonport 1866-68

Seat: Port Eliot, Cornwall (medieval, acq. and remod. 1564, remod. 1804, still own)
Estates: Bateman 12791 (E) 17191
Title: Baron Eliot 1784- GB
Peers: 9 peers 1784-1945
1 in Cabinet 1841-45 1853-55
Notes: 1 Baron succeeded to Kidbrook (Charlton) Manor in Kent 1765 and took the additional name Craggs (see Nugent). 1 Baron and 3 Earl and three others in ODNB.

ELLICE

Origins: Merchants in New York in the 18th century and worked for the Hudson's Bay Company in Canada in the fur trade. In addition, West Indies interests. Edward Ellice MP 1818-63 was also an extremely successful businessman.

1. William Ellice – Great Grimsby 1807-12
2. Edward Ellice – Coventry 1818-26 1830-63
3. Alexander Ellice – Harwich 1837-41
4. Edward Ellice – Huddersfield 1837 St. Andrew's Burghs 1837-80
5. Edward Ellice – St. Andrew's Burghs 1903-06

Seats: Ivergarry House, Inverness-shire (purch. 1860 for £120,000, built 1866-69, sold 1923, hotel); Glenquoich, Inverness-shire (purch. 1840 for £32,000, add. c. 1890, sold c. 1945, demolished 1955); Eastbury Manor, Surrey (acq. c. 1900)
Estates: Bateman 99559 (S) 6771. Rubinstein - Alexander Ellice left £175,000 in probate 1805. Owned 15,000 acres in 1996.
1 in Cabinet 1833
Notes: Two in ODNB.

ELLIOT (Eliott) [Drake, Fuller, Murray-Kynymound, Pollexfen] *SCOTLAND & ENGLAND*

<u>Earl of Minto</u> (1813- UK)

Origins: A border dynasty founded in 15th century by a squire to the Earl of Angus. 17th-century lawyers and a judge.

1. Sir Gilbert Elliot 1 Bt – [Roxburghshire 1703-07]
2. Sir Gilbert Elliot 2 Bt – Roxburghshire 1722-26
3. Sir Gilbert Elliot 3 Bt – Selkirkshire 1753-65 Roxburghshire 1765-77
4. John Elliot – Cockermouth 1767-68

5. Gilbert Elliot 1 Earl of Minto – Morpeth 1776-77 Roxburghshire 1777-84 Berwick-on-Tweed 1786-90 Helston 1790-95
6. Gilbert Elliot-Murray-Kynynmound 2 Earl of Minto – Ashburton 1806-07 Roxburgshire 1812-14
7. Sir George Elliot – Roxburghshire 1832-53
8. William Elliot 3 Earl of Minto – Hythe 1837-41 Greenock 1847-52 Clackmannon & Kinross 1857-59
9. John Elliot – Roxburghshire 1837-41 1847-59
10. Sir George Elliot – Chatham 1874-75
11. Arthur Elliot – Roxburghshire 1880-92 Durham 1898-1906
12. Hugh Elliot N. Div. Ayrshire 1885-92

Seats: Minto House, Roxburghshire (built 16th c., purch. 1703, rebuilt c. 1738-43, rebuilt 1809-14, remod. 1837, fire 1992 and much demolished); Headshaw, Roxburghshire (acq. 1696); Lochgelly House, Fife (inherited by mar. 1778, still own); Melgund Castle, Forfarshire (built 1543, acq. by mar. 1778, ruin)
Estates: Bateman 16071 (S) 15860. Loughgelly estate produced £20,000 pa in coal royalties c. 1914.
Titles: Baron Minto 1797- GB; Viscount Melgund 1813- UK; Baronet 1700-
Peers: 5 peers 1797-1945
2 in Cabinet 1770-77 1806-13 1835-41 1846-52
1 KG 20th
1 KT 19th
Notes: The 1 Earl assumed the name Murray-Kynymound in 1778 on inheriting his mother's estates that included Lochgelly and Melgund. 1 and 2 Earls and fourteen others in ODNB.

Baron Heathfield (1787-1813 UK)

Origins: A junior line of the Elliots of Minto. Lord Heathfield's estates passed to the Drakes on the extinction of the title in 1813. Cousins continued at Wolfelee and Stobs Castle. **First [MP 1641 for Roxburghshire].**

1. Sir Gilbert Eliott 1 Bt – [Roxburghshire 1661-63 1667 1669-74]
2. Sir William Eliott 2 Bt – [Roxburghshire 1689-93]
3. Sir Gilbert Eliott 3 Bt – Roxburghshire 1708-15 1726-27

Seats: Heathfield Park (Bayley Park), Sussex (built 1677, remod. early 18th c., purch. 1760s, add. 1766, sold 1791); Stobs Castle, Roxburghshire (acq. by 1632, built 1792-93, add. 19th c., sold 1905); Wolfelee (Wolflee), Roxburghshire (built 17th c., rebuilt 1825-27, rebuilt 1862, burned 1977); Buckland Abbey, Devon (inher. from Drakes 1794 and passed to descendents, remod. 1796-1810 and 1915, fire 1937, sold 1946, NT 1946)

Estates: Bateman 22375 (S) 13793
Title: Baronet 1666-
Peer: 1 peer 1787-90
Notes: 1 Baron and two others in ODNB.

Drake

Origins: Modestly landed family from the early 15th century. The admiral under Queen Elizabeth, son of a farmer-preacher, built up his own fortune. **First MP 1572. An additional MP 1628**. Bt 1622.

1. Sir Francis Drake 2 Bt – Bere Alston 1646-48 Newport 1660-62
2. Sir Francis Drake 3 Bt – Tavistock 1673-81 1689-1700
3. Sir Francis Drake 4 Bt – Tavistock 1715-34 Bere Alston 1734-40
4. Sir Francis Drake 5 Bt – Bere Alston 1747-71 1774-80
5. Francis Drake – Bere Alston 1771-74
6. Augustus Eliott Fuller – E. Sussex 1841-57

Seats: Buckland Abbey, Devon (medieval, remod. 1576, purch. 1581, remod. 1770, passed by mar. to Lord Heathfield 1794); Nutwell Court, Devon (medieval, acq. by mar. 1732, remod. mid-18th c., passed by mar to Lord Heathfield 1794, rebuilt 1790s, passed to Fuller-Eliott-Drakes 1813, and then by mar. to Lord Seaton in 20th c.)
Estates: Bateman 7665 (E) 9093
Titles: Baronet 1622-1794; 1821-1916
Notes: Related to the Drakes of Ashe and Shardeloes (see). Two in ODNB.

Pollexfen

Origins: The Pollexfens were minor gentry in the late 16th century. They were also merchants in the peninsular trade. The first MP was a lawyer and Lord Chief Justice under William III. The Drakes (see above) inherited Nutwell Court from the Pollexfens in 1732.

1. John Pollexfen – Plympton Erle 1679-81 1689-95
2. Sir Henry Pollexfen – Exeter 1689
3. Nicholas Pollexfen – Great Bedwyn 1705-08

Seats: Nutwell Court (Woodbury), Devon (medieval, purch. 1685, passed by mar. 1732 to Drakes, see above); Sherford, Devon
Notes: Two in ODNB.

Fuller

Origins: The family fortune was established by an iron-maker and gun-founder in the later 17th century. They continued in the business through the 18th century. Thomas Fuller married Elizabeth Rose, the daughter and heiress of a Jamaican planter, and acquired estates in the West Indies. They called the estate they purchased in 1697 Rosehill.

1. John Fuller – Sussex 1713-15
2. John Fuller – Boroughbridge 1754-55
3. Rose Fuler – New Romney 1756-61 Maidstone 1761-68 Rye 1768-77
4. John Fuller – Southampton 1780-84 Sussex 1801-12

Seat: Rosehill (Rose Hill Park, Brightling Park), Sussex (purch. 1697, built 1699, passed out of family 1876, part demolished)
Estates: 5,548 acres in 1777. Worth £4,000-£5,000 pa in 1779. Rubinstein – John Fuller left £160,000 in probate in 1834. Rubinstein – Rose Fuller left £120,000 in probate 1821. Their wealth came from manufacturing, sugar plantations, and landed estates.
Notes: August Fuller inherited the Meyrick estates (see that family) and assumed the name Meyrick. On his death in 1876 they passed to the Tapps-Gervis family (under Meyrick). The Fuller family has an entry in the ODNB and one other biography.

Elliot

Origins: Cadet of the Elliots of Minto and Stobs. The father of the first MP was a lace merchant who made a fortune in London and purchased Wells. His son was an equerry to George II.

1. William Elliot – Calne 1741-54
2. William Elliot – {St. Canice 1796-97 1798-1800} Portarlington 1801-02 Peterborough 1802-18

Seat: Wells (House), Roxburghshire (built c. 1690, sold sec. half 19th c., rebuilt house demolished 1951)

ELLIS

Baron Howard de Walden (1597- E)

Origins: Colonel Ellis went to Jamaica in 1650s and became a planter and member of the Assembly by 1685. Five further generations sat in the Assembly over the course of the 18th century. The next generation returned to England where the granddaughter of the 5 Baron Howard de Walden married the 1 Baron Seaford. Their son succeeded as 6 Baron Howard de Walden.

1. Charles Ellis 1 Baron Seaford – Heytesbury 1793-96 Seaford 1796-1806 East Grinstead 1807-12 Seaford 1812-26
2. George Ellis – Seaford 1796-1802
3. Augustus Ellis – Seaford 1826-31

Seats: Chirk Castle, Denbighshire (medieval, leased 1930s); Seaford House, Sussex; Avington Park, Berkshire (built 16th c., add. 1670s, remod. 18th c., purch. 1952)
Estates: Under 2,000 in the 1870s. In the 1890s the London estate produced revenues of £145,000 pa. The Jamaican plantation was worth £20,000 pa in 1782. The family owned 3,000 acres in the 1990s plus the London estate. Worth £310,000,000 in 1990.
Notes: The Barony of Howard de Walden traveled through a number of families before reaching the Ellises including the Herveys and Howard Earls of Suffolk. In 1879 it passed to a Portland heiress and then to the Ellises, which made the 20th-century Barons immensely rich thanks to the Portland's 110 acre estate in central London. 1 and 2 Barons Seaford and 6 and 8 Barons Howard de Walden in ODNB.

ELPHINSTONE *SCOTLAND*

<u>Baron Elphinstone</u> (1510- S)

Origins: The family held Elphinstone since the 14th century.

1. George Elphinstone 1 Viscount Keith – Dumbartonshire 1781-90 Stirlingshire 1796-1801
2. Charles Elphinstone-Fleming – Stirlingshire 1802-12 1832-34
3. James Buller-Elphinstone – East Looe 1826-29

Seats: Carberry Tower, Midlothian (built mid-16th c., acq. by mar. 1802, add. 19th c., donated 1961, sold, hotel); Trenant Park, Cornwall (built 17th c., remod. 18th c., acq. from Bullers by mar. 1824, sold 19th c., flats); Tulliallan Castle, Fife (built by Admiral Lord Keith 1812-20, sold for institutional use after 1954)
Estates: Under 2,000 acres in the 1870s.
Titles: Baron Kieth 1797-1867 I; Baron Keith 1801-67 UK; Viscount Keith 1814-23 UK; Baron Elphinstone 1859-60 UK; Baron Elphinstone 1885- UK
Peers: [2 peers 1668-69 1703-07] 4 Scottish Rep peers 1784-94 1803-07 1832-35 1847-59 1867-85 4 peers 1801-23 1859-60 1885-1945
3 Lds Lt 18th, 19th
Notes: The 10 Baron succeeded by marriage to a great heiress to the representation of the Earls Mairshal (Keith) and the lands of Wigtoun (Fleming) in 1735. A younger son

was created Viscount Keith in 1814. James Elphinstone MP inherited by marriage in 1824 the Buller seat of Trenant Park (see Buller). Carberry was purchased in the 18th century by John Fullerton whose niece Elizabeth married William Elphinstone, third son of the 10 Baron Elphinstone, and succeeded to Carberry. (see also Keith) 4, 13 Barons and 1 Viscount Keith and four others in ODNB.

Baron Balmerino(ch) (1606-1746 S)

Origins: The 1 Baron was a younger son of the 3 Baron Elphinstone. A younger son of the 1 Baron was created Baron Coupar in 1607. The family was attainted and became extinct in 1746.

No MPs

Seat: Restalrig, Edinburghshire (purch. 1605, forfeited 1746)
Titles: Baron Coupar 1607-1746 S
Peers: [3 peers 1660-89 1660-1707] 1 Scottish Rep peer 1710-15
Notes: The 3 Baron lost most of his land in lawsuits in the late 17th century. 1, 2, 3, 4, and 6 Barons in ODNB

Elphinstone

Origins: Descended from a younger son of Sir William Elphinstone, ancestor of the Lords Elphinstone.

1. Richard Elphinstone – [Stirlingshire 1681]

Seat: Airth Castle, Stirlingshire (built 14th c., acq. 16th c., sold 1717, now hotel)

ELTON

Origins: The 1 Bt was son of a market gardener who became a great merchant in Bristol involved in weaving, iron, glass, and pottery. High Sheriff 1702.

1. Sir Abraham Elton 1 Bt – Bristol 1722-27
2. Sir Abraham Elton 2 Bt – Taunton 1724-27 Bristol 1727-42
3. Sir Arthur Elton 7 Bt – Bath 1857-59
4. Charles Elton – W. Somerset 1884-85 Wells Div. Somerset 1886-92

Seats: Clevedon Court, Somerset (built 1320, add. 1570, purch. 1709, add. 1882, part demolished, NT 1960); Whitestaunton House, Somerset (medieval, remod. 16th c., purch. 1718 for £11,600, remod. early 19th c., sold 1920-25)

Estates: Bateman 6556 (E) 13124 (includes Marwood-Elton Bts)
Titles: Baronet 1717- ; 1838-84
Notes. Inherited Marwood fortune (estimated at half a million pounds in property and £200,000 probate in 1811 – Rubinstein 47). Family stayed engaged in business. 2 Bt Mayor of Bristol 1719. 4 Bt was a barrister and Master of the Merchant Venturers. 6 and 11 Bts and one other in ODNB.

ELWES [Duffield, Meggott]

Elwes

Origins: The grandfather of the 1 Bt made a fortune in trade and became a London Alderman 1605. Robert Meggott, a wealthy brewer, married the sister and heiress of Sir Hervey Elwes 2 Bt. Their son took the name Elwes in 1751 and inherited the estates in 1763.

1. Sir John Elwes – Marlborough 1673-79
2. Sir Gervase Elwes 1 Bt – Sudbury 1677-79 Suffolk 1679 Sudbury 1680-81 Suffolk 1690-98 Sudbury 1700-06
3. Gervase Elwes – Sudbury 1679-81
4. Sir Hervey Elwes 2 Bt – Sudbury 1706-10 1713-22
5. George Meggott – Southwark 1722-23
6. John Meggott Elwes – Berkshire 1772-84

Seats: Stoke College, Suffolk (medieval, purch. c. 1660, rebuilt early 18th c., sold by 1897, school); Marcham Park, Berkshire (Meggots acq. 1717, rebuilt 18th c., passed to Duffields, see below); Congham House, Norfolk (purch. 18th c., rebuilt 1856, burned 1938, still own estate); Colesbourne Park (House), Gloucestershire (built 16th c., remod. 1704, purch. 1790 by John Elwes with 1,515 acres. He built estate up to 6,000 acres - Kingsley, *The Country Houses of Gloucestershire*, II, 281 - rebuilt c. 1853-59, part demolished c. 1958, still own)
Estates: Bateman 3441 (E) 4226 and 4549 (E) 4066 and 3313 (E) 3074. Rubinstein – John Elwes MP, a miser, reportedly left £800,000 in 1789 and John Elwes, another miser, left £250,000 in probate 1817.
Title: Baronet 1660-1779
Notes: A family famous for misers. Two in ODNB.

Duffield

Origins: Abingdon burgesses in the 18th century. Emily Elwes, the heiress to Marcham, married Thomas Duffield MP who succeeded to a portion of the Elwes estates and took the name Elwes.

1. Thomas Duffield – Abingdon 1832-44

Seat: Marcham Park, Berkshire (acq. by mar. 19th c., remod. c. 1820, sold 1947, institutional use)
Estates: Bateman 2521 (E) 3037

ENGLAND

Origins: The grandfather of the first MP was a Yarmouth craftsman, and his father a leading merchant. The first MP was a lawyer. Kt 1671.

1. George England – Great Yarmouth 1679-81 1689-1701
2. Benjamin England – Great Yarmouth 1702-08
3. George England – Great Yarmouth 1710-22

Seat: Stokesby Old Hall, Norfolk (built 16th c., purch. 1710, sold 1725)
Notes: Family bankrupt 1725 and estates sold. One in ODNB.

ERSKINE *SCOTLAND*

Earl of Mar (1404- and 1565- S)

Origins: The Erskine became an important political family in the 14th century, and the Earldom of Mar was the premier peerage of that rank in Scotland. The descent of the title became almost unbelievably complex, and it was alienated and restored and the source of prolonged legal dispute. In 1866 the restored title (which did not pass through the female line) went to a cousin, who also inherited the Earldom of Kellie (which had originally been created for a cadet but passed to the 28 Earl of Mar in 1834). The old Earldom, which did descend through the female line, went to the son of the sister of the 28 Earl. **First [MP 1602]. Three further [MPs in the mid-17th century]**.

1. Sir Alexander Erskine 2 Bt – Fifeshire 1710-15
2. Thomas Erskine Lord Erskine (23 Earl of Mar) – Stirling Burghs 1728-34 Stirlingshire 1747 Clackmannanshire 1747-54
3. James Erskine – Clackmannanshire 1734-41 Stirling Burghs 1741-47
4. John Erskine Lord Erskine – Weston-super-Mare 1922-23 1924-34 Brighton 1940-41

Seats: Alloa House, Clackmannanshire (acq. 1363 and built 14th c., remod. 1672, remod. early 1727, burned 1800, rebuilt 1834-38, remod. c. 1866, fire, sold and much demolished c. 1960, medieval tower remains); Kellie Castle, Fife (built 14th c., add. 1573, remod. 1603-06, purch. 1613, abandoned 1828, sold 1878)

Estates: Bateman 6312 (S) 13091. Rubinstein – Mary Erskine left £120,000 in probate in 1837.
Titles: Baron Erskine before 1429- S; Baron Direlton 1603- S; Viscount Fentoun 1606- S; Earl of Kellie 1619- S; Baronet 1666-1829
Peers: [5 peers 1660-77 1660-89 1696-1707 1698-1707] 7 Scottish Rep peers 1707-15 1790-96 1804-06 1807-28 1869-72 1876-88 1886-1922 1892-1945
3 Lds Lt 19t, 20th
1 in Cabinet Council 1705-09 1713-14
2 KT 18th, 20th
Note: The Earldom was attainted 1715-1824 and estates forfeited but bought back by a brother. The Erskine family has an entry in the ODNB, and the 17, 18, 19, and 22 Earls of Mar and the 1, 6, and 9 Earls of Kellie and four others.

Erskine

Origins: Descended from an illegitimate son of the 9 Earl of Mar. The 9 Earl of Kellie (d. 1828) was a merchant in Sweden.

1. Sir James Erskine – St. George's Div. Westminster 1921-29

Seat: Cambo House, Fife (acq. 1668, built 18th c., forefeited 1745, repurch. 1790s by 9 Earl of Kellie, fire 1878, rebuilt 1879-81, still own)
Estates: Bateman 3523 (S & W) 7297. Rubinstein – Stewart Erskine left £140,000 in probate in 1826.

Earl of Buchan (1469- S)

Origins: The brother of the 20 Earl of Mar married the Countess of Buchan in her own right. Their son succeeded as 7 Earl of Buchan. The 19 Earl of Mar was created Baron Cardross. This title passed to a younger son. On the death of the 8 Earl of Buchan that title passed to the 4 Baron Cardross. A younger son of the 10 Earl was created Baron Erskine.

1. William Erskine – [Culross 1689-96]
2. William Erskine – Perth Burghs 1722-27
3. Charles Erskine – Dumfriesshire 1722-41 Tain Burghs 1741-42
4. Thomas Erskine 1 Baron Erskine – Portsmouth 1783-84 1790-1806
5. Henry Erskine – Haddington Burghs 1806 Dumfries Burghs 1806-07

Seats: Almondell House, Linlithgowshire (built 1786, gutted c. 1950, demolished 1969); Kirkhill, Linlithgowshire (built 1590, remod. 18th c. and 19th c., now flats); Dryburgh Abbey House, Roxburghshire (purch. 1786, sold mid-19th c., hotel)

Estates: Bateman 3071 (S) 5758 plus 3635
Title: Baron Cardross 1610- S
Peers: [5 peers 1660-88 1660-75 1689-93 1694-1707] 1 Scottish Rep peer 1715-34
1 Ld Lt 18th
1 KT 19th
Notes: The 2 and 3 Barons Cardross and 6 and 11 Earls of Buchan and eight others in ODNB.

<u>Baron Erskine</u> (1806- UK)

Origins: See Earl of Buchan above. The 1 Baron was Lord Chancellor.

1. Thomas Erskine 1 Baron Erskine – Portsmouth 1783-84 1790-1806
2. David Erskine 2 Baron Erskine – Portsmouth 1806

Peers: 6 peers 1806-1945
1 in Cabinet 1806-07
Notes: 1 and 2 Barons Erskine in ODNB and three others.

<u>Erskine</u>

Origins: Descended from a younger brother of the 3 Baron Cardross.

1. Sir William Erskine 2 Bt – Fifeshire 1796-1806

Seats: Torry (Torrie) House, Fife (built c. 1785, remod. early 19th c., passed to the Wemyss family 1841, see Wemyss); Dunimarle Castle, Fife (medieval, rebuilt 18th c., rebuilt 1839-40, sold)
Title: Baronet 1791-1839
Notes: One in ODNB.

<u>Erskine</u>

Origins: Descended from the youngest son of the 3 Baron Cardross.

1. John Erskine – Stirlingshire 1865-74

Seat: Cardross House, Perthshire (acq. later 16th c., built 1598, remod. 18th c., add. 1790, add. 1820, sold later in 19th c.)
Estates: Bateman 6285 (S) 4080

Earl of Rosslyn (1801- UK)

Origns: Alexander Wedderburn was created Earl of Rosslyn with a special remainder to his nephew, the son of his sister Janet, who married Sir Henry Erskine 5 Bt of Alva, a descendent of the youngest son of the 9 Earl of Mar.

1. Sir Charles Erskine 1 Bt – [Clackmannanshire 1665 Stirlingshire 1667 1689]
2. Sir John Erskine 3 Bt – [Clackmannanshire 1700-02 Bruntisland Burgh 1703-07] Scotland 1707-08 Clackmannanshire 1713-15
3. John Erskine – [Stirling Burghs 1703-07] Scotland 1707-08 Stirling Burghs 1708-10
4. Charles Erskine – Dumfriesshire 1722-41 Tain Burghs 1741-42
5. Charles Erskine – Ayr Burghs 1747-49
6. Sir Henry Erskine 5 Bt – Ayr Burghs 1749-54 Anstruther Burghs 1754-65
7. James St. Clair-Erskine 2 Earl of Rosslyn – Castle Rising 1782-84 Morpeth 1784-96 Dysart Burghs 1796-1805
8. James St. Clair-Erskine 3 Earl of Rosslyn – Dysart Burghs 1830-31 Great Grimsby 1831-32

Seats: Dysart House, Fife (acq. by Wedderburns 1470, rebuilt 1755-56, acq. by mar. from the Wedderburns 1805, add. 1808-14, sold 1896, convent); Alva House, Clackmannanshire (built by 1542, rebuilt 1636, sold c. 1766, demolished c. 1945); Rosslyn Castle, Edinburghshire (acq. c. 1280, built c. 1330, rebuilt 15th c., burned 1544, rebuilt 1597, remod. 1622-23, dilapidated 18th c., part restored 1982-88, still own)
Estates: Bateman 3310 (S) 10410
Titles: Baron Loughborough 1780-1805 GB; Baron Loughborough 1795- UK; Baronet 1666-
Peers: 5 peers 1780-1939
1 in Cabinet 1829-30 1834
Notes: The St. Clairs acq. Rosslyn c. 1280, and it later passed to the Wedderburns. The name was assumed by the Erskines in 1789. 2 Earl and two others in ODNB.

Erskine

Origins: Descended from a younger brother of the 1 Baron Erskine, ancestor of the Earls of Mar (1390s). **First [MP 1563]. One additional [MP 1630].**

1. David Erskine Lord Dun – [Forfarshire 1689-96]

Seat: Dun House (House of Dun), Forfarshire (purch. 1375, built 16th c., demolished 1723, new house c. 1730-42, remod. early 19th c., remod. 1912, family departed 1939, NT 1980)
Estates: Bateman 3533 (S) 4108

Notes: In 1824 the estate passed by mar. to the 1 Marquis of Ailsa, and a younger son took the additional name Erskine on succeeding as 18 laird of Dun. Erskine family extinct 1980. Two in ODNB.

ESMONDE *IRELAND*

Origins: Seneschal of Wexford 1294. Baron 1622. **First {MP 1613}. One additional {MP 1641}.**

1. Sir Thomas Esmonde 9 Bt – Wexford 1841-47
2. Sir John Esmonde 10 Bt – County Waterford 1852-76
3. Sir Thomas Esmonde 11 Bt – S. Div. County Dublin 1885-92 W. Kerry 1892-1900 N. Wexford 1900-18
4. John Esmonde – N. Tipperary 1910-15
5. Sir John Esmonde 14 Bt – N. Tipperary 1915-18 {TD 1937-51}
6. Sir Osmond Esmonde 12 Bt – {TD Wexford 1923-27}
7. Sir Anthony Esmonde 15 Bt – {TD Wexford 1951-73}
8. John Grattan Esmonde 16 Bt – {TD Wexford 1973-77}

Seats: Ballynastragh, Wexford (acq. and built by 17th c., add. c. 1767, remod. 1803-25, burned 1923, new house 1937, still own); Glenwood, Wicklow; Huntington Castle, Carlow (acq. and built 1625, descendents still own)
Estates: Bateman 8057 (I) 4563
Titles: Baron Esmonde 1622-46 I; Baronet 1629-
Notes: A Roman Catholic family, which excluded them from parliamentary service in the 18th century. The 11 Bt was Senator in the Irish Free State 1922-34. 1 Baron and 11 and 12 Bts in ODNB.

ESTCOURT

Baron Estcourt (1903-15 UK)

Origins: The Estcourts were landed fom the 13th century. **First MP 1563. Three further MPs 1584-1624**. Thomas Estcourt married in 1774 the daughter of Mary Bucknall and their heirs succeeded to the Bucknall estates in 1822. In the 19th century Thomas Estcourt married the daughter and heiress of Frank Sotherton MP (see below) and succeeded to the Sotherton estates in 1839.

1. Thomas Estcourt – Cricklade 1790-1806
2. Thomas Bucknall Estcourt – Devizes 1805-26 University of Oxford 1826-47
3. Thomas Sotherton-Escourt – Marlborough 1829-32 Devizes 1835-44 N. Wiltshire 1844-65

4. James Bucknall-Estcourt – Devizes 1848-52
5. George Sotherton-Estcourt 1 Baron Estcourt – N. Div. Wiltshire 1874-85
6. Thomas Sotherton-Estcourt – Pontefract Div. W. R. Yorkshire 1931-35

Seats: Estcourt Park, Gloucestershire (acq. 1330, medieval house, rebuilt mid-16th c., rebuilt 1776-79, remod. c. 1830, demolished 1964, still own estate); Cam, Gloucestershire; New Park (Roundway Park), Wiltshire (inherit. 1801, sold 1840); Darrington Hall, Yorkshire (demolished 1980s); Lasborough Park, Gloucestershire (built 1598, rebuilt 1794, sold 1826); Newnton Priory (Long Newnton), Wiltshire [in Gloucestershire after 1930) (acq. and rebuilt mid-18th c., remod. 1868, sold 1885)
Estates: Bateman 11551 (E) 18252
Titles: Baronet 1626-84 1903-15
Peer: 1 peer 1903-15
1 in Cabinet 1859
Notes: Two in ODNB.

<u>Bucknall</u>

Origins: A businessman purchased Oxhey in 1667. Kt 1670. Estates passed to Estcourts (see above).

1. Sir William Bucknall – Liverpool 1670-76
2. Sir John Bucknall – Middlesex 1696-98
3. Ralph Bucknall – Petersfield 1701

Seat: Oxhey Park, Hertfordshire (medieval, purch. by Bucknalls 1668, new house 1688, demolished 1799, passed to Estcourts 1829, sold 1866-77)
Notes: Related to the Bucknalls under Grimston.

<u>Sotherton</u> (Sotheron)

Origins: Originally from Suffolk and Norwich in the 16th century. Estates passed to Estcourts, see above.

1. William Sotherton – Pontefract 1784-96
2. Frank Sotherton – Nottinghamshire 1814-31

Seats: Darrington Hall, Yorkshire (acq. 18th c.); Kirklington Hall, Nottinghamshire (built 17th c., remod. 1770s, inher. by mar. 1808, passed out of family 1839, now a school)

Estcourt

Origins: Descended from Edmund Estcourt of Estcourt, the last common ancestor of the two families. **First MP 1628.**

1. Sir William Estcourt – Malmesbury 1679-81

Seat: Newnton Priory (Long Newnton), Wiltshire [in Gloucestershire after 1930] (acq. by senior line 1585, sold 1646, later repurch. by Estcourts of Estcourt)
Title: Baronet 1622-84

Estcourt-Cresswell

Origins: Descended from the most junior line of Edmund Estcourt of Estcourt. Elizabeth Cresswell, daughter and heiress of Sir Thomas Estcourt (d. 1702), succeeded to the Pinkney estate. The Cresswells were gentry by the 17th century. One was a page to Charles I.

1. Sir Thomas Estcourt – Malmesbury 1673-79 1685-87 Bath 1695-98
2. Richard Cresswell – Bridgnorth 1710-13 Wootton Bassett 1713-15
3. Thomas Cresswell – Wootton Bassett 1754-74
4. Estcourt Cresswell – Cirencester 1768-74

Seats: Pinkney Park (Court), Wiltshire (resident 18th and 19th c., sold later 19th c.); Bibury Court, Gloucestershire (built later 16th c., rebuilt 1633, inherited 1756 through the Warnefords from the Sackvilles, remod. c. 1759, sold 1816); Rudge Hall, Shropshire (medieval, acq. by mar. 1709, rebuilt 19th c., sold 1816?); Sidbury, Shropshire (acq. by mar. first half 17th c. and held in 18th c. and 19th c.)
Estates: Bateman 2693 (E) 3007
Notes: Estcourt Cresswell MP fell heavily into debt and sold a large block of the estate in 1816, more sold 1829, leaving a small remainder.

EURE (Evers)

Baron Eure (1544-1690 E)

Origins: Acquired estates in Yorkshire by marriage in the 13th century. William Eure fought at Agincourt. **First MP 1307. Six additional MPs 1542-1658, including several kts of the shire.**

No MPs

Seats: Malton Castle (House), Yorkshire (acq. by mar. 1387, built early 17th c., seized for recusancy 1632, demolished 1675 and passed to remote heirs); Upper Heyford, Oxfordshire (leased 17th c.); Gatley Park, Herefordshire (built 16th c., purch. 1632 for £3450, sold 1679)
Peers: 2 peers 1660-90 One member of Cromwell's House of Lords.
Notes: Recusants early 17th c. but estates pass to Protestants 1650s.

EUSTACE *IRELAND*

Viscount Baltinglass (1541-85 I)

Origins: An Anglo-Norman family that obtained extensive estates in Kildare and Meath in the 15th century thanks to royal service and office holding through a number of generations. Lord Deputy 1454. **First {MP 1559 for County Kildare}. Two additional {MPs in the 1630s}.**

1. Sir Maurice Eustace – {Knocktopher 1664-66 Harristown 1692-93 1695}
2. Charles Eustace – {Clomines 1794-97 Fethard 1797-1800}
3. Henry Eustace – {Clomines 1800}

Seats: Corbally (Gorbally), Queen's County; Robertstown, Kildare (acq. 18th c., resident into 20th c.); Harristown House, Kildare (acq. 1661, sold 1783)
Estates: Bateman 3938 (I) 2236. Held 3,091 acres in 1660.
Titles: Baron Portlester 1492-96 I; Baron Kilcullen 1535-85 I
Notes: Attainted for rebellion and deprived of titles 1585. Family resident in England post 1918. 1 Baron Portlester, 3 Viscount and one other in ODNB.

EVANS *IRELAND*

Baron Carbery (1715- I)

Origins: The Evanses claimed descent from a baronial family at the Conquest (Jones, *Views of the Seats*, 125), but in fact rose by law in the later 17th century. John Evans, the younger son of the 1 Baron, married 1741 Grace daughter of Sir Ralph Freke 1 Bt of Castle Freke. Their grandson succeeded as 6 Baron Carbery. The Frekes came from Devon and rose by office under Henry VIII (see under Pitt). A younger son went to Ireland in the early 17th century. Sheriff 1694.

1. Thomas Evans – {Kilkenny 1661-63}
2. George Evans – {County Limerick 1692-93 Askeaton 1695-99 Charleville 1703-13 1715-20}

3. George Evans 1 Baron Carbery – {County Limerick 1707-14} Westbury 1715-22 1724-27
4. Eyre Evans – {County Limerick 1721-60}
5. Thomas Evans – {Castlemartyr 1737-53}
6. George Evans 2 Baron Carbery – Westbury 1734-47
7. George Evans – {Queen's County 1747-60}
8. William Evans – {Baltimore 1777-83}
9. Sir John Evans-Freke 1 Bt – {Baltimore 1768-77}
10. John Evans-Freke 6 Baron Carbery – {Donegal 1782-90 Baltimore 1790-1800}
11. George Evans – {Baltimore 1797-1800}
12. George Evans 4 Baron Carbery – Rutland 1802-04
13. George Evans – County Dublin 1832-41

Seats: Castle Freke, Cork (originally Rathbarry House/Castle) (15th c. castle, purch. by Frekes 1641, burned c. 1690, new hosue c. 1780s, add. c. 1820, fire 1910, rebuilt, sold 1920s, dismantled 1952, ruin); Bulgaden Hall, Limerick (acq. later 17th c., rebuilt 1790s, burned 1910 and rebuilt, sold 1919, repurchased by family in the 1990s for £360,000 - Hicks, *Irish Country Houses*, 25); Laxton Hall, Northamptonshire (acq. by mar. 1720, built 1759, add. 1806-16, passed by inher. 1889 to the Earl of Bandon, sold 1924); Caharas, Limerick; Portrane (Portraine) House, Dublin (purch. 1725, resident 20th c.)
Estates: Bateman 21246 (I & E) 12850. Evans worth £3,000 pa in 1713, £4,000 pa in 1805; inherited nabob fortune of £80,000 in 1806. Rubinstein – George Freke Evans left £120,000 in probate in 1829.
Title: Baronet 1768-
Peers: {4 peers 1715-83 1798-1800} 2 Irish Rep peers 1823-45 1891-94
Notes: The 1 Baron was supposed to have been elevated to the peerage by George I for his good looks. (Cannon, *Aristocratic Century*, 31) Said to be related to the Earl of Carbery of the first creation (see Vaughan). In Kenya in the 1930s.

Freke

Origins: See above.

1. Arthur Freke – {Clonakilty 1661-66}
2. Sir Percy Freke – {Clonakilty 1692-93 1695-99 Baltimore 1703-06}
3. Sir Ralph Freke 1 Bt – {Clonakilty 1703-17}
4. George Freke – {Clonakilty 1703-27 Bandon 1727-30}
5. Sir Percy Freke 2 Bt – {Baltimore 1721-28}
6. Sir John Freke 3 Bt – {Baltimore 1728-60 Cork 1761-64}

Seats: Castle Freke, Cork (built by Barrys 15th c., purch. by Frekes 1641, old castle fell into ruin later 18th c., passed to Evans 1764); West Bilney Hall, Norfolk (purch. late 17th c., sold by early 19th c.)
Estates: Held 15,276 acres in 18th c. Worth £2,000 pa in 1713 and £7,000 pa in 1750.
Title: Baronet 1713-64
Note: The Senior line of the family descended from the elder brother of the first Freke to go to Ireland (see Pitt).

EVELYN [Boone, Calvert, Glanville]

Evelyn

Origins: Gunpowder manufacturers who made their fortune in the Tudor period with the help of a monopoly. George Evelyn (1530-1603) established three lines of descendents. The senior branch derived from the eldest son, Thomas. They became Baronets in 1683 but were extinct 1692. The youngest line, descended from George's son, Richard, was seated at Wotton House. It also received a Baronetcy in 1713 and became extinct 1848, when the estates passed to the middle branch seated at West Dean, Lee Place, and Nutfield. A younger son of this line married in 1766 the Countess of Rothes. Their son succeeded as 13 Earl of Rothes (see Leslie). The lines are combined here. **First MP 1626**.

1. Sir John Evelyn – Wilton 1626 Ludgershall 1640 1660 Stockbridge 1660
2. Sir John Evelyn – Bletchingley 1628 1640-48 1660
3. George Evelyn – Reigate 1645 Haslemere 1661-79 Surrey 1679-81 1689-90
4. George Evelyn – Bletchingley 1679-81 Gatton 1696-98
5. Sir Edward Evelyn 1 Bt – Surrey 1685-87
6. John Evelyn – Bletchingley 1702
7. George Evelyn – Bletchingley 1705-24
8. Sir John Evelyn 1 Bt – Helston 1708-10
9. Sir John Evelyn 2 Bt – Helston 1727-41 Penryn 1741-47 Helston 1747-67
10. William Evelyn Glanville – Hythe 1728-66
11. William Evelyn – Helston 1767-74
12. William Evelyn – Hythe 1768-1802
13. William Evelyn – W. Surrey 1849-57 Deptford 1885-88

Seats: Nutfield, Surrey (acq. 1602, passed out of the family later in the 17th c.); Wotton House, Surrey (medieval, acq. 1579, built early 17th c., add. 1670, add. 18th c., add. 1864-77, c., fire 1870s, rebuilt 1870s, family departed 1947, sold 1980s, hotel); Sayes Court, Kent (acq. by inher. 17th c., family departed 1680s, sold 18th c., demolished c. 1940); Lee Place, Surrey (acq. 1589, sold 1734); Rook's Nest, Surrey (acq. 17th c., sold 1711); West Dean House, Wiltshire (purch. 1618, sold 1725); St. Clere, Kent (purch. 1723, sold

1878); Send Grove, Surrey (acq. mid-18th c., sold 1783); Godstone Place, Surrey (acq. 1588-91, built c. 1620, sold 1724, demolished 18th c.)
Estates: Bateman 3601 (E) 2971. Wotton line worth £4,000 pa in 1640.
Titles: Baronet 1660-71; 1683-92; 1713-1848
Notes: Inherited Sayes from Brownes, founded by a Tudor official, Kt 1603, **MP 1584**. Four in ODNB.

Glanville

Origins: Merchants in the mid-17th century. Later lawyers. The granddaughter and heiress of William Glanville MP married William Evelyn.

1. William Glanville – Queenborough 1681

Seat: Wonford House, Devon (leased?)
Notes: Probably related to the Glanvilles of Catchfrench, Cornwall. (see Glanville) One in ODNB.

Boone

Origins: Merchants purchased estates 1630. **First MP 1646** was Cromwell's ambassador to Russia. Inherited some Evelyn estates by marriage. Charles Boone MP was Governor of Bombay and a Director of the East India Company 1729-35.

1. Charles Boone – Dartmouth 1689-90
2. Charles Boone – Ludgershall 1727-34
3. Daniel Boone – Ludgershall 1734-41 Grampound 1741-47 Stockbridge 1747-54 Minehead 1754-61
4. Charles Boone – Castle Rising 1757-68 Ashburton 1768-84 Castle Rising 1784-96

Seats: Rook's Nest, Surrey (purch. 1711, sold 1758); Lee Place, Kent (acq. 1734, sold 19th c.); Godstone Place, Surrey (acq. 1734, sold 19th c.); Barking Hall, Suffolk (acq. by mar. 1762, passed out of family 1782); Mount Boone, Devon (purch. 1630, passed out of family 1689)
Estates: Rubinstein – Charles Boone MP left £500,000 in probate 1819.
Notes: In the 18th c. the family produced several colonial governors and inherited some industrial wealth. Probably related to the Glanville family listed above. One in ODNB.

Baron Baltimore (1625-1771 I)

Origins: Rose in royal service; started as a secretary to Robert Cecil. Invested in the East India Company and in Virginia in the early 17th century. Kt 1619. 1 Baron was a lawyer, politician, and diplomat. **First MP 1609 (Yorkshire 1621).** The Calverts inherited Woodcote Park in 1692 under the will of Elizabeth Evelyn, a kinswoman.

1. Benedict Calvert 4 Baron Baltimore – Harwich 1714-15
2. Charles Calvert 5 Baron Baltimore – St. Germans 1734-41 Surrey 1741-51

Seats: Woodcote Park, Surrey (built 1679, acq. by mar. from Evelyns 1692, sold 1768); Kilpin Hall, Yorkshire (tenants there c. 1570, purch. 1619, sold 1722)
Estates: Vast territories in America. Granted 2,300 acres in County Longford 1621.
Notes: Proprietors of Maryland from 1632 to c. 1689. Most of the family were Roman Catholics. Conformed to the Established Church 1713. 1, 2, 4, 5, and 6 Barons and three others in ODNB.

EVERARD I

Origins: Held manorial land from 1482. **First MP 1589. Second MP 1658.**

1. Sir Richard Everard 2 Bt – Westminster 1661-79

Seat: Langleys, Essex (acq. by mar. c. 1515, rebuilt c. 1620, sold c. 1710)
Estates: Worth £500 pa in the early 18th century.
Title: Baronet 1629-1745
Notes: The 3 Bt sold his estates in 1710 to pay debts. The 6 Bt emigrated to America. One in ODNB.

EVERARD II *IRELAND*

Origins: Judge of the Kings Bench in Ireland 1602. **First {MP 1585}. Three further {MPs 1613-34}.**

1. Nicholas Everard – {Fethard 1661-63}
2. Sir Redmond Everard 4 Bt – {Kilkenny 1711-13 Fethard 1713-14

Seats: Fethard, Tipperary; Ballyboy (Balliboye), Tipperary (acq. early 17th c., sold 1750s)
Estates: Held 1743 acres in Tipperary 1702 and more in Waterford. Worth £1,500 pa in 1714.
Title: Baronet 1622-c.1740
Notes: Roman Catholic family. Outlawed 1691, reversed 1702. Created a Viscount in the Jacobite peerage by James III 1722-c.1740. Extinct in male line 1740. Estates sold 1750 to pay debts.

EVERSFIELD

Origins: Acquired considerable estates in the mid-16th century. Also owned ironworks. Sheriff 1599. **First MP 1624. A second MP 1640-44.**

1. Edward Eversfield – Bramber 1660
2. John Eversfield – Steyning 1660
3. Nicholas Eversfield – Bramber 1679
4. Anthony Eversfield – Horsham 1679-81 1685-87 1689-90
5. Sir Charles Eversfield 2 Bt – Horsham 1705-10 Sussex 1710-13 Horsham 1713-15 1721-41 Steyning 1741-47

Seats: Denne Park (Place), Sussex (purch. and built 1604 for £5,500, sold post-1945, flats); Charlton Court, Sussex (purch. 1652, sold 1817); The Grove (Grove House), Sussex (acq. by mar. 1586, declined to a farm house after 1785)
Estates: 3124 (E) 4756
Title: Baronet 1725-84
Notes: The 2 Bt left a substantial part of his property to his natural daughters in 1749.

EWER

Origins: The first MP was a younger son of a family settled at Lea since the first half of the 16th century, but he was a London grocer, Alderman 1741.

1. Charles Ewer – Shaftesbury 1741-42
2. William Ewer – Dorchester 1765-89
3. Thomas Ewer – Dorchester 1789-90

Seat: (The) Lea, Hertfordshire (acq. 1541, sold 1715)
Notes: One in ODNB.

EYRE I *ENGLAND & IRELAND*

Eyre

Origins: Can be traced in Wiltshire back to the reign of Edward II. After two generations as mercers two successful marriages in the 16th century gave them a fortune large enough to become a leading family in the county. **First MP 1558 for Wiltshire. Six additional MPs 1563-1659, two for the county.**

1. Sir Robert Eyre – Salisbury 1698-1710
2. Robert Eyre – Southampton – 1727-29

3. Samuel Eyre – Salisbury 1765-68

Seat: Newhouse (New House), Wiltshire (built c. 1615, purch. 1633, add. mid-18th c., passed by mar. late 18th c. to Matcham family who took the additional name Eyre and in the 20th c. to the Jeffreys, still own)
Estates: Bateman 2814 (E) 2185. Owned 1,300 acres in 1980s. Cousins at Warrens, Wiltshire 2539 (E) 3541. The Eyres still own 190 acres in London worth at least £1,000,000,000, possibly as much as two billion, in 2001. (Cahill, *Who Owns Britain*, 155, 383)
Notes: The Eyres purchased a large London estate in the 18th c., which increased vastly in value. The family produced three judges in the early 18th century. Two in ODNB.

Eyre

Origins: A junior line seated at Brickworth.

1. Henry Eyre – Salisbury 1659 1660 Downton 1675-78
2. Sir Giles Eyre – Downton 1660 Salisbury 1689
3. John Eyre – Downton 1698-1701 1705-15
4. Giles Eyre – Downton 1715-34

Seats: Brickworth House, Wiltshire (purch. and built c. 1605, remod. 1717, passed to Nelsons 1821); Landford, Wiltshire (built 1599, acq. 1715, passed to Nelsons 1821)
Notes: The estates passed in 1821 to the 2 Earl Nelson. One in ODNB.

Earl Nelson (1805- UK)

Origins: Clergy in the 18th century. Admiral Horatio Nelson's heir was created an Earl by a grateful nation and Trafalgar House was purchased for him by Parliament. Brickworth and the Eyre estates passed to the 2 Earl (Thomas Bolton, who took the name of Nelson – his mother was Nelson's sister) by his marriage to the heiress Frances Eyre in 1821.

No MPs

Seats: Trafalgar House (Standlynch Park), Wiltshire (built 1731-33, rebuilt c. 1766-70, purch. 1814, sold 1948); Brickworth House, Wiltshire (acq. by mar. 1821, sold 1917)
Estates: Bateman 7196 (E) 5800. £90,000 to purchase an estate and a perpetual pension of £5,000 were voted by Parliament in 1806. The pension was ended in 1950.
Titles: Baron Nelson 1798-1805 GB; Viscount Nelson 1801-05 UK; Viscount Merton 1805- UK
Peers: 4 peers 1798-1835 1845-1945

Notes: Admiral Nelson was also created Duke of Bronte in the Kingdom of the Two Sicilies and granted the estate of Bronte, which was held by his heirs until its sale in 1969. Trafalgar House passed by inheritance via the 1 Earl's daughter, Lady Bridport, to the Hood family on her death.
One in ODNB.

Baron Eyre (1768-81 I)

Origins: Descended from a younger son of Giles Eyre of Brickworth (died 1628). To Ireland mid-17th c. Sheriff 1681.

1. Edward Eyre – {Galway 1661-66}
2. John Eyre – {Galway 1661-66}
3. John Eyre – {County Galway 1692-93 1695-99 1703-09}
4. Edward Eyre – {Castlebar 1695-99 Galway 1703-13 1716-27}
5. George Eyre – {Banagher 1703-11}
6. Samuel Eyre – {Galway 1713-14}
7. John Eyre – {County Galway 1713-14 Armagh 1716 27 County Galway 1727-45}
8. John Eyre 1 Baron Eyre – {Galway 1745-60 1761-68}
9. Thomas Eyre – {Thomastown 1761-68 Fore 1768-72}

Seats: Eyre Court (Eyrecourt) Castle, Galway (acq. and built 1660s, sold 1928, ruin by 1940); Uppercourt (Upper Court, Upperwood), Kilkenny (built 17th c., rebuilt late 18th c., remod. early 19th c., purch. mid-19th c., sold c. 1929, institutional use); Eyreville, Galway (acq. late 17th c., resident into 20th c.)
Estates: Bateman 5284 (I) 4809. Worth £1,200 pa in 1713. 4,147 acres worth £2,563 pa in 1854.
Peer: {1 peer 1769-81}
Notes: A second Irish line (Hedges-Eyre) was the issue of a younger brother seated at Macroom Castle, Cork, whose estates eventually passed to the 3 Earl of Bantry (see White II).

EYRE II [Archer, Houblon, Wastneys]

Eyre

Origins: Landowners in the Peak region since the reign of Henry III. **First MP 1459 for Derbyshire.**

1. Anthony Eyre – Nottinghamshire 1661-71
2. Gervase Eyre – Nottinghamshire 1698-1704
3. Anthony Eyre – Boroughbridge 1774-84

4. Anthony Eyre – Nottinghamshire 1803-13

Seats: Rampton Manor, Nottinghamshire (medieval, rebuilt 16th c., acq. by mar. and purch. 1624, demolished c. 1730, new house 1853, sold 1893, demolished 1985); Grove Park (Hall), Nottinghamshire (medieval, add. 16th c., purch. 1762, passed to Harcourt Vernons by mar. 1836)
Estates: 1,400 acres sold in 1893. 1,500 acres at Grove.

Archer Houblon

Origins: Protestant refugees from Flanders arrived in Britain 1567. They gained great wealth in the City. Three brothers were founding Directors of the Bank of England. They became country gentlemen in the mid-18th century. A descendent of Roger Eyre of Holme, Derbyshire, ancestor of the Eyres of Rampton, took the name Archer on inheriting Welford Park. Susannah Archer, heiress to Welford, married Jacob Houblon of Hallingbury. John Archer Houblon's eldest son succeeded to Hallingbury while a younger son, Charles Eyre succeeded to Welford.

1. Sir James Houblon – London 1698-1700
2. William Archer (Eyre) – Berkshire 1734-39
3. Jacob Houblon – Colchester 1735-41 Hertfordshire 1741-47 1761-68
4. John Archer Houblon – Essex 1810-20

Seats: Hallingbury Place, Essex (purch. 1729, built 1771, remod. 19th c., sold and demolished 1926); Welford Park, Berkshire (monastic property, acq. by Jones family 1618 and passed through several families by mar. to the Eyres c. 1706, built c. 1660-70, remod. early 18th c., passed by mar. to the Houblons 1770, still own); Culverthorpe Hall, Lincolnshire (built c. 1680, additions, c. 1704, add. 1734, passed by mar. from the Newton family to the Archer Houblons 1743, sold c. 1900)
Estates: Bateman 15515 (E) 19487; at Welford 6146 (E) 7713 – the Welford estate constituted 3,000 acres in the 1980s. Rubinstein – Susannah Houblon Newton left £500,000 in probate in 1837.
Notes: The Jones who purchased Welford was a Lord Mayor of London in the early 17th c. The Eyre who married the Archer heiress to Welford took the name Archer. A continued complex series of inheritances brought the Culverthorpe and Welford estates together in the possession of the Houblons. Two in ODNB.

Wastneys (Wasteneys)

Origins: The Wastneys emerged in the 13th century. Kts 14th century. **First MP 1450 for Nottinghamshire**. On the death of the 4 Bt his estates went to his great niece who married in 1755 Anthony Eyre of Grove Park (see above).

1. Sir Hardolph Wastneys 4 Bt – East Retford 1706-08

Seat: Headon Park (House), Nottinghamshire (there perhaps by r. Edward III, house rebuilt 1710, demolished 1776)
Estates: Worth £500-600 pa in 1625.
Title: Baronet 1622-1742

EYTON *WALES*

Eyton

Origins: A prominent Flint family descended from the princes of North Wales in the early Middle Ages. One fought at Bosworth. **First MP 1614**.

1. Thomas Eyton – Flint Boroughs 1721-27

Seats: Lower Leeswood (Leeswood Isa), Flintshire (held from at least 1431); Leeswood Hall, Flintshire (built 1724-26, purch. 1798, remod. early 19th c., sold early 20th c.)

Eyton

Origins: Cadet.

1. Kenrick Eyton – Flintshire 1660

Seat: Eyton Hall, Denbighshire

Eyton

Origins: Probably related. **First MP 1614**.

1. Peter Eyton – Flint 1874-78

Seat: Englefield House, Flintshire (built 1830)

FABER

Baron Faber (1905-20 UK)

Origins: 1 Baron Faber's mother was a Beckett of Leeds (see Beckett), and he headed Beckett's Bank.

1. George Faber 1 Baron Wittenham – York 1900-10 Clapham 1910-18
2. Edmund Faber 1 Baron Faber – Andover Div. Hampshire 1901-05
3. Walter Faber – Andover Div. Hampshire 1906-18

Seat: Northaw House, Hertfordshire (built late 18th c., acq. mid-19th c., sold c. 1945)
Title: Baron Wittenham 1918-31 UK
Peers: 2 peers 1905-20 1918-31

FAIRFAX

Viscount Fairfax of Emley (1629-1772 I)

Origins: Began as vintners in York under Richard II. Held manorial property since the 13th century. Acquired Gilling 1492, succeeded by marriage to the Etton family heiress. (*Country Life*, 24, p. 416). **First MP 1324 for Yorkshire. Three further MPs 1542-1626, two for Yorkshire.**

No post-1660 MPs

Seats: Gilling Castle, Yorkshire (acq. and built by Ettons from 1349, acq. by Fairfaxes by mar. 1492, add. 1575-85, add. 1715-25, passed to heirs 1793, sold 1895, school 1929); Walton, Yorkshire (acq. c. 1249, passed to Lane-Fox family c. 1800?)
Peers: {4 peers 1660-1772}
Notes: The family remained Roman Catholic in the 17th and 18th centuries. The 1 Viscount "conformed". Related to Baron Fairfax (see Wykeham). Four in ODNB.

FALKINER *IRELAND*

Origins: Settled in Ireland 1651. Merchants in Cork late 17th century and then moved to Dublin. Sheriff 1721. Lord Mayor of Dublin 1735.

1. Daniel Falkiner – {Baltinglass 1727-59}
2. Sir Riggs Falkiner 1 Bt – {Clonakilty 1768-76 Castle Martyr 1776-83}
3. Sir Frederick Falkiner 1 Bt – {Athy 1791-97 County Dublin 1797-1800} 1801-07 Carlow 1812-18

Seat: Anne Mount (Garryhesty House), Cork (acq. and built late 18th c., add. c. 1883, sold 1945, fire 1948, demolished)
Estates: Held 2247 (I) 1658 in 1878. Worth £900 pa in 1817.
Titles: Baronet 1778- ; 1812-15
Notes: Two in ODNB.

FANSHAWE (Fanshaw)

<u>Viscount Fanshawe</u> (1661-1716 I)

Origins: Yeomen in the 15th century. Built up estates from 1456. A Tudor Clerk of the Exchequer acquired additional estates. **The First MP 1571** became King's Remembrancer in 1568. Five members of the family held the office under the Tudors and Stuarts. **Four additional MPs 1589-1643.**

1. Thomas Fanshawe 1 Viscount Fanshawe – Hertford 1624 1625 Preston 1626 Hertford 1628 1640-42 1644 Hertfordshire 1661-65
2. Sir Richard Fanshawe 1 Bt – University of Cambridge 1661-66
3. Thomas Fanshawe 2 Viscount Fanshawe – Hertford 1661-74
4. Henry Fanshawe – Penryn 1685-87
5. Sir Thomas Fanshawe – Essex 1685-87
6. Charles Fanshawe 4 Viscount Fanshawe – Mitchell 1689
7. Simon Fanshawe – Old Sarum 1751-54 Grampound 1754-68
8. Robert Fanshawe – Plymouth 1784-90
9. Guy Fanshawe – Stirling Div. Stirlingshire & Clackmannanshire 1924-29

Seats: Ware Park, Hertfordshire (purch. 1576, sold 1668); Dengie Hall (Manor), Essex (transferred their main seat to Essex and acq. Dengie later 16th c., rebuilt 1700, rebuilt c. 1820-30, sold 1929); Parsloes, Essex (built 16th c., acq. 1619, add. 17th c. and 1814, leased out post 1858, sold 1917, demolished 1927); Fanshawe Gate (Fanshawegate Hall), Derbyshire (original seat late 14th c., dismantled c. 1660, held estate until c. 1950)
Estates: Worth £4,000 pa. later 16th c.; £4,500 c. 1652. Ware sold in 1668 for £26,000
Title: Baronet 1650-94
Peers: {4 peers 1661-74 1687-1716}
Notes: Became Barons of the Russian Empire. 1 and 2 Viscounts and four others in ODNB.

FARMER [Wilshire]

<u>Farmer</u>

Origins: Dyers in London and then engaged with the East India Company.

1. William Farmer – Huntingdon 1807-09
2. Samuel Farmer – Huntingdon 1809-18

Seat: Nonsuch Park, Surrey (built 1731-43, acq. 1799, rebuilt 1802-06, sold 1937)

Estates: Bateman 9495 (E) 8377. Rubinstein – Samuel Farmer left £120,000 in probate in 1839

Wilshire (Wilshere)

Origins: Yeomen at The Frythe from the r. of Richard II. Gradually worked their way up into the gentry through agricultural success. Purchased estates 1546. Continued to add land into the 18th century. (Duncan Warrand, *Hertfordshire Families, Victoria County History*, London 1907, 243-51) A younger son of the Farmers succeeded to the Wilshire estates through the marriage of his aunt Elizabeth Farmer to Charles Wilshire in 1840.

1. William Wilshire – Great Yarmouth 1837-47

Seat: The Frythe, Hertfordshire (medieval, purch. c. 1550, rebuilt 1846, add. 1867, passed by mar. to Farmers 1934, sold c. 1945)
Estates: Bateman 3449 (E) 6347. Rubinstein – William Wilshere left £140,000 in probate 1824.

FARNHAM

Origins: Minor gentry holding Quorndon since the reign of Edward I. Rose as lawyers and royal servants under the Tudors. **First MP 1553. Two additional MPs 1554-71**.

1. Edward Farnham – N. Leicestershire 1837-59

Seat: Quorndon House, Leicestershire (acq. 13th c., sold 1754)

FARQUHAR [Townshend]

Earl Farquhar (1922-23 UK)

Origins: The 1 Bt (1796) was physician to the Prince of Wales. Colonial governor 1810. Bankers in the 19th century. High Sheriff 1859. Royal Household 1901.

1. Sir Robert Townshend-Farquhar 1 Bt – Newton 1825-26 Hythe 1826-30
2. Sir Walter Townshend-Farquhar 2 Bt – Hertford 1857-59 1865-66
3. Sir Horace Townshend-Farquhar 1 Earl Farquhar – W. Marylebone 1895-98

Seat: Castle Rising Hall, Norfolk (leased 19th and early 20th c., demolished c. 1940)
Estates: Rubinstein – 2 Bt left £120,000 in 1836.

Titles: Baron Farquhar 1898-1923 UK; Viscount Farquhar 1917-23 UK; Baronet 1796- ; 1821-1924; 1892-1923
Peer: 1 peer 1898-1923
Notes: 1 Earl died bankrupt and without a male heir. Four in ODNB.

FARRINGTON (Farington)

Farrington

Origins: Medieval family. Originally gentry at Farrington, Lanacashire. **First MP 1529. Another MP 1640 both for Lancashire**. A branch moved to Chichester later 16th century.

1. John Farrington – Chichester 1660 1679-80
2. Sir Richard Farrington 1 Bt – Chichester 1681 1698-1700 1708-10 1710-13 1715-19

Seat: Farrington House, Sussex (built later 17th c., rebuilt early 18th c. sold 1739 and demolished)
Title: Baronet 1697-1719
Notes: One in ODNB.

Farrington

Origins: Cadet of the Lancashire family. The MP below was a London merchant.

1. Thomas Farrington – Malmesbury 1705-12

FAWKES

Origins: Owned Farnley since the 14th century. Stewards of Knaresborough Forest from the 14th century onwards.

1. Thomas Fawkes – Knaresborough 1689-95
2. Francis Fawkes – Knaresborough 1714-15
3. Walter Fawkes – Yorkshire 1806-07
4. Frederick Fawkes – Pudsey & Otley Div. W. R. Yorkshire 1922-23

Seat: Farnley Hall, Yorkshire (acq. 14th c., built 17th c., rebuilt 1786-90, still own)
Estates: Bateman 11850 (E) 12460. 15,000 acres in 1786.
Notes: One in ODNB.

FEILDEN

Origins: Joseph Feilden, a manufacturer, purchased the manor of Blackburn in the late 18th century. His son entered the gentry. The 1 Bt swelled the family fortune by marrying a Jamaica heiress. High Sheriff 1833.

1. Sir William Feilden 1 Bt – Blackburn 1832-47
2. Montagu Feilden – Blackburn 1853-57
3. Joseph Feilden – Blackburn 1865-69
4. Henry Feilden – Blackburn 1869-75
5. Randle Feilden – N. Lancashire 1880-85 Chorley Div. Lancashire 1885-95

Seats: Witton Park, Lancashire (built 1798, demolished c. 1955); Feniscowles Hall, Lancashire (built 1808, overcome by industrial pollution, ruin)
Estates: Bateman 2611 (E) 7314
Title: Baronet 1846-

FEILDING

<u>Earl of Denbigh</u> (1622- E)

Origins: Claimed, falsely, descent from the Habsburgs. (Carpenter, *Locality and Polity*, 258) Country gentlemen from the 14th century. Kt 1420s. High Sheriff reign of Edward IV. **First MP 1449 for Leicestershire. One additional MP 1614 for Rutland.** The 1 Earl made a fortune by marrying the Duke of Buckingham's sister, which brought him offices and cash.

1. Sir Charles Feilding – {Limerick 1692-93 Duleek 1695-99}
2. William Feilding – Castle Rising 1705-23
3. William Feilding Viscount Feilding – Bere Alston 1780-90 Newport 1790-96

Seats: Newnham Paddox, Warwickshire (purch. 1433, built c. 1600, rebuilt 1754-68, enlarged 1820s, remod. 1876-9, family departed 1939, demolished 1952, still own part of the estate); Martinsthorpe, Rutland (acq. 15th c., sold 1750s)
Estates: Bateman 3218 (E & W) 6340
Titles: Viscount Feilding 1620- E; Earl of Desmond 1622- I; Baron St. Liz 1664- E
Peers: 9 peers 1660-1800 1817-1945
2 Lds Lt 17th, 18th
Notes: The 8 Earl converted to Roman Catholicism. 1 and 2 Earls and five others in ODNB, including the novelist Henry Fielding.

FELLOWES [Benyon, Wrighte]

Baron De Ramsey (1887- UK)

Origins: London merchants in the 17th century. A successful barrister (Master in Chancery 1708) inherited a fortune from an uncle and married an heiress. He acquired estates, continued in the next generation by two sons. (*Country Life*, 142, p. 312)

1. Coulson Fellowes – Huntingdonshire 1741-61
2. William Fellowes – Ludlow 1768-74 Andover 1784-96
3. William Fellowes – Huntingdon 1796-1807 Huntingdonshire 1807-30
4. Edward Fellowes 1 Baron De Ramsey – Huntingdonshire 1837-80
5. William Fellowes 2 Baron De Ramsey – Huntingdonshire 1880-85 Ramsey Div. Huntingdonshire 1885-87
6. Ailwyn Fellowes 1 Baron Ailwyn – Ramsey Div. Huntingdonshire 1887-1906

Seats: Ramsey Abbey, Huntingdonshire (built c. 1539, purch. 1737, rebuilt 1837-39, family departed 1931, donated to NT 1952, school); Abbots Ripton Hall, Huntingdonshire (medieval, purch. 1794, rebuilt c. 1800, add. late 19th c., still own); Felthorpe Hall, Norfolk (built c. 1825, purch. soon afterwards by Fellowes family, sold c. 1900); Haveringland (Haverland) Hall, Norfolk (purch. c. 1762, rebuilt 1839-43, sold c. 1930, demolished 1946)
Estates: Bateman 20021 (E) 26203. Rubinstein – W. H. Fellowes MP left £140,000 in probate in 1837. Worth £2,000 pa in 1732. Owned 15,000 acres worth 95 million pounds in 2001.
Title: Baron Ailwyn 1921-88; Baronet 1718-24
Peers: 3 peers 1887-1925 1921-45 1931-45
1 in Cabinet 1905-06

Fellowes

Origins: The descendents of the younger son of the two sons mentioned above.

1. Robert Fellowes – Norwich 1802-07

Seat: Shotesham Park, Norfolk (acq. 1731, built 1785-88, sold 1979)
Estates: Bateman 7759 (E) 11080
Notes: Two in ODNB.

Benyon

Origins: The Benyons rose as nabobs in the 18th century. Richard Benyon was Governor of Fort St. George. Emma Benyon, daughter and heiress of Richard Benyon, married William Fellowes of Ramsey Abbey. Their eldest son was created 1 Baron De Ramsey. Their second son took the name Benyon and succeeded to Englefield House in 1854.

1. Richard Benyon – Peterborough 1774-96
2. Richard Benyon De Beauvoir – Pontefract 1801-06 Wallingford 1806-12
3. Richard Benyon – Berkshire 1860-76
4. William Benyon – Buckingham Div. Buckinghamshire 1970-83 Milton Keynes 1983-92
5. Richard Benyon – Newbury 2005-

Seats: Englefield House, Berkshire (built c. 1558, remod. 1820s, acq. by mar. 1789, still own); Gidea Hall, Essex (built c. 15-16 c., rebuilt c. 1720, purch. 1745, sold 1802, demolished c. 1930); Ufton Court, Berkshire
Estates: Bateman 16007 (E) 20004. Rubinstein – Peter Beauvoir, not a blood relative, left Richard Benyon £720,000 in 1822 including a large London estate. Owned 19,650 acres worth 125 million pounds in 2001.
2 Lds Lt 20th
Notes: Richard Benyon, who inherited Englefield from his half-brother Paulet Wrighte, also succeeded to his grandmother's parents' estates (Tyssens in Hackney and the Beauvoirs of Downham, Essex and Culford, Essex). He married the daughter of another nabob, Sir Francis Sykes of Basildon, thus merging four fortunes. Englefield originally belonged to the Marquess of Winchester (purch. 1635). It passed to a younger son, Lord Francis Paulet. He left it to his daughter Anne who married Nathan Wrighte. He died in 1789, and it devolved on Richard Benyon and his wife, Wrighte. They took the names Paulet Wrighte.

Wrighte

Origins: Sir Nathan Wrighte was the son and grandson of clergymen. He was a Clerk of the Crown in Chancery, Keeper of the Great Seal, and Speaker of the House of Lords without being an MP or peer. His son was the first MP. The son of the Benyon nabob married the mother of Paulet Wrighte, son of her second marriage. Benyon's son succeeded his half-brother to the Wrighte estates.

1. George Wrighte – Leicester 1727-66

Seats: Gayhurst House, Buckinghamshire (purch. 1704); Brooksby Hall, Leicestershire; Caldecote Hall, Warwickshire (built 1st half 17th c.?); Englefield House, Berkshire (acq. by mar., owned by Wrightes 1729-1789, passed to Benyons 1789, see above)
Notes: Spent £50,000 on land in the early 18th century. The last Wrighte heiress died in 1830. Two in ODNB.

FELTON

Origins: Merchants who acquired manorial land in the 15th century. Bt 1620.

1. Sir Henry Felton 2 Bt – Suffolk 1656 1659 1661-79
2. Sir Adam Felton 3 Bt – Orford 1695-97
3. Sir Thomas Felton 4 Bt – Orford 1690-1700 Bury St. Edmunds 1701-09

Seat: Playford Hall, Suffolk (acq. by mar. and built c. 1590, passed by mar. to Hervey family 1719, sold 1951)
Estates: Worth £797 pa in 1637.
Title: Baronet 1620-1719
Notes: Estates passed to the wife of John Hervey, 1 Earl of Bristol (see Hervey), daughter of the 4 Bt, after the death of the last Baronet in 1719. One in ODNB.

FENWICK [Loraine, Smith]

Fenwick

Origins: The family held land in Northumberland since the 13th century. **First MP 1378 for Northumberland. Five further MPs 1431-1656, four kts of the shire**. Bt 1628.

1. Sir William Fenwick 2 Bt – Northumberland 1645 1654 1656 1659 1660-76
2. Sir John Fenwick 3 Bt – Northumberland 1677-81 1685-87
3. Roger Fenwick – Morpeth 1689-95
4. John Fenwick – Northumberland 1741-47

Seats: Wallington, Northumberland (medieval castle, acq. by Strother family 1326, passed by mar. to Fenwicks r. Henry IV, new house mid-16th c., sold 1684 to Blacketts); Stanton Hall, Northumberland (medieval, acq. c. 1530, sold 1730); Bywell Hall (Castle), Northumberland (medieval castle, purch. 1630, remod. 1670, passed out of family by mar. 1809, sold 1820)
Estates: owned c. 20,000 acres c. 1600
Title: Baronet 1628-97
Notes: Attainted 1697. Four in ODNB.

Loraine Smith

Origins: The Loraines claimed ancient ancestry. Emerged in the 15th century as gentry. Bankers in the 19th century.

1. Sir William Loraine 2 Bt – Northumberland 1701-02
2. Charles Loraine Smith – Leicester 1784-90

Seats: Kirkharle Hall, Northumberland (acq. by mar. c. 1400, sold 1834, reduced to a farm house); Styford Hall, Northumberland (built c. 1800)
Estates: In 1834 2,000-3,000 acres. 12 Bt died worth £505,000 in 1961.
Title: Baronet 1664-1961
Notes: 1 Baronet mar. Fenwick heiress. 12 Bt in ODNB.

Fenwick

Origins: Son of Roger Fenwick MP (above) succeeded to Burrow by marriage to a Tatham heiress. He was a successful lawyer. His son was a London barrister.

1. Robert Fenwick – Lancaster 1734-47
2. Thomas Fenwick – Westmorland 1768-74
3. Edward Fenwick – Lancaster 1864

Seats: Burrow Hall, Lancashire (built early 17th c., acq. by mar. 1686, c. 1740, sold 1945); Nunriding, Northumberland (acq. 16th c., rebuilt 17th c., remod. mid-18th c., sold 1839); Claughton Hall (Lonsdale), Lancashire (built 1570-1606, purch. 1702, sold 1898)
Estates: Bateman 4057 (E) 4938
Notes: Estates passed by marriage to the Wilsons of Westmorland who took the name Fenwick, and through an illegitimate daughter, mother of the last MP.

FERGUSON *SCOTLAND*

Origins: Rose through law and business. First MP was a ballie. The second MP was the son of a judge.

1. William Ferguson – [Inverurie 1661-63]
2. James Ferguson – Banffshire 1789-90 Aberdeenshire 1790-1820
3. George Ferguson – Banffshire – 1832-37

Seat: Pitfour House, Aberdeenshire (purch. and built 1764, add. c. 1809, demolished 1927); Inverugie Castle, Aberdeenshire (medieval, rebuilt c. 1660, acq. c. 1746, abandoned 1820, ruin by 1890, demolished 1899)

Estates: Bateman 23150 (S) 19938
Notes: Two in ODNB.

FERGUSSON (Ferguson) *SCOTLAND*

Fergusson

Origins: Old family in Dumfriesshire. At Craigdarroch since at least the 15th century. **First [MP 1640 for Dumfriesshire]**.

1. Robert Fergusson – [Dumfriesshire 1649-51 1661-63 1665 1667 1669-74 1678]
2. Alexander Ferguson – Dumfries Burghs 1715-22
3. Robert Cutlar-Fergusson – Kirkcudbrightshire 1826-38

Seats: Craigdarroch, Dumfriesshire (acq. 15th c., rebuilt 1726-29, add. 1840, fire 1946, repaired); Orraland House, Kirkcudbrightshire (medieval, acq. by mar. 1769 to Cutlar heiress - owners since the 16th c., declined into farm house, new Lodge built 1897, sold 1921)
Estates: Bateman 3803 (S) 3462
Notes: Male line extinct 1900 and estates broken up among multiple heiresses.

Ferguson

Origins: Cadet family.

1. Alexander Ferguson – [Dumfriesshire 1703-07]

Seat: Isle Tower, Dumfriesshire (built 1414, acq. 1580, built 1589, add. mid-18th c., add. 1806, remod. 1882, sold 19th c. or 1955?)

FETHERSTONHAUGH (Fetherston) *ENGLAND & IRELAND*

Fetherstonhaugh

Origins: Medieval gentry. **First MP 1621. One other MP 1621**.

1. Thomas Fetherstonhaugh – County Durham 1679 1681

Seat: Stanhope Hall, Durham (medieval, acq. by mar., built 16th/17th c., sold c. 1704)
Notes: Extinct in male line 1704.

Fetherstonhaugh

Origins: In Newcastle in the 17th century (Mayor 1711) and then London merchants in the 18th century.

1. Sir Matthew Fetherstonhaugh 1 Bt – Morpeth 1755-61 Portsmouth 1761-74
2. Sir Henry Fetherstonhaugh 2 Bt – Portsmouth 1782-96

Seats: Uppark, Sussex (built 16th c., rebuilt c. 1690-94, purch. 1747, remod. 1751 and 1810-13, passed 1893 to Turnors and in 1931 to the Meades, NT 1954, fire 1989, rebuilt 1990-95); Featherstone Castle, Northumberland (medieval, rebuilt early 17th c., purch. 1st half 18th c., sold 1766)
Estates: 5983 (E) 5558. Worth £400,000 in the mid-18th century.
Titles: Baronet 1660-1746; 1747-1846
Notes: The last Fetherstonhaugh of Uppark left his estates to the younger son of an old friend, Kieth Turnour, who took the name Fetherstonhaugh. Through him, again no blood relation, Uppark passed to a younger son of the 4 Earl Clanwilliam (see Meade), who also took the name Fetherstonhaugh. Pronounced "fanshaw".

Fetherstonhaugh

Origins: Cousins.

1. Godfrey Fetherstonhaugh – N. Femanagh 1906-16

Seat: Glenmore, Mayo (purch. 1853, sold 20th c.)
Estates: Bateman 10277 (I) 2381. Cousins at Rockview, Westmeath 3148 (I) 2868

Fetherston

Origins: Cadet to Ireland in the 1650s.

1. Sir Ralph Fetherston 1 Bt – {County Longford 1765-68 St. Johnstown 1768-80}
2. Sir Thomas Fetherston 2 Bt – {St. Johnstown 1783-90 County Longford 1796-1800} 1801-19
3. Sir George Fetherston 3 Bt – County Longford 1819-30

Seat: Ardagh House, Longford (acq. and built late 17th c., add. early-mid-19th c., sold 20th c., institutional use)
Estates: Bateman 8711 (I) 5606. Worth £7,000 pa in 1800. Bracklyn Castle, Westmeath 4711 (I) 2583
Title: Baronet 1776-1923

FFOLKES [Howell]

Ffolkes

Origins: An eminent lawyer acquired Hillington by marriage to a Howell heiress. His son was a barrister. His son was the 1 Bt.

1. Sir Martin Ffolkes 1 Bt – Kings Lynn 1790-1821
2. Sir William Ffolkes 2 Bt – Norfolk 1830-32 W. Norfolk 1832-37
3. Sir Wiliam Ffolkes 3 Bt – Kings Lynn 1880-85

Seat: Hillington Hall, Norfolk (acq. by mar. to later 18th c., rebuilt 1824-30, part demolished 1946, estate passed to Dawnays)
Estates: Bateman 8111 (E) 10139
Title: Baronet 1774-
Notes: One in ODNB.

Howell

Origins: Old family in Norfolk. Kt 14th century.

1. Sir William Howell – Kings Lynn 1661-70

Seat: Hillington Hall, Norfolk (purch. 1610, built 1627, passed to Ffolkes later 18th c.)

FFOLLIOTT (Folliott) *IRELAND*

Baron Ffolliott (1620-1716 I)

Origins: Old Worcestershire family. Bishop of Hereford 1149. Held manorial land from 1346. **First MP 1363**. To Ireland as a soldier, Kt 1599. Granted lands 1611. **First {MP 1613}**. Baron 1620.

1. John Ffolliott – {Ballyshannon 1692-93}
2. Francis Ffolliott – {Ballyshannon 1692-93 1695-99}
3. Henry Ffolloitt 3 Baron Ffolliott – {Ballyshannon 1695-97}
4. John Ffolliott – {Longford 1721-27 Granard 1727-60 Sligo 1761-62}
5. John Ffolliott – {Donegal 1730-60 Kinsale 1761-65}
6. John Ffolliott – County Sligo 1841-50

Seats: Hollybrook House, Sligo (acq. 1659, built 1660s, passed to Harloes via an heiress late 17th c., rebuilt c. 1756, repurch. 19th c., sold 1945); Ballyshannon House, Donegal

(acq. 1613, sold 1718); Wardtown Castle, Donegal (acq. 1613, built 1739-40, abandoned by family later 18th c., ruined 1920s, sold 1933); Four Oaks Hall, Warwickshire (acq. and built 1696, remod. 1740, sold 1744).
Estates: Bateman 7424 (I) 3142
Peers: {2 peers 1660-1716}
Notes: The 3 Lord Ffolliott married a Warwickshire heiress 1696 and established a large English estate to add to his Irish lands. English estates sold in 1744. Two in ODNB.

FIELDEN

Origins: The founder was the son of a yeoman. His son established a cotton factory (he left £200 at his death, Rubinstein, *Men of Property*, 141) where his son, the first MP, began as a spinner. Between 1811 and 1830 it became the largest textile factory in Britain.

1. John Fielden – Oldham 1832-47
2. Joshua Fielden – E. Div. W. R. Yorkshire 1868-80
3. Thomas Fielden – Middleton Div. Lancashire 1886-92 1895-97
4. Edward Fielden – Middleton Div. Lancashire 1900-06 Exchange Div. Manchester 1924-35

Seats: Grimston Park, Yorkshire (old house, rebuilt c. 1840, add. c. 1850, purch. 1872 for £240,000, sold c. 1960, flats); Dobroyd Castle, Lancashire (purch. and built 1865-69, sold c. 1940, institutional use); Nutfield Priory, Surrey (built 1849-54, add. 1855-59, purch. 1866, rebuilt 1870-74, sold 1920, now hotel); Mollington Hall, Cheshire (rebuilt 1756-57, purch. 1796, sold 1906, demolished 1937)
Estates: Bateman 3379 (E) 9000. The first MP left £95,000 in 1849. The second MP left £500,000 in 1887.
Notes: Two in ODNB.

FIENNES

Viscount Saye and Sele (1624-1781 E)

Origins: Claimed to have come over with the Conqueror. Authentic descent from the Norman Counts of Boulogne, prominent under Edward I, whose second wife, Margaret of France, was their kinswomen (Roskell, Clark, and Rawcliffe, *The House of Commons*, III, 71). Summoned to Parliament 1294. Kt 1290s. High Sheriff 1297. Baron 1447. **First MP 1416 for Sussex** fought at Agincourt. **Seven additional MPs 1447-1656, six kts of the shire.**

1. James Fiennes 2 Viscount Saye and Sele – Banbury 1625 Oxfordshire 1626 1628 1640-48 1660
2. Sir Eustace Twisleton-Wykeham-Fiennes 1 Bt – Banbury Div. Oxfordshire 1906-18

Seat: Broughton Castle, Oxfordshire (built c. 1300, purch. 1377 by Wykehams, add. 1406, passed to Fiennes by mar. 1457, add. 1551-4 and 1599, remod. 1780s, restored 1860-85 and 1980s, still own)
Estates: Bateman 6855 (E) 12521
Titles: Baron Saye and Sele (1447-1781, 1603-abeyant 1674, revived 1715- E)
Peers: 13 peers 1661-62 1663-74 1675-96 1699-1788 1795-1844 1846-1945
1 Ld Lt 17th
Notes: The 2 Baron married in 1451 Margaret Wykeham, heiress of Broughton. William of Wykeham was Chancellor of England 1368-71 and 1389-91. The family produced **two MPs 1402-42**. (see Wykeham). The daughter of the 2 Viscount married John Twisleton of Barley, Yorkshire. Their daughter succeeded as Baroness Saye and Sele in her own right. Her son succeeded in 1723 as 11 Baron. A Cromwellian peer. 1 Baron and 1 Viscount and four others in ODNB.

FILMER

Origins: Gentry in medieval period. Purchased Sutton and Kt and official under Elizabeth I. 1 Baronet a barrister.

1. Sir John Filmer 4 Bt – Steyning 1767-74
2. Sir Edmund Filmer 8 Bt – W. Kent 1838-57
3. Sir Edmund Filmer 9 Bt – W. Kent 1859-65 Mid Kent 1880-84

Seat: East Sutton Place (Park), Kent (built 1570, purch. and rebuilt 1610-12, family departed 1939, sold 1945, institutional use)
Estates: Bateman 6608 (E) 9395. Rubinstein – 6 Bt left £100,000 probate in 1810 and Willian Filmer left £120,000 in 1830.
Title: Baronet 1674-1916
Note: Possible **kinsman MP 1701**. Estates passed via an heiress to the Wilsons in 1916 (see Wilson). Male line extinct 1916. Two in ODNB.

FINCH [Banks, Fisher, Hatton]

<u>Earl of Winchilsea</u> (1628- E) and <u>Earl of Nottingham</u> (1681- E)

Origins: Owned manorial land including an ironworks in Sussex from the 1340s. Built up a large fortune by the 16th century and purchased more land after the Dissolution. Married the Moyle heiress to Eastwell in 1547. Rose to great eminence in the 17th century as Speaker of the House of Commons 1626 and held legal office including Lord Privy Seal 1673. **First MP 1485. Eight additional MPs 1572-1642.**

1. Heneage Finch 1 Earl of Nottingham – Canterbury 1660 University of Oxford 1661-73
2. Francis Finch – Winchilsea 1661-77
3. Daniel Finch 2 Earl of Nottingham and 7 Earl of Winchilsea – Great Bedwyn 1673-81
4. William Finch – Great Bedwyn 1679-81
5. Heneage Finch 5 Earl of Winchilsea – Hythe 1685
6. Daniel Finch 8 Earl of Winchilsea and 3 Earl of Nottingham – Rutland 1710-30
7. Henry Finch – Malton 1724-61
8. John Finch – Higham Ferrers 1724-41 Rutland 1741-47
9. William Finch – Cockermouth 1727-54 Bewdley 1755-61
10. Edward Finch-Hatton – University of Cambridge 1727-68
11. George Finch-Hatton – Rochester 1772-84
12. George Finch – Lymington 1820-21 Stamford 1832-37 Rutland 1846-47
13. George Finch-Hatton 11 Earl of Winchilsea and 6 Earl of Nottingham – N. Northamptonshire 1837-41
14. George Finch – Rutland 1867-1907
15. Murray Finch-Hatton 12 Earl of Winchilsea and 7 Earl of Nottingham – S. Lincolnshire 1884-85 Holland & Spalding Div. Lincolnshire 1885-87
16. Harold Finch-Hatton – Newark Div. Nottinghamshire 1895-98

Seats: Eastwell Park, Kent (acq. by mar. 1547, add. 1611, rebuilt 1793-1800, add. 1849, leased out from 1868, sold 1918, fire and demolished 1926, rebuilt 1926-28, hotel); Charlewood, Hertfordshire; The Moat (The Mote), Kent (acq. by mar. c. 1500, sold c. 1700); Kirby Hall, Northamptonshire (built 1570, remod. 1575-80s, add. 1677, inher. by Finches by mar 1762, fell into disuse by 1810s, ruin by 1889, acq. by state 1930); Burley-on-the-Hill, Rutland (purch. 1694 for £50,000 and 30,000 spent on building – Lees-Milne, *English Country Houses: Baroque 1685-1715*, 112, 118 – built 1696-1700, principal seat until 1826, fire 1908, passed by mar. to Hanburys in 1939, sold 1990, flats, still own estate); Haverholme Priory, Lincolnshire (medieval monastic building, add. 1788, passed by mar. 1831, became principal seat 1827, rebuilt 1830-35, sold and demolished 1927)
Estates: Bateman 19396 (E) 29055; Burley line 17332 (E) 28443
Titles: Viscount Maidstone 1623- E; Baron Fitzherbert 1660-1729 E; Baron Finch 1674- E; Baronet 1611- ; 1660-
Peers: 13 peers 1660-89 1673-1769 1693-1712 1726-30 1783-1945
3 Lds Lt 17th, 18th, 19th
4 in Cabinet 1673-82 1681-84 1689-93 1702-04 1711-12 1714-16 1742-44 1757 1765-66
2 KG 18th, 19th

Notes: The wife of Sir Moyle Finch 1 Bt, Elizabeth Heneage (see that family), was created 1 Countess of Winchilsea in her own right. (One Heneage **MP in this line 1629.**) Their eldest son succeeded as 2 Earl. On the death of the 6 Earl the line became extinct and the title passed to a descendent of the 1 Bt's younger son, Sir Heneage Finch, whose son had been created Earl of Nottingham. The titles were merged in 1729 when the 2 Earl of Nottingham succeeded as 7 Earl of Winchilsea. In 1826 the illegitimate son of the 9 Earl of Winchilsea and 4 Earl of Nottingham inherited Burley-on-the-Hill and almost half the family estates. 3, 7, 9, 10 and 12 Earls of Winchilsea and 1 Earl of Nottingham and thirteen others in ODNB.

Viscount Hatton (1683-1762 E)

Origins: The Hattons were an old Cheshire gentry family who in the late-15th c. century acquired Holdenby, Northamptonshire by marriage to an heiress whose family had held it since the 13th century. An Elizabethan courtier became a royal favorite and acquired further land. Kt 1577. Lord Chancellor 1587. **First MP 1571. Five further MPs 1586-1645.** The 7 Earl of Winchilsea married Anne daughter and heiress of Christopher, Viscount Hatton and the estates eventually passed to a younger brother of the 9 Earl who took the additional name Hatton, and then to the 10 Earl.

1. Christopher Hatton 1 Viscount Hatton – Northampton 1663-70
2. Sir Thomas Hatton 2 Bt – Cambridgeshire 1674-79

Seats: Kirby Hall, Northamptonshire (built 1570-75, purch. 1576, remod. 1580s and 1575-80s, passed by inher. to Finch family 1762, see above); Holdenby, Northamptonshire (acq. by mar. late 15th c., rebuilt 1571-83, passed to the Crown 1607, dismantled mid-17th c.); Longstanton (Long Stanton), Cambridgeshire (acq. and built from 1570s, demolished 1851, sold 1874)
Estates: Worth £1,370 pa in 1660s. See Earls of Winchilsea.
Title: Baron Hatton 1643-1762 E
Peers: 4 peers 1660-1706 1711-62
Notes: A cadet line was seated at Longstanton, Baronets 1641-1812 (owned 1,700 acres in the 19th c.). 1 Baron and 1 Viscount and one other in ODNB.

Earl of Aylesford (1714- GB)

Origins: The 1 Earl of Aylesford was a younger son of the 1 Earl of Nottingham.

1. Heneage Finch 1 Earl of Aylesford – University of Oxford 1679
2. Edward Finch – University of Cambridge 1690-95
3. Heneage Finch 2 Earl of Aylesford – Maidstone 1704-05 Surrey 1710-19
4. John Finch – Maidstone 1722-40

5. Heneage Finch 3 Earl of Aylesford – Leicestershire 1739-41 Maidstone 1741-47 1754-57
6. Savile Finch – Maidstone 1757-61 Malton 1761-80
7. Heneage Finch 4 Earl of Aylesford – Castle Rising 1772-74 Maidstone 1774-77
8. Charles Finch – Castle Rising 1775-77 Maidstone 1777-80
9. Edward Finch – Cambridge 1789-1819
10. William Finch – Surrey 1790-94
11. Heneage Finch 5 Earl of Aylesford – Weobley 1807-12
12. Heneage Finch 6 Earl of Aylesford – S. Warwickshire 1849-57

Seats: Packington Hall, Warwickshire (built late 17th c., acq. by mar. 1739, enlarged house 1763-81, fire 1979, still own); The Friars, Aylesford, Kent (acq. by mar. 1699, leased out, fire 1930, repaired, sold 1949, institutional use)
Estates: Bateman 19581 (E) 32620. Rubinstein – 4 Earl left £200,000 probate in 1812. Own 5,000 acres today.
Title: Baron Guernsey 1703- E
Peers: 10 peers 1703-19 1721-1945
1 in Cabinet 1714-16
Notes: 1 Earl and two others in ODNB.

Banks

Origins: Founded by a woolen draper in London in the later 16th century. The 1 Bt was one of the richest merchants in England in the Restoration period. Elizabeth, daughter and heiress of Sir John Banks 1 Bt, married the 1 Earl of Aylesford, who inherited the Banks fortune of between £170,000 and £200,000 in 1699.

1. Sir John Banks 1 Bt – Maidstone 1654-55 1656-58 1659 Winchelsea 1678 Rochester 1679-81 1685-87 1689-90
2. Caleb Banks – Queenborough 1685-87 Maidstone 1689-90 Rochester 1691-95 Queenborough 1695-96

Seat: The Friars, Aylesford, Kent (medieval, remod. 16th c., purch. 1657, remod. 1670s, passed to Finches 1699)
Estates: Worth £600 pa in 1640s. The Banks lent the government £340,000 between 1660-99. The 1 Bt was worth £5,000 pa in land and c. £180,000 in liquid assets in 1699.
Title: Baronet 1661-99

Fisher

Origins: John Fisher who purchased Packington and built the house after the Dissolution was an official and courtier. **First MP 1584**. Mary Fisher, the daughter and heiress of the 3 Bt, married the 2 Earl of Aylesford, who inherited Packington on the extinction of the Fisher family in 1739.

1. Sir Clement Fisher 2 Bt – Coventry 1661-79

Seat: Packington Hall, Warwickshire (acq. 1540s, built house mid -16th c., new house 1670s, rebuilt 1690s, passed to Finch family 1739)
Title: Baronet 1622-1739

FITZCLARENCE

Earl of Munster (1831- UK)

Origins: The 1 Earl was an illegitimate son of King William IV and the actress Mrs. Jordan.

No MPs

Seat: Sandhills, Surrey
Peers: 5 peers 1831-1945
Notes: 1 Earl and two others in ODNB.

FITZGERALD I [De Ros, Deane, Grogan, Petty-Fitzmaurice] *IRELAND & ENGLAND*

Duke of Leinster (1766- I)

Origins: The Geraldines (including the Earls of Desmond and Kildare) were a great Anglo-Norman family that arrived in Ireland 1168. Four served as Justiciar between 1232-1356. Premier Earls of Ireland. **1st MP for an English seat 1563. First {MP 1614}. Two further {MPs 1634-39}.**

1. Wentworth Fitzgerald 17 Earl of Kildare – East Retford 1660
2. Robert Fitzgerald – {County Kildare 1661-66 1692-93 1695-98}
3. George Fitzgerald – {County Kildare 1692-93 1695-98}
4. John Fitzgerald 18 Earl of Kildare – Tregony 1694-95
5. James Fitzgerald 1 Duke of Leinster – {Athy 1741-44}
6. William Fitzgerald 2 Duke of Leinster – {Dublin 1767-73}
7. Charles Fitzgerald 1 Baron Lecale – {County Kildare 1776-90 Cavan 1790-97 Ardfert 1798-1800} Arundel 1807
8. Lord Edward Fitzgerald – {Athy 1783-90 County Kildare 1790-97}
9. Lord Henry Fitzgerald – {Kildare 1783-90 Dublin 1790-97} County Kildare 1807-14

10. Lord Robert Fitzgerald – County Kildare 1802-07
11. Lord William Fitzgerald – County Kildare 1814-31
12. Charles Fitzgerald 4 Duke of Leinster – County Kildare 1847-52
13. Lord Otho Fitzgerald – County Kildare 1865-74

Seats: Carton, Kildare (acq. early Middle Ages, built 17th c., add. 1739, add. 1776, add. 1815, sold 1949, hotel); Kilkea Castle, Kildare (acq. c. 1200 and built castle, moved seat to Carton in the 18th c., restored 1849, sold c. 1960, hotel); Frascati, Dubin (built mid-18th c., add. 1770s, demolished 1981-83); Ballyragget House (Castle), Kilkenny (acq. and built castle 1495, sold 1788); Grangemellon, Kildare; Caversham Park, Oxfordshire (leased in the 17th and 18th centuries)
Estates: Bateman 73100 (I) 55877. Worth £36,000 pa in 1804 but many debts. Owned no land in 2001
Titles: Earl of Kildare 1316- I; Baron Offaly 1620- I; Viscount Leinster 1747- GB; Marquess of Kildare 1761- I; Baron Lecale 1800-10 I; Baron Kildare 1870- UK
Peers: {5 peers 1661-64 1695-1800} 7 peers 1747-1804 1813-74 1870-93 1908-1945
3 Lds Lt 19th, 20th
1 KP 18th-19th
Notes: Leinster House in Dublin is now the home of the Irish Parliament. In an extraordinary episode of financial ineptitude the family estates were lost beginning in the early 20th century. 1, 2, 4, 7, 8, 9, 10, 11, 16 Earls and 1 and 2 Dukes and twenty-four others (including the Desmonds) in ODNB.

Grogan

Origins: John Grogan (1653-1720) married the heiress to Johnstown and succeeded 1682. Granted arms 1757. Sheriff 1746. In the 19th century a Grogan heiress married Lord Maurice Fitzgerald, son of the Duke of Leinster, and he succeeded to Johnstown.

1. John Grogan – {Enniscorthy 1761-68}
2. Cornelius Grogan – {Enniscorthy 1768-76}
3. Hamilton Grogan-Morgan 1 Bt – County Wexford 1841-68

Seat: Johnstown Castle, Wexford (tower house, acq. by 1682, new house built late 17th c., rebuilt 1810, add. c. 1840, donated to the state 1945)
Estates: Bateman 15215 (I) 8840. Worth £6,000 to £7,000 pa in 1798.
Title: Baronet 1859-1923
Notes: A cadet line descended from John Grogan (above) gained a baronetcy 1859-1923. One in ODNB, Cornelieus Grogan, hanged for participating in the 1798 rebellion.

<u>Baron De Ros</u> (1264 or 1299- E)

Origins: The medieval title eventually passed, after descent through a number of families (including the Earls of Rutland and Dukes of Buckingham), to Charlotte Manners Baroness De Ros in her own right who married in 1791 Lord Henry Fitzgerald, younger son of the 1 Duke of Leinster.

1. Henry Fitzgerald-De Ros 21 Baron De Ros – West Looe 1816-18

Seat: Old Court, Down (acq. and built mid-19th c., burned c. 1920, family still resident in a rebuilt house)
Estates: Bateman 4223 (I) 5014
Peers: 3 peers 1831-1907
Notes: 4 KGs 14th-16th c.

<u>Knight of Kerry</u> (1259- I)

Origins: The Knights of Kerry and Glin and the White Knight (designated by Charter from 1259) descended from John FitzThomas ancestor of the attainted Earls of Desmond. **First {MP 1585 for County Kerry}. An additional {MP for Kerry 1634 and another MP 1640}.**

1. John Fitzgerald 15th Knight of Kerry – {Dingle 1728-41}
2. Robert Fitzgerald 17th Knight of Kerry – (Dingle 1741-81}
3. Maurice Fitzgerald 16th Knight of Kerry – {Dingle 1761-76}
4. Maurice Fitzgerald 18th Knight of Kerry – {County Kerry 1795-1800} 1801-31

Seats: Glanleam House, Kerry (leased and built 1775, purch. 1807, new house, 1820, sold 1935); Buckland, Berkshire (rebuilt 1755-9, purch. 1908, enlarged 1910, family departed 1947, sold by descendents 1963); Ballinruddery Castle (House), Kerry (built 15-16 c., forfeited 1637, regained 1665, ruin, house occupied, became seat c. 1821, fire c. 1850, family departed c. 1870); Rahinane Castle, Kerry (built 15th c., principal seat through late 17th / early 18th c., ruin by mid-18th c.); Thurlough Park, Mayo (cadet line, acq. and built c. 1656, new house 1866, sold 1970s?)
Estates: Bateman 16425 (I) 7629
Title: Baronet 1880-
1 in Cabinet 1828-30
Notes: Conformed to state church 1703. The 18th Knight married a banking LaTouche heiress, and the 19th Knight went into the bank. 18, 19 Knights and one other in ODNB.

Knight of Glin (1259-2011 I)

Origins: See Knight of Kerry.

1. Gerald Fitzgerald 17th Knight of Glin – {Limerick 1661-66}
2. Richard Fitzgerald 21st Knight of Glin – {Boyle 1763-76}

Seats: Glin Castle, Limerick (acq. c. 1200, old castle, castle abandoned and house built c. 1675, burned 1740, rebuilt 1780-89, remod. 1820-36, for sale 2015); Castle Ishen (Castleishen House), Cork (acq. c. 1660, cadet line in residence 19th c.)
Estates: Bateman 13547 (I) 13606. Owned less than 700 acres in 2001.
Title: Baronet 1644-91
Notes: Conformed to the Established Church in the 17th century. The male line became extinct with the death of the 29th Knight, Desmond Fitzgerald, ardent leader of the campaign to preserve Ireland's architectural heritage, in 2011. Castle Ishen line extinct 1894.

Baron Fitzgerald (1826-60 I; 1835-43 UK)

Origins: Descended from the White Knight (see Knight of Kerry). James Fitzgerald, a lawyer and son of an attorney in Ennis, married Catherine Vesey. She was created Baroness Fitzgerald in her own right in 1826. Their son was created Baron Fitzgerald. (see Vesey)

1. James Fitzgerald – {Fore 1776-83 Tulsk 1783-97 Kildare 1798-1800} Ennis 1802-08 1812-13
2. William Vesey-Fitzgerald 2 Baron Fitzgerald – Ennis 1808-12 1813-18 County Clare 1818-28 Newport 1829-30 Losthwithiel 1830 Ennis 1831-32
3. William Vesey-Fitzgerald – Horsham 1848 1852-65 1874-75

Seats: Inchicronan, Clare (resident 18th and 19th c.); Croagh, Limerick (purch. by 2 Baron for William V-F); Moyriesk (Mooreask), Clare (built mid-18th c., purch. late 18th c., remod. mid-19th c., passed by mar. to Fosters later 19th c., sold 1932, most demolished); Moyvane, Kerry (acq. 1830s, sold post 1924, demolished); Holbrook House, Sussex (resident 19th c.)
Estates: 2482 (I) 1315 in 1878. The 2 Baron died 1843 worth at least £150,000.
Peer: 1 peer 1835-43
1 in Cabinet 1812-16 1828-30 1841-43
Notes: Letitia Vesey-Fitzgerald, sister of the 2 Baron married John Foster, nephew of Lord Oriel (see Skeffington). Their son was William Foster Vesey-Fitzgerald. William Vesey-Fitzgerald MP 1848-75 above was the illegitimate son of the 2 Baron Fitzgerald. Four in ODNB.

Marquess of Lansdowne (1784- GB)

Origins: A cadet of the Geraldines, the Lords of Kerry were great chieftains in the Middle Ages. Attended the Parliament in Dublin 1295. The 20 Baron Kerry (family name Fitzmaurice) also 1 Earl of Kerry married in 1692 Anne Petty, sister of Charles and Henry Petty, Lords Shelburne. The eldest son inherited the Earldom of Kerry, £300,000, and estates in England. The younger son took the name Petty and was created Earl of Shelburne, from who the Marquesses of Lansdowne descend. On the death of the 3 Earl of Kerry in 1818, the titles were merged, and the family took the name Petty-Fitzmaurice. Sir William Petty MP 1658 was the son of a Hampshire clothier. **First MP 1628**. He began as a merchant, then an Oxford professor of anatomy. He went to Ireland as a land surveyor and official and acquired large amounts of property. He assembled an estate of c. 270,000 acres in County Kerry after the Civil War. (*A Landlord's Garden: Derreen Demesne, County Kerry*, sec. ed., 8)

1. Sir William Petty – West Looe 1658 {Innistioge 1661-66}
2. Edmund Petty – Chipping Wycombe 1660
3. Thomas Fitzmaurice 1 Earl of Kerry – {County Kerry 1692-93 1695-97}
4. William Fitzmaurice – {Dingle 1692-93 1695-99 1703-11}
5. Henry Petty – {County Waterford 1695-99}
6. Henry Petty 1 Baron Shelburne – {Midleton 1692-93 County Waterford 1695-99} Great Marlow 1715-22 Chipping Wycombe 1722-27
7. John Petty 1 Earl of Shelburne – {County Kerry 1743-51} Chipping Wycombe 1754-60
8. William Petty 1 Marquess of Lansdowne – {County Kerry 1761} Chipping Wycombe 1760-61
9. John Petty 2 Marquess of Lansdowne – Chipping Wycombe 1786-1802
10. Henry Petty-Fitzmaurice 3 Marquess of Lansdowne – Calne 1802-06 University of Cambridge 1806-07 Camelford 1807-09
11. William Petty-Fitzmaurice Earl of Kerry – Calne 1832-36
12. Henry Petty-Fitzmaurice 4 Marquess of Lansdowne – Calne 1837-56
13. Edmund Petty-Fitzmaurice 1 Baron Fitzmaurice – Calne 1868-85 Cricklade Div. Wiltshire 1898-1905
14. Henry Petty-Fitzmaurice 6 Marquess of Lansdowne – W. Derbyshire 1908-18

Seats: Bowood, Wiltshire (built early 18th c., purch. 1754, rebuilt 1755-64 and 1768-71, remod. c. 1813, 1818, 1822-24, main house demolished 1956, family live in the very grand stables and still own estate); Lixnaw, Kerry (castle built 1215, principal seat from 13th c., demolished 1600, new house by 1680, add. 18th c., allowed to decay early 19th c., ruin by 1837, estate sold later 19th c.); Wycombe (Loakes House), Buckinghamshire (purch. 1700 by Petty, sold 1798); Leigh House, Wiltshire (acq. early 19th c., still own); Meikleour House, Perthshire (old house, rebuilt 1734, inher. by mar. of 1843 from

Mercers acq. 1392, remod. 1869, still own); Derreen, Kerry (built 14th c., acq. later 17th c., remod. 1858-59, add. 1864-66 and later 19th c., burned 1922, rebuilt 1924, still own)
Estates: Bateman 142916 (E, S, & I) 62025. Owned c. 270,000 acres in Kerry later 17th c. Worth £30,000,000 with 15,000 acres in 1990.
Titles: Baron Kerry r. Richard I- I; Baron Nairn 1681- S; Baron Shelburne 1688-96 I; Baron Shelburne 1699-1751 I; Earl of Shelburne 1719-51 I; Earl of Kerry 1751- I; Viscount Fitzmaurice 1751- I; Earl of Shelburne 1753- I; Baron Wycombe 1760- GB; Baron Fitzmaurice 1906-35 UK; Baronet 1673-
Peers: {8 peers 1661-1747 1688-96 1703-61 1762-1800 1764-1800} 10 peers 1784-1945 1906-35
3 Lds Lt 18th, 19th, 20th
4 in Cabinet 1763 1766-68 1782-83 1806-07 1827-28 1830-34 1835-41 1846-58 1895 1905 1908-09 1915-16
4 KG 18th, 19th, 20th
Notes: The Earl of Shelburne contested Coventry N. E. in 1979. The 8 Marquess was a Minister in the Conservative Government 1962-64. 16, 17, and 18 Barons Kerry and 1, 3, 4, and 5 Marquesses in ODNB and two others.

Earl of Orkney (1696- S)

Origins: The second son of the Earl of Shelburne married 1777 Mary Countess of Orkney in her own right. Their son, John Fitzmaurice became 5 Earl of Orkney. The Earls of Orkney descended from the Dukes of Hamilton (see Hamilton).

1. Thomas Fitzmaurice – {County Kerry 1763-68} Calne 1762-74 Chipping Wycombe 1774-80
2. John Fitzmaurice Viscount Kirkwall – Heytesbury 1802-06 Denbigh 1812-18
3. William Fitzmaurice – Buckinghamshire 1842-47

Seats: Clivedon, Buckinghamshire (built late 17th c., purch. 1696, add. 1706, fire 1795, sold 1824); Glanmore, Tipperary (resident 19th c.); Llewenny Hall, Denbighshire (purch. for £110,000 by a brother of the Earl of Shelburne. Sold 1810 for £209,000 to Edward Hughes of Kinmel)
Estates: Bateman 10958 (I) 5031
Titles: Baron Dechmont and Viscount Kirkwall 1696- S
Peers: [1 peer 1696-1707] 3 Scottish Rep peers 1708-37 1833-74 1885-89
1 Ld Lt 18th
1 KT 18th

Baron Muskerry (1781- I)

Origins: The 1st Deane Bt (b. 1626) settled in Ireland in the mid-17th century at Dromore, Cork. Sheriff 1714. The 1 Baron Muskerry married in 1775 Anne, granddaughter and heiress of John Fitzgerald of Springfield Castle, a nephew of the 1 Earl of Kerry.

1. Sir Matthew Deane 3 Bt – {Charleville 1713-14 County Cork 1728-47}
2. Sir Matthew Deane 4 Bt – {Cork 1739-51}
3. Sir Robert Deane 5 Bt – {Tallow 1757-60 Carysfort 1769-70}
4. Jocelyn Deane – {Baltimore 1773-80} Helston 1780
5. Robert Deane 1 Baron Muskerry – {Carysfort 1771-76 County Cork 1776-81}

Seats: Springfield Castle, Limerick (built 16th c., acq. by mar. to Fitzgeralds 1775, rebuilt early 18th c., add. 19th c., burned 1923, remod., still own); Old Dromore House, Cork (purch. 1687, built c. 1750, rebuilt c. 1781, dismantled 1790s, sold 1803); Castle Cor (Castlecor House), Cork (old castle, purch. and rebuilt c. 1700 by Freeman family, passed to Deanes by mar. of 1754, add. early 19th c., sold 1852, ruin by 1980s, demolished)
Estates: Bateman 15277 (I) 10736. Worth £1,500 pa in 1713. Springfield estate worth £3,000 pa in 1775.
Title: Baronet 1710-
Peers: {1 peer 1781-1800} 1 Irish Rep peer 1892-1929

FITZGERALD II *IRELAND*

Origins: Claimed descent from the Geraldines (*Burke's Peerage and Baronetage*, 1898) but emerged only in the mid-17th century when they acquired Carrigoran.

1. Edward Fitzgerald – {County Clare 1776-90 Castlebar 1790-97}
2. Sir Augustus Fitzgerald 1 Bt – County Clare 1808-18 Ennis 1832
3. Sir John Fitzgerald – Clare 1852-57

Seat: Carrigoran, Clare (castle, acq. 1667, fire 18th c., new house 18th c., sold 1922, institutional use)
Estates: Bateman 16351 (I) 9600
Title: Baronet 1822-1908
Notes: The 1 Bt was a Lt. General and Sir John Fitzgerald MP 1852-57 was a Field Marshal. One in ODNB.

FITZGIBBON *IRELAND*

Earl of Clare (1795-1864 I)

Origins: A Roman Catholic family before the days of forfeiture but rose again by merit in the law. The 1 Earl's father conformed to the Established Church and made a fortune of £100,000 at the bar. Sheriff 1782. Lord Chancellor of Ireland 1789. (Malcolmson, *John Foster: the Politics of the Anglo-Irish Ascendancy,* 5)

1. John Fitzgibbon – {Newcastle 1761-68 Jamestown 1768-76}
2. John Fitzgibbon 1 Earl of Clare – {Dublin University 1778-83 Kilmallock 1783-89}
3. Richard Fitzgibbon 3 Earl of Clare – County Limerick 1818-41

Seat: Mount Shannon, Clare (built mid-18th c., purch. by Fitzgibbons soon after construction, add. c. 1760s, remod. 1813, sold 1893, burned 1920, ruin)
Estates: Bateman 13494 (I) 8120. Worth c. £9,000 pa early 19th c.
Titles: Baron Fitzgibbon 1789-1864 I; Viscount Fitzgibbon 1793-1864 I; Baron Fitzgibbon 1799-1864 GB
Peers: {1 peer 1789-1800} 3 peers 1799-1864
2 Lds Lt 19th
1 KP 19th
Notes: Financial troubles in later 19th c. Contents of Mount Shannon sold 1888. 1 Earl in ODNB.

FITZPATRICK [Vernon Smith] *ENGLAND & IRELAND*

Earl of Upper Ossory (1751-1818 I)

Origins: The 1 Baron Gowran was of uncertain parentage though well connected, possibly to the Fiztpatrick Barons of Upper Ossory (1541-1691). He rose as a Captain in the Royal Navy and was granted land in Ireland by William III. He married the heiress to Farmingwoods. On the death of the last Earl of Upper Ossory in 1818 his Irish estates passed to his illegitmate son, who was created Baron Castletown in 1869. The English estates passed to the Earl's illegitimate daughter who married Robert Vernon Smith (see below).

1. Richard Fitzpatrick 1 Baron Gowran – {Harristown 1703-13 Queen's County 1713-14}
2. John Fitzpatrick 1 Earl of Upper Ossory – Bedfordshire 1767-94
3. Richard Fitzpatrick – {Galway 1761-67}
4. John Fitzpatrick 2 Earl of Upper Ossory – Bedfordshire 1767-94

5. Richard Fitzpatrick – Okehampton 1770-74 Tavistock 1774-1807 {Maryborough 1782-83} Bedfordshire 1807-12 Tavistock 1812-13
6. John Wilson-Fitzpatrick 1 Baron Castletown – Queen's County 1837-41 1847-52 1865-69
7. Bernard Fitzpatrick 2 Baron Castletown – Portarlington 1880-83

Seats: Ampthill Park, Bedfordshire (built c. 1525-50, rebuilt late 1680s, add. 1704-07, purch. 1737, remod. 1769-71, passed by mar. to Lord Holland - see Fox III - 1818); Farmingwoods (Fermyn Woods, Farming Woods) (Hall), Northamptonshire (built 17th c., acq. by mar. later 17th c., remod. 1788, passed by mar. 1841 to the Vernon Smiths see below); Granston Manor, Queen's County (acq. 1696, rebuilt early 19th c., remod later 19th c., sold 1947, burned 1977); Lyveden Old and New Bields, Northamptonshire (built 16th c. and 1615, purch. 1719, passed to Smiths 1841, New Bield NT 1922)
Estates: Bateman 23143 (I & E) 15758. Irish estates worth £7,756 pa in 1801.
Titles: Baron Gowran 1715-1818 I; Baron Upper Ossory 1794-1818 GB; Baron Castletown 1869-1937 UK
Peers: {4 peers 1715-27 1740-58 1766-1800} 3 peers 1794-1818 1869-1937
2 Lds Lt 18th, 19th
1 in Cabinet 1782
1 KP 20th
Notes: 1 Baron and one other in ODNB.

Baron Lyveden (1859- UK)

Origins: The Smiths were London merchants in the 18th century. The first MP went to India and served as Judge Advocate General where he garnered a fortune of £150,000. His son, Robert Vernon Smith married Emma Fitzpatrick in 1823 and inherited Farmingwoods in 1841.

1. Robert Smith – Grantham 1812-18 Lincoln 1820-26
2. Robert Vernon Smith 1 Baron Lyvedon – Tralee 1829-31 Northampton 1831-59
3. Grenville Vernon – S. Div. Ayrshire 1886-92

Seats: Farmingwoods (Fermyn Woods Hall), Northamptonshire (acq. by mar. 1841, remod. c. 1850, sold 1922); Lyveden New Bield, Northamptonshire (built 1615, purch. 1719 by Fitzpatricks, passed to Smiths by mar. 1841, NT 1922)
Estates: Bateman 4138 (E) 5529. 1 Baron left £250,000 in 1873.
Peers: 4 peers 1859-1945
1 in Cabinet 1855-58
Notes: The first MP was the brother of the clergyman and wit Sydney Smith. 1 Baron and two others in ODNB.

FITZWILLIAM *IRELAND & ENGLAND*

Earl of Tyrconnel (1661-67 I)

Origins: To Ireland with King John. Kt 1608. Sheriff 1610. Viscount 1629. **First MP 1539, a kt of the shire for Berkshire. First {MP 1559}.**

1. Richard Fitzwilliam 5 Viscount Fitzwilliam – Fowey 1727-34
2. John Fitzwilliam – New Windsor 1754-68
3. Richard Fitzwilliam 7 Viscount Fitzwilliam – Wilton 1790-1806

Seat: Mount Merrion, Dublin (acq. c. 1610, new house built early 18th c., passed by inher. to Earls of Pembroke 1833, demolished c. 1986)
Estates: Rubinstein – 7 Viscount left £350,000 in probate in 1816.
Title: Viscount Fitzwilliam 1629-1833 I
Peers: {6 peers 1662-67 1710-43 1751-1800}
Notes: A Roman Catholic family that conformed to the Established Church 1710. The last Viscount deposed his estates to his cousin the Earl of Pembroke (see Herbert), but also he left his art collection and £120,000 endowment to Cambridge, where the Fitzwilliam Museum is a crown jewel of the University. 7 Viscount in ODNB.

FLEETWOOD [Fuller]

Fleetwood

Origins: An old Lancashire family seated at Hesketh since the 14th century. They rose to prominence under the patronage of Lord Audley, Lord Chancellor 1532-44 and purchased enough monastic lands to endow three lines in Lancashire, Staffordshire, and Buckinghamshire and Northamptonshire. The family produced a remarkable number of generals, politicans, judges, and bishops in the 17th century and then suddenly decayed, branch after branch, into an almost unique cascading meltdown by the 18th century. (Girouard, *County Life*, 125, pp. 522ff and 596ff) **First MP 1572 for Staffordshire**. (see Hesketh)

1. Edward Fleetwood – Preston 1660 1685-87
2. Richard Fleetwood – Lancashire 1704-05
3. Henry Fleetwood – Preston 1708-22

Seats: Penwortham Priory, Lancashire (acq. c. 1540, rebuilt early 17th c., sold 1748, demolished c. 1922); Rossall (Hall), Lancashire (prob. 16th c., passed by mar. from Fleetwoods to Hesketh (see) mid-19th c., demolished 1928)
Title: Baronet 1611-1802

Notes: Family indebted and sold estates in the mid-18th century. Further losses occurred in the years before 1844 trying to develop the port of Fleetwood. A school was established in the house at Rossall in that year.

Fleetwood

Origins: Cadet line mid-Tudor period. **First MP 1586. Three other MPs 1614-54.**

1. Sir William Fleetwood – New Woodstock 1640 1661-74
2. Miles Fleetwood – Oxfordshire 1656 New Woodstock 1659 Northamptonshire 1678-81

Seat: Aldwinkle All Saints, Northamptonshire (acq. by mar. c. 1627, sold 1693)
Estates: Financial troubles from early 17th c. Worth £140 pa in 1674.
Notes: Charles Fleetwood MP 1646-54 was a Cromwellian peer. His brother was a Swedish baron. Family died out in the early 18th century. "Lord" Fleetwood in ODNB and four others.

Fleetwood

Origins: Cadet line in the mid-Tudor period. Originally seated at The Vache, Buckinghamshire. **First MP 1553. Five further MPs 1558-1628. Three kts of the shire.**

1. John Fleetwood – Buckinghamshire 1713-22

Seat: Great Missenden Abbey, Buckinghamshire (acq. by purch. and marriage 1594, 1684 and 1724 from a family that acq. 1574, passed out of family 1780)
Estates: Worth £1,000 pa in 1691.
Notes: Two in ODNB.

Fuller

Origins: John Fuller of Neston Park succeeded in 1796 to the estates in Sussex of Gerard Dutton Fleetwood, of the Fleetwood of Aldwinkle All Saints family. Gained a fortune as brewers in London.

1. George Fuller – Westbury Div. Wiltshire 1885-95
2. Sir John Fuller 1 Bt – Westbury Div. Wiltshire 1900-11

Seat: Neston Park, Wiltshire (acq. and built 1790s, still own)
Estates: Rubinstein – John Fuller left £120,000 in probate in 1839.
Title: Baronet 1910-

FLEMING I (Le Fleming)

Origins: Important landowners since the 12th century.

1. Sir Daniel Fleming – Cockermouth 1685-87
2. Sir William Fleming 1 Bt – Westmorland 1696-1700 1704-05
3. Michael Fleming – Westmorland 1707-08
4. Sir William Fleming 3 Bt – Cumberland 1756-57
5. Sir Michael Le Fleming 4 Bt – Westmorland 1774-1806

Seats: Rydal Hall, Westmorland (built 16th c., add. late 17th c. and late 18th c., remod. 1824, sold 1969, institutional use); Hill Top (Winster), Westmorland (built 1677 and later 18th c., sold 19th c.)
Estates: Bateman 5442 (E) 3952
Title: Baronet 1705-
1 Ld Lt 20th
Notes: 2 Bt and one other in ODNB.

FLEMING II *SCOTLAND*

Earl of Wigtown (1341-72 S; 1606-1747 S)

Origins: Descended from a Flemish knight granted lands by David I and William the Lion. Prominent from 1320.

No MPs

Seat: Cumbernauld, Dumbartonshire (acq. and built castle c. 1300, new house 1731, passed to Elphinstones by inher. 1747, sold 1875, now offices)
Title: Baron Fleming 1451?-1747 S
Peers: [4 peers 1660-81 1704-07]
Notes: Extinct in male line 1747. The daughter of the 6 Earl married in 1735 the 10 Lord Elphinstone. A younger son took the name Fleming and succeeded to Cumbernauld. 1 Earl of first creation, 1, 4, and 5 Barons and 1 and 2 Earls and six others in ODNB.

FLETCHER *SCOTLAND*

Origins: Merchants. **First [MP 1639 for Dundee].**

1. George Fletcher – [Dundee 1665]
2. James Fletcher – [Dundee 1685-86 1689-1701]

FLOOD [Warden] *IRELAND*

Flood

Origins: Came to Ireland as a Cromwellian officer during the Civil War.

1. Francis Flood – {Callan 1703-05 1713-27}
2. Warden Flood – {Callan 1727-60}
3. Henry Flood – {County Kilkenny 1759-60 Callan 1762-76 Kilbeggan 1783-90} Winchester 1783-84 Seaford 1786-90 (illegitimate)
4. Jocelyn Flood – {Callan 1765-67}
5. John Flood – {Callan 1767-76 Innistioge 1777-83}
6. Warden Flood – {Longford 1769-76 Carysfort 1776-83 Baltinglass 1783-90 Taghmon 1790-97}
7. Sir Frederick Flood 1 Bt – {Enniscorthy 1776-83 Ardfert 1783-90 Carlow 1796-97} County Wexford 1812-18

Seats: Farmley House, Kilkenny (acq. and built early-mid-18th c., add. c. 1850, resident 20th c.); Paulstown Castle, Kilkenny (old tower house, purch. 1742, remod. c. 18th c., resident into 19th c.); Newton Ormond, Kilkenny (acq. 18th c., sold 1897); Banna Lodge, Wexford; Burnchurch House (Castle), Kilkenny (acq. by mar. 1692, sold 1817); Flood Hall, Kilkenny (built late 18th c., remod. early 19th c., add. late 19th c., sold c. 1937, demolished 1950)
Estates: Bateman 6366 (I & E) 7364. Worth £5,000 pa in 1791.
Title: Baronet 1780-1824
Notes: Warden Flood was Lord Chief Justice of Ireland 1760. Two in ODNB.

Warden

Origins: William Warden MP was a Cromwellian Colonel. His granddaughter and heiress married Francis Flood MP.

1. William Warden – {Gowran 1661-66}

Seat: Burnchurch House (Castle), Kilkenny (acq. mid-17th c., passed by mar. to Flood 1692)

FLOWER *IRELAND*

Viscount Ashbrook (1751- I)

Origins: **First MP 1396 for Rutland**, a lawyer and Speaker of the House of Commons. **Two further MPs 1563-93, one for Rutland.** Military officer in Ireland under Elizabeth I and acquired estates there. Kt 1641. Sheriff 1731.

1. Sir William Flower – {Ballynakill 1642-48 St. Canice 1661-63}
2. William Flower 1 Baron Castle Durrow – {County Kilkenny 1715-27 Portarlington 1727-33}

Seats: Castle Durrow (Durrow Castle), Kilkenny (acq. late 17th c., built 1716-18, remod. 19th c., sold 1922, school); Marlingford Hall, Norfolk (leased 20th c.)
Estates: Bateman 23050 (I) 13911. Worth £4,000 pa in 1779 and £7,000 pa c. 1800.
Title: Baron Castle Durrow 1733- I
[4 peers 1733-1800]
Notes: Resident in England by 1930s. One in ODNB.

FLUDYER

Origins: London clothier early 18th century. Sheriff of London 1754, Lord Mayor 1761. Director of the Bank of England 1753-60.

1. Sir Samuel Fludyer 1 Bt – Chippenham 1754-68
2. Sir Thomas Fludyer – Great Bedwyn 1767-68 Chippenham 1768-69
3. Sir Samuel Fludyer 2 Bt – Aldborough 1781-84
4. George Fludyer – Chippenham 1783-1802 Appleby 1818-19

Seats: Lee Place (Park?), Kent (acq. and built mid-18th c. – different than the Boone house – passed to 18 Lord Dacre later 18th c.); Ayston Hall, Rutland (acq. by Brudenells 1510, passed by mar. to the Fludyers, built 1805, passed by mar. to Finch family, sold 1989)
Estates: Bateman 4841 (E & W) 6951. The 1 Baronet left an estate of £900,000 in 1786. (Rubinstein, *Men of Property*, 33). Rubinstein – Henry Fludyer left £100,000 in probate 1817.
Title: Baronet 1759-1922
Notes: One in ODNB.

FOLEY

Baron Foley (1712-66 GB; 1776- GB)

Origins: The father of the first MP was a nail maker and mill owner who purchased Witley for his eldest son and Stoke Edith for his younger sons. Began leasing mills in 1624. High Sheriff 1671. The family became a great dynasty of industrialists (iron-making), landowners, and politicians. They continued in active management of their business operations for over a century while also entering the aristocracy. When the baronial line at Witley became extinct in 1766, the Stoke Edith line gained a Barony and succeeded to Witley. The third line at Prestwood died out and those estates passed to the new junior Stoke Edith branch. All are combined here.

1. Thomas Foley – Worcestershire 1659 Bewdley 1660 1673-77
2. Philip Foley – Bewdley 1679-81 Stafford 1689-90 Droitwich 1690-95 Stafford 1695-1700 Droitwich 1701
3. Paul Foley – Hereford 1679-81 1689-99
4. Thomas Foley – Worcestershire 1679-81 1689-98 Droitwich 1699-1701
5. Robert Foley – Grampound 1685-87
6. Thomas Foley – Weobley 1691-1700 Hereford 1701-22 Stafford 1722-27 1734-37
7. Thomas Foley 1 Baron Foley – Stafford 1694-1712
8. Edward Foley – Droitwich 1701-11 1732-41
9. Richard Foley – Droitwich 1711-32
10. Paul Foley – Aldborough 1713-15 Weobley 1715
11. Thomas Foley – Hereford 1734-41 Herefordshire 1742-47
12. Thomas Foley 1 Baron Foley – Droitwich 1741-47 1754-68 Herefordshire 1768-76
13. Thomas Foley 2 Baron Foley – Herefordshire 1767-74 Droitwich 1774-77
14. Edward Foley – Droitwich 1768-74 Worcestershire 1774-1803
15. Andrew Foley – Droitwich 1774-1818
16. Thomas Foley – Droitwich 1805-07 Herefordshire 1807-18 Droitwich 1819-22
17. John Hodgetts-Foley – Droitwich 1822-34 E. Worcestershire 1847-61
18. Edward Thomas Foley – Ludgershall 1826-32 Herefordshire 1832-41
19. Thomas Foley 4 Baron Foley – Worcestershire 1830-32 W. Worcestershire 1832-33
20. Henry Hodgetts-Foley – S. Staffordshire 1857-68

Seats: Witley Court, Worcestershire (built early 17th c., purch. 1655, add. 1683 and 1735, remod. 1805, sold 1837); Stoke Edith Park, Herefordshire (purch. 1670, built 1690s, fire 1927, demolished 1950s, still own estate); Newport House, Herefordshire (medieval, purch. 1717, rebuilt c. 1720, sold 1863); Prestwood, Staffordshire (built mid-18th c., fire 1921)
Estates: Bateman 8205 (E) 14659; Prestwood 4232 (E) 6690
Peers: 10 peers 1712-66 1776-93 1801-69 1871-1927 1944-45
2 Lds Lt 19th

Notes: Chronic indebtedness forced the Foleys to sell Witley in the 1830s. The Foley family has an entry in the ODNB and the 1 Baron and one other are listed separately.

FONNEREAU [Williams]

Fonnereau

Origins: Huguenots naturalized in 1693. Hamburg merchants who made a fortune in the linen trade. Victulars to the army in the 18th century. Director of the East India Company mid-18th century. Director of the Bank of England 1780s.

1. Thomas Fonnereau – Sudbury 1741-68 Aldeburgh 1773-79
2. Zachary Fonnereau – Aldeburgh 1747-74
3. Philip Fonnereau – Aldeburgh 1761-68
4. Martyn Fonnereau – Aldeburgh 1779-84

Seats: Christchurch Mansion, Suffolk (built 1548-50, remod. c. 1564, 1675, purch. 1732, sold 1894, museum); Dale Hall, Suffolk (purch. c. 1835, owned into 20th c.); The Moat, Suffolk (acq. 19th c.?, owned into 20th c.)
Notes: One in ODNB.

Williams

Origins: The 1 Baronet was a lawyer. On the death of the 3 Bt in 1784 his estates passed to his sister Ann who married in 1758 William Fonnereau.

1. Sir William Williams 2 Bt – New Shoreham 1758-61

Seats: Grey Friars, Sussex (acq. 1736, sold c. 1784); Clapton, Northamptonshire
Title: Baronet 1747-84

FOOT

Baron Caradon (1964-90 UKLife)

Origins: The first MP was the son of a builder and undertaker. He was a solicitor and politician.

1. Isaac Foot – Bodmin Div. Cornwall 1922-24 1929-35
2. Sir Dingle Foot – Dundee 1931-45 Ispwich 1957-70
3. Michael Foot – Plymouth Devonport 1945-55 Ebbw Vale Div. Monmouthshire 1960-83 Blaenau Gwent 1983-92

Title: Baron Foot (1967-99 UKLife)
Notes: Michael Foot was the Leader of the Labour Party 1980-83. His brother, Lord Caradon, was a colonial governor and diplomat. Another brother, Lord Foot, a solicitor and politician. Four in ODNB.

FORBES [Belsches] *SCOTLAND & IRELAND*

Baron Forbes (c. 1445- S)

Origins: Emerged in the 12th century. Lord Provost of Edinburgh 1350. Summoned to Parliament 1436. Sir John Forbes, who lived in the reign of Robert III, established three principal branches among his sons, the most senior, the Lords Forbes, and cadets at Pitsligo and Foveran/Culloden. These in turn also produced cadet lines.

No MPs

Seats: Castle Forbes (Whitehouse), Aberdeenshire (acq. 1411, built c. 1731, rebuilt 1815, still own); Druminnor Castle, Aberdeenshire (built 1440-56, add. 1577, demolished early 19th c., rebuilt 1841-43, demolished 1965)
Estates: Bateman 13621 (S) 5675
Peers: [2 peers 1672-1707] 3 Scottish Rep peers 1806-43 1874-1906 1917-24
1 Ld Lt 18th
Notes: A number of cadet lines seated at Brux, Echt, and Rires elected **four [MPs 1560-1650 for Aberdeenshire].** The Forbes family has an entry in the ODNB, and the 18 and 19 Barons, and three others are listed separately.

Baron Sempill (1488- S)

Origins: Descended from a younger son of the 2 Baron Forbes. The 1 Bt was a merchant in the Baltic trade (known as "Merchant Willie"), who purchased Craigievar. (Young, *The Parliaments of Scotland*, I, 245) **First [MP 1640 for Aberdeenshire].** Sir William Forbes 5 Bt married Sarah the daughter of the 13 Baron Sempill. The 7 Bt succeeded in 1884 as 17 Baron Sempill.

1. Sir John Forbes 2 Bt – [Aberdeenshire 1689-1702]
2. Sir Robert Forbes – [Inverurie Burgh 1693-1702 1703-07]
3. Sir Arthur Forbes 4 Bt – Aberdeenshire 1732-47

Seats: Craigievar Castle, Aberdeenshire (built c. 1600, acq. 1610, remod. 1625-26, NT 1963); Fintray House, Aberdeenshire (old house, acq. 1610, rebuilt 1829-37, rebuilt 1880, requisitioned WWII, demolished 1953)
Estates: Bateman 9347 (S) 8539

Title: Baronet 1630-
Peers: [3 peers 1660-75 1681-84 1703-07] 2 Scottish Rep peers 1910-34 1935-45
Notes: Estate in serious debt 1820s. Recovery came in 1824 with an injection of cash from a younger son in the East India Company service who inherited unexpectedly. 1 Bt in ODNB.

Earl of Granard (1684- I)

Origins: Descended from the third son of the 2 Baron Forbes. To Ireland as a soldier in 1620 where he acquired estates. Baronet 1628.

1. Arthur Forbes 1 Earl of Granard – {County Tyrone 1661-66}
2. George Forbes 3 Earl of Granard – Queenborough 1723-27 Ayr Burghs 1741-47
3. John Forbes – {St. Johnstown 1751-60 Mullingar 1761-68}
4. George Forbes 4 Earl of Granard – {Mullingar 1749-65}
5. George Forbes 5 Earl of Granard – {St. Johnstown 1762-68}
6. John Forbes – {Ratoath 1776-83 Drogheda 1783-96}
7. Arthur Forbes – {Ratoath 1783-88}
8. George Forbes Viscount Forbes – County Longford 1806-32 1833-36

Seat: Castle Forbes, County Longford (acq. 1628, built mid-17th c., fire 1825, rebuilt c. 1830, add. c. 1870, still own)
Estates: Bateman 21294 (I) 9840. Worth £3,000 pa c. 1804.
Titles: Viscount Forbes 1675- I; Baron Granard 1806- UK; Baronet 1628-
Peers: {6 peers 1692-1734 1726-1800} 3 peers 1806-37 1854-89 1895-1945
3 Lds Lt 19th, 20th
1 in Cabinet Council 1685
2 KP 19th, 20th
Notes: 1, 3 and 6 Earls and one other in ODNB.

Forbes

Origins: The founder of this line was the younger son of a laird descended from a younger son of the 1 Baron Forbes who made a fortune in trade in Inverness in the first half of the 17th century and later owned a distillery. **First [MP 1625]**.

1. John Forbes – [Inverness 1646-47 1648-50 Inverness-shire 1669-74]
2. Duncan Forbes – [Nairnshire 1678 1681 Inverness 1689-1702 Nairnshire 1703]
3. John Forbes – [Nairnshire 1704-07] 1713-15 Inverness-shire 1715-22 Nairnshire 1722-27
4. Duncan Forbes – Ayr Burghs 1721-22 Inverness Burghs 1722-37

Seat: Culloden House, Inverness-shire (purch. 1625, rebuilt 1772-78, hotel, still own)
Estates: Bateman 12048 (S) 8367
Notes: Two in ODNB.

Forbes

Origins: Cadet of the same branch as Forbes of Culloden.

1. Sir Samuel Forbes 1 Bt – [Aberdeenshire 1693-1702]

Seat: Foveran House, Aberdeenshire (acq. mid-17th c., sold later 18th c.)
Title: Baronet 1700-c.60

Baron Forbes of Pitsligo (1633-1746 S)

Origins: The third line descended from the 1 Baron Forbes. **First [MP 1612 for Aberdeenshire].**

No post-1660 MPs

Seats: Pitsligo Castle, Aberdeenshire (built 1424, acq. by Forbes 15th c., add. c. 1570, destroyed c. 1746, ruins repurch. late 18th c. but not repaired); Colinton House, Edinburghshire (damaged castle purch. c. 1790, new house c. 1800, sold 1839, now school)
Peers: [2 peers 1661-89 1700-1707]
Notes: Attainted 1746. Estates repurchasd by a son, and the castle repurchased by a banker grandson later 18th c. 4 Baron in ODNB and five others.

Forbes

Origins: Cadet of the Pitsligo line. In 1833 declared heir general to the 3 Baron Forbes of Pitsligo. The 1 Baronet went to India as a merchant and returned a rich nabob.

1. Sir Charles Forbes 1 Bt – Beverley 1812-18 Malmesbury 1818-32
2. John Forbes – Malmesbury 1826-32

Seats: Castle Newe, Aberdeenshire (old Forbes seat, built 1604, purch. by the nabob John Forbes c. 1811, add. 1831, demolished 1929); Edinglassie House, Aberdeenshire (acq. and built early 18th c., add. late 18th c., add. c. 1850, sold 1956)
Estates: Bateman 29238 (S) 5992. Rubinstein – John Forbes (uncle of 1 Bt and also a nabob) left £350,000 in probate in 1821.
Title: Baronet 1823-
Notes: 1 Bt in ODNB.

Belsches

Origins: The estates of a cadet line of the 2 Baron Forbes seated at Monymusk (created Baronets 1626) passed by marriage in 1866 to the 20 Baron Clinton (see Rolle). **First [MP 1560]. Two further [MPs 1639-49].** This line succeeded to the estates of the Belsches of Fettercairn in the 19th century. The 4 Belches Bt succeeded his mother's maternal uncle (Sir William Stuart - originally Wishart - 2 Bt of Colinton) under questionable legal circumstances.

1. Sir John Wishart Stuart Belsches 4 Bt – Kincardineshire 1797-1806

Seats: Fettercairn House, Kincardineshire (built 1670, purch. c. 1783, add. 1826-29, passed to 20 Baron Clinton 1866, add. 1877); Invermay House, Perthshire (old house, remod. late 17th c., rebuilt 1750-70, remod. 1806, passed to 20 Baron Clinton 1866)
Title: Forbes Baronet 1626- ; Wishart-Stuart-Belsches Baronet 1706-1802

Forbes

Origins: Cadet of the Lords Forbes.

1. Francis Forbes – [Forres 1665]

Seat: Thornhill, Elginshire

FORDE *IRELAND*

Origins: Claimed Welsh extraction. In Ireland by the late 16th century. Sheriff 1678. **First {MP mid-17th century}.**

1. Mathew Forde – {County Wexford 1695-99 1703-09}
2. Mathew Forde – {Downpatrick 1703-14}
3. Mathew Forde – {Bangor 1751-60}
4. Mathew Forde – {Downpatrick 1761-76}
5. Mathew Forde – County Down 1821-26
6. William Forde – County Down 1857-74

Seats: Seaforde (Castle Navan), Down (purch. 1637, became main seat early 18th c., built early 18th c., fire 1816, rebuilt 1816-20, remod. later 19th c., resident 20th c.); Coolgreany, Wexford (original seat, purch. 1637)
Estates: Bateman 20106 (I) 15990. Worth £2,100 pa in 1750 and £16,000 pa in 1804.
Notes: One in ODNB.

FORESTER [Weld]

Baron Forester (1821- UK)

Origins: The family has been seated at Wellington since at least the 13th century. They were hereditary foresters of Wellington Hay, hence their name. Tudor courtiers, one gaining the right to remain covered in the presence of the King from Henry VIII. **First MP 1529 for Wenlock. Another in 1554.**

1. Sir William Forester – Wenlock 1679-81 1689-1715
2. William Forester – Wenlock 1715-22 1734-41 1754-58
3. Brooke Forester – Wenlock 1739-68
4. George Forester – Wenlock 1758-61 1768-84 1785-90
5. Cecil Forester – Wenlock 1761-68
6. Cecil Weld-Forester 1 Baron Forester – Wenlock 1790-1820
7. Francis Forester – Wenlock 1820-26
8. John Weld-Forester 2 Baron Forester – Wenlock 1826-28
9. George Weld-Forester 3 Baron Forester – Wenlock 1828-74
10. Cecil Weld-Forester 5 Baron Forester – Wenlock 1874-1885

Seats: Willey Park (Hall), Shropshire (old house, acq. by mar. 18th c., rebuilt 1812-20, still own); Meaford Hall, Staffordshire (acq. by mar. later 19th c., sold 1953, partially demolished); Dothill Park, Shropshire (acq. and built medieval period, rebuilt c. 1626, add. 1763, sold late 19th c., demolished c. 1960); Apley Castle, Shropshire (medieval, rebuilt 1567-1620, new house built 1791-94, purch. late 1840s for £500,000, add. 1856, demolished 1955); Ross Hall (Rossall), Shropshire (built 1677,acq. 18th c., still owned 19th c.); Benthall Hall, Shropshire (built 1572, add. 1610, purch. 1844, sold 1934, NT)
Estates: Bateman 15615 (E) 22581. Rubinstein – George Forester left £175,000 probate in 1811. Owned 7,500 acres in England and 12,000 acres in Zimbabwe in 2001.
Peers: 7 peers 1821-1945
Notes: A very unusual string of MPs for a single constituency ranging over 350 years. Wenlock was disfranchised in 1885, bringing the sequence to an end. Developed iron and coal on estate in 18th c. Two in ODNB.

Weld

Origins: A family of merchants in London (Sheriff 1352) and acquired property in Cheshire from the 14th century. A younger son was a grocer and Lord Mayor of London 1608. He purchased Willey and Lulworth Castle (for £42,860 in 1641) before the Civil war. **First MP 1604. One other MP pre-1660.** Brooke Forester married the daughter and heiress of the last Weld of Willey.

1. George Weld – Wenlock 1661-79 1685-87 1689-1701
2. Sir John Weld – Wenlock 1679
3. George Weld – Wenlock 1701-08 1710-13
4. Thomas Weld – Wenlock 1708-10

Seat: Willey Park, Shropshire (purch. 1641, passed to Foresters 18th c.)
Estates: Worth £1,000 pa in 1660.

Weld

Origins: Cousins of the Welds of Willey. One was Lord Mayor of London 1609.

1. Humphrey Weld – Christchurch 1661-79

Seat: Lulworth Castle, Dorset (built c. 1605, purch. 1641, fire 1929, new house 1975 – Lulworth Manor – built to replace the burned house)
Estates: Bateman 15525 (E) 13854 and 2249 (E) 2941 at Leagram Park, Lancashire (demolished c. 1945, new house)
Notes: The family was Roman Catholic, hence the dearth of MPs. In 1754 they succeeded by marriage with an heiress to Stonyhurst, Lancashire (acq. 13th c., built c. 1372, rebuilt 1592, add. later 17th c., male line died out 18th c. and passed to Welds, given to school 1794) and Leagram Hall, Lancashire (acq. 16th c.) held by the Shirburnes (Sherbourne, Sherborn, Sherburne).
Notes: The Shirburnes **elected two MPs 1420-1558, both for Lancashire**. Baronets 1686-1717. The Welds gave the great house at Stonyhurst to the Jesuits for a school in 1794, but they still own Leagram Hall. Cardinal Weld (19th c.) was a descendent. In the 19th century Thomas Weld succeeded to the Ince Blundell (Blundell seat built 13th c., rebuilt c. 1720, remod. 1802 and 1847-50, became a convent c. 1960) estates in Lancashire. Four in ODNB.

FORRESTER *SCOTLAND*

Baron Forrester of Costorphine (1633- S)

Origins: Merchants in the 14th and 15th centuries and then became officials and royal servants. Kt 1403. Gentry by the 16th century. **First [MP 1560]**, Kt 1568. **One other [MP 1625-33]**.

No post-1660 MPs

Seats: Costorphine Castle, Edinburghshire (acq. 1376, razed 1443, rebuilt, confiscated due to debt 1664, ruins in 18th c., then demolished); Torwoodhead (Torwood) Castle,

Stirlingshire (estate acq. early 13th c. and c. 1450, built 1566, remod. 17th c., sold 1748, ruin)
Peers: [3 peers 1660-1705]
Title: Baronet 1625-52
Notes: Financial crisis in the family in the 1660s continued into the 18th c. and forced sale of most property. The title and estates of the 1 Baron passed to the Baillies of Lamington and later to the Earl of Verulam (see Grimston). The Forrester family has an entry in the ODNB.

FORSTER I

Origins: An old Northumberland family raised to prominence by the illegitimate son of an Elizabethan Warden of the Marches. Lord Chief Justice under Henry VIII. Kt 1640s.

1. William Forster – Northumberland 1698-1700
2. Ferdinando Forster – Northumberland 1701
3. Thomas Forster – Northumberland 1705-08
4. Thomas Forster – Northumberland 1708-16

Seats: Adderstone Hall, Northumberland (there since early 15th c., sold 1709); Bamburgh Castle, Northumberland (site occupied from 1st c. BC, built 11th c. and 12th c., add. 14th c., resident 1541, acq. 1610, ruin later 17th c., sold 1704)
Estates: Worth £1,000 pa in 1660.
Notes: Two families, one at Adderstone and one at Bamburgh, united by marriage in 1681. The Adderstone family was Jacobite. Thomas Forster MP 1708-16 died in exile. Family heavily indebted in the early 18th century. Estates sold 1709. Three in ODNB.

FORSTER II *IRELAND*

Origins: **First {MP 1642}** an Alderman in Dublin.

1. Richard Forster – {Swords 1692-93}
2. John Forster – {Dublin 1703-14}

Seat: Clonsagh, Dublin (acq. 17th c., resident 18th c.)

FORT

Origins: Rich printers in Blackburn from the 18th century. High Sheriff 1854.

1. John Fort – Clitheroe 1832-41

2. Richard Fort – Clitheroe 1865-68
3. Richard Fort – Clitheroe 1880-85
4. Richard Fort – Clitheroe 1950-59

Seats: Read Hall, Lancashire (medieval, purch. 1799, old house demolished and new house built 1818-25, sold 1897); Sedgley Park (Hall), Lancashire (fire 1902)

FORTESCUE [Aland] *ENGLAND & IRELAND*

Earl Fortescue (1789- UK)

Origins: Family established in the reign of King John. Great soldier under Henry V. **First MP 1382. Thirteen additional MPs 1421-1607, five kts of the shire**. Lord Chief Justice of the King's Bench 1442. Hugh Fortescue married Bridget, granddaughter of the 4 Earl of Lincoln. His son inherited the Lincoln barony of Clinton, was summoned to the Lords in 1721, and was created Earl of Clinton but died without a successor in 1751. (see Rolle).

1. Sir Edmund Fortescue 1 Bt – Plympton Erle 1666
2. Hugh Fortescue – Tregony 1689-95 Grampound 1695-98 Truro 1698-1700 Tregony 1701-02 Mitchell 1705-10 Lostwithiel 1710-13
3. William Fortescue – Newport (IoW) 1727-36
4. Theophilus Fortescue – Barnstaple 1727-41 Devon 1741-46
5. Hugh Fortescue 1 Earl Fortescue – Beaumaris 1784-85
6. John Inglett Fortescue – Callington 1801-03
7. Hugh Fortescue 2 Earl Fortescue – Barnstaple 1804-07 St. Mawes 1807-09 Buckingham 1812-17 Devon 1818-20 Tavistock 1820-30 Devon 1830-32 N. Devonshire 1832-39
8. George Fortescue – Hindon 1826-31
9. Hugh Fortescue 3 Earl Fortescue – Plymouth 1841-52 Marylebone 1854-59
10. John Fortescue – Barnstaple 1847-52
11. Dudley Fortescue – Andover 1857-74
12. Hugh Fortescue 4 Earl Fortescue – Tiverton 1881-85 Tavistock Div. Devonshire 1885-92

Seats: Castle Hill, Devon (Filleigh Manor) (acq. mid-15th c., new house built 1684-94 and rebuilt 1730-40, fire 1934, rebuilt 1936, still own); Buckland Filleigh, Devon (acq. by mar. mid-15th c., rebuilt c. 1700, sold 1840s); Exmoor Forest (Simonsbath House built 1654), Devon (purch. 1879, sold 1958); Ebrington Manor, Gloucestershire (built c. 1400?, purch. 1456, rebuilt sec. half of the 16th c., reduced in size c. 1830, add. 1922, fire 1970, still own); Weare Giffard Hall, Devon (acq. by mar. 1454, built 1460-72, add.

1590s, add. 1830-32, sold 20th c. ?); Dropmore, Buckinghamshire (built 1792-94, acq. by mar. from Grenvilles 1864, sold 1943, demolished 1990)
Estates: Bateman 30887 (E & I) 28673. Owned 16,500 acres in 2001. Purchased 20,000 acres of Exmoor for hunting purposes in 1879, sold 1958)
Titles: Baron Fortescue 1746- GB; Earl of Clinton 1746-51 GB; Viscount Ebrington 1789- GB; Baronet 1664-
Peers: 7 peers 1721-1841 1839-61 1859-1945
5 Lds Lt 18th, 19th, 20th
1 in Cabinet 1839-41
1 KG 19th
Notes: George Fortescue MP 1826-31 succeeded in 1864 to his aunt, Lady Grenville's (Pitt) estates at Boconnoc, Cornwall (acq. 1718) and Dropmore, Buckinghamshire (see Grenville). These were given to the second son of the 1 Earl Fortescue. Still own Boconnoc. 2 and 3 Earls and six others in ODNB.

Earl of Clermont (1777-1806 I)

Origins: Descended from a younger grandson of Sir John Fortescue, Lord Chief Justice of the King's Bench (see above). Appointed Lord Chief Justice of the Common Pleas in Ireland 1426. Soldier to Ireland 1598. Lord Deputy of Ireland 1604. On the extinction of the Earldom and Viscountcy, the estates passed to a cadet line who were created Barons Clermont and Barons Carlingford, titles that were later merged.

1. Faithful Fortescue – {County Louth 1727-41}
2. Thomas Fortescue – {Dundalk 1727-60}
3. William Fortescue 1 Earl of Clermont – {County Louth 1745-60 Monaghan 1761-70}
4. Chichester Fortescue – {Trim 1747-57}
5. James Fortescue – {Dundalk 1757-60 County Louth 1761-82}
6. Thomas Fortescue – {Trim 1768-80}
7. Thomas Fortescue – {County Louth 1782-95}
8. William Fortescue 2 Viscount Clermont – {County Louth 1796-1800} 1801-06
9. Sir Chichester Fortescue – {Trim 1797-1800}
10. William Fortescue – {Monaghan 1798-1800}
11. Faithful Fortescue – {Monaghan 1800}
12. Chichester Fortescue – {Hillsborough 1800}
13. Thomas Fortescue 1 Baron Clermont – County Louth 1840-41
14. Chichester Fortescue 2 Baron Clermont – County Louth 1847-74

Seats: Ravensdale Park, Louth (built early/mid-18th c., new house early Victorian, sold c. 1900, burned 1921); Stephenstown, Louth (acq. and built late 18th c., add. c. 1820, sold 1974, derelict); Clermont Hall, Norfolk (built 1776, add. 1806, sold c. 1829)
Estates: Bateman 27075 (I) 21437 (includes Stephenstown line)

Titles: Baron Clermont 1770-1806 I; Viscount Clermont 1776-1829 I; Baron Clermont 1852-98 I; Baron Clermont 1866-87 UK; Baron Carlingford 1874-98 UK
Peers: {1 peer 1773-1800} 2 peers 1866-87 1874-98
1 Ld Lt 19th
1 in Cabinet 1865-66 1868-74 1881-85
2 KP 18th, 19th
Notes: 1 Baron Carlingford in ODNB.

Baron Fortescue of Credan (1746-80 I)

Origins: Descended from Sir John Fortescue (15th c.). **First MP 1553. One additional MP 1593.** 1 Baron was a Justice of the King's Bench and Justice of the Common Pleas 1718-46. His father had married the Aland heiress and took the additional name Aland 1704 and inherited estates.

1. John Fortescue Aland – Midhurst 1715-17

Seat: Knolls Hill (Stapleford Abbots), Essex (acq. 1715, add, 1734, sold 1782, became a farm house, demolished mid-19th c.)
Notes: 1 Baron in ODNB.

FOSTER I

Origins: Manufacturers in Bradford. Owned one of the largest woolen textile mills in the world. Began purchasing estates early-mid 19th century. High Sheriff 1881.

1. William Foster – Lancaster Div. Lancashire 1895-1900
2. Philip Foster – S. W. Warwickshire 1901-06 1909-18
3. John Foster – Coventry 1910

Seats: Hornby Castle, Lancashire (built 13th c., add. 16th c., remod. 1849-52, purch. 1862 for £200,000, remod. 1889, sold post 1945, fire c. 1950); Canwell Hall, Staffordshire (built late 17th c., rebuilt late 18th c., purch. 1872 for £207,000, sold 1920, demolished 1957)
Estates: Bateman 12725 (E) 9098. William Foster d. 1884 worth £1,279,000. The Canwell landed estate alone was valued at £501,000 in 1904.
Notes: One in ODNB.

FOSTER II [Barham] *ENGLAND & WALES*

Origins: Fosters acquired a plantation in Jamaica in the early 18th century and inherited Welsh estates by marriage (1754) to the Vaughans of Trecwn in the later 18th century. They married (1733) into the Barham family, also West Indian planters, and took the additional name Barham. The first MP was called a "West Indian parvenu", but the first and second MPs married into the titled aristocracy and the family held Trecwn for almost four centuries.

1. John Foster Barham – Stockbridge 1793-99 1802-06 Okehampton 1806-07 Stockbridge 1807-22
2. John Foster Barham – Stockbridge 1820-26 1831-32 Kendal 1834-37
3. Charles Foster Barham – Appleby 1832

Seat: Trecwn, Pembroke (built 17th c., passed by mar. to the Foster Barhams 1789, sold 1939, demolished)
Estates: Estate in Jamaica was 6,496 acres. Worth £2,000 pa in 1792 but declined in value to £1,200 pa by 1832. Welsh estate worth £1,381 pa in 1828.
Notes: The male line became extinct in 1878 and the estates passed to a sister's son who took the name Barham. The estate in Pembroke was sold after two sons were killed in a car accident in 1933. The Barhams were related to the Barhams of Barham Court, Kent (see Noel).

FOSTER III

Origins: Ironmasters in the 18th century. The first MP built up the company and became a banker. High Sheriff 1840.

1. James Foster – Bridgnorth 1831-32
2. William Foster – S. Staffordshire 1857-68
3. William Foster – Bridgnorth 1870-85

Seats: Apley Park, Shropshire (Georgian house, rebuilt 1811, purch. 1867, leased to a school after WWII, sold c. 1990, flats); Spratton Grange, Northamptonshire (built 1848, sold 1946?); Stourton Castle, Worcestershire (medieval, rebuilt 1580s, rebuilt 1831-32, purch. lease 1831, sold 1868); Coton Hall, Worcestershire (medieval, rebuilt c. 1800, purch. 1833 for £10,000, add. c. 1860)
Estates: Bateman 21062 (E & I) 28426. The first MP left £700,000 in 1853 (Thompson, "Life after death", 60). The family was worth £2,500,000 in 1899.
Notes: The iron business, Bradley and Company, traded until 1982. The family was related to the Darbys of Coalbrookdale.

FOTHERINGHAM *SCOTLAND*

Origins: Did homage to Edward I in 1296. In Forfar in the 14th century. **First [MP 1482]. Two further [MPs 1560-1621].**

1. David Fotheringham – [Forfarshire 1665]

Seats: Powrie Castle (Wester Powrie), Forfarshire (acq. 1412, rebuilt 16th c., add. 1604); Fotheringham House, Forfarshire (demolished 1859, new house 1859, demolished 1953)
Estates: Bateman 12529 (S) 13399. 20,500 acres in 1996

FOULIS *SCOTLAND & ENGLAND*

Origins: In service to the Stuarts from the 15th century. One was private secretary to James V. Lord of Session 1526. Master of the Mint 17th century. **First [MP 1526 for Edinburgh]. Three further [MPs 1594-1621 for Edinburgh or Edinburghshire]**. Granted an English estate by James VI and I.

1. Sir James Foulis 2 Bt – [Edinburghshire 1645-47 1648-51 1661-63 1665 1667 1672-74 1678 1681]
2. Sir James Foulis 3 Bt – [Edinburghshire 1685-86 1689-93 1704-07]
3. Sir David Foulis 3 Bt – Northallerton 1685-87

Seats: Colinton (Castle) House, Edinburghshire (castle built 1450, purch. 1519, add. c. 1609, wrecked 1650, ruin, sold 1790); Ingleby Greenhow, Yorkshire (built c. 1540s, acq. 1608, remod. late 18th and mid-19th c., passed out of the family 1876)
Estates: Bateman 2804 (S) 2163. Worth £1,000 pa in 1632, later reduced by fines.
Titles: Baronet 1620-1874; 1634- ; 1661-1746
Notes: Became a great legal family. The 2 and 3 Bts Lords of Session 1661 and 1674. 1, 2, 3, and 5 Bts and three others in ODNB.

FOWELL (Vowell) [Champernowne]

<u>Fowell</u>

Origins: **First MP 1455 for Totnes** was a lawyer. **Two further MPs 1529-1648**.

1. Sir John Fowell 2 Bt – Ashburton 1659 1660-77
2. Edmund Fowell – Tavistock 1646-48 Devon 1656 Tavistock 1659 Plymouth 1660
3. Sir John Fowell 3 Bt – Totnes 1689 1690-92

Seats: Fowellscombe, Devon (built 1537, passed to Champernownes 1692, became a ruin later 19th c.); Harewood House, Cornwall (acq. by mar. a lease and then purchased 1647, passed out of family early 18th c.)
Title: Baronet 1661-92
Notes: Represented Totnes over the course of more than two centuries.

Champernowne

Origins: A Norman family that came to England in the 12th century. **First MP 1298 for Devonshire. Seven further MPs 1309-1626, three of whom also sat for the county.** Arthur Champernowne married Margaret, sister and heiress of Sir John Fowell 3 Bt, who died in 1692, when the Champernownes succeeded to Fowellscombe.

1. Arthur Champernowne – Totnes 1715-17
2. Arthur Champernowne – Saltash 1806-07

Seat: Dartington Hall, Devon (built 14th c., acq. 1559, remod. late 16th c., remod. 1846-51, sold 1925, school)
Estates: Bateman 2385 (E) 3388. Worth £6,155 pa in 1828 (Emery, *Dartington Hall*, 88)
Notes: In the 18th century Dartington passed through the female line, the new husband taking the name Champernowne. Three in ODNB.

FOWNES [Luttrell]

Origins: The Fownes were merchants (alderman and mayors) in Plymouth form the 16th century. Henry Fownes married the daughter and heiress of Alexander Luttrell and took the additional name Luttrell in 1747. The Luttrells held property in Somerset from 1232. Kt 1337. **First MP 1363 for Devon. Seven additional MPs 1404-1642, five of them for Minehead.**

1. Francis Luttrell – Somerset 1656 Minehead 1660-66
2. Francis Luttrell – Minehead 1679-81 1685-87 1689-90
3. Narcisus Luttrell – Bossiney 1679-81 Saltash 1691-95
4. Richard Fownes – Corfe Castle 1681 1685-87 1689-1714
5. Alexander Luttrell – Minehead 1690-1708
6. John Fownes – Dartmouth 1714-15
7. John Fownes – Dartmouth 1715-22
8. Alexander Luttrell – Minehead 1727-37
9. Henry Fownes Luttrell – Minehead 1768-74
10. John Fownes Luttrell – Minehead 1774-1806 1807-1816
11. Francis Fownes Luttrell – Minehead 1780-83
12. Thomas Fownes Luttrell – Minehead 1795-96

13. John Fownes Luttrell – Minehead 1812-32
14. Henry Fownes Luttrell – Minehead 1816-22
15. Hugh Fownes Luttrell – Tavistock Div. Devon 1892-1900 1906-10

Seats: Dunster Castle, Somerset (built 11th c., purch. 1376, add. 1420-24, restructured late 16th c. and c. 1617, remod. 1680s and 1868-72, family departed 1974, NT 1976); Nethway House, Devon (built 16th c., fire 1696, rebuilt 1696-99, purch. by Fownes 1699, sold 1874); Kittery Court, Devon (built 16th c., purch. by Fownes 1717, remod. 18th c. and 19th c., sold 1874?); The Court House, East Quantoxhead, Somerset (granted by William I to the Pagnells, medieval house, Luttrells married Pagnell heiress 1232, partly rebuilt 17th c., still own) (Dunning, *Some Somerset Country Houses*, 33)
Estates: Bateman 15528 (E) 22000. Worth £1,500 pa in 1660. Owned 10,000 acres in 2001.
Notes: 15 MPs represented Minehead over two and a half centuries. The Luttrell family has an entry in the ODNB.

FOX I (Foxe)

Origins: The family was prominent in Ludlow from the early 15th century. Purchased estates after the Dissolution. Kt 1603. **First MP 1523 for Ludlow. Three further MPS 1539-1629, two of them for Ludlow.**

1. Somerset Fox – Ludlow 1670-79

Seats: Caynham Court, Shropshire (leased 1536, purch. 1584, sold 1668 for £2,077); Bromfield, Shropshire (leased 1541, medieval buildings remod. 1540s, fire 17th c. and family departed, ruin)
Estates: Acq. 8,000 acres of monastic land.
Notes: One in ODNB.

FOX II *IRELAND*

Origins: The family claimed descent from the first King of Teffia. (*Burke's Landed Gentry*, 1879, I, 594) The first to emerge clearly was Sir Patrick Fox Clerk of the Council and Interpreter of Irish to the States d. 1618. Sheriff of Longford 1633.

1. Patrick Fox – {Kilbeggan 1703-13 Fore 1715-27}
2. Charles Fox – County Longford 1837
3. Richard Fox – County Longford 1847-56

Seats: Fox Hall (Rathreagh), Longford (purch. by Sir Patrick Fox 1560, resident into 20th c., now ruin); Durrow Abbey, King's County (sold 18th c.); Moyvore, Westmeath (resident 18th c.)
Estates: 3085 (I) 1675 in 1878.

FOX III [Horner, Strangways]

Earl of Ilchester (1756- E)

Origins: Sir Stephen Fox, who began life as a borderline peasant (Henning, *The House of Commons*, II, 356), became a court page, rose to the office of Paymaster, which enabled him to amass assets of c. £380,000 by 1686, a Kt and MP. His son became an earl.

1. Sir Stephen Fox – Salisbury 1661-79 Westminster 1679 Salisbury 1685-87 Westminster 1691-98 Cricklade 1699-1702 Salisbury 1714-15
2. Charles Fox – Eye 1680-81 Cricklade 1685-87 1689-98 Salisbury 1698-1713
3. Stephen Fox-Strangways 1 Earl of Ilchester – Shaftesbury 1726-34 Hindon 1734-35 Shaftesbury 1735-41
4. Henry Fox Strangways 2 Earl of Ilchester – Midhurst 1768-74
5. John Fox Strangways – Calne 1836-37 Dorset 1837-41

Seats: Melbury House, Dorset (acq. by mar. to Strangways heiress mid-18th c., still owned by descendents); Abbotsbury Castle, Dorset (acq. by mar. to Strangways heiress mid-18th c., see below, rebuilt mid-18th c., fire 1913); Redlynch House, Somerset (built 1740s, declined to farm house in mid-19th c., restored 1901, sold 1912, fire 1913 restored, now flats); Waterston Manor, Dorset (medieval, rebuilt 1586, purch. 1641, became a farm house, fire 1863, rebuilt 1864, sold 1911); Holland House, Middlesex (Strangways inher. from Holland Fox family to Ilchester line 1859, made uninhabitable by bomb damage 1940, partly demolished, passed to LCC 1952)
Estates: Bateman 32849 (E) 43452. Worth £14,000 pa in 1686. Worth £50,000,000 in 1990 with 15,000 acres.
Title: Baron Ilchester 1741- GB
Peers: 6 peers 1741-1802 1808-65 1868-1945
2 Lds Lt 19th, 20th
Notes: 6 Earl and four others in ODNB.

Strangways (Strangwish)

Origins: Established in Dorset 15th century. Estates enlarged at the Dissolution and acquired Melbury by marriage to an heiress mid-16th century. **First MP 1472. Two further MPs 1529-59**. The 1 Earl of Ilchester married Elizabeth, daughter and heiress of Thomas Strangways Horner of Mells Park and his wife Susanah, daughter and heiress of Thomas Strangways of Melbury House.

1. Sir John Strangways – Dorset 1614 1621 1624 Weymouth & Melcombe Regis 1625 1626 Dorset 1628 Weymouth & Melcombe Regis 1640-42 1644 1661-66

2. Giles Strangways – Bridport 1640-44 Dorset 1661-75
3. John Strangways – Bridport 1661-76
4. Thomas Strangways – Poole 1673-79 Dorset 1679-81 1685-87 1689-1713
5. Wadham Strangways – Bridport 1677-79
6. George Strangways – Weymouth & Melcombe Regis 1685-87
7. Thomas Strangways – Bridport 1705-13 Dorset 1713-26
8. John Strangways – Bridport 1715

Seats: Melbury House, Dorset (medieval, purch. 1500, rebuilt c. 1546, remod. 1692, passed by mar. to Foxes 1726); Abbotsbury Castle, Dorset (purch. 1542, burned 1643, passed by mar. to the Fox family 18th c.)
Estates: Worth £5,000 pa in 1666.
Notes: Two in ODNB.

<u>Horner</u>

Origins: Settled in Somerset since the early 15th century. Acquired Mells at the Dissolution. Sir John Horner married the heiress of Henry VIII's tailor. **First MP 1584. Three additional MPs 1584-1654, two of the kts of the shire**. Thomas Horner MP married 1713 the daughter and co-heiress of Thomas Strangways and took the additional name Strangways, inheriting Melbury 1726. Mells eventually passed back to a junior line of the Horners.

1. Sir George Horner – Somerset 1645-48 1660
2. George Horner – Somerset 1685-87 1689-90
3. Thomas Horner – Somerset 1713-15 Wells 1715-17 Somerset 1727-41

Seat: Mells Park, Somerset (purch. 1543, rebuilt later 16th c., much demolished 1780, restored c. 1900, fire 1917, rebuilt 1925, sold 1939, family still resident in a smaller manor house on estate)
Estates: Bateman 6786 (E) 10184

<u>Baron Holland</u> (1762-1859 GB)

Origins: The 1 Baron Holland was a younger son of the Fox dynasty.

1. Henry Fox 1 Baron Holland – Hindon 1735-41 Windsor 1741-61 Dunwich 1761-63
2. Stephen Fox 2 Baron Holland – Salisbury 1768-74
3. Charles James Fox – Midhurst 1768-74 Malmesbury 1774-80 Westminster 1780-84 Tain Burghs 1784-85 Westminster 1785-1806
4. Henry Fox 4 Baron Holland – Horsham 1826-27

5. Charles Fox – Calne 1831-32 Tavistock 1832-34 Stroud 1835 Tower Hamlets 1841-47

Seats: Holland House, Middlesex (built 1605-06, add. 1638-40, part demolished 1704, leased to Fox family 1746 who purch. 1768, passed to Ilchesters by mar. 1859, see above); Ampthill Park, Bedfordshire (built c. 1525-50, rebuilt late 1680s, add. 1704-07, remod. 1769-71, passed by mar. from Lord Upper Ossory to Lord Holland 1818, sold 1840)
Estates: Bateman 5791 (E) 7457 plus metropolitan rents.
Peers: 4 peers 1763-74 1796-1859
3 in Cabinet 1755-65 1782-83 1806 1806-07 1830-34 1835-40
Notes: 1, 3, and 4 Barons and five others in ODNB.

FRANKLAND [Croke, Hawtrey, Lewis, Payne, Russell, Thurbane] *ENGLAND & WALES*

<u>Frankland</u>

Origins: A London clothworker made a fortune and acquired estates in the reign of Elizabeth I. Granted arms 1569. **First MP 1628 for Thirsk.** Kt 1636. The 7 Bt inherited the Russell estates from his kinsman Sir Robert Greenhill Russell 1 Bt (see below).

1. Sir William Frankland 1 Bt – Thirsk 1671-81
2. Sir Thomas Frankland 2 Bt – Thirsk 1685-87 1689-95 Hedon 1695-98 Thirsk 1698-1711
3. Sir Thomas Frankland 3 Bt – Harwich 1708-13 Thirsk 1713-47
4. Frederick Frankland – Thirsk 1734-49
5. Sir Thomas Frankland 5 Bt – Thirsk 1747-80 1784
6. William Frankland – Thirsk 1768-74
7. Sir Thomas Frankland 6 Bt – Thirsk 1774-80 1796-1801
8. William Frankland – Thirsk 1801-06 Queenborough 1806-07 Thirsk 1807-15
9. Sir Robert Frankland-Russell 7 Bt – Thirsk 1815-34

Seats: Thirkleby Park (Hall), Yorkshire (acq. 1576, built c. late 16th c., new house 1784-87, sold 1919, demolished c. 1927); Chequers Court, Buckinghamshire (built mid-16th c., inher. by mar. 1837, leased out 1909, sold 1917, became prime minister's residence)
Estates: Bateman 2531 (E) 3585 and 2534 (E) 3719
Title: Baronet 1660-
Notes: Thirkleby was left to the 7 Bt's widow who left it to her daughter, Emily Payne-Frankland. One in ODNB.

Greenhill Russell

Origins: Robert Greenhill succeeded to the estates of his kinsman Sir George Russell 10 Bt of Chequers Court and took the name Russell. The 1 Bt below was a lawyer.

1. Sir Robert Greenhill Russell 1 Bt – Thirsk 1806-32

Seat: Chequers Court, Buckinghamshire (built mid-16th c., acq. by mar. from Thurbanes 18th c., passed by mar. to Franklands 1837)
Estates: Rubinstein – 1 Bt left £140,000 in probate in 1836.
Title: Baronet 1831-36

Thurbane

Origins: Prominent in the Cinque Ports since the 14th c. **First MP 1366. Two further MPs 1586-1621.** John Thurbane MP Married the daughter and heiress of Robert Croke of Chequers Court. Thurbane's daughter and heiress married John Russell through whom Chequers passed to the Frankland-Russells.

1. James Thurbane – Sandwich 1656 1659 1660-79
2. John Thurbane – Sandwich 1679-81 1689-95 1698-1700

Seat: Chequers Court, Buckinghamshire (built mid-16th c., acq. by mar. 1681, passed by mar. to the Russells 18th c.)

Croke

Origins: A Clerk of Chancery in the 1520s acquired estates at the Dissolution. Lawyers and judges under Elizabeth I and James I. Speaker of the House of Commons 1601. **First MP 1572** (a lawyer) **for Buckinghamshire**. **Five additional MPs 1584-1640**. Sir Henry Croke married the granddaughter of William Hawtrey of Chequers Court.

1. Robert Croke – Wendover 1640-43 1661-71
2. Sir Richard Croke – Oxford 1654-55 1656-58 1659 1661-79

Seats: Marston (Manor House), Oxfordshire (acq. by mar. and built house 1617, sold 1682); Chequers Court, Buckingamshire (built mid-16th c., acq. by mar. 1637, passed via heiress to Thurbanes 1681, passed by mar. to Russells)
Notes: Estates alienated in 1682, and the last Croke died poor 1728.
Notes: Six in ODNB.

Hawtrey

Origins: Acquired Chequers in the reign of Edward I. **First MP 1563 for Buckinghamshire. Two additional MPs 1572 and 1628.** The MP listed below was from a junior line extinct 1725 seated at Eastcote House. Chequers passed to the Crokes (see above).

1. Ralph Hawtrey – Middlesex 1685-87 1689-95

Seats: Chequers Court, Buckinghamshire (medieval, acq. by mar. late 13th c., rebuilt mid-16th c., passed by mar. to the Crokes via an heiress 1637); Eastcote House, Middlesex (acq. by mar. c. 1525, passed out of family 17th c.)
Notes: One in ODNB.

Baron Lavington (1795-1807 I)

Origins: Settled in St. Kitts 1654 and became rich planters. Chief Justice and Governor of St. Kitts early to mid-18th century. Kt 1728. On the death of Sir Robert Frankland-Russell 7 Bt his estates passed to his daughter who married a Payne.

1. John Willett Payne – Huntingdon 1787-96
2. Peter Payne – Bedfordshire 1831-32
3. Sir William Payne-Gallwey 2 Bt – Thirsk 1851-81

Seats: Tempsford Hall, Bedfordshire (purch. 1768, built 1769, sold 1824); Knuston Hall, Northamptonshire (leased mid-19th c.); Wootton House, Bedfordshire (see Monoux - rebuilt 17th c., acq. through mar. of 1792, sold 1923, now offices)
Estates: Held over 1,000 acres at Tempsford. West Indian estates sold 1892 for £7,500.
Title: Baronet 1737- in dispute from 1828, ceased to use c. 1900; Baronet 1812-2008
Notes: Several lines combined here. 1 Baron and one other in ODNB.

Lewis

Origins: The Lewis family held Harpton from at least the 15th century. **First MP 1545 for New Radnor with another in 1597. A number of MPs also elected by a cadet branch at Gladestry Court, Radnor in the 16th and 17th centuries.** John Lewis of Harpton married the daughter and heiress of Sir Thomas Frankland 6 Bt.

1. Thomas Lewis – New Radnor Boroughs 1715-61
2. John Lewis – New Radnor Boroughs 1768-69 1774-75

3. Sir Thomas Frankland Lewis 1 Bt – Beaumaris 1812-26 Ennis 1826-28 Radnorshire 1828-34 New Radnor Boroughs 1847-55
4. Sir George Cornewall Lewis 2 Bt – Radnor District 1855-63

Seat: Harpton Court, Radnorshire (old house, acq. mid-16th c. or earlier, rebuilt 1750, add. 1805-12, passed to Duff Gordons by mar. 1911, sold 1953 and partly demolished 1956)
Estates: Bateman 10006 (W) 7005
Title: Baronet 1846-1911
1 in Cabinet 1855-63
Notes: 1 and 2 Bts in ODNB.

FRASER I *SCOTLAND*

Baron Saltoun (1445- S)

Origins: Became prominent in the 13th century. Regent of Scotland in the 1280s. At Philorth by the 14th century. The Abernethys were the original Barons Saltoun. Alexander Fraser below succeeded at 10 Baron through his mother. **First [MP 1566].**

1. Alexander Fraser 10 Baron Saltoun – [Aberdeenshire 1643 1648 1661-63]
2. Sir Alexander Fraser 1 Bt – [Kincardineshire 1669-74]
3. William Fraser – Elgin Burgh 1722-25

Seats: Philorth House, Aberdeenshire (acq. by marriage 1375, rebuilt 1666, add. 1874, fire 1915, ruinous); Cairnbulg Castle (also called Philorth), Aberdeenshire (built 13th c., acq. by mar. 1375, add. 1545, sold 1615, abandoned 1799, repaired 1930s, repurch. 1934, still own); Pittulie Castle, Aberdeenshire (built 1596, sold early 18th c., ruin)
Estates: Bateman 10762 (S) 11929
Peers: [2 peers 1660-68 1670-93] 4 Scottish Rep peers 1807-53 1859-86 1890-1933 1935-45
1 KT 19th
Notes: The Lords Lovat were almost certainly related to the Barons Saltoun but the links are not clear. See entry on the Fraser family in the ODNB. 12 and 16 Barons and three other individual entries in ODNB.

FRASER II *SCOTLAND*

Baron Lovat (1460- S; 1837- UK)

Origins: Emerged in the 12th century, Lord in Parliament 1431. **First [MP 1646]. Several cadet lines produced three additional [MPs 1639-51].**

1. Simon Fraser (12 Baron Lovat) – Inverness-shire 1761-82

2. Archibald Fraser (13 Baron Lovat) – Inverness-shire 1782-84
3. John Simon Fraser – Inverness-shire 1796-1802
4. Sir Hugh Fraser – Stone Div. Staffordshire 1945-50 Stafford and Stone Div. Staffordshire 1950-83 Stafford 1983-84

Seats: Beaufort Castle, Inverness-shire (medieval, acq. late 13th c., razed 1746, rebuilt 1839, rebuilt 1880, sold 1994); Lovat Castle, Inverness-shire (medieval, acq. early 17th c., demolished later 17th c.); Strichen House, Aberdeenshire (built 1818-21, sold mid 19th c., ruin 1954)
Estates: Bateman 181791 (S) 30300. Worth £55,000,000 in 1990 with 190,000 acres. (Most of the land subsequently sold due to bankruptcy.)
Peers: [2 peers 1664-72 1687-96] 4 peers 1837-87 1892-1945
2 Lds Lt 18th
1 KG 19th
1 KT 20th
Notes: The title passed through the Mackenzies (see Mackenzie). Lord Lovat was executed after the 1745 Jacobite Rising and the title attainted 1747. The estates were restored 1774 and the title in 1857. Created Duke of Fraser in the Jacobite peerage. Lord Lovat led his troops onto the beaches on D-Day accompanied by his personal piper. Sir Hugh Fraser was Secretary of State for Air 1962-64. Entry for Fraser family in ODNB, and the 11, 14, and 15 Lords and five other individual entries. The family encountered extreme financial difficulties from the 1980s onwards.

Fraser

Origins: Descended from a younger son of the 1 Lord Lovat. Moved to Aberdeenshire 1454. The estates of the Barons Fraser passed to this family in 1716.

1. Sir William Fraser 4 Bt – Barnstaple 1852-53 1857-59 Ludlow 1863-65 Kidderminster 1874-80
2. Sir Charles Fraser – Lambeth N. 1885-91
3. Sir Keith Fraser 5 Bt – Harborough Div. Leicestershire 1918-23

Seats: Carlton Curlieu Hall, Leicestershire (leased 1903 to 1930s); Castle Fraser, Aberdeenshire (granted 1454, built 1575, add. 1617, sold 1922, NT 1976); Kinmundy House, Aberdeenshire (built 18th c., unroofed early 1950s)
Titles: Baron Fraser 1633-1715 S; Baronet 1806-
Peers: [2 peers 1660-74 1695-1715]
Notes: See Mackenzie.

Fraser

Origins: Cadets of Lords Lovat.

1. Hew Fraser – [Inverness-shire 1678]
2. Hew Fraser – [Inverness-shire 1685-86]

Seat: Belladrum, Inverness-shire (built late 18th c., sold early 19th c., demolished 1957)

Fraser

Origins: Cadets of Lords Lovat.

1. Finley Fraser – [Inverness 1669-74]

Seat: Merkinch, Inverness-shire (acq. 1605, sold 1754); Fairfield House, Inverness-shire (built c. 1700, sold later 18th c.)

FREDERICK

Origins: A physician emigrated from the Low Countries in 1580. Merchant 1650s, ship owner, and Lord Mayor of London 1662. Kt 1660.

1. Sir John Frederick – Dartmouth 1660 London 1663-79
2. Thomas Frederick – New Shorham 1734-40
3. Sir John Frederick 4 Bt – New Shorham 1740-41 West Looe 1743-61
4. Charles Frederick – New Shorham 1741-54 Queenborough 1754-84
5. Sir John Frederick 5 Bt – Newport 1774-80 Christchurch 1781-90 Surrey 1794-1807

Seats: Burwood Park, Surrey (purch. 1739, sold c. 1863); Lamport Grange, Northamptonshire
Estates: Worth £2,000 pa in 1660.
Title: Baronet 1723-

FREEMAN-THOMAS

Marquess of Willingdon (1936- UK)

Origins: The Freemans were planters in Antigua from the early 18th century. First MP 1796. Sir George Thomas 1 Bt of Ratton and Yapton founded that family's fortunes as Governor of the Leeward Islands. First MP 1784. His daughter married Arthur Freeman of Antigua. Their son Inigo Freeman took the additional name Thomas.

1. George White Thomas – Chichester 1784-1812
2. Sir George Thomas 3 Bt – Arundel 1790-97
3. Inigo Freeman-Thomas – Weobley 1796-1800
4. Freeman Freeman-Thomas 1 Marquess of Willingdon – Hastings 1900-06 Bodmin Div. Cornwall 1906-10

Seats: Ratton Park, Sussex (acq. 18th c., sold 1902-18); Yapton House (Place), Sussex (purch. 1749, sold c. 1910)
Estates: Bateman 2935 (E) 4122
Titles: Baron Willingdon 1910- UK; Viscount Ratendone 1924- UK; Earl of Willingdon 1931- UK; Baronet 1766-
Peers: 2 peers 1910-45
Notes: The 1 Marquess was an imperial governor, Viceroy of India. 1 Marquess and two others in ODNB.

FREMANTLE [Halford]

Baron Cottesloe (1874- UK)

Origins: Founder a merchant in Lisbon in the early 18th century. His son was a Secretary to the Customs Board. His son was a courtier and another an Admiral (Kt and an Austrian Baron d. 1819). The Fremantles succeeded to the Halford estates in 1897 (see below), and they remained engaged in banking.

1. Sir Thomas Fremantle – Sandwich 1806-07
2. Sir William Fremantle – Enniskillen 1806 Harwich 1806-07 Saltash 1807 Tain Burghs 1808-12 Buckingham 1812-27
3. Thomas Fremantle 1 Baron Cottesloe – Buckingham 1827-46
4. Thomas Fremantle 2 Baron Cottesloe – Buckinghamshire 1876-85
5. Sir Francis Fremantle – St. Albans Div. Hertfordshire 1919-43

Seats: Swanbourne House, Buckinghamshire (purch. 1798, built 1864, still own); Wistow Hall, Leicestershire (built 1621, acq. by inher. 1897, still own)
Estates: Bateman 2683 (E) 5675
Titles: Baronet 1821-
Peers: 3 peers 1874-1945
1 Ld Lt 20th
1 in Cabinet 1844-46
Notes: 1 and 4 Barons and four others in ODNB.

Halford

Origins: The Halfords purchased Wistow 1603. Bt 1641. The Vaughans were from Leicester, where the father of the 1 Bt was a successful physician. The 1 Bt of the 1809 creation inherited the Halford estates on the death of Lady Denbigh, widow of his mother's cousin, Sir Charles Halford 7 Bt, and changed his name to Halford. Sir Henry Halford 1 Bt was physician to King George IV and Queen Victoria.

1. Sir Thomas Halford 3 Bt – Leicestershire 1689-90
2. Richard Halford – Rutland 1698-1713
3. Sir Henry Halford 1 Bt – S. Leicestershire 1832-57

Seats: Edith Weston Hall, Rutland (purch. early 17th c., sold c. 1830, demolished 1954); Wistow Hall, Leicestershire (purch. 1603, descended to Fremantles 1897); Newton Harcourt, Leicestershire (medieval manor house, purch. early 17th c., descended to Fremantles 1897)
Estates: Bateman 3053 (E) 6000
Titles: Baronet 1641-1780; 1809-97
Notes: 1 Bt and three others in ODNB.

FRENCH (Ffrench) [Brewster] *IRELAND*

Baron De Freyne (1839-56 1851- UK)

Origins: Settled in Galway 1425. Acquired 6,000 acres through a Cromwellian grant 1657. **First {MP 1585}.**

1. John French – {Carrick 1695-99 County Galway 1703-13 Carrick 1713-14 Tulsk 1715-27}
2. Arthur French – {Tulsk 1714 County Roscommon 1721-27 Boyle 1727-60}
3. John French – {County Roscommon 1745-75}
4. Arthur French – County Roscommon {1783-1800} 1801-20
5. Arthur French 1 Baron De Freyne – County Roscommon 1821-32
6. Patrick French – County Roscommon 1832-73
7. Charles French – Roscommon 1873-80

Seats: French Park (Frenchpark, Dungar), Roscommon (acq. and built c. 1650-68, rebuilt c. 1729, remod. mid-19th c. and late 19th c., sold 1953, demolished c. 1970); Errit(t) Lodge, Roscommon (acq. by 1837, resident 20th c.)
Estates: Bateman 38788 (I) 15231 and 13573 (I) 3938. Worth £1,000 pa in 1713 and £2,100 pa in 1824.
Peers: 4 peers 1851-68 1876-1913

1 Ld Lt 19th
Notes: Roman Catholic family. Conformed early 18th c. One in ODNB.

Earl of Ypres (1922-88 UK)

Origins: Descended from a younger son.

No MPs

Title: Viscount French 1916- UK
Peers: 2 peers 1916-45
1 in Cabinet 1918-21
1 KP 20th
Notes: 1 Earl in ODNB.

French

Origins: A cadet line.

1. Jeffrey French – Milbourne Port 1741-47 Tavistock 1754

Seat: Cloonyquin, Roscommon (acq. and built 18th c., add. 19th c., sold 1955, demolished)
Estates: Bateman 3701 (I) 2933

French-Brewster

Origins: Descended from an uncle of the 1 Baron De Freyne. His son married Elizabeth Brewster, daughter and heiress of Abraham Brewster of Cloonanatmore, Lord Chancellor of Ireland 1867. The Brewsters settled in Ireland in 1650s or 1660s and acquired estates in Tipperary.

1. Robert French-Brewster – Portarlington 1883-85

Seat: Cloonanatmore, Roscommon (acq. 19th c., family departed by 1918)
Estates: Bateman 2863 (I) 2522
Notes: Resident in England post WWI.

Ffrench

Origins: Descended from Robocke Ffrench (d. 1598), a cadet of the French family of French Park. Galway merchants in the 16th century. Purchased estates in the first decades of the 17th century. Conformed to the Established Church 1709. (Cronin, *A Galway Gentleman in the Age of Improvement*, passim) Sheriff 1774.

1. Patrick Ffrench – {County Galway 1713-14 Blessington 1727-44}
2. Robert Ffrench – {Jamestown 1727-45}
3. Robert French – {County Galway 1753-60 Carrick 1761-68 Galway 1768-76}

Seat: Monivea Castle, Galway (old tower house of O'Kellys, acq. by Frenches before 1619, add. 1713-15, remod. 19th c., family departed 1938, all but tower house demolished c. 1939)
Estates: Batmean 10121 (I) 3703. Worth £300 pa in 1713 and £1,638 pa in 1748.
Notes: Created Marquis de Castelthomond by the Pope in 1896. Male line extinct 1938. One in ODNB.

FRERE

Origins: Old Suffolk family dating to the 14th century. Hookhams were London merchants in the 18th century. **First MP 1653 for Norfolk.**

1. John Hookham Frere – West Looe 1796-1802
2. John Frere – Norwich 1799-1802

Seats: Roydon Hall, Norfolk (purch. 1766, house late-Georgian, sold 1934); Finningham Hall, Suffolk (medieval, acq. 1660, sold 1912)
Estates: Bateman 4512 (E) 6203
Notes: Five in ODNB.

FRESCHEVILLE (Fretchvile)

<u>Baron Frescheville</u> (1665-82 E)

Origins: Norman family. Held land in Derbyshire at least from 1225. Medieval barons (1306), but the title fell into abeyance. **First MP 1300.** Rose again by marriage to an heiress under the Tudors. **Two additional MPs for Derbyshire 1554-1621.**

1. John Frescheville 1 Baron Frescheville – Derbyshire 1628 1661-65

Seat: Staveley Hall, Derbyshire (medieval, acq. by mar. 1301, rebuilt 1603-04, add. 1634, sold 1681, part demolished 1756, now offices)
Estates: 1,767 acres by 1680s.

Peer: 1 Peers 1665-82
Notes: Extinct in the male line 1682. Staveley acquired by marriage to the Mustard heiress 1301. Her family had held it since 1086. Family has an entry in ODNB.

FREWEN [Turner]

Origins: The Frewens were clergy under Elizabeth I and one was Archbishop of York in 1660. A merchant in London inherited the substantial wealth accumulated by his brother the Archbishop in 1664. The Frewens succeeded to the Turner estates in Leicestershire 1753 and took the name Turner. In 1837 they reverted to Frewen.

1. Thomas Frewen – Rye 1679-85 1689 1694-98
2. John Frewen Turner – Athlone 1807-12
3. Thomas Frewen Turner – Leicestershire 1835-36
4. Charles Frewen – E. Sussex 1846-57
5. Moreton Frewen – N. E. Cork 1910-11

Seats: Brickwall House, Sussex (built 16th c., rebuilt early 17th c., purch. 1666, remod. 1680s, 1832, and later 19th c., donated to a school 1974, still own estate); Cold Overton Hall, Leicestershire (built 1664, acq. by Turners early 18th c., passed to Frewens 1753, sold c. 1904); Innishannon, Cork (built mid-18th c., acq. 19th c., burned 1921)
Estates: Bateman 7892 (E) 13431. Estates worth c. £30,000 in 1664.
Notes: Four in ODNB.

FULFORD

Origins: At Fulford by the reign of Richard I. **First MP 1432 (Cornwall). Two other MPs 1553-1625, both for Devon.**

1. George Fulford – Christchurch 1679-81
2. Francis Fulford – Callington 1690-95 1698-1700

Seats: Fulford (Great Fulford), Devon (acq. possibly by 1085 and certainly by late 12th c., built 1534, still own); Toller Fratrum, Dorset (medieval, rebuilt mid-16th c., passed by mar. to the Fulfords from the Samways family who had purch. 1540, sold 1867)
Estates: Bateman 2987 (E) 2289. Worth £100 pa in 1579, £600 pa in 1660.
Notes: Achieved an extraordinary length of tenure for a gentry family at an estate from which they derive their name. Two in ODNB.

FURNESS

Viscount Furness (1918- UK)

Origins: Grocers and from the 1870s steamship company owners.

1. Christopher Furness 1 Baron Furness – Hartlepool 1891-95 1900-10
2. Sir Christopher Furness 1 Bt – Hartlepool 1910-14
3. Sir Stephen Furness – Sunderland 1935-45

Seats: Grantley Hall, Yorkshire (built mid-18th c., add. 1760, remod, early 19th c., purch. mid-19th c., remod. early 20th c., sold 1926); Tunstall Court, Durham (acq. and built 1897, family departed 1920s, sold 1950, demolished 2014)
Estates: 1 Baron owned 30,000 acres and left £1,000,000 in 1912.
Titles: Baron Furness 1910- UK; Baronet 1913-
Peers: 2 peers 1910-40
Notes: 1 Baron in ODNB.

FYDELL

Origins: The first MP, a wine merchant in Boston, was the son of a London brewer.

1. Richard Fydell – Boston 1734-41
2. Thomas Fydell – Boston 1790-1803 1806-12
3. Thomas Fydell – Boston 1803-06

Seats: Kirton House, Lincolnshire (purch. mid-18th and resident in 19th c.); Fydell House, Boston, Lincs. (built c. 1702-03, purch. 1720s, family departed 1816)

GAGE

Viscount Gage (1720- I)

Origins: Emerged in the 13th century. Married the heiress to Firle in 1446. **First MP 1529 for Sussex. Two further MPs 1554 and 1558**. KG 1532.

1. Thomas Gage 1 Viscount Gage – Minehead 1717 Tewkesbury 1721-54
2. Sir William Gage 7 Bt – Seaford 1722-44
3. William Gage 2 Viscount Gage – Seaford 1744-47 1754-80
4. Henry Gage 3 Viscount Gage – Warwick 1790-91

Seats: Firle Place, Sussex (acq. by mar. 1472, built c. 1500, remod. 1713, remod. c. 1744-54, still own); Highmeadow House, Gloucestershire (built 16th c.?, rebuilt 1672, passed by mar. to the Gages 1717, sold 1805, demolished early 19th c.)
Estates: Bateman 12352 (E) 13337
Titles: Baron Gage 1780-91; 1790- GB; Baronet 1622- ; 1662-1872
Peers: 5 peers 1780-1808 1812-1912 1916-45
Notes: The Roman Catholic Hall family built the very grand Highmeadow House, which passed to the Gages via an heiress in 1717. The Gages were also Roman Catholic until the 1 Viscount conformed to the Established Church. The family continued to marry heiresses and accumulated more property and wealth. Ten in ODNB.

GAHAN *IRELAND*

Origins: Claimed descent from ancient Irish princes. Estates forfeited in 1607. Captain Gahan rose as a soldier under the Commonwealth and was granted estates in Tipperary 1666. Sheriff 1699.

1. Daniel Gahan – {Taghmon 1666}
2. Sir Daniel Gahan – {Portarlington 1692-93 Rathcormack 1703-13}
3. Daniel Gahan – {Fethard 1785-97 Wicklow 1797-99}

Seats: Coolquill Castle, Tipperary (old house, acq. and built 1666, passed by mar. to Tighes 1800); Charlestown, King's County (resident 18th until early 19th c.)
Estates: Held 1,000 acres in 1666. Worth between £1,000 and £2,000 pa in late 18th c.

GAPE

Origins: Tanners in St. Albans who had held property there since the 15th century. Many mayors. Granted arms 1684.

1. John Gape – St. Albans 1679
2. John Gape – St. Albans 1701-05 1708-15
3. Thomas Gape – St. Albans 1730-32

Seat: Harpsfield Hall, Hertfordshire (purch. 1676, leased out throughout the 19th c., sold 20th c., demolished 1930)
Estates: Bateman 3246 (E) 3199

GARDNER

Baron Gardner (1800-83 I; 1806-83 UK)

Origins: The founder commanded a company inside the walls at the siege of Derry. His son was a merchant, his son a lt. colonel, and his son an admiral, the 1 Baron.

1. Alan Gardner 1 Baron Gardner – Plymouth 1790-96 Westminster 1796-1806
2. Herbert Gardner 1 Baron Burghclere – Saffron Walden Div. Essex 1885-95
3. Alan Gardner – S. Hertfordshire 1906-07

Seat: Debden Hall, Essex (leased later 19th and early 20th c.)
Estates: under 2000 acres in Bateman. Rubinstein £125,000 probate 1809.
Titles: Baron Burghclere 1895-1921 UK; Baronet 1794-1883
Peers: 4 peers 1806-15 1836-83 1895-1921
Notes: The 1 Baron had two sons and a grandson who were also admirals. The 1 Baron Burghclere was the illegitimate son of the 3 Baron Gardner. 1 Baron Gardner and one other in ODNB.

GARLAND [Lester]

Garland

Origins: The Garlands were merchants engaged in the Newfoundland trade in Poole. High Sheriff of Dorset 1824.

1. George Garland – Poole 1801-07
2. Benjamin Garland Lester – Poole 1809-34

Seat: Leeson House, Dorset (built 1805, purch. early 19th c., sold 1903, institutional use)
Estates: Rubinstein – George Garland MP left £120,000 in probate in 1825.
Notes: The brother of Benjamin Garland Lester MP was Speaker of the Assembly in Newfoundland.

Lester

Origins: Poole merchants and partners with the Garlands. George Garland married the daughter and heiress of Benjamin Lester. Their son succeeded to the Lester estates and took the additional name Lester.

1. Benjamin Lester – Poole 1790-96

GAWDY

Origins: Gentry possibly as early as the late 14th century. Prominent through the law in the 15th century. Justice of the Queen's Bench 1574. **First MP 1545. Ten additional MPs 1553-1648**.

1. Sir William Gawdy 1 Bt – Thetford 1661-69
2. Sir Charles Gawdy 1 Bt – Eye 1678-79 1681 1685-87

Seats: Crow's (Crows) Hall, Suffolk (built 1508, acq. 1595, sold 1723); Berdewell (Berdwell, Bardwell) Hall (West Harling), Norfolk (Bardwells built house 15th c., passed to Gawdys mid-16th c., sold and demolished c. 1723); Gawdy Hall, Suffolk (purch. and built 16th c., passed by mar. out of the family 1662, demolished 1939)
Estates: Worth £1,000 pa in 1630s.
Titles: Baronet 1661-1720; 1663-1723
Notes: Family extinct and estates sold by an heiress 1723. Gawdy family has an entry in the ODNB and four individual entries.

GAYER

Origins: An old Cornish family. The first MP of Trebrace was the son of a lawyer. Robert Gayer MP 1715 was the grandson of a Lord Mayor of London. **First MP 1553** of Foxley, Berkshire. **Another MP 1553-71**.

1. Robert Gayer – Windsor 1715

Seat: Stoke Park, Buckinghamshire (medieval, rebuilt 1555, purch. 1656 for £8,564, sold 1724 for £12,000)
Notes: These MPs were kinsmen but not close relatives. Two in ODNB.

GEERS [Cotterell, Winford]

<u>Geers</u>

Origins: Purchased Bridge Sollers in 1622. The first MP was a lawyer and judge.

1. Thomas Geers – Hereford 1685-87
2. Thomas Geers – Hereford 1727-34 1741-47 Worcester 1747-48

Seats: The Marsh, Bridge Sollers, Herefordshire (purch. 1622); Glasshampton, Worcestershire (inher. by mar. 1731, split among heiresses 1744)

Winford

Origins: 1 Bt a lawyer and official. The Geers family succeeded by marriage to the Winford estates in 1731.

1. Sir Thomas Winford 2 Bt – Worcestershire 1707-10

Seats: Glasshampton, Worcestershire (built c. 1705, passed to Geers family by mar. 1731, see above); Norgrove Court, Worcestershire (built 1649, inher. by mar. 1701, divided into farm houses c. 1823)
Title: Baronet 1702-44
Notes: The 2 Bt succeeded 1701 to the estates of his uncle Sir Thomas Cooke 2 Bt (Bts 1664-1701) of Norgrove, worth £2,500 pa.

Cotterell

Origins: Sheriff of Gloucestershire 1578. Sir John Cotterell (d. 1790) married Ann, the daughter and heiress of John Geers of Garnons and the Cotterells succeeded to the Geers estates.

1. Sir John Geers Cotterell 1 Bt – Herefordshire 1802-03 1806-31
2. Sir Geers Cotterell 3 Bt – Hereford 1857-59

Seat: Garnons, Herefordshire (built c. 1600, rebuilt 1815-20 and c. 1855, most demolished 1957, still own)
Estates: Bateman 5066 (E) 8020
Title: Baronet 1805-
2 Lds Lt 20th

GELL [Thornhill]

Origins: Held Hopton as tenants from 1327 and can be traced back to 1209. Grew rich marketing lead. Granted arms 1575. High Sheriff 1630s. Bt 1642. The estates passed through the female line twice in 1730 and 1842. On the second occasion William Thornhill MP 1853-65 married Isabella Gell, heiress to Hopton, and he took the additional name Gell. The Thornhills were gentry by the 13th century but had decayed to innkeepers by the 17th. They married the heiress to Stanton and revived their fortunes.

1. Sir John Gell 2 Bt – Derbyshire 1654 1656 1659 1689
2. Sir Philip Gell 3 Bt – Steyning 1681 Derbyshire 1689-90
3. Philip Gell – Malmesbury 1807-12 Penryn 1812-18
4. William Pole Thornhill-Chandos-Gell – N. Derbyshire 1853-65

Seats: Hopton Hall, Derbyshire (acq. at least by 1327 and possibly 1209, medieval house, rebuilt late 16th c. and early 18th c., remod. 1760s and 1840 sold 1918, repurch. 1926, sold 1989); Stanton Hall, Derbyshire (medieval, acq. by mar. by Thornhills 1698, add. 1699 and 1799, still own)
Estates: Bateman 3744 (E) 4467; Thornhills 6409 (E) 8007: 5,000 acres in 1991.
Title: Baronet 1642-1719
Notes: The Gells claimed wholly fictitious descent from a Roman soldier called Gellius. The story was prompted by Philip Gell unearthing in the 18th century a Romano-British pot in front of the Hall with the alleged inscription "Gelli". (Craven and Stanley, *The Derbyshire Country House*, 113-15) Six in ODNB.

GERARD [Lake, Mohun]

Earl of Macclesfield (1679-1702 E)

Origins: Major landowners by the 14th century. **First MP 1384 for Lancashire. Ten further MPs 1422-1628, four of who were kts of the shire**.

1. Sir Gilbert Gerard 1 Bt – Northallerton 1661-81
2. Charles Gerard 2 Earl of Macclesfield – Lancashire 1679-81 1689-94
3. Fitton Gerard 3 Earl of Macclesfield – Yarmouth (IoW) 1689-90 Clitheroe 1693-95 Lancaster 1697-98 Lancashire 1698-1700

Seats: Gawsworth Old Hall, Cheshire (medieval, rebuilt 16th c., acq. by mar. 1643, part demolished 1701, Gawsworth estates passed to Lord Mohun 1702, rebuilt 1707-12, sold 1727); Halsall, Lancashire (purch. 1625, estates divided among heiresses 1741); Fiskerton, Lincolnshire (demolished); Brafferton, Yorkshire (acq. by mar. mid-17th c., sold 1691)
Titles: Baron Gerard of Bandon 1645-1702 E; Baronet 1666-1730
Peers: 3 peers 1660-1702
Notes: Held high legal office in the Tudor period. Inherited the estates of the Fittons of Gawsworth by marriage on the death of the 2 Bt 1643. The Fittons elected **three MPs 1406-1589**. Inherited the Almer of Pant Locyn estates (**two MPs 1555-72**), an ancient Welsh family. In 1741 the Lancashire estates passed to the Dukes of Hamilton (see Hamilton I). 1 and 2 Earls and three others in ODNB.

Baron Gerard of Gerard's Bromley (1603-1733 E)

Origins: A cadet line descended from Sir Peter Gerard (d. c.1380), ancestor of the Earls of Macclesfield.

No MPs

Seat: Gerard's Bromley (Bromley Hall), Staffordshire (acq. and built c. 1575, sold and demolished c. 1750)
Estates: Worth £6,000 pa in the early 18th century.
Peers: 3 peers 1660-67 1683-1707
Notes: The family was Roman Catholic. On the death of the 6 Baron Gerard the estates passed by marriage to Charles Fleetwood (d. 1747 in ODNB), who ran through his wealth and died bankrupt. One in ODNB.

Baron Gerard (1876- UK)

Origins: Descended from Thomas Gerard of Bryn, son of Sir Peter Gerard, see previous entry. Medieval kts and sheriffs. **First MP 1563. Two other MPs 1597-1624.**

No MPs

Seats: Garswood Hall, Lancashire (built 1692, purch. mid-18th c., rebuilt 1826, demolished 1921); Eastwell Park, Kent (see Finch - part demolished 1926, ruin); Blakesware, Hertfordshire (built 1876-79, acq. post 1876); Birchley Hall, Lancashire (built 1594, acq. by mar. later 17th c. from Andertons who held it from 1581, sold 1898, now institution); Bryn Hall, Lancashire (acq. by mar. 1250 to Bryn heiress, abandoned 18th c.)
Estates: Bateman 7107 (E) 43671
Title: Baronet 1611-
Peers: 3 peers 1876-1902 1904-1945
Notes: A notable recusant family. Their Roman Catholicism made it impossible for them to elect MPs in the 17th and 18th centuries. Coal was discovered on the estates that made the family very rich in the 18th and 19th centuries.

Baron Mohun (1628-1712 E) [Mohun]

Origins: Norman landowners from the 11th century and barons 13th-15th centuries. The Cornish line was a cadet. **The first Mohun MP was elected in 1547. Four further MPs 1584-1626, one for Cornwall.** On the death of the 3 Earl of Macclesfield in 1702 the Gerard estates passed to the 4 Baron Mohun.

No post-1660 MPs

Seats: Boconnoc, Cornwall (purch. 1579, sold c. 1718); Gawsworth New Hall, Cheshire (Gawsworth estate acq. by mar. from Gerards 1702, New Hall built by 5 Baron Mohun 1707-12, sold 1727)
Title: Baronet 1611-1712
Peers: 3 peers 1660-77 1698-1712

Notes: The 4 Baron killed the 4 Duke of Hamilton and then himself was killed in a duel over the Gerard inheritance. 1 and 4 Barons and five others in ODNB.

<u>Gerard</u>

Origins: Descended from a cadet of Sir Peter Gerard (see above). Officials in 16th c. **First MP 1553. Another 1584-93.**

1. Sir Gilbert Gerard 1 Bt – Wigan 1614 Middlesex 1621 1624 1625 1626 1640-48 Lancaster 1660
2. Sir Francis Gerard 2 Bt – Seaford 1641-48 Middlesex 1659 Bossiney 1660
3. Sir Gilbert Gerard – Westminster 1660
4. Sir Charles Gerard 3 Bt – Middlesex 1685-87 1689-95 Cockermouth 1695-98

Seat: Flambards, Middlesex (purch. from 1552, passed by mar. to Lakes 1716)
Title: Baronet 1620-1716

<u>Viscount Lake</u> (1807-1848 UK)

Origins: The Lakes were shopkeepers in Southampton. One became an **MP 1593** and Secretary of State (1616-19). He purchased Canons in 1604. **Two further MPs 1624-28.** Sir Gilbert Gerard 1 Bt of Flambards (see above) married the heiress of Aston Clinton Park. The daughter and heiress of the 3 Bt, Elizabeth Gerard married Warwick Lake and he succeeded to Flambards on the extinction of the Baronetcy in 1716.

1. Sir Lancelot Lake – Middlesex 1660-79
2. Warwick Lake – Middlesex 1698-1705
3. Gerard Lake 1 Viscount Lake – Aylesbury 1790-1802 {Armagh 1799-1800}

Seats: Aston Clinton Park (House), Buckinghamshire (acq. by mar. 1716, sold 1851, demolished 1958); Canons Park, Middlesex (old house, purch. 1604, rebuilt c. 1605, sold 1709); Flambards, Middlesex (acq. by mar. 1716, sold 1767, demolished 19th c.)
Estates: Land worth £800 pa in 1808 plus a parliamentary annuity of £2,000 pa.
Title: Baron Lake 1804-48 UK
Peers: 3 peers 1808 1810-48
Notes: The 1 Duke of Chandos, who was married to a Lake daughter, purchased Canons in 1709. (see Grenville) 1 Viscount and three others in ODNB.

GIBBS [Hucks]

Baron Aldenham (1896- UK)

Origins: Began as small gentry, physicians, lawyers, merchants, and bankers in the 18th century who became very successful in the 19th century. The first MP was a barrister, Attorney General, and judge, Kt 1805. Later in the century the family made a great fortune in trade with South America in guano and nitrates and as bankers. The partners in the firm were earning up to £100,000 pa c. 1875. (Girouard, *The Victorian County House*, 244)

1. Sir Vicary Gibbs – Totnes 1804-06 Great Bedwin 1807 Cambridge University 1807-12
2. Henry Gibbs 1 Baron Aldenham – City of London 1891-92
3. Vicary Gibbs – St. Albans Div. Hertfordshire 1892-1904
4. Alban Gibbs 2 Baron Aldenham – City of London 1892-1906
5. George Gibbs 1 Baron Wraxall – Bristol West 1906-28

Seats: Aldenham House (Park), Hertfordshire (acq. by mar. 1869, remod. 1870-73, sold 1932, school); Manor House, Clifton Hampden, Oxfordshire (acq. by mar. 1784, built 1843-46, remod. 1902, sold 2000); Briggens, Hertfordshire (built 1719, remod. 1770, remod. 1899, purch. 1908, sold 1979, hotel); Tyntesfield, Somerset (built 1830s, purch. 1843, rebuilt 1863-66 and 1873-75 for £70,000 - Franklin, *The Gentleman's Country House*, 268 - NT acq. at a cost of £35,000,000 for purchase and preservation in 2002); Pytte, Devon (built late 18th c., remod. early 19th c., purch. 1859, remod. late 19th c. and 1911, owned post 1945)
Estates: Bateman 6278 (E) 11128. First Baron Aldenham left £700,000 in addition to landed property.
Titles: Baron Hunsdon 1923- UK; Baron Wraxall 1928- UK
Peers: 6 peers 1896-1945 1923-45 1928-45
Notes: Three separate peerages were conferred on an uncle, nephew, and cousin in a short space of time. 1 Baron Aldenham and 1 Baron Hunsdon and five others in ODNB.

Hucks

Origins: London brewers. The Gibbs family inherited the Hucks estates by marriage in the 19th century.

1. William Hucks – Abingdon 1709-1710 Wallingford 1715-40
2. Robert Hucks – Abingdon 1722-41

Seat: Aldenham House, Hertfordshire (built c. 1672, remod. 18th c., acq. by mar. 1735, passed to Gibbs family 1869)

GIBSON *IRELAND*

<u>Baron Ashbourne</u> (1885- UK)

Origins: Father of 1 Baron was a solicitor in Dublin. 1 Baron was a barrister and politician. Sheriff 1879.

1. Edward Gibson 1 Baron Ashbourne – Dublin University 1875-85
2. John Gibson – Walton Div. Liverpool 1882-88

Seat: Rockforest, Tipperary (acq. 19th c., resident 20th c.)
Estates: Bateman 5214 (I) 2245. The 1 Baron also left £136,000 exclusive of property in 1913.
Peers: 3 peers 1885-1945
1 in Cabinet 1885-89 1895-1905
Notes: 1 Baron in ODNB.

GIFFORD I

<u>Baron Gifford</u> (1824- GB)

Origins: The father of the 1 Baron was a grocer in Exeter. 1 Baron a lawyer, Attorney General, and Lord Chief Justice 1824.

1. Robert Gifford 1 Baron Gifford – Eye 1817-24

Seat: Ampney Park, Gloucestershire (medieval, rebuilt 1628, leased 19th c., hotel)
Estates: Under 2000 in Bateman. 1 Baron left £50,000 and landed estates, which were sold.
Peers: 5 peers 1824-26 1838-1945
Notes: 1 Baron in ODNB.

GIFFORD II (Giffard) *IRELAND*

Origins: To Ireland in the 1590s as a soldier. **First {MP 1639}**. Sheriff 1695.

1. Sir Thomas Gifford 1 Bt – {Trim 1661-62}
2. Duke Gifford – {Philipstown 1692-93 1695-99}

Seat: Castle Jordan, Meath (acq. by mar. early 17th c., resident into 18th c.)
Title: Baronet 1661-62 (assumed 1747-1823)

Notes: Sir John Gifford {MP 1639} inherited Castle Jordan from his mother, the daughter and heiress of Sir Henry Duke. Male line extinct 1823.

GILBERT *IRELAND*

Origins: Went to Ireland 1569. **First {MP 1634}. One further {MP 1644}.**

1. John Gilbert – {Maryborough 1661-66}
2. St. Leger Gilbert – {Maryborough 1692-93 1695-99 1703-13 Old Leighlin 1713-27}
3. Bartholomew Gilbert – {Maryborough 1755-60}
4. William Gilbert – {Maryborough 1761-64}

Seat: Kilminchy (Kilminshy), Queen's County (acq. 1622)
Notes: Extinct in the male line by 1800?

GILMOUR *SCOTLAND*

Baron Gilmour (1992-2007 UKLife)

Origins: The family rose through the law in the late 16th century.

1. Sir John Gilmour – [Edinburghshire 1661-63 1665 1667 1669-72]
2. Sir Alexander Gilmour 1 Bt – [Edinburghshire 1690-1701]
3. Sir Charles Gilmour 2 Bt – Edinburghshire 1737-50
4. Sir Alexander Gilmour 3 Bt – Edinburghshire 1761-74
5. Sir Ian Gilmour 1 Baron Gilmour – Central Norfolk 1962-74 Chesham & Amersham 1974-92

Seats: Craigmillar Castle, Edinburghshire (built from 1374 onwards, acq. and rebuilt c. 1661, ruin); Liberton House, Edinburghshire (inher. from Little family who purch. 1587, built later 17th c., remod. 19th c., sold 20th c.); The Inch (House), Edinburghshire (built 1617, purch. 1660, add. 1660s, became a ruin, restored 1892, sold, institutional use)
Estates: The 1 Baron inherited over £200,000 in the 1950s from the Meux brewery fortune (see Meyrick). Owned 20,000 acres worth 15 million pounds in 2001.
Titles: Baronet 1678-1792; 1926-
1 in Cabinet 1974 1979-81 1989-91
Notes: 1 Baron in ODNB and one other.

GINCKEL [van Reede] *ENGLAND & IRELAND*

Earl of Athlone (1692-1844 I)

Origins: The 1 Earl was the son of Godard van Reede Ginckel, Baron van Reede. He was a military commander from an old Dutch family who accompanied William III in 1688. He campaigned in Ireland and was granted estates there in 1692.

No MPs

Seats: Amerongen Castle and Middachten Castle, The Netherlands
Estates: Granted 40,000 acres in Ireland 1692, sold before 1700. 5 Earl granted an annuity by Parliament 1800.
Titles: Baron van Reede 1645-1844
Peers: {3 peers 1692-1719 1795-1800}
Notes: Family extinct 1844. 1 Baron and 1 and 2 Earls in ODNB.

GIPPS

Origins: The first MP was a hop merchant, apothecary, and banker, son of a soldier and staymaker.

1. George Gipps – Canterbury 1780-96 1797-1800
2. George Gipps – Ripon 1807-26
3. Henry Gipps – Canterbury 1852-53

Seats: Hall Place, Harbledown, Kent (medieval, rebuilt 18th c., lease acq. by mar. 1787, passed out of family by 1800); Howletts, Kent (medieval, rebuilt 1797, acq. 19th c., sold 1913); Thanington Court, Kent (purch. 1775, sold c. 1910)
Estates: Bateman 2910 (E) 2743
Notes: One in ODNB.

GLADSTONE [Glynne, Ravenscroft] *SCOTLAND, WALES, & ENGLAND*

Viscount Gladstone (1910-30 UK) (Gladstones)

Origins: The 1 Bt was a self-made Liverpool merchant and shipowner, with large investments in West Indian plantations and businesses and in India. He died a very rich man.

1. Sir John Gladstone 1 Bt – Lancaster 1818-20 Woodstock 1820-26 Berwick-on-Tweed 1826-27

2. Sir Thomas Gladstone 2 Bt – Queenborough 1830-31 Portarlington 1832-34 Leicester 1835-37 Ipswich 1842
3. William Ewart Gladstone – Newark 1832-45 University of Oxford 1847-65 S. Lancashire 1865-68 Greenwich 1868-80 Midlothian 1880-95
4. John Gladstone – Walsall 1841-42 Ipswich 1842-47 Devizes 1852-57
5. William Gladstone – Chester 1865-68 Whitby 1868-80 E. Worcestershire 1880-85
6. Herbert Gladstone 1 Viscount Gladstone – Leeds 1880-85 W. Leeds 1885-1910
7. William Gladstone – Kilmarnock Burghs 1911-15

Seats: Fasque, Kincardineshire (old house, rebuilt 1809, purch. 1833 for £80,000, add. 1833 and c. 1845-50, sold c. 2007, hotel); Phesdo House, Kincardineshire (built 1814-15, purch. later 19th c.); Harwarden Castle, Flintshire (acq. by mar. 1874, still own, see below); Burton Manor, Cheshire (purch. and built 1904, sold 1926)
Estates: Bateman 45062 (S) 9174 and 6918 (W) 18173. The 1 Bt died worth £746,000 in addition to landed property and £324,000 given to his children during his lifetime. Baron Gladstone of Harwarden died worth close to £500,000 in 1935. The Fasque estate stood at 47,700 acres in 1996. Also owned 7,000 acres in Wales in 2001.
Titles: Baron Gladstone of Harwarden 1932-35 UK; Baronet 1846-
Peers: 2 peers 1910-30 1932-35
4 Lds Lt 19th, 20th
2 in Cabinet 1843-46 1852-55 1859-66 1868-74 1880-86 1892-94 1905-10
Notes: 6 in ODNB.

Glynne

Origins: Descended from Welsh princes. They claimed to be able to trace their descent to the 3rd century (*Country Life*, 174, p. 989). Acquired Glynllifon by marriage in the reign of Edward III. **First MP 1593. Another MP 1624 for Caernarvonshire**.

1. Sir John Glynne – Caernarvon Borough 1640 Westminster 1640-48 Caernarvonshire 1654 1660
2. Sir William Glynne 1 Bt – Caernarvonshire 1659 Caernarvon 1660
3. Sir William Glynne 2 Bt – University of Oxford 1698-1700 Woodstock 1702-05
4. Sir John Glynne 6 Bt – Flintshire 1741-47 Flint Boroughs 1753-77
5. Henry Glynne – Flint Boroughs 1831-32
6. Sir Stephen Glynne 9 Bt – Flint Boroughs 1832-37 Flintshire 1837-47

Seats: Hawarden Castle, Flintshire (built 13th c., slighted 1647-48, acq. by mar. 1653, new house 18th c., remod. 1866, passed to Gladstones by mar. in 1874); Glynllifon (Glynnllivon), Caernarvonshire (passed by mar. c. 1700 to the Wynns, see Williams-Wynn)

Estates: 7,000 acres in 1815. Sir John Glynne MP 1640-60 was said to have made £100,000 in political and legal office-holding.
Title: Baronet 1661-1874
1 Ld Lt 19th
Notes: 3 in ODNB.

Ravenscroft

Origins: Old Cheshire family. Acquired Flint estates c. 1440 by marriage. **First MP 1563 for Flintshire. Three further MPs 1586-1628, two for the county**. On the death of Thomas Ravenscroft MP in 1698 his estates passed to a daughter who married Henry Conway and thence to his son-in-law Sir John Glynne 6 Bt.

1. Hall Ravenscroft – Horsham 1640-53 1659-60
2. Thomas Ravenscroft – Flint Boroughs 1697-98

Seats: Harwarden (Broadlane), Flintshire (acq. c. 1440, built 16th c., passed by mar. to Glynnes 1653); Bretton Hall, Flintshire (acq. c. 1440, passed by mar. to Glynnes 1653 and then Gladstones, sold to Grosvenors)
Notes: One in ODNB.

GLANVILLE [Gregor, Masterman]

Glanville

Origins: An old Devon family. **First MP 1584** was a lawyer and judge, son of a merchant. His son was an **MP from 1614** and Speaker of the House of Commons 1640. **One further MP 1640-44**.

1. Francis Glanville – Malmesbury 1794-96 Plymouth 1797-1802

Seats: Catchfrench, Cornwall (medieval, rebuilt 1580, purch. 1728, remod. late 18th c., sold 1830); Clevancy, Wiltshire (purch. 1640, sold c. 1789); Broad Hinton, Wiltshire (built 16th c., purch. 1628, demolished 1645, sold 1702-09)
Notes: Two in ODNB. Probably related to the Glanville family listed under Evelyn.

Masterman

Origins: Founded by an attorney and merchant who was the son of a tanner. He died worth £125,000. His daughter and co-heiress married in 1790 Francis Glanville MP. The other co-heiress married a Gregor (see below). The Glanvilles eventually succeeded to the whole estate. (Christie, *Myth and Reality in Late Eighteenth Century British Politics*, 232-43)

1. William Masterman – Bodmin 1780-84

Seat: Trinity House (Hall), renamed Restormel House (Park), Cornwall after 1775 (acq. 1775, remod. 1780s, passed to co-heiresses – one a Glanville, 1809)

Gregor

Origins: Merchants in Truro in the 17th century.

1. Francis Gregor – Cornwall 1790-1806

Seat: Trewarthenick, Cornwall (purch. 1640, built later 18th c., add. c. 1825, part demolished 1925, sold 1950s)
Estates: Bateman 4206 (E) 4626
Notes: One in ODNB.

GLEANE

Origins: Draper, mercer, and Mayor of Norwich in the later 16th century. Kt 1615. **First MP 1589. Another MP 1628, both for Norwich**.

1. Sir Peter Gleane 1 Bt – Norfolk 1679-81

Seat: Hardwick Hall, Norfolk (acq. by mar. early 17th c., sold 1686)
Title: Baronet 1666-1745
Notes: Bankrupt 1680-90s.

GLEMHAM

Origins: Held property around Glemham by the early 15th century but did not acquire large estates until the Dissolution. Kt 1591. **First MP 1571. Three additional MPs 1593-1626, one kt of the shire**.

1. Thomas Glemham – Orford 1681 1685-87 1689-95

Seat: Glemham Hall, Suffolk (acq. 1540s, medieval house, rebuilt 16th c., sold 1690)
Estates: £2,000 pa in 1603
Notes: One in ODNB. Male line extinct 1711.

GLYN

Baron Wolverton (1869- UK)

Origins: Dry salter and oilman in the 17th and early 18th century. Banker and active in insurance in London 1750s, Lord Mayor 1758. Continued to be active in banking into the second half of the 20th century. Several branches descended from Sir Richard Glyn 1 Bt of Ewell.

1. Sir Richard Glyn 1 Bt – London 1758-68 Coventry 1768-73
2. Sir Richard Glyn 1 Bt – St. Ives 1796-1802
3. George Glyn 1 Baron Wolverton – Kendal 1847-68
4. George Glyn 2 Baron Wolverton – Shaftesbury 1857-73
5. Sidney Glyn – Shaftesbury 1880-85
6. Pascoe Glyn – E. Div. Dorset 1885-86
7. Ralph Glyn 1 Baron Glyn – E. Stirling and Clackmannon 1918-22 Abingdon Div. Berkshire 1924-53
8. Sir Richard Glyn 9 Bt – N. Dorset 1957-70

Seats: Gaunt's House, Dorset (built 1810, add. 1887, still own); Glyn House (Elwell), Surrey (acq. by mar. mid-18th c., rebuilt 1839, sold 1946); Knapp House, Dorset (built 18th c., remod. 19th c., purch. 19th c., sold); Iwerne Minster House, Dorset (built early 18th c., purch. 1876, rebuilt 1878, sold 1908, now a school); Albury Hall, Hertfordshire (built c. 1780, purch. 1906, demolished c. 1950, sold estate 1981)
Estates: Bateman 9770 (E) 12893. Rubinstein – 1 Bt left £250,000 in probate in 1838. The 1 Baron died in 1873 worth about £1,000,000 and the 2 Baron nearly two million a few years later.
Titles: Baron Glyn 1953- UK; Baronet 1759- ; 1800- ; 1934-
Peers: 5 peers 1869-1945
Notes: Claimed ancestral connection with the Glynnes (see Gladstone). 1 and 2 Bts and 1 and 2 Barons and one other in ODNB.

GODDARD I

Origins: Held land in Wiltshire since the 13th century.

1. Edward Goddard – Marlborough 1679
2. Richard Goddard – Wootton Bassett 1710-13 Wiltshire 1722-27
3. Thomas Goddard – Wiltshire 1767-70
4. Ambrose Goddard – Wiltshire 1772-1806
5. Thomas Goddard – Cricklade 1806-12
6. Ambrose Goddard – Cricklade 1837-41

7. Ambrose Goddard – Cricklade 1847-68 1874-80

Seats: The Lawns (Swindon), Wiltshire (acq. and built 1562, rebuilt late 17th c./early 18th c., sold 1927, demolished 1952); Plwath, Carmarthen
Estates: Bateman 3821 (E) 8162. Worth £3,000 pa in the 1730s.

GODDARD II

Origins: Merchants and mayors in the 16th century. **First MP 1584. Another MP 1589.**

1. Richard Goddard – Winchester 1661-66

Seats: Etchilhampton, Wiltshire (owned 17th and early 18th c., sold); Birchenwood House, Hampshire (purch. 1588 for 1,000 marks, passed to an heiress and sold 1787)

GOLDSMID

Origins: Financiers and bullion brokers in the later 18th and the 19th centuries. An heiress married Count Solomon d'Avigdor, who took the additional name Goldsmid.

1. Sir Francis Goldsmid 2 Bt – Reading 1860-78
2. Frederick Goldsmid – Honiton 1865-66
3. Sir Julian Goldsmid 3 Bt – Honiton 1866-68 Rochester 1870-80 St. Pancras 1885-96

Seats: Somerhill, Kent (built c. 1602-13, add. 1828-38, purch. 1849, remod. later 19th and early 20th c., sold 1979, school); Rendcomb Park, Gloucestershire (built 1660s, purch. 1863, rebuilt 1863-65, sold 1883, now a school)
Estates: Bateman 14273 (E) 35580. Rubinstein – Benjamin Goldschmidt left £100,000 in probate 1813 and Asher Goldsmid left £250,000 in 1822. The 1 and 2 Bts of the 1st cr. were both worth £1,000,000 at their deaths.
Titles: Baronet 1841-96; 1934-
Notes: 1 and 2 Bts of 1st cr. and the 2 Bt of the 2nd cr. and four others in ODNB.

GOODRICKE [Holyoake]

Goodricke

Origins: A successful wool merchant purchased Ribston after the Dissolution. His brother was Bishop of Ely and a Lord Chancellor.

1. Francis Goodricke – Aldborough 1659 1660-73
2. Sir John Goodricke 1 Bt – Yorkshire 1661-70

3. Sir Henry Goodricke 2 Bt – Boroughbridge 1673-79 1685-87 1689-1705
4. Sir John Goodricke 5 Bt – Pontefract 1774-80 Ripon 1787-89
5. Sir Henry Goodricke 6 Bt – Lymington 1778-80

Seat: Ribston Hall, Yorkshire (purch. 1542, sold 1836)
Estates: Worth £7,000 pa c. 1835.
Title: Baronet 1641-1839
Notes: Four in ODNB.

Holyoake

Origins: The 7th Goodricke Baronet, a horseracing maniac, willed his estates to his sporting friend Sir Francis Holyoake, who took the name Goodricke. He was the son of a banker and the Lyttelton heiress to Studley Castle (an estate held since the mid-17th century).

1. Sir Francis Holyoake Goodricke 1 Bt – Stafford 1835 S. Staffordshire 1835-37

Seat: Studley Castle, Warwickshire (passed to Holoakes 1809, new house built 1834-37, sold 1863, now offices)
Estates: In 1847 the Studley estate was 2,000 acres worth £3,377 pa. The house of 1834-37 was said to have cost £120,000 to build (Tyack, *Warwickshire Country Houses*, 186). This must have come from the Goodricke fortune inherited in 1833.
Title: Baronet 1835-88
Notes: The 1 Baronet squandered the Goodricke inheritance and the family bank collapsed in 1847. He died poor in 1865. (Wedgwood, *Staffordshire Parliamentary History*, III, 92-93)

GOODWIN

Origins: **First MP probably/possibly 1302 and another 1432. The first certain MP 1529. Another MP 1626-53, both for East Grinstead.**

1. John Goodwin – Haslemere 1641 East Grinstead 1654 1656 Bletchingley 1660
2. Deane Goodwin – Reigate 1679-81

Seats: Rowfant House, Sussex (built 15th and 1574, acq. c. 1635, passed out of the family by mar. 1711); Horne (Bletchingley), Surrey (resident 16th - 19th c.?)

GORDON I [Coxe, Cumming, Halyburton, Lennox, Morris, Seton, Stuart] *SCOTLAND & ENGLAND*

Duke of Gordon (1684-1836 S)

Origins: Family mentioned in a charter previous to 1180. Statesmen and warriors from the 14th century onwards. Earl of Huntly 1445. **First [MP 1612].**

1. John Gordon – Aberdeen 1708-10
2. Lord Adam Gordon – Aberdeenshire 1754-68 Kincardineshire 1774-88
3. Cosmo Gordon – Nairnshire 1774-77
4. Lord George Gordon – Ludgershall 1774-80
5. Lord William Gordon – Elginshire 1779-84 Inverness-shire 1784-90 Horsham 1792-96
6. George Gordon 5 Duke of Gordon – Eye 1806-07

Seats: Gordon Castle, Banffshire (acq. 14th c., built c. 1480, add. 16th c., rebuilt 1770s, passed to Dukes of Richmond 1836); Cluny (Castle), Aberdeenshire (acq. 16th c. or earlier, built c. 1604, passed through various Gordon branches, add. 1820, fire 1926, restored, still own); The Burn, Kincardineshire (built 1791, sold early 20th c.); Preston Hall (Prestonhall), Edinburghshire (old house, rebuilt c. 1700, purch. 1738, remod. c. 1740, sold 1789)
Estates: Bateman 269292 (S) 60388. Rubinstein – 4 Duke left £122,677 in probate in 1827.
Titles: Baron Gordon 1784-1836 GB; Earl of Norwich 1784-1836 GB; Baronet 1625-
Peers: [1 peer 1689] 2 Scottish Rep peer 1747-52 1767-84 2 peers 1784-1827 1807-36
2 Lds Lt 18th, 19th
4 KT 17th, 18th, 19th
Notes: The Gordon family, the 1, 2, 4, and 5 Dukes, and five others has an entry in the ODNB.

Duke of Richmond, Lennox and Gordon (1675- E; 1675- S; 1876- UK)

Origins: The 1 Duke of Lennox and Richmond was an illegitimate son of King Charles II. The 1 Duke was also made a French Duke (Aubigny, confirmed 1818). The 3 Duke added 16,000 acres to the small estate at Goodwood in the mid-18th c. The 4 Duke married the heiress of the 4 Duke of Gordon. The 5 Duke of Richmond succeeded to the Gordon estates in 1836 (mar. last Duke's sister 1789).

1. Charles Lennox 2 Duke of Richmond – Chichester 1722-23
2. Lord George Lennox – Chichester 1761-67 Sussex 1767-90
3. Charles Lennox 4 Duke of Richmond – Chichester 1790-1806

4. Charles Gordon-Lennox 5 Duke of Richmond – Chichester 1812-19
5. Lord John Gordon-Lennox – Chichester 1819-31 Sussex 1831-32 W. Sussex 1832-41
6. Lord William Lennox – King's Lynn 1831-34
7. Lord Arthur Gordon-Lennox – Chichester 1831-46 Yarmouth 1847-48
8. Charles Gordon Lennox 6 Duke of Richmond – W. Sussex 1841-60
9. Lord Henry Gordon Lennox – Chichester 1846-85
10. Lord Alexander Gordon Lennox – Shoreham 1849-59
11. Lord George Gordon Lennox – Lymington 1860-74
12. Charles Gordon Lennox 7 Duke of Richmond – W. Sussex 1869-85 Chichester Div. Sussex 1885-88
13. Lord Walter Gordon Lennox – Chichester Div. Sussex 1888-94

Seats: Goodwood, Sussex (built 1616-17, purch. 1697, rebuilt 1760s through to 1820, still own); Molecomb, Sussex (purch. 1697, built mid-18th c., still own); Gordon Castle, Banffshire (built c. 1480, add. 16th c., rebuilt 1770s, inher. by mar. 1836, contents sold 1938, requisitioned WWII, large portion demolished 1954, still own)
Estates: Bateman 17119 (E) 19295. Plus Gordon estates in Scotland after 1836. Worth £45,000,000 with 12,000 acres in 1990.
Peers: 9 peers 1693-1750 1756-1945
7 Lds Lt 17th, 18th, 19th, 20th
4 in Cabinet 1766 1782-95 1807-13 1830-34 1867-68 1874-80 1885-86
7 KG 17th, 18th, 19th, 20th
Notes: 1, 2, 3, 4, 5, and 6 Dukes of Richmond and three others in ODNB.

Marquis of Huntly (1559- S)

Origins: The senior line of the Gordons, the Dukes of Gordon, were earlier created Marquises of Huntly. On the death of the 5 Duke of Gordon in 1836, the Marquisate of Huntly and a substantial portion of the estate passed to a descendent of a younger brother of the 3 Marquis, the 5 Earl of Aboyne.

1. Charles Gordon 10 Marquis of Huntly – East Grinstead 1818-30 Huntingdonshire 1830-31
2. Lord Douglas Gordon Halyburton – Forfarshire 1832-41
3. Lord John Gordon – Forfarshire 1841-52
4. Lord Douglas Gordon – W. Aberdeenshire 1876-80 Huntingdonshire 1880-85

Seats: Aboyne Castle, Aberdeenshire (built early 17th c., remod. 1671, add. 1801, remod. 1835 and 1860, sequestered for debts and much land sold 1850s-1920s, still own the house and have rebuilt some of the estate); Orton Hall, Huntingdonshire (built 16th c., add. 18th c., acq. by mar. 1821, rebuilt 1835, add. 1861, sales from 1900 through final

sale 1954, hotel); Huntly Castle, Aberdeenshire (medieval, burned 1594, rebuilt 1602, decayed by early 18th c., ruin by 1746, sold 1923)
Estates: Bateman 85711 (S & E) 19860. 2,000 acres in 1996.
Titles: Earl of Huntly 1445- S; Earl of Enzie 1599- S; Viscount Aboyne 1632- S; Earl of Aboyne 1660- S; Baron Meldrum 1815- UK
Peers: [2 peers 1661-81 1698-1707] 1 Scottish Rep peer 1796-1806 1807-18 4 peers 1815-63 1868-1945
1 Ld Lt 19th
1 KT 19th
Notes: Remained Roman Catholic in the 17th c. Orton Longueville passed from the Cope Baronets (see Cope) to the Gordons in 1821. The 11 Marquis was beset by financial problems from the 1880s. 1, 2, 3, 4, and 5 Earls of Huntly and 1, 2, and 9 Marquises of Huntly, and 2 Viscount Aboyne, and 1 and 2 Earls of Aboyne and five others in ODNB.

Halyburton (Haliburton, Hallyburton)

Origins: Emerged at Dirleton, Haddingtonshire in the 14th century. High Treasurer of Scotland and lords of Parliament in the 15th century. **First [MP 1560]. Two other [MPs 1560-1617].** James Halyburton of Pitcur entailed his estates on his sister, the wife of the 13 Earl of Morton in 1765. May, daughter of the 14 Earl, married the 4 Earl of Aboyne. Their younger son, Lord Douglas Gordon, took the name Halyburton in 1843 and succeeded to Pitcur.

1. James Halyburton – [Forfarshire 1702-07] Scotland 1707-08
2. James Halyburton – Orkney & Shetland 1747-54

Seats: Pitcur, Forfarshire (acq. 1432, passed out of the family by mar. 1765); Halyburton House, Forfarshire
Notes: Family entry and three others in ODNB.

Gordon

Origins: Cadet family.

1. Sir George Gordon – [Banffshire 1681 1685-86]

Seats: Park House, Banffshire (built 1536, add. c. 1723, remod. c. 1750, passed by mar. to Duffs by mar. later 18th c.); Edinglassie, Aberdeenshire (owned 16th-17th c., passed to Forbes family in the 18th c.)
Title: Baronet 1686-1835

Morris

Origins: Staats Long Morris, an American soldier of prominent lineage, married the Dowager (3) Duchess of Gordon and was seated at Gordon Castle during the marriage and gained a place in Parliament through Gordon family influence.

1. Staats Long Morris – Elgin Burghs 1774-84

Seat: Gordon Castle, Banffshire (see Duke of Gordon above)
Notes: Morris in ODNB.

Seton

Origins: The Setons were a powerful family. The senior line were Earls of Winton (see Montgomerie). The Setons of Touch were hereditary armor bearers of the Kings of Scots. One was killed at Flodden 1513. **First [MP 1593 for Dumbartonshire]. Another [MP 1612 for Stirlingshire].** The Setons of Touch were descended from a son of the 1 Earl of Huntly.

1. James Seton – [Stirlingshire 1665 1667 1669-72]
2. James Seton – [Stirlingshire 1673-74 1678 1681 1685-86]

Seat: Touch House, Stirlingshire (acq. c. 1480, built 16th and 17th c., add. 1757, sold 1928)
Estates: Bateman 7474 (S) 5679
Notes: The family finances were saved in the late 18th century by a Seton who worked for the East India Company and returned a nabob. Seton family and one other has an entry in ODNB.

Seton

Origins: Also descended from the 1 Earl of Huntly. This line produced officials and lawyers in the 17th c.

1. Sir Walter Seton 1 Bt – [Linlithgowshire 1665 1667 1669-74]

Seat: Abercorn, Linlithgowshire (acq. 1662 and resident in 18th c.)
Title: Baronet 1663-

Seton

Origins: Also descended from the 1 Earl of Huntly.

1. Sir Alexander Seton 1 Bt – [Aberdeenshire 1681 1685-86]
2. Sir William Seton 2 Bt – [Abderdeenshire 1703-07] Scotland 1707-08

Seats: Pitmedden, Aberdeenshire (acq. by mar. later 16th c., new house mid-17th c., fire 1818, rebuilt 1860s, sold 1894); Cushnie House, Aberdeenshire (built 1707, acq. 19th c., passed out of the family later in the 19th c., ruin by 1901, demolished 1959)
Title: Baronet 1683-

Gordon

Origin: Descended from a younger brother of the 3 Earl of Huntly. This Adam Gordon married Elizabeth Countess of Sutherland in her own right (see Leveson Gower). A junior line of the 12 Earl of Sutherland (Gordon) was seated at Gordonstoun. **First [MP 1630]. Another [MP 1649].**

1. Robert Gordon – [Sutherland 1661-63]
2. Sir Robert Gordon 3 Bt – [Sutherlandshire 1672-74 1678 1681 1685-86]
3. Sir John Gordon – [Sutherlandshire 1685-86]
4. Alexander Gordon – [Sutherlandshire 1700-05]
5. Sir Robert Gordon 4 Bt – Caithness 1715-22

Seat: Gordonstoun, Elginshire (acq. 15th c., built c. 16th c., add. 1616 by 1 Marquis of Huntly, remod. 1730 and 1775, sold 1934, school)
Estates: A junior line at Letterfourie, Banffshire 2331 (S) 2719
Title: Baronet 1625-1795
Notes: Three in ODNB.

Gordon-Cumming (Cuming)

Origins: The Cummings claimed ancient descent from the Comyns of Badenoch (13th century). Rose to importance as a result of the career of an official in the late 17th and early 18th century. Alexander Cumming of Altyre succeeded his cousin Sir William Gordon 6 Bt of Gordonstoun in 1795 and took the name Gordon.

1. Sir Alexander Cumming 1 Bt – Aberdeenshire 1709-22
2. Sir Alexander Cumming-Gordon 1 Bt – Inverness Burghs 1802-03
3. George Cumming – Inverness Burghs 1803—06 1818-26
4. Sir William Gordon-Cumming 2 Bt – Elgin Burghs 1831-32

5. Charles Cumming Bruce – Inverness Burghs 1831-37 Elginshire & Nairnshire 1840-68

Seats: Altyre, Elginshire (old house, add. and remod. late 19th c., demolished 1962); Gordonstoun, Elginshire (see above); Culter House, Aberdeenshire (built 17th c., sold 1725)
Estates: Bateman 38499 (S) 13840. Owned 16,300 acres in 1996.
Title: Baronet 1695-1793; 1804-
Notes: 2 Bt of Culter (of the first creation) ended up in debtors prison and died in an almshouse. Three in ODNB.

Gordon

Origins: Descended from a younger brother of the 1 Earl of Huntly via an illegitimate line.

1. Sir Robert Gordon 2 Bt – [Sutherlandshire 1649-50 1661]
2. Sir John Gordon 3 Bt – [Sutherlandshire 1681 1689-90]
3. George Gordon – [Dornoch Burgh 1685-86 1689-90]

Seat: Embo House, Sutherlandshire (old house 17th c., purch. c. 1777, rebuilt c. 1767, later sold)
Title: Baronet 1631-1956

Viscount Kenmure (1633-1716 1824-1847 S)

Origins: Descended from William Gordon, a younger son of Sir Adam Gordon (14th century). **First [MP 1560]. Another [MP 1612]**. Attainted 1716 but estates (1722) and title (1824) eventually restored.

1. John Gordon 7 Viscount Kenmure – Kirkcudbright Stewartry 1781-82

Seats: Kenmure Castle, Kirkcudbrightshire (acq. 1297, medieval, rebuilt 15th c., purch. early 16th c., rebuilt 1630, add. 18th c., add. 1840, add. 1879, burned 1950, ruin); Overton House Kirkcudbrightshire (rebuilt c. 1900, owned at least until 1929); Lochinvar Castle, Kirkcudbrightshire (acq. and built 1297, sold 1787, ruin); Earlston House (Castle), Kirkcudbrightshire (built late 16th/early 17th c., acq. 1615, add. 1655, demolished 1950)
Estates: Bateman 14093 (S) 4229
Titles: Baron Lochinvar 1633-1716 S; 1824-1847 S; Baronet 1626-1847
Peer: [1 peer 1660-63]
Notes: The 6 Viscount was created Marquis of Kenumre in the Jacobite peerage. He was beheaded on Tower Hill 1716. 1 and 6 Viscounts and three others in ODNB.

Gordon

Origins: A junior line that broke off in the 16th century from the Kenmure Gordons. Robert Gordon of Auchendolly, the son of a Bristol merchant and West Indian planter in Jamaica, married in 1809 Elizabeth Coxe, heiress of Charles Coxe of Kemble House.

1. Robert Gordon – Wareham 1812-18 Cricklade 1818-37 Windsor 1837-41

Seats: Auchendolly, Kirkcudbrightshire (passed to Lord Biddulph 1884); Kemble House, Wiltshire (passed to Lord Biddulph 1884); Leweston House, Dorset; Nether Lypiatt Manor House, Gloucestershire (acq. by mar. from Coxe family 1809, passed to Sheppards 1884, sold 20th c.)
Estates: Bateman 6631 (E) 7853
Notes: The daughter and heiress of Robert Gordon MP above left Auchendolly and Kemble to the 1 Baron Biddulph in 1884 (see Myddelton). She left Nether Lypiatt to other kin, the Sheppard family, who sold it in the 20th century.

Coxe

Origins: Gentry since the 16th century. The first MP became a judge. He purchased Nether Lypiatt, Gloucestershire in 1693.

1. Charles Coxe – Cirencester 1698-1705 1708-13 Gloucester 1713-22
2. John Coxe – Cirencester 1749-54
3. Charles Westley Coxe – Cricklade 1784-85

Seats: Kemble House, Wiltshire; Nether Lypiatt Manor House, Gloucestershire (built early 16th c., inher. by mar. from Freame family, who acq. by 1509, in 1699, rebuilt c. 1708-10, passed to Gordons by mar. 1809); Rosmarton, Gloucestershire (there by late 16th century)
Notes: Last MP was son of a Westley heiress, daughter of a Lord Mayor of London.

Marquis of Aberdeen and Temair (1916- UK)

Origins: John Gordon's (14th century) senior line of descendents became the Dukes of Gordon and the junior line established themselves at Haddo. **First [MP 1617]. Another [MP 1625].**

1. George Gordon 1 Earl of Aberdeen – [Aberdeenshire 1669-74 1678 1681]
2. William Gordon Lord Haddo – Aberdeenshire 1708
3. William Gordon – New Woodstock 1767-74 Heytesbury 1774-80
4. William Gordon – Aberdeenshire 1820-54
5. George Gordon 5 Earl of Aberdeen – Aberdeenshire 1854-60

6. Arthur Hamilton-Gordon 1 Baron Stanmore – Beverley 1854-57
7. Sir Alexander Gordon – E. Aberdeenshire 1875-85

Seats: Haddo House, Aberdeenshire (acq. estate 1469, new house 1732-35, remod. 1822-28, NT 1974); Fyvie Castle, Aberdeenshire (medieval, add. 1598-1603, purch. 1733, passed to a younger son 1745, see below)
Estates: Bateman 62422 (S) 44112. 7,047 acres in 1996.
Titles: Earl of Aberdeen 1682- S; Viscount Gordon 1814- UK; Baron Stanmore 1893- UK; Baronet 1625-1839; 1642-
Peers: [1 peer 1682-89] 3 Scottish Rep peers 1721-27 1747-61 1774-90 1806-14 8 peers 1814-70 1872-1945 1893-1945
3 Lds Lt 19th, 20th
2 in Cabinet 1828-30 1834-35 1841-46 1852-55 1886 1905-15
1 KG 19th
2 KT 19th, 20th
Notes: The 4 Earl was Prime Minister, the 3 Marquis was Chairman of Hadfields, the Sheffield steel company, and President of the Federation of British Industries 1940-43. The 5 Marquis was the BBC producer of the "Week at Westminster" for twenty years and Head of radio talks and documentaries in the 1960s and 1970s. 1 Baron Stanmore and 1 and 4 Earls of Aberdeen, 1 Marquis of Aberdeen, and five others in ODNB.

Duff-Gordon

Origins: Descended from a younger son of the 2 Earl of Aberdeen. Alexander Gordon married the sister and heiress of Sir James Duff 1 Bt of Crombie. Their son succeeded to the Baronetcy by special remainder.

1. Sir William Duff-Gordon – Worcester 1807-18
2. Charles Gordon – Berwick 1859-63

Seats: Fyvie Castle, Aberdeenshire (acq. 1745 from Earl of Aberdeen, see above, add. 1777 and possibly 1798-93, sold 1889); Harpton Court, Radnorshire (built 1750, add. 1805-12, inher. 1911, sold 1953, partly demolished 1956)
Estates: Bateman 13054 (S) 10111
Title: Baronet 1813-

Gordon

Origins: Descended from a common ancestor with the Marquises of Aberdeen.

1. Alexander Gordon – [Aberdeenshire 1703-07]

Seat: Pitlurg House, Aberdeenshire (built 1827, sold c. 1900, fire 1927, ruin)

Gordon

Origins: Descended from a common ancestor with the Marquises of Aberdeen.

1. William Gordon – [Kirkcudbright 1690]

Seat: Craig, Kirkcudbrightshire

Gordon

Origins: Descended from a common ancestor with the Marquises of Aberdeen. One made a fortune in the West Indies in the 18th century, purchased plantations and land in England and died worth £100,000 in addition to the value of the estates in 1822.

1. James Gordon – Stockbridge 1785-90 Truro 1790-96 Clitheroe 1808-12
2. James Gordon – Tregony 1830-32

Seats: Knockspock, Aberdeenshire (inherit. 1836, sold c. 1990); Moor Place, Hertfordshire (built 16th c., purch. 1749, rebuilt 1775-79, sold 1860); Naish House, Somerset (purch. 1790s, passed out of family in mid-19th c., fire 1903); Stockton House, Hertfordshire
Estates: Rubinstein – James Gordon left £100,000 in probate 1822. Said to have owned 1,400 acres in Antigua.
Notes: One in ODNB.

Baron Blantyre (1606-1900 S)

Origins: The 1 Baron was the son of a Provost of Glasgow. The family descended from Sir Thomas Stewart of Dalswinton and Garlies, progenitor of the Earls of Galloway (see Stewart). **Probable MP for Monmouth 1624-25.** The 5 Baron inherited a fortune from his cousin the Duchess of Richmond and Lennox in 1702.

1. James Stuart – Huntingdon 1824-31

Seats: Erskine House, Renfrewshire (medieval, acq. 18th c., rebuilt 1828, derelict from 1900, hospital from 1916 onwards); Lennoxlove (Lethington) House, Haddingtonshire (built 14th c. and 15th c., add. 17th c., purch. 1703, add. early 1828, passed by mar. to the Bairds 1900, sold 1947, hotel)
Estates: Batmean 14061 (S) 20593
Peers: [2 peers 1670-1707] 3 Scottish Rep peers 1710-13 1806-07 1850-92
1 Ld Lt 19th

GORDON II *SCOTLAND*

Origins: Descended from the 1 Earl of Sutherland (see Leveson Gower). Father of 1 Bt was a moneylender. The son was a burgess of Edinburgh and banker in London. He purchased an estate renamed Invergordon.

1. Sir Adam Gordon – [Sutherlandshire 1689-1700]
2. Sir William Gordon 1 Bt – Sutherland 1708-13 1714-27 Cromartyshire 1741-42
3. Alexander Gordon – Inverness Burghs 1722
4. Sir John Gordon 2 Bt – Cromartyshire 1742-47 1754-61

Seats: Invergordon Castle, Cromartyshire (medieval castle, purch. 1704, sold 1780, demolished 1928); Dalpholly, Sutherland (acq. by mar. 1509); Newhall, Ross-shire (acq. by mar. 1674, ruin, rebuilt 1730, add. 1805)
Title: Baronet 1704-1850

GORE I [Booth, Ormsby, Owen, Sankey, Saunders] *IRELAND, WALES & ENGLAND*

Earl of Ross (1772-1802 I)

Origins: The founder of the family was Gerard Gore an Alderman in the City of London. His eldest son Richard was **MP for London 1604**. From a second son, a Lord Mayor of London, descend the Gore-Langtons (see Grenville). Another son, Sir Paul Gore 1 Bt, went to Ireland as a military officer under Elizabeth I and acquired estates. He was elected **{MP Ballyshannon 1613}.** From his eldest son descended the Earls of Ross. The 2 Bt was an **{MP 1639}.**

1. Sir William Gore 3 Bt – {Banagher 1661-66}
2. Sir Ralph Gore 4 Bt – {Donegal 1703-13 County Donegal 1713-27 Clogher 1727-33}
3. Sir St. George Gore 5 Bt – {County Donegal 1741-46}
4. Ralph Gore 1 Earl of Ross – {County Donegal 1741-64}
5. Frederick Gore – {Tulsk 1747-60}
6. Henry Gore – {Killibegs 1749-60 Lanesborough 1761-68}

Seats: Belle Isle (Belleisle) (Ballymacanus), Fermanagh (acq. and built 1598, rebuilt 18th c., became ruinous, sold c. 1818); Manor Gore, Leitrim (acq. later 16th c.); Manor Hamilton, Leitrim (acq. by Hamiltons late 17th c., passed to Gores by mar. 1733, sold by 1807); Dunmore House, Galway (acq. by mar. from St. Georges 17th c., sold late 18th c., now a ruin)
Estates: Bateman 3176 (I) 1384. Held 28,896 acres with an income of £1,200 pa in 1713. Property gradually divested during the 18th c. 9,000 acres sold 1872. The remainder of around 2,500 acres sold in 1916.

Titles: Baron Gore 1764-1802 I; Viscount Belleisle 1772-1802 I; Baronet 1621-
Peer: {1 peer 1772-1800}
Notes: The 4 Baronet married a St. George heiress and inherited Dunmore, Galway. He inherited Hamilton estates (Viscount Boyne) at Manor Hamilton 1733. 4 Bt in ODNB

Earl of Arran (1762- I)

Origins: The second son of Sir Paul Gore 1 Bt (see Earl of Ross) was the ancestor of the Earls of Arran. He settled in Mayo and was created a Bt in 1662. Sheriff 1711.

1. Sir Arthur Gore 1 Bt – {County Mayo 1661-66}
2. Sir Arthur Gore 2 Bt – {Ballynakill 1703-13 Donegal 1713-14 County Mayo 1715-42}
3. Arthur Gore 1 Earl of Arran – {Donegal 1727-58}
4. Arthur Gore – {County Longford 1739-58}
5. Paul Gore – {County Mayo 1751-60 County Sligo 1765-68}
6. Arthur Gore 2 Earl of Arran – {Donegal 1759-60 County Wexford 1761-68 Donegal 1768-73}
7. Richard Gore – {Castlebar 1761-68 Donegal 1769-76}
8. Arthur Gore 3 Earl of Arran – {Baltimore 1783-90 County Donegal 1800} 1801-06
9. Robert Gore – New Ross 1841-47

Seats: Castle Gore (Deel Castle), Mayo (16th c. tower house, acq. c. 1690, add. 18th c., damaged 1798, burned 1922, ruin); Saunderscourt, Wexford (acq. by Saunders 1656, inher. by mar. 1730 by Earl of Arran, house built early to mid-18th c., sold c. 1860, demolished post 1926)
Estates: Bateman 36527 (I) 10112. Worth £7,004 pa in 1787.
Titles: Viscount Sudley 1758- I; Baron Sudley 1884- UK; Baronet 1662-
Peers: {3 peers 1759-1800 1797-1800} 1 Irish Rep peer 1800-21 2 peers 1884-1945
2 Lds Lt 19th, 20th
3 KP 18th, 19th, 20th
Notes: The sister of the 1 Earl of Arran had a son, James Cuffe, who inherited Castle Gore and was created Baron Tyrawley, although the estates eventually reverted to the Earls (see Cuffe). Three in ODNB.

Saunders

Origins: To Ireland mid-17th century in the army. Sheriff 1707. Heiress married 1 Earl of Arran.

1. Richard Saunders – {Taghmon 1703-13 Wexford 1713-14 Taghmon 1715-30}

Seat: Saunderscourt (Saunders Court), Wexford (acq. 1656, passed by mar. to Gores 1730, demolished post 1926)
Estates: Worth £550 pa in 1688, £800 pa in 1713, £1,300 pa in 1727, and £3,500 pa in 1784.

Baron Harlech (1876- UK)

Origins: Descended from the third son of Gerard Gore (see above), whose great-grandson settled in Ireland. The latter's great-granddaughter and heiress married a cadet descendent of the ancestor of the Earls of Arran, William Gore MP. Their son married 1815 Mary Jane Ormsby, daughter and heiress of Owen Ormsby of Willowbrook and Porkington (inherited from Owens), and the Gores assumed the additional name Ormsby. The Ormsbys inherited Porkington c. 1600 and elected their **first MP before the Civil War**. (See Ormsby)

1. William Gore – {Donegal 1695-99 County Leitrim 1703-30}
2. William Gore – {County Leitrim 1720-60 1768-69}
3. William Gore – {Kilkenny 1727-48}
4. Ralph Gore – {Kilkenny 1748-60 1776-78}
5. William Gore – {County Leitrim 1769-76}
6. John Gore – {County Leitrim 1784-90}
7. William Gore – {Carrick 1798-1800}
8. William Ormsby-Gore – County Leitrim 1806-07 Caernarvon 1830-31 N. Shropshire 1835-57
9. John Ormsby-Gore 1 Baron Harlech – Caernarvonshire 1837-41 N. Shropshire 1859-76
10. William Ormsby-Gore 2 Baron Harlech – County Sligo 1841-52 Leitrim 1858-76
11. Seymour Ormsby-Gore – Gainsborough Div. Lincolnshire 1900-06
12. George Ormsby Gore 3 Baron Harlech – W. Oswestry Div. Shropshire 1901-04
13. William Ormsby-Gore 4 Baron Harlech – Denbigh District 1910-18 Stafford 1918-38
14. William Ormsby-Gore 5 Baron Harlech – Oswestry 1950-61

Seats: Brogyntyn (Porkington), Shropshire (acq. by mar. by Owens c. 1600, built c. 1617, rebuilt 1735-36, add. 1814-15, acq. by mar. from the Owens, add. 1870, sold 2001); Woodford, Leitrim (Gore seat 18th c., ruinous by 1835, sold c. 1865); Derrycarne, Leitrim (built and purch. 1814, sold 1924, derelict later 20th c.); Willowbrook, Sligo (built late 17th c., acq, by mar. 1815, fire 1867, ruin)
Estates: Bateman 58357 (E, W, & I) 26400. The 5 Baron died worth £3,300,000 in 1985.
Peers: 4 peers 1876-1945
4 Lds Lt 19th, 20th
1 in Cabinet 1931-38
Notes: The 5 Baron was Ambassador to the United States 1961-65 and close to President Kennedy. 4 and 5 Barons in ODNB.

Owen

Origins: John Owen was an official under Elizabeth I and married the heiress to Clenennau. **First MP 1597. Two further MPs, one for Shropshire before 1660**. The Owen heiress of Porkington married in 1777 an Ormsby of Willowbrook.

1. Sir Robert Owen – Merioneth 1681 Caernarvon 1689-98
2. Francis Owen – Helston 1774

Seats: Porkington (Brogyntyn), Shropshire (acq. by Owens c., 1600, built for Owens c. 1617, rebuilt 1735-36, passed to Ormsbys by mar. 19th c.); Clenennau, Caernarvonshire (Maurice family acq. 1462, Owens acq. by mar. c. 1600, passed by mar. to the Ormsby's by mar. 19th c.)
Notes: Clenennau belonged to Sir William Maurice (Morris) **MP 1593-1604**, descendent of the 12th-century Welsh Prince Owen Gwynedd. He left his estates to the Owens, who became one of the richest families in Caernarvonshire by 1626.
Notes: One in ODNB.

Baron Annaly (1766-84 and 1789-93 I)

Origins: Descended from a younger son of Sir Arthur Gore 1 Bt, grandfather of the 1 Earl of Arran.

1. George Gore – {Longford 1709-20}
2. John Gore 1 Baron Annaly – {Jamestown 1747-60 County Longford 1761-64}
3. Henry Gore 1 Baron Annaly – {County Longford 1758-60 Lanesborough 1761-68 County Longford 1768-89}

Seat: Tenelick (Tennalick), Longford (acq. by mar. 1722)
Estates: Worth £1,000 pa in 1713.
Peers: {2 peers 1767-84 1789-93}
Notes: 1 Baron a judge. 1 Baron in ODNB.

Sankey

Origins: First MP was a professional soldier. Tenelick passed by marriage on first MP's death 1722 to the Gores.

1. Nicholas Sankey – {Lanesborough 1703-13}

Seat: Tenelick (Tennalick), Longford (acq. 1692, passed to Gores by inher. 1722)

Gore-Booth

Origins: Descended from the youngest son of Sir Paul Gore 1 Bt. His grandson married Letitia Booth heiress to considerable estates in Manchester and Salford.

1. Sir Francis Gore – {County Sligo 1661-66}
2. John Gore – {Ennis 1692-93}
3. Francis Gore – {Ennis 1695-99 1713-14 County Clare 1715-25}
4. Sir Robert Gore-Booth 4 Bt – County Sligo 1850-76
5. Constance Gore-Booth Countess de Markievicz – St. Patrick's Div. Dublin 1918

Seats: Lissadell, Sligo (castle 13th c., acq. late 16th c., rebuilt 17th c., rebuilt on new site 1830-35, sold late 20th c.); Ardtermon (Artarman), Sligo
Estates: Bateman 31774 (I) 16346
Title: Baron Gore-Booth 1969-84 UKLife; Baronet 1760-
1 Ld Lt 19th
Notes: Constance Gore-Booth-Markievicz was the first woman elected to the House of Commons and a revolutionary in the Easter Rising. 1 Baron and 3 others in ODNB.

GORE II

Origins: Merchants and attorneys in the 16th century. A mercer became Lord Mayor of London 1701. **First MP 1656 for Hertfordshire**.

1. Sir John Gore – Hertford 1677-79
2. Gerard Gore – Queenborough 1681
3. William Gore – Colchester 1711-13 Cricklade 1713-14 Colchester 1714-15 St. Albans 1722-27 Cricklade 1734-39
4. Thomas Gore – Cricklade 1722-27 Amersham 1735-46 Portsmouth 1746-47 Bedford 1747-54 Cricklade 1754-68
5. Charles Gore – Cricklade 1739-41 Hertfordshire 1741-61 Tiverton 1762-68
6. John Gore – Cricklade 1747-54
7. John Gore – Great Grimsby 1747-61

Seats: Tring Park, Hertfordshire (built 1670s, purch. 1705, sold 1786); Dunstan Park, Berkshire (built 1720, leased?, demolished 1798); Bush Hill Park, Middlesex (built 18th c., leased?, demolished 1927)
Estates: Worth about £5,000 pa in 1709.
Notes: One member of the family married a daughter of the 4 Earl of Northampton in 1705, but William Gore MP 1711-39 was both a merchant and a landed gentleman.

Gore

Origins: John Gore {MP} below was the son of Sir John Gore (MP 1677-79) above, who sold his English estates and whose children emigrated to Ireland in the later 17th c. The other {MPs} below descended from the same family. John was probably a soldier and Francis was a general and his son Arthur was an army captain. Sheriff 1705.

1. John Gore – {Ennis 1692-93}
2. Francis Gore – {Ennis 1695-99 1713-14 County Clare 1715-24}
3. Arthur Gore – {Ennis 1727-31}

Seat: Clonroad, Clare (medieval castle, add. 17th c., acq. 1712, rebuilt 1842, sold 1852)
Estates: Estimated income 1715 was £400 pa.

GORGES *ENGLAND & IRELAND*

Gorges

Origins: The family first gained estates by marriage in the 13th century. Baron by writ 1309. **First MP 1331. Five additional MPs 1432-1639.**

1. Edward Gorges – Somerset 1689

Seat: Charlton House, Somerset (acq. by 1316, passed to Codringtons 1694)
Estates: Worth £600 pa in 1660.
Notes: Sir Ferdinando Gorges (MP 1593) was a colonial pioneer in Barbados and owned the province of Maine. Edward Gorges MP above was the last of the senior line. His daughter and heiress married John Codrington of Dodington (see that family). Three in ODNB.

Baron Gorges of Dundalk (1620-1712 I)

Origins: Cadet of the Gorges of Wraxall. **First MP 1640.**

1. Richard Gorges 2 Baron Gorges – Newton 1661-79

Seats: Longford Castle, Wiltshire (old house, purch. 1573, rebuilt 1576-91, sold 1717); Stetchworth House, Cambridgeshire (built 1640s, purch. 1667, passed out of family 1712, demolished 1796 and rebuilt)
Title: Baronet 1611-1712

Gorges

Origins: Cadet of the Gorges line at Wraxall 16th century. Merchants, lawyers, colonial businessmen. **First MP 1625. Another MP 1654.**

1. Thomas Gorges – Taunton 1654 1656 1659 1660
2. Henry Gorges – Herefordshire 1698-1708 Weobley 1708-10 Leominster 1713-15
3. Richard Gorges – Leominster 1754-61

Seats: Batcombe, Somerset (acq. 16th c., there 17th c., sold c. 1665); Heavitree, Devon (acq. by mar. mid-17th c., sold early 18th c.); The Mynde (Le Minde), Herefordshire (acq. by Pyes (see below) 1433, built late 15th c., add. 16th and 19th c., inher. by mar. to Gorges 1696, remod. c. 1725, sold mid-18th c.); Eye Manor, Herefordshire (built c. 1680, sold 18th c.)
Estates: Worth £1,800 pa in 1718.
Notes: Pye family gentry from 15th c., **first MP 1597. Another MP 1628**. Henry Gorges MP above made his fortune in the slave trade.

Gorges

Origins: Cadet of the Gorges of Longford Castle, to Ireland 1655 as a secretary to Henry Cromwell. Acquired estates in Meath. This entry includes members of two lines that were cousins.

1. Robert Gorges – {Bandon 1661-66 Ratoath 1692-93}
2. John Gorges – {Londonderry 1665-66}
3. Richard Gorges – {Charlemont 1692-93 Bandon 1703-13 Ratoath 1713-27}
4. Hamilton Gorges – {Coleraine 1757-60 Swords 1761-68}
5. Richard Gorges – {Augher 1739-60 Enniskillen 1761-68}
6. Sir Richard Gorges 1 Bt – {Enniskillen 1768-76 Naas 1787-90}
7. Hamilton Gorges – {County Meath 1792-1800} 1801-02

Seats: Rathbe(a)le Hall (House) (St. Catherine's Grove), Dublin (built late 1680s, purch. 1748, add. 1751, sold 1810); Kilbrew House, Meath (built later 18th c., acq. c. 1800, sold before 1837); Ballygawley Park, Tyrone (acq. sec. half 17th c., sold 1811, burned 1920s)
Estates: Worth £7,200 pa in 1713.
Title: Baronet 1787-1821
Notes: Rathbele passed via heiresses to the Merediths and Somervilles, who sold it.

GORING [Fagge (Fagg)]

Earl of Norwich (1644-70 E)

Origins: Achieved gentry status in the 15th century or earlier. **First MP 1467 for Sussex. Seven further MPs 1539-1642, one further for the county**. Master of the Horse to Henry VIII, Privy Councillor, and held financial offices under Elizabeth I and James I that allowed the purchase of extensive estates. Baron 1628.

1. Sir Henry Goring 2 Bt – Sussex 1660 Steyning 1661-79 Sussex 1685-87
2. Percy Goring – Bramber 1661-79 1681
3. Sir Henry Goring 2 Bt – New Shoreham 1673-79 Bramber 1679-81 Steyning 1685-87
4. Sir Charles Goring 3 Bt – Bramber 1689-90
5. Charles Goring – Steyning 1701-08
6. Sir Henry Goring 4 Bt – Horsham 1707-08 Steyning 1709-15 Horsham 1715
7. Charles Goring – New Shoreham 1774-80
8. Sir Harry Goring 6 Bt – New Shoreham 1790-96
9. Sir Henry Goring 8 Bt – New Shoreham 1832-41
10. Charles Goring – New Shoreham 1841-49

Seats: Wiston Manor (Park), Sussex (built 1573-75, acq. by mar. 1743, remod. 1830s, family departed 1926 and leased out, still own, institutional use); Highden, Sussex (acq. 1610, sold 1887); Wappingthorne, Sussex (built early 17th c., purch. 1671, declined to a farm house, for sale 2011)
Estates: Bateman 14139 (E) 13705. Said to have had an income of perhaps £15,000 to 26,800 pa c. late 1630s. Charles Goring left £250,000 in probate in 1829.
Titles: Baron Goring 1628-71 E; Baronet 1622-1724; 1678-
Peers: 2 peers 1660-71
Notes: 1 Earl and one other in ODNB.

Fagge (Fagg)

Origins: The 1 Bt was the richest man in Rye, the son of a successful merchant of the town. Member of the Council of State 1659. Sir Charles Goring 5 Bt married in 1743 Elizabeth Fagge daughter and heiress of Sir Robert Fagge 5 Bt of Wiston Manor.

1. Sir John Fagg 1 Bt – Rye 1645-53 Sussex 1654-59 Steyning 1660-81 1685-87 1689-1701
2. John Fagg – New Shoreham 1667-72
3. Sir Robert Fagg 2 Bt – New Shoreham 1679-81 Steyning 1690-95 1701-02
4. Thomas Fagg – Rye 1701-05
5. Sir Robert Fagge 3 Bt – Steyning 1708-10
6. Sir Robert Fagge 4 Bt – Steyning 1734-40

Seat: Wiston Manor (Park), Sussex (built c. 1578, purch. c. 1630s, passed to Gorings by mar. of 1743)
Estates: Worth £1,000 pa in 1650.
Title: Baronet 1660-
Notes: 1 Bt in ODNB.

GOTT

Origins: The first MP was the son of an ironmonger in London. He became a landowner and iron founder. Peter Gott MP was a Director of the Bank of England.

1. Samuel Gott – Winchelsea 1645 Sussex 1656 Hastings 1659 Winchelsea 1660
2. Peter Gott – Hastings 1690-95 1698-1701 Sussex 1708-10
3. Samuel Gott – Lewes 1708-10

Seats: Battle (a large courtyard house – not the Abbey), Sussex (built mid-16th c., acq. 1654, sold 1671); Stanmer, Sussex (sold c. 1712)
Notes: The male line became extinct in 1725 and estates divided between heiresses.

GOUGH *IRELAND*

Viscount Gough (1848- UK)

Origins: First recorded in Wiltshire in 1562. A Gough went to Ireland as a clergyman in the 1580s. Bishop of Limerick under Charles I. Modest gentry, many soldiers, in the 18th and 19th centuries. **First {MP 1613}.**

No post-1660 MPs.

Seats: Lough Cutra Castle, Galway (built 1811-17, purch. 1854, add. 1856, add. 1900, family departed 1920s, derelict 1940s, sold 1952); St. Helens (Seamount), Dublin (built 1750-54, remod. 1830s, purch. 1851, remod. 1863, sold c. 1895, hotel)
Estates: Bateman 13708 (I) 7903
Titles: Baron Gough 1846- UK; Baronet 1842-
Peers: 4 peers 1846-1945
1 KP 19th
Notes: The 1 Viscount was a Field Marshal in India. 1 Viscount and four others in ODNB.

GOUGH-CALTHORPE [Reynolds]

Baron Calthorpe (1796-1997 GB)

Origins: The Goughs were London merchants in the 15th century. A "great userer" purchased a landed estate early 17th century. **First MP 1659**. The Calthorpes were merchants who acquired Ampton in Suffolk. They inherited Castle Camps, Cambridgeshire in the later 17th century from the Reynolds family (**one MP pre-1660**). Sir Henry Gough 1 Bt married the daughter and heiress of Reynolds Calthorp of Elvantham Park. The 2 Bt succeeded to the Calthorp estates and took the name Calthorpe.

1. Sir Henry Gough – Tamworth 1685-87 1689-1701 Lichfield 1705-08
2. Reynolds Calthorpe – Hindon 1698-1702 1705-10 1715-20
3. Reynolds Calthorpe – Hindon 1713-14
4. Sir Richard Gough – Bramber 1715-28
5. Sir Henry Gough 1 Bt – Totnes 1732-34 Bramber 1734-41
6. Henry Gough – Bramber 1734-51
7. Henry Calthorpe – Hindon 1741-47
8. James Calthorpe – Hindon 1758-61
9. Henry Gough Calthorpe 1 Baron Calthorpe – Bramber 1774-96
10. Frederick Gough 4 Baron Calthorpe – Hindon 1818-26 Bramber 1826-31
11. Arthur Gough-Calthorpe – Bramber 1825-26 Hindon 1826-30
12. Frederick Calthorpe 5 Baron Calthorpe – E. Worcestershire 1859-68

Seats: Elvetham Park, Hampshire (acq. by Calthorpes by mar. later 17th c., rebuilt 1859-62, remod. 1901, add. 1911, still own); Edgbaston Hall, Warwickshire (purch. 1717, built c. 1718, family ceased to live here 1783, leased out and from 1932 a golf club); Oldfallings Hall, Staffordshire (purch. early 17th c., family departed early 19th c., leased out, sold c. 1925); Ampton Hall, Suffolk; Perry Hall, Warwickshire (in Staffordshire until 1927) (purch. 17th c., demolished 1927); Cockthorpe Hall, Norfolk (medieval, inherited by Calthorpes in r. of Henry IV, rebuilt c. 1614, demolished, family still own the living)
Estates: Bateman 6470 (E) with an income of £23,981 in 1850 (Cannadine, *Lords and Landlords*, 128). Owned 5,500 acres with a large urban estate valued at one and a half billion pounds in 2001.
Title: Baronet 1726-
Peers: 8 peers 1796-98 1808-1912 1912-40 1945
Notes: Sir Richard Gough, an East India merchant, purchased Edgbaston in 1717, which produced a large income as Birmingham expanded in the 19th century. 6 Baron and one other and one Gough in ODNB.

GOULD I

Origins: A cadet line of a Devon gentry family became merchants in Dorchester in the mid-17th century.

1. James Gould – Dorchester 1659 1661-76
2. James Gould – Dorchester 1677-81 1690-95
3. Nicholas Gould – Dorchester 1679-81 Weymouth & Melcombe Regis 1690-91

Seats: Upway (Upwey) (both the "Manor" – built 1639, sold 1900 – and the "House", Dorset – built 18th c., add. 1830 and 1880s, sold by 1900 – estate acq. 1678, land held at least until 1921); Stafford House, Dorset (medieval, purch. 1613, remod. 1633, sold 1830); Fleet, Dorset (acq. by mar. 1758, passed out of direct family line 1841)
Estates: Rumored to be worth £10,000 pa c. 1670s.

GOULD II

Origins: Turkey merchants in the 17th century, Chairman of the East India Company and Director of the Bank of England.

1. Sir Nathaniel Gould – New Shoreham 1701-08 1710-28
2. Nathaniel Gould – Wareham 1729-34
3. John Gould – New Shoreham 1727-34

Seats: Woodford, Essex (demolished 1900); Bovingdon, Hertfordshire

GRAHAM I (Graeme) [Murray] *SCOTLAND*

Duke of Montrose (1707- S)

Origins: First recorded in the 12th century. Attended the Parliament of Scone as a lord in 1284 and at the Battle of Dunbar 1296. Earl 1406. **First [MP 1584]. Cadet lines at Inchbraikie and Morphie produced four additional [MPs 1612-44]**.

1. John Graham – [Stirlingshire 1703-07]
2. John Graham – Stirlingshire 1722-27
3. Lord George Graham – Stirlingshire 1741-47
4. James Graham 3 Duke of Montrose – Richmond 1780-84 Great Bedwyn 1784-90
5. James Graham 4 Duke of Montrose – Cambridge 1825-32
6. Lord Montagu Graham – Dumbartonshire 1830-32 Grantham 1852-57 Herefordshire 1858-65

Seats: Buchanan Castle, Stirlingshire (purch. 1682, rebuilt 1724, remod. 1751, add. 1789, fire 1852, rebuilt 1854, family ceased to inhabit 1934, unroofed 1953, now a ruin); Brodick Castle, (Arran) Buteshire (built 13th c., add. 1558 and later 16th c., rebuilt 1844, acq. by mar. to the heiress of the 12 Duke of Hamilton 1906, NT 1958); Mugdock Castle, Stirlingshire (acq. mid-13th c., built mid-14th c., add. late 15th c., sacked 1644, restored c. 1661, abandoned in favor of Buchanan c. 1690s, later sold, ruin); Auchmar House, Stirlingshire (purch. c. 1830, built 1932, still own)
Estates: Bateman 103447 (S) 24872. The Duke owned 8,800 acres in 1996. His two sisters owned 56,000 acres in 2001.
Titles: Baron Graham 1445- S; Earl of Montrose 1503- S; Marquis of Montrose 1644- S; Earl Graham 1722- GB
Peers: [3 peers 1660-69 1678-84 1705-07] 1 Scottish Rep peer 1707-10 1715-34 6 peers 1727-1945
4 Lds Lt 18th, 19th, 20th
3 in Cabinet 1714-15 1804-06 1858-59
3 KT 18th, 19th
1 KG 19th
Notes: The Grahams claimed descent from a Caledonian chief who in the 5th century broke down Agricola's Wall and the gap became known as Graham's Dyke. (Burke, *A Visitation of Seats and Arms of the Noblemen and Gentlemen of Great Britain and Ireland,* sec ser., I, 166). The 6 Duke conceived and designed the first aircraft carrier, HMS Argus (1918). The 7 Duke of Montrose was a senior minister in Ian Smith's government in Rhodesia. His son was the only Duke and one of 90 peers elected by the other hereditary members under the new rules governing membership of the House of Lords to a seat there in 1999. The Graham family has an entry in the ODNB. Also included are the 3 and 4 Earls, 2 and 5 Marquises, 1, 3, 4, 6, and 7 Dukes, 3 Earl of Strathearn and 7 Earl of Menteith, and two others.

<u>Graham</u>

Origins: A cadet line of the Grahams of Inchbraikie (17th century) (see above).

1. Henry Graham – [Orkney & Shetland 1685-86]

Seat: Breckness House, Orkney (built 1633, remod. 18th/19th c., ruin)

<u>Graham</u>

Origins: A cadet of the Grahams of Inchbraikie (16th century) (see above).

1. Alexander Graham – [Fortrose 1661-63]

Seat: Drynie, Cromartyshire (sold 19th c.)
Notes: Family extinct 19th c.

Graeme

Origins: The 1 Bt was a younger son of the 3 Earl of Montrose.

1. Mungo Graeme – [Perthshire 1702-07] Scotland 1707-08 Kinross-shire 1710-11
2. David Graeme – Perthshire 1724-26
3. David Graeme – Perthshire 1764-73

Seats: Orchill House, Perthshire (built mid-18th c., remod. c. 1840); Braco Castle, Perthshire (built from 17th c., sold 1916)
Estates: Bateman 5088 (S) 3211
Title: Baronet 1625-1700
Notes: The first MP served as factor to the Duke of Montrose.

Graham

Origins: Descended from the senior line of the second son of Sir William Graham, ancestor of the Dukes of Montrose. **First [MP 1641]. One additional [MP 1646-48].**

1. John Graham – [Perthshire 1678]
2. David Graham – [Forfarshire 1703-07]

Seat: Fintry (Fintrie) Castle (aka Mains), Forfarshire (medieval, acq. 16th c., built 1480-1580, add. c. 1700, estate sold c. 1800)
Notes: Two in ODNB.

Viscount Dundee (1688-90 S)

Origins: Descended from the junior line of the second son of Sir William Graham, ancestor of the Dukes of Montrose. Kted by Robert III. **First [MP 1628 for Forfarshire].**

No post-1660 MPs

Seat: Claverhouse, Forfarshire (acq. c. 1530, forfeited 1689)
Peer: [1 peer 1688-90]
Notes: Title and estates forfeited 1689-90. Family extinct 1700. 1 Viscount in ODNB.

Baron Lynedoch (1814-43 UK)

Origins: Descended from the youngest branch of the heirs of Sir William Graham, ancestor of the Dukes of Montrose.

1. Thomas Graham 1 Baron Lynedoch – Perthshire 1794-1807

Seats: Balgowan House, Perthshire (built early 18th c., fell into ruin 1860s); Lynedoch, Perthshire (purch. 1787, built c. 1790)
Peer: 1 peer 1814-43
Notes: The 1 Baron was a general. 1 Baron in ODNB.

Viscount Dunedin (1926-42 UK)

Origins: Descended from a cadet of the lairds of Balgowan (see above). Patrick Graeme married Janet Murray granddaughter and heiress of Sir Andrew Murray of Pitlochie. Their son took the additional name Murray and succeeded to Murrayshall (see Murray).

1. Andrew Graham Murray 1 Viscount Dunedin – Buteshire 1891-1905

Seats: Murrayshall, Perthshire (built 1664, sold 1927); Stenton, Perthshire
Title: Baron Dunedin 1905-42 UK
Peer: 1 peer 1905-42
1 Ld Lt 20th
Notes: Succeeded to part of the Balgowan estate in 1859. The 1 Viscount was a judge.

GRAHAM II *IRELAND*

Origins: Merchants and Aldermen of Drogheda who purchased land from the Earl of Athlone in the 1680s. Sheriff 1728.

1. John Graham – {Drogheda 1710-14 1715-17}
2. William Graham – {Drogheda 1727-48}
3. John Graham – {Drogheda 1749-68}

Seat: Platten (Platin) Hall, Meath (old house, purch. c. 1690s, passed out of family 1777, demolished c. 1950)
Notes: Estate left by last Graham to a friend, who sold it post 1800. One in ODNB.

GRAHAM III (Grahme) [Widdrington]

Viscount Preston (1681-1739 S)

Origins: Arose in the Scottish borders; acquired estates at Esk in Cumberland in the early 17th century. **First MP 1626.** Ambassador to France under Charles II.

1. Ranald Grahme – Leominster 1661-79
2. Richard Graham 1 Viscount Preston – Cockermouth 1675-81 Cumberland 1685-87
3. Richard Graham – New Windsor 1685-87
4. James Grahme – Carlisle 1685-87 Appleby 1702-08 Westmorland 1708-27
5. Henry Graham – Westmorland 1701-07

Seats: Nunnington Hall, Yorkshire (medieval, built later 16th c., purch. 1655, part demolished before 1830, declined to farm house, sold 1839, NT 1952); Levens Hall, Westmorland (medieval, rebuilt c. 1580-86, purch. 1686, add. c. 1690s, passed to the Howards (Earls of Suffolk) by inher. 1745)
Estates: Worth £1,000 pa 1690s.
Title: Baronet 1629-
1 Ld Lt 17th
1 in Cabinet Council 1688-89
Notes: 1 Viscount Lord President of the Council under James II. On the death of James Grahme MP (above) in 1730 the estates passed via his daughter to the Earl of Berkshire (see Howard). 1 Viscount and one other in ODNB.

Graham

Origins: Descended from a younger brother of the 1 Viscount Preston.

1. Sir James Graham 1 Bt – Ripon 1798-1807
2. Sir James Graham 2 Bt – Kingston-upon-Hull 1818-20 St. Ives 1820-21 Carlisle 1826-28 Cumberland 1829-32 E. Cumberland 1832-37 Pembroke Boroughs 1838-41 Dorchester 1841-47 Ripon 1847-52 Carlisle 1852-61
3. Sir Fergus Graham 5 Bt – N. Cumberland 1926-35 Darlington 1951-59

Seat: Netherby (Esk), Cumberland (built 15th c., acq. 1624, rebuilt c. 1760, c. 1790, and 1833-36, house sold 1989, still own estate)
Estates: Bateman 25408 (E) 26821
Title: Baronet 1783-
1 in Cabinet 1830-34 1841-46 1852-55
Notes: 2 Bt and one other in ODNB.

Graham

Origins: A younger son of Sir Richard Graham 1 Bt of Esk, grandfather of the 1 Viscount Preston, established a cadet line at Edmond Castle. Several generations were lawyers.

1. Sir James Graham 1 Bt – Cockermouth 1802-05 Wigtown Burghs 1805-06 Cockermouth 1807-12 Carlisle 1812-25
2. Sir Sandford Graham 2 Bt – Aldeburgh 1812 Ludgershall 1812-15 1818-26 1830-32

Seats: Edmond Castle, Cumberland (old house, remod. 1824-29, add. 1844-48, sold. c. 1935); Kirkstall, Yorkshire (acq. by mar. 1781, sold 1889)
Estates: Bateman 7265 (E) 6640
Title: Baronet 1808-95

Baron Widdrington (1643-1716 E)

Origins: The Widdringtons held Widdrington by 1166. **First MP 1295. Six additional MPs 1348-1642, all for Northumberland**. The daughter of the 1 Viscount Preston and sister of the 3 Viscount married the 4 Baron Widdrington. She willed the Widdrington estates to her nephew Ralph Graham. The title was attainted 1716, but the 4 Baron's son continued to be called Lord Widdrington in the Roman Catholic community until his death in 1774.

1. Sir Thomas Widdrington – Berwick-on-Tweed 1640-53 York 1654 Northumberland 1656 Berwick-on-Tweed 1661-64
2. Thomas Widdrington – Morpeth 1660
3. Sir Henry Widdrington – Morpeth 1661-65
4. Ralph Widdrington – Berwick-on-Tweed 1685-87

Seats: Widdrington Castle, Northumberland (acq. by 1166, medieval castle, forfeited 1716, decayed by 1720, pulled down 1767); Cheeseburn Grange, Northumberland (acq. by mar. c. 1600, passed to Riddells by mar. 1762); Swinburne Castle, Northumberland (built c. 1346, ruined, sold 1678, partly demolished 1967); Felton Park (Hall), Northumberland (acq. by mar. 1661, new house built 1732, passed to Riddells by mar. 1762, demolished 1953); Stella Hall, Durham (built 16th c., inher. from Tempests 1698, confiscated 1716, restored 1733, passed to Towneleys 1762, remod. 1813, demolished 1955)
Estate: Cheeseburn Grange line worth £800 pa in 1660s.
Title: Baronet 1642-1774
Peer: 1 peer 1660-75

Notes: The family was Roman Catholic, which reduced its parliamentary representation. The 4 Baron's estates were confiscated after the 1715 Jacobite rising in which the family was active. Granted £12,000 from sale of estates 1723, and the 4 Baron regained his wife's estates in 1733. 1 and 4 Barons and two others in ODNB.

GRANT [Colquhoun, MacDowall, MacPherson, Ogilvy (Ogilvie), Suttie] *SCOTLAND*

Earl of Seafield (1701- S)

Origins: An old family. Sir Duncan Grant was the common ancestor of the various branches. **First [MP 1560].** Sir Ludovick Grant 7 Bt married Margaret Ogilvie, sister and heiress of the 4 Earl of Seafield and 7 Earl of Findlater. Their grandson, the 9 Bt, succeeded as 5 Earl of Seafield in 1811.

1. Ludovic Grant – [Elgin & Forresshire 1681 Inverness-shire 1689-1702 1703-07]
2. Alexander Grant – [Inverness-shire 1702-07] Scotland 1707-08 Inverness-shire 1708-10 Elginshire 1710-19
3. Sir James Grant 6 Bt – Inverness-shire 1722-41 Elgin Burghs 1741-47
4. Sir Ludovick Grant 7 Bt – Elginshire 1741-61
5. Sir James Grant 8 Bt – Elginshire 1761-68 Banffshire 1790-95
6. Francis Grant – Elginshire 1768-74
7. Lewis Grant-Ogilvie 5 Earl of Seafield – Elginshire 1790-96
8. Francis Ogilvie-Grant 6 Earl of Seafield – Elgin Burghs 1802-06 Inverness Burghs 1806-07 Elginshire 1807-32 Elgin & Nairn 1832-40
9. Francis Ogilvie-Grant The Master of Grant – Inverness-shire 1838-40
10. James Ogilvie-Grant 9 Earl of Seafield – Elgin and Nairn 1868-74

Seats: Castle Grant, Elginshire (built 16th c., add. 18th c., decayed and sold 1950); Cullen House, Banffshire (acq. 1600, built c. 1600, add. 1711, remod. 1769, add. 1858-59, family departed 1975, sold 1983, flats, still own estate); Moy House (House of Moy), Elginshire (built 17th c., purch. 1733, rebuilt 1762, sold 1775 to another Grant branch, add. 1870, sold 1922)
Estates: Bateman 305930 (S) 78227; Worth £35,000,000 in 1990. Owned 185,000 acres in 1996.
Titles: Viscount Seafield 1698- S; Viscount Reidhaven 1701- S; Baron Strathspey 1858-84 & 1884 UK; Baronet 1625-
Peers: 2 Scottish Rep peers 1841-53 1853-58 4 peers 1858-81 1882-88 1897-1915
3 Lds Lt 18th, 19th
1 KT 19th
Notes: Grant family has an entry in the ODNB, and the 8 Bt and two others.

Grant

Origins: Cadet of the Grants of Castle Grant (15th century).

1. Sir Alexander Grant 5 Bt – Inverness Burghs 1761-68
2. Sir Alexander Grant 8 Bt – Tregony 1812-18 Lostwithiel 1818-26 Aldborough 1826-30 Westbury 1830-31 Cambridge 1840 1841-43

Seat: Dalvey House, Elginshire (purch. 1749, built c. 1770, sold 1790); Gartenbeg, Elginshire
Estates: Worth over £9,000 pa in 1825 plantation income. 5 Bt died worth £93,000 in 1772.
Title: Baronet 1688-
Notes: The family were Jacobites and suffered accordingly. Their fortunes were revived by the 5 Bt a doctor, planter, and merchant in Jamaica in the 1740s. He returned to Scotland and continued in business. Family was impoverished again c. 1850. The 8th Baronet died insolvent. 5, 8, 10, 12 Bts in ODNB.

Grant

Origins: Cadet of the Grants of Castle Grant (16th century).

1. John Grant – [Nairnshire 1639-41 1661-63]
2. James Grant – [Nairnshire 1667]

Seat: Moynes, Nairnshire

Colquhoun

Origins: At Luss by the 14th century. Lord High Chamberlain of Scotland 1474. **First [MP 1605]. Two subsequent [MPS 1612-47 all for Dumbartonshire].** John Grant 6 Bt of Pluscandine, grandfather of Ludovick Grant 7 Bt (see Seafield above) married Anne, daughter and heiress of Sir Humphrey Colquhoun 5 Bt of Luss. Sir James succeeded to the Colquhoun estates and his son James, uncle of Sir Ludovick, became chief of the Clan Colquhoun, a Baronet, and took the name Colquhoun.

1. Sir John Colquhoun 2 Bt – [Dumbartonshire 1651 1661-63 1665 1667 1669-74]
2. Sir Humphrey Colquhoun 5 Bt – [Dumbartonshire 1703-07]
3. Sir James Colquhoun 3 Bt – Dumbartonshire 1790-1806
4. Sir James Colquhoun 4 Bt – Dumbartonshire 1837-41

Seats: Rossdhu (Castle) House, Dumbartonshire (castle, medieval, acq. 1458, abandoned 1770, new house built 1772-74, family departed 1972, leased to golf club 1980s); Arrochar House, Dumbartonshire (built 1697, sold c. 1785); Camstraddan House, Dumbartonshire (acq. 1458, old tower, rebuilt 1739, still own)
Estates: Bateman 67041 (S) 12845. Worth £25,000,000 in 1990. Owned 50,000 acres in 1996.
Title: Baronet 1625-1704; 1786-
3 Lds Lt 19th, 20th
Notes: Two in ODNB.

Colquhoun

Origins: Cadet of the Colquhouns of Luss (16th Century).

1. William Colquhoun – [Dumbartonshire 1689-98]

Seat: Craigtoun, Dumbartonshire (acq. 16th c., resident into 18th c.)

Campbell Colquhoun

Origins: Cadet of the Colquhouns of Luss (14th century). Estates inherited in 1821 by a Coates, Glasgow merchant in the 18th century (Provost 1784) and plantation owner on St. Kitts, who had taken the name Campbell and whose son was Lord Advocate.

1. Archibald Campbell Colquhoun – Elgin Burghs 1807-10 Dumbartonshire 1810-20
2. John Campbell Colquhoun – Dumbarton 1832 Kilmarnock Burghs 1837-41 Newcastle-under-Lyme 1842-47

Seats: Killermont House, Dumbartonshire (old house, purch. 1747, rebuilt 1805, family depart 1903 and later sold to a golf club); Garscadden House, Dumbartonshire (old house, acq. c. 1664, rebuilt c. 1723-40, sold 1939, fire and demolished 1959)
Estates: Bateman 3879 (S) 9382
Notes: One in ODNB.

Grant

Origins: Senior line of the MacPherson Grants (see below).

1. John Grant – Great Grimsby 1812-18 Tavistock 1819-26

Seat: The Doune of Rothiemurchus, Inverness-shire (built 16th c., acq. 1560s, add. 1780, remod. 1876, family departed 1920s, leased, restored c. 1978, family returned 1991, still own)
Estates: Bateman 24457 (S) 2290. Owned 24,000 acres in 1996.
Notes: Five in ODNB.

MacPherson-Grant

Origins: Descended from a younger son of Sir Duncan Grant (see Seafield above). Acquired Ballindalloch c. 1547. Sir George MacPherson of Invereshie succeeded in 1806 to the estates of his maternal uncle James Grant of Ballindalloch.

1. James Grant – Tain Burghs 1773-80 Sutherlandshire 1787-1802
2. Sir George MacPherson-Grant 1 Bt – Sutherlandshire 1809-12 1816-26
3. Sir George MacPherson-Grant 3 Bt – Elgin & Nairn 1879-86

Seats: Ballindalloch Castle, Banffshire (acq. and built c. 1547, add. 1718, add. 1847, still own); Invereshie House, Inverness-shire
Estates: Bateman 125443 (S) 11546 and 4749 (S) 7092. 100,000 acres sold 1950. Own 25,000 today. (Knox, *The Scottish Country House*, 153)
Title: Baronet 1838-
Notes: 3 Bt and one other in ODNB.

Grant

Origins: A cadet of the Grants of Ballindalloch. First MP son of a tenant farmer, nephew of a rich merchant, was himself a lawyer.

1. Sir William Grant – Shaftesbury 1790-93 New Windsor 1794-96 Banffshire 1796-1812

Seats: Beldornie (Beldorney) Castle, Banffshire (built 16th c., add. 1679, remod. early 18th c., purch. 1790s, add. 1830, sold 1919); Wester Elchies House, Elginshire (old house, remod. 19th c., passed to Earls of Seafield, demolished 1968)
Estates: Bateman 24674 (S) 6667

Grant

Origins: Descended from a younger son of Sir Duncan Grant (see Seafield above). The wife of the 11 Bt was elected to the House of Commons for Aberdeen South 1946-66 and created a Life Peer in 1970.

1. Sir Archibald Grant 2 Bt – Aberdeenshire 1722-32
2. William Grant – Elgin Burghs 1747-54

Seat: Monymusk Castle, Aberdeenshire (built 1587, purch. 1712 for £10,000, still own)
Estates: Bateman 14881 (S) 7698. 5486 acres in 1996
Title: Baronet 1705-
Notes: 2 Bt in ODNB and one other.

Grant-Suttie

Origins: Descended from a cadet of the Monymusk Grants. Sir George Suttie 3 Bt of Balgone married in 1757 the daughter of William Grant Lord Prestongrange (Lord of Session). Their son succeeded to Preston Grange in 1818 and took the additional name Grant.

1. Sir George Suttie 3 Bt – Haddingtonshire 1768-77
2. Sir James Grant-Suttie 4 Bt – Haddingtonshire 1816-26

Seats: Preston Grange, Haddingtonshire (acq. by Suttie family by mar. to Grants 1818, sold 1958); Balgone, Haddingtonshire (built 15th c., acq. by Sutties by mar. 1680, sold 1989)
Estates: Bateman 11066 (S) 12752
Title: Baronet 1702-

Baron Glenelg (1835-66 UK)

Origins: A cadet of Sir Duncan Grant (see Seafield above). The father of 1 Baron was a Director of the East India Company 1794.

1. Charles Grant – Inverness-shire 1802-18
2. Charles Grant 1 Baron Glenelg – Inverness Burghs 1811-18 Inverness-shire 1818-35
3. Sir Robert Grant – Elgin Burghs 1818-20 Inverness Burghs 1826-30 Norwich 1830-32 Finsbury 1832-34

Seat: Glanely, Inverness-shire (sold 1837?)
Estates: The father of the 1 Baron left £50,000 to 60,000. 1 Baron was said to have spent £85,000 on a Highland estate but was forced to sell it later. Wealth at death under £5,000 in 1866.
Peers: 1 peer 1835-66
1 in Cabinet 1818-21 1827-28 1830-39

Notes: A Jacobite family, one killed at Culloden. Family fortunes revived by a nabob, Chairman of the East India Company in 1805. His son was created Baron Glenelg. 1 Baron and five others in ODNB.

MacDowall-Grant (McDowall, McDouall)

Origins: The MacDowalls were an ancient family in Wigtownshire. **First [MP 1643 for Wigtownshire].** David MacDowall married in 1800 Eleanor Grant, daughter and heiress of Alexander Grant of Arndilly, a cadet of the Monymusk line (see above).

1. William MacDowall – [Wigtownshire 1689-1700]
2. William MacDowall – Renfrewshire 1768-74
3. William MacDowall – Renfrewshire 1783-86 Ayrshire 1789-90 Glasgow Burghs 1790-1802 Renfrewshire 1802-10
4. David MacDowall-Grant – Banffshire 1795-96

Seats: Castle Semple, Renfrewshire (built mid-18th c., fire 1937, shell demolished c. 1960s); Garthland (Castle), Wigtownshire (built c. 1211, add. 1274, new house 1796, decayed, family in Canada, still own); Arndilly, Banffshire (built 1750, add. 1850, sold 20th c.)
Estates: Bateman 2825 (S) 2706
1 Ld Lt 18th-19th
Notes: The MacDowalls claimed to be the only family in Galloway of genuine Pictish origin. Their putative ancestor was Lord of Galloway before the time of Christ. They were certainly in Wigtownshire before written records were kept. (C. Hussey, *Country Life*, 116, p. 426)

McDowall

Origins: Cadet of the MacDowalls of Wigtownshire.

1. Uchtred McDowall – [Wigtownshire 1661-63]

Seat: Freuch, Wigtownshire

McDouall (MacDowall)

Origins: Cadet of the MacDowalls of Wigtownshire. At Logan by 1295 and probably earlier.

1. Andrew McDouall – Wigtownshire 1784-96 1802-05

Seat: Logan House, Wigtownshire (acq. by 1295, built 1702, rebuilt 1874-75, sold and much demolished 1952)
Estates: Bateman 21933 (S) 14441
Notes: One in ODNB.

Earl of Findlater (1638-1811 S)

Origins: See under Earl of Seafield above. An Ogilvie was the King's Standard Bearer in 1381, and the family was connected to the Earls of Airlie in the Middle Ages (see below). **First [MP 1543]. Eight additional [MPs 1560–1648].**

1. James Ogilvie 4 Earl of Findlater – [Cullen Burgh 1689-95]
2. Sir Patrick Ogilvie – [Cullen Burgh 1702-07] Scotland 1707-08 Elgin Burghs 1708-10

Seat: Cullen House, Banffshire (acq. 1578, passed to Grants see above); Findlater House, Banffshire (castle acq. by mar. 1437, later a ruin)
Title: Baron Ogilvie 1616-1811 S
Peers: [2 peers 1660-1707] 2 Scottish Rep peers 1707-10 1712-15 1722-30 1734-61
1 in Cabinet Council 1696-1702 1704-05
1 KT 18th
Notes: 1 Earl in ODNB.

Ogilvie

Origins: Cadet line of the Earls of Findlater and Seafield. **First [MP 1644 for Banffshire].**

1. Sir Patrick Ogilvie – [Banffshire 1669-74 1678 1681 1685-86 1689-90]
2. James Ogilvie – [Banffshire 1703-07]

Seat: Boyne Castle (Palace of Boyne), Banffshire (castle 14th c., acq. 1575, rebuilt 1575-80, in use into 18th c., sold 1731, ruin by later 18th c.)
Notes: In financial difficulties by the 1680s. Jacobites who went into exile and were in the French service in the 18th century.
Notes: One in ODNB.

Earl of Airlie (1639- S)

Origins: Emerged in the 12th century. Descended from a younger son of Sir Walter Ogilvie (d. 1391) ancestor of the Earls of Findlater and Seafield. Master of the Household of James I 1430.

1. Sir James Ogilvy – [Forfarshire 1661-63]
2. William Ogilvy – Perth Burghs 1831
3. Donald Ogilvy – Forfarshire 1831-32

Seats: Cortachy (Cortachie) Castle, Forfarshire (acq. 1405, built 15th c., burned 1641, rebuilt, add. 1871, remod. c. 1950s, still own); Airlie Castle, Forfarshire (acq. 1431, built 1432, razed 1641, partly rebuilt 1792-93, still own)
Estates: Bateman 69875 (S) 28592. Worth £25,000,000 with 69,000 acres in 1990.
Title: Baron Ogilvy 1491- S
Peers: [3 peers 1660-93 1703-1707] 4 Scottish Rep peers 1833-49 1850-81 1885-1900 1922-45
2 Lds Lt 19th, 20th
2 KT 19th, 20th
Notes: The family was attainted for Jacobite activity 1717-1826. The Ogilvys claimed Pictish descent. (Millar, *The Historical Castles & Mansions of Scotland*, 319). The 13 Earl of Airlie was a banker and master of Queen Elizabeth II's household as Lord Chamberlain 1984-97. 2 and 6 Earls and two others in ODNB.

Ogilvy

Origins: Cadet of the Earls of Findlater and Airlie. **First [MP 1560]**. A brother of the 10 Bt took the name Hamilton-Nisbet of Biel (see Hamilton). Property developers in the 19th c. Became manufacturers in nearby Dundee.

1. Sir David Ogilvy 2 Bt – [Forfarshire 1665 1678]
2. Sir John Ogilvy 9 Bt – Dundee 1857-74

Seats: Inverquarity Castle, Forfarshire (acq. 1420, built 1440s, sold late 18th c.); Baldovan House, Forfarshire (built 18th c., remod. c. 1825, add. 1831, gutted by fire and derelict 20th c.)
Title: Baronet 1626-

Ogilvy

Origins: A cadet line of the Inverquarity branch (see above). **First [MP 1560].**

1. Sir David Ogilvy – [Forfarshire 1669-74 1681]

Seats: Clova, Forfarshire (acq. 1420, 19th c. house, now hotel); Balnaboth House, Forfarshire (acq. 1470, built 17th c., remod. second half 18th c., descendents still own)
Estates: Bateman 21893 (S) 3515. Hold 5,500 acres today.

GRANTHAM

Origins: Great wool merchants in the 15th century. Entered the gentry in the 16th century. Kt 1603. **First MP 1328. Eight further MPs 1447-1653, five of them for Lincoln and one for Lincolnshire.**

1. Richard Grantham – Lincoln 1710-13 1715-22

Seat: Goltho Hall, Lincolnshire (old house, acq. mid-16th century, sold and demolished 1812, new house built nearby by another family)
Notes: The family was in financial trouble in the 18th century.

GRATWICK [Weekes]

Origins: Yeomen and then ironmasters in the later 16th century. **First MP 1645**. The estates passed by marriage to the Weekes family.

1. Francis Gratwick – Seaford 1670
2. Carew Weekes – Arundel 1701-05

Seat: Tortington (Manor), Sussex (purch. 1587, built 16th c., rebuilt 17th c., passed to Weekes by inher. 1670, sold 1706, declined to a farm house in the 18th c.)
Notes: In financial trouble by 1710.

GRAVES [Sawle]

Baron Graves (1794- I)

Origins: Merchants and tradesmen in the 17th c. A family of amazingly numerous 18th and 19th-century admirals.

1. William Graves – West Looe 1768-74 East Looe 1775-86 1796-98
2. Thomas Graves 1 Baron Graves – East Looe 1775
3. Thomas Graves 2 Baron Graves – Okehampton 1812-18 New Windsor 1819-20 Milborne Port 1820-27

Seats: Thanckes House, Cornwall (medieval, rebuilt 1871, sold 1909, now hotel); Gravesend House, Devon; Bishop's Court (Bishopscourt), Devon (medieval, sold by 1860)
Estates: The 2 Baron was "impoverished". (Fisher, *The House of Commons*, V, 400)
Peer: {1 peer 1794-1800}
Notes: 1 Baron and two others in ODNB.

Graves-Sawle

Origins: The Sawles were an old Cornish family. **First MP 1624.** The heiress of the Sawle family married in 1786 Admiral John Graves. Their son took the additional name Sawle.

1. Joseph Sawle – Tregony 1702-05
2. Sir Charles Graves-Sawle 2 Bt – Bodmin 1852-57

Seats: Penrice House, Cornwall (acq. and built 1620, donated to an institution 1971); Restormel House, Cornwall (acq. 16th c., lease sold mid-18th c., reacquired mid-19th c., passed out of family 1971); Barley House, Devon (built 19th c.)
Estates: Bateman 3391 (E) 12919
Title: Baronet 1836-1932
Notes: Family extinct 1971.

GRAYDON (Grayden) *IRELAND*

Origins: In Ireland by the later 17th century. Sheriff of Wicklow 1703.

1. Robert Graydon – {Harristown 1692-93 1695-99}
2. Alexander Graydon – {Naas 1703-13 Harristown 1713-27}
3. John Graydon – {Harristown 1727-60}
4. Robert Graydon – {Harristown 1768-76 Kildare 1790-97}

Seats: Russelltown (Russellstown), Wicklow (leased at first, purch. freehold 1673, sold 1741); Killashee House, Kildare (owned 17th and 18th c.)

GREENALL

Baron Daresbury (1927- UK)

Origins: Warrington brewers in the 19th century.

1. Peter Greenall – Wigan 1841-45
2. Sir Gilbert Greenall 1 Bt – Warrington 1847-68 1874-92

Seats: Walton Hall, Cheshire (purch. 1812, built 1836-38, add. 1870, house sold and estate much reduced in size 1941, final land sold 2010, museum); Mount Coote, Limerick (built 18th c., purch. c. 1930, sold c. 1940, demolished c. 1960); Clonshire House, Limerick (built c. 1800, acq. mid-19th c., sold 20th c.?); Myddleton Hall, Lancashire (built 1658, acq. early 19th c., sold later in the 19th c.?)

Estates: Peter Greenall MP died worth £35,000 in 1845. Owned 5,500 acres in 2001.
Title: Baronet 1876-
Peers: 2 peers 1927-45
Notes: One in ODNB.

GREENE I *IRELAND*

Origins: Went to Ireland as a soldier in 1649. Acquired estates 1678. Sheriff 1713. The first MP was a barrister.

1. Godfrey Greene – {Dungarvon 1777-90}
2. William Greene – Dungarvon 1802-06
3. John Greene – County Kilkenny 1847-65

Seats: Greenville (Kilcroney), Kilkenny (acq. mid-17th c., sold second half 19th c.); Old Abbey, Limerick (acq. early 17th c., passed out of family by mar. mid 18th c.)

GREENE II

Origins: Brewers in Suffolk the 19th century.

1. Edward Greene – Bury St. Edmunds 1865-85 Stowmarket Div. Suffolk 1886-91
2. Sir Raymond Greene 2 Bt – Chesterton Div. Cambridgeshire 1895-1906 Hackney Div. Middlesex 1910-23
3. Sir Edward Greene 1 Bt – Bury St. Edmunds 1900-06

Seat: Nether Hall, Suffolk (medieval, new house 1622, purch. 1874 or in the 1880s, rebuilt c. 1900, sold 1920)
Estates: The Greene brewery was worth c. £500,000 in the 1880s. The head of the firm drew an income of £20,000 pa in some years just before 1914.
Title: Baronet 1900-
Notes: The Greene family has an entry in the ODNB and four individual entries. Graham Greene, the novelist, was a member of the family.

GREGORY *IRELAND*

Origins: Robert Gregory, whose background was obscure, was born in Galway. He was a nabob who returned from India with a fortune in 1766. Chairman of the East India Company 1782. Sheriff 1799.

1. Robert Gregory – Maidstone 1768-74 Rochester 1774-84
2. William Gregory – {Portarlington 1780}

3. Sir William Gregory – Dublin 1842-47 County Galway 1857-71

Seats: Coole Park, Galway (purch. 1768, built 1770, sold 1927, demolished 1941); Rolls Park, Essex (leased?); Valence, Kent (leased late 1760s)
Estates: Bateman 4893 (I) 2378. Held 15,142 acres in 1857 when much was sold. (Smythe, *Guide to Coole Park*, 33)
Notes: Lady Gregory was a major figure in the Irish Literary Renaissance of the late 19th and early twentieth century. Two in ODNB.

GRENFELL

Baron Desborough (1905-45 UK)

Origins: Merchants in Cornwall in the first half of the 18th century. Became dealers in tin and copper ores in the 1780s. The first two MPs continued to operate the copper smelting business. Active in banking into the 20th century.

1. Pascoe Grenfell – Great Marlow 1802-20 Penryn 1820-26
2. Charles Grenfell – Preston 1847-52 1857-65
3. Charles Grenfell – Sandwich 1847-52 Windsor 1852-59
4. Henry Grenfell – Stoke-on-Trent 1862-68
5. William Grenfell 1 Baron Desborough – Salisbury 1880-82 1885-86 Hereford 1892-93 Wycombe Div. Buckinghamshire 1900-05
6. Cecil Grenfell – Bodmin Div. Cornwall 1910
7. Edward Grenfell 1 Baron St. Just – London 1922-35

Seat: Taplow Court, Buckinghamshire (medieval, purch. 1852, rebuilt 1855-56, sold c. 1945, institutional use)
Estates: Bateman 3195 (E) 7224. Rubinstein – P. Grenfell MP left 140,000 in probate in 1838. 1 Baron St. Just left £880,000 in 1942.
Titles: Baron Grenfell 1902- UK; Baron St. Just 1935- UK
Peers: 5 peers 1902-45 1905-45 1935-41 1944-45
1 KG 20th
Notes: The 1 Baron was a Field Marshal. The Grenfells succeeded to Panshanger, Hertfordshire in 1913, which they broke up and sold over the next 40 years. The Grenfell family has an entry in the ODNB and seven other individuals also included.

GRENVILLE [Brydges, Gore, Halsey, Langton, Temple] *ENGLAND & IRELAND*

Duke of Buckingham and Chandos (1822-89 UK)

Origins: The Temples, tenants at Stowe in the reign of Henry VI, built a fortune in land and sheep under the Tudors. Granted arms 1567. **First MP 1554. Three additional MPs 1589-1654**. Peter Temple of Stow (d. 1577) was the common ancestor of the Viscounts Cobham and Palmerston (see below). The eldest sister of the 1 Viscount Cobham was created Countess Temple in 1749 and married Richard Grenville of Wotton. Several branches derived from this union. The Grenvilles succeeded to Stowe and took the additional name Temple. The Grenvilles were gentry from the reign of Henry II c. 1180. (Beckett, *The Rise and Fall of the Grenvilles*, 9, 13) **First MP 1654**.

1. Sir Richard Temple 3 Bt – Warwickshire 1654-55 1659 Buckingham 1660-81 1685-87 1690-97
2. Richard Temple 1 Viscount Cobham – Buckingham 1697-1702 Buckinghamshire 1704-08 Buckingham 1708-13
3. Richard Grenville – Wendover 1715-22 Buckingham 1722-27
4. Richard Temple-Grenville 2 Earl Temple – Buckingham 1734-41 Buckinghamshire 1741-47 Buckingham 1747-52
5. George Grenville – Buckingham 1741-70
6. Thomas Grenville – Bridport 1746-47
7. Henry Grenville – Bishop's Castle 1759-61 Thirsk 1761-65 Buckingham 1768-74
8. George Grenville-Nugent-Temple 1 Marquess of Buckingham – Buckinghamshire 1774-79
9. Thomas Grenville – Buckinghamshire 1779-84 Aldburgh 1790-96 Buckingham 1796-1810 Buckinghamshire 1813-18
10. William Grenville 1 Baron Grenville – Buckingham 1782-84 Buckinghamshire 1784-90
11. Richard Temple-Nugent-Brydges-Chandos-Grenville 1 Duke of Buckingham – Buckinghamshire 1797-1813
12. George Nugent-Temple 2 Baron Nugent – Buckingham 1810-12 Aylesbury 1812-32 1847-50
13. Richard Temple-Nugent-Brydges-Chandos-Grenville 2 Duke of Buckingham – Buckinghamshire 1818-39
14. Richard Temple-Nugent-Brydges-Chandos-Grenville 3 Duke of Buckingham – Buckingham 1846-57

Seats: Stowe House, Buckinghamshire (purch. 1590 by Temples, new house 1678-83, add. c. 1719-26 and 1733-50, sold 1921, school); Wotton House, Buckinghamshire (Grenvilles there by 1213, rebuilt 1704-14, fire 1820, remod. 1820, fire 1929, sold 1929); Dropmore, Buckinghamshire (built 1792-94, passed by mar. to Fortescues 1864,

demolished 1990); Lillies, Buckinghamshire (built 16th c., sold to Rothschilds mid-19th c., fire and rebuilt 1870); Avington Park, Hampshire (built 16th c., purch. by Brydges 1665, add. 1670s, remod. 18th c., passed to Grenvilles by mar. 1789, sold 1848); Gosfield Hall, Essex, (built c. 1545 and 1691, part rebuilt c. 1720, purch. by Knight 1714, passed by mar. to Nugents 1736, add. 1755, passed to Grenvilles by mar. 1788, sold 1825, now institutional use)
Estates: Bateman 10482 (E) 18080. Temple estates worth £6,000 pa in 1653 and £7,000 in 1749. Grenville estates worth £21,000 pa in 1779.
Titles: Baron Cobham 1714-49 GB; Viscount Cobham 1718- GB; Earl Temple 1749-1889 GB; Marquess of Buckingham 1784-1889 GB; Baron Grenville 1790-1834 GB; Earl Temple of Stowe 1822- UK; Baronet 1611-1786
Peers: 7 peers 1714-49 1752-79 1774-1889 1790-1834
5 Lds Lt 18th, 19th
7 in Cabinet 1756-61 1756-65 1782-83 1782-83 1787-89 1789-1801 1806-07 1806-07 1841-42 1852 1866-67
4 KG 18th, 19th
Notes: The title Viscount Cobham was revived for Sir Richard Temple 4 Bt by virtue of his descent by the marriage of the 2 Bt with Christian Leveson, great-granddaughter of the 10 Baron Cobham (d. 1597). The Cobham Viscountcy passed after the extinction of the Buckingham Dukedom in 1889 to the Lytteltons of Hagley by virtue of the marriage of Sir Thomas Lyttelton to a younger sister of the 1 Viscount Cobham (see Lyttelton). The 1 Marquess of Buckingham married the daughter and heiress of the 1 Earl Nugent. She was created Baroness Nugent in her own right and the title passed to her younger son. The son of a younger son of the 1 Countess Temple was created Baron Glastonbury. A brother of the 1 Marquess was created Baron Grenville. The 1 Duke married Lady Anne Brydges, daughter and heiress of the last Duke of Chandos. She was Baroness Kinloss in her own right by virtue of her descent from Mary Bruce, wife of the 2 Duke of Chandos and daughter of the 4 Earl of Elgin and 6 Baron Kinloss. On the extinction of the Dukedom of Buckingham in 1889 the 3 Duke's daughter, Lady Mary, succeeded as 11 Baroness Kinloss. Massive indebtedness brought down the family during the second half of the 19th c. The 1 Viscount Cobham, 2 Earl Temple, 1 Marquess, 1, 2 and 3 Dukes, 1 Baron Grenville, 2 Baron Nugent, and eight others in ODNB.

<u>Halsey</u>

Origins: The first MP was a self-made brewer. In 1729 his estate passed to his only daughter Viscountess Cobham (see above).

1. Edmund Halsey – Southwark 1712 Buckingham 1717-22 Southwark 1722-29

Seat: Stoke Poges (Stoke Park or Stoke Manor), Buckinghamshire (medieval, rebuilt 1555, purch. 1724 for £12,000, sold 1760, hotel)
Estates: Aside from land Halsey left to his daughter £30,000 from the sale of the brewery (Hayton, *The House of Commons*, IV, 161).

Earl Temple of Stowe (1822- UK)

Origins: The daughter of the 2 Duke of Buckingham married William Gore-Langton. Their son succeeded as Earl Temple of Stowe (created with a special remainder to pass through the female line) on the death of the 3 Duke in 1889. The Gores descended from a younger son of the ancestor of the Earl of Arran (see Gore). A Gore married a Langton heiress in 1783. The Langtons were merchants in Bristol. Purchased Newton Park in 1666.

1. Joseph Langton – Bath 1690-95
2. William Gore-Langton – Somerset 1795-1806 Tregony 1808-12 Somerset 1812-20 1831-32 Somerset 1832-47
3. William Gore-Langton – W. Somerset 1851-59 1863-73
4. William Gore-Langton – Bristol 1852-65
5. William Gore-Langton 4 Earl Temple – Mid Somerset 1878-85

Seats: Newton Park, Somerset (medieval house, purch. 1666, new house built 1762-65, sold c. 1940, now a school); Hatch Beauchamp (Hatch Court), Somerset (medieval, rebuilt c. 1755, acq. by a mar. of 1822, house sold 1922 but estate retained); Barrow Court, Somerset (medieval monastic building, rebuilt c. 1545, add. 1602, purch. 1659, sold 1856); Cold Ashton Manor, Gloucestershire (built 1597-1601, acq. by mar. 1679, sold 1918)
Estates: Bateman 8183 (E) 16233
Peers: 3 peers 1889-1945

Baron Glastonbury (1797-1825 GB)

Origins: A cadet line descended from younger brothers of the 2 Earl Temple.

1. James Grenville – Old Sarum 1742-47 Bridport 1747-54 Buckingham 1754-68 Horsham 1768-70
2. James Grenville 1 Baron Glastonbury – Thirsk 1765-68 Buckingham 1770-90 Buckinghamshire 1790-97
3. Richard Grenville – Buckingham 1774-80

Seat: Butleigh Court, Somerset (acq. by mar. 1738, rebuilt 1845, sold 1947, partially demolished 1952, flats)

Estates: Bateman 3434 (E) 5770. Rubinstein – Richard Grenville left £120,000 in probate in 1823 and 1 Baron Glastonbury left £250,000 in 1825.
Peers: 1 peer 1797-1825
Notes: On the death of the 1 Baron Glastonbury, Butleigh Court passed to the Lords Braybrooke (see Neville), who took the name Grenville.

Duke of Chandos (1719-89 GB)

Origins: The Chandos family emerged as knights in the Marches of Wales in the reign of Edward III. One fought at Agincourt. **Three MPs 1322-95 for Herefordshire**. Called as Baron by writ 1337. The Chandos estates passed to the Brydges family through an heiress in 1428. High Sheriff under Richard III. Courtiers under Henry VIII. Baron 1554. **First MP 1523. Nine further MPs 1529-1628, five of them kts of shire**. The 1 Duke of Chandos, as Paymaster of the Forces, made a huge fortune. He also married an heiress. The daughter of the last Duke of Chandos married the 1 Duke of Buckingham.

1. George Rodney Brydges – Haslemere 1690-98 Winchester 1701-14
2. James Brydges 1 Duke of Chandos – Hereford 1698-1714
3. George Brydges – Whitchurch 1708-10 Winchester 1714-51
4. John Brydges Marquess of Carnarvon – Steyning 1726-27
5. Henry Brydges 2 Duke of Chandos – Hereford 1727-34 Steyning 1734 Bishop's Castle 1741-44
6. James Brydges 3 Duke of Chandos – Winchester 1754-61 Radnorshire 1761-68

Seats: Canons Park, Middlesex (old house, rebuilt c. 1605, purch. 1709, built 1713-25, sold and demolished 1747); Sudeley Castle, Gloucestershire (medieval, rebuilt mid 15th c., acq. c. 1554, remod. 1572 and 1614, slighted 1648-50, passed by mar. to Pitts 1789); Wilton Castle, Herefordshire (medieval, new house built 16th c., purch. 1560s, fire 1645, sold 1781); Avington Park, Hampshire (built 16th c., purch. 1665, add. 1670s, remod. 18th c., passed to Grenvilles by mar. 1789)
Estates: Worth £3,120 pa in 1642.
Titles: Baron Chandos 1554-1789 E; Viscount Wilton and Earl of Carnarvon 1714-89 GB; Marquess of Carnarvon 1719-89 GB; Baronet 1627-1789
Peers: 5 peers 1660-1789
2 Lds Lt 18th
Notes: The 1 Duke of Chandos was a younger son of a family that that had lost status from its earlier grandeur. He achieved great wealth holding the Paymastership, which raised him from gentry status to a Dukedom in one generation. (Mingay, *English Landed Society in the Eighteenth Century*, 74) The 1, 2, 3, 5, and 6 Barons and 1 Duke and three others in ODNB.

Viscount Palmerston (1723-1865 I)

Origins: This branch of the Temple family went to Ireland with Essex in 1599. Provost of Trinity College, Dublin 1609. Kt 1622. **First MP 1597. One additional {MP 1613}.**

1. Sir John Temple – {County Meath 1642} Chichester 1645-48 {Sligo & Roscommon 1654 County Carlow 1661-66} Tregony 1660
2. Sir William Temple 1 Bt – {County Carlow 1661-66} Cambridge 1679-81
3. Henry Temple – {Wicklow 1665-66}
4. Henry Temple 1 Viscount Palmerston – East Grinstead 1727-34 Bossiney 1734-41 Weobley 1741-47
5. Richard Temple – Downton 1747-49
6. Henry Temple 2 Viscount Palmerston – East Looe 1762-68 Southampton 1768-74 Hastings 1774-84 Boroughbridge 1784-90 Newport (IoW) 1790-96 Winchester 1796-1802
7. Henry Temple 3 Viscount Palmerston – Newport (IoW) 1807-11 University of Cambridge 1811-31 Bletchingley 1831-32 S. Hampshire 1832-34 Tiverton 1835-65

Seats: Broadlands, Hampshire (built c. 1540, purch. 1736, rebuilt 1765-74, remod. 1788-92, add. 1859, passed by mar. to Cowpers 1865, passed to Mountbattens 1922); Palmerston (Palmerstown) House, Dublin (sold late 18th c.); Ballycrath, Carlow; Classiebawn Castle, Sligo (built mid-19th c., passed to Mountbattens by mar. 1922)
Estates: 12436 (E & I) 5801. Worth £12,000 pa in 1789.
Titles: Baron Temple 1723-1865 I; Baronet 1666-99
Peers: {2 peers 1723-57 1761-1800}
1 in Cabinet 1809-12 1827-28 1830-34 1835-41 1846-51 1852-65
1 KG 19th
Notes: On the death of the 3 Viscount Palmerston his estates passed to the second son of the 5 Earl Cowper (see Cowper). On his death the estates passed to the third son of the 7 Earl of Shaftesbury and his wife the daughter of the 5 Earl Cowper (Ashley-Cooper). 1, 2, and 3 Viscounts and three others in ODNB.

GREVILLE [Maynard, Nugent] *ENGLAND & IRELAND*

Earl of Brooke (1746- GB) and Warwick (1759- GB)

Origins: Wool merchants from the 13th century. Loaned money to Richard II 1397 and purchased a manor. Soldier and courtiers under the Tudors, and acquired a large estate 1541. **First MP 1414 for Gloucestershire. Seven additional MPs 1420-1628, of which five were kts of the shire**. The Grevilles married the Beauchamp heiress (Dukes of Warwick, extinct 1445).

1. Fulke Greville 5 Baron Brooke – Warwick 1664-77
2. Francis Greville – Warwick 1695-98 1701-10
3. Robert Greville – Warwick 1698-99
4. Algernon Greville – Warwick 1699-1705
5. Dodington Greville – Warwick 1705-27
6. Fulke Greville – Monmouth 1747-54
7. George Greville 2 Earl of Warwick – Warwick 1768-73
8. Charles Greville – Warwick 1774-90
9. Robert Greville – Warwick 1774-80 Windsor 1796-1806
10. Charles Greville – Petersfield 1795-96
11. William Greville – {Granard 1797-98}
12. Henry Greville 3 Earl of Warwick – Warwick 1802-16
13. Sir Charles Greville – Warwick 1816-31 1832-33 1835-36
14. George Greville 4 Earl of Warwick – S. Warwickshire 1845-53
15. Francis Greville 5 Earl of Warwick – E. Somerset 1879-85 Colchester 1888-92

Seats: Warwick Castle, Warwickshire (built 1068 onwards, acq. 1604, restored and rebuilt 1606-17, add. 1669-78, fire 1871, rebuilt 1871, sold 1978); Beauchamp Court, Warwickshire (medieval, acq. by mar. 16th c., fell into decay 17th c., sold, farm house); Easton Lodge, Essex (built later 16th c., rebuilt 1847, passed by mar. to Grevilles 1865, fire 1918, rebuilt c.1920, demolished 1949); Knowle Hall, Warwickshire (acq. 1622, rebuilt mid-17th c., sold 1743, demolished c. 1840)
Estates: Bateman 10102 (E) 18336 and 8621 (I) 7906. Rubinstein – William Greville MP left £160,000 in probate in 1837.
Titles: Baron Brooke 1554-1628 E; 1621- E
Peers: 10 peers 1660-1710 1715-27 1740-1945
5 Lds Lt 17th, 18th, 19th, 20th
2 KT 18th, 19th
Notes: Current Earl lives in Australia. 1 and 2 Barons Brooke and six others in ODNB.

<u>Viscount Maynard</u> (1766-1865 GB)

Origins: First MP a lawyer. Acquired Easton 1590. **First MP 1553. Six additional MPs 1584-1658, one for Essex.** The daughter and heiress of the last Viscount married the 5 Earl of Warwick. She succeeded to the estates in 1865.

1. Banastre Maynard 3 Baron Maynard – Essex 1663-79
2. Sir William Maynard 1 Bt – Essex 1686
3. Thomas Maynard – Eye 1710-15 West Looe 1715-22
4. Sir William Maynard 4 Bt – Essex 1759-72

Seats: Hoxne Hall, Suffolk (medieval, rebuilt c. 1600, remod. 1654, acq. later 17th c., rebuilt 1st half 18th c., sold 1823, demolished c. 1923); Easton Lodge, Essex (medieval, acq. 1582, rebuilt c. 1593, add. 17th c., burned 1847, rebuilt c. 1850, passed by mar. to Grevilles 1865, demolished 1949); Waltons, Essex (built later 16th c., add. 17th c., remod. c. 1730)
Estates: Bateman 13844 (E) 20001
Titles: Baron Maynard 1620-1775 I; Baron Maynard 1628-1775 E; Baronet 1611-1775; 1682-1865
Peers: 7 peers 1660-1865
2 Lds Lt 18th, 19th
Notes: The 1 Viscount left estates to his aunt's grandson, Thomas Hesilrige (see Hazlerigg). He died childless in 1817 when the property reverted to the Maynards. Four in ODNB.

Baron Greville (1869-1987 UK)

Origins: The estates of the 1 Marquess of Westmeath (see Nugent) passed to his daughter in 1871. She married the 1 Baron Greville, who took the additional name Nugent. He was descended from a younger son of the 5 Baron Brooke (see above).

1. Fulke Greville-Nugent 1 Baron Greville – County Longford 1852-69
2. Algernon Greville 2 Baron Greville – Westmeath 1865-74
3. Reginald Greville-Nugent – Longford 1869
4. George Greville – County Longford 1870-74
5. Ronald Greville – East Bradford 1896-1906

Seats: Clonyn Castle, Westmeath (built 19th c., inher. by mar. 1871, resident in 20th c.); Clonhugh, Westmeath (acq. 19th c.?, rebuilt 1858, sold 1917); Polesden Lacy, Surrey (built 1632, rebuilt 1821-24, purch. 1906, NT 1942); Cubberley, Herefordshire (built 1971)
Estates: Bateman 17430 (I) 16113 and 1178 (E) 2081
Peers: 3 peers 1869-1945
1 Ld Lt 19th

GREY I [Bennet, Bull, Fitzroy, Willoughby Gordon]

Earl of Tankerville (1695-1701 E)

Origins: Family emerged in the 13th century. Gentry by early 1300s. One at Agincourt. Earl c. 1400, extinct 1551. KG 1419. **First MP 1397 for Northumberland. Five additional MPs 1449-1624 all for the county.**

1. Edward Grey – Berwick-on-Tweed 1660-76

2. Thomas Grey – Ludgersall 1669-72
3. Ralph Grey 4 Baron Grey of Warke – Berwick-on-Tweed 1679-81

Seats: Chillingham Castle, Northumberland (built 13th c., purch. and rebuilt 1344, Greys acq. by mar. of 1399 in 1420s, damaged 1536, rebuilt later 16th c., remod. 1625-35 and 1650s, passed by mar. to Bennets 1701, add. mid-18th c., add. 1809 and 1873, family departed 1931, decayed, sold 1980s); Warke Castle, Northumberland (medieval castle, restored by Greys 1554, ruin, sold 1920); Horton Hall (Castle), Northumberland (castle acq. and built medieval period, decayed 16th c., restored c. 1740, then abandoned and demolished c. 1815, sold 1870s); Gosfield Hall, Essex (built c. 1545, purch. mid-17th c., sold 1691); Uppark, Sussex (built 16th c., acq. by mar. from the Fords 1690, who acq. it c. 1450, rebuilt c. 1690-94, passed to Bennets 1701)
Estates: Worth £6,000 pa in the 1670s. Held 250,000 acres in late 16th c. (Thrush and Ferris, *The House of Commons 1604-1629*, IV, 475).
Titles: Baron Grey of Warke 1624-1701 E; Baronet 1619-1706
Peers: 4 peers 1660-83 1686-1701 1705-06
1 in Cabinet Council 1700-01
Notes: The 4 Baron Grey of Warke left his estates divided between his cousin, the 6 Baron Lord North (see North) and the Nevilles of Audley End (see Neville). 1 Baron Grey of Warke and 1 Earl in ODNB.

Earl of Tankerville (1714- GB)

Origins: The Bennets were minor gentry in the 16th century and London merchants. Lord Mayor 1604. **First MP 1593. One further MP 1597-1621.** Baronet 1660. Baron 1682. The daughter and heiress of the 1 Earl of Tankerville (extinct 1701, see above) married Charles Bennet 2 Baron Ossulston, who was created Earl of Tankerville and succeeded to Chillingham.

1. John Bennet – Bridgnorth 1660-63
2. Sir Humphrey Bennet – Petersfield 1661-67
3. John Bennet 1 Baron Ossulston – Wallingford 1663-79
4. Thomas Bennet – Marlborough 1679-81 1695-98
5. Sir Levinus Bennet 2 Bt – Cambridgeshire 1679-81 1685-87 1689-93
6. John Bennet – Newton 1691-95
7. Sir John Bennet – Morpeth 1708-10 (possible)
8. Charles Bennet 3 Earl of Tankerville – Northumberland 1748-49
9. Charles Bennet 5 Earl of Tankerville – Steyning 1803-06 Knaresborough 1806-18 Berwick-on-Tweed 1820-22
10. Henry Bennet – Shrewsbury 1806-07 1811-26
11. Charles Bennet 6 Earl of Tankerville – N. Northumberland 1832-59

Seats: Chillingham Castle, Northumberland (acq. by mar. 1701, sold 1932); Uppark, Sussex (see above, acq. by mar. 1701, sold 1747); Babraham Hall, Cambridgeshire (built c. 1580, purch. 1632, sold 1770, see below)
Estates: Bateman 31423 (E) 33650
Titles: Baron Ossulston 1682- E; Baronet 1660-1701
Peers: 9 peers 1682-1945
1 Ld Lt 18th
2 KT 18th
Notes: The 4 Earl (for prowess at cricket) and one other in ODNB.

Duke of Grafton (1675- E)

Origins: Henry Fitzroy 1 Duke of Grafton was an illegitimate son of King Charles II and the Duchess of Cleveland. He married the daughter of Henry Bennet, brother of the 1 Baron Ossulston (see above), who had been created 1 Earl of Arlington. The Fitzroys succeeded to his estate at Euston Hall.

1. Henry Bennet 1 Earl of Arlington – Callington 1661-65
2. Charles Fitzroy Scudamore – Thetford 1733-54 Hereford 1754-68 Heytesbury 1768-74 Thetford 1774-82 (illegitimate son)
3. George Fitzroy Earl of Euston – Coventry 1737-47
4. Lord Augustus Fitzroy – Thetford 1739-41
5. Augustus Fitzroy 3 Duke of Grafton – Boroughbridge 1756 Bury St. Edmunds 1756-57
6. Lord Charles Fitzroy – Bury St. Edmunds 1787-96 1802-18
7. George Fitzroy 4 Duke of Grafton – Thetford 1782-84 University of Cambridge 1784-1811
8. Lord William Fitzroy – Thetford 1806-12
9. Lord John Fitzroy – Thetford 1812-18 Bury St. Edmunds 1820-26
10. Lord Charles Fitzroy – Thetford 1818-30 Bury St. Edmunds 1832-47
11. Henry Fitzroy 5 Duke of Grafton – Bury St. Edmunds 1818-20 1826-31 Thetford 1834-42
12. Lord James Fitzroy – Thetford 1830-34
13. Sir Charles Fitzroy – Bury St. Edmunds 1831-32
14. Robert Fitzroy – Durham 1841-43
15. William Fitzroy 6 Duke of Grafton – Thetford 1847-63
16. Lord Frederick Fitzroy – Thetford 1863-65

Seats: Euston Hall, Suffolk (purch. 1666 by 1 Earl of Arlington, built 1666-70, rebuilt 1750-56, fire 1902, part demolished 1952, still own); Wakefield Lodge, Northamptonshire (old lodge, granted by Charles II 1673, rebuilt 1747, add. 19th c., sold 1921, most demolished 1948)

Estates: Bateman 25773 (E) 39284. Rubinstein – 3 Duke left £175,000 probate in 1811 and Lord Charles Fitzroy left £100,000 in 1829. Worth £37,000,000 with 10,500 acres in 1990.
Titles: Baron Arlington 1664- E; Earl of Arlington and Earl of Euston 1672- E
Peers: 11 peers 1665-90 1704-1945
5 Lds Lt 17th, 18th, 19th
3 in Cabinet 1662-74 1720-57 1765-66 1768-70 1771-75 1782-83
6 KG 17th, 18th, 19th, 20th
Notes: 1 Earl of Arlington and 1, 2, 3, 4 Dukes of Grafton and four others in ODNB.

Baron Southampton (1780- GB)

Origins: The 1 Baron was a grandson of the 1 Duke of Grafton.

1. Charles Fitzroy 1 Baron Southampton – Orford 1759-61 Bury St. Edmunds 1761-74 Thetford 1774-80
2. George Fitzroy 2 Baron Southampton – Bury St. Edmunds 1784-87
3. Henry Fitzroy – Great Grimsby 1831-32 Lewes 1837-59
4. Edward Fitzroy – S. Northamptonshire 1900-06 1910-18 Daventry Div. Northamptonshire 1918-43

Seats: Idlicote House, Warwickshire (built mid-18th c., purch. c. 1896, sold 1952); Whittlebury Lodge, Northamptonshire (built 1865, demolished 1972); Arbury Hall, Warwickshire (inher. by mar. 1936, see Newdigate)
Estates: Bateman 6861 (E) 8858
Title: Viscountess Daventry 1943- UK
Peers: 4 peers 1780-1810 1825-72 1888-1943
1 Ld Lt 19th
Notes: 1 and 2 Barons and one other in ODNB.

Bennet (Bennett)

Origins: The son of Sir Levinus Bennet 2 Bt MP (see above under Earl of Tankerville) left his estates in 1701 to the Alexander family, who took the name Bennet.

1. Richard Alexander Bennett – Newport (IoW) 1770-74
2. Richard Alexander Bennet – Launceston 1802-06 Enniskillen 1807 Launceston 1807-12

Seats: Brabraham Hall, Cambridgeshire (medieval, rebuilt c. 1580, purch. 1632, sold 1770); North Court (IoW), Hampshire (built 1615, acq. by mar. 1st half of 19th c. and passed to Willoughby Gordons, see below)

Bull

Origins: A Turkey merchant in London purchased North Court on the Isle of Wight. His estates passed by marriage to the Bennets of Brabraham (see above).

1. Richard Bull – Newport (IoW) 1756-80

Seat: North Court (Northcourt House), Hampshire (IoW) (built 1615, acq. c. 1795, passed by mar. to Willoughby Gordons 1st half 19th c.)
Estates: Rubinstein £125,000 probate 1809.

Willoughby Gordon

Origins: The North Court estate passed by marriage from the Bennets to Sir James Willoughby Gordon 1 Bt.

1. Sir James Willoughby Gordon 1 Bt – Launceston 1829-31

Seat: North Court, Hampshire (IoW) (built 1615, acq. by mar. 1st half 19th c., sold 1984)
Estates: Bateman 2345 (E) 3419
Title: Baronet 1818-76
Notes: 1 Bt in ODNB.

Earl Grey (1806- UK)

Origins: The Greys of Howick, prominent in Northumberland since the 14th century, were cousins of the Lords Grey of Warke (see above).

1. Sir Henry Grey 2 Bt – Northumberland 1754-68
2. Charles Grey 2 Earl Grey – Northumberland 1786-1807 Appleby 1807 Tavistock 1807
3. Henry Grey 3 Earl Grey – Winchelsea 1826-30 Higham Ferrers 1830-31 Northumberland 1831-32 N. Northumberland 1832-41 Sunderland 1841-45
4. Charles Grey – Chipping Wycombe 1832-37
5. Sir George Grey 2 Bt – Devonport 1832-47 N. Northumberland 1847-52 Morpeth 1853-74
6. Albert Grey 4 Earl Grey – S. Northumberland 1880-85 Tyneside Div. Northumberland 1885-86
7. Edward Grey 1 Viscount Grey of Fallodon – Berwick Div. Northumberland 1885-1916

Seats: Howick House, Northumberland (acq. 1319, medieval tower demolished 1780, new house built 1782 and 1809, fire 1926, rebuilt, still own); Fallodon, Northumberland (built early 18th c., acq. by mar. 1764 from Wood family, fire 1917, rebuilt 1921-24, sold 1946)
Estates: Bateman 18512 (E) 27813. The 4 Earl died in 1918 owning 17,600 acres and £459,000 in liquid assets. The 1 Viscount Grey of Fallodon left £128,000 in 1933.
Titles: Baron Grey 1801- UK; Viscount Grey of Fallodon 1916-33 UK; Baronet 1746- ; 1814-
Peers: 6 peers 1801-1945 1916-33
2 Lds Lt 19th, 20th
4 in Cabinet 1806-07 1830-34 1835-39 1841 1846-52 1854-58 1859-66 1905-16
3 KG 19th, 20th
Notes: The 1 Baronet married the heiress of Fallodon. A younger son was created a Baronet and inherited Fallodon. The Greys produced two exceptionally influential figures between 1807 and 1916, the great Prime Minister the 2 Earl Grey and the Foreign Secretary at the outbreak of the First World War, Sir Edward Grey 3 Bt, 1 Viscount Fallodon. A prominent cadet branch was seated at Dilston, Northumberland. The 1, 2, 3, 4 Earls, 1 Viscount Grey of Fallodon, and eight others in ODNB.

GREY II [Aislabie, Booth, Laurence, Robinson, Vyner, Weddell, Yelverton]

Duke of Kent (1710-40 GB)

Origins: The Greys were an ancient family with many ramifications. They were tenants in chief in the Domesday Book and held the manor on which Wrest Park was built from 1086. They were summoned to Councils from 1258. The senior line, Barons Grey of Wilton, were the ancestors of the Earls of Wilton (see Egerton). Another line became Dukes of Suffolk (1551-54). A younger son, Roger de Grey, Lord Grey of Ruthin (d. 1352) was the ancestor of the 1 Earl of Kent, Lord High Treasurer. **First MP 1472. Four additional MPs 1529-1643, three of them kts of the shire**.

No post-1660 MPs

Seats: Crudwell, Wiltshire (acq. by mar. 1671 from Lucas family seated there since 1552, built early 19th c., passed to the Robinsons by mar. 1833, sold 1919-23); Wrest Park, Bedfordshire (resident since 1086, built 14th c., sold 1507, repurch. 1512, rebuilt 16th c., add. 1672-76, add. 1709-12, remod. 1736, passed by inher. to the Lords Grantham (Robinson) 1833, demolished 1839-40, rebuilt, see below)
Estates: Not rich in the 17th century
Titles: Baron Grey of Ruthin 1325- E; Earl of Kent 1465-1740 E; Baron Lucas 1663- E; Earl of Harold and Marquess of Kent 1706-40 E; Marquess of Kent 1740-97 GB
Peers: 3 peers 1660-1740 1718-23

1 Ld Lt 18th
1 in Cabinet 1719-20
1 KG 18th
Notes: The Grey of Ruthin family has an entry in the ODNB. The 1 and 3 Baron Grey of Ruthin and 1, 2, 3, and 10 Earls of Kent and one other in ODNB.

Earl of Sussex (1717-99 GB)

Origins: The sister of the 8 Earl of Kent married Sir Michael Longueville. Their son succeeded as Baron Grey of Ruthin. His daughter was also Baroness Grey in her own right and married Sir Henry Yelverton. Their younger son, 15 Baron Grey of Ruthin, was created Viscount Longueville. His son was the 1 Earl of Sussex. The 3 Earl's daughter and heiress married Edward Gould. Their son, the 20 Baron Grey of Ruthin, took the name Yelverton. His daughter married the Marquess of Hastings (see Rawdon). Their son succeeded as Marquess of Hastings and Baron Grey de Ruthin. His sister married A. W. Clifton of Lytham Hall, and their son succeeded as Baron Grey (see Rawdon). The Yelvertons were a legal family established in Norfolk in the 14th century that produced several judges in the 15th, 16th, and 17th, centuries. Extended estates to Northamptonshire. **First MP 1435. Five further MPs 1450-1648.**

1. Sir Henry Yelverton 2 Bt – Northamptonshire 1660 1664-70

Seats: Easton Maudit, Northamptonshire (old house, purch. 1578, rebuilt c. 1600, sold 1801, demolished); Brandon Hall, Warwickshire (purch. 1615, built 16th c., demolished and rebuilt early 19th c., sold 1810)
Titles: Viscount de Longueville 1690-1799 E; Baronet 1641-1799;
Peers: 6 peers 1678-79 1685-1704 1711-31 1748-99 1802-10
Notes: Three in ODNB.

Marquess of Ripon (1871-1923 UK)

Origins: The wife of the 11 Earl of Kent (see above) was the daughter and heiress of the 1 Baron Lucas. She was created Baroness Lucas in her own right. This title passed to the daughter of the 1 Duke, who married the 3 Earl of Breadalbane (see Campbell). Their daughter, Lady Jemmima Campbell, was 4 Baroness Lucas. She married the 2 Earl of Hardwicke (see Yorke), who inherited Wrest Park. Their daughter, the 5 Baroness Lucas, was created Countess de Grey in 1816. Her sister married the 2 Baron Grantham (Robinson). Their eldest son was created Earl of Ripon and succeeded to the Kent estate of Wrest Park. The Robinsons descended from a Hamburg merchant. **First MP 1584**. High Sheriff 1630s.

1. Sir Metcalfe Robinson 1 Bt – York 1660-79 1685-87

2. Sir William Robinson 1 Bt – Northallerton 1689-95 York 1698-1722
3. Thomas Robinson 1 Baron Grantham – Thirsk 1727-34 Christchurch 1748-61
4. Thomas Robinson 2 Baron Grantham – Christchurch 1761-70
5. Frederick Robinson – Ripon 1780-87
6. Frederick Robinson 1 Earl of Ripon – Carlow 1806-07 Ripon 1807-27
7. George Robinson 1 Marquess of Ripon – Hull 1852-53 Huddersfield 1853-57 W. R. of Yorkshire 1857-59
8. Frederick Robinson 2 Marquess of Ripon – Ripon 1874-80

Seats: Newby Hall, Yorkshire (built 1690, remod. c. 1767, passed by mar. from Weddells to Robinsons 1792, add. 1807, passed to Vyners 1833, still own); Studley Royal, Yorkshire (medieval, rebuilt c. 1716, inher. by Robinsons through a female descent from the Aislabies 1845, passed by mar. to Vyners 1923, see below); Nocton Hall, Lincolnshire (built c. 1625, acq. by mar. from Hobarts 1814, burned 1834, rebuilt 1841, sold 1886, institutional use from 1936 onwards); Wrest Park, Bedfordshire (Greys resident since the 12th century, rebuilt 16th c., add. 1676, add. 1709-12, passed by inher. to the Lords Grantham (Robinson) 1833, rebuilt 1834-39, passed to the Earls Cowper later 19th c., sold 1917)
Estates: Bateman (Ripon only) 21770 (E) 29126
Titles: Baron Grantham 1761-1923 GB; Earl de Grey 1816-1923 UK; Viscount Goderich 1827-1923 UK; Earl of Ripon 1833-1923 UK; Baronet 1660-89; 1690-1923
Peers: 6 peers 1761-1923
2 Lds Lt 19th, 20th
5 in Cabinet 1754-55 1780-83 1818-28 1830-34 1834-35 1841-46 1841-44 1863-73 1886 1892-95 1905-08
2 KG 19th, 20th
Notes: Extinct in the male line 1923. The 1 and 2 Barons Grantham, 2 Earl de Grey, 1 Earl of Ripon, and 1 Marquess of Ripon in ODNB.

<u>Weddell</u>

Origins: Purchased Newby Hall in 1748 from the Blacketts. On the death of William Weddell in 1792 his estates passed to his cousin the 3 Baron Grantham.

1. William Weddell – Kingston-upon-Hull 1766-74 Malton 1775-92

Seat: Newby Hall, Yorkshire (built 1690, purch. 1748, remod. c. 1767, passed to Robinsons by mar. 1792, see above)

<u>Aislabie</u> (Aislaby)

Origins: Sir William Robinson married Mary Aislabie of Studley Royal. Their son was 1 Baron Grantham. A 17th-century Aislabie, Registrar to the Archbishop of York, married the Mallory heiress of Studley Royal. Merchants in the later 17th century and added to their fortune through the East India trade in the 18th. Chancellor of the Exchequer 1718.

1. John Aislabie – Ripon 1695-1702 Northallerton 1702-05 Ripon 1705-21
2. William Aislabie – Ripon 1719-22
3. William Aislabie – Ripon 1721-81
4. William Aislabie – Ripon 1727-34

Seats: Studley Royal, Yorkshire (Mallorys owned and built from 1452, acq. by Aislabies by mar. 1693, fire and rebuilt c. 1716, remod. 1762, see above); Fountains Hall (Abbey), Yorkshire (built 1598-1604, purch. 1768, passed by inher. to Robinsons 1845, passed to Vyners 1923, sold 1966, NT)
Estates: John Aislabie worth £119,000 in 1718.
Notes: Extinct in the male line 1781. Heiresses held the Studley Royal estate and Fountains until 1845 when it passed to the 1 Earl of Ripon. **Mallory MPs included first MP 1584 for Yorkshire and two more MPs 1601-44**. Three in ODNB.

<u>Laurence</u>

Origins: William Laurence MP, son of a Captain in the Royal Navy, married Anna, daughter and heiress of William Aislabie of Studley Royal.

1. William Laurence – Ripon 1761-68 1775-80 1781-98

Seat: Kirkby Fleetham, Yorkshire (acq. by mar. 1740 by Aislabies, passed to Robinsons 1845)

<u>Vyner</u>

Origins: The daughter and heiress of the 2 Earl de Grey and 3 Baron Grantham, Lady Mary Robinson, married Henry Vyner of Gautby. Their daughter married the 1 Marquess of Ripon. The Vyners rose as goldsmiths and bankers on a grand scale (Lord Mayor of London 1653) to Charles II. Master of the Mint 1660-70. Some sharp practice raised the family to considerable wealth in the late 17th century.

1. Thomas Vyner – Great Grimsby 1699-1701
2. Robert Vyner – Great Grimsby 1710-13 Lincolnshire 1724-61
3. Robert Vyner – Okehampton 1754-61 Lincoln 1774-84 Thirsk 1785-96
4. Robert Vyner – Lincolnshire 1794-1802
5. Reginald Vyner – Ripon 1860-65

Seats: Newby Hall, Yorkshire (built 1690, remod. c. 1767, add. 1807, passed by mar. from Robinsons to Vyners 1833, add. c. 1875, still own); Studley Royal, Yorkshire (Studley Royal, Yorkshire (medieval, rebuilt c. 1716, inher. from the Robinsons 1923, destroyed by fire 1945, sold 1966, NT); Gautby Hall, Lincolnshire (house built by mid-16th c., acq. late 17th c., rebuilt 1757, decayed after mid-19th c., demolished 1874, sold later); Tupholme Hall, Lincolnshire (purch. c. 1661, built before 1726, leased out, sold 1919, demolished 1984)
Estates: Bateman 26705 (E) 37693
Title: Baronet 1661-80; 1666-88
Notes: The last Vyner's daughter married a Compton (Marquess of Northampton), whose sons took the name Vyner. One inherited Studley Royal and the other Newby on the death of the 2 Marquess of Ripon. Two in ODNB.

Earl of Stamford (1628- E) and Warrington (1796-1883 GB)

Origins: Descended from a younger brother of the 1 Earl of Kent. Gained an estate in Essex in 1194. His grandson was Marquess of Dorset in 1475. His grandson was Duke of Suffolk (extinct 1554). The nephew of the Duke was created Earl of Stamford. **First MP 1542. Six additional MPs 1554-1653, four of them kts of the shire**.

1. John Grey – Leicester 1660 1677-81 Staffordshire 1689-98
2. Anchitell Grey – Derby 1665-81 1689-95
3. Harry Grey 4 Earl of Stamford – Leicestershire 1738-39
4. John Grey – Bridgnorth 1754-68 Tregony 1768-74
5. Harry Grey 5 Earl of Stamford – Staffordshire 1761-68
6. Booth Grey – Leicester 1768-84
7. George Grey 6 Earl of Stamford – Aldeburgh 1790-96 St. Germans 1796-1802
8. Booth Grey – Petersfield 1807-12

Seats: Enville Hall, Staffordshire (acq. late 15th c., became principal seat 1719, rebuilt 1750, fire 1904, rebuilt, passed to descendents 1921, still own); Bradgate Park, Leicestershire (park enclosed 1241, house built 1501-30, abandoned by family 1719, ruin, sold 1926); Dunham Massey Hall, Cheshire (acq. by mar. 1758, remod. 1905-07, NT 1976)
Estates: Bateman 30962 (E) 58393. Rentals said to be worth £90,000 pa in 1845 (NT booklet).
Titles: Baron Grey of Groby 1603- E; Baron Delamer 1796-1883 GB
Peers: 10 peers 1660-73 1675-1720 1723-1845 1833-35 1848-83 1892-1910 1918-45
3 Lds Lt 17th, 18th, 19th
1 in Cabinet 1697-1702 1707-11
Notes: 1 Baron Grey of Groby, 1 and 2 Earls of Stamford and four others in ODNB.

Earl of Warrington (1690-1758 E)

Origins: In 1070 Dunham Massey was granted to Hamo de Massey. On the death of the 6 Baron in 1341 it passed by marriage to the Fittons and then to the Venables coming to the Booths by inheritance in 1433. A Booth of Barton in Lancashire was Bishop of Exeter and two Archbishops of York in the 15th century. **First MP 1455 (possible) and 1572 (certain). One additional MP 1624, both for Cheshire**. The daughter and heiress of the last Earl of Warrington married 1736 the 4 Earl of Stamford.

1. George Booth 1 Baron Delamer – Cheshire 1646 1654 1656 Lancashire 1659 Cheshire 1660
2. Henry Booth 1 Earl of Warrington – Cheshire 1678-81
3. John Booth – Weobley 1679-81 (separate branch)
4. George Booth – Dartmouth 1689 Malmesbury 1692-95 Bossiney 1695-98 Losthwithiel 1698-1702
5. Langham Booth – Cheshire 1705-10 1715-22 Liverpool 1723-24
6. Robert Booth – Bodmin 1727-33

Seats: Hawthorne Hall, Cheshire (built c. 1610, remod. 1698, acq. 18th c.?, sold 1800); Dunham Massey Hall, Cheshire (medieval, acq. 1433, new house 1616, remod. 1732-40, passed by mar. to Greys 1758, see above)
Titles: Baron Delamer(e) 1661-1770 E; Baronet 1611-1797
Peers: 3 peers 1661-94 1696-1758
1 Ld Lt 17th
Notes: 1 Baron Delamer and 1 and 2 Earls of Warrington and four others in ODNB.

GRIERSON *SCOTLAND*

Origins: Emerged by 15th century, perhaps earlier. **First [MP 1617 for Dumfriesshire]. Two additional [MPs 1628-49], both for counties**.

1. Sir Robert Grierson 1 Bt – [Dumfriesshire 1678 1681 1685-86]
2. Sir William Grierson 2 Bt – Dumfries 1709-11

Seat: Rock Hall (Rockhall) (Lag Tower), Dumfriesshire (acq. 1408, built c. 1460, remod. 16th and 17th c., 1 Bt abandoned tower house, family ceased residence at Rockhall and sold later 19th or 20th c.)
Estates: Bateman 3713 (S) 3546
Title: Baronet 1685- (dormant 2008)
Notes: The 1 Bt and one other in ODNB.

GRIFFITH I [Wynne] *WALES*

Origins: Landed in the 15th century. Sheriff 1589. **First MP 1603 for Caernarvonshire. Three further MPs 1621-43, two for Caernarvonshire.** The Griffiths inherited Voelas from the Wynnes by marriage in the later 18th century. Both Cefnamwlch and Voelas passed by marriage to the Finches (see that family).

1. William Griffith – Caernarvon 1661-79
2. John Griffith – Caernarvon 1685-87
3. William Griffith – Caernarvon 1708-13 Caernarvonshire 1713-15
4. John Griffith – Caernarvonshire 1715-39
5. Charles Wynne-Griffith – Denbighshire 1818-26
6. Charles Griffith-Wynne – Caernarvonshire 1830-32
7. Charles Griffith Wynne Finch – Caernarvon 1859-65

Seats: Cefnamwlch, Caernarvonshire (acq. by 15th c., built 16-17th c., passed to Wynnes of Voelas by inher. 1794 and then to the Finches by mar. 1811, demolished 1813 and rebuilt, add. 1877, resident at least until 1950s); Voelas, Caernarvonshire (acq. by Wynnes c. 1545, passed to Finches by mar. 1811, resident at least until 1950s)
Estates: Bateman 15158 (W & E) 10772. Cefnamwlch property 4,200 acres worth £4,037. Total income £8,542 in 1830.
Notes: Two in ODNB.

GRIFFITH II [Chicheley, Darby]

<u>Chicheley</u> (Chichele)

Origins: The Chicheley family, successful wool-staplers, produced an Archbishop of Canterbury and a prosperous London grocer (Lord Mayor) in the early 15th century. **First MP 1397. Four additional MPs 1414-1614.** The family seat at Wimpole was sold in 1686, but the family recovered in the 18th century, one was Master General of the Ordnance and Kt 1770. His son married a Griffith heiress (see below).

1. Sir Thomas Chicheley – Cambridgeshire 1640-42 1661-79 Cambridge 1679-81 1685-87 1689-90
2. Sir John Chicheley – Newton 1679-81 1685-87 1689-91

Seat: Wimpole Hall, Cambridgeshire (medieval, acq. 1428, rebuilt c. 1641, sold 1686)
Estates: Worth £2,000 pa in 1660.
1 in Cabinet Council 1682-87
Notes: Two in ODNB.

Griffith

Origins: Rose by successful marriages.

1. Christopher Griffith – Berkshire 1774-76
2. Christopher Griffith – Devizes 1857-68

Seat: Padworth House, Berkshire (medieval and 17th c., purch. 1655 by Brightwells, passed by mar. to Griffiths mid-18th c., rebuilt 1769, remod. 19th c., sold mid-20th c., school)

Darby

Origins: Of obscure origin. The first MP rose through the Royal Navy and marriage. The Griffith estates passed to the Darbys, who also inherited the St. Quintin of Scampston estates 1797, which passed to a younger son. (see St. Quintin).

1. George Darby – Plymouth 1780-84

Notes: One in ODNB.

GRIMSTON [Bucknall, Luckyn]

Earl of Verulam (1815- UK)

Origins: William Luckyn, the son of Sir William Luckyn 3 Bt, succeeded his great uncle, Sir Samuel Grimston in 1700 and took the name Grimston. The Grimstons were an old Yorkshire family settled in Suffolk in the early 15th century. Kt under Henry II. **First MP 1563. Two additional MPs 1614-48**. The Luckyns were yeomen in the 15th century, and became gentry in the early 17th century. **First MP 1624.**

1. Sir Harbottle Grimston 2 Bt – Harwich 1628 Colchester 1640-48 Essex 1656 Colchester 1660-81
2. Sir Capell Luckyn 2 Bt – Harwich 1648 1660 1664-79
3. Sir Samuel Grimston 3 Bt – St. Albans 1668-81 1689-1700
4. William Grimston 1 Viscount Grimston – St. Albans 1710-22 1727-34
5. James Grimston 2 Viscount Grimston – St. Albans 1754-61
6. James Grimston 3 Viscount Grimston – St. Albans 1783-84 Hertfordshire 1784-90
7. William Grimston – St. Albans 1784-90 Appleby 1791-96
8. James Grimston 1 Earl of Verulam – St. Albans 1802-08
9. James Grimston 2 Earl of Verulam – St. Albans 1830-31 Newport 1831-32 Hertfordshire 1832-45

10. Edward Grimston – St. Albans 1835-41
11. James Grimston 3 Earl of Verulam – St. Albans Div. Hertfordshire 1885-92
12. Robert Grimston 1 Baron Grimston of Westbury – Westbury Div. Wiltshire 1931-64
13. John Grimston 6 Earl of Verulam – St. Albans Div. Hertfordshire 1943-45 1950-59

Seats: Gorhambury, Hertfordshire (built later 16th c., purch. 1652, rebuilt 1777-84, still own); Little Waltham, Essex (Luckyns purch. 1624)
Estates: Bateman 10117 (E) 14101. Worth £3,000-£4,000 pa in 1655. Worth c. £8,000 pa. c. 1700. Owned 2,000 acres in 2001.
Titles: Baron Forrester 1633- S; Viscount Grimston 1719- I; Baron Verulam 1790- GB; Baronet 1611-1700; 1629- ; 1661-1700
Peers: [2 peers 1660-79 1698-1705] {3 peers 1719-1800} 5 peers 1790-1945
2 Lds Lt 19th
Notes: The 5 Earl was a successful businessman. 3 Bt, 1 Viscount, and 5 Earl and four others in ODNB.

Bucknall

Origins: The 3 Viscount Grimston inherited 1796 £150,000 from his maternal uncle, J. A. Bucknall. The Bucknalls were London brewers. (see Estcourt)

1. Thomas Bucknall – St. Albans 1796-1802

GROSVENOR [Drax, Erle, Ernle, Kyrle, Sawbridge]

Duke of Westminster (1874- UK)

Origins: The Grosvenors were of Norman descent. Acquired land in Cheshire c. 1160. **First MP 1621 for Cheshire**. Due to the growth in value of their large estate in central London (acq. by mar. 1677) they became among the richest families in the world in the 19th and 20th centuries.

1. Sir Thomas Grosvenor 3 Bt – Chester 1679-81 1685-87 1690-1700
2. Sir Richard Grosvenor 4 Bt – Chester 1715-32
3. Sir Thomas Grosvenor 5 Bt – Chester 1727-33
4. Sir Robert Grosvenor 6 Bt – Chester 1733-55
5. Richard Grosvenor 1 Earl Grosvenor – Chester 1754-61
6. Thomas Grosvenor – Chester 1755-95
7. Robert Grosvenor 1 Marquess of Westminster – East Looe 1788-90 Chester 1790-1802

8. Thomas Grosvenor – Chester 1795-1826 Stockbridge 1826-30
9. Richard Grosvenor 2 Marquess of Westminster – Chester 1818-30 Cheshire 1830-32 S. Cheshire 1832-34
10. Richard Erle-Drax-Grosvenor – New Romney 1819-26
11. Robert Grosvenor 1 Baron Ebury – Shaftesbury 1822-26 Chester 1826-47 Middlesex 1847-57
12. Hugh Grosvenor 1 Duke of Westminster – Chester 1847-69
13. Richard Grosvenor 1 Baron Stalbridge – Flintshire 1861-86
14. Robert Grosvenor 2 Baron Ebury – Westminster 1865-74
15. Norman Grosvenor – Chester 1869-74
16. Robert Grosvenor 5 Duke of Westminster – Fermanagh & S. Tyrone 1955-64

Seats: Eaton Hall, Cheshire (acq. by marriage 15th c., built 1675-82, rebuilt 1804-12, add. 1823-25, remod. 1845-54, rebuilt 1870-82 - at a cost of over £600,000 - abandoned 1939, institutional use until 1960, demolished 1961-65, new house 1970-73, remod. 1990, rebuilt 1989-91, still own); Halkin Lodge (Castle), Flintshire (built 1824-27, still own); Ely Lodge, Fermanagh (built 1830s, demolished 1870, purch. 20th c., surviving stables converted into a house for Duke of Westminster); Moor Park, Hertfordshire (built 1460s, remod. c. 1617, rebuilt 1679-84, rebuilt c. 1720-28 at a cost of £150,000 (Hussey, *English Country Houses: Early Georgian 1715-1760*, 44), add. 1763-65, purch. 1828, sold 1920, golf club); Stalbridge Park, Dorset (built 1638, demolished 1822); Saighton Grange, Cheshire (built c. 1490, purch. c. 1845, add. 1861-76, remod. 1957, school 1977); Motcombe House, Dorset (purch. 1825, rebuilt 1894, residence of the Lords Stalbridge, extinct 1949, now a school); Abbeystead, Lancashire (built 1886, purch. along with 19,000 acres in 1980, still own); Fonthill Abbey, Wiltshire (built 1796, collapsed 1825, purch. and rebuilt 1856-59, demolished 1955)
Estates: Bateman 40140 (E & W) 57439 (not including urban income). The Grosvenor lead mines in North Wales produced £50,000 or more c. 1800 (de Figueirdo and Treuherz, *Cheshire Country Houses*, 87). The London property was worth £250,000-500,000 pa in the 19th century. A huge world empire based on property was built up in the later 19th and throughout the 20th c. The Duke owned 129,300 acres in 2001 worth over eleven billion pounds.
Titles: Baron Grosvenor 1761- GB; Earl Grosvenor 1784- GB; Marquess of Westminster 1831- UK; Baron Ebury 1857- UK; Baron Stalbridge 1886-1949 UK; Baronet 1622-
Peers: 12 peers 1761-1945 1857-1932 1886-1945 1935-45
4 Lds Lt 18th, 19th, 20th
3 KG 19th
Notes: 1, 3 Bts, 1 Earl, 1, 2 Marquesses, 1 Duke, 1 Baron Ebury, 1 Baron Stalbridge and two others in ODNB.

Ernle-Erle (Earle)-Drax

Origins: The daughter of Thomas Erle married Sir Edward Ernle of Maddington. Their daughter succeeded to Charborough. The Erles (minor gentry from the 13th c., who rose high through office, law, and business in the 16th c.) acquired Charlborough c. 1550 by marriage to a Wykeham heiress. **The first Erle MP 1614. Three further MPs 1621-53**. The daughter of the 3rd Ernle Bt married Henry Drax, who succeeded to Charborough. Their granddaughter married Richard Grosvenor in 1788, who took the additional name Erle-Drax. His heiress married John Sawbridge, who took the name Erle Drax (see below). Charborough eventually passed to a younger son of the 17 Baron Dunsany (see Plunkett). The Draxes made a great fortune as sugar planters in Barbados from the 1630s onwards and were the first to introduce sugar cane to the island (Parker, *Sugar Barons*). They returned to England and began marrying into the aristocracy from the 1670s onwards.

1. Sir Walter Erle – Poole 1614 1621 1624 Dorset 1625 Lyme Regis 1626 Dorset 1628 Lyme Regis 1640 Weymouth 1640-48 Dorset 1654 1659 Poole 1660
2. Sir John Ernle – Wiltshire 1654-55 1660 Cricklade 1661-79 New Windsor 1679 Great Bedwin 1681 Marlborough 1689-95
3. Sir Walter Erle 1 Bt – Devizes 1679-81
4. Thomas Erle – Wareham 1679-81 1685-87 1689-98 Portsmouth 1698-1701 Wareham 1701-18 {Cork 1703-13}
5. Sir John Erle – Calne 1685-86
6. Sir Edward Ernle 3 Bt – Devizes 1695-98 Wiltshire 1698-1700 Wareham 1701 Heytesbury 1701-02 Wareham 1704-05 Marlborough 1708-10 Wareham 1710-13 Portsmouth 1715-22 Wareham 1722-29
7. Henry Drax – Wareham 1718-22 Lyme Regis 1727-34 Wareham 1734-48 1751-55
8. Thomas Earle Drax – Corfe Castle 1744-47 Wareham 1747-48 1761-68
9. Edward Drax – Wareham 1755-61
10. Richard Erle-Drax-Grosvenor – New Romney 1819-26
11. Richard Plunkett-Ernle-Erle-Drax – S. Dorset 2010-

Seats: Charborough Park, Dorset (acq. by mar. c. 1550, built c. 1650s, passed to the Drax family 1729, enlarged 1790 and 1810, remod. early 19th c., still own); Swell Court, Somerset (built 15th c., Grosvenors acq. by mar. 1730, passed by mar. to Erle-Drax family, sold 1950); Ellerton Abbey, Yorkshire (acq. by Drax family 1654, built c. 1830, owned into 20th c.); Maddington, Wiltshire (built c. 1600, acq. by Ernles by inher. 1688 and thence to Drax and Grosvenors, new house built 1773, demolished late 19th c., sold 1918)
Estates: Bateman 23587 (E) 23165. Erles held 11,000 acres in 1597, 13,000 acres in the 1950s.
Title: Baronet 1661-1734 or 1787

Notes: The descent of the estates became very complex in the 19th century. Admiral Reginald Plunkett-Ernle-Erle-Drax was Commander-in-Chief The Nore in 1939 and supervised the North Atlantic Convoy Operations during World War II. His grandson was elected to Parliament in 2010. Two Erles and one Ernle in ODNB.

Sawbridge

Origins: John Sawbridge married in 1827 the daughter of Richard Grosvenor (above). The Sawbridges were bankers in the 17th century, and later one was a Director of the South Sea Company. A hop merchant and distiller was Lord Mayor of London 1775.

1. Jacob Sawbridge – Cricklade 1715-21
2. John Sawbridge – Hythe 1768-74 London 1774-85
3. Samuel Sawbridge – Canterbury 1796-97 1807
4. John Sawbridge Erle-Drax – Wareham 1841-57 1859-65 1868-80

Seats: Holnest Park, Dorset (built 1768, purch. 1826 by Sawbridge Drax family, rebuilt 1841-42, sold 1919, flats, fire 2010); Olantigh Towers, Kent (purch. 1720, fire 1903, new house, sold 1935)
Notes: Two in ODNB.

Kyrle

Origins: Sir John Ernle MP married the heiress of Sir John Kyrle 2 Bt and succeeded to The Homme. The Kyrles emerged in the 14th century. **First MP 1571. Another MP 1640.** Bt 1627.

1. Sir John Kyrle 2 Bt – Herefordshire 1668-79

Seats: The Homme (Much Marle), Herefordshire (built c. 1500, purch. 1574, add. late Georgian period, passed by mar. from Kyrles to Ernles 1680, and to Popes who still own it); Walford Court, Herefordshire (acq. 15th c., built 16th c., rebuilt 19th c., sold, now hotel); Fawley Court, Herefordshire (built early 16th c., add. c.1630, purch. 17th c., sold 1931)
Estates: Bateman 4084 (E) 5940
Title: Baronet 1627-80; 1838-43

GROVE [Reynes]

Grove

Origins: The first MP was of humble origins. He was steward to several noble families and purchased landed estates in the mid-16th century. **First MP 1545. One additional MP 1558.**

1. Thomas Grove – Milborne Port 1645 Wiltshire 1654 1656 1659 Shaftesbury 1660
2. Sir Thomas Grove 1 Bt – S. Wiltshire 1865-74 Wilton Div. Wiltshire 1885-92

Seats: Ferne House, Wiltshire (purch. 1563, sold 1890s); Sedgehill Manor, Dorset (purch. 1573, sold 1966)
Estates: Bateman 7655 (E) 7111
Title" Baronet 1874- (dormant 1962)
Notes: See Hawkins, *Grove Diaries 1809-1925*, 1995.

Grove

Origins: Cadet line of above. Acquired Zeals by marriage to a Chafyn heiress in the mid-17th century.

1. William Grove – Shaftesbury 1768-74 Weymouth & Melcombe Regis 1774-81

Seat: Zeals House, Wiltshire (built 14th c., acq. by Chafyns c. 1452, passed to Groves 17th c., passed to cousins 1898, sold 1968)
Estates: Bateman 4307 (E) 6091 and 3699 (E) 5296
Notes: Family extinct 1898.

Reynes (Reymes)

Origins: An old Norfolk family. **First MP 1404 for Norfolk**. Bullen Reynes MP below left his estate to his wife who married Harry Chafyn. He left Waddon to his brother. It then came to his nephew William Grove (d. 1768).

1. Bullen Reynes – Weymouth & Melcombe Regis 1660-72

Seat: Waddon Manor (Whaddon), Dorset (acq. by mar. sec. half 17th c. from a family in possession in 15th c., built sec. half 17th c., passed to the Chafyns by mar. 1695 and to the Groves 1726, add. c. 1700, fire 1704, declined to farm house)

GUEST *ENGLAND & WALES*

Viscount Wimborne (1918- UK)

Origins: Established ironworks in Wales in the 1760s. The family firm became the largest producer of iron in the world by 1840. The family retained control of the company until 1890. High Sheriff 1862.

1. Sir Josiah Guest 1 Bt – Honiton 1826-31 Merthyr Tydvil 1832-52
2. Arthur Guest – Poole 1868-74
3. Montagu Guest – Youghal 1869-74 Wareham 1880-85
4. Ivor Guest 1 Viscount Wimborne – Plymouth 1900-06 Cardiff 1906-10
5. Christian Guest – E. Dorset 1910 Pembroke Boroughs 1910-18 N. Bristol 1922-23 Drake Div. Plymouth 1937-45
6. Frederick Guest – E. Dorset 1910-22 Stroud Div. Gloucestershire 1923-24 N. Div. Bristol 1924-29
7. Oscar Guest – Loughborough Div. Leicestershire 1918-22 Camberwell N. W. 1935-45
8. Ivor Guest 2 Viscount Wimborne – Brecon & Radnor 1935-39

Seats: Ashby St. Ledgers, Northamptonshire (built 15-16th c., remod. mid-17th c., purch. 1903, add. 1909-10, sold 1982, repurch. 1998, still own); Canford Manor, Dorset (medieval, most demolished 1765, rebuilt 1826-36, purch. 1846 for £350,000, add. 1848-52 and 1887-89, sold 1923, now a school); Dowlais House, Glamorganshire (built later 18th c., new house c. 1818, family departed 1852, offices 1894, demolished 1970s); Glencarron Lodge, Ross-shire (purch. and built mid-19th c.)
Estates: Bateman 83539 (E,W,& S) 46756. Worth £32,000,000 with 32,000 acres in 1990.
Titles: Baron Wimborne 1880- UK; Baron Ashby St. Ledgers 1910- UK; Baronet 1838-
Peers: 3 peers 1880-1914 1910-45
2 in Cabinet 1915-18 1921-22
Notes: 1 Viscount and one other in ODNB.

GUINNESS [Channon] *IRELAND & ENGLAND*

Earl of Iveagh (1919- UK)

Origins: Merchants and brewers in Ireland. Purchased brewery in 1759. Also became bankers. Attained great wealth, purchased landed estates, and married into the aristocracy but remained in charge of the business into the 20th century.

1. Richard Guinness – Kinsale 1847-48 Barnstaple 1854-57
2. Sir Benjamin Guinness 1 Bt – Dublin 1865-68
3. Arthur Guinness 1 Baron Ardilaun – Dublin 1868-69 1874-80

4. Walter Guinness 1 Baron Moyne – Bury St. Edmunds 1907-31
5. Rupert Guinness 2 Earl of Iveagh – Haggerston Div. Shoreditch 1908-10 S. Essex 1912-18 Southend 1918-27
6. Thomas Guinness – Bath 1931-45
7. Sir Henry Channon – Southend 1935-58
8. Paul Channon Lord Kelvedon – Southend 1959-97

Seats: Elveden Hall, Suffolk (built c. 1760, remod. 1869-70, purch. 1894, add. 1899-1904, contents sold 1984, still own); Farmleigh, Dublin (built late 18th c., purch. 1873, add. 1881-84, add. 1896-1901, sold 1999); Pyrford Court, Surrey (purch. 1906, built. c. 1910, sold c. 1966); Ashford Castle, Galway (medieval castle, Georgian house, purch. 1855, rebuilt 1870, sold 1939, hotel); St. Anne's (aka Thornhill), Dublin (built 18th c., demolished and rebuilt 1850, add. 1860, passed by mar. to Plunkets 1925, fire 1943, demolished 1968); Knockmaroon, Dublin (built c. 1800, purch. 19th c., still owned mid-20th c.); Kelvedon Hall, Essex (built 18th c., purch. 1937, still own); Luggala, Wicklow (built 1790, purch. 1937, still own); Biddesden House, Wiltshire (built 1711, purch. 1931, still own);
Estates: Bateman 31342 (I) 6573 – owned by Lord Ardilaun. (22,000 acres at Ashford and house sold 1939. 1 Bt worth £1,100,000 in 1869. English estates purchased by Lord Iveagh later. The 1 Earl of Iveagh worth £650,000 pa in 1910. Their English estate was large. Worth £200,000,000 in 1990. Owned 27,270 acres in 2001.
Titles: Baron Ardiluan 1880-1915 UK; Baron Iveagh 1891- UK; Viscount Iveagh 1905- UK; Baron Moyne 1932- UK; Baron Kelvedon 1997-2007 UKLife; Baronet 1867- ; 1885-
Peers: 5 peers 1880-1915 1891-1945 1932-45
2 in Cabinet 1925-29 1941-42 1986-89
1 KP 19th-20th
1 KG 20th
Notes: The 3 Earl of Iveagh was a member of the Irish Senate 1973-77. The 2 Countess of Iveagh was MP for Southend 1927-35, but she is included with her birth family (see Onslow). She was succeeded at Southend by her son-in-law Sir Henry Channon 1935-58, and then by her grandson 1959-97 (first elected at age 23) so that the seat was in the hands of the Guinness family for most of the 20th century (1918-97) The money used by "Chips" Channon to suatin his parliamentary career and to purchase his seat at Kelvedon Hall, Essex came from his wife's Guinness fortune. The 1 Lord Moyne, Minister of State for the Middle East was assassinated by Zionist terrorists in Cairo in 1944. The 3 Baron Moyne was Chairman of the Conservative Party's Monday Club 1972-74. Desmond Guinness founded the Irish Georgian Society, saved many important buildings that were to be demolished, and helped to slow down if not stop the architectural rape of Dublin in the 1960s, 70s, and 80s.
Notes: 1 Baron Ardiluan, 1 and 2 Barons Moyne, and the 1, 2, 3 Earls of Iveagh and six others and two Channons in ODNB.

GUISE (de Gyse)

Origins: Emerged in the 13th century. **First MP 1328 for Gloucestershire. Two further MPs 1491-1654, one for Gloucestershire**.

1. Sir John Guise 2 Bt – Gloucestershire 1679-81 1689-95
2. Sir John Guise 3 Bt – Gloucestershire 1705-10 Great Marlow 1722-27
3. Sir John Guise 4 Bt – Aylesbury 1722-27
4. Sir William Guise 5 Bt – Gloucestershire 1770-83
5. Sir Berkeley Guise 2 Bt – Gloucestershire 1811-32 E. Gloucestershire 1832-34

Seats: Elmore Court, Gloucestershire (acq. 1274, medieval, rebuilt 1570s, remod. 1720s, add. 1807, remod. 1869-70, still own); Highnam Park (Court), Gloucestershire (built 1658, inherited from the Cooke II family 1750 and part purch. 1769, sold c. 1850s); Harleyford, Buckinghamshire (built 16th c., purch. 1719, sold 1735); Ablode's (Abload) Court, Gloucestershire (built c. 1600, acq. lease c. 1629, sold 1705); Rendcomb Park, Gloucestershire (medieval, rebuilt later 16th c., purch. 1635, fire c. 1680s, rebuilt late 1680s, add. 1770s, sold 1864)
Estates: Bateman 2087 (E) 4002. Elmore Court line worth £500 pa in the mid-17th c. Owned 1,200 acres 2007.
Titles: Baronet 1661-1783; 1783-
Notes: The family declined financially in the 19th century and sold all of their houses except Elmore. 3 Bt of 2nd cr. and two others in ODNB.

GULLY

Viscount Selby (1905- UK)

Origins: Coffee planters in the 18th century, returned to England 1814. A son of the returning planter became a physician. The 1 Viscount rose through the law and politics to Speaker of the House of Commons 1895.

1. William Gully 1 Viscount Selby – Carlisle 1886-1905

Seat: Ibornden Park, Kent (leased?)
Estates: 1 Viscount left £62,000 in 1909.
Peers: 3 peers 1905-23 1932-45
Notes: 1 Viscount and one other in ODNB.

GULSTON (Goulston) [Cowell, Stepney] *ENGLAND & WALES*

Gulston

Origins: Merchants and financiers in Portugal in the 17th and 18th centuries. Director of the South Sea Company 1742-60.

1. William Gulston – Bridport 1701-02
2. Joseph Gulston – Tregony 1737-41 Poole 1741-65
3. Joseph Gulston – Poole 1765-68 1780-84

Seats: Dirleton House (later Danyrallt Park), Carmarthenshire (acq. by mar. 1767, sold 1881); Derwydd, Carmarthenshire (acq. by mar. 1767, held at least until 1980s); Ealing Grove, Middlesex (sold 1775 for £12,000)
Estates: Bateman 7154 (W) 10976. Income from a Hertfordshire estate £1,500 pa and £250,000 in funds in 1766. Severe financial difficulties in the late 18th c.
Notes: One in ODNB.

Gulston (Goulston)

Origins: The senior line of the family. A lawyer and legal official who purchased an estate in 1628. **First MP 1659 for Hertfordshire**.

1. Sir William Gulston – Bletchingley 1681 New Romney 1685-87
2. Edward Gulston – New Romney 1701-02
3. Richard Gulston – Hertford 1701-05 1710-15

Seat: Wyddial Hall, Hertfordshire (built early 16th c., purch. 1628, fire and remod. 1733, sold 1780)

Stepney

Origins: Rose by trade in the mid-15th century, and acquired estates at the Dissolution. **First MP 1555**. Moved to Wales 1561. Registrar of the Diocese of St. David's. **Two MPs for Welsh seats including Pembrokeshire 1572-1643**. Sheriff 1573, Kt 1618. Bt 1621. On the death of the 9th and last Baronet the estates were divided between his two sisters. One married Joseph Gulston in 1767 and she brought Dirleton to that family. Her sister married a Cowell, who took the additional name Stepney.

1. Sir Thomas Stepney 5 Bt – Carmarthenshire 1717-22
2. Sir John Stepney 8 Bt – Monmouth 1767-88
3. Sir John Cowell-Stepney 1 Bt – Carmarthen District 1868-74

4. Sir Emile Cowell-Stepney 2 Bt – Carmarthen District 1876-78 1886-92

Seats: Dirleton, Carmarthenshire (acq. 16th c., passed by mar. to Gultsons 1767 see above); Llanelly (Llanelli) House, Carmarthenshire (built 16th c., acq. by mar. 1691, rebuilt 1714, passed to Cowells 1825, sold 1959); Prendergast House, Pembrokeshire (medieval building, acq. by mar. 1565, ruin by 1767)
Estates: Bateman 9847 (W) 7200. 1,400 acres in the 1640s.
Titles: Baronet 1621-1825; 1871-1909
Notes: One in ODNB.

GUMLEY

Origins: A cabinetmaker in the 17th century. The first MP was a plate-glass manufacturer and army contractor.

1. John Gumley – Steyning 1722 27
2. John Gumley – Bramber 1728
3. Samuel Gumley – Hedon 1746-47

Seat: Gumley House, Isleworth, Middlesex (acq. and built 1700, sold 1750, now school)

GURDON [Rebow]

Baron Cranworth (1899- UK)

Origins: Small clothiers who at the end of the 15th century rose in status and acquired Assington in 1556. Gentry by the reign of Elizabeth I, when they inherited Letton from the Bramptons. **First MP 1571. Another MP 1621, both for Sudbury**.

1. John Gurdon – Ipswich 1640-53 Suffolk 1654 Sudbury 1660
2. Philip Gurdon – Sudbury 1689-90
3. John Gurdon – Sudbury 1699-1700
4. Brampton Gurdon – W. Norfolk 1857-65
5. John Gurdon Rebow – Colchester 1857-59 1865-70
6. Robert Gurdon 1 Baron Cranworth – S. Norfolk 1880-85 Mid Norfolk 1885-92 1895
7. Sir William Gurdon – N. Norfolk 1899-1910

Seats: Grundisburgh Hall, Suffolk (built c. 1500, purch. 1771, reduced in size 1960s, still resident); Letton Hall, Norfolk (acq. by mar. later 16th c., built 1783-89, sold c. 1917, institutional use); Assington Hall, Suffolk (medieval, purch. 1556, rebuilt later 16th c., remod. c. 1815, sold 1938, burned 1957); Brantham Court, Suffolk (built 1850-52, sold in 20th c.)

Estates: Bateman 11092 (E) 8758. Worth £1,400 pa in 1655.
Peers: 2 peers 1899-1945
1 KG 20th
1 Ld Lt 20th
Notes: For a family of comparatively modest stature the Gurdons achieved the remarkable feat of electing at least one MP in five successive centuries. Three in ODNB.

Rebow

Origins: Of Flemish extraction settled in Colchester as clothiers in the early 17th century. Granted arms 1685. The first MP was a merchant-clothier. An uncle of the 1 Baron Cranworth married in 1835 the heiress of the Rebows of Wivenhoe Park.

1. Sir Isaac Rebow – Colchester 1689-90 1692-1714 1715-22
2. Isaac Rebow – Colchester 1734-35
3. Isaac Rebow-Martin – Colchester 1755-81

Seat: Wivenhoe Park, Essex (purch. 1733, built 1759, passed to Gurdons by mar. 1845 who took name Rebow, sold 1902, institutional use)
Estates: Bateman 4209 (E) 6889

GUNTER (Gutter) *WALES*

Origins: An old but not rich family. **First MP 1539. One further MP for Monmouthshire 1554.**

1. James Gunter – Monmouthshire 1712

Seats: The Priory, Abergavenny, Monmouthshire; Gunterstone (Tregunter or Gwernyfyd), Breconshire
Notes: The male line became extinct with the death of the last MP. The family claimed to have come over with the Conqueror. (Williams, *The Parliamentary History of the Principality of Wales,* 128) Two in ODNB.

GURNEY

Origins: Originally a gentry family, and elected an **MP for Norfolk in 1399**. Later they became silk merchants in Norwich in the 17th century. Became brewers and bankers in the 18th and 19th centuries.

1. Hudson Gurney – Shaftesbury 1812-13 Newtown (IoW) 1816-32
2. Richard Gurney – Norwich 1818-26 1830-32

3. John Gurney – King's Lynn 1854-65
4. Samuel Gurney – Penryn & Falmouth 1857-65

Seats: Sprowston Hall, Norfolk (built 1560, purch. 1869, rebuilt 1872-76, sold 1973, now hotel); Keswick Hall, Norfolk (purch. c. 1750, built later 18th c., add. 1817, sold c. 1945); Catton Hall, Norfolk (built 1780, owned by Gurneys 1852-66); Colney Hall, Norfolk (built 1834, purch. 1881, passed by mar. to the Barclays, sold 1956) Earlham Hall, Norfolk (built early 17th c., owned by Bacons until 1925, leased by Gurneys 1786-1885); North Runcton Hall, Norfolk (purch. 1816, built 1835, add. 1853, sold 1945, demolished); Northrepps Hall, Norfolk (built 16th c.?, purch. 1794, still own); Nutfield Priory, Surrey (purch. 1855, rebuilt 1858-59, sold 1866)
Estates: Bateman 11714 (E) 6229 and 8703 (E) 8965. Rubinstein – Richard Gurney left £125,000 probate in 1811 and Joseph Gurney £120,000 in 1830. Hudson Gurney MP left £1,100,000 in 1864.
Notes: One of the most eminent Quaker families in England. The Gurney bill-brokering business failed in 1866 with serious consequences for the finances of the family. Nine in ODNB.

GUYBON

Origins: A landed family in the 14th century. **First MP 1504. An additional MP 1597.**

1. Sir Francis Guybon – Thetford 1689-95

Seat: Thursford, Norfolk (built c. 1600, sold 1753, partly demolished post 1918); Heydon's Hall, Norfolk (medieval, purch. 1657, sold 1715)

GWYNNE *WALES*

Origins: Emerged in the 15th century. A Colonel in the Civil War. Lawyer later 17th century. Kt 1680.

1. George Gwynne – Radnorshire 1654 1656 1660
2. Sir Rowland Gwynne – Radnorshire 1679-81 1689-90 Breconshire 1690-95 Bere Alston 1695-98 Breconshire 1698-1702
3. Howell Gwynne – Radnorshire 1755-61 Old Sarum 1761-68

Seats: Garth House (Garth in Llanleonfel), Breconshire (purch. and built 17th c., sold 1823); Llanelwedd House (Hall), Radnorshire (built 16th c., acq. early 18th c., sold early 20th c., fire 1955, rebuilt, institutional use); Pencoyd (Pencoed) Castle, Monmouthshire (built 13th c., ruin, new house 16th c., ruin)
Estates: Worth £1,500 pa in 1660. Held about 1,000 acres in the 19th c.

1 Ld Lt 18th
Notes: Sir Rowland Gwynne greatly diminished the value of the estate by wasteful spending. Sales of land took place later 18th c. One in ODNB.

HADDOCK

Origins: An old seafaring family, mariners from at least 1327. Naval service during the Commonwealth. Flag Captain RN 1660s-70s. Kt 1675. Admirals.

1. Sir Richard Haddock – Aldeburgh 1679 New Shoreham 1685-87
2. Nicholas Haddock – Rochester 1734-46
3. Nicholas Haddock – Rochester 1754-61

Seat: Wrotham Place, Kent (purch. 1723, sold 1790s)
Notes: Family extinct in male line 1792. Two in ODNB.

HALDANE [Duncan] *SCOTLAND*

Haldane

Origins: Seated at Gleneagles since the late 13th century. **First [MP 1630 for Perthshire].**

1. Mungo Haldane – [Perthshire 1681 1685]
2. John Haldane – [Perthshire 1689-93 Dumbartonshire 1700-02 Perthshire 1703-07] Scotland 1707-08
3. Mungo Haldane – Stirlingshire 1715-22 Dumbartonshire 1722-25 Perthshire 1726-27
4. Patrick Haldane – Perth Burghs 1715-22
5. George Haldane – Stirling Burghs 1747-58
6. Robert Haldane – Stirling Burghs 1758-61

Seat: Gleneagles House (Castle), Perthshire (built early 16th c., new house 17th c., new house c. 1750, passed to Duncans later 18th c.)
Estates: see Camperdown
Notes: One in ODNB.

Earl of Camperdown (1831-1933 UK)

Origins: The 1 Viscount Duncan was the son of a Provost of Dundee whose ancestors were merchants who purchased landed property in the mid-17th century. He became a Rear Admiral in 1787, and enjoyed a very successful naval career. On the death of the 17th Haldane laird of Gleneagles in 1767 the estates passed to his daughters, the younger of who married Alexander Duncan, father of the 1 Viscount. The Duncans also succeeded to the Philips estates in Warwickshire (see Philips I).

1. Adam Haldane Duncan 2 Earl of Camperdown – Southampton 1837-41 Bath 1841-52 Forfarshire 1854-59

Seats: Camperdown House, Forfarshire (medieval "Lundie Castle" acq. and demolished in 17th c. by Duncans and replaced by a house, then a new house built 1824-28, sold 1941); Gleneagles House (Castle), Perthshire (built early 16th c., new house 17th c., new house c. 1750, inher. by mar. later 18th c., remod. late 19th c., sold 1924, hotel)
Estates: Bateman 13892 (S) 11720. Owned 4,000 acres in 1996.
Title: Viscount Duncan 1797-1933 GB
Peers: 5 peers 1797-1804 1806-1933
1 KT 19th
Notes: Family extinct in male line 1933. 1 Viscount in ODNB.

Viscount Haldane (1911- UK)

Origins: A Cadet line of the Haldanes of Gleneagles.

1. Richard Haldane 1 Viscount Haldane – Haddingtonshire 1885-1911

Seat: Cloan (Cloanden), Perthshire (built 18th c., purch. 1852, remod. 1865, for sale 2013)
Estates: The 1 Viscount left £69,000 in 1928.
Peers: 1 peer 1911-28
1 in Cabinet 1905-15
1 KT 20th
Notes: 1 Viscount and ten others in ODNB.

HALE

Hale

Origins: A London grocer purchased King's Walden in the later 16th century. High Sheriff 1647.

1. William Hale – Hertfordshire 1669-79 1681
2. William Hale – Bramber 1709-10 St. Albans 1713-17
3. Peggan Hale – Hertfordshire 1747-55

Seat: King's Walden Park, Hertfordshire (purch. 1576, sold 1884, demolished 1958)
Estates: Bateman 7999 (E) 11790
Notes: Three in ODNB.

<u>Hale</u>

Origins: A cadet line. John Hale MP acquired an estate in Devon by marriage 1634.

1. John Hale – Devon 1654 1656 Dartmouth 1660

Seat: Bowringsleigh (Bowrings Leigh), Devon (built 1303, rebuilt later 16th c., acq. by mar. 1634, passed out of family by mar. later 17th c.)

HALES [Pym]

<u>Hales</u>

Origins: The family can be traced to the 14th century. Rose through the law (Master of the Rolls 1536), office (Baron of the Exchequer), and fortunate marriages in the 16th century. **First MP 1512**. Kt 1547. **Six additional MPs 1523-1659, including Kent 1626.**

1. Sir Thomas Hales 2 Bt – Kent 1701-05 Canterbury 1715-34 1735-41 1746-47
2. Sir Thomas Hales 3 Bt – Minehead 1722-27 Camelford 1727-34 Grampound 1734-41 Hythe 1744-61 East Grinstead 1761-62
3. Sir Thomas Hales 4 Bt – Downton 1762-68 Dover 1770-73
4. Sir Philip Hales 5 Bt – Downton 1775-80 Marlborough 1784-90

Seat: Bekesbourne (Beakesbourne), Kent (house called Howletts built 16th c., purch. c. 1620, became ruinous, occupied a different house later 17th c., sold 1787, demolished)
Title: Baronet 1660-1824
Notes: Family extinct in male line 1824. Four in ODNB.

<u>Hales</u>

Origins: Junior line broke off in the 16th century. **First MP 1547. Three additional MPs 1563-1628.**

1. Sir Edward Hales 2 Bt – Maidstone 1660 Queenborough 1661-79
2. Sir Edward Hales 3 Bt – Canterbury 1679-81
3. John Hales – New Shoreham 1679-81
4. Edward Hales – Hythe 1679-81 1689-90

Seats: Hales' Place (Woodchurch), Kent (medieval, acq. by mar. 1602, sold 1680, demolished 1928); Paulerspury, Northamptonshire (acq. by mar. 1644, sold c. 1670-74); Tunstall Place, Kent (medieval, inher. by mar. and rebuilt 1613, held into 18th c.)
Estates: Bateman 2980 (E) 3843
Title: Baronet 1611-1829
Notes: Sir Edward Hales 3 Bt MP was created Earl of Tenterdon in the Jacobite peerage 1692. The family remained Roman Catholic in the 18th century and were not involved in politics.
Notes: 3 Bt in ODNB.

Pym

Origins: The Pyms were gentry from the reign of Edward I when they were first recorded at Brymore. **First MP 1584. Two additional MPs 1621-48.** Sir Thomas Hales 2 Bt of Bekesbourne married in 1688 Mary, daughter and heiress of Sir Charles Pym 1 Bt.

1. Sir Charles Pym 1 Bt – Bere Alston 1641-48 Minehead 1660

Seat: Brymore (Brummer), Somerset (acq. 13th c., medieval house, sold 1729)
Title: Baronet (Cromwellian Bt) and 1663-88
Note: John Pym MP 1621-43 was one of Charles I's most implacable opponents. One in ODNB.

HALL [Herbert, Howe, Jones, Stephens] *WALES & IRELAND*

Baron Llanover (1859-67 UK)

Origins: The grandfather of the first MP was Dean of Llandaff. His son was a barrister and married 1801 into the Crawshay ironmasters family, became a partner in the business in 1803, and inherited considerable industrial wealth. Sold iron interest 1816.

1. Benjamin Hall – Totnes 1806-12 Westbury 1812-14 Glamorganshire 1814-17
2. Benjamin Hall 1 Baron Llanover – Monmouth 1831 1832-34 Marylebone 1837-59
3. Ivor Herbert 1 Baron Treowen – S. Div. Monmouthshire 1906-17

Seats: Llanarth Court, Monmouthshire (medieval, Jones family acq. by mar. c. 15th c., rebuilt c. 1770, rebuilt 1849-50, passed to Herberts 1896, donated 1948, now a hospital, family still own estate); Treowen, Monmouthshire (built 15th c., rebuilt by Jones family 1623-27, family depart 1670s, became a farm house, passed to Herberts 1896, sold 1945); Llanover (Llanofer Court), Monmouthshire (acq. by Hall family 1826, rebuilt 1828, passed to Herberts 1896, still own); Abercarn, Monmouthshire (acq.

1808, passed to Herberts 1896, still own); Hensol Castle, Glamorganshire (built late 17th/early 18th c., add. c. 1735, Halls purch. 1815 for £45,000, sold 1826, now hospital)
Estates: Bateman 4641 (W) 24355; 6533 (W) 8136; 4542 (W) 10623. Still own 5,000 acres 2015. Rubinstein – Benjamin Hall MP left £100,000 probate in 1817.
Titles: Baron Treowen (Herbert) 1917-33 UK; Baronet 1838-67; 1907-33
Peers: 2 peers 1859-67 1917-33
2 Lds Lt 19th, 20th
Notes: On the death of the only Lord Llanover (Hall) in 1867 (family extinct in male line), he left his estates to his wife. In 1896 she was succeeded by her daughter who married 1846 John Jones, who took the name Herbert in 1848, of Llanarth Court, 1 Baron Treowen. Jones family took name Jones in the 16th c. Long a distinguished Roman Catholic family. **First Jones MP 1589**. **Another Jones MP 1614**. First MP, of Treowen, a London grocer, had a brother who was Sherfff of Monmouthshire. 1 Baron Llanover in ODNB.

Earl of Ranelagh (1677-1712 I)

Origins: The family settled in Ireland in the 1570s, Archbishop of Dublin 1605. Became courtiers. Viscount 1628. **First {MP 1634}. That MP also sat for an English seat in the Long Parliament. Another {MP 1639}.** This was the senior line of the Jones family of which the junior was seated at Treowen and Llanarth (see above).

1. Richard Jones 1 Earl of Ranelagh – {Roscommon 1661-66} Plymouth 1685-87 Newtown 1689-95 Chichester 1695-98 Marlborough 1698-1701 West Looe 1701-03
2. William Jones – {Athlone 1703-23}

Seats: Dormstown Castle (Durhamstown), Meath (old castle, acq. later 16th c., sold late 18th c.); Horsham St. Faith, Norfolk (owned by Cornwallis family from 1602, passed by mar. to Jones family, passed out of family in 1885 when the male line became extinct)
Estates: The estate in Ireland was worth £1,200 pa in the 1640s.
Titles: Baron Jones 1628-1885 I; Viscount Ranelagh 1628-1885 I
Peers: {3 peers 1660-1712 1759-97}
Notes: The family fell on hard times in the 18th century and lost its Irish estates. 1 Earl and one other in ODNB.

Stephens

Origins: Cadets of the Stephens family of Eastington Manor, Gloucestershire (see Stephens), gentry in the 12th century. An illegitimate daughter and heiress of Sir Philip Stephens 1 Bt married the 6 Viscount Ranelagh (see above). Stephens Howe rose to Brigadier General through the influence of his maternal uncle Philip Stephens, Chief

Secretary to the Admiralty. He married a Stephens cousin, and had he lived would have succeeded to the Stephens Baronetcy.

1. Sir Philip Stephens 1 Bt – Liskeard 1759-68 Sandwich 1768-1806
2. Stephens Howe – Great Yarmouth 1795-96

Seats: Horsham St. Faith, Norfolk; Somerton Hall, Suffolk (built 18th and 19th c.)
Title: Baronet 1795-1809
Notes: Two Stephens in ODNB.

HALSEY [Whatley]

Origins: A legal family from the early Tudor period. Acquired landed estates in the mid-16th century. Kt 1630. Master in Chancery (d. 1670). High Sheriff under Charles II. Sir Joseph Whatley married Sarah Halsey, heiress to her family's estates, and took the name Halsey.

1. Thomas Halsey – Hertfordshire 1685-87 1695-1705 1708-15
2. Thomas Halsey – Hertfordshire 1768-84
3. Sir Joseph Whatley Halsey – St. Albans 1807-18
4. Thomas Halsey – Hertfordshire 1846-54
5. Sir Frederick Halsey 1 Bt – Hertfordshire 1874-85 Watford Div. Hertfordshire 1885-1906

Seat: Gaddesden Place, Hertfordshire (Great Gaddesden) (acq. 1545, house leased for commercial use 1984, still own estate)
Estates: Bateman 3911 (E) 5839
Title: Baronet 1920-
Notes: One in ODNB.

HAMBRO

<u>Baron Hambro</u> (1994-2002 UKLife)

Origins: Merchants and bankers in Denmark from the 18th century. Founded a London bank 1839. Continued to run the bank until 1998.

1. Baron Charles Hambro – Weymouth 1868-74 1885-91
2. Sir Eric Hambro – Wimbledon Div. Surrey 1900-07
3. Angus Hambro – S. Dorset 1910-22 N. Dorset 1937-45

Seats: Milton Abbey, Dorset (medieval monastic buildings, add. 1498-1525, remod. 1771-76, purch. 1852, sold 1932, now a school); The Hyde, Bedfordshire (built 18th c., add. 19th c., purch. c. 1930, remod. 1952-53, still own); Kidbrooke Park, Sussex (built 1733, remod. c. 1805, add. 1814-15, remod. 1842, add. 1870s, purch. 1921, sold 1938, school)
Estates: Bateman 9622 (E) 12000. Worth £100,000,000 in 1990.
Notes: Danish Barons 1851. Six in ODNB.

HAMILTON I [Arden, Baillie, Dalzell, Douglas, Nisbet, Russell, Stirling] *SCOTLAND, IRELAND & ENGLAND*

Duke of Hamilton (1643- S)

Origins: Walter FitzGilbert Hamilton switched allegiance from Edward II to Robert Bruce after Bannockburn in 1314. He was richly rewarded with land. The 1 Baron Hamilton made the family a preeminent one through his marriage in 1445 to the daughter of James II, Princess Mary. The Earl of Arran was Regent of Scotland 1542-54. **First [MP 1546]. At least nine additional [MPs in the main or closely allied lines between 1560-1649]. At least six additional [MPs remoter kinsmen]. The 2 Duke also sat for Portsmouth in 1640**. The family remained at the center of Scottish life in succeeding centuries. The current Duke carries the Crown of Scotland when the Queen attends the opening sessions of the Scottish Parliament. **One was elected as an MSP in the new Scottish Parliament in 1999-2007 (Lord James Douglas-Hamilton)**. The family spawned a unique and extraordinary number of cadet families that elected **[MPs] in the 16th and 17th centuries (at least 12 pre-1660 [MPs]).**

1. Lord Archibald Hamilton – Lanarkshire 1708-10 1718-34 Queenborough 1735-41 Dartmouth 1742-47
2. Sir James Abercromby 1 Bt – Dysart 1710 (illegitmate son of the 3 Duke)
3. Lord William Hamilton – Lanarkshire 1734
4. Basil Hamilton – Kirkcudbright Stewartry 1741-42
5. William Hamilton – Midhurst 1761-64
6. Archibald Hamilton 9 Duke of Hamilton – Lancashire 1768-72
7. Alexander 10 Duke of Hamilton – Lancaster 1802-06
8. Lord Archibald Hamilton – Lanarkshire 1802-27
9. Douglas Douglas Hamilton 14 Duke of Hamilton – Renfrew East 1930-40
10. Lord Malcolm Douglas-Hamilton – Inverness 1950-54
11. James Douglas-Hamilton 11 Earl of Selkirk – Edinburgh West 1974-97

Seats: Hamilton Palace, Lanarkshire (old house, rebuilt 1693-1701, add. 1718, add. 1822-25, sale of contents 1882, demolished 1919-22); Dungavel House (Castle), Lanarkshire (built 19th c., became principal seat 1919, sold 1947, now a prison); Ashton

Hall, Lancashire (built 14th c., inher. by mar. from Gerards, sold 1853); Brodick Castle, (Arran), Buteshire (the Isle of Arran acq. by marriage to the daughter of James II, built 13th c., add. 1558 and later 16th c., rebuilt 1844, passed by mar. to the Dukes of Montrose 1906); Lennoxlove (Lethington Castle), Haddingtonshire (built 15th c., add. 17th c., purch. 20th c., still own); Kinneil (House), Linlithgowshire (built 1546-53, part destroyed 1570, add. 1677, not much used by family after early 18th c., demolition proposed 1936 but given to a trust for preservation); Easton Park, Suffolk (built c. 1627, acq. by mar. 1830, add. 1875, sold 1919, demolished 1923)
Estates: Bateman 157386 (S) 140642. Reduced to 13,000 acres in the 1980s. (Masters, *The Dukes*, 90) Owned 5,200 acres in 1996.
Titles: Earl of Angus 1389- S; Baron Hamilton 1445-1579 S; Earl of Arran 1503-79 S; Marquis of Hamilton 1599- S; Marquis of Douglas 1633- S; Earl of Lanerick 1639- S; Baron Mordington 1641-1755 S; Marquis of Clydesdale 1643- S; Duke of Douglas 1703-61 S; Duke of Brandon 1711- GB
Peers: [2 peers 1660-94 1698-1707] 1 Scottish Rep peer 1708-12 7 peers 1782-1819 1806-63 1866-1945
5 Lds Lt 18th, 19th
6 KT 18th, 19th
3 KG, 17th, 18th, 19th
Notes: The 14 Duke was the first to fly a plane over Mt. Everest and Rudolf Hess landed his aircraft on the Duke's estate during the Second World War in the hope of using the services of the House of Hamilton to help negotiate a peace between Churchill and Hitler. The 10 Duke succeeded to much of the Beckford possessions via marriage to William Beckford's daughter. Succeeded to the estates of the Earl of Macclesfield in Lancashire in 1744 (see Gerard). Hamilton family and 1 and 2 Marquises and 1, 2, 3, 4, 10, 11, and 14 Dukes and 1 Earl of Orkney and 1, 2 and 3 Earls of Arran and Duchess of Atholl and ten others in ODNB.

Baron Bargeny (1641-1736 S) (Bargany)

Origins: Sir John Hamilton, younger son of the 1 Marquis of Hamilton, was granted Bargeny in 1631. His son was created Baron Bargeny.

No MPs

Seat: Bargany House, Ayrshire (16th c. house, acq. 1631, rebuilt 1681, later passed to Dalrymples)
Peers: [1 peer 1695-1707]
Notes: 2 Baron in ODNB.

Earl of Selkirk (1646-1885 S)

Origins: The husband of Anne, Duchess of Hamilton in her own right, William Douglas, was created Duke of Hamilton for life and Earl of Selkirk. Their eldest son became Duke of Hamilton while the second son inherited the Selkirk title. The third son succeeded his brother as Earl of Selkirk and was created Earl of Ruglen. The latter's daughter succeeded as Countess of Ruglen and the title passed to the Duke of Queensberry. The Selkirk title passed to a great nephew. In 1885 it became dormant. It was revived later and the 10 Earl was a Scottish Representative peer from 1945 and served in the Cabinet in the 1950s while the estates passed to a younger son of the Earl of Hopetoun (see Hope).

No MPs

Seat: St. Mary's Isle, Kirkcudbrightshire (acq. 18th c.)
Estates: Bateman 22264 (S) 21473
Titles: Baron Deer 1646-1885 S; Earl of Ruglen 1697-1810 S
Peers: [2 peers 1688-1707 1697-1707] 4 Scottish Rep peers 1713-15 1722-39 1787-99 1806-18 1831-85
3 Lds Lt 18th, 19th
Notes: 5 and 10 Earls in ODNB.

Duke of Abercorn (1868- I)

Origins: The younger brother of the 1 Marquis of Hamilton was created Baron Paisley in 1587. His son became the 1 Earl of Abercorn. He established a branch of the family in Ulster. **First {MP 1639}.**

1. William Hamilton – {St. Johnstown 1661-66}
2. James Hamilton 6 Earl of Abercorn – {County Tyrone 1692-93 1695-99}
3. George Hamilton – {St. Johnstown 1727-60} Wells 1734-35 1747-54
4. Charles Hamilton – {Strabane 1727-60} Truro 1741-47
5. John James 1 Marquess of Abercorn – East Looe 1783-84 St. Germans 1784-89
6. James Hamilton Viscount Hamilton – Dungannon 1807 Liskeard 1807-12
7. Lord Claud Hamilton – Dungannon 1807-08
8. Lord Claud Hamilton – County Tyrone 1835-37 1839-74
9. James Hamilton 2 Duke of Abercorn – Donegal 1860-80
10. Lord Claud Hamilton – Londonderry 1865-68 Kings Lynn 1869-80 Liverpool 1880-85 West Derby Div. Liverpool 1885-88 S. Kensington 1910-18
11. Lord George Hamilton – Middlesex 1868-85 Ealing Div. Middlesex 1885-1906
12. Lord Frederick Hamilton – S. W. Manchester 1885-86 N. Tyrone 1892-95
13. Lord Ernest Hamilton – N. Tyrone 1885-92

14. James Hamilton 3 Duke of Abercorn – Londonderry 1900-13
15. Douglas Proby – Saffron Walden Div. Essex 1910
16. James Hamilton 5 Duke of Abercorn – Fermanagh & S. Tyrone 1964-70

Seats: Baron's Court (Baronscourt), Tyrone (acq. 1606, built 1779-82, fire 1796, rebuilt 1810, remod. 1836-40, remod. 1946-47, still own); Bentley Priory, Middlesex (medieval, remdo. 16th c., rebuilt later 18th c., purch. 1788, add. c. 1780s-90s, sold 1852, institutional use); Duddingston House, Edinburghshire (purch. 1745, built 1763-68 for £30,000, damaged WWII, offices); Witham Place, Essex (purch. 1720); Bruntstane, Edinburghshire (built 1565, remod. c. 1639, add. 1672, remod. 1744, purch. 1769, sold 1875)
Estates: Bateman 78662 (I & S) 53400. Owned 15,000 acres in 2001.
Titles: Baron Paisley 1587- S; Baron Abercorn 1603- S; Earl of Abercorn 1606- S; Baron Hamilton 1616-91 I; Baron Hamilton 1692- I; Baron Mountcastle and Viscount Strabane 1701- I; Viscount Hamilton 1786- GB; Marquess of Abercorn 1790- GB; Marquess of Hamilton 1868- I; Baronet 1634-
Peers: {5 peers 1660-91 1695-1701 1703-44 1736-89} [1 peer 1706-07] 2 Scot Rep Peers 1734-44 1761-87 5 peers 1786-1818 1832-1945
3 Lds Lt 19th, 20th
2 in Cabinet 1866-68 1874-76 1885-92 1895-1903
4 KG 19th, 20th
Notes: The Scottish Hamiltons were granted lands in Tyrone in the 16th century. The 1 Earl of Abercorn acquired additional land there in 1606. The Abercorns lost their Scottish estates during the Commonwealth because they were Roman Catholics. The 4 Earl followed James II into exile. The 5 Earl declared loyalty to William III and the 6 Earl conformed to the Established Church. Lord Claud Hamilton's son succeeded to the Proby estates in 1909. (see Proby) 1, 6, and 8 Earls and 1 and 2 Dukes and eight others in ODNB.

Hamilton

Origins: Kinsmen of the Dukes of Abercorn. The first {MP} was an agent of the Hollow Blade Company. He was the son and grandson of Archdeacons.

1. Sir Henry Hamilton 1 Bt – {Londonderry 1747-68}

Seat: Castle Conyngham, Donegal (acq. by mar. from Conynghams mid-18th c., sold 1782)
Title: Baronet 1775-82

Hamilton

Origins: Kinsmen of the Dukes of Abercorn.

1. James Hamilton – {Strabane 1660}
2. William Hamilton – {Strabane 1733-62}
3. Sir John Hamilton 1 Bt – {Strabane 1763-97}
4. Claud Hamilton – {Strabane 1769-76}

Seat: Dunnamonagh (Dunamana), Tyrone (resident 18th-19th c.)
Title: Baronet 1781-1818

Hamilton

Origins: Descended from a younger brother of the 6 Earl of Abercorn.

1. Sir Charles Hamilton 2 Bt – St. Germans 1790 Dungannon 1801-02 1803-06 Honiton 1807-12

Seats: Iping Hall (House), Sussex (purch. c. 1800, still owned post WWII); Chilston Park, Kent (built c. 1500, acq. by Hamilton and add. c. 1710-28, add. 1782, sold 1821); Trebinshun House, Breconshire
Estates: Bateman 2969 (E & W) 2785
Titles: Baronet 1776-2008; 1819-2008
Notes: One in ODNB.

Viscount Boyne (1717- I)

Origins: Descended from a younger brother of the 1 Earl of Abercorn. The 4 Viscount succeeded to the Stackallan estates on the death of the 2 Viscount Stackallan. In 1828 the 7 Viscount married the heiress of Matthew Russell of Brancepeth Castle and succeeded to his vast English estates. William Russell was a self-made man (coal mines) in the later 18th century. He was a Sunderland banker, financier, and coal mine owner.

1. Gustavus Hamilton 1 Viscount Boyne – {County Donegal 1692-93 1695-99 1703-13 Strabane 1713-14}
2. Frederick Hamilton – {County Donegal 1707-15}
3. Frederick Hamilton – {Coleraine 1713-27}
4. Gustavus Hamilton – {County Donegal 1716-35}
5. Henry Hamilton – {St. Johnstown 1725-27 County Donegal 1730-43}
6. Gustavus Hamilton 2 Viscount Boyne – Newport (IoW) 1736-41

7. Richard Hamilton 4 Viscount Boyne – {Navan 1755-60}
8. Sackville Hamilton – {St. Johnstown 1780-83 Clogher 1783-95 Armagh 1796-97}
9. Matthew Russell – Saltash 1802-07 1808-22
10. William Russell – Saltash 1822-26 Bletchingley 1826-27 County Durham 1828-32

Seats: Brancepeth Castle, Durham (medieval, purch. by Russells with 4,600 acres in 1796 for £75,000, Russells rebuilt castle 1798-1803 for £120,000, add. 1818-21, inher. by Hamiltons 1850 by mar. of 1828, add. 1860s, abandoned and contents sold 1922, commercial use); Castletown Castle, Louth (acq. 1694, sold c. 1837); Burwarton Hall (House), Shropshire (acq. by Hollands 15th c., passed by mar. to Baughs, and Baugh heiress mar. 6 Viscount Boyne early 19th c., rebuilt 1876-77, partially demolished, still own); Stackallan House (Boyne House), Meath (built 15th c., purch. 1704, built c. 1710, sold 1920)
Estates: Bateman 30205 (E, W, I) 88364. Rubinstein – William Russell left £280,000 in probate in 1817 and Matthew Russell left £220,000 probate in 1822. Owned 8,000 acres in 2001.
Titles: Baron Hamilton 1715- I; Baron Brancepeth 1866- UK
Peers: {5 peers 1715-23 1731-1800} 3 peers 1866-1942
Notes: Family became English in orietation after inheriting Brancepeth in 1850. 1 Viscount in ODNB.

Hamilton

Origins: Cadet line of the main line. **First [MP 1640].**

1. George Hamilton – Anstruther Burgh 1712-13

Seat: Grangemuir House, Fife (acq. 17th c., sold early 18th c.)
Estate: 2,700 acres

Hamilton

Origins: Hamilton cadet. Merchants in Glasgow (Provost 1614). **First [MP 1617].**

1. James Hamilton – [Lanarkshire 1690-1701 1703-07]

Seats: Aikinhead House, Lanarkshire (purch. and built early 17th c., rebuilt 1806, add. 1823, sold c. 1765); Torrance House, Lanarkshire (medieval, acq. by mar. 14th c., rebuilt early 17th c., add. 18th c., remod. 19th c., now golf club)
Notes: Male line extinct 1765.

Hamilton

Origins: Hamilton cadet.

1. Sir William Hamilton – [Queensferry 1689 1690-1702 1703-04]
2. James Hamilton – [Dumfermline 1700-01]

Seats: Bangour, Fife (resident 17th through 19th c.); Old House of Hedderwick, Forfarshire (acq. and built by Scotts mid-17th c., remod. 1740s, farm house by mid-19th c., ruin by 1960s); Ninewar House, Haddingtonshire (resident 16th c. through 19th c.); Whitelaw, Edinburghshire (resident 17th c.)

Hamilton

Origins: Hamilton cadet.

1. Arthur Hamilton – [Irvine 1673-74]

Seat: Auchingrymont, Lanarkshire (resident 17th c.)

Hamilton

Origins: Hamilton cadet.

1. James Hamilton – [Dunbar 1681]

Seat: Mauchlinloll, Ayrshire (resident 17th c.)

Hamilton

Origins: Hamilton cadet.

1. Robert Hamilton – [Banff 1665]

Hamilton

Origins: Hamilton cadet. Settled in Ireland by 1600 and further kin in the early 17th century. A legal family. Became cotton manufacturers in Dublin. Several branches are combined here.

1. Alexander Hamilton – {Killyleagh 1739-60}
2. George Hamilton – {Belfast 1768-76}

3. George Hamilton – {Augher 1776-83}
4. Alexander Hamilton – {Ratoath 1789-90 Carrickfergus 1790-97 Belfast 1798-1800}
5. George Hamilton – Dublin University 1842-59

Seats: Hampton Hall, Dublin (acq. early 18th c.); Cabinteely House (Clare Hill), Dublin (built 18th c., passed by inher. to Orsmby-Hamiltons 1888, sold 20th c.); Tyrella, Down (resident 18th c.)
Notes: Hamilton heiress mar. mid-19th c. Ormsby of Gortner Abbey and Tobervaddy, etc. (see). One in ODNB.

Hamilton

Origins: Descended from an uncle of the 1 Earl of Arran. **First [MP 1597]. One additional [MP 1625].**

1. Sir Robert Hamilton 1 Bt – [Lanarkshire 1661-63 1678]
2. Sir John Hamilton 1 Bt – {Castlebar 1775-76 St. Canice 1776-81}

Seat: Silverton Hill, Lanarkshire (acq. 15th c.)
Estates: 6 Bt died worth £18,671 in 1887.
Title: Baronet 1645-; 1775-82
Notes: One in ODNB.

Baron Hamilton of Dalzell (1886- UK)

Origins: Descended from an uncle of the 1 Earl of Arran, younger brother of the ancestor of the Hamiltons of Silverton Hill (see previous article). Two branches were seated at Orbiston and Dalzell. Eventually Orbiston passed to the Dalzell line. James Hamilton of Orbiston and Dalzell married the Hamilton heiress of Rosehall (see below). **First [MP 1645].**

1. William Hamilton – [Dumbartonshire 1678 Renfrewshire 1681 1685-86]
2. John Hamilton 1 Baron Hamilton of Dalzell – Falkirk Burghs 1857-59 S. Lanarkshire 1868-74 1880-86
3. Archibald Hamilton Baron Hamilton of Epsom – Epsom & Ewell 1978-2001

Seats: Dalzell House, Lanarkshire (acq. 13 c., rebuilt 16th c., acq. 1645, add. 1647, add. 1857, sold 1952, now flats); Orbiston, Dumbartonshire (acq. 1468, sold 1800)
Estates: Bateman 2460 (S) 14959
Title: Baron Hamilton of Epsom 2005- UKLife
2 peers 1886-1945
1 Ld Lt 20th

1 KT 20th
Notes: 2 Baron and four others in ODNB.

Hamilton

Origins: The heiress of Rosehall married James Hamilton of Dalzell and Orbiston.

1. Sir James Hamilton 2 Bt – Lanarkshire 1710-15 1735-50

Seat: Rosehall, Lanarkshire (later named Douglas Support) (built 17th and 18th c., passed to Duchess of Douglas – see Campbell I)
Title: Baronet 1703-55

Earl of Carnwarth (1639-1716 S; 1826-1941 S)

Origins: The sister of the 1 Earl of Carnwarth married John Hamilton of Orbiston (see above), and through this marriage Dalzell passed to the Hamiltons. **First [MP 1605].** The Earldom of Carnwarth was attainted in 1716, restored 1826, and dormant 1941.

1. Sir Robert Dalzell 1 Bt – [Dumfries and Stewartry of Annandale 1665 1667 1669-74 1681 1685]
2. Sir John Dalzell 2 Bt – [Dumfries and Stewartry of Annandale 1686 1689]

Seats: Glenae Tower, Dumfriesshire (built 16th c., ruin); Dalzell, Lanarkshire (acq. 13th c., passed to Hamiltons, see above); Carnwarth House, Lanarkshire (purch. early 17th c., sold later 17th c., demolished 1970)
Estates: Worth £864 pa in 1715
Titles: Baron Dalzell 1628-1716 S; 1826-1841 S; Baronet 1666-1716; 1826-1941
Peers: [4 peers 1660-1707] 2 Scottish Rep peers 1892-1910 1935-41
Notes: 1 and 5 Earls and one other poss. in ODNB.

Baron Belhaven and Stenton (1647-1777 S; 1799- S)

Origins: Descended from a great uncle of the 1 Earl of Arran. The 1 Baron was a judge.

1. William Hamilton – Newport (IoW) 1841-47
2. Edward Hamilton – Salisbury 1865-69

Seat: Wishaw House, Lanarkshire (add. 1825, remod. 1858, demolished 1953)
Estates: Bateman 3043 (S) 24654
Titles: Baron Hamilton 1831-68 UK; Baronet 1635-

Peers: [2 peers 1660-1707] 4 Scottish Rep peers 1715-21 1819-32 1900-20 1922-45 1 peer 1832-68
1 Ld Lt 19th
1 KT 19th
Notes: Large coal seams were discovered under the Wishaw estates, which accounts for the large income derived from relatively small acreage. 2 Baron Belhaven and 1 Viscount Belhaven (Douglas) and one other in ODNB.

Nisbet-Hamilton

Origins: On the death of the 5 Baron Belhaven and Stenton in 1777 his titles passed to the heir male while the estates went to the heir female in entail, Mary Hamilton of Pencaitland, Haddingtonshire. She married William Nisbet of Dirleton. Their son took the name Hamilton-Nisbet in 1797. His brother took the name Nisbet-Hamilton. The Nisbets were in business in Edinburgh, Provost 1597. The daughter of the younger brother above married in 1828 Robert Dundas (see that family), who took the name Nisbet-Hamilton. They had a daughter who married in 1888 Henry Ogilvy of Inverquarty (see that family), who took the name Nisbet-Hamilton.

1. William Nisbet – [Haddingtonshire 1703-07] Scotland 1707-08
2. William Hamilton-Nisbet – Haddingtonshire 1777-80 East Grinstead 1790-96 Newport (IoW) 1796-1800
3. John Nisbet-Hamilton – Haddingtonshire 1786-95
4. Robert Christopher-Nisbet-Hamilton – Ipswich 1827-31 Edinburgh 1831-32 Ipswich 1835 N. Div. Lincolnshire 1837-57

Seats: Biel House, Haddingtonshire (built 14th c., purch. by 1 Baron Belhaven 1647 from the Biels, add. 1760, add. 1814-18, partly demolished 1952); Well Vale Hall, Lincolnshire (built c. 1725, purch. 1836, sold 1919); Winton (Wintoun) House, Haddingtonshire (built 1620, purch. 1779, remod. c. 1800, passed to Oglivys by mar. 1920, still own); Archerfield (Dirleton), Haddingtonshire (purch. 1663, built late 17th c., remod. c. 1745 and 1790, gutted 1962, hotel); Saltcoats, Haddingtonshire (built c. 1590, add. 1690, acq. by mar. c. 1700, ruin from 1810); Bloxholm Hall, Lincolnshire (built mid-17th c., remod. 1772, add. 1827, inherited by mar. c. 1830, sold 1913, demolished after 1973)
Estates: Bateman 27775 (S & E) 41486
1 in Cabinet 1852
Notes: One Nisbet (Lord Dirleton) in ODNB.

Hamilton

Origins: This family shared a common descent with the Lords Belhaven from the great uncle of the 1 Earl of Arran. **First [MP 1628 for Lanarkshire].**

1. Gavin Hamilton – [Lanarkshire 1665 1667]

Seat: Raploch Castle, Lanarkshire (acq. 1441, demolished)
Estates: Bateman 2282 (S) 2759
Notes: One in ODNB.

Hamilton

Origins: Cousins of the Hamiltons of Raploch (above).

1. Claud Hamilton – [Dumbartonshire 1689-1702]

Seat: Cochno House (Barnes – original estate acq. 1575), Dumbartonshire (acq. 17th c., built 1757, add. 1842, sold 1954)

Stirling-Hamilton

Origins: Descended from a younger son of the eldest son of Walter FitzGilbert Hamilton of Cadzow, common ancestor of the Hamiltons. **First [MP 1560]. An additional [MP 1621].**

1. Sir Thomas Hamilton – [Haddington Constabulary 1661-3 1667]

Seat: Preston Tower and House, Haddingtonshire (acq. by mar. late 14th c., built 1450s, add. 1626, burned 1650, restored, burned 1663, new house built, forfeited 1684, recovered 1816, NT 20th c.)
Title: Baronet 1673-
Notes: Two in ODNB.

Earl of Haddington (1627- S)

Origins: Descended from the younger son of Walter FitzGilbert Hamilton of Cadzow, common ancestor of the Hamiltons. They became burgesses in Edinburgh. One fell at Pinkie. Several became Lords of Session in the late 16th and early 17th centuries. Barons 1613. **First [MP 1594]. Another [MP 1628].** The 5 Earl of Haddington married the daughter of the Duke of Rothes, a Countess in her own right. Their eldest child became Earl of Rothes (see Leslie) and the Haddington title passed to a junior line. The son of the 6 Earl married the daughter and heiress of George Baillie of Jerviswood and Mellerstain. The Baillies were successful Edinburgh merchants who purchased landed estates in the mid-17th century. Their estates were confiscated in 1684 and restored 1688.

1. George Baillie – [Berwickshire 1691-1701 Lanarkshire 1703-07] Scotland 1707-08 Berwickshire 1708-34
2. Charles Hamilton Lord Binning – St. Germans 1722-27
3. George Baillie Hamilton – Berwickshire 1796-1818
4. Thomas Baillie-Hamilton 9 Earl of Haddington – St. Germans 1802-06 Cockermouth 1807 Callington 1807-12 Mitchel 1814-18 Rochester 1818-26 Yarmouth (IoW) 1826-27
5. John Baillie-Hamilton – Aylesbury 1839-47
6. Robert Baillie-Hamilton – Berwickshire 1874-80
7. Charles Baillie-Hamilton-Arden – Bath 1929-31

Seats: Tyninghame Castle, Haddingtonshire (medieval, add. 16th c., acq. 1628, remod. 1829-33, sold 1987, flats); Mellerstain (orig. Whitesyde), Berwickshire (medieval, purch. 1642, rebuilt 1725-38 and 1770-79, still own); Jerviswood(e) (Tower), Lanarkshire (old castle, purch. 1636, new house 1630s, later became a farm building); Arderne Hall, Cheshire (built 1863 for £17,500, demolished 1958)
Estates: Bateman 34046 (S & E) 46616. Owned 13,000 acres in 1996.
Titles: Baron Binning 1613- S; Earl of Melrose 1619- S; Baron Melrose 1827-58 UK
Peers: [3 peers 1661-69 1671-85 1702-07] 5 Scottish Rep peers 1716-34 1807-12 1859-1917 1922-45 1 peer 1827-58
4 Lds Lt 18th, 19th, 20th
1 in Cabinet 1835 1841-46
3 KT 18th, 19th, 20th
Notes: One Baillie (Lord Jerviswood) and two others in ODNB. 1, 2, 6, and 9 Earls of Haddington and two other Hamiltons in ODNB.

Baron Alvanley (1801-57 UK)

Origins: The 1 Baron was from a minor gentry family that had held Arderne Hall since the 13th century. **Three or four possible MPs 1295-1450**. He rose through the law and became Attorney General and Chief Justice of the Common Pleas. The estates passed to a niece of the 2 Baron who married the 11 Earl of Haddington, who took the additional name Arden.

1. Richard Arden 1 Baron Alvanley – Newtown (IoW) 1783-84 Aldborough 1784-90 Hastings 1790-94 Bath 1794-1801

Seats: Alvanley, Cheshire (medieval house, held by Ardernes from reign of King John, only a fragment remains); Arderne Hall, Cheshire (medieval, acq. 1630 from the Dones by mar., new house built by Earl of Haddington 1860s, demolished 1958)
Peers: 3 peers 1801-04 1810-57
Notes: 1 Baron in ODNB.

Hamilton

Origins: Descended from a brother of the 1 Earl of Haddington.

1. George Hamilton – Anstruther Easter Burghs 1712-13

Seat: Reidhouse (Red House, Redhouse), Haddingtonshire (built c. 1600, acq. by mar. c. 1609, add. early 17th c., forfeited 1745, ruin)
Notes: Last laird "out" in 1745 and beheaded. Estates confiscated.

HAMILTON II [Blackwood, Jocelyn, Stevenson] *IRELAND*

Earl of Clanbrassil (1647-75 I; 1756-98 I)

Origins: The common ancestor of the Hamiltons was Hans Hamilton of Dunlop, Ayrshire. It was claimed that he was an illegitimate offspring of the ducal house (see Hamilton I) (Nicolson, *The Desire to Please*, 19). His son went to Ireland in 1604 as a soldier and acquired large estates under James I. Kt 1609. Viscount 1622.

1. James Hamilton – {Downpatrick 1692-93 County Down 1695-99}
2. Sir John Hamilton – [Cullen 1696-1702]
3. James Hamilton 1 Earl of Clanbrassil – {Dundalk 1715-19} Wendover 1727-34 1735-41 Tavistock 1742-47 Morpeth 1747-54
4. James Hamilton 2 Earl of Clanbrassil – {Midleton 1755-58} Helston 1768-74

Seats: Tullymore (Tollymore) Park, Down (acq. by mar. 18th c., built mid-18th c., add. 1787, passed to Earl of Roden by mar. 1798, demolished 1952); Dundalk House, Louth (acq. 17th c., built 18th c., sold 19th c., demolished c. 1900); Killyleagh Castle, Down (medieval castle, acq. early 17th c., rebuilt 1610, sold 1705 to Stevesons); Halcraig, Lanarkshire (resident 17th c.)
Titles: Viscount Clandeboye (Claneboye) 1622-75 I; Baron Clandeboye and Viscount Limerick 1719-98 I
Peers: {2 peers 1719-98}
1 KP 18th
Notes: The estates of the last Earl of Clanbrassil were divided and passed to several lines. Hans Hamilton's second son, Archibald, had a granddaughter who married Hans Stevenson. Their granddaughter Dorcos Stevenson was created Baroness Blackwood in her own right and married 1751 Sir John Blackwood. From them descended the Marquesses of Dufferin (see below). Archibald Hamilton's younger son succeeded to Killyleagh. A younger son of Hans Hamilton was the ancestor of the Lords Holm Patrick. The youngest son of Hans Hamilton succeeded to Tullymore Park and from him descended the Earls of Clanbrassil of the second creation. 1 Viscount and one other in ODNB.

Marquess of Dufferin and Ava (1888-1988 UK)

Origins: See above for the Hamilton family's branches. **First {MP 1613}. Three additional {MPs 1613-39}.** The Blackwoods moved from Scotland to Ireland in 1586 and acquired estates in Down. The first Blackwood in Ireland was a merchant and Provost of Bangor. His son was a tenant of the Hamiltons, and acquired the land on which Clandeboye was built by 1688 (sold to pay the debts of the Earl of Clanbrassil). The Hamilton marriage raised them to great wealth and status.

1. William Hamilton – {Bangor 1665-66}
2. Sir James Hamilton – {County Down 1692-95 Bangor 1695-99}
3. Sir John Blackwood 2 Bt – {Killyleagh 1761 68 Bangor 1768-76 Killyleagh 1776-90 Bangor 1790-97 Killyleagh 1797-99}
4. Robert Blackwood – {Killyleagh 1776-86}
5. James Stevenson Blackwood 2 Baron Dufferin – {Killyleagh 1788-1800} Helston 1807-12 Aldeburgh 1812-18
6. Hans Blackwood 3 Baron Dufferin – {Killyleagh 1798-1800}

Seat: Clandeboye (Ballyleidy), Down (acq. and built by Blackwoods by 1688, new house c.1750, rebuilt 1801-04, remod. 1849-50, remod. c. 1865, still own)
Estates: Bateman 18238 (I) 21043 and at Killyleagh 3875 (I) 4523. The 1 Marquess sold 18,000 acres in anticipation of the land acts. Owned 10,000 acres in 2001.
Titles: Baron Dufferin 1800- I; Baron Clandeboye 1850-1988 UK; Earl of Dufferin 1871-1988 UK; Baronet 1763-
Peers: 1 Irish Rep peer 1820-36 4 peers 1850-1945
1 Ld Lt 19th-20th
1 in Cabinet 1869-72
1 KP 19th-20th
Notes: Although the family did not appear in the House of Commons after 1818, it remained very active in national life. The 1 Marquess was a celebrated proconsul and viceroy. The 3 Marquess was Speaker of the Northern Ireland Senate in the 1920s. The 4 Marquess was a Deputy Secretary of State while still in his 20s (1937-40) and died on active service in Burma in 1945. The 5 Marquess was a leader of arts institutions. Both his mother and wife were Guinnesses, which helped the family finances.

Baron Holm Patrick (1897- UK)

Origins: See the Notes under the Earl of Clanbrassil.

1. Sir Hans Hamilton 1 Bt – {County Armagh 1661-66}
2. Hans Hamilton – {Killyleagh 1695-99 Newry 1707-27 Dundalk 1727-28}
3. Sir Hans Hamilton 2 Bt – {County Armagh 1703-13 Carlingford 1713-14}

4. James Hamilton – {Newry 1723-27 Carlow 1727-60}
5. John Hamilton – {Carlow 1725-27 Dundalk 1728-57} Wendover 1728-34
6. Hans Hamilton – {County Dublin 1797-1800} 1801-22
7. James Hamilton – County Dublin 1841-63
8. Ion Hamilton 1 Baron Holm Patrick – County Dublin 1863-85

Seats: Abbotstown House (Sheephill Park), Dublin (acq. partly 18th c. and part 1832, built early to mid-19th c., sold 1947); Baillieboro (Bailieborough) Castle, Cavan (purch. early 18th c., sold later in the 18th c.); Cavandoogan, Armagh
Estates: Bateman 6889 (I) 8869
Titles: Baronet 1662-82; 1683-1730
Peers: 2 peers 1897-98 1907-42
1 Ld Lt 19th

Stevenson

Origins: See Notes under Earl of Clanbrassil. The first {MP} was a Captain in the army and purchased Killyleagh from Sir Hans Hamilton in 1705. Sheriff 1723

1. Hans Stevenson – {Killyleagh 1703-13}
2. James Stevenson – {Killyleagh 1713-14 Randalstown 1715-27 Killyleagh 1727-38}
3. James Stevenson – {Killyleagh 1727-60}

Seats: Ash Park, Londonderry; Killyleagh, Down (purch. 1705, passed to Hamiltons, add. 1847-51, Hamiltons still own)
Estates: Worth £960 pa in 1723.

Earl of Roden (1771- I)

Origins: Gentry in the 14th century. A younger son was Lord Mayor of London 1464. **First MP 1467 for London. Two further MPs 1545-58.** Kt r. Edward VI. High Sheriff 1677. A successful lawyer went to Ireland as Lord Chancellor in 1739. The 1 Earl of Roden married the daughter and heiress of the 1 Earl of Clanbrassil of the second creation.

1. Robert Jocelyn 1 Viscount Jocelyn – {Granard 1725-27 Newtown 1727-39}
2. Robert Jocelyn 1 Earl of Roden – {Old Leighlin 1745-56}
3. Robert Jocelyn 2 Earl of Roden – {Dundalk 1783-97}
4. George Jocelyn – {Dundalk 1783-98}
5. John Jocelyn – {Dundalk 1797-1800} County Louth 1807-09 1820-26
6. Robert Jocelyn 3 Earl of Roden – County Louth 1806-07 1810-20
7. Robert Jocelyn Viscount Jocelyn – Kings Lynn 1842-54

Seats: Tullymore (Tollymore) Park, Down (built mid-18th c., inher. by mar. of 1798, add. 1859, add. 1878, sold 1930 and 1941, demolished 1952); Hyde Hall, Hertfordshire (acq. early 14th c., built 1572, add. c. 1770, add. 1806-07, remod. 1896-1904, sold c. 1940, now flats); Dundalk House, Louth (acq. first half 18th c., sold 19th c., demolished); Brockley Park, Queen's County (built 1768, ceased to use by 1825, sold late 19th c., demolished 1944)
Estates: Bateman 14496 (I & E) 13077
Titles: Baron Newport 1743- I; Viscount Jocelyn 1755- I; Baron Clanbrassil 1821-97 UK; Baronet 1665-
Peers: {3 peers 1755-1800} 2 Irish Rep peers 1801-20 1919-45 3 peers 1821-97
2 KP 19th
Notes: 1 Viscount and 1 and 3 Earls and one other in ODNB.

HAMILTON III *IRELAND*

Origins: Emigrated from Scotland and settled in County Cavan where they acquired estates 1610. Sheriff 1694.

1. Sir Francis Hamilton 1 Bt – {Jamestown 1639 County Cavan 1661-66}
2. Sir Charles Hamilton 2 Bt – {County Donegal 1661-66}
3. Sir Francis Hamilton 3 Bt – {County Cavan 1692-93 1695-99 1703-14}

Seat: Castle Hamilton, Cavan (acq. c. 1610, passed by mar. 1714 to Cecils)
Estates: Worth £1,000 pa in 1713.
Title: Baronet 1628-1714

HAMLYN [Williams] *WALES & ENGLAND*

Origins: The Hamlyns were gentry seated in Devon. Made a fortune by law in London in the early 18th c. The 1 Baronet married in 1795 the Williams heiress to Edwinsford. Originally the seat of the Vaughans in the Middle Ages, it passed to the Williams family by marriage in 1600. The Williams descended from a Welsh warrior and emerged as an important landed family in the 17th century.

1. Sir Nicholas Williams 1 Bt – Carmarthenshire 1724-45
2. Sir James Hamlyn 1 Bt – Carmarthenshire 1793-1802
3. Sir James Hamlyn-Williams 2 Bt – Carmarthenshire 1802-06
4. Sir James Hamlyn-Williams 3 Bt – Carmarthenshire 1831-32 1835-37

Seats: Edwinsford, Carmathenshire (Williams acq. by mar. 1600, built c. 1635, add. 1670s, passed by mar. to Hamlyns 1795, add. 1842 and 1862, ruin, sold 1976); Clovelly

(Clovely) Court, Devon (purch. and rebuilt 1738, passed to the Fanes (see Vane) by mar. with daughter of 3 Bt in the 19th c.)
Estates: The Edwinsford estate consisted of 10,000 acres in the 19th c.
Titles: Baronet 1707-95; 1795-1861
1 Ld Lt 18th
Notes: The 3rd and last Bt died in 1861. He divided his estates among three daughters, who married into the Fane, Davie, and Drummond families.

HANBURY [Bateman, Keck, Kerrison, Tracy, Williams] *WALES & ENGLAND*

Hanbury

Origins: The Hanburys owned land in Worcestershire since the 12th century. They gained great wealth as ironmasters from the 17th century onwards. They remained active businessmen in the 18th century both promoting iron interests and in finance. At the same time they rose high socially – Ambassador to St. Petersburg 1755. **First MP 1628.** The Williams fortune came from a Smyrna merchant who left £70,000 in 1720 to a godson (Hanbury), who took the additional name Williams.

1. John Hanbury – Gloucester 1701-08 Monmouthshire 1720-34
2. Sir Charles Hanbury Williams – Monmouthshire 1735-47 Leominster 1754-59
3. Capel Hanbury – Leominster 1741-47 Monmouthshire 1747-65
4. John Hanbury – Monmouthshire 1766-84

Seat: Pontypool Park, Monmouthshire (purch. 16th c. and built 1659 and 1680s, sold 1920-23, school); Hoarstone, Worcestershire (acq. and built late 16th c., add. 17th c., sold 1920s); Coldbrook Park, Monmouthshire (purch. c. 1720, sold 1888)
Estates: Bateman 10973 (W) 27787
2 Lds Lt 18th, 19th
Notes: Sir John Hanbury-Williams was a major industrialist, Chairman of Courtaulds 1946-63. Three in ODNB.

Viscount Tracy (1643-1797 I)

Origins: A younger son of the Hanburys of Pontypool married in 1798 the daughter and heiress of the 8 Viscount Tracy and took the name Tracy. The Tracys may well be one of the oldest recorded families in England. Their descent can be traced to Henry I, Anglo-Saxon royalty, and even to Charlemagne. (Johnson, *The Gloucestershire Gentry*, 10; Roskell, Clark, and Rawcliffe, *The House of Commons*, IV, 638) **First MP 1313 for Gloucestershire. Eight additional MPs 1358-1640.**

1. Charles Hanbury-Tracy 1 Baron Sudeley – Tewkesbury 1807-12 1832-37

2. Thomas Hanbury-Tracy Leigh 2 Baron Sudeley – Wallingford 1831-32
3. Henry Hanbury-Tracy – Bridgenorth 1837-38
4. Charles Hanbury-Tracy 4 Baron Sudeley – Montgomery 1863-77
5. Frederick Hanbury-Tracy – Montgomery 1877-85 1886-92

Seats: Gregynog Hall, Montgomery (medieval, rebuilt 1577, acq. by Tracys by mar. 1795, rebuilt 1837, much of estate sold 1913, house sold 1920, now institutional use); Toddington Manor, Gloucestershire (built c. 1620s, acq. by Hanburys from Tracys by mar. 1798, rebuilt in 1819-40 for £150,000, sold 1900, institutional use, now a residence again); Morville Hall, Shropshire (built later 16th c., remod. c. 1748, add. 1770, acq. by Hanbury-Tacys 19th c. sold 20th c., NT)
Estates: Bateman 17158 (W) 13539 and 6795 (E) 9800
Titles: Baron Sudeley 1838- UK
Peers: [7 peers 1661-1797} 6 peers 1838-1941
3 Lds Lt 19th
Notes: The family lost all their land in the late 19th and early 20th c. due to extreme indebtedness, precipitated by the cost of rebuilding Toddington. The 4 Baron was twice a bankrupt. 7 Viscount and three others in ODNB.

Tracy

Origins: Descended from a younger son of the 3 Viscount Tracy. Anthony Tracy succeeded to the Keck estates in 1729. Sir Anthony Keck MP was a successful lawyer who purchased substantial estates, Commissioner of the Great Seal 1688. (A third cousin of the Kecks listed under Legh).

1. Sir Anthony Keck – Tiverton 1691-95
2. Robert Tracy – Tewkesbury 1734-41 Worcestershire 1748-54
3. Anthony Tracy Keck – Woodstock 1753-67
4. Thomas Tracy – Gloucestershire 1763-70

Seats: Stanway House (Hall), Gloucestershire (medieval, acq. 1533, expanded c. 1530s, add. c. 1580-90, passed to Earl of Wemyss after 1817); Great Tew Park, Oxfordshire (built early 17th c., add. later 17th c., purch. 1698, sold 1780-93, demolished c. 1800); Sandywell Hall, Gloucestershire (built c. 1704, add. c. 1720s, purch. 1748 for £17,250 - Kingsley, *The Country Houses of Gloucestershire*, II, 219 - passed to another family by inher. 1823)
Title: Baronet 1611-77
Notes: On the extinction of the male line, Stanway passed by marriage to Lady Elcho (see Wemyss) in 1817.

Hanbury

Origins: Descended from a younger son of Richard Hanbury, great-great-great-grandson of John Hanbury of Hanbury.

1. Sir Cecil Hanbury – N. Dorset 1924-37

Seat: Kingston Maurward (Maurwood), Dorset (built c. 1590, new house 1717-20, acq. 1914, sold 1947, institutional use)

Culling-Hanbury

Origins: Cadet of the Dorset Hanburys. Brewers in 19th c.

1. Robert Culling-Hanbury – Middlesex 1857-67

Seats: Poles (Hanbury Manor), Hertfordshire (built 16th c., leased later half 18th c., purch. c. 1800, new house 1890-91 – cost £30,000 – add. 1913, sold 1914); Drumstinchall, Kirkcudbrightshire
Estates: Bateman 2351 (E) 4280

Viscount Bateman (1725-1802 I)

Origins: William Hanbury of Kelmarsh was a cadet of the Worcestershire line whose founder made a fortune as a merchant in London. Knighted by James I. He succeeded to the Bateman estates in 1802 on the death of his cousin the 2nd and last Viscount. Sir James Bateman MP, descended from a Flemish immigrant naturalized under Charles II, was a great financier (Lord Mayor 1716) who at his death in 1718 left a fortune said to be worth £400,000. Charles Bateman-Hanbury succeeded to the Lennox estates in 1862.

1. Sir James Bateman – Ilchester 1711-15 East Looe 1715-18
2. William Bateman 1 Viscount Bateman – Leominster 1721-22 1727-34
3. James Bateman – Carlisle 1722-27
4. John Bateman 2 Viscount Bateman – Orford 1746-47 Woodstock 1747-68 Leominster 1768-84
5. William Bateman – Gatton 1752-54
6. William Bateman-Hanbury 1 Baron Bateman – Northampton 1810-18
7. Charles Bateman-Hanbury-Kincaid-Lennox – Herefordshire 1852-57 Leominster 1858-65

Seats: Shobdon Court, Herefordshire (purch. by Batemans 1705, built soon after, acq. by mar. by Hanburys 1802, remod. 1830-35, fire mid-19th c., rebuilt, demolished 1933); Kelmarsh Hall, Northamptonshire (purch. by Hanbury 1618, rebuilt. 1620, rebuilt c. 1727, sold 1865); Lennox Castle, Stirlingshire (acq. by mar. 1862, sold 1927, derelict); Well Vale Hall, Lincolnshire (acq. and built c. 1725, passed out of the family by mar. later 18th c.)
Estates: Bateman 7253 (E) 12101 and 7686 (S) 8453. The Herefordshire estates were worth £14,000 pa in 1718. (Hayton, *The House of Commons*, III, 149)
Title: Baron Bateman 1837-1931 UK
Peers: 3 peers 1837-45 1847-1931
3 Lds Lt 18th, 19th, 20th
Notes: Brother of the 1 Baron in ODNB (under Hanbury).

Kerrison

Origins: Matthew Kerrison, the son of a yeoman farmer, was a London merchant and canal owner with no education (Rubinstein, *Men of Property*, 128). He died in 1827 said to be worth £1,000,000. He purchased the Cornwallis and Maynard estates. The male line of his descendents became extinct in 1886 and the bulk of his property passed through an heiress, Lady Bateman (see above).

1. Sir Edward Kerrison 1 Bt – Shaftesbury 1813-18 Northampton 1818-20 Eye 1824-52
2. Sir Edward Kerrison 2 Bt – Eye 1852-66 E. Suffolk 1866-67

Seats: Brome Hall, Suffolk (built 16th c., purch. 1823, sold 1919, demolished 1963); Hoxne Hall (renamed Oakley Park), Suffolk (see Maynard under Greville, purch. 1823, remod. 1830s, passed to Batemans by mar. 1886, sold 1919, demolished 1923); Ranworth Old Hall, Norfolk (built 16th c., purch. 1779, sold c. 1900)
Estates: Bateman 11861 (E) 18608. Rubinstein – M. Kerrison left £250,000 in probate in 1827.
Title: Baronet 1821-86
Notes: 1 Bt in ODNB.

HANDCOCK *IRELAND*

Viscount Castlemaine (1822-39 I)

Origins: Came to Ireland in Cromwell's army. Acquired 6,000 acres after the Civil War and purchased more land.

1. William Handcock – {County Westmeath 1661-66 Athlone 1692-93 1695-99 County Westmeath 1703-07}

2. William Handcock – {Boyle 1692-93 Dublin 1695-99}
3. Thomas Handcock – {Lanesborough 1692-93 1695-99}
4. William Handcock – {Athlone 1703-14 County Westmeath 1721-23}
5. Gustavus Handcock – {Athlone 1723-27 1732-51}
6. Robert Handcock – {Athlone 1751-58}
7. William Handcock – {Athlone 1759-83}
8. William Handcock – {Fore 1727-41}
9. John Handcock – {Ballyshannon 1761-66}
10. John Handcock – {Philipstown 1776-83}
11. William Handcock 1 Viscount Castlemaine – {Athlone 1783-1800} 1801-03
12. Richard Handcock 2 Viscount Castlemaine – {Athlone 1800}
13. Richard Handcock 3 Viscount Castlemaine – Athlone 1826-32
14. Henry Handcock – Athlone 1856-57

Seats: Moydrum Castle, Westmeath (built 18th c., rebuilt 1812, burned 1921); The Hare Island, Westmeath (marine villa built early 19th c.); Twyford House, Westmeath (acq. c. 1650, built c. 1760, sold c. 1790)
Estates: Bateman 12041 (I) 8919
Title: Baron Castlemaine 1812- I
Peers: 3 Irish Rep peers 1841-69 1874-92 1898-1937
2 Lds Lt 19th, 20th

HANDLEY

Origins: An old Nottinghamshire family. Their fortunes rose in the 18th century through the efforts of businessmen in Newark (Mayor 1760) and a banker and attorney in Sleaford, Lincolnshire.

1. Henry Handley – Heytesbury 1820-26 S. Lincolnshire 1832-41
2. William Handley – Newark 1831-34
3. Benjamin Handley – Boston 1832-34
4. John Handley – Newark 1857-65

Seats: Leased various houses such as Muskham Grange, Nottinghamshire, Culverthorpe Hall, Lincolnshire, and Wiverton Hall, Nottinghamshire
Notes: The family continued to engage in business in the 19th century. William Handley MP was a banker, brewer, and cotton master. On the extinction of the male line, the family wealth was divided among multiple heiresses.

HANKEY

Origins: London goldsmiths and bankers in the later 17th and the 18th century. Also plantation owners in the West Indies. Governor of the Bank of England 1851.

1. Joseph Hankey – Wareham 1799-1802
2. Sir Richard Hankey – Plympton Erle 1799-1802
3. Thomson Hankey – Peterborough 1853-68 1874-80
4. Frederick Hankey – Chertsy Div. Surrey 1885-92

Seats: Fetcham Park, Surrey (built 1699, purch. c. 1790, add. 1793, remod. 1875, sold 1926, now offices); Balcombe Place, Sussex (built 1856, purch. 1866, add. 1899, sold 1905, institutional use from 1954); Shipborne Grange, Kent
Estates: Bateman 3850 (E) 3942. Thomson Hankey died worth £133,000 in 1893.
Notes: One in ODNB.

HARBORD

Baron Suffield (1786- GB)

Origins: Tenant farmers in the later 16th century. The first MP was a self-made man – solicitor and agent to noblemen – called "a very rich and covetous man." (Burnet, *Country Life*, 183, p. 48). His son married an heiress.

1. Sir Charles Harbord – Launceston 1661-79
2. William Harbord – Dartmouth 1661-79 Thetford 1679-81 Launceston 1689-92
3. Harbord Harbord – Norfolk 1728-34
4. William Morden Harbord 1 Bt – Bere Alston 1734 1741-54 Dunwich 1738-41
5. Harbord Harbord 1 Baron Suffield – Norwich 1756-86
6. William Harbord 2 Baron Suffield – Ludgershall 1790-96 Plympton Erle 1807-10
7. Edward Harbord 3 Baron Suffield – Great Yarmouth 1806-12 Shaftesbury 1820-21

Seats: Gunton Park, Norfolk (acq. 1678, built c. 1742, add. 1781, fire 1882 part destroyed, sold 1980, flats); Stannighall, Norfolk (purch. c. 1648, declined to a farm house)
Estates: Bateman 11828 (E) 15071
Title: Baronet 1746-
Peers: 9 peers 1786-1945
1 Ld Lt 19th
Notes: 3 Baron and one other in ODNB.

HARDIE

Origins: The father of the first MP was a ship's carpenter. The first MP was a coal miner, union organizer, journalist and leading figure in the early years of the Labour Party.

1. James Kier Hardie – West Ham 1892-95 Merthyr Tydfil 1900-15
2. George Hardie – Springburn Div. Glasgow 1922-31 1935-37
3. David Hardie – Rutherglen Div. Lanarkshire 1931
4. Agnes Hardie – Springburn Div. Glasgow 1937-45

Notes: Two in ODNB.

HARDINGE *ENGLAND & IRELAND*

Viscount Hardinge (1846- UK)

Origins: A prosperous yeoman family in the 15th century with 56 acres in 1564 at King's Newton in Derbyshire. Held 108 acres by 1631. Kt and granted arms 1674. Clergy, lawyers and officials in the 18th century. A younger son went to Ireland and was created a Bt 1801. Clerk of the House of Commons 1731. Field Marshal mid-19th c. The 1 Viscount was the son of a clergyman who held a living worth £5,000 pa. He was a soldier, politician and Governor General of India. "Service" nobility.

1. Nicholas Hardinge – Eye 1748-58
2. George Hardinge – Old Sarum 1784-1802
3. Sir Richard Hardinge 1 Bt – {Knocktopher 1796-97 Midleton 1797-99}
4. Henry Hardinge 1 Viscount Hardinge – Durham 1820-30 St. Germans 1830 Newport 1830-32 Launceston 1832-44
5. Charles Stewart Hardinge 2 Viscount Hardinge – Downpatrick 1851-56

Seats: South Park, Kent (built 1773, acq. 1st half 19th c., add. 1844, partly demolished 1989); Belleisle (Belle Isle), Fermanagh (leased? or held briefly in 19th c.); King's Newton Hall, Derbyshire (acq. by 1564, built 16th c., rebuilt c. 1660, passed out of family 1729)
Estates: 108 acres by 1631. Under 500 acres in Bateman. The family never acquired much land. 1 Viscount was granted pensions of £8,000 pa and for two successors £3,000 pa. 1 Viscount also earned large official salaries. The 2 Viscount died worth £91,000 in 1894.
Titles: Baron Hardinge of Penshurst 1910- UK; Baronet 1801-
Peers: 6 peers 1846-1924 1910-45 1926-45
2 in Cabinet 1834-35 1841-44 1910-16

1 KG 20th
Notes: An unusual family in that they rose to high rank without ever accumulating a substantial landed estate. 1 and 2 Barons and 1 and 2 Viscounts and five others in ODNB.

HARDRES

Origins: The family claimed ancestry dating from the Norman Conquest (Burke and Burke, *The Extinct and Dormant Baronetcies of England*, 242). They may well have descended from a Domesday Book tenant. **First MP 1379 for Canterbury** – then a long gap in parliamentary representation.

1. Sir Thomas Hardres – Canterbury 1664-81
2. John Hardres – Canterbury 1705-08 1710-22
3. Sir William Hardres 4 Bt – Kent 1711-13 Dover 1713-15 Canterbury 1727-35

Seat: Hardres Court, Kent (acq. medieval period, estate broken up among multiple heirs 1764)
Title: Baronet 1642-1764
Notes: On the extinction of the male line Hardres Court estate passed to the widow of the last Baronet and was then split up among her heirs. One in ODNB.

HARDY [Gathorne]

<u>Earl of Cranbrook</u> (1892- UK)

Origins: The 1 Earl, a younger son, inherited £250,000 from his father, an ironworks owner in Staffordshire (who married a Gathorne). He rose to a title through the law and politics. The eldest son gained a baronetcy and a second son also purchased a landed estate.

1. John Hardy – Bradford 1832-37 1841-47
2. Gathorne Gathorne-Hardy 1 Earl of Cranbrook – Leominster 1856-65 University of Oxford 1865-78
3. Sir John Hardy 1 Bt – Midhurst 1859 Dartmouth 1860-68 S. Warwickshire 1868-74
4. John Gathorne-Hardy 2 Earl of Cranbrook – Rye 1868-80 Mid Div. Kent 1884-85 Medway Div. Kent 1885-92
5. Alfred Gathorne-Hardy – Canterbury 1878-80 East Grinstead Div. E. Sussex 1886-95
6. Laurence Hardy – S. Kent 1892-1918

Seats: Dunstall Hall, Staffordshire (medieval, new house c. 1566, demolished post WWII); Sandling Park, Kent (built 1779, purch. 1896, bombed 1943, demolished 1945-46, new house); Foston Hall, Derbyshire; Chilham Castle, Kent (medieval, rebuilt 1616, purch. 1861, remod. 1862, sold c. 1880?); Hemsted Park House, Kent (medieval, rebuilt 1786, purch. 1857 for £157,000, rebuilt 1859-62, sold 1912, now Benenden School, 1859 house cost £33,000 to build exclusive of land purchase – Franklin, *The Gentleman's Country House*, 262); Great Glemham Hall, Suffolk (Georgian, purch. after 1912, sold 1923)
Estates: 5188 (E) 6426 (additional branches 3300 (E) 4500 and 2338 (E) 5618). The 1 Earl died leaving £274,000 in 1906.
Titles: Viscount Cranbrook 1878- UK; Baronet 1876-
Peers: 4 peers 1878-1915 1921-45
1 in Cabinet 1866-68 1874-80 1885-92
Notes: 1 Earl in ODNB.

HARE

Earl of Listowel (1822- I)

Origins: Moved from Norfolk to Cork in the 18th century. (Descended from the same family as the Barons Coleraine, see Pakenham). Probably made a fortune in business as Cork merchants and became gentry. Gained a peerage for supporting the Union.

1. William Hare 1 Earl of Listowel – {Cork 1796-97 Athy 1797-1800}
2. Richard Hare Viscount Ennismore – {Athy 1797-1800} County Cork 1812-27
3. William Hare 2 Earl of Listowel – St. Albans 1826-30 1841-46
4. John Hare 1 Viscount Blakenham – Woodbridge 1945-63

Seats: Convamore House, Cork (built 1617, purch. 1800, rebuilt early 19th c., add. 1838, burned 1921, ruin); Ballyhooly Castle, Cork (built 1314, ruin by 1750, acq. and restored 1864, add. 1882, sold 1920s)
Estates: Bateman 35541 (I) 19500; most of the estate sold by 1910. Compensation for the burned house 1921 £85,202. (Blake, *Abandoned Mansions of Ireland II*, 36). 1 Viscount Blakenham left £1,646,000 in 1982.
Titles: Baron Convamore 1800- I; Viscount Ennismore 1816- I; Baron Hare 1869- UK; Viscount Blakenham 1963- UK
Peers: 3 peers 1869-1945
1 in Cabinet 1960-64
2 KP 19th, 20th
Notes: The 6 Earl was one of the hereditary peers elected to continue to sit in the House of Lords post-1999. 1 Viscount Blakenham and 5 Earl and two others in ODNB.

HARLAND *IRELAND*

Origins: Belfast shipbuilders in the 19th and 20th centuries. Began as an engineer and manager in the 1850s.

1. Sir Edward Harland 1 Bt – N. Belfast 1889-95
2. Albert Harland – Ecclesall Div. Sheffield 1923-29
3. Henry Harland – E. Belfast 1940-45

Seat: Glenfarne Hall, Leitrim (purch. 1917, burned 1923)
Title: Baronet 1885-95
Notes: 1 Bt in ODNB.

HARLEY [Bangham] *ENGLAND & WALES*

<u>Earl of Oxford and Mortimer</u> (1711-1853 GB)

Origins: Owned a manor 1221. **First MP 1300 for Shropshire. Two additional MPs 1338-1648, both kts of the shire**.

1. Sir Edward Harley – Herefordshire 1646-48 1656-58 1660 New Radnor 1661–79 Herefordshire 1679-81
2. Sir Robert Harley – New Radnor 1647-48 1660
3. Robert Harley 1 Earl of Oxford – Tregony 1689-90 New Radnor 1690-1711
4. Edward Harley – Droitwich 1695-98 Leominster 1698-1722
5. Thomas Harley – Radnorshire 1698-1715
6. Edward Harley 2 Earl of Oxford – New Radnor 1711-15 Cambridgeshire 1722-24
7. Edward Harley 3 Earl of Oxford – Herefordshire 1727-41
8. Robert Harley – Leominster 1734-47 Droitwich 1754-74
9. Edward Harley 4 Earl of Oxford – Herefordshire 1747-55
10. Thomas Harley – London 1761-74 Herefordshire 1776-1802

Seats: Eywood, Herefordshire (built c. 1705, remod. 1805-07, rebuilt 1898, demolished 1954); Brampton Bryan Hall (Castle), Herefordshire (acq. c. 1309, medieval castle, dismantled 1644, new house 1661, reduced in size 20th c., still owned by Harley descendents); Kinsham Court, Herefordshire (built 18th c., remod. 19th c., sold to Arkwrights early 20th c.); Wimpole Hall, Cambridgeshire (built c. 1640-70, remod. 1693-1705, purch. 1710, add. 1713-30, sold 1740) Berrington Hall, Herefordshire (purch. 1774, built 1778, passed by mar. 1804 to the Rodneys)
Estates: Bateman 10221 (E & W) 11532
Title: Baron Harley 1711-1853 GB
Peers: 6 peers 1711-90 1794-1853

2 Lds Lt 18th, 19th
1 in Cabinet 1704-08 1710-11
1 KG 18th
Notes: A younger son of the 3 Earl of Oxford entered the office of a London merchant and later prospered as a banker. Lord Mayor 1767. His heiress married the 2 Baron Rodney. On the death of the last Earl the estates passed to his eldest sister, Lady Langdale. On her death in 1872 another sister, Lady Charlotte Bacon, inherited. Later sold to the 2 Baron Ormanthwaite in 1892. 1, 2, and 3 Earls and five others in ODNB.

Bangham

Origins: Dyers in Leominster in the 17th century. Their estates passed to Thomas Harley MP by marriage to Edward Bangham's daughter.

1. Edward Bangham – Leominster 1710-12

Seat: Stockton Bury, Herefordshire (built by Harleys 17th c.?, rebuilt 18th c., demolished 1960s)

HARMSWORTH

Viscount Northcliffe (1918-22 UK)

Origins: The father of the 1 Viscount Northcliffe was a failed barrister. His son was a journalist and publisher. The family became the greatest of all English newspaper proprietors in the 20th century.

1. Sir Robert Harmsworth 1 Bt – Caithness 1900-18 Caithness & Sutherland 1918-22
2. Cecil Harmsworth 1 Baron Harmsworth – Droitwich Div. Worcestershire 1906-10 Luton Div. Bedfordshire 1911-22
3. Esmond Harmsworth 2 Viscount Rothermere – Isle of Thanet Div. Kent 1919-29

Seats: Elmwood, Kent (built 16th c., purch. 1890s, sold post 1945); Burghfield House, Sutherland; Mereworth Castle, Kent (built 1720-30, leased 1920s); Stody Lodge, Norfolk (old house, purch. 1932, fire and rebuilt 1933-34, sold 1941); Hemsted Park House, Kent (built 1859-62, purch. and remod. 1912, family departed 1924, became Benenden School)
Estates: The 1 Viscount Northcliffe left £5,250,000 in 1922. Worth £308,000,000 in 1990.
Titles: Baron Northcliffe 1905-22 UK; Baron Rothermere 1914- UK; Viscount Rothermere 1919- UK; Baron Harmsworth 1939- UK; Baronet 1904-22; 1910- ; 1918- ; 1922-
Peers: 4 peers 1905-22 1914-45 1939-45

1 in Cabinet 1918
Notes: 1 Viscount Northcliffe and 1, 2, and 3 Viscounts Rothermere in ODNB.

HARRINGTON (Harington)

Baron Harrington (1603-14 E)

Origins: The family was established in the 14th century. **First MP 1384 for Rutland. Eleven additional MPs 1472-1655, six of them for Rutland. Baron 1326 (extinct 1457)** and 1603. A Lancashire branch of the family was first summoned to Parliament as barons 1326. **First MP for Lancashire 1327. Eight additional MPs 1343-1478.**

1. Thomas Harrington – Grantham 1685-87

Seats: Exton Hall, Rutland (acq. 15th c., sold c. 1613); Boothby Pagnell, Lincolnshire (built c. 1630, sold c. 1690)
Estates: Income of £5,000-7,000 in the early 17th c. but heavily indebted. Most remaining estates sold by 1628.
Title: Baronet 1611-c.1661
Notes: The Baronetcy was forfeited and most of the family estates confiscated in 1661. The author of *Oceana* was a member of the family. Harrington family has an entry and 1 and 2 Barons and two others included in ODNB.

HARRIS I

Origins: An old Devonshire family whose ancestry may have stretched back to the Conquest. One married a Mohun heiress. A lawyer and Recorder of Exeter acquired Hayne in the mid-16th century. **First MP 1529. Five additional MPs 1584-1644.**

1. John Harris – Liskeard 1661-77
2. Sir Arthur Harris 1 Bt – Okehampton 1671-81
3. William Harris – St. Ives 1690-95 Okehampton 1698-1702 1708-09
4. Christopher Harris – Okehampton 1709-22
5. John Harris – Helston 1727-41 Ashburton 1741-67

Seats: Hayne, Devon (acq. mid-16th c., passed to Northcotes by mar. 16th c.); Radford, Devon (medieval, acq. by mar. c. 1413, rebuilt later 16th c., remod. mid-18th c., sold 1914, demolished 1937)
Estates: Hayne line owned 4,200 acres in 1628 and with additional land was worth £1,000 pa in 1644.
Title: Baronet 1673-86

Notes: In 1686 some of the family estates passed by marriage to the Arundells of Trengwaiton and Lifton Park.

HARRIS II [Hooper]

Earl of Malmesbury (1800- GB)

Origins: Emerged in the 16th century. Successful marriages in the 17th century. A lawyer and diplomat in the mid-18th century. Edward Hooper MP of Heron Court left all his property to his cousin the 1 Earl of Malmesbury.

1. Edward Hooper – Christchurch 1734-48
2. James Harris – Christchurch 1761-80
3. James Harris 1 Earl of Malmesbury – Christchurch 1770-74 1780-88
4. James Harris 2 Earl of Malmesbury – Helston 1802-04 Horsham 1804-06 Heytesbury 1807-12 Wilton 1816-20
5. Edward Harris – Christchurch 1844-52

Seats: Heron (Hurn) Court, Hampshire (built later 16th c., purch. 1798, remod. c. 1806, remod. c. 1840, sold c. 1910); Malmesbury House, Wiltshire (medieval, remod. 17th c., purch. 1660, remod. 18th c., leased out through much of 19th c., sold post 1945); Greywell Hill House, Hampshire (built 17th c., purch. 1787, rebuilt c. 1824, passed by mar. to Earl of Malmesbury 1963, still own)
Estates: Bateman 5446 (E) 6304. The 2 Earl received a pension of £1,200 pa and a salary of £1,379 as Governor of the Isle of Wight. 6,750 acres in early 19th c.
Title: Baron Malmesbury 1788- GB
Peers: 5 peers 1788-1945
1 Ld Lt 19th
1 in Cabinet 1852 1858-59 1866-68 1874-76
Notes: 1 and 3 Earls and three others in ODNB.

HARRIS III

Baron Harris (1815- UK)

Origins: The father of the 1 Baron was a poor curate. His son was a general in India and America. He married an heiress, which helped make his fortune, much assisted by his own ability. He received £150,000 from the fall of Seringapatam in 1799.

1. Frederick Harris – Monmouth 1900-01 Dulwich 1903-06

Seats: Belmont, Kent (built 1789-92, purch. 1801, still own); Waterston, Westmeath (built c. 1749, acq. by marriage to Temple heiress 18th c., abandoned 1923, dismantled 1930, ruin)
Estates: Bateman 9572 (E & I) 10528
Peers: 5 peers 1815-1945
Notes: The 2 Baron was a Lt. General, the 3 Baron Governor of Madras 1854-59, and the 4 Baron Governor of Bombay 1890-95. The 2 Baron married in 1824 Isabella Temple. Their younger son succeeded to Waterston and took the name Temple. 1, 2, 3, and 4 Barons in ODNB.

HARRISON I *IRELAND*

Origins: Probably founded by a Cromwellian settler in Ireland. Dublin bankers in 18th century. Sheriff 1677.

1. Matthew Harrison – {Callan 1663-66}
2. Edward Harrison – {Lisburn 1692-93 1695-99}
3. Michael Harrison – {Lisburn 1703-09}
4. Francis Harrison – {Knocktopher 1703-13 Lisburn 1713-14 County Carlow 1715-25}

Seats: Castlemartin, Kildare (acq. and built 1720, sold 1730); Marlea (Magheralave), Antrim (acq. 17th c., sold c. 1725)
Estates: Said to have owned land in four Ulster counties.
Notes: Francis Harrison MP was a Dublin banker. William Harrison {MP Thomastown 1692-93 Bannow 1730-36} may have been a kinsman of Matthew Harrison MP above. He purchased Castle Dodd, Cork and his brother was the ancestor of the Harrisons of Castle Harrison, Cork. Extinct in male line 1725 and estates broken up.

HARRISON II

Origins: A family of obscure origins, probably a clothier in the early 17th c., then an official. Kt 1641. **First MP 1628** (see below) was a government official and financier. **One additional MP 1640-43**.

1. Sir John Harrison – Scarborough 1628 Lancaster 1640-44 1661-69
2. Richard Harrison – Lancaster 1669-79
3. Edward Harrison – Weymouth & Melcombe Regis 1717-22 Hertford 1722-26
4. George Harrison – Hertford 1727-34 1741-59
5. Thomas Harrison – Old Sarum 1728-34

Seat: Balls Park, Hertfordshire (purch. and built 1637-40, remod. 18th c., sold later 18th c.)

Estates: Worth £1,800 pa in 1670.
Notes: Edward Harrison MP was a nabob and Chairman of the East India Company.

HARTLEY [Packer, Winchcombe]

Hartley

Origins: The Hartley founder was from a poor family. He received a scholarship to Oxford in the 1690s and became a clergyman. His son also went to Oxford and became a physician and author. His son, David Hartley MP, was an inventor and politician. The Hartleys inherited the estates of the Winchcombe Baronets via the marriage of Winchcombe Hartley's mother's father, Robert Packer to the heiress of the second and last Winchcombe Baronet.

1. David Hartley – Kingston-upon-Hull 1774-80 1782-84
2. Winchcombe Hartley – Berkshire 1776-84 1790-94

Seats: Bucklebury House, Berkshire (purch. by Winchcombs 1541 and built, and passed by mar. early 18th c. to the Packers and mid-18th c. to the Hartleys, fire 1833, partly demolished, descendents still own); Little Sodbury Manor, Gloucestershire (medieval house, rebuilt 1703, acq. by mar. by the Hartleys second quarter 18th c., became a farm house from 1820s, sold 1911); Lyegrove House, Gloucestershire (acq. and built early 17th c. by Stephens family, passed by mar. to Packers 1728 and then to Hartleys, add. early 18th c., remod. c. 1835 and 1856, sold c. 1900)
Estates: Bateman 7724 (E) 9997
Notes: Two in ODNB.

Packer

Origins: Crown servants and officials in the 17th century who purchased estates. **First MP 1628**. Packers inherited the Winchcombe estates in the early 18th century, and these passed by mar. to the Hartleys later in the century.

1. Robert Packer – Wallingford 1646-48 1660-79
2. Robert Packer – Berkshire 1712-31
3. Winchcomb Packer – Berkshire 1731-46

Seats: Shellingford, Berkshire (purch. 1620, sold 1738 for £8,000); Bucklebury House, Berkshire (acq. by Winchcombes 1541, built 16th c., acq. by mar. from Winchcombes early 18th c., passed to Hartleys by mar. mid-18th c.); Donnington, Berkshire (medieval castle, purch. 1632, dismantled, new house 1648-60, passed to the Hartleys by mar. mid-18th c.); Little Sodbury Manor, Gloucestershire (acq. by mar. from Stephens family

– acq. c. 1608 – by the Packers 1728, from them it passed to the Hartleys second quarter 18th c.)
Notes: One in ODNB.

Winchcombe

Origins: The Winchcombes were rich clothiers (Sheriff of London 1379) who invested heavily in land, purchased Bucklebury in 1540. **First MP 1545. Another MP 1553.**

1. Sir Henry Winchcombe 2 Bt – Berkshire 1689-95

Seat: Bucklebury House, Berkshire (purch. 1541, passed to Packers and Hartleys, see above)
Title: Baronet 1661-1703
Notes: Winchcombe family has an entry in the ODNB and one other biography.

HARTOPP [Cradock]

Hartopp

Origins: The Hartopps were yeomen granted arms 1596. They acquired Freatby in the early 17th century. The 1 Bt was a soldier who fought with Leicester in the Low Countries. Kt 1617. **First MP 1628 for Leicestershire**. The daughter of the last Baronet (d. 1762) married Joseph Hurlock, a Director of the East India Company. Their daughter, Anne, married Edmund Bunney, who took the names Cradock and Hartopp, created a Baronet 1796.

1. Sir William Hartopp – Leicester 1661-79
2. Sir John Hartopp 3 Bt – Leicestershire 1679-81
3. Sir Edmund Cradock-Hartopp 1 Bt – Leicestershire 1798-1806
4. George Fleetwood Hartopp – Dundalk 1820-24

Seats: Four Oaks Hall, Warwickshire (built 1696, remod. c. 1740, purch. 1792, sold 1880, demolished 1899); Freatby (Freeby), Leicestershire (acq. 1598, sold mid-19th c.)
Estates: Bateman 2181 (E) 4110
Titles: Baronet 1619-1762; 1796-
Notes: Four Oaks was too close to expanding Birmingham and in the late 19th c. was demolished and the estate divided up into plots for suburban villas. 3 Bt in ODNB.

Hartopp

Origins: Descended from the fourth son of William Hartopp of Burton-Lazers (16th c.), ancestor of the Hartopps of Four Oaks and Freatby.

1. Edward Hartopp – N. Leicestershire 1859-68

Seat: Dalby Hall, Leicestershire (built 1580, add. 1682 and 1816, remod. 1837, sold 1938, partially demolished 1951)
Estates: Bateman 34190 (E & I) 13845

HARTPOLE *IRELAND*

Origins: To Ireland 1550s. Constables of the Castle of Carlow. Sheriff 1571. Knighted by the Lord Deputy 1603. His son at Shrule d. 1632. Further lands acquired 1685. **First {MP 1585 for Queen's County}. Another {MP 1639}**.

1. George Hartpole – {Portarlington 1761-66}

Seats: Shrule Castle, Queen's County (acq. c. 1580, departed later 18th c.); Monks Grange, Queens County (acq. 1577, ruin 18th c.)
Notes: The family was in financial trouble in the mid 18th c., and parts of the estate were sold. Extinct in male line 1780.

HARTSTONGE *IRELAND*

Origins: Came to Ireland from Norfolk in the 1650s, a lawyer and Baron of the Exchequer. His son was Bishop of Derry 1714. Acquired Bruff by marriage to an heiress.

1. Sir Standish Hartstonge 1 Bt – {Limerick 1661-66}
2. Standish Hartstonge – {Kilkenny 1695-99 1703-25}
3. Sir Standish Hartstonge 2 Bt – {Kilmallock 1695-99 Ratoath 1703-13 St. Canice 1713-27}
4. Price Hartstonge – {Charleville 1727-44}
5. Sir Henry Hartstonge 3 Bt – {County Limerick 1776-90}

Seat: Bruff, Limerick (acq. later 17th, passed to Pery family early 19th c.)
Estates: Worth £1,000 pa in 1713.
Title: Baronet 1681-1797
Notes: Extinct in the male line in 1797. One in ODNB.

HARVEY

Origins: Began as Kentish yeomen. One became a grocer and wealthy merchant. His son (MP 1660) was ambassador to the Ottoman Empire 1668. **First MP 1640**.

1. Sir Daniel Harvey – Surrey 1660
2. Sir Eliab Harvey – Old Sarum 1669-79 Essex 1679 Old Sarum 1679-81 1685-87 Maldon 1689-90 1693-99
3. Edward Harvey – Bletchingley 1679 Clitheroe 1705-13 1715-22
4. Michael Harvey – Weymouth & Melcombe Regis 1679-81 1689-1701
5. Eliab Harvey – Old Sarum 1679
6. William Harvey – Old Sarum 1689-1705 Appleby 1705-08 Old Sarum 1708-10 Weymouth & Melcombe Regis 1711-13 1714-15 Essex 1715-16 1722-27
7. Daniel Harvey – Clitheroe 1707-08 Dunwich 1709-10 Weymouth & Melcombe Regis 1713-14 1715-22
8. William Harvey – Old Sarum 1710-13
9. Michael Harvey – Milborne Port 1717 1722-41 1742-47
10. William Harvey – Essex 1747-63
11. Edward Harvey – Gatton 1761-68 Harwich 1768-78
12. Eliab Harvey – Dunwich 1761-68
13. William Harvey – Essex 1775-79
14. Eliab Harvey – Maldon 1780-84 Essex 1802-12 1820-30

Seats: Rolls Park (Chigwell), Essex (acq. and built c. 1600, remod. mid-18th c., passed to the Lloyds IV [see that family] by a marriage of 1804, passed by mar. to Harveys 1830, demolished 1953); Coombe, Surrey (acq. 1651, sold c. 1753); Clifton Maybank, Dorset (built 1546, acq. 1659, sold 1747, part demolished 1786); Claybury Hall, Essex (medieval, remod. 16th and 17th, purch. 1767, passed to an heiress 1769, sold 1789)
Estates: The Coombe estate was worth £3,100 pa in 1701. Chigwell was worth £5,000-£6,000 pa in the 18th c. Rubinstein – Sir Eliab Harvey left £120,000 in probate in 1830.
Notes: The Harvey of blood circulation was a relative. The family produced a remarkable number of admirals. Seven in ODNB.

HATTON *IRELAND*

Origins: Clergyman from Northamptonshire to Ireland c. 1660. Barrister c. 1745. Sheriff 1758.

1. Henry Hatton – {Wexford 1727-35}
2. Henry Hatton – {Donegal 1783-90 Fethard 1793}
3. George Hatton – {Lisburn 1792-1800} 1801-02
4. Villiers Hatton – County Wexford 1841-47

Seat: Clonard, Wexford (old castle became ruinous, acq. late 17th c., rebuilt 1783, sold 1837)
Estates: 3252 (I) 1953 in 1878. Mostly urban property in Wexford worth £2,000 pa in 1799.

HAWKE

Baron Hawke (1776- GB)

Origins: The father of the 1 Baron was a barrister. The son was an admiral, First Lord of the Admiralty 1766.

1. Edward Hawke 1 Baron Hawke – Portsmouth 1747-76
2. Martin Hawke 2 Baron Hawke – Saltash 1768-74

Seats: Scarthingwell Hall, Yorkshire (acq. by mar. from the Hamonds, who had acq. it in the 17th c., sold 1848, demolished 1948); Womersley Park, Yorkshire (built 16th c., Hawkes acq. by marriage to an heiress 1805, passed by marriage to the 4 Earl of Rosse 1869)
Estates: Bateman 6187 (E) 8007
Peers: 9 peers 1776-1887 1881-1945
1 in Cabinet 1766-71
Notes: 1 and 7 Barons in ODNB.

HAWKINS

Origins: An attorney in the late 17th century became the wealthiest lawyer in Cornwall (handling mining disputes). His son purchased landed estates.

1. Philip Hawkins – Grampound 1727-38
2. Thomas Hawkins – Grampound 1747-54
3. Sir Christopher Hawkins 1 Bt – Mitchell 1784-99 Grampound 1800-07 Penryn 1818-20 St. Ives 1821-28
4. John Hawkins – Mitchell 1830-31 Tavistock 1831-32 Newport 1832-41

Seats: Trewithen, Cornwall (built 1715, acq. 1737, add. c. 1729-40 and c. 1763-64, passed by mar. to the Johnstones 1903, still own); Bignor Park, Sussex (built late 16th c., purch. 1806, rebuilt 1826-29, passed by mar. 1903 to Johnstones, sold 1926); Trewinnard, Cornwall (purch. 1650, passed by mar. to Johnstones 1903)
Estates: Bateman 12119 (E) 14049
Titles: Baronet 1791-1829

Notes: Some of the Hawkins wealth came from mines in which they continued to invest in the 18th and 19th centuries. The daughter of John Hawkins MP married George Johnstone of Alva (see Hope), and the Hawkins estates passed to the Johnstones in 1903 when the Hawkins line became extinct (see Hope).

HAWLEY

Baron Hawley (1645-1790 I)

Origins: The **first MP (1584)** was an official and "creature" of Elizabeth I's favorite, Sir Christopher Hatton. He accepted bribes from pirates. **One additional MP 1586.**

1. Francis Hawley 1 Baron Hawley – Mitchell 1665-79
2. Henry Hawley – {Kinsale 1703-24}
3. Francis Hawley 2 Baron Hawley – Bramber 1713-15

Seat: Buckland House (Priory), Somerset (acq. 1539, sold 1711 and 1725, demolished c. 1800)
Title: Baronet 1643-1790
Peers: {4 peers 1660-84 1690-1743 1751-90}
Notes: Estates heavily mortgaged in the early 18th c.

HAY *SCOTLAND & ENGLAND*

Marquis of Tweeddale (1694- S)

Origins: Of Norman origins. Came to Scotland under King David I. The Hays acquired great estates through a successful series of marriages and held important offices of state in the 12th and 13th centuries. Summoned to Parliament in 1303.

1. Sir James Hay 1 Bt – [Haddingtonshire 1669-74]
2. William Hay – [Selkirkshire 1685-86]
3. Lord Charles Hay – Haddingtonshire 1741-47
4. Lord John Hay – Haddingtonshire 1826-31 Windsor 1847-50
5. George Hay Earl of Gifford – Totnes 1855-62
6. Lord John Hay – Wick 1857-59 Ripon 1866-71
7. William Hay 10 Marquis of Tweeddale – Taunton 1865-68 Haddington Burghs 1878
8. Thomas Hay – S. Norfolk 1922-23

Seats: Yester House, Haddingtonshire (Giffords acq. 12th c., built c. 1267, acq. by mar. to a Gifford heiress at the end of the 14th century, new house 1720s, mid-18th c. and

1789, remod. 1830s, sold 1967); Neidpath Castle, Peeblesshire (built 14th c., add. 1654, passed to Wemyss family 1810)
Estates: Bateman 43517 (S) 26530
Titles: Baron Tweeddale 1488- S; Earl of Tweeddale 1646- S; Earl of Gifford 1694- S; Baron Tweeddale 1881- UK; Baronet 1667-1751
Peers: [2 peers 1661-1707] 4 Scottish Rep peers 1707-08 1715 1722-34 1742-62 1818-76 3 peers 1881-1945
4 Lds Lt 18th, 19th, 20th
1 in Cabinet 1742-46
2 KT 19th, 20th
Notes: Some members of the family remained Roman Catholic, which reduced parliamentary representation. Hay family and 1 and 5 Barons Hay of Yester and 1, 2, 4, 8 and 9 Marquises and seven others in ODNB.

Earl of Erroll (1452- S)

Origins: The 1 Earl was descended from Sir William Hay, ancestor of the Marquis of Tweeddale. Became hereditary High Constables of Scotland. The daughter of the 12 Earl had a daughter who married William Boyd 4 Earl of Kilmarnock. Their son succeeded as 15 Earl of Erroll.

No MPs

Seats: Slains Castle, Aberdeenshire (medieval, demolished 1594, rebuilt 1598, add. 1664, add. 1707, rebuilt 1836, unroofed 1925, ruin); Delgatie (Delgaty), Aberdeenshire (medieval castle, acq. 1314, rebuilt 1570-79, add. early 17th c., add. 1743 and 1768, add. 19th c., decayed early 20th c., restored post-1945, still owned by Hays); Errol House, Perthshire (house there by 17th c., new house later 18th c., fire 1874, rebuilt soon after); The Dean Castle, Ayrshire (acq. by Boyds 1316, built c. 1350, add. c. 1460s, fire 1735, ruin, sold 1746, restored from 1908-46, donated as museum 1975)
Estates: Bateman 8264 (E & S) 9599
Titles: Baron Hay 1450 S; Baron Boyd 1454-1746 S; Earl of Kilmarnock 1661-1746 S; Baron Kilmarnock 1831- UK
Peers: [6 peers 1660-92 1661-1707 1705-07] 4 Scottish Rep peers 1770-74 1796-98 1806-07 1818-19 1823-31 5 peers 1831-1941
1 Ld Lt 19th
2 KT 19th, 20th
Notes: Held the barony of Erroll by knight service from the reign of William the Lion. The Kilmarnock titles were attainted in 1746 for Jacobitism. For a discussion of the decline of the Erroll estates in the 18th century see Callander, *A Pattern of Landownership in Scotland*, 53. Hay family and 9 and 22 Earls in ODNB.

Earl of Kinnoull (1633- S)

Origins: Descended from a younger son of the 1 Earl of Erroll. Summoned to Parliament as a Lord 1598. Kt c. 1600. Comptroller of Scotland 1608. Baron 1615, Earl 1622, and Lord Chamberlain of Scotland 1627. On the death of the 3 Viscount Strathallan in 1711 the estate of Cromlix devolved on the Hays as heirs of Elizabeth, wife of the 7 Earl of Kinnoull, only surviving daughter of the 1 Viscount Strathallan. **First [MP 1644 for Perthshire].**

1. Thomas Hay 7 Earl of Kinnoull – [Perthshire 1693-96]
2. George Hay 8 Earl of Kinnoull – Fowey 1710-11
3. Thomas Hay 9 Earl of Kinnoull – Scarborough 1736 Cambridge 1741-58
4. Claude Hay – Hoxton Div. Shoreditch 1900-10

Seats: Dupplin Castle, Perthshire (medieval castle, rebuilt 1460s, acq. 1623, rebuilt 1688, add. 1720-25, add. c. 1786, add. 1814-15, fire 1827, rebuilt 1828-32, sold 1911, demolished 1967); Balhousie Castle, Perthshire (medieval, rebuilt 17th c., acq. 1625, restored 1863, sold 1926); Broadsworth Hall, Yorkshire (old house, purch. 1713, rebuilt 1714, sold 1790)
Estates: Bateman 12657 (S) 15413; at Cromlix 7683 (S) 5239
Titles: Earl of Carlisle 1623-60 S; Viscount Dupplin 1697- S; Baron Hay 1711- GB
Peers: [1 peer 1660-77] 1 Scottish Rep peer 1710-14 7 peers 1711-1804 1806-1916 1923-38
1 Ld Lt 19th
1 in Cabinet 1758-62
Notes: The third son of the 7 Earl was created Duke of Inverness in the Jacobite peerage. 1 Earl an active businessman and industrialist. 1, 8, and 9 Earls of Kinnoull and 1 Earl of Carlisle and one other in ODNB.

Hay

Origins: Descended from a younger son of the 2 Baron Hay, ancestor of the Marquis of Tweeddale. **First [MP 1628 for Peeblesshire].** Bankers in the 18th and 19th centuries.

1. Adam Hay – Peeblesshire 1767-68 1775
2. Sir Adam Hay 7 Bt – Linlithgow Burghs 1826-30
3. Sir John Hay 6 Bt – Peeblesshire 1831-37

Seats: Smithfield Castle (Venlaw House), Peeblesshire (acq. and built 14th c., rebuilt 16th c., sold c. 1782, hotel); Haystoun, Peeblesshire (acq. 14th c., old tower, add. 1660, add. 18th c., family left 1795 and became farm house); Kings Meadows (Kingsmeadows), Peeblesshire (acq. medieval period, built late 18th c., became main seat 1795, add. 1811 and 1855 and 1890, sold 1920, now flats)
Estates: Bateman 9755 (S) 4514
Title: Baronet 1635 – (dormant 1683-1805)

HAZLERIGG (Hesilrige)

Baron Hazlerigg (Hasilrige) (1945- UK)

Origins: In Leicestershire since the 14th century. Rose in royal service under the Tudors. High Sheriff 1612. **First MP 1589. Two further MPs 1624-54 both kts of the shire. Two possible MPs 14th century.**

1. Sir Thomas Hesilrige 4 Bt – Leicestershire 1690-95

Seat: Noseley Hall, Leicestershire (built 15th c., acq. by marriage 1419, rebuilt 1720s, remod. 1835, many contents sold 1998, house for sale 2011 with 1,300 acres, but still own)
Estates: Bateman 2162 (E) 3837. Owned 2,000 acres in 2001.
Title: Baronet 1622-1817
Peer: 1 peer 1945
Notes: The spelling of the name changed in 1818. Thomas Hesilrige succeeded to the Maynard estates and took the name Maynard (see Greville). But he reverted to his own name on inheriting the Baronetcy. He died childless in 1817. 2 Bt in ODNB.

HEATH

Origins: Robert Heath MP was a great ironmaster.

1. Robert Heath – Stoke-on-Trent 1874-80
2. Sir James Heath 1 Bt – N. W. Staffordshire 1892-1906
3. Arthur Heath – Hanley 1900-06 Leak Div. Staffordshire 1910

Seats: Biddulph Grange, Staffordshire (built 1848-60, purch. 1871, fire 1896, rebuilt 1897, sold 1923, NT); Greenway Bank (Hall), Staffordshire (built 18th c., remod. 19th c., purch. 1871, demolished 1973)
Estates: Bateman 3320 (E) 4800
Title: Baronet 1904-42

HEATHCOAT-AMORY (Heathcote)

Viscount Amory (1960-81 UK)

Origins: The first Amory was a banker in the early 19th century. His son married Anne Heathcoat, heiress and daughter of an MP. The Heathcotes began as lace-makers in the 18th century and founded a major fabric-making firm.

1. John Heathcote – Tiverton 1832-59
2. Sir John Heathcoat-Amory 1 Bt – Tiverton 1868-85
3. Sir Derick Heathcoat-Amory 1 Viscount Amory – Tiverton Div. Devon 1945-60
4. David Heathcoat-Amory – Wells 1983-2010

Seat: Knightshayes Court, Devon (acq. and built 1869-74, NT 1972)
Estates: Bateman 5202 (E) 11057. Owned 13,000 acres in Scotland in 1996.
Title: Baronet 1874-
1 in Cabinet 1951-60
1 KG 20th
Notes: The Heathcoat lace business began in Derbyshire but was moved to Tiverton after the mill was destroyed in 1815 by Luddites. The family continued to manage the company into the 20th c. The 1 Viscount was a government minister in the 1950s. 1 Viscount and one other in ODNB.

HEBBLETHWAITE

Origins: Acquired land under Elizabeth I. Gentry in the 17th century. **First MP 1641**, a lawyer.

1. Sir Thomas Hebblethwaite – Malton 1660-68
2. James Hebblethwaite – Malton 1678-79

Seat: Norton, Yorkshire (acq. r. Elizabeth I, sold later 17th c.?, demolished c. 1970)

HEDGES (Hodges)

Origins: Clothiers in the 16th century. **First MP 1553. One further MP 1640.**

1. Sir Charles Hedges – Orford 1698-1700 Dover 1701 Malmesbury 1701-02 Calne 1702-05 West Looe 1705-13 East Looe 1713-14
2. William Hedges – Calne 1710-15

Seats: Shipton Moyne (Manor House), Gloucestershire (medieval, purch. 1554, rebuilt early 17th c., rebuilt 1724, demolished 1838); Wanborough, Wiltshire (purch. 1704, sold 1768); Alderton, Wiltshire (acq. by mar. 1714 to a Gore heiress, owners since 14th c., passed out of family via heiress 1766)
1 in Cabinet 1700-01 1702-06
Notes: Family died out in the male line 1761. One in ODNB.

HELE (Heale) [Bulteel]

Hele

Origins: The Heles held land in Devon since the reign of Edward I. High Sheriff in the later 16th century. **First MP 1350. Six further MPs 1355-1625.**

1. Sir Thomas Hele 1 Bt – Plympton Erle 1626 1628 1640-44 Okehampton 1661-70
2. John Hele – Reigate 1659 1660
3. Thomas Hele – Plympton Erle 1661-65
4. Richard Hele – Plympton Erle 1701-02 West Looe 1702-03 Plympton Erle 1703-05

Seat: Flete (Fleet) House, Devon (purch. r. Elizabeth I, built late 16th c., passed to Bulteels 1716)
Estates: Worth £1,000 pa in the 1620s. Flete line owned 2,200 acres in 1624, while another branch held 2,500 acres.
Title: Baronet 1627-77
Notes: **Six Heles represented Plympton Erle between 1355 and 1705**. One in ODNB.

Bulteel

Origins: Huguenots who fled France on the Revocation of the Edict of Nantes. Merchants. After the last Hele died in 1716 the estates passed to their kinsman by marriage James Bulteel.

1. John Bulteel – Lostwithiel 1661-69
2. James Bulteel – Tavistock 1703-08 1711-15
3. John Bulteel – S. Devon 1832-34

Seats: Flete House, Devon (built late 16th c., acq. by mar. 1716, sold 1855/63); Pamflete, Devon (built 18th c., add. 19th c., sold 1863)
Notes: One in ODNB.

HELY-HUTCHINSON *IRELAND*

Earl of Donoughmore (1800- I)

Origins: The first Hely was a self-made man, a lawyer and politician in the mid-18th century. He married the Hutchinson heiress to Knocklofty in 1751. The Hutchinsons began with a merchant in mid-17th century Nenagh.

1. John Hely-Hutchinson – {Lanesborough 1759-60 Cork 1761-90 Taghmon 1790-94}

2. Richard Hely-Hutchinson 1 Earl of Donoughmore – {Sligo 1778-83 Taghmon 1783-88}
3. John Hely-Hutchinson 2 Earl of Donoughmore – {Lanesborough 1776-83 Taghmon 1789-90 Cork 1790-1800} 1801
4. Francis Hely-Hutchinson – {Dublin University 1790-97 Naas 1797-1800}
5. Christopher Hely-Hutchinson – {Taghmon 1795-96} Cork 1802-12 1818-26
6. John Hely-Hutchinson 3 Earl of Donoughmore – Tipperary 1826-32
7. John Hely-Hutchinson – Cork 1826-30
8. Maurice Hely-Hutchinson – Hastings 1937-45
9. John Hely-Hutchinson 7 Earl of Donoughmore – Peterborough Div. Northamptonshire 1943-45

Seats: Knocklofty, Tipperary (built 17th c., Hutchinsons acq. 1688, Helys acq. by mar. 1751, add. mid-18th c., add. early 19th c., sold 1983, now hotel); Kilmanahan Castle, Waterford (medieval castle, add. early 19th c., purch. 1855, ruinous 1945, sold and demolished 1952); Palmerstown House, Dublin, (purch. late 18th c., sold c. 1860); Chelwood Beacon, Sussex (built 1882, purch. 1911, sold 1948, institutional use)
Estates: Bateman 11950 (I) 10424. Worth £6,000 pa in 1783.
Titles: Baron Donoughmore 1783- I; Viscount Donoughmore 1797- I; Baron Hutchinson 1801-32 UK; Viscount Hutchinson 1821- UK
Peers: {1 peer 1789-1800} 1 Irish Rep peer 1801-25 5 peers 1825-1945
2 Lds Lt 19th
1 in Cabinet 1859
2 KP 19th, 20th
Notes: The 6 Earl was a member of the Irish Senate 1922-31. He also married an American heiress, which helped improve the family's financial situation considerably. 1, 2, 3, and 6 Earls and four others in ODNB.

HENDERSON I

Baron Faringdon (1916- UK)

Origins: 1 Baron, the son of a printer and proof corrector, was a businessman and financier. Heavily involved in railways and petroleum.

1. Alexander Henderson 1 Baron Faringdon – W. Staffordshire 1898-1906 St. George's Hanover Square 1913-15
2. Harold Henderson – N. Berkshire 1910-16

Seat: Buscot Park, Berkshire (built 1780s, purch. 1889, NT 1949)
Estates: Purchased 3,500 acres in 1889. The family was worth about two and a half million pounds in the 1930s.

Peers: 2 peers 1916-45
1 in Cabinet 1916-17
Notes: 2 Baron was Chairman of the Fabian Society. 1 Baron and one other in ODNB.

HENDERSON II

Baron Henderson (1945-84 UK)

Origins: Arthur Henderson was probably the illegitimate son of a domestic servant. His mother married a policeman. He became an apprentice in a locomotive factory at the age of 12. He rose in trade union work and politics and was Foreign Secretary in the first Labour government.

1. Arthur Henderson – Barnard Castle Div. Durham 1903-18 Widnes Div. Lancashire 1919-22 E. Newcastle 1923 Burnley 1924 1929 Claycross Div. Derbyshire 1933-35
2. William Henderson 1 Baron Henderson – Enfield Div. Middlesex 1923-24 1929-31
3. Arthur Henderson 1 Baron Rowley – S. Cardiff 1923-24 1929-31 Kingswinford 1935-50 Rowley Regis and Tipton 1950-66

Estates: Arthur Henderson was worth the considerable sum of £23,000 at his death in 1935.
Titles: Baron Rowley 1966-68 UKLife
Peers: 1 peer 1945
2 in Cabinet 1916-17 1924 1947-51
Notes: One in ODNB.

HENEAGE [Helyar, Walker]

Baron Heneage (1896-1967 UK)

Origins: The family traced their descent to the 14th century. One served as private secretary to Cardinal Wolsey and was Master of the Household of Henry VIII. He expanded the family estates considerably at the Dissolution. **First MP 1497 for Great Grimsby. Four further MPs 1523-93, two of them for Great Grimsby, two kts of the shire.** The family remained Roman Catholic in the 17th, 18th and into the 19th centuries. The first MP in the 19th century conformed to the Established Church.

1. George Heneage – Great Grimsby 1826-30 Lincoln 1832-34 1852-62
2. Edward Heneage – Great Grimsby 1835-52
3. Edward Heneage 1 Baron Heneage – Lincoln 1865-68 Great Grimsby 1880-92 1893-95
4. Sir Arthur Heneage – Louth Div. Lincolnshire 1924-45

Seat: Hainton Hall, Lincolnshire (acq. early 15th c., rebuilt 16th c., rebuilt c. 1638, remod. 1735-37, enlarged c. 1800, add. 1875, fire 1919, rebuilt, fire 1924, partly demolished 1956, restoration work 1972-75 and 1985, still own)
Estates: Bateman 10761 (E) 15527. Rubinstein – George Heneage left £160,000 in probate in 1833. Held 5,500 acres in 1980s.
Peers: 2 peers 1896-1945
1 in Cabinet 1886
Notes: Four centuries separated the first and last MP from the family for Great Grimsby. The male line of the family remained unbroken from the reign of Edward III through the 20th century. Four in ODNB.

Walker Heneage

Origins: Robert Heneage, younger son of John Heneage of Hainton (d. 1586) had an elder son whose daughter married Sir Moyle Finch 1 Bt and was created Countess of Winchilsea in her own right (see Finch). A younger son, Michael, had a descendent, Cecil, who married John Walker (d. 1793). Their son John Walker Heneage was seated at Compton Bassett.

1. John Walker Heneage – Cricklade 1785-94
2. George Walker Heneage – Devizes 1838-57

Seats: Compton Bassett House, Wiltshire (medieval, remod. 1674, purch. 1768, sold 1918, demolished c. 1930); Coker Court, Somerset (built 15th c., add. early 17th c., add. 1666-70, remod. mid-18th c., acq. by mar. late 19th c., add. 1900, sold 1950)
Estates: Bateman 6513 (E) 9518
Notes: Succeeded in 1917 to the Cathcart of Carelton estates (see Cathcart). Family extinct 1950.

Helyar (Hillyard)

Origins: The first notable member of the family was a clerical pluralist who became Archdeacon of Barnstaple in 1605. Later the family acquired a plantation in Jamaica.

1. William Helyar – Iichester 1689-90 Somerset 1715-22

Seat: Coker Court, Somerset (built 15th c., purch. 1616, additions 1766-70, passed by mar. to Heneages late 19th c.)
Estates: Bateman 3724 (E) 5527

HENLEY [Eden, Holt]

Earl of Northington (1764-86 GB)

Origins: The Henleys produced a prodigious troop of successful lawyers in the 17th century culminating in one becoming Master of the King's Bench. They acquired much property and many honors. The 1 Earl served as Lord Chancellor in the 18th century.

1. Henry Henley – Somerset 1653 Dorset 1654 Lyme Regis 1659 Bridport 1660 Lyme Regis 1661-81
2. Sir Andrew Henley 1 Bt – Portsmouth 1660
3. Sir Robert Henley – Andover 1679-81 Hampshire 1691-92
4. Sir Robert Henley 2 Bt – Bridport 1679-81
5. Henry Henley – Lyme Regis 1690-1700 1702-05 1710-15
6. Robert Henley – Lyme Regis 1695-1701
7. Anthony Henley – Andover 1698-1700 Weymouth 1702-11
8. John Henley – Lyme Regis 1715-22
9. Henry Holt Henley – Lyme Regis 1722-27 1728-48
10. Anthony Henley – Southampton 1727-34
11. Robert Henley 1 Earl of Northington – Bath 1747-57
12. Robert Henley – Lyme Regis 1748-54
13. Robert Henley 2 Earl of Northington – Hampshire 1768-72

Seats: The Grange, Hampshire (acq. c. 1660, built c. 1670, sold 1787); Wootton Abbotts, Dorset (inher. by mar. early 18th c.); Leigh House, Somerset (purc. 1588, built c. 1617, remod. 18th c., remod. 1893, sold 1919); Bramshill, Hampshire (older house, new house built 1605-12, acq. 1640, sold 1700)
Estates: Robert Henley spent £15,000 on land purchases between 1576-1613. The Grange estate worth £3,000 pa in 1692.
Title: Baron Henley 1760-86 GB; Baronet 1660-1740
Peers: 2 peers 1760-86
1 Ld Lt 18th
2 in Cabinet 1757-67 1783-84
1 KT 18th
Notes: 1 and 2 Earls and three others in ODNB.

Holt

Origins: Merchants in Portsmouth, Mayor 1627 and 1641. Purchased landed estates and became country gentlemen in the later 17th century. The daughter and heiress of Richard Holt of Nurstead married Henry Henley.

1. Richard Holt – Lymington 1685-87 1689-90 Petersfield 1690-98

Seat: Nurstead (Nursted) House, Hampshire (built late 17th c., passed by inher. to Henley's 1710, remod. c. 1760)

Baron Henley (1799- I)

Origins: Morton Frederick Eden 1 Baron Henley, younger brother of the 1 Baron Auckland, married the sister and co-heiress of the 2 and last Earl of Northington. The 3 Baron was created Baron Northington. Several members of the Eden family took the name Henley. For Eden see below.

1. Robert Henley 2 Baron Henley – Fowey 1826-30
2. Anthony Eden 3 Baron Henley – Northampton 1859-74

Seat: Watford Court, Northamptonshire (built 1568, purch. 1836, sold c. 1962, demolished 1975)
Estates: Bateman 5366 (E) 8516
Title: Baron Northington 1885- UK
Peers: 4 peers 1885-1945
Notes: 1 and 2 Barons in ODNB.

Earl of Auckland (1839-49 UK)

Origins: The Edens were established in Durham in the 15th century. One was a royalist colonel in the Civil War. His son was a lawyer and created a Baronet.

1. Sir Robert Eden 1 Bt – County Durham 1679 1690-95 1698-1700 1702-13
2. Sir John Eden 2 Bt – County Durham 1713-27
3. Sir John Eden 4 Bt – County Durham 1774-90
4. William Eden 1 Baron Auckland – New Woodstock 1774-84 {Dungannon 1781-83} Heytesbury 1784-93
5. William Eden – New Woodstock 1806-10
6. George Eden 1 Earl of Auckland – New Woodstock 1810-12 1813-14
7. Anthony Eden 1 Earl of Avon – Warwick and Leamington Div. Warwickshire 1923-57
8. John Eden 8 Bt and Baron Eden – Bournemouth West 1954-83

Seats: Windlestone Hall, Durham (built 16th c., acq. c. 1700, rebuilt 1830-34, sold 1957); Beamish Park (Hall), Durham (medieval, rebuilt early 17th c., acq. by mar. 1739, passed via heiress 1803 to Shafto family who took add. name Eden, see Shafto); West Auckland Hall, Durham (built 16th c., rebuilt early 17th c., sold, hotel)
Estates: Bateman 7928 (E) 13227 and 4278 (E) 6885

Titles: Baron Auckland 1789- I; Baron Auckland 1793- GB; Earl of Avon 1961- UK; Baron Eden of Winton 1983- UKLife; Baronet 1672- ; 1776-
Peers: 7 peers 1793-1945
3 in Cabinet 1780-82 1806-07 1830-42 1846-49 1934-38 1940-45
Notes: The 1 Earl of Avon was Prime Minister 1955-57. The 1 and 3 Barons and 1 Earl of Auckland and 1 Earl of Avon and nine others in ODNB.

HENNIKER [Hughan, Major]

Baron Henniker (1800- I)

Origins: Traders and shipbuilders in the 18th century. The 1 Baron was a Russia merchant. The 1 Baron married the heiress of John Major of Worlingworth Hall (iron and timber traders). The 2 Baron took the additional name Major on inheriting by marriage the Major Baronetcy in 1781.

1. John Henniker 1 Baron Henniker – Sudbury 1761-68 Dover 1774-84
2. John Henniker-Major 2 Baron Henniker – New Romney 1785-90 Steyning 1794-1802 Rutland 1805-12 Stamford 1812-18
3. Sir Brydges Henniker 1 Bt – {Kildare 1797-1800}
4. John Henniker-Major 4 Baron Henniker – E. Suffolk 1832-46 1856-66
5. John Henniker-Major 5 Baron Henniker – E. Suffolk 1866-70

Seats: Thornham Hall, Suffolk (built 16th c., purch. by Majors mid-18th c., passed by mar. to Hennikers 1813, remod. 1837-39, leased out after 1895, contents sold 1937, burned 1954); Worlingworth Hall, Suffolk (Hennikers acq. by mar. 1781, family ceased to inhabit by 1830s, declined to a farm house); Yaxley Hall, Suffolk (built 16th c., remod. 18th c., purch. 1880s, major fire 1922 reduced size, sold after fire)
Estates: Bateman 11040 (E) 15357
Title: Baron Hartismere 1866- UK
Peers: 4 peers 1866-1945
Notes: 2 and 3 Barons were both barristers. 2 Baron in ODNB.

Henniker

Origins: A younger son of the 1 Baron Henniker was created a Baronet in 1813.

1. Sir Arthur Henniker-Hughnan 6 Bt – Galloway 1924-25

Seat: Newton Hall, Essex (old house, purch. mid-18th c., rebuilt mid-19th c., sold second half 19th c.)
Notes: 2 and 8 Bts in ODNB.

Major

Origins: The Major family was founded by a successful iron merchant and sea captain who purchased landed estates in the mid-18th century. These passed to the Hennikers, see above.

1. Sir John Major 1 Bt – Scarborough 1761-68

Seat: Worlingworth Hall, Suffolk (medieval, remod. 16th, 17th, 18th c., purch. by Major family mid-18th c., passed to Henniker family by mar. 1781, see above)
Estates: Worth £5,000 pa in the 1760s.
Title: Baronet 1765-

HENRY I *IRELAND*

Origins: The founder was a 17th century Presbyterian clergyman. His son was a merchant and banker in the early 18th century, who purchased estates. Sheriff 1771.

1. Hugh Henry – {Antrim 1713-43}
2. Joseph Henry – {Newtown Limavady 1715-17}
3. Joseph Henry – {Longford 1761-68 Kildare 1769-76}

Seats: Straffan House, Kildare (purch. c. 1710 and built c. 1720, sold 1831); Straffan Lodge (Lodge Park), Kildare (acq. c. 1720, built 1775-77, add. late 19th-early 20th c., sold 1948)
Estates: 4506 (I) 4305. Held 7,000 acres c. 1710 (Bunbury, *The Landed Gentry & Aristocracy: Kildare*, 116). Worth £1,000 pa in 1713.

HENRY II *ENGLAND & IRELAND*

Origins: Alexander Henry MP was born in County Down. He founded a large merchant firm in Manchester, Leeds, and Huddersfield.

1. Alexander Henry – S. Lancashire 1847-52
2. John Henry – S. E. Lancashire 1868-74
3. Mitchell Henry – County Galway 1871-85 Blackfriars Div. Glasgow 1885-86

Seats: Woodlands, Manchester, Lancashire (purch. c. 1860s); Kylemore Castle, Galway (purch. and built 1860, sold 1900)
Estates: 14,000 acres around Kylemore, little income from the Irish estate.
Notes: One in ODNB.

HERBERT [Powell, Sawyer] *ENGLAND, WALES & IRELAND*

Earl of Pembroke and Montgomery (1551- & 1605- E)

Origins: The Herberts were great landowners in Wales by the 14th century, originally seated at Raglan Castle, Montgomeryshire. They inherited this estate by marriage c. 1405 from the Bloats who were granted the castle in 1174. Sir William Herbert of Raglan was created Earl of Pembroke in 1468 (extinct 1491). His daughter and heiress married the Earl of Worcester taking Raglan to that family. The senior line by illegitimate descent was granted a revived Earldom in 1551. The Earls of the second creation became courtiers, acquired large estates at the Dissolution, and became a great Tudor family. **First MP 1460 for Herefordshire. Twenty-seven other MPs 1467-1650, many of them kts of the shire.**

1. William Herbert 6 Earl of Pembroke – Glamorganshire 1661-69
2. Thomas Herbert 8 Earl of Pembroke – Wilton 1679-81
3. Philip Herbert – Rye 1705-07
4. Thomas Herbert – Newport 1726-39
5. William Herbert – Wilton 1734-57
6. Nicholas Herbert – Newport 1740-54 Wilton 1757-75
7. George Herbert 11 Earl of Pembroke – Wilton 1780-84 1788-94
8. Sidney Herbert 1 Baron Herbert – S. Wiltshire 1832-61
9. Sidney Herbert 14 Earl of Pembroke – Wilton 1877-85 Croydon 1886-95
10. Sir Sidney Herbert 1 Bt – Scarborough & Whitby Div. N. R. Yorkshire 1922-31 Abbey Div. Westminster 1932-39

Seats: Wilton House, Wiltshire (medieval monastic building, acq. 1544, remod. soon after, rebuilt 1630-36, remod. 1648-50, 1801-11, and 1913, still own); Mount Merrion, Dublin (built early 18th c., inher. from Viscount Fitzwilliam 1833, sold 19th c., demolished c. 1986)
Estates: Bateman 44806 (E & I) 77720. Rental of £3,600 to £5,400 pa in c. 1600. Total income in c. 1650 was said to be £30,000 pa. Rubinstein – 11 Earl left £600,000 in probate in 1827. Worth £40,000,000 with 16,000 acres in 1990.
Titles: Baron Herbert 1551- E; Baron Herbert 1605- E; Baron Herbert of Lea 1861- UK; Baronet 1937-42
Peers: 12 peers 1660-1827 1833-62 1861-1945
6 Lds Lt 17th, 18th, 19th
2 in Cabinet 1690-1709 1852-55 1859-61
2 KG 18th, 19th
Notes: The 11 Earl left in 1827 the unentailed part of his estate (worth c. £600,000) to his younger son, Lord Herbert of Lea. 1 and 2 Earls of the 1st creation, 1, 2, 3, 4, 5, 7, 8, 9, 10, 11, 13 Earls and 1 Baron Herbert of Lea and two others in ODNB.

Earl of Carnarvon (1793- GB)

Origins: The 1 Earl of Carnarvon was the grandson of the 8 Earl of Pembroke, who married the daughter and heiress of Sir Robert Sawyer of Highclere. The Sawyers were Exchequer officials from the later 16th century, who purchased landed estates in 1623. **First MP 1624**. Speaker 1678 and later Attorney General. The Herberts succeeded to the estates in 1701. The 4 Earl married the sister and heiress of the 7 Earl of Chesterfield and succeeded to Bretby in 1871 (see Stanhope). Auberon Herbert succeeded as 9 Baron Lucas in 1905.

1. Sir Robert Sawyer – Chipping Wycombe 1673-79 University of Cambridge 1689-92
2. John Sawyer – Downton 1713-15
3. Robert Sawyer Herbert – Wilton 1722-68
4. Henry Herbert 1 Earl of Carnarvon – Wilton 1768-72 1772-80
5. Charles Herbert – Wilton 1775-80 1806-16
6. Henry Herbert 2 Earl of Carnarvon – Cricklade 1794-1811
7. Charles Herbert – Wilton 1806-07
8. William Herbert – Hampshire 1806-07 Cricklade 1811-12
9. Henry Herbert 3 Earl of Carnarvon – Wootton Bassett 1831-32
10. Edward Herbert – Callington 1831-32
11. Auberon Herbert – Nottingham 1870-74
12. Aubrey Herbert – S. Somerset 1911-18 Yeovil Div. Somerset 1918-23

Seats: Highclere Castle, Hampshire (Sawyers purch. 1671, built house soon after, passed by a mar. of 1691 to Herberts, remod. 1774-77, rebuilt 1842-50, remod. 1861-62 and 1890s, still own); Christian Malford, Wiltshire (old house, purch. 1749, sold 19th c.)
Estates: Bateman 35583 (E) 37211. Worth £20,000,000 with 10,000 acres in 1990.
Title: Baron Porchester 1780- GB
Peers: 7 peers 1780-1849 1852-1945 1905-16
2 Lds Lt 18th, 19th
2 in Cabinet 1866-67 1874-78 1885-86 1914-15
Notes: A grandson of the 4 Earl of Carnarvon, Auberon Herbert, whose mother was sister to the last Earl Cowper (see Cowper) and also heiress to the de Grey estate of Wrest Park, Bedfordshire, succeeded in 1905 as 8 Baron Lucas and 5 Baron Dingwall. 8 Baron Lucas, the 3, 4, and 5 Earls of Carnarvon and seven others in ODNB.

Marquess of Powis (1687-1748 E)

Origins: Descended from a younger son of the 1 Earl of Pembroke. The sister and heiress of the last Marquess married a Clive, who was created the Earl of Powis of the second creation (see Clive). **First MP 1597. Two further MPs 1620-59.**

1. Francis Herbert – Ludlow 1689-90 1698-1700 1701-05 1715-19
2. Henry Herbert 1 Earl of Powis – Bletchingley 1724-27 Ludlow 1727-43
3. Richard Herbert – Ludlow 1727-41 1743-54
4. Henry Herbert – Montgomery 1747-48
5. Francis Herbert – Montgomery 1748-54

Seats: Powis Castle, Montgomeryshire (medieval, purch. 1587, remod. 17th c. and 18th c., passed by mar of 1784 to the Clives); Oakley Park, Montgomeryshire (acq. by mar. c. 1600, passed to Clives 1784)
Estates: Worth £10,000 pa in 1688.
Titles: Baron Powis 1629-1748 E; Earl of Powis 1674-1748 E and 1748-1801 GB; Baronet 1622-1748
Peers: 6 peers 1660-78 1685-88 1722-48 1743-72 1776-1801
3 Lds Lt 17th, 18th, 19th
Notes: This family succeeded to the estates of the 4 and last Baron Herbert of Cherbury of the first creation in 1691. They remained Roman Catholic until 1748, when the recreated Earldom and estates went to a Protestant heir. The 1 Marquess was titular Duke of Powis in the Jacobite peerage. 2 Baron, 2 Earl, and 1 and 2 Marquesses and three others in ODNB.

Herbert

Origins: Descended from a younger son of the 4 Earl of Pembroke.

1. James Herbert – Wiltshire 1646 Queenborough 1659 1660-77
2. James Herbert – Queenborough 1677-81 Westbury 1685-87 Queenborough 1689-98 Aylesbury 1696-1704
3. James Herbert – Queenborough 1710-13 Amersham 1714-15 Oxfordshire 1715-21
4. James Herbert – Oxford 1739-40
5. Philip Herbert – Oxford 1740-49

Seat: Tythrop House, Buckinghamshire (built early 17th c., acq. by mar. 1650, remod. c. 1660, remod. 18th c., passed by inher. to Viscount Wenman 1749, that family held into 1920s)
Estates: Worth £2,000 pa in the 17th century.

Herbert

Origins: Descended from a younger brother of the 1 Earl of Pembroke of the 1 creation. **First MP 1547 for Monmouthshire. Five additional MPs 1558-1655, four of them kts of the shire**. Sir James Herbert left his estates to his daughter who married in 1698 Sir Thomas Powell 1 Bt (son of a judge).

1. Sir James Herbert – Monmouth 1685-87
2. Sir Thomas Powell 1 Bt – Monmouth 1705-08 Carmarthen 1710-15

Seats: Coldbrook Park, Monmouthshire (Herberts acq. 15th c., acq. by Powells by mar to Herbert heiress 1709, divided among heiresses and sold c. 1720); Broadway, Carmarthenshire (Powell seat, divided among heiresses and sold c. 1720)
Estates: Worth £3,000 pa in 1721.
Title: Baronet 1698-1721
Notes. On the extinction of the Baronetcy the estates were divided between three daughters.

Baron Herbert of Cherbury (Chirbury)
(1629-91 and 1694-1738 E)

Origins: Descended from a younger son of the Herberts of Coldbrook. **First MP 1553. Twelve further MPs 1553-1640, six of them kts of the shire**.

1. Sir Henry Herbert – Montgomery 1626 Bewdley 1640-42 1644 1661-73
2. Henry Herbert 4 Baron Herbert of Cherbury – Montgomery Boroughs 1665-78
3. Henry Herbert 1 Baron Herbert of Cherbury – Bewdley 1677-79 Worcester 1681 Bewdley 1689-94
4. Henry Herbert 2 Baron Herbert of Cherbury – Bewdley 1708-09

Seats: Chirbury, Shropshire (passed to the Powis line by inher. 1691); Montgomery Castle, Montgomeryshire (passed to Powis line by inher. 1691); Ribbesford House, Worcestershire (built c. 1535, purch. 1625, passed by inher. to Powis line 1691, sold 1760); Aston, Montgomeryshire (passed to Powis Line by inher. 1691)
Peers: 4 peers 1660-91 1694-1738
Notes: Title also spelled Chirbury. 1, 2, 3, and 4 Barons and 1 and 2 Barons of 2nd cr. and five others in ODNB.

Herbert

Origins: The founder was a cousin of the 3 Baron Herbert of Cherbury who sent him to Ireland to manage his estates there, acquired c. 1600. Some property purchased in 1656. Sheriff 1659. The family acquired Muckross by marriage to a McCarthy Mor heiress in c. 1700.

1. Edward Herbert – {Innistioge 1749-60 Tralee 1761-70}
2. Edward Herbert – Ludlow 1754-70
3. Thomas Herbert – Ludlow 1770-74
4. Henry Herbert – East Grinstead 1782-86 County Kerry 1806-12 Tralee 1812-13

5. Richard Herbert – {County Kerry 1783-90 Clogher 1790-97 Granard 1800}
6. Henry Herbert – County Kerry 1847-66
7. Sir Thomas Herbert – Dartmouth 1852-57
8. Henry Herbert – County Kerry 1866-80

Seat: Muckross Abbey (House), Kerry (old house, acq. by mar. c. 1700, rebuilt c. 1720-50, new house 1839-43, add. 1870, sold 1899, now owned by government)
Estates: Bateman 47238 (I) 10647. 1839 house cost £30,000.
1 Ld Lt 19th
1 in Cabinet 19th
Notes: Family bankrupt late 19th c. and estates sold. One in ODNB.

Earl of Torrington (1689-1716 E)

Origins: Descended from an uncle of the 1 Baron Herbert of Cherbury.

1. Arthur Herbert 1 Earl of Torrington – Dover 1685-87 Plymouth 1689
2. Charles Herbert – Montgomery 1685-87 1689-91
3. Sir Edward Herbert ("Earl of Portland") – Ludlow 1685

Seats: Oatlands Park, Surrey (built 15th c., rebuilt c. 1540, granted 1696, sold c. 1716); Aston, Montgomeryshire
Estates: Worth £6,000 pa in the early 18th c. Granted 10,000 acres worth £3,000 pa in 1690 by William III.
Peers: 1 peer 1689-1716
1 in Cabinet 1689-90
Notes: The 1 and last Earl left his estates to the 7 Earl of Lincoln (see Pelham). The 1 Earl's brother was the Jacobite Earl of Portland. 1 Earl and one other ODNB.

HERLE

Origins: Acquired Prideaux by marriage at the end of the 14th century. **First MP 1410. Another MP 1558.**

1. Edward Herle – Bossiney 1640 Fowey 1654 1660 Grampound 1689-90
2. Thomas Herle – Grampound 1659 1660 Tregony 1661-79
3. Nicholas Herle – Grampound 1679-81
4. Edward Herle – Launceston 1713-21

Seats: Prideaux, Cornwall (acq. by mar. at the end of the 14th c. and built 14th c., sold 1806); Landrew (Landue), Cornwall (acq. by mar. 1600s, built late 17th c., estate

broken up among heiresses 1737); Trenowth, Cornwall (acq. by mar. mid-16th c., inher. by heiresses 1806)
Estates: Worth £4,753 pa in 1806 including timber and mines (J. Polsue, *A Complete Parochial History of the County of Cornwall*, III, 1870, 190)
Notes: Male line extinct 1737. One in ODNB.

HERNE (Hyrne) [Napier]

Herne

Origins: The founder was a Merchant Taylor and Alderman in London (d. 1625). Another family member was the head of a leading firm in the peninsular trade in the 17th century, Alderman 1686. A number of the MPs below continued to stay engaged in business into the 18th century. **First MP, in a disputed election, 1628.**

1. Sir Nathaniel Herne – Dartmouth 1679
2. Sir Joseph Herne – Dartmouth 1689-99
3. Frederick Herne – Dartmouth 1698-1714
4. Nathaniel Herne – Dartmouth 1701-14
5. Thomas Herne – Bodmin 1706-08 Tregony 1708-10
6. Joseph Herne – Dartmouth 1715-22
7. Francis Herne – Bedford 1754-68 Camelford 1774-76

Seat: Luton Hoo, Bedfordshire (medieval house, acq. by mar. c. 1750, sold 1762 for £94,700)
Estates: In 1699 Sir Joseph Herne was worth £200,000.
Notes: A distant relative (Hyrne), a rich merchant and landowner in Norwich, **MP 1614-26.** Two in ODNB.

Napier

Origins: A cadet of the Napiers of Middlemarsh, Dorset (see Napier). The 4 Bt was the grandson of a successful Turkey merchant and grocer who had purchased Luton Hoo in 1601. Baronet 1611. **First MP 1626.** On the death of the last Napier Baronet Luton Hoo passed to the Hernes by marriage.

1. Sir John Napier 4 Bt – Bedfordshire 1664-78

Seat: Luton Hoo, Bedfordshire (purch. 1601, passed by mar. to Hernes after 1748)
Title: Baronet 1611-1748; 1661-1748
Notes: 1 Bt and two others in ODNB.

HERON

Heron

Origins: A powerful medieval family seated at Chipchase and Ford Castle in Northumberland from at least the 14th century. **First MP 1371 for Northumberland. Five additional MPs 1379-1555.** This line was a cadet of the stem family.

1. Peter Heron – Newton 1806-14

Seats: Moor(e) Hall, Cheshire (built early 18th c., acq. by mar. sec. half 18th c., sold mid-19th c.); Daresbury Hall, Cheshire (purch. c. 1755, built 1759, sold c. 1800)

Heron

Origins: A cadet line that produced local officials in Newark and later moved to Kent. 1 Bt was Chief Secretary to the Lord Lieutenant of Ireland in 1777.

1. Henry Heron – Boston 1713-22 Lincolnshire 1722-27
2. Sir Richard Heron 1 Bt – {Lisburn 1777-83}
3. Sir Robert Heron 2 Bt – Great Grimsby 1812-18 Peterborough 1819-47

Seats: Cressy Hall, Lincolnshire (medieval, acq. 1600, house rebuilt 17th c., burned 1789, sold 1794); Stubton Hall, Lincolnshire (acq. and built 17th c., rebuilt 1813-14, passed out of family 1854, school); Chilham Castle, Kent (medieval, rebuilt 1616, purch. 1775, sold 1794)
Estates: 3601 (E) 5586
Title: Baronet 1778-1854
Notes: On the death of the 2nd and last Bt in 1854 the estates passed to George Neville. 1 and 2 Bts in ODNB.

HERSCHELL

Baron Herschell (1886-2008 UK)

Origins: The 1 Baron was a lawyer and Lord Chancellor. He was the son of a missionary and grandson of a brewer, from a Polish Jewish family. He was born in Poland.

1. Farrer Herschell 1 Baron Herschell – Durham 1874-85

Seat: Manor House, West Hendred, Berkshire (leased)
Estates: 1 Baron left £153,000 in 1899.

Peers: 3 peers 1886-1945
Notes: 1 Baron and one other in ODNB.

HERVEY (Harvey) [Aston, Bathurst, Bruce, Carr, Davers, Jermyn] *ENGLAND & IRELAND*

Marquess of Bristol (1826- UK)

Origins: Emerged in Bedfordshire in the 13th century. **First MP 1386 for the county. Seven additional MPs 1472-1628.** Married the heiress to Ickworth 1467. Rose high in royal service under Henry VIII.

1. John Hervey – Hythe 1661-79
2. Sir Thomas Hervey – Bury St. Edmunds 1679-81 1685-87 1689-90
3. John Hervey 1 Earl of Bristol – Bury St. Edmunds 1694-1703
4. Carr Hervey Baron Hervey – Bury St. Edmunds 1713-22
5. John Hervey Baron Hervey – Bury St. Edmunds 1725-33
6. Thomas Hervey – Bury St. Edmunds 1733-47
7. Felton Hervey – Bury St. Edmunds 1747-61
8. Augustus Hervey 3 Earl of Bristol – Bury St. Edmunds 1757-63 Saltash 1763-68 Bury St. Edmunds 1768-75
9. Frederick Hervey 1 Marquess of Bristol – Bury St. Edmunds 1796-1803
10. Frederick Hervey 2 Marquess of Bristol – Bury St. Edmunds 1826-59
11. Lord Alfred Hervey – Brighton 1842-57 Bury St. Edmunds 1859-64
12. Frederick Hervey 3 Marquess of Bristol – W. Suffolk 1859-64
13. Lord Augustus Hervey – W. Suffolk 1864-75
14. Lord Francis Hervey – Bury St. Edmunds 1874-80 1885-92
15. Frederick Hervey 4 Marquess of Bristol – Bury St. Edmunds 1906-07

Seats: Ickworth, Suffolk (acq. by mar. 1467, rebuilt 1794-1830, remod. 1907-09, NT 1956); Ballyscullion, Londonderry (built sec. half 18th c. but not complete, passed to Bruce family 1803, demolished soon after); Downhill House (Castle), Londonderry (built 1776-85, passed to Bruce family 1803, dismantled 1950, ruin); Rushbrooke Hall, Suffolk (built c. 1550, remod. 18th c., acq. by mar. 1806, exchanged for another estate 1808, abandoned, fire and demolished 1961)
Estates: Bateman 32014 (E) 41270. Income of over £10,000 pa in 1775. Worth £20,000,000 or more with 4,500 acres in 1990. Bankrupt in 1999. 20,000 acres of the Hervey estates were saved from the wreckage caused by the 7 Marquess's outrageous behavior and are under the control of the trustees of the 8 Marquess.
Titles: Baron Hervey 1620-42 I; Baron Hervey 1703- E; Earl of Bristol 1714- GB; Earl Jermyn 1826- UK; Baronet 1619-42
Peers: 9 peers 1703-51 1733-1945

1 Ld Lt 19th, 20th
3 in Cabinet 1740-42 1766-67 1766-67 1768-70
Notes: From 1628 every direct male descendent of Sir William Hervey down to the 4 Marquess of Bristol in 1907 sat for Bury St. Edmunds or Suffolk with the exception of the 4 Earl. The 6 and 7 Marquesses were imprisoned as criminals in the 20th c. 1 Baron (of Kidbrooke), 1, 2, 3 and 4 Earls and 2 Baron (of Ickworth) and 7 Marquess and eight others in ODNB.

<u>Hervey-Bathurst</u>

Origins: Descended from a younger son of the 1 Earl of Bristol. They inherited property by marriage from the Bathursts (see Bathurst).

1. Sir Frederick Hervey-Bathurst 4 Bt – S. Wiltshire 1861-65

Seat: Clarendon Park, Wiltshire (acq. by Bathursts c. 1710, built 1717-37, passed Herveys by mar. 1801, remod. 1814, sold c. 1920)
Estates: Bateman 10012 (E) 8936
Title: Baronet 1818-

<u>Earl of St. Albans</u> (1660-84 E)

Origins: Old gentry who rose high as courtiers and through royal favor under the early Stuarts. **First MP 1584 for Suffolk. Five additional MPs 1589-1659, three of them for Bury St. Edmunds**. On the death of the 1 Earl of St. Albans, the Barony of Jermyn passed to his nephew. His daughter married Sir Robert Davers 2 Bt of Rougham Hall. Cheveley Park passed to the Dukes of Rutland (see Manners). The rest of the Jermyn estates passed to the Earls of Bristol by the marriage with Elizabeth Davers, sister of the 5 Bt.

1. Thomas Jermyn 2 Baron Jermyn – Bury St. Edmunds 1679-81

Seats: Cheveley Park, Cambridgeshire (acq. 17th c.?, rebuilt 1670s, passed to Manners family 1750); Rushbrooke Hall, Suffolk (acq. by 1286, built c. 1550, passed to Davers by mar. 1708, passed to Rushbrookes in 1806, sold 1919, destroyed by fire 1961); Torksey Castle, Lincolnshire (acq. and built c. 1560s, wrecked 1640s, ruin, sold 1743)
Estates: Worth £15,000 pa in 1703.
Titles: Baron Jermyn 1643-1708 E; Baron Dover 1685-1708 E
Peers: 3 peers 1660-1708
1 Ld Lt 17th
1 KG 17th
Notes: 3 Baron and 1 Earl and 2 others in ODNB.

Davers

Origins: Went to Barbados in the mid-17th century and became leading planters with estates worth £30,000. Returned to England in 1680 and purchased Rougham. Succeeded to part of the Jermyn inheritance through marriage (see above).

1. Sir Robert Davers 2 Bt – Bury St. Edmunds 1689-1701 1703-05 Suffolk 1705-22
2. Sir Jermyn Davers 4 Bt – Bury St. Edmunds 1722-27 Suffolk 1727-43
3. Sir Charles Davers 6 Bt – Weymouth & Melcombe Regis 1768-74 Bury St. Edmunds 1774-1802

Seats: Rougham Hall, Suffolk (built 16th c., purch. 1680, sold c. 1705, bombed 1940); Rushbrooke Hall, Suffolk (built c. 1550, acq. by mar. 1708, remodel. 1730s, passed by mar. to 1 Marquess of Bristol 1806, - another source says Rushbrookes acq. it 1806)
Title: Baronet 1682-1806

Aston

Origins: An old gentry family. **First MP 1604 for Cheshire. One additional MP 1640**. A younger son of the 1 Earl of Bristol married Catherine Aston and took the name Aston in 1730. Their descendents lived at Aston Hall from 1744.

1. Sir Thomas Aston 4 Bt – Liverpool 1729-34 St. Albans 1734-41
2. Sir Willoughby Aston 5 Bt – Nottingham 1754-61

Seats: Aston Hall, Cheshire (built 1577, rebuilt 1668, passed by inher. to Chetwynd-Talbots 1839, demolished 1938); Risley Hall, Derbyshire (built c. 1513 by Willoughbys, passed to Astons 1723, demolished 1757, sold 1770)
Title: Baronet 1628-1815
Notes: 1 Bt and two others in ODNB.

Bruce

Origins: A younger son of the Bruces of Stenhouse emigrated from Scotland to Ireland as a clergyman and settled in County Down in the early-mid 17th century. His great-grandson married 1762 the youngest daughter of a younger son of the 1 Earl of Bristol. The 4 Earl (Bishop) of Bristol left his Irish estates to his cousin the 1 Bruce Bt. The 3 Bt married the heiress to Clifton Hall in 1842.

1. Sir Stewart Bruce 1 Bt – {Lisburne 1798-1800}
2. Sir Henry Bruce 3 Bt – Coleraine 1862-74 1880-85

Seats: Downhill (Castle), Londonderry (built 1776-85, inher. from Herveys 1803, burned 1851, rebuilt 1870-74, family departed 1922, sold 1946, dismantled 1950, NT ruin); Ballyscullion, Londonderry (inher. 1803, dismantled 1813, new house c. 1850, sold 20th c.); Clifton Hall, Nottinghamshire (inher. by mar. 1869, sold 1958, school)
Estates: Bateman 21514 (I) 12409
Title: Baronet 1804- ; 1812-41
2 Lds Lt 19th, 20th
Notes: The 3 Bt married in 1842 Marianne Clifton eventual heiress to Clifton Hall in 1869 (see Clifton). A Bruce younger son in the 17th established a cadet line at Benburb (The Manor House), Tyrone 9230 (I) 8322.

Carr (Carre)

Origins: The founder was a merchant of staple who acquired a Lincolnshire estate in 1503. As local officials they used their influence to gain further property at the Dissolution. On the death of the last Carr Bt his estates passed by marriage to the 1 Earl of Bristol by his wife, sister of the 4 Bt. **First MP 1559**.

1. Sir Robert Carr 3 Bt – Lincolnshire 1665-81

Seat: Aswarby Hall, Lincolnshire (purch. and built late 17th c., passed to Herveys 1695, demolished 1952)
Estates: Worth £4,000 pa in 1660.
Title: Baronet 1611-95

Hervey (Harvey)

Origins: The founder was a lawyer in the later 16th century. **First MP 1597**. The family acquired recognition from the Herveys of Ickworth as "cousins". (Hayton, *The House of Commons*, IV, 351)

1. Stephen Hervey – Reigate 1698-1707
2. John Hervey – Reigate 1739-41 Wallingford 1754-64

Seat: East Betchworth (Beechworth), Surrey (acq. part of manor 1409, house built mid-17th c., manor acq. by mar. 1750, passed to the Bouveries 1786)
Notes: One in ODNB.

HESKETH [Fermor, Fleetwood]

Baron Hesketh (1935- UK)

Origins: The Hesketh acquired Rufford by a marriage of 1276. A Hesketh fought at Crécy in 1346. **First MP 1360 for Lancashire. Two additional MPs 1586-1611, both for the county**. The 5 Bt married in 1846 Lady Anna Fermor daughter and co-heir of the 5 Earl of Pomfret. The family assumed the name Fermor-Hesketh and inherited Easton Neston.

1. Thomas Hesketh – Preston 1722-27
2. Sir Thomas Hesketh 5 Bt – Preston 1862-72
3. Thomas Fermor-Hesketh 1 Baron Hesketh – Enfield Div. Middlesex 1922-23

Seats: Rufford Hall, Lancashire (estate acq. by mar. 1276 c., Old Hall built 1490-1523, reconstructed 1662, remod. 1821-22, given to NT 1936. New Hall built in park 1761, remod. 1789, sold later 1930s, hospital); Easton Neston, Northamptonshire (medieval, built c. 1682-1711, inher. by mar. from Fermors 1857, sold 2005); Martholme, Lancashire (acq. 1289, medieval and c. 1500, remod. 1561, 1577, and 1607, became farm house, sold 1818)
Estates: Bateman 15193 (E) 31633
Title: Baronet 1761-
Peers: 2 peers 1935-45
Notes: Remained Roman Catholic in the 16th and 17th centuries, hence the dearth of MPs. Conformed late 17th c. Two in ODNB.

Hesketh-Fleetwood

Origins: A Hesketh of Rufford married the Fleetwood heiress in 1733. (see Fleetwood)

1. Sir Peter Hesketh Fleetwood 1 Bt – Preston 1832-47
2. Roger Fleetwood-Hesketh – Southport 1952-59

Seats: Rossall, Lancashire (built prob. 16th c., remod. 18th c., passed by mar. from Fleetwoods to Hesketh mid-19th c., demolished 1928); Meols Hall, Lancashire (built late 12th c., passed by inher. via mar. ever since, Hesketh acq. 1563, add. 1695, Fleetwoods in 1733 when the old house demolished, farm house, add. 1938, reconstructed 1960-64, still own)
Estates: Bateman 2069 (E) 4322. Owned 6,000 acres in 2001.
Titles: Baronet 1611-1802; 1838-80
Notes: Family nearly bankrupted through speculation and much land sold mid-19th c. 1 Bt 2nd cr. and two others in ODNB.

Earl of Pomfret (1721-1867 GB)

Origins: Originally clothiers at Witney, Oxfordshire in the late 15th century. In the early 16th century made a fortune in wool and silks as a Merchant of Staple of Calais and made two good marriages. Amassed large estates. High Sheriff 1557. **First MP 1539. Five further MPs 1553-1621, three kts of the shire**.

1. William Fermor 1 Baron Leominster – Northampton 1670-79

Seat: Easton Neston, Northamptonshire (medieval, purch. 1535, rebuilt c. 1682-1711, passed by mar. to Hesketh's 1857, see above)
Titles: Baron Leominster 1692-1867 E; Baronet 1641-1867
Peers: 6 peers 1692-1711 1719-85 1789-1833 1845-67
Notes: 1 Bt and 1 Baron and 4 Earl and four others in ODNB.

HEVENINGHAM

Origins: At Heveningham since the reign of King John. **First MP 1399 for Suffolk. Two further MPs 1628-53, one for Norfolk.**

1. Henry Heveningham – Thetford 1685 Dunwich 1695-1700

Seats: Hockwold (Hockwood) Hall, Norfolk (built 16th c., confiscated 1660); Heveningham Hall, Suffolk (acq. r. King John, confiscated 1660); Ketteringham, Norfolk (acq. 15th c., sold 1717)
Notes: William Heveningham was a regicide and his estates were confiscated 1660. The family became extinct in the male line in 1700. Two in ODNB.

HEWITT I (Hewett)

Viscount Hewitt of Gowran (1689-89 I)

Origins: Lord Mayor of London 1559. The father of the 1 Viscount was a London merchant and moneylender. Sheriff 1638. Kt 1641. **First MP 1624 for Windsor. One additional MP 1628 also for Windsor**.

1. Joseph Hewitt – {Belfast 1745-56}

Seat: Pishiobury, Hertfordshire (built 1608, purch. 1635 for £16,500, sold c. 1689)
Title: Baronet 1660-89
Peer: {1 peer 1689}
Notes: Pishiobury passed to the sister of the 1 Viscount, Lady Reade, who sold it.

HEWITT II *IRELAND*

Viscount Lifford (1781- I)

Origins: The 1 Viscount was the son of a Coventry draper. Lawyer. Lord Chancellor of Ireland 1768. Sheriff 1815.

1. James Hewitt 1 Viscount Lifford – Coventry 1761-66
2. Joseph Hewitt – {Belfast 1784-91}

Seat: Meenglas (Meen Glas), Donegal (acq. later 18th c., 19th c. house, demolished 1948); Newtonpark, Dublin
Estates: 11755 (I) 1148 in 1878
Title: Baron Lifford 1768- I
Peers: {2 peers 1768-1800} 1 Irish Rep peer 1856-87
Notes: 1 Viscount in ODNB.

HEYGATE *ENGLAND & IRELAND*

Origins: To Ireland with the military in 1596. Businessmen in the 18th century, first in hosiery manufacture and then banking. Purchased landed estates in Essex and Leicestershire. The first MP was a banker and Lord Mayor of London 1822.

1. Sir William Heygate 1 Bt – Sudbury 1818-26
2. Sir Frederick Heygate 2 Bt – County Londonderry 1859-74
3. William Heygate – Leicester 1861-65 Stanford 1868 S. Leicestershire 1870-80

Seats: Bellarena, Londonderry (Gages acq. mid-17th c. and passed by mar. 1851 to Heygates, sold post 1975); Holwood House, Kent (built 1823-26, leased only)
Estates: Bateman 8845 (I) 4287
Title: Baronet 1831-
Notes: The widow of the 1 Bt divided the family estates among four children, which suggests that the English estates were either sold or parceled out in small units. One in ODNB.

HEYSHAM

Origins: The first MP was a Barbados merchant in London and eminent agent for the colony c. 1700. Alderman 1720. The second MP was also a West Indian merchant.

1. Robert Heysham – Lancaster 1698-1715 London 1715-22
2. William Heysham – Lancaster 1705-16
3. William Heysham – Lancaster 1716-27

Seat: Stagenhoe Park, Hertfordshire (built mid-17th c., purch. 1703, fire 1737, rebuilt c. 1740, sold 1833)
Estates: The first MP was worth £45,000 in 1723 (about a third of the value invested in land). Estates passed by mar. to Thorntons, who took name Heysham 1734.

HICKS-BEACH (Hickes)

<u>Earl of St. Aldwyn</u> (1915- UK)

Origins: The first Hicks of note was the son of an ironmonger and mercer in London in the 16th c. **MP 1626**. He was a barrister and secretary to Lord Burghley. Kt 1604. A younger brother, a mercer and moneylender, was created Viscount Campden 1628 (see Noel). He married an heiress worth £100,000. The elder brother was the ancestor of the Hicks-Beach line. A younger son of the 6 Baronet married 1779 Henrietta Beach, an heiress. Their grandson succeeded as 8 Baronet. He assumed the name Hicks-Beach in 1790. His uncle took the name Beach only and was seated at Oakley Hall.

1. John Hicks – Fowey 1701-08 (possible)
2. Michael Hicks Beach – Cirencester 1794-1818
3. William Beach – Malmesbury 1812-17
4. Sir Michael Hicks-Beach 8 Bt – E. Gloucestershire 1854
5. William Beach – N. Hampshire 1857-85 Andover Div. Hampshire 1885-1901
6. Michael Hicks-Beach 1 Earl of St. Aldwyn – E. Gloucestershire 1864-85 W. Bristol 1885-1906
7. Michael Hicks-Beach Viscount Quenington – Tewkesbury Div. Gloucestershire 1906-16
8. William Hicks-Beach – Tewkesbury Div. Gloucestershire 1916-18
9. William Hicks-Beach – Cheltenham 1950-64

Seats: Williamstrip Park, Gloucestershire (built c. 1600, rebuilt c. 1720, add. c. 1771, purch. 1785, remod. 1791, expanded 1896, partially demolished 1946, still own); Witcombe Park, Gloucestershire (acq. early 17th c., built 1704, demolished 1880s, rebuilt 1891, still own); Netheravon House, Wiltshire (Beach seat acq. by mar. 1779, built c. 1780, add. 1791, sold 1898); Oakley Hall, Hampshire (Bramston family acq. 18th c. and built house 1795, passed to Beach family by inher. 1832, sold 1940, hotel); Keevil House, Wiltshire (purch. by Beach family 1681, later Hicks Beach, sold 1911)
Estates: Bateman 11334 (E) 10467 and 7051 (E) 8692. Owned 3,000 acres in 1973.
Titles: Viscount St. Aldwyn 1906- UK; Baronet 1619-
Peers: 2 peers 1906-16 1936-45
1 in Cabinet 1874-80 1885-92 1895-1902
Notes: 1 Viscount Campden and 1 and 2 Earls and one other in ODNB.

HILL I [Blundell, Brand, Dunbar, Ellis, Ellys, Hampden, Hobart, Lear, Morley, Sandys, Tipping, Trevor] *IRELAND, ENGLAND & WALES*

Marquess of Downshire (1789- I)

Origins: Moyses Hill, younger son of a Devon gentry family, went to Ireland as a soldier 1573. He gained his first grant of land 1592. Judicious marriages followed. Provost Marshall of Ulster under James I. Leased and purchased more land, building up a great estate. His son expanded the family holdings through speculation and political adroitness. His son married two heiresses. (Maguire, *The Downshire Estates*, 2-7) **First {MP 1634}. One additional {MP 1654}.**

1. Moyses Hill – {Drogheda 1661-66}
2. William Hill – {Ballyshannon 1661-66}
3. Arthur Hill – {County Down 1661-66}
4. Conway Hill – {County Antrim 1665-66}
5. Michael Hill – Saltash 1692-95 {Hillsborough 1695-99}
6. Arthur Hill – {Carlingford 1703-04}
7. Trevor Hill 1 Viscount Hillsborough – {Hillsborough 1713-15 County Down 1715-17} Aylesbury 1715-22 Malmesbury 1722
8. Wills Hill 1 Marquess of Downshire – Warwickshire 1741-56
9. Arthur Hill 2 Marquess of Downshire – Lostwithiel 1774-80 {County Down 1776-93} Malmesbury 1780-84
10. Arthur Hill 2 Baron Sandys – County Down 1817-36
11. Lord George Hill – Carrickfergus 1830-32
12. Marcus Hill 3 Baron Sandys – Newry 1832-34 Evesham 1837-41
13. Arthur Hill 4 Marquess of Downshire – County Down 1836-45
14. Arthur Hill-Trevor 1 Baron Trevor – County Down 1845-80
15. Lord Arthur Hill-Trevor – County Down 1880-85 W. Down 1885-98 1907-08
16. Arthur Hill-Trevor – W. Down 1898-1905

Seats: Hillsborough Castle, Down (purch. 1616, fort built 1630, house built later 17th c., fire c. 1730, rebuilt 1749, add. 1797, add. 1830s-40s, sold 1922 to government); Murlough, Down (built 1860, resident to 1970s, donated to Church as a retreat late 20th c.); Easthampstead Park, Berkshire (passed by mar. from Trumbulls (see) who had acq. it in 1629 to the Hills 1769, became principal residence later 19th c., demolished 1860, rebuilt 1864, leased out early 20th c., sold after 1945, institutional use); Blesington, Wicklow (built c. 1670, acq. by mar. from Dunbars 1778, burned 1798); Edenderry (Blundell Manor), King's County (built 17th c., demolished 1691, estate inher. by mar. from Blundells via Sandys family 1786, held into 20th c.); Dundrum Castle, Down (medieval, Blundell seat from 1636, slighted mid-17th c., passed to Sandys and thence

to Downshires 1797 by inher., sold to state 1954); Clifton Castle, Yorkshire (built 1802-10, purch. 1963, still own)
Estates: Bateman 120189 (E & I) 96691. Worth £4,000 pa in 1713 and £40,000 pa in 1800. Held 50,825 acres 1790.
Titles: Viscount Hillsborough 1717- I; Earl of Hillsborough 1751- I; Baron Harwich 1756- GB; Earl of Hillsborough 1772- GB; Baron Sandys 1802- UK; Baron Trevor 1880- UK
Peers: {3 peers 1717-1800} 14 peers 1756-1801 1809-74 1836-1945 1880-1945 1892-1945
1 Ld Lt 19th
1 in Cabinet 1763-66 1768-72 1779-82
1 KP 19th
Notes: The family continued to make large purchases of land in the 18th century and beyond. The 3 Marquess spent £176,000 on expansion in the first half of the 19th century. 1 Marquess and one other in ODNB.

Dunbar

Origins: The first eminent Dunbar was Archbishop of Armagh 1682-1702. Charles Dunbar {MP} left his estates to the 1 Earl of Hillsborough to whom he was related through his grandmother.

1. David Dunbar – {Blessington 1719-27}
2. Charles Dunbar – {Blessington 1771-78}

Seat: Blesington, Wicklow (built c. 1670, acq. by mar. from Stewart Earls of Blesington – see Boyle – 1769, passed by mar. to Hills 1778, burned 1798)
Estates: Worth £10,000 pa. in 1778.

Viscount Dungannon (1662-1706 I and 1766-1862 I)

Origins: The Trevors descend from Tudor Trevor (fl. 940) reputed King of much of Wales. His son inherited the estate that is now Brynkinalt (d. 1037). Sir Edward Trevor, who built Brynkinalt House, went to Ireland in 1598 and acquired estates there. His son was created Viscount Dungannon in 1662. (*Dictionary of Welsh Biography*, 978ff.) **First {MP 1613}. Two additional {MPs 1634-39}.** Anne Trevor, heiress of the last Trevor of Brynkinalt, married Michael Hill of Hillsborough. Their son Trevor Hill was 1 Viscount Hillsborough (see above). A younger son, Arthur, was 1 Viscount Dungannon of the second creation. On the extinction of this line in 1862 the estates passed to Lord Arthur Hill, younger son of the 3 Marquess of Downshire, who was created Baron Trevor in 1880 (see above).

1. Marcus Trevor 1 Viscount Dungannon – {County Down 1639 1661-62}
2. Marcus Trevor – {County Down 1665-66}

3. Sir John Trevor – Castle Rising 1673-79 Bere Alston 1679-81 Denbighshire 1681 Denbigh 1685-87 Yarmouth (IoW) 1690-95 {Newry 1692-93}
4. Arthur Hill-Trevor 1 Viscount Dungannon – {Hillsborough 1715-27 County Down 1727-66}
5. Arthur Trevor – {Hillsborough 1761-68 1769-70}
6. Arthur Hill-Trevor 3 Viscount Dungannon – New Romney 1830-31 Durham 1831-32 1835-41 1843

Seats: Brynkinalt, Denbighshire (acq. medieval period, built 1612, remod. 1808, still own); Ros(e)trevor, Down (owned from early 17th c., sold 1850); Belvoir Park, Down (built 1740s, sold 1811, demolished 1961); Wicken Park, Northamptonshire (built 1717, add. 1765, leased 1830s)
Estates: Bateman 23694 (E, W, & I) 17700. Irish estates worth £6,000 pa in 1833.
Title: Baron Trevor 1662-1706 I
Peers: {4 peers 1662-70 1695-1706 1766-71 1784-1800} Irish Rep peer 1855-62
Notes: It was said (*Country Life*, 22, p. 348) that the Trevor genealogy "soars into the clouds like Jack's beanstalk, and a body climbing it to the top might find himself in Eden garden." In fact, only a few other existing families in the British Isles or Europe can trace a more ancient trajectory – the O'Neills and Tracys and perhaps one or two others. Trevors also proliferated in England in the Tudor and Stuart period as soldiers, sea captains, and a judge in the Ship Money case.

Viscount Hampden of Glynde (1776-1824 GB)

Origins: The Hampdens were seated at Hampden since before the Conquest (Roskell, Clark, and Rawcliffe, *The House of Commons*, III, 277). **First MP 1351 for Buckinghamshire. Fourteen additional MPs 1399-1643, nine of them for Buckinghamshire**. A younger line of the Trevors of Brynkinalt inherited the estates of John Hampden "The Patriot" after his male descendents became extinct. Sir John Trevor married Anne Hampden of Hampden. The elder branch descended from this marriage was seated at Glynde, Sussex and inherited from the Morleys (see below). The Trevors of Trevelyan of ancient lineage (cadet of the Brynkinalt family c. 1500, see also Boscawen) **elected six MPs 1593-1659**.

1. Sir John Trevor – Flintshire 1646-48 1654 1656 1659 Arundel 1660 Great Bedwyn 1663-72
2. Richard Hampden – Buckinghamshire 1656 Wendover 1660-81 Buckinghamshire 1681 Wendover 1685-87 1689-90 Buckinghamshire 1690-95
3. John Hampden – Buckinghamshire 1679-81 Wendover 1681 1685-87
4. Thomas Trevor 1 Baron Trevor – Plympton 1692-98 Lewes 1701

5. Richard Hampden – Wendover 1701-08 Buckinghamshire 1708-10 Berwick-on-Tweed 1711-15 Buckinghamshire 1715-22 Wendover 1722-27 Buckinghamshire 1727-28
6. John Trevor – Sussex 1705-08 Lewes 1712-19
7. John Hampden – Wendover 1734-54
8. John Trevor – Lewes 1738-43
9. John Trevor 3 Baron Trevor – New Woodstock 1746-53
10. Thomas Trevor Hampden 2 Viscount Hampden – Lewes 1768-74

Seats: (Great) Hampden House, Buckinghamshire (acq. pre-Conquest, medieval house, new house built 14th c., add. later 16th c., rebuilt 17th c., remod. 18th c., passed to Earls of Buckinghamshire by mar. (of 1655) in 1824, see below); Glynde Place, Sussex (built c. 1569-79 by Morleys, estate passed to Trevors by mar. 1679, remod. 18th c., passed to Brands by mar. 1824, see below); Plas Teg, Flintshire (purch. and built 1610, sold 1930); Trevalyn Hall, Denbighshire (acq. by mar. late 15th c., built 1576, sold 20th c., now flats)
Estates: Worth £1,500 pa in 1643. Rubinstein – 2 Hampden Viscount and 5 Baron Trevor left £160,000 in probate in 1824 and 3 Viscount and 6 Baron left £250,000 also in 1824.
Titles: Baron Trevor 1712-1824
Peers: 6 peers 1712-1824
1 in Cabinet 1668-72 1726-30
Notes: The last Trevor died in 1743. The Welsh estates passed to sisters. Glynde went to a second cousin once removed, Richard Trevor, Bishop of St. Davids. His brother was 1 Viscount Hampden in 1776. The last Viscount bequeathed Glynde to Henry Brand 21 Baron Dacre, great grandson of John Morley Trevor.

<u>Morley</u>

Origins: The Morleys acquired Glynde in the mid-15th century by marriage with the heiress of the Waleys, there by the 12th century. **First MP 1435. Five additional MPs 1553-1648**. They were active in the iron industry in the 16th century. The last Morley bequeathed all his property to his maternal cousin John Trevor (see above).

1. Robert Morley – Lewes 1640-53 Rye 1654 Sussex 1654 1656 1659 Rye 1660 1661-67
2. Robert Morley – Seaford 1671
3. William Morley – Lewes 1679

Seat: Glynde Place, Sussex (built c. 1579, passed by mar. to Trevors 1679).

Earl of Buckinghamshire (1746- GB)

Origins: The ancestors of the Hobarts can be traced to 1389. Granted arms in the 15th century. **First MP 1467. Four additional MPs 1589-1647.** Numerous lawyers in the 16th century and first half of the 17th century. Attorney General to Henry VII 1486. Lord Chief Justice 1611. Sat in Cromwell's House of Lords. Sir John Hobart 2 Bt married Mary Hampden. Their descendent, the 5 Earl of Buckinghamshire, succeeded to the Hampden estates on the extinction of the Viscounts Hampden of Glynde in 1824.

1. Sir John Hobart 3 Bt – Norfolk 1654 1656 1673-81
2. Sir Henry Hobart 4 Bt – Kings Lynn 1681 Norfolk 1689-90 Bere Alston 1694-95 Norfolk 1695-98
3. John Hobart 1 Earl of Buckinghamshire – St. Ives 1715-27 Norfolk 1727-28
4. John Hobart 2 Earl of Buckinghamshire – Norwich 1747-56
5. George Hobart 3 Earl of Buckinghamshire – St. Ives 1754-61 Bere Alston 1761-80
6. Henry Hobart – Norwich 1786-99
7. Robert Hobart 4 Earl of Buckinghamshire – {Portarlington 1784-90 Armagh 1790-97} Bramber 1788-90 Lincoln 1790-96
8. George Hobart 5 Earl of Buckinghamshire – St. Michael 1812-13
9. Sir Henry Ellis – Boston 1820-21 (illegitimate son of 4 Earl of Buckinghamshire)
10. Sir Robert Hobart 1 Bt – New Forest Div. Hampshire 1906-10

Seats: Blickling Hall, Norfolk (medieval, purch. 1616, built 1619-28, remod. c. 1765 and c. 1785, passed 1793 by heiress to the Suffields and then in 1850 to the 8 Marquess of Lothian (see Kerr), NT 1940); (Great) Hampden House, Buckinghamshire (acq. by mar. 1824 – see above, remod. 18th c., family depart 1938, sold 1985, offices); Fordell Castle (House), Fife (built c. 1567-80, rebuilt c. 1760, add. c. 1855, inher. by mar. 1903 from a family that had held the estate since the beginning of the 16th c., sold, demolished 1963); Hales Hall, Norfolk (medieval, acq. 1478, built 16th c., sold 1647); Intwood House, Norfolk (built c. 1550, purch. c. 1680s, sold 1779); Nocton Hall, Lincolnshire (orig. built 16th c., rebuilt c. 1625, inher. by mar. by the Hobarts 1742, passed to Robinson (1 Earl of Ripon) family by mar. 1816)
Estates: Bateman 5207 (E & I) 5890
Titles: Baron Hobart 1728- GB; Baronet 1611- ; 1914-
Peers: 8 peers 1728-1804 1798-1945
1 Ld Lt 18th
2 in Cabinet 1777-80 1789-93 1801-05 1812-16
Notes: Sat in Cromwell's House of Lords as Lord Hobart. In 1903 the Hobarts inherited Fordell Castle from the Hendersons of Fordell (began as merchants in Edinburgh in the 14th and 15th c.). Two Hendersons served as **Scottish MPs [1506] and [1543 and 1546].** In 1793, the 2 Earl of Buckinghamshire divided the family estates among his four daughters. His half-brother, the 3 Earl, was rescued by inheriting the Ellys estates

and by his wife's skill at gambling. 1 and 3 Bt and 1, 2, 3, and 4 Earls and five other Hobarts in ODNB. Henry Ellis in ODNB.

Ellys

Origins: Seated at Wyham since the reign of Elizabeth I. **First MP 1597**, a lawyer and judge. On the death of the 3 Bt in 1742 the Ellys estates passed to his cousins the Hobarts.

1. Sir William Ellys – Boston 1679
2. Sir William Ellys 2 Bt – Grantham 1679-81 1689-1713
3. Sir Richard Ellys 3 Bt – Grantham 1701-05 Boston 1719-34
4. Thomas Ellys – Wendover 1708-09

Seats: Nocton Hall, Lincolnshire (purch. and rebuilt c. 1625, passed to the Hobarts 1742, see above); Wyham House, Lincolnshire (built 14th c., acq. sec. half 16th c., remod. 17th c., passed to Hobarts 1742 and sold)
Estates: Worth £5,000 pa in 1742.
Title: Baronet 1660-1742
Notes: 3 Bt in ODNB.

Viscount Hampden (1884- UK)

Origins: Gertrude Roper, Baroness Dacre in her own right, married in 1771 Thomas Brand of The Hoo. Their son succeeded as 20 Baron Dacre. Baroness Dacre's mother was the daughter and heiress of John Trevor of Glynde (see above), which passed to the Brands in 1824. The 23 Baron Dacre was created Viscount Hampden.

1. Thomas Brand – New Shoreham 1741-47 Tavistock 1747-54 Gatton 1754-68 Okehampton 1768-70
2. Thomas Brand Hollis – Hindon 1774-75
3. Thomas Brand – Arundel 1774-80
4. Thomas Brand 20 Baron Dacre – Helston 1807 Hertfordshire 1807-19
5. Thomas Trevor 22 Baron Dacre – Hertfordshire 1847-52
6. Henry Brand 1 Viscount Hampden – Lewes 1852-68 Cambridgeshire 1868-84
7. Henry Brand 2 Viscount Hampden – Hertfordshire 1868-74 Stroud 1880-86
8. Arthur Brand – Wisbech Div. Cambridgeshire 1891-95 1900-06

Seats: The Hoo, Hertfordshire (built 1656, purch. 1732, sold 1938, demolished 1958); Glynde Place, Sussex (inher. by mar. from Hampdens above 1824, still own)
Estates: 22163 (E) 24753
Titles: Baron Dacre 1321- E; Baron Brand of Eydon 1946-63 UK

Peers: 6 peers 1819-90 1884-1945
3 Lds Lt 19th, 20th
Notes: 1 and 2 Viscounts and one other in ODNB.

Baron Sandys (1523-1683 E; 1743-97 GB)

Origins: An old north country family. Archbishop of York 1576. However, another family of the same name seated in Hampshire, which rose in service via a soldier under the Black Prince, not related to this family, was given parliamentary patronage by the Archbishop. They were created Baron Sandys in 1523. The daughter of the 4 Baron married Sir Edwin Sandys of the Archbishop's family, and their grandson was allowed to succeed to the peerage even though not a blood relation, the title being counted as one by writ heritable through the female line. The Hampshire family **first MP 1381 for Hampshire. Two further MPs 1414-1529 both for the county.** The Barons of the second creation **first MP 1563. Eleven further MPs 1563-1628, three kts of the shire**. On the extinction of the Barony of Sandys of the second creation in 1797 the family estates passed to the Marchioness of Downshire. She was created Baroness Sandys in her own right with special remainder to her younger sons (see above). Two cadet lines are included here, one of which produced a modern Cabinet minister.

1. Samuel Sandys – Droitwich 1640-42 1660 Worcestershire 1661-81
2. William Sandys – Evesham 1640-41 1661-69
3. Samuel Sandys – Droitwich 1661-81 1685-87 1689-90
4. Edwin Sandys – Worcestershire 1695-98
5. Samuel Sandys 1 Baron Sandys – Worcester 1718-43
6. Edwin Sandys 2 Baron Sandys – Droitwich 1747-54 Bossiney 1754-61 Westminster 1762-70
7. Thomas Sandys – Bootle Div. Lancashire 1885-1911
8. George Sandys – Wells Div. Somerset 1910-18
9. Duncan Sandys Lord Duncan-Sandys – Norwood Div. Lambeth 1935-45 Streatham Div. Wandsworth 1950-74
10. Laura Sandys – South Thanet 2010-

Seats: Ombersley Court, Worcestershire (acq. 1614, rebuilt 1723-26, passed 1797 to the Downshires by mar. and a junior line stayed here, remod. 1808, add. 1812-14, still own); Graythwaite Hall, Lancashire (built 16th c., acq. 19th c., add. c. 1840 and 1887-90, still own); Misarden Park, Gloucestershire (purch. 1616, built c. 1620, sold 1862); Dundrum Castle, Down (acq. by mar. from Blundells 1756, passed to Marquess of Downshire 1797, see above)
Estates: Bateman 5890 (E) 10663. Worth £1,125 pa in 1690s.
Titles: Lord Duncan-Sandys 1975-87 UKLife

Peers: 4 peers 1660-79 1743-97
2 in Cabinet 1742-43 1761-63 1957-64
Notes: Archbishop and 1 Baron 1st cr. and 2nd cr. and 1 Baroness and Lord Duncan-Sandys and two others in ODNB.

Viscount Blundell (1720-56 I)

Origins: Tudor yeomen. Sir Francis Blundell was appointed Secretary for Irish Affairs, created a Baronet in 1620, and granted an estate in King's county. The 2 Bt married the Colley heiress to Edenderry. **First {MP 1613}. Another {MP 1634}. First English MP 1621**. The daughter and heiress of the 1 Viscount Blundell (d. 1756) married William Trumbell. Their only child married Martin Sandys, and their only child was the Marchioness of Downshire, who was created Baroness Sandys. (see above).

1. Sir George Blundell 2 Bt – {Dingle 1639 Philipstown 1661-66}
2. Sir Francis Blundell 3 Bt – {King's County 1692-93 1695-99 1703-07}
3. Montague Blundell 1 Viscount Blundell – Haslemere 1715-22

Seats: Blundell Manor (Edenderry), King's County (acq. 1st half 17th c., passed to Hills by mar. 1786, see above); Dundrum Castle, Down (acq. 1636, passed to Sandys by mar. 1756 and thence to the Marquess of Downshire by inher.)
Title: Baronet 1620-1756

Tipping

Origins: Emerged in the early 16th century. The 1 Baron Sandys of the second creation married Letitia Tipping, sister and heiress of the 2 and last Tipping Bt.

1. Sir Thomas Tipping 1 Bt – Oxfordshire 1685 Wallingford 1689-90 1695-1701

Seat: Wheatfield (Whitfield), Oxfordshire (acq. c. 1576, sold 1727)
Estates: Letitia Tipping brought a fortune of £170,000 to the 1 Baron Sandys. (*Country Life*, 113, p. 94)
Title: Baronet 1698-1725
Notes: Serious financial difficulties early 18th c. One in ODNB.

Lear

Origins: The 1 Bt was son of a farmer and became a planter in Barbados and West Indian merchant. He purchased estates in Devon, High Sheriff 1673, and passed his fortune on to his nephew, the 1 Bt of the second creation. On the death of the 2 Bt in 1736 his estates passed through his daughter and heiress by her marriage to Sir Thomas Tipping 2 Bt (see above).

1. Sir John Lear 1 Bt – Ashburton 1701-05

Seat: Lindridge House, Devon (built 17th c., purch. 1660, remod. 1673, passed out of family 1736, fire 1963, ruin)
Titles: Baronet 1660-83 1683-1736

HILL II [Noel, Strode]

<u>Viscount Hill</u> (1842- UK)

Origins: Sir Rowland Hill, of a gentry family at Hawkestone from the 15th century, was a successful merchant and mercer, Lord Mayor of London 1549. **First MP 1553 for London**. One of his brothers established the branch at Hawkestone and another brother founded the Court of Hill line.

1. Samuel Hill – Lichfield 1715-22
2. Sir Rowland Hill 1 Bt – Lichfield 1734-41
3. Sir Richard Hill 2 Bt – Shropshire 1780-1806
4. Rowland Hill 1 Viscount Hill – Shrewsbury 1812-14
5. Rowland Hill 2 Viscount Hill – Shropshire 1821-32 N. Shropshire 1832-42
6. Rowland Hill 3 Viscount Hill – N. Shropshire 1857-65
7. Sir Clement Hill – Shrewsbury 1906-11

Seats: Hawkestone Park (Hall), Shropshire (acq. and rebuilt c. 1720, add. c. 1750, sold 1906); Shenstone Park, Staffordshire (purch. and rebuilt 1717, sold later 18th c., demolished 1930s); Willenhall, Warwickshire (purch. 1722, sold c. 1809); Hardwicke Grange, Shropshire (built 1st half 19th c., sold later 19th c., demolished 1931); Peplow Hall, Shropshire (medieval, rebuilt 1725, acq. by mar. 1831, sold 1873)
Estates: Bateman 16554 (E) 21000. £15,000 pa in 1783.
Titles: Baron Hill of Almaraz 1814-42 UK; Baron Hill 1816- UK; Baronet 1727-
Peers: 6 peers 1814-1945
1 Ld Lt 19th
Notes: The 1 Viscount was a general. 2 Viscount married the Clegg heiress (daughter of Joseph Clegg of Peplow Hall, whose father – made a fortune in cotton in Manchester - left £380,000 in probate in 1831 - Rubinstein). 3 Viscount bankrupt by 1895. 1 Viscount and four others in ODNB.

Baron Berwick (1784- GB)

Origins: Cousins of the Hills of Hawkestone. The estates passed through the female line to the Haywards (Harwood). Thomas Harwood (Hill) MP below was the son of a Shrewsbury draper by the daughter of Richard Hill of Hawkestone, nephew and heir of Sir Richard Hill. He was apprenticed as a banker and made a fortune before he inherited another and took the name Hill.

1. Thomas Harwood Hill – Shrewsbury 1749-68
2. Noel Hill 1 Baron Berwick – Shrewsbury 1768-74 Shropshire 1774-84
3. William Noel-Hill 3 Baron Berwick – Shrewsbury 1796-1812

Seats: Attingham Park (Tern Hall), Shropshire (acq. c. 1680, built c. 1683, rebuilt 1783-85, add. 1805, NT 1947)
Estates: Bateman 5553 (E) 10461
Peers: 8 peers 1784-89 1794-1945
Notes: 3 Baron in ODNB.

Hill

Origins: Shared a common ancestry with the Hills of Hawkestone (see above).

1. Andrew Hill – Bishop's Castle 1741-47
2. Thomas Hill – Leominster 1774-76

Seats: Court of Hill, Shropshire (acq. c. 1221, later remod., sold 20th c.); Walthamstow, Essex; Whitton Court, Shropshire (built 14th, 15th, 16th and 17th c., purch. 1835, sold 20th c.)
Estates: Considerable wealth derived from lime workings and quarries in the 18th century.

Strode

Origins: Originally from Strode, Devon circa the reign of Henry III; a wealthy stannery family from the Tudor period onwards. **First MP 1437 for Plympton. Six further MPs 1512-1645, five of them for Plympton and one sat for the county**. Dorothea Strode, sister and heiress of the last Strode (d. 1874), died in 1894. Her sister married Arthur Lowe, son of Thomas Hill-Lowe of the Court of Hill family (see above). Their son took the name Strode and succeeded to the estates.

1. William Strode – Plympton Erle 1660-76
2. Richard Strode – Plympton Erle 1685-87 1690

Seats: Newnham Park, Devon (medieval, acq. by mar. 1410, rebuilt 15th c., new house built c. 1700, passed to Lowes – took name Strode – by mar. 1896, descendents still own)
Estates: Bateman 3254 (E) 3489. Owned 1,550 acres in 2014.
Notes: Three in ODNB.

HILL III *IRELAND*

Origins: To Ireland in 1642 as a soldier and granted lands by Cromwell. Also acquired estates by marriage to an heiress. Sheriff 1727.

1. Rowley Hill – {Ratoath 1734-39}
2. Sir Hugh Hill 1 Bt – {Londonderry 1768-95}
3. Sir George Hill 2 Bt – {Coleraine 1791-95 Londonderry 1795-98} County Londonderry 1801-02 Londonderry 1802-30

Seats: Brook Hall, Londonderry (resident in the 18th c., new house c. 1800 at a cost of £12,000, sold 1858); Culmore House, Londonderry (acq. by Rowley later 17th c., passed 1701 by mar. to Hill family, rebuilt 1805, resident into 19th c.)
Estates: 1199 (I) 1010 in the 1870s
Title: Baronet 1779-
Notes: One in ODNB.

HILLERSDEN

Origins: Minor gentry by the 15th century. **First MP 1478**, a lawyer.

1. Richard Hillersden – Plympton Erle 1679
2. William Hillersden – Bedford 1707-10 Bedfordshire 1715-22

Seats: Elstow Place, Bedfordshire (acq. 1616, built 17th c., family depart 1790, ruin, estate sold c. 1800); Membland, Devon (built 18th c., sold by early 19th c.)
Estates: Bateman 2966 (E) 4724
Notes: On the death of William Hillersden MP in 1725 his estates passed to a daughter Elizabeth who married a cousin Denis Farrer of Cold Brayfield, Buckinghamshire, (estates listed above) who took the name Hillersden. Male line extinct later 18th c. For Farrer see also Boteler.

HIPPISLEY COXE (Hypsley, Cox)

Origins: Although the family claimed Norman lineage, the first significant Hippisley was Recorder of Bristol in the mid-16th century, the son of a sheep farmer who leased Ston Easton in c. 1524. **First MP 1558. Two further MPs 1621-54**. The daughter and heiress of Preston Hippisley of Ston Easton married at the end of the 17th century John Coxe, whose descendents took the additional name Hippisley.

1. John Cox – Milborne Port 1715-17
2. Richard Hippisley Coxe – Somerset 1768-84
3. Sir John Hippisley Coxe 1 Bt – Sudbury 1790-96 1802-18
4. Henry Hippisley Coxe – Somerset 1792-95

Seats: Ston Easton, Somerset (purch. 1544, house built, add. 17th c., enlarged mid-18th c., sold 1956, now hotel); Lamborne (Lambourn) Place, Berkshire (medieval, rebuilt 16th c., inher. by mar. after 1610, new house built 1843, sold 1886, demolished 1938)
Estates: Bateman 4216 (E) 7845 and 4078 (E) 5364
Title: Baronet 1796-1867
Notes: The 1 Bt was in the service of the East India Company and a diplomat. 1 Bt in ODNB.

<u>Northleigh</u>

Origins: Merchants. Gentry by early 17th c. Owned urban property and a country estate.

1. Henry Northleigh – Okehampton 1677-79 1689-94
2. Stephen Northleigh – Totnes 1713-22

Seat: Peamore House, Devon (built 16th c., acq. by mar. c. 1600 from family that purch. mid-16th c., declined to farm house, passed by mar. 1739 to Hippisley Coxes, sold c. 1800)
Notes: Estates indebted c. 1700. Male line extinct 1731. One in ODNB.

HOARE I *IRELAND & ENGLAND*

<u>Hoare</u>

Origins: To Ireland as a soldier under Cromwell. Merchant and Mayor of Cork. Bankers. Sheriff of Cork 1684. This is the senior line descended from Edward Hoare of Togher Castle, Cork (d. 1690).

1. Edward Hoare – {Cork 1710-27}
2. Sir Joseph Hoare 1 Bt – {Askeaton 1761-1800}
3. Sir Edward Hoare 2 Bt – {Carlow 1768-76 Banagher 1790-1800}

Seats: Annabella Park, Cork (built c. 1750, purch. c. 1770s, sold c. 1814, demolished c. 1860s); Factory Hill, Cork (acq. and built c. 1670s, sold c. 1954)

Estates: Worth £1,200 pa in 1713.
Title: Baronet 1784-
Notes: Resident in London 20th c. 1 Bt was a barrister.

Viscount Templewood (1944-1959 UK)

Descended from a younger son of Edward Hoare (see above) established in London 18th c. A line of bankers.

1. Joseph Hoare – Hull 1859
2. Sir Samuel Hoare 1 Bt – Norwich 1886-1906
3. Samuel Hoare 1 Viscount Templewood – Chelsea 1910-44

Seats: Templewood, Norfolk (acq. 19th c., built 1938, sold 1960s); Sidestrand Hall, Norfolk (built 18th c. purch. 1836, add. soon after, sold 1935)
Estates: Rubinstein – Samuel Hoare left £250,000 in probate in 1825.
Title: Baronet 1899-1959
Peer: 1 peer 1944-45
1 in Cabinet 1922-29 1931-40
Notes: Quaker family. 1 Viscount and one other in ODNB.

HOARE II

Hoare

Origins: The Hoares (the founder was the son of a horse-dealer) began as goldsmiths (bankers) associated with the Childs. Their first ledger was dated 1673. Lord Mayor of London 1712 and 1745. Never broke away from the family bank even in the 20th century.

1. Sir Richard Hoare – London 1710-15
2. Henry Hoare – Salisbury 1734-41
3. Sir Henry Hoare 5 Bt – Windsor 1865-66 Chelsea 1868-74
4. Peter Hoare – Southampton 1868-74

Seats: Stourhead, Wiltshire (medieval castle called Stourton, ruin by 1644, purch. 1717, old house demolished and rebuilt 1719-25, add. 1793-95 and 1840-41, fire 1902, rebuilt, NT 1946); Wavendon House, Buckinghamshire (built 16th c., remod. 18th c., purch. 1798, remod. 19th c., still own); Luscombe Castle, Devon (purch. 1797, built 1799-1804, still own)
Estates: Bateman 13987 (E) 16088; 3258 (E) 4964; 3275 (E) 7144
Title: Baronet 1786-
Notes: 2 Bt and seven others in ODNB.

Hoare

Origins: The senior branch of the family. Bankers.

1. Hugh Hoare – Chesterton Div. Cambridgeshire 1892-95

Seats: Iden Park and Staplehurst Park, Kent (Staplehurst old manor house – medieval and later, purch. 1835, Iden a new house built 1840-66, both sold 1904-13)
Notes: Financial crisis early 20th c. for family.

HOBHOUSE

Baron Broughton (1851-69 UK)

Origins: Bristol merchants, bankers, and brewers in the 18th century. The first MP was a barrister, Chief Secretary of the Board of Control 1801.

1. Sir Benjamin Hobhouse 1 Bt – Bletchingley 1797-1802 Grampound 1802-06 Hindon 1806-18
2. John Hobhouse 1 Baron Broughton – Westminster 1820-33 Nottingham 1834-47 Harwich 1848-51
3. Thomas Hobhouse – Rochester 1837-41 Lincoln 1848-52
4. Henry Hobhouse – Hereford 1841
5. Henry Hobhouse – E. Somerset 1885-1906
6. Sir Charles Hobhouse 4 Bt – E. Wiltshire 1892-95 E. Bristol 1900-18
7. Sir Arthur Hobhouse – Wells Div. Somerset 1923-24

Seats: Manor House, Monckton Farleigh, Wiltshire (built 16th c., add. 17th c., add. 18th c., purch. 1873, still own); Westbury College, Gloucestershire (leased 19th c.); Hadspen Hall, Somerset (built c. 1676, purch. 1785 for £19,500, add. 1886 and 1900, for sale 2012)
Estates: Rubinstein – 1 Bt left £250,000 in probate in 1830. Held 4,000 acres in the 1980s. Worth nearly £4 million in 2004.
Titles: Baron Hobhouse 1885-1904 UK; Baron Hobhouse of Woodborough 1998-2004 UKLife; Baronet 1812-
Peers: 2 peers 1851-69 1885-1904
2 in Cabinet 1851-69 1885-1904
Notes: 1 Baron Broughton was a politician and one of the men who burned Byron's memoirs. 1 and 4 Bts and 1 Baron Broughton and 1 Baron Hobhouse and Baron Hobhouse of Woodborough and seven others in ODNB.

HOBY

Origins: Claimed ancient Welsh descent (Radnorshire). Rose in the Household of Henry VIII with the help of the Cecils and Russells. Acquired land at the Dissolution. (*Country Life*, 17, pp. 908-09) **First MP 1547 for Cardiff. Two further MPs 1572-1628.**

1. Peregrine Hoby – Great Marlow 1641-48 1660-79
2. Thomas Hoby – Great Marlow 1681 Salisbury 1689-98
3. John Hoby – Great Marlow 1689
4. Sir Thomas Hoby 4 Bt – Great Marlow 1732-44

Seats: Bisham Abbey, Berkshire (medieval, acq. 1553, add. 1559, sold 1768); Breamore House, Hampshire (built 1580-83, sold 1748); Somerley, Hampshire (acq. by mar. by 1728, sold by c. 1750)
Estates: Worth £1,000 pa in the 1660s.
Title: Baronet 1666-1766
Notes: Some estates passed to the Mills in 1766 (see under Knollys).
Notes: Three in ODNB.

HODGE [Hermon]

Baron Wyfold (1919- UK)

Origins: Edward Hermon MP was a Lancashire cotton manufacturer, the owner of one of the largest mid-19th century textile businesses. His daughter married 1877 the 1 Baron Wyfold who took the additional name Hermon.

1. Edward Hermon – Preston 1868-81
2. Robert Hodge 1 Baron Wyfold – N. E. Lancashire 1886-92 S. Oxfordshire 1895-1906 Croydon 1909-10 S. Oxfordshire 1917-18

Seat: Wyfold Court, Oxfordshire (acq. and built by Hermons 1872-76, in 1881 passed by mar. to Robert Hodge 1 Baron Wyfold, sold 1919, now flats)
Estate: 1,700 acres in 1880s
Title: Baronet 1902-
3 peers 1919-45

HODSON [Cardwell]

Hodson

Origins: Merchant family in Wigan in the 18th century. Established cotton mills in the 1790s. Went into partnership with the Cardwells in the 19th century. Purchased landed property from 1799 onwards.

1. John Hodson – Wigan 1802-20
2. James Hodson – Wigan 1820-31

Seat: Ellerbeck Hall, Lancashire (purch. 1799, built 1807, passed to Cardwells 1855)
Estates: Worth up to £200,000 by 1806.

Viscount Cardwell (1874-86 UK)

Origins: Wigan merchants in partnership with the Hodsons in the early 19th century. The 1 Viscount was a nephew of John Hodson and inherited the Ellerbeck estate from the Hodsons in 1855.

1. Edward Cardwell 1 Viscount Cardwell – Clitheroe 1842-47 Liverpool 1847-52 Oxford 1852-74

Seat: Ellerbeck Hall, Lancashire (built 1807, inher. by mar. 1855, demolished 1920s-30s)
Estates: Bateman 4557 (E) 8861
Peer: 1 peer 1874-86
1 in Cabinet 1859-66 1868-74
Notes: 1 Viscount and one other in ODNB.

HODY

Origins: The son of an agricultural laborer acquired a small fortune as a clerical lawyer and another son, also a lawyer, administered the estates of a noble family. His two sons were also lawyers, one knighted and Chief Justice of the King's Bench 1440. In the next generation a Chief Baron of the Exchequer 1486. **First MP 1421, kt of the shire for Somerset. Four further MPs 1429-1589, one other sitting for Somerset.**

1. John Hody – Ilchester 1681

Seat: Northover, Somerset (built 15th c., purch. 1650, declined to a farm house after 1729)
Notes: Family in decline 16th c. Extinct in male line 1729. Two in ODNB.

HOEY *IRELAND*

Origins: The family was in Ireland before 1634. The second {MP} was a soldier granted land in Longford for military service in 1660. **First {MP 1634}.** Sheriff 1666.

1. Sir John Hoey – {Naas 1661-65}
2. William Hoey – {Naas 1665-66 Carysfort 1695-98}
3. William Hoey – {County Wicklow 1725-46}

Seats: Cotlandstowne, Longford (acq. later 17th c., resident 18th c.); Dunganstown, Wicklow (acq. c. 1660, departed c. 1760s)
Notes: Extinct in male line 1763?

HOGG *ENGLAND & IRELAND*

Viscount Hailsham (1929- UK)

Origins: The family emigrated from Scotland to Ireland at the end of the 17th century. The 1 Baronet was a barrister in India 1814 and Chairman of the East India Company. He returned to Britain with a nabob fortune. (J. Phillips, *The Great Reform Bill in the Boroughs*, 225 n. 26) In the 19th century West Indies sugar merchants.

1. Sir James Hogg 1 Bt – Beverley 1834-47 Honiton 1847-57
2. James McGarel-Hogg 1 Baron Magheramorne – Bath 1865-68 Truro 1871-85 Hornsey Div. Middlesex 1885-87
3. Douglas Hogg 1 Viscount Hailsham – St. Marylebone 1922-28
4. Mavis Hogg – W. Div. Willesdon 1931-35 Frome 1935-45
5. Quinton Hogg 2 Viscount Hailsham – Oxford 1938-50 St. Marylebone 1963-70
6. Douglas Hogg 3 Viscount Hailsham – Grantham 1979-1997 Sleaford and North Hykeham 1997-2010

Seat: Magheramorne, Antrim (inher. from McCarels by mar. and built 1880, sold 20th c., hotel)
Estates: Bateman 3541 (I) 4083. 1 Bt left £350,000 in 1876. 1 Baron Magheramorne left £200,000 in 1890. 1 Viscount left £225,000 in 1950. The 2 Viscount left £4,600,000 in 2001.
Titles: Baron Magheramorne 1887- UK; Baron Hailsham 1928- UK; Baron Hailsham of Marylebone UKLife 1970-2001; Baronet 1846-
Peers: 5 peers 1887-1945 1928-45
3 in Cabinet 1924-29 1931-38 1956-64 1970-74 1979-87 1995-97
1 KG 20th

Notes: 1 Baron Magheramorne was Chairman of the Metropolitan Board of Works 1870. Resident permanently in England post WWI. 1 and 2 Viscounts were Lord Chancellors. 1 Bt and 1 Baron Magheramorne and 1 and 2 Viscounts and one other in ODNB.

HOGHTON (de Hoghton, Houghton) [Bold, Patten]

Hoghton

Origins: Claim to have been at Hoghton in the 11th century. They were landowners in the 12th century and acquired Hoghton by the early 14th century. **First MP 1315 for Lancashire. Eight additional MPs 1322-1656, all for Lancashire**.

1. Sir Charles Hoghton 4 Bt – Lancashire 1679-81 1689-90
2. Sir Henry Hoghton 5 Bt – Preston 1710-13 1715-22 East Looe 1724-27 Preston 1727-41
3. Sir Henry Hoghton 6 Bt – Preston 1768-95
4. Sir Henry Hoghton 7 Bt – Preston 1795-1802

Seats: Hoghton Tower, Lancashire (acq. c. 1300 or earlier, rebuilt 1561-65, add. c. 1700, decayed later 18th and early 19th c., restored 1860s and 1901, still own); Walton Hall, Lancashire (acq. 16th c., became principal seat in the 18th c. until 1860s, rebuilt 1830, demolished late 19th c.)
Estates: Bateman 47000 (E) 13397. Owned 4,000 acres in 2001.
Title: Baronet 1611-
Notes: The family resumed their medieval name "de Hoghton" in 1862. 5 and 6 Bts and two others in ODNB.

Baron Winmarleigh (1874-92 UK)

Origins: The Bolds were at Bold by 1212. **First MP 1584 for Lancashire**. The Pattens married the Bold heiress in the 18th century. A Patten heiress carried the Bold-Patten estates by marriage to the Wilsons in 1800. They took the name Patten in 1823. The Pattens were merchants in the 16th century who made a fortune with copper smelting furnaces in the late 17th century. Mayor of Preston c. 1650s. The first MP 1689 was a barrister. They also patented a roller machine, which they manufactured. The 8th Hoghton Bt married the Patten-Bold-Wilson heiress.

1. Peter Bold – Lancashire 1679
2. Thomas Patten – Preston 1689-90
3. Richard Bold – Lancashire 1701-04
4. Peter Bold – Wigan 1727-34 Lancashire 1736-41 1750-61
5. Peter Patten-Bold – Newton 1797-1806 Lancaster 1807-12 Malmesbury 1813-18
6. Thomas Wilson-Patten – Stafford 1812-18

7. John Wilson Patten 1 Baron Winmarleigh – Lancashire 1830-31 N. Lancashire 1832-74

Seats: Bold Hall, Lancashire (acq. 1212, new house 1728-30, remod. c. 1800, sold 1858, pulled down 1900); Winmarleigh Hall, Lancashire (purch. 1744 by Pattens, built 1871, sold 1912, institutional use); Bank Hall (Warrington), Lancashire (built by Pattens 1750, became surrounded by industrial workings so that the family built the new house at Winmarleigh in 1871, became Warrington Town Hall, 1872)
Estates: Bateman 5338 (E) 8852. Rubinstein – Anna Bold left £100,000 in probate 1813 and Everilda Bold left £100,000 in 1837 and her sister Anna Maria Patten left £100,000 in 1837.
Peers: 1 peer 1874-92
Notes: The park at Bold Hall was the largest in Lancashire after Knowsley. The Patten family remained active in manufacturing. The 1 Baron Winmarleigh was a partner in the industrial firm. 1 Baron and two others in ODNB.

HOLDEN

Baron Holden (1908- UK)

Origins: The 1 Bt, son of a mine foreman, worked 14 hours a day in a cotton mill. He then became a teacher, bookkeeper in a worsted mill, manager, and finally partner in the mill c. 1835 onwards. He invented a wool-combing machine in 1848. Eventually he owned the world's largest wool-carding business.

1. Sir Isaac Holden 1 Bt – Knaresborough 1865-68 W. Riding Yorkshire 1882-85 Keighley 1885-86
2. Angus Holden 1 Baron Holden – East Bradford 1885-86 Buckrose Div. E. R. Yorkshire 1892-1900

Seats: Oakworth House, Yorkshire (built first half 19th c., purch. and rebuilt by Holdens 1864-74 at a cost of £80,000, burned down 1907, park donated c. 1925 to local council); Appleton House, Yorkshire (purch. 1894, sold 1913, demolished c. 1945)
Estates: 1 Bt left over £300,000 in 1897.
Title: Baronet 1893-
Peers: 3 peers 1908-45
Notes: 1 Bt in ODNB.

HOLLAND I [Hibbert, Parker]

Viscount Knutsford (1895- UK)

Origins: The 1 Bt was appointed a royal physician in 1853. The family was engaged in business in Cheshire and Lancashire. They came to London as merchants and bankers.

1. Henry Holland 1 Viscount Knutsford – Midhurst 1874-85 Hampstead 1885-88
2. Lionel Holland – Bow & Bromley Div. Tower Hamlets 1895-99

Seats: Munden House, Hertfordshire (passed by mar. to Hollands 1874, remod. late 19th c., still own); Kneesworth Hall, Cambridgeshire (built c. 1600, purch. 1900, sold 1948)
Estates: The 1 Bt left £140,000 in 1873 and inherited more than 1,000 acres in Hertfordshire. 200 acres in Cambridgeshire in early 20th c.
Titles: Baron Knutsford 1888- UK; Baronet 1853-
Peers: 4 peers 1888-1945
1 in Cabinet 1887-92
Notes: The 1 Viscount inherited the Parker estates in Hertfordshire through marriage to a Hibbert heiress (see below). See Malchow, *Gentleman Capitalists*, 19, 54. 1 Bt and 1 and 2 Viscounts and two others in ODNB.

Holland

Origins: Cousins of above. Owned real estate in Liverpool and involved in slate quarries in Wales. May have been Liverpool merchants in the late 18th century.

1. Samuel Holland – Merioneth 1870-85

Seats: Noddfa, Merionethshire (acq. mid 19th c., add. 1850, sold later 19th c.); Caerdeon, Merionethshire (purch. second half 19th c., sold c. 1900)
Estates: Rubinstein – Swinton Holland left £180,000 in probate 1827.

Parker

Origins: Burgesses in Peterborough. Inherited land in Lincolnshire in the 17th c. and in 1750 in Hertfordshire from John Rogers, a London mercer. High Sheriff Northamptonshire 1727.

1. Charles Parker – Peterborough 1710-22
2. Armstead Parker – Peterborough 1734-47 1761-68

Seats: Munden House, Hertfordshire (purch. and built 1715 by Rogers and passed by mar. to Parkers 1750, passed by mar. to Hibberts 1828); Burghberry Manor, Peterborough, Northamptonshire
Estates: Parkers worth £600-700 pa in 1700. Rubinstein – Rogers Parker left £140,000 in probate in 1828.

Hibbert

Origins: Father of first MP a Manchester merchant. The MP was a dock owner and successful West India merchant in London. He was a leading figure in the London commercial world.

1. George Hibbert – Seaford 1806-12

Seat: Munden House, Hertfordshire (acq. by mar. to Parkers 1828, add. 1829, passed to Hollands by mar. 1874)
Estates: Rubinstein – Robert Hibbert left £250,000 in probate in 1835.
Notes: Some of the Hibberts were also planters in Jamaica. Three in ODNB.

HOLLAND II

Origins: Rose in the 16th century as a retainer of the Howards (Dukes of Norfolk). Kt c. 1600. **First MP 1621 (1624 for Norfolk)**. Bt 1629.

1. Sir John Holland 1 Bt – Norfolk 1640 Castle Rising Norfolk 1640-48 1660 Aldeburgh 1661-79
2. Sir John Holland 2 Bt – Norfolk 1701-10

Seat: Quidenham Hall, Norfolk (acq. 1572, built 1606, sold c. 1740)
Title: Baronet 1629-1729
Notes: 1 Bt in ODNB.

HOLMES *IRELAND*

Origins: Moved to Ireland mid-17th century, founded by a legal official 1646. His sons were also law clerks. Sheriff 1707. Owned only a small property but controlled a borough seat.

1. Peter Holmes – {Banagher 1713-14 Athlone 1727-32}
2. George Holmes – {Banagher 1727-34}
3. Galbraith Holmes – {Banagher 1734-35}
4. Peter Holmes – {Banagher 1761-90 Kilmallock 1790-97 Doneraile 1798-1800}

Seat: Peterfield (Johnston), Tipperary (acq. early 18th c., built later 18th c., now a ruin)
Estates: Worth £300 pa in 1713. Sold Banagher for £10,000 in 1788.
Notes: Extinct in the male line 1802.

HOLTE [Brereton] *ENGLAND & WALES*

Holte

Origins: Important landowners by the 14th century. **First MP 1378. Three additional MPs 1421-1571, one kt of the shire.**

1. Sir Robert Holte 2 Bt – Warwickshire 1661-79
2. Sir Charles Holte 3 Bt – Warwickshire 1685-87
3. Sir Lister Holte 5 Bt – Lichfield 1741-47
4. Sir Charles Holte 6 Bt – Warwickshire 1774-80

Seats: Aston Hall, Warwickshire (acq. 1367, medieval house, rebuilt 1618-35, sold 1818, now owned by Birmingham Corp.); Erdington Hall, Warwickshire (purch. 1647, built 1662, sold 1817, demolished 1912); Brereton Hall, Cheshire (built 1585-86, acq. by mar. 1722, sold 1817)
Estates: Worth £1,000 pa in 1618 and £4,000 pa in 1729
Title: Baronet 1611-1782
Notes: 1 Bt in ODNB.

Baron Brereton of Laghlin (1624-1722 I)

Origins: At Brereton since the 13th century. Soldiers in the medieval period. Lord Chief Justice of Ireland (d. 1541). **First MP 1547 for Cheshire. Four additional MPs 1597-1640, three for the county**. On the death of the 3 Baron in 1772 the male line failed after 500 years. The estates passed to Sir Charles Holte 3 Bt, a nephew (see above).

1. William Brereton 3 Baron Brereton – Newton 1659 Bossiney 1660
2. Wiliam Brereton 2 Baron Brereton – Cheshire 1661-64
3. Edward Brereton – Denbigh Boroughs 1689-1705

Seats: Brereton Hall, Cheshire (acq. 12th c., rebuilt 1585-86, passed to Bracebridges by mar. 1722, sold 1817); Borras Hall, Denbighshire (acq. by mar. and built 15th c., rebuilt early 17th c., sold 1789)
Notes: One in ODNB.

HOME (Hume) [Campbell, Dick, Douglas, Hepburn, Macartney, Milne, Scott, Thriepland] *SCOTLAND & IRELAND*

Earl of Home (1604- S)

Origins: The family was first mentioned in a charter of 1138. The common ancestor of the Homes was Sir Thomas Home, living in the 14th century. His eldest son was 1 Baron Home. The daughter of the 1 Baron Douglas, heir of the Dukes of Douglas and the Baron Montagu of Boughton, married the 11 Earl of Home, who took the additional name Douglas. He inherited the Douglas estates in 1857 and was created Baron Douglas in 1875. The second son, David Home of Wedderburn, was the ancestor of the other branches at Wedderburn and Polwarth (Marchmont). **First [MP 1560]. One other [MP 1572].**

1. Alexander Douglas-Home 14 Earl of Home – Lanark Div. Lanarkshire 1931-45 1950-51 Kinross & W. Perthshire 1963-64

Seats: The Hirsel, Berwickshire (built 17th c., became main seat c. 1650, add. 1739-41, add. 1813-18, remod. 1858, remod. 1958-59, still own); Douglas Castle, Lanarkshire (medieval, razed 1644, fire 1758, rebuilt 1760s, passed to Earl of Home by mar. 1877, add. 1883, unroofed and then demolished 1938); Bothwell Castle, Lanarkshire (medieval castle, inher. by mar. from Douglas family, abandoned in 18th c., ruin. given to state 1935)
Estates: Bateman 106550 (S) 62248. Worth £21,000,000 and 20,000 acres in 1990.
Titles: Baron Home 1473- S; Baron Douglas 1875- UK; Baron Home 1970-95 UKLife
Peers: [4 peers 1661-1707] 4 Scottish Rep peers 1710-13 1741-61 1807-41 1842-74 3 peers 1875-1945
1 in Cabinet 1955-57 1960-64 1970-74
5 Lds Lt 18th, 19th, 20th
2 KT 19th, 20th
Notes: Home is pronounced Hume. The 14 Earl was Foreign Secretary 1960-63 and 1970-74 and Prime Minister 1963-64. Hume (Home) family has an entry and 1, 3, 4, and 5 Barons and 1, 3, 8, and 14 Earls and three others in ODNB.

Milne-Home

Origins: The senior line descended from David Home of Wedderburn. **First [MP 1560]. Two further [MP 1590-1650].** David Milne married in 1832 Jean, daughter and heiress of William Home of Wedderburn and Paxton House. The Milnes were merchants in Edinburgh in the early 18th century.

1. Patrick Home – Berwickshire 1784-96

2. Sir David Milne – Berwick-on-Tweed 1820
3. David Milne-Home – Berwick-on-Tweed 1874-85

Seats: Wedderburn Castle, Berwickshire (acq. 1413, built 17th c., rebuilt 1770-76, still own but commercial use); Paxton House, Berwickshire (acq. 1413, rebuilt 1758-66, add. 1812-13, given to charitable trust 1988)
Estates: Bateman 9144 (S) 16500
Title: Baronet 1638-1715
Notes: Between 1413 and 1576 every laird died in battle or died a prisoner. (*Country Life*, 57, p. 446) Sir David Milne MP was an admiral. The family went through a melodramatic series of episodes of the loss and recovery of estates due to Jacobitism (*Country Life*, 142, p. 365). David Milne Home and one other in ODNB.

Earl of Dunbar (1605-11 S)

Origins: Descended from Alexander Home the second son of David Home of Wedderburn (see above). **First [MP 1560]. Two further [MPs 1593-1633].**

1. George Home – [New Galloway 1703-07]
2. Sir Patrick Home 1 Bt – [Berwickshire 1703-07]

Seats: Lumsden, Berwickshire (acq. 17th c., sold later 18th c.; Manderston, Berwickshire (acq. later 17th c., sold later 18th c.)
Title: Baronet 1697-1783
Notes: 1 Earl in ODNB.

Home

Origins: Descended from the third son of David Home of Wedderburn. **First [MP 1617 for Berwickshire]. Two further [MPs 1643-47 both for the county].**

1. Sir John Home 2 Bt – [Berwickshire 1690-1701 1703-05]

Seat: Blackadder House, Berwickshire (medieval, acq. by mar. 1518, rebuilt 1782-84, sold 1836, demolished c. 1923)
Title: Baronet 1671-
Notes: One in ODNB.

Earl of Marchmont (1697-1794 S)

Origins: Descended from a younger son of the Wedderburn line. The 1 Baronet 1637 was Solicitor General of Scotland. **First [MP 1590]. Two additional [MPs 1617-30].**

The 2 Earl of Marchmont married the heiress of the Campbells of Cessnock and took the additional name Campbell (see Campbell). The sister of the 3 Earl married the 4 Purves Bt, who took the additional names Hume-Campbell.

1. Patrick Hume 1 Earl of Marchmont – [Berwickshire 1665 1667 1669-74 1689-90]
2. Alexander Hume-Campbell 2 Earl of Marchmont – [Kirkwall 1698-1702 Berwickshire 1706-07]
3. Sir Andrew Hume – [Kirkcudbright Burghs 1700-07] Scotland 1707-08
4. Hugh Hume-Campbell 3 Earl of Marchmont – Berwick-on-Tweed 1734-40
5. Alexander Hume-Campbell – Berwickshire 1734-41 1742-60
6. Sir Hume Purves-Hume-Campbell 7 Bt – Berwickshire 1834-47

Seats: Marchmont House, Berwickshire (acq. by 16th c., built 1750-54, remod. 1834-42, sold 1913); Redbraes Castle, Berwickshire (acq. and built by c. 16th c., remod. 1709, remod. 1726-35, family ceased to use 1750s, ruin, sold 1913); Purves Hall, Berwickshire (purch. and built 17th c. by Purves family, much altered, acq. by mar. 18th c., new house Victorian, sold 19th-20th c.)
Estates: Bateman 20180 (S) 17976
Titles: Baron Polwarth 1690- S; Baron Hume 1776-81 GB; Baronet 1637-1794; 1665-1960
Peers: [1 peer 1690-1707] 2 Scottish Rep peers 1727-34 1750-84 1 peer 1776-81
1 KT 18th
Notes: 2, 3 Earls and two others in ODNB.

<u>Baron Polwarth</u> (1690- S)

Origins: The Scotts were an old Border family, cadets of the Dukes of Buccleuch (see Monatgu). **First [MP 1640 for Selkirkshire]. Two other [MPs 1650 for Selkirkshire and Roxburghshire].** Created Earl of Tarras 1660-93. Lady Diana Hume-Campbell 5 Baroness Polwarth in her own right, the daughter of the 3 Earl of Marchmont (see above), married in 1822 Walter Scott of Harden. Their son, Hugh Hepburn-Scott succeeded as 6 Baron Polwarth.

1. Sir William Scott – [Selkirkshire 1689-93]
2. John Scott – [Roxburghshire 1693-1702]
3. Walter Scott – Roxburghshire 1747-65
4. Hugh Hepburn-Scott 6 Baron Polwarth – Berwickshire 1780-84
5. Henry Hepburn-Scott 7 Baron Polwarth – Roxburghshire 1826-32
6. Francis Hepburn-Scott – Roxburghshire 1841-47 Berwickshire 1847-59

Seats: Harden, Roxburghshire (Scotts acq. 1501, demolished 1590, rebuilt c. 1630, add. 1680, became a farm house in 18th c., add. 1864, became main seat again 1913, still own); Mertoun House, Berwickshire (main seat until 1912, acq. 1641, old house

1677, rebuilt 1703, remod. 1843, sold 1912, partly demolished 1953); Humbie House, Haddingtonshire (acq. by mar. 1677, resident 20th c.)
Estates: Bateman 10664 (S) 15243
Titles: Earl of Tarras 1660-93 S
Peers: [1 peer 1660-93] 3 Scottish Rep peers 1843-67 1882-1900 1929-44
3 Lds Lt 19th, 20th
Notes: 1 Earl of Tarras and one other in ODNB.

Hepburn

Origins: The Hepburns rose high in the peerage during the Middle Ages: Baron Hailes 1452, Earl of Bothwell 1485, and Duke of Orkney 1567, all extinct 1578. **They also elected an [MP 1483-89]**. The Hepburns at Humbie were a cadet line. **They elected two [MPs 1643-51].** In 1820 Hugh Scott 6 Baron Polwarth took the additional name Hepburn on succeeding his cousin James Hepburn at Humbie.

1. Sir Thomas Buchan-Hepburn 3 Bt – Haddingtonshire 1838-47

Seat: Smeaton, Haddingtonshire (acq. 16th c., rebuilt 1790, sold 1948)
Estates: 2772(S) 8512
Title: Baronet 1815-

Hepburn

Origins: Cadet of Smeaton.

1. William Hepburn – [Haddington Constabulary 1693-1701]

Seat: Benistoun, Haddingtonshire
Notes: Benistoun passed to another Hepburn line. One in ODNB.

Hume Dick

Origins: The Hume family descended from a younger son of the 3 Baron Polwarth (see above). To Ireland in the first half of the 17th century, and purchased land in Tipperary 1641 and 1660 and in Wicklow in 1704. Sheriff 1769. William Hume married Charlotte Dick, heiress of the Dicks of Dublin. They emigrated from Scotland to Antrim in the 17th century and became East India merchants. Later they were involved in insurance and banking, one being a founder and Governor of the Bank of Ireland (1797-99). The Humes took the additional name Dick in 1864.

1. William Hume – {County Wicklow 1790-98}

2. William Hume – {County Wicklow 1799-1800} 1801-15
3. Quinton Dick – {Dunleer 1800} West Looe 1803-06 Cashel 1807-09 Orford 1826-30 Maldon 1830-47 Aylesbury 1848-52
4. Hugh Dick – Maldon 1827-30
5. William Hume Dick – County Wicklow 1852-80

Seats: Humewood Castle, Wicklow (purch. 1704 and built house, new house built 1867-70, sold 1992); Layer Marney Tower, Essex (built c. 1510s-20s, purch. by Dicks 1835, sold later 19th c.)
Estates: Bateman 4770 (I) 2534. Worth £2,000 pa in 1814. The Dick fortune c. 1800 was valued at £400,000, and they were worth £15-20,000 pa in 1826. Rubinstein – James Dick left £140,000 in probate in 1828. By 1858 worth 2 to 3 million pounds in stocks and land. (Fisher, *The House of Commons*, IV, 918)
Notes: James and Quinton Dick were West India merchants. One in ODNB.

Earl Macartney (1794-1806 I)

Origins: The 1 Earl's great-grandfather owned a small property in Kirkcudbrightshire. He departed Scotland in 1649 for Ulster. He became a merchant and Mayor of Belfast and purchased land, but he divided his estates among numerous sons. Sheriff 1688. Two became lawyers and MPs, one a judge and the other married two heiresses in succession, acquiring a large landed estate, which was built up further over many years. (Roebuck, *Macartney of Lisanoure 1737-1806*, 1-7) Elizabeth Balaguier, niece and adopted daughter of the 1 Earl Macartney, married Travers Hume, a younger son of the Humes of Humewood. On the Earl's death in 1806 his estates passed to his great nephew, George Hume, who took the name Macartney.

1. George Macartney – {Belfast 1692-93}
2. James Macartney – {Belfast 1692-93 1695-99}
3. George Macartney – {Limavady 1703-13 Donegal 1713-14 Belfast 1715-57]
4. James Macartney – {Longford 1713-27 Granard 1727-60}
5. George Macartney – {Belfast 1721-24}
6. Francis Macartney – {Blessington 1749-59}
7. George Macartney 1 Earl Macartney – {Armagh 1768-76} Cockermouth 1768-69 Ayr Burghs 1774-76 Bere Alston 1780-81
8. George Macartney – Antrim 1852-58

Seats: Lis(s)anoure Castle, Antrim (14th c., purch. 1730s, built c. 1770, rebuilt 1829, add. 1847, fell into ruin, owned demense until sold 1943); Auchinleck, Kirkcudbrightshire (acq. 16th c.); Lowther Lodge, Dublin (Filgate family acq. mid-17th c., passed by mar. to Macartneys 19th c., still resident 20th c.)
Estates: Bateman 13118 (I) 6783

Titles: Baron Macartney 1776-1806 I; Viscount Macartney 1792-1806 I; Baron Macartney 1796-1806 GB
Peers: {1 peer 1788-1800} 1 peer 1796-1806
1 in Cabinet 1769-72
Notes: The 1 Earl rose through government service, diplomacy, and East India Company and imperial governorships. He made £16,000 pa as President of Fort St. George in India and added more land to the family estates. (Roebuck, *Macartney*, 280) Family extinct 1943. 1 Earl and one other in ODNB.

Thriepland

Origins: The family began as burgesses in Perth. The 1 Bt was Provost of the city. Kt 1674. The Scotts of Thirlestaine, Roxburghshire, a cadet of the Scotts of Harden (see above), succeeded to the Thriepland estates by marriage (see Napier I).

1. Sir Patrick Thriepland 1 Bt – [Perth 1661-63 1665 1667 1669-74]

Seat: Fingask Castle, Perthshire (built 1594, purch. 1671, add. 1670s, confiscated 1715, repurch. 1783, remod. 18th and 19th c., sold 1920, reduced in size 1925, repurch. 1968, sold 1990s)
Estates: 13738 (S) 5096. The Thrieplands purch. 45,000 acres in Caithness in the 1990s.
Title: Baronet 1687-1882
Notes: The Thrieplands were attainted and their estates annexed in 1716 after the Jacobite rising. They went into exile in France after the 1745. They repurchased the estates in 1782 and the Baronetcy was restored in 1826 by an Act of Parliament.

Scott

Origins: A cadet line of the Scotts of Harden (see above).

1. Hugh Scott – [Selkirkshire 1681]
2. Sir James Scott – [Roxburghshire 1698-1701]

Seat: Gala House, Selkirkshire (built 16th c., family departed later 19th c.)
Estates: 3790 (S) 3546

HONYMAN *SCOTLAND*

Origins: The first MP entered the Royal Navy as a Captain's servant and rose to admiral. The 1 Bt was a Lord of Session.

1. Robert Honyman – Orkney & Shetland 1796-1806

2. Robert Honyman – Orkney & Shetland 1806-07
3. Sir Richard Honyman 2 Bt – Orkney & Shetland 1812-18

Seats: Armadale, Sutherland (purch. 1779 and built, sold 1813 for £25,000); Graemsay, Orkney (purch. 1699); Coton Hall, Shropshire (built c. 1800, add. 1860, purch. 1821, sold 20th c.)
Estates: Coton Hall estate was 5,000 acres in 1821.
Title: Baronet 1804-1911
Notes: 4 Bt in ODNB.

HONYWOOD (Honeywood, Honywode) [Sandford]

Honywood

Origins: Kentish family. The **first MP 1393 for Hythe**, a trader in sheep and cattle. **Next MP 1397, also for Hythe**, was a butcher. **Eight additional MPs, five of them for Hythe, 1447-1659**. Became bankers in London in the 17th century.

1. Sir William Honywood 2 Bt – Canterbury 1685-87 1689-98
2. Sir John Honywood 4 Bt – Steyning 1784-85 1788-90 Canterbury 1790-96 1797-1802 Honiton 1802-1806

Seats: Evington Place, Kent (acq. late 15th c., demolished 1938); Malling Abbey, Kent (acq. and built mid-18th c., sold 1892)
Estates: Bateman 5601 (E) 5876
Title: Baronet 1660-
Notes: One in ODNB.

Honywood

Origins: Cadet line that acquired property in Essex in the early 17th century. **First MP 1654**.

1. John Honeywood – Essex 1679-81 1693-94
2. Robert Honywood – Essex 1716-27
3. Philip Honywood – Appleby 1754-84
4. Frazer Honywood – Steyning 1759-64
5. Filmer Honywood – Steyning 1774-80 Kent 1780-96 1802-06
6. William Honywood – Kent 1806-12
7. William Honywood – Kent 1818-30

Seats: Marks Hall, Essex (acq. 1605, rebuilt c. 1609, rebuilt c. 1754, sold after 1895, demolished 1951); Hull Place, Kent (acq. 18th c.); Sibton Park, Kent (built 1602, purch. 1786, remod. 18th c., sold 1898); Howgill Castle, Westmorland (built 14th c., add. late 17th c., passed to Honywoods 1723, add. 1733, sold c. 1780)
Estates: Bateman 7459 (E) 9155
Notes: Sir Robert Honywood sat in the Cromwellian House of Lords. The family encountered financial difficulties and the estate was declared insolvent in 1834. Three in ODNB.

Sandford

Origins: A family of some eminence in the Middle Ages. **First MP 1320 for Westmorland. Seven additional MPs 1332-1413, three of them for the county.** Howgill Castle originally belonged to the Crackenthorpes (Crackanthorpe) (**six MPs 1382-1456, all of whom sat for Westmorland)**. A Crackenthorpe heiress brought it to Sir Thomas Sandford by marriage in the mid-16th century. On the death of the 3 Bt the estates passed to his sister 1723, wife of Robert Honywood of Marks Hall.

1. Sir Richard Sandford 3 Bt – Westmorland 1695-1700 1701-02 Morpeth 1701 1705-13 Appleby 1713-23

Seat: Howgill Castle, Westmorland (built 14th c., acq. by Crackenthorpes 15th c. then to Sandfords, add. late 17th c., passed to Honywoods 1723)
Title: Baronet 1641-1723
Notes: The Crackenthorpes were seated at Newbiggin Hall, Westmorland from the reign of Edward III and still owned that estate in the later 19th c. (Bateman 2265 E 2008).

HOOD [Acland, Fuller, Palmer]

Viscount Hood (1796- GB)

Origins: A great naval family that began with a clergyman's son who served as a purser.

1. Samuel Hood 1 Viscount Hood – Westminster 1785-88 Reigate 1789-90 Westminster 1790-96

Seats: Catherington House, Hampshire (acq. and built later 18th c., add. 19th c., sold 19th c.); Whitley Abbey (Hall), Warwickshire (built early 17th c., acq. by mar. early 19th c., add. c. 1808, sold 1867, demolished 1953)

Estates: Bateman 2600 (E) 5311. 1 Viscount left his widow an income of only about £800 pa. A state pension of £2,000 pa was granted in 1800.
Titles: Baron Hood 1782- I; Baronet 1778-
Peers: {1 peer 1782-1800} 6 peers 1796-1846 1859-1945
Notes: 1 Viscount and three others in ODNB.

Viscount Bridport (1800-1814 UK; 1868- UK)

Origins: Samuel Hood was the father of two admirals, Viscount Hood and Viscount Bridport. The Bridport title passed by special remainder to a younger son of the 2 Viscount Hood.

1. Alexander Hood 1 Viscount Bridport – Bridgwater 1784-90 Buckingham 1790-96
2. Samuel Hood 2 Baron Bridport – Heytesbury 1812-18
3. Arthur Hood 2 Viscount Hood – W. Somerset 1868-80

Seat: Cricket St. Thomas House, Somerset (medieval, purch. 1775 for £14,000, remod. c. 1800, sold 1898, hotel)
Estates: Bateman 5512 (E) 8098
Titles: Baron Bridport 1794- I; Baron Bridport 1796-1814 GB; Duke of Bronte (cr. 1799 - Two Sicilies) from 1873, inherited from a maternal ancestor, Viscount Nelson
Peers: 4 peers 1796-1814 1868-1945
Notes: 1 Viscount in ODNB.

Baron St. Audries (1911- UK)

Origins: Cousins of the Hood Viscounts. The 3 Baronet married in 1849 the daughter and heiress of Sir Palmer Fuller-Palmer-Acland. Their son succeeded to the Palmer estates (see Acland). He was created 1 Baron St. Audries.

1. Sir Samuel Hood 1 Bt – Westminster 1806-07 Bridport 1807-12
2. Sir Alexander Hood 2 Bt – West Somerset 1847-51
3. Sir Alexander Fuller-Acland-Hood 3 Bt – W. Somerset 1859-68
4. Sir Alexander Fuller-Acland-Hood 1 Baron St. Audries – W. Somerset 1892-1911

Seats: St. Audries Park, Somerset (medieval, purch. 1835 by Fuller-Acland-Palmers, Hoods acq. by mar. 1849, remod. 1835-70, rebuilt c. 1870-72, sold 1925, hotel); Fairfield, Somerset (remod. 1815, inherit. from the Palmers via the Aclands 1849, still own); Wootton House, Somerset (built 17th c., add. 1722, remod. mid-18th c., acq. by mar. 1792 from families who held it since the 16th c., add. c. 1802 and 1843, part demolished c. 1885, still own)
Estates: Bateman 11337 (E) 17431

Titles: Baron Hood of Avalon 1892-1901 UK; Baronet 1809-
Peers: 3 Peers 1892-1901 1911-45
Notes: 1 Baron Hood in ODNB.

Palmer

Origins: The Palmers were gentry in Sussex by the 14th century. Courtiers and soldiers under the Tudors gained lucrative offices. **First MP 1529. Five additional MPs 1553-1601, four of them kts of the shire**. They acquired property in Somerset by marrying a Verney heiress c. 1580 (whose family had held it since the beginning of the 13th century). Estates passed via an heiress to the Hoods in the mid-19th century (see Baron St. Audries above).

1. Peregrine Palmer – Bridgwater 1669-79
2. Thomas Palmer – Minehead 1679-81
3. Nathaniel Palmer – Minehead 1685-87 1689-90 Somerset 1690-95 Bridgwater 1695-98 Somerset 1699-1708 Bridgwater 1710-15
4. Thomas Palmer – Bridgwater 1715-27 1731-35
5. Peregrine Palmer – University of Oxford 1745-62

Seat: Fairfield, Somerset (medieval house, add. 16th and 17th c., remod. 1780, passed by mar. to Aclands in the 18th c.)

Earl of Castlemaine (1661-1705 I)

Origins: The Palmer Baronets of Wingham, Kent were a cadet of the Palmers of Sussex and Somerset (see above). **First MP 1614-44. One further MP 1621-26**. A younger son of the 1 Bt became a courtier under James I, and his younger son, the husband of Charles II's mistress, the Duchess of Cleveland, was created Earl of Castlemaine.

1. Roger Palmer 1 Earl of Castlemaine – Newton 1640-44 Windsor 1660
2. Sir Thomas Palmer 4 Bt – Kent 1708-10 Rochester 1715-22 1722-23

Seats: Llanfyllin Hall, Montgomeryshire (built 16th c., remod. 1832); Wingham, Kent (purch. 1553, passed to an illegitimate son and then out of the family 1723); Dorney Court, Berkshire (built late 15th c., purch. 1624, add. early early-mid-16th c., remod. 1733, 1840s, 1867, c. 1905-10, descendents still own)
Estate: Worth £1,500 pa in 1705
Title: Baronet 1621-1838
Notes: 1 Bt and 1 Earl and three others in ODNB.

HOOKE

Hooke

Origins: Bristol merchants in the early 17th century. Granted arms 1600. **First MP 1640**.

1. Sir Humphrey Hooke – Bristol 1666-77

Seat: King's Weston, Gloucestershire (built c. 1580s, purch. early 17th c., sold 1679)

Hooke

Origins: Cousins of the Hookes of Bristol. Founder of this line was a merchant.

1. John Hooke – Haslemere 1659 Winchester 1660

Seat: Bramshott Place, Hampshire (purch. and built 1594, sold 1685, demolished mid-19th c.)

HOPE [Beresford, Bruce, Johnstone, Vanden-Bempde, Vere (Weir), Wallace] *SCOTLAND & ENGLAND*

Hope

Origins: The common ancestor of the Hopes was Henry Hope father of Sir Thomas Hope 1 Bt of Craighall, ancestor of the Hopes of Culdraines, the Marquises of Linlithgow, and the Beresford-Hopes. He may have come from France with James V in the mid-16th century. Merchant in Edinburgh under Queen Mary. The 1 Bt was Lord Advocate, and the 2 Bt was a very successful lawyer, Lord of Session, who purchased large estates. **First [MP 1650].** The 4 Bt married the daughter and heiress of Sir William Bruce of Kinross 8 Bt (see Brudenell).

1. Sir Archibald Hope – [Fifeshire 1706]
2. Thomas Hope – [Fifeshire 1706-07]
3. John Bruce-Hope 7 Bt – Kinross-shire 1727-34 1741-47
4. Sir John Hope 11 Bt – Edinburghshire 1845-53
5. Sir John Hope 16 Bt – Midlothian 1912-18 N. Div. Midlothian and Peebles 1918-22

Seats: Culdraines, Kinross-shire (acq. by mar. 1729, passed out of family 1766); Craighall, Fife (medieval castle, purch. and built early 17th c., remod. 1697-99, sold to the Earl of Hopetoun 1729, demolished 1955); Pinkie House, Edinburghshire (built mid-16th c., rebuilt 1613, purch. 1788, add. early 18th c., remod. 19th c., sold 1950, school)

Title: Baronet 1628-
Notes: 1, 7, and 8 Bts and six others in ODNB.

Marquis of Linlithgow (1902- UK)

Origins: Descended from a younger son of Sir Thomas Hope 1 Bt of Craighall. Developed great mining interests in Lanarkshire in the 17th c. **First [MP 1639]. Two further [MPs 1649-50].** The 3 Earl of Hopetoun succeeded in 1792 to the estates of George Marquis of Annandale, his grand uncle. The Marquis's daughter and heiress married William Hope of Craigie Hall and inherited those estates.

1. John Hope – [Linlithgowshire 1681]
2. Charles Hope 1 Earl of Hopetoun – [Linlithgowshire 1703]
3. John Hope 4 Earl of Hopetoun – Linlithgowshire 1790-1800
4. Charles Hope – Dysart Burghs 1790-96 Haddingtonshire 1800-16
5. Sir Alexander Hope – Dumfries Burghs 1796-1800 Linlithgowshire 1800-34
6. Charles Hope – Dumfries Burghs 1802 Edinburgh 1803-04
7. Sir George Hope – East Grinstead 1815-18
8. John Hope – Gatton 1830-31 Okehampton 1831-32
9. James Hope-Wallace – Linlithgowshire 1835-38
10. George Hope – Weymouth 1837-42 Southampton 1842-47 Windsor 1859-63
11. Charles Hope – Linlithgowshire 1838-45
12. Thomas Hope – Linlithgow 1893-95
13. James Hope 1 Baron Rankeillour – Brightside Div. Sheffield 1900-06 Central Div. Sheffield 1908-29
14. Arthur Hope 2 Baron Rankeillour – Nuneaton Div. Warwickshire 1924-29 Aston Div. Birmingham 1931-39
15. John Hope 1 Baron Glendevon – N. Midlothian Div. Midlothian and Peebles 1945-50 Pentlands Div. Edinburgh 1950-64

Seats: Hopetoun House, Linlithgowshire (purch. 1678, built 1699-1703, add. 1721-58, add. 1774, still own); Niddry (Niddrie) Castle, Linlithgowshire (built 15th c., acq. 1676, decayed, sold and restored 1980s); Ormiston Hall (House), Haddingtonshire (medieval castle now offices, new house purch. and built 1747, partly demolished 1940, still own); Luffness Castle, Haddingtonshire (built 15th c., add. 16th c., purch. 1739, still own); Over Rankeillour House, Fife (purch. later 17th c., built new house 1796-1800, remod. c. 1833, sold later 19th c.)
Estates: Bateman 42507 (S) 43491. Owned 21,300 acres in 1996; Luffness line 5710 (S) 11235
Titles: Earl of Hopetoun 1703- S; Baron Hopetoun 1809- UK; Baron Niddry 1814- UK; Baron Rankeillour 1932- UK; Baron Glendevon 1964- UK; Baronet 1698-1763

Peers: [1 peer 1704-07] 2 Scottish Rep peers 1722-42 1784-90 1794-96 8 peers 1809-16 1814-43 1852-73 1881-1945 1932-45
7 Lds Lt 18th, 19th, 20th
1 in Cabinet 1905
3 KT 18th, 19th
Notes: The Marquis of Linlithgow was Viceroy of India in the 1930s. 1, 3, and 4 Earls and 1 and 2 Marquises, and 1 Baron Rankeillor and fourteen others in ODNB.

Baron Wallace (1828-44 UK)

Origins: Thomas Wallace founded the family in the early 17th century by marrying an heiress. He purchased some land in 1637. His great-grandson was an attorney, whose son, the first MP, was Attorney General in 1780. He married the heiress to Carleton Hall (Simpson). The 1 Baron Wallace left his estates to his wife's nephew, John Hope, who took the additional name Wallace 1844 (see above).

1. James Wallace – Horsham 1770-83
2. Thomas Wallace 1 Baron Wallace – Grampound 1790-96 Penryn 1796-1802 Hindon 1802-06 Shaftesbury 1807-12 Weymouth 1812-13 Cockermouth 1813-18 Weymouth 1818-28

Seats: Featherstone Castle, Northumberland (medieval, rebuilt early 17th c., purch. 1766, extended 1828, sold 1950); Carleton Hall, Cumberland (purch. and built c. 1700 by Pattisons from who it passed by mar. to the Wallaces, remod. late 18th c., sold 1828); Asholme, Northumberland (acq. 1637, declined to farm house later 18th c.)
Estates: Worth under £3,000 pa in Bateman.
Peer: 1 peer 1828-44
Notes: 1 Baron and one other in ODNB.

Hope-Vere

Origins: The second son of the 1 Earl of Hopetoun succeeded to Craigie Hall in 1730, inheriting it from his uncle the 2 Marquis of Annandale. He spent time in London as a merchant. He succeeded to Blackwood House by marriage in 1733 to the daughter and heiress of Sir William Weir 2 Bt and took the additional name Weir (Vere). The Weir family emerged in the 12th century.

1. Charles Hope Vere – Linlithgowshire 1743-68
2. John Hope – Linlithgowshire 1768-70
3. James Hope-Vere – Ilchester 1830-31 Newport (IoW) 1831-32

Seats: Craigie Hall (Craigiehall), Linlithgowshire (built 1695, inher. 1730, in possession of the army 20th c.); Blackwood House, Lanarkshire (Weirs acq. by 1404, sold 1930s)
Estates: Bateman 8289 (S) 15949
Notes: Three in ODNB.

Weir (Vere)

Origins: Cadets of the Blackwood line who acquired estates in the 15th century.

1. Daniel Weir – Linlithgow Burghs 1722-24
2. James Vere – Lanarkshire 1754-59

Seat: Stonebyres, Lanarkshire (acq. 15th c., built 16th c., sold mid-19th c., demolished 1939)

Marquis of Annandale (1701-92 S)

Origins: First recorded as a Scottish baron who swore fielty to Edward I in 1296. His great-grandson was prominent under David II and Robert II. Sir James Johnstone was Warden of the West Marches 1597. His son was created Baron Johnstone in 1633. **First [MP 1560]. One further [MP 1609]**. The estates of the 2 Marquis passed to the Earls of Hopetoun (see above).

1. James Johnstone – [Dumfriesshire 1690]
2. James Lord Johnstone – Dumfriesshire 1708 Dumfriesshire & Linlithgowshire 1708
3. Lord John Johnstone – Dumfries Burghs 1741-42

Seats: Craigie Hall (Craigiehall), Linlithgowshire (built 1695, passed to Hopes 1730); Lochwood Castle (Tower), (Johnstoun, Johnstone) Dumfriesshire (medieval, abandoned early 18th c., ruin)
Estates: The estate of the last Marquis was valued at £415,000.
Titles: Baron Johnstone 1633-61 S; Earl of Hartfell 1643-61 S; Earl of Annandale and Hartfell 1661-1792 S
Peers: [2 peers 1660-72 1685-1707] 1 Scottish Rep peer 1708-13 1715-21
1 Ld Lt 18th
1 in Cabinet 1705
1 KT 18th
Notes: 1 Marquis in ODNB.

Hope-Johnstone

Origins: The daughter of the 3 Earl of Hopetoun and heiress of the 2 Marquis of Annandale, Anne of Annandale, married Sir William Hope, a cousin, younger son of the Craigie Hall line. She succeeded to the Annandale estates in 1818.

1. Sir William Johnstone-Hope – Dumfries Burghs 1800-02 Dumfriesshire 1804-30
2. John Hope-Johnstone – Dumfriesshire 1830-47 1857-65
3. John Hope-Johnstone – Dumfriesshire 1874-80

Seats: Raehills House, Dumfriesshire (built 1782-92, add. 1829-34, still own); Moffat House, Dumfriesshire (built 1762-67, now hotel); Knockdrin Castle, Westmeath (leased 19th c., see Levinge)
Estates: Bateman 65366 (S) 28236
Notes: One in ODNB.

Johnstone

Origins: After the death of the last Marquis of Annandale the Johstones of Westerhall became the chiefs of the clan. The 5 Bt married the daughter of Daniel Pulteney, first cousin of the Earl of Bath and took the name Pulteney when he inherited the estates of Lord Bath in 1767. Their daughter was created Countess of Bath in 1803. (see Murray of Dunerne). On her husband's death the estates (said to be worth £50,000 pa) were divided among the Johnstones, Sir Robert Sutton, and the Earl of Darlington (Duke of Cleveland).

1. Sir James Johnstone – [Dumfries 1689-98]
2. Sir John Johnstone 1 Bt – [Dumfriesshire 1700-07] Scotland 1707-08
3. Sir William Johnstone 2 Bt – [Annan Burgh 1698-1707] Dumfries Burghs 1708-10 1713 Dumfriesshire 1713-22
4. Sir Johnstone 3 Bt – Dumfries Burghs 1743-54
5. George Johnstone – Cockermouth 1768-74 Appleby 1774-80 Lostwithiel 1780-84 Ilchester 1786-87
6. Sir William Johnstone-Pulteney 5 Bt – Cromartyshire 1768-74 Shrewsbury 1775-1805
7. Sir James Johnstone 4 Bt – Dumfries Burghs 1784-90 Weymouth & Melcombe Regis 1791-94
8. Sir John Johnstone 6 Bt – Weymouth & Melcombe Regis 1810-11
9. Sir George Johnstone 7 Bt – Weymouth 1832-35
10. Sir Frederic Johnstone 8 Bt – Weymouth 1874-85

Seat: Westerhall House, Dumfries (built 17th c., add. early 18th c., add. 1783, fire 1873, restored, fire 1955, restored, still own)
Estates: Bateman 17264 (S) 9550 and held plantations in the WI and large tracts of land in North America.
Title: Baronet 1700-
Notes: 5 Bt, who took the name Pulteney, and six others in ODNB.

Johnstone

Origins: Descended from a younger brother of the 5 Bt of Westerhall. John Johnstone MP 1774-80 worked for the East India Company and returned from India with a fortune of £300,000.

1. John Johnstone – Dysart Burghs 1774-80
2. James Johnstone – Clackmannan & Kinross 1851-57
3. John Johnstone – Horsham Div. Sussex 1893-1904

Seat: Alva House, Clackmannanshire (built before 1542, rebuilt 1636, purch. c. 1766, add. c. 1820, sold 1929, demolished c. 1945)
Estates: Bateman 15541 (S) 7230
Notes: The Johnstones inherited the Hawkins estates 1903 (see Hawkins). One in ODNB.

Baron Derwent (1881- UK)

Origins: The brother of the 3 Bt of Westerhall married the daughter and heiress of John Vanden-Bempde (she was the Dowager Marchioness of Annandale) of Hackness Hall. Their son Richard Vanden-Bempde-Johnstone (not a Johnstone, but a uterine brother of the last Marquis) was created a Baronet and succeeded to Hackness Hall. The Bempde's came to England in the reign of Henry VIII as merchants. Kted by the King. They purchased Hackness in 1707.

1. John Vanden-Bempde – Aldborough 1690
2. Sir Richard Vanden-Bempde-Johnstone 1 Bt – Weymouth & Melcombe Regis 1790-96
3. Sir John Johnstone 2 Bt – Yorkshire 1830-32 Scarborough 1832-37 1841-69
4. Harcourt Johnstone 1 Baron Derwent – Scarborough 1869-80
5. Harcourt Johnstone – E. Willseden 1923-24 South Shields 1931-35 Middlesborough W. 1940-45

Seat: Hackness Hall, Yorkshire (built 16th c., purch. 1707 for £31,000, built 1790-96, fire 1910, rebuilt, still own)
Estates: Bateman 12764 (E) 10026. Owned 12,000 acres worth 72 million pounds in 2001.
Title: Baronet 1795-
Peers: 3 peers 1881-1945

Hope

Origins: Began with of the 1 Bt of Craighall (see above) who married the 1 Baron Decies. The Hopes migrated to the Netherlands in the 17th century and became merchants in Rotterdam. They began the creation of a great fortune by founding a bank in Amsterdam in 1731, sold to the Barings in 1814. They moved to England in 1794.

1. Henry Hope – East Looe 1829-32 Gloucester 1833-41 1847-52
2. Alexander Beresford-Hope – Maidstone 1841-52 1857-59 Stoke 1865-68 Cambridge University 1868-87

Seats: The Deepdene, Surrey (built early 17th c., rebuilt 1769-75, purch. 1807, rebuilt 1802-29, add. c. 1836-40, passed to the 8 Duke of Newcastle, leased out, sold 1920, demolished 1969); Trenant Park, Cornwall (built early 17th c., purch. and remod. 1829, sold mid-19th c., add. mid-19th c., flats); Bedgebury Park, Kent (classical style, purch. by Viscount Beresford 1836, passed by inher. to the Hopes 1854, remod. c. 1854-55, sold 1899, owned by state); Rushton Hall, Northamptonshire (built early 16th c., add. 1626-31, purch. 1828, remod. mid-19th c., sold 1855, from 1940 institutional use); Hope Castle (Blayney Castle), Monagahan (built 17th c., purch. 1853, passed by inher. 1861 to Duke of Newcastle)
Estates: Bateman 22430 (E & I) 22138. Rubinstein – Henry Hope left £500,000 in probate in 1821 and Thomas Hope £180,000 in 1831.
Notes: The estates were left to a daughter in 1862 who married the 6 Duke of Newcastle (see Pelham). The Hope family has an entry in the ODNB and three others also included.

HOPKINS

Origins: Drapers and Mayors in Coventry since the 15th century. **First MP 1614 for Coventry**.

1. Richard Hopkins – Coventry 1660
2. Richard Hopkins – Coventry 1670-81 1690-95 1698-1700
3. Thomas Hopkins – Coventry 1701
4. Edward Hopkins – Coventry 1701-02 1707-10 Eye 1713-27 {Dublin 1721-27}
5. Richard Hopkins – Dartmouth 1766-80 Thetford 1780-84 Dartmouth 1784-90 Queenborough 1790-96 Harwich 1796-99
6. Benjamin Hopkins – Great Bedwyn 1771-74

Seat: Oving House, Buckinghamshire (purch. 1756, sold 1862)
Notes: Oving passed to the granddaughter of Richard Hopkins, who married Lord Boston (who sold in 1862, see Irby under Paget).

HOPTON

Origins: Can be traced to 1408, but only emerge as significant in the mid-16th century with Sir Richard Hopton "the Userer". Kt c. 1600.

1. Sir Edward Hopton – Hereford 1661
2. Richard Hopton – Herefordshire 1715-22
3. Edward Hopton – Hereford 1841-47

Seats: Cannon ffrome (Frome) Court, Herefordshire (built 17th c., acq. by mar., rebuilt 1786, sold 1948); Kemerton Court, Worcestershire (16th-17th c., inher. by mar. from the Parsons, sold 20th c.)
Estates: Bateman 5532 (E) 7700

HORDE

Origins: Prominent burgesses in Bridgnorth in the 15th and 16th centuries. **First MP 1391 for Bridgnorth. Seven MPs 1414-1601, six of them for Bridnorth, on kt of the shire**. In 1400 they succeeded to the property of the Palmers of Bridgnorth. **First MP 1311 for Bridgnorth. Five further MPs 1315-99 all for Bridgnorth**. Hence the family represented the town for three centuries. Successful Tudor lawyer purchased Cote House. The MP below was from the branch of the family that became important country gentry. (Cox, *Victoria County History, Shropshire*, 242)

1. Thomas Horde – Oxfordshire 1679-81

Seats: Horde (Hoards) Park, Shropshire (acq. mid-15th c., built 16th c., sold 1619); Cote House, Brampton, Oxfordshire (medieval, purch. and rebuilt 1553, remod. c. 1600, remod. c. 1700, leased out from mid-18th c., passed by inher. to Hippisleys 1836, sold 1920)
Notes: Male line extinct 1785.

HORE *IRELAND*

Earl of Gowrie (1581-1600 S; 1945- UK)

Origins: The Hores acquired land in Ireland beginning in 1547. **First {MP 1559 for County Wexford}. An additional {MP 1634}**. In 1806 Walter Hore married Mary Baroness Ruthven in her own right. Their son took the name Hore-Ruthven and was created 1 Baron Ruthven. The family claimed Saxon descent, settling in Scotland under David I. The first Lord of Parliament 1488, killed at Flodden. **First [MP 1567]. An additional [MP for Perthshire 1639]**. Earls of Gowrie 1581-84 and 1586-1600 S.

1. William Hore – {County Wexford 1709-13}
2. William Hore – {Taghmon 1727-46}
3. Walter Hore – {Taghmon 1746-60}
4. Walter Hore – {Taghmon 1761-68}

Seat: Harperstown House, Wexford (old castle, acq. and rebuilt later 17th c., family departed 1860s, estates sold off, house neglected and became a ruin late 19th early 20th c.)
Estates: Bateman 7624 (I & S) 10981
Titles: Baron Ruthven 1651- S; Baron Ruthven 1919- UK; Baron Gowrie 1935- UK
Peers: [2 peers 1661-1701] 3 peers 1919-45 1935-45
Notes: The Hores were in extreme financial difficulty later 19th c. The 1 Earl of Gowrie was Governor General of Australia during World War II and the 2 Earl was a Minister in the 1980s. The 1 and 2 Barons Ruthven and 1 Earl of Forth and 1 and 3 Earls of Gowrie of the 1st creation (Ruthven) and the 1 Earl of the 2nd creation (Hore-Ruthven) and three others in ODNB.

HORNBY

Origins: The first MP was the son of a cotton manufacturer. He was a lawyer.

1. John Hornby – Blackburn 1841-52
2. William Hornby – Blackburn 1857-69
3. Edward Hornby – Blackburn 1869-74
4. Sir William Hornby 1 Bt – Blackburn 1886-1910

Seats: Poole Hall, Cheshire (old house, rebuilt 1812-17, leased later 19th c.); Raikes Hall, Lancashire (built c. 1760, purch. 1820, sold 1860); Shrenbridge Hall, Cheshire (owned 19th c.); Ribby Hall, Lancashire (purch. and built 1795, sold 1916, now flats)
Title: Baronet 1899-
Notes: Two in ODNB.

HOSKYNS (Hoskins) [Wren]

<u>Hoskyns</u>

Origins: Yeomen under the Tudors. **First MP 1604** a lawyer (his elder brother was a draper). **Another MP 1646 and 1654**. The 1 Bt was a barrister. Chandos Wren-Hoskyns married Sir Christopher Wren's daughter and heiress to Wroxall Abbey (see Wren).

1. Sir John Hoskyns 2 Bt – Herefordshire 1685-87
2. Sir Hungerford Hoskyns 4 Bt – Herefordshire 1717-22
3. Charles Wren-Hoskyns – Hereford 1869-74

Seats: Harewood Park, Herefordshire (built 16th c., purch. 1654, rebuilt 18th c. and early 19th c., house sold c. 1918, estate sold 1941, demolished 1952); Wroxall Abbey, Warwickshire (acq. by Wren marriage 1828, sold 1861); Morehampton Park, Herefordshire (purch. 1621 for £3,000, declined into a farm, house demolished early 19th c.)
Title: Baronet 1676-
Notes: 1, 2, and 13 Bts and three others in ODNB.

Hoskins

Origins: Cadet line.

1. Kedgwin Hoskins – Herefordshire 1831-47

Seat: Strickstenning (Much Birch), Herefordshire (built 17th c., resident 19th c.)

HOTHAM

Baron Hotham (1797- I)

Origins: The Hothams descended from Sir John de Trehouse, who came from Normandy with the Conqueror (Fisher, *The House of Commons*, V, 713). Seated at Scorborough since the 12th century. **First MP 1307 for Yorkshire. Five additional MPs 1378-1643, two knights of the shire**. Achieved one of the great fortunes in Yorkshire in the early 17th century by means that remain mysterious (English, *The Great Landowners of East Yorkshire*, 19).

1. Sir John Hotham 2 Bt Beverley 1660-81 1689
2. Sir John Hotham 3 Bt – Beverley 1689-90
3. Sir Charles Hotham 4 Bt – Scarborough 1695-1702 Beverley 1702-23
4. Sir Charles Hotham 5 Bt – Beverley 1723-27 1729-38
5. Sir Charles Hotham 8 Bt – St. Ives 1761-68
6. Beaumont Hotham 2 Baron Hotham – Wigan 1768-75
7. Beaumont Hotham 3 Baron Hotham – Leominster 1820-41 E. R. Yorkshire 1841-68

Seats: (South) Dalton Hall, Yorkshire (purch. 1680, built c. 1705, add. c. 1730, rebuilt 1770s, remod. 1870s, still own); Scorborough Hall, Yorkshire (original seat acq. 13th c., built c. 1600, burned c. 1705); Hotham House, Yorkshire (built c. 1721, sold 1766, demolished c. 1768); Humbleton (Hall, Manor), Yorkshire (acq. by mar. 1764, medieval manor house demolished late 18th c., the Hall – built 1811-24 – purch. 1866, estate and Hall sold 1908-19)

Estates: Bateman 20352 (E) 26126. Worth £3,000 pa in 1645. Rubinstein – 1 Baron left £125,000 probate in 1813.
Title: Baronet 1621-
Peers: {1 peer 1797-1800}
Notes: The family encountered major problems during the Civil War, both father and son were executed, but the estates survived intact. (Roebuck, *Yorkshire Baronets*, 62ff.) Became a naval family that produced several admirals in the 18th century. The 7 Bt married the Thompson heiress of Humbleton, Yorkshire in the mid-18th century (see Thompson I). The Hothams expanded their holdings at Humbletom by large purchases of land 1870s and 1880s. 1 Bt and 1, 2, and 3 Barons and six others in ODNB.

HOWARD I [Fitzalan, FitzHerbert, Gally Knight, Griffin, Jerningham, Knight, Stafford, Stephenson, Talbot, Vyse]

<u>Duke of Norfolk</u> (1483- E)

Origins: Began as burgesses or yeomen in Norfolk. A successful lawyer, who purchased landed estates was appointed Chief Justice Common Pleas 1297. **First MP 1295. Nine additional MPs 1328-1640, six of them kts of the shire.** High Sheriff 1317. Married a Mowbray (Dukes of Norfolk) heiress in the 15th century. Baron 1470. Became the premier noble family in England (Robinson, *The Dukes of Norfolk*).

1. Lord Frederick Howard – {Duleek 1716-27}
2. Charles Howard 11 Duke of Norfolk – Carlisle 1780-86
3. Lord Henry Howard-Molyneux-Howard – Arundel 1790-95 Gloucester 1795-1818 Arundel 1818-20 Steyning 1820-24
4. Henry Howard – Steyning 1824-26 Shoreham 1826-32
5. Henry Howard 13 Duke of Norfolk – Horsham 1829-32 W. Sussex 1832-41
6. Henry Stephenson – Westbury 1831-32 (illegitimate son of the 11 Duke of Norfolk)
7. Henry Howard 14 Duke of Norfolk – Arundel 1837-51 Limerick 1851-52
8. Edward Fitzalan-Howard 1 Baron Howard of Glossop – Horsham 1848-52 Arundel 1853-68
9. Sir Edward Howard – E. Cumberland 1876-85 Thornbury Div. Gloucestershire 1885-86
10. Henry Howard – Penrith Div. Cumberland 1885-86
11. Edmund Howard Talbot 1 Viscount Fitzalan – Chichester Div. Sussex 1894-1921

Seats: Arundel Castle, Sussex (built soon after 1066, add. c. 1138, acq. by Fitzalans 1234, passed by mar. to Dukes of Norfolk 1556, slighted 1654, ruin by mid-18th c., reconstruction 1787-1812, rebuilt 1875-1903, still own); Worksop Manor, Nottinghamshire (built 1595, acq. by mar. 17th c., fire 1761, rebuilt 1767, sold 1840 and demolished); Beech Hill, Yorkshire (built 16th c., rebuilt c. 1830, add. 1859, in use in 20th c., now institutional use);

Duke's Palace, Norwich, Norfolk (built early 16th c., demolished 1662, rebuilt and used until 1708, demolished again); Derwent Hall, Derbyshire (built 1670s, remod. 1692, purch. 1876, add. 1877-81, leased out from 1932, flooded by reservoir 1945); Fornham Hall, Suffolk (built 1770s, purch. 1789, add. c. 1800, sold 1842, demolished 1951); The Deepdene, Surrey (acq. and built early 17th c., rebuilt 1769-75, sold c. 1800); Greystoke Castle, Cumberland (medieval, passed by mar. from the original grantees after the Norman Conquest via the Greystokes and Dacres to the Howards 1595, fire c. 1675, held by the brother of the 6 Duke of Norfolk whose descendent became 10th Duke, then to a brother of the 12th Duke and his descendents, Lords Howard of Penrith, remod. 1670s, much demolished 1789, remod. 1837-48, fire 1868 and rebuilt 1875-78, huge park of 5,000 acres, still own); Thornbury Castle, Gloucestershire (medieval, rebuilt 1507-21, purch. 1727, sold 1960s, now hotel); Glossop Hall (Royle Hall), Derbyshire (acq. by Talbots 15th c., passed by mar. to Howards 1604, built early 18th c., rebuilt 1850, sold 1925, demolished 1956); Catterlen Hall, Cumberland (medieval, add. 1577 and 1652, purch. by Howards of Greystoke mid-18th c., sold c. 1890); Albury Park, Surrey (medieval, acq. 1641, rebuilt mid to later 17th c., fire 1697, sold 1685)
Estates: Bateman 49866 (E) 75596. The 2 Duke was worth £4,500 pa in the 1520s. Howard of Greystoke 17540 (E) 9249 and Lord Howard of Glossop 17911 (E&S) 13102. Rubinstein – 11 Duke left £140,000 in probate in 1815. Owned 46,000 acres worth 210 million pounds in 2001.
Titles: Earl of Arundel 1433- E; Earl of Surrey 1483- E; Earl of Norfolk 1644- E; Baron Howard of Castle Rising 1669- E; Earl of Norwich 1672- E; Baron Howard of Glossop 1869- UK; Viscount Fitzalan of Derwent 1921- UK; Baron Howard of Penrith 1930- UK
Peers: 15 peers 1660-77 1669-1701 1786-1815 1829-60 1868-1917 1869-1945 1921-45 1929-45 1930-45
4 Lds Lt 17th, 18th, 19th, 20th
1 in Cabinet 1921-22
6 KG 17th, 18th, 19th, 20th
Notes: The Dukes of Norfolk hold the hereditary office of Earl Marshal of England (from 1483), which places them at the center of royal ceremonial, particularly the conduct of coronations. They also hold one of the two hereditary seats remaining in the House of Lords after the reforms of the 1990s. The 4 Duke of Norfolk married Lady Mary FitzAlan, heiress to Arundell Castle (1 Earl of Arundell c. 1138 or 1139, head of a great Norman family). The family also became and remain the leading Roman Catholic family in England, although a few members have conformed to the established church. This greatly reduced the number of MPs the family elected until after 1828. The Barony of Greystoke and the associated Castle in Cumberland was granted to the Norman Earl of Northumberland after the Conquest. It passed through the de Greystokes. The last of these, an heiress, married Sir Thomas Dacre, Lord Dacre in the early 16th century. His daughter Anne married the eldest son of the 4 Duke of Norfolk. It descended to a cadet line in the 17th century, which itself succeeded to the Dukedom in 1777. It was left to a younger brother of the 12 Duke. Younger sons also succeeded to Thornbury Castle

and Glossop Hall. Baronies were created for these cadets. The brother of the 15 Duke succeeded to the estates of the 17 Earl of Shrewsbury (see Talbot I) and was created Viscount Fitzalan. The estates of all the cadet lines except for the Talbots are included in the totals above. The brother of the 11 Duke, Edward Howard, was a successful chemist, who by 1816 was deriving an income of £30,000 pa from his patents. The 18th and 19th c. Dukes made a vast fortune in the textile trade in Derbyshire, which they promoted. Their agent built one of the largest mills in the area near Manchester on the estate. They also owned urban and industrial property in Sheffield. (Robinson, *Felling the Ancient Oaks*, 103-04.) 13, 14, and 15 Earls of Arundell and 1, 2, 3, 4, 6, 7, 10, 11, 12, 13, 14, 15, 16, and 17 Dukes and 1 Earl of Northampton and 1 Baron Howard of Glossop and 1 Baron Howard of Penrith and 1 Viscount Fitzalan and fourteen others in ODNB.

<u>Earl of Suffolk and Berkshire</u> (1603- and 1625- E)

Origins: The 1 Earl of Suffolk was a younger son of the 4 Duke of Norfolk. He inherited Audley End from the 1 Baron Audley, whose daughter had married the Duke. The 1 Baron Audley was Speaker of the House of Commons in 1529. A younger son of the 1 Earl of Suffolk was created Earl of Berkshire. The 4 Earl of Berkshire succeeded to the Suffolk title in 1745. Another younger son of the 1 Earl of Suffolk was created Baron Howard of Escrick. **First MP 1604. Ten additional MPs followed 1605-51.** Audley End passed to the daughter of the 3 Earl of Suffolk, who married the 1 Baron Griffin (see Neville). The Griffins had acquired Braybrooke in the 14th century from an heiress whose family had held it from 1232. An important legal family under the Tudors. Barons 1688.

1. William Howard 3 Baron Howard of Escrick – Winchelsea 1660
2. George Howard – Tavistock 1660-71
3. Sir Robert Howard – Stockbridge 1661-79 Castle Rising 1679-81 1689-98
4. Philip Howard – Malmesbury 1662-79 Westminster 1689-90
5. Thomas Howard – New Woodstock 1674-79
6. Thomas Howard – Castle Rising 1685-87 Bletchingley 1689-98 Castle Rising 1698-1701
7. James Griffin 2 Baron Griffin – Brackley 1685-87
8. Henry Howard 6 Earl of Suffolk – Arundell 1694-98 Essex 1705-06
9. Craven Howard – Malmesbury 1695-98
10. Henry Howard 10 Earl of Suffolk – Bere Alston 1728-33
11. William Howard Viscount Andover – Castle Rising 1737-47
12. Thomas Howard 14 Earl of Suffolk – Castle Rising 1747-68 Malmesbury 1768-74 Mitchell 1774-79
13. John Griffin 4 Baron Howard de Walden (1 Baron Braybrooke) – Andover 1749-84
14. Thomas Griffin – Arundell 1754-61
15. Thomas Howard 16 Earl of Suffolk – Arundell 1802-06

16. Charles Howard 17 Earl of Suffolk – Malmesbury 1832-41
17. James Howard – Malmesbury 1841-52
18. Henry Howard – Cricklade 1841-47
19. Henry Howard 18 Earl of Suffolk – Malmesbury 1859-68
20. Charles Howard – Bilston Div. Wolverhampton 1922-24 Chelmsford Div. Essex 1926-31
21. Greville Howard – St. Ives 1950-66

Seats: Audley End, Essex (medieval, acq. by Audley 1538, inher. by Howards mid-century, rebuilt 1603-14, remod. 17th and 18th c., sold and repurch. part demolished c. 1720 and 1750, passed to Griffins); Charlton Park, Wiltshire (acq. by mar. 1598 from a family that purch. at the Dissolution, add. early 17th c., add. 1772-76, family departed 1945, now flats but family still retain the estate and a residence); Ashstead Park, Surrey (purch. 1680, passed out of family by mar. 1783); Elford Hall, Staffordshire (old house, acq. by mar. 1683, rebuilt 1710, sold 19th c., demolished 1964); Castle Rising Hall, Norfolk (castle built 12th c., granted to the Dukes of Norfolk, 1544, and descended through this branch of the Howards who still own it; the Hall was built in the 19th c., demolished c. 1940)
Estates: 11098 (E) 14209. Audley End was said to have cost £200,000 to build in 1603, a staggering sum. (Kenworthy-Browne, et. al., *Burke's and Savills Guide to Country Houses: East Anglia*, III, 36)
Titles: Viscount Andover (1621- E); Baron Howard of Escrick (1628-1715 E); Baron Griffin (16888-1742 E); Earl of Bindon (1706-22 E); Baron Howard of Rising 2004- UKLife
Peers: 25 peers 1660-69 1660-1725 1660-1709 1678-1715 1689-90 1731-45 1762-1917 1784-97 1927-41
5 Lds Lt 17th, 18th
2 in Cabinet 1715-18 1771-77
2 KG 17th, 18th
Notes: Lord Suffolk built an enormous house at Audley End, eventually sold to Charles II in 1669. The house was returned to the Suffolks in 1701. It later passed to the Griffins and then the Nevilles. The daughter and heiress of the 11 Earl of Suffolk brought Levens Hall, Westmorland to the Howards in 1745. In 1809 it passed by mar. to the Uptons of Castle Upton (see that family). Richard Bagot (son of Sir Walter Bagot 5 Bt) married 1783 the sister of the 12 Earl of Suffolk and inherited Ashstead, Elford, Levens, and Castle Rising from the Earl of Berkshire and took the name Howard. Rubinsteon – Richard Bagot Howard left £350,000 in probate in 1818. His heiress married an Upton. 1 and 3 Barons Howard of Escrick and 4 Baron Howard de Walden and 1, 2, 3 and 12 Earls of Suffolk and eight others in ODNB.

Earl of Carlisle (1661- E)

Origins: Descended from the third son of the 4 Duke of Norfolk who married a Dacre heiress and acquired in the later 16th century Naworth Castle and the site of Castle Howard (Henderskelfe). The Dacres had acquired Naworth in 1335. **First MP 1442 for Cumberland. Five additional MPs 1447-1563, all kts of the shire.**

1. Charles Howard 1 Earl of Carlisle – Westmorland 1653 Cumberland 1654 1656 1660
2. Sir Philip Howard – Malton 1659 1660 Carlisle 1661-81
3. Charles Howard 2 Earl of Carlisle – Morpeth 1666-79 Cumberland 1679 Carlisle 1681
4. Charles Howard 3 Earl of Carlisle – Morpeth 1689-92
5. William Howard – Carlisle 1695-1700 Northumberland 1701
6. Philip Howard – Morpeth 1698-1700 Carlisle 1701-02
7. Henry Howard 4 Earl of Carlisle – Morpeth 1715-38
8. Charles Howard – Carlisle 1727-61
9. Charles Howard Viscount Morpeth – Yorkshire 1741
10. George Howard 6 Earl of Carlisle – Morpeth 1795-1806 Cumberland 1806-20
11. William Howard – Morpeth 1806-26 1830-32 Sutherlandshire 1837-40
12. George Howard 7 Earl of Carlisle – Morpeth 1826-30 Yorkshire 1830-32 W. R. Yorkshire 1832-41 1846-48
13. Frederick Howard – Morpeth 1832-34
14. Edward Howard 1 Baron Lanerton – Morpeth 1833-37 1840-52
15. Fredeick Howard – Youghal 1837-41
16. Charles Howard – Cumberland 1840-79
17. George Howard 9 Earl of Carlisle – E. Cumberland 1879-80 1881-85
18. Charles Howard 10 Earl of Carlisle – S. Birmingham 1904-11
19. Geoffrey Howard – Eskdale Div. Cumberland 1906-10 Westbury Div. Wiltshire 1911-18 Luton Div. Bedfordshire 1923-24

Seats: Castle Howard, Yorkshire (medieval, inher. by mar. from Dacres 1571, rebuilt 1683, fire 1693, rebuilt 1693-1730, add. 1753-59 and 1800, remod. 1875-78, fire 1940, rebuilt after war, still own); Naworth Castle, Cumberland (acq. by Dacres 1317 and built 1335, add. 1515-25, acq. by Howards by mar. 1571, remod. 1602-33 and 18th c., fire 1844, remod. 1844-51, add. 1881-86, still own); Calthwaite Hall, Cumberland (sold 1791); Askerton Castle, Cumberland (de Vaux family acquired 1157, passed to Lord Dacre 1317, built 14th c., add. 1500-10, passed to the Earls of Carlisle later 16th c., descendants still own)

Estates: Bateman 78540 (E) 49601. The Earl of Carlisle at Naworth was worth £42,000,000 with 10,000 acres in 1990. Simon Howard of Castle Howard owned 13,000 acres in 2001.

Titles: Baron Lanerton 1874-80 UK; Lord Howard of Henderskelfe 1983-84 UKLife

Peers: 12 peers 1661-1758 1769-1912 1874-80 1916-45
7 Lds Lt 17th, 18th, 19th, 20th
4 in Cabinet 1701-02 1715 1779-83 1827 1830-34 1835-41 1846-49 1850-52 1855-58 1859-64
4 KG 18th, 19th
Notes: The Naworth (Earl of Carlisle) and Castle Howard estates were split between two lines in 1921. Lord Howard of Henderskelfe (of Castle Howard) was Chairman of the BBC 1980-83. 1, 3, 4, 5, 6, 7, 9, and 10 Earls and Baron Howard of Henderskelfe and six others in ODNB.

Howard

Origins: A younger son of the first Howard at Naworth, a younger son of the 4 Duke of Norfolk, acquired Corby Castle, Cumberland. The 11 Duke of Norfolk left the family some property.

1. Philip Howard – Carlisle 1830-47 1848-52

Seats: Corby Castle, Cumberland (built 13th c., purch. 1611 and 1624, add. late 17th c., rebuilt 1812-17, sold 1994); Foxcote, Warwickshire (built early 18th c., acq. by mar. 1843, sold 1960); Middleton Lodge, Shropshire (built 18th c., acq. by mar. 1843, remod. mid-19th c., sold 1945)
Estates: Bateman 7297 (E) 8163
Notes: A Roman Catholic family, which explains the dearth of MPs. One in ODNB.

Earl of Stafford (1688-1792 E)

Origins: The Staffords were an ancient and powerful family. Lords in the 12th century. They built Stafford Castle soon after the Conquest. **First MP 1290 for Staffordshire. At least 18 MPs 1301-1547, many for the county and for Worcestershire.** Earl of Stafford 1351. They were Dukes of Buckingham 1444-1521. Mary Stafford succeeded to the estates in 1637 and married William Howard, younger son of the 14 Earl of Arundel and uncle of the 5 Duke of Norfolk. He was created Viscount Stafford. The family was Roman Catholic and attainted in 1680, restored to an Earldom in 1688. The title became extinct in 1762. Mary Stafford Howard, sister of the last Earl, married Francis Plowden. Their daughter and heiress married Sir George Jerningham 5 Bt, who inherited the Stafford estates in 1769. The Jernighams were an early medieval family. **First MP 1553. One other MP 1553.** A reversal of the attainder restored the Barony of Stafford in 1825. The Fitzherberts of Swynnerton inherited as heirs general in 1913.

1. William Stafford – Stamford 1661-65
2. Henry Stafford Jerningham 3 Baron Stafford – Pontefract 1830-34
3. Sir Hubert Jerningham – Berwick-on-Tweed 1881-85

Seats: Costessey Hall (Park), Norfolk (medieval, acq. 1555, rebuilt 1564, rebuilt c. 1826-55, sold 1913, dismantled c. 1920-25); Meretown House, Shropshire (sold); Shifnal Manor, Shropshire (medieval, inher. from Earls of Shrewbury, hotel); Stafford Castle, Staffordshire (medieval, demolished 1643-45, rebuilt 1813-17, occupation ceased 1950, most demolished 1961); Swynnerton Park, Staffordshire (acq. by the FitzHerberts mar. to the Swynnertons in the later 16th c., rebuilt c. 1713, passed by mar. to Jerninghams 1825, passed to Fitzherberts 1913); Longridge Towers, Northumberland (acq. by mar. mid-19th c., rebuilt 1870s, sold 1920s, school); Thornbury Castle, Gloucestershire (medieval, acq. by mar. 1347, rebuilt 1507, sold 1727)
Estates: Bateman 13622 (E) 31374
Titles: Baron Stafford 1640- E; Viscount Stafford 1640-1762 E; Baronet 1621-1937
Peers: 7 peers 1660-78 1829-84 1892-1941
Notes: Coal and iron on the Shropshire estates raised income in the later 18th c. Henry O'Brien married the Stafford heiress of Blatherwycke Park and their son succeeded to that estate in the early 18th century (see O'Brien). 10 Baron Stafford and 1, 2, and 3 Dukes of Buckingham and eleven others in ODNB.

<u>FitzHerbert</u>

Origins: Basil FitzHerbert of Swynnerton married the Jerningham heiress in 1858 (see above) and their son succeeded as Baron Stafford. The Tissington FitzHerberts were cousins. **First MP 1447. Four additional MPs 1553-93**. The FitzHerberts held Norbury for 770 years.

1. William FitzHerbert – Bramber 1761-62 Derby 1762-72
2. Alleyne FitzHerbert 1 Baron St. Helens – {Carysfort 1788-90}

Seats: Swynnerton (Swinnerton) Park, Staffordshire (acq. by mar. to the Swynnertons in the later 16th c., rebuilt c. 1725-29, passed by mar. to Jerninghams 1825); Norbury Hall (Manor), Derbyshire (acq. 1125, built 1252, add. 1473-83, add. 16th c., add. 1680, ceased to be a family residence mid-18th c., sold 1881, NT 1988); Tissington Hall, Derbyshire (acq. by mar. from descendant of holders in 1086 in the Middle Ages, purch. additional parts of the estate later, medieval house, rebuilt 1609, remod. mid-18th c., add. c. 1802 and 1910, still own); St. Helen's House, Derbyshire (medieval, acq. c. 1660s, add. later 17th c., sold 1800 and demolished); West Farleigh House (Smiths Hall), Kent (built 1719, purch. 1838, sold 1949); Claughton Hall (Garstang), Lancashire (old house demolished, mid-18th c. passed by mar. to FitzHerberts from Brockholes, who held it from the 13th c., rebuilt 1816-17, demolished 1955, rebuilt c. 1956)
Estates: Bateman 20197 (E) 27856 (includes FitzHerbert-<u>B</u>rockholes of Claughton). Owned 2,500 acres in 2001.
Titles: Baron St. Helens 1791-1839 I and 1801-39 UK; The family succeeded to the Barony of Stafford (cr. 1640 E) in 1913. Baronet 1784-

Peers: 1 peer 1802-39
Notes: The Tissington line of FitzHerberts conformed to the Established Church, unlike other branches of the family that remained Roman Catholic. (*Country Life*, 160, p. 159) Cadet line at Black Castle, Meath (acq. 1722, sold 1946) 4398 (I) 5377 1 Bt and 1 Baron and three others in ODNB.

Gally Knight

Origins: The Gallys took the additional name Knight in 1768 when they inherited Langold Park via marriage to a Knight heiress. The Gallys were French Huguenot refugees. The great grandfather of the first MP was a prominent clergyman. Henry Gally Knight MP left the main part of his estate to the FitzHerberts in 1846. His father married the daughter of William FitzHerbert MP above.

1. John Gally Knight – Aldborough 1784-96
2. Henry Gally Knight – Alborough 1814-15

Seats: Firbeck Hall, Yorkshire (built 1594, purch. 1800, sold 1846); Langold Park, Yorkshire (purch. 1760s, sold 1846)
Notes: On the death of the last MP Langold was sold to provide an inheritance for friends, while Firbeck was sold to benefit religious charities. Two in ODNB.

Earl of Effingham (1731-1816 E and 1837- UK)

Origins: The 1 Baron Howard was a younger son of the 2 Duke of Norfolk. His son was created Earl of Nottingham in 1597 (extinct 1681). The Barony passed to a cousin, whose line became Earls of Effingham. **First MP 1559. Five additional MPs 1563-1628.**

1. Richard Howard 4 Earl of Effingham – Steyning 1784-90
2. Henry Howard 2 Earl of Effingham – Shaftesbury 1841-45

Seats: Tusmore House (Park), Oxfordshire (built 1766-79, purch. 1857, sold 1929, demolished 1961, rebuilt 1964, rebuilt 2004); Barbot Hall, Yorkshire; Thundercliffe Grange, Yorkshire (built 16th c., purch. 1770s, rebuilt 1777, sold, now flats)
Estates: Bateman 5731 (E) 7942
Titles: Baron Howard of Effingham 1554- E; Earl of Nottingham 1597-1681 E
Peers: 12 peers 1660-81 1689-95 1703-63 1768-1945
Notes: The 2 Baron was Commander of the British fleet in the Armada campaign 1588. 1 Baron and 1 Earl of Nottingham and 1 Earl of Effingham and one other in ODNB.

Howard-Vyse

Origins: Richard Vyse married in 1780 Anne Howard heiress of Sir George Howard of Stoke Place, who was a nephew of the 5 Lord Howard of Effingham. The first Vyse of eminence was Dean of Lichfield in the 18th century. The first MP was a Lt. General 1801.

1. Sir George Howard – Lostwithiel 1761-66 Stamford 1768-96
2. Richard Vyse – Beverley 1806-07
3. Richard Howard-Vyse – Beverley 1807-12 Honiton 1812-18
4. Richard Howard-Vyse – S. Northamptonshire 1846-57 Windsor 1863-65

Seats: Stoke Place, Buckinghamshire (built 1690, purch. 1764, add. 1760s, sold 1963, hotel); Boughton Hall, Northamptonshire (medieval, remod. late 17th c. and 1718, inher. by mar. 1791, demolished c. 1810)
Estates: Bateman 3288 (E) 11290
Notes: Three in ODNB.

HOWARD II [Forward] *IRELAND*

Earl of Wicklow (1793-1983 I)

Origins: To Ireland in the mid-17th century. A physician in the 1660s. Sheriff 1679. His son was Bishop of Elphin 1683. The 1 Viscount Wicklow married in 1755 Alice, daughter and heiress of William Forward of Castle Forward. She was created Countess of Wicklow in her own right. The Forwards emigrated from England to Donegal in the 1660s.

1. John Forward – {St. Johnstown 1692-93}
2. William Forward – {St. Johnstown 1715-68}
3. William Howard – {Dublin 1727}
4. Ralph Howard 1 Viscount Wicklow – {County Wicklow 1761-76}
5. Hugh Howard – {St. Johnstown 1769-83 Athboy 1783-99}
6. Robert Howard 2 Earl of Wicklow – {St. Johnstown 1776-89}
7. William Howard 3 Earl of Wicklow – {St. Johnstown 1783-1800}
8. Hugh Howard – {St. Johnstown 1790-1800}
9. Sir Ralph Howard 1 Bt – County Wicklow 1829-52

Seats: Shelton Abbey, Wicklow (leased from mid-17th c., purch. 1697, built early 18th c., new house 1770, remod. c. 1819, add. 1840, sold 1951, institutional use); Castle Forward, Donegal (resident and built 18th c., demolished 20th c.); Bushy Park, Wicklow

(acq. 19th c., sold after 1873); Castle Howard, Wicklow (purch. 1811, rebuilt 1828, sold later 19th c.)
Estates: Bateman 28713 (I) 15717. Howards held 8,025 acres in the 18th c. worth £5,007 pa in 1760 and £11,377 in 1788. The Forward estates were worth £4,519 in 1785 and £16,000 to £20,000 pa in 1816.
Titles: Baron Clonmore 1776- I; Viscount Wicklow 1785- I; Baronet 1838-73
Peers: {1 peer 1776-89} 5 Irish Rep peers 1801-15 1821-69 1872-81 1888-91 1905-45
2 Lds Lt 19th
1 KP 19th
Notes: The 7 Earl was a Senator of the Irish Free State 1922-27 while the Countess of Wicklow was a member of the Seanad of the Republic in 1948. Viscount and three others in ODNB.

HOWARTH *WALES AND ENGLAND*

Origins: The cadet line of an old Herefordshire family that settled in Radnorshire. The family had a somewhat checkered career. The first MP held the office of Receiver of Crown Rents in Cheshire 1714-30, and sold most of the family estates after a bankruptcy. The second MP recovered ground as a King's Counsel and Recorder of Abingdon, while the third MP became a minor nabob.

1. Sir Humphrey Howarth – Radnorshire 1722-55
2. Henry Howarth – Abingdon 1782-83
3. Humphrey Howarth – Evesham 1806-07 1808-20

Seats: Maesllwch Castle, Radnorshire (medieval acq. early 18th c., by mar. from a family resident in 16th c., rebuilt 1715, sold c. 1750, partly demolished c. 1965); Banstead, Surrey

HUBBARD

Baron Addington (1887- UK)

Origins: The father of the 1 Baron was a Russia merchant. The 1 Baron was a banker.

1. John Hubbard 1 Baron Addington – Buckingham 1859-68 City of London 1874-87
2. Egerton Hubbard 2 Baron Addington – Buckingham 1874-80 Buckingham Div. Buckinghamshire 1886-89
3. Evelyn Hubbard – Brixton Div. Lambeth 1896-1900

Seats: Addington Manor, Buckinghamshire (purch. and built 1856, family departed 1915, sold soon after, demolished 1926); Leonardslee, Sussex (built 1853, sold 1889)
Estates: Bateman 2576 (E) 4887. In addition to landed estates the 1 Baron left £110,000 in assets in 1889.
Peers: 3 peers 1887-1945
Notes: The incompetence of the 2 Baron and his brother brought the family business to ruin. 1 Baron and one other in ODNB.

HULSE [Lethieullier]

Hulse

Origins: The first Hulse was a Court physician to the Prince of Orange in Holland. His son was doctor to George I and George II and purchased landed estates. The first four generations of the family all married money. The 3 Bt married the Lethieullier heiress in 1769.

1. Sir Charles Hulse 4 Bt – West Looe 1816-32
2. Sir Edward Hulse 6 Bt – Salisbury 1886-97

Seats: Breamore House, Hampshire (built 1580-83, purch. 1748, remod. c. 1750, fire 1856, rebuilt soon after, still own); Loxford Hall, Essex (medieval and 16th c., acq. by Lethieulliers in 18th c., passed to Hulse by mar. 1769, rebuilt 1830, add. 1860s, sold later 19th c., institutional use)
Estates: Bateman 6952 (E & I) 13712
Notes: 1 Bt and two others in ODNB.

Lethieullier (Lethuillier)

Origins: A Huguenot family that arrived in London in 1605 and became successful merchants and bankers.

1. Benjamin Lethieullier – Andover 1768-97

Seats: Belmont, Middlesex (resident 18th c.); Aldersbrook (Addersbrooke), Essex (built 16 c., part demolished by 1670, purch. 1693, remod. mid-18th c., passed to Hulse by inher. 1769, sold 1786 by the Hulses and demolished)
Estates: Owned large estates in Essex. Sir John Lethieuller left £100,000 in 1719.

HUNGERFORD

Baron Hungerford (1426-61 1485-? E)

Origins: The family was established in Wiltshire in the 12th century, and then were noble servants and estate stewards at Hungerford in Berkshire in the 14th century, when their real rise to prominence began. Speaker of the House of Commons 1377 and 1414. The family divided into several branches. The Barony was forfeited in 1461, revived in 1485 and after c. 1533 merged with other titles in the Hastings family, and eventually fell into abeyance. Sir Walter Hungerford MP fought at Agincourt and another Sir Walter at Bosworth. The original Speaker "became wealthy by capitalizing upon connections formed with those in authority." (Roskell, Clark and Rawcliffe, *The House of Commons*, III, 444) **First MP 1332. At least 26 further MPs 1335-1648, many kts of the shire**. The family went into decline after the Restoration.

1. Henry Hungerford – Great Bedwyn 1646 Wiltshire 1656 Marlborough 1659 1660
2. Sir Edward Hungerford – Chippenham 1659 1660 1661-81 New Shoreham 1685-87 1689-95 Steyning 1695-1705
3. Sir Giles Hungerford – Whitchurch 1661-79 Devizes 1679-81

Seats: Corsham, Wiltshire (medieval, ruin by 1541, rebuilt 1582, purch. 1602, sold later 17th c.); East Coulston (Coulston Manor), Wiltshire (medieval, purch. 1669 and 1678, passed out of family by mar. 1711); Freefolk, Wiltshire (acq. by mar. mid-16th c., passed out of the family by mar. 1711); Farleigh (Farley) (Hungerford) Castle, Somerset (medieval, acq. 14th c., sold 1686 for £56,000, stripped and a ruin by 1701)
Estates: Worth £128 pa in 1397, £1,800 in 1448, £900 pa in 1459, £1,000 pa in 1530s.
Notes: Sir Edward Hungerford, who wasted his inheritance and sold Farleigh Hungerford to pay debts, died in 1711 in poverty. 1, 2, and 3 Barons and seven others in ODNB.

Hungerford

Origins: Cadet line descended from Sir Edmund Hungerford of Down Ampney (MP 1491).

1. Sir George Hungerford – Cricklade 1661-79 Calne 1679 1681 Wiltshire 1695-1701
2. George Hungerford – Calne 1695-98
3. Walter Hungerford – Calne 1701- 1734-47

Seats: Studley House, Wiltshire (medieval, acq. 1468, fire c. 1800, sold mid-18th c.); Cadenham (Cadnam) House, Wiltshire (medieval, purch. 1468, decayed 1670s, rebuilt sec. half 17th c., sold mid-18th c.)

Estates: Worth £1,000 pa c. 1660s.
Notes: The estates of the senior line at Down Ampney passed to the Dunch family in the mid-17th century (see Dunch) when the male line of Hungerfords became extinct. Financial difficulties and a diminished estate first half of the 17th c.

Hungerford

Origins: A cadet of the Down Ampney line.

1. John Hungerford – Scarborough 1692-95 1702-05 1707-29

Seat: Hungerford, Wiltshire (purch. 1721, sold mid-18th c.)
Notes: One in ODNB.

HUNTER BLAIR *SCOTLAND*

Origins: The Hunters were cadets of the gentry family Hunters of Hunterston breaking away in the 16th century. A younger son was a merchant and his son became a banker in Edinburgh in the mid-18th century (first MP). Lord Provost 1785. In 1770 he married Jean Blair, daughter and heiress of John Blair of Dunskey, and succeeded to the Blair estates in 1777 and took the additional name Blair.

1. Sir James Hunter Blair 1 Bt – Edinburgh 1781-84
2. James Hunter Blair – Wigtownshire 1816-22
3. James Hunter Blair – Ayrshire 1852-54

Seats: Abbotshill, Ayrshire (purch. 1549, sold 1772); Blairquhan (Park), Ayrshire (built 14th c., add. 1573, purch. 1798, rebuilt 1820-24, remod. 1967, still own); Dunskey Castle, Wigtownshire (medieval, add. 1630s, acq. mid-17th c., family departed 1570s, ruin by 1684)
Estates: Bateman 21672 (S) 12892. Owned 2,700 acres in 1996.
Title: Baronet 1786-
Notes: 1 Bt in ODNB.

HURD

Baron Hurd (1964-66 UKLife; 1997- UKLife)

Origins: The first MP, the son of a solicitor, was a journalist.

1. Sir Percy Hurd – Frome Div. Somerset 1918-23 Devizes Div. Wiltshire 1924-45
2. Anthony Hurd 1 Baron Hurd – Newbury Div. Berkshire 1945-64

3. Douglas Hurd 1 Baron Hurd – Mid-Oxfordshire 1974-83 Witney 1983-97
4. Nick Hurd – Ruislip-Northwood 2005-

1 in Cabinet 1984-95

HURST

Origins: The family held land as farmers within what became Horsham Park from the 13th century (T. P. Hudson, ed., *A History of the County of Sussex*, *VCH*, VI, part 2, (1986) 156-66). The first MP was a barrister and electoral agent to the Duke of Norfolk. He made a fortune and purchased a large landed estate.

1. Robert Hurst – Shaftesbury 1802-06 Steyning 1806-12 Horsham 1812-29
2. Robert Hurst – Horsham 1832-41 1844-47
3. Robert Hurst – Horsham 1865-74 1875-76

Seats: Horsham Park, Sussex (built 17th c., add 1720, pieced together by purch. between 1790 and 1856, sold 1928, public park); Barrington Grove, Gloucestershire (built 17th c., inher. by mar. 1873, add. c. 1900, passed to another family by mar. 1948)
Estates: 4333 (E) 6098
Notes: Male line extinct 1948. One in ODNB.

HUSSEY

Baron Hussey (1529-37 E)

Origins: Sir William Hussey was the founder of the family. He was Lord Chief Justice of the King's Bench 1481 and fought for Henry VII at the Battle of Stoke 1487. His son was a courtier and created a Baron 1529 (attainted 1537). **First MP 1460. Nine further MPs** in several branches 1472-1641. Two branches were created Bts, the two titles eventually merging into one line, which are combined here.

1. Sir Charles Hussey 1 Bt – Lincolnshire 1656 1661-64
2. Sir Thomas Hussey 2 Bt – Lincoln 1681 Lincolnshire 1685-87 1689-98
3. Sir Edward Hussey 3 Bt – Lincoln 1689-95 1698-1705

Seats: Doddington Hall, Lincolnshire (medieval, purch. by Tailors 1593, rebuilt 1593-1607, passed by mar. 1653 to Husseys, passed by mar. to Appreece family 1706); Honington, Lincolnshire (medieval, acq. 15th c., passed to Apreece family by mar. 1706); Caythorpe Hall, Lincolnshire (medieval, acq. by 15th c., passed to the Packes 1734, see below)

Estates: The Tailor estate rose to 9,000 acres. Worth £5,000 pa c. 1537. In the 17th c. each of the two titled branches worth about £2,500 pa in the 1660s.
Titles: Baronet 1611-1734; 1661-1734
Notes: Thomas Tailor acquired a fortune as an ecclesiastical official. He purch. Doddington, which passed via marriage in 1610 to Sir Edward Hussey 1 Bt. Husseys extinct in male line 1734.
Notes: 1 Baron and two others in ODNB.

<u>Apreece</u> (ap Rice)

Origins: Of Welsh origin, became an established family in Huntingdonshire by the early 16th century. **First MP 1542 for Huntingdonshire**. The family's Roman Catholicism continued for nearly a century. Conformed mid-17th c. The 2 Hussey Bt (d. 1706) left Doddington and Honington to his daughter Sarah who married Robert Apreece of Washingley.

1. Robert Apreece – Huntingdonshire 1673-79 1698

Seats: Washingley Hall, Huntingdonshire (medieval, acq. c. 1500, rebuilt early 17th c., remod. mid-18th c., sold 1859, demolished c. 1951); Honington, Lincolnshire (acq. by mar. 1706, sold 1851, demolished 1951); Doddington Hall, Lincolnshire (acq. by mar. 1706, passed out of family to Delavals by mar. 1749); Mamhead, Devon (acq. by inher. from Balles 1749, sold c. 1750, see below)
Estates: Worth £1,500 pa in the mid-17th century.

<u>Balle</u> (Ball)

Origins: The Balles were settled in Devon in the 13th century. **First MP 1626**, Attorney General to the Queen 1640. Thomas Balle bequeathed Mamhead to his mother's nephew Thomas Hussey Apreeece of Honington, who sold it.

1. Robert Balle – Ashburton 1708-10
2. Thomas Balle – Exeter 1734-41

Seat: Mamhead, Devon (purch. 1547, built 16th c., rebuilt c. 1700, passed by inher. to Appreece family 1749)
Title: Baronet 1672 (seems never to have passed the Great Seal)
Notes: Extinct in the male line 1749. Three in ODNB.

Pochin

Origins: Acquired estates through several successful marriages from the mid-15th century or earlier onward. (see Packe below)

1. Wiliam Pochin – Leicestershire 1780-98
2. Charles Pochin – Enniskillen 1807-1812

Seats: Barkby Hall, Leicestershire (acq. 15th c., old house, rebuilt c. 1810, fire 1847, part demolished 1870, still own); Edmondthorpe Hall, Leicestershire (built 1621, purch. 1762, fire 1942, ruin by 1960s)
Estates: Bateman 7791 (E) 14282

Packe

Origins: London draper and merchant adventurer (Lord Mayor 1654) **MP 1656**, became a member of Cromwell's House of Lords. Charles Packe of Prestwold married 1750 Charlotte Pochin (see above), the daughter of Thomas Pochin by his wife the half sister of Sir Edward Hussey 3 Bt, sole heiress of the Husseys and to Caythorpe.

1. Charles Packe – S. Leicestershire 1836-37
2. George Hussey Packe – S. Lincolnshire 1859-68

Seats: Prestwold Hall, Leicestershire (purch. 1650, rebuilt mid-18th c., remod. 1805, rebuilt 1843, remod. 1875, passed out of family by mar. 1936 took add. name Packe, descendents still own); Caythorpe Hall, Lincolnshire (medieval, acq. by mar. 1734, rebuilt by Packes 1824-27, owned at least until mid-20th c.)
Estates: Bateman 6234 (E) 11807
Title: Bt 1666 (but never passed the Great Seal).
Notes: George Hussey Packe MP was a founder of the Great Northern Railway. Four in ODNB.

HUTCHINSON I

Origins: Gentry rose in the 16th century. **First MP 1626 for Nottinghamshire**.

1. John Hutchinson – Nottinghamshire 1646 Nottingham 1660
2. Charles Hutchinson – Nottingham 1690-95

Seat: Owthorpe Hall, Nottinghamshire (purch. early 16th c., sold 1773, later demolished)
Estates: c. 3,000 acres in 1640

Notes: The family was loaded with debt and "vanished into obscurity". (Henning, *The House of Commons*, II, 624). One in ODNB.

HUTCHINSON II *SCOTLAND*

Origins: The father of the first MP was a Presbyterian minister who married an heiress with an estate in Argyllshire.

1. Sir George Clark Hutchinson – N. Midlothian 1922-23 1924-28
2. Sir George Clark Hutchinson – W. Edinburgh 1941-59
3. Michael Clark Hutchinson – S. Edinburgh 1957-79

Seat: Eriska House, Argyllshire (built 1884, early 20th c., acq. by mar., sold 1973)

HUTTON

Origins: Lancashire husbandman's son became Archbishop of York 1596. **First MP 1626.**

1. John Hutton – Richmond 1701-02

Seat: Marske, Yorkshire (purch. 1596, rebuilt c. 1600, rebuilt c. 1735, family departed for Marske Lodge c. 1900, estate sold 1960, flats)
Estates: As much as £1,500 pa by 1620s.
Notes: The family produced a second Archbishop of York 1747 (and of Canterbury 1757). So two family members sat in the Commons and two in the Lords. The Huttons seemed an exceptional case and are included in the study, even though they elected only two MPs. Four in ODNB.

HYDE *IRELAND & ENGLAND*

Origins: Originally seated at South Denchworth, Berkshire (sold 1617) and Kingston Lisle, Berkshire. **First MP 1553 for Berkshire. Three additional and possibly more MPs 1558-1621.** Emigrated to Ireland under Elizabeth I. Sheriff 1670.

1. Arthur Hyde – {Tralee 1703-13 Middleton 1713-14 Youghal 1715-20}
2. Arthur Hyde – {Youghal 1721-27 County Cork 1747-60}
3. Arthur Hyde – {Youghal 1758-60}
4. John Hyde – {County Carlow 1767-68 County Cork 1768-76}
5. John Hyde – Youghal 1820-26
6. Sir Clarendon Hyde – Wednesbury 1906-10

Seats: Castle Hyde, Cork (medieval, acq. 1588, rebuilt 1670, rebuilt c. 1801, sold under Encumbered Estates Commission 1851); Cregg Castle, Cork (old tower house, acq. 1588, new house mid-18th c., sold by 20th c.)
Estates: Bateman 8919 (I) 3524. The original grant in 1588 was 12,000 acres. Worth £8,000 pa in 1803.
Notes: Family in financial diffculties by mid-19th c. Douglas Hyde served in the Irish Senate and then as first President of Ireland 1938-45. One in ODNB.

ILIFFE

Baron Iliffe (1933- UK)

Origins: The 1 Baron was the son of a printer and a magazine and local newspaper publisher. The next generation became proprietors of the *Birmingham Post* and later became partners with the owners of the *Daily Telegraph*. Also involved in insurance.

1. Edward Iliffe 1 Baron Iliffe – Tamworth 1923-29

Seats: Allesley Hall, Warwickshire (built mid-17th c., purch. and rebuilt 1909, donated to Coventry City Council 1937); Basildon Park, Berkshire (built 1776, purch. c. 1953, 1978 given to NT)
Estates: Worth £200,000,000 in 2006.
Peers: 1 peer 1933-45
Notes: Three members of the family have now held the peerage.

INGOLDSBY *ENGLAND & IRELAND*

Ingoldsby

Origins: Gentry by the 15th century. **One MP 1658**. This line descended from the eldest son of Sir Richard Ingoldsby (d. 1656).

1. Sir Richard Ingoldsby – Wendover 1647 Buckinghamshire 1654 1656 Aylesbury 1660-81
2. Thomas Ingoldsby – Aylesbury 1730-34

Seats: Waldridge Manor, Buckinghamshire (built late 16th c., remod. early 17th c., purch. 1650); Lenborough, Buckinghamshire (acq. 15th c., sold 1670s)
Notes: Two brothers were members of Cromwell's House of Lords. Three in ODNB.

Ingoldsby

Origins: Descended from a younger son of Sir Richard Ingoldsby (see above). To Ireland with Cromwell. Acquired landed estates.

1. Sir Henry Ingoldsby 1 Bt – {County Clare 1661-66 1689 1695-99}
2. Richard Ingoldsby – {Limerick 1703-12}
3. Henry Ingoldsby – {Limerick 1713-14 1727-31}

Seats: Beggstown Castle, Meath (acq. mid-17th c.); Ballybricken Castle, Limerick (acq. mid-17th c., ruin)
Estates: £1,200 pa in 1714.
Title: Baronet 1661-1726
Notes: Male line extinct 1726. 1 Bt and one other in ODNB.

IRVINE I *SCOTLAND*

Origins: The first [MP] was a wine merchant and importer. Burgesses in Dumfries. **First [MP 1617]. Another [MP 1630].**

1. John Irvine – [Dumfries 1661 1665 1667 1669-74]

IRVINE II *IRELAND*

Origins: Granted lands in Fermanagh in the early 17th century and acquired more in 1666. Sheriff 1690.

1. Christopher Irvine – {County Fermanagh 1695-99 1703-13}
2. William Irvine – {Ratoath 1769-76 1790-97}
3. Henry Irvine – {Tulsk 1797-1800}

Seat: Castle Irvine (Irvinestown Castle, Necarne Castle), Fermanagh (acq. and built 1629, burned by rebels 1641, rebuilt 1831, sold 1925, empty shell)
Estates: Bateman 6190 (I) 5547
Title: Baronet 1677-89
Notes: Cadet line at Killadeas Manor (aka Rockfield), Fermanagh 14114 (I) 6806.

ISHAM

Origins: Very possibly of Saxon origin. Can be traced back to the 12th century. A younger son who went to London as an apprentice and made a fortune as a mercer, wool merchant, and maker of loans purchased Lamport in 1560. He reentered the gentry after 1572 and his descendents increased the estate through marriage and sheep farming. High Sheriff 1581. Bt 1627. (Finch, *The Wealth of Five Northamptonshire Families*, 4-24). **First MP 1554.**

1. Sir Justinian Isham 2 Bt – Northamptonshire 1661-75
2. Sir Justinian Isham 4 Bt – Northampton 1685-87 1689-90 1694-98
3. Sir Justinian Isham 5 Bt – Northamptonshire 1730-37
4. Sir Edmund Isham 6 Bt – Northamptonshire 1737-72

Seat: Lamport Hall, Northamptonshire (purch. 1560, built 1568, add. 1654-55, remod. 1732-42, add. 1819-21, charitable trust 1974)
Estates: Bateman 4230 (E) 7343. Perhaps worth £1,600 pa in the later 17th c.
Title: Baronet 1627-
Notes: 2, 3, and 10 Bts and three others in ODNB.

JACKSON I *IRELAND*

Origins: The Rev. Richard Jackson of Kirby Lonsdale in Westmorland had a son Captain William Jackson, a tenant of the London Company in Coleraine, Ulster 1663. His son and grandson built up the estate. "Men of energy and resource." (Mullin, *Coleraine in Bygone Centuries*, 156)

1. William Jackson – {Coleraine 1666}
2. Samuel Jackson – {Coleraine 1695-99}
3. William Jackson – {County Londonderry 1697-99} (possible kinsman)
4. Thomas Jackson – {Coleraine 1728-51}
5. Richard Jackson – {Coleraine 1751-89 Lisburn 1776 Randalstown 1783}
6. George Jackson – {Coleraine 1789-96 Randalstown 1797-1800}

Seat: Jackson Hall (later The Manor House, Coleraine), Londonderry (acq. 1662, built 1680, add. 1770s, sold c. 1800, demolished in 20th c.)
Estates: Worth £563 pa in 1717, £1,003 in 1736 pa, £2,689 pa in 1770, and £4,200 pa in 1801.
Title: Baronet 1813-51

JACKSON II

Baron Allerton (1902- UK)

Origins: 1 Baron was the son of an inept tanner and leather merchant in Leeds. The former built up the business into a great enterprise. Mayor of Leeds 1895.

1. William Jackson 1 Baron Allerton – Leeds 1880-85 N. Div. Leeds 1885-1902
2. Francis Jackson – Howdenshire Div. E. R. Yorkshire 1915-26

Seats: Loddington Hall, Leicestershire (built late 16th c., add. late 17th c., purch. 1934, trust 1992, for sale 2012); Allerton Hall, Yorkshire (demolished 1968)
Estates: 1 Baron purchased landed estates but lived at Allerton Hall in Leeds. 1 Baron left £250,000 in 1917.
Peers: 3 peers 1902-45
1 in Cabinet 1891-92
Notes: The tannery was closed in 1912 on the 1 Baron's retirement. None of his sons followed him into business. 1 Baron and one other in ODNB.

JAMES [Head]

Baron Northbourne (1884- UK)

Origins: The Heads began as Yorkshire yeomen who entered the gentry in the early 16th century seated at Langley. High Sheriff 1698. In 1791 the Heads succeeded to the property of the Jameses of Denford via marriage 1778 and took the name James and were created Baronets. Father of the 1 Baron was Minister to the Netherlands. They inherited urban and industrial property in Gateshead and 4,300 acres from the Ellisons in the mid-19th century (see Carr Ellison).

1. John Head – Stockbridge 1685-87
2. Walter James 1 Baron Northbourne – Hull 1837-47
3. Walter James 2 Baron Northbourne – Gateshead 1874-93
4. Cuthbert James – Bromley 1919-30

Seats: Betteshanger Park (House), Kent (built 1825, purch. 1850, remod. 1856 and 1886, sold 1933, now a school); Northbourne Court, Kent (built early 17th c., fire 1750, ruin, rebuilt 19th c., purch. 1895, still own); Langley Hall, Berkshire (built 17th c., acq. by Heads c. 1650, remod. 18th c., transferred seat to Denford c. 1791, institutional use); Denford Court, Berkshire (acq. by Jameses 1778, passed by mar. to Heads, sold 1810); Evistones, Northumberland
Estates: Bateman 6617 (E) 12949. Rubinstein – 1 Bt left £200,000 in probate in 1829.
Title: Baronet 1791-
Peers: 4 peers 1884-1945
Notes: 1 Baron in ODNB.

JANSSEN

Origins: Flemish Protestants settled in France came to England in 1683. The 1 Bt was one of the most eminent merchants and financiers of his era, a founding Director of the Bank of England and the South Sea Company. Kt 1698. Bt. 1715.

1. Sir Theodore Janssen 1 Bt – Yarmouth (IoW) 1717-21
2. Sir Abraham Janssen 2 Bt – Dorchester 1720-22
3. Sir Stephen Janssen 4 Bt – London 1747-54

Seat: Wimbledon House, Surrey (built c. 1585-88, remod. 1639-42, purch. and demolished 1717, sold 1723)
Estates: Worth £200,000 in 1721.
Title: Baronet 1715-77
Notes: 1 Bt lost heavily in the South Sea Bubble. 1 Bt in ODNB.

JEFFREYS [Price] *ENGLAND & WALES*

Jeffreys (Jeffres)

Origins: A Brecon mercer before the Civil War and merchants in London in the American trade afterwards. Became very rich. Still active in business in the early 18th century.

1. John Jeffreys – Breconshire 1661-62 Brecon 1679-81 1685-87
2. Sir Jeffrey Jeffreys – Brecon 1690-98 1701-09
3. John Jeffreys – Radnorshire 1692-98 Marlborough 1701-02 Breconshire 1702-05 Marlborough 1705-08
4. Edward Jeffreys – Marlborough 1702-05 Brecon 1709-13
5. John Jeffreys – Breconshire 1734-47 Dartmouth 1747-66

Seats: The Priory, Brecon, Breconshire (inher. by mar. 1678 from Price family, sold to a different branch of family 1689, they sold early 18th c.); Pencoed Castle, near Newport in Gwent (built 13th c., now a ruin, new house built 16th c., purch. 1701, sold 1749)
Estates: Worth £600 pa in 1660. Sir Jeffrey Jeffreys owned several thousand acres in Breconshire and was worth £300,000 c. 1699.
Notes: On the death of the last male Jeffreys the estates passed via an heiress to the 1 Earl Camden (see Pratt).
Notes: Two in ODNB.

Price (Prise)

Origins: Claimed descent from a medieval Welsh king and a hero at Agincourt. Landowners since Tudor times. Did well out of the Dissolution. **First MP 1547 for Breconshire. Two additional MPs 1571-1626 also for the county**. Related to the Prices of Foxley (see Price III). The Price estates, including The Priory, passed to their cousins by marriage the Jeffreys family in 1689.

1. Sir Herbert Price 1 Bt – Brecon 1640-43 1661-78
2. Thomas Price – Herefordshire 1661-79
3. John Price – Herefordshire 1708-13

Seats: The Priory, Brecon, Breconshire (purch. c. 1540s, passed to Jeffreys 1678); Wistaston Court, Herefordshire (acq. 17th c., sold early 18th c., fire c. 1910)
Estates: Worth £135 pa in 1555 and £300 pa in the 1640s.
Title: Baronet 1657-89 (Cromwellian)
Notes: Sold much land in the 1680s and met final financial ruin in the early 18th century. Related to Price III (see). One in ODNB.

JENISON

Jenison

Origins: An old Newcastle merchant family that entered the gentry through profits of office. **First MP 1571 for Newcastle-on-Tyne. An additional MP 1601**.

1. Ralph Jenison – Northumberland 1724-41 Newport (IoW) 1749-58

Seat: Walworth Castle, Durham (medieval, acq. 1579, rebuilt later 16th c., remod. 1740s, sold c. 1759, now hotel)
Notes: Some Jenisons remained Roman Catholic. In the later 18th c. one moved to Germany, where he was a diplomat and made a Count. Four in ODNB.

Jenison

Origins: Cadet of the Newcastle family (16th century). Were merchants in Nottingham from the 1580s; rose to gentry status c. 1660. High Sheriff 1684.

1. Sir Matthew Jenison – Newark 1701-05

Notes: Estates passed to a cousin, Elizabeth Bradford, in 1734.

JENKINSON [Foljambe, Medley, Shuckburgh, Thornhaugh]

Earl of Liverpool (1796-1851 GB; 1905- UK)

Origins: Merchants in Bristol and agents for the Muscovy Company in the 16th century. Granted arms 1568. Knighted by James I. Purchased land in Oxfordshire and Gloucestershire before the Civil War. Gentry by the 1620s. **First MP 1654.**

1. Sir Robert Jenkinson 2 Bt – Oxfordshire 1689-1710
2. Sir Robert Jenkinson 3 Bt – Oxfordshire 1710-17
3. Sir Robert Bankes Jenkinson 4 Bt – Oxfordshire 1717-27
4. Charles Jenkinson 1 Earl of Liverpool – Cockermouth 1761-66 Appleby 1767-72 Harwich 1772-74 Hastings 1774-80 Saltash 1780-86
5. John Jenkinson – Corfe Castle 1768-80
6. Robert Jenkinson 2 Earl of Liverpool – Rye 1790-1803
7. Sir Charles Jenkinson 10 Bt – Dover 1806-18
8. Charles Jenkinson 3 Earl of Liverpool – Sandwich 1807-12 Bridgnorth 1812-18 East Grinstead 1818-28
9. Sir George Jenkinson 11 Bt – N. Wiltshire 1868-80
10. Cecil Foljambe 1 Earl of Liverpool – N. Nottinghamshire 1880-85 Mansfield Div. Nottinghamshire 1885-92

Seats: Hawkesbury, Gloucestershire (medieval, purch. 1621, demolished 1770s,); Eastwood Park, Gloucestershire (old house, purch. 1688, rebuilt 1820 and c. 1865, sold 1916); Hartsholme Hall, Lincolnshire (built 1862, purch. 1909, sold 1939, demolished 1951); Walcot, Oxfordshire (built 16th c., acq. early 17th c., remod. early 17th c., sold 1759); Coombe Wood (Coombe House), Surrey (owned early 19th c., institutional use); Pitchford Hall, Shropshire (purch. by Ottleys 1473, built c. 1549, passed by mar. to Jenkinsons 18th c., passed by mar. to Cotes 19th c.); Buxted Park, Sussex (built 1722, ad. 1810, inher. by mar. from Shuckburghs 1814, passed out of family by mar. 1871, hotel)
Estates: Bateman 3624 (E) 5517. Rubinstein – 1 Earl left £200,000 probate 1809 and the 2 Earl £120,000 in 1828.
Titles: Baron Hawkesbury 1786-1851 GB; Baron Hawkesbury 1893- UK; Baronet 1661-
Peers: 6 peers 1786-1808 1803-51 1893-1945
2 in Cabinet 1778-82 1786-1804 1801-27
1 KG 19th
Notes: 1, 2, and 3 Earls of 1st cr. and three others in ODNB.

Foljambe

Origins: The Foljambes claimed descent from a companion of the Conqueror. Owned Tideswell, Derbyshire from the 11th century. (Roskell, Clark, and Rawcliffe, *The House of Commons*, III, 98) Baliffs of the Peak in the medieval period. Expanded estates at the Dissolution. **First MP 1297 for Derbyshire. Five further MPs 1338-1626, three of them for the county**. One of a cadet line married the daughter and heiress of the last Earl of Liverpool (d. 1851), and the title was revived for this family in 1905.

1. Frances Foljambe – Yorkshire 1784 Higham Ferrers 1801-07
2. Francis Savile Foljambe – East Retford 1857-85

Seats: Aldwarke Hall, Yorkshire (acq. and built early 17th c., rebuilt c. 1720, family departed, pulled down c. 1880/99, new house); Osberton Hall, Nottinghamshire (acq. from Thornhaughs by mar. 1774, rebuilt c. 1798, add. 1830 and 1840s, add. 1880s, sold post 1986)
Estates: Bateman 14498 (E) 20140. 12,000 acres in the 1980s.
Title: Baronet 1622-40
Notes: The Foljambes acquired Aldwarke and the Earl of Southampton's estates by marriage to an heiress. That family elected many pre-1660 MPs. Aldwarke was engulfed by industrial growth in the second half of the 19th c. and abandoned by the family.

Thornhaugh

Origins: Wealthy country gentry seated at Fenton since the reign of Henry VI. **First MP 1604. Another MP 1640**. Mary Thornhaugh, heiress of John Thornhaugh and Arabella, heiress of Sir George Savile 8 Bt of Rufford Abbey, married Francis Foljambe of Aldwarke.

1. John Thornhaugh – East Retford 1689-1702 Nottinghamshire 1704-10
2. John Thornhaugh – Nottinghamshire 1747-74

Seats: Osberton, Nottinghamshire (acq. 1682, passed to Foljambes by mar. later 18th c.); Shireoakes Hall, Nottinghamshire (purch. by Hewetts mid-16th c., built 1612-17, remod. 1719-26, acq. by inher. 1726, fire 1811, sold 1812); Fenton Hall, Nottinghamshire (acq. 15th c., passed out of family by mar. 1787)
Notes: John Thornhaugh of Osberton inherited the estates of his godfather Sir Thomas Hewett of Shireoaks, Nottinghamshire in 1726. Male line extinct 1787.

Shuckburgh

Origins: Settled at Shuckburgh since the beginning of the 13th century. Sheep farmers in 16th century. High Sheriff 1568. Kt 1642. **First MP 1640 for Warwickshire.** The 3 Earl of Liverpool married Julia Shuckburgh-Evelyn, sole heiress of Sir George Shuckburgh-

Evelyn 6 Bt. Their daughter married George Savile Foljambe of Aldwarke, whose son was created Earl of Liverpool in 1905.

1. Sir Charles Shuckburgh 2 Bt – Warwickshire 1698-1705
2. Sir George Shuckburgh-Evelyn 6 Bt – Warwickshire 1780-1804

Seats: Shuckburgh Hall (Park), Warwickshire (acq. early 13th c., built c. 1500, remod. c. 1600, late 17th c. and 1844, still there); Bourton Hall, Warwickshire (medieval, purch. c. 1590, rebuilt late 18th c., add. 1875-85, sold 1906, now offices); Buxted Place, Sussex (acq. by mar. 1797 from Medleys, passed to Jenkinsons 1814, see above)
Estates: Bateman 3502 (E) 6290
Title: Baronet 1660-
Notes: 6 Bt and four others in ODNB.

<u>Medley</u>

Origins: Founder a wine merchant in Portugal and subsequently country gentleman in Sussex mid-18th century. Suffered heavy losses in the Lisbon earthquake of 1755. Sir George Shuckburgh-Evelyn 6 Bt married Julia, daughter and heiress of John Evelyn of Felbridge, Surrey and heiress in 1796 of her uncle George Medley MP.

1. George Medley – Seaford 1768-80 Esat Grinstead 1783-90

Seats: Buxted Place (Park), Sussex (purch. and built 1722, passed by mar. to Shuckburghs 1797 see above); Hever Castle, Kent
Estates: Wife of George Medley, née Waldo, inheritor of Hever Castle had passed Hever to a cousin - in Bateman 2798 (E) 3837. Rubinstein – Jane, widow of George Medley, left £180,000 in probate in 1829.
Notes: Waldos were probably London merchants.

JENNINGS I

Origins: Granted arms 1641. Kt 1660. High Sheriff 1675. The first MP was a government official and Mayor of Ripon.

1. Sir Edmund Jennings – Ripon 1659 1660 1673-79 1685 1690-91
2. Sir Jonathan Jennings – Ripon 1659 1689-95
3. Jonathan Jennings – Ripon 1691-1701

Notes: Residents of Ripon.

JENNINGS II

Origins: In London in business in the 16th century. Gentry by 1640. **First MP 1640**. Sir John Jennings MP was an admiral. Kt 1704.

1. Sir John Jennings – Queenborough 1705-10 Portsmouth 1710-11 Rochester 1715-34
2. Edward Jennings – East Looe 1713-15
3. Philip Jennings – Queenborough 1715-22
4. George Jennings – Whitchurch 1757-68 St. Germans 1768-74 Thetford 1784-90
5. Sir Philip Jennings-Clerke 1 Bt – Totnes 1768-88

Seats: Duddleston Hall, Shropshire; Newsells Park, Hertfordshire (built 17th c., fire c. 1943, new house)
Title: Baronet 1774-88
Notes: 1 Bt and one other in ODNB.

JERVIS

Earl St. Vincent (1797-1823 GB)

Origins: An old but impoverished family settled in Staffordshire by the 17th century. A number were lawyers. The 1 Earl, son of a barrister and counsel to the Admiralty, was a celebrated admiral. On the death of the 1 Earl, the Viscountcy passed by special remainder to a nephew through the female line.

1. John Jervis 1 Earl St. Vincent – Launceston 1783-84 Great Yarmouth 1784-90 Chipping Wycombe 1790-94

Seats: Little Aston Hall, Staffordshire (built c 1730, purch. 19th c., remod. 1857, sold c. 1900); Park Hall, Staffordshire (acq. by Parkers early 17th c., built early-mid-17th c., fire 1791, rebuilt 1790s, passed to Jervis by mar. c. 1810, family departed 1890s, fire 1970); Norton Disney, Lincolnshire (medieval, rebuilt 18th c., acq. by mar. mid-19th c., sold c. 1900); The Hall (Sutton Hall), Sutton-on-Derwent, Yorkshire (medieval, acq. by mar. 1857, sold 1948); Meaford Hall, Staffordshire (purch. and built later 17th c., remod. 19th c., sold 1943)
Estates: 12676 (E) 20963
Title: Viscount St. Vincent 1801- UK
Peers: 7 peers 1797-1945
1 in Cabinet 1801-04
Notes: 1 Earl in ODNB.

Jervis

Origins: The senior line of the Jervis family of which the Earl was a cadet. First MP was a leading barrister, his son, also an MP, became Chief Justice of the Common Pleas 1850.

1. Thomas Jervis – Great Yarmouth 1802-06
2. Sir John Jervis – Chester 1832-50
3. Swynfen Jervis – Bridport 1837-41
4. John Jervis – Horsham 1847-48

Seats: Darlaston Hall, Staffordshire (late medieval, purch. 1685, sold 1880, demolished 1953); Chatcull Hall, Staffordshire (medieval, still owned later 19th c.)
Notes: Two in ODNB.

JERVOISE [Clarke, Purefoy]

Jervoise

Origins: The grandfather of the first MP was a mercer and Alderman of London in the 16th century. Purchased an estate 1538. **First MP 1621. Another MP 1640**.

1. Thomas Jervoise – Hampshire 1680-81 1689-90
2. Thomas Jervoise – Stockbridge 1691-95 Hampshire 1698-1702 Plympton 1702-03 Hindon 1704-05 Hampshire 1705-10
3. George Purefoy-Jervoise – Salisbury 1813-18 Hampshire 1820-26

Seats: Herriard House (Park), Hampshire (purch. 1538, rebuilt 1703-06, demolished 1965); The Moat (Moat House), Wiltshire (purch. 1542, built 17th c., remod. 1766, remod. early 19th c., still owned mid-19th c.)
Estates: Bateman 9846 (E) 10057
Notes: Herriard was acquired by the Cowdray family c. Edward III. An heiress married a younger son of Lord St. John (Paulet). A Paulet (see Powlett) heiress married 1601 Thomas Jervoise MP and carried the estates to that family. The Jervoise family succeeded 1762 by marriage to the Purefoy of Shalstone House, Buckinghamshire estates (first MP 1654). They eventually passed by the marriage in 1832 of a Jervoise heiress to Thomas Fitzgerald (in Bateman 5475 (E) 5586).

Clarke-Jervoise

Origins: On the death of Thomas Jervoise MP (1691-1710) (see above) of Herriard, Jervoise Clarke took the additional name Jervoise on inheriting the estates from his maternal grandfather. The Clarkes descended from Sir Samuel Clarke, a skinner and Lord Mayor of London, Kt 1712.

1. Jervoise Clarke-Jervoise – Yarmouth (IoW) 1768-69 1774-79 Hampshire 1779-90 Yarmouth 1791-1808
2. Thomas Clarke-Jervoise – Yarmouth 1787-90
3. Sir Jervoise Clarke-Jervoise 2 Bt – S. Hampshire 1857-68

Seat: Idsworth Park, Hampshire (built mid-16th c., remod. 18th c., purch. 1790, abandoned due to railway encroachment, new house on new site built 1852, add. 1912, sold 1974, flats)
Estates: Bateman 8932 (E) 5413
Titles: Baronet 1813-1933

JODRELL [Lombe]

Jodrell

Origins: Three generations of barristers led to the first MP. The Jodrells succeeded to the Lombe Baronetcy by special remainder through marriage to an heiress.

1. Paul Jodrell – Old Sarum 1751
2. Richard Paul Jodrell – Seaford 1790-92 1794-96
3. Henry Jodrell – Great Yarmouth 1796-1802 Bramber 1802-12

Seats: Bayfield Hall, Norfolk (medieval, rebuilt c. 1740, purch. 1766, passed to Cokes by mar. 1929); Salle Park, Norfolk (built 1761, acq. by mar. 1817, sold 1890); Duffield, Derbyshire (purch. and built early 18th c., still resident early 19th c., house leased or sold by mid-19th c.)
Estates: Bateman 5972 (E) 6735 and 2407 (E) 3081 and 13832 (E) 17789 (Evans-Lombe). 2 Bt left £250,000 plus land in 1861.
Title: Baronet 1784-1929
Notes: 2 Bt and two others in ODNB.

Lombe

Origins: The father of the first MP was born a Beevor who took the name Lombe on inheriting Great Melton in 1817 (probably an illegitimate son). The Lombes were textile manufacturers who introduced a new technique of silk throwing in the early 18th century. The first mill was built in Derby in 1715, which continued to operate until 1908. Kt 1727. The first Lombe Bt was formerly named Hase, and succeeded to the Lombe estates in 1762.

1. Edward Lombe – Arundel 1826-30

Seat: Great Melton Hall, Norfolk (built 1611, purch. 1713, abandoned 1899, derelict, became a ruin, still own estate); Bylaugh Hall, Norfolk (won by gambling from Lloyd famly 1794, built 1847-52, sold 1917, gutted 1952, restored c. 2000s, hotel)
Estates: Sir Thomas Lombe left £120,000 in 1739. Rubinstein - 1 Bt. left £160,000 in probate 1817. The rebuilding of Bylaugh c. 1850 may have cost £38,000. (Franklin, *The Gentleman's Country House*, 258)
Title: Baronet – see above
Notes: Three in ODNB.

JOICEY

Baron Joicey (1906- UK)

Origins: The father of the 1 Baron was a mining engineer who invested in coal mines 1828. 1 Baron was Chairman of the firm that managed the largest coalfield in Durham and also manufactured wire rope. They were also involved with the railways.

1. John Joicey – N. Durham 1880-81
2. James Joicey 1 Baron Joicey – Chester-le-Street 1885-1905

Seats: Ford Castle, Northumberland (medieval, ruined and rebuilt by 1509, ruined c. 1648, remod. 1694, rebuilt 1761-1800, rebuilt 1861-65, purch. 1907, remod. 1938, donated to local council for institutional use 1970s); Newton, Northumberland (resident second half 19th c.); Longhirst Hall, Northumberland (purch. 1890s, still own)
Estates: Bateman 7854 (E) 7563. The 1 Baron left £1,500,000 in 1936. Owned 16,000 acres in 2015.
Title: Baronet 1893-
Peers: 3 peers 1906-45
Notes: 1 Baron in ODNB.

JOLLIFFE

Baron Hylton (1866- UK)

Origins: Robert de Hylton was summoned to Parliament as Baron Hylton in 1295, but the descent became confused. The *de jure* heirs, who did not use the titles, died out in 1746. Anne Hylton, the heiress to Hylton Castle, Durham married a Musgrave Baronet of Hayton Castle, Cumberland (see Musgrave). Her granddaughter, Eleanor Hylton married William Jolliffe. Eleanor's grandson was created Baron Hylton in 1866. (see Musgrave)

1. John Jolliffe – Heytesbury 1660-79
2. William Jolliffe – Poole 1698-1705
3. Sir William Jolliffe – Petersfield 1734-41
4. John Jolliffe – Petersfield 1741-54 1761-68
5. William Jolliffe – Petersfield 1768-1802
6. Thomas Jolliffe – Petersfield 1780-87
7. Hylton Jolliffe – Petersfield 1796 1802-34
8. William Jolliffe 1 Baron Hylton – Petersfield 1830-32 1837-38 1841-66
9. Gilbert Jolliffe – Petersfield 1830-31
10. Hedworth Jolliffe 2 Baron Hylton – Wells 1855-68
11. William Jolliffe – Petersfield 1874-80
12. Hylton Jolliffe 3 Baron Hylton – Wells Div. Somerset 1895-99

Seats: Ammerdown Park (House), Somerset (purch. and built 1788, add. 1855 and 1877, remod. 1901, still own); Merstham House, Surrey (purch. and built 1788, demolished c. 1834, new house built, sold 1899, demolished 1950s); Crofton Hall, Worcestershire (medieval, acq. by mar. 1633, fire 1645, rebuilt, passed out of the family by mar. 1758); Trotton Place, Sussex (purch. 1779, sold 1786); Botham Hall, Staffordshire (purch. c. 1600, passed out of family by mar. 1712, demolished early 19th c.); Caverswall Castle, Staffordshire (built 13th c., decayed 16th c., new house c. 1615, purch. 1655, passed out of family by mar. 1712); Hayton Castle, Cumberland (built 15th c., rebuilt 1609, passed to Joliffes by mar. c. 1815, leased to farmers, sold 1903)
Estates: Bateman 10058 (E) 17072
Title: Baronet 1821-
Peers: 4 peers 1866-1945
Notes: John Hylton of Hylton Castle, Durham (medieval, extended c. 1700, burned 1856, rebuilt 1863-69, ruin 20th c., engulfed by urban area), the last of the male line died in 1746. His niece married a Musgrave, and the Castle was sold 1758 to the Bowes family of Gibside (see Lyon). 1 Baron and one other in ODNB.

JONES I *IRELAND*

Origins: A Welsh family moved to Ireland 1606, bishop 1632 - acquired estates from 1622. Rose through the military, the law, office, marriage, and the Church. (Burtchaell, *Genealogical Memoirs of the Members of Parliament for the County and City of Kilkenny,* 63) Sheriff 1682. **First {MP 1639}. Another {MP 1656}.**

1. Sir Theophilus Jones – {Meath 1660-61}
2. Oliver Jones – {Knocktopher 1661-64}
3. Nicholas Jones – {Sligo 1692-93 County Leitrim 1695-99 1703-42}
4. Theophilus Jones – {County Leitrim 1761-68 Coleraine 1769-76 County Leitrim 1776-83 Monaghan 1783-90 County Leitrim 1790-1800} 1801-02

5. Walter Jones – {Coleraine 1798-1800} 1801-09
6. Theobald Jones – County Londonderry 1830-57

Seats: Headfort House, Leitrim (acq. late 17th c., still resident in 20th c.); Cork Abbey, Wicklow; Hayle Place, Kent (built mid-18th c., add. 1830); Bealanamore, Dublin; Bovagh House, Londonderry (built c. 1740, resident first half 19th c.)
Estates: Bateman 9904 (I) 4702. Worth £1,200 pa in 1713. Held 14,000 acres worth between £5,000 and £9000 pa in 1803.
Notes: The Jones estates were broken up among three heiresses in 1839. One married a younger son of the Earl of Romney (see Marsham), who succeeded to Headfort and took the name Jones. Five in ODNB.

JONES II *WALES*

Origins: The first MP was a lawyer of obscure origin. Became leading gentry in the late 17th century. **First MP 1654 for Breconshire.**

1. Edward Jones – Breconshire 1685-87 1689-90 1695-96
2. Roger Jones – Brecon 1713-22

Seat: Buckland Hall, Breconshire (medieval, rebuilt early 17th c., purch. 1709, sold by heirs 1756)
Notes: Male line extinct 1741.

JONES III *ENGLAND & WALES*

Origins: Prominent in Shrewsbury from the reign of Elizabeth I. **First MP 1656 for Shrewsbury. Another MP 1659.** The second MP was a barrister and then Lord Chief Justice.

1. Sir Thomas Jones – Shrewsbury 1660-76
2. Thomas Jones – East Grinstead 1685-87
3. Thomas Jones – Shrewsbury 1710 1713-15

Seats: Cerreghwfa (Carreghofa, Carreghova), Montgomeryshire (medieval castle, acq. mid-17th c., resident 18th c.); Caneghora, Denbighshire

JONES-PARRY *WALES*

Origins: The Joneses were seated at Llwyn Onn from the Middle Ages. Margaret Parry married in 1780 Thomas Jones of Llwyn Onn and the Parry estates passed to the Joneses. The first Parry was a Colonel under Cromwell and married an heiress.

1. John Parry – Caernarvonshire 1780-90
2. Sir Love Jones-Parry – Horsham 1807-08 Caernarvonshire 1835-37
3. Sir Thomas Jones-Parry 1 Bt – Caernarvonshire 1868-74 Caernarvon District 1882-86

Seats: Wernfawr (Wern Fawr), Caernarvonshire (Jones seat); Llwyn (Lwyn) Onn, Denbighshire (Jones seat from Middle Ages, sold 1910); Madryn Castle (Park), Caernarvonshire (acq. by Parrys by mar. 1708, passed to Jones family by mar. 1780, sold 1910)
Estates: Bateman 10025 (W) 5750 and 4699 (W) 2626
Title: Baronet 1886-91
Notes: One in ODNB.

KAVANAGH *IRELAND*

Origins: "The MacMorrough". Kings of Leinster and High Kings of Ireland down to the reign of Henry VIII. Protestant by 1641. Remained one of the great Gaelic families of Ireland into the 20th century. **First {MP 1541}. Two other {MPs 1613-34}**.

1. Bryan Kavanagh – {Kilkenny 1796-97}
2. Thomas Kavanagh – {Kilkenny 1797-99} County Carlow 1826-31 1835-37
3. Arthur Kavanagh – County Wexford 1866-68 County Carlow 1869-80
4. Walter Kavanagh – County Carlow 1908-10

Seats: Borris House, Carlow (acq. 13th c.?, castle, rebuilt c. 1720-41, damaged 1798, rebuilt c. 1820, still own); Ballyraggert, Kilkenny
Estates: Bateman 29025 (I) 15608
1 Ld Lt 19th
Notes: Two in ODNB.

KAYE [Lister]

Origins: Acquired Woodsome (resident there since 14th century) c. 1520 and added gradually to their estates through piecemeal accumulation of property over four generations between c. 1550-1662, moving from modest to greater gentry. They worked to increase their fortune both through the textile business and the iron industry. (Cliffe, *The Yorkshire Gentry from the Reformation to the Civil War*, 96-97) They also mined coal. The Kayes inherited the Lister estates by marriage in 1745. **First MP 1610**.

1. Sir John Kaye 2 Bt – Yorkshire 1685-87 1689-98 1701 1702-06
2. Sir Arthur Kaye 3 Bt – Yorkshire 1710-26
3. Sir John Lister-Kaye 4 Bt – York 1734-41

Seats: Woodsome Hall, Yorkshire (medieval, acq. c. 1520 and built soon after, add. 17th c., passed out of the family by mar. 1726); Fairfield Hall, Yorkshire (built 16th-17th c., rebuilt 1720s, purch. by Listers 1805, sold 1906); Denby Grange, Yorkshire (Kayes acq. 16th c., enlarged 1636, rebuilt mid-18th c., sold 1948, demolished 1950)
Estates: Bateman 15019 (E & S) 10641
Title: Baronet 1642-1809; 1812-
Notes: For the Cunliffe-Lister-Kays, see Cunliffe-Lister.

KEANE *IRELAND*

Baron Keane (1839-1901 UK)

Origins: Acquired Belmont and Cappoquin in 1737. How? Sheriff 1780, The 1 Baron was Commander in Chief in India.

1. Sir John Keane 1 Bt – {Bangor 1791-97 Youghal 1797-1800} 1801-06 1807-18
2. Sir Richard Keane 2 Bt – County Waterford 1832-35

Seats: Cappoquin House, Waterford (old house, purch. 1737, rebuilt 1779, burned 1923, rebuilt, still own); Castletown House, Wexford; Belmont, Waterford (acq. 1737, sold 1st half 19th c.); Belleville (Bettyville) Park, Waterford (built late 18th c., acq. 19th c.)
Estates: Bateman 8909 (I) 3237. Reportedly worth £14,000 pa in c. 1800. The Cappoquin estate consted of 7,213 acres in 1737.
Title: Baronet 1801-
Peers: 3 peers 1838-1901
Notes: 1 Baron in ODNB.

KEATING (Keatinge) *IRELAND*

Origins: Possibly Anglo-Norman in origin. Acquired estates 1662. Chief Justice of the Common Pleas in Ireland 1679. The relationships of the MPs below are not fully delineated. **First {MP 1642}.**

1. Maurice Keating – {Ballynakill 1661-66}
2. Maurice Keating – {Athy 1695-99 1703-27}
3. John Keating – {Trim 1715-17}
4. Maurice Keating – {Kildare 1725-27 County Kildare 1727-60 Naas 1761-68 Kildare 1768-69}
5. Michael Keating – {Harristown 1776-81}
6. Maurice Keating – {Harristown 1776-77}
7. Maurice Keating – {County Kildare 1790-1800} 1801-02

Seats: Millicent, Kildare (purch. 1662, built c. 1700, sold 1813); Castle Mey, Kildare; Narraghmore, Kildare (built 17th c., new house built late 18th c., burned 1798, sold 1813)
Estates: Some estates sold in 1766. The rest in 1813 for £93,000.
Notes: The last male Keating died in 1835. Two in ODNB.

KEITH-FALCONER *SCOTLAND*

Earl Marischal of Scotland (prior to 1458-1716 S)

Origins: The Keiths held the title of Marischal of Scotland from 1294. Represented Scotland in the English Parliament 1305. Signed the Declaration of Arbroath 1320. **First [MP 1625].** A younger son of the 6 Earl Marischal was created Earl of Kintore. A daughter of the 2 Earl married the 4 Baron Falconer. A grandson succeeded as 7 Baron Falconer and 5 Earl of Kintore. The Falconers acquired estates in the 13th century. **First [MP 1482], another [MP 1617]. An additional [MP 1643].** The Falconers of Phesdo, a cadet line, died out in 1764, and their estates passed to a son of the 5 Baron Falconer.

1. George Keith 8 Earl Marischal – [Aberdeenshire 1661-63]
2. Sir David Falconer – [Kincardineshire 1667]
3. Sir John Falconer – {Kincardineshire 1678 1681 1685]
4. Sir Alexander Falconer 1 Bt – [Kincardineshire 1678 1681 1685-86]
5. Sir David Falconer – [Forfarshire 1685]
6. Sir James Falconer – [Kincardineshire 1703-04]
7. John Falconer – Kincardineshire 1734-41

Seats: Dunnottar (Dunottar) Castle, Kincardineshire (built 13th c., acq. c. 1395, add. c. 1400, add. c. 1580s-1610s, family abandoned due to the Countess not liking the noise of the seals, damaged 1651, forfeited and dismantled 1716-18, ruin); Keith Hall, Aberdeenshire (purch. and built c. 1662, add. 1700, sold 1984, flats); Phesdo House, Kincardineshire (built 1814-15, sold mid-19th c.); Inverugie Castle, Aberdeenshire (built 12th c., acq. mid-14th c., rebuilt c. 1660, forfeited 1746, ruin); Fetteresso Castle, Kincardineshire (built early 16th c., destroyed 1645, rebuilt 1671, forfeited 1716); Inglismaldie, Kincardineshire (built late 16th c., purch. 1693, add. mid-18th c., fire 1882, rebuilt, sold 1925, derelict by 1950s)
Estates: Bateman 25433 (S) 29551. The 3 Earl Marischal was said to be the richest man in Scotland (d. 1581). Estate totaled 18,000 acres in 1914 and 635 in 1965 (Sayer, *The Disintegration of a Heritage*, 116)
Titles: Baron Keith c. 1430-1716 S; Baron Falconer 1646- S; Earl of Kintore 1677- S; Baron Kintore 1838- UK; Baronet 1625-1716, 1663-90
Peers: [6 peers 1660-94 1660-84 1677-1707 1698-1707] 1 Scottish Rep peer 1710-12 4 peers 1838-1945
2 Lds Lt 18th, 19th

1 KT 20th
Notes: The 6 Earl was forced to sell much land after 1660 due to heavy fines and expenses during the Civil War, and the 9 Earl impaired the remaining estates by high living, while the 10 Earl was a Jacobite who was attainted 1716 and exiled. Some estates were repurchased in 1764. Lady Mary Keith, sister of the last Earl Marischal, married the Earl of Wigtown. Their daughter Clementine married the 10 Lord Elphinstone, who was created Viscount Keith. (see Elphinstone). The last Earl sold Dunnottar to Alexander Keith of Edinburgh, who claimed descent from the family, which, apparently, the Earl acknowledged. However, this line later deferred to another branch of the family as senior. The Keith family (six biographies) has an entry in the ODNB plus the 3, 4, 5, 6, and 10 Earls Marischal and 1 Earl of Kintore and five others and three under Falconer.

Keith

Origins: Descended from a younger son of the 2 Earl Marischal.

1. James Keith – [Kintore Burghs 1660-63]

Seat: Auquhorsk (Aquhorsk, Afforsk) (Old House of), Aberdeenshire (owned 16th-18th c.)

Falconer

Origins: Cadet line.

1. Alexander Falconer – [Nairn 1685-86]

KEKEWICH

Origins: Gentry by the Tudor period, but never rich. Originally at Catchfrench in Cornwall. **First MP 1553. Another MP 1640.** Samuel Kekewich MP was a merchant and in the 18th century the family was involved in insurance. The 1 Bt was a barrister.

1. Samuel Kekewich – Sudbury 1698-1700
2. Samuel Kekewich – Exeter 1826-30 S. Devon 1858-73
3. Sir George Kekewich 1 Bt – Exeter 1906-10

Seat: Peamore House, Devon (built 16th-17th c., purch. c. 1800, remod. c. 1810, sold 1952, flats)
Estates: Bateman 4734 (E) 5942
Title: Baronet 1921-32
Notes: Three in ODNB.

KEMP

Origins: Acquired Gissing by marriage in 1324. **First MP 1584**. The 1 Bt was a courtier.

1. Sir Robert Kemp 2 Bt – Norfolk 1675-79 Dunwich 1679-81
2. Sir Robert Kemp 3 Bt – Dunwich 1701-05 1708-09 1713-15 Suffolk 1732-34
3. Sir Robert Kemp 4 Bt – Orford 1730-34

Seats: Gissing Hall, Norfolk (acq. by mar. 1324, medieval house, demolished c. 1700, rebuilt 19th c., sold 1936); Ubbeston Hall (aka Harefield House), Suffolk (Harefield built 1641, purch. 1674, demolished, Ubbeston built, 18th c., sold 1784); Mergate Hall, Norfolk (acq. by mar. late 15th c., built 16th c., sold 1936); Flordon Hall, Norfolk (built 16th c., sold 1936)
Estates: Bateman 2133 (E) 3163
Title: Baronet 1642-1936
Notes: One in ODNB.

KENDALL

Origins: Established at Treworgey in the early 14th century. A number of lines are combined here. **First MP 1330. Nine additional MPs 1365-1640**.

1. John Kendall – East Looe 1659 West Looe 1660 East Looe 1681
2. Thomas Kendall – Dartmouth 1664-66
3. Walter Kendall – Lostwithiel 1679-81 1689-95
4. James Kendall – West Looe 1685-87 1689-90 1695-1702 Lostwithiel 1706-08
5. Nicholas Kendall – E. Cornwall 1852-68

Seats: Pelyn (House), Cornwall (medieval, acq. early 16th c., rebuilt 1601, add. 18th c., add. 19th c., sold and repurch. post 1945, still own); Treworgey, Cornwall (acq. early 14th c., remod. 18th c., sold 1748); Killigarth, Cornwall (medieval, acq. by mar. 17th c., sold 18th c., demolished after 1820, rebuilt 1872)
Estates: Bateman 2276 (E) 2341
Notes: Eight members of the family represented Lostwithiel in each of the five centuries between the 14th and the 18th, and the family produced MPs in six successive centuries. James Kendall MP 1685-1708 owned West Indian estates.

KENNARD

Origins: The founder was a banker in the early 19th century. His son was a merchant.

1. Robert Kennard – Newport (IoW) 1847 1859-68

2. Edmund Kennard – Beverley 1868-69 Lymington 1874-85
3. Coleridge Kennard – Salisbury 1882-85

Seat: Fernhill, Hampshire (acq. 19th c., fire 1938)
Title: Baronet 1891-1999

KENNEDY *SCOTLAND & ENGLAND*

Marquis of Ailsa (1831- UK)

Origins: Claimed very ancient Gaelic descent. The family emerged into history in the 12th century as members of the retinue of the Earls of Carrick, to whose lands and offices they eventually succeeded. The first recorded Kennedy was Steward of Carrick 1367, and they acquired Cassillis in the same period. His grandson married a daughter of King Robert III in 1407. The 1 Earl fell at Flodden. The title passed to a remote descendent in the 18th century. **First [MP 1571]. One additional [MP 1599].**

1. Thomas Kennedy – Ayr Burghs 1720-21
2. David Kennedy 10 Earl of Cassiliis – Ayrshire 1768-74
3. Archibald Kennedy 2 Marquis of Ailsa – Evesham 1830

Seats: Culzean Castle, Ayrshire (acq. 15th c., medieval with add., rebuilt 1776-82, add. 1875-78, NT 1945); Cassillis (Cassilis) Castle (House), Ayrshire (acq. 1367, building in the 14th and 15th c., add. 1673-74, add. 1830-32, family departed 2007 and sold c. 2009); Castle Kennedy, Wigtownshire (built 1607, fire 1716, ruin)
Estates: Bateman 76015 (S) 35825. 250,000 acres in 1755. 10,000 acres in 1996.
Titles: Baron Kennedy 1458- S; Earl of Cassillis 1509- S; Baron Ailsa 1806- UK; Baronet 1682-1792
Peers: [2 peers 1661-1701] 3 Scottish Rep peers 1774-75 1776-90 1796-1806 5 peers 1806-1945
2 Lds Lt 19th, 20th
2 Kt 19th
Notes: The Kennedy family has an entry in the ODNB plus the 2, 3, 4, 5, 6, 7, 9, and 10 Earls and five other biographies.

Kennedy

Origins: Descended from a cadet line in the 14th century.

1. Thomas Kennedy – Ayr District Burghs 1818-34

Seats: Dunure Castle, Ayrshire (acq. mid-14th c., built 15th c., add. late 16th c., ruin by 1696, new house c. 1800); Dalquharran Castle, Ayrshire (built 15th c., add. c. 1679, new house 1782-90, add. c. 1881, now ruin)
Estates: Bateman 4141 (S) 5990
Notes: One in ODNB.

Kennedy

Origins: Another cadet line.

1. Myles Kennedy – Lonsdale Div. Lancashire 1922-23

Seat: Stone Cross, Lancashire (built 1874, now a school)

KENT I

Origins: This family was established in Reading from the early 15th century: clothiers and involved in other businesses. A number served as Mayors. The Bt line moved to London and was engaged in distilling, insurance and the South Sea Company. Several lines combined here. **First MP 1383 for Reading. Two further MPs 1421-50.**

1. Walter Kent – Ludgershall 1698-1700 1705-08
2. Clement Kent – Wallingford 1705-08 Reading 1722-27
3. Samuel Kent – Ipswich 1734-59
4. Sir Charles Kent 1 Bt – Thetford 1784-90 (son of Samuel's daughter, took name Kent)

Seats: Fornham Hall, Suffolk (old house, purch. 1731, built 1770s, sold 1789, demolished 1951); Poynton House, Lincolnshire (acq. 1811); Cookham, Berkshire; Goring, Oxfordshire (owned 18th c.)
Estates: Rubinstein – 2 Bt left £140,000 in probate in 1834
Title: Baronet 1782-1848
Notes: The heiress of Samuel Kent MP married Charles Egleton, a London goldsmith, who took the name Kent and inherited the Fornham estate in 1760.

KENT II

Origins: Moved from Cheshire to Wiltshire 1585. The first MP was a noble servant, town clerk, and attorney. Became gentry. **First MP 1597. Two additional MPs 1614-28.**

1. John Kent – Devizes 1661-69
2. Richard Kent – Chippenham 1685-87 1690

Seats: Winsley, Wiltshire (purch. c. 1612, sold c. 1690); Boscombe House, Wiltshire (purch. 1628, sold to cousin 1676 sold out of family 1733)
Notes: Most estates sold c. 1690.

KENYON *ENGLAND & WALES*

Baron Kenyon (1788- UK)

Origins: Settled in Lancashire since the reign of Henry III. Minor gentry in the 17th century. A barrister, grandson of a barrister, became Master of the Rolls and Lord Chief Justice 1788. He made a great fortune through the law.

1. Roger Kenyon – Clitheroe – 1690-95
2. George Kenyon – Wigan 1713-15
3. Lloyd Kenyon 1 Baron Kenyon – Hindon 1780-84 Tregony 1784-88
4. Lloyd Kenyon 3 Baron Kenyon – St. Michael's 1830-32
5. George Kenyon – Denbigh District 1885-95 1900-06

Seats: Gredington Hall, Flintshire (inherited by 1 Baron's mother 1730, sales of land from 1920s onwards, demolished 1978); Parkhead, Lancashire; (Kenyon) Peel Hall, Lancashire (built 1631-34, acq. by mar. of 1657 add. 1741, restored c. 1890, undermined by mining subsidence, demolished 1950s, still own estate)
Estates: Bateman 7941 (E & W) 12297. The 1 Baron left £260,000 plus landed estates in 1802. The 5 Baron left nearly £3 million in 1993.
Title: Baronet 1784-
Peers: 5 peers 1788-1869 1885-1927 1938-45
2 Lds Lt 18th, 20th
Notes: 1, 2, and 5 Barons and three others in ODNB.

Kenyon-Slaney

Origins: William Kenyon, son of a younger son of the 1 Baron Kenyon married Frances Slaney of Hatton Grange. Their son succeeded to the Slaney estates 1862. The Slaneys were originally from Yorkshire and settled in Shropshire where they made a long series of purchases of land completed in the 1680s. They owned forges and leased mineral rights into the 19th century.

1. Robert Slaney – Shrewsbury 1826-35 1837-41 1847-52 1857-62
2. William Kenyon-Slaney – Newport Div. Shropshire 1886-1908
3. Philip Kenyon-Slaney – Tavistock Div. Devon 1924-28

Seats: Hatton Grange, Shropshire (purch. 1650-80, built 1764-68, remod. c. 1900, still own); Walford Manor, Shropshire (Slaney acq. by mar. early-19th c., built 1831, sold 1920)
Estates: Bateman 2809 (E) 4860
Notes: One in ODNB.

KEPPEL

Earl of Albemarle (1696- E)

Origins: Medieval nobles in Holland. The 1 Earl accompanied William III from the Netherlands as a soldier in 1688 and stayed in England.

1. George Keppel 3 Earl of Albemarle – Chichester 1746-54
2. Augustus Keppel 1 Viscount Keppel – Chichester 1755-61 New Windsor 1761-80 Surrey 178-82
3. William Keppel – Chichester 1767-82
4. Augustus Keppel 5 Earl of Albemarle – Arundel 1820-26
5. George Keppel 6 Earl of Albemarle – E. Norfolk 1832-35 Lymington 1847-50
6. William Keppel 7 Earl of Albemarle – Norwich 1857-59 Wick 1860-65 Berwick-on-Tweed 1868-74
7. Arnold Keppel 8 Earl of Albemarle – Birkenhead 1892-94

Seats: Quidenham Hall, Norfolk (built 1606, add. c. 1750, purch. 1762, remod. later 18th c., sold 1948, now a convent); Lexham Hall, Norfolk (built early 18th c., purch. 1806, sold 1912)
Estates: Bateman 9846 (E & I) 8356; at Lexham Hall, Norfolk 3155 (E) 5566. Succeeded to large Egerton estate in 1958.
Title: Viscount Keppel 1782-86 GB
Peers: 10 peers 1697-1718 1723-72 1782-86 1793-1891 1876-1945
1 in Cabinet 1782-83
3 KG 18th
Notes: 1, 2, 3, 6, and 7 Earls and 1 Viscount and two others in ODNB.

KER *IRELAND*

Origins: Emigrated from Scotland mid-17th century. Settled first in Antrim and then Down. A linen merchant and banker purchased estates in the later 18th and early 19th centuries. Sheriff 1852.

1. David Ker – {Blessington 1796-97}
2. Richard Ker – Newport (IoW) 1802-06

3. David Ker – Athlone 1820-26 Downpatrick 1835-41
4. Richard Ker – Downpatrick 1847-51 1857-59
5. David Ker – County Down 1852-57 Downpatrick 1859-67
6. Richard Ker – County Down 1884-85 E. Div. County Down 1885-90

Seats: Montalto, Down (built mid-18th c., purch. 1802 from E. of Moira, remod. early 19th c., add. 1837, add. later 19th c., sold 1912, part demolished 1952); Portavo (Portavoe), Down (built c. 1650, purch. 1765, remod. 1817, fire 1844, rebuilt 1884, sold 1980); Red Hall, Antrim (acq. and built 1609, purch. for £24,500 in 1783, add. later 18th c., sold 1868)
Estates: Bateman 20544 (I) 22196. Worth £4,000 pa in 1793, £15,000 pa in 1800 and £20,000 pa in 1814.

KERR (Carr, Ker) [Cross, Innes, McDonnell] *SCOTLAND & IRELAND*

Duke of Roxburghe (1707- S)

Origins: The Kerrs were an Anglo-Norman family settled in the Scottish borders in the 13th century. They held land in Roxburghshire from 1357. Acquired additional estates in the 15th and 16th centuries. Lords of Session 1569 and 1589. **First [MP 1560]. An additional [MP 1597].** The daughter of a younger son the 1 Earl of Roxburghe married the 22nd Innes laird (3 Bt). The Inneses were a medieval family. **First [MP 1560]. An additional [MP 1612].** The 6 Bt succeeded after much litigation as 5 Duke of Roxburghe in 1812.

1. Sir Robert Innes 2 Bt – [Elgin & Forresshire 1661-63 1678]
2. Sir Robert Innes – [Elgin & Forresshire 1665]
3. Sir Henry Innes 4 Bt – [Elgin & Forresshire 1704-07]
4. William Kerr – Berwick-on-Tweed 1710-13 Dysart Burgh 1715-22 Aberdeen Burghs 1722 Berwick 1723-27
5. James Innes-Kerr 7 Duke of Roxburghe – Roxburghshire 1870-74

Seats: Floors (Fleurs) Castle, Roxburghshire (acq. by Kers 16th c., built 1721-26, passed in 1812 by mar. to Innes family, add. 1837-43, remod. early 20th c., still own); Innes (House), Elginshire (acq. by Innes family – Innes of that Ilk - 1157, rebuilt 1640-53, sold early 20th c.)
Estates: Bateman 60418 (S) 50917. Worth £70,000,000 with 56,000 acres in 1990. Owned 65,600 acres in 1996.
Titles: Baron Kerr 1600- S; Earl of Roxburghe 1616- S; Baron Bellended 1661-1805 S; Earl Ker 1722-1804 GB; Earl Innes 1837- UK
Peers: [5 peers 1661-1707 1661-75 1678-82 1701-07

2 Scottish Rep peers 1707-10 1715-27 1818-20 6 peers 1730-55 1761-1804 1837-92 1897-1932 1934-45
5 Lds Lt 18th, 19th, 20th
1 in Cabinet 1704 1716-25
3 KT 18th, 19th, 20th
2 KG 18th, 19th
Notes: The daughter of the 1 Earl of Roxburghe married the 2 Earl of Perth (see Drummond). Their eldest son succeeded as Earl of Perth while the Roxburghe peerage went to a younger son. The Drummond-Kerr line became extinct in 1805, which is when the Dukedom passed to the Inneses. 1 Earl and 1, 3, and 5 Dukes and one other in ODNB.

Ker(r)

Origins: Cadet line descended from Andrew Ker (d. 1481) the common ancestor of the family. **First [MP 1645 for Roxburghshire]**.

1. Sir Andrew Kerr 2 Bt – [Roxburghshire 1669-74]
2. Sir William Kerr 3 Bt – [Roxburghshire 1685-86 1702-07] Scotland 1707-08

Seat: Greenhead, Roxburghshire (owned 16th-17th c.)
Title: Baronet 1637-1776

Innes-Cross

Origins: A cadet of the Inneses. To Ireland c. 1660. Merchants in Belfast and Dublin.

1. Arthur Innes-Cross – Newry 1865-68

Seat: Dromantine (Glen Manor), Down (acq. mid-18th c., resident through 19th c.)
Estates: Bateman 3237 (I) 4522

Innes

Origins: Cadet line.

1. Sir Alexander Innes 1 Bt – [Elgin & Forresshire 1685-86]

Seat: Coxton, Elginshire (16th c. tower burned 1584, rebuilt 1644, sold 18th c.)
Title: Baronet 1686-1882

Marquis of Lothian (1701- S)

Origins: Descended from a younger son of Sir Andrew Ker (d. 1526), ancestor of the Dukes of Roxburghe. **First [MP 1560]. Four additional [MPs 1597-1649]. The 1 Earl of Ancrum sat for an English seat 1628.** The father of the 1 Earl developed coal mines, saltpans, and large-scale sheep ranching on his estates in the second half of the 16th century.

1. Charles Kerr 2 Earl of Ancrum – Mitchell 1647 Thirsk 1660 Wigan 1661-81 1685-87
2. William Kerr 4 Marquis of Lothian – Richmond 1747-63
3. John Kerr 7 Marquis of Lothian – Huntingdon 1820-24
4. Charles Kerr 1 Baron Teviot – Montrose 1932-40
5. Michael Kerr 13 Marquis of Lothian – Berwickshire and East Lothian 1974 Edinburgh S. 1979-87 Devizes 1992-2010

Seats: Monteviot (House), Roxburghshire (built 1740, add. c. 1830, remod. 1960, still own); Blickling Hall, Norfolk (built 1619-28, passed by mar. from the Hobarts to the Suffields in 1793 and then in 1850 to the 8 Marquis of Lothian, left to the NT 1940 by the 11 Marquis); Newbattle Abbey, Midlothian (built 1140, rebuilt 1385, acq. 1547, remod. 1550s, remod. 18th c., add. 1836, 1858, 1875, and 1886, institutional use from 1930s); Ferniehirst Castle, Roxburghshire (built 1470, rebuilt 1598, abandoned 18th c., reroofed and repaired c. 1830, restored c. 1890, youth hostel from 1934-85, restored as family seat 1988, still own); Melbourne Hall, Derbyshire (acq. by mar. from the Earls Cowper 1905, still own)
Estates: Bateman 32361 (E & S) 45203. Owned 18,000 acres in 1996.
Titles: Baron Newbattle 1591- S; Earl of Lothian 1606- & 1631- S; Baron Jedburgh 1622- S; Earl of Ancrum 1633- S; Baron Kerr 1821- UK; Baron Teviot 1940- UK; Lord Kerr of Monteviot 2010- UKLife
Peers: [5 peers 1660-90 1662-1703 1670-1707] 5 Scottish Rep peers 1708-09 1715-22 1731-61 1768-74 1778-90 1817-24 8 peers 1821-41 1853-1940 1940-15 1943-45
2 Lds Lt 19th
1 in Cabinet 1931
6 KT 18th, 19th, 20th
Notes: The 6 Marquis married in 1793 the heiress of the 2 Earl of Buckinghamshire (see Hill I) and succeeded to Blickling Hall. The 11 Marquis served until his death in the key post of Ambassador to the United States in the early part of the Second World War. The 13 Marquis was Chairman of the Conservative Party 1998-2001 and Shadow Foreign Secretary 2001-03. 1 and 3 Earls of Lothian and 1 Earl of Ancram and 1, 2, 4, 9, and 11 Marquises and six others in ODNB.

Marquess of Antrim (1644-82 1789-91 I)

Origins: The McDonnells (MacDonnell) descended from the Lords of the Isles and married the Irish heiress to the Glens of Antrim in the 15th century. King James I granted the family a vast estate of over 300,000 acres in 1603. (Perceval-Maxwell, *The Scottish Migration to Ulster*, 48) The eldest daughter of the 1 Marquess of Antrim succeeded as Countess of Antrim in her own right and married Sir Henry Vane Tempest. Their daughter inherited the Tempest estates and married the 3 Marquess of Londonderry (see Vane). The second daughter succeeded her sister as Countess of Antrim and married Lord Mark Kerr, son of the Marquis of Lothian. Their son succeeded as 4 Earl of Antrim.

1. William McDonnell 1 Marquess of Antrim – {County Antrim 1768-75}
2. Angus McDonnell – Dartford Div. Kent 1924-29

Seats: Glenarm Castle, Antrim (castle built mid-13th c., acq. by mar. c. 1427, castle destroyed 1597, new house built 1603, burned 1642, ruin until rebuilt c. 1750, remod. 1770s, remod. 1823-24, fire 1929, rebuilt, still own); Dunluce Castle, Antrim (built 14-17th c., acq. c. 1555, damaged 1642, abandoned 1690, given to state 1928)
Estates: Bateman 34404 (I) 20910. 333,000 acres in 1606. Held 148,497 acres in 1734. Worth £9,774 pa 1798. Held 44,066 acres in 1812. Owned 7,500 acres in 2001.
Titles: Viscount Dunluce 1618-1791 I; Earl of Antrim 1620-1791 I; Earl of Antrim 1785- I; Baronet 1627-90
Peers: {5 peers 1660-99 1701-21 1734-91}
1 KP 18th
Notes: A Roman Catholic family through the 17th century. Estates confiscated during the Civil War, restored 1661. Outlawed 1689. Estates restored 1697, but value much reduced and greatly indebted. 1, 3, and 8 Earls and 1 Marquess in ODNB.

KILLIGREW

Origins: Held manorial property in the 13th century. **First MP 1553. Five additional MPs 1572-1644, two of them kts of the shire**.

1. Sir William Killigrew – Penryn 1628 Richmond 1664-79
2. Sir Peter Killigrew – Orkney, Shetland & Caithness 1659 Helston 1661-68
3. Sir Peter Killigrew 2 Bt – Camelford 1660
4. Henry Killigrew – Stockbridge 1702-05 St. Albans 1705-08

Seats: Arwenick (Arwennack) House, Cornwall (acq. by mar. 1385, rebuilt c. 1567, fire c. 1650, mostly ruinous early 18th c.); Hanworth Park, Middlesex (acq. 1570s, sold 18th c.)

Title: Baronet 1660-1705
Notes: Estate gradually grew impoverished in the later 16th and early 17th c. Male line extinct 1705. Eleven in ODNB.

KING I [Fenton, Harman, Parsons, Tenison] *IRELAND*

Earl of Kingston (1768- I)

Origins: Emigrated from Yorkshire to Ireland in 1585 as secretary to the Governor of Munster. Received grants of land under Elizabeth I and James I. Married heiress of the 12th White Knight. Royal officials and PC Ireland 1609. **First {MP 1613}. One further {MP 1634-56}**.

1. Sir Robert King 1 Bt – {Ballyshannon 1661-66 County Roscommon 1692-93 1695-99 Boyle 1703-07}
2. Sir William King – {County Limerick 1661-66 1692-93 1695-99}
3. Sir John King 2 Bt – {Boyle 1695-99 1703-14 County Roscommon 1715-21}
4. Sir Henry King 3 Bt – {Boyle 1707-27 County Roscommon 1727-41}
5. George King – {County Limerick 1713-14 Kilmallock 1715-22}
6. Edward King 1 Earl of Kingston – {Boyle 1749-60 County Sligo 1761-64}
7. Robert King 1 Baron Kingsborough – {Boyle 1744-48}
8. Henry King – {Boyle 1761-1800}
9. Charles King – {Swords 1776-83 Belturbet 1797-99}
10. Robert King 2 Earl of Kingston – {County Cork 1783-97 Boyle 1776-83}
11. Robert King 1 Viscount Lorton – {Jamestown 1796-97 Boyle 1798-1800}
12. George King 3 Earl of Kingston – {County Roscommon 1797-99}
13. John King – {Clogher 1800}
14. Edward King – County Roscommon 1802-06
15. Edward King Viscount Kingsborough – County Cork 1818-26
16. Sir Henry King – County Sligo 1822-31
17. Robert King 4 Earl of Kingston – County Cork 1826-32
18. Robert King 6 Earl of Kingston – Roscommon 1826-30

Seats: Mitchelstown Castle, Cork (medieval castle passed on death of 12th White Knight 1611 via two heiresses to 1 Baron Kingston, destroyed 1641, new house by 1750, new house built 1776, demolished 1823 and new house built at a cost of £100,000, which helped bankrupt estate, burned 1922); Kilronan Castle, Roscommon (built 18th c., acq. by mar. 1872, ruin 20th c.); Boyle Abbey, Roscommon (granted by Eliz. I, family moved to Rockingham and house abandoned early 18th c.); King House, Roscommon (built 17th c., fire, rebuilt early 18th c., abandoned by family early 19th c., became barracks, now decayed); Oakport, Roscommon; Rockingham House, Roscommon (acq. under

James I, built 17th c., rebuilt 18th c., new house 1810, add. 1822, fire 1863, rebuilt, burned 1957, sold, demolished)
Estates: Bateman 24671 (I) 17951 and 21307 (I) 9064. Large land sales 1844 and c. 1907 to clear debts.
Titles: Baron Kingston 1660-1761 I; Baron Kingsborough 1748-55 I; Baron Kingston 1764- I; Viscount Kingsborough 1766- I; Baron Erris 1800- I; Viscount Lorton 1806- I; Baron Kingston 1821-69 UK; Baronet 1682-
Peers: {7 peers 1660-76 1692-93 1697-1715 1728-61 1764-1800} 3 Irish Rep peers 1807-21 1823-54 1887-96 1 peer 1821-39
3 Lds Lt 19th
Notes: 1 and 2 Barons and 2 Earl of Kingston and six others in ODNB.

Tenison

Origins: First emerged in the 1520s. To Ireland to serve the Earl of Strafford 1640s. Archbishop of Canterbury 1694. Several cousins were Irish bishops 1690s and 1730s. Commissioner of the Revenue for Ireland 1703. The daughter of the 1 Earl of Kingston married Thomas Tenison of Castle Tenison. Their son succeeded as Edward King-Tension. The King-Tenison estates passed to the 8 Earl of Kingston 1872.

1. Henry Tenison – {County Monaghan 1695-99 County Louth 1703-09}
2. Richard Tenison – {Dunleer 1715-25}
3. William Tenison – {Dunleer 1727-28}
4. Thomas Tenison – {Dunleer 1728-61}
5. Thomas Tenison – {County Monaghan 1775-83}
6. Thomas Tenison – {Boyle 1792-97}
7. Edward King-Tenison – Leitrim 1847-52

Seats: Kilronan Castle (Tenison Castle or Castle Tenison), Roscommon (acq. and built 18th c., add. early 19th c., passed to Kings by mar. 1872, ruin 20th c.); Lough Bawn, Louth (acq. and built, 1695, fire 1795, rebuilt early 19th c., resident into 20th c.)
Estates: Lough Bawn line 2696 (I) 2013
1 Ld Lt 19th
Notes: Three in ODNB.

Fenton

Origins: The Fentons went to Ireland in 1580 from Nottinghamshire: Sir Geoffrey Fenton, Principal Secretary State for Ireland. Kt 1589. His daughter married the 1 Earl of Cork in 1603. His son Sir Maurice Fenton married 1614 to the Fitzgibbon heiress of the White Knight of Mitchelstown Castle. The 1 Baron Kingston married the daughter of Sir William Fenton of Mitchelstown and his wife Margaret Fitzgibbon, sister and heiress of the White Knight.

1. Sir Maurice Fenton 1 Bt – {Fethard 1661-66}

Seat: Mitchelstown, Cork (see above)
Title: Baronet 1661-71
Notes: One in ODNB.

Harman

Origins: Henry Harman was Clerk of the Council under Henry VIII. Nicholas Harman settled in Ireland in the early 17th century. Acquired estates 1607. The heiress of Cutts Harman of Newcastle married in 1742 Sir Lawrence Parsons of Birr Castle. Their son, Lawrence Parsons-Harmon, 1 Earl of Rosse, married in 1772 Lady Jane King, daughter of the 1 Earl of Kingston. The Rosse title passed by special remainder to a Parsons nephew (see below). The Harman estates passed to the Earl's daughter Frances Parsons-Harman, who married in 1799 the 1 Viscount Lorton, younger son of the 2 Earl of Kingston. The 2 Viscount succeeded as 6 Earl of Kingston. His younger brother took the name King-Harman and succeeded to Newcastle and Rockingham. **The first Harman {MP 1614}. Two further {MPs 1634-39}**.

1. Sir Thomas Harman – {County Carlow 1659 Kildare 1661-66}
2. Wentworth Harman – {County Longford 1695-99 Granard 1703-13 Lanesborough 1713-14}
3. Wentworth Harman – {Lanesborough 1715-27}
4. Robert Harman – {Kildare 1755-60 County Longford 1761-65}
5. Caleb Harman – {County Longford 1793-96}
6. Edward King-Harman – County Sligo 1877-80 County Dublin 1883-85 Isle of Thanet 1885-88

Seats: Rockingham, Roscommon (see under King); Newcastle, Longford (acq. by Sheppards later 17th c., built early 18th c., passed by mar. 1691 of Sheppard heiress to Harmans 1738, passed by mar. to Earl of Rosse 1784 and then to King-Harmans, remod. early 19th c., sold c. 1950, hotel)
Estates: Bateman 72913 (I) 40105
Title: Baronet 1914-
2 Lds Lt 19th

Earl of Rosse (1718-64; 1806- I)

Origins: To Ireland as an adventurer from Leicestershire c. 1590. Became Surveyor General 1602 and aggressively sought landed property. Kt 1612. **First {MP 1613}. Two further {MPs 1613-40}.** Birr acquired 1619.

1. Sir William Parsons 2 Bt – {King's County 1692-93 1695-99 1703-41}
2. Sir Lawrence Parsons 3 Bt – {King's County 1741-56}
3. Sir William Parsons 4 Bt – {King's County 1757-91}
4. Wentworth Parsons – {County Longford 1766-68}
5. Lawrence Parsons-Harmon 1 Earl of Rosse – {County Longford 1775-92}
6. Lawrence Parsons 2 Earl of Rosse – {Dublin University 1782-90 King's County 1791-1800} 1801-07
7. John Parsons – King's County 1818-21
8. William Parsons 3 Earl of Rosse – King's County 1821-34

Seats: Birr Castle, King's County (acq. 1619, built 1620-27, burned 1643, rebuilt, remod. c. 1801, fire 1825, add. c. 1830, remod. 1908, still own); Heaton Hall, Yorkshire (inher. by Parsons by mar. 1837 from the Field family who acq. it in the 16th c., sold 1911, demolished 1939); Tullynisk Park, King's County (built early 19th c.); Womersley Park, Yorkshire (built 16th c., passed by marriage to the 4 Earl of Rosse 1869, sold 2004)
Estates: Bateman 26486 (I & E) 15549. Worth £2,300 pa in 1738, £8,000 pa 1790, £10,000 pa in 1812. Owned 5,000 acres in 2001.
Titles: Viscount Rosse 1681-1764 I; Baron Oxmantown 1792- I; Viscount Oxmantown 1795-1807 I; Baronet 1620-1764; 1677-
Peers: {3 peers 1681-96 1703-64} 5 Irish Rep peers 1801-07 1809-41 1845-1908 1911-18
3 Lds Lt 19th, 20th
2 KP 19th, 20th
Notes: Sir Charles Parsons, a younger son of the Earl of Rosse, invented the steam turbine and left an estate of close to a million pounds in the early 20th c. (Roberts, *Lost Country Houses of Suffolk*, 37). 1 Bt and 1 Bt and 2, 3, and 4 Earls and one other in ODNB.

Sheppard

Origins: To Ireland from Suffolk mid 17th century. Sheriff 1734. Estates pass to Harmans (see above) 1738.

1. Anthony Sheppard – {County Longford 1703-13 1715-38}
2. Anthony Sheppard – {Newcastle 1726-27 Longford 1727-37}

Seat: Newcastle, Longford (acq. later 17th c., built early 18th c., passed via marriage 1691 to Sheppard heiress to Harmans 1738, see above)

KING II *IRELAND*

King

Origins: To Ireland as Bishop of Elphin 1611. Sheriff 1657. **First {MP 1657}.**

1. John King – {Jamestown 1703-14 1721-37}
2. Gilbert King – {Jamestown 1709-21}
3. John King – {Jamestown 1721-39}
4. Gilbert King – {Jamestown 1737-60}
5. Edward King – {Carrick 1781-93}
6. Robert King – {Jamestown 1790-97}
7. Sir Gilbert King 1 Bt – {Jamestown 1797-1800}
8. John King – {Jamestown 1797-1800}

Seat: Charlestown, Roscommon (acq. mid-17th c., rebuilt late 18th c., still resident 1930s)
Estates: Bateman 6666 (I) 3728
Title: Baronet 1815-
Notes: Family in Canada c. 2000.

King

Origins: Descended from a younger son of Gilbert MP {1709-21} of Charlestown.

1. John King – King's County 1865-68

Seat: Ballylin, King's County (acq. 18th c., built late 18th c., remod. late 19th c., add. early 20th c., later demolished)
Estates: Bateman 11196 (I) 5517

KINGSMILL

Origins: The family emerged in the 15th century. A Judge of the Common Pleas 1504. Kt 1530. Sheriff 1538. Acquired estates at the Dissolution and later. **First MP 1472. Five additional MPs 1491-1586.**

1. Sir Robert Kingsmill 1 Bt – Yarmouth 1779-80 Tregony 1784-90
2. William Kingsmill – Yeovil Div. Somerset 1945-51

Seat: Sydmonton (Sidmontan) Court, Hampshire (acq. and built 1540s, add. early 18th c., sold 1978); Highclere, Hampshire (purch. 1577, in 1600 passed to an heiress to Lucys who sold it 1671)
Estates: Bateman 5361 (E) 4630
Title: Baronet 1800-23
Notes: The male line died out in 1766. The daughter of the last Kingsmill married 1764 Admiral Sir Robert Brice. He took the name Kingsmill. Later the estates passed through another heiress. The Kingsmill family has an entry in the ODNB plus three other biographies.

KINNAIRD *SCOTLAND & ENGLAND*

Baron Kinnaird (1682- S)

Origins: Granted the barony of Kinnaird c. 1180 and held for seven centuries. **First [MP 1625 for Perthshire].** The family became bankers from the 18th century onwards.

1. George Kinnaird 1 Baron Kinnaird – [Perthshire 1661-63]
2. Charles Kinnaird 8 Baron Kinnaird – Leominster 1802-05
3. Douglas Kinnaird – Bishop's Castle 1819-20
4. Arthur Kinnaird 10 Baron Kinnaird – Perth 1837-39 1852-78

Seats: Rossie Priory, Perthshire (built 1807-15, add. 1839 and 1866, most demolished c. 1949); Drimmie House, Perthshire (old house, replaced by Rossie Priory)
Estates: Bateman 11818 (S & E) 17003
Titles: Baron Rossie 1831-78 UK; Baron Kinnaird 1860- UK
Peers: [3 peers 1682-1707] 2 Scottish Rep peers 1787-90 1 peer 1831-78
2 Lds Lt 19th, 20th
1 KT 19th
Notes: From 1837 the 10 Baron was a banker, succeeding his uncle Douglas Kinnaird as head of Ransome & Co. The 11 Baron succeeded him. The 11 Baron also played in eleven FA Cup finals, a record never surpassed since. 1, 8, 9, 10, and 11 Barons and four others in ODNB.

KIRKBY

Origins: Established at Kirkby Ireleth by the 12th century. **First MP 1640**.

1. Ricahrd Kirkby – Lancaster 1661-81
2. Roger Kirkby – Lancaster 1685-87 1689-1702

Seat: Kirkby Ireleth, Lancashire (acq. 12th c., unable to recover after mortgage of 1689)

Estates: Worth £1500 pa c. 1660.
Notes: Became indebted in the later 17th century and then financial collapse. A younger son, Captain in the RN, was executed for cowardice in battle in 1703. One in ODNB.

KIRKPATRICK *SCOTLAND*

Origins: Witnessed a charter 12th century. **First [MP 1593 for Dumfriesshire]. One other [MP 1641 also for the county].**

1. Sir Thomas Kirkpatrick 1 Bt – [Dumfriesshire 1593]
2. William Kirkpatrick – Dumfries Burghs 1736-38

Seats: Closeburn Castle, Dumfriesshire (acq. 1232, built late 14th c., new house 17th c., fire 1748, remod. old castle c. 1750, remod. and add. 19th c., sold 1783); Capenoch House, Dumfriesshire (built 1780, sold 1847)
Title: Baronet 1685-
Notes: In Kenya in 20th century.

KITSON

Baron Airedale (1907-96 UK)

Origins: The grandfather of the first Baron was a publican. (Morris, *Class, Sect, and Party*, 34) The father of the 1 Baron founded a great locomotive manufacturing firm in 1837.

1. James Kitson 1 Baron Airedale – Colne Valley Yorkshire 1892-1907

Seats: Elmete Hall, Yorkshire (purch. and built mid-19th c., add. 1885, sold 1920); Gledhow Hall, Yorkshire (built 1601, remod. 1768, purch. 1883, sold 1922-23, now flats)
Estates: 1 Baron left £1,000,000 in 1911.
Title: Baronet 1886-1996
Peers: 3 peers 1907-45

KNATCHBULL [Hugessen]

Baron Brabourne (1880- UK)

Origins: Emeregd as landowners in Kent under Edward III. At Mersham le Hatch since 1485. **First MP 1609**.

1. Sir Norton Knatchbull 1 Bt – Kent 1640 New Romeny 1640-48 1661-79

2. Sir John Knatchbull 2 Bt – New Romney 1660 Kent 1685-87 1689-95
3. Sir Edward Knatchbull 4 Bt – Rochester 1702-05 Kent 1713-15 1722-27 Lostwithiel 1728-30
4. Sir Edward Knatchbull 7 Bt – {Armagh 1727-60}
5. Sir Wyndham Knatchbull Wyndham 6 Bt – Kent 1760-63
6. Sir Edward Knatchbull 8 Bt – Kent 1790-1802 1806-19
7. Sir Edward Knatchbull 9 Bt – Kent 1819-31 E. Kent 1832-45
8. Edward Knatchbull-Hugessen 1 Baron Brabourne – Sandwich 1857-80
9. Sir Wyndham Knatchbull 12 Bt – E. Kent 1875-76
10. Herbert Knatchbull-Hugessen – Feversham Div. Kent 1885-95
11. Edward Knatchbull-Hugessen 2 Baron Brabourne – Rochester 1889-92
12. Michael Knatchbull 5 Baron Brabourne – Ashford Div. Kent 1931-33

Seats: Mersham le Hatch, Kent (purch. 1485, rebuilt 1762-72, remod. 1819-49, leased out 1980s, still own); Smeeth Paddocks, Kent
Estates: Bateman 4638 (E) 7224; 483 (E) 930; 4173 (E) 5646. Worth £2,000 pa in c. 1600. The 9 Baron left £3 million in 2006. Owned 2,700 acres 2015.
Title: Baronet 1641-
Peers: 7 peers 1880-1939 1943 1945
1 in Cabinet 1834-35
Notes: 1, 4, and 9 Bts and 1 and Barons and two others in ODNB.

<u>Knatchbull</u>

Origins: Descended from a younger son of the 4 Bt.

1. William Knatchbull – E. Somerset 1852-65

Seat: Babington House, Somerset (built c. 1705, inher. by mar. and remod. 1790, sold 1952)
Estates: Bateman 2513 (E) 3719

KNIGHT [King]

<u>Earl of Catherlough</u> (1770-72 I)

Origins: The Knights were yeomen from Worcestershire and Warwickshire in the 16th century. The 1 Earl was the son of a South Sea Company cashier who fled to France in 1721, having lost £200,000 when the "Bubble" burst, and became a banker in Paris.

1. Robert Knight 1 Earl of Catherlough – Great Grimsby 1734-47 Castle Rising 1747-54 Great Grimsby 1762-68

2. Henry Knight – Great Grimsby 1761-62
3. Robert Knight – Wootton Bassett 1806-07 1811-12 1823-26 Wallingford 1826-32 (illegitimate son)

Seats: Barrells Hall, Warwickshire (acq. mid-16th c. and house built, purch. by 1 Earl 1730, enlarged 1792-94, sold 1856, fire 1933, demolished 1954); Luxborough Hall, Essex (built 16th c., acq. c. 1710, rebuilt 1716-20, sold and demolished c. 1800)
Estates: 400 acres in 1681. Owned c. 1,000 acres at Barrells 1856. (Tyack, *Warwickshire Country Houses*, 30)
Title: Baron Luxborough 1745-72 I
Notes: 1 Earl and one other in ODNB.

King

Origins: Edward King MP married in 1828 the daughter and heiress of Robert Knight MP (illegitimate son of the Earl of Catherlough) and succeeded in 1855 to the Knight estates at Chadshunt, purchased by the Earl of Catherlough.

1. John King – Enniskillen 1806
2. Edward Bolton King – Warwick 1831-37 S. Warwickshire 1857-59

Seats: Chadshunt Hall, Warwickshire (built early 18th c., purch. by Knights 1772, rebuilt 1841-6, inher. by Kings 1855, sold c. 1920); Umberslade Hall, Warwickshire (built 1693-8, purch. 1826 for £76,000, sold 1858)
Estates: Bateman 2994 (E) 3837
Notes: A King stood for Parliament in 1901 and lost.

KNIGHTLEY

Baron Knightley (1892-95 UK)

Origins: The Knightleys could trace their descent from Nicholas Mauconvenant, one of the followers of William the Conqueror (Roskell, Clark, and Rawcliffe, *The House of Commons*, III, 529). Held estates in Staffordshire in the 12th century. A successful Staffordshire lawyer and King's Serjeant purchased Fawsley in Northamptonshire in 1416. **First MP 1325 for Staffordshire. Nine further MPs 1373-1628, seven of them kts of the shire**.

1. Sir Richard Knightley – Northampton 1640-48 Northamptonshire 1659 St.Germans 1660
2. Valentine Knightley – Northamptonshire 1748-54
3. Lucy Knightley – Northampton 1763-68 Northamptonshire 1773-84
4. Sir Charles Knightley 2 Bt – S. Northamptonshire 1834-52

5. Rainald Knightley 1 Baron Knightley – S. Northamptonshire 1852-92

Seats: Fawsley Hall, Northamptonshire (medieval, purch. 1416, rebuilt c. 1500, add. 1732, remod. early 19th c., remod. 1860s, unoccupied after 1913, passed by mar. to Viscount Gage 1938, derelict, part demolished 1966, sold 1975, restored as a hotel); Offchurch Bury, Warwickshire (purch. 1542, remod. 1560s, add. 1655, passed to Earls of Aylesford by mar. 1829, later demolished)
Estates: Bateman 8041 (E) 13182. Said to have been worth £13,000 pa in 1566.
Title: Baronet 1798-1938
Peer: 1 peer 1892-95
Notes: 1 Baron and four others in ODNB.

KNOLLYS [Mill]

Earl of Banbury (1626-32 E)

Origins: Grocer and Lord Mayor of London 1399. Purchased manorial property in Hertfordshire c. 1390. **First MP 1416. Nine additional MPs 1529-1648, five of them kts of the shire**. Courtiers under Elizabeth I.

1. William Knollys – Oxfordshire 1663
2. William Knollys (titular) 5 Earl of Banbury – Banbury 1733-40
3. Charles Knollys (reputedly illegitimate son of titular 5 Earl) – Gatton 1749-52

Seats: Rotherfield Greys (built c. 1347, acq. 1514, new house later 16th c., rebuilt early 17th c., alienated 1686); Boughton Hall, Northamptonshire (medieval, inher. 1662, sold 1686); Great Harrowden Hall, Northamptonshire (medieval, inher. by mar. 1662 from Lord Vaux, sold 1693)
Estates: Worth £800 pa in 1660
Titles: Baron Knollys 1603-32 E; Viscount Wallingford 1616-32 E; Baron Knollys 1902- UK; Viscount Knollys 1911- UK
Peers: 3 peers 1660 1902-45
Notes: The son of the 1 Earl was of questionable legitimacy, and the title not recognized, although the titular Earl was summoned to the Convention Parliament. The claim of the descendents to the Earldom was rejected by the House of Lords in 1813. 1, 3, "4" and "8" Earls and 1 and 2 Viscounts and four others in ODNB.

Knollys

Origins: Cadet line.

1. Fancis Knollys – Reading 1701

2. Francis Knollys – Oxford 1722-34
3. Sir Francis Knollys 1 Bt – Reading 1761-68

Seats: Thame Park, Oxfordshire (medieval and early 16th c. monastic buildings, acq. after Dissolution 1540, passed by mar. later 16th to Williams family (see Wenman)); Lower Winchendon, Buckinghamshire (acq. 16th c., sold 18th c.)
Estates: Worth £1,700 pa in 1722.
Title: Baronet 1754-72

Knollys

Origins: Cadet branch in Hampshire since the reign of Henry VIII.

1. Thomas Knollys – Southampton 1659 1670-79
2. Henry Knollys – St. Ives 1722-34

Seat: Grove Place, Hampshire (medieval, rebuilt mid to later 16th c., acq. 1630, passed out of family 1751, add. 18th c.)
Title: Baronet 1642-48
Notes: Male line extinct 1751.

Mill

Origins: Held estates in Sussex from before 1476 and acquired larger holdings at the Dissolution. **First MP 1529. Four (possibly five) additional MPs 1547-1640.** On the extinction of the Knollyses of Grove Place (see above) their estates passed by marriage to the Mills of Mottisfont.

1. Sir Richard Mill 5 Bt – Midhurst 1721-22 1729-34 Penryn 1734-41 Horsham 1741-47
2. Sir Richard Mill 6 Bt – Hampshire 1765-68

Seat: Mottisfont Abbey (Montisford), Hampshire (medieval and 1521-36, remod. c. 1538, purch. 1684, remod. 1740s, sold c. 1934)
Estates: Bateman 5040 (E) 5751
Title: Baronet 1619-1835; 1836-60
Notes: In the 16th century a Mill married the Lewknor heiress of Camois Court, Sussex (family summoned to Parliament by Richard II as Lord Camois). The 7 Bt succeeded to the Bisham estate of Sir Philip Hoby 5 Bt and took the name Hoby 1766 (see Hoby). On the death of the 10 Bt his estates passed to a nephew, son of his sister Mary by her husband John Barker of Wareham, Dorset. The son took the name Mill in 1835 and was created a Baronet.

KNOX [Gore] *IRELAND*

Earl of Ranfurly (1831- I)

Origins: Glasgow merchants in the 16th century settled in Ireland post 1660. Lord Mayor of Dublin 1685-86.

1. Thomas Knox – {Newtown 1692-93 Dungannon 1695-99 1703-27}
2. Thomas Knox – {Dungannon 1731-69}
3. Thomas Knox 1 Viscount Northland – {Dungannon 1755-81}
4. John Knox – {Dungannon 1769-76}
5. Thomas Knox 1 Earl of Ranfurly – {Carlingford 1776-83 Dungannon 1783-90 County Tyrone 1790-97} 1806-12
6. John Knox – {Killibegs 1777-83 Dungannon 1790-94 1800} 1801
7. George Knox – {Dungannon 1790-97 Dublin University 1797-1800} 1801-07
8. Charles Knox – {Dungannon 1797-99}
9. Thomas Knox 2 Earl of Ranfurly – County Tyrone 1812-18 Dungannon 1818-30 1837-38
10. John Knox – Newry 1826-32
11. John Knox – Dungannon 1830-37
12. Thomas Knox 3 Earl of Ranfurly – Dungannon 1838-51
13. Brownlow Knox – Marlow 1847-68
14. William Knox – Dungannon 1851-74
15. Edmund Knox – W. Cavan 1890-95 Londonderry 1895-99
16. Sir Alfred Knox – Wycombe Div. Buckinghamshire 1924-45

Seat: Northland House (Dungannon Park), Tyrone (purch. 1692, rebuilt 1785, add. c. 1840, abandoned by family by 1930s, demolished)
Estates: Bateman 10153 (I) 11237. Worth £1,000 pa in 1713.
Titles: Baron Wells 1781- I; Viscount Northland 1791- I; Baron Ranfurly 1826- UK
Peers: {1 peer 1781-1800} 1 Irish Rep peer 1800-18
6 peers 1826-58 1870-75 1877-1933 1934-45
Notes: Family resident in England after WWI. Three in ODNB.

Knox

Origins: The senior line descended from Uctred Knox, whose younger son was the ancestor of the Earls of Ranfurly. To Ireland 1610 as Bishop of Raphoe.

1. George Knox – {County Donegal 1735-41}
2. Andrew Knox – {County Donegal 1743-60 1761-68}
3. Andrew Knox – {Strabane 1798-1800}

Seat: Prehen, Londonderry (acq. by mar. early 18th c., built mid-18th c., sold 1914)
Estates: 4528 (I) 2673

Knox [Gore]

Origins: Descended from an older brother of the ancestor of the Earls of Ranfurly. Mary Gore, heiress of Belleek Manor (descended from a brother of the 1 Earl of Arran, see Gore), married Francis Knox of Rappa. One of their sons succeeded to Rappa and another took the additional name Gore and was seated at Belleek.

1. Francis Knox – {Philipstown 1797-1800}
2. James Knox-Gore – {Taghmon 1797-1800}

Seats: Rappa Castle, Mayo (Knox acq. mar. Gore heiress 1761, family departed 1920s, part demolished 1937, ruin); Moyne Abbey, Mayo (medieval, burned 1590, partly restored, acq. mid-17th c., now a ruin); Belleek Manor (Abbey, Castle), Mayo (rebuilt 1831, sold c. 1942, hotel)
Estates: Bateman 30592 (I) 11082 and at Rappa 10722 (I) 2788 (five younger sons given 1,128 acres worth £408 pa each in mid-19th c.)
Title: Baronet 1868-90
1 Ld Lt 19th

Knox

Origins: Cadet of the Rappa line.

1. John Knox – {Dongeal 1761-68 Castlebar 1768-74}
2. Lawrence Knox – Sligo 1868-69

Seat: Mount Falcon, Mayo (acq. 19th c., built 1876, sold 20th c., hotel)
Estates: Bateman 5589 (I) 2246. Still owned 93 acres in 2001.

LA TOUCHE *IRELAND*

Origins: Huguenot refugees who came from Amsterdam to Ireland with William III's army. One fought at the Boyne. Sheriff 1797. They operated a poplin factory in Dublin from 1694 and then became bankers (1712) and country gentlemen simultaneously in the 18th and 19th centuries. Several branches are combined here.

1. James La Touche – {Dublin 1727-49}
2. David La Touche – {Dundalk 1761-68 Longford 1769-83 Belturbet 1783-90}

3. John La Touche – {Newcastle 1783-90 Newton 1796-97 County Kildare 1797-1800} 1801-02
4. Peter La Touche – {County Leitrim 1783-97}
5. David La Touche – {Newcastle 1790-1800} County Carlow 1802-16
6. Robert La Touche – {Harristown 1794-1800} County Kildare 1802-30
7. John La Touche – {Newtown 1796-97 Harristown 1797-1800} Dublin 1802-06 County Leitrim 1807-20
8. Peter La Touche – County Leitrim 1802-06
9. Robert La Touche – County Carlow 1816-18

Seats: Marley (Marlay), Dublin (built early 18th c., purch. and rebuilt 1760, sold 1867); Harristown House, Kildare (acq. and buult 1783, fire and rebuilt c. 1900, sold 1946); Bellevue, Wicklow (purch. 1753, house built 1754 for £30,000, remod. 1790s, add. ealy 19th c., sold c. 1915, demolished early 1950s); Belfield, Dublin; Williamrow, Carlow; Drumhierny Lodge, Leitrim (acq. early 18th c., sold 1912, became a ruin); Luggala, Wicklow (acq. 1788 and built c. 1790s, sold 1857)
Estates: Bateman 15311 (I) 10160 and 11379 (I) 7557. Bank income may have totaled £30,000 pa by the later 18th c. but then declined. (O'Byrne, *Luggala Days*, 36) Harristown rental £6-7,000 pa in 1800. Still held 1,024 acres at Harristown in 1928 (Bunbury, *The Landed Gentry & Aristocracy: Kildare*, 137).
Notes: One in ODNB.

LAMBART (Lambert) *IRELAND & ENGLAND*

<u>Earl of Cavan</u> (1647- I)

Origins: Claimed lineal descent from Ralphe de Lambart, who fought at the Battle of Hastings. (ODNB) Founder a goldsmith in London in the 1540s. To Ireland 1580 and again in 1599 as a soldier. Kted at the storming of Cadiz 1596. Governor of Connaught 1601, acquired estates. PC Ireland 1603. The 1 Baron lost or mortgaged most of his estates, but the 1 Earl gained further property 1622, although he too, was in financial trouble by 1660. **First MP 1597 for Southampton and {1613 for County Cavan}. Two additional MPs one for Southampton 1601 and one for Bossiney 1626-29**. The family kept one foot on each island.

1. Frederick Lambart 9 Earl of Cavan – S. Div. Somerset 1885-92

Seats: Wheathampstead House (Hall), Hertfordshire (acq. and built 19th c., sold after 1946); Stone Court, Surrey; Lambarton Park (House), Queen's County (acq. c. 1622, sold mid-18th c.); Eaglehurst, Hampshire (built 1780, purch. 1803, add. c. 1810, sold 1844); Sharpham Park, Somerset (built 16th c., acq. by mar. 1794, part demolished 1799-1826, became a farm house, sold between 1906-23)

Estates: Bateman 2731 (E & I) 2099. Estimated income c. 1600 between £1,700 and £2,600.
Title: Baron Lambart 1618- I
Peers: {6 peers 1689 1692-1778 1786-1800} 1 Irish Rep peer 1915-45
2 KP 19th, 20th
Notes: The 10 Earl was a field marshal. 1 Baron and 1, 7, and 10 Earls and one other in ODNB.

Lambart

Origins: Descended from a younger son of the 1 Earl of Cavan. **First {MP 1647 for Kilbeggan}.**

1. Walter Lambart – {Kilbeggan 1661-65}
2. Oliver Lambart – {Kilbeggan 1661-66 1692-93 1695-99}
3. Charles Lambart – {Kilbeggan 1695-99 1703-13 Cavan 1713-14 Kilbeggan 1715-53}
4. Charles Lambart – {Kilbeggan 1727-40}
5. Charles Lambart – {Kilbeggan 1727-40}
6. Gustavus Lambart – {Kilbeggan 1741-76}
7. Hamilton Lambart – {Kilbeggan 1753-60}
8. Charles Lambart – {Kilbeggan 1768-83}
9. Gustavus Lambart – {Kilbeggan 1797-1800}

Seats: Beauparc (Beau Parc), Meath (acq. early 17th c., built 1755, add. c. 1778, held until 1930s); Hayes, Meath
Estates: 1405 (I) 1794
Title: Baronet 1911-86

LAMBTON

Earl of Durham (1833- UK)

Origins: The Lambton's have held Lambton since at least the mid-14th century, possibly much earlier. Mined coal before 1600, and by 1640 were exporting 30,000 tons a year. (*Country Life*, 139, p. 665). Coal provided a great fortune by the 19th century. **First MP 1431 for Northumberland**.

1. William Lambton – County Durham 1685-87 1689-98 1701-02 1710-13
2. Henry Lambton – Durham 1734-61
3. John Lambton – Durham 1762-87
4. William Lambton – Durham 1787-97
5. Ralph Lambton – Durham 1798-1813

6. John Lambton 1 Earl of Durham – County Durham 1813-28
7. Hedworth Lambton – N. Durham 1832-47
8. Frederick Lambton 4 Earl of Lambton – S. Durham 1880-85 S. E. Durham 1900-10
9. Sir Hedworth (Lambton) Meux – Portsmouth 1916-18
10. Antony Lambton 6 Earl of Durham – Berwick-on-Tweed 1951-73

Seats: Lambton Castle, Durham (originally Harraton Hall – old house, rebuilt later 17th c. for the Hedworths, passed to Lambtons by mar. in part 1688 and rest by purch. from co-heirs 1714, pulled down 1796 and rebuilt as Lambton Castle 1796-1802, vastly enlarged 1820s and 1857-65, radically reduced in size 1932, still own); Old Lambton Hall, Durham (on opposite side of river from Harraton, pulled down 1797); Biddick Hall, Durham (medieval, add. 16th c., purch. 1610, rebuilt 1721-23, add. 1954-55, present seat)
Estates: Bateman 30471 (E) 71671. The 6 Earl left £11,800,000 in 2006. Owned 9,500 acres in 2001.
Title: Baron Lambton 1828- UK
Peers: 5 peers 1828-40 1849-1945
2 Lds Lt 19th, 20th
1 in Cabinet 1830-33
1 KG 20th
Notes: The 6 Earl of Durham was involved in a sex scandal with security implications when serving as a junior minister in the Ministry of Defense and was obliged to resign in 1973. The Meux estates (brewers, perhaps close to one million pounds) passed to the Lambtons in 1911 (see Meyrick). 1 and 6 Earls and four others in ODNB.

LAMONT *SCOTLAND*

Lamont

Origins: First mentioned in a charter 1238. This line held the chiefship of the clan. **First [MP 1630 for Argyll]. An additional [MP 1639 also for Argyll].**

1. Archibald Lamont – [Argyll 1685-86]

Seat: Ardlamont House, (Inveryne) Argyllshire (built 1325, acq. 1646, rebuilt 1819-20, sold 1893)

Lamont

Origins: A cadet line were Jacobites and became West Indian proprietors in Trinidad. Repurchased estates in Scotland 1753.

1. Norman Lamont – Wells 1832-34
2. Sir James Lamont 1 Bt – Buteshire 1865-68
3. Sir Noman Lamont 2 Bt – Buteshire 1905-10

Seat: Knockdow House (Kilmichael), Argyllshire (acq. 1554, repurch. 1753, built c. 1765, add. c. 1815, add. c. 1870, remod. 1921-25, sold 1954)
Estates: Bateman 6775 (S) 2427
Title: Baronet 1910-
Notes: The Lamonts remodled Knockdow in the 1920s with exotic hardwoods from their estates in Trinidad, which they still owned.
1 Bt in ODNB.

LAMPLUGH

Origins: Settled at Lamplugh since the 12th century. Every head of the family was High Sheriff of Cumberland from the 15th to the 18th century. **First MP 1384 for Cumberland. One additional MP 1421 also for the county**.

1. Richard Lamplugh – Cumberland 1679
2. Thomas Lamplugh – Cockermouth 1702-08

Seats: Lamplugh Hall, Cumberland (acq. and built late 12th c., add. 1595, burned mid 18th c.); Ribton Hall, Cumberland (purch. mid-17th c., rebuilt later 17th c., sold 1722, demolished)
Estates: Worth £1,000 pa in 1660. Owned 6,000 acres in the 19th c.
Notes: Thomas Lamplugh MP died 1737 leaving the estates to his daughter, who married Richard Briscoe (see Briscoe). One in ODNB.

LANE-FOX [Benson]

Baron Bingley (1713-31 GB; 1762-73 GB; 1933-47 UK)

Origins: Robert Benson of Bramham Park, the son of a Yorkshire attorney "of mean extraction" (*The Complete Peerage*, II, 177), was grasping and ambitious, and became a financier and purchased estates. He became Chancellor of the Exchequer and was created Baron Bingley 1713. George Fox married his daughter and heiress in 1731 and the Barony of Bingley was revived for him. The first Fox MP was the son of a mercer. Thomas's nephew Henry Fox married 1691 the sister and heiress of the 2 Viscount Lanesborough (see below). Their eldest son, George Fox, 1 Baron Bingley of the second creation, took the additional name Lane. George Fox was succeeded by his nephew for whose descendent the Baronry was revived for a third time.

1. Thomas Fox – Tamworth 1659 1660
2. Robert Benson 1 Baron Bingley – Thetford 1702-05 York 1705-13
3. George Lane-Fox 1 Baron Bingley – Hindon 1734-41 York 1742-61
4. Robert Lane – York 1761-68
5. James Lane-Fox – Horsham 1796-1802
6. George Lane-Fox – Beverley 1820-26 1837-40
7. Sackville Lane-Fox – Helston 1831-34 Beverley 1840-41 Ipswich 1842-47 Beverley 1847-52
8. George Lane-Fox 1 Baron Bingley – Barlston Ash Div. Yorkshire 1906-31

Seats: Bramham Park, Yorkshire (acq. and built 1703-10, burned 1828, rebuilt 1906, still own); Hope Hall, Yorkshire; Moat House, Staffordshire; Oran House, Yorkshire (built 1830); Red Hall, Yorkshire
Estates: Bateman 42529 (E & I) 34538. The father of the 1 Baron Bingley was worth perhaps as much as £3,000 pa in 1676. The 1 Baron left large estates and £100,000 to his heiress in 1731. Rubinstein – James Lane Fox left £120,000 in probate in 1821.
Title: Baroness Lane-Fox 1981-88 LifeUK
Peers: 4 peers 1713-31 1762-73 1859-88 1933-45
1 in Cabinet 1711-13
Notes: Sackville Lane Fox succeeded his maternal uncle the 3 Duke of Leeds in 1859 as 12 Baron Conyers and 15 Baron Darcy, but the titles passed again through the female line out of the family in 1888. Augustus Lane-Fox inherited the estates in 1880 of the 6 Baron Rivers (see Pitt). Baroness Lane-Fox, Robert Benson 1 Baron Bingley, and two others in ODNB.

Viscount Lanesborough (1676-1724 I)

Origins: The father of the 1 Bt went to Ireland in the later 16th c. as a soldier and was granted estates. Sheriff 1651. Kt 1657. The 1 Bt married an heiress and the 2 Bt was a politician and created a Viscount. The estates passed by marriage to the Fox family 1724 (see above).

1. George Lane 1 Viscount Lanesborough – {County Roscommon 1662-66}
2. Sir Richard Lane 1 Bt – {Tuam 1665-66}

Seats: Tulske Castle, Roscommon (acq. c. 1600, castle demolished in 1651); Rathcline Castle (Lanesborough), Longford (medieval, acq. 1664, rebuilt 1660s, damaged 1690, passed to Lanes-Foxes 1724, sold 1770, ruin today)
Estates: At least 10,000 acres in 1660s worth £2,000 to £3,000 pa (ODNB).
Title: Baronet 1661-1724
Peers: {2 peers 1676-1724}
Notes: 1 Viscount in ODNB.

LANGFORD

Origins: At Langford by the 13th century. Warden of the Isle of Wight 14th c. **First MP 1355. Three further MPs 1373-1601, one kt of the shire.**

1. Humphrey Langford – Camelford 1685

Seats: Langford, Devon; Langford Hill, Cornwall (acq. 13-14th c., medieval, passed by mar. from Cornish Langfords to Devon Langfords 1686); Chale, Hampshire (IoW) (acq. 13th c., built c. 1330, sold 1562); Bradfield, Berkshire (acq. by mar. mid-14th c., passed out of family 16th c.)

LANGHAM

Origins: The family began with a son of a yeoman apprenticed to a Turkey merchant. Became involved in the East India Company in the 1620s, and became one of the wealthiest merchants of his day. Sheriff of London 1642. Purchased landed estates in the 1630s.

1. Sir John Langham 1 Bt – London 1654 Southwark 1660
2. Sir James Langham 2 Bt – Northamptonshire 1656 Northampton 1659 1661-62
3. Sir William Langham 3 Bt – Northampton 1679-81 1689-95
4. Sir James Langham 7 Bt – Northamptonshire 1784-90
5. Sir James Langham 10 Bt – St. Germans 1802-06

Seats: Cottesbrooke Hall, Northamptonshire (purch. 1637, built 1702-12, remod. 1775-79, sold 1911); Walgrave Hall, Northamptonshire (purch. 1655 for £8,600, built 17th c., still owned 1937); Tempo Manor, Fermanagh (acq. by mar. 1893, still own)
Estates: Bateman 9669 (E) 14883
Title: Baronet 1660-
Notes: Sir John Langham spent more than £50,000 on the purch. of land in Northamptonshire by 1665. (Heward and Taylor, *Country Houses of Northamptonshire*, 141)

<u>Tennent</u>

Origins: Belfast merchants 18th-19th centuries (distilling, banking, insurance). The Tennent heiress married an Emerson, who took the name Emerson-Tennent (1834).

1. Sir James Emerson Tennent 1 Bt. – Belfast 1832-45

Seat: Tempo Manor, Fermanagh (purch. 1815, built 1863, passed by mar. 1893 to Langhams)
Title: Baronet 1867-76
Notes: One in ODNB.

LASCELLES

Earl of Harewood (1812- UK)

Origins: A Lascelles family held estates in the Middle Ages but the modern line cannot demonstrate the connection. The latter emerged c. 1600. One served as a colonel in the Civil War and went to Barbados in the mid-17th century. The family engaged in trading, planting, and office-holding which led to the accumulation of large plantations. They returned to England rich in the mid-18th century and engaged in slave trading, supplying army contracts and banking (Kennedy, *Harewood*, 13-42).

1. Francis Lascelles – Thirsk 1645 N. R. Yorkshire 1653 1654 1656 Northallerton 1660
2. Thomas Lascelles – Northallerton 1660 1689-97
3. Daniel Lascelles – Northallerton 1702
4. Edwin Lascelles 1 Baron Harewood – Scarborough 1744-54 Northallerton 1754-61 Yorkshire 1761-80 Northallerton 1780-90
5. Henry Lascelles – Northallerton 1745-52
6. Daniel Lascelles – Northallerton 1752-80
7. Edward Lascelles 1 Earl of Harewood – Northallerton 1761-74 1790-96
8. Edward Lascelles Viscount Lascelles – Northallerton 1796-1814
9. Henry Lascelles 2 Earl of Harewood – Yorkshire 1796-1806 Westbury 1807-12 Yorkshire 1812-18 Northallerton 1818-20
10. William Lascelles – Northallerton 1820-26 East Looe 1826-30 Northallerton 1831-32 Wakefield 1837-41 1842-47 Knaresborough 1847-51
11. Henry Lascelles 3 Earl of Harewood – Northallerton 1826-31
12. Edwin Lascelles – Ripon 1846-57
13. Egremont Lascelles – Northallerton 1866-68

Seats: Harewood House, Yorkshire (purch. 1739, built 1759, remod. 1765-71 and 1843-50, still own); Goldsborough Hall, Yorkshire (medieval, burned 16th c., rebuilt 1601, purch. 1753, remod. 1750s, family departed 1939, sold 1951); Stank Hall, Yorkshire (built 15th c., resident 16th c., purch. 1608, remod. 17th c., sold 19th c.)
Estates: Bateman 29620 (E) 38118. Henry Lascelles after a career as a West India merchant died in 1753 worth nearly £400,000. Rubinstein – 1 Earl left £250,000 in probate 1820. Worth £50,000,000 in 1990. Owned 10,000 acres in 2001.
Titles: Baron Harewood 1790-95 GB; Baron Harewood 1796- GB
Peers: 7 peers 1790-1945

4 Lds Lt 19th, 20th
1 KG 20th
Notes: The 6 Earl succeeded to the large fortune (two and a half million pounds) of the 2 and last Marquess of Clanricarde and married the Princess Royal, daughter of King George V. Sir Alan Lascelles was Private Secretary to George VI and Elizabeth II. 2 and 6 Earls and three others in ODNB.

LAURIE *SCOTLAND*

Origins: Merchants in the 17th century. Purchased estates 1611. **First [MP 1643 for Dumfriesshire].**

1. Sir Robert Laurie 4 Bt – Dumfries Burghs 1738-41
2. Sir Robert Laurie 5 Bt – Dumfriesshire 1774-1804

Seat: Maxwelton House (Glencairn Castle), Dumfries (built 1370, purch. 1611, built 17th c., later add., sold 1966)
Titles: Baronet 1685-1848
Notes: In 1848 the estates passed to the Fectors via an heiress, bankers in Dover who took the name Laurie.

LAW

Earl of Ellenborough (1844-71 UK)

Origins: Yeomen in the 17th century. Then a clergyman. His son was Bishop of Carlisle 1768, his two sons were both bishops 1782 and 1812. In the next generation the 1 Baron, was a barrister and Lord Chief Justice 1802. 1 Earl Governor General of India. The first MP was a nabob who left an estate worth £70,000.

1. Ewan Law – Westbury 1790-95 Newtown (IoW) 1802
2. Edward Law 1 Baron Ellenborough – Newtown 1801-02
3. Edward Law 1 Earl of Ellenborough – Mitchell 1813-18
4. Charles Law – University of Cambridge 1835-50

Seats: Windlesham Court, Surrey (leased); Southam Delabere, Gloucestershire (built c. 1500, purch. 1839, add. 1840, sold 1947, became a school); Prescott House, Gloucestershire (built 17th c., purch. 1848, add. 1860, sold 1872)
Estates: Under 2000 acres in Bateman. The 1 Baron left £240,000 in 1818 (Rubinstein £200,000).
Title: Baron Ellenborough 1802- UK
Peers: 7 peers 1802-1945

2 in Cabinet 1806-07 1828-30 1834-35 1841 1846 1858
Notes: 1 Baron and 1 Earl and eleven others in ODNB.

LAWLESS *IRELAND*

Baron Cloncurry (1789-1929 I; 1831-1929 UK)

Origins: The father of the 1 Baron was a Roman Catholic and made a fortune in the woolen trade as a blanket manufacturer in Dublin in the 18th century. The 1 Baron, who conformed, was also a businessman. The creation of the peerage scandalized Dublin. Purchased estates in the mid-18th century. Sheriff 1838.

1. Nicholas Lawless 1 Baron Cloncurry – {Lifford 1776-89}
2. Cecil Lawless – Clonmell 1846-53

Seats: Lyons Castle, Kildare (medieval castle, purch. 1796, built new house 1797, add. 1802, sold 1962); Maretimo, Dublin (built c. 1800, remod. 19th c., demolished 20th c.); Abington, Limerick (purch. 1776, held into 20th c.)
Estates: Bateman 12487 (I) 10443
Title: Baronet 1776-1929
Peers: {2 peers 1789-1800} 3 peers 1831-1929
Notes: The new house of the 1 Baron Cloncurry at Lyons was said to have cost £200,000. 2 Baron and two others in ODNB.

LAWRENCE I [Smith]

Lawrence

Origins: Builders in London. Sheriff of London 1849. Lord Mayor 1868.

1. Sir William Lawrence – London 1865-74 1880-85
2. Sir James Lawrence 1 Bt – Lambeth 1865 1868-85
3. Sir Edwin Durning-Lawrence 1 Bt – Truro Div. Cornwall 1895-1906

Seat: King's Ride, Berkshire (acq. by mar. 1879, sold early 20th c.)
Title: Baronet 1869-97; 1898-1914

Smith

Origins: Sir Edwin Lawrence 1 Bt married Edith Smith, daughter and heiress of John Smith MP and Jemima Durning. John B. Smith was a merchant and President of the

Manchester Chamber of Commerce 1839-41. He was First Chairman of the Anti-Corn Law League.

1. John B. Smith – Stirling District 1847-52 Stockport 1852-74

Seat: King's Ride, Berkshire (purch. 1860, built 1863, passed to heiress who mar. Lawrence 1879)

LAWRENCE II

Baron Lawrence (1869- UK)

Origins: The 1 Baron was the son of a lt. col. in the army from Yorkshire. He rose in the Indian Civil Service to become Viceroy of India 1864-69, a rare appointment for a non-aristocrat. A younger son became a railway chairman and peer in his own right in 1923.

No MPs.

Estates: Under 2000 in Bateman. 1 Baron left £140,000 and a government pension for his son's lifetime.
Title: Baron Lawrence of Kingsgate 1923-27 UK; Baronet 1858-
Peers: 4 peers 1869-1945 1923-27
Notes: 1 Baron and four others in ODNB.

LAWSON I

Origins: Rose by fortunate marriages in the second half of the 16th century. **First MP 1563 for Northumberland. Another MP 1593 for Cumberland.** Kt 1604.

1. Wilfred Lawson – Cockermouth 1659 1660
2. Sir Wilfred Lawson 1 Bt – Cumberland 1659 1660 Cockermouth 1661-79
3. Sir Wilfred Lawson 2 Bt – Cockermouth 1690-95
4. Sir Wilfrid Lawson 6 Bt – Cumberland 1701-05 1708-34
5. Sir Wilfred Lawson 3 Bt – Boroughbridge 1718-22 Cockermouth 1722-37
6. Sir Wilfred Lawson 8 Bt – Cumberland 1761-62
7. Sir Wilfred Lawson 2 Bt – Carlisle 1859-65 1868-85 Cockermouth Div. Cumberland 1886-90 Cambourne Div. Cornwall 1903-06
8. Sir Wilfred Lawson 3 Bt – Cockermouth Div. Cumberland 1910-16

Seats: Brayton House (Hall), Cumberland (acq. c. 1705, remod. 1800, rebuilt 1820s, remod. later 19th c., burned 1940); Isel Hall, Cumberland (Leighs acq. 1313, built 15th

c., add. 1540, acq. by mar. from Leghs (Leigh) 1573, family owned into the 1970s, part demolished); Hesket Hall, Cumberland (built early 17th c., passed by mar. to Wyberghs in 1806)
Estates: Bateman 8294 (E) 14752
Title: Baronet 1688-1806; 1831-1959
Notes: The Leighs of Isel produced an **MP for Cumberland 1423.** On the death of the last Bt of the first creation in 1806 the estates passed to Thomas Wybergh (of Clifton Hall, Westmorland and Borrans Hill, Cumberland) son of Lady Lawson's sister. He took the name Lawson. His brother of Brayton was created a Bt in 1831. The Wyberghs were a medieval family (Shirley, *The Noble and Gentle Men of England*, 282). 2 Bt in ODNB.

LAWSON II

Viscount Burnham (1919-33 UK)

Origins: The family name was originally Levy, borne by a London merchant who died in 1830. His son Moses Levy founded the *Daily Telegraph* (sold 1927, but the 4 Baron managed it until 1961) and took the name Lawson 1875. Sheriff 1886.

1. Harvy Lawson 1 Viscount Burnham – W. St. Pancras 1885-95 Mile End Div. Tower Hamlets 1905-06 1910-16

Seat: Hall Barn Park, Buckinghamshire (purch. 1881, still own)
Estates: 3207 (E) 3802. Moses Levy left £100,000 in probate in 1830. 6,000 acres in the 20th c. In addition to the landed estate the 4 Baron left half a million pounds in 1963. The 1 Baron left £267,000 and land in 1916.
Title: Baron Burnham 1903- UK; Baronet 1892-
Peers: 3 peers 1903-45
Notes: 1 and 4 Barons and 1 Viscount in ODNB.

LAWSON III [Wilkinson]

Origins: Merchants in York, Lord Mayor of York and Kt 1530. Mayor of York again 1741. Inherited Wilkinson estates by marriage 1805. **First MP 1529 for York.**

1. Marmaduke Lawson – Boroughbridge 1818-20
2. Andrew Lawson – Knaresborough 1834-37 1841-47
3. Sir John Lawson 1 Bt – Thirsk and Malton Div. N. R. Yorkshire 1892-1906

Seats: Aldborough Manor, Yorkshire (built early 18th c., acq. by mar. from Wilkinsons 1805, still own); Boroughbridge Hall, Yorkshire (acq. by mar. 1805 from Wilkinsons, sold 1980, flats)
Bateman 2672 (E) 4305
Title: Baronet 1905-
Notes: Some members of the family remained Roman Catholic into the 19th century.

Wilkinson

Origins: The father of the first MP was the estate agent to the Dukes of Newcastle.

1. Thomas Wilkinson – Boroughbridge 1715-18
2. Andrew Wilkinson – Aldborough 1735-65 1768-72
3. Charles Wilkinson – Aldborough 1774-77

Seats: Aldborough (Aldburgh) Hall (Manor), Yorkshire (purch. 1654, built early 18th c., passed by mar. 1805 to Lawsons); Boroughbridge Hall, Yorkshire (purch. 1654, built later 17th c., remod. c. 1730, add. 1770s, passed by mar 1805 to Lawsons)

LAWTON

Origins: The family took their name from the manor where they resided from at least the reign of King John. **First MP 1584-1606**.

1. John Lawton – Newcastle-under-Lyme 1689-90 1695-98 1706-08 1709-10
2. John Lawton – Newcastle-under-Lyme 1734-40

Seat: Lawton Hall, Cheshire (medieval, purch. 1541, rebuilt early 17th c., remod. mid-18th c., add. 1830s, sold 2003)
Estates: Bateman 2556 (E) 7492. Worth £1,800 pa c. 1730s.

LE HUNTE *IRELAND*

Origins: A Captain in Cromwell's bodyguard settled in Ireland. Sheriff 1657. The first MP married an heiress.

1. Richard Le Hunte – {Cashel 1661-66}
2. Richard Le Hunte – {Enniscorthy 1713-47}
3. Thomas Le Hunte – {Wexford 1735-68 Newtown 1769-75}
4. Richard Le Hunte – {Wexford 1768-83}

Seat: Artramont (Artramon, Ardtramont) House, Wexford (acq. mid-18th c., built c. 1770-80, burned 1923, sold, rebuilt 1928-32)
Estates: Bateman 3834 (I) 2675
Notes: One in ODNB.

LEADER [Maberly]

Leader

Origins: The father of the first MP was coachmaker to the Prince of Wales. His son was a malt distiller and MP.

1. William Leader – Camelford 1812-18 Winchelsea 1823-26
2. John Leader – Bridgwater 1835-37 Westminster 1837-47

Seat: Lower House, Putney, Surrey
Estates: Rubinstein - first MP died worth £300,000 in probate in 1828.
Notes: Male line extinct 1903. One in ODNB.

Maberly

Origins: The Maberlys were curriers in London and inherited part of the Leader fortune by marriage. Became ordnance manufacturers and contractors to the army.

1. John Maberly – Rye 1816-18 Abingdon 1818-32
2. William Leader Maberly – Westbury 1819-20 Northampton 1820-30 Shaftesbury 1831-32 Chatham 1832-34

Seat: Shirley House, Surrey
Notes: The first MP went bankrupt 1832. Male line extinct 1885? One in ODNB.

LECHMERE [Charlton]

Baron Lechmere (1721-27 GB)

Origins: The first recorded mention of the Lechmere family is 1272, although it is possible that Severn End has descended almost from the time of the Conquest (*Country Life*, 158, p. 194). The 1 Baron rebuilt the family fortunes after the Civil War through a career in the law. **First MP 1654**. Owned a bank in the 19th century.

1. Nicholas Lechmere 1 Baron Lechmere – Appleby 1708-10 Cockermouth 1710-17 Tewkesbury 1717-21

2. Anthony Lechmere – Bewdley 1710 Tewkesbury 1714-17
3. Edmund Lechmere – Worcestershire 1734-47
4. Nicholas Lechmere-Charlton – Worcester 1774
5. Edmund Lechmere – Worcester 1790-96
6. Sir Edmund Lechmere 3 Bt – Tewkesbury 1866-68 W. Worcestershire 1876-85 Bewdly Div. Worcestershire 1885-92 Evesham Div. Worcestershire 1892-94

Seats: Rhydd Court, Worcestershire (acq. land medieval period, built c. 1800, add. 1863, family departed 1915, sold c. 1919); Severn End, Worcestershire (acq. by 12th c., medieval, rebuilt 1660-7, fire 1896, rebuilt 1899, still own, leased out 1976); Ludford House, Shropshire (inher. by mar. 1784, sold by 1840)
Estates: Bateman 5752 (E) 11608. Own 1,500 acres today.
Title: Baronet 1818-
Peer: 1 peer 1721-27
1 in Cabinet 1717-27
Notes: Two in ODNB.

Charlton

Origins: Old Shropshire gentry. The founder of this cadet line rose from being a fishmonger and goldsmith in the early 17th century to Speaker of the House of Commons 1673. The estates of the 4 and last Bt passed in 1784 to a nephew Nicholas Lechmere, son of his sister who married Edmund Lechmere.

1. Sir Job Charlton 1 Bt – Ludlow 1659 1660-79
2. Sir Francis Charlton 2 Bt – Ludlow 1679-81 Bishop's Castle 1685-87
3. William Charlton – Ludlow 1685
4. Job Charlton – Newark 1741-61
5. Edmund Charlton – Newark 1835-37

Seats: Ludford House, Shropshire (built c. 1600, remod. 1761, passed by mar. to Lechmeres 1784); Whitton Court, Shropshire (built 14th, mid-15th, and c. 1550, purch. 1635, add. c. 1635, sold 1835) (*Country Life*, 143, p. 1511); Staunton Hall, Nottinghamshire (Stauntons held estate from at least the 12th c., medieval house, rebuilt 16th c., damaged in mid-17th c., remod. early 18th c. and 1778-80, passed by mar. to Charltons 1784, passed to cousins, the Broughs who took the name Staunton, still own); Blunden Hall, Shropshire (built mid-16th c, add. 17th c., acq. by mar. 1646)
Estates: Worth £1,748 pa in the late 17th c.
Title: Baronet 1686-1784
Notes: Job Charlton MP succeeded to the Staunton estates of Staunton Hall belonging to his mother. Later heirs resumed the name Staunton and are still resident at Staunton Hall (held 1,500 acres in 1980s). Sir Job Charlton married the daughter and heiress of

the Blunden estates 1646. (Blundens **one MP 1625-26**). Another branch of the family can be found under Meyrick. 1 Bt and two others in ODNB.

LEE [Antonie]

Origins: Settled in Buckinghamshire from the 15th century. Acquired Hartwell by marriage 1617.

1. Sir Thomas Lee 1 Bt – Aylesbury 1660-81 Buckinghamshire 1689-90 Aylesbury 1690-91
2. Sir Thomas Lee 2 Bt – Aylesbury 1689-99 1701-02
3. Sir Thomas Lee 3 Bt – Chipping Wycombe 1710-22 Buckinghamshire 1722-27 1729-41
4. William Lee – Chipping Wycombe 1727-30
5. Sir George Lee – Brackley 1733-42 Devizes 1742-47 Liskeard 1747-54 Launceston 1754-58
6. John Lee – Malmesbury 1747-54 Newport 1754-61
7. William Lee – Appleby 1754-56
8. William Lee Antonie – Great Marlow 1790-96 Bedford 1802-12

Seats: Hartwell House, Buckinghamshire (built c. 1600, passed by mar. to Lees 1617, add. c. 1755-63, sold 1938, hotel); Totteridge Park, Hertfordshire (purch. 1748, passed to Fiott family by inher. 1827, sold after 1866); Colworth House, Bedfordshire (built later 16th c., purch. by Antonie family 1714, rebuilt 1714-18, passed to Lees by mar. 1771 who took name Antonie, add. 1771-75, add. 1810-12, sold 1826, now offices)
Estates: Bateman 2086 (E) 5495
Title: Baronet 1660-1827
1 in Cabinet 1754
Notes: Connected to the Lees of Ditchley (see Dillon). Claimed descent from the Leghs of Lyme. Hartwell was acquired by the Hampdens in the 15th century (kin of the Hampdens of Hampden [see Hill I]). In 1827 the Lee estates passed to Dr. John Fiott (son of a merchant), who took the name Lee. He was a nephew and heir of William Lee Antonie of Colwick, Bedfordshire. The Antonies were Huguenots. The purchaser of Colwick in 1714 was the steward of the Duke of Montagu. Four Lees and one Fiott in ODNB.

LEESON [Turton] *IRELAND & ENGLAND*

Earl of Milltown (1763-1891 I)

Origins: Settled in Ireland in the reign of Charles I. The father of the 1 Earl was a brewer and banker. Purchased a landed estate 1741. Sheriff 1756.

1. Joseph Leeson 1 Earl of Milltown – {Rathcormack 1743-56}
2. Joseph Leeson 2 Earl of Milltown – {Thomastown 1757-60}

Seat: Russborough House, Wicklow (purch. 1741, built 1741-48, passed to Turtons by mar. 1891)
Estates: Bateman 5042 (I) 2597
Titles: Baron Russborough 1756-1891 I; Viscount Russborough 1760-1891 I
Peers: {2 peers 1756-1800} 1 Irish Rep peer 1881-90
1 Ld Lt 19th
2 KP 19th

Turton

Origins: Edmund Peters MP (below), son of an artist turned clergyman, took the name Turton in 1817 on succeeding to the Turton estates. The Turton fortune was made by a royal physician in the second half of the 18th century, himself the son of a physician. On the death of the last Earl of Milltown the Irish estates passed to his nephew, a Turton of Upsall Castle.

1. Edmund Peters Turton – Hedon 1818-19
2. Sir Edmund Turton – Thirsk and Malton Div. N. R. Yorkshire 1915-29
3. Robert Turton Baron Tranmire – Thirsk and Malton Div. N. R. Yorkshire 1929-74

Seats: Upsall Castle, Yorkshire (built c. 1500, damaged 1640s, estate purch. 1773, house built 1872-76, burned 1918, rebuilt 1924, still own); Kildale Hall, Yorkshire (built c. 1810, acq. by mar. later 19th c., still own); Russborough House, Wicklow (acq. by mar. 1891, sold 1931); Brasted Park, Kent (purch. c. 1780s, built 1784)
Title: Baron Tranmire 1974-94 UKLife
Estates: Bateman 9887 (E) 5649 and 3792 (E) 2425. The royal doctor left £9,000 pa in land and £60,000 in funds in 1806 to Edmund Peters.
1 in Cabinet 1955-57
Notes: One Turton in ODNB.

LEGARD

Origins: The founder was a younger son of a minor gentry (arms 1564) family who became a London haberdasher (d. 1587). **First MP (for Scarborough) 1625** (but the MP declined to serve).

1. Sir John Legard 1 Bt – Scarborough 1660
2. Sir Charles Legard 11 Bt – Scarborough 1874-80

Seats: Ganton Hall, Yorkshire (purch. 1583, rebuilt 1863, family departed 1910); Alnaby, Yorkshire (purch. early 16th c., rebuilt c. 1680, add. early 18th c., remod. 19th c., engulfed by Hull 19th c.); Storrs Hall, Westmorland (purch. and built 1781, sold 1805)
Estates: Bateman 6407 (E) 7751
Title: Baronet 1660-
Notes: Family inherited Scampston Hall, Yorkshire in the 20th century and still live there in the old St. Quintin seat.

LEGGE [Bilson, Dutton, Forster, Gounter, Naper, Nicoll, Stawell, Tonson] *ENGLAND & IRELAND*

Earl of Dartmouth (1711- GB)

Origins: In business in London in the 14th century, Lord Mayor 1346. Soldiers and courtiers under Charles I. Offered an earldom 1660 by Charles II.

1. William Legge – Southampton 1661-70
2. George Legge 1 Baron Dartmouth – Ludgersall 1673-79 Portsmouth 1679-81
3. William Legge – Portsmouth 1685-87
4. George Legge Viscount Lewisham – Great Bedwyn 1727-29
5. Henry Bilson Legge – East Looe 1740-41 Orford 1740-59 Hampshire 1759-64
6. Edward Legge – Portsmouth 1747
7. George Legge 3 Eral of Dartmouth – Plymouth 1778-80 Staffordshire 1780-84
8. William Legge 4 Earl of Dartmouth – Milborne Port 1810
9. Heneage Legge – Banbury 1819-26
10. Arthur Legge – Banbury 1826-30
11. William Legge 5 Earl of Dartmouth – S. Staffordshire 1849-53
12. William Legge 6 Earl of Dartmouth – W. Kent 1878-85 Lewisham 1885-91
13. Heneage Legge – St. George's, Hanover Square 1900-06
14. William Legge 7 Earl of Dartmouth – West Bromwich 1910-18
15. Sir Edward Legge-Bourke – Isle of Ely 1945-73

Seat: Patshull House, Staffordshire (built 1730s, purch. 1848, sold 1960s, commercial use)
Estates: Bateman 19518 (E) 58657 and 4023 (E) 4282
Titles: Baron Dartmouth 1682- E; Baron Stawell 1780-1820 GB
Peers: 10 peers 1682-91 1693-1750 1752-1945 1780-1820
3 Lds Lt 17th, 19th, 20th
4 in Cabinet 1710-14 1739 1754-61 1765-66 1772-82 1801-02
1 KG 19th
Notes: The current Earl has been an MEP since 2009. 1 Baron and 1, 2, and 3 Earls and six others in ODNB.

Bilson

Origins: Emigrated from Germany in the 16th century. Brewers in Winchester. Bishop of Winchester 1597. Purchased estates 1605. Kt 1613. **First MP 1614**. The fourth son of the 1 Earl of Dartmouth married a Bilson heiress and succeeded to the Bilson estates. Henry Bilson Legge married the daughter and heiress of the last Baron Stawell of the first creation and was created Baroness Stawell.

1. Leonard Bilson – Petersfield 1677-81
2. Thomas Bilson – Petersfield 1685-87 1689-90
3. Leonard Bilson – Petersfield 1704-15

Seat: West Mapledurham House, Hampshire (purch. 1605, demolished 1829)
Notes: One in ODNB.

Baron Stawell (1683-1755 E)

Origins: The Stawells were settled in Somerset soon after the Conquest (Roskell, Clark, and Rawcliffe, *The House of Commons*, IV, 470). Prudent marriages assisted their rise. **First MP 1420, for Somerset**. The daughter and heiress of the last Baron married a younger son of the 1 Earl of Dartmouth (see above).

1. Sir John Stawell – Somerset 1625 1640-42 1661-62
2. Ralph Stawell 1 Baron Stawell – Bridgwater 1679-81

Seats: Cothelstone House, Somerset (acq. 12th c., sold 1792, demolished 1968); Somerton, Somerset (acq. 1683, sold 1692); Low Ham, Somerset (built from c. 1690, never completed)
Estates: Worth £6,000 pa in c. 1600. Estates worth £63,000 in 1651.
Titles: Baroness Stawell 1760-1820
Peers: 4 peers 1683-92 1704-55
1 Ld Lt 17th
Notes: Male line extinct 1755. Overspent and gradually became improverished later 17th c. onwards. One in ODNB.

Forster

Origins: Landed by the 15th century. **First MP 1467. Two further MPs 1572-97, all three kts of the shire**. On the death of the last Bt Aldermaston passed to a niece, the wife of the 3 Baron Stawell.

1. Sir Humphrey Forster 3 Bt – Berkshire 1677-79 1685-87 1690-1702

Seat: Aldermaston, Berkshire (medieval, acq. by mar. 16th c., rebuilt c. 1636, passed out of family by mar. 1752)
Title: Baronet 1620-1711.
Notes: Male line extinct 1752.

Stawell

Origins: Cadet line of the Barons Stawell. Went to Ireland 17th century.

1. Jonas Stawell – {Kinsale 1692-93}
2. Jonas Stawell – {Kinsale 1745-60}

Seats: Kilbrittain Castle, Cork (built 16th c., purch. c. 1703, rebuilt first half 18th c., rebuilt mid-19th c., sold before 1920, burned 1920); Lisnagar (Lisnegar), Cork (built early 18th c., add. early 19th c., acq. by inher. 1861 from Tonsons, sold 20th c.)
Estates: Bateman 11654 (I) 6752
Notes: On inheriting the estates of an uncle, the 3 Baron Riversdale (Tonson see below) took the name Riversdale. In 20th c. became Alcock-Stawell-Riversdale.

Stawell

Origins: The junior line of the Stawells.

1. William Stawell – Ashburton 1677-79 1681 1685-87 1690-1702

Seat: Parke, Devon (medieval, sold later 17th c., demolished late 19th c.)

Baron Riversdale (1783-1861 I)

Origins: Major Richard Tonson acquired land in Cork in the period after the Restoration. Further estates were purchased by his son and grandson. The latter, the, first MP, was a businessman of questionable ethics and a banker. (Johnston, *Great Britain and Ireland, 1760-1800*, 253). The 1 Baron was his illegitimate son. The 3 Baron devised his estates to his kinsman William Stawell of Kilbrittain Castle (see above), who took the name Riversdale in 1861.

1. Richard Tonson – {Baltimore 1727-73}
2. William Tonson 1 Baron Riversdale – {Tuam 1768-76 Rathcormack 1776-83}

Seats: Lisnagar (Lisnegar), Cork (medieval castle, part demolished mid-18th c., rebuilt early 18th c., purch. 1775 for £68,000, add. early 19th c., passed to nephew 1861 Stawell-Riversdale, sold 20th c.); Dunkettle, Cork (resident 17th-18th c.)

Estates: Worth £10,000 pa. in mid-18th c. Worth £11,000 to £12,000 pa in 1774.
Peers: {2 peers 1783-87 1796-1800}

Baron Sherborne (1784-1985 GB)

Origins: Landowners at least from the 15th century. Successful marriages with commercial wealth in the 16th century enlarged landed property. **First MP 1624, for Gloucestershire.** The 2 Baron married Mary daughter and heiress of Henry Bilson Legge 2 Baron Stawell and inherited Hinton Ampner.

1. Sir Ralph Dutton 1 Bt – Gloucestershire 1679-81 1689-98
2. Sir John Dutton 2 Bt – Gloucestershire 1727-34
3. James Dutton 1 Baron Sherborne – Gloucestershire 1781-84
4. Ralph Dutton – S. Hampshire 1857-65 Cirencester 1865-68

Seats: Sherborne Park (House), Gloucestershire (medieval, purch. 1551 for £3,000, rebuilt 1651-53, remod. 18th c. and 1829-42 at a cost of £40,000 – Kingsley, *The Country Houses of Gloucestershire*, III, 221 - sold 1980, school, estate NT); Timsbury Manor, Hampshire (acq. sec. half 18th c., built 1840s, sold 1901); Hinton Ampner House, Hampshire (acq. by Stekeleys 1597, passed through Stawells to Duttons early 19th c., rebuilt c. 1800, add. 1864, rebuilt c. 1936-37, fire 1960, rebuilt 1963, NT 1985); Bibury Court, Gloucestershire (built 1633, purch. 1816, sold 1920s)
Estates: Bateman 15923 (E) 21445; 4750 (E) 6033; 5124 (E) 6970
Title: Baronet 1678-1743
Peers: 6 peers 1784-1945
Notes: Dutton family has an entry in the ODNB.

Naper (Napier)

Origins: The founder was a younger son of the Dorset Napiers (see Napier) settled in Ireland at Loughcrew (d. 1676). Sheriff 1671. James Naper married Anne Dutton and succeeded to Sherborne in 1743. Their son took the name Dutton and a grandson was created 1 Baron Sherborne (see above). His younger brother retained Loughcrew.

1. James Naper – {Enniscorthy 1661-66}
2. William Naper – {Trim 1695-99 1703-08}
3. James Naper – {Athboy 1695-99 Trim 1703-13 1715-19}
4. Robert Naper – {Athboy 1727-39}
5. James Naper – {County Meath 1733-60}
6. William Naper – {Athboy 1748-60}
7. James Naper – Weobley 1813-18

Seat: Loughcrew, Meath (old castle, acq. by 1671, rebuilt 1823-25, fire 1888, rebuilt, fire 1960, family still lives in the Orangery)
Estates: Bateman 19039 (I) 15658. Worth £5,350 pa in 1787.

Gounter Nicoll (Gunter)

Origins: The Gounters were at Racton by 1327. **First MP 1442.** The daughter and heiress of Sir Charles Gounter Nicoll married the 2 Earl of Dartmouth.

1. George Gounter – Chichester 1685-87
2. Sir Charles Gounter Nicoll – Peterborough 1729-33

Seat: Racton, Sussex (acq. by 1327, passed to Earls of Dartmouth by mar. 1755 with a dowry of £100,000, still owned 1950s)

LEGH (Lee, Leigh) [Hare, Keck, Towneley]

Baron Leigh (1643-1786 E; 1839- UK)

Origins: A medieval family. A younger son of the Leighs of High Leigh, Cheshire came to London and worked as a clerk for Sir Rowland Hill (see Hill II) and rose to become Lord Mayor in 1558 (Kt). He married a niece and heiress of Hill and together with Hill purchased monastic lands at Stoneleigh Abbey and in Gloucestershire. **First MP 1584. Four further MPs 1592-1628, two for Warwickshire.** Baronet 1611. Baron 1628. Earl of Chichester 1644-53. On the extinction of the Barony of Leigh 1786 the estates passed (1806) to descendents of the 1 Baronet seated at Adlestrop, for whom the barony was recreated in 1839.

1. Sir Thomas Leigh – Staffordshire 1661-62
2. Charles Leigh – Warwick 1710-13 Higham Ferrers 1714-22 Bedfordshire 1722-27 1733-34
3. James Leigh – Marlborough 1802-06 Great Bedwyn 1806-18 Winchester 1818-23
4. Gilbert Leigh – S. Warwickshire 1880-84
5. Sir Thomas Leigh Hare 1 Bt – S. W. Norfolk 1892-1906

Seats: Stoneleigh Abbey, Warwickshire (12th c., 14th c., mid-16th c., purch. 1561, add. c. 1600, rebuilt 1714-26, add. 1851, fire 1960, restored 1982-4, sold 1993, flats); Fletchhampstead Hall (Park), Warwickshire (purch. and built 1564, declined to farm house by 1830, now gone); Adlestrop House (Park), Gloucestershire (purch. mid-16th c., became a residence c. 1650, remod. c. 1690 and 1754-63, add. 1796-99, post 1945 a school)
Estates: Bateman 20965 (E) 32013. Owned at least 2,000 acres in 2001.

Titles: Baron Dunsmore (1628-53) and Earl of Chichester (1644-passed out of family 1653); Baronet 1611-1786; 1618-53; 1818- ; 1905-
Peers: 8 peers 1660-1749 1764-86 1839-1945
2 Lds Lt 19th, 20th
Notes: Edward Leigh of Stoneleigh married the heiress of the Hare Baronets of Stow Bardolph, and their descendents took the name Hare (see Pakenham). A line of the family (Legh/Lee) established in Cumberland at St. Bees, Isel (acq. r. Edward II, passed to Lawsons c. 1600), and Calder Abbey (acq. 1536, sold 1730) elected **seven MPs 1423-1585**. 1 Baron first cr. and 1 Baron sec. cr. in ODNB.

<u>Baron Newton</u> (1892- UK)

Origins: The Leghs, a junior line of the Leighs, acquired Lyme by marriage to an heiress in 1388. Piers Legh fought at Agincourt. **First MP 1491, for Lancashire. Four additional MPs 1584-1642, two kts of the shire**. They first represented Newton in 1658.

1. Richard Legh – Cheshire 1656 1659 Newton 1660-79
2. Thomas Legh – Liverpool 1685-87
3. Peter Legh – Newton 1685-87
4. Thomas Legh – Newton 1698-1703
5. Thomas Legh – Newton 1701-13
6. Peter Legh – Newton 1743-74
7. Anthony James-Keck – Leicester 1765-68 Newton 1768-80
8. Thomas Legh – Newton 1780-97
9. George Legh-Keck – Leicestershire 1797-1818 1820-31
10. Thomas Legh – Newton 1814-32
11. William Legh 1 Baron Newton – S. Lancashire 1859-65 E. Cheshire 1868-85
12. Thomas Legh 2 Baron Newton – Newton Div. Lancashire 1886-98
13. Peter Legh 4 Baron Newton – Petersfield Div. Hampshire 1951-60

Seats: Lyme Park, Cheshire (medieval, acq. by mar. 1388, rebuilt c. 1570, remod. c. 1660s, add. 1727-38 and 1813-22, NT 1946); Haydrock Lodge, Lancashire (old house, rebuilt c. 1795, add. mid-19th c., institutional use most of 20th c., demolished c. 1991); Golborne Park, Lancashire (built c. 1737, fire c. 1920); Ridge, Cheshire (acq. r. Henry VI, sold c. 1703); Bank Hall (Bretherton), Lancashire (built 1608, add. 1832-33, passed to Powys family 1860); Calveley Hall, Cheshire (built late 17th c., acq. 1705 by mar. to Calveley heiress, sold, demolished); Bradley Old Hall, Lancashire (built mid-14th c., acq. by mar. in the 15th c., add. late 15th c., abandoned in favor of Haydock in the 18th c., demolished)
Estates: Bateman 13800 (E) 45000. Worth c. £2,600 in 1662.
Peers: 3 peers 1892-1945

Notes: In the 19th c. the Leghs profited greatly from the expansion of Wigan over their land. Thomas Legh married a Fleetwood heiress and acquired Bank Hall. The heiress of Peter Legh of Lyme married into the Keck family of Stoughton Grange (see Hanbury), one of who sat for the Legh borough of Newton. The Kecks at Stoughton Grange, Leicestershire (Bateman 6529 E 12156) acquired Stoughton Grange Hall from the Beaumonts by marriage (see Beaumont) and on the death of George Legh-Keck in 1860 it passed to the Powys family, Lords Lilford, who also inherited Bank Hall (see that family). 2 Baron and two others in ODNB.

Leigh

Origins: The most senior line of the Leighs, holding the original seat at High Leigh (Legh), which it was claimed they had held before the Conquest (old DNB), and with more certainty since the reign of William II. **First MP 1442.**

1. George Legh – N. Cheshire 1841-47 1848-68 Mid. Div. Cheshire 1868-73
2. Egerton Leigh – Mid Cheshire 1873-76
3. Sir Edward Egerton Leigh – Gainsborough 1983-

Seats: (West Hall), High Leigh (Legh), Cheshire (rebuilt c. 1814, fire 1891, rebuilt 1893, sold 1924, demolished 1935); (East Hall), High Leigh (Legh), Cheshire (built later 16th c., rebuilt 1781-84, remod. 1797-1818, demolished c. 1963, still own estate); Jodrell Hall, Cheshire (built 1779 for the Jodrells, passed to Leghs, sold 1939); Broadwell House, Gloucestershire (inherited 1777, sold 1970); Bulcote Lodge, Nottinghamshire (built 17th c. remod. early 18th c., and c. 1800, acq. by mar. 1842, sold)
Estates: Bateman 3946 (E) 8391; 3377 (E) 6223
Notes: A line of cousins was created Bts in 1773-1870 seated at Brownsover Hall, Warwickshire. An heiress brought their estates to the Ward Broughton (Leigh) family of Guilsborough Hall and Great Addington Hall, Northamptonshire (see Boughton). Charles Cornwall-Legh of High Legh, was recognized as 5 Baron Grey of Codnor in 1989, succeeding to the barony created in 1397 and in abeyance since 1496. One in ODNB.

Legh

Origins: Senior line of the Leghs.

1. Peter Legh – Ilchester 1765-74

Seat: Norbury Booths Hall, Cheshire (acq. r. Edward I, medieval, rebuilt 1745, add. 1845, sold 1917)
Estates: Bateman 2979 (E) 5588

Legh

Origins: The senior line of the Leghs of Lyme.

1. John Legh – Bodmin 1715-22

Seats: Adlington Hall, Cheshire (medieval, acq. 1315, add. 1505 and 1581, add. 1740s and 1747, reduced in size 1929, still own); Bonis Hall, Cheshire (built 17th c.?, purch. 1746, sold 20th c., offices); Booths Hall, Cheshire (built 1745, remod. 1860s, sold c. 1900)
Estates: Bateman 5829 (E) 11324 and at Booths 2979 (E) 5588

Leigh

Origins: A cadet of the Leghs of Adlington. Roger Leigh MP was the adopted (illegitimate?) son of Sir Robert Holt Leigh 1 Bt (see Pemberton).

1. Roger Leigh – Rochester 1880-85

Seats: Barham Court, Kent (old house, rebuilt early 18th c., purch. 19th c., damaged by fire 1930s, offices); Hindley Hall, Lancashire (purch. 1721, passed to Pembertons c. 1800, now golf club); Whitley Hall (Leigh Place), Lancashire (acq. 1775, still owned 1830s, flats)
Estates: Bateman 4607 (E) 30703
Notes: The huge income was due to mining royalties. (see also Pemberton)

Towneley

Origins: John Legh, a kinsman of the Leghs of Lyme, married Cecilia Towneley and took the name Towneley on inheriting the estates. The Towneleys claimed descent from Alfred the Great (Bevan, *The Parliamentary Representation of Lancashire, 1258-1885*, 33). **First MP in the 13th century, one additional MP 1360, for Lancashire**. A Towneley fought at Agincourt.

1. John Towneley – Beverley 1841-52
2. Charles Towneley – Sligo 1848 1852-53

Seats: Towneley Hall, Lancashire (acq. 13th c., built 1400, add. 15th c., 17th c., 1726, 1736, 1851, sold 1902, family still own part of estate); Stella Hall, Durham (built 16th c., acq. by mar. 1762, remod. 1813, sold 1850, demolished 1955); Town Head, Lancashire (built early 19th c., still own)
Estates: Bateman 24167 (E) 12324

Notes: A Roman Catholic family. In the late 19th century the estates were divided between three heiresses. Three in ODNB.

Towneley (Townley)

Origins: A cadet of the Towneleys of Towneley had descended to the occupation of mercer in the early 18th century. One became a steward to the Butterworths, who left him Belfield Hall, Lancashire in 1728. Acquired Beaupré Hall by marriage to a Greaves heiress, who had inherited it by marriage from the Bells (**three MPs 1563-1626, one for Norfolk**) who had inherited it from a Beaupré heiress (mar. 1559).

1. Richard Towneley – Cambridgeshire 1831-41 1847-52

Seats: Fulbourn Manor House, Cambridgeshire (built 17th c., purch. by Greaves 1742, passed to Towneleys by mar. 1787, still own); Beaupré Hall, Norfolk (see above) (built early 16th c., passed by mar. through several families to the Towneleys, sold c. 1900, demolished 1966); Belfield Hall, Lancashire (medieval, rebuilt c. 1619, acq. 1728, remod. 1752, sold c. 1855, ruin by 1900, demolished 1916)

LEICESTER (Leycester) [Byrne, O'Byrne, Revell, Warren] *ENGLAND & IRELAND*

Baron de Tabley (1826-95 UK)

Origins: Emerged before 1380. The daughter of Sir Francis Leicester 3 Bt (d. 1742) married Sir John Byrne 3 Bt of Timogue (see below). Their son took the name Leicester in 1744, and his descendent was created Baron de Tabley.

1. Sir Francis Leicester 3 Bt – Newton 1715-27
2. Sir Peter Leicester 4 Bt – Preston 1767-68
3. John Leicester 1 Baron de Tabley – Yarmouth (IoW) 1791-96 Heytesbury 1796-1802 Stockbridge 1807

Seat: Tabley House, Cheshire (acq. 1272, Old Hall built c. 1380, add. 1619, collapsed 1927, demolished c. 1950; new house 1761-69, family departed 1975, museum)
Estates: The 1 Baron's income was £12,000 from land and salt mines. However, the estate suffered under a heavy burden of debt. The 2 Baron inherited £250,000 from Viscountess Bulkeley in 1825.
Notes: On the extinction of the de Tabley barony the estates passed via an heiress to the Leighton Bts in 1895 (see Leighton). 1 and 3 Barons and one other in ODNB.

Byrne

Origins: Descended from an Irish sept chief (see above).

1. Sir Gregory Byrne 1 Bt – {Ballynakill 1689}

Seat: Cullenagh Castle (Timogue), Queen's County (Pierce Byrne MP mar. a Barrington widow 1676 and gained residence at Timogue – the castle passed to his Barrington stepson thereafter – see Barrington III)
Title: Baronet 1671-1895
Notes: The 4 Bt succeeded to Tabley House and took the name Leicester. Created Baron de Tabley (see above).

O'Byrne

Origins: Junior line of the family (see above). **First {MP 1613}. Four additional [MPs 1613-34}.**

1. William O'Byrne – County Wicklow 1874-80

Seat: Cabinteely House (Clare Hill), Dublin (built 18th c., passed to O'Byrnes by inher. 1888, passed to Ormsby-Hamiltons late 19th c.)
Estates: Bateman 2658 (I) 2679

Warren

Origins: Gentry by 18th century. The 2 Baron de Tabley was a cousin of Elizabeth Warren, daughter of Sir George Warren. She married the 7 Viscount Bulkeley, who took the name Warren-Bulkeley (see Bulkeley). On her death the estates passed to the 2 Baron de Tabley.

1. Sir George Warren – Lancaster 1758-80 Beaumaris 1780-84 Lancaster 1786-96

Seat: Poynton Towers and Lodge (Hall), Cheshire (Poynton Towers built mid-16th c., passed to 2 Baron de Tabley 1825, demolished 1935, new house 1750s, demolished c. 1935)
Estates: £6,500 c. 1755 (including income from coal mines)
Notes: Poynton was originally owned by the Stockport family and passed via an heiress to the Eton family and then to the Warrens. The estate was owned by the ancestors of the Warrens from the r. of Edward III, and the house was built in the r. of Edward VI. (See Vernon I)

Revell

Origins: Founded by a victualling agent in Lisbon and for Gibraltar who made a fortune out of army contracts. His daughter and heiress married Sir George Warren.

1. Thomas Revell – Dover 1734-52

Seat: Fetcham Park, Surrey (built c. 1700, remod. early 18th c., purch. 1737, sold 1788, business)
Estates: Thomas Revell was worth upwards of £200,000 and £4,000 pa in land.

Leycester

Origins: A cadet of the de Tabley line (14th c.). **First MP 1559 for Cheshire. Two further MPs 1589-97.**

1. Hugh Leycester – Milbourne Port 1802-12
2. Ralph Leycester – Shaftesbury 1821-30
3. Edward Leycester Penrhyn – Shaftesbury 1830-32

Seat: Toft Hall, Cheshire (acq. by mar. c. 1380, rebuilt c. 1700, remod. 1809-13, add. 1850, sold 1977, offices, family still owns estate)
Estates: Bateman 3970 (E & W) 10,000; inherited £120,000 in 1816.
Notes: A Leycester married a Toft heiress c. 1380 (Tofts there in the 12th c.). A younger son was a minor nabob with the East India Company and then inherited the Toft estate in 1809. £30,000 was spent of Toft 1809-13 (de Figueiredo and Treuherz, *Cheshire Country Houses*, 187). Edward Leycester inherited in 1816 a fortune from his aunt, Lady Penrhyn (wife of Lord Penrhyn who left his own estates to the Pennants – see Douglas), who had her own fortune, and he took the name Penrhyn.

LEIGH I *IRELAND*

Origins: An indigenous Irish family. Obtained estates, in the 16th century after the Dissolution. One served as an interpreter to the Dublin administration under Elizabeth I.

1. Francis Leigh – {Kildare 1689}
2. John Leigh – {New Ross 1727-58}
3. Robert Leigh – {New Ross 1759-1800} 1801-02
4. Francis Leigh – {Wexford 1785-97 1800} 1801 New Ross 1821-24
5. Charles Leigh – New Ross 1806-07 1812-18

Seats: Rosegarland, Wexford (built 16th c., acq. 1668, new house early 18th c., add. later 18th c., add. 1800, add. 1874, still own); Rathanagan, Kildare; Rathbridge, Kildare
Estates: Bateman 8280 (I) 4052. Worth £6,000 pa in 1810.

LEIGH II

Origins: Held manorial land since the 14th century. **First MP 1478. Two additional MPs 1529-1625.**

1. Sir Francis Leigh – Kent 1702-05
2. Richard Leigh – East Looe 1770-72

Seats: Hawley House (Sutton-at-Hone), Kent (acq. 1695, passed out of the family by mar. 1873); Addington Place (Park), Surrey (acq. 1447, sold 1767, demolished)
Notes: Male line extinct 1841.

LEIGH III

Origins: Yeomen farmers in the early 16th century. Leased a manor in 1530 and rose to Deputy Lieutenant in the third generation at the end of the century. Kt by James I.

1. Sir John Leigh – Yarmouth (IoW) 1640-48 1660
2. John Leigh – Newport (IoW) 1679-81
3. John Leigh – Newtown (IoW) 1702-05

Seat: North Court, Hampshire (IoW) (medieval, purch. 1586, rebuilt 1615, sold c. 1790)
Notes: Another branch of the Leighs of the Isle of Wight became the richest landowners on the island in the 16th century (see Worsley).

LEIGHTON

Origins: An ancient gentry family seated in Shropshire before 1155. Married a great Welsh heiress in the 15th century and served on the Court of the Marches of Wales. **First MP 1313, for Shropshire. Five additional MPs 1460-1601, all kts of the shire. Twelve generations of the family sat as MPs.** The 8 Baronet married the daughter and heiress of the 2 Baron de Tabley (see Leicester) and succeeded to the Leicester estates in 1895.

1. Robert Leighton – Shrewsbury 1661-78
2. Sir Edward Leighton 1 Bt – Shropshire 1698-1700 1709-10
3. Daniel Leighton – Hereford 1747-54
4. Sir Charlton Leighton 4 Bt – Shrewsbury 1774-75 1780-84

5. Sir Baldwyn Leighton 7 Bt – S. Shropshire 1859-65
6. Stanley Leighton – N. Shropshire 1876-85 Oswestry Div. Shropshire 1885-1901
7. Sir Baldwyn Leighton 8 Bt – S. Div. Shropshire 1877-85
8. Bertie Leighton – Oswestry Div. Shropshire 1929-45

Seats: Loton Park, Shropshire (acq. 1468, built c. 1665, became main seat after 1711, remod. 1773-74, 1838-39 and 1870s, still own); Wattlesborough Castle, Shropshire (medieval, acq. 1468, became a farm house after 1711); Sweeney Hall, Shropshire (built 1805 by Parkers and passed by mar. to the Leightons 1832, sold 1960s, hotel); Bragginton Hall, Shropshire (built 17th c., passed by mar. to Owen family 1614, add. 1675, repurch. 1849, demolished c. 1968)
Estates: Bateman 4096 (E) 5421 (does not include the de Tabley inheritance of 1895). Owned 2,000 acres in 1980s.
Title: Baronet 1693-
Notes: Three in ODNB.

LEITH *SCOTLAND & ENGLAND*

Baron Leith of Fyvie (1905-25 UK)

Origins: The Leiths began as medieval shipowners and merchants in Aberdeen. **First [MP 1357 for Aberdeen].** John Leith married Mary Hay of Rannas. Their grandson took the name Leith Hay thanks to the Hay's purchase of Leith to clear it of debts and then returned to the Leiths in 1789. His eldest son established the Leith-Hays of Leith Hall. His younger son married the Forbes heiress of Blackford. The Forbes family began with a Lord Provost of Edinburgh in 1350. A junior line became the Lords Forbes (see that family). Later one son became the 1 Baron Leith of Fyvie. He married an American heiress and became President of a large steel company in Illinois in 1885. He bought back the ancestral estate of Fyvie for £175,000 in 1890. His daughter married Sir Charles Burn 1 Bt, who took the name Forbes Leith.

1. Sir Andrew Leith Hay – Elgin & District Burghs 1832-38 1841-47
2. Sir Charles Forbes Leith 1 Bt – Torquay Div. Devon 1910-23

Seats: Leith Hall, Aberdeenshire (acq. by Leiths and built c. 1650, add. 1756 and 1796, add. 1868, add. 1900, NT 1945); Fyvie Castle, Aberdeenshire (medieval, add. 1598-1603, add. 1777, purch. 1889, add. 1890-99, NT 1984)
Estates: Bateman 12546 (S) 7916. 18,100 acres in 1996.
Title: Baronet 1923-
Peer: 1 peer 1905-25
Notes: Three in ODNB.

Baron Burgh (1529- E)

Origins: A son of John Leith (see above) established a line that succeeded to the Burgh Barony in 1916 through the female line.

No MPs

Seats: Freefield, Aberdeenshire; Glenkindie, Aberdeenshire
Peers: 2 peers 1916-26 1927-45

Leith

Origins: Descended from an uncle of John Leith (see above). Provost of Aberdeen (d. 1763). His son, a soldier, was created a Baronet.

1. Sir Alexander Leith 1 Bt – Tregony 1774-78

Seat: Drygrange, Dumbartonshire (acq. by mar. 1864)
Estates: Bateman 4535 (S) 3837
Title: Baronet 1775-

Leith

Origins: A cadet of Leith of Leith.

1. John Leith – Aberdeen 1872-80

Seat: St. Mary's Priory, Essex (resident 19th c.)

LEKE (Leake)

Earl of Scarsdale (1645-1736 E)

Origins: Settled in the north Midlands since the mid-12th century. **First MP 1362 for Nottinghamshire. Eight additional MPs 1386-1601, six kts of the shire**.

1. Sir Francis Leke 1 Bt – Nottinghamshire 1666-79
2. Robert Leke 3 Earl of Scarsdale – Newark-on-Trent 1679

Seats: Sutton Hall (Sutton Scarsdale), Derbyshire (medieval, acq. by mar. 1403 from a family who held it by 1226, rebuilt 1594, rebuilt 1724-27, sold 1736); Pilsley Old Hall, Derbyshire (purch. before 1505, built 16th c., sold 1736-43, demolished 1968)

Titles: Baron Deincourt 1624-1736 E; Baronet 1611-1736
Peers: 3 peers 1660-81 1680-1736
2 Lds Lt 17th, 18th
Notes: Sutton Scardsdale was granted to Peter de Hareston by Henry III in 1255. An heiress carried it to Richard de Grey. A Grey heiress married Edward Hilary, who took the name Grey. It passed through another heiress to the Lekes 1403. On the extinction of the Earldom in 1736 the estates were sold to pay debts.

LENNARD [Barrett, Cator, Roper] *ENGLAND & IRELAND*

Earl of Sussex (1674-1715 E)

Origins: The Dacres acquired Askeaton Castle, Cumberland by marriage in 1317 (original grant 1157). It passed with Naworth Castle to the Howards (see that family). Margaret Baroness Dacre in her own right married in 1564 a lawyer, Samson Lennard. The Lennards were settled in Kent by 15th century as yeoman farmers. A successful lawyer purchased Wicken Court in the later 16th century. **First MP 1571. Three further MPs 1597-1654, one for Essex**. Their eldest son succeeded as 12 Baron Dacre and married the heiress of the Barretts of Belhus, Essex (**first MP 1614**). The great-grandson of this union was raised to the Earldom of Sussex (seated at Chevening, Kent). The Earl's daughter married the 8 Baron Teynham (see below). Their granddaughter, Gertrude Baroness Dacre, married Thomas Brand of The Hoo, whose descendents were created Viscounts Hampden (see Hill I). The Barrett Lennard Baronets below were illegtimate descendents of the 17 Baron Dacre in the 18th century.

1. Richard Barrett – {Carrick 1661-66}
2. Dacre Barrett – {County Monaghan 1692-93}
3. Thomas Barrett Lennard – Ipswich 1820-26 Maldon 1826-37 1847-52
4. Sir Thomas Barrett Lennard 1 Bt – S. Essex 1832-35

Seats: Belhus, Essex (acq. by mar. 1397, built by the Barretts c. 1500, passed to Lennards 1644, remod. 1744-77, sold 1923, demolished 1957); Horsford Manor, Norfolk (acq. by Cheyneys by time of Domesday, passed by inheritance through a number of families to the Barret Lennards, who moved there when they abandoned Belhus in the 1920s, sold cricket venue); Dacre Castle, Cumberland (built mid-14th c., remod. 1675, sold 1716); Chevening, Kent (built 1616-30, sold 1717)
Estates: Bateman 14412 (E & I) 18525
Titles: Baron Dacre 1321- E; Baron Barrett 1627-44 S; Baronet 1628-44; 1801-
Notes: 14 Baron Dacre and one other Lennard and one Barrett in ODNB.

Lennard

Origins: Descended from a younger brother of the 12 Baron Dacre, see above. Mary Lennard, daughter and heiress of Stepehn Lennard, illegitimate son of Sir Samuel Lennard 3 Bt, married Sir John Farnaby 6 Bt (see Radcliffe). He devised Wicken Court to his nephew Sir John Farnaby Lennard 1 Bt, the eldest son of Sir William Cator by one of his daughters.

1. Sir Stephen Lennard 2 Bt – Winchelsea 1681 Kent 1698-1700 1708-09
2. Sir Samuel Lennard 3 Bt – Hythe 1715-27

Seat: Wickham (Wicken) Court (West Wickham), Kent (built 1469, purch. 1580, remod. 1625, passed to Farnabys by mar. late 18th c., passed out of the family 1861, add. 1866, sold c. 1900?, institutional use in 20th c.)
Estates: Bateman 4870 (E) 7636
Titles: Baronet 1642-1727

Cator

Origins: Quaker timber merchants in Southwark in the 18th century. A Cator married a Farnaby, who had inherited the Lennard estates and took the name Lennard, see above.

1. John Cator – Wallingford 1772-80 Ipswich 1784 Stockbridge 1790-93
2. John Cator – S. Div. Huntingdon 1910-18

Seats: Woodbastwick Hall, Norfolk (built 1819, fire and rebuilt 1889, demolished 1971, still own estate); Beckenham Place, Kent (purch. 1773, built soon after, sold 1928, golf club)
Estates: Bateman 4136 (E) 19296
Title: Baronet 1880-1936

Baron Teynham (1616- E)

Origins: The Roper family claimed medieval descent but rose to prominence under the Tudors by law and office-holding. **First MP 1529. Two further MPs 1553-58**. They inherited Waterperry from the Curson Baronets (1661-1765) and took the additional name Curson in 1787.

No post-1660 MPs.

Seats: The Lodge, Linstead (Lynsted Park), Kent (acq. 15th c., built 1599, add. 17th c., major part demolished 1829, resident to early 20th c., still own); Teynham, Kent (acq. by mar. 16th c., still own); Waterperry House, Oxfordshire (medieval, purch. 1517 and 1562, rebuilt 17th c. by Cursons, rebuilt 1713, inher. by Ropers by mar. 1787, sold 1815 for £100,000, educational use)
Peers: 11 peers 1660-88 1716-23 1781-1945
Notes: The Cursons and Ropers were Roman Catholic until they conformed to the Established Church in 1781. Four in ODNB.

LENTHALL

Origins: Acquired landed estates 15th century. A younger son rose as a lawyer and Speaker of the House of Commons 1640.
First MP 1624. Cromwellian peer 1657.

1. Sir John Lenthall – Gloucester 1645 Abingdon 1659 1660
2. William Lenthall – Wallingford 1679-81 Cricklade 1681

Seats: Burford Priory, Oxfordshire (medieval, rebuilt 1580s, purch. 1634, sold 1828); Besselsleigh, Berkshire (purch. 1634, still owned 1920s); Lachford (Latchford), Oxfordshire (acq. by mar. 15th c., passed out of family 1702)
Notes: The family went bankrupt c. 1708. Two in ODNB.

LESLIE (Lesley) [Melville] *SCOTLAND & IRELAND*

Duke of Rothes (1680-81 S)

Origins: Claimed descent from Attila the Hun and Roman emperors. More credibly a lineage can be traced to a Hungarian nobleman who attended an Anglo-Saxon princess at the court of Henry II of the Holy Roman Empire. The first Leslie arrived in Scotland in 1067. (Pielou, *The Leslies of Tarbert*) Baron 1445 (one of the first to elevated to the new rank of Lord of Parliament). **First [MP 1621 for Fife]**. The daughter of the 1 Duke married the 5 Earl of Haddington (see Hamilton I). One son succeeded as Earl of Haddington and the other as the 9 Earl of Rothes.

1. Thomas Leslie – Dysart Burghs 1734-41 Perth Burghs 1743-61

Seats: Leslie House, Fife (acq. 1283, built 1667-74, fire 1763, rebuilt 1765-77, remod. 1906-07, fire 2009, retirement home); Ballinbreich Castle, Fife (acq. and built 14th c. add. 15th c., sold 1760s, became a ruin)
Estates: Bateman 3562 (S) 7347. The 6 Earl died 1641 worth £55,283 Scots.
Titles: Baron Leslie 1445- S; Earl of Rothes 1458- S

Peers: [2 peers 1660-81 1700-07] 5 Scottish Rep peers 1708-10 1715-22 1723-34 1747-67 1812-17 1906-23 1931-45
1 KT 18th
Notes: The 10 and 11 Barons of Balquhain, Leslie kinsmen, were **[MPs 1593-1617].** 1, 2, 4, 5, 6, 9, and 10 Earls and 1 Duke and seven others in ODNB.

Baron Lindores (1606-1813 S)

Origins: The 1 Baron was a younger son of the 5 Earl of Rothes.

No MPs

Seat: Pitcairly (Pitcairlie) House, Fife (acq. 1312, built after 1550, sold 1667)
Titles: Baron Newark 1661-94 S
Peers: [3 peers 1660-1707]
Notes: 1 Baron Newark in ODNB.

Earl of Leven and Melville (1641- S; 1690- S)

Origins: A junior line of the Earls of Rothes. The granddaughter of the 1 Earl of Leven married the 1 Earl of Melville. Their son succeeded as 5 Earl of Leven and 2 Earl of Melville. The Melvilles emerged in the 13th century. Ambassador to England 1562. Baron 1616. **First Melville [MP 1594]. Two others 1602-05].**

No post-1660 MPs

Seats: Glenferness, Nairnshire (built 1844, purch. and remod. 1869, still own); Balgonie Castle, Fife (built 15th c., purch. by 1 Earl of Leven 1635, add. 1650s, add. 1706, sold 1829); Melville House, Fife (built 14th c. (Monimail Tower), Melvilles purch. 1592, rebuilt 1697-1703, sold 1949); Roehampton House, Surrey (built c. 1620, rebuilt 1710-13, purch. 1837, sold 1908, flats)
Estates: Bateman 8824 (S) 3078. The 12 Earl of Leven left an estate of £1,300,000 in 1906. Owned 6,500 acres in 2001.
Title: Baron Melville 1616- S
Peers: [4 peers 1660-64 1660-1707 1681-1707] 9 Scottish Rep peers 1707-10 1747-54 1806-07 1831-60 1865-76 1880-89 1891-1906 1910-13 1922-45
1 Ld Lt 20th
1 in Cabinet 1689-91
1 KT 20th
Notes: On the death of the 8 Earl the titles went to the male heirs while the estates were left to his daughter. The 9 Earl recouped his financial position by marrying a great banking heiress (Thornton) and the 10, 11, and 12 Earls became rich investment bankers.

Melville estates in Bateman passed to the Cartwrights by marriage (2464 [S & E] 3703). 1 Earl of Levan and 1 Baron and 1 and 2 Earls of Melville and five other Melvilles in ODNB.

Melville

Origins: Cadet founded by a son of the 1 Earl of Melville.

1. James Melville – [Fifeshire 1690-1702 Kinghorn Burgh 1703-05]

Seat: Hall Hill, Fife

Leslie

Origins: A Leslie cadet went to Ireland as a colonel under Charles I. His cousin was Bishop of Orkney translated to Ireland as Bishop of Raphoe 1633-61 and Clogher 1661-71. He purchased Castle Leslie. The son of the Colonel became a clergyman and inherited the Bishop's estates.

1. Charles Leslie – {Hillsborough 1771-76 County Monaghan 1783-1800}
2. Charles Leslie – County Monaghan 1801-26 New Ross 1830-31
3. Charles Leslie – County Monaghan 1842-71
4. Sir John Leslie 1 Bt – County Monaghan 1871-80

Seat: Glasslough House (Castle Leslie), Monaghan (old house, purch. 1664, new house 1874, still own)
Estates: Bateman 44481 (I) 16579. Owned 700 acres in 2001.
Title: Baronet 1876-
2 Lds Lt 19th, 20th
Notes: Shane Leslie was Winston Churchill's first cousin. One in ODNB.

LESTRANGE (L'Estrange) *ENGLAND & IRELAND*

L'Estrange

Origins: First recorded in 1122. Acquired manorial lands in the 12th and 13th centuries. Baron 1299. The title passed to the Earls of Derby on the death of the 9 Baron Strange. Another Barony was created in 1309 but became abeyant in 1349. Yet another was created in 1349, which passed via an heiress to the Furnivals in the 1380s. **First MP 1388 for Norfolk. Five additional MPs 1404-1625, four of them kts of the shire**.

1. Sir Nicholas L'Estrange 4 Bt – Castle Rising 1685-87
2. Roger L'Estrange – Winchester 1685-87

Seats: Hunstanton Hall, Norfolk (Le Stranges mar. heiress of Domesday owner, medieval house, add. c. 1500 and 1623, fire 1853, add. later 19th c., house sold 1949, fire 1950, still own estate); Snettisham Old Hall, Norfolk (built late 17th c. by the Stylemans who later took the name Le Strange, sold c. 1860); East Barsham Manor, Norfolk (built 1520-30 by Fermors from whom it passed by inher. eventually to L'Estranges in 1720, passed to Astleys 1762)
Estates: Bateman 7803 (E) 12413. Estates worth £3,000 pa. in 1654.
Title: Baronet 1629-1762
Notes: The heir of the 4 Bt became a Roman Catholic, which brought an end to the family's participation in Parliament. East Barsham belonged to the Fermors, who inherited it from the Wodes (fl. 1480s), and then to the L'Estranges. On the death of the last Baronet in 1760 East Barsham and possibly other estates passed to his nephew Sir Edward Astley 4 Bt of Melton Constable (see Astley). It was sold 1914. Snettisham and Hunstanton went to another family as co-heirs, the Stylemans, who took the name Le Strange in 1839. Eight in ODNB.

Lestrange

Origins: Richard Lestrange (MP 1559-63, see above) went to Ireland, and his descendents purchased Moystown. **First {MP 1585}.** Sheriff 1684.

1. Henry Lestrange – {King's County 1661-66}
2. Thomas Lestrange – {Banagher 1692-93 1695-99 1703-13 1715-27}
3. Henry Lestrange – {Banagher 1735-60}

Seats: Moystown, King's County (acq. c. 1660, sold 1853); Castle Strange, Roscommon (built 16th c., acq. late 16th or early 17th c., new house 18th c., resident in 18th c., burned 1918)
Estates: Moystown was sold for £6,360 under encumbered estates act in 1853 (Lyons, *Illustrated Incumbered Estates, Ireland, 1850-1905*, 54-55).

LEVESON GOWER [Gresham, Sutherland] *ENGLAND & SCOTLAND*

Duke of Sutherland (1833- UK)

Origins: The Levesons held property in Wolverhampton from the reign of Edward I and acquired great wealth in the wool trade in the 16th century, investing heavily in land, especially after the Dissolution, including Trentham and Lilleshall. **First MP 1432. Five other MPs 1584-1644, four kts of the shire.** In the later 17th century a Gower married the Leveson heiress and inherited Trentham. Their properties were merged in 1689. The Gowers were seated at Sittenham, Yorkshire from at least 1167 and held manorial land from soon after the Conquest. **First MP 1338. Three further MPs 1435-**

68. Like the Habsburgs the family rose to the apex of wealth and status through a series of spectacular marriages to heiresses (see Richards, *Leviathan of Wealth*, 5). After the Leveson Gower union came marriage with a daughter of the Duke of Rutland, who brought a large dowry. Then a marriage with the sister and heiress of the Duke of Bridgewater (see Egerton). The family inherited the Duke's famous canal in 1803. Finally, in 1785 came the alliance with the Countess of Sutherland (see below), which catapulted the Leveson Gowers into the stratosphere of the British peerage as the largest landowners and one of the two or three richest families in the United Kingdom and in Europe. The heiress of the Earls of Cromartie (see Mackenzie) married 1861 the 3 Duke of Sutherland. Their second son, Lord Francis Leveson Gower, succeeded to a revived title as Earl of Cromartie.

1. Sir Thomas Gower 2 Bt – Malton 1661-72
2. Sir William Leveson Gower 4 Bt – Newcastle-under-Lyme 1675-81 Shropshire 1681 Newcastle 1689-91
3. Richard Leveson – Lichfield 1685-87 Newport (IoW) 1692-95
4. William Gower – Ludlow 1690 1698-99 1701
5. John Leveson Gower 1 Baron Gower – Newcastle-under-Lyme 1692-1703
6. William Leveson Gower – Staffordshire 1720-56
7. Thomas Leveson Gower – Newcastle-under-Lyme 1722-27
8. Baptist Leveson Gower – Newcastle-under-Lyme 1727-61
9. Granville Leveson Gower Marquess of Stafford – Bishop's Castle 1744-47 Westminster 1747-54 Lichfield 1754
10. Richard Leveson Gower – Lichfield 1747-53
11. George Leveson Gower 1 Duke of Sutherland – Newcastle-under-Lyme 1779-84 Staffordshire 1787-99
12. John Leveson Gower – Appleby 1784-90 Newcastle-under-Lyme 1790-92
13. Granville Leveson Gower 1 Earl Granville – Lichfield 1795-99 Staffordshire 1799-1815
14. John Leveson Gower – Truro 1796-1802
15. Frederick Leveson Gower – Truro 1802-07 Mitchell 1807
16. George Sutherland Leveson Gower 2 Duke of Sutherland – St. Mawes 1808-12 Newcastle-under-Lyme 1812-15 Staffordshire 1815-20
17. Granville Leveson Gower 2 Earl Granville – Morpeth 1837-40 Lichfield 1841-46
18. Edward Leveson Gower – Derby 1847 Stoke-upon-Trent 1852-57 Bodmin 1859-85
19. George Leveson Gower 3 Duke of Sutherland – Sutherlandshire 1852-61
20. Granville Leveson Gower – Reigate 1863-66
21. Lord Ronald Sutherland Leveson Gower – Sutherlandshire 1867-74
22. Cromartie Leveson Gower 4 Duke of Sutherland – Sutherlandshire 1874-86
23. George Leveson Gower – N. W. Staffordshire 1885-86 Stoke-upon-Trent 1890-95
24. Frederick Leveson Gower 6 Duke of Sutherland – Sutherlandshire 1900-06

Seats: Trentham, Staffordshire (medieval, purch. 1540, rebuilt early 17th c., rebuilt early 18th c., add. 1759-76, rebuilt 1834-40, demolished 1910-12, estate sold 1919); Dunrobin Castle, Sutherlandshire (acq. 1211, built 13th c. onwards, add. 1641-44, restored c. 1682, passed to Leveson Gowers by mar. 1785, remod. c. 1789, rebuilt 1845-51, fire 1915, remod. 1915-21, school 1965-72, still own); Cliveden, Buckinghamshire (built late 17th c., fire 1795, rebuilt after 1824, purch. 1849, fire c. 1850, rebuilt 1850-51, add. 1862, sold 1893); Lilleshall Hall, Shropshire (built 1829, sold 1919, institutional use); Carbisdale Castle, Sutherlandshire (built 1906-17, sold 1933); Mertoun House, Roxburghshire (built 1703, purch. 1912, reduced in size 1956, current seat)
Estates: Bateman 1,358,545 (S & E) 141,667. Worth £6,000 pa. in 1710. Gross income of £200,000 pa in late 1820s. Rubinstein – at his death in 1833 the 1 Duke was probably worth 7 million pounds. Large land sales 1912-13. The Earl of Granville owned 62,200 acres in Scotland in 1996. Most of the remaining landed property passed to the Countess of Sutherland in 1963, when the Earldom was separated from the Dukedom that went to a remote male heir. The Duke of Sutherland owned 12,000 acres in 2001.
Titles: Baron Gower 1702- E; Earl Gower 1746- GB; Marquess of Stafford 1786- GB; Viscount Granville 1815- UK; Earl Granville 1833- UK; Baronet 1620-
Peers: 13 peers 1703-09 1715-1803 1799-1833 1815-91 1826-1945 1893-1945
7 Lds Lt 18th, 19th, 120th
5 in Cabinet 1702-06 1742-43 1744-54 175-57 1767-79 1783-94 1809 1851-66 1868-74 1880-86
6 KG 18th, 19th, 20th
1 KT 20th
Notes: In 1825 the 1 Duke purchased a fifth of the shares in the Liverpool Manchester railway for £100,000. These rose greatly in value in later years. Other similar investments were made that added hugely to the income of the family. The surname is pronounced "Looson Gore". 1 Baron Gower, 1 Earl Gower, 1 Marquess of Stafford, 1 Earl of Ellesmere, and 2 Earls Granville and 1 and 3 Dukes of Sutherland and nine others in ODNB.

Earl of Sutherland (1235- S)

Origins: One of the most ancient families in Scotland. Large grants of land by David I, confirmed under William the Lion 1196. Lord of Sutherland 1214 and Earl 1235, "a length of succession unparalleled in the peerage of this country." (Richards, *Leviathan of Wealth*, 9, quoting an observer in 1822). The title of Earl of Sutherland and 1,000,000 acres went to the Leveson Gowers when the Countess of Sutherland in her own right married Earl Gower in 1785.

1. William Sutherland Lord Strathnaver – Tain Burghs 1708
2. William Sutherland 17 Earl of Sutherland – Sutherland 1727-33

Seat: Dunrobin Castle, Sutherlandshire (acq. 1401, see above)

Estates: 1,000,000 acres. The Countess of Sutherland (see above for the separation of the earldom and dukedom in 1963) owned 83,239 acres in 1996.
Peers: [3 peers 1660-79 1689-1707] 3 Scottish Rep peers 1707-08 1715-33 1734-47 1763-66
1 Ld Lt 18th
1 KT 18th
Notes: The Sutherland family has an entry and 11, 12, 14, 16 Earls and 19 Countess and one other in ODNB.

Gresham

Origins: Landowners in Norfolk by 1442 and granted arms. The founder of the family fortunes was a younger son apprenticed to a mercer. He became a mercer, ship owner, loansman to Henry VIII, and Lord Mayor of London 1537. His son was also a mercer and Lord Mayor 1547. They purchased landed estates, and speculated in monastic property on a large scale. **First MP 1539. Two further MPs 1586-1625, one for Norfolk**. The daughter and heiress of the 6 and last Baronet married in 1804 William Leveson Gower who established a cadet line.

1. Sir Marmaduke Gresham 1 Bt – East Grinstead 1660 Bletchingley 1685-87
2. James Gresham – Haslemere 1661 1679
3. Sir Edward Gresham 2 Bt – Bletchingley 1701-02

Seats: Titsey Place, Surrey (purch. 1534, rebuilt later 16th c., rebuilt 1775, passed to Leveson Gowers by mar. 1804, add. 1826, remod. 1856, given to a foundation 1992); New Hall, Surrey (acq. and built 16th c.); Limpsfield (Lynsfield), Surrey (acq. 16th c., passed to Leveson Gowers 1804, still owned c. 1900)
Estates: Bateman 7113 (E) 5500. Worth £800 pa in the mid-16th century. Still held 3,000 acres in 1945 (C. Knight, *London's Country Houses*, Chichester, 2009, 280).
Title: Baronet 1660-1801
Notes: Male line extinct 1804. Serious indebtedness in the 18th c. Three in ODNB.

Baron Duffus (1650-1827 S)

Origins: These Sutherlands were descended from a younger son of the 4 Earl of Sutherland. **First [MP 1560]. One additional [MP for Sutherland 1646-47].** The daughter of Sir William Dunbar 1 Bt of Hempriggs and Ackergill (see Dunbar) married James Sutherland, second son of the 2 Baron Duffus. He succeeded to Hempriggs Castle, was created a Bt in 1706, and took the name Dunbar.

1. William Sutherland – [Elgin Burgh 1703-07]
2. Sir James Sutherland Dunbar 1 Bt – Caithness-shire [1706-07] 1710-13

Seats: Duffus House (Castle), Morayshire (acq. and built 12th c., castle rebuilt mid-15th c., abandoned about 1705, ruin, Duffus House built by Sutherland-Dunbars early 18th c., add. 1840, leased to school from 1930s, still own estate); Ackergill Tower, Caithness-shire (built late15th/early 16th c., acq. 1711, remod. 1851-52, sold 1980, now conference center); Hempriggs Castle (House), Caithness-shire (built 1692, inherited 1711, add. 1875, sold 1981)
Peers: [3 peers 1660-1707]
Title: Baronet 1706-
Notes: The barony of Duffus was attainted in 1716 and restored in 1826.

LEVINGE *IRELAND & ENGLAND*

Origins: Rose in the 16th century by law and land (arms granted 1611). **First MP for Derby 1621.** The 1 Bt was a younger son of a Derbyshire squire who went to Ireland as a legal official in 1690: Speaker of the Irish House of Commons 1692, Chief Justice of the Common Pleas in Ireland 1720.

1. Sir Richard Levinge 1 Bt – Chester 1690-95 {Blessington 1692-93 Longford 1698-99 1703-13 Kilkenny 1713-14} Derby 1710-11
2. Sir Richard Levinge 2 Bt – {County Westmeath 1723-27 Blessington 1727-48}
3. Sir Richard Levinge 4 Bt – {Duleek 1768-76}
4. Sir Richard Levinge 7 Bt – Westmeath 1857-65

Seats: High Park (Mullalea) renamed Knockdrin Castle 19th c., Westmeath (acq. later 17th c., built c. early 18th c., rebuilt c. 1810, principal seat until c. 1830, ceased residence before 1939, sold 1946); Levington Park, Westmeath; Parwich Hall, Derbyshire (purch. 1606, built c. 1610, rebuilt c. 1747, sold 1814)
Estates: Bateman 5018 (I & E) 3377. Worth £400 pa in 1714.
Title: Baronet 1704-
Notes: 1 and 7 Bts in ODNB.

LEWIS I *WALES*

Origins: The Mortimers held manorial land in the 13th century. Their estates passed by marriage of an heiress in the late 16th century to the Lewis family of Abernart-bychan. **First Lewis MP 1604 for Cardiganshire. One other MP 1624-58 also for the county**.

1. John Lewis – Cardiganshire 1685-87 1689-90 Cardigan Boroughs 1693-98 Cardiganshire 1698-1700 Cardigan Boroughs 1701

Seats: Coedmawr (Coedmor), Cardiganshire (acq. 13th c., sold early 18th c.); Abernant-bychan (Aber Nante Bechan), Cardiganshire (acq. 16th c., passed to Langtons by mar.

1701, that male line extinct 1739, and then passed by inher. to Pryse of Gogerddan); Hurst, Berkshire (leased?)
Estates: Worth £700 pa in the late 17th century.
Notes: John Lewis MP 1685-1701 was the last of the line.

LEWIS II *WALES*

Baron Merthyr (1911- UK)

Origins: Coal owners and iron masters in the 19th century. 1 Baron the son of a mining engineer and apprenticed as an engineer himself. He worked for the Bute estate. High Sheriff 1884. Kt 1885. Baronet 1896.

No MPs

Seat: Hean Castle, Pembrokeshire (first mentioned 1295, rebuilt later, purch. by 1 Baron 1899, still own)
Estates: 1 Baron left an estate worth £615,522 plus land in 1914. Owned 2,000 acres in 2001.
Title: Baronet 1896-
Peers: 3 peers 1911-45
Notes: 1 Baron in ODNB.

LIDDELL [Bright]

Earl of Ravensworth (1874-1904 UK)

Origins: Began with an Elizabethan merchant adventurer. Alderman of Newcastle-upon-Tyne c. 1600. Purchased estates. Granted arms 1615. Bt 1642. **First MP 1640**. Wealth based on coalmining. Industrialists in the 19th century.

1. Sir Henry Liddell 3 Bt – Durham 1689-90 1695-98 Newcastle-upon-Tyne 1701-10
2. John Liddell-Bright – Pontefract 1698-1701
3. Thomas Liddell – Lostwithiel 1715-18
4. George Liddell – Berwick-on-Tweed 1727-40
5. Henry Liddell 1 Baron Ravensworth – Morpeth 1734-47
6. Thomas Liddell 1 Baron Ravensworth – County Durham 1806-07
7. Henry Liddell 1 Earl Ravensworth – Northumberland 1826-30 N. Durham 1837-47 Liverpool 1853-55
8. Henry Liddell 2 Earl of Ravensworth – S. Northumberland 1852-78

Seats: Ravensworth Castle, Durham (built 14th c., purch. 1607, new house 1724, rebuilt 1811-46, contents sold 1920, subsidence, demolished 1952-53); Eslington Park, Northumberland (medieval castle, purch. 1718, built c. 1720, add. 1796, still own); Newton Hall, Durham (built c. 1730, sold 1812, demolished 1926)
Estates: Bateman 13851 (E) 39164
Titles: Baron Ravensworth 1747-84 GB; Baron Ravensworth 1821- UK; Baronet 1642-
Peers: 8 peers 1747-84 1821-1945
Notes: 1 Baron and 1 Earl and four others in ODNB.

<u>Bright</u>

Origins: The Brights settled in the Pontefract area in the 15th century. Grandfather of the 1 Baronet was a yeoman farmer. Father of the 1 Bt was baliff of the Earls of Arundel, and he used profits from that office to build up an estate worth £600 pa during the first half of the 17th century. **First MP 1654**. Estates passed via a daughter and heiress to the Liddells.

No post-1660 MPs

Seat: Badsworth, Yorkshire (purch. for £8,600 in 1653, passed by mar. in the early 18th c. to the Rockinghams (Watson), demolished).
Estates: Worth £1,000 pa by mid 17th c. Estate tripled in value between 1642 and 1660. Worth £3,210 pa in 1688.
Title: Baronet 1660-88

LINDSAY [Bradshaigh, Crawford, Loyd] *SCOTLAND & ENGLAND*

<u>Earl of Crawford and Balcarres</u> (1398- S)

Origins: The Lindsays acquired land by c. 1200. Chamberlain of Scotland 1255. Ambassador to England 1357. Earl 1398. The 1 Earl married c. 1384 a daughter of King Robert II. The 5 Earl was created Duke of Montrose 1488. The first non-royal Scottish Duke. The descendents of Sir David de Lindsay were Earls of Crawford while a younger son became Earl of Balcarres. The titles were merged from 1652 to 1808. **First [MP 1568]. One other [MP 1575].**

1. John Crawford 1 Viscount Garnock – [Ayrshire 1693-1703]
2. Patrick Lindsay – Edinburgh 1734-41
3. James Lindsay 24 Earl of Crawford – Wigan 1820-25
4. Hugh Lindsay – Perth Burghs 1820-30
5. James Lindsay – Wigan 1825-31 Fifeshire 1831-32
6. Hugh Lindsay – Sandwich 1841-47

7. James Lindsay – Wigan 1845-57 1859-65
8. Robert Lindsay 1 Baron Wantage – Berkshire 1865-85
9. Charles Lindsay – Abingdon 1865-74
10. James Lindsay 26 Earl of Crawford – Wigan 1874-80
11. David Lindsay 27 Earl of Crawford – Chorley Div. Lancashire 1895-1913
12. David Lindsay 28 Earl of Crawford – Lonsdale Div. Lancashire 1924-40
13. Sir George Broun-Lindsay – Patrick Div. Glasgow 1924-29
14. James Lindsay – N. Devon 1955-59
15. Robert Lindsay 29 Earl of Crawford – Hertford 1955-74

Seats: Haigh Hall, Lancashire (medieval house collapsed due to mine subsidence 1827, rebuilt 1827-40, family departed 1940, sold 1947); Balcarres House, Fife (purch. 1586, built 1595, add. 1838-43, still own); Dun Echt (Dunecht) House, Aberdeenshire (add. c. 1866-71, sold 1908); Kilconquhar House (Castle), Fife (Earl of Lindsay) (built 13th c., acq. 17th c., rebuilt 1831, sold)
Estates: Bateman 13480 (E, S, & W) 39252 and 5288 (S & E) 104999. Ubinstein – 23 Earl of Crawford left £100,000 in probate 1825 (owned 4,000 acres in 1996); 2205 (S) 5548 Earl of Lindsay
Titles: Baron Lindsay 1444- S; Duke of Montrose 1488-95 S; Baron Spynie 1590-1671 S; Earl of Lindsay 1633- S; Earl of Balcarres 1650- S; Viscount Garnock 1703- S; Baron Wigan 1826- UK; Baron Wantage 1885-1901 UK; Baronet 1821-1913; 1836-
Peers: [6 peers 1661-63 1663-70 1689-89 1678-1707 1700-07 1703-07] 6 Scottish Rep peers 1707-10 1732-49 1734-36 1784-96 1802-25 1885-94 1917-39 6 peers 1826-1945 1885-1901
2 Lds Lt 19th, 20th
1 in Cabinet 1916-22
1 KT 19th-20th
Notes: After inheriting the Bradshaigh estates in 1770 the Earls of Crawford became the active managers of a vast industrial complex of coal mines and steel works, which they operated into the 20th century. The 24 Earl spent £100,000 rebuilding Haigh Hall in the 1820s (Robinson, *A Guide to the Country Houses of the North West*, 190) The Lindsay family has an entry plus the 10, 11, 16, 17, 18, 20, 23, 25, 26, 27, and 28 Earls of Crawford and the 3 Earl of Balcarres and seventeen others in ODNB.

<u>Bradshaigh</u>

Origins: Acquired Haigh by marriage to an heiress 1295. **First MP 1313 for Lancashire**. Became very rich from coal mines in the 16th century. The 23 Earl of Crawford married in 1780 the granddaughter and heiress of the last Bardshaigh Bt of Haigh Hall and gained the great mineral wealth of the family.

1. Sir Roger Bradshaigh 1 Bt – Lancashire 1660-79
2. Sir Roger Bradshaigh 2 Bt – Wigan 1679 Lancashire 1685-87

3. Sir Roger Bradshaigh 3 Bt – Wigan 1695-1747
4. Henry Bradshaigh – Wigan 1708-12

Seat: Haigh Hall, Lancashire (medieval, acq. by mar. 1295, passed by mar. to Earls of Crawford 1780)
Title: Baronet 1679-1779
Notes: Remained Roman Catholics into the 17th century. 1 and 3 Bts and one other in ODNB.

Lindsay

Origins: Descended from the 9 Earl of Crawford. **First [MP 1597]. One additional [MP 1649]**.

1. David Lindsay – [Forfarshire 1678]

Seat: Edzell Castle, Forfarshire (medieval, acq. by mar. 1358, add. late 16th c., sold 1715, ruin)
Notes: Estates sold to pay debts 1715. Extinct 1744.
Notes: Four in ODNB.

Baron Overstone (1850-83 UK)

Origins: The 1 Baron Overstone was the son of a Welsh Dissenting minister and the daughter of a Manchester banker. The minister gave up his clerical life to go into the bank. They moved to London and created a huge fortune in the 1820s and 1830s. A nephew of the 24 Earl of Crawford married the daughter and heiress of the 1 Baron Overstone in 1858. He took the name Loyd and was created 1 Baron Wantage (see above).

1. Samuel Loyd 1 Baron Overstone – Hythe 1819-23
2. Arthur Loyd – Abingdon Div. Berkshire 1921-23

Seats: Lockinge House, Berkshire (purch. 1854, demolished 1947); Overstone Park (Hall), Northamptonshire (rebuilt 1861-62, became a school and hotel, burned 2001, part ruin)
Estates: Bateman 20528 (E) 26492 and 30849 (E) 58098. The Lloyds spent £1,670,000 on purchasing land 1825-83, and the 1 Baron left land and other wealth worth over £5,000,000 in 1883.
Peers: 1 peer 1850-83
1 Ld Lt 20th
Notes: 1 Baron and one other in ODNB.

LINGEN

Origins: The family held the manor of Lingen in the Domesday Book (Bindoff, *The House of Commmons*, II, 534). Kt 1256. **First MP 1373 for Herefordshire. At least one additional MP 1539 also for the county. Possibly more.**

1. Sir Henry Lingen – Hereford 1660-62

Seats: Stoke Edith, Herefordshire (purch. 17th c., sold 1670); Radbrooke Manor, Gloucestershire (acq. by mar. early 18th c., built c. 1720s, passed by inher. to the Burtons 1742)
Estates: Family suffered heavy financial losses due to the Civil War. Stoke Edith was sold in 1670 for £6,100.
Notes: The family remained Roman Catholic in the later 16th century. Thomas Lingen married in 1732 Ann Burton, heiress to Longnor Hall, Shropshire, and he took the additional name Burton in 1748. One in ODNB.

LISTER

<u>Baron Ribblesdale</u> (1797-1925 GB)

Origins: Merchants in Hull in the 16th century, involved in smelting and the largest exporters of lead from the port. Mayor of Hull 1595, 1618. Kt 1628. Purchased landed estates in several counties. **First MP 1601 for Hull. Five additional MPs 1604-58.**

1. Christopher Lister – Clitheroe 1695-1701
2. Thomas Lister – Clitheroe 1713-45
3. Thomas Lister – Clitheroe 1745-61
4. Nathaniel Lister – Clitheroe 1761-73
5. Thomas Lister 1 Baron Ribblesdale – Clitheroe 1773-90

Seats: Gisburn(e) Park, Yorkshire (purch. 1614, rebuilt 1724, sold 1925 and 1944, institutional use); Westby Hall, Yorkshire (medieval?, abandoned c. 1720, ruin)
Estates: Bateman 4719 (E) 6980; senior line at Muckton, Lincolnshire 2116 (E) 2786
Peers: Four peers 1797-1832 1849-1925
Notes: 4 Baron and one other in ODNB.

LIVINGSTON I (Livingstone) *SCOTLAND & ENGLAND*

Earl of Linlithgow (1600-1716 S) and Earl of Callender (1641-1716 S)

Origins: Prominent from the 14th century. Guardian of James II in the 1430s. Justiciar of Scotland 1449. The 1 Earl of Linlithgow's eldest son succeeded to his father's titles. A younger son was created Earl of Callender. The 4 Earl of Callender succeeded to the Linlithgow Earldom. **First [MP 1560]. Two further [MPs 1605-30]**.

No post-1660 MPs

Seat: Callendar House, Stirlingshire (acq. 1345, built 14th c., rebuilt 17th c., forfeited 1716)
Estates: 8,000 acres in 1716
Titles: Baron Livingston 1458-1716 S; 1633-1716 S; Baronet 1625-34
Peers: [5 peers 1660-85 1660-90 1688-1706] 1 Scottish Rep peer 1713-15
Notes: The 4 Earl of Linlithgow was elected to the Scottish Convention in 1689 for Linlithgow but was not allowed to take his seat as he was the eldest son of a peer. Both Earldoms were attainted in 1716 and the line became extinct in 1723. 1 and 5 Barons and 1, 3 and 4 Earls of Linlithgow and 1 Earl of Callender and four others in ODNB.

Campbell-Livingstone

Origins: The 1 Bt (Livingstone) of Glentirran was the illegitimate son of the 2 Earl of Callender (see above). The 2 Bt married the daughter and heiress of Sir James Campbell Bt of Ardkinglas (see Campbell I).

1. Adam Livingston – Argyllshire 1772-80
2. Sir James Campbell-Livingstone 3 Bt – Stirlingshire 1747-68

Seats: Glentirran, Stirlingshire (acq. by Livingstons in early 16th c., demolished); Ardkinglas, Argylshire (acq. and built 1396, acq. by mar. from Campbells 1752, rebuilt c. 1795, derelict 1822, fire 1831, stables adapted as house, sold 1905)
Estates: Bateman 52271 (S) 7511
Title: Baronet 1685-1810

Earl of Newburgh (1660- S)

Origins: Probable cousins of the Earls of Linlithgow (15th century). Provost of Stirling 1553. Courtiers under Queen Mary (Master Stabler) and in the 17th century.

1. James Livingston 1 Earl of Newburgh – Cirencester 1661-70

2. Charles Livingston 2 Earl of Newburgh – Cirencester 1685-87

Seat: Kinnaird House (Tower), Perthshire (medieval, acq. 1618, sold before 1674)
Estates: Worth £411 pa in 1656.
Titles: Viscount Newburgh 1647-94 S; Viscount Kynnaird 1660- S; Baronet 1627-94
Peers: [2 peers 1660-94]
Notes: Kinnaird Tower was built by the Livingstons in the 15th c., sold 1674 to the Threiplands. The Earldom passed through the Radclyffe and Clifford families before landing in the Italian aristocracy where it has remained. The manor of Cirecester passed to the 1 Earl of Newburgh via a marriage connection with the Pooles in the mid-17th c. Poole **– see Poole for MPs.** 1 Earl and two others in ODNB.

LIVINGSTON II *SCOTLAND*

Viscount Kilsyth (1661-1715 S)

Origins: Lord of Session under James I. **First [MP 1599].**

1. Sir James Livingston – 1 Viscount Kilsyth – [Stirlingshire 1661]
2. William Livingston – 3 Viscount Kilsyth – [Stirlingshire 1685-86 1702]

Seat: Kilsyth Castle, Stirlingshire (acq. 14th c., forfeited 1715)
Peers: [2 peers 1664-1707] 1 Scottish Rep peer 1710-14
Notes: Attainted 1715. 3 and last Viscount died in exile in Rome 1733. 1 Viscount in ODNB.

LLOYD I *IRELAND & WALES*

Origins: A medieval Welsh family that rose to prominence under the Tudors largely due to successful marriages. Sheriff 1583. Kt 1586. Sir John Lloyd (d. 1606) went to Ireland with Sir Richard Trevor and acquired an estate near Newry c. 1600. His grandson married the Medhop heiress in 1639 who brought estates in King's County and Tipperary. **First MP 1584 for Denbighshire. One additional MP 1597 also for the county.**

1. Trevor Lloyd – {Newry 1661-66}
2. Trevor Lloyd – {King's County 1741-47}
3. John Lloyd – {King's County 1768-90 Innistioge 1790-97}
4. Hardess Lloyd – King's County 1807-18

Seats: Gloster (Glasterrymore, Glosterboy), King's County (acq. by Medhop family c. 1640, built 17th c., passed by inher. to Lloyds 1696, add. before 1730, sold 1958,

convent); Bodidris Hall, Denbighshire (built later 16th c., remod mid-17th c., sold 19th c., part demolished 1958)
Estates: 4628 (I) 1526. Worth £3,500 pa in 1775.
Title: Baronet 1647-1700

LLOYD II [Adams] *WALES*

Origins: Founder a judge in the early 17th century (Kt 1622). Marriage to an heiress in 1713 lifted the family to the rank of leading figures in the county. (Howell, *Patriarchs and Parasites*, 11) **First MP 1640. One additional MP 1659.**

1. Sir Charles Lloyd 1 Bt – Cardigan 1698-1700
2. Henry Lloyd – Cardigan 1701-05
3. Walter Lloyd – Cardiganshire 1734-42
4. John Lloyd – Cardiganshire 1747-55
5. Sir Herbert Lloyd 1 Bt – Cardigan Boroughs 1761-68

Seats: Peterwell, Cardiganshire (purch. by Evan family c. 1630s), passed by mar. to Lloyds 1713, passed to Adams by mar. 1769, sold 1776); Maesyfelin, Cardiganshire (inher. by marriage to Evans heiress 1713, passed to Adams by mar. 1769, sold by 1781); Voelallt, Cardiganshire
Titles: Baronet 1708-50; 1763-69
Notes: Became heavily indebted mid-18th c. Male line extinct 1769. One in ODNB.

Adams

Origins: John Adams acquired wealth and position by marriage to the Lloyd heiress to Peterwell, to which he succeeded in 1769.

1. John Adams – Carmarthen 1774-80

Seat: Peterwell, Cardiganshire (acq. by mar to Lloyd heiress 1769, sold 1776-81)
Notes: John Adams overspent his inheritance and the estates were sold.

LLOYD III

Baron Lloyd (1925-85 UK)

Origins: The Lloyds claimed ancient descent. They were resident at Dolobran in the early 15th century. They built an iron forge on the estates c. 1720 and moved to Birmingham in c. 1733. They lost money in their industrial enterprises and sold Dolobran c. 1780s. However, Sampson Lloyd founded Lloyd's Bank in the later 18th century, and the family became wealthy in the 19th and 20th centuries as bankers and industrialists, repurchasing their ancestral estate (*Dictionary of Welsh Biography*, 570-71).

1. Thomas Lloyd – Barnstaple 1863-64
2. Sampson Lloyd – Plymouth 1874-80 S. Warwickshire 1880-85
3. Wilson Lloyd – Wednesbury 1885-86 1892-95
4. George Lloyd 1 Baron Lloyd – W. Staffordshire 1910-18 Eastbourne 1924-25

Seats: Dolobran (Hall), Montgomeryshire (early 15th c., remod. late 17th c., sold c. 1780s, part demolished, repurchased 1877-78, still resident 1969); The Priory, (Warwick Priory) Warwickshire (built 16th c. and 1620, purch. 1865, sold and demolished 1925); Budbrooke House, Warwickshire (acq. 19th c., owned into 20th c.)
Peers: 2 peers 1925-45
Notes: A Quaker family. 1 Baron and three others in ODNB.

LLOYD IV

Origins: The first MP was a judge. Kt 1677. **First MP 1656.**

1. Sir Richard Lloyd – Durham 1679-81 1685-86
2. Francis Lloyd – Ludlow 1691-95
3. Robert Lloyd – Shropshire 1699-1702 1705-08
4. Robert Lloyd – Shropshire 1710-13 1722-27

Seats: Aston Hall, Shropshire (built 1789-93, remod. 19th c., still own); Rolls Park, Essex (built c. 1600, remod. mid-18th c. acq. by mar. 1804, passed by mar. to Harveys 1830, demolished 1953)
Estates: Bateman 3978 (E) 6772
Notes: Married Harvey heiress to Rolls Park (see Harvey).

LLOYD GEORGE *WALES*

Earl Lloyd George of Dwyfor (1945- UK)

Origins: The 1 Earl was the son of a schoolmaster and farmer. David Lloyd George rose through the law and politics.

1. David Lloyd George 1 Earl Lloyd George – Caernarvon District 1890-1945
2. Gwilym Lloyd George 1 Viscount Tenby – Pembrokeshire 1922-24 1929-50 Newcastle-upon-Tyne 1951-57

3. Lady Megan Lloyd George – Anglesey 1929-51 Carmarthen Div. Carmarthenshire 1957-66

Seat: Ty Nwewydd, Caernarvonshire (built 15th c., later remod., purch. 1942, sold post 1945)
Title: Viscount Tenby 1957- UK
Peers: 1 peer 1945
Estates: The 1 Earl left £141,000 in 1945. Owned 2,500 acres in 2001.
2 in Cabinet 1905-22 1951-57
Notes: The 3 Viscount Tenby was elected as one of the hereditary peers to remain in the House of Lords in 1999. 1 Earl and 1 Viscount Tenby and one other in ODNB.

LOCH *SCOTLAND & ENGLAND*

Baron Loch (1895- UK)

Origins: Merchants in the Baltic trade in Edinburgh in the 16th century. Purchased landed estates in the 17th century but became impoverished due to Jacobitism and most estates sold. James Loch became a lawyer and was called to the English Bar in 1806. He became the agent (a major executive position) to the Marquess of Stafford and the great Sutherland estates in 1812 (see Leveson Gower). (Richards, *Leviathan of Wealth*, 19-25)

1. James Loch – St. Germans 1827-30 Tain Burghs 1830-36 Wick District 1832-52
2. John Loch – Hythe 1830-32
3. George Loch – Wick District 1868-72

Seats: Stoke College, Suffolk (built early 18th c., purch. mid-19th c., remod. 1897, now a school); Drylaw House, Midlothian (purch. 1641, rebuilt 1718, sold 1786)
Estates: 1 Baron left £100,000 and property in 1900.
Peers: 3 peers 1895-1945
Notes: 1 Baron and two others in ODNB.

LOCKHART [Macdonald] *SCOTLAND*

Lockhart

Origins: The Lockharts were at The Lee from the 13th century. Ambassador to France in the 1650s. Lords of Session in the 17th century. The daughter and heiress of John MacDonald of Largie Castle married Charles Lockhart of Carnwarth. Their son took the name Macdonald-Lockhart and was created a Baronet. The 1 Bt had a son who succeeded to Lee Castle. **First [MP 1607 for Lanarkshire]. Cadet line at Bar 3 [MPs 1567-1612].**

1. Sir James Lockhart – [Lanarkshire 1628-33 1645-47 1648 1660-63 1665 1667 1669-70]
2. Sir William Lockhart – [Lanarkshire 1654 1656 1672]
3. Cromwell Lockhart – [Lanarkshire 1678 1681 1685-86]
4. Sir George Lockhart – [Lanarkshire 1681 1685-86]
5. Sir John Lockhart – [Lanarkshire 1693]
6. Richard Lockhart – [Lanarkshire 1695]
7. George Lockhart – [Edinburghshire 1703-07] 1708-15
8. James Lockhart – Lanarkshire 1715-18
9. Sir Alexander Macdonald-Lockhart 1 Bt – Berwick-on-Tweed 1807-12
10. Alexander Macdonald-Lockhart – Lanarkshire 1837-41

Seats: Lee Castle (The Lee), Lanarkshire (acq. 1272 and built 1297, rebuilt 1817, add. 1834-45, sold 1948); Carnwath House, Lanarkshire (medieval, remod. 16th c., add. 17th c., purch. 1681, remod. 19th c., golf club from 1907, demolished 1970); Largie Castle, Argyllshire (old house, acq. by mar. 1837, rebuilt 1857-59, demolished 1953)
Estates: Bateman 32274 (S) 22387 plus 869. Owned 12,500 acres in 1996; at Largie 12775 (S) 4025
Title: Baronet 1806-1919
Notes: Member of the Cromwellian House of Lords 1657-58. The daughter of the 1 Bt married in 1837 Augustus Moreton, a younger son of the Earl of Ducie (see Moreton) and succeeded to Largie Castle. A cadet line at Balnagown Castle, Ross-shire (see Ross II). Five in ODNB.

<u>Lockhart</u>

Origins: Cadet line 15th century. **First [MP 1485].** A Lockhart heiress married William Eliott of Borthwickbrae in 1792. He took the additional name Lockhart. The family claimed descent from the Eliotts of Stobs (see Elliot).

1. William Eliott Lockhart – Selkirkshire 1806-30
2. Alan Eliott Lockhart – Selkirkshire 1846-61

Seats: Cleghorn, Lanarkshire (acq. and built 15th c., fire c. 1740, rebuilt); Borthwickbrae, Selkirkshire
Estates: Bateman 7142 (S) 4642
1 Ld Lt 19th

LOCKWOOD [Wood]

Baron Lambourne (1917-28 UK)

Origins: Gentry in Northamptonshire in the 17th century. High Sheriff 1695. The first MP was a successful Turkey merchant in the early 18th century. J. Lockwood of Dews Hall married in 1816 the daughter and heiress of Sir Mark Wood 1 Bt of Gatton Park (see below). Their son took the name Wood in 1838. The name Lockwood was resumed in 1876.

1. Richard Lockwood – Hindon 1713-15 London 1722-27 Worcester 1734-41
2. Amelius Lockwood 1 Baron Lambourne – E. Epping Div. Essex 1892-1917
3. John Lockwood – Hackney Central 1931-35 Romford 1950-55

Seats: Bishop's Hall, Essex (Lambourne Hall) (built 1571, Lambourne purch. 1782, leased 1818, passed to Woods by mar. 1838, sold 1929, demolished 1936); Dews Hall, Essex (medieval, part of same site as Bishop's Hall, purch. 1735, add. 1740s, demolished before 1841); Gayton Manor, Northamptonshire (built c. 1600, acq. early 17th c., add. 18th c.)
Estates: Bateman 4966 (E) 9200
Peers: 1 peer 1917-28
1 Ld Lt 20th
Notes: 1 Baron in ODNB.

Wood

Origins: The Woods arose in Scotland via a naval commander who acquired estates in 1483 and an official overseeing public works and vendor of stores. He built castles and became a royal advisor and man of business for the King. His son was secretary to the Regent Moray (d. 1570). Sir Mark Wood succeeded to Largo, Fife (purch. 1483) but made a fortune in the East India Company. **First Wood [MP 1560]. Another [MP 1590].**

1. James Wood – Gatton 1806-07
2. Sir Mark Wood 1 Bt – Milborne Port 1794-96 Newark 1796-1802 Gatton 1802-18
3. Sir Mark Wood 2 Bt – Gatton 1816-18

Seats: Gatton Park, Surrey (medieval, later add., purch. 1808 for £90,000, rebuilt early 19th c., sold 1830, fire 1934, school); Largo House, Fife (purch. 1483, built 1491, sold 17th c., add. 17th c., rebuilt 1750, ruin)
Estates: The 1 Bt was said to have returned from India with a fortune of £200,000 in 1793.

Title: Baronet 1808-37
Notes: Three in ODNB.

LODER

Baron Wakehurst (1934- UK)

Origins: Russia merchant in the 19th century. High Sheriff 1877. 1 Baron was a barrister.

1. Sir Robert Loder 1 Bt – Shoreham 1880-85
2. Gerald Loder 1 Baron Wakehurst – Brighton 1889-1905
3. John Loder 3 Baron Wakehurst – E. Leicester 1924-29 Lewes Div. Sussex 1931-36

Seats: Whittlebury Park, Northamptonshire; Leonardslee, Sussex (built 1853, purch. 1889, sold 2010); Wakehurst Place, Sussex (built 16th c., purch. 1903, donated 1963 NT)
Estates: Bateman 10241 (E) 11527. The Russia merchant left £2,900,000 in 1871.
Title: Baronet 1887-
Peers: 2 peers 1934-45

LOFTUS [Hopkins, Hume, Tottenham] *IRELAND*

Marquess of Ely (1801- UK)

Origins: The family moved from Yorkshire to Ireland in the 16th century. Archbishop of Armagh 1562. Lord Chancellor of Ireland 1578 and 1619. **First {MP 1613}. Five additional {MPs 1613-48}**. Sheriff 1674. The titles were recreated several times and assumed by junior lines when more senior branches became extinct. The sister and heiress of the 1 Earl of Ely married Sir John Tottenham 1 Bt (see below) in 1736. Their son took the name Loftus and was created 1 Marquess of Ely in 1801.

1. Nicholas Loftus – {County Wexford 1634 1639 Fethard 1661-66}
2. Dudley Loftus – Wicklow 1659 {Naas 1642-48 Bannow 1661-66 Fethard 1692-93}
3. Adam Loftus 1 Viscount Lisburne – {Lismore 1661-66}
4. Sir Nicholas Loftus – {Fethard 1661-66 1695-99}
5. Henry Loftus – {Clomines 1692-93 1695-99}
6. Nicholas Loftus 1 Viscount Loftus – {Fethard 1710-13 Clomines 1713-14 County Wexford 1715-51}
7. Thomas Loftus – {Clomines 1727-60}
8. Nicholas Hume-Loftus 1 Earl of Ely – {Bannow 1737-60 Fethard 1761-63}
9. Henry Loftus 1 Earl of Ely – {Bannow 1747-68 County Wexford 1768-69}
10. Nicholas Hume-Loftus 2 Earl of Ely – {Fethard 1759-66}

11. Charles Tottenham 1 Marquess of Ely – {Clomines 1761-76 Fethard 1776-83 Wexford 1783-85}
12. Sir Edward Loftus 1 Bt – {Jamestown 1761-68}
13. Arthur Loftus – {Fethard 1768-76 Clomines 1776-81}
14. Henry Loftus – {Clomines 1768-76 Bannow 1776-90}
15. Nicholas Loftus Tottenham – {Bannow 1776-90 Clomines 1790-97}
16. Thomas Loftus – {Clomines 1781-90 Fethard 1790-92}
17. John Loftus 2 Marquess of Ely – {County Wexford 1791-1800} 1801-06
18. William Loftus – {Fethard 1796-97 Bannow 1797-1800} Great Yarmouth 1796-1802 Taymouth 1802-12 Great Yarmouth 1812-18
19. John Loftus 3 Marquess of Ely – Woodstock 1845
20. Pierse Loftus – Lowestoft Div. Suffolk 1934-45

Seats: Loftus Hall (orig. Redmond Hall), Wexford (old castle, purch. 1666, built late 17th-early 18th c., new house 1871, sold 1917, institutional use); Ely Lodge (Castle Hume), Fermanagh (acq. and built by Hume Bts, 1727-29, passed by mar. to Loftus family 1750, rebuilt 1830s, demolished 1810, sold); Rathfarnham Castle, Dublin (acq. and built 1583, remod. 1770-71, sold 1837); Kearsney Abbey, Kent (old house, rebuilt c. 1820, purch. c. 1878, sold c. 1899); Mount Loftus (Dunroe, Mount Eaton), Kilkenny (acq. late 17th c., built 1750, passed to an illegitimate daughter 1864, repurch. by Loftus family 1903, demolished 1906, new house built 1909, fire 1934, servants wing converted into house, sold 1995)
Estates: Bateman 48992 (I & E) 23751 and 13625 (I) 5678
Titles: Viscount Loftus 1622-1725 I; Viscount Lisburne 1685-91 I; Baron Loftus 1751-83 I; Viscount Loftus 1756-83 I; Earl of Ely 1766-69 I; Earl of Ely 1771-83 I; Baron Loftus 1785- I; Viscount Loftus 1789- I; Earl of Ely 1794- I; Baron Loftus 1801- UK; Baronet 1768-1864; 1780-
Peers: {8 peers 1660-1725 1685-91 1756-83 1785-1800} 7 peers 1801-57 1870-1945
3 KP 18th, 19th
Notes: 1 Viscount and three others in ODNB.

<u>Tottenham</u>

Origins: The family settled in Ireland under James I from Cambridgeshire. Sheriff 1737. One succeeded to the Loftus estates by marriage. (see above)

1. Charles Tottenham – {New Ross 1727-58}
2. Charles Tottenham – {Fethard 1755-61 New Ross 1761-68 Bannow 1768-76 Clomines 1776-90 Fethard 1790-95}
3. Sir John Tottenham 1 Bt – {New Ross 1768-1800}
4. Charles Tottenham – {New Ross 1768-1800}

5. Ponsonby Tottenham – {Fethard 1779-90 Bannow 1790-97 Clomines 1797-1800} Wexford 1801-02 New Ross 1805-06
6. Charles Tottenham – New Ross 1802-05
7. Charles Tottenham – New Ross 1831 1856-63
8. Charles Tottenham – New Ross 1866-68 1878-80

Seats: Tottenham Green, Wexford (purch. and built later 17th c., add. c. 1712, sold 1783, demolished c. 1950); Ballycurry, Wicklow (built 18th c., acq. by mar. 1772, rebuilt c. 1808, resident into 20th c.)
Estates: Bateman 11517 (I) 12679. 9,377 acres in 1828.
Title: Baronet 1780-
Notes: One in ODNB.

Tottenham

Origins: A cadet line in the 19th century.

1. Arthur Tottenham – Leitrim 1880-87

Seats: Glenfarne Hall, Leitrim (acq. 19th c., sold later 19th c.); Tudenham Park (House) (previously Rochfort House), Westmeath (built c. 1742, remod. c. 1790, purch. 1836 by Hopkins family who left it to Tottenhams 1860, abandoned 1939, unroofed 1957)
Estates: Bateman 14818 (I) 4431

Hopkins

Origins: Came to Ireland with Cromwell and acquired Athboy. 1 Bt a lawyer.

1. Sir Francis Hopkins 1 Bt – {Kilbeggan 1797-1800}

Seats: Athboy Lodge, Meath (acq. mid-17th c., sold c. 1860); Rochfort (Tudenham Park), Kerry (purch. 1836, passed to Tottenhams by mar. to sister of last Bt 1860)
Estates: 2,588 acres worth £1,739 pa in 1878. Worth £5,560 pa in 1816.
Title: Baronet 1795-1860
Notes: Extinct in the male line 1860. Estates broken up among several heiresses.

Hume

Origins: In Ireland by the beginning of the 17th century. **First {MP 1634}.** The heiress of Sir Gustavus Hume 3 Bt married Nicholas Loftus in 1736. The latter succeeded to Castle Hume in 1750.

1. Sir Gustavus Hume 3 Bt – {County Fermanagh 1713-31}

Seat: Castle Hume, Fermanagh (old castle, rebuilt 1727-28, passed to Loftus family 1750 and renamed Ely Lodge, see above, demolished 1810)
Estates: Worth £3,000 pa in 1729.
Title: Baronet 1671-1750

LONG I [Chaloner, Child, Tylney]

Viscount Long (1921- UK)

Origins: The father of the first MP was of humble origins. The family were clothiers and then landowners. **First MP 1414. Eight additional MPs 1433-1626, three of them kts of the shire**.

1. Richard Long – Chippenham 1694-95
2. Richard Long – Chippenham 1734-41
3. Walter Long – Calne 1701
4. Richard Long – Wiltshire 1806-18
5. Walter Long – N. Wiltshire 1835-65
6. Richard Long – Chippenham 1859-65 N. Wiltshire 1865-68
7. Walter Long 1 Viscount Long – N. Wiltshire 1880-85 Devizes Div. Wiltshire 1885-92 Liverpool 1893-1900 S. Bristol 1900-06 S. County Dublin 1906-10 Strand Div. Middlesex 1910-18 St. George's Hanover Square 1918-21
8. Richard Long 2 Viscount Long – Westbury Div. Wiltshire 1927-31

Seats: South Wraxall Manor, Wiltshire (purch. by 1429 and built, enlarged c. 1478-85, add. c. 1598-1611, remod. c. 1700, leased out from 1820, restoration 1900-02, sold 1966); Rood (Rowde) Ashton House, Wiltshire (built 1806, add. 19th c., gutted 1950); Whaddon, Wiltshire (purch. 1544-55, built 16th c., acq. by Longs of Wraxall 1748 - see Parker II - fire 1835, sold 1911-19); Dolforgan Hall, Montgomeryshire (built 17th c. or earlier, rebuilt. c. 1790, acq. by mar. 1846, sold 1870, flats)
Estates: Bateman 15404 (E & W) 23213; Rubinstein – Catherine Long left £175,000 in probate in 1814; junior line at Preshaw House, Hampshire 4798 (E) 6983
Title: see Parker II
Peers: 3 peers 1921-45
1 Ld Lt 20th
2 in Cabinet 1905 1916-21
Notes: Four and half centuries separated the first and last member of the family sitting for Westbury. See Parker II for Long Bts. 1 Viscount and one other in ODNB.

Baron Gisborough (1917- UK)

Origins: Began as mercers and merchants in London in the early 16th century. Two served as ambassadors later in the Tudor period. Gained monastic land to form an estate. Kt 1547. **First MP 1545. Three additional MPs 1555-1658.** Margaret Chaloner, daughter and heiress of Robert Chaloner of Gisborough married William Hume of Humewood (see Home). Their daughter married Richard Long of Wraxall (see above). A younger son succeeded to Gisborough and took the name Chaloner.

1. Robert Chaloner – Richmond 1810-18 York 1820-26
2. Richard Chaloner 1 Baron Gisborough – Westbury Div. Wiltshire 1895-1900 Abercromby Div. Liverpool 1910-17

Seats: Gisborough (Gisboro) Hall, Yorkshire (acq. 1547-58, built c. 1560, demolished early 19th c., rebuilt 1856, passed to Longs 1888, family departed 1939, still own but leased for business use); Long Hull (Longhull), Yorkshire (acq. early 19th c.)
Estates: Bateman 3551 (E) 5949
Title: Baronet 1620-81
Peers: 2 peers 1917-45
Notes: The family remained engaged in business, opening alum mines in Yorkshire c. 1600 and engaged in banking in the early 19th century.
Notes: Four in ODNB.

Long

Origins: Sir Walter Long divided his estates in two, establishing the senior line at Wraxall and a junior line at Draycot Cerne in 1610. **First MP 1442. Six additional MPs 1529-1626.** Sir Robert Long 6 Bt married the daughter of the 1 Earl Tylney. The 7 Bt succeeded to the estates of the 2 Earl Tylney in 1784 and took the additional name Tylney. The Tylneys were established gentry by the early 17th century, whose estates were merged with those of the Childs, a great merchant family (see below).

1. Sir Robert Long 1 Bt – Devizes 1626 1628 Midhurst 1640 Boroughbridge 1661-73
2. Sir James Long 2 Bt – Malmesbury 1679-81 1690-92
3. Sir James Long 5 Bt – Chippenham 1705-13 Wootton Bassett 1715-22 Wiltshire 1727-29
4. Sir Robert Long 6 Bt – Wootton Bassett 1734-41 Wiltshire 1741-67
5. Sir James Tylney-Long 7 Bt – Marlborough 1762-80 Devizes 1780-88 Wiltshire 1788-94

Seat: Draycot Cerne (Draycot Park/House), Wiltshire (acq. by mar. 1438, rebuilt mid-18th c., passed to Wellesleys by mar. – see below, demolished c. 1955)

Estates: See Earl Cowley under Wellesley
Title: Baronet 1662-1805
Notes: The daughter and heiress of Sir James Tylney-Long 7 Bt married the 4 Earl of Mornington (see Wellesley). The 5 Earl of Mornington left Draycot to his cousin the 1 Earl Cowley. Two in ODNB.

Earl Tylney (1731-84 I)

Origins: The estates of Frederick Tylney MP (below) passed to his niece, who married Sir Richard Child 3 Bt. He was created Earl Tylney in 1731. The merged estates eventually passed 1784 to the Longs of Draycot Cerne (see above). The Childs rose from humble beginnings in business in naval supplies to become Mayor of Portsmouth 1658. Their fortune was expanded by the Chairmanship of the East India Company and banking.

1. Sir Josiah Child 1 Bt – Petersfield 1658-59 Dartmouth 1673-79 Ludlow 1685-87
2. Frederick Tylney – Winchester 1690-1700 Stockbridge 1701-02 Southampton 1702-05 Whitchurch 1708 1710-15 1721
3. Sir Josiah Child 2 Bt – Wareham 1702-04
4. Richard Child 1 Earl Tylney – Maldon 1708-10 Essex 1710-22 1727-34
5. John Child-Tylney 2 Earl Tylney – Malmesbury 1761-68

Seats: Wanstead House, Essex (built 16th c., purch. 1673, rebuilt 1715-22, passed by mar. to the Longs 1784 and to the Wellesleys 1812, sold and demolished 1823); Tylney Hall (Park), Hampshire (built 1561, acq. 1629, built early 18th c., passed to Wellesleys by mar., demolished, sold 19th c., hotel)
Estates: Worth £200,000 in 1699 and £10,000 pa in the 18th century.
Titles: Baron Newton and Viscount Castlemaine 1718-84 I; Baronet 1678-1784
Notes: 1 Bt in ODNB.

LONG II

Baron Farnborough (1826-38 UK)

Origins: The Longs were merchants and owned the largest plantation in Jamaica. They held the offices of Chief Justice and Speaker of the Assembly in the colony. They purchased an estate in Suffolk.

1. Charles Long – Dunwich 1715-22
2. Dudley Long-North – St. Germans 1780-84 Great Grimsby 1784-96 Banbury 1796-1806 Newtown (IoW) 1807-08 Banbury 1808-12 Richmond 1812-18 Haddington Burghs 1818-20 Newtown 1820-21

3. Charles Long 1 Baron Farnborough – Rye 1789-96 Midhurst 1796-1802 Wendover 1802-06 Haselmere 1806-26
4. Samuel Long – Ilchester 1790-96

Seats: Hurts Hall, Suffolk (built 1803, fire 1889, rebuilt 1893, sold post 1945); Carshalton Park (not House), Surrey (acq. 18th c., passed out of the family by mar. early 19th c.); Bromley Hill Place, Kent (purch. and built early 19th c., sold mid-19th c.?)
Estates: Bateman 3634 (E) 4790 and 3917 (E) 5563. Rubinstein – 1 Baron left £120,000 in 1838.
Peers: 1 peer 1826-38
1 in Cabinet 1805-06
Notes: The Longs would have been a good deal richer but for heavy losses in the South Sea Bubble crash of 1721. The 1 Baron divided his estates among multiple heirs. 1 Baron and five others in ODNB.

LONGFIELD *IRELAND*

Viscount Longueville (1800-11 I)

Origins: Went to Ireland as an official in the Dublin administration 1652. Acquired estates in the 1680s.

1. Richard Longfield 1 Viscount Longueville – {Charleville 1761-68 Clonakilty 1768-76 Cork 1776-83 Baltimore 1783-90 Cork 1790-95}
2. Mountifort Longfield – {Enniscorthy 1776-97 Cork 1797-1800} 1801-18
3. Robert Longfield – {Donegal 1777-78}
4. John Longfield – {Mallow 1790-1800} 1801-02
5. John Longfield – {Philipstown 1795-97 Ballynakill 1797-1800}
6. Richard Longfield – County Cork 1835-37
7. Robert Longfield – Mallow 1859-65

Seats: Longueville, Cork (purch. 1702, built c. 1720, add. c. 1800-05, add. c. 1866, sold 1938, hotel); Castle Mary, Cork (old castle, acq. by cadet line c. 1680, rebuilt c. 1685, add. early 18th c., rebuilt 19th c., burned c. 1920, ruin, family lived in stables, sold 1978)
Estates: Bateman 13120 (I) 6054 and 10813 (I) 7885. Worth £7,000 pa in 1779 and £20,000 pa c. 1810.
Title: Baron Longueville 1795-1811 I
Peers: {1 peer 1795-1800} 1 Irish Rep peer 1801-11
Notes: See also Conner. One in ODNB.

LONGVILLE (Longueville)

Origins: Held Little Billing estate from 1301. **First MP 1298. Six additional MPs 1311-1475, two of them kts of the shire.**

1. Charles Longueville – Downton 1715-22 Great Bedwyn 1722-27 East Looe 1727-41

Seats: Bradwell (Abbey), Buckinghamshire (sold 1650); Little Billing Priory, Northamptonshire (acq. 1301, sold c. 1701, demolished in 20th c.)
Notes: Heavily indebted by the Civil War. One in ODNB.

LOPES

Baron Ludlow (1897-1922 UK)

Origins: Portuguese Jews established in Jamaica as planters and London merchants. Purchased English estates in the late 18th century. Baronet 1805. High Sheriff 1869.

1. Sir Manasseh Lopes 1 Bt – New Romney 1802-06 Evesham 1807-08 Barnstaple 1812-19 Westbury 1820-29
2. Sir Ralph Lopes 2 Bt – Westbury 1814-19 1831-37 1841-47 S. Devon 1849-54
3. Sir Massey Lopes 3 Bt – Westbury 1857-68 S. Devon 1868-85
4. Henry Lopes 1 Baron Ludlow – Launceston 1868-74 Frome 1874-76
5. Henry Lopes 1 Baron Roborough – Grantham 1892-1900

Seats: Maristow House, Devon (medieval, rebuilt c. 1560, rebuilt mid-18th c., purch. 1798, remod. 1907-09, family depart 1939, institutional use, fires 1952 and 1981-82, much demolished, flats); Manor House, Westbury, Wiltshire (purch. 1810, sold 1920); Heywood House, Wiltshire (acq. by mar. 1876, sold c. 1922); Roborough House, Devon (purch. 1798, sold post 1945, hotel)
Estates: Bateman 12103 (E) 10668. The 1 Bt purchased Maristow for £100,000 and left £800,000 in stock and land in 1831. Rubinstein – 1 Bt left £160,000 in probate in 1830. Worth £33,000,000 with 12,000 acres in England in 1990. Owned 34,000 acres in Scotland in 1996.
Titles: Baron Roborough 1938- UK; Baronet 1805-
Peers: 4 peers 1897-1922 1938-45
1 Ld Lt 20th c.
Notes: The family renounced Judaism in the later 18th century. The 1 Bt was imprisoned for electora1 corruption. Baron and 1 and 3 Bts in ODNB.

LOVELACE

Origins: Held property in Kent from the 14th century. Kt. 1497. **First MP 1563. Two other MPs 1614-21.**

1. Francis Lovelace – Canterbury 1661-64

Seat: Lovelace Place, Kent (purch. 1367, sold later 17th c.)

LOWE

Origins: The first MP was a barrister, and the second son of a London merchant. **First MP 1597. An additional MP 1625-28, both for Calne.**

1. George Lowe – Calne 1640-44 1661-79

Resident in Calne, Wiltshire
Notes: The family dropped into obscurity in the 18th century.

LOWNDES [Selby]

Origins: An old gentry family that came to prominence produced a Secretary to the Treasury in the early 18th century. William Lowndes succeeded to the Whaddon estates of the Selbys in 1813, though they were not kinsmen, on the condition of taking the name Selby.

1. William Lowndes – Seaford 1695-1715 St. Mawes 1715-22 East Looe 1722-24
2. Richard Lowndes – Buckinghamshire 1741-74
3. Charles Lowndes – Bramber 1768-69
4. William Selby-Lowndes – Buckinghamshire 1810-20

Seats: Whaddon Hall, Buckinghamshire (medieval, acq. 1813, rebuilt 1820, fire 1976, flats); The Bury (Bury House) (Chesham), Buckinghamshire (purch. 16th c., rebuilt 1712-16, sold and donated late 1940s/ early 1950s, flats); Winslow House (Hall), Buckinghamshire (purch. 1697, rebuilt 1698-1702, sold 1898)
Estates: Bateman 7537 (E) 11923
Notes: One in ODNB.

LOWRY-CORRY [Leslie, Lyster] *IRELAND & ENGLAND*

Earl of Belmore (1797- I)

Origins: The Lowrys emigrated from Scotland to Ireland before 1641. Sarah, heiress of John Corry, married Galbraith Lowry, who took the additional name Corry. The Corrys emigrated from Dumfriesshire to Belfast 1649 where they made a fortune as merchants and began acquiring estates in the 1650s. Sheriff 1666. The sister of Sarah Corry married Edmund Leslie, who took the additional name Corry.

1. James Corry – {County Fermanagh 1692-93 1695-99 1703-18}
2. John Corry – {Enniskillin 1711-13 County Fermanagh 1719-26}
3. Edmund Leslie-Corry – {Newtown-Limavady 1742-64}
4. Leslie Corry – {Killybegs 1739-41}
5. Galbraith Lowry-Corry – {County Tyrone 1748-68}
6. Robert Lowry – {Strabane 1761-64}
7. Armar Lowry-Corry 1 Earl of Belmore – {County Tyrone 1768-81}
8. Somerset Lowry-Corry 2 Earl of Belmore – {County Tyrone 1797-1800} 1801-02
9. Armar Lowry-Corry 3 Earl of Belmore – County Fermanagh 1823-31
10. Henry Lowry-Corry – County Tyrone 1825-73
11. Henry Lowry-Corry – County Tyrone 1873-80

Seats: Castle Coole (Castlecoole), Fermanagh (castle built 1613, burned 1641, purch. by Corrys 1656, repaired and burned again 1689, new house 1709, burned 1797, new house 1790-98 cost over £70,000, NT 1951, retained residence and land); Edwardstone Hall, Suffolk (built early 17th c. and 1840s, acq. by mar. 1853, owned by a younger son and his descendants, demolished 1952); Rowton Castle (built c. 1700, Lord Rowton inher. by mar. mid-19th c., sold early 20th c.); Melbury, Tyrone (acq. 17th c., sold 1774)
Estates: Bateman 19429 (I) 11015; 3141 (I) 2348 at Rockdale, Tyrone; 8158 (I) 3848 at Pomeroy House, Tyrone. Held 53,000 acres in 1800, but land sold to pay debts thereafter. Worth £16,645 pa in 1800 and £26,849 pa in 1816. Owned 6,500 acres in 2001.
Titles: Baron Belmore 1781- I; Viscount Belmore 1789- I; Baron Rowton 1880-1903 UK
Peers: {1 peer 1782-1800} 2 Irish Rep peers 1819-41 1857-1913 1 peer 1880-1903
1 Ld Lt 19th-20th
1 in Cabinet 1867-68
Notes: Castle Coole is one of the most perfect late classical houses in the British Isles. 1 Baron Rowton and one other in ODNB.

Lyster

Origins: Seated at Rowton since the end of the 15th century. **First MP (probable) 1572.** A younger son of the Earls of Belmore succeeded by marriage to Rowton Castle and was created Baron Rowton in 1880.

1. Richard Lyster – Shrewsbury 1722-23 1727-34 Shropshire 1740-66
2. Richard Lyster – Shrewbury 1814-19

Seat: Rowton Castle, Shropshire (built c. 1700, add. 1809-12 and 1824, passed to Lord Rowton by mar. mid-19th c., see above)
Estates: Bateman 6297 (E) 5642

LOWTHER [Crofton, Preston, Turner] *ENGLAND & IRELAND*

Earl of Lonsdale (1784-1802 GB; 1807- UK)

Origins: A lawyer and King's Serjeant 1290-92 built up a landed estate. Kt 1293. Geoffrey and Hugh Lowther fought at Agincourt. **First MP 1305 for Westmorland. Fifteen additional MPs 1322-1640, ten of them kts of the shire.**

1. Sir John Lowther 1 Bt – Westmorland 1628 1660
2. Sir William Lowther – Pontefract 1660-79
3. John Lowther – Appleby 1661-68
4. Sir John Lowther 2 Bt – Cumberland 1665-81 1685-87 1689-1700
5. John Lowther 1 Viscount Lonsdale – Westmorland 1677-79 1681 1689-96
6. Anthony Lowther – Appleby 1679-81
7. Richard Lowther – Appleby 1689-90
8. William Lowther – Carlisle 1692-94
9. Sir James Lowther 4 Bt – Carlisle 1694-1702 Cumberland 1708-22 Appleby 1723-27 Cumberland 1727-55
10. Sir William Lowther – Pontefract 1695-98
11. Sir William Lowther 1 Bt – Pontefract 1701-10 1716-29
12. Sir William Lowther 1 Bt – Lancaster 1702-05
13. Robert Lowther – Westmorland 1705-08
14. Anthony Lowther – Cockermouth 1721-22 Westmorland 1722-41
15. Sir Thomas Lowther 2 Bt – Lancaster 1722-45
16. John Lowther – Pontefract 1722-29
17. Sir William Lowther 2 Bt – Pontefract 1729-41
18. James Lowther 1 Earl of Lonsdale – Cumberland 1757-61 Westmorland 1761-62 Cumberland 1762-68 Cockermouth 1769-74 Cumberland 1774-84
19. Robert Lowther – Westmorland 1759-61 1763

20. James Lowther – Westmorland 1775-1812 Appleby 1812-18
21. William Lowther 1 Earl of Lonsdale – Carlisle 1780-84 Cumberland 1784-90 Rutland 1796-1802
22. Sir John Lowther 1 Bt – Cockermouth 1780-86 Carlisle 1786 Haselmere 1786-90 Cumberland 1796-1831
23. William Lowther 2 Earl of Lonsdale – Cockermouth 1808-13 Westmorland 1813-31 Dunwich 1832 Westmorland 1832-41
24. Henry Lowther – Westmorland 1812-67
25. Sir John Lowther 2 Bt – Cockermouth 1816-26 Wigton Burghs 1826-31 Cockermouth 1831-32 York 1835-47
26. Henry Lowther 3 Earl of Lonsdale – W. Cumberland 1847-72
27. James Lowther – York 1865-80 N. Lincolnshire 1881-85 Isle of Thanet Div. Kent 1888-1904
28. William Lowther – Westmorland 1868-85 Appleby Div. Westmorland 1885-92
29. James Lowther 1 Viscount Ullswater – Rutland 1883-85 Mid-Cumberland 1886-1921
30. Claude Lowther – Eskdale Div. Cumberland 1900-06 1910-18 Londsdale Div. Lancashire 1918-22
31. Henry Lowther – Appleby Div. Westmorland 1915-18 Penrith & Cockermouth Div. Cumberland 1921-22
32. Christopher Lowther – N. Div. Cumberland 1918-22

Seats: Lowther Castle (Hall), Westmorland (built 14-15th c., remod. 1631, remod. 1642 and 1655, demolished 1690, rebuilt 1692-95, fire 1718 and ruinous for nearly a century, rebuilt 1800-22, abandoned mid-1930s, unroofed 1957, still own); Marske Hall, Yorkshire (built 1625, purch. 1649, sold 1762); Whitehaven Castle (Flatt Hall), Cumberland (purch. and built 1675, rebuilt 1766-69, sold 1920s, now hospital); Swillington House, Yorkshire (purch. 1663, rebuilt 1690s, 1738, 1803, sold due to being undermined by coal mine c. 1945, demolished 1950); Askham Hall, Westmorland (built 14th c., add. 1570s, remod. c. 1685-1700, purch. 1815, since 1957 principal seat); Barleythorpe Hall, Rutland (purch. early 19th c., sold before 1939, institutional use); Campsea Ashe High House, Suffolk (seat of Viscounts Ullswater with 2,700 acres worth £3,700 pa in 1949) (built early 17th c., rebuilt 1864, purch. 1883, sold 1949, ruin 1950s)
Estates: Bateman 68065 (E) 71333; Swillington line 6085 (E) 18572. Worth £570 pa early 17th c., £1,450 pa in 1637, c. £25,000 pa in the 1730s and £45,000 pa in 1756. Worth £72,000,000 with 80,000 acres in 1990. Owned 72,000 acres in 2006. Another 3,000 acres for sale 2014. (*Country Life*, 208, p. 92).
Titles: Viscount Lonsdale 1696-1751 E; Viscount Lonsdale 1794- GB; Viscount Ullswater 1921- ; Baronet 1638-1802; 1642-1755; 1715-63; 1824-; 1914-
Peers: 10 peers 1696-1700 1715-51 1784-1945 1921-45
9 Lds Lt 17th, 18th, 19th, 20th
4 in Cabinet 1690 1699-1700 1733-35 1852 1878-80
2 KG 19th, 20th

Notes: **Thirteen Lowthers represented Cumberland between 1324 and 1922 and sixteen Westmorland 1300-1892. Eleven sat for Appleby 1318-1918.** The family refreshed and greatly enlarged its fortune with coalmining and the development of Whitehaven in the 17th-19th centuries. Many younger sons were merchants. One was a successful draper in London who purchased Marske in 1649. A son became an MP and his heir married the heiress to Holker Hall (see below) and was created a Bt. His brother was a Danzig merchant and inherited Marske. Another line of merchants in Leeds also gained a Baronetcy in 1715 and established the Swillington branch of the family. The Lowther family has an entry in ODNB and the 1 Viscount Ullswater and the 1 and 3 Viscounts Lonsdale and 1, 2, and 5 Earls and twelve others.

Lowther

Origins: Descended from a younger son of the grandfather of the first Lowther Bt (1638), who became a merchant. Sir William Lowther married the daughter and heiress of Thomas Preston of Holker Hall. The Prestons gained monastic estates after the Dissolution.

1. Thomas Preston – Lancashire 1665-79
2. Thomas Preston – Lancaster 1689-97
3. Sir Thomas Lowther 2 Bt – Lancaster 1722-45
4. Sir William Lowther 3 Bt – Cumberland 1755-56

Seat: Holker Hall, Lancashire (originally built by the Prestons c. 1540, rebuilt early 17th c., inher. by the Lowthers via mar. 17th c., passed to Cavendishes by mar. 1794)
Estates: Worth £2,000 pa in 1660.
Title: Baronet 1697-1753

Lowther

Origins: Descended from a younger brother of the grandfather of the first Lowther Bt. To Ireland before c. 1600. **First {MP 1613}.** Purchased estates in County Meath 1702.

1. George Lowther – {Ratoath 1705-13 Coleraine 1713-14 Ratoath 1715-16}
2. Gorges Lowther – {Ratoath 1739-60 County Meath 1761-92}
3. George Lowther – {Ratoath 1761-68 Ardee 1768-76 Newtown 1783-84}
4. Gorges Lowther – {Ratoath 1790-98}

Seats: Shrigley Park (Hall), Cheshire (built c. 1820, acq. later 19th c., sold 1930s, institutional use); Kilbrew House, Meath (acq. 1702, rebuilt later 18th c., sold c. 1800)
Estates: Bateman 2118 (E) 3547. Worth £800 pa in 1713.
Notes: Lowthers moved to England later 18th c. and held only English land in the 19th c.

Turner

Origins: The first MP was a calico printer whose mills were located in Blackburn. He purchased Shrigley. He left it to his granddaughter Ellen Legh, who brought it to Brabazon Lowther of Kilbrew (see above).

1. William Turner – Blackburn 1832-41

Seat: Shrigley Park (Hall), Cheshire (purch. 1818, built c. 1825, passed to Lowthers by mar. later 19th c.)

Baron Crofton (1798- I)

Origins: A Crofton emigrated to Ireland as Escheator-General in 1584. **First {MP 1585}.** Sheriff 1606. **Two additional {MPs 1613-39}**. Sir Marcus Lowther 1 Bt, a younger son of the Lowthers of Kilbrew, took the additional name Crofton in 1745 on the death of his wife's brother, Sir Edward Crofton 4 Bt of Mote Park. Their son, Sir Edward Crofton 2 Bt married an heiress, Anne Croker, who was created Baroness Crofton in 1798.

1. Sir Edward Crofton 1 Bt – {Lanesborough 1665-66}
2. Sir Edward Crofton 2 Bt – {Boyle 1695-99 County Roscommon 1703-29}
3. Sir Edward Crofton 3 Bt – {Roscommon 1713-39}
4. Sir Edward Crofton 4 Bt – {Roscommon 1735-45}
5. Sir Marcus Lowther-Crofton 1 Bt – {Ratoath 1753-60 Roscommon 1761-68 Ratoath 1769-76}
6. Sir Edward Crofton 2 Bt – {County Roscommon 1775-77 1778-97}

Seat: Mote Park, Roscommon (acq. 17th c., rebuilt 1777-87, add 1816, fire 1865, rebuilt, sold 1950s, demolished c. 1958); Galey (Gailey), Roscommon (resident 19th c.)
Estates: Bateman 11053 (I) 7332; Worth £4,483 pa in 1783.
Title: Baronet 1661-1780; 1758-
Peers: 3 Irish Rep peers 1840-69 1873-1912 1916-42

Crofton

Origins: Descended from a younger son of John Crofton (d. 1610), ancestor of the Lords Crofton.

1. Hugh Crofton – {County Leitrim 1743-60}
2. Sir Hugh Crofton 2 Bt – {Tulsk 1786-90}

Seat: Mohill Castle, Leitrim (acq. and built 1622, resident into 20th c.)

Estates: Bateman 11469 (I) 6222. Worth £1,476 pa in 1760.
Title: Baronet 1801-

LUBBOCK

Baron Avebury (1900- UK)

Origins: The father of the founder was a clergyman in the 18th century. His son was a merchant and banker, created Bt 1806.

1. Sir John Lubbock 1 Bt – Bossiney 1796-1802 Leominster 1802-12
2. Sir John Lubbock 2 Bt – Leominster 1812-20
3. John Lubbock 1 Baron Avebury – Maidstone 1870-80 London University 1880-1900
4. Eric Lubbock 4 Baron Avebury – Orpington 1962-70

Seat: High Elms, Kent (purch. 1840, built c. 1845, sold 1938, fire 1967)
Estates: Rubinstein 1 Bt left £120,000 in probate in 1816, and the 1 Baron died 1913 worth £315,000.
Title: Baronet 1806-
Peers: 3 peers 1900-45
Notes: The 2 Bt was a banker, the 3 Bt a scientist, and the 1 Baron a politician. A younger son Edgar Lubbock served as Managing Director of Whitbreads brewery, a Director of the Bank of England, and Master of the Blankney Foxhounds. He built Caythorpe Court, Lincolnshire for hunting in 1899 (sold 1946). (Franklin, *The Gentleman's Country House*, 33) So, like the Barings, the Lubbocks combined business with an aristocratic style of life a century or more after gaining entry into landed society. 1 Bt and 1 Baron and one other in ODNB.

LUCY

Origins: The Lucys have held Charlecote since at least the early 13th century. Kt 1233. **First MP 1312, for Warwickshire. Eleven further MPs 1336-1659, seven of them kts of the shire**.

1. Richard Lucy – Warwickshire 1653 1654 1656 1659 Yarmouth (IoW) 1660-77
2. Sir Fulke Lucy – Warwick 1659 Cheshire 1664-77
3. Sir Kingsmill Lucy 2 Bt – Andover 1673-78
4. Thomas Lucy – Yarmouth (IoW) 1678-79 Warwick 1679-81
5. George Lucy – Fowey 1818-19 1820-30

Seats: Charlecote Park, Warwickshire (acq. 1189, built c. 1558, add. 1829-36 and 1853-67, NT 1945); Maxton, Roxburghshire; Faccombe, Hampshire (purch. 1655, passed out of family by mar. 1759)
Estates: 5883 (E) 12087. Wealth in 1640 £3,500 pa.
Titles: Baronet 1617-1759 1836-
Notes: 1 Bt and four others in ODNB.

LUKE

Origins: The founder was a Tudor judge. Acquired Woodend by marriage in the reign of Henry VIII. **First MP 1584 for Bedfordshire. Two additional MPs 1597-1648, one for Bedfordshire**.

1. Sir Samuel Luke – Bedford 1641-48 1660

Seat: Woodend, Bedfordshire (acq. by mar. 1st half 16th c., sold 1686)
Estates: 6,000 acres in 1613
Notes: The family fortunes declined after the Civil War and estates were sold. One in ODNB.

LUMLEY [Saunderson, Savile, Wray]

Earl of Scarborough (1690- E)

Origins: The Lumley's claimed Saxon descent. When told of their lineage, James I exclaimed: "Oh mon! gang na further. I maun digest the knowledge I ha' this day gained, for I did na ken Adam's ither name was Lumley." (*Country Life*, 171, p. 346) Kt 12th century. Baron 1385. **First MP 1467 for Northumberland. Another MP 1495 also for the county**.

1. Henry Lumley – Sussex 1701 1702-05 Arundel 1715-22
2. Henry Lumley Viscount Lumley – Arundel 1708-10
3. Richard Lumley 2 Earl of Scarborough – East Grinstead 1708-10 Arundel 1710-15
4. Thomas Saunderson Lumley 3 Earl of Scarborough – Arundel 1722-27 Lincolnshire 1727-40
5. Charles Lumley – Chichester 1727-28
6. John Lumley – Arundel 1728-39
7. James Lumley – Chichester 1729-34 Arundel 1741-47
8. George Lumley-Saunderson 5 Earl of Scarborough – Lincoln 1774-80
9. Richard Lumley-Savile 6 Earl of Scarborough – Lincoln 1784-90
10. John Lumley-Savile 8 Earl of Scarborough – Nottinghamshire 1826-32 N. Nottinghamshire 1832-35

11. Lawrence Saunderson Lumley 11 Earl of Scarborough – E. Div. Hull 1922-29 York 1931-37

Seats: Sandbeck Park, Yorkshire (acq. by Lumleys by mar. from Saundersons – see below – 1723, rebuilt 1760s, still own); Lumley Castle, Durham (acq. at an early date, built c. 1389 or earlier, remod. 1570-80, 1721-28, 1732-33, post WWII institutional and commercial use); Stansted Park, Sussex (medieval house, acq. by mar. later 16th c., remod. mid-16th c., new house built 1688, sold 1778); Glentworth Hall, Lincolnshire (inher. by mar. 1720, rebuilt 1753, sold c. 1945, ruin); Tickhill Castle, Yorkshire (built 11th c., add. 12th c., decayed 16th c.); Rufford Abbey, Nottinghamshire (acq. from Saviles by mar. 1784, passed to illegit. son of 8th Earl, sold 1938, part demolished 1950s, public ownership)
Estates: Bateman 21698 (E) 31567. Rubinstein – the 7 Earl left £340,000 in probate in 1835. Hold 5,000 acres today.
Titles: Baron Lumley 1385-1537 [1609] E; Viscount Scarborough 1628- I; Baron Lumley 1547-1609 E; Baron Scarborough 1681- E; Viscount Scarborough 1689- E; Baron Savile 1888-96
Peers: {1 peer 1671-1721} 10 peers 1681-1945
5 Lds Lt 17th, 18th, 19th, 20th
1 in Cabinet 1716-17
2 KG 18th, 20th
Notes: Stanstead Park, Sussex was held from 1244 by the FitzAlans, Earls of Arundel (see Howard I). It passed to the Lumleys by right of a wife (d. 1576) who was the sister of the last FitzAlan Earl of Arundel. It passed to the Earl of Halifax in 1766. The Lumleys were recusants, hence the gap in MPs. The 1 Earl coverted to Protestantism in 1687. 3, 5 and 6(1) Barons and 1 Baron Savile and 1 Viscount and 1 and 11 Earls and four others in ODNB.

Earl of Castleton (1720-23 E)

Origins: Yorkshire yeomen gradually built up an estate and rose to prominence in the mid-16th century. (Bearstall, *North Country Estate*, 8-9) Kt. 1603. **First MP 1589. One additional MP 1593 (Lincolnshire 1625)**. On the death of the 1 Earl of Castleton in 1723 his estates passed to the 3 Earl of Scarborough, a cousin by marriage through the Belasyse family, who took the additional name Saunderson.

1. George Saunderson 5 Viscount Castleton – Lincolnshire 1660-81 1685-87 1689-98
2. Nicolas Saunderson – Thirsk 1679-81 Newark 1689-92
3. James Saunderson 1 Earl of Castleton – Newark 1698-1700 1701-10

Seats: Sandbeck Park, Yorkshire (medieval, acq. by Saundersons 1549, house rebuilt 1626, passed to Lumleys by mar. 1723, see above); Fillingham, Lincolnshire (purch.

mid-16th c., passed to Wrays 1714); Saxby, Lincolnshire (purch. later 16th c., built late 18th c., passed to the Earls of Scarborough 18th c.); Glentworth Hall, Lincolnshire (purch. and built c. 1570, passed to Earls of Castleton later 17th c., passed to Earls of Scarborough by mar. 1720); Reasby Hall, Lincolnshire (built 16th c., passed to Earls of Scarborough 1720)
Estates: Worth £500 later 16th c., £3,000 pa by 1630, and £8,000 pa in 1723.
Titles: Baron Saunderson and Viscount Castleton 1627-1723 I; Baron Saunderson 1714-23 GB; Viscount Castleton 1716-23 GB
Peers: {1 peer 1660-61} 1 peer 1714-23

Wray

Origins: The founder was Lord Chief Justice of the Queen's Bench 1575. Speaker of the House of Commons. High Sheriff 1594. Kt 1596. **First MP 1553. Five additional MPs 1584-1653, three of them kts of the shire**. The 1 Earl of Castleton married Elizabeth Wray and through her succeeded to Glentworth and Fillingham.

1. William Wray – Great Grimsby 1654 1656 1659 1660
2. Sir Christopher Wray 2 and 6 Bt – Great Grimsby 1675-79
3. Sir Cecil Wray 13 Bt – East Retford 1768-80 Westminster 1782-84

Seats: Ashby, Lincolnshire; Fillingham Castle, Lincolnshire (inher. from Saudersons 1714, built 1760, passed out of family by mar. 1825); Glentworth Hall, Lincolnshire (purch. and built c. 1570, passed to Earls of Castleton later 17th c., passed to Lumleys 1720)
Estates: Worth £2,500 pa in 1655. Rubinstein – Lady Esther Wray (wife of 13th Bt) left £120,000 in probate in 1825.
Title: Baronet 1611-1809
Notes: Estates divided 1805. 2, 9, and 13 Bts and two others in ODNB.

LUSHINGTON

Lushington

Origins: The Lushingtons purchased manorial property c. 1700. The family produced barristers, clergymen, and professors in the 18th and 19th centuries. The eldest son of Stephen Lushington of Sittingbourne, Kent (late 17th century) established this branch of the family. Stephen Lushington MP (below) was Governor of Madras 1827-32.

1. Stephen Lushington – Rye 1807-12 Canterbury 1812-30 1835-37
2. James Lushington – Petersfield 1825-26 Hastings 1826-27 Carlisle 1827-31
3. Charles Lushington – Canterbury 1854-57

Seats: Park House, Kent (purch. and built 1792, resident at least until 1893); Aldington Court, Kent (resident 19th c.); Norton Court, Kent (acq. late 18th c., passed by mar. to Wildmans 1868 – see Wildman)
Notes: Four in ODNB.

Lushington

Origins: Descended from a younger son of Stephen Lushington of Sittingbourne, Kent (see above). The 1 Bt was Chairman of the East India Company 1790.

1. Sir Stephen Lushington 1 Bt – Hedon 1783-84 Helston 1790-96
2. William Lushington – London 1795-1802
3. Stephen Lushington – Great Yarmouth 1806-08 Ilchester 1820-26 Tregony 1826-30 Winchelsea 1831 Ilchester 1831-32 Tower Hamlets 1832-41
4. Charles Lushington – Ashburton 1835-41 Westminster 1847-52

Seats: South Hill Park, Berkshire (built 1760, leased?); Merry Hill (Meryhill, Merryhill), Hertfordshire
Estates: Stephen Lushington MP left c. £100,000 in 1893.
Title: Baronet 1791-
Notes: Five in ODNB.

LUTTRELL [Olmius] *IRELAND & ENGLAND*

Earl of Carhampton (1785-1829 I)

Origins. Falsely claimed descent from the Luttrells of Dunster Castle (see Fownes). Settled at Luttrellstown near Dublin from the 15th century. Acquired English property in the 18th century. They also owned a Jamaican plantation. **First {MP 1613}. One additional {MP 1643}**. The 1 Earl was an adventurer and corrupt politician.

1. Simon Luttrell 1 Earl of Carhampton – Mitchell 1755-61 Wigan 1761-68 Weobley 1768-74 Stockbridge 1774-80
2. Henry Luttrell 2 Earl of Carhampton – Bossiney 1768-69 Middlesex 1769-74 Bosiney 1774-84 {Old Leighlin 1783-87} Plympton Erle 1790-94 Ludgershall 1817-21
3. John Luttrell-Olmius 3 Earl of Carhampton – Stockbridge 1774-75 1780-85
4. Temple Luttrell – Milborne Port 1775-80
5. James Luttrell – Stockbridge 1775-80 Dover 1784-88
6. Henry Luttrell – {Clomines 1799-1800}

Seats: Luttrellstown Castle (Woodlands), Dublin (medieval castle, acq. 15th c., remod. 18th c., sold 1799); Four Oaks Hall, Warwickshire (built 1696, remod. c. 1740, purch. 1744, remod. 1770s, sold 1778); Painshill, Surrey (built 1774, leased)
Estates: 4,000 acres in Ireland 1717.
Titles: Baron Irnham 1768-1829 I; Viscount Carhampton 1781-1829 I
Peers: {2 peers 1768-1800}
Notes: Simon Luttrell was a member of James II's Irish Parliament of 1689. 2 and 3 Earls and seven others in ODNB.

Baron Waltham (1762-87 I)

Origins: Founded by a Dutch merchant who purchased estates in Essex. His grandson, the 1 Baron, was Deputy Governor of the Bank of England. The sister and heiress of the 2 Baron Waltham married John Luttrell.

1. John Olmius 1 Baron Waltham – Weymouth & Melcombe Regis 1737-40 Colchester 1741-42 1754-61
2. Drigue Olmius 2 Baron Waltham – Weymouth & Melcombe Regis 1768-74 Maldon 1784-87

Seat: New Hall, Essex (built 13th c., new house c. 1518, add. c. 1573, purch. 1737, sold 1798, became a school)
Peers: {2 peers 1762-87}

LUTWYCHE

Origins: The family was seated at Lutwyche from at least 1418. **First MP 1586**.

1. Sir Edward Lutwyche – Ludlow 1685-86
2. Thomas Lutwyche – Appleby 1710-22 Callington 1722-27 Amersham 1728-34

Seat: Lutwyche Hall, Shropshire (built 1587, sold late 18th c.)
Notes: The last two MPs were successful lawyers. Two in ODNB.

LYELL *SCOTLAND*

Baron Lyell (1914- UK)

Origins: Began as farmers and then merchants in the mid-18th century. Acquired a fortune in China and returned home to purchase Kinordy c.1790.

1. Leonard Lyell 1 Baron Lyell – Orkney & Shetland 1885-1900

2. Charles Lyell – East Div. Dorset 1904-10 S. Div. Edinburgh 1910-17

Seat: Kinnordy House, Forfarshire (purch. 1782, still own)
Estates: Bateman 8313 (S) 10363. 10,500 acres in 1996.
Title: Baronet 1864-75; 1894-
Peers: 2 peers 1914-43
Notes: The great geologist was a member of the family. 1 Bt and one other in ODNB.

LYGON (Ligon)

Earl Beauchamp (1815- UK)

Origins: The Lygons, medieval gentry, married well. William Lygon, son of a lawyer, succeeded in 1451 to Madresfield Court via an heiress of the Bracy family (Kt 1196). They rose further through a marriage to Anne Beauchamp, daughter of the 2 and last Lord Beauchamp of Powyke (d. 1496). The Beauchamps held the Earldom of Warwick (Duke 1445) from 1268, and were one of the great families of medieval England with many MPs. Later the Lygons succeeded to the estates of other families. **First MP 1467 for Worcestershire. One additional MP 1589-1608 also for the county**.

1. William Lygon 1 Earl Beauchamp – Worcestershire 1775-1806
2. William Lygon 2 Earl Beauchamp – Worcestershire 1806-16
3. Henry Lygon 4 Earl Beauchamp – Worcestershire 1816-31 W. Worcestershire 1832-53
4. Edward Lygon – Callington 1818-20
5. Henry Lygon 5 Earl Beauchamp – W. Worcestershire 1853-63
6. Frederick Lygon 6 Earl Beauchamp – Tewkesbury 1857-63 W. Worcestershire 1863-66
7. William Lygon 8 Earl Beauchamp – E. Norfolk 1929-38

Seats: Madresfield Court, Worcestershire (built 15th c., add. later 16th c., remod. 1863-85 and 1913, still own); Springhill (Spring Hill) House, Worcestershire (built 1763, purch. and remod. 1830)
Estates: Bateman 17634 (E) 24941. 1 Earl left £760,000 in probate 1816.
Title: Baron Beauchamp 1806- UK
Peers: 8 peers 1806-91 1893-1945
2 Lds Lt 19th, 20th
1 Cabinet 1910-15
1 KG 20th
Notes: 1, 6, and 7 Earls in ODNB.

LYNCH [Blosse] *IRELAND*

Origins: Mayor of Galway in the late 16th century. **First {MP 1559}. Five additional {MPs 1559-1639}**. The 6 Bt married in 1749 the heiress of Tobias Blosse and took the additional name Blosse.

1. Sir Henry Lynch-Blosse 7 Bt – {Tuam 1776-83}

Seats: Athaville, Mayo (acq. 18th c., sold 20th c., institutional use); Castle Carra, Mayo (acq. 1676, still resident into 20th c.)
Estates: Bateman 22658 (I) 9274. Held 6,400 acres in Mayo by 1676.
Title: Baronet 1622-

LYNDON *IRELAND*

Origins: A younger son of a Somerset gentleman became Mayor of Carrickfergus. Granted arms 1639. First MP a lawyer.

1. John Lyndon – {Killybegs 1665-66}
2. Edward Lyndon – {Armagh 1692-93 Carrickfergus 1703-13 1719-27}
3. John Lyndon – {Carrickfergus 1727-41}

LYON [Bowes] *SCOTLAND & ENGLAND*

<u>Earl of Strathmore and Kinghorne</u> (1606- and 1672- S)

Origins: A courtier (Lord Chamberlain of Scotland 1377) to Robert II granted the Thanage of Glamis 1372. Baron 1445. **First [MP 1630 for Forfarshire]. One additional [MP 1644 also for the county].**

1. Patrick Lyon – [Forfarshire 1703-07]
2. Thomas Lyon 8 Earl of Strathmore – Forfarshire 1734-35
3. Thomas Lyon – Aberdeen Burghs 1768-78
4. John Bowes – S. Durham 1832-47 (illegitimate son of 10 Earl)

Seats: Glamis Castle, Forfarshire (medieval, acq. 1372, add. early 15th c., remod. 1621 and 1679, remod. 19th c., still own); Castle Huntly, Forfarshire (built 1452, purch. 1615, sold late 18th c.); Streatlam Castle, Durham (built medieval by Bowes, wrecked 1569, restored later 16th c., inher. 1885, part demolished 1920, sold 1922-27, demolished 1959); St. Paul's Walden Bury, Hertfordshire (purch. and built early 18th c. by Gilberts, passed by mar. from Gilberts to Bowes 1762, to Lyons and remod. 1767, still own)
Estates: Bateman 24686 (S & E) 28502. 17,300 acres in 1996.

Titles: Baron Glamis 1445- S; Baron Bowes 1815-20 UK; Baron Bowes 1887- UK; Earl of Strathmore 1937- UK
Peers: [2 peers 1664-1707] 4 Scottish Rep peers 1767-76 1796-1812 1852-65 4 peers 1815-20 1887-1945
2 Lds Lt 19th, 20th
1 KG 20th
1 KT 20th
Notes: Three brothers of the 4 Baron died at Flodden. Lady Elizabeth Bowes-Lyon married King George VI and became Queen Consort in 1936 and Queen Mother in 1952. Queen Elizabeth and the 1, 2, 3, 7, and 8 Barons and 3, 9, and 14 Earls and four others and John Bowes in ODNB.

Bowes

Origins: The Bowes held Streatlam from 1310. Chief Justice of the Common Pleas 1331. Married an heiress. **First MP 1362. Nine additional MPs 1422-1628** (possibly one other 1601). Kt 1424. Great coal mine owners. The 9 Earl of Strathmore married Mary Bowes, heiress to the Bowes estates, although the property was held by an illegitimate line until the later 19th century.

1. Sir William Bowes – County Durham 1679-81 1695-98 1702-07
2. George Bowes – County Durham 1727-60
3. Andrew Bowes – Newcastle-upon-Tyne 1780-84

Seats: Streatlam Castle, Durham (medieval, acq. by mar. 1310, rebuilt, 1450 and 1717-20, passed to Strathmores 1885, demolished from 1920 and 1959); Gibside, Durham (estate passed by inher. from first owners c. 1200 to the Bowes in 1713 and to the Strathmores in 1800, house built c. 1625, abandoned by family from 1860, gutted 1920, fittings removed to Glamis); Cold Pike Hill, Durham (acq. by mar. 1768)
Estates: Bateman 43200 (E) 21071. One estimate of the Bowes wealth in 1760 was one million pounds.
Notes: Seven in ODNB.

Lyon

Origins: Descended from Sir Thomas Lyon, the Master of Glamis (d. 1608). West Indian merchants and slave owners in the later 18th and 19th century.

1. William Lyon – Seaford 1831-32
2. David Lyon – Bere Alston 1831-32

Seats: Goring Hall, Sussex (old house demolished, purch. and rebuilt 1834, fire 1888, rebuilt, family departed 1906, leased to tenants, now hospital); Balintore (Balentore) Castle, Forfarshire (purch. and built 1860, abandoned 1960s, sold, ruin)
Estates: Bateman 7354 (E & S) 4538. Rubinstein – David Lyon left £600,000 in probate in 1827.

LYONS *IRELAND*

Origins: To Ireland early 17th c. The first MP was a land speculator. Sheriff 1715.

1. John Lyons – {Athy 1713-14}
2. Colley Lyons – {King's County 1727-41}
3. Henry Lyons – {King's County 1748-68}

Seats: Ledwithstown (Ladestown, Ledestown, Ledwichtown), Westmeath (tower house, purch. 1715, rebuilt 1746, rebuilt 1823, not occupied by family from late 19th c., derelict 20th c., demolished); River Lyons, King's County (acq. late 17th c., unoccupied after 1798, passed by mar. to Champagne family, ruin)
Estates: 1356 (I) 1046 in 1878.
Notes: One in ODNB.

LYSAGHT *IRELAND*

Baron Lisle (1758- I)

Origins: Founder a 17th–century soldier. Fought in the rebellion of 1641 and at the Boyne with William III. Sheriff 1731.

1. John Lysaght 1 Baron Lisle – {Charleville 1727-58}
2. John Lysaght 2 Baron Lisle – {Castlematyr 1753-60 County Cork 1765-68}
3. James Lysaght – {Charleville 1768-76 Castlematyr 1776-83}
4. Nicholas Lysaght – {Tallow 1768-82}
5. Joseph Lysaght – {Youghal 1768-76 Cashel 1797-99}

Seats: Mount North (Mountnorth Court), Cork (acq. and built mid-17th c., resident 19th c. but abandoned, ruin); Hazlewood House, Cork (acq. and built 1819, add. 1917 and 1922, part demolished early 1960s, still own); Kenton House, Devon (resident 19th c.)
Estates: Bateman 5408 (I) 1988. Worth £2,500 pa in mid-18th c.
Peers: {2 peers 1759-98}
Notes: Edward Lysaght was a member of the Irish Senate 1922-25 and Chief Herald.

LYTTELTON [Brouncker, Littleton]

Lyttelton

Origins: The family emerged in the 13th century. Judge 1464. Four lines descended from Sir Thomas Lyttelton (15th century), a celebrated lawyer. **First MP 1316 for Worcestershire. Six additional MPs in the most senior line 1491-1640, four for the county.**

1. Sir Henry Lyttelton 2 Bt – Lichfield 1678-79
2. Sir Charles Lyttelton 3 Bt – Bewdley 1685-87

Seat: Frankley Hall, Worcestershire (acq. by mar. 13th c., destroyed 1642)
Title: Baronet 1618-1779
Notes: The estate of Hagley and the Baronetcy passed from this line to the more junior branch, Lords Lyttelton (see below) in the 1690s. Three in ODNB.

Baron Hatherton (1835- UK)

Origins: This branch of the family separated in the 15th century. **First MP 1529 for Staffordshire. Two further MPs 1604-44, both for the county.**

1. Sir Edward Littleton 2 Bt – Staffordshire 1663-79
2. Edward Littleton – Staffordshire 1685-87
3. Sir Edward Littleton 4 Bt – Staffordshire 1784-1812
4. Edward Littleton 1 Baron Hatherton – Staffordshire 1812-32 S. Staffordshire 1832-35
5. Edward Littleton 2 Baron Hatherton – Walsall 1847-52 S. Staffordshire 1853-57

Seats: Teddesley Park (Hall), Staffordshire (built 1757, sold 1953, demolished 1954); Pillaton Hall, Staffordshire (medieval, acq. by mar. 1502, add. early 18th c., transferred principal seat to Teddesley 1750s, decayed, part restored 1884-88 and 1979, still own); Hatherton Hall, Staffordshire (medieval, rebuilt 1817, sold 2000)
Estates: Batmean 14901 (E) 23196
Title: Baronet 1627-1812
Peers: 5 peers 1835-45
1 Ld Lt 19th
1 in Cabinet 1833-34
Notes: On the death of the 4 Bt the estates passed to the Walhouse family of Hatherton by marriage. Edward Walhouse took the name Littleton and became 1 Baron Hatherton. 1 Baron in ODNB.

Baron Lyttelton (1641-45 E)

Origins: The next most junior line descended from Sir Thomas Lyttelton in the 15th century. **First MP 1614 (1624 for Staffordshire).**

1. Sir Thomas Littleton 2 Bt – Much Wenlock 1640-44 1661-79 East Grinstead 1679 Yarmouth (IoW) 1681
2. Sir Timothy Littleton – Ludlow 1660-69
3. Sir Thomas Littleton 3 Bt – Woodstock 1689-1702 Castle Rising 1702-05 Chichester 1705-07 Portsmouth 1708-09
4. James Littleton – Weymouth & Melcombe Regis 1710-11 1713-15 Queenborough 1722-23
5. Thomas Littleton – Weymouth & Melcombe Regis 1715-22

Seats: North Ockenden Hall, Essex (acq. by mar. 1632, passd out of family by mar. 1723, sold 1758); Lingfield, Surrey (acq. by mar. c. 1700, passed out of the family 1723)
Estates: Worth £4,000 pa c. 1709.
Title: Baronet 1642-1709
Notes: Acquired North Ockenden by marriage to a Poyntz heiress 1618 century (see Browne II). Male line extinct 1723. Five in ODNB.

Viscount Cobham (1718- GB)

Origins: The most junior line of the family. For the inheritance of the Cobham Viscountcy, see Grenville. The 3 Bt of Frankley (see above) settled at Hagley 1690s.

1. Sir Thomas Lyttelton 4 Bt – Worcestershire 1721-34 Camelford 1734-41
2. George Lyttelton 1 Baron Lyttelton – Okehampton 1735-56
3. Sir Richard Lyttelton – Brackley 1747-54 Poole 1754-61
4. William Lyttelton 1 Baron Lyttelton – Bewdley 1748-55 1774-90
5. Thomas Lyttelton 2 Baron Lyttelton – Bewdley 1768-69
6. George Lyttelton 2 Baron Lyttelton – Bewdley 1790-96 {Granard 1797-1800}
7. William Lyttelton 3 Baron Lyttelton – Worcestershire 1806-20
8. Charles Lyttelton 8 Viscount Cobham – E. Worcestershire 1868-74
9. Alfred Lyttelton – Warwick & Leamington 1895-1906 St. George's Hanover Square 1906-13
10. John Lyttelton 9 Viscount Cobham – Droitwich Div. Worcestershire 1910-16
11. Oliver Lyttelton 1 Viscount Chandos – Aldershot Div. Hampshire 1940-54

Seats: Hagley Hall, Worcestershire (purch. 1564, built 1560s, new house built 1753-60, fire 1926, restored, still own); Arley Castle, Worcestershire (built 16th c., add. early 17th

c., passed on death of 2 Baron Lyttelton 1779 to his sister Viscountess Valentia (see Annesley), demolished c. 1960).
Estates: Bateman 6939 (E) 10263
Titles: Baron Lyttelton 1756-79 GB; Baron Westcote 1776- I; Baron Lyttelton 1794- GB; Viscount Chandos 1954- UK; Baronet 1618-1779
Peers: 8 peers 1756-79 1794-1945
3 Lds Lt 19th, 20th
3 in Cabinet 1755-56 1903-05 1940-45
Notes: 1, 2, and 4 Barons Lyttelton, 1 and 3 Barons Westcote, and 1 Viscont Chandos and six others in ODNB.

Viscount Brouncker (1645-88 I) (Brouncher)

Origins: The family entered the gentry in the 16th century. Lord President of Munster and a courtier under Charles I. Purchased an Irish peerage in 1645. **First MP 1572. One additional MP 1572 (Wiltshire 1586-93).** On the extinction of the Viscountcy in 1688 the 3 and last Viscount left all his property to his old Civil War comrade Sir Charles Lyttelton (under Viscount Cobham).

1. William Brouncher – Westbury 1660
2. Henry Brouncker 3 Viscount Brouncker – New Romney 1665-68

Seats: Sheen Abbey (Priory), Surrey (leased 1675-88); Newcastle Lyons Castle, Dublin (acq. 17th c., ruinous from 1642)
Notes: 2 and 3 Viscounts in ODNB.

LYTTON [Bulwer, Robinson] *ENGLAND & WALES*

Earl of Lytton (1880- UK)

Origins: The Lyttons were among the leading gentry of Hertfordshire from the later 15th century. The son of a Derbyshire landowner fought at Bosworth and became a favorite of Henry VII. **First MP 1491 (Hertfordshire 1495). Two additional MPs 1585-1648, both also for the county**. William Bulwer of Heydon Hall (gentry by 14th century) married the Lytton heiress in 1798. The second son was created Baron Dalling and his younger brother Baron Lytton.

1. Sir Rowland Lytton – Hertfordshire 1656 1659 1660
2. John Robinson-Lytton – Bishop's Castle 1747-54
3. Henry Lytton Bulwer 1 Baron Dalling – Wilton 1830-31 Coventry 1831-34 Marylebone 1835-37 Tamworth 1868-71

4. Edward Lytton-Bulwer 1 Baron Lytton – St. Ives 1831-32 Lincoln 1832-41 Hertfordshire 1852-66
5. Edward Lytton Viscount Knebworth – Hitchin Div. Hertfordshire 1931-33

Seats: Knebworth House, Hertfordshire (purch. and built 1492, drastically reduced in size 1814, enlarged and remod. c. 1840, still own); Wood Dalling, Norfolk (Bulwers purch. 1566, built c. 1582, sold 1632, Bulwers repurch. c. 1790, sold later 19th c. /20th c.); Heydon Hall, Norfolk (built 1581-84, Earles purch. 1650, acq. by Bulwers via marriage from the Earles 1780, add. 1797 and 19th c., Bulwer-Longs still own)
Estates: Bateman 4863 (E) 5366 and 9051 (E) 11027
Titles: Baron Lytton 1866- UK; Baron Dalling 1871-72 UK; Baronet 1838-
Peers: 4 peers 1866-91 1871-72 1897-1945
1 in Cabinet 1858-59
1 KG 20th
Notes: Active in government and literature later 19th and 20th centuries. 1 Baron Lytton and 1 Baron Dalling and 1, 2, and 3 Earls and five others in ODNB.

Robinson

Origins: The direct Lytton line died out in 1705. An heiress married Sir Nicholas Strode, who took the name Lytton. The estates and name passed through the Strode family to William Robinson of Guersylt in 1710. The Robinsons rose in the Tudor period. One was Bishop of Bangor 1566-85, who increased the family estate at the Dissolution.

1. John Robinson – Beaumaris 1661-79
2. William Robinson – Denbigh Boroughs 1705-08

Seats: Monachty (Mynachdy) Grange, Anglesey (purch. mid-16th c., sold 1737); (Upper) Gwersyllt (Guersylt) Hall (Park), Denbighshire (acq. mid-16th c., sold after 1739, collapsed due to mining subsidence 20th c.)
Estates: Worth £800 pa in 1660.
Notes: The main line of the family died out in 1737 and the estates were sold to pay debts. Three in ODNB.